BIRNIE, BOYLE & REDGWELL'S INTERNATIONAL LAW AND THE ENVIRONMENT

BIRNIE, BOYLE & REDGWELL'S INTERNATIONAL LAW AND THE ENVIRONMENT

Fourth Edition

ALAN BOYLE

CATHERINE REDGWELL

OXFORD
UNIVERSITY PRESS

OXFORD
UNIVERSITY PRESS

Great Clarendon Street, Oxford, OX2 6DP,
United Kingdom

Oxford University Press is a department of the University of Oxford.
It furthers the University's objective of excellence in research, scholarship,
and education by publishing worldwide. Oxford is a registered trade mark of
Oxford University Press in the UK and in certain other countries

First Edition 1992
Second Edition 2002
Third Edition 2009

Impression: 1

Published in the United States of America by Oxford University Press
198 Madison Avenue, New York, NY 10016, United States of America

British Library Cataloguing in Publication Data
Data available

Library of Congress Control Number: 2021932661

ISBN 978–0–19–959401–6

Printed in Great Britain by
Ashford Colour Press Ltd, Gosport, Hampshire

PREFACE

It is 29 years since the Rio Conference established the current architecture of international environmental policy, law and institutions. The Rio principles and the now extensive architecture of multilateral environmental agreements have been supplemented and amplified by customary international law, soft law, and the decisions of international courts and treaty bodies. The great wave of treaty-making that characterized global environmental governance from the 70's to the early millennium has largely ended, but it leaves behind a complex structure of international regulation that addresses in some form most of the world's main environmental problems. The great wave of cases before international courts and tribunals that started with *Gabčíkovo* in 1997 may also have ended: at the time of writing there were no new environmental disputes before any international adjudicatory body. But the jurisprudence we now have goes far to turn the Rio Declaration and the environmental work of the International Law Commission into law, giving structure and coherence to the subject and its relationship to international law as a whole.

The conclusions of this new edition are nevertheless sobering. Put simply, although we have far more law and policy than a quarter of a century ago, the global environment is in a much worse state now than it was then, whether we look at the poor health of the oceans, or climate change, or the growing loss of biodiversity and ecosystems or the other effects of human mismanagement of our global ecosystem including global pandemics. This outcome reflects a serious political failure on the part of global policy-makers. They have legislated for the global environment, but they have not made that legislation strong enough and in implementing it they have not pursued policies that match the science. This is the Greta Thunberg point. She is right to be deeply sceptical, and the evidence supports her.[1]

The previous edition of *International Law and the Environment* came out in 2009 and this edition has been too long delayed, so there are numerous changes. The most significant legal development reflected throughout the revised the text has been the many new cases before international courts and tribunals, starting with *Pulp Mills on the River Uruguay* in 2010, but including many others before the International Court of Justice, the International Tribunal for the Law of the Sea, international arbitrations, and human rights courts and treaty bodies. Other important developments considered in the relevant chapters are the UN's 2015 Sustainable Development Goals and the 2015 Paris Agreement on climate change. We have also taken the opportunity to rewrite substantially the chapters on non-state actors (expanding the human rights section), biodiversity and wildlife conservation (now merged into a single chapter), and international trade law (restructured and refocused).

[1] See in particular Chs 6 and 11 *infra*.

We are indebted to several colleagues for their generous contributions to bringing the text up to date: the specialist expertise of Navraj Ghaleigh, James Harrison, Lavanya Rajamani, and Annalisa Savaresi will be apparent in various chapters. Early in her PhD studies Justine Bendel delivered an invaluable literature survey that has informed many of our footnotes. We have tried to incorporate new legal material available up to December 2019 but it has also been possible to note some later developments.

As usual we must also thank Caroline Boyle and our OUP editors Lucy Read and Liana Green for their ever patient support and assistance in bringing this edition to a conclusion.

This is the first edition to which Patricia Birnie has not contributed. Sadly, she died on 7 February 2013. Her contribution to developing international environmental law makes her one of the more visionary international lawyers of our time, well ahead of many others in seeing what was needed. Pat led by example and was unstinting in her support and encouragement for those she saw as the next generation of scholars and practitioners. She gave freely of her expertise in support of various organizations dealing with the law of the sea and protection of the environment, including the Advisory Committee on Pollution of the Sea, whose legal committee she chaired, and the International Law Association British Branch, whose environment committee she also chaired. Her expertise on the law of whaling made her a frequent participant in meetings of the International Whaling Commission. But she was not starry-eyed about her role. She was a shrewd and hard-headed lawyer, who knew well that to do good requires professionalism as much as it requires idealism, that saying something should be law does not make it so, and that working with BP is as important as working with Greenpeace. Pat was a remarkable human being and this edition is dedicated to her memory.

Alan Boyle & Catherine Redgwell
Edinburgh & Oxford
December 2020

NEW TO THIS EDITION

The fourth edition has been completely revised and updated to include coverage of key legal developments and case law since 2009:

- Discussion on key cases before the International Court of Justice, the International Tribunal for the Law of the Sea, international arbitrations, human rights courts and treaty bodies.
- Analysis of the *Pulp Mills on the River Uruguay* case.
- Coverage of the UN's 2015 Sustainable Development Goals and the 2015 Paris Agreement on climate change.
- Substantial revisions to Chapter 5 on non-state actors to expand the coverage of human rights, and Chapter 13 on international trade law.
- Improvements to coverage of biodiversity and wildlife conservation issues, placing coverage of these topics in a single chapter (Chapter 11).

ACKNOWLEDGEMENTS

Grateful acknowledgement is made to the authors and publishers of copyright material which appears in this book, and in particular to the following for permission to reprint material from the sources indicated:

Duncker & Humblot GmbH: for extracts from Boyle, A. 'Progressive Development of International Environmental Law: Legislate or Litigate?' (2021). German Yearbook of International Law, 62 (1), pp. 305–334.

CONTENTS

CLR	*Commonwealth Law Reports*
CMLR	*Common Market Law Review*
CMS	*Convention on Migratory Species*
Cornell ILJ	*Cornell International Law Journal*
COP	*Conference of the Parties*
CRAMRA	*Convention on the Regulation of Antarctic Mineral Resource Activities*
CSD	*Commission on Sustainable Development*
CWILJ	*California Western International Law Journal*
CWRJIL	*Case Western Reserve Journal of International Law*
CYIL	*Canadian Yearbook of International Law*
Dal LJ	*Dalhousie Law Journal*
Den JILP	*Denver Journal of International Law and Politics*
DLR (AD)	*Dominion Law Reporter (Appellate Division)(Bangladesh)*
Duke LJ	*Duke Law Journal*
ECHR	*European Convention on Human Rights Reports*
ECtHR	*European Court of Human Rights*
ECJ	*European Court of Justice*
ECLAC	*Economic Commission for Latin America and the Caribbean*
ECOSOC	*Economic and Social Council of the United Nations*
ECR	*European Court Reports*
EEZ	*Exclusive Economic Zone*
EHRR	*European Human Rights Reports*
EIA	*Environmental Impact Assessment*
EJIL	*European Journal of International Law*
ELQ	*Environmental Law Quarterly*
ELR	*European Law Review*
EMEP	*Programme for Monitoring and Evaluation of Long-range Transmission of Air Pollutants in Europe*
Ency of Pub Int L	*Encyclopaedia of Public International Law*
ENMOD	*Environmental Modification Convention*
EPA	*Environmental Protection Agency*
EPL	*Environmental Policy and Law*
ESCAP	*Economic and Social Commission for Asia and the Pacific*
EUETS	*EU Emissions Trading System*
Eur Env LR	*European Environmental Law Review*
FAO	*Food & Agriculture Organisation*
FC	*Federal Courts (Canada)*
Fordham ELJ	*Fordham Environmental Law Journal*
GAOR	*General Assembly Official Records*
GATT	*General Agreement on Tariffs and Trade*
GEF	*Global Environment Facility*
Georgia LR	*Georgia Law Review*
Georgetown IELR	*Georgetown International Environmental Law Review*

LIST OF ABBREVIATIONS

AC	*Appeal Cases (House of Lords) (UK)*
ACHPR	*African Convention on Human and Peoples' Rights*
All ER	*All England Reports*
AFDI	*Annuaire Français de Droit International*
African HR LJ	*African Human Rights Law Journal*
Afr J Int'l & Comp L	*African Journal of International and Comparative Law*
AIR	*All India Reports*
AJIL	*American Journal of International Law*
ALJ	*Australian Law Journal*
ALJR	*Australian Law Journal Reports*
ALR	*Australian Law Reports*
AMRC	*Antarctic Meteorological Research Centre*
Ann Rev Ecol Syst	*Annual Review of Ecological Systems*
Ann Inst DDI	*Annuaire de l'Institut de Droit International*
Ann Suisse DDI	*Annuaire Suisse de Droit International*
AO	*Advisory Opinion*
AOSIS	*Alliance of Small Island States*
Asia Pacific JEL	*Asia Pacific Journal of Environmental Law*
AUJILP	*American University Journal of International Law and Politics*
AULR	*American University Law Review*
AYIL	*Australian Yearbook of International Law*
BAT	*Best Available Techniques*
BIT	*Bilateral Investment Treaty*
Boston CICLJ	*Boston College International and Comparative Law Journal*
Boston Coll Env Aff LR	*Boston College Environmental Affairs Law Review*
Brooklyn JIL	*Brooklyn Journal of International Law*
BYIL	*British Yearbook of International Law*
CBD	*Convention on Biological Diversity*
CCAMLR	*Convention for the Conservation of Antarctic Marine Living Resources*
CCLR	*Climate Change Law Review*
CDM	*Clean Development Mechanism*
CEDAW	*Convention on the Elimination of All Forms of Discrimination Against Women*
CITES	*Convention on International Trade in Endangered Species*
Colorado JIELP	*Colorado Journal of International Environmental Law and Policy*
Columbia JTL	*Columbia Journal of Transnational Law*
Columbia JEL	*Columbia Journal of Environmental Law*
CLP	*Current Legal Problems*

GESAMP	*Group of Experts on the Scientific Aspects of Marine Environmental Protection*
GHG	*Greenhouse Gas*
GYIL	*German Yearbook of International Law*
Hague YIL	*Hague Yearbook of International Law*
Harv ELR	*Harvard Environmental Law Review*
Harv ILJ	*Harvard International Law Journal*
Harv LR	*Harvard Law Review*
HRLJ	*Human Rights Law Journal*
HRR	*Human Rights Reports*
HumEcol Risk Assess	*Human and Ecological Risk Assessment*
IACHR	*Inter-American Convention on Human Rights*
IACtHR	*Inter-American Court of Human Rights*
IACommHR	*Inter-American Commission on Human Rights*
IAEA	*International Atomic Energy Agency*
ICC	*International Criminal Court*
ICCAT	*International Commission for the Conservation of Atlantic Tunas*
ICCPR	*International Covenant on Civil and Political Rights*
ICES	*International Conference on Environmental Science*
ICESCR	*International Covenant on Economic, Social and Cultural Rights*
ICJ	*International Court of Justice*
ICLQ	*International and Comparative Law Quarterly*
ICRC	*International Committee of the Red Cross*
ICRP	*International Commission on Radiological Protection*
ICRW	*International Convention for the Regulation of Whaling*
ICSID	*International Centre for the Settlement of Investment Disputes*
ICSU	*International Council for Science*
Idaho LR	*Idaho Law Review*
IFAW	*International Fund for Animal Welfare*
IFC	*International Finance Corporation*
IJC	*International Joint Commission*
IJECL	*International Journal of Estuarine and Coastal Law*
IJMCL	*International Journal of Marine and Coastal Law*
ILA	*International Law Association*
ILC	*International Law Commission*
ILM	*International Legal Materials*
ILR	*International Law Reports*
IMO	*International Maritime Organisation*
Ind JIL	*Indian Journal of International Law*
Int Affairs	*International Affairs*
Int Env L Reps	*International Environmental Law Reports*

Int Org	*International Organisation*
IOC	*Intergovernmental Oceanographic Commission*
IPBES	*Intergovernmental Science-Policy Platform on Biodiversity and Ecosystem Services*
IPCC	*Intergovernmental Panel on Climate Change*
ISA	*International Seabed Authority*
Ital YIL	*Italian Yearbook of International Law*
ITLOS	*International Tribunal for the Law of the Sea*
ITPGR	*International Treaty on Plant Genetic Resources for Food and Agriculture*
ITTA	*International Tropical Timber Agreement*
ITTO	*International Tropical Timber Organisation*
IUCN	*International Union for Conservation of Nature*
IWC	*International Whaling Commission*
Jap Ann IL	*Japanese Annual of International Law*
JEL	*Journal of Environmental Law*
JHRE	*Journal of Human Rights and the Environment*
JI	*Joint Implementation*
JLS	*Journal of Law and Society*
JMLC	*Journal of Maritime Law and Commerce*
JIDS	*Journal of International Dispute Settlement*
JIEL	*Journal of International Economic Law*
JIML	*Journal of International Maritime Law*
JIWLP	*Journal of International Wildlife Law and Policy*
J Transnatl L & Pol	*Journal of Transnational Law and Policy*
JWT	*Journal of World Trade Law*
JYIL	*Japanese Yearbook of International law*
LGERA	*Local Government and Environment Reports of Australia*
LNTS	*League of Nations Treaty Series*
Loyola ICLJ	*Loyola University International and Comparative Law Journal*
LOSB	*Law of the Sea Bulletin*
LRTAP	*Long-range Transboundary Air Pollution*
LULUCF	*Land Use. Land Use Change and Forestry*
McGill LR	*McGill Law Review*
Mar Pol	*Marine Policy*
MARPOL	*International Convention for the Prevention of Pollution from Ships*
MEA	*Multilateral Environmental Agreement*
MEPC	*Marine Environment Protection Committee*
MJGT	*Minnesota Journal of Global Trade*
MLR	*Modern Law Review*
MOP	*Meeting of the Parties*
MPA	*Marine Protected Area*

MSC	*Maritime Safety Committee*
NAAEC	*North American Agreement on Environmental Cooperation*
NDCs	*Nationally Determined Contributions*
NEA	*Nuclear Energy Agency*
NGO	*Non-Governmental Organisation*
NIEO	*New International Economic Order*
NILR	*Netherlands International Law Review*
NLB	*Nuclear Law Bulletin*
NPT	*Non-Proliferation Treaty*
NRJ	*Natural Resources Journal*
NYIL	*Netherlands Yearbook of International Law*
NYJILP	*New York Journal of International Law and Policy*
NYUEnvLJ	*New York University Environmental Law Journal*
NZLR	*New Zealand Law Reports*
OAS	*Organisation of American States*
O&C Man	*Ocean and Coastal Management*
Ocean YB	*Ocean Yearbook*
ODIL	*Ocean Development and International Law*
OGTLR	*Oil and Gas Taxation Law Review*
OHCHR	*Office of the High Commissioner for Human Rights*
OJ	*Official Journal (of the European Union)*
Oregon LR	*Oregon Law Review*
OHLJ	*Osgoode Hall Law Journal*
OSPAR	*Convention for the Protection of the Marine Environment of the North-East Atlantic*
Otago LJ	*University of Otago Law Journal*
PCA	*Permanent Court of Arbitration*
PCIJ	*Permanent Court of International Justice*
PIC	*Prior Informed Consent*
POPs	*Persistent Organic Pollutants*
Proc ASIL	*Proceedings of the American Society of International Law*
RBDI	*Revue Belge de Droit International*
RECIEL	*Review of European Community and International Environmental Law*
REDE	*Revue Européen du Droit de l'Environnement*
Rev jurid de l'env	*Revue juridique de l'environment*
RGDIP	*Revue General de Droit International Public*
RIAA	*Reports of International Arbitration Awards*
SALJ	*South African Law Journal*
Scal LR	*Southern California Law Review*
SCAR	*Scientific Committee on Antarctic Research*
SCC	*Supreme Court Cases (India)*

S Ct	*Supreme Court (US)*
San Diego LR	*San Diego Law Review*
SDGs	*Sustainable Development Goals*
SERAC	*Social and Economic Rights Action Centre*
SOLAS	*International Convention for the Safety of Life at Sea*
Stanford JIL	*Stanford Journal of International Law*
Stanford ELJ	*Stanford Environmental Law Journal*
Sydney LR	*Sydney Law Review*
Texas ILJ	*Texas International Law Journal*
Tulane ELJ	*Tulane Environmental Journal*
UBCLR	*University of British Columbia Law Review*
UCLA J Envtl L & Pol'y	*University of California at Los Angeles Journal of Environmental Law and Policy*
UKSC	*United Kingdom Supreme Court*
UNCC	*United Nations Compensation Commission*
UNCED	*United Nations Conference on Environment and Development*
UNCESCR	*United Nations Committee on Economic, Social and Cultural Rights*
UNCHE	*United Nations Conference on the Human Environment*
UNCITRAL	*United Nations Commission on International Trade Law*
UNCLOS	*United Nations Convention on the Law of the Sea*
UNCOPUOS	*United Nations Committee on the Peaceful Uses of Outer Space*
UNCSD	*United Nations Conference on Sustainable Development*
UNCTAD	*United Nations Conference on Trade and Development*
UNDP	*United Nations Development Programme*
UN Doc	*United Nations Document*
UNEA	*United Nations Environment Assembly*
UNECE	*United Nations Economic Commission for Europe*
UNESCO	*United Nations Educational, Scientific and Cultural Organisation*
UNEP	*United Nations Environment Programme*
UNFCCC	*United Nations Framework Convention on Climate Change*
UNGA	*United Nations General Assembly*
UNGAOR	*United Nations General Assembly Official Records*
UNHRC	*United Nations Human Rights Commission*
UNSC	*United Nations Security Council*
U Penn LR	*University of Pennsylvania Law Review*
UPOV	*International Union for the Protection of New Variants of Plants*
US	*United States Reports*
UTLJ	*University of Toronto Law Journal*

Vand JTL	*Vanderbilt Journal of Transnational Law*
VCLT	*Vienna Convention on the Law of Treaties*
VELJ	*Virginia Environmental Law Journal*
VJIL	*Virginia Journal of International Law*
VUWLR	*Victoria University of Wellington Law Review*
Wash & Lee LR	*Washington and Lee Law Review*
WCED	*World Commission on Environment and Development*
WEO	*World Energy Outlook*
WHO	*World Health Organisation*
WIPO	*World Intellectual Property Organisation*
Wis ILJ	*Wisconsin International Law Journal*
WLR	*Weekly Law Reports (England)*
Wm & Mary Envtl L & Pol'y Rev	*William and Mary Environmental Law & Policy Review*
Yale LJ	*Yale Law Journal*
Ybk of the AAA	*Association of Attenders and Alumni of the Hague Academy of International Law Year Book*
YEL	*Yearbook of European Law*
YbIEL	*Yearbook of International Environmental Law*
ZAÖRV	*Zeitschrift für Ausländisches und Öffentliches Recht und Völkerrecht*

TABLE OF CASES

TABLE OF MAJOR TREATIES AND OTHER INSTRUMENTS

Only those treaties and other instruments which are cited frequently in the text or are of particular significance are listed here. References to other treaties will be found in the footnotes. 'Not in force' indicates that the treaty had not come into force by 31 December 2019. Most of the major agreements can be found in Birnie and Boyle, *Basic Documents on International Law and the Environment* (Oxford, 1995) (hereafter '*B&B Docs*'). Almost all of these treaties and other instruments are easily accessible on the internet via a Google search.

1

INTERNATIONAL LAW AND THE ENVIRONMENT

'The Court also recognizes that the environment is not an abstraction but represents the living space, the quality of life and the very health of human beings, including generations unborn.'[1]

1 INTRODUCTION

The development of modern international environmental law, starting essentially in the 1960s, has been one of the more remarkable exercises in contemporary international law-making. Over twenty years ago Dupuy drew attention to 'la grande fertilité de cette branche du droit international,'[2] but more recent scholarship continues to emphasize the normative and institutional transformation that has taken place since the Rio UN Conference on Environment and Development in 1992('UNCED') The law which has emerged from this creative process is increasingly sophisticated, though unsurprisingly it has significant weaknesses, as we will see. It might of course be possible to argue that other approaches to global environmental management would have been more efficacious than the focus on international law-making. But to say that economic or political models have as much or more to contribute to the solution of global environmental problems is merely to observe that protecting the environment is not exclusively, or even predominantly, a problem for lawyers. It would be naïve to expect international law to remedy problems of the scale, seriousness, and complexity the global environment now faces without an underlying political, scientific, and economic commitment on the part of states, and a corresponding response in national legal and political systems. Whether that commitment and response are currently more than superficial or symbolic remains an open question. Certainly, while there

[1] *Nuclear Weapons Advisory Opinion*, ICJ Reports (1996) 241–2, para 29.

[2] Dupuy, 101 *RGDIP* (1997) 873, at 900 Kerbrat etc. infra, n.57.

are success stories, it is far from clear that humanity is grappling effectively with global environmental problems that are entirely of its own making.[3]

It is not the purpose of this book to explore the place of international environmental law within this larger context, nor do we attempt to answer the question whether the law we now have serves the needs of environmental justice or fairness among nations, generations, or peoples.[4] We do attempt to show, inter alia, how international law has developed a framework for cooperation on environmental matters between developed and developing states; for the adoption of measures aimed at control of pollution and conservation and sustainable use of natural resources; for the resolution of international environmental disputes; for the promotion of greater transparency and public participation in environmental decision-making; and for the adoption and harmonization of national environmental law. These developments and others covered in subsequent chapters have created the system of international environmental law and regulation that we examine in this book.

We have sought to provide only an overview of international environmental law as a whole, written from the perspective of generalist international lawyers; the subject is now so large that it is not possible to cover every topic or aspect in detail, but our choice of topics is intended to illustrate the major techniques and approaches. For those who require more detail there is a burgeoning literature on most of the specialist topics, including climate change, the marine environment, conservation of wildlife and biological diversity, and the environmental aspects of human rights and World Trade Organization ('WTO') law. We can only hope to reflect some of that literature in the following chapters.

1(1) WHAT IS INTERNATIONAL ENVIRONMENTAL LAW?

A number of preliminary problems arise in any attempt to identify 'international environmental law'.[5] Although international courts make use of the term,[6] some scholars initially avoided doing so,[7] arguing that there is no distinct body of 'international environmental law' with its own sources and methods of law-making deriving from principles peculiar or exclusive to environmental concerns. Rather, they stressed the application of rules and principles of general international law to environmental problems.[8]

[3] See *infra*, section 1(6).

[4] See Ebbesson and Okowa (eds), *Environmental Law and Justice in Context* (Cambridge, 2009); French (ed) *Global Justice and Sustainable Development* (Leiden, 2010); Michelot (ed) *Equité et environnement: Quel(s) modèle(s) de justice environnementale?* (Brussels, 2012), and generally Franck, *Fairness in International Law and Institutions* (Oxford, 1998); Ratner, *The Thin Justice of International Law* (Oxford, 2015).

[5] See generally Bodansky, *The Art and Craft of International Environmental Law* (London, 2010) Ch 1.

[6] See e.g *Gabčíkovo-Nagymaros Case*, ICJ Reports (1997) 7, paras 92, 104, 141; *Iron Rhine Arbitration*, PCA (2005) paras 58, 222–3.

[7] E.g. Brownlie, *Principles of Public International Law* (6th edn, Oxford, 2005) Ch XII, but compare now Crawford's 8th edition of *Brownlie's Principles of Public International Law* (8th edn, Oxford, 2012), Ch 15 of which does refer to 'international environmental law.'

[8] See Brownlie, ibid, and Dupuy, 101 *RGDIP* (1997) 873, 899.

Judicial decisions and later chapters in this book will indeed show that international environmental law is part of international law as a whole,[9] not a separate, self-contained discipline.[10] The problem with over-emphasizing the role of general international law, however, is that 'the traditional legal order of the environment is essentially a *laissez-faire* system. . . . Such limitations on freedom of action as do exist have emerged in an *ad hoc* fashion and have been formulated from perspectives other than the specifically environmental.'[11] This traditional perspective has not been true for some time: as environmental problems have risen in importance it has been necessary to develop a large body of law more specifically aimed at protection of the environment. A study of contemporary international environmental law thus requires us to consider this evolving body of specifically environmental law, as well as the application of general international law to environmental problems, and their interaction. Moreover, international environmental law also includes relevant aspects of private international law, and in some instances has borrowed from national law.

In this work the expression 'international environmental law' is used as a convenient way to encompass the entire corpus of international law, public and private, relevant to environmental problems. It has become common practice to refer to international environmental law in this way.[12] The term 'global environmental law' is also used in some of the literature, but it differs from international environmental law in taking a broader, more pluralistic approach to global environmental problems. Global environmental law is thus a 'field of law that is international, national and transnational in character all at once' and comprises 'the set of legal principles developed by national, international and transnational environmental regulatory systems to protect the environment and manage natural resources' with a view to 'increasingly affecting private behaviour.'[13] Since international environmental law also ultimately seeks to affect private behaviour, there is an overlap between these two schools of thought; what global environmental law adds is a stronger focus on comparative environmental law.

'International environmental law' is of course different from international human rights law, the law of the sea, natural resources law or international economic law, *inter*

[9] See in particular Chs 3, 4 and 5.

[10] But compare Crawford and Koskenniemi (eds), *The Cambridge Companion to International Law* (Cambridge, 2012) 12, who in their introduction refer to Charlesworth's chapter for the remarkable proposition that international environmental law is 'more or less self-contained, even self-sufficient', although Charlesworth in fact makes no such claim.

[11] Schneider, *World Public Order of the Environment: Towards an Ecological Law and Organization* (Toronto, 1979) 30. See also Fitzmaurice, 25 *NYIL* (1994) 181; Chinkin, in Jewell and Steele (eds), *Law in Environmental Decision-making* (Oxford, 1998) Ch 8; Bodansky, Brunnée and Hey (eds), *The Oxford Handbook of International Environmental Law* (Oxford, 2007) Ch 1.

[12] See e.g. Kiss and Shelton, *International Environmental Law* (3rd edn, New York, 2004); Louka, *International Environmental Law* (Cambridge, 2006); Beyerlin and Marauhn, *International Environmental Law* (2nd edn, Oxford, 2016); Sands and Peel, *Principles of International Environmental Law* (4th edn, Cambridge, 2018); Dupuy and Viñuales, *International Environmental Law* (2nd edn, Cambridge, 2018); Beurier, *Droit international de l'environnement* (Paris, 2017).

[13] Morgera, 23 *EJIL* (2012) 744, citing Yang and Percival, 36 *Ecol LQ* (2009) 615, and see generally Walker, *Intimations of Global Law* (Cambridge, 2015).

alia, but there are significant overlaps and interactions with these categories, and the categorization is in some cases a matter only of choice and perspective. Our chapters on the protection of the marine environment, or the conservation of marine living resources, would not be out of place in books on the law of the sea.[14] Our discussion of environmental rights in Chapter 5 draws heavily on international human rights law, but books on that subject more rarely address its environmental implications. The interplay of international trade law and international environmental law is considered in Chapter 13 but many of the issues covered in other chapters could equally well be addressed from the perspective of international economic law, including climate change and sustainable use of natural resources. Much of contemporary international environmental law deals with sustainable use of fresh water, forests, biological diversity, fisheries, or endangered species. This is natural resources law—or perhaps elements of the law of sustainable development—from another perspective. Moreover, even within otherwise discrete bodies of law, specifically environmental norms or applications can also be found. Part XII of the 1982 UN Convention on the Law of the Sea ('UNCLOS') deals with 'Protection and Preservation of the Marine Environment' and is one of the most important environmental agreements currently in existence. The Preamble to the 1994 Agreement Establishing the World Trade Organization refers to 'sustainable development', and to that extent encompasses environmental concerns, as do the exceptions listed in Article XX of the General Agreement on Tariffs and Trade ('GATT').[15] Human rights law has an increasingly important environmental dimension.[16] There is no magic in any of these categorizations.

What matters, as Chapter 3 and later chapters try to make clear, is that the resolution of international environmental problems, however categorized, entails the application of international law as a whole, in an integrated manner. In the real world, it is not possible to address many of the legal issues posed by international environmental problems without also considering the law of treaties, state responsibility, jurisdiction, the law of the sea, natural resources law, dispute settlement, private international law, human rights law, international criminal law, and international trade law, to name only the most obvious. All of these topics have environmental dimensions or affect the resolution of environmental problems and disputes. Bearing that in mind, it is worth re-emphasizing that 'international environmental law' is nothing more, or less, than the application of public and private international law to environmental problems.[17]

A more difficult issue is the distinction, if there is one, between international law relating to the environment, and international law relating to sustainable development. The 1992 Rio Declaration on Environment and Development ('Rio Declaration') refers to the 'further development of international law in the field of sustainable

[14] See e.g. O'Connell, *The International Law of the Sea* (Oxford, 1984) vol ii, Chs 14 and 25; Churchill and Lowe, *The Law of the Sea* (3rd edn, Manchester, 1999) Chs 14 and 15; Rothwell and Stephens, *The International Law of the Sea* (2nd edn, Oxford, 2016) Ch 15; Tanaka, The *International Law of the Sea* (3rd edn, Cambridge, 2019) Ch 8.

[15] See *infra*, Ch 13.

[16] *Infra*, Ch 5.

[17] Dupuy, 101 *RGDIP* (1997) 873, at 899.

development',[18] and it is sometimes suggested that this has subsumed international environmental law. A more nuanced approach was endorsed by the UN Environment Programme ('UNEP'), whose 1997 Nairobi Declaration refers to 'international environmental law aiming at sustainable development.' [19] In subsequent chapters of this book a great deal of attention will be paid to the concept of sustainable development, whose importance for the resolution of environmental problems is undisputed. Yet, although much of international environmental law could be regarded as law 'in the field of' or 'aiming at' sustainable development,[20] there remain important differences. International environmental law encompasses both more and less than the law of sustainable development. There is a major overlap in rules, principles, techniques and institutions, but the goals are by no means identical. Most obviously, sustainable development is as much about economic and social development as about environmental protection;[21] while these goals have to be integrated, they remain distinct. Moreover, not all environmental questions necessarily involve sustainable development, or vice versa. We may wish to preserve Antarctica, or endangered species such as the great whales or the giant panda, for reasons that have little or nothing to do with sustainable development, or put another way, we may wish to preserve them *from* sustainable development. In this sense, international law may in some cases reflect environmental concerns that override or trump development, however sustainable. At the same time, developmental priorities may in other cases override environmental concerns without thereby ceasing to be 'sustainable development'. Of course, much depends on what is meant by sustainable development.[22] Once again the question is not whether there is law in the field of sustainable development, but the perspective from which one looks at the existing law. Our principal concern in this book is to show how international law deals with problems which can plausibly be seen as environmental, while accepting that many of these are also problems of sustainable development. To that extent, this is indeed also a book about international environmental law 'aiming at sustainable development.'

1(2) WHAT IS MEANT BY 'THE ENVIRONMENT'?

Defining the term 'environment' presents further difficulties. None of the major treaties, declarations, codes of conduct, guidelines, etc. referred to throughout this work attempts directly to do so. No doubt this is because it is difficult both to identify and to restrict the scope of such an amorphous term, which could be used to encompass anything from the whole biosphere to the habitat of the smallest creature or organism. Dictionary definitions range from 'something that environs' to 'the whole

[18] Principle 27. See *infra*, Ch 3, section 2.

[19] Adopted by UNEP Governing Council decision 19/1 (1997). See *infra*, Ch 2, section 3 (3).

[20] See Sands, 65 *BYIL* (1994) 303.

[21] See discussion of the UN Sustainable Development Goals, *infra*, Ch 2, section 2(5).

[22] See *infra*, Ch 2, section 2.

complex of climatic, edaphic and biotic factors that act upon an organism or an ecological community and ultimately determine its form or survival; the aggregate of social or cultural conditions that influence the life of an individual or a community'[23] or, more simply, 'The surroundings or conditions in which a person, animal, or plant lives or operates.'[24] The Declaration of the 1972 Stockholm Conference on the Human Environment ('UNCHE') merely referred obliquely to man's environment, adding that 'both aspects of man's environment, the natural and the man-made, are essential for his well-being and enjoyment of basic human rights'.[25] The World Commission on Environment and Development ('WCED') relied on an even more succinct approach; it remarked that 'the environment is where we all live'.[26] The 1992 Rio Declaration refers at many points to environmental needs, environmental protection, environmental degradation and so on, but nowhere identifies what these include. it eschews the term entirely in Principle 1, declaring instead that human beings 'are entitled to a healthy and productive life *in harmony with nature*.' Most attempts at description emphasize the comprehensive character of the term and its 'combination of elements whose complex inter-relationships make up the settings, the surroundings and the conditions of life of the individual and of society as they are and as they are felt'.[27] Many conventions avoid the problem, however, no doubt because, as Caldwell remarks 'it is a term that everyone understands and no one is able to define'.[28]

Some understanding of what 'the environment' may encompass can be discerned from other treaty provisions, however. Those agreements which define 'environmental effects', 'environmental impacts' or 'environmental damage' typically include harm to flora, fauna, biodiversity, soil, water, air, landscape, cultural heritage, and any interaction between these factors.[29] Others take an approach that additionally introduces the equally problematic concept of ecosystem protection, albeit defined differently for the purposes of each treaty.[30] Although conventions limited to the 'marine

[23] Webster's *New World Dictionary* (3rd edn, Cleveland, 1988) 454.

[24] *Concise Oxford Dictionary* (11th edn, Oxford, 2006).

[25] Stockholm Declaration, Preamble, para 1, in UN, *Rept. of UN Conference on the Human Environment*, A/CONF. 48/14/Rev. 1 (New York, 1972) 3, and see *infra*, Ch 2, section 2(1).

[26] WCED, *Our Common Future* (Oxford, 1987) xi. The WCED's Legal Expert Group on Environmental Law did not define the terms; see Munro and Lammers, *Environmental Protection and Sustainable Development* (Dordrecht, 1986).

[27] See Gilpin *EIA for the 21st century*, (CUP, 1995), Ch 1 and compare also Council Regulation (EEC) No 1872/84 on Action by the Community Relating to the Environment, OJL 176 (1984) 1.

[28] Caldwell, *International Environmental Policy and Law* (1st edn, Durham, NC, 1980) 170.

[29] 1992 Convention on the Transboundary Effects of Industrial Accidents, Article 1 (c); 1992 Convention on the Protection and Use of Transboundary Watercourses and International Lakes, Article 1 (2); 1993 Convention on Civil Liability for Damage Resulting from Activities Dangerous to the Environment, Article 2 (7) and (10); *Border Activities Case (Compensation)*, ICJ Reports (2018), esp. sep op Judge Donoghue. See also Payne, in Stahn, Iverson and Easterday (eds), *Environmental Protection and Transitions from Conflict to Peace: Clarifying Norms, Principles, and Practices* (Oxford, 2017) 40–70, and *infra*, Ch 3, section 9.

[30] See e.g. 1982 UNCLOS, Article 194(5); 1992 CBD, Article 8; 1997 UN Watercourses Convention, Articles 20 & 22, and *infra*, Chs 9, 10 and 11.

environment' avoid defining that term,[31] it seems to have been generally understood at the third UN Conference on the Law of the Sea that it included the atmosphere and marine life, as well as 'rare and fragile ecosystems'.[32] Likewise, none of the agreements forming the Antarctic Treaty System defines the Antarctic environment, but all the relevant ones include 'dependent and associated ecosystems' within that term. Thus the 1980 Convention on the Conservation of Antarctic Marine Living Resources applies to the Antarctic marine ecosystem, defined for this purpose as 'the complex of relationships of marine living resources with each other and with their physical environment',[33] while the 1988 Convention on the Regulation of Antarctic Mineral Resource Activities defined damage to the Antarctic environment or dependent or associated ecosystems as 'any impact on the living or non-living components of that environment or those ecosystems, including harm to atmospheric, marine or terrestrial life . . . '.[34] The 1991 Protocol on Environmental Protection to the Antarctic Treaty also adds 'the intrinsic value of Antarctica, including its wilderness and aesthetic values'.[35] Probably the broadest approach is found in the 1992 UN Framework Convention on Climate Change ('UNFCCC'), which defines adverse effects on the environment to include 'changes in the physical environment or biota, resulting from climate change, which have significant deleterious effects on the composition, resilience and productivity of natural and managed ecosystems, or on the operation of natural and managed ecosystems or on the operation of socio-economic systems or human health and welfare'.[36] While there are obvious patterns discernible from these treaty provisions, there is a danger of reading too much into what are intended only as definitions for the different purposes of each treaty.[37]

Another indication of what the environment encompasses at an international level is given by the broad range of issues now addressed by international environmental law, including conservation and sustainable use of natural resources and biodiversity; conservation of endangered and migratory species; prevention of deforestation and desertification; preservation of Antarctica and areas of outstanding natural heritage; protection of oceans, international watercourses, the atmosphere, climate and ozone layer from the effects of pollution; safeguarding human health and the quality of life.[38] Inevitably, any definition of 'the environment' will have the Alice-in-Wonderland quality of meaning what we want it to mean. This should be borne in mind in later chapters.

[31] As in the 1982 UNCLOS although Malta had proposed that the term 'comprises the surface of the sea, the air space above, the water column and the sea-bed beyond the high-tide mark including the bio-systems therein or dependent thereon'. See Nordquist (ed), *The United Nations Convention on the Law of the Sea: A Commentary* (Dordrecht, 1991) iv, 42–3.

[32] *Ibid*, and see Article 194 (5) and *infra*, Ch 9, section 2.

[33] Article 1.

[34] This Convention was replaced by the 1991 Protocol on Environmental Protection to the Antarctic Treaty without entering into force.

[35] Article 3(1).

[36] Article 1(1). This is an expanded version of a very similar definition used in Article 1 (2) of the 1985 Vienna Convention for the Protection of the Ozone Layer: see *infra*, Ch 6.

[37] See *infra*, Ch 3, section 9.

[38] See *Iron Rhine Arbitration*, PCA (2005) para 58.

1(3) WHY PROTECT THE ENVIRONMENT?

Quite apart from the obvious difficulty posed by the previous section, this is too large a question to be answered simply. Much depends on the context. The ethical, aesthetic, cultural or symbolic reasons for saving the great whales, world heritage sites, or Antarctica from exploitation are quite different from the economic and health related objectives behind pollution regulation. However, almost all justifications for international environmental protection are predominantly or in some sense anthropocentric.[39] This is true especially of the 1972 Stockholm Declaration on the Human Environment ('Stockholm Declaration'), which focused explicitly on protecting 'the human environment', and proclaimed:

> Man is both creature and moulder of his environment, which gives him physical sustenance and affords him the opportunity for intellectual, spiritual, moral and social growth. . .[40]

Likewise, the 1992 Rio Declaration asserts that 'Human beings are at the centre of concerns for sustainable development.'[41]

As we shall see in Chapter 5, the emergence of an environmental dimension in human rights law has a strongly anthropocentric motivation, most notable in attempts to develop a new human right to a healthy or sustainable environment. Some advocates assert that such a right is indispensable for the enjoyment of other human rights and freedoms,[42] but they usually fail to explain how competing environmental, economic and social priorities can be accommodated in what necessarily becomes a judgment about what we value most. A more explicit relativism characterizes most environmental measures aimed at protecting human health or safety, including those in which responsibility for the welfare of future generations is a prominent feature, such as the conventions on climate change or nuclear safety.[43] In this context the principal question is the level of socially acceptable risk, but the underlying objective is nevertheless anthropocentric. Economic justifications are also strongly anthropocentric, focusing partly on efficiency considerations and the sustainable use of resources, partly on the perceived desirability of 'internalizing' the true economic costs of pollution damage and control, and partly on the need to minimize the competitive disadvantages of failure to harmonize national environmental policy and law.[44]

Nature, ecosystems, natural resources, wildlife, and so on, are thus of concern to international law-makers primarily for their value to humanity. This need not be limited to economic value, although most of the early wildlife treaties were so limited but, as in the 1972 Convention Concerning the Protection of the World Cultural and

[39] See generally Gillespie, *International Environmental Law, Policy and Ethics* (Oxford, 1997); Eckersley, *Environmentalism and Political Theory* (London, 1992); Redgwell, in Boyle and Anderson (eds), *Human Rights Approaches to Environmental Protection* (Oxford, 1996) Ch 4.

[40] Declaration, Preamble, para 1.

[41] See *infra*, Ch 2, section 2.

[42] E.g. Pathak, in Brown Weiss (ed), *Environmental Change and International Law* (Tokyo, 1993) Ch 8.

[43] See *infra*, Chs 6 and 7.

[44] See e.g. Jacobs, *The Green Economy* (London, 1991); Gillespie, *International Environmental Law, Policy and Ethics*, Ch 3.

Natural Heritage, can include aesthetic, amenity or cultural value, or be motivated by religious or moral concerns.[45] The Preamble to the 1992 Convention on Biological Diversity ('CBD') evinces the complex mixture of objectives which characterizes much of contemporary international environmental law:

> *Conscious* of the intrinsic value of biological diversity and of the ecological, social, economic, scientific, educational, cultural, recreational and aesthetic value of biological diversity and its components,
>
> *Conscious also* of the importance of biological diversity for evolution and for maintaining life-sustaining systems of the biosphere....

The last part of this extract illustrates what can be referred to as a 'holistic' approach to environmental protection, a recognition of the interdependence of humanity and the entire natural world, expressed most characteristically in the notion of the world as a 'biosphere', and implicit in both the 1992 CBD and the Convention on Climate Change.

But other, potentially non-anthropocentric, justifications are apparent here, in references to the 'intrinsic value' of biodiversity, or of Antarctica and other wilderness areas. Intrinsic value and the 'moral considerability' of animals also provide arguments for international attempts to regulate cruelty and protect endangered species.[46] Such ecological or ecocentric perspectives can lead to a different vision of respect for the natural world than those which typify most of international environmental law. Apart from their potential for incoherence, claims based on the intrinsic value of nature, at their most extreme, pose the question 'how does humanity fit within such an ethical view of the world'? [47] It is clear from the opening paragraph of the Rio Declaration quoted above that the international community has not truly embraced this alternative vision of the purposes of environmental protection, but has at most sought to ensure that ecological concerns are accommodated and given weight within a broader process of balancing which remains essentially anthropocentric.[48]

1(4) THE ENVIRONMENT AS A PROBLEM OF INTERNATIONAL CONCERN

International law addresses environmental issues at several levels. Transboundary problems, such as air or water pollution, or conservation of migratory animals, provide examples of the earliest and most developed use of international law to regulate environmental concerns. In many cases these problems are regional in extent, and are regulated by regional organizations and regional agreements, particularly in Europe and North America, or in regional seas such as the Mediterranean or Caribbean.[49] Some environmental problems, for example climate change or depletion of the stratospheric ozone layer, are inherently global in character and affect all

[45] Gillespie, *op.cit,* Chs 4 and 5. See also *infra*, Ch 11, section 3(2). [46] Gillespie, *Id*, Ch 9.
[47] *Id*, at 173. [48] See *infra*, Ch 2, section 2. [49] *Infra*, Chs 6, 8, 10.

states, not necessarily equally, but at least to the extent that impacts are global and global solutions are required. The 1992 Climate Change Convention, the 1985 Vienna Convention on the Protection of the Ozone Layer ('Ozone Convention'), the 1992 CBD, and their respective protocols, typify the emergence of such global regulatory regimes.[50] Increasingly, international law addresses national or domestic environmental problems, whether through international human rights law, conservation of biological diversity, protection of natural heritage areas, or promotion of sustainable development. There is thus no single sense in which an environmental issue can be described as 'international': it could be global, regional, transboundary, domestic, or a combination of all or any of these. All that can be said for the purposes of this book is that, potentially, international environmental law covers any environmental question governed by international law.

What must be appreciated, however, is that the law governing these rather different contexts is likely itself to differ, both in the content of any applicable rules, and in the form they take. Some of the law relating to transboundary problems takes the form of customary or general international law, while very little customary law applies to global environmental concerns, where regulatory treaties instead provide most of the substantive content. Such differences also affect the processes by which disputes are settled or compliance enforced. Transboundary disputes are more likely to be suitable for adjudication or arbitration than global or regional environmental problems. These differences are more fully explored in Chapters 3 and 4.

1(5) THE ROLE OF LAW IN INTERNATIONAL ENVIRONMENTAL PROTECTION

The role played by international law in protecting the environment is not fundamentally different from, or any less varied than, domestic environmental law. Nor, in many cases, is it necessarily any less sophisticated; indeed rather the reverse is true in the case of some countries.

First, in its constitutional role international law provides mechanisms and procedures for negotiating the necessary rules and standards, settling disputes, and supervising implementation and compliance with treaties and customary rules. In this context it facilitates and promotes cooperation between states, international organizations, and non-governmental organizations, and constitutes the processes of international environmental governance, international law-making and regulation and, in a few cases, of international trusteeship.[51] Although international environmental law has historically been focused mainly on inter-state relations and the rights and duties of states, the human rights dimensions have become increasingly prominent.[52] NGO participation has also given non-state actors significant influence in environmental treaty negotiations and the environmental agenda of international bodies. In a very real sense modern international environmental law is no longer made by states alone.

[50] *Infra*, Chs 6 and 11. [51] See *infra*, Ch 2. [52] See *infra*, Ch 5.

Secondly, like national environmental law, much of international environmental law is concerned with regulating environmental problems, providing common standards and practices for prevention or mitigation of pollution, or promoting conservation and sustainable use of natural resources and biodiversity. This requires a flexible rule-making process which allows for easy and regular amendment in the light of technological developments and advances in scientific and other knowledge. Most of this regulatory system is based on multilateral treaties, but softlaw instruments, including declarations, codes of conduct, guidelines and recommendations, are also employed.[53] Implementation of these international regulatory regimes depends ultimately on the adoption of the necessary national policies and laws.

Thus, a third purpose or effect of some multilateral environmental agreements is to harmonize national laws, either globally or regionally. Treaties on civil liability for nuclear accidents or oil pollution damage at sea afford the best examples of such harmonization: in effect national law will largely replicate the provisions of these treaties and will essentially be the same in each state party. Here the objective is to facilitate access to justice for litigants who have suffered loss in large-scale international accidents. Regulatory treaties have different objectives in mind when seeking to harmonize national law: the economic impact of implementing environmental protection measures may be such that states are willing to participate in such treaties once they can be assured that the same regulatory standards will prevail in competitor states. This will not always be possible, and as we shall see, developing states often insist on differential standards[54].

Finally, reinstatement of the environment or compensation for environmental damage is a more limited but still important function of the international legal system. It is more limited because only those who suffer damage can secure such redress, whether they are states relying on the international law of state responsibility,[55] or individuals relying in various ways on their right to bring transboundary actions in national law,[56] and because not all environmental damage is necessarily capable of reinstatement or has an economically assessable value. We explore these questions in Chapter 5.

1(6) DOES INTERNATIONAL LAW ADEQUATELY PROTECT THE ENVIRONMENT?

This is an important question to which there is no easy or single answer. International environmental law has evolved at a time when the heterogeneity of the international community is greater than ever before and when, simultaneously, the economic challenges and development needs and aspirations of developing states have become more prominent. Given this context, the progress made in creating a body of international

[53] See *infra*, section 2(1). [54] See *infra*, section 2, and Ch 3. [55] See *infra*, Ch 4.
[56] See *infra*, Ch 5.

law with an environmental focus is a remarkable achievement.[57] At the same time, although we have far more law and policy than we had a quarter of a century ago, the global environment is in a much worse state now than it was then, whether we look at the oceans, or climate change, or biodiversity and ecosystems.[58]

In part this failure to protect the global environment illustrates the ambiguous character of sustainable development, the key policy established by the 1992 Rio Conference and endorsed by later UN conferences.[59] More fundamentally it reflects a serious political failure on the part of global policy-makers and national governments. We have legislated for the global environment, but we have not made that legislation strong enough, and governments have not implemented the policies they endorsed with sufficient vigour. This is the Greta Thunberg point.[60] Ultimately, whether the protection offered to the environment by international law is 'adequate' is of course a value judgment, which will depend on the weight given to the whole range of competing social, economic and political considerations. All that this book can do is to try help the reader understand what the existing international legal system does or does not provide, and how far it has been effective.

Some attempt is made by the UN, treaty bodies, and experts to measure the effectiveness of multilateral environmental agreements ('MEAs'),[61] but this is not an easy task. Effectiveness in this context has multiple meanings: it may mean solving the problem for which the regime was established (for example restoring the ozone layer); or achieving goals set out in the constitutive instrument (for example attaining a set percentage reduction of sulphur emissions); or achieving sustainability in accordance with the UN's sustainable development goals, or altering behaviour patterns (for example moving from fossil fuels to solar or wind energy production); or enhancing national compliance with rules in international agreements, such as those restricting trade in endangered species. Some of the literature tends to see 'effectiveness' as a function of regime design; the underlying hypothesis is that if we learn the lessons of older regimes we can improve the effectiveness of newer ones.[62] This is true up to a

[57] See Kerbrat and Sandrine-Maljean (eds), *The Transformation of International Environmental Law*, Foreword.

[58] See in particular UN Environment, *Global Environmental Outlook 6: Summary for Policy Makers* (Nairobi, 2019); IPBES, *Global assessment report on biodiversity and ecosystem services of the Intergovernmental Science-Policy Platform on Biodiversity and Ecosystem Services* (Bonn, 2019); IPCC, *Special Report on the Ocean and Cryosphere in a Changing Climate* (2019); IPCC, *Climate Change 2014: Impacts, Adaptation, and Vulnerability* (Cambridge, 2014); UNEP/GPA, *The State of the Marine Environment* (Nairobi, 2006), and *infra*, Chs 6, 9, 11 and 12.

[59] *Infra*, Ch 2.

[60] Thunberg, *No-one is Too Small to Make a Difference* (London, 2018).

[61] See *infra*, Ch 4, section 3.

[62] See generally Doussis, 28 *YbIEL* (2017) 3; Bodansky, *The Art and Craft of International Environmental Law* 252–66; Mehling, 13 *Finnish YB Intl L* (2002) 129; Leary and Pisaputi (eds), *The Future of International Environmental Law* (Tokyo, 2010) Ch 1; Chambers and Green (eds), *Reforming International Environmental Governance: from Institutional Limits to Innovative Reforms* (Tokyo, 2005); Victor, Raustiala, and Skolnikoff (eds), *The Implementation and Effectiveness of International Environmental Commitments* (Cambridge, Mass, 1998); Sand, *Lessons Learned in Global Environmental Governance* (Washington DC, 1990) and *infra*, Ch 4, section 3.

point but, as we will see in subsequent chapters, the effectiveness of different regulatory and enforcement techniques is also determined by the objectives of the MEA in question and the willingness of governments to implement the measures necessary in national law and policy to achieve those objectives. What works in one case may not work in others. Chapter 6 illustrates the point: the MEAs governing ozone depletion and climate change are structurally similar and both are reasonably sophisticated, but while the ozone regime works well and has been effective, however defined, the climate regime has not reduced greenhouse emissions at all, and certainly not to the levels necessary to avoid catastrophic climate change. But this is because the commitments undertaken by the parties under the UNFCCC regime have so far been too weak.[63] This may change; as we note in Chapter 6, the 2015 Paris Agreement could succeed in restraining the increase in global temperatures to less than 2° C if the key states respond urgently and fully, or it could fail entirely if states continue to prioritize short-term economic development. Which outcome prevails will depend largely on the policy choices made by governments in implementing the Paris Agreement in national law and policy, not on the legal character of the agreement.

Nor is the problem necessarily one of compliance; all parties have complied with the 1997 Kyoto Protocol and even the US has reduced its own emissions significantly, despite non-participation.[64] Fundamentally we have made no progress on climate change because China, India and a number of other developing states have massively increased greenhouse gas emissions over the twenty years since the climate regime entered into force, as they are entitled to under the 1997 Kyoto Protocol, and because developed economies have not taken the measures necessary to abate their own production and consumption emissions. This outcome is not evidence of institutional or legal failure; it is the product of a conscious political choice which is fully reflected in the design of the 1997 Kyoto Protocol.[65] But in making that choice governments have failed to address the problem of climate change adequately. For economic and political reasons they have not been willing to go further or faster. The same can be said about the growing problem of plastic pollution in the oceans, or domestic air pollution, or the loss of biodiversity and ecosystems.[66] If international agreements are weak that is because states want them to be weak. Redesigning them will work only if governments want them to work and if they take the measures necessary to make them work. Ultimately this is a political challenge, not a legal one.[67]

Some fundamental questions thus resonate throughout this book: if we are failing to tackle global environmental problems effectively is that because the institutions of global governance (the UN system) or the network of autonomous regulatory regimes (MEAs) or the system of international courts and tribunals (International Court of Justice ('ICJ'), the International Tribunal for the Law of the Sea ('ITLOS'),

[63] See *infra*, Ch 6, section 4. [64] *Ibid.*

[65] See Boyle and Ghaleigh, in Carlarne et al (eds), *Oxford Handbook of Climate Law* (Oxford, 2016) 26–54, and *infra*, Ch 6.

[66] See *infra*, Chs 8, 11, and 12. [67] See Dupuy, 30 *EJIL* (2019) 1441.

the Permanent Court of Arbitration ('PCA'), the WTO etc.) are too fragmented and poorly structured?[68] Or is it because the global law-makers (states) are unable to agree on and implement policies—and laws—that are strong enough to deliver real solutions to global environmental problems? Have we paid too much attention to promoting economic development since the seminal UNCED at Rio in 1992, and not enough attention to protecting the environment which sustains humanity?[69] The reader will have to make his or her own judgment in the light of the chapters that follow, but it seems unlikely that more law or more litigation can solve many of the global environmental problems that have worsened over the past thirty years.

2 LAW-MAKING PROCESSES AND SOURCES OF LAW

2(1) INTERNATIONAL LAW-MAKING PROCESSES

Crucial to any assessment of the current state of international environmental law is an understanding of the sources and the law-making processes from which it derives. Although there is no international legislature as such, there are generally accepted sources from which international law derives, and a variety of processes through which new law is made or existing law changed. Much of international environmental law is the product of an essentially legislative process involving international organizations, conference diplomacy, codification and progressive development, international courts, and a relatively subtle interplay of treaties, non-binding declarations or resolutions ('soft law'), and customary international law.[70] The process may be 'ad hoc and piecemeal'[71] but there is nevertheless a process.

Recognition of the need to protect the global environment as a whole, and to lay down new law on certain priority issues, has required that international environmental law be developed more quickly and in a more flexible manner than in the past, entailing the adoption of new concepts and principles, and taking into account the imperatives of sustainable development. The corpus of environmental treaties, custom and soft law that has developed in the last fifty years reflects these imperatives.[72] It also reflects how profoundly developing states have influenced the development of international environmental law from the 1972 UNCHE onwards.[73] At the same time, there is no evidence that international environmental law is any less universal in scope than the rest of international law; to say that the rules sometimes differentiate the needs

[68] See *infra*, Chs 2 and 4. [69] See *infra*, Ch 2, section 2(5).

[70] See Bodansky, *The Art and Craft of International Environmental Law* and generally Boyle and Chinkin, *The Making of International Law* (Oxford, 2007).

[71] Desai, 30 *YbIEL* (2020) 1, 30.

[72] See generally Fitzmaurice, 25 *NYIL* (1994) 181, and *infra*, section 2 (6).

[73] See *infra*, Chs 2, 3 and 6, and for fuller accounts see Alam et al (eds), *International Environmental Law and the Global South* (Cambridge, 2015); Anand, *International Environmental Justice: A North-South Dimension* (Aldershot, 2004).

and capabilities of developed and developing states does not alter the commitment of international society as a whole to a common vision of international environmental law.[74] Three features have helped to make this law-making process both inclusive and relatively rapid.

First, international institutions, including the United Nations ('UN') and its specialized and regional agencies and programmes, have played a leading role in setting law-making agendas and providing negotiating forums and expertise. The indispensable involvement of these bodies, and of the intergovernmental law-making conferences they have convened, is considered more fully in Chapter 2.

Secondly, following the model of the third UN Conference on the Law of the Sea, the use of consensus negotiating procedures and 'package deal' diplomacy has created a real potential for securing general acceptance of negotiated texts.[75] In a world of almost two hundred states with disparate interests, and sometimes sharp differences on environmental issues, such techniques have been essential to securing agreement on measures to tackle global environmental problems. UNCED and the negotiation of the Conventions on Climate Change and Ozone depletion illustrate particularly well the importance of a process capable of securing universal, or near universal, participation and support.[76]

Thirdly, the use of 'framework treaties' has given the law-making process a dynamic character through regular meetings of the parties or intergovernmental organizations. They provide a basis for progressive action to be taken as scientific knowledge expands, and as regulatory priorities evolve or change. Such treaties usually set out broad principles while providing for detailed rules and measures to be elaborated in successive protocols, annexes and related softlaw instruments. Protocols or annexes of this kind are not necessarily binding on all the parties to a treaty; in many cases states may opt out either by withholding their consent or by objecting within the time allowed.[77] Overuse of this facility, as in the fisheries agreements reviewed in Chapter 12, may undermine the effectiveness of the regulatory system, but this is not often the case.

Examples of this 'framework treaty' approach to law-making include the 1992 UNFCCC, the 1985 Ozone Convention, and the 1979 Geneva Convention on Long-range Transboundary Air Pollution ('LRTAP Convention'), all of which have been amplified by later protocols.[78] Implementation of the 1979 Bonn Convention on the Conservation of Migratory Species of Wild Animals requires the listing of species

[74] See *infra*, Ch 3, section 1(1).

[75] See UNGA Res. 2750 XXV (1970) and 3067 XXVIII (1973); UN, *Official Text of the 1982 UNCLOS* (New York, 1983) Introduction, xix-xxvii, and Final Act; Buzan, 75 *AJIL* (1981) 529; Caminos and Molitor, 79 *AJIL* (1985) 871; Boyle and Chinkin, *The Making of International Law*, Ch 3; Harrison, *Making the Law of the Sea* (Cambridge, 2011), and *infra*, Ch 9.

[76] See generally Susskind, *Environmental Diplomacy* (Oxford, 1994). On the Rio Conference see *Rept. of the UNCED*, UN Doc. A/CONF.151/26/Rev.1, vol. 1; Sand, 3 *YbIEL* (1992) 3; Freestone, 6 *JEL* (1994) 193, and *infra*, Ch 2, section 2. On the Climate Change and Ozone Conventions see Mintzer and Leonard, *Negotiating Climate Change* (Cambridge, 1994); Benedick, *Ozone Diplomacy* (Cambridge, Mass., 1991) and *infra*, Ch 6.

[77] See *infra*, Ch 2, section 5(2)(d).

[78] See *infra*, Ch 6.

on its appendices and conclusion of separate agreements between the relevant 'range states' for its effective operation.[79] These framework MEAs, together with the institutions they create, have become regulatory regimes,[80] giving substance to the obligation 'to take measures' or 'all practicable measures'. As a result, what may begin as a very bare outline agreement, such as the 1985 Ozone Convention, can become a complex system of detailed law with its own machinery for ensuring compliance and implementation.[81]

Regulatory treaties can also be concluded in the form of an 'umbrella' instrument consisting of a general convention linked to one or more treaties on specific issues. The 1982 UNCLOS is an example. Although lacking any formal provision for the adoption of further protocols or annexes, it makes frequent reference to 'generally accepted international rules and standards,'[82] it envisages the adoption of regional agreements on various matters,[83] and it must be read together with subsequently adopted 'implementation agreements', including the 1994 Agreement Relating to Part XI,[84] and the 1995 UN Agreement on Straddling Fish Stocks and Highly Migratory Fish Stocks ('UN Fish Stocks Agreement').[85] Rather like protocols to a framework convention, these agreements interpret, amplify and develop the existing provisions of UNCLOS. They also provide alternative models for what is in effect, although not in form, *inter se* amendment of the Convention.[86] Unlike protocols to environmental framework treaties, however, implementing agreements can be freestanding treaties, independent of participation in UNCLOS itself.

The law-making processes referred to above represent a real vehicle for law-making by diplomatic means rather than through codification and progressive development by lawyers, although the International Law Commission ('ILC') and judicial decisions do play a part in affirming the status of customary rules and general principles, leading in some cases to modest evolution in international law.[87] Moreover, even where, as in the Stockholm and Rio Declarations, the instruments adopted are not formally binding on states, they have in many cases contributed to the development of consistent state practice, or provided evidence of existing law, or of the law-making intention which is necessary for the evolution of new customary international law, or

[79] See *infra*, Ch 11, section 3(3). [80] See *infra*, Ch 2, section 5. [81] See *infra*, Ch 6, section 3.

[82] See *infra*, Ch 9. [83] E.g. fisheries conservation, on which see *infra*, Ch 12.

[84] See Anderson, 43 *ICLQ* (1994) 886; Charney, 35 *VJIL* (1995) 381.

[85] See FAO, *Structure and Process of the 1993–1995 UN Conference on Straddling Fish Stocks and Highly Migratory Fish Stocks* (Rome, 1995) and *infra*, Ch 12.

[86] The use of an 'implementing agreement' was deliberately intended to avoid 'amendment' of the Convention. Nevertheless, the 1994 Agreement on Part XI looks very like amendment in practice. The 1995 UN Fish Stocks Agreement neither specifically amends UNCLOS nor does it prevail over it, but it does make significant changes in the applicable law.

[87] See especially *Gabčíkovo-Nagymaros Case*, ICJ Reports (1997) 7; Boyle, 8 *YbIEL* (1997) 13; Viñuales, 32 *Fordham ILJ* (2008–9) 232. Later cases amplify but do not significantly add to the existing law. See *infra*, Ch 3, sections 5–8.

have led to the negotiation of binding treaty commitments.[88] While it is not yet the case that states can 'declare' new law, it is clear from the development of international environmental law, and from other branches of international law, that a relatively dynamic and creative approach to international environmental law-making is possible.[89]

States parties to MEAs will often have considerable discretion in the methods of implementation they use, and possibly also in the standards and timetables they set. Not surprisingly some treaties have for these reasons proved difficult to implement in a coordinated, consistent way.[90] The degree and form of national implementation will largely determine how successful the treaty is as an instrument of change, assuming its objectives and techniques are themselves realistic, and that the parties intend to make more than symbolic gestures. This is why so much attention has been paid since UNCED to the methods and institutions which can be used to supervise compliance with environmental treaties and ensure through international inspection and reporting procedures that they are adequately implemented.[91]

Should international environmental agreements therefore aim to lay down more detailed and precise rules and try to ensure greater harmonization of national law and practice? The problem is that this is unlikely to be either possible or desirable in some cases. It may not be possible because a degree of flexibility is often the price that has to be paid to secure international agreement. Much will then depend on how far the parties are prepared subsequently to adopt more specific rules. But greater harmonization may also be undesirable. Because environmental problems tend to require flexible solutions to allow for changing scientific evidence, new control technologies, new political priorities, and the differing circumstances of various states, a treaty which casts precise rules in stone may be hard to renegotiate and thus too inflexible to respond to changing conditions.

The need for agreement on the rules is essentially the core of the problem: whereas the European Union ('EU') has the competence to legislate on environmental matters by qualified majority for all its member states, more orthodox treaty-based institutions are merely coalitions of the willing. Harmonization of national law is possible, based on rules agreed within such a treaty, but since the rules may themselves be controversial, as in the case of the 2015 Paris Agreement on climate change,[92] it is no easy task to bring this about. Inevitably therefore, a lot of discretion is often left to governments as the only way to achieve agreement on something.

88 See *infra*, section 2(4).

89 See especially Charney, 87 *AJIL* (1993) 529; Szasz, in Brown-Weiss (ed), *Environmental Change and International Law* (Tokyo, 1992) 61; Brölmann, 74 *Nordic JIL* (2005) 383; and Boyle and Chinkin, *The Making of International Law* (Oxford, 2007) Chs 3–5.

90 See e.g. the 1997 Kyoto Protocol, *infra*, Ch 6, and treaties on land-based sources of marine pollution, *infra*, Ch 8.

91 See *infra*, Ch 4.

92 See *infra*, Ch 6.

2(2) SOURCES OF INTERNATIONAL LAW FROM AN ENVIRONMENTAL PERSPECTIVE

The sources of international environmental law are, of course, the same as those from which all international law emanates, since international environmental law is, as we have seen, simply a branch of general international law.[93] But international environmental law is also rich in illustrations of the problems posed by taking too narrow a view of the traditional sources of international law.[94] Treaties and custom have historically been the main sources of binding international law, augmented since the adoption of Article 38(1) of the Statute of the Permanent Court of International Justice ('PCIJ') in 1920 by general principles of law and, as secondary sources, judicial decisions and the teachings of the most highly qualified publicists.[95] Though drafted before the growth in the number and diversity of states, or the emergence of environmental concerns, Article 38(1) remains the only generally accepted statement of the sources of international law to be applied by the ICJ. There is no mention in it, however, of UN General Assembly Resolutions, Declarations of Principles adopted by the UN or by *ad hoc* conferences, or draft articles and conventions adopted by the ILC. These informal sources have nevertheless played a significant role in the development of international environmental law, and they are frequently cited throughout this book. Their legal status is considered below in the context of a discussion of custom and soft law.

(a) Treaties

Treaties remain the most frequently used instruments for creating generally applicable multilateral rules relating to the environment[96]. The 1992 CBD and the Convention on Climate Change , or the 1982 UNCLOS, are in this sense law-making treaties.[97] They create regimes to which almost all states are party and from which no reservations or derogations are possible unless expressly authorized. Treaties of this kind are the most important basis for international environmental law.

Essentially a treaty is a written agreement between states, or between states and international organizations, governed by international law.[98] The terminology is immaterial: the variety of alternatives includes treaty, convention, protocol, covenant, pact, act, etc. There are no rules prescribing their form but the 1969 Vienna Convention

93 See generally Thirlway, *The Sources of International Law* (Oxford, 2014) or for succinct accounts of sources and analysis of Article 38 of the ICJ Statute, see Evans (ed), *International Law* (5th edn, Oxford, 2018) Ch 4; *Brownlie's Principles,*, Ch 2; Pellet, *The Statute of the ICJ* (Oxford, 2006) Commentary on Article 38; Higgins, *International Law and How We Use it* (Oxford, 1994) Ch 2.

94 See in particular the discussion of soft law, *infra*.

95 See now Statute of the International Court of Justice, Article 38(1).

96 See *Brownlie's Principles*, Ch 16; Aust, *Modern Treaty Law and Practice* (2nd edn, Cambridge, 2007); Sinclair, *The Vienna Convention on Treaties* (2nd edn, Manchester, 1984); Reuter, *Introduction to the Law of Treaties* (2nd edn, London, 1995).

97 On law-making treaties see Brölmann, 74 *Nordic JIL* (2005) 383; Boyle and Chinkin, *The Making of International Law*, Ch 3.

98 1969 VCLT , Article 2(1)(a).

on the Law of Treaties ('VCLT') codifies the law applicable to written treaties concluded after its entry into force in 1980. Whilst not all provisions of the 1969 VCLT have necessarily attained the status of customary law, in practice it has been applied as custom in many international and national judicial decisions.[99] The 1969 VCLT deals with such matters as entry into force, reservations, interpretation, termination, and invalidity. Some agreements are executed in a simplified form, by exchange of notes or letters, and become binding on signature without the need for ratification. Others, concluded at the administrative level in the form of Memoranda of Understanding are not necessarily binding but they may still be taken into account or create good faith expectations.[100]

A brief summary of the process of concluding a treaty will assist the uninitiated reader. The underlying principle is that *pacta sunt servanda* (treaties are made to be kept).[101] Treaties are normally opened for signature following their adoption, but unless there is specific agreement to be bound by signature, it is not until instruments of ratification or accession have subsequently been deposited (which generally requires approval by national parliamentary or other internal processes) and any other requirements for entry into force have been fulfilled (for example a specified number of ratifications) that the treaty enters into force and becomes binding on the parties.[102] Delays can occur at this stage, and some of the treaties we discuss in this book have never entered into force, but the rapid entry into force of the 2015 Paris Agreement indicates that multilateral treaties can take effect quickly when necessary.

The 1969 VCLT liberalized treaty-making in a number of ways. In particular, it allowed states to participate *à la carte*—i.e. with reservations excluding provisions to which they objected, subject only to consistency with the treaty's object and purpose.[103] However, most global environmental treaties prohibit all reservations in order to preserve the integrity of what is usually a 'package deal' compromise text,[104] or they permit only certain kinds of reservations.[105] The possibility of making reservations normally encourages wider participation in treaties; it is partly their impermissibility under the 1982 UNCLOS that delayed this treaty achieving the sixty ratifications required for entry into force and that has kept the US out of several environmental agreements. On the other hand, reservations also undermine the effectiveness of treaties by enabling states to protect their own economic and other interests. In practice, most multilateral environmental treaties are very widely ratified despite the ban on reservations. But as we saw earlier most also allow any party to opt out of detailed

[99] See in particular *Gabčíkovo-Nagymaros Case*, ICJ Reports (1997) 7.

[100] *Iron Rhine Arbitration*, PCA (2005) paras 142, 157. See generally Aust, 35 *ICLQ* (1986) 787.

[101] 1969 VCLT, Article 26. [102] 1969 VCLT, Articles 11–16, 24–25.

[103] 1969 VCLT, Articles 19–23. See *Reservations to the Genocide Convention Case*, ICJ Reports (1951) 15; Redgwell, 64 *BYIL* (1993) 245.

[104] E.g. 1982 UNCLOS, Articles 309–10; 1985 Ozone Convention, Article 18; 1989 Convention on Transboundary Movements of Hazardous Wastes, Article 26; 1992 Climate Change Convention, Article 24; 1992 CBD, Article 37; 1994 Desertification Convention, Article 37.

[105] E.g. 1946 International Convention for the Regulation of Whaling.

regulatory annexes, amendments or additional protocols.[106] This weakness is especially pertinent to adoption of stronger control measures or the listing of additional polluting substances or endangered species.[107] These details matter; participation in an empty framework treaty amounts to little more than symbolic commitment to a process unless the substantive regulations are also accepted subsequently.

So far as interpretation of treaties is concerned, the 1969 VCLT's provisions include all three schools of thought on the subject—the textual, the 'effective', and the teleological approaches.[108] Thus, the ordinary meaning of the words to be interpreted must first be sought but in their broad context in the convention. The interpretation must be made in good faith, be compatible with the objects and purposes of the convention, and so far as possible make it effective.[109] If the wording is ambiguous, recourse may be had to the *travaux préparatoires* (the negotiating record) to verify an interpretation derived from the above process. Although the 1969 VCLT formally applies only to treaties concluded by parties after its entry into force, its provisions on interpretation have been treated by all international courts as customary law, and on that basis they have been used to interpret earlier treaties or treaties between states not party to the 1969 VCLT.[110]

The 1969 VCLT's articles on interpretation provide one of the most important techniques for integrating different treaties or bodies of law. The subsequent practice of the parties, or any agreement regarding interpretation of a treaty, must be taken into account.[111] The task of giving guidance on or amplifying the terms of environmental treaties is performed most frequently by resolutions, recommendations and decisions of international organizations and conferences of parties to treaties. These instruments often provide the detailed rules or standards of best practice to be achieved by the parties in implementing their treaty obligations and are essential in giving hard content to the open-textured terms of framework environmental treaties.[112] Thus UNEP's Cairo Guidelines on the Transport of Hazardous Wastes[113] can be regarded as an amplification of the obligation of 'environmentally sound management' provided for in Article 4 of the 1989 Basel Convention on the Control of Transboundary Movements of Hazardous Wastes and their Disposal ('Basel Convention'). The advantages of

106 *Infra*, Ch 2, section 5.

107 E.g. the 1997 Kyoto Protocol, *infra*, Ch 6; 1998 PIC Convention, *infra*, Ch 8; 1973 CITES, *infra*, Ch 11; 1946 Whaling Convention, *infra*, Ch 12.

108 1969 VCLT, Articles 31–3; Sinclair, *The Vienna Convention on Treaties*, 114–58.

109 See e.g. the *Iron Rhine Arbitration*, PCA (2005) paras 45–8, 85–91.

110 *Territorial Dispute (Libyan Arab Jamahiriya/Chad)* ICJ Reports (1994) 6, para 41; *Kasikili/Sedudu Island(Botswana/Namibia)* ICJ Reports (1999) 1045, para 18; *Sovereignty over Pulau Ligitan and Pulau Sipadan (Indonesia/Malaysia)* ICJ Reports (2002) 625, paras 37–38; *Iron Rhine Arbitration (Belgium/Netherlands)* PCA (2005) para 45.

111 1969 VCLT, Articles 31(3)(a) and (b). See also ILC, 'Subsequent Agreements and Subsequent Practice: Draft Conclusions', GAOR (2016) A/CN.4/L.874.

112 See Contini and Sand, 66 *AJIL* (1972) 37; Bodansky, 98 *Proc ASIL* (2004) 275.

113 UNEP/WG.122/3 (1985) *infra*, Ch 8.

regulating environmental risks in this way are that the detailed rules and standards can easily be changed or strengthened as scientific understanding develops or as political priorities change.

Article 31(3)(c) of the 1969 VCLT additionally provides that in interpreting a treaty account shall also be taken of any other 'relevant rules of international law applicable in the relations between the parties.'[114] Changes in international law can be taken into account and reflected in the jurisprudence, a point particularly well observed in international human rights law,[115] but also relevant in environmental law, where older treaties may need to be interpreted in the light of more modern developments. Doing so may help to avoid conflicts between treaties, or save agreements from premature obsolescence, or the need for constant amendment.[116]

How far, if at all, might re-interpretation of a treaty be possible under this provision in order to give it a 'greener' tinge? The terms within which 'evolutionary interpretation' is permissible under Article 31(3)(c) have been narrowly circumscribed in the jurisprudence, and over-ambitious attempts to reinterpret or 'cross-fertilize' treaties by reference to later treaties or other rules of international law have had only limited success.[117] Nevertheless, while accepting 'the primary necessity of interpreting an instrument in accordance with the intentions of the parties at the time of its conclusion,' the ICJ has acknowledged that treaties must be 'interpreted and applied within the framework of the entire legal system prevailing at the time of the interpretation.'[118] The ICJ's approach, combining both an evolutionary and an intertemporal element, reflects the ILC's commentary to what became Article 31(3)(c).[119] In the *Pulp Mills Case*—an environmental dispute—the court emphasized that 'there are situations in which the parties' intent upon conclusion of the treaty was, or may be presumed to have been, to give the terms used or some of them a meaning or content capable of evolving, not one fixed once and for all, so as to make allowance for, among other things, developments in international law.'[120] On that basis it interpreted broadly worded provisions of a river treaty concluded in 1975 to include an obligation of environmental impact assessment derived from current international law.[121] The WTO Appellate Body has given a similarly evolutionary interpretation to certain

114 See McLachlan, 54 *ICLQ* (2005) 279; French, 55 *ICLQ* (2006) 281.

115 See *infra*, Ch 5, n 45 but compare Rachovitsa, 66 *ICLQ* (2017) 557, where the limitations are explored.

116 For a particularly good environmental example see the *Iron Rhine Arbitration*, PCA (2005) paras 58–9.

117 E.g. Ireland's unsuccessful attempt to rewrite UNCLOS in the *Mox Plant Arbitration* (PCA, 2002). For a contrary but unpersuasive view see Sands, in Boyle and Freestone (eds), *International Law and Sustainable Development*, 39.

118 *Namibia Advisory Opinion*, ICJ Reports (1971) 16, 31; *Aegean Sea Continental Shelf Case*, ICJ Reports (1978) 3, 32–3.

119 See ILC, 'The law of treaties,' commentary to draft Article 27, para (16) in Watts (ed), *The International Law Commission 1949–1998* (Oxford, 1999) vol II, 690.

120 *Pulp Mills Case*, ICJ Reports (2010) 14, para 204, citing *Dispute Regarding Navigational and Related Rights*, ICJ Reports (2009) 213, para 64.

121 See *infra*, Ch 3, section 7.

terms in the GATT Agreement. In the *Shrimp-Turtle* decision, for example, it referred *inter alia* to the 1992 Rio Declaration , the 1982 UNCLOS, the 1973 Convention on International Trade in Endangered Species of Wild Fauna and Flora ('CITES'), the 1979 Convention on Conservation of Migratory Species and the 1992 CBD in order to determine the present meaning of 'exhaustible natural resources.'[122] It follows that the interpretation of a treaty may change over time.

In all of these cases the question at issue was not general revision or re-interpretation of the treaty. Rather, each case was concerned with the interpretation of particular provisions or phrases, such as 'natural resources,' or 'jurisdiction,' which necessarily import—or at least suggest—a reference to current general international law. Ambulatory incorporation of the existing law, whatever it may be, enables treaty provisions to change and develop as the general law itself changes, without the need for any amendment. As the ICJ points out in the *Oil Platforms Case*, such treaty provisions are not intended to operate independently of general international law.[123] Evolutionary interpretation is thus a relatively limited task, usually justified by reference to the wording of the treaty and its object and purpose. It does not entitle a court or tribunal to engage in a process of constant revision or updating every time a newer treaty is concluded that relates to similar matters.[124] On this view, interpretation is interpretation, not amendment or rewriting of treaties. The result must remain faithful to the ordinary meaning and context of the treaty, 'in the light of its object and purpose.'[125]

Whether another treaty is regarded as an agreement on interpretation, or as a guide to the interpretation of inherently evolutionary provisions, or as evidence of a common understanding of comparable provisions, the level of participation cannot be ignored. Some authors read Article 31(3)(c) as referring only to rules applicable between all the parties to a treaty *dispute,* rather than all the parties to a treaty. Apart from being inconsistent with the ILC commentary to Article 31(3) this interpretation leaves unanswered the question how the article should be applied in other contexts, e.g. by treaty Conferences of the Parties ('COPs'), the UN, or foreign ministries, and risks a serious Balkanization of global treaties implemented by regional agreements. It is true that under many treaties individual states are free to agree alternative interpretations *inter se*, within the terms of Article 41 of the 1969 VCLT.[126] However, where there is a clear need for uniform interpretation, given the express terms of Article 31(3) and the ILC commentary thereto, the stronger argument is that a treaty cannot realistically be regarded as an agreement on interpretation or as a 'relevant rule applicable in relations between the parties' unless it has the consensus support of all the parties to that treaty, or

122 *Import Prohibition of Certain Shrimp and Shrimp Products*, WTO Appellate Body (1998) WT/DS58/AB/R, paras 130–1.

123 ICJ Reports (2003) paras 40–1. See also *Gabčíkovo-Nagymaros Case*, ICJ Reports (1997) 7, paras 140–1.

124 Bedjaoui, *Gabčíkovo-Nagymaros Case*, sep op, para 12. See also *SW Africa Case*, ICJ Reports (1966) 3, 48.

125 1969 VCLT, Article 31(1). See *OSPAR Arbitration*, PCA (2003) paras 101–5; *Iron Rhine Arbitration*, PCA (2005) paras 47, 81, 221.

126 See e.g. Bartels, 36 *JWT* (2002) 353, 361, and see the next section.

there is no objection.[127] This does not necessarily mean that all the parties to one treaty would have to be party to the other treaty. The 1994 Agreement on the Implementation of UNCLOS is assumed to be effective on the basis that non-parties have tacitly consented to or acquiesced in the revision of UNCLOS.[128] Alternatively, a treaty rule may also be binding in customary international law and become relevant on that basis. Thus, in *Shrimp-Turtle* the WTO Appellate Body noted that although not a party to UNCLOS, the US did accept the relevant provisions as customary law. These are significant qualifications to the ILC's general principle regarding universality of participation.

An agreement lacking such general support will no longer fall strictly within the obligatory terms of Article 31(3)(a) or (c) and its persuasive force as a basis for evolutionary interpretation will necessarily be weaker the fewer parties there are. In the *OSPAR Arbitration* the arbitrators declined even to take into account a convention which was not in force, and which Ireland had not ratified, although the better view is probably that such an agreement may nevertheless provide some guidance.[129] In practice much will depend on whether other non-parties acquiesce or not, and on the issue in dispute. In *Shrimp-Turtle* the United States ('US') did not object to the Appellate Body taking the 1992 CBD into account. It is difficult to see how it could do otherwise, given the almost universal participation by other states in this treaty and the specific reasons for US non-participation.

Treaties do not bind non-parties, unless the intention to do so is clearly expressed and the state concerned expressly accepts the benefits or obligations in question; in the latter case this must be done in writing.[130] This is relatively unusual. More commonly treaty provisions bind non-parties through their evolution into customary international law, an argument considered in the next section. To be capable of so doing 'It would in the first place be necessary that the provision concerned should, at all events potentially, be of a fundamentally norm-creating character such as could be regarded as forming the basis of a general rule of law.'[131] As we shall see in Chapter 3, this first requirement is one reason for doubting the status of sustainable development or the precautionary principle as 'rules' of customary international law. The second requirement laid down by the ICJ in the *North Sea Continental Shelf Cases* is that the provision in question should have been adopted in the practice of a sufficiently widespread and representative number of states, including those that are *not* parties to the treaty.[132] Moreover, the requirement of *opinio juris*, which establishes the legally binding character of state practice in customary law, must also be satisfied.[133] These two constitutive elements of custom—state practice and *opinio juris*—are considered further below.

[127] ILC commentary in Watts (ed), *The ILC*, vol II, 688–9 and see *EC—Measures Affecting the Approval and Marketing of Biotech Products*, WTO Panel Reports (2006) WT/DS291/2/3/R, paras.7.65–7.89. The arguments are reviewed extensively by Pauwelyn, 95 *AJIL* (2001) 535, 575–6; McLachlan, 54 *ICLQ* (2005) 279, 315, para 16, (but note his qualifications at para 17); French, 55 *ICLQ* (2006) 300–7.

[128] Boyle, 54 *ICLQ* (2005) 563.

[129] Griffith, sep.op, *OSPAR Arbitration*, PCA (2003) paras 101–5, and see also *EC—Measures Affecting the Approval and Marketing of Biotech Products*, WTO Panel Reports (2006) WT/DS291/2/3/R, paras 7.90–7.96.

[130] 1969 VCLT, Articles 34–6.

[131] *North Sea Continental Shelf Cases*, ICJ Reports (1969) 3, para 72.

[132] Paras 70–81.

[133] *Ibid.*

(b) Custom

Although treaties are the most frequently used form of international environmental law-making, customary international law remains important, especially when treaties have to be interpreted by reference to general international law, as in the *Pulp Mills Case* referred to in the previous section.[134] Customary rules may more easily acquire universal application, since acquiescence will often be enough to ensure that 'the inactive are carried along by the active',[135] a particular advantage in environmental matters. Although most writers consider that it is not necessary for a state to have expressly or impliedly consented to a rule of customary law that *has* crystallized as such in order to be bound by it, the creation of new customary rules does in the end depend on some form of consent or acquiescence, and this remains a limitation of some importance.

Article 38(1) of the ICJ Statute instructs the Court to apply 'international custom, as evidence of a general practice accepted as law'. This formulation focuses on the process whereby state practice supported by *opinio juris* (the conviction that conduct is motivated by a sense of legal obligation) provides the evidence necessary to establish a customary rule. On this view it is 'axiomatic that the material of customary international law is to be looked for primarily in the actual practice and *opinio juris* of states'.[136] Identifying state practice usually involves an examination of official statements, unilateral and multilateral declarations, bilateral agreements, national legislation, law enforcement actions, and judicial decisions.[137] The acts of non-state bodies are more difficult to categorize in the custom-creating process. Here it is more a question of states' reaction to acts of their nationals—whether they approve or authorize them or reject or prosecute them—that is significant. Thus, although individuals may form non-governmental pressure groups, such as Greenpeace, that actively campaign for development of or change in the law to protect the environment, it is the adoption of their proposals by states or the significance attributed to them by international courts that is determinative, not the views or actions of the non-governmental organizations ('NGOs') themselves.[138] The identification of customary law always has been, and remains, a task requiring research and the exercise of judgment. This is where codification, judicial decisions, or scholarship can be particularly helpful. However, deciding which norms have crystallized into customary law is not just a matter of inquiry but of policy choice.[139]

134 *Brownlie's Principles*, Ch 2; Roberts, 95 *AJIL* (2001) 757; Akehurst, 43 *BYIL* (1974–5) 1.

135 Meijers, 9 *NYIL* (1978) 4.

136 *Libya/Malta Continental Shelf Case*, ICJ Reports (1985) 29–30. See also *North Sea Continental Shelf Cases*, ICJ Reports (1969) 3, 32–3, 47, 53, and in an environmental context Bodansky, *The Art and Craft of IEL*, Ch 9.

137 *Jurisdictional Immunities Case*, ICJ Reports (2012) 3, paras 55 and 97. See also *Pulp Mills Case*, ICJ Reports (2010) 14, paras 204–5.

138 On the role of NGOs in international law-making see Boyle and Chinkin, *The Making of International Law*, Ch 2.

139 Jennings, 37 *Ann Suisse de Droit Int* (1981) 67.

Judge Jennings pointed out many years ago that much new international law is not customary law in the orthodox sense set out above: 'it is recent, it is innovatory, it involves topical policy decisions, and it is the focus of contention'.[140] Moreover, without some means of bringing about coordination, the practice of individual states would be difficult to reconcile even on questions of general principle, let alone on specific details, and customary law would emerge or change only slowly, if at all.

In practice, new customary international law relating to the environment has first been negotiated by states through the medium of multilateral treaties, UN conference declarations or General Assembly resolutions, or various forms of non-binding soft law, and only later might it begin to affect the practice of states. Here it is the *opinio juris* to create new law that generates the practice rather than the other way round. Two of the most important examples relied on in this work illustrate the point: the 1982 UNCLOS (a binding treaty) and the 1992 Rio Declaration (a non-binding soft law instrument). Both were negotiated by consensus, that is without opposition, and reflect a series of interlocking compromises and concessions involving participants with a variety of different interests and priorities. The law-making effect of such negotiated instruments can be very powerful.[141] We will see several examples in Chapter 3.

The point is that although a multilateral treaty such as UNCLOS does not *per se* 'make' customary law it can facilitate the process of customary norm creation in the right circumstances. In the *North Sea Continental Shelf Cases* the ICJ accepted that a normatively worded provision of a multilateral treaty can contribute to the formation of a new rule of customary law if the law-making intent of the parties is supported by the subsequent practice of a sufficiently widespread and representative selection of parties and non-parties conforming to the treaty.[142] In this case, however, the treaty provision was contested and could not itself be evidence of *opinio juris*, nor was it consistently reflected in state practice, so the treaty did not create new custom. But where the negotiated text is not controversial—for example where it is adopted by consensus—the process of creating new custom is easier. The leading example is the *Nicaragua Case*, where the ICJ found that a widely supported multilateral treaty (the UN Charter) and UN General Assembly resolutions (soft law) constituted evidence of the 'subjective element' (*opinio juris*) recognizing the treaty-based rule as customary law.[143] While 'the shared view of the parties as to the content of what they regard as the rule is not enough' to create new custom, it will do so if 'the existence of the rule in the *opinio juris* of states is confirmed by practice'.[144] The practice in these circumstances

[140] Jennings, ibid. For a more sceptical view see Bodansky, *The Art and Craft of IEL*, Ch 9, but he focuses on state practice as the key determinant of custom, and misses the point that in an environmental context the process of negotiating consensus rules may be more significant than state practice in generating custom binding on all or most states.

[141] See generally Boyle and Chinkin, *The Making of International Law*, Ch 3.

[142] ICJ Reports (1969) 3. See also *Jurisdictional Immunities Case*, ICJ Reports (2012) 3, para 55.

[143] *Nicaragua Case*, ICJ Reports (1986) 14, para 185.

[144] *Ibid*, para 184. See also *Chagos Advisory Opinion*, ICJ Reports (2019) paras 150–160.

does not need to be 'in absolutely rigorous conformity with the rule', provided inconsistent conduct is treated by the states concerned as a breach of the rule, not as an indication of a new rule.[145] In this context only conduct amounting to an outright rejection of the alleged rule will constitute genuinely inconsistent practice. The *Nicaragua Case* also recognized that the embodiment of a rule in a treaty provision does not preclude the continued existence or further development of a comparable rule of customary international law.[146]

The Court's findings of law in *Nicaragua* do not rest only on the normative impact of the UN Charter. As this case shows, the *opinio juris* of states may also be evidenced by the consensus adoption of comparable resolutions in the UN General Assembly.[147] Although the Court is careful to avoid any suggestion that custom can be established by states simply declaring the law in treaties and soft law instruments, the only significant caveat is that there must be no *inconsistent* state practice.[148] This reverses the approach taken in the *North Sea Cases*, where the court emphasized the need for *consistent* state practice. The circumstances of the two cases are different, however. In *North Sea*, the equidistance rule set out in the 1958 Convention on the Continental Shelf was not acceptable to a number of states, and certainly not to Germany, nor was the practice of many non-parties to the treaty consistent with it. By contrast, both parties in the *Nicaragua Case* consistently expressed support for the same rule on the use of force, even in the face of flagrant violations. Moreover, it should not be forgotten that the US is a party to the UN Charter, even if in the circumstances of the *Nicaragua Case* the Court was precluded from applying the Charter to the dispute. Finally, the use of force in violation of international law contravenes a norm of *ius cogens*. By definition, such rules are recognized by the international community as a whole and cannot be derogated from. The delimitation of seabed boundaries on the basis of equidistance is not in the same category.

What conclusions about the normative force of multilateral environmental treaties can we draw from the ICJ case law? First, the Court has no difficulty accepting that appropriately worded treaties 'may have an important role in recording and defining rules deriving from custom, or indeed in developing them.'[149] Secondly, the cases accept that there may be a law-making intention behind the negotiation of multilateral treaties. This law-making intention can constitute evidence of *opinio juris* in favour of new general rules of international law, especially if the treaty was negotiated by consensus or has the consistent support of a large majority of states.[150] Thirdly, we can see that support for a treaty rule, however widespread, cannot by itself create 'instant' law. Such treaties will only create new law if supported by state practice over a period of time. That practice can in appropriate cases consist mainly of acquiescence, or the

145 *Ibid*, para 186. 146 *Ibid*, paras 174–9.

147 See also *Chagos Advisory Opinion*, ICJ Reports (2019) paras 150–160. 148 See also *ibid*, para 150.

149 *Tunisia/Libya Continental Shelf Case*, ICJ Reports (1982) para 27.

150 *Malta/Libya Continental Shelf Case*, ICJ Reports (1985) at 35–6. See also *Chagos Advisory Opinion*, ICJ Reports (2019) paras 150–160.

absence of protest or inconsistent practice. How long a time is required will depend on the circumstances. It may be very short if the subsequent practice is widespread and consistent, as in the case of the exclusive economic zone,[151] or if the treaty is a codification treaty, as we will see below when considering the *Gabčíkovo Case*.[152] Fourthly, as the UNCLOS cases show, it evidently matters little whether the treaty is in force, but the more widely supported the treaty text is shown to be, the easier it will be to establish its law-making effect. The longer it takes to establish consistent *opinio juris* or consistent state practice the harder it will be to establish a new rule of customary law. All of these points are further developed below in the discussion of UN declarations and soft law.[153]

While it is clear that multilateral treaties—even those that are not yet in force—can initiate the development of new customary international law, and in that sense some of them can be described as 'law-making', it does not follow that law which develops in this fashion will necessarily bind all states. Apart from the obvious proviso that customary law may be regional or local rather than global, certain states may also object to attempts to change the law. They may do so in the form of reservations, or they may remain non-parties and oppose the treaty, even if they participated in its consensus negotiation—a position in which the US frequently finds itself. Either way, if they maintain their persistent objection to new rules that emerge from a treaty, these rules will not apply against those states.[154] Charney argues that persistent objectors can at best maintain this position only while the status of a new rule is in doubt; they will be bound once the rule is firmly established.[155] As a matter of diplomatic reality this may be true in many cases, including those on which Charney relies, but much depends on the circumstances and the states involved. Moreover, if customary law can be local or regional in scope, there is no inherent reason why persistent objectors cannot successfully remain bound by the old rules, unless one accepts the possibility that majorities make law for minorities.[156] There is no support for such a majoritarian position in the present case law of the ICJ or other international tribunals.

(c) General Principles of Law

General principles of law[157] are important in the current development of international environmental law because there now exist an increasing number of instruments expressed as 'Declarations of Principles', including the Stockholm and Rio Declarations, the World Charter for Nature, and UNEP's various sets of Principles

[151] *Tunisia/Libya Continental Shelf Case*, ICJ Reports (1982) para 27. See also *Libya/Malta Continental Shelf Case*, ICJ Reports (1985) 29–30.

[152] *Infra*, section 2(3).

[153] *Infra*, sections 2(4) and (5).

[154] See *Fisheries Jurisdiction Case*, ICJ Reports (1974) 3, at 6–7, 22–35. See also *Brownlie's Principles*, Ch 2.

[155] Charney, 58 *BYIL* (1987) 1.

[156] See Charney's discussion of the literature.

[157] See *Brownlie's Principles*, Ch 2; Cheng, *General Principles of International Law* (London, 1953); Higgins, *Problems and Process*, 219–230; Friedmann, 57 *AJIL* (1963) 279; Redgwell in Vogenauer and Wetherill (eds), *General Principles of Law: European and Comparative Perspectives* (Oxford, 2017) Ch 2.

on, for example, the use of shared natural resources.[158] We have to ask whether these are the kind of principles referred to in Article 38(1)(c) of the ICJ Statute or whether a narrower view limiting the role of general principles to common legal maxims is all that was intended?

Article 38(1)(c) allows the International Court to apply 'the general principles of law recognized by civilized nations'. It is unclear whether the principles referred to are merely those commonly applied in all municipal legal systems, such as the maxims relied on to ensure a fair legal process—*audi alteram partem, res judicata,* etc.—or whether they also include 'principles' recognized by international law itself—for example, the basic principles of human rights; the freedom of the seas; the need for good faith evidenced in the maxim *pacta sunt servanda*, and so on. The ambiguity arises from the need to compromise, which arose in the early 1920s when the Statute of the PCIJ was being drafted. One group on the relevant preparatory committee thought that the traditional sources of custom and treaty should be expanded to enable the Court to apply 'the rules of international law as recognized by the *legal conscience* of civilized nations',[159] based on the concept that certain principles existed in so-called 'natural law'. The purpose of this group has been described as revolutionary, namely to place as a 'wedge between the crevices of existing law principles derived from Western civilization',[160] since the principles would not rest on the consent of states in general. The rival group adopted the traditional 'positivist' approach, namely that the Court should apply only rules and principles derived from the will of states. This view has been supported in more recent times by lawyers from developing countries and formerly by the Soviet bloc. The compromise adopted in Article 38(1)(c) was regarded by this group as referring only to general principles accepted by all nations *in foro domestico*.

In the few cases where it has relied on general principles of national law, the International Court has not considered in detail the practice of domestic courts but has drawn on its own jurisprudential perceptions, mainly to support conclusions rather than as the sole basis of decision.[161] Tribunals have not mechanically borrowed from domestic law 'lock, stock and barrel', but have invoked elements of legal reasoning and private law analogies 'as an indication of policy and principles rather than as directly importing these rules and institutions.'[162] As early as 1937, in the *Diversion of Water from the Meuse Case*,[163] the PCIJ considered that equitable principles might be derived from 'general principles of law recognized by civilized nations'. In the *Chorzow Factory Case*[164] the same court enunciated the general principles of state responsibility

[158] Draft Principles of Conduct in the Field of the Environment for the Conduct of States on the Conservation and Harmonious Utilization of Natural Resources Shared by Two or More States, UNEP/I.G. 12/2 (1978) and see *infra*, Ch 3, section 3.

[159] Cassese, *International Law in a Divided World*, 170, citing Lord Phillimore; emphasis added.

[160] *Ibid*, 171.

[161] Cassese, *International Law in a Divided World*, at 174. Relevant cases include the *Chorzow Factory Case (Indemnity) (Jurisdiction)* PCIJ Ser. A, No. 8/9 (1927) 31; *Corfu Channel Case*, ICJ Reports (1949) 18; *South West Africa Case (Second Phase)* ICJ Reports (1966) 294–9.

[162] Lord McNair, *South West Africa Case*, ICJ Reports (1950) 128 at 148.

[163] PCIJ Ser. A/B No. 70 (1937) 4, at 73 and 76.

[164] See *infra*, Ch 4, section 2.

and reparation, including the principle of *restitutio in integrum*, while in the *Free Zones Cases*[165] it made reference to the doctrines of abuse of rights and good faith. In the *South West Africa Case*[166] one judge considered that elements of natural law were inherent in general principles and could provide a foundation for human rights. Most importantly, general principles of national law were relied on in the *Trail Smelter Arbitration* to support a finding that 'no state has the right to use or permit the use of its territory in such a manner as to cause injury by fumes in or to the territory of another.'[167] Nonetheless, it has to be recognized that general principles derived by analogy from domestic law have so far only been marginally useful in an environmental context. They are more important in other contexts, such as international criminal law.

Of greater significance in an environmental context are general principles found in the 1992 Rio Declaration, other soft law instruments and certain treaties, including the 1992 UNFCCC. The precautionary principle, the polluter pays principle, the principle of common but differentiated responsibility have all been endorsed by states in this form.[168] Such general principles do not have to create rules of customary law to have legal effect, nor do they need to be incorporated in treaties or reflect national law. They cannot override or amend the express terms of a treaty,[169] so their importance derives principally from the influence they may exert on the interpretation, application, and development of treaties in accordance with Article 31(3) of the 1969 VCLT. General principles of this kind may also influence the interpretation and application of customary law. Thus the precautionary principle, considered further in Chapter 3, has influenced state practice, the negotiation of treaties, and the judgments of international courts. What gives these general principles their authority and legitimacy is the endorsement of states—*opinio juris* in other words.[170] Such principles have legal significance in much the same way that Dworkin uses the idea of constitutional principles.[171] They lay down parameters which affect the way courts decide cases or how an international institution exercises its discretionary powers. They can set limits, or provide guidance, or determine how conflicts between other rules or principles will be resolved. They may lack the supposedly harder edge of a 'rule' or 'obligation', but they should not be confused with 'non-binding' or emerging law. The ICJ's references to the 'concept' or 'objective' of sustainable development in the *Gabčíkovo-Nagymaros* and *Pulp Mills Cases* remain perhaps the best illustration of the role of internationally

165 *Free Zones Case (Second Phase)* Final Order, PCIJ Ser. A, No. 24 (1932) 12, and *Free Zones Case* (Merits) Ser. A/B, No. 46 (1932) 167.

166 ICJ Reports (1966) 294–9.

167 35 *AJIL* (1941) 716. See *infra*, Ch 3, section 5.

168 See *infra*, Chs 3 and 5.

169 *Beef Hormones Case* (1998) WTO Appellate Body, paras 124–5.

170 Lowe, in Boyle and Freestone (eds), *International Law and Sustainable Development* (Oxford, 1999) 33, dispenses even with *opinio juris*, but unless such norms emerge from thin air at the whim of judges the endorsement of states must be a necessary element. All the norms Lowe relies on do in fact have such endorsement.

171 Dworkin, *Taking Rights Seriously* (London, 1977). This argument is developed by Sands, in Lang (ed), *Sustainable Development and International Law* (London, 1995) Ch 5.

endorsed principles in international environmental law.[172] What these examples show is that subtle changes in the existing law and in existing treaties may come about through the application of such general principles.

d) Judicial Decisions

The reference in Article 38(1)(d) of the ICJ Statute to judicial decisions as a 'subsidiary means' for determining the law is apt to mislead. In reality the ICJ and other international tribunals have an important role in pronouncing on matters of international law in contentious cases and advisory opinions[173]. Judicial decisions are not a formal source of international law as such, since even in contentious cases 'The decision of the Court has no binding force except between the parties and in respect of that particular Case,'[174] while advisory opinions merely give advice on the law to the organ requesting them.[175] Nevertheless, in performing the 'normal judicial function of ascertaining the existence or otherwise of legal principles and rules' courts necessarily provide authoritative evidence of what the law is.[176] In doing so, courts can exercise a formative influence by affirming and giving substance to new norms and principles endorsed by a consensus of the international community, whether in the form of multilateral treaties, custom or soft law.[177] The result may not be especially innovative, but it is not the job of international courts to be especially innovative.[178]

While there is no doctrine of precedent in the ICJ, or in other international courts and tribunals, these courts will not lightly disregard their own pronouncements,[179] though they will find ways of distancing themselves from outdated or erroneous decisions.[180] Thus a body of jurisprudence accumulates and contributes to the development of law. As we will see in Chapter 3, a growing number of ICJ, ITLOS and arbitral decisions and advisory opinions are directly relevant to environmental issues. Other courts whose decisions will be considered in later chapters include the African, European, and Inter-American Courts of Human Rights, the WTO Appellate Body, and national courts. Though decisions of these bodies are not all of equal weight and significance they may be persuasive precedents and provide evidence of general international law.

172 ICJ Reports (1997) 7, para 140; *Pulp Mills Case*, ICJ Reports (2010) 14, at para 177. See *infra*, Ch 3, section 2.

173 See Boyle and Chinkin, *The Making of International Law*, Ch 6; Fitzmaurice, *Symbolae Verzijl* (1958) 174; *Brownlie's Principles*, Ch 2, Jennings, 45 *ICLQ* (1996) 1, Guilllaume,1 *JIDS* (2011)1.

174 Statute of the ICJ, Article 59. See also Statute of the ITLOS, 1982 UNCLOS, Annex VI, Article 33(2).

175 *Namibia Advisory Opinion*, ICJ Reports (1971) 16, para 32.

176 *Nuclear Weapons Advisory Opinion*, ICJ Reports (1996) 226, para 18.

177 See e.g. *Gabčíkovo-Nagymaros Case*, ICJ Reports (1997) 7, *infra*, section 2(3) and others cited *infra*, Ch 3.

178 See Boyle, 63 *GYIL* (2020) section 3.

179 *Cameroon-Nigeria Maritime Boundary Case (Preliminary Objections)*, ICJ Reports (1998) 292, para 28; *Croatian Genocide Case (Preliminary Objections)*, ICJ Reports (2008) 412, para 53.

180 E.g. other tribunals have declined to follow the controversial and widely criticized interpretation of UNCLOS Article 281 adopted by the *Southern Bluefin Tuna Arbitration* (2000) ICSID: see *South China Sea Arbitration*, PCA (2015) paras 223–6.

(e) Writings of Publicists

The ICJ Statute also cites 'the teachings of the most highly qualified publicists of the various nations' as a 'subsidiary means for the determination of rules of law'.[181] The works and views of some writers have been referred to in the ICJ and other tribunals and are especially cited by law officers and counsel preparing opinions, or pleadings for court cases; arbitrators and, especially, municipal courts less familiar with the concepts and practice of international law are perhaps more inclined to give weight to writers than is the ICJ.[182] As we have seen, reports of international codification bodies are also much quoted and relied on for this purpose. These include the reports and articles drafted by the ILC, and the reports and resolutions of the Institute of International Law, the International Law Association ('ILA'), the WCED, and IUCN.[183]

2(3) CODIFICATION AND PROGRESSIVE DEVELOPMENT

The ILC's work on the codification of international law is generally regarded as providing good evidence of the existing law:[184] courts, governments and international organizations make use of its draft conventions, principles, and commentaries on that basis. The ILC was established in 1947 with the object of promoting 'the progressive development of international law and its codification.'[185] Since then it has worked on nearly thirty topics and produced conventions on a wide range of issues including the law of treaties, law of the sea, state responsibility, international watercourses, diplomatic immunity and the statute of an international criminal court.[186] Many of its codifications have become widely regarded as authoritative statements of the law and are relied on by international courts, international organizations and governments. Some, including those on international watercourses, state responsibility and transboundary risk are directly relevant to this study, and are considered in detail in later chapters.

Because the ILC has never drawn a sharp distinction between codification ('the more precise formulation and systematization of rules of international law in fields where there already has been extensive state practice, precedent, and doctrine') and progressive development ('the preparation of draft conventions on subjects which have not yet been regulated by international law or in regard to which the law has not yet been sufficiently developed in the practice of states')[187] it has been possible for it to engage in a certain amount of creative law-making or law reform. This has also enabled the ICJ and other tribunals to rely on ILC conventions without overtly enquiring whether particular articles represent existing law or a development of the

181 See Sivakumaran, 66 *ICLQ* (2017) 1. 182 See *Brownlie's Principles*, Ch 2.
183 See *infra*, Ch 3, section 1, and on IUCN, see *infra*, Ch 2, section 7 (2).
184 Pursuant to Article 38(1)(d) of the ICJ Statute. 185 ILC Statute, Article 1.
186 See Anderson et al (eds), *The International Law Commission and the Future of International Law* (London, 1998); Ago, 92 *RGDIP* (1988) 532f; Sinclair, *The International Law Commission* (Cambridge, 1987); Boyle and Chinkin, *The Making of International Law*, Ch 4.
187 Statute, Article 15.

law. Moreover, the deliberative and sometimes slow pace of its work allows states to influence, appreciate, and in some cases apply the law as articulated and shaped by the Commission. Use by foreign ministries of the 1969 VCLT and the draft articles on state responsibility are the most obvious examples, but by no means the only ones. Although the ILC does not 'make' international law it has become a significant part of the subtle process by which international law both changes and comes into being.

The best example is the *Gabčíkovo-Nagymaros Case*,[188] decided by the ICJ in 1997. Here the Court showed remarkably little inclination to search for evidence of widespread, consistent, and prolonged state practice as it did for example in its judgment in the *North Sea Continental Shelf Cases*.[189] Instead, on questions of treaty law, the law relating to international watercourses, state responsibility and state succession, it relied more heavily than in any previous case on the work of the ILC as representing customary law. The ILC's work on state responsibility was then incomplete, its articles on watercourses had only just been adopted as a treaty, and its convention on state succession had not been widely ratified. Here we can see very clearly the interplay of codification by the ILC, re-negotiation and revision of the text by states in a diplomatic forum, and application of that revised text by an international court, even though it was not in force or binding on the parties. Moreover, the fortuitous conjunction of litigation so soon after the UN's adoption of the 1997 UN Watercourses Convention resulted in a rapid endorsement of its efforts at redrafting the law in a more integrated and systematic way. It also helped that although the Watercourses Convention was not adopted by consensus, very few states opposed the text as a whole and only a handful voted against individual articles.[190] Thus the Commission's work has a potential double impact: on the one hand it may provide evidence of the existing law, on the other it helps constitute new law, sometimes quite quickly. There are few better examples of the process of international law-making.[191]

At the same time, as one study of the ILC shows, the very subtlety of its approach may have precluded the Commission from contributing in a more overtly creative way to the development of those new and important areas of international law which have emerged since 1945.[192] In advancing the process of codification it may have diminished the scope for progressive development in its work and thereby limited its own role in the contemporary law-making process. The resulting displacement of the ILC by other law-making bodies can be observed very clearly in the development of international environmental law. The ILC has played no part in creating what might be called the architecture of this subject: sustainable development, global environmental responsibility, and environmental rights. It has instead confined itself to the more modest role of refining those elements which have become established law—in practice the law relating to transboundary risk.[193] Even then, its early efforts were deeply

188 ICJ Reports (1997) 7. 189 ICJ Reports (1969) 3. 190 *Infra*, Ch 10, n 7.

191 See Boyle and Chinkin, *The Making of International Law*, Ch 4, where the point is elaborated.

192 Anderson *et al* (eds), *The International Law Commission and the Future of International Law*.

193 See *infra*, Ch 3, sections 5–8.

confused, and inevitably raised the question whether the Commission should have any role in the development of new areas of environmental law. Perhaps not surprisingly the UN gave UNEP, not the ILC, responsibility for developing international law relating to sustainable development.[194] The ILC's current (2019) work on 'protection of the environment in relation to armed conflict' is, however, a creditable attempt to develop international environmental law in a novel context (internal armed conflict) where the creative use of human rights law, corporate responsibility, international criminal law and the law of armed conflict is required.[195]

2(4) UN CONFERENCE DECLARATIONS AND GENERAL ASSEMBLY RESOLUTIONS

With minor exceptions, Article 10 of the UN Charter gives the UN General Assembly power only to adopt non-binding resolutions; it has no legislative power as such. UN General Assembly resolutions and declarations by states at UN-sponsored conferences may however have legal effects.[196] Whether they codify or provide evidence of existing law, or constitute the *opinio juris* necessary for new customary law, or legitimize the development of state practice, will depend on various factors which must be assessed in each case. A law-making resolution or declaration need not necessarily proclaim rights or principles as law, but as with treaties, the wording must be 'of a fundamentally norm-creating character such as could be regarded as forming the basis of a general rule of law.'[197] Declarations or resolutions setting out agreed norms or general principles 'will usually have greater influence than recommendations.'[198] The context within which resolutions are negotiated and the accompanying statements of delegations will also be relevant if assessing the *opinio juris* of states. Lastly, the degree of support is significant. A resolution adopted by consensus—without a vote and without objections—or by unanimous vote will necessarily carry more weight than one supported only by a two-thirds majority of states. Resolutions opposed by even a small number of states may have little effect if those states are among the ones most immediately affected.[199] The unsuccessful attempt by the General Assembly in the 1970s to change the law on expropriation of foreign investments is a well-known example of the inability of majorities of states to legislate for minorities in this fashion.[200]

[194] See *infra*, Ch 2, section 3(3). [195] See *infra*, Ch 3, section 10.

[196] See e.g. Sloan, 58 *BYIL* (1987) 39; Brownlie, 162 *Recueil des Cours* (1979) 245, at 261; Virally, *AFDI* (1956) 66–99.

[197] *North Sea Continental Shelf Cases*, ICJ Reports (1969) 3, para 72. On UNGA resolutions see also *Nuclear Weapons Advisory Opinion*, ICJ Reports (1996) 226, para 70; *Chagos Archipelago Advisory Opinion*, ICJ Reports (2019), paras 152–3.

[198] Schermers and Blokker, *International Institutional Law* (The Hague, 1995) 777.

[199] See the cautionary dissent of Schwebel in the *Nuclear Weapons Advisory Opinion*, ICJ Reports (1996) 226, 318–9.

[200] See Charter of Economic Rights and Duties of States, UNGA Res 3281 XXX (1974) and *Texaco v Libya*, 53 ILR (1977) 422, paras 80–91. 120 states voted for the resolution, six voted against, ten abstained.

The ban on deep seabed mining outside the framework of UNCLOS is another.[201] In this case the minority of objecting states maintained their own parallel regime until eventually an agreement was reached.

In an international system where the consent or acquiescence of states is still an essential precondition for the development of new law or changes to existing law, these examples show that opposing votes matter. Even if such resolutions can change the law for states which vote in favour, it is clear that they do not do so for the dissenting minority.[202] Adoption by consensus may give a suitably worded resolution greater normative impact, but not if accompanied by statements which seriously qualify what has been agreed, or if it simply papers over an agreement to disagree without pressing matters to a vote.[203] For all these reasons, the adoption of resolutions by international organizations or of declarations by states should not be confused with law-making *per se*.

Despite these reservations, however, it has to be acknowledged that though resolutions are not *per se* binding they may help make new law. At the very least, consensus resolutions may create strong expectations of conforming conduct and by these means come to have some law-making significance, especially when resolutions are repeated or acquiesced in with sufficient frequency.[204] In the *Nicaragua* case, the ICJ accepted, in the context of the obligation not to use force, that *opinio juris* may, 'though with all due caution', be deduced from the attitude of states towards certain General Assembly resolutions and, in particular, from a resolution adopted without a vote and expressed in the form of a Declaration of Principles interpreting the UN Charter.[205] Consent to such a resolution expressed in the Court's view not merely reiteration of the treaty commitment laid down in the Charter, but acceptance of the rules concerned, separately from the relevant Charter provisions. On this view the attitudes of states expressed in the debates of the UN or other international bodies and their voting on resolutions may be regarded as constituting the *opinio juris* required to confirm a customary rule as set out in the resolution or declaration.

The *Nicaragua* case is not without its critics; it has been contended that the court completely reversed the normal process for formation of custom based on actual state practice accompanied by a psychological element of legal conviction, that is, that it took account of state practice only after first using the UN resolutions as evidence of the *opinio juris*.[206] But this argument ignores the reality that once there is international

201 The Declaration of Principles Governing the Seabed and Ocean Floor etc, UNGA Res 2749 XXV (1970) was adopted by 108 votes in favour with fourteen abstentions.

202 *Texaco v Libya*, 53 ILR (1977) 422. But for a different view compare Charney (1987) *BYIL* 1.

203 See Boyle and Chinkin, *The Making of International Law*, Ch 3. On the evolution of consensus decision-making in the UN see Peterson, *The General Assembly in World Politics* (Boston, 1986) 81–90; Schermers and Blokker, *International Institutional Law*, 506–15.

204 Higgins, *The Development of International Law through the Political Organs of the United Nations* (Oxford, 1963); *id*, in Cheng, *International Law: Teaching and Practice*, 27–44.

205 *Nicaragua Case*, ICJ Reports (1986) 14, para 188. See also *Nuclear Weapons Advisory Opinion*, ICJ Reports (1996) 226, para 70.

206 See in particular D'Amato, 81 *AJIL* (1987) 101.

consensus on the basic rule, it is highly unlikely that any state will object if it is then implemented, however rarely, in state practice.[207] Insofar as custom represents observable social norms it is the agreement on the rules rather than the practice itself that matters most: custom in that sense is first negotiated, then implemented.[208] To that extent the *Nicaragua Case* reflects rather better than the *North Sea Cases* the Court's general treatment of customary international law.

As we shall see, law-making in the environmental field now includes a large number of UN resolutions and declarations, most notably the 1992 Rio Declaration. The Rio Declaration remains the most authoritative general statement of the core rules and principles of international environmental law, comparable in its legal status to the 1948 Universal Declaration of Human Rights.[209] It is not an instrument that lawyers can ignore. Although such normative instruments may in part codify existing law, they may also authorize, even if they do not oblige, states to act upon the basis of the newly articulated rules or principles; they may to that extent have law-making effect in customary law, though they will often require further elaboration through treaties or state practice.[210] From that perspective UN General Assembly resolutions and UN declarations fall into the larger category of 'soft law', considered in the next section.

2(5) SOFT LAW

From a law-making perspective the term 'soft law' is a convenient description for a variety of non-legally binding but normatively worded instruments used in contemporary international relations by states and international organizations.[211] As we saw above, it encompasses *inter alia* inter-state conference declarations with a law-making character, such as the 1992 Rio Declaration , and UN General Assembly resolutions, but the concept also extends to the codes of conduct, guidelines, and resolutions of UN programmes and specialized agencies and other international treaty bodies, including UNEP, the International Maritime Organization ('IMO'), the International Atomic Energy Agency ('IAEA'), the Food and Agriculture Organization ('FAO'), and the International Whaling Commission ('IWC'). Like UN General Assembly resolutions these soft law instruments are not law in the sense used by Article 38(1) of the ICJ Statute, but they are usually negotiated and drafted with care, sometimes in great

[207] Chinkin, 38 *ICLQ* (1989) 850, 866.

[208] See for example the Court's treatment of self-determination in the *Chagos Archipelago Advisory Opinion*, ICJ Reports (2019) paras 150–161.

[209] See *infra*, Ch 3, sections 1(2) and (3).

[210] See generally *Brownlie's Principles*, Ch 2; Boyle, in Evans (ed), *International Law*, Ch 5.

[211] See especially Baxter, 29 *ICLQ* (1980) 549–566; Abbott and Snidal, 54 *Int Org* (2000) 421; Barrelli, 58 *ICLQ* (2009) 957; Boyle, in Malone, Chesterman and Villalpando (eds), *Oxford Handbook of UN Treaties* (Oxford, 2018); Hillgenberg, 10 *EJIL* (1999) 499; Dupuy, 12 *Michigan JIL* (1991) 420; Chinkin, 38 *ICLQ* (1989) 850; Elias and Lim, 28 *NYIL* (1997) 3; Shelton (ed) *Commitment and Compliance: The Role of Non-binding Norms in the International Legal System* (Oxford, 2000). For more sceptical views see Weil, 77 *AJIL* (1983) 413; Klabbers, 67 *Nordic JIL* (1998) 381–91.

detail, and are intended in many cases to have normative significance despite their non-binding, non-treaty form.[212] There is at least an element of good faith commitment,[213] an expectation that they will be adhered to if possible, and in many cases, a desire to influence the development of state practice or the interpretation and application of a treaty. Soft law in this sense can be contrasted with hard law, which is always binding. Seen from this angle, the legal form is decisive: customary international law and treaties which have entered into force are by definition hard law. But the key point is that, in international environmental law, custom, treaties and soft law cannot be viewed in isolation: they interact to form a complex regulatory system that has to be capable of sometimes rapid evolution as the science, the policies and the priorities of governments evolve and change. Soft law has to be a significant part of that system for two main reasons.

First, it may be easier to reach agreement when the form is non-binding. This enables states to take on commitments that otherwise they would not, or to formulate them in a more precise and detailed form that could not at that point be agreed in a treaty. The softlaw approach thus allows states to tackle a problem collectively at a time when they do not want to shackle their freedom of action too firmly. On environmental matters this might be because scientific evidence is not conclusive or complete, but nonetheless a precautionary approach is required,[214] or because the economic costs are uncertain or potentially over-burdensome. With soft law their legal commitments, and the consequences of any non-compliance, are more limited. Soft law has thus been a useful instrument for gradually developing the law in relatively new fields such as human rights or environmental protection. This helps explain why in its early years UNEP made extensive use of soft law instruments.[215] To take only one of many examples, its guidelines on environmental impact assessment have influenced national law, treaties, the ILC, and the ICJ,[216] and thereby stimulated the widespread state practice which has established Environmental Impact Assessment ('EIA') as 'a requirement under general international.'[217] Although not all 'soft' instruments necessarily lend themselves to becoming 'hard' law, the very existence of such an instrument encourages the trend towards hardening the international legal order. Once the principles are accepted by states in soft law form, it becomes easier to incorporate them in a treaty when the need arises. Thus IAEA Guidelines formed the basis for the rapid adoption of the 1986 Convention on Early Notification of a Nuclear Accident following the

212 See previous section.

213 *AO on Voting Procedure on Questions relating to Reports and Petitions concerning the Territory of South West Africa*, Sep Op Lauterpacht, ICJ Reports (1955) 118: 'The State in question, while not bound to accept the recommendation, is bound to give it due consideration in good faith.' See also Virally, *AFDI* (1956) 85–91. A soft law declaration may result in binding unilateral obligations: see *OSPAR Arbitration* (2003) PCA, para 90.

214 See e.g. the Declaration adopted by the 1990 Third North Sea Ministerial Conference, which incorporated the 'precautionary principle', accepting that states may need to take measures before clear scientific proof of harmful effects is obtainable, on which see *infra*, Ch 8, section 3(2).

215 *Infra*, Ch 2, section 3(3).

216 *Infra*, Ch 3, section 7.

217 *Pulp Mills Case*, ICJ Reports (2010) 14, para 204.

Chernobyl accident;[218] UNEP's EIA Guidelines were substantially incorporated in the 1991 Espoo Convention;[219] and UNEP's Guidelines on Land-based Sources of Marine Pollution provided a model for regional seas treaties.[220]

Secondly, soft law instruments will normally be easier to supplement, amend or replace than treaties, since all that is required is the adoption of a new resolution by the relevant international institution.[221] Treaties take time to replace or amend, and the attempt to do so can result in an awkward and overlapping network of old and new obligations between different sets of parties. The important point is that soft law is often relied on to provide the detailed technical rules and standards required to implement international regulatory regimes concerned with safety, pollution, resource conservation and so on. Because they are normally based on expert advice, and may need to change frequently to reflect changes in policy or in the underlying science, there is little point putting these rules and standards into the text of a treaty which would soon require successive amendments. The ILC commentary to what is now Article 31(3)(a) of the 1969 VCLT notes that '. . .an agreement as to the interpretation of a provision reached after the conclusion of the treaty represents an authentic interpretation by the parties which must be read into the treaty for purposes of its interpretation.'[222] That agreement does not have to be binding.[223] Soft law resolutions cannot change the object and purpose of a treaty nor can they formally amend it,[224] but provided they are adopted by consensus, soft law resolutions may constitute either a subsequent agreement on interpretation of a treaty, or subsequent practice, pursuant to Articles 31(3)(a) and (b) respectively.[225] If the parties wish to add to or change their previous interpretation or practice they are free to do so by the simple expedient of adopting another resolution.

Through the technique of incorporation by reference soft law standards may also become part of a binding treaty regime. Non-binding World Health Organization ('WHO') and FAO standards thus constitute 'international standards, guidelines or recommendations' for the purpose of judging compliance with the WTO Sanitary and Phytosanitary Agreement.[226] In the *Pulp Mills Case*, the ICJ had to interpret references to 'guidelines and recommendations of international technical bodies' in Article 41 of the 1975 Statute of the River Uruguay. The parties relied inter alia on WHO standards for air and water pollution. These are not binding on states, but as the ICJ indicated they are 'to be taken into account by the State so that the domestic rules and regulations

[218] *Infra*, Ch 7. [219] *Infra*, Ch 3, section 7.

[220] See e.g. 1990 Kuwait Protocol for the Protection of the Marine Environment Against Marine Pollution from Land-based Sources, *infra*, Ch 8, section 3(1).

[221] Aust, 35 *ICLQ* (1986) 787.

[222] ILC, 'The Law of Treaties,' commentary to Article 27, at para (14) in Watts, *The International Law Commission* (1999, OUP) vol. II, 689.

[223] See *Kasikili/Sedudu Island Case*, ICJ Reports (1999) 1075–76, paras 47–51 and the case-law cited at para 50. See also, 'Treaties over Time,' ILC Report (2011) GAOR A/66/10, 281–284.

[224] *Whaling in the Antarctic Case*, ICJ Reports (2014) 226, para 56.

[225] *Ibid*, paras 46, 83. [226] 1994 SPS Agreement, Article 3, and *infra*, Ch 13.

and the measures it adopts are compatible with those guidelines and recommendations.'[227] The Preamble to the 1994 Nuclear Safety Convention also recognizes that internationally formulated safety guidelines 'can provide guidance on contemporary means of achieving a high level of safety.' IAEA nuclear safety standards would be the obvious starting point for determining what constituted the 'appropriate steps' with regard to safety controls required by Articles 10–19 of the Convention.[228] Soft law has also played an important role in implementing the fisheries provisions of the 1982 UNCLOS by the FAO.[229]

These internationally agreed standards are essential in giving hard content to the overly-general and open-textured terms of regulatory or framework treaties.[230] The examples given above point to the conclusion that the non-binding force of softlaw can be over-stated. States are not free in these cases to disregard applicable softlaw instruments: even when not incorporated directly into a treaty, compliance with the soft law may be necessary in order to comply with the treaty. Although 'soft law' has been described by one writer as no more than 'a convenient shorthand to include vague legal norms',[231] this is a very serious misreading of the concept and is contradicted by many of the examples referred to in this book.[232] Nor does it follow that soft law instruments are unenforceable; some have been made the subject of international supervisory and reporting processes.[233] As later chapters will show, environmental soft law has made an important contribution to establishing a new legal order in a fast-growing and initially unsettled field. Without soft law, we could scarcely have a functioning regulatory system for international environmental problems.

3 OVERVIEW

Writers and environmentalists have sometimes been critical of international law's ability to provide adequate protection for the environment and to respond quickly to the changes required as scientific knowledge advances. Much of this criticism is misconceived. It is true that international environmental law has developed on a sectoral basis, often in response to disasters, and that it does not always reflect the interdependence of the various issues and their solutions, but this failing does not derive from the inherent nature and structure of international law—municipal legal systems have also not developed on a holistic basis so far as environmental protection is concerned. International law offers many vehicles for its own evolution—custom, treaty,

227 ICJ Reports (2010) 14, at para 62. See also para 197.

228 *Infra*, Ch 7.

229 *Infra*, Ch 2, section 4(3).

230 Contini and Sand, 66 *AJIL* (1972) 37.

231 Gruchalla-Wesierski, 30 *McGill LJ* (1984) 44.

232 See also Boyle, in Evans (ed) *International Law*, Ch 5, where the analysis is more fully developed.

233 Shelton (ed) *Commitment and Compliance: The Role of Non-binding Norms in the International Legal System*, and see *infra*, Ch 4.

soft law, general principles, framework agreements and so on—which can be used in a variety of ways to develop and revise the law to meet new environmental perspectives. This development does not have to be slow; progress depends on the willingness of states to resort to these processes. The speed with which they do so depends not only on the competing social, economic, and political priorities of governments, but also on the availability and reliability of scientific information. Soft law solutions may sometimes enable agreement to be reached more quickly but, as the following chapters show, there has since the Stockholm Conference been a remarkable growth not only in legally binding measures of environmental protection, but also in new legal concepts and principles which increasingly call into question traditional boundaries between 'public' and 'private' international law, and between national and international law.

Since the Rio Conference in 1992, international environmental law as a whole has come of age. Its gestation may have been slow, but it has proved to be a very vigorous plant. If the 1990s are best remembered for 'treaty congestion' because of the large number of multilateral environmental agreements under negotiation,[234] the new millennium has seen an unparalleled growth in the environmental jurisprudence of international tribunals. No longer is it necessary to squeeze every drop of life out of the immortal trio of arbitrations—*Behring Sea Fur Seals, Trail Smelter* and *Lac Lanoux*—which sustained international environmental law throughout most of its earlier existence. A modern account now has at least twenty inter-state cases between 1996 and 2018 on which to draw.[235] By any measure this is a substantial jurisprudence. Equally remarkable are the number of courts and tribunals which have contributed to the jurisprudence and its overall coherence.

The growing case law affords little comfort for those who have sometimes doubted the very existence of international law dealing with the environment, or who tend to see it all as soft law or comprised only of specific treaty regimes. Judicial decisions have applied rules of customary law to the control of transboundary environmental risks, protection of the global environment, and the conservation and sustainable use of shared or common resources.[236] In this respect they have drawn heavily on the work of the ILC and the provisions of the 1992 Rio Declaration. The Rio Declaration has also stimulated the development of new general principles with direct relevance to the global environment—the precautionary principle, the polluter pays principle, common but differentiated responsibility, and sustainable development.[237] While the status of all of these principles in customary law is doubtful or disputed, they have nevertheless become important modifiers of existing rules and treaties, or influenced the negotiation and elaboration of treaty regimes. As principles endorsed by consensus they are too important for courts, governments or international organizations and treaty bodies to ignore.

The recognition that human rights law has an environmental dimension—both internally and in a transboundary context—is shown by the developments taking place

[234] See Anton, in Alam et al (eds), *Routledge Handbook of IEL* (Abingdon, 2013) Ch 36.

[235] See *infra*, Ch 3. [236] *Infra*, Ch 3, sections 3–8. [237] *Ibid.*

in this context since the second edition of this book.[238] Civil and political rights have been the focus of the strongest environmental claims. Economic and social rights provide a less well-established basis for environmental protection, but even they have become significant in African and Latin American litigation. Moreover, the emergence of specifically environmental rights is evidenced by the 1998 UNECE Convention on Access to Information, Public Participation in Decision-making and Access to Justice in Environmental Matters ('Aarhus Convention') and the ILC's support for non-discriminatory access to effective remedies for transboundary environmental nuisances. International environmental law has thus moved well beyond its original focus on inter-state problems, while placing humans 'at the centre of concerns for sustainable development' and giving some substance to Principle 1 of the Rio Declaration.

What these developments have done, as we will see in Chapters 3 and 5, is to change the basis and perspective of international environmental law.[239] Having started as a set of rules limited largely to state responsibility for transboundary harm, resource allocation, and the resolution of conflicting uses of common spaces, international environmental law now accommodates a preventive and precautionary approach to the management of environmental risk and the protection of the environment on a global level. This is a necessary and inevitable development if international law is to address major global and regional environmental issues. It involves greater emphasis on environmental regulation and gives less prominence to liability for damage as the law's main response to environmentally harmful activities. To this extent, the development of international environmental law reflects the comparable transformation in national environmental law throughout much of the developed, industrialized world. As a consequence, the most convincing characterization is no longer that of neighbourly relations, but of environmental trusteeship, with certain institutional similarities to the protection of social and economic rights, and a comparable concern for community interests at a global level, not merely those of states *inter se*.[240] However, the system still displays a largely anthropocentric perspective—the environment as such does not have rights and there is little support for giving it 'intrinsic value' beyond the protection of 'charismatic megafauna', biological diversity, or the wilderness value of Antarctica.[241]

Participation in the multilateral treaty regimes which constitute the main element of this system of environmental governance is sufficiently widespread that they represent applicable law for most states. Their growing sophistication testifies to their character

238 *Infra*, Ch 5.

239 See also Bodansky, Brunnée, Hey (eds), *The Oxford Handbook of International Environmental Law* (Oxford, 2007) Ch 1.

240 See e.g the treatment of the marine environment in the *South China Sea Arbitration (Jurisdiction and Merits)* PCA (2016) *infra*, Ch 9, and generally Kerbrat, Maljean-Dubois, Mehdi (eds), *Le Droit International Face aux Enjeux Environnementaux* (Paris, 2010), 17, who refer to 'Le passage d'un droit international de bon voisinage plutôt bilateral, territorial et fondé sur la reciprocité des droits et obligations, à un droit international plutôt multilateral, global, dans le cadre duquel les obligations sont souscrites au nom d'un intérêt commun...'

241 *Supra*, section 1(3).

as evolutionary regimes. At the same time the explosion of treaty-making has visibly diminished. Many of the newer treaties deal with matters of detail rather that broader issues of principle, suggesting that the era of environmental law-making has reached a plateau. The focus of international attention has shifted instead towards a stronger emphasis on treaty ordination, effectiveness, and compliance. Although there is little evidence of systematic non-compliance by states parties with most MEAs, some MEAs are inadequate, ineffective, and constrained by the competing demands of economic development.[242] A few, including the fisheries provisions of the 1982 UNCLOS, may have made matters worse.[243] This mixed record should not be surprising. A focus on sustainable development, as we note in Chapter 2, does not inevitably mean giving greater weight to environmental protection, or nature conservation, or environmental rights. It highlights the difficulty that integrating the needs of environmental protection and economic development poses, not merely for lawyers, but above all for politicians and law-makers.

We explain in Chapter 4 how multilateral supervisory institutions constitute the predominant model of environmental regulation and compliance control. By and large the non-compliance procedures established under most MEAs have functioned successfully, despite their non-confrontational, non-judicial character. The role of courts is inevitably secondary in this context, limited to settling bilateral problems or providing judicial review of the operation of treaty regimes and international institutions. While international courts do have power to act in the public interest in environmental matters, for example in the protection of common spaces, such proceedings should preferably be initiated by states or international organizations, rather than by NGOs.[244] But even if their role were to be widened it is still difficult to envisage courts doing more than supplementing the work of other international institutions. Thus the primary concern of future development should properly be to address the inadequacy of existing environmental regimes, not to introduce radical innovations in global governance or the judicial machinery and process.

From this perspective, the problems of effectiveness which are now so obvious in the major global environmental regimes are essentially political and policy-oriented in character. They are best seen as a reflection of the difficulties of securing international agreement on global environmental management within a complex and diffuse structure of political authority, and of the deeply conflicting policy priorities among developed and developing states. As Hurrell and Kingsbury observe:

> Collective environmental management poses a severe and therefore politically sensitive challenge because it involves the creation of rules and institutions that embody notions of shared responsibilities and shared duties that impinge very heavily on the domestic structures and organization of states, that invest individuals and groups within states with rights and duties and that seek to embody some notion of a common good for the planet as a whole.[245]

242 Pallemaerts, *Toxics and Transnational Law* (Oxford, 2003) Ch 2, and see *infra*, Chs 6, 8 and 11.

243 See *infra*, Ch 12.

244 See the discussion of public interest litigation *infra*, Ch 4, section 3.

245 Hurrell and Kingsbury, *The International Politics of the Environment* (Oxford 1992) 6.

Some environmentalists have argued for the radical restructuring of international governance, abandoning the present model of cooperation between sovereign states in favour of some form of majoritarian decision-making. Perhaps the most far-reaching proposal in this respect is to invest the UN Security Council, or some other UN organ, with power to act in the interests of 'ecological security', taking universally binding decisions in the interests of all mankind and the environment.[246] Other proposals, firmly rejected by the UN, would have turned UNEP into an international environmental organization modelled on the WTO.[247]

Yet the major virtue of the present international political system is precisely that in matters of global interdependence, such as protection of the environment, it compels the negotiation of a balance of interests and requires consensus if a framework of rules is to attain global acceptance. No state or group of states, including the smaller developing nations, is deprived of influence in this system, as it might well be under a majoritarian model of decision-making; competing priorities, including those of economic development, must be fully addressed and accommodated. Negotiating the 1982 UNCLOS on a consensus basis represents the kind of bargaining process arguably essential if global environmental needs are to command a global response. Moreover, as the experience of the EU illustrates, it is by no means clear that a supranational model of interstate regulation necessarily leads to better environmental management in the face of equally pressing claims to higher priority for other issues, or that it generates environmental law more quickly than the present decentralized international system. It took the EU longer to decide how to implement the 1989 Basel Convention than it took for the convention itself to be drafted, negotiated and enter into force, and similar problems have been encountered in attempts to negotiate EU directives on ocean dumping or liability for environmental harm.

If states have generally preferred to avoid resort to supranational law-making institutions, or supranational enforcement, it does not follow that their sovereignty has remained unaffected by the growth of international environmental law and the emergence of the environment as an issue of global concern. Not only are states subject to obligations of restraint and control over the extra-territorial effects of activities within their jurisdiction or control, as well as in the exploitation of shared natural resources and common spaces but, more significantly, notions of common heritage, common interest, common concern and inter-generational equity have extended the scope of international law, and the legitimate interest of other states, into the management of every state's domestic environment, at least in respect of issues such as global climate change and conservation of wildlife and biodiversity.[248] Moreover, the characterization of environmental quality as a human rights issue, potentially affording individuals a claim to protection in national and international law against their own government and those of other states, has effected another radical transformation in the nature of sovereignty or sovereign rights over natural resources and the

[246] See *infra*, Ch 2. [247] See *infra*, Ch 2. [248] *Infra*, Ch 3, section 3.

environment in general.[249] These developments indicate that while sovereignty may remain a focus of conflict and resistance to further encroachments on national autonomy, it is not and never has been a decisive objection.[250]

International law empowers, constrains and compels governments in various ways and at various levels. Its impact on environmental protection policies and laws is complex. For example, a country that enters into free trade agreements gains economic advantages it would not otherwise enjoy, but at the same time its freedom to pursue other policies will be affected. Parts of its economy may develop more rapidly, putting pressure on land, natural resources, water supply and air quality, leading to unsustainable development, environmental degradation, and poorer conditions of health. It may thus be harder to meet commitments undertaken in the International Covenant on Economic, Social and Cultural Rights (ICESCR'), or at UNCED. Equally, those same commitments may restrict certain forms of economic development and limit the ability to benefit from free trade in natural resources. Ultimately, governments make policy choices about how to balance competing objectives of this kind on political, social, economic or ethical grounds. These choices will be reflected in the agreements they sign or in the state practice that contributes to general international law. The relationship between environmental concerns, international trade policy and human rights law is best negotiated by states acting through the UN, the WTO and other international organizations. However, few governments can foresee in detail all the consequences of the commitments they make; even when they do foresee them, it is not always possible to secure the agreement of other governments on how to address whatever tensions may arise out of the interaction of commitments into which they have entered.

Neither conflict nor fragmentation are necessary consequences of the interaction of international environmental law with other branches of international law. In practice, international tribunals have usually found various ways of applying international law as an integrated whole, except where the parties themselves have made this difficult through the Balkanization of dispute settlement and the selective choice of applicable law. Rules of interpretation, priority of treaties, or a balancing of competing interests, have generally provided an ample range of techniques for promoting coherence in the application of international law.[251]

This does not mean there are no problems. On the contrary, there will always be uncertainty about how different legal regimes or different bodies of law interact. Our examination of the interrelationship of environment, trade, and human rights law shows that difficult judgments have to be made, and there remains much for lawyers to argue over.[252] Do these regimes interact at all? How do they interact with customary

[249] *Infra*, Ch 5. [250] Handl, 1 *YbIEL* (1990) 3.

[251] See ILC, 'Fragmentation of International Law', GAOR (2006) A/CN.4/L.682; Simma, 20 *EJIL* (2009) 265; Webb, *International Judicial Integration and Fragmentation* (2013, Oxford) but contrast Koskenniemi, 70 *MLR* (2007) 4–19.

[252] *Infra*, Chs 5 and 13, and see Francioni (ed) *Environment, Human Rights and International Trade* (Oxford, 2001); Young (ed) *Regime Interaction in International Law* (Cambridge, 2015).

international law? Has the right balance between environmental regulation and individual rights been maintained? Are the terms of a treaty inherently evolutionary? Are environmental measures a *lex specialis* or a *lex generalis*, or do they form part of an integral, non-derogable, regime that will prevail over subsequent agreements? What law is applicable in any dispute? Which dispute settlement forum has jurisdiction, if any? The answers to such questions will rarely be obvious and the outcomes are unlikely to be predictable with certainty. For those reasons, these are in practice some of the more challenging questions any international lawyer advising on environmental issues will have to deal with. They illustrate perfectly why international environmental law requires a well-grounded understanding of international law as a whole. It is not a subject for narrow specialists, and it most certainly is neither 'more or less self-contained' nor even 'self-sufficient'.[253]

[253] *Supra*, n 12.

2

INTERNATIONAL GOVERNANCE AND THE FORMULATION OF ENVIRONMENTAL LAW AND POLICY

1 INTRODUCTION

In this chapter* we consider the institutions of global governance responsible for formulating and implementing international environmental policy and law. Global governance has been defined as 'a continuing process through which conflicting or diverse interests may be accommodated and cooperative action may be taken. It includes formal institutions and regimes empowered to enforce compliance, as well as informal arrangements. . . .here is no single model or form of global governance, nor is there a single structure or set of structures. It is a broad, dynamic, complex, process of interactive decision-making'.[1] Although their powers vary widely, the UN, its specialized

* We are grateful to Dr Annalisa Savaresi, University of Stirling, for her contribution to revising this chapter.

[1] Commission on Global Governance, *Our Global Neighbourhood* (Oxford, 1995) 2–4. For a succinct account of 'governance' in international relations see Toope, in Byers (ed), *The Role of Law in International Politics* (Oxford, 2000) 94–9, and generally Hurrell, *On Global Order* (Oxford, 2007) esp. Ch 9. In relation to the environment see in particular Sand, *Lessons Learned in Global Environmental Governance* (New York, 1990); Young, Demko and Ramakrishna, *Global Environmental Change and International Governance* (Dartmouth, 1991); Haas, Keohane and Levy (eds), *Institutions for the Earth: Sources of Effective Environmental Protection* (Cambridge, Mass, 1993); Winter (ed),*Multilevel Governance of Global Environmental Change* (Cambridge, 2006); Axelrod, VanDeveer, Downie (eds) *The Global Environment: Institutions, Law, and Policy* (Washington, 2011) Chs 1–5; Kötze, *Global Environmental Governance* (Cheltenham, 2012).

agencies, and other international bodies have become important institutions of global and regional environmental governance.

Used in this sense, the term 'governance' when applied to the UN and its agencies implies rather less than global government, a task for which no international organization is equipped,[2] but more than just the power to determine policy or initiate the process of international law-making. At the very least it captures the idea of a community of states with responsibility for addressing common problems through a variety of political processes which are inclusive in character, and which to some degree 'embody a limited sense of a collective interest, distinct in specific cases from the particular interests of individual states'.[3] Such bodies may potentially be universal in membership, like the UN or the WTO, or regional, like the Council of Europe or the Organization of American States ('OAS'), or have limited membership based on common interests, as in the Organisation for Economic Co-operation and Development ('OECD'). They may operate on the basis of one- member-one-vote, as in the UN General Assembly or the WTO, or votes may be weighted on some other basis, as in the World Bank, controlled by major donor states, or the UN Security Council, dominated by the five permanent members, or the Council of the IMO, where the major flag states enjoy a privileged position.

The UN and other organizations considered in this chapter are only part of this process of international environmental governance. Equally important is the extensive network of conferences of the parties, commissions and supervisory bodies established by environmental treaties. These autonomous treaty bodies have been likened to a species of international organization, whose main role is to promote implementation of, and compliance with, specific regulatory regimes.[4] They have also contributed to the evolution of what has been termed 'global administrative law'.[5] In contrast, the most valuable contribution made by the UN and related international organizations considered in this chapter has been their ability to determine the international policy-making agenda, and to initiate or facilitate many of the most important law-making developments. Nevertheless, there is, as we shall see, a considerable overlap between conventional international organizations and autonomous treaty bodies, and too sharp a distinction between their respective law-making and implementation roles would be misleading. In reality, both types of institution perform both functions, and the difference between them is largely one of degree. Thus, some intergovernmental

[2] *Our Global Neighbourhood*, 4; Roberts and Kingsbury (eds), *United Nations, Divided World* (2nd edn, Oxford, 1993) 14–17.

[3] Roberts and Kingsbury, *United Nations, Divided World*, 16–17, and see generally, *Our Global Neighbourhood*, 2–6 and Hey, in Bodansky, Brunnée and Hey (eds), *Oxford Handbook of International Environmental Law* (Oxford, 2007) 750–69.

[4] Churchill and Ulfstein, 94 *AJIL* (2000) 623, at 658–9, and see *infra*, section 5.

[5] Kingsbury, Krisch and Stewart, 68 *Law & Cont.Problems* (2005) 15.

organizations, such as the IMO, also offer a means of promoting implementation and compliance with regulatory treaties and other international standards.[6] The range and diversity of organizations and institutions involved in some aspect of global environmental governance point to one obvious problem: the difficulty of ensuring coordination and consistency within such a diffuse and multi-layered system.[7] This is an issue to which we return later.

Intergovernmental organizations such as the UN, the IMO, the FAO[8] and the IAEA[9], among others, have provided the principal fora in which much of the inter-state cooperation necessary for developing international environmental policy and regulatory regimes has been realized. UN conferences, and especially UNCHE and UNCED'), have set agendas for the environment-related work of these bodies. Intergovernmental and non-governmental organizations have also been influential across a broad spectrum of environmental policy and law-making; they have become an important part of the law-making process, even if they are not in themselves *the* process.[10] The most notable are UNEP[11] and the International Union for the Conservation of Nature ('IUCN').[12] International and non-governmental organizations also provide a reservoir of legal and technical expertise and diplomatic machinery not always possessed by individual governments. For many developing states, these organizations thus offer an important source of 'capacity-building' and personnel training, a role which UNCED attributed to the UN Development Programme ('UNDP'), the World Bank, and regional development banks.[13]

In this context the most obvious and indispensable role of the UN and other bodies is to provide a permanent forum where states and other participants can engage in dialogue and negotiations, facilitating the compromises necessary for law-making by states at very different stages of economic and social development. Brunnée and Toope argue that periodic meetings of the parties to multilateral treaties—and by extension the argument must also apply to intergovernmental organizations and law-making conferences such as the third UN Conference on the Law of the Sea—constitute 'on-going, interactional processes,' and that 'It is this broader process and not the formal act of consent that infuses the legal norms generated within [a multilateral agreement] with the ability to influence state conduct.'[14] Their central point is that a law-making

[6] See *infra*, section 4 (4).

[7] See generally Dunoff, in Bodansky, Brunnée and Hey, *Handbook of IEL*, 85–106.

[8] See *infra*, section 4 (3). [9] See *infra*, section 4 (5).

[10] See generally Boyle and Chinkin, *The Making of International Law* (Oxford, 2007) Ch 3.

[11] *Infra*, section 3(3). UNEP is now known as 'UN Environment'.

[12] Membership of IUCN is open both to governments and non-governmental bodies: see *infra*, section 7(2).

[13] UNCED Agenda 21, Ch 37, para 9. See *infra*, section 4(7).

[14] Brunnée and Toope, 39 *Columbia JTL* (2000) 19. See also Brunnée, 15 *LJIL* (2002) 1, 6, and *id*, *Legitimacy and Legality in International Law* (Cambridge, 2010). The arguments in Bodansky, 93 *AJIL* (1999) 596, have general relevance. See also Charlesworth and Coicaud (eds), *Fault Lines of International Legitimacy* (Cambridge, 2010) Chs 1–3.

process perceived as legitimate by states and other relevant actors is more likely to be an effective process. An illegitimate process will either fail to make law at all or will undermine the likelihood of compliance with adopted rules or standards. Moreover, if law-making is the product of interactive processes, then the question who participates in these processes assumes added importance.[15]

It is important to recall, however, that although many intergovernmental organizations will have a legal personality separate from their member states,[16] they have few, if any, powers of independent action, and progress in the development of policy and law depends entirely on the willingness of member states to adopt and implement whatever is proposed. What emerges from any international organization will inevitably reflect the interests and concerns of its members, as well as the voting structure within each organization, and may not always coincide with the priorities of the international community of states as a whole, still less with those of environmental NGOs or scientific experts. The IAEA and IMO a both illustrate the influence wielded by states representing important industries.[17] International organizations are not immune from the phenomenon of 'agency capture' well documented by administrative lawyers.[18]

The significance of viewing any of these bodies as processes of international governance is twofold. First, it suggests an understanding of international society as 'something more than a crucible for the resolution of competitive state interests, with law the mere handmaiden of power'.[19] Whether this is true of international environmental relations will have to be judged on the evidence of subsequent chapters, but it is certainly true that major environmental treaties, like the 1992 CBD and the 1992 Climate Change Convention, or the 1982 UNCLOS, cannot easily be explained by conventional realist conceptions of an international society dominated by great powers. In this respect the role played by international organizations in institutionalizing co-operation on the basis of a community of interest has been crucial.

Secondly, governance implies a more cosmopolitan notion of international society than one composed solely of states. Most notions of governance thus envisage participation by other entities, including NGOs, , industry and business, and civil society in general.[20] Here too, international organizations have been notably progressive, especially in environmental affairs. One of the most striking features of modern international law-making is the interaction of states, inter-governmental organizations ('IGOs') and NGOs in what have been described as 'epistemic communities' or 'transnational

[15] See Boyle and Chinkin, *The Making of International Law*, Ch 2, and *infra*, sections 5 and 7.

[16] *Reparations for Injuries Case*, ICJ Reports (1949) 174.

[17] See *infra*, Chs 7 and 9, respectively.

[18] For a succinct account see Baldwin and McCrudden (eds), *Regulation and Public Law* (London, 1987) 9–12, and literature at 333–4.

[19] Toope, in Byers (ed), *The Role of Law in International Politics*, 96.

[20] Commission on Global Governance, *Our Global Neighbourhood*, 253–60; and Boyle and Chinkin, *The Making of International Law*, Ch 2. On NGO participation in the work of international organizations see *infra*, section 7. Higgins, *Problems and Process: International Law and How We Use it* (OUP, 1994) Ch 3, argues strongly that discussion of the 'subjects' of international law is outmoded and should be replaced by 'participants'. On participation by individuals see 1998 Aarhus Convention, and 1989 ILO Convention No.169 Concerning Indigenous and Tribal Peoples, *infra*, Ch 5.

networks' of officials, experts and interest groups whose quasi-autonomous character allows them to constitute a broader international community than the states that nominally make the decisions.[21] This perspective helps explain why some states—or their representatives—appear to have more (or less) influence on outcomes than the relative size or importance of that state might suggest. But studying the list of observers at meetings of parties to environmental treaties is also instructive. To take just one example, the sixth COP of the 1989 Basel Convention was attended by observers from the Association of Plastics Manufacturers, the International Council on Mining and Metals, and no fewer than nine electronics or mobile phone companies, including Nokia, Sony, LG Electronics and Motorola.[22] What was on the agenda? Negotiation of an end-of-life management agreement with the manufacturers of mobile phones. There were also two environmental NGOs present—World Wide Fund for Nature ('WWF') and the Basel Action Network. Knowing who participates in such meetings is essential to an understanding of the politics of international law-making. In some treaty bodies, environmental NGOs and industry observers are more active and influential than many of the states that participate as full members.[23]

Two objections are commonly made to the involvement of intergovernmental bodies in international governance. First, they may be seen as fundamentally undemocratic in taking power away from elected governments and national legislatures, locating it instead in unaccountable institutions where decisions are taken by national representatives insulated from public scrutiny, and promoting an elitist vision of globalization remote from the concerns of ordinary people.[24] Such a 'democratic deficit' is only partially mitigated by greater transparency and the growing involvement of NGOs and business in the work of some intergovernmental bodies. From this perspective conceptions of a more cosmopolitan international order may appear essentially false. Secondly, without real law-making authority or, in most cases, the ability to take binding decisions by majority vote, they lack the necessary power to take effective action for the common good and to impose their collective will on individual states. From this perspective the problems international organizations encounter in addressing environmental issues may be seen as evidence of the continuing power of national sovereignty or of a need to transcend the outdated structures of an international society dominated by states. Although both characterizations are widely prevalent, they are also mutually incompatible, and in any case considerably over-simplified.[25]

[21] Haas, in Bodansky, Brunnée and Hey (eds), *Handbook of IEL*, 791; Szasz, in Joyner (ed), *The UN and International Law*, 34–5; Slaughter, 76 *Foreign Affairs* (1997) 183; Walker, *Intimations of Global Law* (Cambridge, 2015) 42–54.

[22] 1989 Basel Convention, *Rept. of 6th COP*, UNEP/CHW.6/40 (2003) para 21.

[23] For examples see *infra*, sections 5(2) and 7.

[24] The arguments reviewed in Bodansky, 93 *AJIL* (1999) 596, have general relevance.

[25] Koskenniemi, *From Apology to Utopia: The Structure of International Legal Argument* (Helsinki, 1989) and Allott, *Eunomia* (Oxford, 1990) exemplify the opposing arguments in a much more sophisticated form. See also Toope, in Byers (ed), *The Role of Law in International Politics*, 99–104; Roberts and Kingsbury, *United Nations, Divided World*, Ch 1; Alvarez, *International Organizations as Law-makers* (Oxford, 2005) Chs 5 and 6.

Nevertheless, they do capture the dilemma of how to address the evident need for more effective means of promoting international cooperation to tackle global problems within a politically legitimate and publicly accountable process.[26] Despite these concerns, in an environmental context it will be seen in later chapters that the role and form of cooperation through international organizations has evolved well beyond its rudimentary origins and has at least to some extent been responsive to the needs of contemporary international society.

2 THE DEVELOPMENT OF INTERNATIONAL ENVIRONMENTAL POLICY

2(1) 1972 UN CONFERENCE ON THE HUMAN ENVIRONMENT

It was pressure from NGOs, especially in the US, that led to the convening of the first intergovernmental conference devoted to environmental issues, the 1972 Stockholm Conference on the Human Environment.[27] A preliminary meeting of experts drew particular attention to the developmental aspects of the problem.[28] This report encouraged many developing countries to participate in the Conference on the understanding that any environmentally protective measures resulting from it would not be used as the medium for inhibiting their economic development.

The Conference resulted in four major initiatives which together provided the driving force for developments in UN environmental policy during the next decade and beyond.[29] The first was the adoption of the 1972 Stockholm Declaration, intended to 'inspire and guide the peoples of the world in the preservation and enhancement of the human environment'.[30] The second was the establishment of UNEP, later rechristened 'UN Environment'.[31] The third was the adoption of the Stockholm Action Plan for the development of environmental policy, to be administered by UNEP, and finally the institution, by voluntary contributions, of an Environment Fund.

[26] The literature is too extensive to cite but see in particular Brunnée and Toope, 39 *Columbia JTL* (2000) 19; Franck, *Fairness in International Law and Institutions* (Oxford, 1995).

[27] A number of seminal books had stimulated awareness, including Carson, *Silent Spring* (New York, 1962); Commoner, *The Closing Circle* (New York, 1971); Falk, *This Endangered Planet* (Toronto, 1971); Meadows et al, *The Limits to Growth* (London, 1972).

[28] *Development and Environment: Report and Working Papers of Experts Convened by the Secretary-General of the United National Conference on the Human Environment*, Founex, Switzerland, 4–12 June 1971.

[29] The *Report of the Conference on the Human Environment,* together with the Action Plan, is found in UN Doc. A/CONF. 48/14/Rev. 1 (1972). For a full account see Caldwell, *International Environmental Policy* (3rd edn, Durham NC, 1996) Chs 2 and 3.

[30] *Reports of the Preparatory Committee* relevant to the Declaration are in UN Doc. A/CONF. 48/PC 9, 13 and 17. The *Final Report of the Working Group on the Declaration* is in UN Doc. A/CONF. 48/14/Rev. 1/ Annex II. See Sohn, 14 *Harv. ILJ* (1973) 423.

[31] See *infra*, section 3(3).

The human rights perspective with which the 1972 Stockholm Declaration opens was innovative at the time; although not repeated in the same terms in the 1992 Rio Declaration, developments in human rights law since then reflect the influence of Stockholm.[32] The responsibility for future generations also articulated in Principle 1 was not entirely novel, and has subsequently become an important element of the 1992 Rio Declaration and the concept of sustainable development.[33] The key normative provision in the 1972 Stockholm Declaration, Principle 21, was drawn from existing treaty and customary law. While recognizing both sovereignty and developmental concerns, it makes clear that transboundary environmental harm must be controlled. Principle 21 was repeated almost verbatim in the 1992 Rio Declaration and has been regarded as customary international law by the ILC and ICJ.[34]

Other provisions of the 1972 Stockholm Declaration were more policy-oriented, but they point to later normative developments. The term 'sustainable development' was not used, but Principles 2 to 5 proclaimed that the Earth's natural resources 'must be safeguarded for the benefit of present and future generations', 'that its capacity to produce vital renewable resources must be maintained and, if practical, restored or improved', and that humans have a responsibility to 'safeguard and wisely manage the heritage of wildlife and its habitat'. Principles 6 and 7 relate to pollution control, calling for cessation of the discharge of toxic and other substances in quantities that exceed of the capacity of the environment to render them harmless, to ensure that no irreversible damage is inflicted on ecosystems, and to prevent pollution of the sea. Stockholm thus initiated a process of international law-making on pollution control which is still evolving.[35] The reference to preservation of ecosystems was considered a significant step at the time, long advocated by NGOs, but subsequently included in the 1980 Convention for the Conservation on Antarctic Marine Living Resources, the 1982 UNCLOS, the 1992 CBD, and many later treaties.[36] In deference to the economic concerns of developing countries, Principles 8 to 11 recognize *inter alia* that economic and social development is essential, and that environmental policies should 'enhance and not adversely affect the present or future development potential of developing countries.' Principles 12 to 17 set out policies on environmental and resource management that are in many respects repeated twenty years later in the 1992 Rio Declaration, as well as in a series of multilateral environmental agreements. These include the need for capacity-building and financial assistance for developing states (Principle 12); integration of development planning and environmental protection (Principles 13 & 14); adoption of policies on urbanization and population planning (Principles 15 & 16),[37] and the creation of national institutions with responsibility for 'enhancing environmental quality.' Finally, Principle 22 requires states to further develop international

[32] See *infra*, Ch 5, section 2.
[33] See *infra*, Ch 3, section 2 (2).
[34] See *infra*, Ch 3, section 5.
[35] See *infra*, Ch 6 (air pollution), Ch 7 (radioactive pollution), Ch 8 (toxic substances), Ch 9 (pollution from ships) and Ch 10 (pollution of watercourses).
[36] See *infra*, Chs, 9, 11, 12.
[37] No comparable provisions were included in the 1992 Rio Declaration: see *infra*, section 2(2).

law on liability and compensation for pollution and other forms of environmental damage to areas beyond their jurisdiction.[38]

2(2) 1992 UN CONFERENCE ON ENVIRONMENT AND DEVELOPMENT

(a) The negotiations

Following Stockholm, IUCN began to promote *sustainable* use of resources,[39] but it was not until the WCED published the 'Brundtland Report' calling for a new approach, articulated as 'sustainable development', that a turning point in UN policy was reached.[40] The Brundtland Report recommended that the UN transform its conclusions into a Programme of Action on Sustainable Development, hold a conference to review implementation of this programme, and institute follow-up arrangements to 'set benchmarks and maintain human progress within the guidance of human needs and natural law'. The UN General Assembly decided to convene a UN Conference on Environment and Development (UNCED) in 1992, and it established a Preparatory Commission in which most of the negotiations took place.[41] Political objections from developing countries ensured that intergovernmental negotiating committees established by the UN General Assembly were given responsibility for drafting conventions on climate change and biological diversity, rather than UNEP, the World Meteorological Organization ('WMO') or the FAO.[42] Developing states also worked hard to coordinate their negotiating position,[43] although in the intergovernmental negotiating committee on climate change they could not agree on a common position and separated into different groups.[44] Despite these various disagreements,

[38] See *infra*, Chs 4, 5, 6, 7, 8 and 9.

[39] *World Conservation Strategy: Living Resource Conservation for Sustainable Development* (1980) prepared by the IUCN in collaboration with UNEP, the WWF, the FAO and UNESCO; see also the updated version prepared for the UNCED, *Caring for the Earth: A Strategy for Sustainable Living* (1991).

[40] WCED, *Our Common Future* (Oxford, 1987); see also report of the WCED's Legal Expert Group on Environmental Law, in Munro and Lammers (eds), *Environmental Protection and Sustainable Development* (London, 1986). See generally Ginther, Denters and De Waart (eds), *Sustainable Development and Good Governance* (Dordrecht, 1995) esp. Ch by Matsui; Schrijver, *Sovereignty over Natural Resources* (Cambridge, 1997) esp. Ch 4; Bugge and Voigt (eds), *Sustainable Development in International and National Law* (Groningen, 2008) esp. Chs 1 and 2, and see *infra*, Chs 3 and 11.

[41] UNGA Res 44/228 (1989). On the negotiations and the conference see Campiglio et al (eds), *The Environment after Rio* (London, 1994); Spector, Sjöstedt, Zartman (eds), *Negotiating International Regimes: Lessons Learned from the UNCED* (London, 1994); Johnson (ed), *The Earth Summit* (London, 1993); Sand, 3 *YbIEL* (1992) 3; Freestone, 6 *JEL* (1994) 193; 'Symposium: UNCED', in 4 *Colorado JIELP* (1993) 1ff; and report in 22 *EPL* (1992) 204–225.

[42] See Bodansky, *Yale JIL* (1993) 451, 471–92.

[43] See Beijing Ministerial Declaration on Environment and Development, UN Doc. A/CONF.151/PC/85 (1991); South Centre, *Environment and Development: Towards a Common Strategy of the South in the UNCED Negotiations and Beyond* (Geneva, 1991); Mensah, in Campiglio *et al*, *The Environment after Rio* (London, 1994) 33–54.

[44] Bodansky, *Yale JIL* (1993) 451.

a declaration on environment and development, a detailed programme of action, known as Agenda 21, and framework conventions on climate change and biological diversity, were adopted by consensus.

Two unusual features of UNCED were: first, its sponsorship not only by states but also by major companies (e.g. ICI) and foundations (e.g. the MacArthur and Rockefeller Foundations) and, secondly, the fact that NGOs were allowed to play a major role in the preparatory committees. The negotiating climate in these meetings was often hostile, as major differences emerged on such basic questions on the weight to be accorded to development and the environment; whether the two could be separated; and the content of 'sustainable development.' As in earlier negotiations, developing states characterized the environmental crisis as a long-term developmental one, while developed states saw it as a more immediate technical problem. The former thus endeavoured to direct discussion, as in the 1974 debates on the 'New International Economic Order,' towards reform of the international economic system as a prerequisite for effective environmental action. Major differences thus again arose along a North-South divide on issues relating to sovereignty over natural resources, economic costs, equitable burden-sharing, funding, the role of multilateral institutions, transfer of technology, climate change, biological diversity, and deforestation. The North's proposals on the last two issues, in particular, were regarded as a threat to the sovereignty of developing states over their own natural resources, while pressure for global action on climate change was seen as an inequitable attempt to force developing states to share the costs and burdens of a problem created almost entirely by the industrialized states.

Many governments and NGOs expressed regret that UNCED was not asked to adopt the more ambitious proposals for an Earth Charter, that the 1992 Climate Change Convention was weakened, that many crucial issues were removed from or diluted in the final conference text, and that the US refused to sign the 1992 CBD in order to protect its pharmaceutical industry.[45] A proposed treaty on forests was blocked by the opposition of developing states,[46] while developed ones only made vague commitments on provision of financial resources and debt reduction. Despite these deficiencies, some spirit of solidarity (referred to as the 'Spirit of Rio') did prevail, enabling new instruments and an agenda for future action (Agenda 21) to emerge from the negotiations. A Commission on Sustainable Development ('CSD') was established, with responsibility for keeping under review 'the implementation of Agenda 21, recognizing that it is a dynamic programme that could evolve over time. . . .'[47] A contributing factor was the unprecedented level of NGO participation in the negotiations leading up to UNCED, the vast number of NGO observers who were present in Rio to lobby government delegates, and the presence of so many heads of state and government.

45 On the UNCED negotiations see references cited *infra*, Ch 3, fn 45.
46 Sand, 8 *J Nat Resources & Env L* (1992) 209, at 9–10.
47 UNGA Res 47/191 (1992) para 4 (c).

(b) UNCED instruments

UNCED adopted a range of instruments whose legal status and implications we explore in greater depth in later chapters.

(i) *The Rio Declaration on Environment and Development.* This set of twenty-seven principles, finely balanced between the priorities of developed and developing states, sets out the principal contours of sustainable development as now endorsed by UN member states, but it also has much greater legal significance than its 1972 predecessor. It is examined in detail in Chapter 3.[48]

(ii) *Agenda 21*,[49] a programme of action covering many issues, including climate change, deforestation, desertification and protection of the oceans. Although not legally binding it is potentially relevant to interpretation of treaties and other instruments adopted in accordance with its provisions. It recognizes more explicitly than the Stockholm Action Plan the interconnections between economic, environmental, social, and development issues, and endeavours to integrate these objectives. Agenda 21 is directed primarily at states, but it also gives international agencies, including the UN and the World Bank, a role in supporting and complementing action by states, including the promotion of enhanced international cooperation and capacity building.

(iii) *The Framework Convention on Climate Change and the Convention on Biological Diversity.* These important agreements create new regulatory regimes for two of the most significant problems facing contemporary society: anthropogenic climate change caused mainly by consumption of fossil fuels, and large-scale species extinction and ecosystem depletion resulting in a worldwide loss of biological diversity. Despite their adoption by consensus, both treaties exemplify the difficult policy choices facing governments trying to integrate economic and environmental considerations. Even though ratification is virtually universal, the continuing inability to achieve the objectives of either agreement illustrates the gulf between commitment in principle to sustainable development and implementation in practice in national law and economic policy. The climate change and the biodiversity agreements are considered in more detail in Chapters 6 and 11 respectively.

(iv) *Non-legally Binding Authoritative Statement of Principles for a Global Consensus on the Management, Conservation and Sustainable Development of all Types of Forests.* UNCED's mandate only made generic reference to deforestation as an issue 'of major concern in maintaining the quality of the Earth's environment and especially in achieving environmentally sound and sustainable development in all countries.'[50]

48 Section 1(2).

49 UN, *Report of the UN Conference on Environment and Development* I, UN Doc. A/CONF.151/rev.1 (1992) ['UNCED Report']. Agenda 21 is so called because implementation of the plan would extend well into the 21st century.

50 UNGA Res 44/228 (1989) at 12.

Proposals for a forest agreement were put forward,[51] but the most that could be agreed after strong opposition from developing countries was the Statement of Principles referred to above, now known as the Forest Principles (or the Rio Forest Principles).[52] The Forest Principles laid out key notions that have influenced subsequent negotiations within and outwith the UN, including re-negotiation of the 1983 International Tropical Timber Agreement ('ITTA') in 1994 and 2006.[53] The importance of these developments is the endorsement of sustainable management as the core principle applicable to forests.

2(3) 2002 WORLD SUMMIT ON SUSTAINABLE DEVELOPMENT

The third UN conference on environment and development convened at Johannesburg in 2002. Like the others, the World Summit on Sustainable Development ('WSSD') adopted a declaration and an action plan, known respectively as the Johannesburg Declaration on Sustainable Development and the Johannesburg Plan of Implementation.[54] Unlike the earlier conferences neither document articulates new principles or policies, nor do they specifically set an agenda for further law-making. Their value lies mainly in the reaffirmation and refinement of existing policies and principles, and in giving a little more substance to the contours of sustainable development as a concept. They are best seen as a modest programme of incremental progress towards strengthening implementation of goals and commitments previously endorsed. Of particular environmental significance are the paragraphs in both documents on protection and management of natural resources, trade and environment, energy efficiency, and strengthening the CSD. Otherwise, for lawyers, their main importance is that they reiterate the precautionary principle, the polluter pays principle and public participation.

If the WSSD has generally been seen as a disappointment for environmental policy, it should be recalled that environmental protection is but one of the objectives of 'special significance' to which international policy-making and the attention of the UN is devoted, together with 'development and poverty eradication,' 'peace and security,' and 'human rights, democracy and good governance.'[55]

[51] Proposal for an International Convention on Conservation and Development of Forests, FAO Committee on Forestry, 10th Session, Rome, 24–8 September 1990, FAO Doc COFO-90/3(a).

[52] UNCED, *Report* I (1992), 480. See Palmer, 70 *Wash ULQ* (1992) 1005, at 1020; Schally, 4 *YbIEL* (1993) 30; Tarasofsky (ed), *Assessing the International Forests Regime* (IUCN, 1999).

[53] A revised Non-Legally Binding Instrument on All Types of Forests was adopted in 2007: see UNGA Res 62/98 (2007). It is now known as the UN Forest Instrument.

[54] UN, *Report of the WSSD*, UN Doc. A/Conf.199/20 (2002) Resolution 1 and Annex. See Beyerlin and Reichard, 63 *ZAÖRV* (2003) 213–38. For background see Dodds (ed), *Earth Summit 2002* (London, 2001).

[55] UN Millennium Declaration, UNGA Res 55/22 (2000) para 7. See also World Summit Outcome Document, UNGA Res 60/1 (2005) para 16; and Galizzi, 29 *Fordham ILJ* (2006) 952–1008.

2(4) 2012 UN CONFERENCE ON SUSTAINABLE DEVELOPMENT

To mark the 20th anniversary of UNCED, the UN General Assembly decided to convene the UN Conference on Sustainable Development ('UNCSD') in Rio de Janeiro, with the objective of securing 'renewed political commitment for sustainable development, assessing the progress to date and the remaining gaps in the implementation of the outcomes of the major summits on sustainable development and addressing new and emerging challenges.'[56] The conference was prepared in the aftermath of the 2008 financial crisis and the ensuing economic recession which especially affected developed countries in the Northern hemisphere. It is perhaps unsurprising that, together with the 'institutional framework for sustainable development,' the main theme of the conference was 'a green economy in the context of sustainable development and poverty eradication.'[57]

Most of the negotiations again took place in a Preparatory Commission, which held multiple sessions between 2010 and 2012. They were marred by familiar North-South divides on the interpretation of fundamental principles, including common but differentiated responsibility and the transfer of funding and technology.[58] The significant change in circumstances since 1992 was palpable, with emerging economies, including Brazil, China and India, playing a leading role in negotiations, while economic recession reinforced developed countries' reluctance to live up to the requests of their developing counterparts concerning finance and technology transfer.

In preparation for the conference, UNEP, OECD and the World Bank promoted a 'green economy' as a new paradigm for sustainable development,[59] but this quickly reopened unresolved questions about the very notion of sustainable development.[60] While some developed countries proposed the adoption of indicators to measure progress toward the green economy and the establishment of a capacity development scheme, developing countries largely resisted these suggestions, arguing that the green economy should not turn into a 'normative straightjacket.'[61] The guidance on the green economy eventually included in the conference outcome document ('*The Future We Want*') thus represents only a minimalist common denominator between largely opposing views.[62] It affirms that the green economy is but 'one' of the tools available to achieve sustainable development, and should not be regarded as a 'rigid set of rules.'[63] All countries are encouraged to consider its implementation in a manner

56 UNGA Res 64/236 (2010) para 20(a). 57 *Ibid.*

58 See generally Morgera and Savaresi, 22 *RECIEL* (2012) 14 and other articles in this special issue of RECIEL.

59 UNEP, *Global Green New Deal* (Nairobi, 2009) and UNEP, *Towards a Green Economy: Pathways to Sustainable Development and Poverty Eradication* (Nairobi, 2011); OECD, *Towards Green Growth* (Paris, 2011); and World Bank, *Inclusive Green Growth* (Washington, 2012).

60 Morgera and Savaresi, 22 *RECIEL* (2012) 14, at 22–24.

61 Earth Negotiations Bulletin, *Summary of the First PREPCOM for the UN Conference on Sustainable Development*: 17–19 May 2010, at 5.

62 UNCSD, *The Future We Want*, UN Doc A/CONF.216/L.1 (2012) and UNGA Res 66/288 (2012) Annex. For analysis, see Morgera and Savaresi, 22 *RECIEL* (2012) 14.

63 *The Future We Want*, para 56.

that 'endeavours to drive sustained, inclusive and equitable economic growth and job creation.'[64] The emphasis here is not on long-term sustainability of natural capital but on short term economic growth.

While *The Future We Want* merely reasserted existing principles and policies on sustainable development, it did take steps to consolidate and strengthen the institutional framework, emphasising the need for policy coherence and coordination. First, it replaced the CSD with an intergovernmental High-Level Political Forum.[65] Secondly, it expressed a commitment to 'strengthen' the UN Economic and Social Council ('ECOSOC') as the 'principal organ' with responsibility for furthering the outcomes of all major UN conferences and summits in economic, social, and environmental fields.[66] Thirdly, the UN General Assembly was mandated to 'strengthen and upgrade' UNEP.[67] *The Future We Want* also identified a framework for further action in various thematic areas, including biodiversity, climate change, energy, water, oceans and seas. The most important and potentially meaningful measure to emerge, however, was the establishment of an intergovernmental working group to elaborate 'universally applicable' goals 'for pursuing focused and coherent action on sustainable development.'[68] The outcome was the adoption by the UN General Assembly of 17 'Sustainable Development Goals' and a '2030 Agenda for Sustainable Development'.[69]

At the time of writing, most of this work remains ongoing and an assessment of its impact is premature. It nevertheless seems clear that UNCSD has not engendered a radical departure from the *status quo* but rather exposed the faltering political will generally affecting international environmental governance. With 44,000 participants, however, UNCSD also provided a concrete manifestation of the increasingly prominent role played by NGOs, business, and local and regional governments. Building upon sustainable development 'partnerships' launched at the 2002 WSSD, 'voluntary commitments' were undertaken at UNCSD by a variety of non-state actors.[70] Together with the development of sustainable development goals, considered in the next section, this recognition of a bottom-up, multi-stakeholder approach to sustainable development may be the most important legacy of UNCSD.

2(5) THE CONCEPT OF SUSTAINABLE DEVELOPMENT

With the adoption of the Rio instruments at UNCED, sustainable development became and has remained the leading concept of international environmental policy. While some have argued that sustainable development may be regarded as a principle

[64] *Ibid*, para 62. [65] *Ibid*, para 84, and see *infra*, section 3(2)(c).

[66] *Ibid*, para 83, and see *infra*, section 3(2)(c).

[67] *Ibid*, para 88; and UNGA Res 67/213 (2012). See *infra*, section 3(3). [68] *Ibid*, paras 246 and 248.

[69] *Transforming our World: the 2030 Agenda for Sustainable Development*, UNGA Res 70/1 (2015).

[70] *The Future We Want*, para 283. In preparation for WSSD, UNGA Res 56/226 encouraged 'global commitment and *partnerships*, especially between Governments of the North and the South, on the one hand, and between Governments and major groups on the other.'

of international law,[71] or even of customary international law,[72] the ICJ has more cautiously referred to it as an 'international objective.'[73] The legal status of sustainable development is considered in Chapter 3.

The Brundtland Report characterized sustainable development as a process that 'meets the needs of the present without compromising the ability of future generations to meet their own needs.'[74] According to UNEP's Governing Council this platitudinous formulation 'does not imply in any way encroachment upon national sovereignty.'[75] Although 'sustainable development' is referred to throughout the 1992 Rio Declaration and Agenda 21, it was not until the 2002 WSSD that anything approaching a UN definition of the concept could be attempted. Three 'interdependent and mutually reinforcing pillars of sustainable development' were identified in the Johannesburg Declaration—economic development, social development and environmental protection.[76] In 2015 the UN went further and adopted an ambitious set of Sustainable Development Goals ('SDGs').[77] The vision of sustainable development set out in the 2015 SDGs and the accompanying 2030 Agenda for Sustainable Development ('2030 Agenda') focuses mainly on economic and social development. Reduction of poverty and hunger are the pre-eminent objectives, but the goals cover almost every aspect of international policy, including well-being for all ages, gender equality, safer cities, better sanitation, sustainable consumption, access to justice, and so on.

While the Preamble to the 2030 Agenda fully recognizes the seriousness of the environmental challenge—including threats to the climate, biodiversity, water resources, and the marine environment—only four of the seventeen 2015 SDGs are of particular relevance to the environment. SDG 12 commits states to 'ensure sustainable consumption and production patterns' and reiterates existing commitments on management of hazardous wastes and chemicals.[78] SDG 13 calls for 'urgent action' to deal with climate change and its impacts, and, at least in form, they have since done so, by adopting the 2015 Paris Agreement.[79] SDG 14 addresses conservation and sustainable use of the oceans and marine resources.[80] SDG 15 aims to conserve and sustainably manage terrestrial ecosystems such as forests and wetlands, combat desertification, and halt loss of biodiversity.[81] None of this adds anything new to international environmental policy or law, but it does serve to reaffirm existing commitments within the context of a process whose outcomes ECOSOC will keep under review.[82]

[71] See e.g. Voigt, *Sustainable Development as a Principle of International Law: Resolving Conflicts Between Climate Measures and WTO Law* (Leiden, 2009).

[72] Barral, 23 *EJIL* (2012) 377, at 388.

[73] *Pulp Mills Case*, ICJ Reports (2010) 14, at 177. See *infra*, Ch 3, section 2.

[74] WCED, *Our Common Future*, at 43.

[75] Annex II to UNEP GC decision 15/2, May 1989; Thacher, in Hurrell and Kingsbury (eds), *The International Politics of the Environment: Actors, Interests and Institutions* (Oxford, 1992) 183–211, 190.

[76] UN, *Report of the WSSD*, UN Doc. A/CONF.199/20 (2002) Resolution 1, para 5.

[77] *Transforming Our World: the 2030 Agenda for Sustainable Development*, UNGA Res 70/1 (2015).

[78] See *infra*, Ch 8. [79] See *infra*, Ch 6. [80] See *infra*, Chs 9 and 12.

[81] SDG 15. See *infra*, Ch 11.

[82] UNGA Res 70/1 (2015) paras 72–91; UNGA Res 71/313 (2017), and see *infra*, section 3(2)(c).

The expectation is that the process of reporting will engender peer pressure, leading states to deliver on the 2030 Agenda.[83] Reporting and review of non-binding targets and goals have become trademarks of international environmental law and policy—as exemplified by the Aichi Targets adopted under the 1992 CBD, or the global temperature goal enshrined in the 2015 Paris Agreement. Their effectiveness has yet to be demonstrated. When compared with earlier UN conferences, the 2015 SDGs and the 2030 Agenda unequivocally acknowledge that global environmental problems cannot be solved without the cooperation of business and industry, whose commitment to tackling climate change, mercury pollution or the spread of plastic litter, may matter more than that of states.

In spite of the adoption of the 2015 SDGs and of the 2030 Agenda, it seems fair to say that, more than thirty years on from the Brundtland Report the concept of sustainable development remains almost infinitely malleable.[84] Social, political and economic choices abound: what weight should be given to natural resource exploitation over nature protection, to industrial development over air and water quality, to land-use development over conservation of forests and wetlands, to energy consumption over the risks of climate change, among others. These choices may result in wide diversities of policy and interpretation, as different governments and international organizations pursue their own priorities and make their own value judgments, moderated only to some extent by international agreements on such matters as climate change and conservation of biological diversity. The 2030 Agenda recognizes that it is for each state to make these choices, provided they also make progress towards achieving the agreed goals.

Whatever else it means, therefore, sustainable development does not imply zero growth.[85] Nor do the 1992 Rio Declaration and subsequent UN conferences envisage such an outcome. International policy has taken an approach to sustainable development which emphasizes the fundamental importance of equity within the economic system. This equity is both inter-generational, in seeking a fair allocation of costs and benefits across succeeding generations,[86] and intra-generational, in that it seeks to redress the imbalance in wealth and economic development between the developed and developing worlds by giving priority to the needs of the poor.[87] Put simply, development will only be 'sustainable' if it benefits the disadvantaged, without disadvantaging

[83] Norichika and Biermann, *Governing through Goals—Sustainable Development Goals as Governance Innovation* (Cambridge, Mass, 2017).

[84] See generally Redclift, *Sustainable Development: Exploring the Contradictions* (London, 1987); Pearce, Markandya and Barbier, *Blueprint for a Green Economy* (London, 1989); Jacobs, *The Green Economy* (London, 1991); Reid, *Sustainable Development* (London, 1995); Moffat, *Sustainable Development: Principles, Analysis and Policies* (London, 1995) esp. Ch 3; Goldin and Winters (eds), *The Economics of Sustainable Development* (OECD, Cambridge, 1995); Dresner, *The Principles of Sustainability* (2nd edn, London, 2008); Neumayer, *Weak Versus Strong Sustainability* (4th edn, Cheltenham, 2013); Dernbach and Cheever, 2 *Transnational Env L* (2015) 247; Helm, *Natural Capital: Valuing the Planet* (London, 2016).

[85] Helm, *Natural Capital: Valuing the Planet*, 14–15.

[86] 1992 Rio Declaration, Principle 3, and see Brown-Weiss, *In Fairness to Future Generations* (Dobbs Ferry, NY, 1989).

[87] WCED, *Our Common Future*, 44–5; 1992 Rio Declaration, Principle 5.

by Helm, who observes that 'It is not hard to make the case that the process of destruction [of natural capital] has gone too far, and that renewable natural capital as a whole is already well below the optimal level. . . .The state of core ecosystem services, from climate to fresh water and soils, is already a serious cause for concern.'[105]

Helm's conclusion is amply borne out by later chapters of this book. If sustainability truly entails a balance between economic development and environmental protection then that balance remains heavily tilted towards development. Rio's long-term contribution to global environmental policy and thus to the evolution of international law is at best an ambiguous one: it may have slowed things down, but it has not fundamentally changed the direction of travel.

3 THE UN AND ENVIRONMENTAL GOVERNANCE

3(1) THE UN'S ENVIRONMENTAL COMPETENCE

The UN has become the most significant political embodiment of the international community, 'a central institution in the conduct of international relations'.[106] Nevertheless, although the UN Charter expressed the UN's aims and purposes in far wider terms than those of the League of Nations, nowhere is there any explicit reference to the aim of protecting, preserving or conserving the natural environment or promoting sustainable development. This is hardly surprising. There was little awareness in 1945 of any need to protect the environment, except on a limited and *ad hoc* basis, and it was not anticipated that UN action would be needed. Thus, the subsequent evolution of the UN's power to adopt policies or take measures directed at environmental objectives has to be derived from a broad interpretation of the UN Charter and of the implied powers of the organization. Article 1 includes among the purposes of the UN the furtherance of 'international cooperation in solving international problems of an economic, social, cultural, or humanitarian character, and in promoting and encouraging respect for human rights. . .'. Article 55 also requires the UN to promote conditions of economic and social progress and development, solutions to international economic, social, health and related problems, and observance of human rights and fundamental freedoms.

In the *Reparations for Injuries Case* the ICJ held that 'the rights and duties of an entity such as the Organization must depend upon its purpose and functions as specified or implied in its constituent documents and developed in practice'.[107] It can readily be assumed that environmental protection is an essential element in the promotion of social progress and in solving economic and social problems as referred

105 Helm, *Natural Capital: Valuing the Planet*, 63.

106 See Roberts and Kingsbury, *United Nations, Divided World*, 1.

107 ICJ Reports (1949) 174, at 180.

to in Articles 1 and 55.[108] On that basis UNEP was established in 1972 following the Stockholm Conference, and the CSD in 1992 following UNCED. Both bodies reported to ECOSOC, and so do their successors. The same articles of the UN Charter also support the environmental work of the regional UN Economic Commissions.[109]

An important feature of the UN system has been the establishment of various specialized agencies. Like the UN, these organizations were not originally endowed with explicit power over environmental matters, but they have had to develop such a competence through interpretation and practice.[110] Those whose responsibilities for environmental protection or sustainable use of natural resources have evolved in this way include the IMO, FAO, World Bank, and the UN Educational, Scientific and Cultural Organization ('UNESCO').[111] The IAEA is an independent international organization related to the UN system; it too has acquired an environmental dimension through interpretation of its constituent instrument.[112] The same is true of the WTO and OECD.[113]

The powers of all these bodies are necessarily more limited than those of the UN. In its *Advisory Opinion on the Legality of the Threat or Use of Nuclear Weapons*,[114] the ICJ distinguished the general power of the UN General Assembly from the exclusively health-related powers of the WHO and denied the latter body the competence to seek an advisory opinion on the legality of nuclear weapons, notwithstanding their obvious potential for harming human health and the natural environment. This decision illustrates how closely the express and implied powers of specialized agencies must be related to their specific objects and purposes. Thus the IMO's environmental competence is confined to marine pollution from ships, the FAO deals with the environment as an aspect of sustainable use forests, fisheries and so on.

3(2) UN PRINCIPAL ORGANS AND PROTECTION OF THE ENVIRONMENT

(a) The General Assembly

The General Assembly, the Security Council, and ECOSOC, are amongst the 'principal organs' of the UN.[115] Every member state has one vote in the General Assembly, giving developing states an overwhelming majority. The General Assembly has limited power, but may discuss any matter within the scope of the Charter, and make

[108] On the interpretation of these articles see Simma et al (eds), *The Charter of the United Nations: A Commentary* (3rd edn, Oxford, 2012).

[109] See *infra*, section 4(2).

[110] See Werksman (ed), *Greening International Institutions* (London, 1996); White, *The Law of International Organisations*, Ch 10; Desai, *Institutionalizing International Environmental Law* (Ardsley, 2004) Ch 5.

[111] *Infra*, section 4. [112] *Infra*, section 4(5). [113] *Infra*, sections 4(6) and (8).

[114] ICJ Reports (1996) 66 (WHO) and 226 (UNGA).

[115] UN Charter, Article 7. The others are the Trusteeship Council, the ICJ and the Secretariat.

recommendations to member states or to the Security Council.[116] In particular, Article 13 provides that it 'shall initiate studies and make recommendations' for the purpose of promoting political cooperation, encouraging the progressive development and codification of international law, promoting international cooperation in the economic, social, cultural, education and health fields and assisting in the realization of human rights. The General Assembly is thus the UN's most important political body.

While the General Assembly has no law-making power as such, its ability to adopt resolutions, convene law-making conferences and initiate codification projects has given it a central role in the development of international policy and law relating to many aspects of the environment.[117] As we shall see in later chapters, General Assembly resolutions on the legal status of the deep-seabed, natural resources, and the global climate have influenced the evolution of treaties and customary law on these matters, as has the General Assembly endorsement of the Stockholm and Rio Declarations. Decisions to convene the UN Conferences on, *inter alia*, the Human Environment (Stockholm, 1972) the Law of the Sea (Caracas, 1973), Environment and Development (Rio de Janeiro, 1992), and most recently, Sustainable Development (Rio de Janeiro, 2012) were taken by the General Assembly. With regard to the codification of international law, the General Assembly usually acts through the ILC or ad hoc committees. Over the years the ILC has considered a number of topics of particular relevance to the environment, including non-navigational uses of international watercourses; transboundary aquifers; the prevention of transboundary harm; the protection of the environment during armed conflict; and the protection of the atmosphere.[118]

Even when it does not itself promote the negotiation of new treaties or other instruments, the General Assembly's power to coordinate the legal and policy agendas of specialized agencies and other UN bodies gives it a continuing role at the heart of the law-making process. With so many different bodies potentially involved in international law-making, the task of allocating responsibilities and coordinating policy is an important feature of the General Assembly's role. Where, for example, should responsibility for developing international law relating to forests be located? The FAO's agricultural mandate covers forestry, while promoting trade in timber is the main objective of the International Tropical Timber Organization ('ITTO'). The 1972 Convention for the Protection of the World Cultural and Natural Heritage ('World Heritage Convention') adopted by UNESCO protects some forest areas, while forests generally are also covered by the 1992 CBD. Sustainable use of natural resources falls within the mandate of UNEP, while the management of forest carbon stocks is a significant issue for parties to the 1992 Climate Change Convention and the 1997 Kyoto

[116] UN Charter, Article 10. See generally Peterson, *The General Assembly in World Politics* (London, 1986); *id*, in Weiss and Daws (eds), *The Oxford Handbook on the UN* (Oxford, 2007) Ch 5.

[117] On the UN's general contribution to international law see Joyner (ed), *The United Nations and International Law* (Cambridge, 1997) and on the environment see Birnie, in Roberts and Kingsbury, *United Nations, Divided World*, Ch 10.

[118] See *infra*, Chs 3 and 10.

Protocol. Where such cross-cutting areas of policy are involved, no single forum is self-evidently the right one to undertake the development of new law. Yet the choice of forum may affect not only the perspective from which the issues are approached but also the constituencies most likely to become involved and whose interests are most strongly favoured by the governmental representatives concerned. To give responsibility for a convention on forests to the FAO, for example, would tend to favour the perspectives of agriculture and forestry ministries and the relevant industries. To give it to UNEP would be more likely to favour environmental ministries and organizations. In either case, the influence of developing countries may not be as strong as it is in the General Assembly, and forests are a matter of strong interest to a number of important developing states. In such circumstances there is a tendency for the UN General Assembly to take upon itself responsibility for coordinating action.[119]

Moreover, even a specialized agency with undisputed competence may not be the best forum to take the relevant measures. Specialized agencies, both national and international, tend to be strongly influenced by special interests and particular ministries. For instance, the IMO, dominated by shipping states, has been notably reluctant to strengthen international law relating to flag of convenience vessels.[120] The FAO, in which fishing states have a powerful voice, has been slow to react to unsustainable practices such as drift-netting or flag of convenience trawling. In all of these cases it may become necessary for the General Assembly with its universal membership and broader view to take action, as it did when adopting a ban on driftnet fishing,[121] or establishing an inter-agency task force on flags of convenience in response to lobbying by Greenpeace, IUCN and the International Transport Workers' Federation.[122]

Moreover, the UN's endorsement of global policies necessarily affects other international organizations. Thus, when the General Assembly endorsed the 1992 Rio Declaration, referring to its 'fundamental principles for the achievement of sustainable development,' it also called on the CSD and the UN Secretary-General to promote incorporation of the principles of the declaration in the implementation of Agenda 21 and in UN programmes and processes, and urged governments to promote their widespread dissemination.[123] The Rio agenda has gradually affected the application and development of law and policy by most of the relevant international organizations, including the FAO, IMO, World Bank, and the WTO, as well as by treaty bodies such as the ITTO and the European Energy Charter.[124] International law-making by

[119] Via the UN Forum on Forests and the Non-Legally Binding Instrument on All Types of Forests, UNGA Res 62/98 (2007). For another example see UNGA Res 59/25 (2004) which gives directions on fisheries policy to FAO, IMO and UNEP.

[120] See *infra*, section 4.

[121] UNGA Res 44/225 (1989); 45/197 (1990); 46/215 (1991); 59/25 (2004). See Rothwell, in Shelton (ed), *Commitment and Compliance* (Oxford, 2000) 121–145.

[122] Consisting of the UN, FAO, IMO, UNEP, UNCTAD, International Labour Organization ('ILO'), and OECD. See UN Doc A/59/63 (2004) *Rept of the Consultative Group on Flag State Implementation.*

[123] UNGA Res 47/190 (1992) and 48/191 (1993).

[124] See *infra*, Ch 3, section 2(3).

all of these organizations on issues such as the precautionary approach, sustainable use of natural resources, and environmental impact assessment reflects the changes brought about through UN soft law since 1992. The same can be said for the treaty bodies which administer MEAs.[125]

The point is not that the General Assembly has usurped the powers of other bodies, nor does it have the constitutional power to direct the policies of autonomous bodies such as the WTO, World Bank, or *ad hoc* treaty COPs and commissions. Rather, it can perform a necessary role in seeking to bring some measure of coherence to the policies and law-making activities of an otherwise diverse range of organizations.

(b) The Security Council

The Security Council has more power, but a narrower role, than the UN General Assembly. Composed of 15 states, its decisions on measures to restore international peace and security under Chapter VII of the UN Charter are binding on all UN member states unless vetoed by one of the five permanent members.[126] Its post-Cold War practice shows how broad an interpretation can be given to the phrase 'international peace and security'.[127] Although the Security Council is not formally a law-making body, since 9/11 it has used its mandatory powers to adopt a number of binding resolutions on anti-terrorism measures laying down general rules for all states.[128] There are some obvious advantages to Security Council law-making rather than the more formal processes of negotiation through the UN General Assembly or a treaty conference. First, all UN Member States are bound to comply with Chapter VII resolutions—there is no room for opt-outs or reservations. Secondly, such resolutions prevail over other international agreements and they do not have to conform to existing general international law.[129] Security Council law-making could thus enhance the coherence of international law if used appropriately.[130] To that extent the Security Council could become an instrument of law reform, overcoming the problem of the 'persistent objector' in customary law and the 'free-rider' in multilateral treaties.

Some authors have used the concept of 'environmental security' to envisage a greater role for the Security Council in dealing with environmental threats and emergencies, including climate change.[131] Measures to promote environmental protection

125 See e.g. the renegotiation of regional seas agreements after 1992, *infra*, Ch 8.

126 UN Charter, Articles 23–5, 27, 41–2.

127 For differing views of the limits to Security Council powers see chapters by Gowlland-Debbas and Nolte in Byers (ed), *The Role of Law in International Politics* (Oxford, 2000) and generally Alvarez, *International Organizations as Law-makers* (Oxford, 2005) 184–217.

128 UNSC resolutions 1373 (2001) and 1540 (2005) and see generally Boyle and Chinkin, *The Making of International Law*, Ch 3, section 4.

129 *Lockerbie Case (Provisional Measures)* ICJ Reports (1992) 114, para 42; UN Charter, Article 103, and commentary in Simma (ed), *The Charter of the United Nations* (3rd edn, Oxford, 2012).

130 But compare Bianchi, 13 *EJIL* (2002) 263.

131 Timoshenko, in Weiss (ed), *Environmental Change and International Law* (Tokyo, 1992) Ch 13; Elliott, in Chambers and Green (eds), *Reforming International Environmental Governance: from Institutional Limits to Innovative Reforms* (Tokyo, 2005); Hulme, 20 *YbIEL* (2010) 41; Boyle, in Cassese (ed)*Realizing Utopia* (Oxford, 2012) 172. For contrary views see Szasz, in Brown Weiss, *Environmental Change and International Law*, 359–361; Tinker, 59 *Tennessee LR* (1992) 787.

may in some circumstances be necessary for the maintenance of international peace and security, thus giving the Security Council power to take mandatory action under Chapter VII, although 'the language of the Charter, not to speak of the clear record of the original meaning, does not easily lend itself to such an interpretation'.[132] The Council has acted cautiously with respect to environmental matters, using its Chapter VII powers only once, to hold Iraq responsible in international law for environmental damage inflicted on Kuwait during the 1991 Gulf war.[133] In 2007 the Council also held its first debate on climate change. At present no consensus exists on addressing climate change within the Security Council, although it seems likely that it could do so if the need arose.[134] To give the Security Council an enhanced role as an international legislator in areas such as climate change would be a tenable option only if the process can be legitimized and made generally acceptable to States.[135]

(c) UN Economic and Social Council

ECOSOC is the principal UN organ responsible for the promotion of international cooperation on economic and social matters.[136] It has in the past been notoriously 'unable to rise to this task,'[137] but UNCSD expressed a commitment to strengthen ECOSOC as the 'principal organ in the integrated and coordinated follow-up of the outcomes of all major UN conferences and summits.'[138] It now has a leading role in integrating the three dimensions of sustainable development, identifying emerging challenges, and 'promoting innovative thinking'.[139] The new High-Level Political Forum on Sustainable Development has been created in order to provide stronger political leadership and make recommendations for sustainable development.[140] It will have a central role in the follow-up and review of the 2030 Agenda and the 2015 SDGs.[141] The Forum replaces the CSD which achieved little in its twenty-year existence; whether a Forum with much the same mandate will do any better remains to be seen. Other subsidiary bodies of ECOSOC include the UN Forum on Forests. ECOSOC is also the body to which UN specialized agencies, commissions and programmes report, and with which NGOs may have consultative status.[142]

132 Szasz, *loc cit*, 359.

133 UNSC Res 687. See *infra*, Ch 4, section 2.

134 Gray, in Rayfuse and Scott (eds), *International Law in the Era of Climate Change* (Cheltenham, 2012) 219. For a comprehensive treatment of the UNSC's potential with respect to climate change see Scott and Ku (eds), *Climate Change and the UN Security Council* (Cheltenham, 2018) esp. Ch 6.

135 Caron, 87 *AJIL* (1993) 552; Szasz, 96 *AJIL* (2002) 901, but contrast Sato, in Coicaud and Heiskanen, *The Legitimacy of International Organisations* (Tokyo, 2001) 327–9.

136 UN Charter, Articles 55, 62. See generally Rosenthal, in Weiss and Daws, *Oxford Handbook on the UN*, Ch 7.

137 Chambers and Green (eds), *Reforming International Environmental Governance,* 35.

138 *The Future We Want*, para 83.

139 UNGA Res 68/1 (2013).

140 *The Future We Want*, para 84; UNGA Res 67/203 (2012); UNGA Res 67/290 (2013).

141 UNGA Res 70/299 (2016).

142 UN Charter, Articles 64, 71.

3(3) UN ENVIRONMENT (PROGRAMME)

(a) UN Environment's mandate

UNEP, or UN Environment as it is now known, is the only UN body with a mandate to focus specifically and exclusively on environmental issues. Although only a 'programme' it has been the most active UN body in the development of environmental soft law and multilateral environmental agreements, as well as promoting treaty implementation and coordinating some of the growing number of treaty bodies. It was established by the UN General Assembly in 1972, following the Stockholm Conference.[143] UNEP's original terms of reference envisaged a limited role:

> To promote international co-operation in the field of the environment and to recommend, as appropriate, policies to this end; [and] to provide general policy guidance for the direction and co-ordination of environmental programmes within a United Nations System.[144]

It was thus expected to act as a catalyst in developing and coordinating an environmental focus in the programmes of other UN bodies, rather than initiating action itself. Its first director said its role was 'to complexify', that is, to 'remind others of, and help them to take into account all the systems, interactions and ramifications implied in their work'. He observed that it was the lack of this cross-sectoral, cross-disciplinary view that had led to many environmental problems.[145]

The status and future role of UNEP were the subject of debate before, during and after UNCED in 1992.[146] Although its activities had to some extent helped in 'greening' specialized agencies, including the World Bank, and resulted in some important law-making innovations, it had not succeeded in coordinating the environmental work of the UN and other bodies. UNEP did not have a clear role in the 1992 Rio Conference. Proposals for transforming it into a specialized agency like the FAO or IMO attracted little support.[147] Instead, there was more support for strengthening UNEP in its existing role. In addition to UNEP's original mandate, Agenda 21 gave priority, *inter alia*, to developing international environmental law, environmental impact assessment and auditing, providing advice and support to governments, and promoting regional and sub-regional cooperation.[148] Yet another priority was accorded to coordinating

143 See Birnie, 20 *Melb ULR* (1995) 80–93.

144 UNGA Res 2997 (XXVII)(1972).

145 UNEP Governing Council, *Introductory Statement by the Executive Director* (11 February 1975) UNEP/GC/31; UNEP/GC/31/Add.1; UNEP/GC/31/Add.2; UNEP/GC/31/Add.3.

146 See Tarasofsky in Chambers and Green (eds), *Reforming International Environmental Governance*, 66; Desai, *Institutionalizing International Environmental Law*, 166–88; Kimball, *Forging International Agreements: Strengthening Intergovernmental Institutions for Environment and Development* (Washington, 1992); Szasz, in Brown Weiss (ed), *Environmental Change and International Law* (Tokyo, 1992) 340; Thacher, in Hurrell and Kingsbury (eds), *The International Politics of the Environment*, 183; Sand, *Lessons Learned in Global Environmental Governance* (Washington DC, 1990).

147 See Birnie in Roberts and Kingsbury (eds), *United Nations, Divided World*, 373–9

148 UNCED Agenda 21, Ch 38, para H. See also UNGA Res S/19-2 (1997); 1997 Nairobi Declaration on the Role and Mandate of UNEP, adopted by UNEP Governing Council decision 19/1 (1997); UNGA Res 53/242 (1999).

('clustering') the growing number of environmental treaties, and their secretariats.[149] At the same time, the creation of the CSD, the GEF, and an Inter-agency Committee on Sustainable Development added yet more competing institutions with overlapping responsibilities, diluting UNEP's influence within the UN system, and reinforcing the 'sense of policy incoherence among the different international bodies dealing with environmental issues.'[150]

The UNCSD in 2012 once again rejected proposals for the establishment of a UN specialized agency for the environment,[151] opting instead to further 'strengthen and upgrade' UNEP by, *inter alia*, establishing universal membership in its Governing Council (now rechristened the 'UN Environment Assembly' or 'UNEA'), increasing its budget, strengthening its engagement in UN coordination bodies, and empowering it to lead efforts to formulate UN system-wide strategies on the environment.[152] UNEA's establishment may be viewed as part of a process to render the UN bureaucracy more transparent and inclusive, whilst at the same time giving greater prominence to the environmental pillar of sustainable development. Its first meeting set new priorities for tackling air pollution, chemicals, and illegal trade in wildlife, but it has also drawn attention to new challenges, such as the spread of plastic in the marine environment.[153] An obvious question remains: how will the UNEA interact with the High-Level Political Forum on Sustainable Development? Will these bodies cooperate or will they pursue different agendas, as has happened before?

(b) UNEP's Role in Developing International Environmental Law

Although UNEP was not initially given a specific mandate to develop international environmental law, the necessity for promotion of binding and non-binding instruments to achieve its purposes was appreciated from the outset. An ambitious environmental law programme (the 'Montevideo Programme') has been revised periodically in response to UNCED and subsequent reviews.[154] Agenda 21 expressly mandated UNEP to undertake further development of international environmental law, as well as promoting its implementation and coordinating the growing number of treaty secretariats and meetings of parties.[155] One reading of the revised mandate concludes that it is 'wider than just the coordination of the environmental conventions' secretariats,

[149] *Ibid*, Ch 38, para H, and UNGA Res 55/198 (2001). See Von Moltke, in Winter (ed), *Multilevel Governance of Global Environmental Change* (Cambridge, 2006) 409–29; Oberthur in Chambers and Green (eds), *op cit*, 40–65; Caddell, 22 *YbIEL* (2011) 37.

[150] Tarasofsky in Chambers and Green (eds), *Reforming International Environmental Governance*, 70.

[151] UNCSD, Co-Chairs' paper 'The Future We Want: Zero Draft of the Outcome Document,' 10 January 2012, para 51 sets out the two options.

[152] *Ibid*, para 88; and UNGA Res 67/213 (2012). See also *infra*, section 3(3).

[153] See resolutions adopted at the meetings in 2014, 2016, and 2017.

[154] UNEP/Env. Law/2/3 (1991); UNEP/Env.Law/4/4 (2001); UNEP/GC/25/INF/15 (2008).

[155] Agenda 21, Ch 38, para H (1)(h); UNGA Res S/19-2 (1997); UNGA Res 53/242 (1999); Desai, 40 *Ind JIL* (2000) 455. See also the 1997 Nairobi Declaration on the Role and Mandate of UNEP, adopted by UNEP Governing Council decision 19/1 (1997) which refers to 'international environmental law aiming at sustainable development'.

and includes the coordination of the whole process of international law-making in the field of sustainable development.'[156]

UNEP's achievements are considerable, if measured purely by the number and importance of the legal instruments for which it has been responsible, but its catalytic role was clearly strongest during its first two decades. Its contribution to international law-making can be grouped loosely into three categories: (i) conclusion of international agreements;[157] (ii) development of soft law principles, guidelines, and standards;[158] (iii) provision of assistance for drafting of national environmental legislation and administration in developing countries.[159] It pioneered both the use of so-called 'framework treaties' and 'soft law' instruments.[160] The Regional Seas Programme introduced some innovatory concepts, such as specially protected areas, and now covers some fourteen regions.[161] UNEP guidelines provided the basis for negotiation of the 1989 Basel Convention, resulted in the adoption of further regional agreements, and (with the FAO) the Rotterdam Convention on the Prior Informed Consent Procedure for Certain Hazardous Chemicals and Pesticides in International Trade ('Rotterdam Convention on Prior Informed Consent').[162] Guidelines on environmental impact assessment have resulted in refinement and adoption of the concept in national law and their elaboration in the 1991 Espoo Convention on Environmental Impact Assessment in a Transboundary Context ('Espoo Convention').[163] More recently, UNEP has played a crucial role in establishing the processes that lead to the adoption of the 2013 Minamata Convention on Mercury.[164]

We will examine in later chapters the results of UNEP's law-making efforts. Not every UNEP soft law instrument is necessarily intended to be normative in character.[165] For example, the UN General Assembly only asked states to use the UNEP Principles

[156] Timoshenko and Berman, in Werksman (ed), *Greening International Institutions*, at 43.

[157] These include the so-called 'Regional Seas Conventions', on which see *infra*, Ch 9; 1979 Convention on the Conservation of Migratory Species of Wild Animals 1979, *infra*, Ch 11; 1985 Ozone Convention, *infra*, Ch 6; 1989 Basel Convention, *infra*, Ch 8; 1992 CBD, *infra*, Ch 11; 1998 Rotterdam Convention on Prior Informed Consent (in collaboration with the FAO) *infra*, Ch 8; 2001 Convention on Persistent Organic Pollutants and 2013 Convention on Mercury, *infra*, Ch 8.

[158] These include the 1978 Principles of Conduct in the Field of the Environment for the Guidance of States in the Conservation and Harmonious Utilization of Natural Resources Shared by Two or More States; 1985 Montreal Guidelines for the Protection of the Marine Environment against Pollution from Land-based Sources; 1987 Conclusions on Legal Aspects Concerning the Environment related to Offshore Mining and Drilling Carried Out Within the Limits of National Jurisdiction; 1987 Cairo Guidelines and Principles for the Environmentally Sound Management of Hazardous Waste; 1987 Goals and Principles of Environmental Impact Assessment; 1989 London Guidelines for the Exchange of Information on Chemicals in International Trade; 1995 Global Programme of Action for the Protection of the Marine Environment from Land-based Activities; 2002 Guidelines on Compliance with and Enforcement of MEAs; 2010 Guidelines for the Development of National Legislation on Access to Information, Public Participation and Access to Justice in Environmental Matters.

[159] See UNEP, *New Directions in Environmental Legislation and Administration Particularly in Developing Countries* (Nairobi, 1989) and *Environmental Law in the UNEP*, 36–40.

[160] *Supra*, Ch 1, section 2. [161] *Infra*, Ch 9. [162] *Infra*, Ch 8. [163] *Infra*, Ch 3, section 7.

[164] Tsioumani, 43 *EPL* (2013) 90. [165] On soft law see *supra*, Ch 1, section 2.

on Shared National Resources as 'guidelines and recommendations in formulating conventions'; states and international organizations were asked to 'take. . .into account' the Montreal Guidelines for the Protection of the Marine Environment from Land-based Sources of Pollution when developing agreements and national legislation.[166] The Cairo Guidelines on Waste Management were addressed to states 'with a view to assisting them in the process of developing *policies*' for this purpose.[167] Assessing the legal significance of any of these non-binding instruments depends, as we saw in Chapter 1, on their relationship to related treaties, subsequent state practice, and *opinio juris*.

3(4) A GLOBAL ENVIRONMENTAL ORGANIZATION?

Should UN Environment have been turned into a fully-fledged UN specialized agency as a number of states and writers had proposed?[168] Protagonists rightly pointed to fragmentation of UN structures dealing with the environment, the relative weakness of UNEP as the principal UN body with general environmental competence, and the powerful focus the IMF, World Bank, UNDP and the WTO bring to economic development. Sceptics regarded the creation of a new international organization as politically unrealistic and unnecessary.[169] As we saw above, UNEP's existing status as a UN programme has not stopped it from performing a considerable law-making role or providing an effective forum for treaty negotiations and coordination. A UN environment agency could not easily take over the environmental responsibilities of other specialized agencies, such as the FAO or the IMO:[170] the work of these bodies has an important environmental dimension which cannot be separated from their general responsibilities. Nor is it evident how coordination of environmental treaty regimes would be any easier if UN Environment were a specialiszd agency instead of a programme. The failure of the WTO to achieve anything comparable on trade since 1994 makes that comparison look increasingly hollow. Reforms introduced since the UNCSD have enhanced UN Environment's role in the UN system and addressed many of the earlier criticisms, at least to some extent. The problem of coordination of the UN's still diverse environmental structures remains, but the real challenge for UN Environment is not structural, but whether it continues to have a useful role in a global environmental agenda rightly dominated by sustainable development, climate change, and the marine environment.

166 UNEP GC Decision 13/18 (II) (1985).

167 UNEP GC Decision 14/30 (1987) emphasis added

168 On proposals for a new UN environmental agency see Palmer, 86 *AJIL* (1992) 259; Esty, *Greening the GATT: Trade, Environment and the Future* (Washington, 1994); Dunoff, 19 *Harv ELR* (1995) 241, 257–70; Ayling, 9 *JEL* (1997) 243; Desai, 40 *Ind JIL* (2000) 455; Charnovitz in Chambers and Green (eds), *Reforming International Environmental Governance*, 93–123; Desai, *Institutionalizing International Environmental Law*, Ch 6.

169 The arguments are comprehensively reviewed in Biermann and Bauer, *A World Environment Organization* (Aldershot, 2005).

170 A point illustrated by the exclusion of aviation and shipping carbon emissions from the 1997 Kyoto Protocol and the Paris Agreement in deference to ICAO and IMO: see Martinez Romera 25 *RECIEL* (2016) 215.

4 OTHER INTERNATIONAL ORGANIZATIONS

4(1) UN SPECIALIZED AGENCIES AND RELATED BODIES

Space does not permit a detailed explanation of the environment-related work of all the agencies which, through agreements with ECOSOC, have entered into a special relationship with the UN.[171] For our purposes the most directly relevant are the FAO, IMO, the World Bank, and other related organizations, including the IAEA, the WTO, and the OECD. There are also a number of UN regional bodies with environmental responsibilities. Within the UN system specialized agencies and regional commissions are the principal repositories and disseminators of technical expertise, and it is this attribute which arguably constitutes their most significant contribution to the law-making process. Moreover, NGOs and national experts often work closely with specialized agencies, sometimes to a greater extent than is possible in the UN itself.

The range of law-making activities undertaken by the specialized agencies and related bodies is very varied. Their most important role is best understood as international standard setting.[172] The adoption of soft law codes and guidelines on nuclear installations by the IAEA, the Codex Alimentarius of the WHO and FAO, the radiological protection standards established by the International Commission on Radiological Protection (ICRP'), or the annexes to IMO treaties on ship safety and pollution typify this aspect of their work.[173] Essentially technical in character, these instruments seek to establish internationally agreed minimum standards for the regulation of internationally important industries. Their precise legal status will depend on the organization involved, the basis on which the standards are adopted and the form of the instrument.

Specialized agencies and regional commissions also negotiate and adopt multilateral treaties. In many cases, these treaties provide the legal framework for international regulatory regimes which provide the basis for standard-setting, monitoring processes, and compliance mechanisms. The regulation of maritime and nuclear safety, security and liability by the IMO and IAEA respectively are among the most important examples of this genre. Both organizations are responsible for adopting new treaties and treaty amendments, revising or adding annexes, and setting additional soft law standards on related matters. In effect they each constitute a standing diplomatic forum, whose ongoing oversight enables law-making to evolve relatively quickly in response to new problems, priorities, or opportunities. Less convincingly, they also enable member states to exercise some degree of oversight over implementation and compliance by member states.

Lastly, major UN agreements such as the 1982 UNCLOS and the 1992 CBD, or policy statements such as Agenda 21, often require further implementation by specialized agencies.

[171] E.g. the WHO, the WMO and the ILO. The work of these bodies is referred to when appropriate in later chapters.

[172] The seminal study is Contini and Sand, 66 *AJIL* (1972) 37.

[173] See Kirgis in Joyner (ed), *The UN and International Law*, 82–88.

4(2) UN REGIONAL COMMISSIONS

There are five UN regional economic commissions. While the UN Economic and Social Commission for Asia and the Pacific ('ESCAP') has attracted attention for its work on green growth,[174] only UNECE has made a significant contribution to the development of regional environmental law. However, the Economic Commission for Latin America and the Caribbean ('ECLAC') has begun to follow suit.[175]

UNECE's most important environmental achievement is the creation of a framework for environmental cooperation and the harmonization of environmental law in Eastern Europe and the former Soviet Union, thus ensuring greater compatibility with standards in Western Europe. The first substantive achievement was the negotiation of the 1979 LRTAP Convention.[176] The end of the Cold War brought rapid progress, including the 1991 Espoo Convention, the 1992 Convention on the Transboundary Effects of Industrial Accidents, the 1992 Convention on the Protection and Use of Transboundary Watercourses and Lakes, and the 1998 Aarhus Convention in addition to the adoption of further protocols to the 1979 LRTAP Convention.[177] The impact of some of these agreements has been significant, notably in harmonizing legislation and practice on EIA, access to justice and public participation,[178] and in the negotiation of further agreements covering environmental protection of the Rhine, Meuse, Scheldt and Danube.[179]

4(3) THE FOOD AND AGRICULTURE ORGANIZATION

The FAO was created for the purpose, *inter alia*, of improving efficiency in the production of food and agricultural produce.[180] Broadly defined, its mandate also covers fisheries, marine products, forestry and forestry products.[181] It is empowered to collect information, promote research, furnish assistance to governments, and make recommendations on conservation of natural resources and other matters. The FAO's governing bodies include a Conference of member states, a Council which exercises powers delegated by the Conference, and various committees.

Within its specialized sphere, the FAO has promoted international environmental law-making in various ways.[182] Article XIV of the FAO Constitution empowers the Conference to approve conventions and agreements relating to food and agriculture. While the majority of Article XIV treaties mainly establish regional fisheries commissions rather than adding to the corpus of international law, a few have laid down rules of more general significance, most notably the 1993 Agreement to Promote Compliance

[174] See Morgera and Savaresi, 22 *RECIEL* (2012) 14.

[175] In 2018 ECLAC adopted an Agreement on Access to Justice, Information and Participation in Decision-making on Environmental Matters: see *infra*, Ch 5, section 2.

[176] *Infra*, Ch 6.

[177] *Infra*, Chs 3, 5, 6 and 10. For an overview see Schrage et al, 18 *YbIEL* (2008) 3.

[178] *Infra*, Ch 3, section 7, and Ch 5, section 2(6).

[179] *Infra*, Ch 10.

[180] 1945 Constitution of the FAO, Article 2.

[181] 1945 Constitution of the FAO, Article 1,

[182] See Dobbert in Schachter and Joyner (eds), *United Nations Legal Order* (ASIL, 1995) 902.

with International Conservation and Management Measures by Fishing Vessels on the High Seas ('Compliance Agreement') and the 2001 International Treaty on Plant Genetic Resources for Food and Agriculture ('ITPGR'). The FAO provided expert and influential advice in the negotiation of the 1958 Geneva Convention on Fishing and Conservation of the Living Resources of the High Seas, the 1982 UNCLOS, and the 1995 UN Fish Stocks Agreement. It collaborated with UNEP in the negotiation of the 1998 Rotterdam Convention on Prior Informed Consent. Finally, when the adoption of binding agreements is not possible, the FAO has made some use of non-binding agreements, including the 1983 International Undertaking on Plant Genetic Resources, now superseded by the 2001 treaty considered below, and others relating to fisheries, also considered below.

The FAO played only a limited role in the negotiation of the 1992 CBD but it has subsequently been involved in implementation of the Convention and related elements of Agenda 21. To this end, the ITPGR adopted in 2001 replaced the earlier non-binding 1983 Undertaking and created a multilateral scheme for access to certain agricultural crops, an issue not specifically dealt with in the 1992 CBD.[183] Negotiations were initiated by the FAO Council and conducted mainly in the Commission on Genetic Resources for Food and Agriculture, in which a large number of states participated, together with observers from the World Intellectual Property Organization ('WIPO'), the CBD Secretariat, the International Union for the Protection of New Varieties of Plants ('UPOV'), and a variety of NGOs and agricultural research institutes. Moreover, the negotiations straddled issues of concern to several other international bodies, including UNEP, the WTO, the UN Conference on Trade and Development ('UNCTAD'), the WIPO and the COP to the 1992 CBD.[184] The FAO's work on the ITPGR therefore had to secure 'harmony'[185] with work carried out under the 1992 CBD—which eventually led to the adoption of the 2010 Nagoya Protocol on Access and Benefit Sharing ('Nagoya Protocol') to the 1992 CBD[186]—as well as complementarity with the work of the WIPO Intergovernmental Committee on Intellectual Property and Genetic Resources, Traditional Knowledge and Folklore, established in 2000. The treatment of genetic resources under these instruments is a good example of how the same issue can be addressed by different processes, in different ways and with different but largely compatible outcomes, depending on the objectives and the interests they set out to protect.[187]

Since its inception the FAO has been the principal UN body responsible for establishing regional fisheries agreements, developing international fisheries law and promoting implementation of the fisheries provisions of the 1958 Geneva Convention on Fishing and Conservation of the Living Resources of the High Seas, the 1982

183 See Dobbert, *loc cit*, 930–8; Raustiala and Victor, 58 *Int Org* (2004) 277.

184 See Petit et al, *Why Governments Can't Make Policy: The Case of Plant Genetic Resources* (Lima, 2001) 6; Chambers, 6 *J World Intellectual Property* (2003) 311.

185 International Treaty on Plant Genetic Resources for Food and Agriculture, Article 1.

186 *Infra*, Ch 11.

187 Savaresi, 9 *JHRE* (2018) 32.

UNCLOS, the 1995 UN Fish Stocks Agreement, and Agenda 21 of the 1992 UNCED.[188] It has employed a mixture of hard and soft law for this purpose, including the 1993 Compliance Agreement, the 1995 Code of Conduct on Responsible Fishing, the 2001 Reykjavik Declaration on Sustainable Fisheries, the 2009 Agreement on Port State Measures, and various voluntary undertakings.[189] All of these fisheries instruments were considered initially by a 'technical consultation' of industry and government experts; they were then negotiated by consensus in the Committee on Fisheries before adoption by the FAO Council. Here we can see how, in the framework of a UN law-making treaty—the 1982 UNCLOS—a specialised agency can further develop the law within its own special field in response to emerging needs and priorities. At the same time, we can also see that a variety of law-making instruments allows added flexibility and increases the likelihood of reaching agreement.

Not all agreements on marine living resources come under the FAO's jurisdiction however. It is notable that the International Whaling Commission ('IWC'), which the US had at the outset thought should be incorporated into the FAO, voted against such a move when the opportunity arose. More recently regional fisheries agreements involving 'fishing entities' (i.e. Taiwan) have been concluded outside the FAO in deference to Chinese wishes.[190]

Faced with the disparate national interests of its members—which include developed and developing states, coastal, artisanal, and distant water-fishing states—the FAO has eschewed any attempt at a global or regional managerial role, confining itself instead to promoting effective management by states and fisheries commissions. A Committee on Fisheries ('COFI') and various committees of independent experts advise the Director General. Their reports have shown the unreliability of estimates of maximum sustainable yield ('MSY'), the unsustainability of many fisheries, and the manifestation of biological degradation and economic waste.[191]

These considerations resulted in a reassessment of international fisheries policy and law during and after the 1992 Rio Conference. Placing international fisheries policy in a broader environmental context, Agenda 21 gave new vigour to the importance of sustainable use and conservation of marine living resources and recognized once more the need for more effective regional cooperation. The FAO has played a leading role in the negotiation of agreements on straddling and highly migratory fish stocks, sustainable fishing, and compliance with regional fisheries agreements. Intended to supplement the existing provisions of the 1982 UNCLOS, these agreements underline the FAO's importance in the process of reforming international fisheries law.[192]

[188] See Edeson, in Boyle and Freestone (eds), *International Law and Sustainable Development* (Oxford, 1999) Ch 8; Harrison, *Making the Law of the Sea* (Cambridge, 2011) Ch 9; and *infra*, Ch 12.

[189] E.g. the 2001 International Plan of Action on Illegal, Unreported and Unregulated Fishing. For others see *infra*, Ch 12, section 3.

[190] See Edeson, 22 *IJMCL* (2007) 485.

[191] FAO, *State of World Fisheries and Aquaculture* (Rome, 2016) 38–45, and see *infra*, Ch 12.

[192] See in particular Edeson, in Boyle and Freestone (eds) *International Law and Sustainable Development*, Ch 8; Moore, in Hey (ed), *Developments in International Fisheries Law*, 55ff; Reyfuse, ibid, 107ff; and *infra*, section 5.

In particular, the 1995 UN Fish Stocks Agreement has for the first time provided a framework for regional agreements, revising those already in existence and requiring the negotiation of new ones. We return to this important development in Chapter 12.

4(4) THE INTERNATIONAL MARITIME ORGANIZATION

The IMO is the principal body responsible for the international regulation of shipping and thus for the prevention of pollution of sea by ships. Its role as 'the competent organization' in this respect is referred to implicitly in several articles of the 1982 UNCLOS.[193] It is empowered to promote 'the general adoption of the highest practicable standards in matters concerning the maritime safety, efficiency of navigation and prevention and control of marine pollution from ships'.[194] Responsibility for regulatory developments is divided between a Maritime Safety Committee ('MSC'), a Marine Environment Protection Committee ('MEPC'), established following a recommendation of the 1972 Stockholm Conference,[195] and a Legal Committee.[196] The IMO Council, whose forty members are drawn on an equitable geographical basis from the largest maritime states and other states with a 'special interest in maritime transport and navigation', supervises the work of these bodies. As a result, the Council is dominated by shipping states,[197] but all member states are represented in the Assembly, the governing body of the organization, and in the various committees referred to above. Coastal states and those with limited maritime interests can thus participate fully in the Organization's main rule-making bodies; however, it does not follow that they will necessarily be influential.

Agenda 21 re-iterated the need for the IMO to adopt further regulatory measures to address 'degradation of the marine environment', and this is reflected in its subsequent work, which addresses a broader range of environmental concerns than hitherto, including protection of sensitive sea areas and regulation of air and ballast-water pollution from ships.[198] The 1997 Kyoto Protocol identified the IMO as the forum to pursue limitation or reduction of emissions of greenhouse gases from marine bunker fuels not controlled by the 1987 Montreal Protocol on Substances that Deplete the Ozone Layer ('Montreal Protocol').[199]

193 Notably Articles 211, 217, 218. See IMO, *Implications of the Entry into Force of the UNCLOS for the IMO*, LEG/MISC/2 (1997) and Harrison, *Making the Law of the Sea* (Cambridge, 2011) Ch 6.

194 Article 1, 1948 Convention Establishing the International Maritime Consultative Organization (changed to IMO in 1982) ('IMO Convention').

195 IMO Res A297 (VIII)(1973). See de La Fayette, 16 *IJMCL* (2001) 155.

196 See Gaskell, 18 *IJMCL* (2003) 155.

197 See M'Gonigle and Zacher, *Pollution, Politics and International Law* (London, 1979); Tan, *Vessel-Source Marine Pollution* (Cambridge, 2006) 29–102.

198 Agenda 21, Ch 17.30. See *Report of the IMO to the Commission on Sustainable Development*, IMO Doc MEPC 37/Inf (1995) and *Report on Follow-Up Action to UNCED*, MEPC 37/10/1 (1995). On subsequent IMO regulatory developments see Nordquist and Moore (eds), *Current Maritime Issues and the International Maritime Organisation* (The Hague, 1999); Harrison, *Saving the Oceans through Law* (Oxford, 2017) Ch 6, and *infra*, Ch 9.

199 1997 Kyoto Protocol, Article 2(2). See *infra*, Ch 9, section 4.

The IMO has negotiated almost 40 conventions, as well as adopting non-binding codes, recommendations and guidelines on related matters. For environmental purposes the most important regulatory treaties are the 1973/78 Convention for the Prevention of Marine Pollution from Ships ('MARPOL'), the 1974 Convention on the Safety of Life at Sea ('SOLAS') and the 2004 Convention for the Control and Management of Ships' Ballast Water.[200] These agreements establish internationally recognized standards for the construction and operation of ships and the prevention of pollution at sea. The principal regulations are found not in the text of the Conventions themselves but in annexes which are easily and regularly supplemented or amended by decision of the MEPC or MSC.[201] Apart from their character as treaty law, many of the relevant provisions of these annexes have become 'generally accepted international rules and standards' for the purposes of the 1982 UNCLOS.[202] Another important role for IMO law-making is the development of treaty regimes whose principal purpose is to harmonize and progressively develop national law on liability for marine pollution.[203] Some states have questioned whether these agreements are too favourable to the interests of the shipping and oil industries.[204]

Another criticism of the IMO has been the failure to give enough attention to non-implementation and non-compliance with existing conventions and standards, especially by flag states, many of which are members of the IMO Council. Although there is now a Sub-committee on Flag State Implementation, and a periodic audit scheme under which national laws and policies are reviewed, the IMO's powers as a supervisory body remain more limited that the non-compliance procedures established under most MEAs.[205]

The IMO exhibits many of the strengths and weaknesses of international regulatory agencies. In its favour it enables the law-making process to draw upon appropriate technical expertise and it is rather more than a forum within which interested states negotiate and revise global standards. Industry associations, mainly representing shipping companies, seafarers and insurers, participate actively and they are often influential, as are some environmental NGOs.[206] Bodies typically involved include the International Chamber of Shipping, the International Confederation of Trade Unions, P&I Clubs, Friends of the Earth International and IUCN. Among its weaknesses, the IMO inevitably finds it difficult to act against the opposition of flag of convenience states, many of which coordinate their positions in advance and are influential members of the IMO Council. This has been a significant factor in its inability to deliver stronger regulation and better compliance mechanisms. Like some other regulatory

200 See *infra*, Ch 9, section 4.

201 But only the states parties have a vote: see 1973/78 MARPOL Convention, Article 16; 2004 Ballast Water Convention, Article 19.

202 See *infra*, Ch 9, section 2.

203 See *infra*, Ch 9, section 8.

204 See e.g. the discussion of the 2004 Ballast Water Convention in Tsimplis, 19 *IJMCL* (2004) at 444–5.

205 See *infra*, Ch 9, section 4(3)(d).

206 Gaskell, 18 *IJMCL* (2003) 172–4; de La Fayette, 16 *IJMCL* (2001) 213–6; Tan, *Vessel-Source Marine Pollution*, 34–46.

agencies the IMO is thus open to the criticism that it too often serves the interests of the industry it is meant to regulate.[207] Pressure for action on flags of convenience has thus come from the UN General Assembly rather than from the IMO. Lastly, the whole process of negotiating and renegotiating maritime conventions can be very slow. The 1989 Salvage Convention took eleven years to negotiate, the 1996 HNS Liability Convention almost twenty; in 2019 the latter was still not in force. In this respect IMO compares unfavourably with the work of the Comité Maritime International ('CMI') in the years prior to IMO's involvement in maritime law-making.[208] The IMO can act quickly, as its response to disasters such as the sinking of the *Torrey Canyon*, the *Erika* or the *Prestige* shows.[209] Nevertheless, given the IMO's failure to take significant action in relation to pressing matters falling squarely within its remit, it is unsurprising if some states opt for unilateral measures rather than waiting for the IMO.[210]

4(5) THE INTERNATIONAL ATOMIC ENERGY AGENCY

The IAEA was established principally to facilitate dissemination of nuclear technology for peaceful purposes and to prevent the proliferation of nuclear weapons.[211] It has over 100 member states, meeting annually in a General Conference, and a Board of Governors, which must include the ten members most advanced in the technology of atomic energy or production of its source materials, and representatives of the eight major UN regions, if not already included. Although the agency is associated with the UN, it is an independent intergovernmental organization without specialized agency status. It is responsible, *inter alia*, for setting international standards on nuclear safety, a task which became more important following the Chernobyl disaster in 1986. Conventions on nuclear safety, radioactive waste, liability for nuclear accidents, and notification and cooperation in emergencies have all been negotiated through IAEA. It is thus the principal international regulatory agency for civil nuclear activities. Its role is considered in more detail in Chapter 7.

4(6) THE WORLD TRADE ORGANIZATION

The WTO is not part of the UN system. It was created by an inter-governmental conference in 1994 for the purpose of furthering free trade and facilitating implementation and operation of the GATT. and other related agreements.[212] Like the IMO and various other international organizations, it is in effect a regulatory agency; unlike other international organizations it is also responsible for settling disputes between

[207] See Hayashi, 16 *IJMCL* (2001) 501; de La Fayette, 16 *IJMCL* (2001) 215–20.

[208] Gaskell, 18 *IJMCL* (2003) 212–4.

[209] See de La Fayette, 16 *IJMCL* (2001) 195–6; Frank, 20 *IJMCL* (2005) 1, 62–4.

[210] See *infra*, Ch 9, section 5(2) and see also Martinez Romera, 25 *RECIEL* (2016) 215.

[211] 1956 IAEA Statute. See *infra*, Ch 7.

[212] 1994 Marrakesh Agreement Establishing the World Trade Organization.

member states. All WTO members must sign up to all the main agreements adopted in 1994. While many of these agreements are detailed and comprehensive, some are little more than an outline or framework requiring further negotiations, while the whole package of WTO law assumes the need for continued evolution. In this respect the WTO is the forum for agenda-setting and policy review, as well as the negotiation, adoption, amendment and authoritative interpretation of WTO agreements.[213] For these purposes all members are represented on the General Council and the Ministerial Conference, the two main political organs of the organization. The 1947 GATT allowed decisions to be taken by majority vote,[214] but the parties have normally operated on the basis that consensus is desirable (defined for this purpose to mean the absence of objections by any member present when a decision is taken) and that practice is retained expressly in the WTO Agreement.[215] Voting is thus allowed only if the objections of a member government cannot otherwise be overcome.

What can the WTO legitimately regulate? The Agreement Establishing the WTO envisages that it will provide a 'common institutional framework for the conduct of trade relations among its Members. . . . . . .'[216] At the same time, in the Preamble to the Marrakesh agreement the members recognized the need to do so in accordance with sustainable development and protection and preservation of the environment. Despite this explicit reference, the Organization has shown great reluctance to reflect environmental concerns in its law-making agenda, and it is largely through decisions of its quasi-judicial Dispute Settlement Body that serious conflict between trade law and international environmental law has so far been avoided.[217] Moreover, trade regulation is not the exclusive preserve of the WTO, and there is nothing in the WTO Agreement which gives WTO treaties priority over other treaties. A small number of non-WTO multilateral treaties thus regulate environmentally harmful forms of international trade. These include the 1988 UN Convention against Illicit Traffic in Narcotic Drugs, the 1973 CITES and the Basel Convention negotiated by UNEP in 1973 and 1989 respectively, and a protocol on trade in genetically modified organisms adopted by the parties to the 1992 CBD.[218] Provided any trade restraints they adopt are non-discriminatory and not a 'disguised restriction on international trade,'[219] there is no obligation for states to choose WTO as the forum in which to conduct negotiations on such matters. At the same time, since trade regulation is the central purpose of all of these agreements there is no reason in principle why the WTO should not address similar concerns. Because the WTO is not a UN specialized agency, its law-making activities cannot easily be coordinated or dictated by the UN General Assembly. Member governments are largely free therefore to decide for themselves what the scope of WTO law-making should be.

A more difficult question is whether the WTO can also regulate issues that do not themselves involve trade, but which have a direct impact on conditions of trade.

[213] 1994 Agreement, Articles 3, 9–10. [214] Article 25(4). [215] Article 9(1).
[216] Article 2(1). [217] See Charnovitz, 8 *YbIEL* 98 (1998) and *infra*, Ch 13, section 8.
[218] 2000 Protocol on Biosafety. [219] See especially 1992 Rio Declaration, Principle 12.

Obvious examples would include the establishment of health, safety or environmental standards for goods or agricultural produce traded internationally. In all these examples other international bodies with primary responsibility for international regulation already exist, including the FAO, WHO and the various treaty COPs. There are no hard and fast jurisdictional boundaries between these organizations and the WTO, and it is possible to advance policy arguments for and against the WTO taking on a more expansive role in regard to the regulation of these matters and many others.[220] It might well make sense, for example, to link negotiations on trade issues with setting standards for reducing CO2 emissions and promoting energy efficiency, since it is far from obvious why a country that subsidizes pollution by failing to take action on climate change should reap the benefits of free trade. We should not assume therefore that such trade-related issues could not be dealt with by the WTO.[221]

Ultimately it is for the contracting parties to decide on the forum in which they wish to negotiate, and if, for example, they choose to conclude the Agreement on Trade-Related Aspects of Intellectual Property Rights ('TRIPS Agreement') in a WTO context rather than at WIPO they are free to do so. This is no different from the similar choices made when preferring to negotiate a plant genetic resources agreement at the FAO rather than the 1992 CBD, or a tobacco convention at the WHO rather than the FAO or WTO. In all these cases states have treated the question as essentially a pragmatic one: which forum is more appropriate and why? The answer in many instances is best understood in political rather than jurisdictional or constitutional terms.[222] But, while the boundaries between different organizations cannot be laid down in a systematic way, the need for a supportive relationship between the WTO and other international bodies is obvious.[223]

The substantive law of the WTO and its relationship to environmental concerns are dealt with more fully in Chapter 13.

4(7) THE WORLD BANK AND THE GLOBAL ENVIRONMENT FACILITY

(a) The World Bank

The World Bank and its private finance arm the International Finance Corporation ('IFC') fund long-term capital loans that will lead to economic growth in developing countries or that support reconstruction and development projects. Its mandate, like that of most of the regional development banks, requires it to facilitate investment, economic growth, and international trade, but does not as such mention protection

220 See Alvarez and others, 96 *AJIL* (2002) 1–158. 221 See *infra*, Ch 13.

222 See generally Boyle and Chinkin, *The Making of International Law* (Oxford, 2007) Ch 3.

223 See in particular Cass, *The Constitutionalization of the WTO* (Oxford, 2005) who argues against expansion of the role of WTO.

of the environment or sustainable development.[224] Some of its more grandiose projects, such as the funding of power stations, dams, pipelines, or the building of roads through forests, have caused serious environmental harm and dislocated the lives of many local people. Although the 1992 UNCED started the process of 'greening' the Bank, one early study concluded that the Bank's approach 'demonstrated that environmental sustainability cannot be added on [to] the "business-as-usual" approach to development.'[225] Largely through strong NGO and US Congressional pressure the Bank has become increasingly responsive to the environmental impacts of its activities.[226] Over the past twenty years it has developed sophisticated 'safeguard policies' requiring it to avoid, mitigate or minimize adverse social and environmental impacts of its lending decisions.[227] For that purpose it subjects most major projects to a process of environmental impact assessment.[228] Thus it is most unlikely now to fund projects which would be likely to cause significant transboundary environmental harm. The Bank was also instrumental in establishing a prototype carbon fund and other mechanisms designed to assist in implementing the 1997 Kyoto Protocol and promoting clean energy.[229]

The IFC has developed its own 'sustainability framework' under which borrowers must similarly assess environmental and social impacts.[230] The IFC performance standards are designed to avoid or minimize pollution and greenhouse gas emissions 'in line with internationally disseminated technologies and practices'; to promote sustainable use of natural resources, including living resources, water and energy; and to protect and conserve biodiversity and maintain ecosystem services.[231] In practice meeting IFC standards will require compliance with a range of international environmental agreements and customary obligations.[232] The evidence that it complied with

[224] World Bank, Articles of Agreement, Article I; Inter-American Development Bank Agreement, Article I; Asian Development Bank Agreement, Article 2. Only the European Bank for Reconstruction and Development has an explicit obligation to promote 'environmentally sound and sustainable development': Agreement Establishing the EBRD, Article 1 (vii). See also African Development Bank Agreement, Article 1: 'The purpose of the Bank shall be to contribute to the sustainable economic development and social progress of its regional members individually and jointly'. See generally Handl, *Multilateral Development Banking* (The Hague, 2001); Freestone, *The World Bank and Sustainable Development* (Leiden, 2013).

[225] Fox and Brown (eds), *The Struggle for Accountability: the World Bank, NGOs and Grassroots Movements* (Cambridge, Mass, 1998) 9, citing a WWF assessment.

[226] *Ibid.*

[227] See World Bank, 2013 Operational Manual, OP/BP 4.00-37; Di Leva, 4 *Laws* (2015) 674; Handl, in Krämer and Orlando (eds), *Principles of Environmental Law* (Cheltenham, 2018) 627–643.

[228] See *infra*, Ch 3, section 7.

[229] See Freestone, *The World Bank and Sustainable Development* (Leiden, 2012) Chs 3 and 7.

[230] For the current standards see IFC, *Performance Standards on Environmental and Social Sustainability* (2012) Overview, para 1, and Performance Standard 1.

[231] 2012 Performance Standards 3 and 6, at para 2.

[232] These include 1979 LRTAP Convention; 1987 Montreal Protocol; 1989 Basel Convention; 1992 CBD; 1992 UNFCCC and 1997 Kyoto Protocol; 1998 Rotterdam Convention on Prior Informed Consent; 2001 Stockholm Convention on Persistent Organic Pollutants. See in particular Performance Standards 3, 4, and 6. See also Morgera, 18 *Colorado JIELP* (2007) 151.

this element of IFC standards was helpful to Uruguay in the *Pulp Mills* litigation.[233] Borrowers must also comply with national law, 'including those laws implementing host country obligations under international law,'[234] or with the World Bank's own environmental, health and safety standards if these are higher.[235]

An Inspection Panel provides affected groups or communities a means of challenging any failure by the World Bank to observe its own operational policies and procedures.[236] This innovative method for introducing a measure of public accountability to the operations of an international organization has since been adopted by other bodies.[237] The IFC's equivalent was involved in assessing complaints during the *Pulp Mills* dispute.[238] Operational policies and procedures of World Bank and its partner organizations have nevertheless continued to remain at the centre of sustained criticism, especially from human rights bodies.[239]

(b) The Global Environment Facility

The World Bank acts as trustee for the GEF, which provides funding to developing states and has become an important environmental institution in its own right. The GEF was established in 1991 by the World Bank, UNEP, and UNDP. Following decisions taken at UNCED to restructure the GEF in accordance with principles of 'universality, transparency and democracy', a new instrument was adopted by the three implementing agencies. It has since been further revised.[240] Currently the GEF's general function is to provide funds to enable developing countries to meet 'agreed incremental costs' of measures intended to achieve 'agreed global environmental benefits' with regard to climate change, biological diversity, international waters, deforestation and desertification, and chemicals and wastes. It works closely with other international bodies and regional development banks and also funds related IUCN and NGO activities. It has also been designated as the financial mechanism under the Conventions on Biological Diversity, Desertification, Persistent Organic Pollutants, and Mercury. Under the climate regime, however, the GEF has largely been replaced by the Green Climate Fund.[241]

233 See *Pulp Mills Case*, ICJ Reports (2010) 14.

234 2012 Performance Standard 1, para 6.

235 2012 Performance Standard 3, paras 4–5.

236 Res 93/10 (1993). See Schlemmer-Schulte, 58 *ZAÖRV* (1998) 353; Shihata, *The World Bank Inspection Panel in Practice* (Oxford, 2000); Orakhelashvili, 2 *Int Orgs LR* (2005) 57; Nurmukhametova, 10 *Max Planck YbUNL* (2006) 397.

237 See, for example, the Green Climate Fund's environmental and social management system.

238 The Compliance Advisor/Ombudsman (CAO) is independent of IFC management and reports directly to the President of the World Bank Group.

239 Letter from the UN Human Rights Council to the World Bank President on the World Bank's draft Environmental and Social Framework, 14 December 2014.

240 1994 Instrument for the Establishment of the Restructured Global Environment Facility, as revised 2002, 2006, 2011, 2015. See generally Freestone, *The World Bank and Sustainable Development*, Chs 5–6.

241 *Infra*, nn 245–6.

The GEF is a separate and distinct entity from the World Bank and its partners.[242] Representation on the Council and a qualified majority voting structure were designed to avoid the World Bank's pattern of dominance by Western donor countries.[243] The GEF Instrument specifies that GEF grants made from the financial mechanisms referred to above 'shall be in conformity with the eligibility criteria decided by the Conference of the Parties of each convention'.[244] However, the GEF voting structure 'does not preclude the possibility of conflict between the objectives of the Conventions, the implementing agencies, and the GEF in the context of particular decisions.'[245]

The GEF is thus an important instrument for promoting participation by developing countries in policies and conventions intended to protect the global environment, and for assisting their implementation through capacity-building, as envisaged in Agenda 21. As such, it funds measures that do not necessarily benefit the country concerned, but which do benefit the international community as a whole. Its creation and remit reflect notions of 'common but differentiated responsibility' and 'additionality' in funding allocations which are core elements of the equitable treatment of developing countries in the 1992 Rio Declaration and the two Rio Conventions.[246] The scale and impact of GEF funding have been substantial. *Inter alia* it has become the principal instrument for funding biodiversity conservation in developing countries, it has supported negotiation and implementation of MEAs, including the elimination of ozone depleting substances, and helped to promote the objectives of the 1982 UNCLOS, Agenda 21 and the Rio Conventions.[247] The GEF has not been immune from criticism. Developing countries' dissatisfaction with its operation led to the establishment of the Green Climate Fund,[248] which has rapidly become the largest global institution disbursing climate finance.[249] It remains to be seen whether it will manage to overcome the legitimacy and accountability difficulties experienced by the GEF.

4(8) THE ORGANISATION FOR ECONOMIC CO-OPERATION AND DEVELOPMENT

The OECD is an economic grouping of industrialized states, not a UN agency. It has thirty-five member states, mainly European, but also including Australia, Canada, Japan, Chile, Mexico, South Korea and the US. Recognizing the economic interdependence of its members, its objectives are to promote growth, help less developed states, and encourage world trade. On this basis, and because its members undertake to 'promote the efficient use of their economic resources' and in scientific and

[242] Werksman, 6 *YbIEL* (1995) 55–58 reviews the legal status of the GEF.

[243] 2015 Instrument, para 25(b).

[244] 2015 Instrument, para 9(a).

[245] Werksman, 6 *YbIEL* (1995) at 60.

[246] See *infra*, Ch 3, section 4 (3).

[247] For a detailed assessment see GEF, *5th Overall Performance Study* (2014) and Freestone, *The World Bank and Sustainable Development*, Chs 5–6.

[248] Yamineva and Kulovesi in Hollo, Kulovesi, Mehling (eds), *Climate Change and the Law* (Berlin, 2013) 191.

[249] Climate Policy Initiative, *Global Landscape of Climate Finance 2017* (2017) 4.

technological fields to encourage research,[250] the OECD has been a pioneer in the development of environmental policy and the promotion of sustainable development. Its Nuclear Energy Agency has played a significant role in the development of national and international nuclear law in Europe.[251] More generally, the OECD has been an important forum in which to coordinate policy on environmental matters among the developed economies, and its expertise gives it significant influence in global environmental negotiations.

The OECD has performed three principal tasks with respect to the environment. First, it has developed some important principles of environmental law that have subsequently been adopted into national and international law. It was the OECD that first endorsed the polluter pays principle,[252] and the principles of non-discrimination and equal access for transboundary claimants to national judicial remedies, administrative procedures and information.[253] International support for transboundary EIA originated in a series of OECD recommendations which relied on the principle of non-discrimination.[254] The OECD has also promoted public participation in environmental decision-making, access to environmental information held by public bodies, and access to justice.[255] These instruments apply the basic principles now found in the 1998 Aarhus Convention.

Secondly, the OECD's membership and expertise have given it significant influence in shaping global environmental negotiations and international law relating to transboundary problems. The obligation of states to cooperate in managing transboundary environmental risks through notification, consultation and negotiation was recognized in OECD principles as early as 1974.[256] The formative influence of this precedent on general international environmental law should not be underestimated.[257] OECD principles on transfrontier movements of hazardous waste also provided the model on which the 1989 Basel Convention is largely based.[258] A later decision establishes agreed standards for implementation of the 1989 Basel Convention's requirement for environmentally sound management of hazardous waste.[259]

250 Article 2, OECD Constitution. 251 *Infra*, Ch 7.

252 OECD, Recommendations C(72) 128 (1972); C(74) 223 (1974) reprinted in OECD, *OECD and the Environment*, (Paris, 1986) and C(89) 88 (1988). Most of these instruments are collected in OECD, *OECD and the Environment* (Paris, 1986). See *infra*, Ch 5, section 4(4).

253 OECD Council Recommendations C (74) 224 (1974); C (77) 28 (1977); C (78) 77 (1978); C (79) 116 (1979). See *infra*, Ch 5, section 3(2).

254 See *infra*, Ch 3, section 7.

255 Decision-Recommendation C(88)85 (1988) Provision of Information to the Public and Public Participation in Decision-making Processes related to the Prevention of, and Response to, Accidents Involving Hazardous Substances; Recommendation C(98) 67 (1998) on Environmental Information. See *infra*, Ch 5, section 2(6).

256 Recommendation C(74)224 on Principles concerning Transfrontier Pollution; OECD, *Legal Aspects of Transfrontier Pollution* (Paris, 1977).

257 See *infra*, Ch 3, section 8.

258 Decisions C(83)180 and C(88)90 on Transfrontier Movements of Hazardous Waste. See *infra*, Ch 8.

259 Recommendation C(2004)100 on Environmentally Sound Management of Waste.

Thirdly, the Environment Policy Committee of the OECD periodically reviews the environmental performance of its member states and makes recommendations on matters of environmental policy.[260] One review concluded that 'The Committee's work provides major and sometimes the only references in this policy field.'[261] The OECD also contributed to the debate on green growth in preparation for UNCSD.[262]

It is evident, however, that although climate change and natural resources management have 'become an increasingly higher priority for members',[263] and the OECD is doing an increasing amount of work in this area, the focus of the OECD's environmental instruments remains relatively narrow, reflecting the environmental agenda of the 1970s and 80s and mainly dealing with domestic and transfrontier environmental problems. Only a handful of the OECD's instruments have anything to say on global environmental issues such as climate change, loss of biological diversity or protection of the marine environment. None of the OECD's instruments addresses sustainable use of natural resources; again, this topic is mostly covered by multilateral agreements. The OECD's committees have reviewed member state policies on sustainable fisheries, and on climate change, but no law-making initiatives or recommended principles have so far emerged.

In the environmental field the OECD's legal instruments are overwhelmingly in the form of non-binding 'recommendations'. A few are described as 'Declarations', including Declaration C(2006)94 on Integrating Climate Change Adaptation into Development Co-operation. A small minority are binding 'decisions' or 'decision – recommendations', mainly relating to the transfrontier movement of hazardous wastes, provision of environmental information, and radiation protection norms. At the same time, the OECD's recommendations on transfrontier pollution, equal access, non-discrimination, and environmental impact assessment have become established as general international law or are incorporated in UN or UNECE treaties.[264] Their non-binding form is from that perspective largely immaterial. The binding status of decisions on waste puts this topic in a different category, but that may simply reflect the non-participation of the US in the 1989 Basel Convention and the consequent need for a parallel regime governing waste movements between the US and other developed economies.

5 INTERNATIONAL REGULATORY REGIMES

5(1) INTRODUCTION

Often referred to as 'international regimes', MEAs with their related protocols and soft law have been employed by states and international institutions to provide a regulatory

[260] See OECD, *Environmental Performance Review of OECD Countries* (Paris, 1998).

[261] OECD, *In-depth Evaluation of the Environment Policy Committee*, C(2012)14 at 3.

[262] OECD, *Towards Green Growth* (Paris, 2011). For an analysis, see Morgera and Savaresi, 22 *RECIEL* (2012) at 18.

[263] *Ibid*, 22, para 63.

[264] See *infra*, Ch 3.

system capable of dynamic evolution.[265] The strength of this model of governance is the provision of multilateral solutions to environmental problems and the negotiated application and development of international legal standards. It enables states to exercise a fiduciary or trusteeship role in the protection of the environment, other species, and future generations. No other model of governance offers adequate solutions to the problem of controlling phenomena of global character, such as climate change or ozone depletion, where no single state's acts are responsible and where the interests of all are at stake. While some theorists see international regimes creating 'epistemic communities' of experts and interest groups,[266] others argue that they offer a new basis for integrating international law and international relations.[267]

The application of regime theory to environmental relations can be observed in numerous treaties considered in later chapters, including the 1946 International Convention for the Regulation of Whaling ('ICRW'), the 1972 London Dumping Convention ('London Convention') (replaced in 1996 by a new protocol), the 1973 CITES, the 1985 Ozone Convention, and the 1992 Convention on Climate Change, as well as many regional agreements. Both the 1985 Ozone Convention and the 1992 Climate Change Convention have evolved into complex regulatory regimes following regular meetings of the parties, with additional protocols, amendments, adjustments and decisions.[268] In order to facilitate this further development most MEAs establish regulatory institutions, usually intergovernmental and autonomous in character,[269] but in a few cases this role is performed by existing international organizations such as the IMO or the IAEA. The autonomous treaty bodies created by these agreements have become the international community's primary institutional model for the regulation and control of environmental risks. Even when the problems are regional, such as the conservation of fish stocks, the allocation of water resources, or transboundary air pollution, some form of international management and cooperation will usually facilitate the equitable allocation and conservation of such resources. In the following sections we consider the role and powers of these international regulatory bodies.

Whether they are autonomous bodies or part of an international organization, the essential elements of environmental treaty institutions are threefold. First, and most importantly, the parties must meet regularly. Conferences or meetings of the parties

265 See Bodansky, *The Art and Craft of International Environmental Law* (Cambridge, Mass, 2010); Jacur, *The Dynamics of Multilateral Environmental Agreements* (Naples, 2013); Schiele, *Evolution of International Environmental Regimes* (Cambridge, 2014) and generally Boyle and Chinkin, *The Making of International Law* (Oxford, 2007) Ch 4, section 4.

266 Haas, in Bodansky, Brunnée and Hey (eds), *Handbook of IEL*, 791; Szasz, in Joyner (ed), *The UN and International Law*, 34–5; Slaughter, 76 *Foreign Affairs* (1997) 183; Walker, *Intimations of Global Law*, 42–54.

267 See Rittberger (ed), *Regime Theory and International Relations* (Oxford, 1993); Slaughter, 87 *AJIL* (1993) 205; Byers, *Custom, Power and the Power of Rules* (Cambridge, 1999) Ch 2.

268 For comprehensive studies see Brunnée and Toope, *Legitimacy and Legality in International Law* (Cambridge, 2010) Ch 4; Bodansky, Brunnée, Rajamani, *International Climate Change Law* (Oxford, 2017); Yoshida, *The International Legal Regime for the Protection of the Stratospheric Ozone Layer* (2nd edn, Leiden, 2019) and *infra*, Ch 6.

269 Churchill and Ulfstein, 94 *AJIL* (2000) 623; Brunnée, 15 *LJIL* (2002) 1; Ulfstein, in Bodansky, Brunnée and Hey, *Handbook of IEL*, 878; French, 21 *JEL* (2009) 255.

('COPs/MOPs') may be provided for in the treaty itself or may be convened by the UN or one of its specialized agencies, or by a commission established to manage the treaty. It is this ongoing role which institutionalizes these gatherings. Secondly, it will usually be the responsibility of the parties to keep the relevant treaty under review and take whatever measures they are empowered to adopt to further its object and purpose. Some treaties, usually described as 'framework' or 'umbrella' treaties, are specifically designed to facilitate further development through the addition of protocols, annexes, additional agreements, amendments, decisions or recommendations which give detailed content to the outline legal regime created by the treaty.[270] COPs are usually the fora in which these measures are negotiated and adopted, and it is in this sense that they are law-making bodies. Thirdly, they will usually be assisted by expert bodies providing scientific, technical and legal advice where appropriate. These bodies may be the source of recommendations for further regulation, or they may be concerned with treaty implementation, or they may have other functions. Additionally, some treaty bodies also have a responsibility for supervising compliance with the treaty regime, but this is not a necessary feature of a law-making agreement.[271]

In general, effective treaty institutions are those which combine political direction and inclusive, transparent, informed decision-making processes with the availability of technical, financial and capacity-building support for developing state parties from UN specialized agencies, the GEF, or developed states.[272] In all these respects environmental treaties have been notably innovative. Not all such bodies have been a success, however. Some lack a wide enough remit, or sufficient resources. In a few cases they have been unable to ensure the full participation of all the states most closely concerned. Rather than any failure to ensure compliance with agreed standards of environmental protection, MEA institutions are most likely to fail when seeking consensus on the more stringent measures that may be needed to tackle environmental problems effectively. Such bodies are often open to the criticism that their decisions represent only the lowest common denominator of agreement: the climate change regime considered in Chapter 6 and the Conventions on toxic chemicals considered in Chapter 8 are good examples. Those failings are the product of political choice, or the lack of adequate political commitment, rather than of inherent institutional weakness. In that respect they are no different from the UN, or from any of the other political institutions considered earlier in this chapter.

Thus, a commitment to a multilateral approach may in some cases prove an obstacle to stronger action. The IMO, whose record was considered above, is perhaps the best current example of this phenomenon. The true role of such bodies may in some cases be closer to legitimation of policies acceptable to the relevant industry than to acting as a trustee for the interests of the environment. For the same reasons, it does

[270] *Supra*, Ch 1, section 2(1). [271] See *infra*, Ch 4, section 3.

[272] See Sand, 56 *ZAöRV* (1996) 754; Gündling, *ibid*, 796; Victor, Raustiala and Skolnikoff (eds), *Implementation and Effectiveness of International Environmental Commitments*, Ch 16; Wettestad, *Designing Effective Environmental Regimes* (Cheltenham, 1999).

not follow that replacing the present fragmented structure of treaty supervision with a single global environmental organization would necessarily improve the effectiveness of international environmental regimes. As one experienced participant observes, 'each IEA [international environmental agreement], regardless of how superficially similar, develops its own unique sense of what is politically possible'.[273]

5(2) AUTONOMOUS TREATY BODIES

Two principal models of governance are found in the majority of MEAs. One consists of regular meetings of the parties, with institutional continuity usually provided by a permanent secretariat.[274] This model is adopted by the 1985 Ozone Convention and the 1992 Climate Change Convention (see Chapter 6), the 1972 London Convention (see Chapter 8), the UNEP Regional Seas Conventions (see Chapter 8), the 1959 Antarctic Treaty,[275] and the 1973 CITES (see Chapter 12). The alternative approach is to establish a commission in which member states are represented. This model is employed by the 1974 and 1992 Paris Conventions and the Helsinki Convention on the Protection of the Baltic Sea (see Chapter 8) the 1976 and 1999 Rhine Conventions (see Chapter 10) and, as we shall observe in Chapter 13, it is common in the case of multilateral fisheries or marine living resources treaties, including the 1980 Convention for the Conservation of Antarctic Marine Living Resources ('CCAMLR') and the 1946 ICRW.

The International Joint Commission ('IJC') established by the US and Canada in the 1909 Boundary Waters Treaty represents a third model, unique among environmental bodies in exercising quasi-judicial functions and having a composition independent of its member governments.[276] It is noteworthy, however, that these states have been reluctant to allow the IJC to perform a truly regulatory role, probably because of its independent structure. In all other cases considered in this work the regulatory body, whether a meeting of the parties or a commission, is in substance no more than a diplomatic conference, and the existence in some cases of a separate legal personality does not alter the reality that these institutions are in no sense independent of their member states.[277] This is not necessarily a weakness, however. Because the development of regulatory standards and further measures is essentially a political task, entailing adoption and implementation by governments, in practice it can only be performed by an intergovernmental body with appropriate negotiating authority. The idea of an 'independent' regulatory agency in this context is thus an unhelpful analogy.

This does not mean that questions of structure and process are unimportant.[278] Several general considerations apply. First, community interests will only be protected

273 Werksman, 6 *YbIEL* (1995) at 62.

274 See Werksman (ed), *Greening International Institutions* (London, 1996) Ch 4.

275 See Gautier, in Francioni and Scovazzi, *International Law for Antarctica* (2nd ed, The Hague, 1996) Ch 2.

276 See *infra*, Ch 10, section 3(2).

277 But see *infra*, section 6 on scientific bodies, and Ch 4, section 3 on non-compliance bodies.

278 See Bodansky, *The Art and Craft of International Environmental Law*, Chs 6–8, and generally Kingsbury, Krisch and Stewart, 68 *Law & Cont. Problems* (2005) 34ff.

if the right community of interest is defined. Institutions whose membership is too narrowly drawn are more likely to legitimize pollution or the over-exploitation of resources than to tackle them. Secondly, transparency is an essential ingredient if these institutions are to be made responsive to a wider community. That may, thirdly, entail a greater willingness to facilitate NGO participation, and to publish reports and findings. Fourthly, decision-making within treaty bodies must be inclusive and effective. Majority voting will not necessarily achieve either objective. Fifthly, the problem of 'free-riders'—states whose non-participation may undermine the effectiveness of the regulatory regime—needs to be addressed in some fashion. Finally, scientific recommendations, verification and review of national reports and environmental data, compliance procedures and inspection regimes will not be successful if the subsidiary bodies which carry them out do not have a measure of independence from the political organs. These functions must be carried out with objectivity and detachment and the institution must therefore be structured in such a way as to facilitate this goal.[279]

(a) Membership

The effectiveness of treaty bodies is significantly affected by their composition. A crucial question is whether membership is limited to those who benefit from the activity or resource in question, as in the consultative meetings of the Antarctic Treaty system and most regional fisheries agreements, or whether membership is drawn from a wider category including those who may be adversely affected by the activity in question. Examples of the latter are the 1972 London Convention Consultative Meeting, and the IWC, which any state may join.[280] Both of these bodies now contain a preponderance of members opposed respectively to dumping and whaling and this has greatly facilitated gradual progress towards the decision to phase out dumping and impose a moratorium on whaling, despite inconclusive scientific evidence in both cases. These are institutions in which community pressure is arguably at its strongest because of their broadly drawn membership and because they have allowed significant NGO involvement at meetings of the parties: they have substantially answered the question who may speak for the global commons in their respective areas of competence, and can be regarded as bodies which have fulfilled a fiduciary role on behalf of the environment. Up to a point the same could be said of the 1985 Ozone and 1992 Climate Change Conventions and their associated protocols.[281]

Where membership and functions are too narrowly defined the wrong states may then address the issues from the wrong perspective. One of the reasons for the ineffectiveness of fisheries commissions is that their membership is drawn exclusively from those states participating in the exploitation of a particular area or stock. As Koers has observed, 'such restrictions on membership may also result in the organization becoming an instrument to further the interests of its members rather than

[279] On the role of scientific bodies in MEAs see *infra*, section 6 and Ch 4, section 3(3).

[280] See *infra*, Chs 8 and 12.

[281] See *infra*, Ch 6.

as an instrument to regulate marine fisheries rationally'.[282] Despite radical changes made by the 1995 UN Fish Stocks Agreement, the right to participate in a regional fisheries agreement remains limited to 'states having a real interest in the fisheries concerned'.[283] The same problem affects the ITTA and commissions on land-based sources of marine pollution. Only timber producing and consuming states may join the former.[284] In the latter case a regional approach is dictated both by geopolitical considerations and the special ecological needs of enclosed or semi-enclosed seas,[285] but it has the effect of leaving environmental protection in the hands of those whose economic and industrial activities would be most affected by high standards or strict enforcement of pollution controls. What is lacking in these cases is a constituency of outside states able to speak for the environmental interests of a wider community. For this reason, some regional seas treaties now combine responsibility for pollution control and ecosystem protection, as envisaged by Article 194(5) of the 1982 UNCLOS.[286]

In spite of difficulties in their practical operation, there are advantages in a regional approach to some environmental issues. Such arrangements facilitate policies and rules appropriate to the needs of particular areas. Political consensus may be obtainable at a regional level which could not be achieved globally. Cooperation in enforcement, monitoring, and information exchange may be easier to arrange. These advantages are recognized in a number of treaties, including the 1982 UNCLOS, whose environmental provisions assume the need for appropriate regional action. But it is important not to overlook the weaknesses of many regional regimes, or the benefits to be derived from ensuring that such regimes are structured within a framework of minimum global standards with some oversight and supervision at global level. Chapter 8 shows clearly the benefits of coordinating regional action within a global framework such as the 1972 London Convention, and the limitations of leaving the problem to regional solutions alone, as in the case of land-based sources of marine pollution.

(b) NGO participation

Non-governmental organizations play an increasingly important role in environmental treaty bodies.[287] NGOs can turn the fear of adverse publicity into a weapon for putting pressure on states to agree stricter standards or ensure better compliance.

282 Koers, *International Regulation of Marine Fisheries*, 126. For a current example see discussion of ICCAT, *infra*, Ch 12, section 2(3).

283 Article 8(3). See Molenaar, 15 *IJMCL* (2000) 475. But see also Article 12, which gives NGOs a right to participate.

284 Article 4. See Savaresi, in Morgera and Razzaque (eds), *Encyclopaedia of Environmental Law: Biodiversity and Nature Protection Law* (Cheltenham, 2017) 203 at 207.

285 See *infra*, Ch 8.

286 See *infra*, Ch 9, section 3.

287 See Morgenstern, *Legal Problems of International Organisations* (Cambridge, 1986) 86ff; Kimball, in Soons (ed), *Implementation of the Law of the Sea Convention through International Institutions* (Honolulu, 1989) 139; Sands, 30 *Harv ILJ* (1989) 393; Victor, Raustiala and Skolnikoff (eds), *Implementation and Effectiveness of International Environmental Commitments*, 664–8; Charnovitz, 18 *Mich JIL* (1997) 183, and *infra*, section 7.

The climate regime in particular has witnessed unprecedented levels of civil society involvement, with a staggering 22,000 observers attending the Copenhagen Climate Conference in 2009. Some studies have suggested that this sizeable civil society involvement has exerted some influence on the evolution of the climate regime.[288]

There is now widespread provision for NGOs qualified in relevant fields to be accorded observer status at meetings of the parties to MEAs.[289] While there is no general right to observer status, and some treaties continue to exclude NGOs,[290] the usual empowering formulation presumes admission unless at least one third of member states object.[291] Unusually, relevant NGOs have a right to take part in the meetings of regional fisheries bodies by virtue of Article 12 of the 1995 UN Fish Stocks Agreement, but there is no comparable provision in the 1997 UN Watercourses Convention.

NGOs serve four main functions as participants in MEA institutions.[292] First, although they cannot vote as full members, their observer status allows them in many cases to make proposals, to influence other parties, and to join actively in the negotiating process. Their influence on policy in the development of treaty regimes such as 1973 CITES and the 1992 Climate Change Convention has been substantial, often more so than the contribution of many states. Secondly, NGOs can to some extent further the interests of public participation and transparency in decision-making by treaty bodies. The 1998 Aarhus Convention recognizes the importance of NGOs in this respect.[293] Thirdly, NGOs may be a source of technical and scientific expertise, and for that reason are sometimes given observer status or even full membership in advisory committees established by several treaties.[294] Fourthly, NGOs such as Greenpeace have on some occasions helped monitor implementation and compliance

[288] Savaresi in Francioni and Bakker (eds), *The EU, The US and Global Climate Governance* (Farnham, 2014); Arts, *The Political Influence of Global NGOs: Case Studies on the Climate and Biodiversity Conventions* (Utrecht, 1998) at 155; Carpenter, 77 *Int Affairs* (2001) 313, at 321; Betsill, Hochstetler and Stevis, *Advances in International Environmental Politics* (Basingstoke, 2005) Ch 7, at 191; Andresen and Gulbrandsen, *The Role of Green NGOs in Promoting Climate Compliance* (Lysaker, 2003) at 13.

[289] See e.g. 1972 World Heritage Convention, Article 8(3); 1973 CITES, Article 11(7); 1979 Migratory Animals Convention, Article 7(9); 1985 Ozone Convention, Article 6(5); 1987 Montreal Protocol, Article 11 (5); 1989 Basel Convention, Article 15(6); 1991 Antarctic Protocol, Articles 11–12; 1991 Convention on the Protection of the Alps, Article 5; 1992 Climate Change Convention, Article 7(6); 1992 CBD, Article 23(5); 1992 Paris Convention, Article 11; 1994 Desertification Convention, Article 22(7); 1995 Agreement on the Conservation of African-Eurasian Migratory Water Birds, Article 7; 1996 Agreement on the Conservation of Cetaceans, Article 3(4). NGO observers have also been admitted to meetings of the parties to the 1946 ICRW and the 1972/1996 London Convention even though there is no specific treaty provision: see Victor *et al* (eds), *Implementation and Effectiveness etc*, Chs 10 and 11.

[290] See e.g. the 1994 Nuclear Safety Convention.

[291] See Article 11(7) of the 1973 CITES and Article 6(5) of the 1987 Montreal Protocol, which are the two principal provisions repeated in many later treaties.

[292] See Bodansky, *The Art and Craft of International Environmental Law* (Cambridge, Mass, 2010) 123–30.

[293] Article 3(7). See *infra*, Ch 5, section 2(6).

[294] See e.g. the 1991 Antarctic Protocol, Articles 11–12 (Scientific Committee on Antarctic Research). IUCN is specifically given observer status by several treaties, including the 1972 World Heritage Convention. The 1995 Agreement on African and Eurasian Migratory Water Birds, Article 7, makes it a full member of that agreement's Technical Committee.

with treaty commitments by exposing, for example, illegal nuclear waste dumping in the Barents Sea.[295] However, one study concluded that NGOs perform this function only rarely.[296]

(c) Transparency

The functionalist view of transparency visible in national law-making is equally relevant to international law-making: it has become an indispensable element of legitimacy and accountability.[297] This is partly a consequence of wider participation, but it also reflects a significant change in the way governments and international organizations view their role as international law-makers. Transparency is perceived as an essential ingredient if these institutions are to be made responsive to a wider public. That entails a willingness to facilitate NGO participation, to make information available, and to publish reports and findings. Quite apart from the publicity generated by press reporting and NGOs, international organizations and treaty secretariats put enormous amounts of material into the public domain via websites. Transparency of this kind can be seen as enhancing both the effectiveness of MEAs and the legitimacy of international regulatory institutions in exercising responsibility for global environmental governance. It is notable, for example that the GEF was restructured in accordance with principles of 'universality, transparency and democracy'.[298]

The importance of transparency is recognized in at least two important treaties which lay down general principles. Article 12 of the 1995 UN Fish Stocks Agreement requires that states 'shall provide for transparency in the decision-making process and other activities of...fisheries management organizations.' The 1998 Aarhus Convention commits UNECE member states to 'promote the application of the principles of this Convention in international environmental decision-making processes and within the framework of international organizations in matters relating to the environment'.[299] Some treaties provide for reports to be made public, while only a few insist on the maintenance of confidentiality.[300] However, there is remarkably little identifiable international law underpinning this rather significant constitutional development. It is easy enough to identify the principle that law-making should be transparent. It is harder to translate this conclusion into something an international lawyer can work with.

295 See Stokke, in Victor *et al* (eds), *Implementation and Effectiveness etc*, 475.

296 Victor *et al* (eds), *Implementation and Effectiveness etc*, 667–8.

297 Bianchi and Peters (eds), *Transparency in International Law* (Cambridge, 2013) especially Boyle and McCall-Smith at 419.

298 1994 Instrument for the Establishment of the Restructured Global Environment Facility, as revised; see *supra*, section 4(7).

299 Article 3 (7). See Ebbesson, 8 *YbIEL* (1997) 51, at 57, and *infra*, Ch 5.

300 Compare 1973 CITES, Article 8 (8) [reports of parties to be made public]; 1991 Antarctic Protocol, Article 11 (5) [reports of the Committee on Environmental Protection to be made public], with 1994 Convention on Nuclear Safety, Article 27 [reports and meetings to be confidential].

(d) Regulatory decision-making

The form in which detailed environmental rules and standards are adopted varies widely. In some cases new treaties may be required. As we have seen, the Antarctic Treaty system has extended its regulatory scope mainly in this way. Other treaties provide for the negotiation of protocols to lay down detailed standards. The 1979 LRTAP Convention and the 1985 Ozone Convention have relied on this method.[301] In some treaties specific technical standards are found in annexes: the 1973/78 MARPOL Convention regulates various aspects of pollution from ships in this way. These annexes can easily be amended by a vote of the parties in the IMO without having to amend the treaty itself. The 1982 UNCLOS indirectly incorporates regulations drawn from IMO regulatory treaties among the category of 'generally accepted international rules and standards' to which Part XII refers.[302] More informal methods of rule-making, such as recommendations, resolutions, codes of practice, and guidelines all fall into the category of soft law but they are nevertheless an important means by which states undertake further measures of treaty implementation. The legal status of these instruments was considered in Chapter 1.

Whether formally binding or not, all of these various methods of rule-making have in common that no obligation may be imposed on any state without its consent. Differences exist in the manner in which this is achieved. Where consensus is required for any decision, as in the climate change regime, or in the listing of additional chemicals in the 1998 Rotterdam Convention on Prior Informed Consent, one state can block the adoption of a new treaty, protocol or amendment by expressing its opposition.[303] Where consensus is not required for decisions to be taken, a two-thirds or three-quarters majority vote of the parties will typically be enough for the adoption of decisions. The benefit of the consensus model is that it allows complex, comprehensive and inclusive agreements to be negotiated, relying on the politics of interdependence that characterizes regulation of world trade, the oceans, or the global environment. As with the UNCED and UNCLOS III conferences, the consensus negotiating procedure generates a greater need to engage in diplomacy, to listen, and to bargain than would be the case when decisions are taken by majority vote.[304] Every state or group of states has to be accommodated in this process—none can be ignored. Powerful states cannot simply dictate what should be in an agreement without risking ultimate breakdown. This explains the influence of the Alliance of Small Island States ('AOSIS') during the UNFCCC negotiations, but also the need to keep the US on board. The consensus negotiating model does not always facilitate agreement, however: if the compromises necessary to engineer consensus cannot be reached then nothing will be agreed, and

[301] See *infra*, Ch 6. [302] See *infra*, Chs 8 and 9.

[303] On the PIC Convention see *infra*, Ch 8, section 2(2); on the problems faced by the UNFCCC see Boyle and Ghaleigh in Carlarne et al (eds), *The Oxford Handbook of International Climate Change Law* (Oxford, 2016) Ch 2.

[304] See Boyle and Chinkin, *The Making of International Law* (Oxford, 2007) Ch 3.

some way must be found to overcome that outcome, as the failure of the 2009 Climate Change Conference in Copenhagen so spectacularly demonstrated.

Whether to join in a consensus is thus a potentially delicate decision. A state that refuses to do so may find itself ignored, as Bolivia was during the climate negotiations in Cancun, or it may be part of a tiny minority if it forces matters to a vote, a position in which the US sometimes finds itself. But if the participation of that state is essential to the deal under discussion then other states may have no option but to keep negotiating if stalemate is to be avoided. Any climate negotiations would be pointless unless the US, China, and India, the largest greenhouse gas emitters, are part of the deal. The difficulty of bringing them on board is one of the reasons why negotiation of the 2015 Paris Agreement took so long, and why that agreement says so little of substance.[305]

However adopted, entry into force of new agreements or amendments will normally follow only if enough states then decide to ratify or accede. This often slow 'opt-in' process can be a serious impediment to law-making, since, as we saw in Chapter 1, states which fail to ratify will not be bound. An alternative approach relies on tacit consent or non-objection to bring amendments to technical annexes into force within a set time-limit. This method of amendment reverses the normal procedure and is now widely used for annexes to treaties such as the 1973/78 MARPOL Convention, the 1989 Basel Convention, the 1973 CITES, the 2001 Stockholm Convention on Persistent Organic Pollutants ('POPS Convention') and most fisheries conventions, since it enables schedules of protected species, prohibited substances, or conservation regulations to be changed speedily as circumstances require. The procedure has enabled parties to the 1973 CITES to list and de-list protected species easily and regularly.[306] The success of the parties to the 1972 London Convention and the 1989 Basel Convention in progressively adopting stricter standards leading to the elimination of hazardous waste exports for dumping at sea or disposal in developing countries shows how in the right conditions substantial changes can come about within the terms of an existing treaty.[307] Although states still remain free to opt out of these measures if they object within the prescribed time limit, the onus is on them to do. In many cases simple inertia operates in favour of stronger regulation covering more states than an opt-in procedure would capture.

Inertia does not always work, however. Much depends on the politics of each treaty body. A willingness to object has enabled a small number of whaling states to delay or opt out of proposals adopted by large anti-whaling majorities in the IWC.[308] For the same reason some fisheries commissions have had difficulty setting appropriate catch quotas.[309] The so-called 'Turbot war' in 1994 between Canada and Spain resulted from the abuse by the European Community of its power to object to quotas set under

305 See generally Boyle and Ghaleigh, *op cit*, Ch 2, and *infra*, Ch 6.

306 Sand, 8 *EJIL* (1997) 29, and see *infra*, Ch 11, section 3(4).

307 *Infra*, Ch 8.

308 E.g. the inability of the IWC to persuade Japan to terminate its programme of 'scientific' whaling: see *Whaling in the Antarctic Case*, ICJ Reports (2014) 226.

309 See *infra*, Ch 12, section 3(3)(d).

the 1978 Northwest Atlantic Fisheries Convention.[310] In an attempt to overcome this problem the 1995 UN Fish Stocks Agreement now requires parties to regional fisheries agreements to 'agree on decision-making procedures which facilitate the adoption of conservation and management measures in a timely and effective manner'.[311] Any failure to do so in respect of fishing for straddling or highly migratory fish stocks on the high seas could be dealt with by the FAO or the UN General Assembly recommending international minimum standards which become binding under Article 10.[312]

The 1987 Montreal Protocol shows that a more radical approach to the problem of regulatory opt-outs is possible. Combined majorities of industrialized and developing states are empowered to amend standards set by the protocol for production and consumption of controlled ozone-depleting substances.[313] Once adopted, these adjustments are automatically binding on all parties to the protocol. Withdrawal from the protocol is then the only option left for those states which find such an amendment unacceptable. The result is to make isolated opposition to majority decisions as difficult and costly as possible. In practice such opposition is pointless and it has never been necessary to adopt amendments using this procedure. However, the 1987 Montreal Protocol precedent is unique among environmental agreements.[314]

(e) Non-participants

Treaties or regulations adopted under them cannot bind states which refuse to participate in the treaty.[315] In order to tackle this potential challenge to the universality of major global environmental agreements, various techniques have been employed to minimize non-participation or objection. Diplomatic and economic pressure applied by other states may help to make objectors comply with majority decisions; such pressure was successfully used by the US to persuade Japan to accept the whaling moratorium adopted by the IWC in 1982. Japan has remained in the 1946 ICRW ever since. Through the Marine Mammal Protection Act, the High Seas Driftnet Fisheries Enforcement Act, the Packwood-Magnuson and Pelly amendments to its fisheries laws, and the Sea Turtle Conservation amendments to the Endangered Species Act, the US has made extensive use of trade restrictions to enforce compliance with international conservation agreements, or with its own national conservation objectives.[316] Unilateral measures of this kind will not always be consistent with international trade agreements, however, nor are they endorsed by Principle 12 of the 1992 Rio Declaration.[317] But the *Shrimp-Turtle* case shows that where Article XX of the GATT

[310] See Davies, 44 *ICLQ* (1995) 927.

[311] Article 10(j). See *infra*, Ch 12, section 3(3)(d). For an analysis of what this might mean see McDorman, 20 *IJMCL* (2005) 423.

[312] See *infra*, Ch 12, section 5(3).

[313] Article 2(9) as amended 1990. See *infra*, Ch 6, section 2.

[314] But see also UN Charter, Article 27, which allows the UNSC to adopt binding resolutions on matters of international peace and security by majority vote.

[315] 1969 VCLT, Article 34.

[316] Zoller, *Enforcing International Law Through US Legislation* (Dobbs Ferry, 1985); Wolfrum, 272 *Recueil des Cours* (1998) 62–65.

[317] Opposition to the adoption of unilateral measures has been reiterated in multiple fora, including in 'The Future We Want', paras 26 and 57(h).

can be invoked, and the other party refuses to negotiate, trade sanctions aimed at encouraging treaty participation remain permissible in accordance with GATT rules.[318]

Other forms of pressure or persuasion have also been built into some treaty regimes: in effect a mixture of carrots and sticks.[319] The 1985 Ozone and 1992 Climate Change Convention and the 1992 CBD, and their protocols, employ trust funds, technology transfer provisions, and other capacity-building measures in order to encourage participation by developing states. All of these agreements use 'common but differentiated responsibility' to place fewer burdens on developing states. The 1992 CBD goes further than most such agreements in encouraging participation. It seeks to provide resource-rich developing countries with additional economic incentives through the sharing 'in a fair and equitable way' of the benefits arising from the utilization of genetic resources.[320] In much the same way the 1982 UNCLOS was widely ratified by developing states because of the benefits from deep seabed mining and the exclusive economic zone which at one time it appeared to offer them. Non-participants thus deprive themselves of whatever potential benefits any of these treaties may provide.

Some treaties also impose constraints on non-parties. Trade with non-parties is restricted under the 1987 Montreal Protocol, the 1989 Basel Convention, the 1973 CITES, and the 1946 ICRW. Article 10 of the 1980 CCAMLR allows its Commission to put pressure on non-parties whose activities affect implementation of the Convention. This attempt to involve non-parties is a distinctive feature of the Antarctic Treaty system, but it is probably too limited in scope and insufficiently supported by acquiescence to constitute an assertion of jurisdiction or to create an objective regime binding on all states.[321] However, parties to the 1995 UN Fish Stocks Agreement must now participate in regional fisheries agreements such as 1980 CCAMLR if they wish to continue high seas fishing,[322] and even non-parties to such regional agreements must comply with their rules and may be subject to compulsory dispute settlement under Part XV of the 1982 UNCLOS if they refuse to cooperate.[323]

5(3) INTERNATIONAL RESOURCE MANAGEMENT BODIES

Exceptionally, a small number of international institutions perform functions more appropriately described as international resource management. Their responsibilities include protection of the environment but they differ from other treaty bodies in that

318 See *United States—Import Prohibition of Certain Shrimp and Shrimp Products* (*'Shrimp/Turtle Case'*) WTO Appellate Body (1998) WT/DS58/AB/R, *infra*, Ch13.

319 See generally Wolfrum, 272 *Recueil des Cours* (1998) 110–145.

320 See 1992 CBD Articles 1, 15(7) 19(1) and (2); 2010 Nagoya Protocol, and *infra*, Ch 11.

321 On the status of the Antarctic Treaty system against third states see Charney and Brunner, in Francioni and Scovazzi (eds), *International Law for Antarctica* (2nd edn, The Hague, 1996) Chs 3 and 4. For other examples see the 1978 Convention for Future Co-operation in Northwest Atlantic Fisheries, Article 19; 1982 North Atlantic Salmon Convention, Article 2(3); 1995 UN Fish Stocks Agreement, Article 33.

322 1995 UN Fish Stocks Agreement, Article 8.

323 *Infra*, Ch 12.

the right of individual states to exploit the resource is subordinated to the authority of collective decision-making. These institutions thus possess stronger powers than is normally the case, since exploitation may take place only with their prior consent and subject to rules some of which are established by qualified majorities which bind all participants. The most prominent example is the International Seabed Authority ('ISA'), designed as a means of implementing the concept of the common heritage of mankind which the 1982 UNCLOS applies to deep seabed mineral resources.[324]

The ISA is concerned only with exploration for and exploitation of deep seabed mineral resources; earlier proposals to include management of high seas fisheries and protection of the whole marine environment within its mandate were not pursued.[325] More recently it has been suggested that it might take on the role of regulating access to and conservation of deep seabed biological resources and bio-prospecting, although that would probably require an amendment of the Convention or an implementing protocol.[326] Article 157 of the 1982 UNCLOS provides that the ISA '. . .is the organization through which States Parties shall. . .organize and control activities in the [deep seabed] Area, particularly with a view to administering the resources of the Area.' No exploitation of these resources may take place outside the control and administration of this body, which is given the duty to adopt appropriate rules, regulations, and procedures for ensuring effective protection of the marine environment.[327] Although seabed mining is carried out by companies sponsored by member states, the Convention as amended in 1994 also provides for the ISA to enter into joint ventures with mining companies, so there is some potential for a conflict of interest with its role as a regulator.[328]

The ISA comprises several elements, including the Assembly, a political organ consisting of all member states, to which other organs of the authority are responsible. Its approval is necessary for the adoption of regulations governing exploitation and exploration of the deep seabed, including environmental protection measures, and it also approves arrangements for the equitable sharing of benefits derived from seabed activities. The second component is the Council, a small executive body reflecting a balance of geographical, political, and economic groupings, whose functions are, *inter alia*, to establish specific policies, to supervise and coordinate the implementation of the Convention's provisions on the deep seabed, to approve proposed plans

[324] Articles 156–70, and Annexes III-IV. These provisions must now be read together with the 1994 Agreement Relating to Implementation of Part XI. See Nandan, in Freestone, Barnes and Ong (eds), *The Law of the Sea* (Oxford, 2006) Ch 5.

[325] See Carroz, 21 *San Diego LR* (1984) 516–17; Kenya, Draft Articles for the preservation and protection of the marine environment, UN Doc A/CONF. 62/C3/L/2 (1974).

[326] See *infra*, Chs 9 and 12.

[327] UNCLOS Article 143; Annex II, Article 17; 1994 Agreement on Implementation, Annex, Section 1.5. On the environmental regulations adopted by the ISA see *infra*, Ch 9.

[328] UNCLOS Article 170 as modified by 1994 Implementation Agreement, Annex, section 2. See ISA, Legal and Technical Commission, *Issues relating to the operation of the Enterprise, in particular the legal, technical and financial implications for the Authority and for States parties*, ISBA/20/LTC/12 (2014).

for exploration and exploitation, and to make recommendations to the Assembly.[329] Both bodies are empowered to take decisions on most questions by qualified majority, although in a few instances consensus is required (e.g. amendments to Part XI of the Convention).[330]

For reasons partly of political, economic, and ideological opposition, internationalized management of natural resources has had a troubled history. Establishment of the International Seabed Authority was only possible following reforms agreed in the 1994 Implementation Agreement intended to reduce its bureaucratic complexity and possible expense. The very similar Antarctic Mineral Resources Commission ('AMRC') was stillborn, following French and Australian opposition to the Convention for the Regulation of Antarctic Mineral Resource Activities ('CRAMRA'),[331] which never entered into force. CRAMRA was replaced in 1991 by the Antarctic Protocol, which bans all Antarctic mineral resource activities for fifty years, designates Antarctica as a natural reserve, and lays down new rules for the protection of the Antarctic environment and the management of activities in Antarctica.[332] However, the 1991 Antarctic Protocol creates no management institutions with distinctive powers comparable to those of the AMRC or the ISA. A Committee on Environmental Protection is established, within the framework of the Antarctic Treaty Consultative Meetings, but it performs only the usual supervisory and regulatory functions associated with other environmental treaty institutions. Although a case can still be made for regarding Antarctica as part of the 'common heritage' of mankind,[333] managed by the Consultative Parties to the 1959 Antarctic Treaty under a form of international trusteeship, regulatory 'measures' under the 1991 Antarctic Protocol can only be adopted, or the Protocol amended, by unanimous agreement.[334] Thus, although the 1991 Antarctic Protocol otherwise establishes a strong environmental regime, application of the Treaty's unanimity requirement to decision-making by the parties leaves Antarctica in quite a different category from the ISA.

The significance of international management for environmental protection and resource conservation is that it represents a model of international trusteeship which,

329 UNCLOS Article 161, as revised by 1994 Implementation Agreement, Annex, section 3.15.

330 Articles 159(8) [the Assembly] and 161(8) [the Council].

331 1988 CRAMRA, Articles 18–33. See Watts, 39 *ICLQ* (1990) 169; Stokke and Vidas (eds), *Governing the Antarctic* (Cambridge, 1996); Wolfrum, *The Convention on the Regulation of Antarctic Mineral Resource Activities* (Berlin, 1993).

332 Redgwell, 43 *ICLQ* (1994) 599; Pineschi, in Francioni and Scovazzi (eds), *International Law for Antarctica* (2nd edn, The Hague, 1996) Ch 9; Francioni (ed), *International Environmental Law for Antarctica* (Milan, 1992) Ch 1; Vidas (ed), *Implementing the Environmental Protection Regime for the Antarctic* (The Hague, 2000); Triggs and Riddell (eds), *Antarctica: Legal and Environmental Challenges for the Future* (London, 2007); Saul and Stephens (eds), *Antarctica in International Law* (Oxford, 2015).

333 Francioni, in Francioni and Scovazzi (eds), *International Law for Antarctica* (2nd edn) 9–10, but compare Charney, *ibid*, 75–80, and Baslar, *The Concept of the Common Heritage of Mankind*, Ch 7.

334 1991 Antarctic Protocol, Articles 9 and 10, applying Articles 9 (4) and 12 (1) of the 1959 Antarctic Treaty. Even the annexes can only be amended unanimously, unless the annex itself provides otherwise. On the question whether 'measures' are legally binding see Gautier, in Francioni and Scovazzi (eds), *International Law for Antarctica*, Ch 2.

by taking away from individual states' control over resource allocation and regulation of the environment, overcomes the two central problems confronting the more limited regulatory and supervisory institutions established under other treaties. Crucially, it substitutes an obligation to comply with majority decisions for an obligation merely to cooperate in reaching decisions. As Wijkman points out, the latter type of voluntary agreement under which international fisheries commissions have typically operated has proved economically inefficient in utilizing common property resources or arresting the 'tragedy of the commons'. He concludes that: 'When many governments share a resource, the management authority must be given power to determine harvesting limitations unilaterally and to enforce the observance of national quotas allocated within this general limit'.[335] If this cannot be achieved, it may be preferable to remove the resource from a common property regime entirely, as has now happened for fish stocks falling within the exclusive economic zone.[336] A similar inability to make international control of the high seas environment fully effective has also resulted in the transfer to coastal states of pollution jurisdiction in the exclusive economic zone.[337] However, as we shall see in Chapters 9 and 12, it is not clear that this transfer has been wholly successful.

Proposals to give the UN Trusteeship Council responsibility for management of the global commons were not adopted at UNCED and no other UN body has a mandate to manage common areas on behalf of the international community. Thus the ISA remains a uniquely powerful resource management and environmental regulatory body within its very specific and limited sphere.

5(4) INTERNATIONAL REGIMES: CONCLUSIONS

There has plainly been a need for improvements in environmental treaty regimes, which themselves represent a pragmatic attempt to find workable answers to difficult problems affecting many states with diverse and competing interests. The essential modesty of what has been achieved falls well short of international management of the global environment and remains heavily dependent on progress by consensus. Measures of the type considered earlier in this chapter may increase the costs of isolated opposition to majority decisions, but they cannot guarantee either participation or adherence to treaty regimes by all states. Resort to soft-law techniques only partially resolves this dilemma, since there may be no obligation to comply. The more radical alternative of allowing majorities of states to impose regulations on dissenting minorities is at variance with the philosophy of consent on which the international legal order is based and would accentuate the problem of democratic legitimacy in international governance. Nevertheless, the problem of dissentient minorities must be

335 Wijkman, 36 *Int Org* (1982) 511; Koers, *International Regulation of Marine Fisheries: A Study of Regional Fisheries Organizations* (London, 1973).

336 1982 UNCLOS, Articles 61–70; see *infra*, Ch 12.

337 1982 UNCLOS, Articles 56, 207–12; see *infra*, Ch 9, section 5(3).

addressed if environmental protection regimes are to deliver common rules and implement collective policies followed by all states.[338] It is for this reason that the tentative steps towards majority decision-making in the 1987 Montreal Protocol and more extensively in Part XI of the 1982 UNCLOS remain of particular significance, since they eliminate opt-outs and increase the likelihood of more stringent standards being adopted and enforced. It is notable, however, that no subsequent MEA has followed these precedents. For the rest, consensus decision-making or ad hoc opt outs continue to be the preferred options.

Improving and measuring the performance of environmental treaty bodies was an item on the UNCED agenda in 1992. The conference considered the facilitation of wider participation, especially by developing countries, the provision of better financing arrangements, and improvements in the rule-making and amendment procedures.[339] We have seen in this chapter that, although there have been improvements, some of those issues remain under discussion. Perhaps the most important development, however, has been the creation of a growing number of non-compliance procedures. These are considered further in Chapter 4.

6 SCIENTIFIC ORGANIZATIONS

Many intergovernmental organizations and treaty bodies have established their own scientific advisory committees; depending on the quality of the science these can provide vital input into environmental policy-making.[340] A number of international bodies exist specifically to provide independent scientific advice and research on matters of environmental importance.[341] The value of most of these bodies is that they represent 'a diversity of knowledge and expertise',[342] and provide an independent or neutral source of publicly accessible data. Scientists cannot be expected to take policy decisions that are ultimately the responsibility of politicians; rather their role as experts is 'to refine problem definition and to identify and expand the range of response options', setting out uncertainties, assumptions, and the probable consequences of action or inaction.[343]

338 See McDorman, 20 *IJMCL* (2005) 423 who looks at the problem from the perspective of fisheries commissions.

339 See e.g. Sand, *Lessons Learned in Global Environmental Governance* (New York, 1990) 6–20; UNCED, *The Effectiveness of International Agreements* (Cambridge, 1992).

340 See *infra*, Ch 4, section 3(3).

341 See generally Andresen et al (eds), *Science and Politics in International Environmental Regimes* (Manchester, 2000).

342 Kimball, *Treaty Implementation: Scientific and Technical Advice Enters a New Stage* (Washington, 1996) at 7. See also Andresen and Skjaerseth, in Bodansky *et al*, *Handbook of IEL*, 183ff.

343 *Ibid.*

One of the most active is the International Council for Exploration of the Seas ('ICES').[344] ICES was founded informally by scientists in 1902 but put on a treaty basis in 1964. It is open to any state approved by its members, though its scope is limited to the Atlantic Ocean and adjacent seas. Its aim is to promote, encourage, and organize research and investigation for the study of the sea, especially its living resources, and to disseminate the results. It has a coordinating, not a managerial or law-making, role but gives advice on request or by formal agreement to such bodies as the FAO, IMO, UNESCO, WHO, UNEP, the EU, the North-East Atlantic Fisheries Commission, and the Helsinki and Paris Commissions. It has interpreted its mandate broadly to cover not only fisheries but also pollution from various sources. It can make recommendations, drawing attention to management and legislative needs, indicating whether species or pollutants should be added to regulatory annexes. The Antarctic Treaty system generally makes use of the Scientific Committee on Antarctic Research ('SCAR'), an independent scientific NGO, to provide advice.[345]

UNESCO's Intergovernmental Oceanographic Commission ('IOC') is also active in structuring and coordinating marine scientific research projects and has increasingly involved developing countries in joint research programmes.[346] It is notable that the US and United Kingdom ('UK'), even when they withdrew from UNESCO, continued to participate in and support the work of the IOC. Scientific research is conducted at the regional level through intergovernmental commissions, such as those dealing with land-based pollution, pollution from dumping and fisheries discussed in later chapters. The IOC works closely with an inter-agency Group of Experts on the Scientific Aspects of Marine Pollution ('GESAMP') whose reports have provided invaluable information on the state of the marine environment.[347]

Other non-governmental groups providing independent, authoritative advice include the International Council for Science ('ICSU') which has various environmental programmes and has cooperated *inter alia* with the WMO, UNEP and UNESCO in scientific studies relating to climate change and in organizing scientific conferences calling for policy decisions from governments.[348] The ICSU is also prominent in the provision of scientific advice to the Antarctic Treaty system, through the SCAR. The Intergovernmental Panel on Climate Change ('IPCC'), an independent scientific body established by UNEP and the WMO, now has the principal responsibility for scientific assessment of climate change science and policy.[349] Climate change deniers have sought to undermine the IPCC's credibility, and in response it has strengthened the robustness of its peer review process. As Ghaleigh observes, 'while. . .the COP was under

344 1964 Convention for the International Council for the Exploration of the Seas. See Kimball, *Treaty Implementation*, 187–8.

345 1991 Antarctic Environment Protocol, Articles 11–12.

346 See Bernal, in Nordquist et al (eds), *Law, Science and Ocean Management* (Leiden, 2007) 21–63.

347 See *infra*, Ch 9.

348 Kimball, *Treaty Implementation*, 188–9.

349 UNFCCC, Article 21; 1997 Kyoto Protocol, Articles 3(4) 5, and 10. See Ghaleigh, in Carlarne, Gray and Tarasofsky (eds), *The Oxford Handbook of International Climate Change Law*, Ch 3, and *infra*, Ch 6.

no binding obligation to follow IPCC recommendations, UNFCCC decision-making processes de facto regarded the IPCC as singular in its expertise, independence and legitimacy.'[350] The IPCC's 'remarkable success'[351] has prompted the establishment in 2010 of the Intergovernmental Science-Policy Platform on Biodiversity and Ecosystem Services ('IPBES') which has been entrusted to assesses the state of biodiversity and of the ecosystem services in response to state requests.

7 NON-GOVERNMENTAL ORGANIZATIONS

7(1) ROLE OF NGOS IN GENERAL

Some of the earliest NGOs were formed to protect birds, the first in 1867. In the US the Sierra Club was founded in 1892. The movement to save whales began at the 8th International Zoological Congress in 1910.[352] NGOs continue to play an important role in contemporary environmental governance.[353] This is evident in the presence of many NGOs at the 1992 UNCED and in the references to NGOs in Agenda 21.[354] NGOs have influenced the development of international environmental law, whether by promoting or opposing particular initiatives, but not all were established purely for purposes of environmental protection. Japanese fishermen's unions have attended IWC meetings alongside conservationist NGOs. Organizations representing oil companies and the car industry are as active as environmentalist NGOs at meetings of the parties to climate change treaties.

By allowing alternative views distinct from those of states to be heard, NGO participation can be seen as democratizing and helping to legitimize the processes of international law-making.[355] In some cases NGOs have provided an effective voice because of their freedom from governmental control and ability to influence public opinion and supranational bodies. Increasingly they have networked their activities, and since the adoption of Agenda 21 their presence at UN conferences on the environment and development has become institutionalized.[356] At the same time some NGOs may be little more than self-appointed elites from developed states, addressing a limited range of issues, and unresponsive to the broader compromises required by any

350 Ghaleigh, *loc cit*, 61. 351 *Ibid*, 70–1.

352 See McCormick, *The Global Environmental Movement* (London, 1989) esp. 1–24.

353 See Charnovitz, 18 *Mich JIL* (1997) 183; *id*, 100 *AJIL* (2006) 348; Spiro, in Bodansky, Brunnée and Hey, *Handbook of IEL*, 771–90; Gupta, 63 *ZAöRV* (2003) 459; Bodansky, *The Art and Craft of International Environmental Law*, 123–30.

354 UN, *Report of the UNCED* (New York, 1993) paras 27.9 and 13; and 38, 42–43.

355 Crawford, 64 *BYIL* (1993) 113; Anderson, 11 *EJIL* (2000) 91; Held, *Democracy and the Global Order: From the Modern State to Cosmopolitan Governance* (Cambridge, 1995); Reus Smit (ed), *The Politics of International Law* (Cambridge, 2004) 35; Boyle and Chinkin, *The Making of International Law*, Ch 2.

356 See e.g. UNGA Res 64/236, paras 21–22.

modern society. There is no guarantee that the views expressed by even high-profile environmental NGOs are representative, nor do they command the democratic legitimacy which most governments can rightly claim.[357]

NGOs' aims and activities are diverse and so is their impact on the real world. Some are international professional bodies, usually in the scientific field, such as the ICSU; some have exclusively educational or research purposes, such as the World Resources Institute. Others are campaigning organizations advocating particular courses of action, such as Friends of the Earth International, Greenpeace International, the International Fund for Animal Welfare ('IFAW'), and the WWF. Most of the major international environmental NGOs are headquartered in developed states, but their regional and national offices play an increasingly important role in developing countries.

Despite the prevalence of NGOs in UN fora, participation falls within the discretion of each organization or treaty body, and no general principle can be identified.[358] In accordance with Article 71 of the UN Charter, ECOSOC defines the terms on which NGOs whose mandates are 'in conformity with the spirit, purposes and principles of the UN Charter'[359] may be accorded consultative status with the UN. *Inter alia* they must have a democratically adopted constitution, representative structure, appropriate mechanisms for ensuring accountability to members and transparent decision-making processes.[360] Different categories of NGO status determine the level of participation.[361] The practice of most UN specialized agencies, such as the IMO and FAO, is similar: NGOs participate in meetings as observers only if they are concerned with matters within the competence of the relevant organ or organization. NGO participation remains controversial in the IAEA and WTO, due to opposition from some member states.[362]

7(2) INTERNATIONAL UNION FOR THE CONSERVATION OF NCATURE

The IUCN is not an NGO but it merits special mention in this section because of its broad environmental mandate and hybrid character. Founded in 1948, the diversity of its membership is unique, comprising over 200 governmental agencies, over 1100 national and international NGOs, and some 10,000 experts. As such it is neither

[357] Anderson and Rieff, in Anheier, Glasius and Kaldor (eds), *Global Civil Society* (London, 2005) 26, 33–35; Boyle and Chinkin, *op cit*, Ch 2, section 3.3.

[358] Boyle and Chinkin, *The Making of International Law*, at 57, but see Klabbers, Peters and Ulfstein, *The Constitutionalisation of International Law* (Oxford, 2011) 219–39.

[359] ECOSOC, Resolution 1296 (XLIV) 1968.

[360] ECOSOC, Consultative Relationship between the United Nations and Non-Governmental Organizations, Resolution 1996/31 (1996).

[361] Chinkin, in Norton, Andenas, Footer (eds), *The Changing World of International Law in the 21st Century* (The Hague, 1998) 48–50.

[362] On WTO see Marceau and Pedersen, 33 *JWT* (1999) 5–20; Esty, 1 *J Int Econ L* (1998) 123.

exclusively intergovernmental nor wholly non-governmental in character. Of particular note is the IUCN Environmental Law Centre, which performs advisory activities and, together with the FAO and UNEP, maintains the ECOLEX database, a repository of information on environmental law. The Species Survival Commission oversees the compilation of the IUCN Red List of Threatened Species, one of the most comprehensive information sources on the conservation status of species and subspecies, highlighting those threatened with extinction.

IUCN's hybrid character has helped it to play a catalytic role in initiating or supporting new legal developments. It perceived the need to link environment and development and prepared the IUCN/WWF/UNEP World Conservation Strategy.[363] IUCN was also instrumental in drafting the World Charter for Nature.[364] It did preparatory work on the 1992 CBD and the Earth Charter proposed for UNCED, and contributed to the negotiation of the 1971 Convention on Wetlands of International Importance, the 1972 World Heritage Convention, the 1973 CITES and the 1979 Convention on Conservation of Migratory Species of Wild Animals.[365] As an international organization IUCN also has the ability to participate in ICJ or ITLOS advisory proceedings if requested.[366] This makes it unique among international environmental organizations but, as a mainly expert body, IUCN tends to avoid politically controversial cases.

IUCN's most ambitious but so far unsuccessful undertaking has been the drafting of an International Covenant on Environment and Development, a detailed and comprehensive attempt to codify and progressively develop international environmental law.[367] A less ambitious attempt to synthesize international environmental law in a binding treaty ('Global Pact for the Environment') was launched by IUCN and UNEP in 2018, but negotiations ended without success a year later. The Global Pact resembled what the WCED attempted when international environmental law was in its infancy.[368] Many of the states and NGOs most supportive of global environmental initiatives were lukewarm. It always seemed unlikely that this idea would advance the subject.

8 CONCLUSIONS

In his book, *On Global Order*, Hurrell refers without much enthusiasm to the 'technocratic and interest-driven literature on global governance.'[369] Much of that literature focuses on process rather than outcomes. Hurrell prefers to emphasize 'the need to

363 See *infra*, Ch 11. 364 *Ibid.*

365 On all these agreements see *infra*, Ch 11.

366 See ICJ Statute, Article 66 and *Advisory Opinion on Responsibilities of States for Activities in the Area*, ITLOS (2011).

367 The 5th edition was published in 2015. On the earlier versions see Robinson, 13 *Pace ELR* (1995) 133; Boyle and Freestone, *International Law and Sustainable Development*, Ch 4.

368 For the draft text see https://www.unenvironment.org/events/conference/towards-global-pact-environment. On the WCED Legal Principles see *infra*, Ch 3, n 3.

369 Hurrell, *On Global Order*, 2.

capture shared and common interests, to manage unequal power, and to mediate cultural diversity and value conflict.'[370] From that perspective the core question in concluding this chapter is whether 25 years after the first Rio Conference the institutional structure of global environmental governance is still an important part of the problem. Has it addressed our shared and common interest in saving the planet from environmental catastrophe? Despite successive attempts at reform, it is probably still true that the UN and its agencies have not generated a system of governance that is well suited to synthesizing environmental and developmental goals, a fusion that UNCED identified as the key issue in the achievement of sustainable development.[371] But as we saw when assessing proposals for a global environmental organization, what really matters is whether better institutional structures would generate better environmental outcomes. That is far from obvious.[372] Climate change, the health of the oceans, and loss of biodiversity on a global scale continue to worsen despite the effort devoted to institutional and policy reform, but these are complex problems any system of global governance would struggle with, however structured. If the system as a whole has failed, the most convincing explanations in the following chapters are that key environmental problems have not been given sufficient priority, or the measures agreed have been too weak, not that global governance institutions have been inadequate.

Anyone who compares the 1st edition of this book (1992) with the present text cannot fail to observe that there is a great deal more international environmental policy and law today than 25 years ago and it is much more sophisticated than it was then. Much of that law and policy has been negotiated and developed in the UN, its specialized agencies, and treaty conferences. Whatever the perceived imperfections of the UN system as a whole, it has not been idle or unproductive if measured by this record. What UNCED and subsequent conferences have produced is a set of policies and tools for achieving the goal of sustainable development in the long term. Much depends, as always, on the political will of states to use these tools effectively. As Hurrell and Kingsbury have pointed out, 'It would be wrong to assume . . . that the universal rhetoric of ecological interdependence translates readily into effective international action.'[373] The debate on the green economy at UNCSD has shown signs that the international community is increasingly aware of the inherent non-sustainability of present economic development patterns. The question remains: can the world do enough to remedy these problems before it is too late? This a profound political and economic challenge; it seems likely that only at the margins might the solutions lie in further international institutional reform.

Since the Rio Conference sustainable development has provided a unifying concept for the utilization of natural resources and the integration of environment and development, but it nevertheless requires concrete political action if it is to be implemented as

370 *Ibid.* 371 See discussion of ECOSOC, *supra*, section 3(2)(c).

372 See in particular Kötze, *Global Environmental Governance*, Ch 1.

373 Hurrell and Kingsbury (eds), *The International Politics of the Environment*, 47.

envisaged in the 2015 SDGs. In Chapter 3 we will explore further the contours and legal implications of the concept, as well as the 1992 Rio Declaration's codification and development of certain principles of international law relating to sustainable development and environmental protection. We will see that from a legal perspective sustainable development is as much about process as about outcomes. Integration, environmental impact assessment, access to information and public participation in policy formation and environmental governance are among the more important elements of that process.[374] Nevertheless, it is worth repeating the obvious point: process without substance risks merely legitimizing unsustainable outcomes. Giving real substance to the environmental elements of the sustainable development goals thus matters. Later chapters will show that while much of value has been achieved, much remains to be done if the global environment is to survive in anything like its present form.

[374] See Principles 4, 10 and 17, and *supra*, Ch 3 and *infra*, Ch 5.

3

RIGHTS AND OBLIGATIONS OF STATES CONCERNING PROTECTION OF THE ENVIRONMENT

1 CODIFICATION AND DEVELOPMENT

1(1) INTRODUCTION

Although '[t]here is considerable debate as to what, within the field of environmental law, constitutes "rules" or "principles"; what is "soft law"; and which environmental treaty law or principles have contributed to the development of customary international law',[1] the main argument in this and the following two chapters is that rules and principles of general international law concerning protection of the environment can be identified.[2]

It must be remembered, as we saw in Chapter 1, that 'international environmental law' is not a separate or self-contained field of law, nor is it comprehensively codified

[1] *Iron Rhine Arbitration*, PCA (2005) para 58.

[2] See generally Dupuy, 101 *RGDIP* 873 (1997); Bodansky, Brunnée, Hey (eds), *Oxford Handbook of International Environmental Law* (Oxford, 2007) and other texts cited *supra*, Ch 1, at n 15.

or set out in a single treaty or body of treaties comparable to the 1982 UNCLOS or the 1994 WTO Agreement and its related instruments.[3] In some respects international environmental law is merely the application of established rules, principles and processes of general international law to the resolution of international environmental problems and disputes, without the need for creating new law, or even for developing old law. A good example is the defence of necessity in the law of state responsibility. Once it is appreciated that states also have environmental as well as other interests to protect within the terms of the existing rule, the application of this defence in such cases is neither problematic nor innovative.[4]

Modern environmental problems have also necessitated the creation of much new law, and the partial codification and progressive development of existing law. The 1992 Rio Declaration does all of those things and it has come to be regarded as an articulation of the basic rules and general principles of the subject.[5] No other instrument has the same overarching significance, comparable in that respect to the 1948 Universal Declaration of Human Rights. The most widely ratified multilateral environmental agreements, including inter alia the conventions and related agreements or protocols on the Law of the Sea, Biological Diversity, Climate Change and Ozone Depletion, constitute a *lex specialis* on these subjects for the very large number of states parties. Some of their provisions also reflect or have become customary international law.[6] Further evidence of existing or developing international environmental law can be found in the work of UN specialized agencies and programmes,[7] and of bodies such as the ILC,[8] the ILA,[9] and the Institut de Droit International (IDI).[10]

In our earlier discussion of regulatory and framework treaties it was noted that the ongoing evolution of successive treaties, protocols and related instruments on

[3] But see WCED, Legal Experts Group, Draft Convention on Environmental Protection and Sustainable Development, in Munro and Lammers, *Environmental Protection and Sustainable Development: Legal Principles and Recommendations* (London, 1986) and IUCN, *Draft International Covenant on Environment and Development* (5th edn, Gland, 2015).

[4] *Gabčíkovo-Nagymaros Case*, ICJ Reports (1997) 7, paras 49–58.

[5] *Infra*, section 1(2).

[6] Notably the 1982 UNCLOS, on which see Chs 8, 9 and 13.

[7] The most important of these is UNEP/UN Environment, on which see *supra*, Ch 2, section 3.

[8] See 2001 Articles on the Prevention of Transboundary Harm from Hazardous Activities, and commentary, *infra*, section 5; on environmental crimes see *infra*, Ch 5, section 6; on international watercourses see *infra*, Ch 10, and on allocation of loss *infra*, Ch 5, section 4.

[9] For the ILA's early work see *Rept of 55th Conference* (1972) 468–500; *57th Conference* (1976) 564–87; *58th Conference* (1978) 383–422. For the Montreal Rules on Transfrontier Pollution see *60th Conference* (1982) 1; transboundary air pollution: *65th Conference* (1992); water pollution: *67th Conference* (1996) 401–15; marine pollution: *69th Conference* (2000) 443–512; sustainable development: *69th Conference* (2000) 655–710; water resources: *71st Conference* (2004) 334–65; transnational enforcement: *72nd Conference* (2006) 655–91; sustainable development: *74th Conference* (2012) 821–67; climate change: *76th Conference* (2014) 330–77. See generally Boyle and Freestone, *International Law and Sustainable Development*, Ch 4.

[10] IDI, *Rept of the Athens Session* (1979) I, 193–380 and II, 197 (pollution of rivers and lakes); id, *Rept of the Cairo Session* (1987) I, 159–294 and II, 296 (transboundary air pollution); IDI, 1997 Resolutions on (i) Environment, (ii) Procedure for the Adoption and Implementation of Rules in the Field of Environment, and (iii) Responsibility and Liability for Environmental Damage, on which see Sands, 30 *RBDI* (1997) 512. He rightly condemns the Institute's 1997 resolutions as 'rubble rather than architecture'.

the same subject has been a distinctive feature of international environmental law.[11] Even treaties not directly related in this sense may nevertheless overlap or affect the same issue. As we shall see in later chapters, it is not possible, for example, to discuss the law relating to the marine environment without taking into account both the 1982 UNCLOS and the 1992 CBD. The application of international law dealing specifically with environmental problems may also have to take into account the law on sustainable development, human rights, international watercourses, law of the sea, armed conflict or world trade, inter alia. How different norms affecting the same issue interact remains a matter for judgment and debate, especially if a treaty contains no express provision on the matter. Interpretation can only take the systematic integration of treaties so far,[12] and it cannot readily deal with genuine conflicts. How conflicting treaties interrelate cannot be determined in any *a priori* sense. In general international law the relationship between treaties is partly governed by the intention of the parties as expressed in the text, partly determined by the nature of the treaty, partly regulated by the relationship between special (*lex specialis*) and general rules, partly determined by residual rules based on the time of conclusion of incompatible treaties, and partly dictated by operation of law.[13] What cannot be supposed is that environmental treaties or rules of customary law have any inherent priority over others save in the exceptional case of *ius cogens* norms.[14] The principle characteristic of a *ius cogens* rule is that 'it may not be trumped by another rule that is not itself *ius cogens*'.[15] No such norms of international environmental law have yet been convincingly identified,[16] nor is there an obvious case for treating them in this way.[17]

Because a treaty has to be interpreted and applied in the light of other rules of international law, including new norms of environmental law,[18] an understanding of contemporary customary international law and general principles is essential even when the applicable law is treaty-based. Since 1992, but especially in the present decade, environmental disputes have formed a significant proportion of the case load of the International Court of Justice (ICJ),[19] the Dispute Settlement Body of the WTO ,[20]

[11] *Supra*, Ch 2, section 2. [12] *Supra*, Ch 1, section 2(2)(a).

[13] 1969 VCLT, Articles 30, 41, 53. See Pauwelyn, *Conflict of Norms in Public International Law* (Cambridge, 2003) Chs 6 and 7; Aust, *Modern Treaty Law and Practice* (2nd edn, Cambridge, 2007) Ch 12; Czaplinski and Danilenko, 21 *NYIL* (1990) 3; Jenks, 30 *BYIL* (1953) 401; Boyle and Chinkin, *The Making of International Law* (Oxford, 2007) 250–3.

[14] See *Indus Waters Kishenganga Arbitration (Final Award)* PCA (2013) para 112.

[15] Seiderman, *Hierarchy in International Law* (Antwerp, 2001) 35–6.

[16] In *Gabčíkovo-Nagymaros*, para 97, the Court impliedly accepted Slovakia's argument that none of the norms of environmental law on which Hungary relied was *ius cogens*.

[17] Orakhelashvili, *Peremptory Norms in International Law* (Oxford, 2006) 65, suggests otherwise, but while certain norms considered in this chapter may apply *erga omnes*, it does not follow that they are therefore also *ius cogens*. On the contrary, there is no necessary connection between these two categories. See generally Seiderman, op cit, 123–9.

[18] 1969 VCLT, Article 31(3) and *supra*, Ch 1, section 2. [19] See *infra*, sections 5–8.

[20] See *infra*, Ch 13.

the ITLOS,[21] and arbitration tribunals.[22] This growing body of case law provides authoritative evidence for the present status of customary international law and general principles concerning protection of the environment and has begun to answer some of the previously contested questions referred to in the opening quotation from the *Iron Rhine Arbitration*. The progressive development of international environmental law has not been led by courts or tribunals; neverthless, the important role of courts in this context has been to affirm that law has been made and to give it coherence within the overall system of international law.[23] Moreover, the case law of the ICJ and of other international tribunals shows that where possible they prefer an integrated conception of international law to a fragmented one.[24] Apart from highlighting the formative role of international courts in determining the applicable law, this conclusion points again to the danger of viewing any part of international law in isolation from the whole. Not only are the rules dynamic, but potentially so is their interaction.

To say that we can identify rules and principles of international environmental law does not mean that the law is always the same for all states regardless of their capabilities or differing circumstances. In the development of international environmental law the different priorities of mainly southern hemisphere less-developed countries have been given 'special consideration'.[25] For many of these countries poverty and the need for economic development have been perceived as the main 'environmental' problem.[26] As we saw in Chapter 2, their concerns have been a central feature of environmental diplomacy since the 1972 UNCHE. In this context the particular significance of the Rio Declaration and other insruments adopted by the 1992 UNCED is that they are not simply expressions of the views of developed northern-hemisphere countries, but also reflect the concerns of a broad coalition of developing states.[27] This is clear if we look at the near universal participation of developing states in treaty regimes of

21 At least four can be regarded as environmental: *Southern Bluefin Tuna Cases (Provisional Measures)* ITLOS Reports (1999); *MOX Plant Case (Provisional Measures)* ITLOS Reports (2001); *Case Concerning Land Reclamation by Singapore in and around the Straits of Johor (Provisional Measures)* ITLOS Reports (2003) ['*Land Reclamation Case*']; *Advisory Opinion on Responsibilities and Obligations of States Sponsoring Persons and Entities with Respect to Activities in the Area*, ITLOS Seabed Disputes Chamber (2011) ['*AO on Activities in the Area*'].

22 *MOX Plant Arbitration*, PCA (2003); *Land Reclamation Arbitration*, PCA (2005); *Iron Rhine Arbitration*, PCA (2005); *Indus Waters Kishenganga Arbitration (Partial Award and Final Award)* PCA (2013) ['*Kishenganga Arbitration*']; *Chagos Marine Protected Area Arbitration*, PCA (2015); *South China Sea Arbitration (Jurisdiction and Merits)*, PCA (2016).

23 See Simma, 20 *EJIL* (2009) 265; Harrison, 25 *JEL* (2013) 501; Viñuales, 32 *Fordham ILJ* (2008–9) 232.

24 Stephens, 25 *Australian YIL* (2004) 226, 270. See *Gabčíkovo-Nagymaros Case*, ICJ Reports (1997) 7, paras 112, 140; *Nuclear Weapons AO*, ICJ Reports (1996) 226; *Oil Platforms Case*, ICJ Report (2003) 161, paras 31–45; *Shrimp-Turtle Case* (1998) WT/DS58/AB/R, paras 131–3; *Iron Rhine Arbitration*, PCA (2005) and generally Simma, 20 *EJIL* (2009) 265.

25 For a recent assessment see Alam et al (eds), *International Environmental Law and the Global South* (Cambridge, 2015).

26 See Anand, *International Environmental Justice: A North-South Dimension* (Aldershot, 2004).

27 See *supra*, Ch 2.

global significance, such as the 1985 Ozone Convention, the 1982 UNCLOS, the 1992 Convention on Climate Change and the 1992 CBD, or the 2001 POPS Convention, or at international litigation and regional treaties involving developing states.[28]

Moreover, as the more advanced developing states have begun to suffer the environmental consequences of industrialization, their interest in international environmental law has also evolved.[29] At the same time, ongoing climate negotiations have exposed policy differences between developing states: the position of newly-industrialized states such as China, India, Nigeria and Brazil has little in common with that of small-island or low-lying states, for example.[30] For many of the latter the environmental threat to their existence and sustainability outweighs any concern about restraining economic development elsewhere. Against this background it is no longer plausible simply to assume that developing states share a common position with each other on environmental protection, or that their priorities necessarily differ from those of developed economies.[31]

Various ways of reconciling the competing priorities of north and south have been employed. The concept of sustainable development,[32] economic assistance and capacity-building through the GEF and other trust funds,[33] alterations in the lending policies of the World Bank and other capital providers,[34] and the concept of 'common but differentiated responsibility' have helped to mediate North–South disagreements by recognizing different contributions to the generation of environmental problems and different capacities for resolving them.[35] The UN General Assembly has also been careful to formulate the 'right to development' in terms requiring respect for international law on friendly relations and cooperation, as well as sustainable development.[36] UN resolutions, the Stockholm and Rio Declarations, and other international instruments have consistently recognized that although states have permanent sovereignty over their natural resources and the right to determine their own environmental and developmental policies, they are not free to disregard protection of the environment of common spaces or of other states.[37] When litigating against each other developing states have shown no desire to argue for or tolerate lower standards of environmental protection.[38]

[28] See e.g. the *Pulp Mills Case*, ICJ Reports (2010) 14; human rights cases (Ch 5), regional agreements on the marine environment (*infra*, Ch 9), international watercourses (Ch 10), and fisheries (Ch 12).

[29] See for example the treatment of environmental issues under the 1969 Inter-American Convention on Human Rights, *infra*, Ch 5 andthe 1991 African Convention on Transboundary Movement of Hazardous Waste, *infra*, and the ASEAN practice on transboundary air pollution referred to in Ch 6.

[30] See *infra*, Ch 6.

[31] See Cullet, in Fitzmaurice et al (eds), *Research Handbook on International Environmental Law* (Cheltenham, 2010) 175–7.

[32] *Supra*, Ch 2, section 2(5) and *infra*, section 2.

[33] *Supra*, Ch 2, section 4(7).

[34] *Ibid*.

[35] See *infra*, section 4(3).

[36] See *infra*, section 2(3).

[37] See *infra*, section 5(1).

[38] See e.g. *Pulp Mills Case*, ICJ Report (2010) 14.

In contrast to many developing states, and unlike other developed states, the reluctance of the US to be bound by more recent environmental agreements casts some doubt on the extent to which it is subject to contemporary international environmental law.[39] The US will normally participate in environmental negotiations and advance its own position strongly, but the rarity with which it then ratifies or supports the outcome is noticeable. Its most consistent objective is to protect free trade and its own autonomy. In deference to opposition in the senate, the US is not a party to the 1992 CBD, the 1997 Kyoto Protocol, the 2001 POPS Convention, the 1989 Basel Convention, the 1998 Rotterdam Convention on Prior Informed Consent or the 1982 UNCLOS, although in practice it treats the latter agreement as largely customary law and it has been an active promoter of the 1995 UN Fish Stocks Agreement and of marine conservation in general. The only UNECE treaty to which it is a party is the 1979 LRTAP Convention and its Gothenburg Protocol.[40] It does not participate in any environmental liability treaties, although it has ratified the Vienna Convention on Supplementary Compensation for Nuclear Damage. The US supported the Rio Declaration, but with extensive reservations, and it remains particularly doubtful how far it accepts the precautionary approach as a general principle of international law.[41] It is not subject to the compulsory jurisdiction of the ICJ or the International Criminal Court ('ICC') and is not a party to the 1969 Inter-American Convention on Human Rights. The only fora in which it could until recently be sued in environmental disputes were the WTO and the North American Free Trade Agreement ('NAFTA') arbitral tribunals.[42] The *Trail Smelter Arbitration*, the 1972 UNCHE and the 1985 Ozone Convention remain as testimony to American dynamism in an earlier era of progressive environmentalism; only in the final years of the Obama presidency did the US show signs of re-engagement with the development of international law-making on environmental issues.[43] President Trump reversed that policy. At the same time, the US has until recently taken seriously its treaty obligations; this cannot always be said for parties such as China.[44]

39 See Brunnée, 15 *EJIL* (2004) 617–649, and generally Murphy, *The US and the Rule of Law in International Affairs* (Cambridge, 2005) 325ff.

40 See *infra*, Ch 6, section 2.

41 See *infra*, section 6.

42 See e.g. *Shrimp/Turtle Case*, WTO Appellate Body (1998) WT/DS58/AB/R; *Methanex Corporation v United States of America*, UNCITRAL Final Award (2005).

43 The US was the first to ratify the 2013 Mercury Convention; one of the first to ratify the 2015 Paris Agreement on climate change; and it ratified the 1999 Gothenburg Protocol to the 1979 LRTAP Convention in 2017.

44 Contrast China's complete disregard for 1982 UNCLOS environmental obligations in the South China Sea, its poor record of good faith compliance with the 1973 CITES, and its failure to tackle transboundary air and water pollution. See Mushkat, 34 *Env L & P* (2010) 493.

1(2) THE 1992 RIO DECLARATION ON ENVIRONMENT AND DEVELOPMENT

The Rio Declaration,[45] adopted by consensus at UNCED in 1992, remains the most significant universally endorsed statement of general rights and obligations of states affecting the environment. Despite its apparently soft law status it should not be underestimated by lawyers. The Declaration is in part a restatement of existing customary law on transboundary matters, partly an endorsement of what were at the time new or developing principles of law concerned with protection of the global environment, and partly a statement of policies and ideals set out more fully in Agenda 21, the programme of action for tackling environmental problems also adopted by the Conference, and whose implementation has led to further law-making. This does not mean that the Declaration itself is binding law. Its value, like certain other soft law declarations, is evidential: it tells us what states believe the law to be in certain cases, or in others what they would like it to become or how they want it to develop. The Declaration's legal significance can therefore only be properly appreciated in conjunction with an examination of the pre-existing customary law, and the subsequent development of state practice, further treaties, protocols, regulations, and judicial decisions. As we shall see in the following sections, the Declaration has had significant impact on the drafting or re-drafting of environmental treaties;[46] many of the principles have been referred to by the ILC in support of its codification of the law relating to transboundary harm;[47] and it appears to be one of the 'great number of instruments' setting out norms of international environmental law to which the ICJ referred in the *Gabčíkovo-Nagymaros Case*, and on which the Court also relied explicitly in its *Nuclear Weapons Advisory Opinion*.[48]

Three factors give the Rio Declaration significant authority and influence in the articulation and development of contemporary international law relating to the environment. First, unlike the earlier Stockholm Declaration of 1972, it is expressed mainly

[45] UN, *Report of the UN Conference on Environment and Development* I, UN Doc A/CONF 151/rev 1 (1992) 3. For *Reports of the Preparatory Committee*, see UN Doc A/CONF 151/PC/L 31, Annex (1991); A/CONF 151/PC/78 (1991); A/CONF 151/PC/WG 111.2 (1991); A/CONF 151/PC/WG 111/L5, L6, L8/Rev 1, L 20–8 (1991–2) in Robinson, *Agenda 21 and the UNCED Proceedings* (6 vols, New York, 1992–3). On the Rio Declaration see Sand, 3 *Colorado JIELP* (1992) 1; id, 3 *YbIEL* (1992) 3; Mann, *Proc ASIL* (1992) 405; Sands (ed), *Greening International Law* (London, 1993) 1–34; Kiss and Doumbe-Bille, 38 *AFDI* (1992) 823; Kamto, 1 *Rev Jur de l'Environnement* (1993) 11; Kiss, in Campiglio et al, *The Environment after Rio* (London, 1994) 55; various authors 4 *Colorado JIELP* (1993) 1–215; Wirth, 29 *Georgia LR* (1995) 599; Malanczuk, in Ginther, Denters, and de Waart (eds), *Sustainable Development and Good Governance* (Dordrecht, 1995) Ch 2; Viñuales (ed), *The Rio Declaration on Environment and Development: A Commentary* (Oxford, 2015).

[46] See *infra*, sections 4, 6 and 7.

[47] The commentaries to the 2001 Articles on Transboundary Harm and the 2006 Principles on the Allocation of Loss draw upon Principles 2, 7, 10, 11, 13, 15, 16, 17, 18, and 19. See *ILC Rept* (2001) GAOR A/56/10; id (2006) GAOR A/61/10, paras 51–67.

[48] ICJ Report (1996) 226, paras 29–30, and dissenting opinions of Judges Weeramantry and Palmer in the *Request for an Examination of the Situation*, ICJ Report (1995) 288. See also *Iron Rhine Arbitration*, PCA (2005) para 59; *Kishenganga Arbitration (Partial Award)* PCA (2013) para 449.

in obligatory terms. Although some principles use the words 'States should ......', most start with the injunction 'States shall ...'.[49] Many of its carefully drafted terms are capable of being and were intended to be norm creating or to lay down the parameters for further development of the law. The UN General Assembly endorsed the Declaration, referring to it as containing 'fundamental principles for the achievement of sustainable development, based on a new and equitable global partnership'; it also called on the CSD and the UN Secretary General to promote incorporation of the principles of the Declaration in the implementation of Agenda 21 and in UN programmes and processes, and urged governments to promote their widespread dissemination.[50] These commitments were reaffirmed by the Rio+20 Conference and the UN General Assembly in 2012.[51]

Secondly, the Declaration's twenty-seven principles represent a 'package deal', negotiated by consensus, like the 1982 UNCLOS,[52] and must be read as a whole. The Rio Declaration has thus been called:

> a text of uneasy compromises, delicately balanced interests, and dimly discernible contradictions, held together by the interpretative vagueness of classic UN-ese.[53]

Principle 2 (prevention of transboundary harm) repeats a key provison of the Stockholm Declaration (Principle 21) that was accepted at the time as customary law. The remainder of the Rio Declaration goes well beyond what had been endorsed twenty years before. Some provisions reflect the interests of developed states, such as Principles 4 (integration of environmental protection and development), 10 (public participation), 15 (the precautionary approach), and 17 (environmental impact assessment). Others were more strongly supported by developing states, including Principle 3 (right to development), Principles 6 and 7 (special needs of developing states and common but differentiated responsibility), and Principles 5 and 9 (poverty alleviation and capacity building). One illustration of the Declaration's package-deal character is the conjunction of Principles 3 and 4, which together form the core of the principle of sustainable development. Throughout, the principal concern of the Declaration, and of those who negotiated it, was to integrate the needs of economic development and environmental protection in a single, if not wholly coherent, ensemble. The implications of this interdependence are also apparent in the concept of 'common but differentiated responsibility' referred to in Principle 7 and in the 1992 Climate Change Convention and are considered further below.

Thirdly, as we have seen, the Declaration reflects a real consensus of developed and developing states on core principles of law and policy concerning environmental protection, sustainable development, and their interrelationship. Despite certain

49 On the difference between 'should' and 'shall' see Nordquist (ed), *UNCLOS 1982: A Commentary* (Dordrecht, 1993) II, xlv–xlvi.

50 UNGA Res 47/190 and 191 (1992) and 48/190 (1993).

51 See *The Future We Want*, UNGA Res 66/288 (2012) Annex.

52 On the package deal consensus character of the third UN Conference on the Law of the Sea see *supra*, Ch 1, section 2(1). On the Rio negotiations see *supra*, Ch 2, section 2(2).

53 Porras, in Sands (ed), *Greening International Law*, 20.

reservations on the part of the US,[54] the principles and rules it contains have a universal significance and cannot be dismissed as the work of one segment of international society. Indeed, 'insofar as there is evidence of a shift away from the practice of developed country dominance of the process of dictating international norms and priorities',[55] Rio marks the emergence of developing countries as a real and substantial influence on the making of international environmental law. The legally important elements of the Declaration are more fully discussed in the following sections of this chapter.

Also worth noting are those matters which the Rio Declaration does not address, mainly at the insistence of developing countries. The human right to a decent environment articulated in Principle 1 of the Stockholm Declaration is not repeated.[56] Unlike the Stockholm Declaration, the Rio Declaration is explicitly anthropocentric in character (Principle 1) and makes no reference to animal rights, or the conservation of flora, fauna, habitats, and ecosystems.[57] It does not deal with environmental crimes.[58] On liability for environmental damage it merely reiterates the need to develop the law (Principle 13). Lastly, it calls for the further development not of international law relating to the environment but of international law 'in the field of sustainable development' (Principle 27).[59] Moreover, Principle 12 on trade policy and Principle 16 on the polluter-pays principle are, unusually, expressed in aspirational rather than obligatory terms, suggesting a rather weaker commitment on these economic issues than developed states would have liked to see.[60]

Despite these qualifications, it is right to view the Rio Declaration in generally positive terms. A quarter of a century after its adoption it can be seen that it was not a backward step in the development of international environmental law, as at least one writer suggested.[61] On the contrary, the Declaration has articulated the shared expectations of developed and developing states and brought together an important body of new and existing law. Freestone rightly argued after the Rio Conference that 'a system of international environmental law has emerged, rather than simply more international law rules about the environment'.[62] The Declaration's contribution to the codification and progressive development of international law relating to the environment has been and is likely to remain considerable and significant.

[54] The US joined in the consensus but subject to reservations with regard to Principles 3, 7, 12 and 23. See *UNCED*, UN Doc A/CONF 151/26/Rev 1 (Vol II) (1993) para 16.

[55] Porras, in Sands (ed), *Greening International Law*, 20. But contrast Hey, 34 *NYIL* (2003) 3, although her comments relate mainly to international financial institutions.

[56] See *infra*, Ch 5.

[57] See Schrijver, *Sovereignty over Natural Resources* (Cambridge, 1997) 139–40. But the Rio + 20 Declaration more than rectifies this omission: see UNGA Res 66/288 (2012) annex, paras 4, 30, 40, 61, 111, 113, 122, inter alia.

[58] See *infra*, Ch 5.

[59] On the difference between international environmental law and the law of sustainable development, see *supra*, Ch 1.

[60] On trade and environment see *infra*, Ch 13.

[61] For earlier more pessimistic assessments see Pallemaerts, in Sands (ed),*Greening International Law*, 1–19 and Wirth, 29 *Georgia LR* (1995) 599.

[62] 6 *JEL* (1994) 193. See also Porras, in Sands (ed), *Greening International Law*, 20.

2 SUSTAINABLE DEVELOPMENT: LEGAL IMPLICATIONS

2(1) A RIGHT TO SUSTAINABLE DEVELOPMENT?

There is no explicit reference to a 'right to sustainable development' in the Rio Declaration—nor is there an explicit right to its mirror image, a healthy, sustainable and ecologically sound environment.[63] Looked at as a whole, however, it can be seen that the Rio Declaration is consistent with the proposition that international law affords states a right to sustainable development; at the same time there is no right to development that is unsustainable. Thus, economic development is not an unqualified right. While endorsing the 'right to development', Principle 3 emphasises that it 'should be fulfilled so as to meet equitably the developmental and environmental needs of present and future generations'.[64] Principle 2 affirms both the sovereign right of states to exploit their own resources 'pursuant to their own environmental and developmental policies' and their responsibility 'to ensure that activities within their jurisdiction or control do not cause damage to the environment of other states or of areas beyond the limits of national jurisdiction'. As we will see later in this chapter, Principle 2 is neither an absolute prohibition on global or transboundary environmental damage, nor does it confer on states absolute freedom to exploit natural resources or pursue economic development without regard for the environment.[65] The case law shows that it requires integration or accommodation of economic development and environmental protection, and Principle 4 reiterates that point expressly. Similarly, Article 1 of the 1966 UN Covenants on Civil and Political Rights ('ICCPR') and Economic, Social and Cultural Rights ('ICESCR') proclaims the right of all peoples to pursue economic development, and to dispose freely of their natural wealth and resources, but at the same time regional human-rights treaties in Africa and Latin America also recognize a right to some degree of environmental protection and so does the case law of the 1950 European Convention of Human Rights ('ECHR').[66]

The essential point of each of these examples is that, while recognizing that the right to pursue economic development is an attribute of a state's sovereignty over its own natural resources and territory, it cannot lawfully be exercised without regard for the detrimental impact on human rights or the environment. Equally, as we will see later in this chapter and again in Chapter 5, neither environmental protection nor human rights necessarily trump the right to economic development. Such potential conflicts have not led international courts to employ the concept of *ius cogens* or to give human rights, environmental protection or economic development automatic priority. Instead, the case law has concentrated on questions of balance, necessity, and the degree of interference. It shows that few rights are ever absolute or unqualified. It is in this sense that we can talk about a 'right to sustainable development' and that

[63] See *infra*, Ch 5. [64] See *infra*, section 2(3). [65] See *infra*, section 5. [66] See *infra*, Ch 5.

the International Court has used the concept. In the *Gabčíkovo-Nagymaros Case* the ICJ referred for the first time to 'this need to reconcile economic development with protection of the environment [which] is aptly expressed in the concept of sustainable development'.[67] Its order in the first *Pulp Mills Case* illustrates the essentially relative character of these competing interests:

> Whereas the present case highlights the importance of the need to ensure environmental protection of shared natural resources while allowing for sustainable economic development; whereas it is in particular necessary to bear in mind the reliance of the Parties on the quality of the water of the River Uruguay for their livelihood and economic development; whereas from this point of view account must be taken of the need to safeguard the continued conservation of the river environment and the rights of economic development of the riparian States . . .[68]

From this perspective, one of the main attractions of sustainable development as a concept is that both sides in any legal argument will be able to rely on it.

2(2) THE ELEMENTS OF SUSTAINABLE DEVELOPMENT

Sustainable development contains both substantive and procedural elements.[69] The substantive elements are set out mainly in Principles 3–8 of the Rio Declaration. They include the integration of environmental protection and economic development; the right to development; the sustainable utilization of natural resources; the equitable allocation of resources both within the present generation and between present and future generations (intra- and inter-generational equity). None of these concepts is new, but the Rio Declaration brings them together in a more systematic form than hitherto. The principal procedural elements are found in Principles 10 and 17 dealing with public participation in decision-making and environmental impact assessment. Again, these are not new, but they have never before secured such widespread support across the international community.

(a) Integration of environmental protection and economic development

Principle 4 of the Rio Declaration provides that 'environmental protection shall constitute an integral part of the development process and cannot be considered in isolation from it'. Sands rightly argues that Principle 4 'creates the possibility of moving environmental considerations and objectives from the periphery of international

[67] ICJ Report (1997) 7, para 140. See also *Iron Rhine Arbitration*, PCA (2005) para 59; Lowe and Higgins, in Boyle and Freestone (eds), *International Law and Sustainable Development* (Oxford, 1999) Chs 2 and 5; French, in Fitzmaurce et al (eds), *Research Handbook on IEL*, 51.

[68] *Pulp Mills Case (Provisional Measures)* ICJ Report (2006) para 80. See also *Pulp Mills Case (Merits)* ICJ Report (2010) paras 75–6, 177.

[69] Compare Sands, 65 *BYIL* (1994) 303 and ILA, 2002 Conference Rept, 'Declaration of Principles of International Law Relating to Sustainable Development', 22–9. See generally Atapattu, *Emerging Principles of International Environmental Law* (Ardsley, 2006) Ch 2; Barral, *Le Développement Durable en Droit International* (Brussels, 2016) and *infra*, section 2(4).

relations to the economic core, probably the most important long-term contribution which UNCED will make to international affairs'.[70] Integration permeates the Rio instruments,[71] as well as Agenda 21,[72] and it is reflected in subsequent agreements and declarations including the 1994 Convention to Combat Desertification,[73] the 1995 Washington Declaration on Protection of the Marine Environment from Land-based Activities,[74] and the Rio+20 Declaration.[75] Integration has also been incorporated in certain regional agreements.[76]

As we have seen, the need to integrate environmental protection and economic development was regarded by the ICJ as one of the decisive elements of the *Gabčíkovo-Nagymaros Case*, even for activities 'begun in the past'.[77] In the *Iron Rhine Arbitration*, Principle 4 was regarded as 'a principle of general international law' which 'applies not only in autonomous activities but also in activities undertaken in implementation of specific treaties between the Parties'.[78] The relevant treaty in this case dated from 1839, so the intertemporal implications of Principle 4 for treaty interpretation are plainly significant.

The purpose of Principle 4 is to ensure that development decisions do not disregard environmental considerations. Integration of these competing values is fundamental to the concept of sustainable development and has implications across a broad range of national and international policy, as can be seen from Agenda 21, which refers to the 'more systematic consideration of the environment when decisions are made on economic, social, fiscal, energy, agricultural, transportation, trade and other policies'.[79] Since 1989 the World Bank and other multilateral development banks have sought to integrate environmental assessment into their lending policies.[80] The integration of environmental considerations is also an issue affecting international trade, although here there remains significant scope for improvement. While Principle 12 of the Rio Declaration reflects the concerns of free trade advocates that environmental restrictions should not constitute disguised or arbitrary interference with free trade, the WTO has been slower to take full account of the needs of environmental protection.[81] The relationship between environmental protection and the GATT is considered further in Chapter 13.

As later chapters will also show, most of the main global and regional treaties which deal with environmental protection already evidence integration of the concerns of

70 65 *BYIL* (1994) 324.

71 1992 Convention on Climate Change, Preamble and Article 3(4); 4(1)(f); 1992 CBD, Article 6(b); 10(a).

72 See Agenda 21, Ch 8. See also the Rio + 20 declaration, UNGA Res 66/288 (2012).

73 Article 4(2). See *infra*, Ch 11.

74 UNEP/OCA/LBA/IG 2/L 4 (1995). See *infra*, Ch 8.

75 *The Futue We Want*, UNGA Res 66/288 (2012) Annex.

76 On integrated water resource management see *infra*, Ch 10; on integrated coastal zone management see *infra*, Ch 8. See also 1978 Treaty for Amazonian Cooperation, Preamble; 1978 Kuwait Regional Convention for Cooperation on the Protection of the Marine Environment from Pollution, Preamble; 1985 ASEAN Agreement on the Conservation of Nature and Natural Resources, Article 2(1).

77 ICJ Report (1997) 7, para 140. See also *Kishenganga Arbitration (Partial Award)* PCA (2013) para 449.

78 PCA (2005) para 59. See also *Kishenganga Arbitration (Partial Award)* paras 451–2.

79 Agenda 21, Chapter 8.2.

80 See *infra*, section 7.

81 But see the Appellate Body's decision in the *Shrimp-Turtle Case, infra*, Ch 13.

business, industry, and government with regard to economic development.[82] In some cases, such as the regulation of nuclear energy, it may be thought that too little attention has been paid to environmental concerns. One criticism of Principle 4 is that it 'ambiguously stands as much for the subordination of environmental policies to economic imperatives in the eyes of some, as for the converse to others'.[83] But this is to view integration in isolation from the broader context of the Rio Declaration as a whole. The subsequent jurisprudence and *The Future We Want* emphasize the need for balance between competing objectives, consistent with the objective of sustainable development.[84] The criticism should remind us that the concept of sustainable development is not intended to serve purely 'environmental' values, but if integration may not be a panacea, it remains the most likely means to secure environmental needs within competing priorities.[85]

A 'balanced integration of the economic, social and environmental dimensions of sustainable development' is thus an intrinsic feature of international environmental regulation.[86] To this extent the real implications of Principle 4 are more to be found in its impact on developing countries, where environmental considerations have historically not been prominent in development planning, and in the World Bank and other development agencies. The establishment of environmental standards by the Bank and its agencies is thus an important contribution to the promotion of sustainable development.[87] The *Pulp Mills Case* provides clear evidence of the impact this 'greening' of the Bank can have in encouraging governments to take environmental protection seriously when promoting foreign investment in natural resource exploitation.[88]

(b) The right to development

Principle 3 of the Rio Declaration is the first example of the international community fully endorsing the previously controversial concept of a 'right to development'.[89] Critics have argued that this is not a right at all and point to its uncertain character in the 'Declaration on the Right to Development' adopted by the UN General Assembly

[82] See e.g. regional agreements on land-based sources of marine pollution, *infra*, Ch 8, and nuclear energy, *infra*, Ch 9.

[83] Pallemaerts, in Sands (ed), *Greening International Law*, 17.

[84] See e.g. *Pulp Mills Case*, ICJ Report (2010) paras 175–7; *Iron Rhine Arbitration*, PCA (2005) para 59; and UNGA Res 66/288 (2012) annex.

[85] French, in Fitzmaurice et al, *Research Handbook on IEL*, 59; Barral and Dupuy, in Viñuales (ed), *The Rio Declaration on Environment and Development*, 163–4.

[86] A point emphasized throughout *The Future We Want*, UNGA Res 66/288 (2012).

[87] See *supra*, Ch 2, section 4(7).

[88] The need for IFC funding ensured that Uruguay and the developer had to take environmental protection seriously.

[89] See Dupuy (ed), *Le Droit au Développement au Plan International* (Dordrecht, 1980); Alston, 1 *Harv HRYb* (1988) 21; Rich, in Crawford (ed), *The Right of Peoples* (Oxford, 1988) Ch 3; Chowdury, Denters and de Waart (eds), *The Right to Development in International Law* (Dordrecht, 1992); Rosas, in Eide, Krause and Rosas (eds), *Economic, Social and Cultural Rights: A Textbook* (Dordrecht, 1995) Ch 16, and references cited there; Schrijver, in Bugge and Voigt (eds), *Sustainable Development in International and National Law* (Groningen, 2008) Ch 2; Galizzi and Herklotz, in Fitzmaurice et al (eds), *Research Handbook on IEL*, Ch 4.

in 1986, and reiterated in the 1993 Vienna Declaration on Human Rights.[90] This amorphous concept embraces not just the promotion of economic development by states but also the social and cultural aspects of human development found in the 1966 ICESCR.[91] Once referred to by its proponents as a 'third generation' human right, others see it as unnecessary and unhelpful to the promotion either of development or of human rights.[92] Although partly drawn from existing UN General Assembly resolutions and conventions on economic and social rights, the legal status of the right to development has been and remains contested. Inclusion in the Rio Declaration represents a success for developing country advocates and reflects concerns that environmental protection should not outweigh their need for economic development. It was thus intended as a counterweight to Principle 4. At the same time, Principle 3 introduces the further important limitation that the right to development must be fulfilled 'equitably' so as to meet both developmental and environmental needs of present and future generations.[93]

The point has already been made that 'development' is not an absolute right but one whose scope is defined only in relation to other competing factors. This may help explain why the US asserted that development is not a right at all but only a 'goal'.[94] Moreover, as we saw earlier, the right to develop requires 'full respect for the principles of international law concerning friendly relations and cooperation among states in accordance with the Charter of the United Nations'.[95] To that extent it cannot override, but must be integrated with, existing international law concerning protection of the environment and human rights.[96] From that perspective, 'Environmental law and the law on development stand not as alternatives but as mutually reinforcing, integral concepts, which require that where development may cause significant harm to the environment there is a duty to prevent, or at least mitigate, such harm'.[97]

(c) Sustainable utilization and conservation of natural resources

Although an important element of sustainable development, sustainable utilization is an autonomous concept best understood in the context of international law concerning the conservation of natural resources and it is considered in the section 3 below and again in Ch 11.

90 UNGA Res 41/128 (1986) adopted by 146 votes to 1 (USA) with 8 abstentions (Denmark, FRG, Finland, Iceland, Israel, Japan, Sweden, UK); 1993 World Conference on Human Rights: Vienna Declaration and Programme of Action, 32 *ILM* (1993) 1661, adopted by consensus. For an account of the subsequent work of the Working Group on the Right to Development see Rosas, *supra*, n 89.

91 Barral and Dupuy, in Viñuales (ed), *The Rio Declaration on Environment and Development*, 163–4.

92 Alston, 1 *Harv HRYb* (1988) 21. But for a spirited defence see Mansell and Scott, 21 *JLS* (1994) 171. See generally Andreassen and Marks (eds), *Development as a Human Right* (Cambridge, Mass, 2006).

93 For an attempt at judicial elaboration see *Centre for Minority Rights Development (Kenya) and Minority Rights Group International on behalf of Endorois Welfare Council v Kenya*, ACHPR (2009) para 748, where the African Commission found a violation of the right to development enshrined in Article 22 of the 1981 African Charter on Human and Peoples' Rights.

94 *UNCED*, UN Doc A/CONF 151/26/Rev 1 (Vol II) (1993) para 16.

95 Declaration on the Right to Development, UNGA Res 41/128 (1986) Article 3(2).

96 *The Future We Want*, UNGA Res 66/288 (2012) Annex; *Pulp Mills Case, supra*, section 2(1). On human rights aspects see *infra*, Ch 5.

97 *Iron Rhine Arbitration*, PCA (2005) para 59, and see *infra*, section 5. See generally Schrijver, in Bugge and Voigt (eds), *Sustainable Development in International and National Law*, Ch 2.3.

(d) Inter-generational equity

The theory of inter-generational equity has been advanced to explain the optimum basis for the relationship between one generation and the next. The theory requires each generation to use and develop its natural and cultural heritage in such a manner that it can be passed on to future generations in no worse condition than it was received.[98] Central to this idea is the need to conserve options for the future use of resources, including their quality, and that of the natural environment. The Brundtland Commission's definition of sustainable development as 'development that meets the needs of the present without compromising the ability of future generations to meet their own needs' begs elaboration, but it does emphasize the importance of inter-generational equity.[99] However, although the idea of moral responsibility to future generations is well established in the writings of Rawls and other philosophers, it is less easy to translate into law, or more specifically, into rights for future indeterminate generations.[100]

As early as 1946, the ICRW recognized the interest of the nations of the world in safeguarding whale stocks for 'future generations'. The same generational perspective underlies references in the 1972 Stockholm Declaration to man's responsibility to protect the environment and the Earth's natural resources.[101] Inter-generational equity is explicitly referred to in Principle 3 of the 1992 Rio Declaration, which provides for the right to development to be fulfilled 'so as to equitably meet developmental and environmental needs of present and future generations', and is reiterated in the same terms in the 1993 Vienna Declaration on Human Rights. These international declarations and the growing number of treaties which reflect an inter-generational perspective indicate the importance now attached in international policy to the protection of the environment for the benefit of future generations.[102] The point is well illustrated by Article 3(1) of the 1992 Convention on Climate Change, which calls for inter-generational equity to be taken into account in decisions of the parties.

98 Brown Weiss, *In Fairness to Future Generations* (Dobbs Ferry, 1989); 1988 Goa Guidelines on Inter-generational Equity, *ibid*, Appendix A. Lowe provides a critique of the theory as expounded by Brown Weiss in Boyle and Freestone, *International Law and Sustainable Development*, Ch 2. See also Redgwell, *Intergenerational Trusts and Environmental Protection* (Manchester, 1999); id, in Carlarne et al (eds), *The Oxford Handbook of International Climate Change Law* (Oxford, 2016) Ch 9; Molinari, in Viñuales (ed), *The Rio Declaration on Environment and Development* (Oxford, 2015) 139–56; Brown Weiss in Fitzmaurice et al, *Research Handbook on IEL*, Ch 5; Fitzmaurice, in Hafner and Buffard (eds), *International Law between Universalism and Fragmentation: Festschrift in Honour of Gerhard Hafner* (Leiden, 2008) 195–229; Agius et al, *Future Generations and International Law* (London, 1998); Supanich, 3 *YbIEL* (1992) 94; D'Amato, 84 *AJIL* (1990) 190; Gundling, *ibid*, 207.

99 WCED, *Our Common Future* (Oxford, 1987) 43. See *supra*, Ch 2.

100 Rawls, *A Theory of Justice* (Oxford, 1972); D'Amato, 84 *AJIL* (1990) 190; Gillespie, *International Environmental Law, Policy and Ethics* (Oxford, 1997) Ch 6; Shue, *Climate Justice: Vulnerability and Protection* (Oxford, 2015), esp Chs 8, 11 and 12.

101 Principles 1 and 2. See also 1968 African Convention on the Conservation of Nature and Natural Resources.

102 UN, *Intergenerational solidarity and the needs of future generations: Rept of the Secretary General*, GAOR A/68/322 (2013) para 36. See also *The Future We Want*, UNGA Res 66/288 (2012).

Brown Weiss argues that inter-generational equity is already part of the fabric of international law.[103] It is true that the policy which underlies a number of global environmental treaties is the avoidance of irreversible harm, as in the 1985 Ozone Convention, the 1992 CBD and the 1992 Convention on Climate Change.[104] It is also possible to point to fisheries conservation treaties which require cooperation in the management of stocks and ecosystems for the purpose of maintaining sustainable utilization.[105] The phasing out of dumping at sea, particularly of radioactive waste, the elaboration of a comprehensive regime of ecosystem protection for Antarctica, including the prohibition on mineral extraction and the designation of the continent as a world park, and the adoption of stringent controls on whaling through the IWC and regional conventions, also demonstrate a real concern for the interests of future generations.[106] Future generations will benefit to the extent that these regimes are successful, and the record of actual practice will doubtless demonstrate the level of commitment to any theory of inter-generational equity. What these examples do not demonstrate is that future generations have been endowed with justiciable rights in international law.[107]

But the essential point of the theory, that mankind has a responsibility for the future, and that this is an inherent component of sustainable development, is incontrovertible, however expressed. The question then becomes one of implementation.[108] The examples cited above show that some international institutions have made efforts to accommodate the interests of future generations. The creation of the CSD and the GEF might also be said to reflect the evolution of a more fiduciary or trusteeship model of man's relationship with the environment, which could enhance inter-generational perspectives.[109] Sceptics will point to the limited impact of the first of these bodies, and to the evident failure of the UN and its member states to grapple with climate change.[110]

Representation of future generations in legal proceedings is a less well-developed possibility. What is lacking is a theory of representation before international tribunals capable of according standing to future generations independently of the states and international institutions which are at present the only competent parties in

[103] *Supra*, n 98. See also Judge Weeramantry in *AO on Nuclear Weapons*, ICJ Reports (1996) 266.

[104] *Infra*, Chs 6, 11.

[105] See 1995 UN Fish Stocks Agreement, *infra*, Ch 12.

[106] *Infra*, Chs 8, 11, 13.

[107] Supanich, 3 *YbIEL* (1992) 94, but compare Agius et al, *Future Generations and International Law* (London, 1998) and Pathak, in Brown Weiss (ed), *Environmental Change and International Law* (Tokyo, 1992) 226ff. On the failure of the Rio Declaration to give prominence to human rights approaches see *infra*, Ch 5.

[108] Gundling, 84 *AJIL* (1990) 207; Ward, 22 *YbIEL* (2012) 3.

[109] On the GEF and CSD see *supra*, Ch 2. A proposal to establish the CSD with stronger powers of guardianship on behalf of future generations was not adopted: see UN Doc A/CONF 151/PC/WG III/L 8/Rev 1/Add 2 (1992). See also the earlier institutional proposals of the WCED in Munro and Lammers, *Environmental Protection and Sustainable Development*, and Redgwell, *Intergenerational Trusts and Environmental Protection*, Ch 6. The Secretary General's Rept, GAOR A/68/322 (2013) again called for consideration of institutional arrangements.

[110] For specific proposals see Ward, 22 *YbIEL* (2012) 3.

international litigation. Although some interstate or advisory proceedings before the ICJ can be interpreted as involving generational responsibilities, as can a few international human-rights decisions, these cases all involve the present generation suing in respect of the misdeeds of the past, rather than a future generation challenging those of the present.[111] Moreover, in none of these cases has an international court expressly recognized the rights of future generations.[112] There is, however, no inherent reason why national courts should not permit representative proceedings on behalf of the unborn, as is not uncommon in English trust law, but much will turn on the procedural rules and the context in each legal system and no generalizations with regard to generational rights in national law are possible.[113] In the Philippines Supreme Court plaintiffs seeking to challenge the grant of timber licences were held to have standing on behalf of themselves and future generations, but this precedent was not followed in comparable proceedings before the Supreme Court of Bangladesh.[114]

The theory of inter-generational equity provides an essential reference point within which future impacts and concerns must be considered and taken into account by present generations, and there are instititutional processes in which these and other concerns can be addressed. Nevertheless, viewing inter-generational equity as an element of sustainable development does not resolve the argument for stronger generational rights or international guardianship, nor does it determine the optimal balance between this generation and its successors. Moreover, while accepting the right of present generations to use resources for economic development, it fails to answer the question how we should value the environment for the purpose of determining whether future generations will be worse off.[115] Nor does concentration on relations between one generation and the next convincingly answer the equally pressing question of how benefits and burdens should be shared within each generation.[116] Thus, although the content of the theory is well defined, it rests on some questionable assumptions concerning the nature of economic equity.

[111] See *Phosphate Lands in Nauru Case*, ICJ Reports (1993) 322; *AO on Nuclear Weapons*, ICJ Reports (1996) 266; and *LCB v United Kingdom* (1999), 27 EHRR 212, in which the respondent government was held to owe a duty to protect the offspring of servicemen engaged in nuclear tests. On the possible international legal capacity of future generations see Agius et al, *Future Generations and International Law*, Chs 5–7.

[112] Brown Weiss, in de Chazournes and Sands (eds), *International Law, the ICJ and Nuclear Weapons* (Cambridge, 1999) 338. See also Lowe, in Boyle and Freestone (eds), *International Law and Sustainable Development*, Ch 2.

[113] Brown Weiss reviews national precedents in Fitzmaurice et al, *Research Handbook on IEL*, Ch 5.

[114] *Minors Oposa v Secretary of the Department of Environment and Natural Resources*, 33 *ILM* (1994) 173; *Farooque v Government of Bangladesh* (1997) 49 *DLR (AD)* 1.

[115] Redgwell, in Churchill and Freestone (eds), *International Law and Global Climate Change*, Ch 3; Christenson, 1 *YbIEL* (1990) 392. For an economist's analysis of how to value the environment on a sustainable basis, see Pearce, *Blueprint for a Green Economy* (London, 1989) and on climate change see Stern, *Ethics, equity and the economics of climate change*, Centre for Climate Change Economics and Policy Working Paper No. 97 (2012).

[116] Gundling, 84 *AJIL* (1990) 211.

(e) Intra-generational equity

If the theory of inter-generational equity can be criticized for neglecting intra-generational considerations, the same cannot be said of the concept of sustainable development. Both in the Brundtland Report, and in Agenda 21, there is no doubt that redressing the imbalance in wealth between the developed and developing worlds and giving priority to the needs of the poor are important policy components of sustainability. Unlike inter-generational equity, intra-generational equity addresses inequity within the existing economic system.

The Rio Declaration does not refer by name to any concept of intra-generational equity, but several of its substantive provisions, and of the 1992 Climate Change Convention and the 1992 CBD, imply that intra-generational concerns are now an element in the contemporary development of international environmental law. Apart from Principle 5, which calls for cooperation to eradicate poverty, intra-generational equity is served mainly by a recognition of the special needs of developing countries and by provisions on access and benefit sharing in a few treaties.[117] In global environmental conventions such as the 1985 Ozone and 1992 Climate Change Conventions this takes the form of financial assistance, capacity-building and the principle of common but differentiated responsibility. These elements are considered below. The CBD, unusually, goes further by establishing a framework under which developing countries are entitled to a 'fair and equitable' sharing of the benefits arising from the use of genetic resources found in their territory.[118] In effect, a trade-off between conservation and economic equity is at the core of this Convention, although troubled by unsettled questions concerning intellectual property rights and the feasibility of controlling the activities of multinational drug companies.[119] Similarly, 'The Nagoya Protocol is basically premised on the . . .principle of intra-generational equity.'[120]

Equity and equitable utilization are well-established general principles of international law;[121] their use in an intra-generational context is less often acknowledged explicitly. At present it cannot easily be argued that intra-generational equity has any applicability outside the limited context of the instruments in which it has so far been employed.[122] However, human rights law up to a point provides another way of looking at intra-generational equity, insofar as it focuses in cases like *Ogoniland* and *Hatton* on the balance between the benefits of economic development for the wider community and the harmful impact on the human rights of those most adversely affected.[123]

[117] See Morgera, 27 *EJIL* (2016) 353.

[118] Article 15(7). See also UNCED Agenda 21, Ch 15.4(d); 2010 Nagoya Protocol on Access and Benefit Sharing; Morgera et al, *Unravelling the Nagoya Protocol* (Leiden, 2014).

[119] See *infra*, Ch 11.

[120] Morgera et al, *Unravelling the Nagoya Protocol* at 375.

[121] See *infra*, section 3(2).

[122] But see Morgera, 27 *EJIL* (2016) 353, who suggests that fair and equitable sharing of natural resources may be a new general principle.

[123] See *infra*, Ch 5, section 2(4).

(f) Procedural elements of sustainable development

No discussion of sustainable development should overlook the procedural elements which facilitate implementation at national level. Cooperation between states, environmental impact assessment, public participation in environmental decision-making, and access to information perform the function of legitimizing decisions and, if properly employed, may also improve their quality. Their role is not limited to the pursuit of sustainability, however, but has equal relevance to global and transboundary environmental law and they are further discussed below.[124]

2(3) THE INFLUENCE OF SUSTAINABLE DEVELOPMENT ON THE LAW

As we saw in the previous chapter, the concept of 'sustainable development' had already begun to emerge prior to UNCED in 1992, but its defining role in the evolution of international law and policy on protection of the environment secured near universal endorsement at Rio and in subsequent UN conferences.[125] Sustainable development informs much of the Rio Declaration, as well as the 1992 Convention on Climate Change and the 1992 CBD, and it is central to the elaboration of global environmental responsibility by these and other instruments.[126] Agenda 21, the non-binding programme of action adopted by the Rio Conference, also refers in its Preamble to the need for a 'global partnership for sustainable development', and most of its provisions are intended to promote the concept. Since Rio, sustainable development has been adopted as a policy by numerous governments, both at national and regional level. It has influenced the application and the development of law and policy by various international organizations, including the World Bank, the FAO, the WTO, and UNDP, as well as treaty bodies such as the ITTO and the European Energy Charter. Various studies have assessed the relevance of the concept to international law.[127]

As we also saw earlier, Principle 27 of the Rio Declaration and Chapter 39 of Agenda 21 call specifically for further development of international law 'in the field

[124] *Infra*, section 2(4). On cooperation and EIA see *infra*, sections 7 and 8. On access to information and participation in decision-making see *infra*, Ch 5.

[125] *Supra*, Ch 2, section 2.

[126] See 1992 Convention on Climate Change, Article 3; 1992 CBD, Articles 8 and 10; 1994 Convention to Combat Desertification, Articles 4, 5; 2010 Nagoya Protocol on Access and Benefit Sharing, Preamble.

[127] See Sands, 65 *BYIL* (1994) 303; Lang (ed), *Sustainable Development and International Law* (London, 1995); Ginther, Denters and de Waart (eds), *Sustainable Development and Global Governance* (London, 1995); McGoldrick, 45 *ICLQ* (1996) 796; Boyle and Freestone (eds), *International Law and Sustainable Development* (Oxford, 1999); Cordonnier Segger (ed), *Sustainable Development Law: Principles, Practices and Prospects* (Oxford, 2004); Schrijver and Weiss (eds), *International Law and Sustainable Development: Principles and Practice* (Leiden, 2004); French, *International Law and Policy of Sustainable Development* (Manchester, 2005); Bugge and Voigt (eds), *Sustainable Development in International and National Law* (Groningen, 2008); Schrijver, *The Evolution of Sustainable Development in International Law* (Leiden, 2008); Barral, *Le Développement Durable en Droit International* (Brussels, 2016).

of sustainable development'.[128] The impact of sustainable development on the evolution of international law can be observed in the *Gabčíkovo-Nagymaros* and *Pulp Mills Cases*. The Court's judgments go some way towards modernizing international watercourses law along the lines indicated by the ILC and the 1997 UN Convention on the Non-Navigational Uses of International Watercourses.[129] The latter Convention was amended in its final drafting stages to take explicit account of the principle of sustainable utilization,[130] which is also one of the new principles applied to high seas fisheries by the 1995 Agreement Relating to the Conservation and Management of Straddling and Highly Migratory Fish Stocks.[131] Together these treaties have redefined existing legal concepts of equitable utilization of shared resources and freedom of fishing on the high seas, and for the first time they introduce important environmental constraints into international law relating to shared and common property natural resources. Older treaties are likely to be interpreted accordingly, especially where they impose obligations of 'optimum and rational use' or similar phraseology.[132]

The most potentially far-reaching aspect of sustainable development is that for the first time it makes a state's management of its own domestic environment a matter of international concern in a systematic way.[133] This is most apparent in the 1992 CBD and the 2006 ITTA,[134] but the point is evident throughout Agenda 21, the Rio+20 Declaration, and the 2015 SDGs.[135] It also has potential implications for the future development of national and international human rights law, as we shall see in Chapter 5.

However, as we noted in Chapter 2, there remain fundamental uncertainties about the concept of sustainable development which the Rio Declaration does not resolve, but which have a direct bearing on the question whether it can in any sense be considered a legal principle. If, as the 2015 SDGs assume, it is to be interpreted, applied, and achieved primarily at national level by individual governments, there may be only a limited need for international definition and oversight, a task which can appropriately be performed by the High-Level Political Forum created for this purpose.[136] If, however, it is intended that states should be held legally accountable for achieving sustainability, whether globally or nationally, then the criteria for measuring this standard must be made clear, as must the evidential burden for assessing the performance of individual states. Whether international courts can perform this role remains to be considered in the following section.

128 UNEP GC Decision 18/9 (1995); Working Papers UNEP/IEL WS/1/2 (1995) UNEP/IEL WS/2/1 (1995) and *Final Rept of the Expert Group on International Law Aiming at Sustainable Development* UNEP/IEL/WS/3/2 (1996). See also UN, Dept for Policy Co-ordination and Sustainable Development, *Rept of the Expert Group Meeting on Identification of Principles of International Law for Sustainable Development* (Geneva, 1995) prepared for 4th Meeting of the CSD.

129 *Infra*, Ch 10.

130 Compare Article 5 of the ILC Draft Convention, UN Doc A/CN 4/L492 and Add 1 (1994) with Article 5 of the 1997 Convention as finally adopted

131 Articles 5 and 6. See Freestone and Makuch, 7 *YbIEL* (1996) 3 and *infra*, Ch 12.

132 See e.g. *Pulp Mills Case*, ICJ Reports (2010) 4, paras 170–177 (1975 Statute of the River Uruguay); *Kishenganga Arbitration (Partial Award)* PCA (2013) paras 449–453 (1960 Indus Waters Treaty).

133 See *infra*, section 4.

134 On which see *infra*, Ch 11.

135 *Supra*, Ch 2, section 2.

136 On the SDGs see *supra*, Ch 2, section 2.

2(4) AN OBLIGATION TO DEVELOP SUSTAINABLY?

No easy answer can be given to the question whether international law now requires that all development should be sustainable, or if so, what that would mean in specific normative terms.[137] It is clear, given the breadth of international endorsement for the concept, that few states would quarrel with the proposition that development should in principle be sustainable and that natural resources should be managed in this way. The Rio+20 Declaration refers to an 'economically, socially and environmentally sustainable future for our planet and for present and future generations,' and it sets out an elaborate programme of objectives.[138] As we saw in Chapter 2, these have since been supplemented by a set of SDGs. Given the social, political and economic value judgments involved in deciding what is sustainable, and the necessity of weighing conflicting factors, of which environmental protection is only one, it is difficult to see an international court reviewing national action and concluding that it falls short of a standard of 'sustainable development', save possibly in an extreme case. The ICJ did not do so in the *Gabčíkovo-Nagymaros Case*,[139] preferring instead to address more readily justiciable questions such as the equitable allocation of water flow or the applicability of international environmental standards in the operation of the hydroelectric system. Nor did it do so in *Pulp Mills*, where it focused on compliance with the procedural and substantive requirements of the River Uruguay Statute, not on the sustainability of an economic policy based on the development of a pulp mill industry.[140] The adoption by the UN of sustainable development 'goals', whose attainment will be reviewed by a 'High-Level Political Forum' makes the point: sustainable development does not look like a legal concept to be interpreted and argued over by international lawyers.[141] That may help explain why the ICJ cautiously referred to it in *Pulp Mills* only as an 'international objective.'[142]

This is not the end of the matter, however, for two reasons. First, courts can review the sustainability of economic development by reference to the detriment to human rights, including the right to life, private life or property, or economic, social, and cultural rights such as health and the right to water.[143] Thus, in the *Ogoniland*

137 See in particular, Lowe, in Boyle and Freestone, *International Law and Sustainable Development*, Ch 2; French, *International Law and Policy of Sustainable Development*, Ch 3; Sands, 65 *BYIL* (1994) 303, but contrast Barral, 23 *EJIL* (2012) 377; id, *Le Développement Durable en Droit International*, 161–211 and 439–43.

138 *The Future We Want*, UNGA Res 66/288 (2012) annex.

139 ICJ Reports (1997) 7. See to the same effect *Indus Waters Kishenganga Arbitration (Final Award)* PCA (2013) para 112.

140 ICJ Reports (2010) 14.

141 See Handl, in Lang (ed), *Sustainable Development and International Law*, 35–43; Dernbach and Cheever, 2 *Transnational Env L* (2015) 247, but compare Barral, 23 *EJIL* (2012) 377, at 388. For the argument that sustainable development could or should be treated as an economic and social human right see *infra*, Ch 5, section 2.

142 *Pulp Mills Case*, ICJ Reports (2010) 14, at para 177. See also Judge Kooijmans, 56 *ICLQ* (2007) 751.

143 See *infra*, Chs 5 and 10, section 2(5).

Case, after noting '[t]he destructive and selfish role played by oil development in Ogoniland, closely tied with repressive tactics of the Nigerian Government, and the lack of material benefits accruing to the local population', the African Commission on Human and Peoples' Rights found, inter alia, that the right of peoples to dispose freely of their own natural resources had been violated as well as their right to 'ecologically sustainable development'.[144] Here, in contrast to the *Gabčíkovo-Nagymaros Case*, we can see an international tribunal taking a critical view of the merits of economic development, albeit in an admittedly extreme case. Any challenge to the sustainability of economic development on this basis will be most effective if focused on the long-term impact on the environment on which those most affected depend for their livelihood. The SDGs will be relevant to the interpretation of states' human rights obligations in this context.[145] Other cases in the Inter-American and European Courts of Human Rights exemplify the same argument,[146] which we explore more fully in Chapter 5.

Secondly, although international law may not require development to be sustainable, the precedents suggest that it does require development decisions to be the outcome of a process which promotes sustainable development and respects international obligations of environmental protection. Specifically, if states do not carry out EIAs, or they refuse to cooperate in the management of global and transboundary risks or the conservation of natural resources, or they fail to integrate development and environmental considerations in their decision-making, or they do not take account of the needs of intra- and inter-generational equity, they will have failed to implement the main tools employed by the Rio Declaration and other international instruments for the purpose of facilitating sustainable development. There is, as we shall see below, ample state practice to support the normative significance of most of these elements. An interpretation which makes the process of decision-making the key legal test of sustainable development, rather than the nature of the development, is implicitly supported by the *Gabčíkovo-Nagymaros* and *Pulp Mills Cases*. In *Gabčíkovo*, while not questioning whether a project conceived in 1977 was sustainable, the ICJ required the parties in the interests of sustainable development to 'look afresh' at the environmental consequences and to carry out monitoring and abatement measures to contemporary standards set by international law.[147] In *Pulp Mills* the Court examined in detail the EIA carried out by Uruguay and the evidence establishing that agreed water quality standards had been complied with.[148] Such an approach enables international courts to further the objective of sustainable development in accordance with the Rio

144 *Social and Economic Rights Action Center and Center for Economic and Social Rights v Nigeria*, ACHPR Communication 155/96 (2002) paras 52–5.

145 See e.g. Committee on Elimination of Discrimination against Women ('CEDAW'), Concluding Observations on Oman and Nigeria (2017); Committee on the Rights of the Child, Concluding Observations on Haiti (2016) and Vanuatu (2017).

146 Compare *Maya Indigenous Community of the Toledo District v Belize*, IACHR (2004) and *Hatton v UK* [2003] ECtHR (Grand Chamber) *infra*, Ch 5.

147 ICJ Reports (1997) 7, para 140.

148 ICJ Reports (2010) 14, paras 190–259.

Declaration while relieving them of the impossible task of deciding what is and what is not sustainable.

An argument of this kind would thus focus on the components of sustainable development, rather than on the concept itself. Even if there is no legal obligation to develop sustainably, there may nevertheless be law 'in the field of sustainable development'.[149] Moreover, a court or international institution can also ensure that elements such as inter-generational equity, or integration of environment and development, or sustainability of natural resources and ecosystems, are taken account of in decision-making, even if it cannot review judgments made in the light of them. Principles of this kind may be 'soft', but as Lowe convincingly demonstrates, sustainable development and its components are very relevant when courts or international bodies have to interpret, apply, or develop, treaties or general international law.[150] That is perhaps the most important lesson to be drawn from the ICJ's references to sustainable development in the *Pulp Mills* and *Gabčíkovo-Nagymaros Cases* and from the WTO Appellate Body's decision in the *Shrimp-Turtle Case*.[151] Sustainable development represents a policy objective which can influence the outcome of cases, the interpretation of treaties, and the practice of states and international organizations, and has led to significant changes and developments in the existing law.[152] In that very important sense, international law requires states and international bodies to take account of the objective of sustainable development, and to employ appropriate processes for doing so.

3 CONSERVATION AND SUSTAINABLE USE OF NATURAL RESOURCES

3(1) LEGAL STATUS OF NATURAL RESOURCES

The legal status of natural resources varies according to whether the resource is under the sovereignty of one state, shared by several states, or held in common for the benefit of all. These categorizations have different impacts on the freedom of states to exploit a resource, and they have continuing relevance to an understanding of the law on conservation and sustainable use of natural resources.[153]

[149] Sands, 65 *BYIL* (1994) 303.

[150] Lowe, in, Boyle and Freestone, *International Law and Sustainable Development*, Ch 2; Sands, in Lang (ed), *Sustainable Development and International Law*, 53–66; Barral, *Le Développement Durable en Droit International*, 439, but for more cautious views see Handl, in Lang (ed), *op cit*, 35–43 and Mann, *ibid*, 67–72.

[151] *Pulp Mills Case*, ICJ Reports (2006) paras 68–84 and (2010) paras 75–6 &177; *Gabčíkovo-Nagymaros Case*, ICJ Reports (1997) para 140; *Shrimp/Turtle Case*, WTO Appellate Body (1998) WT/DS58/AB/R, paras 126–30; *Iron Rhine Arbitration*, PCA (2005) paras 81, 221–3, and *Kishenganga Arbitration (Partial Award)* PCA (2013) paras 449–50.

[152] See in particular Barral, *Le Développement Durable en Droit International*, 439–43.

[153] See generally Brownlie, 162 *Recueil des Cours* (1979) 245; Schrijver, *Sovereignty over Natural Resources* (Cambridge, 1997); Schachter, *Sharing the World's Rsources* (New York, 1977).

(a) Permanent sovereignty over natural resources

In general, it was assumed in the early development of international law that control of natural resources depended on the acquisition of sovereignty over territory and territorial seas.[154] Resolution of disputes concerning resources thus often took the form of boundary delimitations, as in the *Norwegian Fisheries Case*,[155] or centred on the status of a resource as shared or common property falling outside the exclusive control of any one state, as in the *Behring Sea Fur Seals* arbitration,[156] or the *Icelandic Fisheries Cases*.[157] No distinction existed in this respect between sovereignty over living resources, or non-renewable resources such as minerals.[158] Once a resource fell within the category of exclusive sovereignty, such as forests, international law placed few limitations on its use.

The principle of permanent sovereignty over natural resources which developed after 1945 was mainly a response by newly independent developing states to the problem of foreign ownership of their mineral resources, notably oil. Their efforts resulted in the adoption in 1962 by the UN General Assembly of resolution 1803 XVII.[159] It proclaimed 'The right of peoples and nations to permanent sovereignty over their natural wealth and resources', and the Preamble recommended that 'the sovereign right of every state to dispose of its natural wealth and resources should be respected . . . in accordance with their national interests'. This resolution draws no distinction between living and non-living resources and makes no reference to any duty of conservation, although it does recognize the desirability of promoting international cooperation for the economic development of developing countries and the benefits 'derivable' from the exchanges of technical and scientific information in the development and use of resources. Resolution 1803 was regarded by some states as declaratory of existing law; it has also been referred to as such by international arbitral tribunals.[160]

Two years after the Stockholm Conference, the UN General Assembly adopted two further resolutions. The Declaration on the Establishment of a New International Economic Order ('NIEO')[161] reaffirmed permanent sovereignty over natural resources and the right to nationalize them. The 1974 Charter of Economic Rights and Duties of States asserted that 'Every state has and shall freely exercise full permanent sovereignty

154 Brownlie, 162 *Recueil des Cours* (1979) 272–86.

155 ICJ Reports (1951) 116. See also *Jan Mayen Case*, ICJ Reports (1991) 38.

156 Moore, 1 *Int Arb Awards* (1898) 755, repr in 1 *Int Env L Reps* (1999) 43, and see *infra*, Ch 12.

157 ICJ Reports (1974) 3, 175. See *infra*, Ch 12.

158 See e.g. 1958 Continental Shelf Convention, which defines 'natural resources' as consisting of 'the mineral and other non-living resources of the seabed and subsoil, together with living organisms belonging to a sedentary species'.

159 For drafting history see Schrijver, *Sovereignty over Natural Resources*, Ch 2.

160 *Texaco v Libya*, 53 ILR (1977) 389; *BP v Libya*, 53 ILR (1977) 297. See generally Brownlie, 162 *Recueil des cours* (1979) 245; Schachter, *Sharing the World's Resources* 124, and Schrijver, *Sovereignty over Natural Resources*, 82ff.

161 UNGA Res 3201 (S-VI) (1974). See Schrijver, *Sovereignty over Natural Resources*, Ch 3.

including possession, use and disposal, over all its natural resources'.[162] By emphasizing the apparently untrammelled sovereignty of states over natural resources, these resolutions might be thought to imply that any restrictions would for the most part require agreement between the states concerned. In reality, however, these resolutions, and the strong support given by developing states to the concept of permanent sovereignty, were primarily directed at asserting the right to nationalize or control foreign-owned resources and industries, free from some of the older rules which protected foreign investments. They have not constrained the development of treaties and rules of customary international law concerning conservation of natural resources and environmental protection that qualify national sovereignty. On the contrary, as we shall see below in our discussion of the Rio Conference and sustainable development, the NIEO has 'evolved into a general approach to the making of international environmental law aimed at solidarity and cooperation to the benefit of the least-favoured countries.'[163]

Nor has the concept of permanent sovereignty prevented resource conservation within a state's territory from being treated as a question of common concern for all states. Treaties such as the 1968 African Convention on the Conservation of Nature, the 1972 World Heritage Convention, the 1973 CITES and the 1992 CBD exemplify this point.[164] That is not to say that sovereignty does not remain the cornerstone of the rights and duties of states over natural resources within their own territory.[165] It is reiterated, as we saw earlier, in Stockholm Principle 21 and Rio Principle 2, and in the 1992 CBD and other agreements, albeit qualified by responsibilities for the protection of other states and common spaces. But as Schrijver observes, 'It is clear that sovereignty has become pervaded with environmental concerns'.[166] Contemporary sovereignty is in no sense absolute or unfettered. As many writers have argued, new concepts of resource utilization based on notions of sustainable development, sustainable use, ecosystem protection, benefit sharing, and common interest involve a redefinition of sovereignty itself, so that it is no longer a basis for exclusion of others, but entails instead 'a commitment to cooperate for the good of the international community at large'.[167] As we saw in the previous section of this chapter, sovereignty must be exercised responsibly, in accordance with internationally agreed policies and principles of sustainable development and environmental protection.[168]

[162] Article 2, UNGA Res 3281 XXIX (1974). The US and a number of other Western states voted against this resolution or abstained. See *Texaco v Libya*, 53 ILR (1977) 389; Brownlie, 162 *Recueil des Cours* (1979) 267–9; White, 24 *ICLQ* (1975) 542; Chatterjee, 40 *ICLQ* (1991) 669; Schrijver, *Sovereignty over Natural Resources*, Ch 3.

[163] Morgera, 27 *EJIL* (2016) 353, 358–9; Maljean-Dubois, in Michelot (ed), *Equité et environnement* (Brussels, 2012) 355, at 358–359, and see generally Salmon, 62 *ICLQ* (2013) 31.

[164] See *infra*, Ch 11.

[165] Schrijver, *Sovereignty over Natural Resources*, 250.

[166] *Ibid*, 168. See in particular his Chs 4, 8.

[167] Handl, 1 *YbIEL* (1990) 32. See also Schrijver, *Sovereignty over Natural Resources*, Ch 1; Morgera, 27 *EJIL* (2016) 353 at 359; Brownlie, 162 *Recueil des cours* (1979) 282; Kiss, 175 *Recueil des cours* (1982) 229ff; and see *infra*, Chs 12, 13.

[168] See in particular *The Future We Want*, UNGA Res 66/288 (2012).

(b) Shared natural resources

'Shared natural resources' represent an intermediate category.[169] These resources do not fall wholly within the exclusive control of one state, but neither are they the common property of all states. The essence of this concept is a limited form of community interest, usually involving a small group of states in geographical contiguity, which exercise shared rights over transboundary resources. Examples considered in later chapters include international watercourses (Ch 10), regional air masses (Ch 6), and migratory species (Ch 11). Insofar as resources are shared or held in common, utilization has to be both equitable and sustainable.

A succession of UN General Assembly resolutions has recognized the general principle that states do not have unlimited sovereignty with regard to shared resources. Article 3 of the 1974 Charter of Economic Rights and Duties of States set out the basic principle: 'In the exploitation of natural resources shared by two or more countries each state must cooperate on the basis of a system of information and prior consultation in order to achieve optimum use of such resources without causing damage to the legitimate interests of others'.[170]

These resolutions formed the basis for the adoption by the Governing Council of UNEP in 1978 of the 'Principles of Conduct, etc in the Conservation and Harmonious Utilization of Natural Resources Shared by Two or More States'.[171] The UN General Assembly took note of these 'Principles', including the statement that they are 'without prejudice to the binding nature of those rules already recognized as such in international law', and it called on states to use them as 'guidelines and recommendations' in the formulation of bilateral or multilateral conventions, in such a way as to enhance the development and interests of all states, in particular developing countries.[172]

Although, these principles are relevant to mineral and water resources, they can also apply to protection of migratory species of animals and transboundary nature reserves and parks.[173] They require cooperation in conservation and use, conclusion of agreements, creation of institutions, EIA, joint research, exchange of information, and notification and consultation on the basis of good faith and good neighbourliness. They have to be applied in a way that enhances development, based on the concept of equitable utilization.

The legal status of these and similar sets of principles was discussed in Chapter 1; they exemplify the soft law approach to law-making often favoured by UNEP. However, the analysis provided in Chapters 10 and 11 indicates that the UNEP Principles are to a remarkable degree reflected in the provisions of the major wildlife and international

169 See generally Brownlie, 162 *Recueil des Cours* (1979) 289ff.

170 UNGA Res 3281 (XXIX)(1974). See also UNGA Res 3129 (XXVIII) (1973) and generally de Arechaga, 159 *Rec des Cours* (1978) I, 297–310; White, 16 *Virginia JIL* (1975–6) 323–45.

171 17 *ILM* (1978) 1091. See the Working Group's Rept (UNEP.IG.12/2) and government comments (UN document A/34/557 and Corr.l); Schrijver, *Sovereignty over Natural Resources*, 129–33; Sand, in R-J Dupuy, *The Future of International Law of the Environment* (Hague Academy, Dordrecht, 1984) 51–72; Adede, 5 *EPL* (1979) 6; Lammers, *Pollution of International Watercourses* (Dordrecht, 1984) 335–8.

172 UNGA Res 34/186 (1979).

173 On which see *infra*, Ch 11.

watercourse conventions, and although some have not been acted upon, most have, and in certain important respects they reflect existing customary law.

The UN General Assembly's reluctance to give its full endorsement to the 1978 UNEP Principles, and the use of language which avoids the implication of altering existing legal obligations, stems from the controversy and opposition earlier resolutions on the subject had aroused.[174] Continued opposition to the concept of 'shared natural resources' led to the removal of all reference to it in the ILC's codification of the law relating to international watercourses.[175] Even today, the word 'shared' does not appear in the ILC's Articles on Transboundary Aquifers.[176] Moreover, the most notable omission from the UNEP Principles and UN resolutions is the failure to define what resources should be treated as shared. The Executive Director of UNEP indicated his belief that at least the following are 'shared natural resources': river systems, enclosed and semi-enclosed seas, air sheds, mountain chains, forests, conservation areas, and migratory species.[177] Another proposed definition refered to 'an element of the natural environment used by man which constitutes a bio-geophysical unity, and is located in the territory of two or more states'.[178] The working group drafting the Principles did not discuss the issue or reach any conclusions, however.

Whatever the legal position may have been in 1978, UNEP's Principles are today largely reflected in the law of international watercourses codified by the 1997 UN Watercourses Convention, in the 1992 Rio Declaration,, and in the jurisprudence of international courts considered in later sections of this chapter. The long-established legal principle is that transboundary resources must be used equitably.[179] Equitable utilization entails a balancing of interests and consideration of all relevant factors. What these factors are, and how they should be balanced depends entirely on the context of each case.[180] No useful purpose can be served by attempting generalized definitions of what is essentially an exercise of discretion, whether by judges or other decision-makers. This discretion can be structured, however, and rendered more predictable, by careful analysis of international practice or by explicit recognition of relevant criteria in treaties or other instruments.[181] Moreover, as later chapters will show, the negotiation of equitable entitlements to the exploitation of natural resources can be facilitated by cooperation through intergovernmental institutions.[182]

174 Five states voted against UNGA Res 3129; 43 abstained, and 77 voted for. See also II *YbILC* (1983) Pt 1, 195, and Adede, 5 *EPL* (1979) 6. The WCED Experts Group preferred the term 'transboundary natural resources'.

175 UNEP IG/12/2 (1978) para 15, and see *infra*, Ch 10.

176 2008 ILC Articles on Transboundary Aquifers, GAOR, 63rd Session, Supp 10 (2008).

177 UNEP/GC/44 (1975) para 86.

178 UNEP/IG/12/2 (1978) para 16.

179 UNEP Principles, Principle 1; 1997 UN Watercourses Convention, Article 6, *infra*, Ch 10; 2008 ILC Articles on Transboundary Aquifers, Article 4.

180 See *infra*, Ch 10.

181 See e.g. the 1997 UN Watercourses Convention, *infra*, Ch 10, but cf Brownlie, 162 *Recueil des Cours* (1979) 287. Brownlie is too dismissive of equity as a major source of principles for resource allocation. Cf Schachter, *Sharing the World's Resources*, 64–83.

182 Schachter, *Sharing the World's Resources*, 70, and see *infra*, Chs 10 and 12.

Apart from its generality, and limited capacity for prescribing predictable outcomes, equitable utilization is deficient insofar as it addresses resource exploitation solely from the perspective of those states sharing sovereignty over the resource. It is thus less well suited to accommodating environmental concerns or ensuring sustainable use. The key point, reflected in references to sustainable use in the 1997 UN Watercourses Convention, is that equitable use of an exhaustible resource is not necessarily sustainable use.[183] We return to this point below.

(c) Common property

Common property, in international law, refers primarily to areas beyond national jurisdiction, of which the high seas and superjacent airspace are the most important examples. These common spaces are free for equitable and reasonable use by all states, and may not be appropriated to the exclusive sovereignty of any one state.[184] As we will see later in this chapter, the principles of international law which require states to prevent and control pollution and environmental damage have been extended to protect these common spaces, which are now regulated by a series of multilateral treaties for this purpose.[185]

The common property doctrine extends to most of the living resources of the high seas, including fish and mammals, which must be shared equitably.[186] Birds and other species of wildlife that inhabit common spaces or migrate through them are similarly regarded. Once living resources are held in common in this way, no single user can have exclusive rights over them, nor the right to prevent others from joining in their exploitation: they must be shared equitably. Such living resources do, however, become exclusive property once reduced into possession by capture or taking. The common property doctrine is not to be confused with the 'common heritage' concept, a specialized regime applied to certain mineral resources and considered below.

An important factor contributing to the classification of high seas living resources as common property is that they have historically been so plentiful that the cost of asserting and defending exclusive rights exceeds the advantages to be gained. A regime of open access was to everyone's advantage. However, as Hardin observed in a famous article,[187] the 'inherent logic of the commons remorselessly generates tragedy.' The availability of a free resource leads to over-exploitation and minimizes the interest of any individual state in conservation and restraint. Common property resources cannot be protected effectively without the cooperation of all states exploiting the resource; this has generally been difficult to obtain once resource exploitation becomes

183 See *infra*, Ch 10.

184 1958 Convention on the High Seas, Articles 1–2; 1982 UNCLOS, Articles 87, 89. See also 1967 Outer Space Treaty, Article 2.

185 See *infra*, Chs 8, 9 and 10.

186 *Behring Sea Fur Seals Arbitration* (1896) 1 *Int Env LR* 43; *Icelandic Fisheries Cases*, ICJ Reports (1974) 3 & 175; 1982 UNCLOS, Articles 89, 116; *infra*, Ch 12.

187 162 *Science* (1968) 1243–8. See also Wijkman, 36 *Int Org* (1982) 511, and *infra*, Ch 12.

established.[188] Moreover, as with shared resources, equitable use of common property by all the interested states is not necessarily sustainable use.[189]

(d) Common heritage

Although the term 'common heritage' is sometimes used loosely to refer to all the living and non-living resources of nature or to the global environment as an ecological entity, for legal purposes the term is currently confined to the narrow meaning attributed to it in two conventions, the 1979 Moon Treaty and the 1982 UNCLOS.[190] The concept was put forward by Malta at the UN General Assembly as the basis of a new regime for exploiting the resources of the deep seabed.[191] It was included in a 'Declaration of Principles Governing the Sea-bed and Ocean Floor',[192] and in Articles 136 and 137 of the 1982 UNCLOS, which pronounce the deep seabed beyond national jurisdiction (the Area) and its mineral resources to be 'the common heritage of mankind', on whose behalf an International Seabed Authority (ISA) established under the UNCLOS shall act.

As employed in the 1979 Moon Treaty and the 1982 UNCLOS, the concept of common heritage implies that these areas and their mineral resources cannot fall within the sovereignty or sovereign rights of states but must be conserved and exploited for the benefit of all states. The concept thus differs from common property in allowing all states to share in the rewards of resource exploitation, even if they are unable to participate in the actual process of extraction. The ISA represents an elaborate form of international management and regulation in order to control the allocation of exploitation rights and the equitable sharing of benefits.[193] The establishment of some form of international management is also envisaged by the 1979 Moon Treaty.[194] Both schemes require the states concerned to take measures of environmental protection. Article 145 of the 1982 UNCLOS gives the ISA authority to adopt 'appropriate rules regulations and procedures' to prevent, reduce, and control pollution or 'interference with the ecological balance of the marine environment', and to protect natural resources, flora and fauna.[195] Article 209 requires states to adopt laws and regulations 'no less effective' than the rules approved by the ISA. Common heritage resources, unlike common property, are thus subject to regulation by a strong international authority, which, as we saw in Chapter 2, is in this respect unique among international institutions with environmental responsibilities.

[188] See *infra*, Ch 12, especially section 4 on whaling.

[189] Contrast 1995 UN Fish Stocks Agreement, *infra*, Ch 12.

[190] See generally Lodge, 27 *IJMCL* (2012) 733; Egede, *Africa and the Deep Seabed: Politics and International law of the Common Heritage of Mankind* (Berlin, 2011); Baslar, *The Concept of the Common Heritage of Mankind in International Law* (The Hague, 1998); Cheng, *Studies in International Space Law* (Oxford, 1997) 365–80; Pardo and Christol, in Macdonald and Johnston (eds), *Structure and Process of International Law* (The Hague, 1983) 643.

[191] Permanent Mission of Malta to the UN Sec Gen, *Note verbale,* 17 Aug 1967, UN Doc A/6095. See Ogley, *Whose Common Heritage? Creating a Law for the Sea-bed* (Guildford, 1975) 17–25.

[192] UNGA Res 2749 XXV (1970) adopted 108 to none, with 14 abstentions.

[193] *Supra,* Ch 2.

[194] Article 11(5).

[195] See *infra*, Ch 9, section 6.

Although, in convening the third UNCLOS, the UN General Assembly stated that it was 'conscious that the problems of ocean space are closely related and need to be considered as a whole',[196] the 1982 UNCLOS neither applied the common heritage regime to the waters above the deep seabed, nor to the living resources found anywhere in the oceans. Nor, apart from the Moon, has the concept found any further explicit applications, although proposals have been made to apply it to seabed genetic resources.[197] It was not employed in the 1985 Ozone Convention or the 1992 Convention on Climate Change.[198] The UN General Assembly declined to adopt a Maltese proposal to designate the global climate as the common heritage of mankind, preferring instead to describe it as a matter of 'common concern'. Similarly, the parties to the Antarctic Treaty system have adopted a comprehensive regime for the protection of that area and its dependent and associated ecosystems 'in the interest of mankind as a whole',[199] but they have avoided direct analogy with the Moon or deep seabed. A case can be made for the proposition that Antarctica nevertheless has many of the features of a common heritage regime, but such a view does not take full account of the complex legal and political status of that continent.[200]

Some conventions do use terms such as the 'world heritage of mankind' in their preambles.[201] But these are better viewed, like the term 'common concern' as expressions of the common interest of all states in certain forms of ecological protection, and not as attempts to internationalise ownership of resources. Common heritage is important, however, in providing one of the most developed applications of trusteeship over natural resources,[202] and in that sense it represents a significant precedent. But we should not suppose that transferring resources from a common property regime to a common heritage regime will necessarily improve the environment: the ISA exists to facilitate seabed mining, not to promote an environmentalist vision of the oceans.[203]

3(2) THE OBLIGATION OF CONSERVATION AND SUSTAINABLE USE

(a) The legal precedents

As early as 1898, in the *Behring Fur Seals Arbitration*, the need to conserve living resources was recognized.[204] Similarly, in the *Icelandic Fisheries* cases, the ICJ held that 'the former laissez-faire treatment of the living resources of the sea in the high seas has been replaced by a recognition of a duty to have due regard to the rights of

196 UNGA Res 2750 XXV (1970) adopted by 108 to 7, with 6 abstentions.

197 See *infra*, Ch 12, section 2(2)(e).

198 See *infra*, Ch 6.

199 1991 Protocol to the Antarctic Treaty on Environmental Protection, Preamble, on which see *supra*, Ch 2, section 5.

200 See Francioni and Scovazzi (eds), *International Law for Antarctica* (2nd edn, The Hague, 1996).

201 E.g. 1972 World Heritage Convention.

202 Kiss, 175 *Recueil des Cours* (1982) 99, and see *supra*, Ch 2, section 5.

203 See *infra*, Ch 9, section 6.

204 *Behring Fur Seals Arbitration* (1896) 1 *Int Env LR* 43, at 70.

other States and the needs of conservation for the benefit of all'.[205] Older agreements on natural resources use various terms, including 'conservation', 'optimum and rational utilization', or 'optimum sustainable productivity'.[206] Underlying all of these phrases is a concern for the more balanced use of natural resources,[207] and a desire to strengthen existing conservation law.

In 1982 the World Charter for Nature called for 'All areas of the earth, both land and sea' to be subject to principles of conservation.[208] It required 'Special protection' to be given to unique areas, representative ecosystems, and habitats of rare or endangered species; ecosystems and land, atmospheric and marine resources had to be managed to achieve 'optimum sustainable productivity' without endangering other ecosystems or species. Living resources were not be used in excess of their capacity for regeneration, and irreversible damage to 'nature' was to be avoided. On this view, 'conservation' of living resources includes both their protection and sustainable use. That remains the dominant conception of 'conservation' in contemporary international law,[209] subject of course to the need to protect and preserve endangered species, ecosystems and areas of natural beauty and cultural importance.[210] Even the great whales may be used sustainably for commercial purposes if sufficiently abundant.[211]

The 1992 Rio Declaration contains nothing so specific in regard to natural resources, ecosystems or endangered species. Principle 8 talks only of the need to 'reduce and eliminate unsustainable patterns of production and consumption'. Nevertheless, the idea that sustainable development involves limits on the utilization of natural resources, and some commitment to the conservation of natural ecosystems, can be observed in the 1982 UNCLOS,[212] and in the 1992 CBD and the 1992 Climate Change Convention.[213] The terms 'sustainable utilization' or 'sustainable use' or 'sustainable management' are expressly employed in the 1992 CBD and in post-Rio agreements.[214]

205 *Fisheries Jurisdiction Case (UK v Iceland)* ICJ Reports (1974) 3, para 72.

206 The World Charter for Nature refers to 'optimum sustainable productivity' (para I 4); the 1958 Geneva Convention on Fishing and the Conservation of the Living Resources of the High Seas uses the term 'optimum sustainable yield' (Article 2); the 1982 UNCLOS refers to 'maximum sustainable yield' (Article 61). On MSY see *infra*, Ch 12, section 3(3)(b), and for a scientific perspective Hilborn, Walters and Ludwig, 26 *Ann Rev Ecol Syst* (1995) 45–67.

207 *Pulp Mills Case*, ICJ Reports (20101) para 175: 'The Court considers that the attainment of optimum and rational utilization requires a balance between the Parties' rights and needs to use the river for economic and commercial activities on the one hand, and the obligation to protect it from any damage to the environment that may be caused by such activities, on the other.'

208 See *infra*, Ch 11.

209 Confirmed repeatedly by the *The Future We Want*, UNGA 66/288 (2012).

210 On which see inter alia the 1992 CBD and other treaties considered in Ch 11.

211 See 1946 ICRW, Preamble, and the *Whaling in the Antarctic Case*, ICJ Reports (2014) paras 56–8.

212 Article 194(5) and *South China Sea Arbitration*, PCA (2016) paras 945, 956–60.

213 1992 UNFCCC, Preamble, Articles 2 & 3; 1992 CBD, Preamble, Articles 2, 6, 8 & 10.

214 1994 Desertification Convention, Articles 2 and 3; 1995 UN Fish Stocks Agreement, Articles 2 and 5; 1997 UN Watercourses Convention, Article 5(1); 2006 ITTA, Article 1; 2010 Nagoya Protocol on Access and Benefit Sharing, Article 1. See Wälde, in Schrijver and Weiss, *International Law and Sustainable Development*, Ch 6; Rayfuse, *ibid*, Ch 19; Beyerlin, 63 *ZAÖRV* (2003) 417; Epiney, *ibid*, 377; Bekhechi, 101 *RGDIP* (1997) 101; Morgera et al, *Unravelling the Nagoya Protocol*, 48–58.

Article 2 of the CBD defines sustainable use as 'use. . . . in a way and at a rate that does not lead to long-term decline of biological diversity.'[215] The 1995 UN Fish Stocks Agreement also refers to 'measures to ensure the long-term sustainability of straddling fish stocks and highly migratory fish stocks,'[216] and it creates an elaborate regime for that purpose. The 1997 UN Watercourses Convention does not define sustainable use, but it has provisions on vital human needs, ecosystem protection, and prevention of pollution.[217]

The concepts of conservation and sustainable use evidenced in more detail in the treaties discussed in chapters 10–12. None of these treaties makes any presumption in favour of the preservation of a resource regardless of conservation status. Thus, although the 1992 CBD differentiates between the conservation of biological diversity on the one hand and the 'sustainable use of the components of biological diversity' on the other,[218] this language leaves no doubt that it permits the use of biological resources in a manner which 'avoid[s] or minimize[s] adverse effects on biological diversity.'[219] Most of the leading treaties take the same approach, including the 1980 CCAMLR, and the 1995 UN Fish Stocks Agreement.[220] It is also implicit in the fisheries articles of the 1982 UNCLOS,[221] the 1973 CITES,[222] and the 1971 Ramsar Convention on Wetlands of International Importance ('Ramsar Convention').[223] The conservation measures required by all of these treaties thus depend on the conservation status of the target species. Only one treaty, the 1979 Bonn Convention on Migratory Species, attempts to define what 'favourable' conservation status would look like: it requires population dynamics which indicate that the species is 'maintaining itself on a long-term basis as a viable component of its ecosystems', not likely to be reduced in the long-term, with sufficient habitat, and that abundance approaches historic levels (Article I(1)(c)). The focus here is on long-term sustainability; any taking of Appendix II species must be viewed from that perspective.

While the precise meaning of these different phrases may not be the same, the idea of sustainability over time is common to all of them. Three elements can be identified. First, sustainable use implies that consumptive uses are permitted, at least in principle, whether the resources in question are national, shared, or common property.[224]

215 See also 2004 Addis Ababa Principles and Guidelines for the Sustainable Use of Biodiversity, CBD COP Decision VII/12, Annex II, at para. 2 and *infra*, Ch 11.

216 1995 Fish Stocks Agreement, Article 5(a); *infra*, Ch 12.

217 *Infra*, Ch 10.

218 Article 1. See also the 2010 Nagoya Protocol on Access and Benefit Sharing.

219 Article 10(b).

220 See *infra*, Ch 12, section 5.

221 See *infra*, Ch 12, section 3.

222 See *infra*, Ch 11, section 3(4). CITES Resolution 13.2 recognizes that '[a]lthough CITES does not have a definition of sustainable use, the case studies show that the elements of the *Addis Ababa Principles and Guidelines for the Sustainable Use of Biodiversity* that are generally relevant to CITES are either already implicit in the language of CITES or are promoted by CITES.' The resolution urges parties to 'make use of' the Addis Ababa Principles and Guidelines while 'taking into account scientific, trade and enforcement considerations determined by national circumstances.'

223 See *infra*, Ch 11, section 3(1).

224 See e.g. 2006 ITTA, Article 1; 1997 UN Watercourses Convention, Article 5; 1992 CBD Articles 3, 10, 15; 1982 UNCLOS, Articles 62, 116–9.

Secondly, the extent to which utilization is allowed will depend on the status of the resource and the demands upon it at any particular time: 'Sustainable use is not a fixed state, but rather the consequence of balancing an array of factors, which vary according to the context of the use. In addition, sustainability of uses cannot be expressed with certainty, but rather as a probability that may have to change if the conditions in which management is taking place change.'[225] Thirdly, the precautionary principle, as endorsed by Principle 15 of the Rio Declaration, is an important element of sustainable utilization, because it addresses the key question of uncertainty in predictions of sustainability.[226]

How far international law now imposes on states a general obligation of conservation and sustainable use of natural resources and the natural environment depends largely on the extent to which the 1982 UNCLOS, the 1992 CBD, and the 1992 Climate Change Convention can be said to have created such a regime.[227] As we have seen, the *Icelandic Fisheries Cases*,[228] the 1982 UNCLOS and related agreements,[229] and the *South China Sea Arbitration*,[230] support the existence of an obligation to cooperate in the conservation and sustainable use of marine ecosystems, biodiversity and living resources.[231] In *South China Sea* the arbitrators also found that Chinese fishing methods were unsustainable.[232] Treaties forming the Antarctic Treaty system have established a reasonably comprehensive system for conservation of wildlife and ecosystems in that area.[233] To these precedents must be added the references to ecosystem protection and sustainable use in the 1997 UN Watercourses Convention.[234]

Even for natural resources which fall wholly within national boundaries, such as forests, the principle that they should be managed sustainably has been accepted.[235] The Rio+20 Declaration provides explicit political support for conservation and sustainable use of natural resources and ecosystems, biodiversity, and mountain ecosystems, and for sustainable management of forests.[236] The provisions of a growing body of global and regional treaties concerned with biological diversity, wildlife

[225] Note by the Executive Secretary, CBD Subsidiary Body on Scientific, Technical and Technological Advice, Document UNEP/CBD/SBSTTA/9/9, contained in COP Decision VII/12, Annex I, at para. 11. See also Glowka et al, *A Guide to the Convention on Biological Diversity*, IUCN Environmental Policy and Law Paper No. 30 (IUCN, 1994) 57.

[226] See *infra*, sections 3(2)(b) and 6.

[227] See *infra*, Chs 6, 7, 11 and 12.

[228] *Fisheries Jurisdiction Cases*, ICJ Reports (1974) 3, paras 71–2, and 175, para 77.

[229] 1982 UNCLOS, Arts 61, 117; 1995 UN Fish Stocks Agreement, Articles 5–7.

[230] PCA (2016) paras 956–60.

[231] See also *Request for an Advisory Opinion by the Sub-Regional Fisheries Commission*, ITLOS Reports (2015) paras 214–16; *Chagos MPA Arbitration*, PCA (2015) paras 320 and 538; and *infra*, Chs 8, 9, and 12.

[232] *South China Sea Arbitration*, PCA (2016) para 970.

[233] See 1959 Antarctic Treaty; 1980 Convention for the Conservation of Antarctic Marine Living Resources; 1991 Protocol on the Antarctic Environment, and *infra*, Ch 11.

[234] See *infra*, Ch 10, section 2(4).

[235] See 2006 ITTA, Article 1; Non-Legally Binding Instrument on all Types of Forests, UNGA Res 62/98 (2007)q on which see *infra*, Ch 11.

[236] *The Future We Want*, UNGA Res 66/288 (2012).

conservation, habitat protection, endangered species, specially protected areas, and cultural and natural heritage suggest that conservation and sustainable use of natural resources and ecosystems have acquired a wider legal significance beyond that implied in the *Icelandic Fisheries Cases*.[237] In particular, the 1992 CBD affirms that States 'are responsible for conserving their biological diversity and using their biological resources in a sustainable manner' and that 'the fundamental requirement for the conservation of biological diversity is the in-situ conservation of ecosystems and natural habitats. . . .'[238] Other conventions deal with particular aspects of the conservation problem, as in the 1973 CITES, or the 1994 Desertification Convention.

The evidence of these treaty commitments,[239] and indications of supporting state practice,[240] could be said to crystallize conservation and sustainable use of natural resources and ecosystems into an independent norm of international law. This appears to be the implication of the *Indus Waters Kishenganga Arbitration*, which noted that 'a series of international conventions, declarations and judicial and arbitral decisions have addressed the need to manage natural resources in a sustainable manner.'[241] At the same time, as we saw earlier, it is clear that states retain substantial discretion in giving effect to sustainable development, unless specific international action has been agreed. Thus, to return to the example of tropical forests, little of value can be inferred from a broad principle of conservation and sustainable use (or sustainable management) without reference to state practice and the practice of international organizations such as the ITTO, the UN Forum on Forests, and the UN-REDD programme.[242] How the obligation of conservation and sustainable use is applied in specific contexts is considered further in Chapters 10–12.

(b) The precautionary approach and sustainable use

The precautionary principle or approach is considered fully in section 6 below, but it is no less relevant to sustainable use of living resources, including fisheries, endangered species, biological diversity and forests. The moratorium on commercial whaling is one of the earliest examples of a precautionary approach to resource conservation.[243] Similarly, the 'Berne Criteria' for the listing and de-listing of endangered species under the 1973 CITES require de-listing to be 'approached with caution' and on the basis of 'positive scientific evidence that the plant or animal can withstand the exploitation resulting from the removal of protection'.[244] The ninth Conference of the Parties

[237] See *infra*, Chs 11, and 12.

[238] 1992 CBD, Preamble. See *infra*, Ch 11.

[239] See *infra*, Chs 10, 11, and 12.

[240] See e.g. Wales, Environment Act, 2016, ss 3, 4, 9; Croatia, Nature Protection Act, 2013; New Zealand, Resources Management Act, 1991, based explicitly on the WCED'S concept of sustainable development.

[241] *Indus Waters Kishenganga Arbitration (Partial Award)* PCA (2013) para 449.

[242] See in particular the guidelines, criteria and indicators on sustainable forest management adopted by the ITTO, the UNFF's Global Objectives on Forests, and the UN Non-Legally Binding Instrument on All Types of Forests, UNGA Res 62/98 (2007). On UN-REDD see *infra*, Ch 6, section 4.

[243] The 1994 Revised Management Procedure also exemplifies a precautionary approach to the resumption of commercial whaling. See *infra*, Ch 12, section 4(3).

[244] *Infra*, Ch 11, section 3(4).

in 1994 resolved to apply the precautionary approach 'so that scientific uncertainty should not be used as a reason for failing to act in the best interests of conservation of the species'.[245] Both examples show how Rio Principle 15 has come to influence the interpretation and application of multilateral conservation treaties concluded many years earlier.

What action states should take when they decide to adopt precautionary conservation measures varies just as much in this context as in any other. For example, application of a precautionary approach to high seas fisheries is justified not only by the level of uncertainty surrounding fisheries data, but also by the lack of EIA procedures for exploitation of fish stocks, the political misuse of scientific input, and the historically weak compliance and enforcement regime for high seas fishing. Article 6 of the 1995 UN Fish Stocks Agreement seeks to remedy these deficiencies by improving data collection and techniques for dealing with risk and uncertainty. The precautionary approach and other provisions of the Agreement have for the first time given international fisheries law an environmental and inter-generational aspect consistent with the pursuit of sustainable utilization.[246] At the same time, the parties resisted any suggestion that new or exploratory high seas fishing could not take place in the absence of adequate scientific knowledge. Such fisheries are subject to 'cautious conservation and management measures' until the impact on long-term sustainability can be assessed properly. Moreover, it is the parties to regional fisheries agreements who decide whether threatened stocks should be subject to a moratorium on fishing. Even if fully implemented, the principal impact of applying a precautionary approach as defined in Article 6 will only be to 'improve decision-making for fishery resource conservation and management'. Any wider implications for the level of fisheries protection, or the stringency of conservation measures, will flow from changes in the attitude and policies of fishing states, or from other provisions of the Agreement, not from any commitment they may have made to 'apply the precautionary approach'.

Thus, while it is clear that the precautionary principle or approach is now part of international law on sustainable use of natural resources, its precise implications can only be understood in the context of specific treaties.

(c) Cooperation in the conservation and sustainable use of natural resources

Cooperation is as fundamental in the law of natural resources as it is in respect of transboundary pollution. It is inherent in the principle of equitable utilization, in the 1997 UN Watercourses Convention, the 1995 UN Fish Stocks Agreement, the 1982 UNCLOS, and in UNEP's 1978 Principles of Conduct. The precedents considered in section 8 below apply equally in this context.

245 Resolution Conf. 9.24, Annex 4, as revised by COP16 (2013).

246 See also *Southern Bluefin Tuna Case (Provisional Measures)* (1999) ITLOS Reports, paras 77–9, and Garcia, in, FAO, *Precautionary Approach to Fisheries*, Technical Paper 350/2 (Rome, 1996) 3; Boyle and Freestone, *International Law and Sustainable Development*, Ch 7; Hewison, 11 *IJMCL* (1996) 301, and *infra*, Ch 12, section 4.

4 PRINCIPLES OF GLOBAL ENVIRONMENTAL RESPONSIBILITY

4(1) THE ENVIRONMENT AS A 'COMMON CONCERN'

As we saw earlier, the 1992 Rio Conference on Environment and Development marked a distinctive evolution in the scope of international environmental law. For the first time, the Rio instruments set out a framework of global environmental responsibilities, as distinct from those responsibilities which are merely regional or transboundary in character, such as air or river pollution, or which relate to common spaces, such as Part XII of the 1982 UNCLOS. Whereas the 1972 Stockholm Declaration had simply distinguished between responsibility for areas within and beyond national jurisdiction,[247] the Rio treaties use the concept of 'common concern' to designate those issues which involve global responsibilities.[248] Thus climate change and biological diversity are each expressly denominated as the 'common concern of mankind' and have become the subject of global regulatory treaties.[249]

(a) The global environment

The features which appear important in defining climate change and biological diversity as global concerns are their universal character and the need for common action by all states if measures of protection are to work.[250] Global environmental responsibility is not necessarily confined to these two phenomena, however. Although the ozone layer is nowhere referred to as a 'common concern', it is in substance treated by the 1985 Ozone Convention and the 1987 Montreal Protocol in essentially the same way.[251] Many of the elements of global responsibility can also be identified in provisions of the 1982 UNCLOS dealing with protection of the marine environment, in the 1995 UN Fish Stocks Agreement, and in Chapter 17 of Agenda 21, which refers to the oceans, seas and adjacent coastal areas as an 'integrated whole that is an essential component of the global life-support system'.[252] In this context territorial sovereignty or the legal status of any part of the oceans are immaterial: the obligation to protect the marine environment as a whole is what matters.[253]

[247] Principle 21.

[248] See also UN General Assembly Resolution 43/53 (1989) on Global Climate Change; Noordwijk Declaration of the Conference on Atmospheric Pollution and Climate Change, 19 *EPL* (1989) 229; UNEP GC Resolution 15/36 (1989). Note, however, that the Rio Declaration does not itself use the term. The ILC has also avoided using the term in its work on protection of the atmosphere: see ILC Rept (2015) GAOR A/70/10, Ch V.

[249] 1992 Convention on Climate Change, Preamble; 1992 CBD, Preamble.

[250] See the Preambles to both Conventions.

[251] *Infra*, Ch 6.

[252] See also Preamble to the 1982 UNCLOS: '*Conscious* that the problems of ocean space are closely interrelated and need to be considered as a whole', and see *infra*, Chs 8, 9, and 13.

[253] *South China Sea Arbitration*, PCA (2016) paras 939–41.

(b) The domestic environment of states

In certain contexts it might also be arguable that the management of a state's own domestic environment is a matter of international concern independently of any transboundary effects. Even before the Rio Conference, multilateral treaties dealing with wildlife conservation,[254] world heritage areas,[255] disposal of hazardous wastes,[256] and human rights[257] had already touched on the international regulation of matters internal to the states concerned. The Rio Declaration significantly extends the domestic reach of international environmental law by requiring states to enact effective environmental legislation (Principle 11), to facilitate access for individuals to information, decision-making processes and judicial and administrative proceedings at national level (Principle 10), to apply the precautionary approach 'widely' (Principle 15), and to undertake environmental impact assessment 'as a national instrument'(Principle 17). Some authors see the precautionary principle as the basis for comprehensive environmental protection both nationally and internationally.[258] It has also been suggested that the so-called 'preventive principle' applies to domestic environmental harm, requiring states to regulate and control pollution regardless of possible global or transboundary effects.[259] This has certainly been the conclusion of human rights case law, which now addresses domestic environmental concerns at both the substantive and procedural level.[260] The 2001 POPS Convention and protocols on various forms of air pollution exemplify this approach.[261] Moreover, to the extent that sustainable development can be regarded as a legal principle involving some degree of international supervision—and as we saw earlier this is not certain—it might be said that this aspect of domestic environmental protection may by implication also be a matter of 'common concern', although the Rio Declaration itself does not say so.

(c) Implications of 'common concern'

Although in some cases the developments just referred to are tentative and of uncertain legal status and scope, they do point to a 'globalization' of international environmental law, in the sense of addressing contemporary needs for global cooperation to deal with global environmental problems.[262] What is clear after Rio is that for this reason it is no longer possible to characterize international environmental law as no more than a system governing transboundary relations among neighbouring states. It is in this context that the concept of common concern becomes important.

'Common concern' is not a concept previously employed in international law and its present legal implications remain unsettled. The choice of language was itself the

254 *Infra*, Ch 11, section 3.

255 1972 World Heritage Convention.

256 *Infra*, Ch 8.

257 *Infra*, Ch 5.

258 E.g. Trouwborst, *Evolution and Status of the Precautionary Principle in International Law*, 284.

259 De Sadeleer, *Environmental Principles*, Ch 2, 64ff.

260 *Infra*, Ch 5, section 2.

261 See *infra*, Chs 6, 8.

262 Kiss, 32 *GYIL* (1989) 241; Handl, 1 *YbIEL* (1990) 3; Bowman, in Fitzmaurice et al (eds), *Research Handbook on IEL* (Cheltenham, 2010) Ch 23.

outcome of political compromise, agreed after initial proposals using the term 'common heritage of mankind' for the global climate and biological diversity encountered predictable opposition.[263] Nonetheless, 'common concern' indicates a legal status both for climate change and biological resources which is distinctively different from the concepts of permanent sovereignty, common property, shared resources, or common heritage which generally determine the international legal status of natural resources.[264] In relation to climate change, UN General Assembly Resolution 43/53 and the 1992 Climate Change Convention do not make the global atmosphere common property beyond the sovereignty of individual states, but like the ozone layer, they do treat it as a global unity insofar as injury in the form of global warming or climate change may affect the community of states as a whole. It is thus immaterial whether the global atmosphere comprises airspace under the sovereignty of a subjacent state or not: it is a 'common resource' of vital interest to mankind.[265] By approaching the matter from a global perspective, the UN has acknowledged not only the artificiality of spatial boundaries in this context but also the inappropriateness of treating the phenomena of global warming and climate change in the same way as transboundary air pollution, which is regional or bilateral in character.[266] Similarly the 1992 CBD does not internationalize biological resources in the same way that the 1982 UNCLOS treats mineral resources of the deep seabed; still less does it turn them into common property accessible for exploitation by all states.[267]

If 'common concern' is neither common property nor common heritage, and if it entails a reaffirmation of the existing sovereignty of states over their own resources, what legal content, if any, does this concept have? Its main impact appears to be that it gives the international community of states both a legitimate interest in resources of global significance and a common responsibility to promote their sustainable development.[268] Moreover, insofar as states continue to enjoy sovereignty over their own natural resources and the freedom to determine how they will be used, this sovereignty is not unlimited or absolute, but must now be exercised within the confines of the global responsibilities set out principally in the 1992 Climate Change Convention and the 1992 CBD, and also in the Rio Declaration and other relevant instruments.

[263] The original Maltese draft of UNGA Resolution 43/53 on Climate Change used the term 'common heritage'; early drafts of the Biological Diversity Convention also referred to the 'common heritage of all peoples': see UNEP, Ad hoc Working Group of Experts on Biological Diversity, 2nd session, Geneva, February 1990, para 11. The draft convention was amended following Brazilian opposition to the possibility that this might be seen as conferring rights on indigenous peoples.

[264] *Infra*, section 3, and see Bowman, in Fitzmaurice et al (eds), *Research Handbook on IEL*, Ch 23.

[265] See recommendations of the International Meeting of Legal and Policy Experts, Ottawa, Canada, 19 *EPL* (1989) 78. On the status of the ozone layer, see *infra*, Ch 6.

[266] See Boyle, in Churchill and Freestone, *International Law and Global Climate Change*, Ch 1.

[267] *Infra*, section 3.

[268] *South China Sea Arbitration*, PCA (2016) paras 939–41. See also UNEP, *Rept of the Group of Legal Experts to Examine the Concept of the Common Concern of Mankind in Relation to Global Environmental Issues* (1990); Boyle, in Churchill and Freestone, *International Law and Global Climate Change*; Kirgis, 84 *AJIL* (1990) 525; but for a more sceptical view see Brunnée, 49 *ZAÖRV* (1989) 791.

Global responsibility differs from existing transboundary environmental law in three respects. First, like human rights law, the global responsibilities in question may have an *erga omnes* character, owed to the international community as a whole, and not merely to other states inter se. Secondly, although held in common by all states, global environmental responsibilities are differentiated in various ways between developed and developing states, and contain strong elements of equitable balancing not found in the law relating to transboundary harm. Thirdly, although the commitment to a precautionary approach is now relevant to many aspects of environmental law, it is particularly evident in matters of global concern.

4(2) ERGA OMNES STATUS OF GLOBAL ENVIRONMENTAL RESPONSIBILITY

International lawyers have traditionally distinguished between legal obligations owed to another state, which can be enforced only by that state, and legal obligations owed to the whole international community of states, which can be enforced by or on behalf of that community. The latter are sometimes referred to as *erga omnes* obligations. It was this distinction which the ICJ had in mind in the *Barcelona Traction Case,*[269] when it contrasted interstate claims for the taking of property, which could only be brought by the state of nationality of the claimant, and claims based on a violation of international human-rights law, which could be brought by any state. The same distinction is reflected in the ILC's Articles on the law of state responsibility, which recognize explicitly that any state may bring an international claim in respect of the breach of an obligation owed to the international community of states as a whole.[270]

There are now two cases in which environmental obligations have been given erga omnes effect.[271] In the *Whaling Case*, Judge Trindade noted that 'The [ICRW] concerns a matter of general or common interest, and is to be implemented collectively by States Parties, thus contributing to the public order of the oceans.'[272] The Court's judgment did not question Australia's standing to bring the case, which concerned compliance with the 1946 ICRW. In the *South China Sea Arbitration* obligations with respect to the marine environment under Part XII of of the 1982 UNCLOS were found to apply 'to all States with respect to the marine environment in all maritime areas, both inside the national jurisdiction of States and beyond it.'[273] Once again the standing of the applicant state party with respect to these claims was not questioned.

[269] ICJ Reports (1970) 3. See also *East Timor Case*, ICJ Reports (1995) 2, para 29, where the Court holds that self-determination has an *erga omnes* character.

[270] *ILC Rept* (2001) GAOR A/56/10, Article 48. See *infra*, Ch 4, section 2(5) and *Obligation to Prosecute or Extradite (Belgium v Senegal)* (2012) ICJ Reports, paras 68–70.

[271] See also Juge Weeramantry, dissenting, *Gabčíkovo-Nagymaros Case*, ICJ Reports (1997) 7.

[272] Separate Opinion, *Whaling Case, Declaration of Intervention by New Zealand*, Order of 6 February 2013, at para. 71.

[273] *South China Sea Arbitration*, PCA (2016) paras 939–41.

For various reasons considered more fully in Chapter 4, it may be right to take a cautious view of the *erga omnes* character of environmental obligations when the question to be determined is one of standing to bring proceedings before an international court, but the case law shows that treaty provisions and customary obligations which concern protection of the global environment will have an *erga omnes* character.[274]

The idea that some legal obligations are owed to the international community as a whole can be viewed from a broader perspective, however. Characterization of issues such as climate change and biological diversity as the 'common concern of humankind' is important in this context because it places them on the international agenda and declares them to be a legitimate object of international regulation and supervision, thereby overriding the reserved domain of domestic jurisdiction or the possible contention that they relate to economic activities and resources which fall mainly within the exclusive territorial sovereignty of individual states.[275] The concept is more than a rhetorical gesture, moreover. What gives such obligations a real *erga omnes* character is not that all states have standing before the ICJ in the event of breach, but that the international community can hold individual states accountable for compliance with their obligations through institutions such as the COP to the 1992 Climate Change Convention,[276] or other comparable bodies endowed, whether by treaty or UN General Assembly resolution, with supervisory powers.[277] The 1985 Ozone Convention and 1987 Montreal Protocol provide perhaps the best-developed examples of the exercise of *erga omnes partes* rights through the institutions set up by those agreements.[278] The concept of the common heritage of mankind represents another parallel development in the international management of mineral resources of the deep seabed, outer space, and possibly, Antarctica.[279] Multilateral accountability of this kind is considered more fully in Chapter 4, but it is clearly central to the notion of *erga omnes* global environmental responsibilities considered here.

4(3) COMMON BUT DIFFERENTIATED RESPONSIBILITY

It should not be assumed that international law always applies equally to all states. In practice, distinctions have been drawn most often between developed and developing states. Usually this entails acknowledging contextual differences, notably the differing capabilities of states and the level of diligence which can reasonably be expected when controlling environmental risks;[280] more rarely the normative treatment of developed and developing states is specifically differentiated, as in the principle of 'common but differentiated responsibility' elaborated by Principle 7 of the Rio Declaration in the following terms:

> States shall co-operate in a spirit of global partnership to conserve, protect and restore the health and integrity of the Earth's ecosystem. In view of the different contributions to global

274 See *infra*, Ch 4, section 2(5).

275 *Supra*, section 3(1)(c).

276 Article 7(2)(e) and Article 10; *infra*, Ch 6.

277 See *infra*, Ch 4.

278 *Infra*, Ch 4, section 3(3).

279 See *infra*, section 3(1) and Kiss, 175 *Recueil des Cours* (1985) 99.

280 E.g. in the 1992 CBD, on which see below, and in Rio Principle 2 on which see *supra*, section 2.

environmental degradation States have common but differentiated responsibilities. The developed countries acknowledge the responsibility that they bear in the international pursuit of sustainable development in view of the pressures their societies place on the global environment and of the technologies and financial resources they command.[281]

This provision is principally an obligation to cooperate in developing the law, but it has significant normative value in setting parameters within which responsibilities are allocated between developed and developing states in the subsequent negotiation of further implementing agreements or in the interpretation of existing agreements.[282]

Common but differentiated responsibility can thus be seen to define an explicit equitable balance between developed and developing states in at least two senses: it allows for different standards for developing states and it makes their performance dependent on the provision of solidarity assistance by developed states. In international environmental law the evolution of 'common but differentiated responsibility' can best be observed in the 1985 Ozone and 1992 Climate Change Conventions and the 1992 CBD.[283] The commitments undertaken in these treaties are dependent on further elaboration and agreement in protocols and agreements such as those concluded at Montreal in 1987, Kyoto in 1997, Nagoya in 2010 and Paris in 2015. The very widespread ratification of all these treaties, and the terms on which subsequent negotiations have been conducted, point to near universal acceptance of the principle of common but differentiated responsibility for global environmental change, but there are disagreements on how it should be implemented.

Those disagreements are most evident in the post-Kyoto climate change negotiations. The concept of common but differentiated responsibility is one of the cornerstones of the 1992 UNFCCC and 1997 Kyoto Protocol.[284] In that context it has relieved developing States of any obligation to constrain greenhouse gas emissions, including the rapidly rising CO2 emissions generated by China and India, but the science shows that climate change cannot be averted on this basis. Thus a key issue in the climate negotiations which culminated in the 2015 Paris Agreement was whether to preserve the architecture of historic responsibility agreed at Kyoto, or to rethink assumptions about who must take responsibility for reducing greenhouse gas emissions in future. In order to stabilize anthropogenic emissions and constrain further rises in global temperature significant restructuring of the existing regime was essential.[285]

The 2015 Paris Agreement recognizes as much. All parties agreed to make 'ambitious efforts' 'to aim to reach global peaking of greenhouse gas emissions as soon as

[281] See also Convention on Climate Change, Article 3(1) and 1987 Montreal Protocol, Article 5.

[282] On the role of principles in structuring the negotiation of further agreements see *supra,* Ch 1. On the influence of the Principle 7 in negotiation of the 1997 Kyoto Protocol see *infra,* Ch 6.

[283] The most comprehensive treatment is Rajamani, *Differential Treatment in International Environmental Law* (Oxford, 2006). See also Cullet, 10 *EJIL* (1999) 549; id, in Fitzmaurice et al, *Research Handbook on IEL,* Ch 8; id, in Viñuales (ed), *The Rio Declaration etc,* 229–244; French, 49 *ICLQ* (2000) 35; Atapattu, *Emerging Principles of IEL,* Ch 5; Hey, in Wolfrum (ed), *Max Planck Encyclopedia of Public International Law* (2010) 447.

[284] See generally Rajamani, *Differential Treatment,* especially Ch 6, and *infra,* Ch 6.

[285] Young, in Dryzek et al, *Oxford Handbook of Climate Change and Society,* 629, and see *infra,* Ch 6.

possible'.[286] Developing State parties, including China, for the first time accepted a commitment to reduce their own emissions by making 'nationally determined contributions.'[287] This is less specific than the commitments made by 1992 UNFCCC Annex I parties, but it is significantly more than non-Annex I parties are required to do by Kyoto. To that extent common but differentiated responsibility no longer means no emissions reductions by developing States: it means a commitment to different levels of reduction at different speeds, but with a common goal that all must contribute towards.[288] As Rajamani explains, 'symmetry rather than differentiation is intended to be the central organizing principle of the future climate regime.'[289] What this shows is that the principle of common but differentiated responsibility is not set in stone, but can evolve as circumstances change.

(a) Differentiated responsibility

Although responsibility for global environmental change is common to all states, developed and developing alike, higher standards of conduct are explicitly set for developed states on the grounds that they have contributed most to causing problems such as ozone depletion and climate change and that they also possess greater capacity to respond than is generally available to developing states. The differentiation of standards of conduct between developed and developing states is most apparent in Article 4 of the 1992 Climate Change Convention and Article 5 of the 1987 Montreal Protocol (see Chapter 6). Under the former all parties are required to undertake certain measures, mainly concerned with cooperation and information exchange, while only developed countries and others listed in an annex are bound by any commitments to takes measures to deal with greenhouse gases. The same broad distinction is maintained in the 1997 Kyoto Protocol. The 2015 Paris Agreement makes important changes to this regime, however.[290] Under Article 5 of the 1987 Montreal Protocol all parties are bound by the same commitments but developing country parties are given a longer timescale within which to phase out production and consumption of ozone depleting substances. In some cases these states may even increase production and consumption within that period.

Although the phraseology of Principle 7 is not repeated in the 1992 CBD or in the 1982 UNCLOS, nor is there any explicit differentiation in these treaties between the responsibilities of developed and developing states, in practice contextual differences are recognized. Thus there are frequent references to what is 'possible and appropriate' throughout the 1992 CBD, and Article 6 allows account to be taken of the 'particular conditions and capabilities' of each party.[291] Article 194(2) of the 1982 UNCLOS uses similar terminology, whose practical effect is to require less from developing states

286 2015 Paris Agreement, Articles 3, 4(1). 287 *Infra*, Ch 6. 288 *Infra*, Ch 6.

289 Rajamani, 61 *ICLQ* (2012) 501, at 502. See also McGee and Steffek, 28 *JEL* (2016) 37–63.

290 See previous section.

291 *Infra*, Ch 11 and see Boyle, in Bowman and Redgwell, *International Law and the Conservation of Biological Diversity*, 44–7.

in protecting the marine environment than from developed states.[292] The equitable differentiation of responsibilities is evidently less strong in these two treaties than in those dealing with climate change and ozone depletion, but it is still apparent, and they share some of the elements of solidarity and conditionality.

(b) Solidarity and conditionality

In addition to setting higher standards for developed states, Principle 7 of the Rio Declaration also entails obligations of solidarity assistance to developing states in the form of access to new and additional funds and the transfer of environmentally sound technologies or substitutes. Provisions on all of these matters are found in the Climate Change, Biological Diversity and Ozone Conventions and Protocol, and to a more limited extent in the deep seabed provisions of the 1982 UNCLOS.[293] Their purpose is to help developing countries implement their commitments by meeting the incremental costs and building up their capacity to do so. Trust funds and the GEF [294] provide access to funding for these purposes and for projects likely to result in global benefits, including protection of the marine environment.

The extent of this commitment to solidarity should not be exaggerated. Not surprisingly, the developed states which would have to provide the necessary resources under these treaties have been carefully ambiguous about the terms of any commitments they have made. For example, under the 1992 CBD the undertaking to provide or facilitate access to technology is in most cases dependent on mutual agreement of terms and conditions,[295] making it uncertain how far any real obligations or rights are created. Nor is the provision of financial resources open-ended. The incremental costs to be covered under Article 21 must also be agreed between the developing states in question and the financial mechanism created by the convention. The view of many developed states is that contributions to this fund are in effect voluntary and determined by each party.[296] Similar comments can be made about technology transfer and funding provisions of the 1987 Montreal Protocol and the 1992 Climate Change Convention.[297] It is doubtful whether at best these represent more than very weak commitments on the part of developed states.

Developing states have, however, found a much better solution to the problem of financial assistance and technology-transfer which obviates the need to express their

[292] *Infra*, Chs 8, 9. See also *Advisory Opinion on Activities in the Area*, ITLOS Reports (2011) para 161, holding that 'requirements for complying with the obligation to apply the precautionary approach may be stricter for the developed than for the developing sponsoring States', but compare paras 158–60.

[293] Convention on Climate Change, Articles 4(1)(c) 4(3) 4(5) 11; 1992 CBD, Articles 16, 20, 21; 1987 Montreal Protocol, Articles 10 and 10A; 1982 UNCLOS, Part XI, on which see *Advisory Opinion on Activities in the Area*, ITLOS Reports (2011) paras 151–7. See Rajamani, *Differential Treatment*, 108–18.

[294] *Supra*, Ch 2, section 4(7).

[295] Article 16.

[296] The UK and nineteen other states made declarations on signature asserting that the amount, nature, frequency and size of contributions under Articles 20 and 21 are to be determined by individual states, not by the COP. See Boyle in Bowman and Redgwell, *International Law and the Conservation of Biological Diversity*, 46–7.

[297] See *infra*, Ch 6.

expectations in terms of strong obligations or solidarity rights. A common feature of the 1987 Montreal Protocol, the 1992 CBD and the 1992 Climate Change Convention is that the obligations of developing states to comply with these conventions 'will depend upon' the effective implementation of their provisions on financial assistance and transfer of technology by developed states.[298] While this might just be a statement of the obvious, it could also be read as making implementation of these conventions by developing countries conditional on receipt of assistance from developed states.[299] Agenda 21 makes the same point with regard to the marine environment. It provides that implementation of its provisions by developing countries:

> shall be commensurate with their technological and financial capacities and priorities in allocating resources for development needs and ultimately depends on technology transfer and financial resources required and made available to them.[300]

The effect of making obligations conditional in this way is to give developing states the means to put pressure on developed states. From this perspective it becomes irrelevant whether developed states have a legal duty to provide assistance: if they want developing states to participate actively in securing the goals of each agreement they must honour the expectation that the necessary resources will be provided.[301] It is in this sense that solidarity is a key element of the common but differentiated responsibility of the parties.

(c) An assessment of Principle 7

Principle 7 of the Rio Declaration has to be viewed in the context of negotiated global regulatory regimes, rather than as a principle of customary international law, but it is nonetheless legally significant. It may not provide a basis for interstate claims for global environmental damage,[302] but it does provide an equitable basis for cooperation between developed and developing states on which the latter are entitled to rely in the negotiation of new law to address global environmental concerns. In this sense it is far from being merely soft law but can be regarded as a 'framework principle', as we saw in Chapter 1.

Acceptance of the principle of common but differentiated responsibility was one of the conditions for ensuring the widest possible participation by developing countries in the Rio instruments. It is this consideration which provides the main justification

298 1992 CBD, Article 20(4); 1992 Convention on Climate Change, Article 4(7); 1987 Montreal Protocol, Article 10.

299 Contrast Article 13(2) of the 2013 Convention on Mercury: 'The overall effectiveness of implementation of this Convention by developing country Parties will be related to the effective implementation of this Article.'

300 Agenda 21, Ch 17.2.

301 In 1995 the G77 developing countries expressed concern that 'effective implementation of Agenda 21 on developing countries is severely jeopardized by the insufficient transfer of financial and technological resources from developed to developing countries', 26 *EPL* (1996) 59.

302 A point stressed by the US at Rio and Johannesburg: see UN Doc A/Conf 151/26, vol iv (1992) 20 and UN Doc A/Conf 199/20 (2002) 146.

for differentiation. Consensus on common higher standards would have been impossible to achieve; consensus based on common lower standards would, at least in the case of climate change, have meant failure to achieve any notable advance on the status quo. Principle 7 is undoubtedly preferable to either of these outcomes. At the same time there is a loss of legal uniformity, which may entail higher costs and ultimately weaken the legitimacy and credibility of global environmental regimes.[303] Some of these considerations underlay the US insistence at Kyoto, and subsequently, that developing states should accept greater responsibility for averting climate change in future negotiations. As we will see in Chapter 6, acceptance of that argument is reflected in the 2015 Paris Agreement.

The idea of differentiated responsibility is not entirely new in international environmental law. The obligation to use due diligence in mitigating and controlling transboundary environmental risks already takes account of the differing capabilities of individual states,[304] although to a more limited extent and without the elements of conditionality and solidarity found in Principle 7 and the 1992 Climate Change and 1985 Ozone Conventions. But it should not be assumed that differentiated responsibility applies universally to all environmental risks. On the contrary, it finds no place in regulatory treaties dealing with nuclear safety,[305] pollution from ships,[306] the regulation of dumping at sea,[307] trade in endangered species,[308] or the conduct of activities in Antarctica, outer space, or on the deep seabed.[309] In all these cases observance of common international standards is essential for effective international regulation. In its *Advisory Opinion on Activities in the Area*, the ITLOS emphatically rejected arguments to the contrary: 'the general provisions [of UNCLOS Part XI] concerning the responsibilities and liability of the sponsoring State apply equally to all sponsoring States, whether developing or developed.'[310] Although Common But Differentiated Responsibility ('CBDR') is referred to in the Preamble to the 2013 Convention on Mercury, no differentiation is evident in the substance of the agreement. It is also evident that in the 1992 CBD the element of common but differentiated responsibility is more attenuated than in other global conventions.

Moreover, it would clearly be wrong to suggest that the obligations of developing states in cases of transboundary risk are in any sense conditional on the provision of technical and financial assistance by their neighbours. Any such view would not only be subversive of existing law on transboundary risks but would be detrimental to the interests of developing states themselves. Common but differentiated responsibility is based on the perception that global environmental risks, such as climate change, have

303 Handl, 1 *YbIEL* (1990) 8–10, but cf Sand, *Lessons Learned in Global Environmental Governance* (Washington, 1990) who points out that asymmetrical standard-setting may be the best way of avoiding consensus on the lowest acceptable standards.

304 *Infra*, section 5(2)(g).

305 1994 Nuclear Safety Convention, *infra*, Ch 9.

306 1973/78 Convention on the Prevention of Marine Pollution from Ships, *infra*, Ch 9.

307 1996 Protocol to the 1972 London Convention, *infra*, Ch 8.

308 1973 CITES, *infra*, Ch 11.

309 1991 Protocol to the Antarctic Treaty on Environmental Protection; 1979 Moon Treaty; 1982 UNCLOS, Part XI.

310 ITLOS Reports (2011) paras 158–160, and see *infra*, section 5(5).

mainly been caused by and should therefore be tackled primarily by developed states. It was never intended to be a justification for developing states dumping pollution on each other. Cases involving developing countries, such as *Pulp Mills, Indus River* or *San Juan River*, do not suggest otherwise.[311]

4(4) THE PRECAUTIONARY APPROACH AND GLOBAL ENVIRONMENTAL RESPONSIBILITY

The precautionary approach is a common feature of all the Rio and post-Rio global environmental agreements. Its purpose is to make greater allowance for uncertainty in the regulation of environmental risks and the sustainable use of natural resources. Principle 15 of the Rio Declaration requires that a precautionary approach 'shall be widely applied by states according to their capabilities'. Like sustainable development, the precautionary approach is not limited to global environmental concerns, but encompasses in addition transboundary and domestic environmental harm, and for this reason the principle and its legal status is considered below.[312] For present purposes it is necessary only to note that a precautionary approach is of particular importance in cases of global environmental concern, such as ozone depletion, climate change, or protection of the marine environment, because of the seriousness and possible irreversibility of the risks involved. Its adoption in this context confirms the status of the precautionary approach as an important principle of global environmental regulation.

5 PREVENTION OF TRANSBOUNDARY POLLUTION AND ENVIRONMENTAL HARM

International law does not allow states to conduct or permit activities within their territories, or in common spaces, without regard for the rights of other states or for the protection of the global environment. This point is sometimes expressed by reference to the maxim *sic utere tuo, ut alienum non laedas* or 'principles of good neighbourliness', but the contribution of contemporary customary law in environmental matters is neither as modest nor as vacuous as these phrases might suggest. Two rules can be regarded as customary international law:

(i) States have a duty to take appropriate measures to prevent, reduce, and control transboundary pollution and environmental harm resulting from activities within their jurisdiction or control.

[311] See *infra*, section 5(3). [312] *Infra*, section 6.

(ii) States also have a duty to cooperate in mitigating transboundary environmental risks and emergencies, though notification, consultation, negotiation, and in appropriate cases, environmental impact assessment.

Both rules are reflected in the 1992 Rio Declaration ;[313] in the ILC's 2001 Draft Articles on Prevention of Transboundary harm;[314] in the 2010 *Pulp Mills Case*,[315] and in the 2011 *Advisory Opinion with Respect to Activities in the Area*.[316] It should be noted immediately that neither rule prohibits all transboundary harm, and it is erroneous (and deeply confusing) to refer to a 'no harm' rule in this context.[317] The obligation is one of conduct, not of result. The precedents reviewed below confirm this observation.

5(1) THE RIO DECLARATION AND TRANSBOUNDARY ENVIRONMENTAL HARM

Although as we saw above the Rio Declaration is primarily concerned with sustainable development and the global environment, three of its 'principles' apply specifically to transboundary harm and environmental risks. Principle 2 requires states to ensure that activities within their jurisdiction do not cause harm to the environment of other states or of common spaces; Principle 18 requires them to notify emergencies likely to affect the environment of other states, and Principle 19 requires them to give prior notification and consult in good faith before undertaking activities that may have significant adverse transboundary environmental effects.

On these matters the more convincing view is that the Rio Declaration is restating existing law;[318] it is neither soft law nor mere aspiration. A number of other Rio Principles, although not limited to transboundary risks, are also important in that context: Principle 10 on public participation, Principle 15 on the application of the precautionary approach, and Principle 17 on environmental impact assessment. These principles all reflect more recent developments in international law and state practice, but the evidence of consensus support provided by the Rio Declaration, subsequent codification by the ILC, and the case law of international tribunals, are an important indication of their present status as general international law.[319] Taken as a whole, the Rio Declaration is a more significant statement of the law on transboundary environmental harm than the Stockholm Declaration, and it has provided a strong starting point for the further elaboration of this part of international environmental law by the ILC and ICJ.

[313] See *infra*, section 5(1). [314] See *infra*, section 5(2). [315] ICJ Reports (2010) 14, para 101.

[316] ITLOS Reports (2011) paras 110–150.

[317] See e.g. *Iron Rhine Case*, PCA (2005) para 59; *Indus Waters Kishenganga Arbitration*, PCA (2013) Partial Award, para 451, and Final Award, para 112; *Border Activities/San Juan River Case*, ICJ Reports (2015) 665, para 118, and *infra*, section 5(4) and literature cited there.

[318] See *infra*, sections 5–8.

[319] On Principle 10 see *infra*, Ch 5. On Principles 15 and 17 see *infra*, sections 6 and 7.

5(2) THE INTERNATIONAL LAW COMMISSION

Transboundary environmental harm first featured on the agenda of the ILC in 1978 under the improbable title of 'Liability for Injurious Consequences of Acts Not Prohibited by International Law'.[320] The Commission's early work on this topic was fundamentally misconceived, and is of no real value to an understanding of the subject,[321] but Draft Articles proposed in 1996 afforded a more realistic view of the law.[322] There were three elements—prevention, cooperation, and strict liability for damage. In the absence of any consensus on the latter topic, the Commission decided to postpone further work on liability. Amended Articles on the Prevention of Transboundary Harm from Hazardous Activities were finally adopted in 2001 and recommended to the UN General Assembly.[323]

The 2001 Articles largely codify existing obligations of environmental impact assessment, notification, consultation, monitoring, prevention, and diligent control of activities likely to cause transboundary harm. These Articles are based on existing precedents. They draw on case law, treaties, the Rio Declaration, the quite elaborate regime established for the marine environment by the 1982 UNCLOS, the 1991 Espoo Convention, and the ILC's own Articles on protection of international watercourses. The Articles on non-discriminatory access to justice and other procedures in transboundary cases and on provision of information to the public also reflect developments in state practice, treaties, and in other codifications.[324] On all of these matters the 2001 Articles offer an authoritative exposition. Not surprisingly, they have been heavily cited by parties to international environmental litigation.[325]

The 2001 Articles apply to all activities within the jurisdiction or control of states which involve a risk of causing significant transboundary harm, including environmental harm. Risk is broadly defined to include both the possibility of unlikely but disastrous accidents, such as exploding nuclear power plants (e.g. Chernobyl) and more probable but smaller scale harm, such as industrial air pollution (e.g. *Trail Smelter*).[326]

320 See II *YbILC* (1980) Pt1, 160, paras 138–9; I *YbILC* (1981) 224, para 10; the special rapporteur's first schematic outline in II *YbILC* (1982) Pt 1, 62 and II *YbILC* (1983) Pt 1, 204, para 10; the special rapporteur's 4th and 5th Reports in (1983) II *YbILC* 201; II *YbILC* (1984) Pt 1, 155 and the *Survey of State Practice Relevant to International Liability for Injurious Consequences (etc)* (1984) UN Doc ST/LEG/15.

321 For critical analysis see Akehurst, 16 *NYIL* (1985) 8; Boyle, 39 *ICLQ* (1990) 1; Fitzmaurice, 25 *NYIL* (1994) 181; for more favourable views see Magraw, 80 *AJIL* (1986) 305; Lefeber, *Transboundary Interference and the Origin of State Liability*, Ch 6; Handl, 16 *NYIL* (1985) 49.

322 *Rept of the Working Group on International Liability*, in *ILC Rept* (1996) GAOR A/51/10, Annex 1, 235.

323 See *ILC Rept* (2001) GAOR A/56/10, 366. [Hereafter referred to as '2001 Articles on Transboundary Harm']. For drafting history see Special Rapporteur's *1st Rept* (1998) UN Doc A/CN 4/487/Add 1; *2nd Rept* (1999) UN Doc A/CN 4/501; *3rd Rept* (2000) UN Doc A/CN 4/510 and Boyle and Freestone (eds), *Sustainable Development and International Law* (Oxford, 1999) Ch 4.

324 On all these issues see *infra*, Ch 5.

325 See e.g. the pleadings in the *MOX Plant Arbitration* (2003) PCA and the *Pulp Mills Case* (2010) ICJ Reports 14. But cf Judge Donoghue's more cautious reference in the *Border Activities/San Juan River Cases*, ICJ Reports (2015) sep op, para 19.

326 Article 2, and commentary, *ILC Rept* (2001) GAOR A/56/10, 387 paras (3) & (4).

Whether there is such a risk has to be determined objectively: 'as denoting an appreciation of possible harm resulting from an activity which a properly informed observer had or ought to have had'.[327] Thus the Articles would not apply to an activity not reasonably foreseeable as potentially harmful. Hypothetical risks do not fall within this standard.[328] Harm is 'significant' if it is 'more than detectable', but it need not be 'serious' or 'substantial'; what is significant depends on the circumstances of each case, and may vary over time.[329] Trivial or speculative harm will not be covered: '[t]he harm must lead to a real detrimental effect on matters such as, for example, human health, industry, property, environment or agriculture in other states. Such detrimental effects must be susceptible of being measured by factual and objective standards.'[330] The Articles do not cover prohibited activities, although there is no reason why a more comprehensive codification should not do so. Ocean dumping of waste, or the export of waste to developing countries, both of which international law now prohibits,[331] would thus not be included. However, the Commission no longer took the erroneous view that activities which cause transboundary harm are for that reason prohibited, a fallacy which underlay its earlier efforts.[332] Most industrial activities which cause environmental harm are not prohibited; what is needed is a legal regime to regulate the risks and consequences of those activities. This the 2001 Articles provide.

The second element of the ILC's codification of the law on transboundary harm takes the form of Principles on Allocation of Loss, adopted in 2006. These complete its previous work on liability and are examined in more detail in Chapter 5. Additionally, Article 5 also reiterates the requirement that states notify and consult their neighbours and take appropriate response measures when accidents involving hazardous activities occur. This Article builds on state practice and the development of specific environmental response regimes for Antarctica, industrial accidents, accidents at sea, and nuclear incidents.[333]

The ILC's work thus reflects the relevant provisions of the Rio Declaration, notably Principles 2, 10, 11, 17, 18, and 19, but formulates them in greater detail. Inter alia, the 2001 Articles recognize the freedom of states to carry on or permit activities under their jurisdiction subject to the obligations set out (preamble)[334] all appropriate measures must be taken to prevent or minimize the risk of transboundary harm or to minimize its effects (Article 3); states must cooperate to this end (Article 4); no such activity may be undertaken without prior impact assessment and authorization by the state in which it is to be conducted (Articles 6 and 7); states likely to be affected must

[327] *ILC Rept* (2001) GAOR A/56/10, 385 para (15).

[328] See *Japan—Measures Affecting the Import of Apples*, WT/DS245/AB/R (2003) para 202.

[329] *ILC Rept* (2001) GAOR A/56/10, 389 para (7). [330] *Id*, para (4). [331] See *infra*, Ch 8.

[332] Boyle, 39 *ICLQ* (1990) 1. In his *3rd Rept* the special rapporteur noted that 'none of the authorities he had surveyed had indicated that non-compliance with the obligation of due diligence made the activity itself prohibited': *ILC Rept* (2000) GAOR A/55/10, para 678.

[333] See *infra*, section 8.

[334] But see Articles 9 and 10, and the discussion of equitable balancing, *infra*, section 5.

be notified and consulted with a view to agreeing measures to minimize or prevent the risk of harm (Articles 8 and 9); relevant information on the risks must be given to the public likely to be affected (Article 14); and measures must be taken to deal with and notify other states of any emergency (Articles 16 and 17).

5(3) INTERNATIONAL JURISPRUDENCE RELATING TO PREVENTION OF ENVIRONMENTAL HARM

Until 1996, international courts had contributed very little to the evolution of international environmental law.[335] Since then, the ICJ, ITLOS, and arbitral tribunals have added significantly to the jurisprudence.[336] Five cases are especially important to the prevention of transboundary environmental harm.

In its *Advisory Opinion on the Legality of the Threat or Use of Nuclear Weapons* the Court took the opportunity to affirm for the first time that:

> The existence of the general obligation of states to ensure that activities within their jurisdiction and control respect the environment of other states or of areas beyond national control is now part of the corpus of international law relating to the environment.[337]

It held that states had an obligation to protect the natural environment against widespread, long-term and severe environmental damage in times of armed conflict and to refrain from methods of warfare or reprisals intended to cause such damage. Although treaties on protection of the environment did not take away or restrict a state's right of self-defence if attacked, states must nevertheless take environmental considerations into account when assessing what is necessary and proportionate in the pursuit of legitimate military objectives.[338]

The Court's first contentious judgment on the merits in a transboundary environmental dispute was the *Case Concerning the Gabčíkovo-Nagymaros Dam*.[339] In this dispute Hungary argued that a treaty to build a series of hydroelectric dams on the Danube had been terminated on a number of grounds, including ecological necessity. It also alleged that in unilaterally implementing the project Slovakia had failed to take account of the ecological problems or to do an adequate EIA. The Court accepted that grave and imminent danger to the environment could constitute a state of necessity,

[335] See *Nuclear Tests Cases*, ICJ Reports (1974) 253 and 457, and *infra*, Ch 9; *Fisheries Jurisdiction Cases*, ICJ Reports (1974) 3 and 175, and *infra*, Ch 11; *Request for an Examination of the Situation in Accordance with the Court's Judgment in the Nuclear Tests Case*, ICJ Reports (1995) 288. Two other cases with potential importance for the development of international environmental law were settled: *Certain Phosphate Lands in Nauru*, ICJ Reports (1993) 322; *Case Concerning Passage Through the Great Belt*, ICJ Reports (1991) 12 and *ibid*, (1992) 348.

[336] In addition to those reviewed below, see also *Border Activities/San Juan River Cases*, ICJ Reports (2015); *Indus Waters Kishenganga Arbitration (Partial Award and Final Award)* PCA (2013); *Chagos Marine Protected Area Arbitration*, PCA (2015); *Iron Rhine Arbitration*, PCA (2005). For a sharp critique of the *Border Acticivies/San Juan River Cases* see Brent, 20 *Asia Pacific JEL* (2017) 28.

[337] ICJ Reports (1996) 226, para 29 ['*Nuclear Weapons AO*'].

[338] See *infra*, section 10.

[339] ICJ Reports (1997) 7 ['*Gabčíkovo-Nagymaros Case*']. See 'Symposium' in 8 *YbIEL* (1997) 3–50.

but it found no such danger to exist in this case. The contention that the treaty between the parties had terminated was also rejected, but the Court held that in operating the works the parties were obliged to apply new norms of international environmental law, not only when undertaking new activities but also when continuing activities begun in the past. The Court referred, as we saw earlier, to the concept of sustainable development and concluded that the parties must negotiate in good faith, 'look afresh' at the effects on the environment and find an agreed solution consistent with the objectives of the treaty and the principles of international environmental law and the law of international watercourses. The effect of the judgment is to require the parties to co-operate in joint management, and to institute a continuing process of environmental protection and monitoring, although only Judge Weeramantry draws this conclusion explicitly. Slovakia's abstraction of over 80 per cent of the flow of water was found to be inequitable and required adjustment.[340] *Gabčíkovo* is still the ICJ's most innovative decision on environmental issues,[341] and no subsequent case comes closer to refashioning the law, but even *Gabčíkovo* decides nothing not already endorsed by the Rio Conference, the ILC, or the UN General Assembly. As we saw in Chapter 1, there are few better examples of courts affirming progressive development of the law not independently but as an integral part of the process of international law-making.[342]

The *Pulp Mills Case*[343] provided another opportunity to affirm the importance of integrating sustainable development and environmental protection.[344] Although ostensibly a dispute about the interpretation and application of the 1975 Statute of the River Uruguay, this decision is important because it addresses all of the main elements of customary international law relating to transboundary harm. The Court thus made findings concerning the obligation to consult and negotiate,[345] and the content of the due diligence standard in customary law.[346] It read into the Statute a requirement to carry out an EIA,[347] which it regarded as general international law. Lastly, the Court stressed the obligation of each party to protect the river environment and its flora and fauna, and to take the measures required by the treaty for that purpose.[348] The burden of proof was on the party asserting the facts, even in environmental cases,[349] although the Court was much less clear on the standard of proof required.[350] The judgment largely reflects the ILC's view of the law, notwithstanding the lukewarm reception the ILC's Draft Articles on Transboundary Harm have received from states. The Court has been criticized for not being radical enough in *Pulp Mills*,[351] but in reality both

340 See *infra*, Ch 10. 341 See Stephens, in Klein (ed),, *Litigating International Law Disputes*, 297–9.

342 *Supra*, Chapter 1, section 2(4).

343 Provisional Measures Order, ICJ Reports (2006) 113 and Judgment on the Merits, ICJ Reports (2010) 14 ['*Pulp Mills Case*']. See Maljean-Dubois, 115 *RGDIP* (2011) 39; Zhu and He, 23 *YbIEL* (2013) 106; Rieu-Clarke, 24 *YbIEL* (2014) 102; Payne 109 *Proc ASIL* (2015) 193.

344 ICJ Reports (2006) para 80 and (2010) paras 75–6, 177, 184. See also *Indus Waters Kishenganga Arbitration (Partial Award)* PCA (2013) paras 445–453.

345 *Pulp Mills Case*, ICJ Reports (2010), paras 146–147. 346 *Ibid*, para 197.

347 *Ibid*, para 204. 348 *Ibid*, paras 169–266. 349 *Ibid*, para 162.

350 See *infra*, Ch 4, section 4(4). 351 See e.g. Plakokefalos, 26 *IJMCL* 169 (2011).

parties largely agreed on the law as reflected in the judgment, which was followed, and in certain respects clarified in the *Border Activities/San Juan River Cases.*[352]

In its *Advisory Opinion on Responsibilities and Obligations of States Sponsoring Persons and Entities with Respect to Activities in the Area*[353] the Seabed Disputes Chamber of the ITLOS sets out its interpretation of the responsibilities of States under Part XI of the 1982 UNCLOS for protecting the marine environment from activities on the deep seabed in areas beyond national jurisdiction. The opinion closely follows the judgment of the ICJ in the *Pulp Mills Case*, reiterating its conclusions on due diligence and environmental impact assessment.[354] It notes how the precautionary approach endorsed by Rio Principle 15 has altered the interpretation of treaties and rules of customary law.[355] The advisory opinion is the only judicial decision to address the liability of States for environmental damage caused by corporate actors.[356] Consistently with the law on state responsibility, liability of a State under UNCLOS 'arises from the failure of the sponsoring State to carry out its own responsibilities. The sponsoring State is not, however, liable for the failure of the sponsored contractor to meet its obligations.'[357] In addition, as the ITLOS reiterates: 'there must be a causal link between the failure of that State and the damage caused by the sponsored contractor'.[358] This case decides nothing new, but, like *Pulp Mills*, it reaffirms basic principles the ILC had previously codified.

Finally, in the *South China Sea Arbitration*, an arbitral tribunal interpreted and applied Part XII of the 1982 UNCLOS to large scale dredging of coral reefs and other activities harmful to the marine environment of the South China Sea. It found that 'Although phrased in general terms, the Tribunal considers it well established that Article 192 does impose a duty on States Parties, the content of which is informed by the other provisions of Part XII and other applicable rules of international law.'[359] This general obligation extended both to 'protection' of the marine environment from future damage and 'preservation' in the sense of maintaining or improving its present condition.' Part XII is 'not limited to measures aimed strictly at controlling marine pollution. . .', but extends to protection of marine ecosystems, endangered species, and conservation of fish stocks and biodiversity.[360] In this respect China's failure to enforce its own laws on fishing and endangered species was an important element of its responsibility for environmental harm.[361] China had also violated Articles 123 and 197 by failing to cooperate with other states,[362] and Article 206 by failing to communicate an EIA to the competent international organization.[363]

Judgments of international courts and arbitral tribunals provide the most authoritative guidance on the state of the law at the time they are decided. The jurisprudence

352 ICJ Reports (2015). See *infra*, sections 5 and 7.

353 ITLOS Reports (2011). See French, 26 *IJMCL* (2011) 525, and *infra*, sections 5(2) and 6.

354 Paras 110–116, 145–9.

355 Paras 125–135.

356 Paras 170–207. See *infra*, Ch 4.

357 Para 172.

358 Para 181.

359 PCA (2016) paras 939–46.

360 *Ibid*, paras 945, 956–60.

361 *Ibid*, paras 961–66.

362 *Ibid*, paras 984–86.

363 *Ibid*, paras 947–8, 987–91.

affirms the existence of a legal obligation to take appropriate measures to prevent, reduce and control transboundary environmental harm; to apply a precautionary approach where the science is uncertain but the risk of harm is serious or irreversible; to cooperate in the management of transboundary environmental risks; to utilize shared natural resources equitably and sustainably; and to carry out transboundary environmental impact assessment and monitoring.

Equally importantly, states parties to litigation before international tribunals, including the ICJ and the ITLOS, have not sought to argue that general international law does not require them to control transboundary pollution, or to carry out EIAs, or to cooperate in the management of transboundary risks or shared natural resources. They have not challenged the standard textbook accounts of the subject or the ILC's codification of the law relating to transboundary harm.[364] Rather, the focus of most of the litigation has been on the adequacy or inadequacy of the measures states have taken, or failed to take—on whether, for example, an appropriate EIA has been carried out, or diligent pollution control laws exist or have been enforced, not on whether they are necessary at all. Moreover, as we saw in Chapter 1, international courts and tribunals have not been unsympathetic to the needs of international law-making on environmental matters using soft law and other declaratory processes. Nor have they been unresponsive to the claims of sustainable development, as we saw earlier in this chapter.[365]

5(4) THE DUTY TO PREVENT, REDUCE AND CONTROL TRANSBOUNDARY ENVIRONMENTAL HARM

It is beyond serious argument that states are required by international law to regulate and control activities within their territory or subject to their jurisdiction or control that pose a significant risk of global or transboundary pollution or environmental harm.[366] This is an obligation to take appropriate measures to prevent or minimize as far as possible the risk of significant harm, not merely a basis for reparation after the event.[367] It follows that states must also take measures to identify such risks, for example by environmental impact assessment or monitoring.[368] The obligation is a

364 With the exception of Colombia in the *Aerial Spraying Case*.

365 *Supra*, section 2(1).

366 See *infra*. On the meaning of 'jurisdiction or control' see ILC Rept (2001) GAOR A/56/10, 383–5. In addition to the state's own territory it includes ships, aircraft, spacecraft, and occupied territory.

367 Article 3, ILC 2001 Articles on Transboundary Harm. See generally Duvic-Paoli, *The Prevention Principle in International Environmental Law* (Cambridge, 2018); Handl in Bodansky, Brunnée, and Hey, *Oxford Handbook of IEL*, 532; Plakokefalos, 23 *YbIEL* (2013) 3; Jayakumar et al (eds), *Transboundary Pollution* (Cheltenham, 2015); Duvic Paoli and Viñuales in Viñuales (ed),, *The Rio Declaration etc*, 107–38. On the origins of this rule see Dupuy in OECD, *Legal Aspects of Transfrontier Pollution* (Paris, 1977) 345; Smith, *State Responsibility and the Marine Environment* (Oxford, 1988) 36ff, 72ff; Quentin-Baxter, II *YbILC* (1980) Pt 1, 246–62; Lefeber, *Transboundary Environmental Interference and the Origin of State Liability*, Ch 2; Xue, *Transboundary Damage in International Law* (Cambridge, 2003); Bratspies and Miller (eds), *Transboundary Harm in International Law* (Cambridge, 2006).

368 *ILC Rept* (2001) GAOR A/56/10, 391, para (5). On EIA see *infra*, section 7.

continuing one: 'It implies the need for States to review their obligations of prevention in a continuous manner to keep abreast with the advances in scientific knowledge.'[369] Although some writers and treaties use the term 'preventive principle',[370] the obligation referred to here is more than a principle—in regard to transboundary environmental risks it is both an obligatory rule of customary international law and the core obligation of most environmental treaties. It has been identified as such in arbitral and judicial decisions, in a wide range of global and regional treaties, and in the Stockholm and Rio Declarations.[371] The 'preventive principle' is derived from EU law where it is not limited to global or transboundary harm. The ICJ referred to the 'preventive principle' in the *Pulp Mills Case*, but not in later cases.[372]

The origins of a rule on prevention of transboundary harm can be traced to the well-known *Trail Smelter Arbitration*,[373] in which a tribunal awarded damages to the US and prescribed a regime for controlling future emissions from a Canadian smelter which had caused air pollution damage in the US. It concluded that 'no state has the right to use or permit the use of its territory in such a manner as to cause injury by fumes in or to the territory of another or the properties or persons therein, when the case is of serious consequence and the injury is established by clear and convincing evidence'.[374] This finding relied mainly on the *Alabama Claims Arbitration* for the proposition that 'A state owes at all times a duty to protect other states against injurious acts by individuals from within its jurisdiction',[375] and on the US Federal case law dealing with interstate air and water pollution, which it held 'may legitimately be taken as a guide in this field of international law. . . where no contrary rule prevails'.[376] Reliance on domestic case law by analogy was *not* required by the *compromis*, which called for application of US law and practice only in respect of issues of proof of damage, indemnity, and the regime of future operations of the smelter.[377] The tribunal's use of domestic law analogies is better treated as an invocation of 'general principles of law' referred to in Article 38(1) of the Statute of the ICJ.

This key obligation was first codified in Principle 21 of the 1972 Stockholm Declaration on the Human Environment and then reiterated with minor amendments

369 *ILC Rept* (2001) para (7). See *Gabčíkovo-Nagymaros Case*, ICJ Reports (1997) 7, para 140.

370 See e.g. de Sadeleer, *Environmental Principles*, Ch 2; Crawford, *Brownlies' Principles of Public International Law* (8th edn, Oxford, 2012) 356 (supposedly an 'emergent legal principle'); 1999 Rhine Convention, Article 4.

371 See following discussion.

372 ICJ Reports (2010) 14, para 101.

373 33 *AJIL* (1939) 182 and 35 *AJIL* (1941) 684. See Read, 1 *CYIL* (1963) 213; Rubin, 50 *Oregon LR* (1971) 259; Kirgis, 66 *AJIL* (1972); Smith, *State Responsibility*, 72ff; Quentin-Baxter, II *YbILC* (1981) Pt 1, 108ff; Bratspies and Miller (eds), *Transboundary Harm in International Law: Lessons from the Trail Smelter Arbitration* (Cambridge, 2006).

374 35 *AJIL* (1941) at 716.

375 (1872) Moore, 1 *International Arbitrations*, 485. Eagleton, *Responsibility of States in International Law* (1928) 80, was also cited.

376 35 *AJIL* (1941) at 714. For criticism of the tribunal's approach, see Rubin, 50 *Oregon LR* (1971) 267; Goldie, 14 *ICLQ* (1965) 1229, and for explanation, see Read, 1 *CYIL* (1963) 213.

377 35 *AJIL* (1941), 698.

by Principle 2 of the 1992 Rio Declaration and other Rio and post-Rio instruments.[378] Principle 2 provides that:

> States have, in accordance with the Charter of the United Nations and the principles of international law, the sovereign right to exploit their own resources pursuant to their own environmental and developmental policies, and the responsibility to ensure that activities within their jurisdiction or control do not cause damage to the environment of other states or of areas beyond the limits of national jurisdiction.

Although, as Professor Sohn has observed (with respect to Principle 21) the first part of this principle comes 'quite close' to asserting that a state has unlimited sovereignty over its environment,[379] the totality of the provision, including its reference to environmental damage, was regarded by many states present at the Stockholm Conference, and subsequently by the UN General Assembly, as reflecting customary international law.[380] Subsequent case law appears to agree. In the *Pulp Mills Case*, the ICJ held that 'A State is thus obliged to use all the means at its disposal in order to avoid activities which take place in its territory, or in any area under its jurisdiction, causing significant damage to the environment of another State.'[381] It reiterated that this obligation 'is now part of the corpus of international law relating to the environment'.[382] The Court noted that 'the principle of prevention, as a customary rule, has its origins in the due diligence that is required of a State in its territory. It is "every State's obligation not to allow knowingly its territory to be used for acts contrary to the rights of other States" (*Corfu Channel (United Kingdom* v. *Albania) Merits, Judgment, I.C.J. Reports 1949*, p. 22).'[383]

Moreover, whereas older formulations of the preventive obligation, in cases such as *Trail Smelter*, had dealt only with transboundary harm to other states, Stockholm Principle 21, Rio Principle 2 and multilateral environmental agreements point to international acceptance of the proposition that states are also required to protect global common areas, including Antarctica and other areas beyond the limits of national jurisdiction, such as the high seas, deep seabed, the global atmosphere, and

[378] See 1992 CBD, Article 3; and the Preambles to the 1992 UNFCC; 1994 Convention to Combat Desertification; 2001 POPS Convention; 2006 ITTA; 2007 Non-Legally Binding Instrument on all Types of Forests, UNGA Res 62/98.

[379] Sohn, 14 *Harv ILJ* (1973) 491ff.

[380] See Canadian and US Comments in UN Doc A/CONF 48/14/Rev 1, 64–6. UNGA Res 2996 (XXVII) (1972) asserts that Principles 21 and 22 of the Stockholm Declaration 'lay down the basic rules governing the matter'. See also *Kishenganga Arbitration (Partial Award)* PCA (2013) para 448; UNGA Res 2995 XXVII (1972); 2996 XXVII (1972); 3281 XXIX (1974); 34/186 (1979); UNEP Principles of Conduct in the Field of the Environment Concerning Resources Shared by Two or More States, Principle 3, UNEP/IG/12/2 (1978).

[381] ICJ Reports (2010) 14, para 101. See also *Border Activities/San Juan River Cases*, ICJ Reports (2015) 665, para 118.

[382] *Ibid*, citing *AO on Nuclear Weapons*, ICJ Reports (1996) 242, para 29. See also *Iron Rhine Arbitration*, PCA (2005) paras 222–3.

[383] ICJ Reports (2010) 14, para 101.

outer space.[384] Articles 145, 192 and 194(2) of the 1982 UNCLOS make the same point in relation to the protection and preservation of the marine environment. At the Stockholm Conference, the US stated that Principle 21 did not in any way diminish existing international responsibility for damage to areas beyond national jurisdiction; in its view it 'affirmed existing rules'.[385] The UN General Assembly also resolved that in the exploration, exploitation, and development of their natural resources, 'states must not produce significant harmful effects in zones situated outside their national jurisdiction'.[386] An important consequence of this changed perspective, again reiterated in Rio Principle 2, is that the obligation to prevent, reduce and control environmental harm is no longer solely bilateral in character but in relation to the marine environment or the global atmosphere it benefits the international community as a whole and to that extent operates *erga omnes*.[387]

Principle 2 is neither an absolute prohibition on environmental damage, nor does it confer on states absolute freedom to exploit natural resources. The reference to a state's own developmental policies confirms an existing and necessary reconciliation with the principle of sustainable development and the sovereignty of states over their own natural resources. It is an exaggeration to see this qualification as eviscerating the responsibility of states in international law for the control and prevention of environmental harm.[388] Like sustainable development, it requires integration or accommodation of both economic development and environmental protection.[389] This feature of Principle 2 must be taken into account when interpreting both parts of the rule which it articulates.

In practice, the relationship between the sovereign use of resources and the responsibility for environmental protection has usually been negotiated in the context of specific sectoral treaty regimes, and it may differ in different contexts. Treaties dealing with climate change or land-based sources of marine pollution thus allow more latitude for resource use which causes environmental damage than do those concerned with pollution from ships or nuclear accidents.[390] In its work on international watercourses the ILC found it a challenge to determine the right balance between the freedom to make equitable use of an international watercourse and the obligation to prevent harm to other riparian states.[391] Both the need for balance and

[384] 1967 Outer Space Treaty; 1979 Moon Treaty; 1982 UNCLOS, Articles 145, 192, 194; 1985 Ozone Convention, Article 2; 1991 Protocol to the Antarctic Treaty on Environmental Protection; 1992 Climate Change Convention, Articles 2, 4. See Sohn, 14 *Harv ILJ* (1973) 423; Smith, *State Responsibility and the Marine Environment* (Oxford, 1988) 76ff; Charney, in Francioni and Scovazzi (eds), *International Responsibility for Environmental Harm* (Dordrecht, 1991) 149; Pineschi, in Francioni and Scovazzi (eds), *International Law for Antarctica* (2nd edn, The Hague, 1996) 261; Mayer, 5 *Climate Law* (2015) 1.

[385] *Rept of the UN Conference on the Human Environment*, UN Doc A/CONF/48/14/Rev 1, (1972) para 327.

[386] UNGA Res 2995 XXVII (1972).

[387] *Supra*, section 4(2) on *erga omnes* obligations.

[388] *Contra*, Pallemaerts, in Sands, *Greening International Law*, 5–7.

[389] *Supra*, section 2(1).

[390] *Infra*, Chs 6–9.

[391] Compare Articles 5 and 7 of the 1997 UN Watercourses Convention with the same articles in the ILC's 1994 Draft Convention, UN Doc A/CN 4/L492 and Add 1 and the ILA's 1966 Helsinki Rules, Article 10(1) and *infra*, Ch 10.

its context-specific nature in individual situations make it more difficult, but certainly not impossible, to apply Principle 2 in legal disputes between states. Despite its age, the *Trail Smelter Arbitration* illustrates very well how a judicial or arbitral tribunal can find ways of reconciling the prevention of transboundary harm with economic development. In the following sections we consider how this can be achieved, and how Principle 2 should be interpreted.

5(5) THE OBLIGATION TO USE DUE DILIGENCE

Whatever the significance of *Trail Smelter* and older judicial precedents may have been, the primary purpose of Principle 2 and of treaties such as the 1982 UNCLOS, the 1997 Kyoto Protocol, or the 1994 Convention on Nuclear Safety is to ensure that states take measures to prevent or minimize harm to the environment of other states or the global environment.[392] The ILC Draft Articles require states to take 'all appropriate measures to prevent or minimise the risk of significant transboundary harm'.[393] In its *Pulp Mills* judgment the ICJ reaffirmed that a state must use 'all of the means at its disposal' for this purpose.[394] Even in *Trail Smelter*, Canada was ordered by the tribunal to take measures to prevent or reduce future injury.[395] What these formulations imply is an obligation to act with due diligence.[396]

What does the exercise of due diligence entail? Due diligence is a 'variable concept' which may change over time and differ in respect of different risks,[397] but the case law has identified the following elements:[398]

- 'adoption of reasonably appropriate rules and measures'
- 'a certain level of vigilance in their enforcement'
- 'the exercise of administrative control applicable to public and private operators, such as the monitoring of activities undertaken by such operators'
- 'careful consideration of the technology to be used'
- 'the standard of due diligence has to be more severe for the riskier activities.'

[392] See e.g 1982 UNCLOS, Article 194; 1991 Convention on Transboundary Environmental Impact Assessment, Article 2(1) and later chapters, especially 6, 7, 8, 9, and 10.

[393] 2001 ILC Articles on Prevention of Transboundary Harm, Article 3, *ILC Ybk* 2001 Vol II (2) 144–170.

[394] ICJ Reports (2010) para 101. See also *AO with Respect to Activities in the Area*, ITLOS Reports (2011) paras 110–12.

[395] See final award at 35 *AJIL* (1941) 684.

[396] *ILC Rept* (2000) GAOR A/55/10, para 718: 'the special rapporteur was of the opinion that "all appropriate measures" and "due diligence" were synonymous'. See also *Pulp Mills Case*, ICJ Reports (2010) para 101.

[397] *AO with Respect to Activities in the Area*, para 117.

[398] *Pulp Mills Case*, ICJ Reports (2010) 14, paras 197, 204 and 223; *Advisory Opinion with Respect to Activities in the Area*, ITLOS Reports (2011) paras 110–120, 131–35; 145–9; *Border Activities/San Juan River Cases*, ICJ Reports (2015) 665, paras 104, 153, 168. See also *AO Submitted by the Sub-Regional Fisheries Commission*, ITLOS Reports (2015) para 129; *South China Sea Arbitration*, PCA (2016) paras 744–57.

Moreover, both the ICJ and the ITLOS have adopted a broad view of what due diligence requires, incorporating within it the precautionary approach, the obligation to carry out an environmental impact assessment, and the obligation to notify and consult other states whenever activities pose a risk of significant transboundary harm.[399]

The ILC commentary summarizes the key points:

'The standard of due diligence against which the conduct of State of origin should be examined is that which is generally considered to be appropriate and proportional to the degree of risk of transboundary harm in the particular instance. For example, activities which may be considered ultra-hazardous require a much higher standard of care in designing policies and a much higher degree of vigour on the part of the State to enforce them. Issues such as the size of the operation; its location, special climate conditions, materials used in the activity, and whether the conclusions drawn from the application of these factors in a specific case are reasonable, are among the factors to be considered in determining the due diligence requirement in each instance. What would be considered a reasonable standard of care or due diligence may change with time; what might be considered an appropriate and reasonable procedure, standard or rule at one point in time may not be considered as such at some point in the future. Hence, due diligence in ensuring safety requires a State to keep abreast of technological changes and scientific developments.'[400]

Due diligence will thus require in many cases the introduction of policies, legislation, and administrative controls which are capable of preventing or minimizing the risk of transboundary harm to other states or the global environment, and it can be expressed as the conduct to be expected of a good government.[401] This is an obligation of conduct, not an obligation of result: 'The duty of due diligence . . . is not intended to guarantee that significant harm be totally prevented, if it is not possible to do so.'[402] In *Pulp Mills* the ICJ rejected Argentina's argument to the contrary.[403] To that extent it remains lawful to operate inherently harmful or risky activities such as nuclear power plants provided they are appropriately regulated and the risks adequately controlled. The same view is taken in the *Advisory Opinion on Activities in the Area*: 'The sponsoring State's obligation "to ensure" is not an obligation to achieve, in each and every case, the result that the sponsored contractor complies with the aforementioned obligations. Rather, it is an obligation to deploy adequate means, to exercise best possible efforts, to do the utmost, to obtain this result.'[404]

399 *Pulp Mills Case*, para 204; *AO with Respect to Activities in the Area*, para 131; *Border Activities/San Juan River Cases*, paras 104, 153, 168. See below, sections 5(3) and 6.

400 *ILC Rept* (2001) GAOR A/56/10, 394, para (11).

401 ILC 2001 Articles, Article 3 and commentary, *ILC Rept* (2001) GAOR A/56/10, 393–5, paras (10)–(17); OECD, *Legal Aspects of Transfrontier Pollution*, 385f; Dupuy, *ibid*, 369ff; Smith, *State Responsibility and the Marine Environment*, 36–42; Pisillo-Mazeschi, 35 *GYIL* (1992) 9.

402 *ILC Rept* (2001) GAOR A/56/10, 391–2, para (7).

403 *Pulp Mills Case*, para 187.

404 Para 110. See also *ILC Rept* (2001) GAOR A/56/10, 391–2, para (7) and to the same effect but in another context, *Bosnian Genocide Case*, ICJ Reports (2007) para 430. See Handl in Bodansky, Brunnée, and Hey, *Oxford Handbook of IEL*, 538–40, and Dupuy, 10 *EJIL* (1999) 371–85.

Although states are responsible only for their own failure to act diligently, not for any failure by the operator of a risky activity to do so,[405] it is the state's responsibility to require the operator to follow national laws and regulations and to enforce those laws. A failure to monitor compliance or to enforce the law is in many respects the simplest and most easily proved failure of due diligence. [406]

Due diligence entails an evolving standard of technology and regulation. This is commonly expressed by reference to the use of 'best available techniques,' 'best practicable means,' or 'best environmental practices'.[407] Comparison with national standards adopted by other states may be a good guide in this context. This approach allows for the standard of diligence to change as technology and operating techniques develop and for new industrial plants to operate to higher standards than existing plants. In the *Pulp Mills Case*, Uruguay accepted that its newly built mill would have to operate to the highest international standards (in that case the EU's) and that it should employ the most up-to-date technology, whereas Argentina's older mills most probably could not be expected to do so.[408]

Another way of identifying what due diligence requires is to look at standards established by international regulatory bodies such as IMO or IAEA. They may be contained in technical annexes or appendices to treaties.[409] The 1982 UNCLOS in effect incorporates the annexes to the 1973/78 MARPOL Convention and the 1972 London Convention by requiring states to give effect to 'generally accepted international rules and standards', whether or not they are independently binding on parties.[410] Alternatively the agreed standards may be found in soft law codes of conduct, guidelines, or safety recommendations adopted by the appropriate international organization or treaty body. IAEA safety standards are a good example. Although non-binding, these are directly relevant to interpreting the phrase 'appropriate steps' used throughout the 1994 Nuclear Safety Convention.[411] Comparable examples in the outer space context include the 2007 Space Debris Mitigation Guidelines,[412] and the 2009 Safety Framework for Nuclear Power Source Application in Outer Space.[413] These can all be easily updated. Industry standards provide a further possible point of reference in the absence of anything else.[414]

405 *AO with Respect to Activities in the Area*, paras 107–110; *ILC Rept* (2001) GAOR A/56/10, 399, para (3).

406 See *South China Sea Arbitration*, PCA (2016) paras 745–57, 960–66. In the *Aerial Spraying Case* Ecuador's principal complaint was that Colombia had failed to enforce its own rules on aerial spraying. Many of the environmental cases before human rights courts are similarly based on lack of enforcement: see e.g. *Lopez Ostra v. Spain* (1994) 20 EHRR 277; *Guerra v. Italy* [1998] 26 EHRR 357; *Fadeyeva v. Russia* [2007] 45 EHRR 10, and *infra*, Ch 5.

407 For a comprehensive definition of the terms 'best available techniques' and 'best environmental practices' see Article 5(f) and Annex C of the 2001 POPS Convention, and Article 2 of the 2013 Convention on Mercury.

408 See the argument of the parties, ICJ Reports (2010) 14. See also 1994 Nuclear Safety Convention, Article 6.

409 See *supra*, Ch 2, section 5.

410 Articles 210–11. See *infra*, Chs 8, 9.

411 See *infra*, Ch 9.

412 Endorsed by UNCOPUOS, 50th session, UN Doc. A/62/20, annex.

413 Endorsed by UNCOPUOS, 52nd session, UN Doc. A/AC.105/934.

414 Roht-Arriaza, 6 *YbIEL* 107 (1995).

In the *MOX Plant Case* the core of the UK's response to Ireland's claims was that it had fully complied with the relevant international standards established by the IAEA. For its part Ireland pointed instead to applicable regional standards, including EU law.[415] In *Pulp Mills*, Uruguay successfully built its case around the argument that waste discharges from the mill complied in every respect with water quality standards established by the River Uruguay Commission and with Uruguay's own discharge limits.

At the same time, reliance on internationally agreed standards has drawbacks. The most obvious is that states may have agreed standards which represent the lowest common denominator rather than the best available techniques. This has sometimes been a problem with IMO's regulation of shipping standards,[416] and it is true of climate change.[417] The argument that compliance with agreed standards of pollution control is not necessarily enough to satisfy the more general duty of due diligence has been tried and, so far, it has not been successful.[418] The more subtle objection is that overly prescriptive regulation can become an impediment to further technological advance, in some cases resulting in fossilization rather than evolution.[419]

By requiring states to use the 'best practicable means at their disposal and in accordance with their capabilities' Article 194(1) of the 1982 UNCLOS illustrates how the concerns of less developed states about older technology and lack of regulatory capacity can also be accommodated within a flexible model of due diligence. Similarly, Article 2 of the 1972 London Convention required parties to take effective measures 'according to their scientific, technical and economic capabilities', while the 2013 Convention on Mercury defines best available techniques ('BAT') by reference to 'economic and technical considerations for a given Party'.[420] However, there are dangers in pressing this point too far if the result is that developing states remain free to pollute other developing states. In the *Pulp Mills Case*, Uruguay—a developing state—made no attempt to dispute Argentina's claim that the applicable standard was state-of-the-art technology that would meet the most demanding regulatory requirements anywhere else. The standard of comparison was the EU, Canada and the US, not other developing countries.[421] The 1982 UNCLOS recognizes the same point by allowing parties less flexibility under Article 194 where the harm is to other states than in cases of pollution affecting common spaces. The argument that developing countries should be free to operate substandard oil tankers or nuclear power plants is even less attractive, and it finds no support in IMO or IAEA regulations, the 1973/78 MARPOL

415 But the EC disagreed: see *Commission of the European Communities v Ireland*, Case-459/03 (2006).

416 *Infra*, Ch 9.

417 E.g. the 1997 Kyoto Protocol, on which see *infra*, Ch 6.

418 See Argentina's oral argument in the *Pulp Mills Case*, ICJ Reports (2010) 14.

419 For a cogent exposition of this point see US Congress, *Rept from the National Commission on the BP Deepwater Horizon Oil Spill and Offshore Drilling*, Washington, 11th January 2011.

420 Article 2(b).

421 Similarly, the US has consistently sought to ensure that industrial plants in Mexico operate to the same standards as in the US: see 1993 North American Agreement on Environmental Cooperation. But for examples of a 'double standard' in practice, see *infra*, Chs 6, 8.

Convention, or the 1994 Nuclear Safety Convention.[422] The ITLOS has also rejected a differential standard for seabed mining activities.[423] In the Tribunal's view: 'Equality of treatment between developing and developed sponsoring States is consistent with the need to prevent commercial enterprises based in developed States from setting up companies in developing States, acquiring their nationality and obtaining their sponsorship in the hope of being subjected to less burdensome regulations and controls. The spread of sponsoring States "of convenience" would jeopardize uniform application of the highest standards of protection of the marine environment, the safe development of activities in the Area and protection of the common heritage of mankind.'[424]

5(6) EQUITABLE BALANCING AND IMPERMISSIBLE TRANSBOUNDARY RISKS

As we have seen, the exercise of due diligence will not necessarily prevent accidents or harmful emissions. An important question not addressed directly by the ILC is whether there is ever a point at which activities are so risky to other states that they must not be carried out at all if they cannot be rendered harmless or moved elsewhere. To their codification of existing law the ILC's 2001 Articles on Transboundary Harm add the important modification that states have a duty to negotiate an equitable balance of interests in accordance with factors set out in Article 10.[425] These factors include the degree of risk of transboundary or environmental harm; the possibility of prevention, minimization, or repair; the importance of the activity in relation to the potential harm; the economic viability of the project if preventive measures or alternatives are undertaken; the willingness of states likely to be affected to contribute to the cost of preventive measures; and the standards of prevention applied by those states and in regional or international practice. This is not an exhaustive list and it assigns no particular priority or weight to any factor. The parties remain free to take into account whatever they deem relevant, subject only to their over-riding duty to negotiate in good faith. This approach is more than procedural, however. While not prohibiting all risk creation, it requires the parties to establish an equitable balance of interests as the price for undertaking risky activities.[426] The rapporteur noted that the Commission's work was 'guided by the need to evolve procedures enabling States to act in a concerted manner . . .' and he accepted that in this respect the draft convention was progressive development of the topic.[427] If the parties cannot agree an equitable solution, however,

[422] See *infra*, Chs 7, 9. [423] *AO on Activities in the Area*, ITLOS Reports (2011) paras 158–62.

[424] *Ibid*, para 159. [425] Article 9(2).

[426] See *ILC Rept* (2001) 413ff. See also id, (1996) *Rept of the Working Group*, 306–16; Quentin-Baxter's 'Schematic Outline', II *YbILC* (1983) Pt 1, 223, section 6, and compare 1991 Convention on Transboundary EIA, and ILA, Montreal Rules on Transfrontier Pollution. The ILA's approach is criticized by Quentin-Baxter, II *YbILC* (1983) Pt 1, 209. Compare human rights cases which require states to maintain a fair balance between the interests of affected individuals and the community: see *Hatton v UK*, *infra*, Ch 5.

[427] *ILC Rept* (2000) GAOR A/55/10, para 675.

it would remain open to the proposing state to proceed, even if harm is unavoidable.[428] This does not look like a prohibition on risk creation, but it is possible that certain risks can never be rendered equitable if the costs to other states seriously outweigh the benefits to the state undertaking the project. The argument has been made, unsuccessfully on the facts, in both *MOX Plant* and *Pulp Mills*.[429]

The Commission's commentary is unable to cite any significant international practice in support of a requirement of equitable balancing of transboundary risk other than the *Donauversinkung Case*,[430] and some equally old US domestic cases.[431] There is no doubt that the *Behring Sea Fur Seals* and *Trail Smelter* arbitrations resulted in equitable solutions because that is what the parties asked the arbitrators to indicate in their awards.There is also some evidence that states have, even in more modern times, negotiated what might be seen as equitable solutions to transboundary disputes: agreements concerning French potassium emissions into the Rhine,[432] pollution of US–Mexican boundary waters,[433] and North American and European acid rain[434] all display elements of this kind.

On the other hand it is far from clear that the parties to any of these precedents were acting out of any sense of legal obligation to reach an 'equitable' solution.[435] They may be more convincingly explained as cases in which the parties decided that their interests were better served by negotiating compromise outcomes than by insisting on their strict legal rights. Support for a legal obligation to negotiate an equitable solution can be found in the law of international watercourses, the law of high seas fisheries, and the law relating to maritime boundary delimitation.[436] Whether it is permissible to generalize from these precedents a broader rule applicable to transboundary risk depends ultimately on whether transboundary environmental relations are more appropriately based on equitable balancing than on legal rules in which a balance between environmental protection and economic development is already inherent, but which afford states a more predictable basis on which to protect their own interests.

428 Article 9(3). Compare Draft Article 20, UN Doc A/CN 4/428 (1990) which had provided that 'If an assessment of the activity shows that transboundary harm cannot be avoided or cannot be adequately compensated, the state of origin shall refuse authorization for the activity unless the operator proposes less harmful alternatives.'

429 See *MOX Plant Case (Provisional Measures)* ITLOS Reports (2001); *Pulp Mills Case*, ICJ Reports (2010) 14.

430 In 1 *Int Env LR* (1999) 444.

431 *ILC Rept* (2001) 413–4.

432 1976 Convention for the Protection of the Rhine from Pollution by Chlorides, with 1991 Protocol; *infra*, Ch 10.

433 1973 Agreement on the Permanent and Definitive Solution of the International Problem of the Salinity of the Colorado River; *infra*, Ch 10.

434 1979 LRTAP Convention; 1991 Agreement between the US and Canada on Air Quality, *infra*, Ch 6.

435 See *infra*, section 9(2).

436 *Gabčíkovo-Nagymaros Case*, ICJ Reports (1997) 7; *Icelandic Fisheries Cases*, ICJ Reports (1974) 3 and 175; *North Sea Continental Shelf Case*, ICJ Reports (1969) 3. The Commission's analogy is Article 6 of the 1997 UN Watercourses Convention, on which see *infra*, Ch 10.

There are arguments for and against the Commission's proposed solution. The main argument in favour is that it places some degree of restraint on the permissibility of any activity which poses an inequitably large risk for other states with little or no compensating benefit for the host state. Such activities might even be characterized as unsustainable development. We return to this question in our discussion of nuclear power in Chapter 9. If in these situations equity functions as an element additional to the protection offered by other rules of law, then it can only be beneficial to potentially affected states. If, however, it subsumes and weakens existing rules of law then it may not be so benign, and will tend to favour the more powerful states, even the polluting ones.[437] From this perspective it is worth noting the rapporteur's view that equitable balancing is not intended to dilute the obligation of due diligence.[438] Article 18 also provides that 'The present articles are without prejudice to any obligation incurred by states under relevant treaties or rules of customary law.' Moreover, as in other contexts, equitable balancing may be hard to achieve without compulsory third-party dispute settlement. Many states, especially in the developing world, may feel that they are not well served by a regime which offers little certainty and only the limited assurance of compulsory fact-finding in the event of a dispute.[439] Disputes may also be referred to the ICJ, arbitration, or any other means of settlement but only if the parties can agree.

5(7) ALTERNATIVES TO DUE DILIGENCE: NON-DISCRIMINATION

Non-discrimination is not referred to in the Rio Declaration, but it is listed in the Preamble of the 1992 Convention on the Transboundary Effects of Industrial accidents among 'principles of international law and custom'. In a more limited form it is codified in Article 15 of the ILC's 2001 Articles on Transboundary Harm.[440] At least one writer argues that, in a transboundary environmental context, it is an emerging general principle, widely accepted in Europe and North America, and, albeit with reservations, in relations with developing states.[441] As defined by the OECD, where the environmental application of the concept originated, it entails giving equivalent treatment to the domestic and transboundary effects of polluting or environmentally harmful activities.[442] This is not a restatement of the obligation of due diligence, but neither does it represent a lower standard: in effect it requires states with higher domestic standards to apply the same legal standards to activities with external effects.

437 For critical assessments see Okowa, 67 *BYIL* (1996) 311–14; Boyle and Freestone (eds), *International Law and Sustainable Development*, 79–84. For a more positive view see Ellis, in Bratspies (ed), *Transboundary Harm in International Law* (Cambridge, 2006) 62–64.

438 *ILC Rept* (2000) GAOR A/55/10, para 676. See also the rapporteur's *3rd Rept*, UN Doc A/CN 4/510 (2000).

439 Article 19. For a good illustration of how compulsory dispute settlement can work in these situations see the *Pulp Mills Case*, ICJ Reports (2010) 14.

440 *ILC Rept* (2001) GAOR A/56/10, 427–9.

441 Smets, *Rev Eur Droit de l'Env* (2000) 1. See also Knox, 96 *AJIL* (2002) 291.

442 OECD Council Recommendations C (74) 224 (1974); C (77) 28 (1977); C (78) 77 (1978); C (79) 116 (1979) collected in *OECD and the Environment* (Paris, 1986).

One example of such a requirement is found in Article 2 of the 1974 Nordic Convention on Protection of the Environment, which obliges parties to equate domestic and transboundary nuisances when considering the permissibility of environmentally harmful activities. The principle need not be limited to transboundary pollution, however; in OECD recommendations and decisions it has also been applied to export of hazardous wastes and products, export of dangerous installations, and development aid.[443] Potentially it could have implications for such problems as trade in alien or endangered species, export of genetically modified organisms, or sustainable use of natural resources.

The strongest evidence for a principle of non-discrimination in international environmental law will be found in Chapter 5. Outside the context of transboundary access to information, decision-making, and justice, however, the evidence for a broader application of the principle is sparse. There are some parallels with the principle of national treatment in international trade law, and non-discrimination is also a principle of the law of the sea[444] and international human-rights law.[445] The obvious limitation of non-discrimination as a principle of environmental law is that it provides no basis for restraining transboundary effects of harmful activities in states with weak environmental controls.

6 THE PRECAUTIONARY PRINCIPLE AND FORESEEABILITY OF HARM

As we have seen, the rule that states must not cause or permit serious or significant harm to other states or to common spaces is not simply one of responsibility for injury *ex post facto*. It is primarily an obligation of diligent regulation and control of foreseeable risks, and in this sense it can be said that international law already adopts a 'precautionary approach'. The question then arises: at what point does this obligation of diligent control and regulation arise?

This is a question which can only be answered by reference to the foreseeability or likelihood of harm and of its potential gravity. Some states have in the past asserted that they are not bound to take action to control possible global or transboundary risks until there is 'clear and convincing' scientific proof of actual or threatened harm. As we shall see in Chapter 6, this argument has been used at various times to delay the negotiation of measures to tackle the risk of global climate change, ozone depletion and acid rain. It reflects the formulation of international law in the *Trail Smelter Arbitration*[446] and the *Corfu Channel Case*[447] where there was a known risk to other states. But this formulation makes no allowance for the reality of scientific uncertainty

443 Smets, *Rev Eur Droit de l'Env* (2000) 1, 20–7.

444 1982 UNCLOS, Articles 24, 227.

445 *Infra*, Ch 5.

446 *Supra*, n 371.

447 ICJ Reports (1949) 18–22. See also *Bosnian Genocide Case*, ICJ Reports (2007) para 432.

in matters of causation and prediction of long-term effects, or for the different context of cases concerned principally with responsibility for actual damage. If the high standard of proof applied in *Trail Smelter* were required in contemporary international law, irreversible or very serious harm might occur before the causes could be fully understood or preventive action initiated. This is one of the problems with some of the formulations used by the Court in the *Pulp Mills Case*. In the Court's assessment of the evidence Argentina had failed to provide 'clear,' 'convincing,' 'conclusive' or 'sufficient' evidence of any contravention of the agreed water quality standards.[448] At the same time some states may understandably be reluctant to undertake expensive and possibly futile measures to deal with problems whose origin and character remained uncertain. Others may object to measures intended to protect the environment if there is no adequate scientific basis—trade bans on GMOs for example.

In contemporary international law foreseeability of harm, in the sense of an objectively determined risk, will usually be sufficient to engage the state's duty of regulation and control. This is the position adopted by the ILC, whose 2001 Articles on Transboundary Harm define risk to encompass both 'a low probability of causing disastrous harm', and 'a high probability of causing significant harm'.[449] Thus, both the magnitude and probability of harm are relevant factors; what is objectively foreseeable may vary over time, and will depend on the state of knowledge regarding the risk posed by the activity in question at the time when it has to be appreciated.[450] Moreover, the existence of a risk is not exclusively a scientific question:

> It is essential to bear in mind that the risk that is to be evaluated in a risk assessment under Article 5.1 is not only risk ascertainable in a science laboratory operating under strictly controlled conditions, but also risk in human societies as they actually exist, in other words, the actual potential for adverse effects on human health in the real world where people live and work and die.[451]

These precedents show that a state cannot be required to regulate activities of which it is not and could not reasonably have been aware; equally clearly the same must be true of activities which the state did not know, and could not reasonably have known, to be potentially harmful. Thus, if no state could have foreseen the ozone-depleting potential of chlorofluorocarbons ('CFCs') when first introduced, no duty of diligent regulation and control would arise at that time regardless of their eventual impact. So much is common sense, subject to what is said below concerning a duty to enquire further by

[448] ICJ Reports (2010) 14, paras 225, 228, 254, 259, 262, 264, 265. Compare the approach of Judge Greenwood, who employs a balance of probabilities test.

[449] Article 2 and commentary in *ILC Rept* (2001) GAOR A/56/10, 387 paras (2)–(3). For the ILC's earlier approach, which lists categories of 'activities involving risk' see Barboza, *6th Rept*, draft Article 2, UN Doc A/CN 4/428 (1990). Compare the approach to risk assessment adopted by the WTO Appellate Body in *EC Measures Concerning Meat and Meat Products*, WT/DS26/AB/R (1998) para 184: 'Although the utility of a two-step analysis may be debated, it does not appear to us to be substantially wrong.'

[450] *ILC Rept* (2001) GAOR A/56/10, 385, paras (14)–(15) 387, paras (1)–(3).

[451] *EC Measures Concerning Meat and Meat Products*, WT/DS26/AB/R (1998) paras 179–86, referring to Article 5 of the SPS Agreement.

conducting environmental impact assessments. Risk is a complex concept, however, entailing judgments not only about the probability and scale of harm, but about the causes of harm, the effects of the activities, substances or processes in question, and their interaction over time. These are not easy questions to answer with certainty, even for scientists. Very often, they can be understood, if at all, only after prolonged enquiry and monitoring, as in the *Trail Smelter* case.

6(1) PRINCIPLE 15 OF THE RIO DECLARATION

Determining what the standard of proof should be in the above situations, or who bears the burden of proof of risk, are questions of immense practical importance. It is in this context that the so-called precautionary principle or approach has acquired special significance.[452] Inspired by its use in Swedish and German environmental law and policy,[453] the precautionary principle was first employed internationally in the North Sea Conference in 1984 and later affirmed by EC governments in the 1990 Bergen Ministerial Declaration on Sustainable Development. Based on these precedents, a text proposed by the EU[454] secured global endorsement in the 1992 Rio Declaration in the following terms:

> *Principle 15*: In order to protect the environment, the precautionary approach shall be widely applied by states according to their capabilities. Where there are threats of serious or irreversible damage, lack of full scientific certainty shall not be used as a reason for postponing cost-effective measures to prevent environmental degradation.

At US insistence this formulation favours the term 'precautionary approach' rather than 'precautionary principle' and it requires a high threshold of serious or irreversible harm. During negotiation of the 1995 UN Fish Stocks Agreement the term 'precautionary approach' was again preferred, in the belief that the 'approach' offers greater flexibility and will be less potentially restrictive than the 'principle'.[455] Few commentators regard the difference in terminology as significant,[456] although one

452 For a succinct overview see de Sadeleer in Fitzmaurice et al, *Research Handbook on IEL*, Ch 9. See also Viñuales, 43 *Vand JTL* (2010) 437; de Chazournes, in Ndiaye and Wolfrum (eds), *Law of the Sea, Environmental Law and Settlement of Disputes* (Leiden, 2007) 21; Wiener, in Bodansky, Brunnée, and Hey (eds), *Handbook of International Environmental Law*, Ch 25; Atapattu, *Emerging Principles of IEL*, Ch 3; Böckenförde, 63 *ZAÖRV* (2003) 313; de Sadeleer, *Environmental Principles* (Oxford, 2002) Ch 3; Bechmann and Mansuy, *Le Principe de Précaution* (Paris, 2002); Trouwborst, *Evolution and Status of the Precautionary Principle in International Law* (The Hague, 2002); Martin-Bidou, 103 *RGDIP* (1999) 631; Freestone and Hey, *The Precautionary Principle and International Law* (The Hague, 1996); O'Riordan and Cameron (eds), *Interpreting the Precautionary Principle* (London, 1994).

453 Sand, 6 *Hum & Ecol Risk Assessment* (2000) 445, 448; Boehmer-Christiansen, in O'Riordan and Cameron, op cit, 31; Von Moltke, in Royal Commission on Environmental Pollution, *12th Rept* (1988) Annex 3, 57.

454 For the EC's initial draft see UN Doc A/Conf 151/PC/WG 111/L 8/Rev 1 (1991).

455 See FAO, *The Precautionary Approach to Fisheries with Reference to Straddling Fish Stocks and Highly Migratory Stocks* (1994) UN Doc A/Conf 164/INF/8.

456 See e.g. Freestone, 6 *JEL* (1994) 212; Hey, 4 *Georgetown IELR* (1992) 303.

view is that the precautionary *principle* applies in situations of high uncertainty with a risk of irreversible harm entailing high costs, whereas the precautionary *approach* is more appropriate, it is argued, where the level of uncertainty and potential costs are merely significant, and the harm is less likely to be irreversible.[457] However, actual use of the terms in treaties contradicts any such distinction and reveals instead that European treaties and EU law generally refer to the precautionary principle,[458] whereas global agreements more often refer to the precautionary approach or precautionary measures.[459]

Nevertheless, the attempt to distinguish the 'approach' from the 'principle' points to the reality that the concept of precaution appears to mean different things in different contexts. This is not a subject on which consensus is identifiable.[460] Much of the confusion surrounding it stems from a failure to distinguish the identification of risk from the entirely separate question of how to respond to that risk. Thus to suggest that states shall 'apply a precautionary approach (or principle)' may mean that when faced with scientific uncertainty they must be more cautious about identifying risks, or it may mean that they must act more cautiously by taking measures to deal with those risks. Used in the former sense, the precautionary principle is a potentially transformative development in international environmental law, whose principal effect is to reinterpret the concept of environmental risk in treaties and customary international law.[461] Used in the latter sense, however, it is not clear how 'precautionary action' or 'precautionary measures' differ from the customary obligation of due diligence codified in Principle 2 of the Rio Declaration and considered earlier.[462]

Whether viewed as a principle or as an approach, the essence of precaution is succinctly explained by Freestone:

> The precautionary approach then is innovative in that it changes the role of scientific data. It requires that once environmental damage is threatened action should be taken to control or abate possible environmental interference even though there may still be scientific uncertainty as to the effects of the activities.[463]

457 See Garcia, in FAO, *Precautionary Approach to Fisheries*, Technical Paper 350/2 (Rome, 1996) 53–5 for the most detailed elaboration of the distinction.

458 See e.g. 1992 Paris Convention for the Protection of the Marine Environment of the Northeast Atlantic, Article 2; 1992 UNECE Convention for the Protection of Transboundary Watercourses and Lakes, Article 2(5); 1992 Maastricht Treaty on European Union, Article 174; 1994 Danube Convention, Article 2(4); 1999 Rhine Convention, Article 4.

459 See e.g. 1992 Convention on Climate Change, Article 3; 1992 CBD, Preamble and 2000 Protocol on Biosafety; 1994 Sulphur Protocol, 1998 Heavy Metals Protocol, and 1998 Persistent Organic Pollutants Protocol to the 1979 LRTAP Convention; 1996 Protocol to the 1972 London Convention, Article 3; 2001 POPS Convention, Article 1.

460 See Bodansky, in Caron and Scheiber (eds), *Bringing New Law to Ocean Waters* (Leiden, 2004) 381.

461 *Pulp Mills Case*, ICJ Reports (2010) 14, para 164. See also *Advisory Opinion on Activities in the Area*, ITLOS Reports (2011) para 131.

462 De Sadeleer in Fitzmaurice et al, *Research Handbook on IEL*, Ch 9.

463 Freestone, 6 *JEL* (1994) 211.

This does not mean that science ceases to be relevant in judging the existence of risk, or that states are required or permitted to act on the basis of mere hypothesis or purely theoretical assessments of risk. On the contrary:

> Recourse to the precautionary principle presupposes that potentially dangerous effects deriving from a phenomenon, product or process have been identified, and that scientific evaluation does not allow the risk to be determined with sufficient certainty.[464]

Thus there still has to be *some* scientific basis for predicting the possibility of harmful effects, some 'reason to believe' or 'reasonable grounds for concern'.[465] As the European Court of Justice put it in the *Pfizer Case*, 'a preventive measure cannot properly be based on a purely hypothetical approach to risk, founded on mere conjecture which has not been scientifically verified'.[466] At the same time, the evidence of risk need not necessarily be based on the majority of expert opinion: 'the very existence of divergent views presented by qualified scientists who have investigated the particular issue at hand may indicate a state of scientific uncertainty'.[467]

To summarize the position: if the evidence is sufficiently conclusive to leave little or no room for uncertainty in the calculation of risk, then there is no justification for the precautionary principle to be applied at all.[468] Rio Principle 15 requires only that *uncertainties* regarding, for example, the capacity of the environment to assimilate pollution, or of living resources to sustain exploitation, or the impact of proposed activities, or any other relevant factor, should be acknowledged and taken into account when determining what the risks of harm may be and what controls are needed. If assumptions about harmful effects are to be made they should, in other words, be more cautious, allowing for the possibility of error or ignorance, and in that sense reflecting a better understanding of science, not less science.[469] Another way of explaining the point is to say that the environment should be given the benefit of the doubt.[470] The main

464 EC, *Communication on the Precautionary Principle*, COM (2000)1, 4.

465 See *EC Measures Concerning Meat and Meat Products* (1998) WTO Appellate Body, paras 120–5; 1996 Protocol to the 1972 London Convention, Article 3(1) ('reason to believe'); 1992 Paris Convention for the Protection of the NE Atlantic, Article 2 ('reasonable grounds for concern'); 1992 Helsinki Convention on the Protection of the Baltic Sea Area, Article 3(2) ('reason to assume') and see Gray and Bewers, 32 *Mar Poll Bull* (1996) 768–71 who criticize some uses of the precautionary principle for relying on unsustainable suspicion rather than scientific evidence.

466 *Pfizer Animal Health v Council of the EU* (2002) II ECR 3305, para 143.

467 *EC Measures Concerning Meat and Meat Products* (1998) WTO Appellate Body, para 194. But dissent is not necessarily evidence of risk: it is usually possible to find a scientist to oppose any conclusion of a body of experts.

468 *MOX Plant Case (Provisional Measures)* ITLOS Reports (2001) paras 71–81. See also Uruguay's argument in the *Pulp Mills Case*.

469 Gray and Bewers, 32 *Mar Pol Bull* (1996) 768–71. On the role of science and the precautionary principle see Calman and Smith, 79 *Pub Admin* (2001) 185; O'Riordan and Cameron, *Integrating the Precautionary Principle*, 69; Freestone and Hey, *The Precautionary Principle and International Law*, 97–146; FAO, *Precautionary Approach to Fisheries*, Technical Papers 350/1&2 (Rome, 1996).

470 *Landelijke Vereniging tot Behoud van de Waddenzee, Nederlandse Vereniging tot Bescherming van Vogels v Staatssecretaris van Landbouw, Natuurbeheer en Visserij*, I ECR (2004) 7405, para 10 ('*Waddenzee Case*').

effect of Principle 15 in international law therefore is to lower the standard of proof of risk. Where there is *some* evidence of a risk of serious or irreversible harm, even if uncertainty exists, appropriate action may be called for and 'Lack of full scientific certainty shall not prevent the proposal [to control potentially harmful chemicals] from proceeding'.[471]

Principle 15 stresses that the precautionary approach must be 'widely applied by states according to their capabilities'. This includes application to problems of global environmental risk, such as climate change and biological diversity, as well as to transboundary and national environmental risks, in furtherance of the objective of sustainable development. The 1985 Ozone Convention and its 1987 Montreal Protocol are perhaps the best examples of the application of the precautionary principle or approach in the form found in Principle 15 of the Rio Declaration because they required action on the part of states before the causal link between ozone depletion and CFCs had been conclusively demonstrated.[472] Since 1990 the precautionary principle or approach has also been adopted by a growing number of treaty institutions, or incorporated in the text of treaties, dealing with marine pollution,[473] international watercourses,[474] persistent organic pollutants,[475] air pollution and climate change,[476] transboundary trade in hazardous waste[477] and endangered species,[478] biosafety,[479] and the conservation of biological diversity and marine living resources.[480] In each of these cases uncertainty in the identification of causes and the prediction of long-term effects has induced the parties to adopt precautionary policies, including the phasing out of industrial waste-dumping at sea, the adoption of clean or low-waste technology, the elimination of persistent organic pollutants, and a revised formulation of sustainable yields in international fisheries. Without a precautionary approach, regulatory action might have been delayed pending more compelling evidence of a risk of harm.

[471] See 2001 POPS Convention, Article 8(7)(a) dealing with listing of harmful chemicals. See also 2000 Biosafety Protocol, Article 11(8).

[472] *Infra*, Ch 6.

[473] 1992 Helsinki Convention on the Protection of Baltic Sea Area, Article 3(2); 1992 Paris Convention for the Protection of the NE Atlantic, Article 2; 1996 Protocol to the 1972 London Convention, Article 3; 1996 Syracuse Protocol for the Protection of the Mediterranean Against Pollution from Land-based Activities, Preamble. See MacDonald, 26 *ODIL* (1995) 255 and *infra*, Ch 8.

[474] 1992 UNECE Convention on Transboundary Watercourses and Lakes, Article 2(5); 1994 Danube Convention, Article 2(4); 1999 Rhine Convention, Article 4. The principle is *not* included in the 1997 UN Watercourses Convention.

[475] 2001 POPS Convention, Article 1; 2001 Convention on the Control of Harmful Anti-fouling Systems on Ships.

[476] 1994 Sulphur Protocol, Preamble; 1998 Heavy Metals Protocol, Preamble; 1998 Persistent Organic Pollutants Protocol, Preamble; 1992 Convention on Climate Change, Article 3. See also 1991 European Energy Charter, Article 19.

[477] 1991 Bamako Convention, Article 4(3)(f); *infra*, Ch 8. The 1989 Basel Convention does not refer to the precautionary principle, but the ban on waste trade between developed and developing states adopted in 1994 may be seen as precautionary: see Ch 8.

[478] See *infra*, Ch 11.

[479] 2000 Biosafety Protocol, Articles 1, 10(6) 11(8).

[480] 1992 CBD, Preamble; 1995 FAO International Code of Conduct for Responsible Fisheries, General Principles and Article 6(5); 1995 UN Fish Stocks Agreement, Articles 5, 6, and *infra*, Ch 11.

6(2) BURDEN OF PROOF OF RISK

It is sometimes asserted that the precautionary principle requires the promoter of a potentially harmful activity to prove that there is no risk of harm.[481] It is true that, for example, pharmaceutical companies or aeroplane manufacturers must normally show that their products meet acceptable safety standards before they can be licensed for public use. But this has been true for many years; it is not a consequence of any application of Rio Principle 15 and long predates the invention of the precautionary principle. No one would fly or use medicines unless they had been tested and shown to be within acceptable safety standards.

In international law, who bears the burden of proving that a risk exists cannot be answered dogmatically but will depend on the context in which the question arises. International courts have generally required the party alleging a risk of serious environmental harm to adduce enough evidence to establish at least a prima facie case. They have not taken the view that the precautionary principle necessarily shifts the burden of proof to the party proposing to undertake potentially harmful activities. In *Pulp Mills* the ICJ held that 'while a precautionary approach may be relevant in the interpretation and application of the provisions of the Statute, it does not follow that it operates as a reversal of the burden of proof'.[482] The court rejected Argentine arguments to the contrary. On this view the function of the precautionary approach in international law is not to compensate for uncertainties or deficiencies in the applicant's evidence by shifting the burden of proof. If harm or a risk of harm is alleged it must be proved, to the standard required by international courts, by the party alleging it.[483]

Provisional measures were thus refused in the *MOX Plant Arbitration* and the *Pulp Mills Case* because the applicants failed to establish a serious risk, despite their reliance on the precautionary principle, but granted in *Land Reclamation* and *Southern Bluefin Tuna* because they could do so.[484] But these cases also show that where an environmental impact assessment has not been carried out the promoter of a potentially harmful activity will find it more difficult to rebut evidence of risk, however slender. Similarly, the 2000 Biosafety Protocol is significant mainly because it requires

481 Argentina made this argument in the *Pulp Mills Case*. Compare the EC *Communication on the Precautionary Principle* (2000) 5, which notes that there is no general rule to this effect, but that requirements of prior approval for products deemed dangerous '*a priori* reverse the burden of proving injury, by treating them as dangerous unless and until businesses do the scientific work necessary to demonstrate that they are safe'.

482 ICJ Reports (2010) 14, para 164. The ECtHR'has taken the same view: see *Pfizer Animal Health v Council of the EU*, II ECR (2002) 3305, paras 136–48, 164–73. So has the WTO: see *EC Measures Concerning Meat and Meat Products* WT/DS26/AB/R (1998) paras 97–109

483 See *Pulp Mills Case*, ICJ Reports (2010) 14, paras 162–168, and Separate Opinion of Judge Greenwood, paras 25–26; *Application of the Convention on the Prevention and Punishment of the Crime of Genocide*, ICJ Reports (2007) 75, para 204; *Military and Paramilitary Activities in and against Nicaragua*, ICJ Reports (1984) 437, para 101.

484 *MOX Plant Arbitration (Jurisdiction and Provisional Measures)* paras 53–5; *Pulp Mills Case (Provisional Measures)* (2006) paras 73–7; *Southern Bluefin Tuna Cases (Provisional Measures)* para 79; *Land Reclamation Case (Provisional Measures)* para 96.

the exporting state to carry out a risk assessment: it does not place the burden of doing so on the importing state. None of these precedents suggests that international law requires a state to prove that activities within its jurisdiction or control are environmentally 'safe'—that is not the purpose of an EIA or risk assessment and if it were the operation of oil tankers and nuclear power plants would be illegal—but there is ample evidence that international law does require environmental risks to be assessed, as we will see in the next section.

Nevertheless, there are some circumstances where states have agreed that an activity will be impermissible unless it can be shown that it will *not* cause harm to the environment. Examples include the ban on industrial waste dumping at sea,[485] and the moratorium on whaling, which can be recommenced only with the approval of the parties to the Whaling Convention.[486] The main effect of the precautionary principle in these situations is to require states to submit proposed activities affecting the global commons to international scrutiny and demonstrate that they will not cause harm. This reversal of the burden of proof is exceptional, however. It was quite deliberately not adopted when a precautionary approach to fisheries conservation was elaborated in some detail by Article 6 of the 1995 UN Fish Stocks Agreement,[487] nor does the 2001 Convention on Persistent Organic Pollutants reverse the burden of proof,[488] notwithstanding that both treaties are expressly based on the precautionary approach set out in Principle 15 of the Río Declaration.

6(3) LEGAL STATUS AND IMPLICATIONS OF THE PRECAUTIONARY PRINCIPLE OR APPROACH

How far the precautionary principle as found in Principle 15 of the Rio Declaration must now be applied by all states as a matter of international law is a question which cannot be answered dogmatically or simply. On the one hand, it is formulated in obligatory terms in the Rio Declaration; it is very widely endorsed by states, most notably in Agenda 21; it has been applied or adopted by a growing number of international organizations and treaty bodies both as a matter of policy and in legally binding treaty articles and subsidiary rules. At the domestic level it informs environmental policy and law in Australia, France, Germany, the UK, the EU and certain other states, although the position in US law is less certain.[489] It has also been described as a principle

485 1996 Protocol to the 1972 London Convention; 1992 OSPAR Convention, Article 4. See *infra*, Ch 8.

486 See *infra*, Ch 12, section 4(3).

487 See *infra*, Ch 12, section 3(3).

488 See *infra*, Ch 8, section 2.

489 On the application of the principle in national law see de Sadeleer, *Environmental Principles*, 124–49; Freestone and Hey, *The Precautionary Principle and International Law*, 38–40, 187–230; O'Riordan and Cameron, *Interpreting the Precautionary Principle*, 203–61; Sand, 6 *Hum & Ecol Risk Assessment* (2000) 445; Barton, 22 *Harv ELR* (1998) 509. For the EU's policy on the application of the precautionary principle, see EC, *Communication on the Precautionary Principle*, COM (2000)1; Fisher, in Vos, Everson, and Scott (eds), *Uncertain Risks Regulated: National, EU and International Regulatory Models Compared* (London, 2007); Zander, *The Application of the Precautionary Principle in Practice* (Cambridge, 2010).

of international law or applied as such by the Supreme Courts of India and Pakistan.[490] How the precautionary principle is used in each of these countries will differ according to the context and legal culture, however.[491] It should not be assumed that national law and international law on the subject are necessarily the same.

On the other hand, although the precautionary principle was relied on by Hungary in *Gabčíkovo-Nagymaros* and was referred to with approval by Judge Weeramantry in his dissent, the ICJ made no reference to it, despite a willingness to apply new norms of international environmental law. It is not clear whether the court felt that the environmental risks were sufficiently certain to require no reliance on the precautionary principle or whether it did not regard the principle as having any legal status. Both views are plausible. In the *Beef Hormones Case*[492] the WTO Appellate Body concluded that the applicable agreement incorporated precautionary elements, but it found the legal status of the precautionary principle in general international law uncertain. The EU had argued that it was a principle of customary law, or alternatively a general principle of law; Canada accepted that it was an emerging principle of international law, but the US denied that it had any legal status at all. In the *Southern Bluefin Tuna Cases*,[493] the ITLOS relied on scientific uncertainty surrounding the conservation of tuna stocks to justify the grant of provisional measures to protect the stock from further depletion pending resolution of the dispute. This can be regarded as an application of the precautionary approach, but it can also be explained on the basis that the 1982 UNCLOS in effect requires a precautionary approach to fisheries conservation, or alternatively that a precautionary approach is inherent in the award of provisional measures.[494] The Tribunal took no view on the precautionary principle or approach in general international law, although its references to scientific uncertainty do focus directly on the core element of the precautionary approach as set out in Principle 15 of the Rio Declaration.

There are good reasons for this judicial hesitation. The precautionary approach is not universally applied: states have been selective, adopting it in the 1992 Climate Change Convention and the 1992 CBD, but not in the 1994 Nuclear Safety Convention, the 1995 Washington Declaration on the Protection of the Marine Environment from Land-based Activities, or the 1998 Rotterdam Convention on Prior Informed Consent. There are various ways of responding to scientific uncertainty.[495] There are also different thresholds of potential harm: Rio Principle 15 and the 1992 Climate Change Convention require a risk of 'serious or irreversible harm' before the principle

490 India: *A P Pollution Control Board v Nayudu* (2001) 2 SCC 62; *A P Pollution Control Board (I) v Naidu* (1999) 2 SCC 710; *Jagannath v Union of India* (1997) 2 SCC 87; *M C Mehta v Union of India* (1997) 2 SCC 353; *Vellore Citizens Welfare Forum v Union of India* (1996) 7 SCC 375; Pakistan: *Shehla Zia v WAPDA* (1994) SC 693.

491 Fisher, *supra*, n 487.

492 *Measures Concerning Meat and Meat Products* (1998) WTO Appellate Body, paras 120–5. See Cheyne, 19 *JEL* (2007) 155.

493 *Southern Bluefin Tuna Cases (Provisional Measures)* ITLOS Reports (1999) paras 77–9.

494 See Judges Shearer, Laing, paras 16–19, Treves, para 9.

495 Viñuales, 43 *Vand JTL* (2010) 437, and see *infra*.

becomes applicable, but treaties on the marine environment do not. In some cases, as we have seen, there is a reversal of the burden of proof, while in others it merely lowers the standard of proof, but to what level remains uncertain. A precautionary approach can also be characterized in different ways.[496] Does it require states to act? Does it empower them to act? Does it merely encourage them to be more cautious?

In its *Advisory Opinion on Activities in the Area*, the Seabed Disputes Chamber made three distinct findings about the legal status of the precautionary approach. First, it held that 'the precautionary approach is also an integral part of the general obligation of due diligence of sponsoring States.'[497] This is hardly a controversial proposition. The ILC rapporteur concluded that the precautionary principle is already included in the principles of prevention and prior authorization, and in environmental impact assessment, 'and could not be divorced therefrom'.[498] For Professor Brownlie 'The point which stands out is that some applications of the [precautionary] principle, which is based on the concept of foreseeable risk to other states, are encompassed within existing concepts of state responsibility.'[499] Secondly, the ITLOS chamber also observed that 'the precautionary approach has been incorporated into a growing number of international treaties and other instruments, many of which reflect the formulation of Principle 15 of the Rio Declaration.[500] Again, this is obvious. Thirdly, it concluded that 'this has initiated a trend towards making this approach part of customary international law.' [501] The last proposition is the most debatable.

The view that the precautionary principle or approach is a rule of customary international law is quite widely held.[502] Nevertheless, the uncertainties in its meaning, application, and implications outlined above suggest that the proposition that it is, or that it is not, customary international law is too simplistic. It is far from evident that the precautionary approach as articulated in Principle 15 of the Rio Declaration has or could have the normative character of a rule of law. It is phrased in very general terms and says only that scientific uncertainty is not to be used as a reason for postponing cost-effective measures; it does not say anything about what those measures should be.

Of course, a pattern of treaty provisions elaborating 'precautionary measures' might enable a new and more specific customary rule to emerge.[503] A number of treaties dealing with the marine environment do have such provisions, including the 1992 Convention for the Protection of the Marine Environment of the North-East

[496] See Wiener in Bodansky, Brunnée, and Hey, *Handbook of International Environmental Law*, 604–7.

[497] ITLOS Reports (2011) para 131.

[498] *ILC Rept* (2000) GAOR A/55/10, para. 716.

[499] *Principles of Public International Law* (6th edn, Oxford, 2003) 276. The point is missing from later editions however.

[500] ITLOS Reports (2011) para 131. [501] *Ibid.*

[502] See e.g. the EU's argument in the WTO *Asbestos* case; McIntyre and Mosedale, 9 *JEL* (1997) 221, and Trouwborst, *Evolution and Status of the Precautionary Principle*, 284. Trouwborst sees the principle as the basis for comprehensive environmental protection both nationally and internationally.

[503] But compare Daillier and Pellet, *Droit International Public* (7th edn, Paris, 2002) 1308, who draw attention to 'leur fréquente imprécision'.

Atlantic ('OSPAR Convention')[504] and the 2001 POPS Convention,[505] but in essence these agreements strengthen the existing obligation to take preventive measures or eliminate certain pollutants. They are best understood as an elaboration of the obligation of due diligence, not as some separate species of rule.

More fundamentally, the consequences of applying a precautionary approach also differ widely. This should not be surprising. As formulated in Principle 15 of the Rio Declaration, the precautionary approach helps us identify whether a legally significant risk exists by addressing the role of scientific uncertainty, but it says nothing about how to control that risk, or about what level of risk is socially acceptable.[506] Those are policy questions which in most societies are best answered by politicians and by society as a whole, rather than by courts or scientists. The point was well expressed by the French Prime Minister, M Jospin: 'Appliquer le principe de précaution, enfin, implique que la décision soit prise par le politique. Si le politique doit se fonder pour préparer sa décison sur l'analyse du scientifique, il est le seul à devoir décider. Seuls ceux qui sont responsables devant le peuple sont en situation de faire les choix dont dépend la sécurité sanitaire des citoyens . . .'[507] In the *Indus Waters Kishenganga Arbitration* the arbitrators thus declined 'to adopt a precautionary approach and assume the role of policymaker in determining the balance between acceptable environmental change and other priorities.'[508]

The same point is implicit in the EU's assertion that, in applying a precautionary approach to trade, each WTO member state has the right to establish whatever level of health and environmental protection it deems appropriate within its own borders.[509] It is also reflected in treaty formulations such as the 1992 Helsinki Convention on the Protection of the Baltic, which requires the parties to be 'guided by' the precautionary principle, but leaves them free to decide what action to take.

In some cases states have been more specific. Agenda 21, for example, sets out a list of precautionary measures intended to strengthen protection of the marine environment:

> A precautionary and anticipatory rather than a reactive approach is necessary to prevent the degradation of the marine environment. This requires, inter alia, the adoption of precautionary measures, environmental impact assessments, clean production techniques, recycling, waste audits and minimization, construction and/or improvement of sewage treatment

504 1992 OSPAR Convention, Article 2(2)(a). See also the 1995 Revised Convention for the Protection of the Mediterranean Sea Against Pollution, Article 4(3)(a); 1996 Protocol for the Protection of the Mediterranean Sea against Pollution from Land-based Sources and Activities, Preamble.

505 2001 POPS Convention, Article 1.

506 See especially EC Court of 1st Instance in *Pfizer Animal Health v Council of the EU*, II ECR (2002) 3305, paras 135–73; Douma, 15 *JEL* (2003) 394.

507 *Le Figaro*, 16 March 2001.

508 *(Final Award)* PCA (2013) para 112.

509 EC, *Communication on the Precautionary Principle*, (COM (2000)1, 3. The proposition was accepted by the CFI in *Pfizer Animal Health v Council of the EU*, II ECR (2002) 3305, para 151. See also 2000 Cartagena Protocol on Biosafety, Articles 10 and 11 and *infra*, Ch 13, section 4(1).

facilities, quality management criteria for the proper handling of hazardous substances, and a comprehensive approach to damaging impacts from air, land and water.[510]

Commitments of this kind do show that governments may be expected to negotiate 'precautionary measures' in response to perceived risks, but there is no general principle for determining what measures to adopt.

Although taking a precautionary approach has led to a ban or moratorium on ocean dumping, commercial whaling, and driftnet fishing, it has resulted only in more cautious criteria for exploitation of straddling and highly migratory fish stocks.[511] The precautionary measures required by the 2001 POPS Convention involve stricter controls and reductions in the use of chemicals such as dioxin with the aim of ultimate elimination, but the Convention does not ban them outright or require states to show that they are harmless.[512] The 2000 Biosafety Protocol subjects international trade in living modified organisms to a precautionary regime of risk assessment and prior consent from the importing state, but this is no different from the 1989 Basel Convention, which makes no reference to a precautionary approach.[513] Despite a commitment to take precautionary measures in Article 3 of the 1992 Climate Change Convention there remains great difficulty in persuading states to agree on measures to implement this article.[514] Invoking the precautionary principle or approach cannot of itself determine what those measures should be, or how strong they should be. In the context of climate change the measures adopted so far have been woefully inadequate.

There are comparable differences in national law. Whereas Indian and Pakistani courts are prepared to apply the precautionary principle as law imposing duties on governments, and to spell out precise consequences, most national legal systems view it only as a principle which governments and legislatures may lawfully take into account or be guided by. It has thus been relied on by national courts when considering the legality of laws or decisions or when interpreting and applying them, but not normally as a legal obligation which can be used to direct or require stronger action by governments.[515]

If the precautionary approach is viewed not as a rule of customary law but as a general principle of law then its use as an interpretative tool by national and international

[510] UNCED, *Agenda 21*, Ch 17, para 21. [511] See *infra*, Ch 12, section 3.

[512] 2001 Convention on Persistent Organic Pollutants, Article 5 and Annex C.

[513] *Infra*, Ch 8. [514] *Infra*, Ch 6.

[515] Australia: *Leatch v National Parks and Wildlife Service*, 81 Local Govt & Env Reps of Australia (1993) 270; *Nicholls v DG of National Parks and Wildlife*, 84 *LGERA* (1994) 397; England: *Gateshead Metropolitan Council v Secretary of State for the Environment* (1995) *JPL* 432; *R v Secretary of State for Trade and Industry ex parte Duddridge*, 2 *CMLR* (1996) 361; European Community: *United Kingdom v EC Commission*, I ECR (1998) 2265; *Pfizer Animal Health v Council of the EU*, II ECR(2002) 3305, paras 139–44; *Waddenzee Case*, I ECR (2004) 7405; France: *World Wildlife Fund Geneva v France* ['*Superphenix Case*'] (1997) *Cahiers Juridique de l'Electricité et Gaz* 217; Germany: *Kalkar Case* 49 *Entscheidungen des Bundesverfassungsgerichts* (1979) 89; *Augsburg v Federal Republic of Germany* ['*Waldsterben Case*'] 103 *Deutsches Verwaltungsblatt* (1988) 232. Failure to take account of the principle may be a ground for judicial review, however: see *Association Greenpeace France v France, Novartis and Monsanto* ['*Transgenic Maize Case*'] 2/IR Recueil Dalloz (1998) 240.

courts and by international organizations is easy to explain.[516] In this context the precautionary approach has a legally important core on which there is international consensus—that in performing their obligations of environmental protection and sustainable use of natural resources states cannot rely on scientific uncertainty to justify inaction when there is enough evidence to establish the possibility of a risk of serious or irreversible harm, even if there is as yet no conclusive proof. As a general principle, the precautionary approach may be relied upon by decision-makers and courts in much the same way that they may be influenced by the principle of sustainable development.[517]

It follows that, as in the *Pulp Mills Case*,[518] the transformative importance of the precautionary approach is that it redefines existing rules of international law on control of environmental risks and conservation of natural resources and brings them into play at an earlier stage than before. No longer is it necessary to prove that serious or irreversible harm is certain or likely before requiring that preventive measures be taken. Evidence that such harm is possible will be enough to trigger an obligation or to empower states to act.[519] That was the conclusion of the ITLOS in its *Advisory Opinion on Activities in the Area*: 'The due diligence obligation of the sponsoring States requires them to take all appropriate measures to prevent damage that might result from the activities of contractors that they sponsor. This obligation applies in situations where scientific evidence concerning the scope and potential negative impact of the activity in question is insufficient but where there are plausible indications of potential risks. A sponsoring State would not meet its obligation of due diligence if it disregarded those risks. Such disregard would amount to a failure to comply with the precautionary approach.'[520] To that extent the precautionary approach has redefined the applicable customary international law on prevention of harm.

But in determining whether and how to apply 'precautionary measures', states have evidently taken account of their own capabilities, their economic and social priorities, the cost-effectiveness of proposed measures, and the nature and degree of the environmental risk when deciding what preventive measures to adopt. They have in other words made value judgments about how to respond to environmental risks and have been more willing to be more precautionary about ozone depletion, dumping at sea, or whaling, than about fishing or industrial activities which cause air, river, or marine pollution. They have adopted quite different versions of the principle in the WTO's SPS Agreement and in the 2000 Cartagena Protocol on Biosafety.[521] This does not imply that Principle 15 is not a principle of international law, only that it may mean different

[516] Nollkaemper, in Freestone and Hey (eds), *The Precautionary Principle and International Law: The Challenge of Implementation* (The Hague, 1996) 80.

[517] See *Gabčíkovo-Nagymaros Case*, ICJ Reports (1997) 7; Lowe, in Boyle and Freestone, *International Law and Sustainable Development*, Ch 2, and *supra*, section 2(3). For an example, see the ECJ Preliminary Ruling in the *Waddenzee Case*, I ECR (2004) 7405.

[518] ICJ Reports (2010) para 164.

[519] See *Pfizer Animal Health v Council of the EU* (2002) II ECR 3305, paras 135–73.

[520] ITLOS Reports (2011) para 131.

[521] See *infra*, Ch 11, section 4(1).

things in different contexts and that its implications should not be exaggerated by attempting to turn it into an obligation of precautionary conduct with specific normative implications quite separate from those already required by Principle 2 of the Rio Declaration. Thus, to reiterate, while the precautionary approach helps determine whether a risk is sufficiently foreseeable and serious to require a response, regardless of conclusive proof, it cannot determine what that response should be.

6(4) CONCLUSIONS

There can be little doubt that the need for a more precautionary approach to international risk management now underpins an increasing number of multilateral environmental agreements. In that sense the precautionary approach or principle has become one of the central concepts for organizing, influencing, and explaining contemporary international environmental law and policy.[522] States, acting in their role as international regulators, have to some extent taken it seriously. They have become more cautious about some environmental risks, and the use or misuse of scientific evidence. But unlike national regulators who are subject to judicial review, and who must demonstrate both an evidential basis and proportionality in the measures they adopt,[523] the community of states can neither be challenged when they decide to adopt a precautionary approach in an MEA, nor when they fail to do so. In this context the role of the precautionary principle is essentially rhetorical rather than normative. Uniformity of application is not a necessary outcome and may not be a desirable one given the many different contexts.

The precautionary approach has also had an impact on the way treaties and other rules of law are interpreted and applied. In this context, it is a principle with a genuine place in international legal discourse, whether in interstate relations or in international litigation. Lawyers and courts can, and do, make use of it. Beyond that, the evidence does not support some of the more radical characterizations. In particular, the common but essentially incoherent belief that the principle shifts the burden of proof and requires states to prove that development projects pose no risk of harm misunderstands both the nature of the precautionary principle and its relationship to other rules of international law on risk management. EIA (interpreted in accordance with the precautionary principle), transparency, and public participation all play a more important role in identifying environmental risk and the measures necessary to manage it in a socially acceptable manner. These have proved significantly more effective weapons in interstate environmental disputes or in the hands of NGOs than the precautionary principle ever could. The precautionary principle has been of no value to litigators in any ICJ, ITLOS or PCA case, mainly because none of the cases has involved genuine scientific uncertainty about environmental risk.

522 See in particular de Sadeleer, *Environmental Principles*, esp Ch 4.

523 Compare *Pfizer Animal Health v Council of the EU* (2002) II ECR 3305.

7 ENVIRONMENTAL IMPACT ASSESSMENT (EIA) AND MONITORING

7(1) THE EVOLUTION OF EIA IN INTERNATIONAL LAW

EIA is 'a procedure for evaluating the likely impact of a proposed activity on the environment'.[524] Since its adoption in the US National Environmental Policy Act of 1969, EIA has become an important tool of domestic environmental management worlwide. The object of an EIA is to provide decision-makers with information about possible environmental effects when deciding whether to authorize a potentially harmful activity. An EIA is fundamental to any regulatory system which seeks to identify environmental risks, integrate environmental concerns into development projects, and promote sustainable development. The value of an effective EIA is that it provides an opportunity for public scrutiny and participation in decision-making,[525] it introduces elements of independence and impartiality to the process,[526] and it should facilitate better-informed judgments by decision-makers. It is not a process for deciding whether a project should proceed or how it should be regulated. Those decisions are for the relevant public authority, balancing the information provided by the EIA against whatever other considerations are considered decisive, including economic development. Seen from this angle, it is clear that an EIA need not show that there will be no environmental harm. It will be sufficient if it follows the proper process and provides the necessary information about the project's likely impact.

At an international level an EIA alerts other governments and international organizations to the likelihood of transboundary harm or harm to the global commons. Without the benefit of an EIA the duty to notify and consult other states in cases of transboundary risk would in many cases be meaningless.[527] Although US experience shows that the process can be cumbersome, expensive and cause delay, when done properly an EIA should, inter alia, help governments to foresee and avoid international environmental disputes or harmful consequences for which they might otherwise be held legally responsible.

524 1991 Espoo Convention, Article 1(vi). See generally Wathern (ed), *EIA: Theory and Practice* (London, 1988); Glasson, Therivel, and Chadwick, *Introduction to EIA* (2nd ed, London, 2005); Wood, *EIA: A Comparative Review* (2nd ed, Harlow, 2003) Ch 1; Holder, *Environmental Assessment* (Oxford, 2004); Holder and McGillivray (eds), *Taking Stock of Environmental Assessment* (London, 2007); UNEP, *Environmental Impact Assessment and Strategic Environmental Assessment: Towards an Integrated Approach* (Nairobi, 2004).

525 1991 Convention on EIA, Articles 2(6) 3(8); 1987 UNEP Goals and Principles of EIA, Principle 7; Glasson, Therivel and Chadwick, *Introduction to EIA*, Ch 6. On public participation see *infra*, Ch 5.

526 1987 UNEP Goals and Principles of EIA, Principle 6: 'The information provided as part of the EIA should be examined impartially prior to the decision'.

527 See next section, *infra*.

(a) Rio Principle 17

Rio Principle 17 affords the strongest evidence of international support for EIA. It is formulated in the broadest of terms:

> Environmental impact assessment, as a national instrument, shall be undertaken for proposed activities that are likely to have a significant impact on the environment and are subject to a decision of a competent national authority.[528]

This would appear to entail a process focused on impacts on the domestic and transboundary environment,[529] on sustainable development,[530] specially protected areas and wildlife,[531] and probably also on global environmental impacts, such as climate change and loss of biological diversity, albeit in highly qualified terms.[532] There is also an obligatory and detailed EIA scheme in the 1991 Antarctic Protocol, focused on 'the Antarctic environment or on dependent or associated ecosystems', which could include both the marine environment and global climatic impacts.[533]

The practice of international lending agencies supports a broad interpretation of Principle 17.[534] The World Bank's Environmental Assessment Directive was first issued in 1989,[535] since when Bank-funded projects have routinely been screened for their potential domestic, transboundary, and global environmental impacts. These assessments are meant to ensure that 'development options are environmentally sound and sustainable' and that 'any environmental consequences are recognized early in the project cycle and taken account of in project design'.

The most sophisticated national legislation is found in the US,[536] Canada,[537] and the EU.[538] Through the efforts of UNECE the practice is increasingly common in Eastern

528 See Craik, in Viñuales (ed), *The Rio Declaration etc*, 451–470.

529 See *infra*.

530 UNEP, *Environmental Impact Assessment and Strategic Environmental Assessment: Towards an Integrated Approach* (Nairobi, 2004) and the numerous references to EIA in Agenda 21, *Rept of the UN Conference on Environment and Development* (1992) UN Doc A/CONF 151/26/Rev 1, but especially Chapter 8.4(d) which calls for regular monitoring and evaluation of the state of the environment and natural resources. See also Weeramantry in *Gabčíkovo-Nagymaros Case*, ICJ Reports (1997) 7, 111–13.

531 1985 ASEAN Agreement on the Conservation of Nature and Natural Resources, Article 14; 1990 Kingston Protocol Concerning Specially Protected Areas and Wildlife, Article 13; 1989 Protocol for the Conservation and Management of Protected Marine and Coastal Areas of the SE Pacific, Article 8.

532 1982 UNCLOS, Article 206; 1992 Climate Change Convention, Article 4(1)(f); 1992 CBD, Article 14.

533 Article 8 and Annex I. See Bastmeijer and Koivurova (eds), *Theory and Practice of Transboundary EIA* (Leiden, 2008) Ch 9.

534 Bastmeijer and Koivurova (eds), *Theory and Practice of Transboundary EIA*, Chs 12–14, and on bilateral aid see Wathern, *EIA: Theory and Practice*, Chs 15–17.

535 See now OP 4.01: Environmental Assessment (2013).

536 See Karkkainen, in Holder and McGillivray (eds), *Taking Stock of Environmental Assessment*, Ch 3; Craik, in Bastmeijer and Koivurova (eds), *Theory and Practice of Transboundary EIA*, Ch 5. NEPA applies only to 'major Federal actions significantly affecting the quality of the human environment'. Projects not regulated by Federal agencies are thus not covered by NEPA but may be subject to state law.

537 Canadian Environmental Assessment Act, SC 1992, c 37; Wood, *EIA: A Comparative Review*, Ch 5; Craik, in Bastmeijer and Koivurova (eds), *Theory and Practice of Transboundary EIA*, Ch 5.

538 EC Directive 85/337, OJ 1985 L175, 40 as amended by EC Directive 97/11, OJ 1997 L73, 5. See Kramer in Holder and McGillivray (eds), *Taking Stock of Environmental Assessment*, Ch 5.

Europe,[539] while UNEP and the World Bank have promoted its adoption in developing states, particularly in Asia and Latin America.[540] China adopted a law on EIA in 2002.[541] Although there are differences in the frequency and sophistication with which EIA is used across this range of jurisdictions, there has been a worldwide sharing of methodology and the basic features of most schemes are similar.[542]

It might be said that the practice of states or international banks when dealing with impacts that are solely of domestic concern is not evidence of an international legal obligation to conduct an EIA. Evidence of *opinio iuris* for domestic EIA is confined to Principle 17 of the Rio Declaration, UNEP's soft law Goals and Principles of EIA, and the rather lukewarm reference to EIA in Article 14 of the 1992 CBD.[543] Subject to what is said below about strategic environmental assessment, and excluding specific treaty commitments such as the 1992 UNFCCC or the 1982 UNCLOS, it seems necessary to conclude that at present general international law does not require states to assess effects wholly within their own borders. Moreover, the assessment of global impacts is referred to in such qualified terms by the 1992 Climate Change Convention and the 1992 CBD that it too may be difficult to translate into customary law.[544]

(b) Strategic environmental assessment ()

Principle 17 and most of the treaty provisions on EIA refer only to planned 'activities' or 'projects'. These terms embrace, inter alia, the licensing or approval of industrial, energy and transport undertakings,[545] but would not cover government plans, programmes or policies of a more general kind—whether to develop nuclear energy, or encourage the building of coal-fired power stations, for example. However, at the domestic level strategic environmental assessment ('SEA') of this broader kind has been developed in some of the more advanced jurisdictions.[546] Canada and the US have, for example, subjected free-trade agreements to an EIA.[547] The EU has a directive on

[539] Most East European states are parties to the 1991 Espoo Convention. See generally Winter (ed), *European Environmental Law: A Comparative Perspective* (Aldershot, 1996) Ch 5.

[540] See Wathern, *EIA: Theory and Practice*, Ch 13; Lin and Kurukulasuriya (eds), *UNEP's New Way Forward: Environmental Law and Sustainable Development* (UNEP, 1995) 259.

[541] 2002 Law of the People's Republic of China on the Evaluation of Environmental Effects, with implementing regulation of 2006 on public participation. See *South China Sea Arbitration*, PCA (2016).

[542] Robinson, 19 *Boston Coll Env Aff LR* (1992) 594; Bastmeijer and Koivurova (eds), *Theory and Practice of Transboundary EIA*, Ch 15. For a comprehensive study see UNEP, *Assessing Environmental Impacts: A Global Review of Legislation* (Nairobi, 2018).

[543] *Border Activities/San Juan River Cases*, ICJ Reports (2015) 665, para 163: Article 14 of the CBD 'does not create an obligation to carry out an environmental impact assessment before undertaking an activity that may have significant adverse effects on biological diversity.'

[544] But for the contrary conclusion on climate change see Mayer, 68 *ICLQ* (2019) 271, and see also *infra*, Ch 6, section 4(6).

[545] See the activities listed in the 1991 Convention on Transboundary EIA, Annex 1.

[546] See generally UNEP, *EIA and SEA: Towards an Integrated Approach* (Nairobi, 2004); Sadler et al (eds), *Handbook on SEA* (2010, London); Fischer, *Theory and Practice of SEA: Towards a More Systematic Approach* (London, 2007); Dalal-Clayton and Sadler, *SEA: A Sourcebook and Reference Guide to International Experience* (London, 2005).

[547] US Executive Order 13141 (1999) 39 *ILM* (2000) 766. Canada also conducted an EIA of the NAFTA.

SEA.[548] China and a number of developing countries have laws on the subject.[549] A Protocol on Strategic Environmental Assessment has extended the scope of the 1991 EspooConvention.[550]

Article 2(7) of the 1991 Espoo Convention provided for parties to 'endeavour' to apply EIA to 'policies, plans and programmes', but the 2003 Protocol has significantly broadened the obligations of states parties in this respect. It applies in full only to 'plans and programmes', but 'policies and legislation' are covered to a more limited extent.[551] Unlike the Convention, which applies only to 'any impact, *not exclusively of a global nature*, within an area under the jurisdiction of a party. . . .,'[552] the protocol is not limited to transboundary effects.[553] Article 4 requires an SEA for plans and programmes, relating inter alia to energy, forestry, and industry, which are likely to have 'significant effects' on inter alia health, climate, water, and biodiversity,[554] so its potential relevance to climate change is obvious. The 1992 UNFCCC also requires parties to take climate change into account when formulating 'social, economic and environmental policies and actions'.[555]

The 2003 Protocol additionally requires parties to promote SEA in international organizations and 'decision-making processes' (presumably treaty conferences).[556] The protocol's strong provision for public participation will represent a considerable expansion of environmental democracy in many states and international organizations if fully implemented.[557]

7(2) TRANSBOUNDARY EIA

International support for transboundary EIA[558] originated in a series of OECD recommendations which relied on the principle of non-discrimination.[559] UNEP also included an article in its 1987 soft law guidelines.[560] Article 12 provided for neighbouring states to be notified when an EIA indicates the likelihood of significant transboundary environmental effects. Many states now make some provision for transboundary

[548] Directive 2001/42/EC, OJ l 197 (2001). In *R (ex parte Greenpeace Ltd) v Secretary of State for Trade and Industry* [2007] EWHC 311 the UK's plans for nuclear power were successfully challenged.

[549] OECD, *SEA in Development Practice: A Review of Recent Experience* (OECD, 2012) 26–8.

[550] See De Mulder, 20 *RECIEL* (2011) 232; Marsden and De Mulder 'SEA and Sustainability in Europe' in Marsden and Koivurova (eds), *Transboundary EIA in the EU: The Espoo Convention and its Kiev Protocol on SEA* (London, 2011) 219.

[551] Article 13.

[552] Article 1(viii)

[553] Article 10.

[554] See the definition of environmental effects in Article 2(7).

[555] Article 4(1)(f).

[556] Articles 3(5), 4.

[557] See Article 8. On public participation see *infra*, Ch 5.

[558] See Bastmeijer and Koivurova (eds), *Theory and Practice of Transboundary EIA* (Leiden, 2008); Craik, *The International Law of Environmental Impact Assessment* (Cambridge, 2008); Elias, in Fitzmaurice et al, *Research Handbook on IEL* (Cheltenham, 2010) Ch 11.

[559] OECD Council Recommendations C (74) 224 (1974) para 6; C (77) 28 (1977) paras 8–10; C(78) 77 (1978); C (79) 116 (1979) collected in *OECD and the Environment* (Paris, 1986). Reliance on non-discrimination as a basis for transboundary EIA in North America is reviewed by Knox, 96 *AJIL* (2002) 291. However, this article's view of the relationship between EIA and Stockholm Principle 21 should be treated with caution.

[560] 1987 Goals and Principles of EIA, Principle 12.

EIA.[561] US courts have allowed standing for Canadian plaintiffs affected by oil development in Alaska to challenge the adequacy of an EIA under the NEPA.[562] They have also held that the legislation applies to Federal actions abroad, including waste disposal in Antarctica, highway construction in Central America, and the spraying of herbicides on marijuana and poppy crops in Mexico.[563] In Canada a federal court granted mandamus requiring extraterritorial impacts of a dam to be assessed.[564] Both states are party to an Air Quality Agreement of 1991 which requires them to assess any activity likely to cause transboundary air pollution,[565] while the 1993 North American Agreement on Environmental Cooperation ('NAAEC') commits Canada, the US, and Mexico to assess transboundary environmental effects when 'appropriate',[566] but no progress has yet been made in negotiating an agreement.[567]

The 1991 Espoo Convention remains the most comprehensive agreement on the subject.[568] At the time of writing it had forty-five mainly European parties, including the EU, but also Canada and Kazakhstan.[569] It has provided a model for amendment of the EU directive on EIA,[570] and for some harmonization of European law and practice on transboundary EIA.[571] UK regulations now require assessment of extraterritorial impacts, but in practice these had previously been considered where relevant. When a public hearing was held into the licensing of a proposed nuclear waste dump at Sellafield, bordering the Irish Sea, Ireland made representations.[572] The evidence of possible transboundary effects was one factor in the British government's decision to refuse the plant a licence.

561 See UN, *Current Policies, Strategies and Aspects of Environmental Impact Assessment in a Transboundary Context* (New York, 1997). International and regional practice is reviewed in Bastmeijer and Koivurova (eds), *Theory and Practice of Transboundary EIA*.

562 *Wilderness Society v Morton* 463 F 2d 1261 (1972).

563 *Environmental Defense Fund Inc v Massey* 986 F 2d 528 (1993); *Sierra Club v Adams* 578 F 2d 389 (1978); *National Organization for the Reform of Marijuana Laws v US Dept of State* 452 F Supp 1226 (1978). But other cases take different views: see *Natural Resources Defense Council Inc v Nuclear Regulatory Commissions* 647 F 2d 1345 (1981); *NEPA Coalition of Japan v Aspin* 837 F Supp 466 (1993); *Greenpeace v Stone* 748 F Supp 749 (1990); *People of Saipan v US Dept of Interior* 356 F Supp 645 (1973) and Knox, 96 *AJIL* (2002) 298–9 who reviews the literature.

564 *Canadian Wildlife Federation v Minister of Environment and Saskatchewan Water Comp* (1989) 3 FC 309 (TD). The 1992 Environmental Assessment Act (s 47) now applies to extraterritorial effects.

565 *Infra*, Ch 6.

566 Article 2(1)(e). However, no agreement has yet been reached on how to implement this commitment.

567 See Knox, 96 *AJIL* (2002) 305–8; Craik, in Bastmeijer and Koivurova (eds), *Theory and Practice of Transboundary EIA*, Ch 5.

568 Craik, *op cit*, Ch 2.

569 The US and Russia are not parties. An amendment permitting non-UNECE states to accede entered into force in 2014. None has so far done so.

570 Council Directive 97/11/EC 1997 OJ L 73/5.

571 See e.g. Austria, Federal Act Concerning Environmental Impact Assessment and Public Participation, s 10; Germany, 1990 Act Concerning EIA (amended 2006); Finland, 1994 Act on EIA Procedure and Decree on EIA Procedure.

572 See Statements by and on behalf of the Minister of State of the Department of Transport, Energy and Communications, Ireland, to the Public Inquiry Concerning an Appeal by UK Nirex Ltd, 12 January 1996. See now UK, 1999 Town and Country Planning (EIA) Regulations, SI 1999/293.

The 1982 UNCLOS is also relevant. Article 206 requires states to assess activities likely to affect the marine environment and to report their findings to the relevant international organization.[573] Regional and global treaties reflect Article 206.[574] In the *South China Sea Arbitration* this provision was applied to Chinese dredging and construction activities on coral reefs.[575] Detailed regulations adopted by the ISA also apply Article 206 to seabed mining, but in its *Advisory Opinion on Activities in the Area* the ITLOS went further and held that 'the obligations of the contractors and of the sponsoring States concerning environmental impact assessments extend beyond the scope of application of specific provisions of the Regulations.'[576]

Drawing on Rio Principle 17, the UNEP Guidelines, and national precedents, an Article on transboundary EIA formed part of the long-standing work of the ILC. Article 7 of the 2001 Articles on Transboundary Harm provides that 'Any decision in respect of the authorization of an activity within the scope of the present articles shall, in particular, be based on an assessment of the possible transboundary harm caused by that activity, including any environmental impact assessment.'[577]

These precedents undoubtedly influenced the International Court's landmark judgment in *Pulp Mills Case*.[578] This case is the first of several in which an international court has held that prior assessment of transboundary impacts is not merely a treaty-based obligation but a requirement of general international law.[579] It is also the first case to consider the content of such an EIA. The case arose out of the construction of a wood pulp mill in Uruguay. Effluent from the mill would be discharged into the River Uruguay, which forms the border with Argentina. There is no reference to EIA in the 1975 Statute of the River Uruguay, the applicable law in the dispute, nor are Argentina or Uruguay parties to the 1991 Espoo Convention.

573 *Infra*, Ch 8, section 3(3).

574 See 1983 Convention for the Protection and Development of the Marine Environment of the Wider Caribbean Region, Article 12; 1986 Convention for the Protection of the Natural Resources and Environment of the South Pacific Region, Article 16; 1985 Convention for the Protection, Management and Development of the Marine and Coastal Environment of the Eastern African Region, Article 13; 1990 Kuwait Protocol for the Protection of the Marine Environment against Pollution from Land-based Sources, Article 8; 1992 Convention on the Protection of the Marine Environment of the Baltic Sea Area, Article 7; 1992 Convention on the Protection of the Black Sea Against Pollution, Article 15(5). In effect Annex II of the 1996 Protocol to the 1972 London Convention requires prior EIA before a permit to dump may be granted: see *infra*, Ch 8.

575 PCA (2016) paras 947–48, 987–91.

576 ITLOS Reports (2011) paras 141–150.

577 For commentary see *ILC Rept* (2001) GAOR A/56/10, 402–7. For earlier drafts see Barboza, *5th Rept on International Liability*, UN Doc A/CN 4/423 (1989) 26–33; Draft Articles on International Liability, Article 11, UN Doc A/CN 4/428 (1990); id, Article 10, UN Doc A/CN 4/L 5333 (1996).

578 ICJ Reports (2010) 14, paras 203–219.

579 Para 204. See also *Advisory Opinion on Activities in the Area*, ITLOS Reports (2011) paras 145–8; *Kishenganga Arbitration (Partial Award)* PCA (2013) para 450; *Border Activities/San Juan River Cases*, ICJ Reports (2015) paras 104 and 153. The point was argued but not decided in four earlier cases: see *Request for an Examination of the Situation*, ICJ Reports (1995) 288; *Gabčíkovo-Nagymaros Case*, ICJ Reports (1997) 7; *MOX Plant Case*, ITLOS Reports (2001); *Land Reclamation Case*, ITLOS No 12 (2003). See generally Craik, *The International Law of Environmental Impact Assessment*, especially Ch 4; Atapattu, *Emerging Principles of IEL*, Ch 4, but their assessment predates *Pulp Mills*.

Accepting the arguments of both parties on this point, and in accordance with the1969 VCLT, Art 31(3)(c) the International Court found that: 'the obligation to protect and preserve, under Article 41(a) of the Statute [of the River Uruguay], has to be interpreted in accordance with a practice, which in recent years has gained so much acceptance among States that it may now be considered a requirement under general international law to undertake an environmental impact assessment where there is a risk that the proposed industrial activity may have a significant adverse impact in a transboundary context, in particular, on a shared resource. Moreover, due diligence, and the duty of vigilance and prevention which it implies, would not be considered to have been exercised, if a party planning works liable to affect the régime of the river or the quality of its waters did not undertake an environmental impact assessment on the potential effects of such works.'[580]

This finding treats transboundary EIA as a distinct and freestanding obligation in international law[581]—reflecting Principle 17 of the Rio Declaration, the 1991 Espoo Convention, and Article 7 of the ILC Articles on Transboundary Harm. Nevertheless, the court also endorsed the view that EIA is a necessary element of the general obligation of due diligence in the prevention and control of transboundary harm,[582] suggesting that the content of the obligation may evolve over time and will reflect the capabilities of the party concerned and the particular circumstances of the case. Either way, the Court has now confirmed that where there is a risk of significant transboundary harm an EIA must be carried out *prior to the authorization or implementation* of the project or activity in question.[583]

The International Court's conclusion that transboundary EIA is a requirement of customary or general international law is no surprise given the growing body of treaties and soft law that provide for one, as well as the instances of state practice and the policies of international lending agencies. In the real world few states faced with litigation are likely to deny that there is an obligation in international law to carry out a transboundary EIA and Uruguay did not do so in *Pulp Mills*. What states may do instead is deny that the circumstances require an EIA (no risk of transboundary harm) or argue that an EIA was carried out. In *Pulp Mills* Uruguay chose the latter option. Argentina responded by arguing that the EIA was inadequate: that various matters had been overlooked or inadequately evaluated. The significant question in the case was thus not the obligation to do an EIA but what that obligation entailed. We return to that issue in section 7(5) below.

580 Para 204, endorsed in the *Advisory Opinion on Activities in the Area*, paras 145–8, and the *Border Activities/San Juan River Cases*, ICJ Reports (2015) paras 104 and 153.

581 On the distinction between EIA as an independent obligation and an attribute of due diligence see Judge Dugard, *Border Activities/San Juan River Cases*, sep op, para 11, but compare Judge Donoghue's sep op. For a nuanced critique of the ICJ judgment see Brunnée, 5 *ESIL Reflections* (2016) Issue 6; Brent, 20 *Asia Pacific JEL* (2017) 28; Craik, 69 *ICLQ* (2020) 239.

582 An argument articulated by Okowa, 72 *BYIL* (1996) 280; Handl, 1 *YbIEL* (1990) 21 and reiterated in the *Border Activities/San Juan River Cases*, paras 104 and 154.

583 ICJ Reports (2010) paras 120 and 205; see *infra*, section 7(3).

7(3) WHEN IS A TRANSBOUNDARY EIA REQUIRED?

Principle 17 of the Rio Declaration calls for EIA to be undertaken for 'proposed activities that are likely to have a significant adverse impact on the environment'. The majority of precedents follow this formulation and limit the scope of the obligation in two ways.[584] First, it does not apply to minor or transitory impacts—the potential harm must be significant, the threshold adopted by the ILC in its 2001 Articles on Transboundary Harm,[585] and in the jurisprudence.[586] Secondly, a threshold of foreseeable risk must be met in order to trigger the obligation to do an EIA. Herein lies a potential weakness of EIA as a tool of international environmental management and transboundary cooperation. The reason for doing an EIA is to find out whether harm is likely; yet, under some treaties the obligation to do one and to notify other states only arises once it is shown that harm *is* likely, or even that it *will* occur.[587] This is both circular and potentially self-defeating if taken literally, and it is not consistent with the precedents discussed below or with the jurisprudence.[588] Moreover, although the proponent of the activity in question must exercise good faith in making this determination 'on the basis of an objective evaluation of all the relevant circumstances,'[589] the potentially affected state, lacking the necessary information, may find it hard to challenge that determination or justify a request for an EIA if it has to prove actual or likely harm.

In practice, the evidential standard in this context is unlikely to be so onerous. Some treaties expressly set a low threshold of foreseeable risk: for example Article 206 of the 1982 UNCLOS requires only 'reasonable grounds for believing that planned activities. . . . *may* cause substantial pollution of or significant harmful changes'.[590] The precautionary approach as defined in Rio Principle 15 might also be invoked when interpreting references to the likelihood of harm in Principle 17 or in treaty formulations.[591] The practice of the parties in the *MOX Plant* and *Pulp Mills* cases suggests that where large-scale industrial activities with a known risk of potentially significant pollution are involved the necessity of an EIA can be presumed, even if the likelihood of actual harm is small.

584 ILC, 2001 Articles on Transboundary Harm, Articles 1, 2(a) 7; 1987 UNEP Goals and Principles of EIA, Principle 1; 1982 UNCLOS, Article 206; 1991 Convention on Transboundary EIA, Article 2(3); 1992 CBD, Article 14; 1992 Convention on the Protection of the Baltic Sea Area, Article 7; 1989 Protocol for the Conservation and Management of Protected Marine and Coastal Areas of the South East Pacific, Article 89. See Craik, *The International Law of EIA*, Ch 5.

585 *Supra*, section 5(1).

586 *Pulp Mills Case*, ICJ Reports (2010) para 204; *Border Activities/San Juan River Cases (Merits)* ICJ Reports (2015) paras 105, 153–5.

587 See e.g. 1990 Kingston Protocol on Specially Protected Areas and Wildlife, Article 13: 'activities that *would* have a negative environmental impact *and* significantly affect areas or species that have been afforded special protection'.

588 See in particular *Border Activities/San Juan River Cases*, Judge Dugard, sep op, para 19.

589 *Border Activities/San Juan River Cases (Merits)* ICJ Reports (2015) para 153.

590 See also 1990 Kuwait Protocol for the Protection of the Marine Environment from Land-based Sources, Article 8: 'projects . . . which *may* cause significant risks of pollution'.

591 *supra*, section 6.

In less obvious cases it may be necessary to infer evidence of risk. In the *Border Activities/San Juan River* cases the existence or non-existence of a 'risk' of significant transboundary harm triggering an EIA was determined by reference to 'the nature and magnitude of the project and the context in which it was to be carried out.'[592] The context in this case included the ecological sensitivity of the receiving environment.[593] The court held that an EIA was required in one case, but not in the other. Crucially, as Judge Dugard observed, a party could not justify its initial failure to carry out an EIA by showing that no significant harm had subsequently occurred; an EIA should have been carried out if prior to authorization of the project there was a risk of significant transboundary harm.[594]

Another option is to follow the example of the 1991 Antarctic Protocol: except in *de minimis* cases, an 'initial environmental examination' is required for all activities covered by the protocol. Only if the likely impact is found to be more than minor is a comprehensive environmental examination then required.[595] In the *Border Activities/San Juan River Cases* the ICJ accepted that 'to conduct a preliminary assessment of the risk posed by an activity is one of the ways in which a State can ascertain whether the proposed activity carries a risk of significant transboundary harm.'[596] UNEP's EIA Principles similarly distinguish between an initial and a comprehensive assessment but also call for criteria and procedures to be defined clearly by legislation so that 'subject activities can quickly and surely be identified'.[597] In particular, the UNEP Principles suggest that activities likely to cause harm should be listed, as they are in the 1991 Convention on Transboundary EIA. However, an EIA is only necessary under this convention when listed activities are 'likely' to cause significant adverse transboundary impact.[598] While there is thus no presumption that a transboundary EIA is required for all listed activities, in case of dispute other states may invoke an inquiry procedure to determine the question.[599] This procedure has been employed by Romania and Ukraine—the inquiry report in effect constituted an EIA of the proposed project and made various recommendations.[600] The 1991 Convention also provides for activities which are not listed to be the subject of prior assessment if the parties agree, and it sets out criteria to assist in making this judgment, based on the size, location, and possible effects of the proposed project. The ICJ used comparable criteria in the *Border Activities/San Juan River Cases*.[601]

An EIA will normally have to take place before *authorization* for the project is granted and must also be notified to neighbouring states. In *Pulp Mills* the Court held that this notification must take place 'before the State concerned decides on the

592 ICJ Reports (2015) 665, paras 104–5, 153–5.

593 *Ibid*, para 155, and see also Judge Dugard. One of the areas likely to be affected was a Ramsar wetland.

594 *Ibid*, sep op, para 19.

595 1991 Protocol to the Antarctic Treaty on Protection of the Environment, Article 8 and Annex I.

596 Para 154.

597 Principles 1, and 2.

598 Article 2(2).

599 Appendix IV.

600 Espoo Inquiry Commission Rept on the Danube–Black Sea Navigation Route (2006).

601 See paras 154–5, and Judge Dugard, sep op, paras 19 and 32.

environmental viability of the plan, taking due account of the environmental impact assessment submitted to it.'[602] The court's subsequent reference to an EIA taking place before *implementation* of the project[603] leaves open the possibility that an EIA may occur in several stages. In cases involving complex projects, where the time between initial authorization and eventual operation is prolonged, it may be necessary to conduct several EIAs—or at least to review and revise the initial EIA—before a plant is authorized to commence operations. Whether an EIA has been carried out is a question of fact to be proved by the state whose duty it is to conduct one. It is not enough to assert that an EIA has been conducted, even if accompanied by a summary of the alleged conclusions. The documentary evidence must be produced.[604]

We can observe from the *Southern Bluefin Tuna, Land Reclamation,* and *Pulp Mills Cases* that, in the absence of any inquiry process comparable to the Espoo Convention, provisional measures applications to international courts may be the best remedy available to a potentially affected state seeking to enforce the obligation to carry out a transboundary EIA. In *Pulp Mills,* Argentina failed in its attempt to secure provisional measures from the ICJ once Uruguay showed that it had carried out an EIA.[605] In the other two cases the ITLOS found that the risk of harm to the marine environment could not be excluded;[606] in *Land Reclamation* it expressly ordered the parties to assess the risks and effects of the works, while in *Southern Bluefin Tuna* the effect of its order was that catch quotas could only be increased by agreement after further studies of the state of the stock. The outcome in all three cases suggests that if an EIA has not been undertaken and there is some evidence of a risk of significant harm to the environment—even if the risk is uncertain and the potential harm not necessarily irreparable—an order requiring the parties to cooperate in prior assessment is likely to result even at the provisional measures stage.[607]

7(4) THE EIA PROCESS

An EIA is 'a national procedure for evaluating the likely impact of a proposed activity on the environment'.[608] The protection which an EIA affords other states is essentially procedural: it enables them to be better informed about what is planned and what its transboundary effects may be, to be consulted when the EIA shows that they may be affected, and to try to influence the outcome of any decision which takes

602 *Ibid*, para 120. See also *Border Activities/San Juan River Cases,* ICJ Reports (2015) 665, paras 159 and 161.

603 *Ibid*, para 205.

604 *Border Activities/San Juan River Cases,* ICJ Reports (2015) 665, para 154.

605 *Pulp Mills (Provisional Measures)* ICJ Reports (2006) 113.

606 *Southern Bluefin Tuna (Provisional Measures)* ITLOS Reports (1999) para 79; *Land Reclamation (Provisional Measures)* ITLOS Reports (2003) para 96.

607 See also *Border Activities/San Juan River Cases (Provisional Measures),* ICJ Reports (2013) 398, para 54.

608 1991 Convention, Article 1(vi). See to the same effect Rio Principle 17; *ILC Rept* (2001) 402, emphasising that the state of origin carries out the EIA.

the EIA into account. It is not a process of prior joint approval. As we will see in the next section, international law gives affected states no veto on proposed activities, nor does the existence of an adverse EIA place any duty on the proposing state to refrain from proceeding with a project, although in the final decision 'due account' must be taken of the findings of the EIA.[609] However, failure to act in accordance with an EIA may then make it more difficult for a state to show that it has acted with due diligence.

In most cases the Espoo Convention thus gives a potentially affected state the right to participate in a national EIA only to the extent of providing information and making representations.[610] It also has the right to receive EIA documentation and to be informed of the final decision, including the reasons and considerations on which it is based; thereafter, it is entitled to be consulted regarding measures to reduce or eliminate any transboundary impact.[611] Neighbouring states should therefore be fully aware of the risks, the benefits, and the possible alternatives revealed by the EIA. The Espoo Convention also envisages the possibility that joint or multilateral assessment and monitoring may be appropriate where data and information might otherwise be incompatible.[612] The scientific enquiries instituted by agreement of the parties in the *Trail Smelter Arbitration* or the *Land Reclamation Case* exemplify such a joint process.[613] Conducting a transboundary EIA may in some cases be impossible without securing the cooperation of the neighbouring state.[614]

The process for carrying out a transboundary EIA is not set out in any international instrument, and the ICJ has been careful not to prescribe one.[615] Some states rely on the operator or developer to do the EIA, subject to approval by an environmental agency or ministry. This was the model adopted by Uruguayan law and challenged unsuccessfully in *Pulp Mills*. In other legal systems a more formal process is conducted by independent inspectors. This model is the one used by the IFC, also challenged unsuccessfully in *Pulp Mills*. National EIA procedures typically provide for some element of public participation. The 1991 Convention on Transboundary EIA expressly applies this requirement on a non-discriminatory basis to the public in other states likely to be affected,[616] but other formulations are narrower.[617]

609 1991 Convention, Article 6. See also UNEP 1987 Goals and Principles, Principles 6–8.

610 Articles 3(5)–(6). No such rights are identified in the 1987 UNEP Goals and Principles.

611 1991 Convention, Articles 4–7; 1987 UNEP Goals and Principles, Principle 12.

612 Article 3 and Appendix VI. See also 1997 Korea–China Agreement on Environmental Cooperation, Article 2(4); 1994 Israel–Jordan Peace Treaty, Annex IV.

613 See also the *Gabčíkovo-Nagymaros Case* in which the parties were ordered to cooperate in monitoring.

614 *Border Activities/San Juan River Cases (Provisional Measures)*, ICJ Reports (2013) 398, Judge Donoghue, sep op, paras 21–2. See also Craik, 69 *ICLQ* (2020) 239.

615 *Ibid*, Judge Donoghue, sep op, para 14.

616 Articles 2(6) 3(8). See also 2003 Protocol on Strategic EA, Article 10(4).

617 See UNEP EIA Goals and Principles, Principle 5 ['appropriate opportunity to comment on the EIA'] and ILC, 2001 Articles on Transboundary Harm, Article 13 ['provide . . . relevant information'], and commentary, *ILC Rept* (2001) 422–5.

Compliance with international human-rights law also necessitates notification to the public and participation in an 'informed process' wherever environmental impacts may seriously affect life, health, private life, or property.[618] In *Pulp Mills* the Court found that there had in fact been public consultation open to Argentines, but it nevertheless went on to hold that 'no legal obligation to consult the affected populations arises for the parties from the instruments invoked by Argentina.'[619] This conclusion goes beyond what Uruguay had argued, and it seems tenable only if confined literally to the instruments invoked by Argentina.[620] Properly argued there should have been no difficulty persuading the court of the general principle that public consultation is a necessary element of the EIA process, as it is under Article 2(6) of the Espoo Convention.

7(5) THE SCOPE AND CONTENT OF AN EIA

What constitutes an EIA is a question of law, for lawyers to answer, not experts. The ILC's 2001 Articles require only that an EIA should include an evaluation of the possible impact on persons, property and the environment of other states, but otherwise they leave the detailed content for individual states to determine.[621] In its *Pulp Mills* judgment the Court also concluded that 'it is for each State to determine in its domestic legislation or in the authorization process for the project, the specific content of the environmental impact assessment required in each case, having regard to the nature and magnitude of the proposed development and its likely adverse impact on the environment as well as to the need to exercise due diligence in conducting such an assessment.'[622]

This paragraph makes two related points. First, an EIA need not be specifically required by law, but can be required as part of the authorization or permitting process. What matters is that some means exists to ensure that an EIA is carried out. Secondly, while the 'specific content' (or 'scope') of each EIA is for the host state to determine, there must be an EIA and it must have regard to 'the nature and magnitude of the proposed development and its likely adverse impact on the environment'. Thus, the reference to domestic law 'does not relate to the question of whether an environmental impact assessment should be undertaken.'[623] Nor is the Court saying that the scope or content of an EIA is for the state to decide in its sole discretion: there is no renvoi to national law.[624] On the contrary, it is reflecting the views of the ILC and the arguments

[618] See *Taskin v Turkey* [2004] ECHR, paras 113–9; *Tatar v. Romania* [2009] ECHR, para 88; *Kichwa Peoples of the Sarayaku Community v Ecuador* (2012) IACtHR Sers C, No 145, paras 204–7, and *infra*, Ch 5.

[619] ICJ Reports (2010) para 216.

[620] Only one irrelevant human rights case was cited.

[621] Article 7 and commentary in ILC Rept (2001) 405, paras (7) (8).

[622] ICJ Reports (2010) para 205.

[623] *Border Activities/San Juan River Cases (Provisional Measures)*, ICJ Reports (2013) 398, para 157.

[624] *Ibid*, Judge Donoghue, sep op, para 14 and Judge Dugard, sep. op, para 18.

of the parties based on that commentary. The ILC 2001 Commentary contains the following explanation:

> '(7) The specifics of what ought to be the content of assessment is left to the domestic laws of the State conducting such assessment. [*fn omitted*] For the purposes of article 7, however, such an assessment *should contain an evaluation of the possible transboundary harmful impact of the activity*. In order for the States likely to be affected to evaluate the risk to which they might be exposed, they need to know what possible harmful effects that activity might have on them.
>
> (8) The assessment *should include the effects of the activity not only on persons and property, but also on the environment of other States*. The importance of the protection of the environment, independently of any harm to individual human beings or property is clearly recognized.'[625]

It is apparent from this commentary that whatever the scope of an EIA required by national law, international law requires *at a minimum* that an EIA assess possible effects on people, property and the environment of other states likely to be affected. If national law does not ensure that such an assessment is carried out—for whatever reason—then there is inevitably a breach of the obligation to do a transboundary EIA. Both these points have been affirmed in subsequent cases.[626] The scope or content of an environmental impact assessment should thus be determined 'in light of the specific circumstances of each case.'[627]

Unlike most treaty provisions on EIA or the ILC's Draft Articles, the 1991 Convention on Transboundary EIA and UNEP's EIA Goals and Principles specify in some detail the type of information which an EIA should contain. This includes a description of the activity and its likely impact, mitigation measures and practical alternatives, and any uncertainties in the available knowledge.[628] In *Pulp Mills* the extensive EIA documentation covered inter alia the choice of technology; the long-term impact of effluents on the river ecosystem, including compliance with agreed air and water quality standards; the potential for transboundary impact; the regulatory process and pollution monitoring arrangements; the suitablility of the chosen site and the possible alternative. If the costs and benefits of a large-scale industrial project are to be assessed then information of this kind will typically be a necessary aid to decision-makers. Given the wealth of national practice and literature on what an

625 *ILC Rept* (2001) GAOR A/56/10, commentary to Article 7, at pp. 402–5, emphasis added. Article 7 provides: 'Any decision in respect of the authorization of an activity within the scope of the present articles shall, in particular, be based on an assessment of the possible transboundary harm caused by that activity, including any environmental impact assessment.'

626 *Border Activities/San Juan River Cases (Provisional Measures)*, ICJ Reports (2013) 398, paras 104, 157; *South China Sea Arbitration*, PCA (2016) paras 987–991.

627 *Border Activities/San Juan River Cases*, ICJ Reports (2013) 398, para 104.

628 UNEP EIA Principles, Principle 4; 1991 Convention on Transboundary EIA, Article 4(1) and Appendix II, and for more detailed guidance see UNEP, *Environmental Impact Assessment and Strategic Environmental Assessment: Towards an Integrated Approach* (Nairobi, 2004).

EIA requires,[629] the ILC's cautious approach is arguably misplaced. UNEP's definition of the minimum content of an EIA more closely and convincingly reflects national practice. Moreover, the consistent elaboration of the term 'EIA' at the international level may have given it a specialized meaning in international law, based on the UNEP Principles.[630]

7(6) JUDICIAL REVIEW

How far, if at all, is an EIA open to challenge in an international court on the ground that its content is inadequate or its conclusions unfounded? That question was posed in the *MOX Plant* and *Pulp Mills* disputes. In both cases the complainants favoured a prescriptive approach, drawing on detailed standards from EU law or the 1991 Convention on Transboundary EIA to fill out the applicable treaty provisions. Like the Statute of the River Uruguay, Article 206 of UNCLOS is silent about what is required in an EIA, and in contrast to Articles 207–11 it makes no reference to internationally agreed rules and standards. The respondent states in both cases argued that their EIAs already met the highest international standards and they relied on scientific evidence and the judgment of independent bodies—the European Commission and the World Bank respectively—to justify the conclusion that other states were not at risk.

Using litigation to challenge the adequacy and conclusions of an EIA is not unknown in national law. The national caselaw tends to emphasise that an EIA need not address every aspect of a project in depth, and that its purpose is to assist the decision-maker and alert the public, not to test every possible hypothesis or provide detailed solutions to problems that have been identified.[631] UNEP's Goals and Principles say only that '[t]he environmental effects in an EIA should be assessed with a degree of detail commensurate with their likely environmental significance' (Principle 5). Plainly this involves an exercise of judgment. In *Pulp Mills*, Argentina devoted a great deal of energy to pointing out alleged inadequacies, mistakes, and flaws in the various environmental assessments carried out on the Botnia proposal. It argued that key issues were ignored in the EIA, in particular the choice of alternative sites. It appeared to be inviting the Court to hold that both the Botnia EIA and the IFC EIA were insufficient and did not sustain the decision to authorise the plant.

EIAs on such large projects are often the focus of intense controversy, both in national courts and increasingly in international courts. Those opposed will rarely be satisfied by an EIA, however voluminous and detailed. Uruguay responded that the relevant question was whether the assessments actually undertaken provided evidence

[629] Wood, *EIA: A Comparative Review*, 143; Wathern, *EIA: Theory and Practice*, 6–7.

[630] Craik, *The International Law of EIA*, 126–7, relying on Article 31(4) of the VCLT.

[631] See *Prineas v Forestry Commission of New South Wales*, 49 LGERA (1983) 402; *Belize Alliance of Conservation Non-Governmental Organisations v Dept. of Environment*, UKPC (2003) No.63; *Marsh v Oregon Natural Resources Council*, 490 US 360 (1989); *Robertson v Methow Valley Citizens Council*, 490 US 332 (1989).

on which it was reasonable to base the decisions taken by its environment agency (DINAMA) the Environment Ministry, and the IFC with respect to the likely impacts on the river or Argentina. It also argued that an EIA is not required to assess risks that are too remote or are merely speculative. The EIA, in its final form as approved by DINAMA, inter alia covered the possible transboundary impact of the Botnia plant, the river's flow characteristics (including reverse flow) air pollution, water quality, biodiversity, eutrophication and the occurrence of algae blooms, and alternative sites.[632] On this basis Uruguay argued that Dinama had been duly diligent in considering all the relevant matters before the decision to authorise the plant was taken.

The Court noted that neither the Espoo Convention nor the UNEP EIA guidelines specifically required assessment of alternative sites, but it went on to find that Uruguay had in fact assessed other sites.[633] It accepted Uruguay's arguments, based on the ILC commentary, that the scope and content of an EIA are not specified by general international law, but are to be determined on a case by case basis 'having regard to the nature and magnitude of the proposed development and its likely adverse impact.'[634] This formulation and the finding on alternative sites appears to leave open the possibility of reviewing the adequacy of an EIA in appropriate cases, and it would not be unreasonable to conclude that the Court did so here but found nothing wrong with the EIA undertaken by Uruguay, apart from the failure to make timely notification to Argentina as required by the Statute.

On this basis it seems unlikely that an international court would be prepared to set aside a well-reasoned EIA carried out in good faith on the basis of substantial scientific and technical evidence. It may well do so, however, if the EIA is demonstrably inadequate or tendentious in its analysis of the risks, a conclusion supported by the *Whaling Case*.[635] While in that case the ICJ refrained from passing judgment on differences of scientific opinion, it found that important elements of a research plan lacked transparency, were unsupported by adequate reasoning or evidence, were not consistently explained, employed incompatible methodology, and did not support the sample size regarded by Japan as necessary for its scientific research programme. The WTO Appellate Body has similarly reviewed the adequacy of risk assessments under the SPS Agreement. In *Japan—Measures Affecting the Import of Apples*,[636] it held that 'Under the SPS Agreement, the obligation to conduct an assessment of "risk" is not satisfied merely by a general discussion of the disease sought to be avoided by the imposition of a phytosanitary measure.' The Appellate Body found the risk assessment at issue in *EC—Hormones* not to be 'sufficiently specific' even though the scientific articles cited by the importing state had evaluated the 'carcinogenic potential of entire categories of hormones, or of the hormones at issue in general.'[637]

632 DINAMA, Botnia EIA Rept, *Uruguay Counter Memorial*, Vol II, Annex 20.

633 Paras 205, 210.

634 ICJ Reports (2010) para 205.

635 ICJ Reports (2014) 226, paras 67, 172, 179, 181, 188, 193–8, 212, 227.

636 WTO Appellate Body, WT/DS245/AB/R (2003) para 202.

637 *US—Continued Suspension of Obligations in the EC Hormones Dispute*, WT/DS320/AB/R (2008) para 557.

The ICJ was reluctant in *Pulp Mills* to be drawn into reviewing the conclusions of EIAs conducted in good faith by Botnia and the IFC. The Court probably does not want to encourage such challenges and it seems right in principle to give considerable deference to EIAs that are well-reasoned and supported by substantial evidence. But the Court's treatment of the issue in *Pulp Mills* and its willingness in *Whaling* to consider whether the evidence supported the scientific conclusions shows that an EIA is not a mere formality. While judicial review of a transboundary EIA will require a good case to be successful, it is potentially available in any international court with jurisdiction over an environmental dispute.

7(7) MONITORING

Monitoring is another aid to decision-making whereby states 'observe, measure, evaluate and analyze, by recognized scientific methods, the risks or effects' of pollution or environmental harm.[638] Unlike prior EIA, monitoring is undertaken both before and after the project has begun to operate; its purpose is to check initial EIA predictions and provide information to enable national regulatory agencies to determine whether further measures are needed in order to abate or avoid pollution or environmental harm. It is necessarily on ongoing process, which will have to continue over the life of a project and in some cases beyond.[639] A failure to institute proper monitoring, like a failure to undertake an EIA, will necessarily constitute a failure to act with due diligence.[640] At the same time, as the *Pulp Mills Case* illustrates, if an activity has been well planned and properly regulated, effective monitoring should provide the best evidence that there is no pollution and no significant harm to the environment.

Gabčíkovo-Nagymaros remains the most important case. The judgment stresses that new environmental norms and standards have to be taken into account 'not only when States contemplate new activities but also when continuing activities begun in the past'.[641] The court's approach treats prior EIA and subsequent monitoring of the ongoing environmental risks and impacts (or 'post project analysis') as a continuum which will operate throughout the life of the project. This view of the relationship between EIA and monitoring reflects best practice in many national systems and in the provisions of modern treaties,[642] including the 1991 Convention on Transboundary EIA.[643]

638 1982 UNCLOS, Article 204. See Wathern, *EIA: Theory and Practice*, Ch 7; Wood, *EIA: A Comparative Review*, Ch 13.

639 *Pulp Mills*, paras 205, 266.

640 *Pulp Mills*, paras 204–5.

641 At para 140.

642 See e.g. 1982 UNCLOS, Article 204; 1992 Convention on the Protection and Use of Transboundary Watercourses and Lakes, Articles 4, 11; 1991 Antarctic Protocol, Article 3(2)(d) and (e).

643 Article 7. On the relationship between EIA and monitoring see Wathern, *EIA: Theory and Practice*, Ch 7 and Wood, *EIA: A Comparative Review*, Ch 14.

8 PROCEDURAL OBLIGATIONS AND TRANSBOUNDARY COOPERATION

8(1) TRANSBOUNDARY COOPERATION

If due diligence is the first rule of transboundary environmental risk management, co-operation is the second. The 1972 Stockholm Conference recognized that cooperation through multilateral or bilateral arrangements or other appropriate means is essential to the control of adverse transboundary environmental effects resulting from human activities, in such a way that due account is taken of the sovereignty and interests of all states.[644] In endorsing this declaration, the UN General Assembly noted that it should not be construed as enabling other states to delay or impede programmes and projects of exploration, exploitation, and development of natural resources within the territory of states, but that it did require the exchange of information 'in a spirit of good neighbourliness'.[645] At that time, agreement could not be reached on more detailed rules and these formulations fall short of explicitly requiring consultation and negotiation with other states, but the broad contours of 'good neighbourliness' can be identified in subsequent legal developments.

In contrast to the Stockholm Declaration, an obligation to cooperate permeates the 1992 Rio Declaration.[646] It is reiterated in Article 5 of the 1992 CBD, in Article 4 of the 1992 Convention on Climate Change and in many other agreements. Transboundary cooperation is the foundation for the equitable utilization and conservation of shared natural resources:

> 'The Court observes that it is by co-operating that the States concerned can jointly manage the risks of damage to the environment that might be created by the plans initiated by one or other of them, so as to prevent the damage in question, through the performance of both the procedural and the substantive obligations laid down by the 1975 Statute.'[647]

The obligation of states to cooperate through notification, consultation, and negotiation is clearly articulated in the *Lac Lanoux Arbitration*,[648] and in various regional treaties, including the 1991 Espoo Convention and the 1975 Statute of the River Uruguay at issue in the *Pulp Mills Case*.[649] The ILC's 2001 Articles on Transboundary Harm also address procedural issues.[650] Article 4 requires cooperation in good faith.[651] Article 8 requires the contents of any EIA indicating a risk of significant transboundary harm

644 1972 Stockholm Declaration, Principle 24.

645 UNGA Res 2995 XXVII (1972).

646 See Principles 7, 9, 12, 13, 14, 18, 19, 27.

647 *Pulp Mills*, para 77. See also UNEP, 1978 Principles of Conduct, etc in the Conservation and Harmonious Utilization of Natural Resources Shared by Two or More States, and *supra*, section 3.

648 See *infra*. See also *Gabčíkovo-Nagymaros Case*, paras 140–7.

649 *Pulp Mills*, paras 75, 81, 102–113.

650 Articles 9–13 and see commentary in *ILC Rept* (2001) GAOR A/55/10.

651 Article 4 provides: 'States concerned shall cooperate in good faith and, as necessary, seek the assistance of one or more competent international organizations in preventing significant transboundary harm or at any event in minimizing the risk thereof.'

to be communicated to the affected states.[652] Article 9 requires consultations on preventive measures.[653] Finally, Article 12 requires an ongoing exchange of information in a timely manner not only at the planning stage but also while the activity is being carried out.[654] A particular feature of these articles is the continuing character of the obligation to cooperate even after a project has come into operation.[655]

The ILC Commentary notes that 'The principle of cooperation between States is essential in designing and implementing effective policies to prevent significant transboundary harm or at any event to minimize the risk thereof. The requirement of cooperation of States extends to all phases of planning and of implementation.'[656] It explains that Article 8, together with Articles 9, 11, 12 and 13, provide for 'a set of procedures essential to balancing the interests of all the States concerned by giving them a reasonable opportunity to find a way to undertake the activity with satisfactory and reasonable measures designed to prevent or minimize transboundary harm.'[657] In the Commission's view, '[t]he obligation to notify other States of the risk of significant harm to which they are exposed is reflected in the *Corfu Channel* case, where the International Court of Justice characterized the duty to warn as based on elementary considerations of humanity.'[658] Its commentary also draws upon Articles 3(1) and 5 of the 1991 Espoo.[659] The purpose of consultations, it explains, 'is for the parties to find acceptable solutions regarding measures to be adopted in order to prevent significant transboundary harm, or at any event to minimize the risk thereof.'[660] The objective is to accommodate any conflict of rights and interests, not to stifle initiative.[661] In particular, states are not debarred from creating sources of risk to others, even where, as in the case of nuclear installations, these involve the possibility of serious harm.

An obligation to cooperate is less clearly set out in the 1982 UNCLOS. Article 123 somewhat weakly says that states bordering enclosed or semi-enclosed seas 'should' cooperate with each other, while Part XII requires states to cooperate, but mainly in the task of adopting global and regional rules and standards.[662] However, the ITLOS has held that 'the duty to cooperate is a fundamental principle in the prevention of pollution of the marine environment under Part XII of the Convention and general international law and that rights arise therefrom which the Tribunal may consider appropriate to preserve under Article 290 of the Convention'.[663] In *MOX Plant* and

652 Article 8. 653 Article 9. 654 Article 12.

655 See especially Articles 11 and 12, and commentary, *ILC Rept* (2001) 418–21. See also *Pulp Mills*, paras 266, 281.

656 *ILC Rept* (2001) 396, para 1. See also Craik, 69 *ICLQ* (2020) 239.

657 *ILC Rept* (2001) 406, para 1. 658 *ILC Rept* (2001) 406, para 3.

659 Article 3(1) and Article 5. 660 *ILC Rept* (2001) 411, para 5.

661 UNGA Res 2995 XXVII (1972); 1991 Convention on Transboundary EIA, Article 6.

662 Article 197. In the *South China Sea Arbitration*, PCA (2016) paras 984–85, China was found to have violated Articles 123 and 197.

663 *MOX Plant Case (Provisional Measures)* ITLOS Reports, para 82; *Land Reclamation (Provisional Measures)* ITLOS Reports, para 92; *Request for an Advisory Opinion by the Sub-Regional Fisheries Commission*, ITLOS Reports (2015) para 140.

Land Reclamation the parties were thus ordered to improve their cooperation, and to consult, exchange information, and monitor or assess the risks and effects of their activities,[664] notwithstanding that irreparable harm was neither imminent nor likely. Similarly, in *Southern Bluefin Tuna* the Tribunal emphasized the need for greater co-operation to ensure conservation and optimum utilization, and it ordered the parties to resume negotiations for that purpose 'without delay'.[665]

8(2) NOTIFICATION AND CONSULTATION IN RESPECT OF TRANSBOUNDARY RISK

Although some writers have doubted whether it is possible to generalize customary procedural rules for transboundary environmental risk from the treaties, case law, and limited state practice,[666] a strong provision was included in the Rio Declaration. Principle 19 provides:

> States shall provide prior and timely notification and relevant information to potentially affected states on activities that may have a significant adverse transboundary environmental effect and shall consult with those states at an early stage and in good faith.

This provision reflects the common elements of the precedents referred to below. Moreover, even if notification and consultation in cases of transboundary risk are not independent customary rules, non-compliance with them is likely to be evidence of a failure to act diligently in protecting other states from harm under Rio Principle 2.[667] Once notified, a state which raises no objection may find itself estopped from future protest; there are thus significant legal benefits to be gained from following the requirements of Principle 19.

A requirement of prior consultation based on adequate information has a substantial pedigree of international support and is a natural counterpart of the concept of equitable utilization of shared resources. The *Lac Lanoux Arbitration*[668] shows how the rule has been applied in the law of international watercourses. The tribunal held that France had complied with its obligations under a treaty and customary law to consult and negotiate in good faith before diverting a watercourse shared with Spain. It noted that conflicting interests must be reconciled by negotiation and mutual concession.[669] France had to inform Spain of its proposals, allow consultations, and give reasonable

664 See also *Chagos MPA Arbitration*, PCA (2015) paras 519, 534.

665 *Southern Bluefin Tuna (Provisional Measures)* para 78 and operative para (e).

666 Okowa, 67 *BYIL* (1996) 275, 317–22. But for a more positive view see Kirgis, *Prior Consultation in International Law* (Charlottesville, Va, 1983). See now de Chazournes and Sangbana, in Viñuales (ed), *The Rio Declaration etc*, 493–508.

667 Okowa, 67 *BYIL* (1996) 332–4. See *Pulp Mills Case*, paras 101–2; *Border Activities/San Juan River Cases*, ICJ Reports (2015) 665, para 168, and Judge Donoghue, sep op, para 20, and Rieu-Clarke, 24 *YbIEL* (2014) 102.

668 24 ILR (1957) 101. On the question whether this award is based solely on the 1866 Treaty of Bayonne, or also on customary law, see *infra*, Ch 10.

669 24 ILR (1957) 119.

weight to Spain's interests, but that did not mean that it could act only with Spain's consent: 'the risk of an evil use has so far not led to subjecting the possession of these means of action to the authorization of states which may possibly be threatened'.[670] Spain's rights were thus of a procedural character only; it enjoyed no veto and no claim to insist on specific precautions. In the absence of agreement, it was for France to determine whether to proceed with the project and how to safeguard Spain's interests, provided it gave a reasonable place to those interests in the solution finally adopted.[671]

Treaties and state practice apply the basic principles of the *Lac Lanoux* case to the management of transboundary risks posed by hazardous or potentially harmful activities, including nuclear installations near borders,[672] continental-shelf operations and other sources of marine pollution, including dumping and land-based activities,[673] long-range transboundary air pollution,[674] and industrial accidents.[675] An obligation to consult states affected by the introduction of a marine protected area has also been read into the relevant provisions of 1982 UNCLOS.[676] In each of these situations although some measure of prior notification and consultation is called for, neighbouring states are not given a veto over potentially harmful developments: prior consultation does not mean prior consent.

The 1991 Espoo Convention was the first regional agreement to make detailed provision for transboundary procedural obligations in cases of environmental risk. As we saw in the previous section, it applies to a range of proposed activities, including oil refineries, power stations, nuclear installations, smelters, and waste disposal installations 'that are likely to cause significant adverse transboundary impact'. Other states likely to be affected must be notified and given the opportunity to enter into consultations and make representations on the environmental impact assessment, so under this convention the obligation to notify arises *before* the EIA is carried out, not after.[677]

The ILC's 2001 Articles on Transboundary Harm incorporate the requirement of notification and consultation, but only *after* the EIA, if any, has demonstrated a risk of significant transboundary harm.[678] In the *Border Activities/San Juan River Cases* the ICJ treated this as general international law.[679] Judge Donoghue rightly points out that a requirement to notify might arise prior to carrying out an EIA,[680] as envisaged in the 1991 Espoo Convention. The treatment of EIA and transboundary notification in the Rio Declaration ('prior and timely notification. . .at an early stage') could point in

670 *Ibid*, 126. 671 *Ibid*, 128–30, 140–1. 672 See *infra*, Ch 9.

673 On continental-shelf operations see 1983 Canada–Denmark Agreement for Cooperation Relating to the Marine Environment, 23 *ILM* (1984) 269; 1988 Kuwait Protocol Concerning Marine Pollution Resulting from Exploration and Exploitation of the Continental Shelf, 19 *EPL* (1989) 32; 1981 UNEP Principles Concerning the Environment Related to Offshore Drilling and Mining Within the Limits of National Jurisdiction, 7 *EPL* (1981) 50. On dumping and land-based sources of marine pollution see *infra*, Ch 8.

674 1979 LRTAP Convention, Articles 5, 8, *infra*, Ch 6.

675 1992 Convention on Transboundary Effects of Industrial Accidents, especially Article 4.

676 *Chagos MPA Arbitration*, PCA (2015) para 322. 677 Articles 3, 5, 6.

678 Articles 9–13 and see commentary in *ILC Rept* (2001) GAOR A/55/10.

679 Paras 104 and 168. 680 Sep. op, paras 21–2.

either direction: a likelihood of harm that requires an EIA under Principle 17 may also make it 'timely' to notify other states under Principle 19 before the EIA is carried out, but only if transboundary harm is a foreseeable risk in all the circusmstances.

The ILC also requires that information be given to the public likely to be affected in other states, not just to other governments.[681] Subject to one qualification considered later, the ILC articles otherwise follow closely the main principles of the *Lac Lanoux Arbitration* and are comparable to the relevant articles of the 1997 UN Watercourses Convention, which in the ILC's view reflect well-established international practice.[682] As the *Lac Lanoux Arbitration* and the *Nuclear Tests Cases* indicate, Principle 19 and the ILC Articles enjoy support in state practice.[683] Although the *Pulp Mills* and *MOX Plant Cases* both arose out of allegations of failure to cooperate fully under applicable treaty provisions, all of the parties sought to interpret those provisions by reference to the ILC articles and the precedents referred to here.

In the *Pulp Mills Case*, the ICJ concluded that Uruguay had failed to notify the river commission of its plans and communicate the EIA before authorising construction work.[684] The court noted that 'the obligation to notify is therefore an essential part of the process leading the parties to consult in order to assess the risks of the plan and to negotiate possible changes which may eliminate those risks or minimize their effects.'[685] This failure was a violation of the Statute's express provisions on notification and consultation. The court regarded these procedural rules as part of the obligation of prevention,[686] and in general international law the parties had a duty to cooperate in good faith.[687] Consequently, 'in the opinion of the Court, as long as the procedural mechanism for cooperation between the parties to prevent significant damage to one of them is taking its course, the State initiating the planned activity is obliged not to authorize such work and, *a fortiori*, not to carry it out.'[688]

The court nevertheless rejected Argentina's argument that a failure to notify and consult made construction of the plant illegal and that it should be pulled down. It concluded that there was no obligation not to build once the consultation period had passed. In this respect the court followed the views of the ILC that breach of these procedural requirements does not make what follows illegal.[689] This may not be the right answer in all circumstances, but it would have been a grossly disproportionate remedy in *Pulp Mills* to compel Uruguay to dismantle the mill in order to vindicate a right to prior notification and consultation. An order to resume cooperation through the river commission (CARU) would safeguard Argentina's interests without any further remedy. Similarly, in the *Chagos MPA Arbitration*, although the arbitral tribunal

681 Article 13. But in *Pulp Mills* the ICJ disagreed: see supra, section 7(4).

682 See *infra*, Ch 10.

683 On the *Nuclear Tests Cases*, see the French note of 19 Feb 1973, in NZ Ministry of Foreign Affairs, *French Nuclear Testing in the Pacific* (Wellington, 1973) 42. On state practice, see generally Kirgis, *Prior Consultation in International Law*; but for a more sceptical view see Okowa, 67 *BYIL* (1996) 275.

684 ICJ Reports (2010) 14, paras 121–2.

685 Para 115.

686 Paras 101–2.

687 Paras 145–6.

688 Para 144.

689 Paras 154–7, 275. See infra, Ch 4, section 8.

found that the UK had failed adequately to notify and consult Mauritius about its proposed marine protected area ('MPA') this failure did not invalidate the MPA. The parties were instead left to conduct 'the negotiations that the Tribunal would have expected prior to the proclamation of the MPA, with a view to achieving a mutually satisfactory arrangement for protecting the marine environment...'[690] In the *Border Activities/San Juan River Cases* the court likewise held that, in the absence of any proof of significant damage, 'restoring the original condition of the area where the road is located would not constitute an appropriate remedy for Costa Rica's breach of its obligation to carry out an environmental impact assessment.'[691] All three cases show that, where no actual harm results, breach of procedural obligations will not lead to a restoration of the status quo ante.[692] Where harm does result, the outcome could be different.[693]

Moreover, it does not follow that identical procedural obligations will apply to every case of environmental risk. First, the risk must be significant. This, as we have seen, implies both a degree of probability and a threshold of harm, although the risk does not have to be ultra-hazardous in character.[694] Secondly, as with other elements of the obligation of diligent control, much will depend on the circumstances of each case. Procedural obligations in regard to nuclear power, for example, have been narrowly construed, and applied only to border installations, despite the continental implications of accidents at reactors such as Chernobyl.[695] The practice of consultation and notification in respect of activities which affect only common spaces is also more limited in scope.[696]

Lastly, it must be recalled that these procedural rules usually lead only to an obligation to negotiate in good faith. Negotiations must be 'meaningful' and each side must be willing to listen and take account of the other's interests.[697] Subject to what is said below about equitable balancing, however, they will not necessarily result in substantive limitations on the activities which states propose to undertake, nor are states required to refrain from acting if negotiations prove unsuccessful, since that would enable others to obstruct or veto any proposed development.[698] At most, the purpose of negotiation is to provide the opportunity for accommodating any conflict of rights

690 *Chagos MPA Arbitration*, PCA (2015) para 544.

691 Para 226.

692 On remedies for breach of obligation see *infra*, Ch 4, section 2.

693 Although, in the *South China Sea Arbitration*, PCA (2016) the tribunal did not order restoration of the status quo ante, the applicant state (the Philippines) did not request it to do so.

694 ILC, 2001 Articles on Transboundary Harm, Articles 2, 3; 1982 UNCLOS Articles 206, 210(5); 1991 Convention on Transboundary EIA, Article 2; 1997 UN Watercourses Convention, Article 12.

695 See *infra*, Ch 9. However, Appendix III of the 1991 Espoo Convention requires the parties also to consider 'more remote proposed activities which could give rise to significant transboundary effects far removed from the site of the development'.

696 See *infra*, Ch 8, sections 2(4) and 3(7).

697 *North Sea Continental Shelf Cases*, ICJ Reports (1969) 46–7, paras 83–5; *Icelandic Fisheries Cases*, ICJ Reports (1974) 32ff; *Gabčíkovo-Nagymaros Case*, ICJ Reports (1997) 7, para 141.

698 2001 Articles on Transboundary Harm, Article 9(3) and commentary, paras (2) (10) *ILC Rept* (2001) 409–11 and see earlier discussion of *Lac Lanoux Arbitration*. See also the arguments of the parties on this point in the *Pulp Mills* litigation.

and interests which may exist, not to stifle initiative.[699] In particular, states are not debarred from creating sources of risk to others, even where, as in the case of nuclear installations, these involve the possibility of serious harm.

The most obvious flaw in this approach, therefore, is that in disputes concerning the acceptability and mitigation of transboundary environmental risks, finding a solution may depend on the ability to negotiate one. The potential difficulties are illustrated by the continuing frustration of the parties to the *Gabčíkovo-Nagymaros Case*. The ICJ judgment required them to in the joint management of the project, and to institute a process of environmental protection and monitoring. No such agreement has yet been concluded and in 2019 the case remained formally pending before the court. This outcome may be exceptional, however. The practical outcome of the *Pulp Mills Case* was to enable the parties to resume their normal cooperation through the river commission. The *Land Reclamation Case* shows how obligations of transboundary cooperation can also be enforced using court-ordered provisional measures. In addition to requiring the parties to cooperate in establishing an independent study, exchanging information and assessing the risks, the Tribunal noted that in the course of the hearing Singapore had given assurances that it would notify, consult, and negotiate with Malaysia before proceeding with further works, while giving it the opportunity to comment and produce new evidence.[700] Without any decision on the merits, Malaysia thus secured commitments that in substance addressed all of its rights to cooperation under 1982 UNCLOS and general international law. Precedents also exist for successful court-imposed regulatory regimes in similar circumstances, as in the *Behring Sea Fur Seals* and *Trail Smelter* arbitrations.[701] In both cases the parties had jointly requested the arbitrators to indicate an equitable solution. Aided by appropriate scientific investigations, the arbitrators were thus empowered to substitute their own judgment for that of the parties in order to resolve the disputes.

8(3) EMERGENCY NOTIFICATION, RESPONSE, AND ASSISTANCE

The customary obligation of cooperation in the management of environmental risks extends to accidents and emergencies likely to cause transboundary harm. Article 17 of the 2001 ILC Articles on Prevention of Transboundary Harm provides that 'The State of origin shall, without delay and by the most expeditious means, at its disposal, notify the State likely to be affected of an emergency concerning an activity within the scope of the present articles and provide it with all relevant and available information.' As we saw earlier, the *Corfu Channel Case* provides an early example of judicial application of this duty to warn. In that case British warships were damaged by mines in

699 See *infra*, Chs 6, 8, 9, 10; UNGA Res 2995 XXVII (1972); and 1991 Convention on Transboundary EIA, Article 6.

700 *Land Reclamation Case*, ITLOS Reports (2003) paras 76–8.

701 *Behring Sea Fur Seals Arbitration*, Moore, 1 *Int Arb Awards* (1898) 755, repr in 1 *IELR* (1999) 43; *Trail Smelter Arbitration*, *supra*, n 371.

Albanian territorial waters. Giving judgment on this point for the UK, the Court noted: 'The obligations incumbent upon the Albanian authorities consisted in notifying for the benefit of shipping in general, the existence of a minefield in Albanian territorial waters and in warning the approaching British warships of imminent danger to which the minefield exposed them'.[702] Although the context of this case involved interference with freedom of maritime communication, the Court expressly based its conclusion on additional grounds of more general application, namely elementary considerations of humanity and the obligation referred to earlier that a state should not knowingly allow its territory to be used for acts contrary to the rights of other states. As we have seen, these include the right to protection from environmental harm. For this reason, it is legitimate to view the *Corfu Channel Case* as authority for a customary obligation to give warning of known environmental hazards.

Treaties and state practice support this conclusion. It is unequivocally applied to marine pollution by the 1982 UNCLOS and other treaties now widely ratified.[703] The 1986 Convention on Early Notification of Nuclear Accidents, and a network of bilateral agreements apply the same rule to transboundary releases of radioactivity,[704] and it is found in treaties dealing with pollution of international watercourses,[705] in the ILA Montreal Rules on Transfrontier Pollution,[706] and in OECD principles.[707] In all of these instruments the object of notification is the same: states should be given sufficient information promptly enough to enable them to minimize the damage and take whatever measures of self-protection are permitted by international law. Principle 18 of the Rio Declaration codifies this duty to warn other states in situations where 'natural disasters or other emergencies' are likely to produce 'sudden harmful effects' on their environment.[708]

Modern treaties tend also to require states to make contingency plans for environmental emergencies and to cooperate in their response.[709] The ILC has adopted comparable provisions in its articles on transboundary harm.[710] A typical example is Article 199 of the 1982 UNCLOS which requires states to make joint plans. Practice in this respect is well developed in the maritime field.[711] A multilateral convention and a network of bilateral agreements also facilitate emergency cooperation in cases of nuclear accidents.[712] Only in the law of the sea, however, have states assumed a power

702 ICJ Reports (1949) 4, 22.

703 1982 UNCLOS, Articles 198, 211(7) and others cited *infra*, Ch 9. See also 1989 Basel Convention on the Control of Transboundary Movements of Hazardous Wastes, Article 13.

704 See *infra*, Ch 9.

705 E.g. 1976 Convention on the Protection of the Rhine Against Chemical Pollution, Article 11; 1997 UN Watercourses Convention, Article 28, *infra*, Ch 10; 2003 UNECE Protocol on Civil Liability and Compensation for Damage Caused by Accidents on Transboundary Waters.

706 Article 5.

707 Council Recommendation C (74) 224 (1974) Annex, Part F.

708 See Okowa, in Viñuales (ed), *The Rio Declaration etc*, 471–92.

709 1990 Convention on Oil Pollution Preparedness and Response; 1992 UNECE Convention on the Transboundary Effects of Industrial Accidents; 2005 Annex VI to the Antarctic Environmental Protocol.

710 2001 Articles, Article 16; 2006 Principles on Allocation of Loss, Principle 5.

711 See *infra*, Ch 9.

712 See *infra*, Ch 7.

to intervene unilaterally to forestall accidental harm emanating from outside their territory,[713] although in other cases the defence of necessity may provide some basis for emergency measures of ecological protection taken in violation of the sovereignty of other states.[714] Such measures must be the only means of protecting an essential interest of the state from a grave and imminent peril and must not seriously impair the essential interests of the other state affected.[715]

Where accidents do pose an environmental risk for other states or the global commons, the obligation of due diligence, considered earlier, will additionally require the source state to take whatever measures are necessary to forestall or mitigate their effects. Thus, states do not discharge their duty merely by seeking to prevent accidents, or by giving notification of an emergency.[716] It is in this context that treaty obligations to maintain contingency plans and respond to pollution emergencies must be seen: they are part of a state's duty of diligence in controlling sources of known environmental harm.

9 DEFINING 'ENVIRONMENTAL DAMAGE' AND 'POLLUTION'

9(1) ENVIRONMENTAL HARM OR DAMAGE

There is no doubt that injury to persons or property falls within the scope of the obligation to prevent or control transboundary harm.[717] In this context harm can also be defined in human rights terms—i.e. adverse impacts on the right to life, private life, and property, including indigenous peoples' lifestyles.[718] The more difficult question is the extent to which protection of the environment or the prevention of environmental harm also do so. Both *Trail Smelter* and the early civil liability conventions took a narrow view, compensating for injury to persons or property but appearing to exclude wider environmental interests such as wildlife, aesthetic considerations, or the unity

713 1969 Brussels Convention Relating to Intervention on the High Seas in Cases of Oil Pollution Casualties; 1982 UNCLOS, Article 221; see *infra*, Ch 9.

714 ILC, 2001 State Responsibility Articles, Article 25. Bilder, 14 *Vand JTL* (1981) 63ff, suggests a broader principle of unilateral action to protect a state from environmental damage caused by another's breach of duty not to cause serious harm to other states.

715 *Gabčíkovo-Nagymaros Case*, ICJ Reports (1997) 7, paras 49–59. See Jagota, 16 *NYIL* (1985) 269, and Brown, 21 *CLP* (1968) 113.

716 1997 UN Watercourses Convention, Article 28(3). The *Corfu Channel Case* refers only to notification of the danger, but this must be read in the context of that case: notification would of itself have been sufficient to avert the disaster.

717 *ILC Rept* (2001) GAOR A/56/10, 388 para (4); *Trail Smelter Arbitration*, *supra*, section 5(2).

718 See the ICJ claim Ecuador filed against Colombia in 2008. On human rights impacts see *infra*, Ch 5, section 2, and Handl, in Bowman and Boyle (eds), *Environmental Damage in International and Comparative Law* (OUP, 2002) 85–110.

and diversity of ecosystems.[719] Modern civil-liability conventions and protocols now recognize environmental damage as a distinct interest covered by international tort law.[720] Security Council resolution 687, imposing international liability on Iraq for environmental damage in Kuwait, is another important precedent pointing in the same direction.[721]

When viewed from the perspective of international regulatory conventions, rather than responsibility for environmental damage, it can be seen that the older approach is outdated and inappropriate. In contrast, Principle 21 of the Stockholm Declaration and Principle 2 of the Rio Declaration refer explicitly to responsibility for controlling 'damage to the environment' of other states or of areas beyond national jurisdiction. So does the ICJ in its *Advisory Opinion on Nuclear Weapons*, while the ILC specifically includes 'the environment' within the scope of its 2001 Articles on Transboundary Harm. Articles 145 and 194 of the 1982 UNCLOS articulate the obligation to protect the marine environment in particularly broad terms. It includes measures to protect and preserve the 'ecological balance', marine flora and fauna, and 'rare and fragile ecosystems as well as the habitat of depleted, threatened or endangered species and other forms of marine life'.[722] Moreover the convention's definition of pollution in Article 1(4) includes the introduction of substances which may cause 'harm to living resources and marine life'. Similarly, the 1995 Washington Declaration on Protection of the Marine Environment from Land-based Activities refers to 'Setting as their common goal sustained and effective action to deal with all land-based *impacts* upon the marine environment', including 'physical alteration and destruction of habitat'. Instead of 'land-based sources of marine pollution' it uses a broader concept: 'land-based activities that degrade the marine environment'.[723]

Taken together, these provisions indicate that the scope of the obligation to protect the marine environment is not limited to actual or intended human usage of the sea and its contents but focuses instead on the interdependence of human activity and nature. Other treaties adopt an even broader perspective. Thus, the 1991Antarctic Protocol protects not only the Antarctic environment, 'dependent and associated

[719] Rubin, 50 *Oregon LR* (1971) 272–4. On this issue the *Trail Smelter* tribunal was required to follow US law. US tort law is now more generous in allowing for restoration of ecological loss: see *Commonwealth of Puerto Rico v SS Zoe Colocotroni*, 628 F 2d 652 (1980); Schoenbaum, in Wetterstein (ed), *Harm to the Environment* (Oxford, 1997) Ch 9, and Brans, *Liability for Damage to Public Natural Resources* (The Hague, 2001) Ch 4.

[720] 1992 Convention on Civil Liability for Oil Pollution Damage, *infra*, Ch 9; 1993 ECE Convention on Civil Liability for Damage Resulting from Activities Dangerous to the Environment, *infra*, Ch 5; 1997 Vienna Protocol on Civil Liability for Nuclear Damage and 1997 Vienna Convention on Supplementary Compensation for Nuclear Damage, *infra*, Ch 9. See generally de La Fayette, in Boyle and Bowman (eds), *Environmental Damage in International and Comparative Law* (Oxford, 1999) Ch 9; Brans, *Liability for Damage to Public Natural Resources*, Ch 7.

[721] See also *Border Activities Case*, ICJ Reports (2018), *infra*, Ch 4, section 2(6).

[722] 1982 UNCLOS, Articles 145, 194(5); see *infra*, Ch 9.

[723] ILC draft guidelines on protection of the atmosphere also refer to 'atmospheric degradation': *ILC Rept* (2015) GAOR A/70/10, Ch V.

ecosystems and the intrinsic value of Antarctica, including its wilderness and aesthetic values', but it also covers a very broad range of 'adverse effects' which must be avoided by activities planned to take place there. These include effects on climate and weather, air and water quality, marine and terrestrial environments, fauna and flora, as well as endangered species, and biological diversity.[724] Both the 1985 Ozone Convention and the 1992 Climate Change Convention likewise apply, inter alia, to controlling adverse effects on 'the composition, resilience or productivity of natural and managed ecosystems'.[725] Protection of the marine environment under Part XII of UNCLOS also includes protection of marine ecosystems.[726]

As these examples indicate, what is meant by 'the environment', and therefore by 'environmental harm', may differ in individual treaties, and will depend on what each treaty is intended to regulate and protect. It is thus not possible to give a generic definition. What does seem tenable, however, is that while prospective material injury of some kind is a necessary element of the customary obligation to prevent transboundary harm,[727] this is not limited to the loss of resources or amenities of economic value to man but can extend to the intrinsic worth of natural ecosystems, including biological diversity[728] and areas of wilderness or aesthetic significance. Studies conducted for UNEP and the ILC both concluded that the 'environment' covers at least air, water, soil, flora, fauna, ecosystems, and their interaction and noted that some agreements also include cultural heritage, landscape, and amenity values.[729]

The most radical view, supported by a number of treaties,[730] points to the need to move beyond a focus on the territory of other states in favour of an ecosystem approach, emphasizing 'consideration of whole systems rather than individual components'.[731] The 1991 Antarctic Protocol is to date the largest, most comprehensive, and significant example in which an entire continent and the surrounding marine environment have been protected on such an ecosystem basis.[732] However, whether put in holistic terms, or merely in terms of its component elements, there is now substantial consensus

724 1991 Antarctic Protocol, Article 3.

725 1985 Ozone Convention, Article 1(2); 1992 UNFCC, Article 1(1); *ILC Rept* (2015) GAOR A/70/10, Ch V. On the 1982 UNCLOS see *Chagos MPA Arbitration*, PCA (2015) paras 320 and 538.

726 *South China Sea Arbitration*, PCA (2016) paras 945, 959–83.

727 Handl, 69 *AJIL* (1975) 50. In this respect the obligation is an exception to the proposition advanced by some writers and adopted by the ILC that harm is not a necessary element of state responsibility. See Boyle, 39 *ICLQ* (1990) 16.

728 See *Border Activities Case*, ICJ Reports (2018) and *infra*, Ch 4 section 2(6).

729 UNEP, *Rept of the Working Group of Experts on Liability and Compensation for Environmental Damage arising from Military Activities*, 1996; ILC, *11th Rept on International Liability for Injurious Consequences*, UN Doc A/CN 4/468 (1995). Cultural heritage and landscape are included in the 1992 ECE Convention on the Transboundary Effects of Industrial Accidents and the 1993 ECE Convention on Civil Liability for Damage Resulting from Accidents Dangerous to the Environment.

730 E.g. 1992 CBD, *infra*, Ch 11; 1995 UN Fish Stocks Agreement, *infra*, Ch 12; 1997 UN Watercourses Convention, Article 20, *infra*, Ch 10.

731 Brunnée and Toope, 5 *YbIEL* (1994) 55.

732 See Vidas (ed), *Protecting the Polar Marine Environment* (Cambridge, 2000) Chs 1, 4; Redgwell, in Boyle and Freestone, *International Law and Sustainable Development*, Ch 9.

behind the proposition that international law protects the environment of other states and common spaces from harm.[733]

9(2) THRESHOLDS OF SERIOUS OR SIGNIFICANT HARM

Determining the threshold at which harm to the environment becomes a breach of obligation is a question on which there are several possible views. While the *Trail Smelter Case* referred to 'serious' injury,[734] suggesting a relatively high threshold, the ILC initially preferred the term 'appreciable' to qualify the degree of harm.[735] The Commission changed its mind in 1994, however, after analysis of 'more than sixty international instruments' had shown a clear preference for the term 'significant' or equivalents,[736] and this is the term now used in the 1997 UN Watercourses Convention and the 2001 Articles on Prevention of Transboundary Harm. The commentary to both texts notes that significant harm need not be substantial but must be 'more than trivial'.[737] In *Pulp Mills* the ICJ adopted the ILC formulation and applied the customary rule to the prevention of 'significant damage to the environment of another State'.[738] Both the 1985 Ozone and 1992 Climate Change Conventions also use 'significant' to qualify references to deleterious effects but the latter treaty then sets a higher threshold of threats of 'serious or irreversible damage' when introducing the precautionary principle.[739]

Apart from obvious difficulties of definition and assessment of the threshold in individual cases, other formulations, such as Principle 21 of the Stockholm Declaration and Principle 2 of the Rio Declaration, omit any qualifying reference to the level of harm or damage.[740] It should also be noted that none of the relevant civil-liability conventions requires environmental harm to be serious or significant, while the 1994 Nuclear Safety Convention merely refers to protection from the 'harmful effects' of radiation without any further explicit threshold.

More problematic is the view that any threshold of harm is essentially relative and conditional on equitable considerations or a balance of interests between the states concerned.[741] This could allow the utility of the activity to outweigh the seriousness

733 See ILC 2001 Articles on Transboundary Harm, Article 2(b).

734 35 *AJIL* (1941) 716. See also 1992 ECE Convention on the Transboundary Effects of Industrial Accidents, Article 1.

735 ILC, Draft Articles on International Liability, UN Doc A/CN 4/428 (1990) and on International Watercourses, II *YbILC* (1984) Pt 1, 112.

736 II *YbILC* (1993) Pt 2, 93, para 410; II *YbILC* (1994) Pt 2, 102–3. See generally Sachariew, 37 *NILR* (1990) 193.

737 UNGA, *Rept of the 6th Committee*, UN Doc A/51/869 (1997) 5; *ILC Rept* (2001) 388, paras (4)–(7).

738 Para 101. This is also the term used in the 1975 River Uruguay Statute, however.

739 Article 1 of both conventions and 1992 UNFCCC, Article 3(3).

740 See also 1974 Charter of Economic Rights and Duties of States, Article 30; 1978 UNEP Principles of Conduct Concerning Resources Shared by Two or More States, Principle 3; 1982 UNCLOS, Article 194. Compare however UNGA Res 2995 XXVII (1972) which refers to 'significant harmful effects'. Views differ on whether omission of an explicit threshold is intended to change earlier practice: cf Handl, 26 *NRJ* (1986) 412ff, and Pallemaerts, *Hague YIL* (1988) 206.

741 Handl, 13 *CYIL* (1975) 156; *id*, 26 *NRJ* (1986) 405; Quentin-Baxter, II *YbILC* (1981) Pt 1, 112–119; McCaffrey, II *YbILC* (1986) Pt 1, 133–4; Lefeber, *Transboundary Environmental Interference and the Origin of State Liability*, 86–9; Wolfrum, 33 *GYIL* (1990) 308.

of the harm and have the effect of converting an obligation to prevent harm into an obligation to use territory equitably and reasonably or into a constraint on abuse of rights.[742] Thus Lefeber argues that the threshold requirement represents a 'balance of interests between the sovereign right of states to develop . . . and the duty to prevent transboundary interference'.[743] There is some support for equitable balancing as a test of the permissibility of harmful effects on shared resources, such as international watercourses.[744]

While states may choose to regulate transboundary harm in this way,[745] neither the international case law nor treaty definitions of harm referred to above support thresholds determined by equitable balancing. The only balancing of interests in *Trail Smelter* related not to the question whether Canada was in breach of its obligations but to the determination of a regime for the future operation of the smelter.[746] Moreover, although the relationship between harm prevention and equitable utilization was the subject of prolonged controversy in the ILC's work on international watercourses,[747] Article 7 of the 1997 UN Watercourses Convention as finally adopted requires watercourse states to 'take all appropriate measures to prevent the causing of significant harm to other watercourse states', without subordinating this obligation to any threshold of equitable balancing.

This is almost certainly the correct conclusion, since the case for making the customary threshold of harm dependent on an equitable balance of interests is not a strong one.[748] The notion that states must act with due diligence to prevent significant harm is a formula which already allows for flexibility in individual cases, including taking account of the more limited technical and economic capacity of developing states, while excluding *de minimis* pollution. To add yet more variables would be subversive of efforts to establish minimum standards of environmental protection and prove much too favourable to the polluter. Only if the obligation to prevent harm is an absolute one, rather than an obligation of diligence, might it be justifiable to resort to equitable manipulation of the threshold of harm to mitigate the rigours of what would then be an extreme rule.

9(3) POLLUTION

'Pollution' is a narrower concept than environmental harm, as can be seen clearly when Articles 1 and 2 of the 1985 Ozone and 1992 Climate Change Conventions are compared with Article 1 of the 1979 LRTAP Convention.[749] As a concept it has

742 On abuse of rights see Boyle and Redgwell, *International Law and the Environment*, 3rd edn, 204, and *South China Sea Arbitration*, PCA (2016) paras 1166–73.

743 *Transboundary Environmental Interference*, 86–7.

744 *Infra*, Ch 10.

745 Possible examples include the 1979 LRTAP Convention and its protocols, dealing with European acid rain, on which see *infra*, Ch 6, and the 1976 Convention for the Protection of the Rhine from Chlorides, on which see *infra*, Ch 10. See also the *Trail Smelter Arbitration* in which the parties requested an equitable solution.

746 Read, 1 *CYIL* (1963) 213.

747 *Infra*, Ch 10.

748 Handl, 26 *NRJ* (1986) 416–21.

749 See *ILC Rept* (2015) GAOR A/70/10, Ch V, commentary on guideline 1.

increasingly been displaced in favour of the broader 'impacts' or 'adverse effects' or 'degradation' referred to in newer treaties. Nevertheless, pollution represents an important form of environmental harm and many agreements are concerned solely or mainly with its prevention, reduction, and control.[750]

Although several formulations are used, treaty definitions of pollution adopted following the 1972 Stockholm Conference are considerably wider than the *Trail Smelter* approach. The unifying feature of these definitions is their focus on a detrimental alteration in quality, but this can be expressed narrowly, in terms of impact on resources or amenities useful to man, or more broadly, in terms of environmental conservation or amelioration.[751] The narrow approach is represented by the definition of marine pollution initially adopted by the Group of Experts on Scientific Aspects of Marine Pollution ('GESAMP') which referred only to 'harm to living resources, hazard to human health, hindrance to marine activities including fishing, impairment of quality for use of sea water and reduction of amenities'.[752] The broader approach is found in most subsequent definitions of marine pollution, including the 1982 UNCLOS.[753] The important point is that these definitions, although similar to the GESAMP definition, also include harm or the risk of harm to marine ecosystems, endangered species, and other forms of marine life.[754] As Tomczak observes, this makes the definition independent of actual or intended human usage of the sea and its contents and focuses instead on the interdependence of human activity and nature. This broader formulation presents a much more clearly environmental perspective,[755] which now predominates.

Pollution cannot be defined simply in terms of its effects, however. All definitions confine the term to the introduction by man of substances or energy, whether directly or indirectly, into the environment. It is the relationship between these substances and their effects which together constitute pollution. This has several implications. First, it means that over-use of resources, or the impact of urban development on ecosystems, however harmful, is not 'pollution'. Some other concept, such as 'unsustainable utilization' or 'adverse effects', must be found for these problems. Secondly, despite the apparent breadth of conventional definitions, what constitutes pollution will often be limited in practice by reference to the substances whose discharge states have specifically agreed to control. Thus the annexes of prohibited or controlled substances found in treaties concerned with air pollution or land-based sources of pollution are crucial

750 See in particular Chs 8, 9, and 10.

751 See Springer, 26 *ICLQ* (1977) 531; Tomczak, 8 *Marine Policy* (1984) 311; Springer, *International Law of Pollution* (Westport, 1983).

752 See e.g. 1974 Paris Convention on Prevention of Marine Pollution from Land-based Sources, Article 1; 1976 Barcelona Convention for the Protection of the Mediterranean Sea Against Pollution, Article 2(a); 1977 OECD Recommendation C (77) 28 (Final) on Implementing a Regime of Equal Access and Non-Discrimination.

753 Article 1(1)(4). See *infra*, Ch 9.

754 See e.g. 1979 LRTAP Convention, Article 1; 1992 OSPAR Convention, Article 1(d); 1995 Barcelona Convention for the Protection of the Mediterranean Sea Against Pollution, Article 2(a) and Tomczak, 8 *Marine Policy* (1984) 317.

755 Tomczak, *ibid*, 319–21.

in determining what it is states are meant to regulate.[756] The annexes can be amended, however, so the general concept of pollution serves mainly as a residual category which can be invoked when necessary to deal with additional substances, and which allows the application of a precautionary approach to the listing of potential new pollutants.

Thus, it is only when discharges reach a certain level of seriousness, either in volume or in the context of their location, that they will constitute pollution. In *Pulp Mills* there was no 'pollution' as defined by the Statute of the River Uruguay because waste emissions to the river did not exceed applicable discharge and water quality standards.[757] Treaties on land-based sources of marine pollution show considerable diversity in the range and volume of toxic emissions treated as pollution in different seas.[758] An extreme case is Principle 6 of the Stockholm Declaration, which refers to the discharge of toxic substances 'in such quantities or concentrations as to exceed the capacity of the environment to render them harmless'. Here the damage must be irreversible. Few treaties dealing with toxic substances have taken this approach, however.[759] A more recent development adopts the opposite approach by banning all discharges except those identified as harmless and listed accordingly. This form of 'reverse listing' is found in the 1996 revision of the 1972 London Convention. In effect it treats all waste dumping as 'pollution' unless it can be proved harmless, thus reversing the burden of proof.[760] In some cases any level of discharge will be presumed harmful and banned outright. A good example of this category is the treaty prohibition of any disposal of high-level radioactive material into the global commons.[761]

We can see that what 'pollution' means is, like 'environmental damage', significantly dependent on context and objective. While it is possible to talk of an obligation to prevent 'pollution', or to protect 'the environment', there is little point attempting a global definition of what are essentially terms with a variable content. The meaning which these terms have acquired will become more apparent in later chapters.

10 MILITARY ACTIVITIES AND THE ENVIRONMENT

A number of multilateral conventions have sought to place limitations on the infliction of environmental damage for military purposes or during armed conflict.[762] Limited protection is afforded by restraints on methods of warfare and the infliction

756 See *infra*, Chs 6, 8.

757 See paras 198–9 and 229–265; 1975 Statute of the River Uruguay, Article 40.

758 *Infra*, Ch 8.

759 Contrast both the 2001 POPS Convention and the 2013 Convention on Mercury, *infra*, Ch 8.

760 *Infra*, Ch 8.

761 *Infra*, Ch 9.

762 See generally *ILC Report* (2019) Ch VI on Protection of the Environment in Relation to Armed Conflicts; Rayfuse (ed), *War and the Environment: New Approaches to Protecting the Environment in Relation to Armed Conflict* (Leiden, 2015); Droege and Tougas, 82 *Nordic JIL* (2013) 21; Breau, in Alam et al (eds), *Routledge Handbook of IEL* (Abingdon, 2013) Ch 34; Hulme, in Fitzmaurice et al, *Research Handbook on IEL*, Ch 27; Low and Hodgkinson, 35 *VJIL* (1995) 405; Greenwood in Grunawalt, King and McClain (eds), *Protection of the Environment During Armed Conflict* (US Naval War College, 1996) 397; Tarasofsky, 24 *NYIL* (1993) 17; Bothe, 34 *GYIL* (1992) 54; Kalshoven, *Constraints on the Waging of War* (Dordrecht, 1987); Aldrich, 85 *AJIL* (1991) 1; *id*, 26 *VJIL* (1986).

of unnecessary suffering found in the Hague Conventions, and in the 1949 Geneva Conventions.[763] Only the more recent agreements make explicit reference to the environment, however. Partly inspired by the use of toxic defoliation chemicals during the Vietnam War, the 1976 Environmental Modification Convention prohibits the hostile use of environmental modification techniques having 'widespread, long-lasting *or* severe effects'. This convention is in force and has been ratified by major military powers, although not by Iraq, whose actions in setting fire to Kuwaiti oil wells in 1991 might arguably have been a violation. Violations of the UN Charter will, however, entail responsibility under international law to make reparation, and Security Council Resolution 687 (1991) held Iraq liable on this ground for 'direct loss, damage, including environmental damage and depletion of natural resources' arising out of its conflict with Kuwait.[764]

Also adopted in 1977, Additional Protocol I to the 1949 Geneva Conventions prohibits 'methods or means of warfare which are intended or may be expected to cause widespread, long-term and severe damage to the natural environment',[765] and it requires parties to take care to protect the natural environment against such damage.[766] Unlike the 1976 Environmental Modification Convention ('ENMOD Convention') a breach does not occur unless the environmental damage is widespread, long-term, *and* severe. The Protocol also places limits on the circumstances in which 'works or installations containing dangerous forces', including dams and nuclear power plants, can be made the object of attack.[767] The terminology used in Articles 35 and 55 was understood to be directed at high-level policy-makers authorizing the use of unconventional weapons such as chemical agents or herbicides, and not at incidental or collateral environmental damage caused by those conducting conventional warfare.[768] These articles set a very high threshold of environmental harm which is unlikely to be met in real-world conflicts unless chemical or nuclear weapons are employed.[769] After the 1991 invasion of Kuwait unsuccessful proposals were made for the adoption of a fifth Geneva Convention, intended to cover protection of the environment in times of armed conflict.[770] The International Committee of the Red Cross ('ICRC') decided that no convention was needed, but it did adopt a set of Guidelines for inclusion in military manuals.[771] The 1998 Statute of the ICC also treats armed attacks causing

[763] See 1899 Hague Convention II with respect to the Laws and Customs of War on Land; 1907 Hague Convention IV respecting the Laws and Customs of War on Land; 1949 Geneva Conventions relating to the Protection of Victims of Armed Conflicts. See also 1972 World Heritage Convention, Article 6.

[764] See *infra*, Ch 4, section 2.

[765] Article 35(3).

[766] Article 55(1). See also Protocol II on non-international armed conflict. The protocols are very widely ratified, but not by the US.

[767] Article 56(1).

[768] See Aldrich, 26 *VJIL* (1986) 711; Tarasofsky, 24 *NYIL* (1993) 48–54.

[769] See Tomuschat, 26 *EPL* (1996) 242; Breau, *supra*, n 760, at 622–3 and references cited there.

[770] See Gasser, 89 *AJIL* (1995) 637. For the opposite view see Plant (ed), *Environmental Protection and the Law of War* (London, 1992) and IUCN/ICEL, 1991 Munich Consultation Recommendations, 22 *EPL* (1992) 63. See also UN, *Rept of the SG on the Protection of the Environment in Times of Armed Conflict*, UN Doc A/48/269 (1993); Lijnzaad and Tanja, 40 *NILR* (1993) 169.

[771] ICRC Guidelines on Protection of the Environment during Armed Conflict, UN Doc A/49/323 (1994) annex.

widespread, long term and severe harm to the environment as war crimes.[772] More recently UNEP has again recommended that Articles 35 and 55 of Protocol I be clarified and that other changes be made to the current law.[773] The matter is now on the agenda of the ILC.[774]

It should not be assumed, however, that rules of customary international law do not protect the environment in times of armed conflict. Principle 24 of the 1992 Rio Declaration asserts that 'States shall . . . respect international law providing protection for the environment in times of armed conflict and cooperate in its further development, as necessary'. UN General Assembly Resolution 47/37 (1992) also states that 'destruction of the environment not justified by military necessity and carried out wantonly, is clearly contrary to existing international law'. In the *Nuclear Weapons Advisory Opinion*, the ICJ referred to both these instruments and held that as a matter of general international law:

> States must take environmental considerations into account when assessing what is necessary and proportionate in the pursuit of legitimate military objectives. Respect for the environment is one of the elements that go to assessing whether an action is in conformity with the principles of necessity and proportionality.[775]

It seems highly probable that even if Iraq's attacks on Kuwaiti oil wells in 1991 would not meet the high threshold set out in Protocol I, they would neverthless fail the tests of necessity or proportionality which govern all military actions in general international law.[776] Moreover, as against states not parties to an international armed conflict, belligerents enjoy no special privileges and remain bound by general rules of international law.

Few environmental treaties make explicit provision for derogation or suspension during an armed conflict; the general rule is one of non-suspension of such treaties unless a contrary intention is express or implied.[777] As the ICJ pointed out in the *Nuclear Weapons Advisory Opinion*, however, environmental treaty obligations cannot have been intended to deprive a state of its right of self defence under international law.[778] Where relevant, environmental treaties may contain clauses which preclude

772 See *infra*, Ch 5, section 6(3).

773 UNEP, *Protecting the Environment during Armed Conflict* (Nairobi, 2009); Breau, *supra*, n 760, at 630–1.

774 ILC, *2nd Rept of the SR on protection of the environment in relation to armed conflicts*, GAOR A/CN.4/728 (2019) and see proposed draft articles and commentary in Ch VI of the 2019 *ILC Report*.

775 ICJ Reports (1996) 226, paras 30–2. See Gardam and Momtaz in de Chazournes and Sands (eds), *International Law, the ICJ and Nuclear Weapons* (Cambridge, 1999) 275 and 355.

776 See Tarasofsky, 24 *NYIL* (1993) 23–26, 29–30, 38–9. On the environmental aspects of the Gulf war, see Roberts, in, Grunawalt et al, *Protection of the Environment During Armed Conflict*, 222. See also 1994 *San Remo Manual on International Law Applicable to Armed Conficts at Sea*, Article 11.

777 See ILC Rept, GAOR A/66/10 (2011) Ch VI, 'Effects of Armed Conflicts on Treaties', draft Articles 4–7 and Annex, and Bothe, Cassese, Kalshoven, Kiss, Salmon, and Simmonds, *Protection of the Environment in Times of Armed Conflict*, European Parliament (1985) section 3; Tarasofsky, 24 *NYIL* (1993) 62–67.

778 ICJ Reports (1996) 226, para 30.

their application to ships or aircraft entitled to sovereign immunity, including the 1989 Salvage Convention, the 1969/92 Conventions on Civil Liability for Oil Pollution Damage, and the London and Oslo Dumping Conventions. Some treaties, while denying jurisdiction over foreign vessels entitled to immunity, require their parties to ensure as far as possible that their sovereign vessels act in a manner consistent with the treaty's requirements. Both the 1973/78 MARPOL Convention, and the marine pollution provisions of the 1982 UNCLOS are in this category.[779] Moreover, although the 1969 Intervention Convention does not apply to military vessels, several parties to the 1986 Convention on Early Notification of Nuclear Accidents have given notice when nuclear powered military submarines encountered difficulties at sea, although the latter convention is not explicitly applicable to military facilities.[780] Conventions dealing with nuclear safety and liability for nuclear accidents do not apply to military facilities, but, like the 1969 Oil Pollution Convention, the operator or owner is relieved of all liability for incidents due to armed conflict, hostilities, civil war, or insurrection.[781]

Even if international law does not relieve states of their obligations of environmental protection during conflicts, and, as in the case of Iraq, responsibility may be imposed for environmental injury, this does not of itself afford adequate assurance of military restraint. Obligations of prior environmental impact assessment, consultation, and cooperation are inherently difficult to apply in an armed conflict. Certain measures can be taken, however, to ensure that the more precautionary or preventive approach which now characterizes environmental law-making is also applied to the military sphere.[782] Partly because of their obvious potential for environmental harm a number of treaties place limitations on chemical and biological weapons.[783] The control of environmental risks posed by the military use of nuclear power and nuclear weapons remains unsatisfactory, however, partly because it falls largely outside the existing regulation of civil uses of nuclear energy.[784] More fundamentally, the *Nuclear Weapons Advisory Opinion* demonstrates that although international law constrains the use of environmentally destructive weaponry to some extent, it does not prohibit the use of nuclear weapons, or of other weapons not specifically banned by international agreements.[785]

What does need to be emphasized is the importance of making environmental consequences a serious concern in military operations, including military operations by non-state actors.[786] Sites of special cultural or ecological significance can be protected

779 1973/78 MARPOL Convention, Article 3(3); 1982 UNCLOS, Article 236.

780 *Infra*, Ch 9. 781 *Ibid.*

782 See commentary in Plant, *Environmental Protection and the Law of War*, Ch 9.

783 1972 Convention on Biological Weapons; 1976 Environmental Modification Convention; 1993 Convention on the Prohibition of Chemical Weapons. See generally Tarasofsky, 24 *NYIL* (1993) 54–61.

784 On nuclear weapons, see de Chazournes and Sands (eds), *International Law, the International Court of Justice and Nuclear Weapons*.

785 ICJ Reports (1996) 226, para 33.

786 For a comprehensive overview see ILC, *2nd Rept on protection of the environment in relation to armed conflicts*, GAOR A/CN.4/728 (2019).

from attack or military use, and for this purpose the 1972 World Heritage Convention remains relevant,[787] although world heritage status has not protected ancient sites such as Palmrya from deliberate destruction.[788] The active role of the Security Council during the 1991 Gulf conflict, and its appreciation of the environmental implications, does offer some means of ensuring that pressure for compliance with the rules governing armed conflict is applied to the parties involved. Moreover, the Gulf conflict also involved UNEP and IMO in coordinating international action to mitigate some of the more serious environmental effects. This is a role for appropriate international institutions which could also usefully be developed. In short, the continued relevance of international law governing protection of the environment, and of environmental institutions, in situations of armed conflict needs to be stressed.[789]

11 CONCLUSIONS

This chapter has attempted to draw from the relevant cases, general principles of law and the growing body of treaties, soft law instruments, and state practice indications of the main thrust of international law governing the protection of the environment. The extent to which international courts, the ILC, and states themselves, have identified customary international law relating to the environment is noteworthy. Nevertheless, the precedents accumulated here do not necessarily reflect the actual practice of all states in all circumstances. Some of the treaties considered here and in later chapters reflect the continued operation of a process of codification and law-making which will be complete only when supported by the evidence of state practice normally required for creation of customary international law.[790] Others, such as the 1982 UNCLOS, largely meet these conditions, and are generally accepted even by non-parties to represent international law.[791]

Caution is also needed before drawing general conclusions from the limited context of certain precedents, such as fisheries treaties and the *Icelandic Fisheries Case*. While the law may be well established in areas such as the conservation of marine living resources, it is still necessary to ask what evidence there is for the application of some of these rules to more novel situations. It remains important to consider in subsequent chapters how far the general norms identified here codify existing law or have

[787] Article 6(3).

[788] See AAAS, *Ancient History, Modern Destruction: Assessing the Current Status of Syria's World Heritage Sites* (2014). Many of Iraq's ancient sites, including Nimrud and Babylon, are not listed under the World Heritage Convention. Both have been heavily damaged in recent conflicts.

[789] ILC, *2nd Rept on protection of the environment in relation to armed conflicts*, GAOR A/CN.4/728 (2019). The ILC adopted draft articles in 2019.

[790] *Supra*, Ch 1.

[791] See *infra*, Ch 9. Thus, the US and Iran both accept that UNCLOS restates customary international law in their dealings with other states.

influenced the practice of states. This observation applies with equal force to 'soft law' instruments, such as UNEP's Goals and Principles of EIA, or its Montreal Guidelines for the Prevention of Pollution from Land-based Sources. Such instruments, although lacking legal force, have nevertheless had an impact on the development of state practice, or have led to the conclusion of further regional or global treaties. They should not be dismissed as being of no legal significance, and to this extent their use by UNEP for law-making purposes has significantly assisted the process of progressive development.

The importance of the customary international law and general principles outlined in this chapter should not be under-estimated when interpreting and applying environmental treaties.[792] The two go together and interact. Nevertheless, the rather general framework provided by customary international law and general principles has to be supplemented and implemented through soft law and bilateral or multilateral environmental agreements. Much of the more important work of developing precise rules and standards has fallen in practice to the institutions and autonomous intergovernmental bodies which these environmental treaties have created, and whose operation is examined in later chapters.

As we saw in Chapter 1, it would be misleading to view orthodox, customary law-making—the slow accretion of state practice supported by *opinio juris*—as an apt description of the process just described. Rather, what has occurred is an accretion of law-making experience and regulatory techniques over more than forty-five years since the Stockholm Conference. The most notable feature of environmental treaties over this period has been their increasing sophistication, characterized by the greater attention now paid to questions of effective supervision and compliance, the position of non-parties, and the problems of amendment and flexibility. The 1989 Basel Convention, the 1987 Montreal Protocol, the 1992 Convention on Climate Change, the 2001 POPS Convention, and the 2013 Convention on Mercury represent some of the most developed examples of this sort of international regulatory regime.[793] Within their own sphere, these treaties are more important than customary law, and the key question is less their contribution to precedent, although that too is important, than their effectiveness in securing objectives. For this reason subsequent chapters will attempt not merely to review the content of these treaties, but to assess their operation. In those areas where no such formal structure of regulation and supervision exists, the role of international law is necessarily weaker. Even where the problem of identifying the rules can be resolved, the remedies and processes then available for securing compliance or settling disputes present their own difficulties, which we will explore in Chapters 4 and 5.

792 See in particular the *Pulp Mills Case*, ICJ Reports (2010) 14.

793 See *infra*, Chs 6 and 8.

4

STATE RESPONSIBILITY, TREATY COMPLIANCE, AND DISPUTE SETTLEMENT

1 INTRODUCTION

In this chapter we look at the various means that can be employed to secure compliance with international environmental law. The more traditional approach to this subject is the familiar one of interstate claims for breach of international obligations, employing the variety of forms of dispute settlement machinery contemplated in Article 33 of the UN Charter. There are various disadvantages to enforcing international environmental law in this way, particularly if it involves compulsory resort to judicial institutions.[1] These disadvantages include the adverse effect on relations between the states concerned; the complexity, length, and expense of international litigation; the technical character of environmental problems and the difficulties of proof which legal proceedings may entail, and uncertainty concerning jurisdiction and applicable law in legally complex disputes.

Perhaps the most significant objection is that the traditional model exemplified by the *Trail Smelter Case* is concerned largely with affording reparation as a response to violations of international law rather than preventing environmental harm before it happens. Such a system is inherently bilateral and confrontational in character: it assumes that 'injured states' whose rights are affected are the primary actors in seeking

[1] See generally UNEP, *Study on Dispute Avoidance and Dispute Settlement in International Environmental Law*, UNEP/GC 20/INF/16 (1999); Bilder, 144 *Recueil des Cours* (1975) 141; Cooper, 24 *CYIL* (1986) 247; Okowa, in Evans (ed), *Remedies in International Law* (Oxford, 1998) 157; Koskenniemi, 60 *Nordic JIL* (1991) 73; Sand, *Lessons Learned in Global Environmental Governance* (Washington, 1990); de Chazournes, 99 *RGDIP* (1995) 37; Stephens, *International Courts and Environmental Protection* (Cambridge, 2009); Boyle and Harrison, 4 *JIDS* (2013) 245.

compliance with legal standards of environmental protection. Its closest analogy in national legal systems is tort law, and adjudication is the method of dispute settlement to which it is most suited.

Claims for transboundary damage are thus the most obvious application for this approach, yet in practice states have preferred to avoid inter-state litigation and the law of state responsibility for damage, and have relied instead on other methods of establishing liability using national law, considered in the next chapter. No modern pollution disaster, including Chernobyl, Sandoz, or *Amoco Cadiz*, has resulted in the adjudication of an international claim for transboundary damage against the state concerned. Ecuador's claim against Colombia for transboundary air pollution damage was settled without a hearing.[2] The only precedents which hold a state unequivocally responsible for environmental damage in international law are Security Council Resolution 687, adopted following Iraq's invasion and occupation of Kuwait in 1991, and the *Border Activities Case*.[3]

The main reason for discussing state responsibility for environmental damage is because an understanding of its limitations is essential to an explanation of other developments in the international legal system that have largely taken its place. However, the possibility that states might have recourse to international claims against their neighbours for environmental damage may itself exercise an influence on the negotiation of environmental agreements and the settlement of disputes.[4] It is thus not to be discounted.

As we saw in Chapter 3, modern international law focuses principally on the control and prevention of environmental harm and the conservation and sustainable use of natural resources and ecosystems. A preventive, or regulatory, regime of this comprehensive character requires a more sophisticated approach to enforcement and compliance than one based primarily on interstate claims for environmental damage. It must be capable, first, of ensuring compliance with the obligations of pollution control, resource conservation, transboundary risk management and cooperation considered in the previous chapter. Secondly, the emergence of problems of a global character, affecting the atmosphere, oceans, and natural resources, necessitates an appropriately multilateral response. A perspective which accords rights only to 'injured states' after the event will be inappropriate to the polycentric character of global environmental problems involving a range of actors and a multiplicity of complex interrelated issues,[5] or for the protection of common interests, common property resources,

[2] See *Aerial Spraying Case*, ICJ Order of 13 September 2013.

[3] *Certain Activities carried out by Nicaragua in the Border Area (Costa Rica* v *Nicaragua)* [Hereafter '*Border Activities Case*'] ICJ Reports (2015) para 229, section 5, and for the compensation decision see ICJ Reports (2018), discussed *infra*.

[4] See for example the *Aerial Spraying Case (Ecuador/Colombia)* ICJ application 2007, where Ecuador sought cessation and compensation. The case was settled without a hearing in 2013: see Boyle in Jayakumar, Koh, Beckman, Phan (eds), *Transboundary Pollution: Evolving Issues of International Law and Policy* (Cheltenham, 2015) Ch 9.

[5] Fuller, 92 *Harv LR* (1978) 353. See *infra*, Chs 6, 10, 12, 13 for examples.

or future generations. Thirdly, many environmental problems involve harm which is subtle, cumulative, and manifest only after a long period of time; in these circumstances 'only equitable and preventative remedies may be capable of providing an effective solution'.[6]

Judicial tribunals are not necessarily the right institutions to provide these solutions. Their limitations can be observed in two important decisions of the ICJ concerned with control of environmental risks. In the *Nuclear Weapons Advisory Opinion* the ICJ showed that it is possible to accommodate public-interest multi-party litigation within the procedure for giving advisory opinions,[7] but its authoritative exposition of the law did not alter the need for negotiations to bring about further progress on nuclear disarmament. The *Gabčíkovo-Nagymaros Dam Case*[8] is notable as the first contentious case tried by the ICJ in which environmental monitoring and risk management were central to the court's decision, and as the first in which NGOs sought (unsuccessfully) to file an *amicus* brief.[9] However, it too ended in a judgment requiring the parties to negotiate a solution. Not surprisingly, in cases where the dispute is multilateral, or involves fundamental issues of social, economic, and political choice, states will usually prefer to resolve such problems by negotiations, allowing room for flexible regulation or equitable solutions not necessarily dictated by international law, but accommodating as far as possible the interests of all parties.

In Chapter 2 we noted how states increasingly rely on intergovernmental commissions and meetings of treaty parties as a means of coordinating policy, developing the law, supervising its implementation, putting community pressure on individual states, and resolving conflicts of interest. These bodies also have greater flexibility and may be better at securing compliance than traditional forms of dispute settlement. In place of more confrontational approaches, such regimes facilitate 'dispute avoidance', and promote 'alternative dispute resolution' whose purpose is not to penalize states, but to facilitate and promote compliance.[10]

The weakness of this approach, however, is that since in most cases it relies for effectiveness on the operation of community pressure, it may be thought to lack real enforcement power. Moreover, its essentially political character may dilute the force of legal standards,[11] and may legitimize practices otherwise insupportable from an environmental viewpoint. The first of these criticisms misconceives the nature of the international legal system. The resolution of environmental disputes by interstate litigation, as in the *Gabčíkovo Case*, is itself substantially dependent on the consent and good faith of the states concerned. International courts and tribunals do not enforce the law; they merely decide what it is, apply it to the facts, and make appropriate findings and orders, which it is the responsibility of the parties to carry out. Diplomatic pressure remains in practice the only real sanction for ensuring compliance.

[6] Bilder, 144 *Recueil des Cours* (1975) 225.
[7] ICJ Reports (1996) 226. See *infra*, section 4(1).
[8] ICJ Reports (1997) 7.
[9] On NGO participation in litigation see *infra*, section 4(1).
[10] See *infra*, section 3.
[11] Koskenniemi, 3 *YbIEL* (1992) 123.

What institutional supervision offers, whether through international organizations, or autonomous treaty bodies, is the opportunity to organize this pressure on a multilateral basis.[12] The second criticism begs the question whether maintaining normative coherence and strict adherence to law are more important than finding mechanisms that settle disputes and secure compliance with agreed commitments. On this question the international legal system has always been pragmatic rather than principled.[13]

2 STATE RESPONSIBILITY AND LIABILITY FOR ENVIRONMENTAL DAMAGE

2.1 THE BASIS OF STATE RESPONSIBILITY

The law of state responsibility regulates the accountability of states under international law.[14] The foundation of responsibility lies in the breach of obligations undertaken by states or imposed on them by international law.[15] Responsibility in environmental cases will normally arise either because of the breach of one or more of the customary obligations referred to in Chapter 3 or because of a breach of treaty.[16] The concept is not limited to liability for environmental damage, but has a wider application in the enforcement of international obligations concerning protection of the environment and prevention of transboundary harm. It is thus an important element in the *Gabčíkovo-Nagymaros, Pulp Mills* and *MOX Plant Cases*, even without proof of actual or imminent damage.

Only the state's own obligations are in issue here. Private parties or companies are not in general bound by public international law although, as we shall see in Chapter 5, the practice of channelling environmental liability towards private

[12] For a particularly good overview see Bodansky, *The Art and Craft of International Environmental Law* (Cambridge, Mass, 2010) Ch 11.

[13] See Article 33 of the UN Charter, and Bodansky, op cit.

[14] See ILC 2001 Articles on State Responsibility ['ILC Articles'], *ILC Report* (2001) GAOR A/56/10, 43–365, reproduced in Crawford (ed), *The ILC's Articles on State Responsibility* (Cambridge, 2002). This final draft reflects important changes made in 1998 and 2000: see Crawford et al, 94 *AJIL* (2000) 660 and 96 *AJIL* (2002) 874. In Resolution 56/83 (2001) the UN General Assembly 'took note' of the draft articles. See generally de Arechaga, in Sorensen (ed), *Manual of Public International Law* (London, 1968) 530; *id*, 159 *Recueil des Cours* (1978) 267; Crawford, Pellet, Olleson (eds), *The Law of International Responsibility* (Oxford, 2010); Crawford, *State Responsibility* (Cambridge, 2013).

[15] Articles 1–3, ILC Articles; Crawford, *State Responsibility*, 49–51.

[16] See Xue, *Transboundary Damage in International Law* (Cambridge, 2003) Ch 8; Scovazzi, 12 *YbIEL* (2001) 43; Lefeber, *Transboundary Environmental Interference and the Origin of State Liability* (The Hague, 1996) esp Ch 4; Francioni and Scovazzi (eds), *International Responsibility for Environmental Harm* (Dordrecht, 1991) esp chapter by Mazzeschi; Okowa, *State Responsibility for Transboundary Air Pollution in International Law* (Oxford, 2000); Smith, *State Responsibility and the Marine Environment* (Oxford, 1988); Dupuy, *La Responsabilité internationale des états pour les dommages d'origine technologique et industrielle* (Paris, 1976); *id*, in OECD, *Legal Aspects of Transfrontier Pollution* (Paris, 1977).

actors in national law is now a widely developed alternative to the international responsibility (or 'liability') of states in cases of environmental damage. But the problem of attributing private conduct to states will seldom impinge on responsibility in international law for non-performance of the state's own environmental obligations. Even where an activity causing environmental harm is conducted by private parties, as in the *Trail Smelter* or *Pulp Mills Cases*, the issue remains one of the state's responsibility for prevention, cooperation, and notification, which cannot be avoided by surrendering the activity itself into private hands.[17] In this chapter, therefore, it is important to remember that we are not concerned with the conduct of individual polluters, fishermen, or multinational enterprises, but with states themselves, and in particular with their obligations of due diligence and cooperation. Only in this sense is the state a guarantor of private conduct, but its responsibility is direct, not vicarious.

2(2) FAULT AND DUE DILIGENCE

To describe the responsibility of states in international law as based on fault is misleading and liable to confuse. Both the *Corfu Channel Case*,[18] and the manner in which writers have subsequently interpreted that judgment, illustrate the dangers of trying to make general propositions on this subject. Two points must be borne in mind regarding 'fault' in international law. The term can be used subjectively, requiring intention, malice, or recklessness on the part of the state or its agents,[19] or it can be used objectively, meaning simply the breach of an international obligation.[20] Used in the subjective sense, 'fault' is almost never the basis of responsibility in environmental disputes, although the reckless or intentional infliction of environmental damage in situations such as the Iraqi attack on Kuwait in 1991 could be said to involve subjective fault.[21] But the point is that fault of this subjective kind is not a necessary condition of responsibility. Jiménez de Arechaga aptly explains this view: 'The decisive consideration is that unless the rule of international law which has been violated specifically envisages malice or culpable negligence, the rules of international law do not

17 See *Advisory Opinion on the Responsibilities and Obligations of States with Respect to Activities in the Area*, ITLOS Reports (2011) paras 172–177 ['*AO on Activities in the Area*']; *Bosnian Genocide Case*, ICJ Reports (2007) 43, paras 390–415; ILC Articles 4–11 and commentary in Crawford (ed), *The ILC's Articles on State Responsibility*.

18 ICJ Reports (1949) 4. See *infra*.

19 For example genocide, which requires proof of intention to destroy a particular group: *Bosnian Genocide Case*, ICJ Reports (2007) 43, paras 186–7.

20 Brownlie, *System of the Law of Nations: State Responsibility* (Oxford, 1983), 38–48, observes: 'The approach adopted by the majority of the Court [in Corfu Channel] fails to correspond with either the *culpa* doctrine or the test of objective responsibility' (p 47).

21 *Supra*, Ch 3, section 5.

contain a general floating requirement of malice or culpable negligence as a condition of responsibility'.[22]

Used in the objective sense of breach of obligation, however, 'fault' is essentially tautologous, unless the particular obligation itself incorporates subjective elements. While it is not erroneous to describe the breach of an objective standard of diligent control of harmful activities as amounting to 'fault' it adds little to our understanding of the concept of responsibility to do so. Far more significant, as we saw in Chapter 3, is the question how due diligence is to be defined.[23] For this purpose what matters is that there is no additional requirement of intention, malice, or recklessness on the part of the state. References to 'fault' in this chapter are thus to be understood as meaning simply a failure to act with due care or diligence, or a breach of treaty, or the commission of a prohibited act.

Putting all this in an environmental context, the key point is that we can take it for granted that states are responsible ('liable') in international law to make reparation for transboundary damage, or the risk of damage, resulting from their own failure to regulate and control potentially harmful activities to the standard of due diligence required by international law, or from their failure to cooperate.[24] This follows inevitably from the general law of state responsibility codified by the ILC as applied to breach of the obligations outlined Chapter 3. The more difficult question we have to consider in the next section is whether states are also liable in international law for transboundary damage caused *without* breach of obligation or fault in the sense just defined. This form of responsibility is sometimes referred to as strict or absolute liability, by analogy with the same concepts in national law and civil-liability treaties. 'Strict liability' differs from 'absolute liability' only in the greater range of defences which may preclude wrongfulness[25]—but in both cases acting with due diligence will *not* be a defence. Causing foreseeable harm will be enough.

2(3) LIABILITY OF STATES FOR ENVIRONMENTAL DAMAGE IN INTERNATIONAL LAW

Liability for loss or damage is an elementary feature of a legal system; it remains an important part of most systems of environmental law even when supplemented or in part superseded by regulatory regimes, risk avoidance procedures, and criminal penalties.

[22] In Sorensen, *Manual of Public International Law*, 535. See *ILC Report* (1998) Ch VIII, para 340: 'There was no general requirement of fault or damage for a State to incur responsibility for an internationally wrongful act.' See also Brownlie, *State Responsibility*, 44 ff; Smith, *State Responsibility and the Marine Environment*, 15–20, but contrast the dissent of Judge Krylov, *Corfu Channel Case*, ICJ Reports (1949) 72, requiring *dolus* or *culpa*, and Oppenheim, *International Law* (5th edn, London, 1955) vol I, 343: 'An act of state injurious to another is nevertheless not an international delinquency if committed neither wilfully and maliciously nor with culpable negligence.'

[23] *Supra*, Ch 3, section 5(2). [24] *Ibid*.

[25] Compare liability for oil pollution damage, *infra*, Ch 9, and nuclear accidents, *infra*, Ch 7.

In international law, liability for transboundary damage, based on analogies going back to Roman law, is one of the oldest concepts available in interstate disputes. The *Trail Smelter* arbitral award delivered in 1938 and 1941, and involving a transboundary air pollution dispute between the US and Canada, remains the seminal judicial contribution to the international law on the subject.[26] After awarding compensation for damage already proved, the arbitrators ordered payment of further compensation if harm subsequently occurred notwithstanding Canada's compliance with the regime of control laid down in the award. This order can be read in support of a general principle of liability without fault, but the failure of many writers to identify precisely which principle the case supports indicates the difficulty of drawing firm conclusions from it. Because Canada's liability for proven damage was accepted by the parties at the outset, the award was not concerned with establishing a standard of responsibility in international law. It does not provide a strong affirmation of liability without fault as a general principle.

Nevertheless, despite the limited range of national and international sources on which the tribunal relied in determining rules of international law, there is no reason to doubt that states remain responsible in international law for harm caused in breach of obligation by transboundary air pollution.[27] Moreover, modern monitoring and sampling techniques have made it possible to calculate with reasonable accuracy the amounts of transboundary air pollution emanating from individual countries and to identify the areas where it is deposited.[28] Furnishing the necessary proof, even to the 'clear and convincing' standard demanded by the tribunal in the *Trail Smelter Case*, need no longer be a potential obstacle to the attribution of responsibility for long-range transboundary air pollution.[29]

(a) When are states liable for environmental damage?

Since *Trail Smelter* there has been little or no judicial elaboration of liability for transboundary damage in international law, and the precise character of this elementary concept remains unsettled. Academic literature remains deeply divided, with some authors emphasizing the prohibition of transboundary harm, while others, including the present authors, stress the failure to regulate and control the source of harm.[30] It seems generally accepted that no responsibility of any kind will attach to harm resulting from risks of which the state concerned was not and could not have been objectively aware. This was an essential condition of Albania's responsibility in the *Corfu Channel Case*.[31] However, the common assumption that international law simply

26 *Supra*, Ch 3, section 5(2).

27 See Boyle in Jayakumar, et al (eds), *Transboundary Pollution: Evolving Issues of International Law and Policy*, Ch 9, discussing the *Aerial Spraying Case (Ecuador/Colombia)*, and *infra*, Ch 6.

28 Sand, in Helm (ed), *Energy: Production, Consumption and Consequences* (Washington, DC, 1990) 247.

29 Handl, 26 *NRJ* (1986) 440–7; Kirgis, 66 *AJIL* (1972) 294.

30 For example, contrast Scovazzi, 12 *YbIEL* (2001) 43, with the views of the present authors. The disagreements on this subject transcend the divide between civil law and common law.

31 ICJ Reports (1949) 18–22. See *ILC Report* (2001) GAOR A/56/10, 385, para (14) and *supra*, Ch 3, section 5(1).

prohibits states from causing or permitting transboundary environmental harm is not reflected in state practice or in the work of the ILC, as we have already observed in Chapter 3. If it were true that transboundary harm is prohibited, there would then be no need to regulate transboundary or global environmental risks and this book could end at Chapter 5.

On the most widely held view states are liable only if the harm is directly caused by a failure of due diligence, or by some other breach of obligation, such as a violation of the UN Charter prohibition on use of force or the illegal occupation of territory.[32] As Dupuy points out, whatever the *Trail Smelter Case* decides, it must be read in the light of subsequent state practice, which in his view favours liability in such cases if there is a failure to act with due diligence, but not liability without fault.[33] Reviewing the proceedings of the Preparatory Committee for the Stockholm Conference, Handl concluded that they too provide little or no support in favour of any specific theory.[34] Viewed in isolation, Principle 21 of the 1972 Stockholm Declaration and Principle 2 of the 1992 Rio Declaration are thus an inconclusive guide to the precise contours of liability for environmental damage, and must be interpreted within the framework of customary rules on which both are based. As we saw in Chapter 3, their incorporation in environmental treaties points clearly in the direction of a due diligence obligation—an obligation of conduct (regulation and control) rather than result (no transboundary harm). Only exceptionally do treaties adopt a form of state liability for damage without fault.[35] More often, as in Articles 139 and 235 of the 1982 UNCLOS, they specify expressly that only for the non-fulfilment of international obligations will states parties be responsible.[36]

Some writers have argued, however, that a form of strict or absolute liability for environmental harm arises independently through general principles of law, equity, sovereign equality, or good neighbourliness.[37] Jenks identified ultra-hazardous activities as a distinct category for which strict or absolute liability is justified as a means of shifting the burden of proof and ensuring a more equitable distribution of loss.[38]

32 See Lefeber, *Transboundary Environmental Interference*, 172–6; and *Border Activities Case (Compensation)*, ICJ Reports (2018) where responsibility arose from damage caused by illegal occupation of territory.

33 Dupuy, in Bothe (ed), *Trends in Environmental Policy and Law* (Gland, 1980) 373. See also Kiss and Shelton, in Ndiaye and Wolfrum (eds), *Law of the Sea, Environmental Law and Settlement of Disputes* (Leiden, 2007) 1131–2.

34 74 *AJIL* (1980) 535–40 and see also Jiménez de Arechaga, 159 *Recueil des cours* (1978) 272; Dupuy, *La responsabilité internationale etc*, 355–8.

35 See Lefeber, *Transboundary Environmental Interference*, 159–66.

36 See *AO on Activities in the Area*, ITLOS Reports (2011) paras 188–211. See also 1961 Treaty Relating to the Cooperative Development of the Water Resources of the Columbia River Basin, Article 18; 1988 Convention for the Regulation of Antarctic Mineral Resource Activities, Article 8; 2005 Antarctic Protocol, Liability Annex VI, Article 10.

37 Lefeber, *Transboundary Environmental Interference and the Origin of State Liability*, esp Ch 5, reviews the literature comprehensively. See also Scovazzi, 12 *YbIEL* (2001) 43 and Kiss and Shelton, in Ndiaye and Wolfrum (eds), *Law of the Sea, Environmental Law and Settlement of Disputes*, 1131–51.

38 117 *Recueil des cours* (1966) 105. See also Hardy, 36 *BYIL* (1960) 223; Smith, *State Responsibility and the Marine Environment*, 112–25; Handl, 13 *CYIL* (1975) 68ff; and Brownlie, *State Responsibility*, 50.

In defining what constitutes 'ultra-hazardous activity' most attempts focus more on the potential harm than on the likelihood of the risk occurring. One candidate is the risk posed by nuclear power plants.[39] Beyond that, the boundaries are more questionable and views are divided on whether the category should extend to activities whose effects are only cumulatively harmful, as in the *Trail Smelter Case*. An alternative approach to the problem of definition is to require specific agreement, but the only clear example is the 1972 Space Objects Liability Convention, under which states bear direct and absolute liability for damage on earth.[40] Significantly, treaties concerned with nuclear accidents and oil pollution at sea do not follow this example.[41] They focus instead on the liability of the owner or operator, although states may be involved in the provision of insurance or supplementary compensation.

Nor do state claims in general support any particular standard of liability for environmental damage. This can be observed most clearly in respect of nuclear accidents or tests. Only the *Cosmos 954* claim[42] brought by Canada explicitly adopts the view that states are absolutely liable for ultra-hazardous activities as a matter of general principle, but this claim was also based on the 1972 Space Objects Liability Convention and was settled *ex gratia* by the Soviet Union. Other examples of *ex gratia* payments in respect of oil pollution at sea, nuclear tests, or explosions at borders do not afford evidence of *opinio iuris* regarding an explicit standard of liability.[43] In cases where damage is caused by pollution of international watercourses, states have preferred to channel claims through national courts, relying on principles of civil liability. The Sandoz accident and other cases of Rhine pollution have been dealt with in this manner, and not by interstate claims.[44] The *Trail Smelter Case* remains the only example of an interstate claim for air-pollution damage. If that dispute were to arise today, it seems more likely that it too would be resolved by transboundary civil litigation.[45]

Thus, even if states might in theory be held liable for transboundary damage caused by activities within their territory or control when they are not at fault, the examples remain at best exceptional or questionable. After undertaking the most comprehensive review of the precedents Lefeber reluctantly concluded that 'a positivist approach to international law cannot but lead to the rejection of an absolute obligation to prevent transboundary environmental interference causing significant harm or liability *sine delicto*'.[46]

(b) Liability of states under general principles of law

The argument that a standard of liability for environmental damage can be inferred by analogy from general principles of law rests on the use of strict liability in national legal systems and in civil-liability treaties, particularly those dealing with oil pollution

39 Scc *infra*, Ch 7.

40 Article II. See Cheng, *Studies in International Space Law* (Oxford, 1997) Ch 11.

41 See *infra*, Chs 7, 9.

42 *Claim for damage caused by Cosmos 954*, 18 *ILM* (1979) 902; Schwartz and Berlin, 27 *McGill LJ* (1982) 676 and see *infra*, Ch 7 for other state claims concerning nuclear accidents.

43 Lefeber, *Transboundary Environmental Interference*, who reviews other examples at 166–77.

44 See *infra*, Ch 10.

45 See *infra*, Ch 5.

46 *Transboundary Environmental Interference*, 187.

at sea and nuclear accidents.[47] It is true that many legal systems entertain strict liability in certain cases. The common law principle employed in *Rylands v Fletcher*[48] and in certain nuisance cases is also found in many civil-law systems, especially in situations of ultra-hazardous activities.[49] There are, however, significant differences in the scope of strict liability. In French law strict liability is an accepted principle of governmental liability, while in England activities conducted by public bodies under statutory authority are usually excluded from *Rylands v Fletcher*.[50] English common law also excludes from its rules on strict liability damage which could not reasonably have been foreseen, thus significantly limiting the utility of no-fault liability in cases of historic pollution damage.[51] Moreover, although there is a legislative trend to create special rules of strict liability for pollution damage or activities dangerous to the environment,[52] these precedents are 'far from presenting a homogeneous approach to the mechanisms for remedying environmental damage'.[53] National legal systems differ not only in their acceptance of strict liability, but also in the extent to which they allow recovery for environmental damage, that is for losses such as wildlife that are not property or have no accepted economic value.[54]

Attempts have been made to harmonize the general law on liability for environmental damage, most comprehensively in the 1993 Lugano Convention on Civil Liability, but this treaty has not been widely adopted and has had no impact on existing national law.[55] Some writers have concluded that the analogy of international liability

[47] Goldie, 14 *ICLQ* (1965) 1189; Kelson, 12 *Harv ILJ* (1972) 197; Gaines, 20 *Harv ILJ* (1989) 311 and see *infra*, Chs 7, 9.

[48] (1868) LR 3 HL 330, and see Waite, 18 *JEL* (2006) 423. Not all common law jurisdictions follow *Rylands v Fletcher*: see the High Court of Australia's decision in *Burnie Port Authority v General Jones Pty Ltd* (1994) 179 CLR 520, rejecting strict liability in favour of 'ordinary negligence'.

[49] Lawson and Markesinis, *Tortious Liability for Unintentional Harm in the Common Law and Civil Law* (Cambridge, 1981) vol I, Ch 4; Reid, 48 *ICLQ* (1999) 731; Van Dam, *European Tort Law* (2nd edn, Oxford, 2013) Ch 10.

[50] *Dunne v Northwestern Gas Board* [1964] 2 QB 605 and see Brown and Bell, *French Administrative Law* (5th edn, Oxford, 1997) 193–201; Van Dam, *European Tort Law*, Ch 10.

[51] *Cambridge Water Co v Eastern Counties Leather plc* [1994] 1 All ER 53; *The Wagon Mound (No 2)* [1967] 1 AC 67, per Lord Reid. See Ogus, 6 *JEL* (1994) 151; Wilkinson, 57 *MLR* (1994) 799; Brearley, 7 *JEL* (1995) 119.

[52] E.g. China, Environmental Protection Law, Article 41; Brazil, 1980 Constitution, Article 262(3); USA, 1980 Comprehensive Environmental Response, Compensation and Liability Act; Portugal, 1986 Law No 11, Article 41; Sweden, 1986 Environmental Damage Act; Greece, Law No 1650, Article 29; Germany, 1990 Environmental Liability Act, Article 1; Norway, 1989 Pollution Control Act; Russia, 1991 Law on the Protection of the Environment, Articles 89–90; Finland, 1994 Environmental Damage Compensation Act. Not all countries have followed this trend: compare Italy, 1986 Law No 349, Article 18; Chile, 1994 Law on the Environment, Article 52. See Bianchi, 6 *JEL* (1994) 21; Wetterstein, 3 *Env Liability* (1995) 41; Hoffman, 38 *NILR* (1991) 27.

[53] EC, *Green Paper on Remedying Environmental Damage*, COM (93) 47 (1993) para 2.2.1. See also Van Dam, *European Tort Law*, Ch 10; Lefeber, *Transboundary Environmental Interference and the Origin of State Liability* (The Hague, 1996) 182–3, 276–9.

[54] For reviews of different national and international approaches to the inclusion of 'environmental damage' within the scope of liability for damage see Wetterstein (ed), *Harm to the Environment* (Oxford, 1997) especially Chs 2, 6–9; Bowman and Boyle (eds), *Environmental Damage in International and Comparative Law* (Oxford, 2002) Chs 11–18.

[55] See *infra*, Ch 5, section 3(2).

with municipal law is both inappropriate and 'does not, as yet, seem to support the extension of the standard of no-fault liability to all environmentally hazardous activities'.[56] Similarly, although widespread, the use of strict or absolute liability in civil-liability treaties and in the ILC's 2006 Principles for the Allocation of Loss is normally part of a complex scheme whose principles cannot easily be replicated in public international law.[57] These treaties were in any case intended to channel limited liability to the private party responsible for the activity in question: they tell us little or nothing about state liability in international law. Most are not in force and their impact on national law is negligible.[58]

These observations are not necessarily an obstacle to an international court relying on general principles to found a principle of state liability in international law.[59] Given that the decision is thus one of legal policy, an argument based on strict liability as a general principle of law cannot be dismissed. But international courts have been cautious in making use of this source of law, mainly because it constitutes a form of judicial lawmaking independent of the will of states. References to national law in the *Trail Smelter Case* were carefully controlled by the *compromis* and agreed by the parties.[60] Where this is not the case, it seems likely that an international court would hesitate to impose a general principle of strict or absolute liability on states, however widely evidenced in national law, in the face of the contrary evidence of state claims and treaty formulations referred to earlier. For this reason objective responsibility for breach of obligation remains a firmer foundation for a standard of state liability for environmental damage in international law. As we will see below, that also appears to represent the final view of the ILC.

2(4) DEVELOPING THE LAW OF STATE LIABILITY FOR DAMAGE

(a) Who should be liable for transboundary harm: states or private parties?

With the deficiencies of the existing law in mind, the UNCHE in 1972 called on states 'to develop further the international law regarding liability and compensation for the victims of pollution and other environmental damage caused by activities within the jurisdiction or control of such states . . . '.[61] Six years later, the ILC embarked on a twenty-nine-year odyssey entitled 'Liability for Injurious Consequences of Acts Not Prohibited by International Law'.[62] In this guise, the Commission slowly and

[56] Lefeber, *Transboundary Environmental Interference*, 182–3, 276–9.

[57] See *infra*, Ch 5, section 4; Handl, 92 *RGDIP* (1988) 35ff; Lefeber, *Transboundary Environmental Interference*, Ch 7; Doecker and Gehring, 2 *JEL* (1990) 1; Brans, *Liability for Damage to Public Natural Resources* (The Hague, 2001) Ch 7.

[58] Churchill, 12 *YbIEL* (2001) 3. But this comment does not apply to the oil pollution and nuclear liability treaties.

[59] See Judge McNair, *South West Africa Case*, ICJ Reports (1950) 128, 148.

[60] See the tribunal's award at 35 *AJIL* (1939) 698, 714ff.

[61] 1972 Stockholm Declaration , Principle 22.

[62] See Quentin-Baxter, II *YbILC* (1981) Pt 1, 112–22; Barboza, 6th *Report*, UN Doc A/CN 4/428 (1990) with draft articles 1–33 and, *ILC Report* (1990) GAOR A/45/10, 242; Lefeber, *Transboundary Environmental Interference*, Ch 6.

uncertainly grappled with the task identified by the Stockholm Conference and reiterated in 1992 by the Rio Conference on Environment and Development.[63]

Why should the ILC address the question of liability for transboundary damage and is its concluded work on state responsibility and the management of transboundary risk not sufficient for the purpose? As we saw above, transboundary environmental damage resulting from the activities of industry or business will not in normal circumstances be attributable to the source state in international law.[64] State liability for such activities based on a failure to regulate and control will not cover damage that is unforeseeable or unavoidable.[65] In these circumstances the state itself is not at fault and the loss will not be recoverable in international law.[66] The ILC's work thus proceeded from the entirely reasonable assumption that transboundary damage may still happen, however diligent the state has been in regulating and controlling the harmful activity, and that some alternative form of redress is desirable. The Commission had two possible options.

First, even though it may not be at fault in such cases, arguments can be made for shifting the burden of loss back to the source state, particularly where the source is an ultra-hazardous activity such as a nuclear power plant. In the absence of reciprocal acceptance of risk, or some common benefit, making the victim state suffer in the event of unforeseeable or unavoidable harm is not an attractive policy.[67] The underlying assumption here is that it is inequitable to leave the burden to lie where it falls merely because the source state has acted with all due diligence. The injured state can neither control the activities which cause such harm nor does it necessarily benefit from them, however socially or economically desirable they may be to the source state. The problem of inequity can readily be observed in the relationship between states using nuclear power and those non-nuclear states which cannot avoid the risks posed by nuclear accidents such as Chernobyl: the latter have no veto over their neighbours and no guarantee of indemnity for accidental harm beyond the limits of what may be available under nuclear civil-liability conventions.[68] Nor is due diligence always an easy standard to administer unless clearly accepted international standards defining the content of this duty can be identified.[69] Accidents can happen even in the best-regulated and managed installations; their occurrence does not necessarily indicate any fault by the state. A heavy burden of proof will be placed on whoever has to establish a failure of due diligence. In the case of complex processes, such as nuclear reactors, this will be especially difficult unless liberal inferences of fact are allowed, or the burden of proof is placed on the source state.[70] These arguments all pointed the ILC towards affirming that states are and should be liable without fault in such cases.

[63] Rio Declaration, Principle 13.

[64] *Supra*, section 2(1).

[65] See e.g. *Corfu Channel Case* (1949) ICJ Reports 1; 1982 UNCLOS, Article 139.

[66] *ILC Report* (2004) GAOR A/59/10, 166, commentary to Principle 1, para 8.

[67] Quentin-Baxter, II *YbILC* (1981) Pt 1, 113–8; Barboza, II *YbILC* (1986) Pt 1, 160; Handl, 92 *RGDIP* (1988) 50.

[68] See *infra*, Ch 7.

[69] For example in the 1994 Convention on Nuclear Safety, *infra*, Ch 7.

[70] Cf *Corfu Channel Case*, ICJ Reports (1949) 1, 18 where the court did allow certain inferences from the fact of Albania's exclusive territorial control. McCaffrey, II *YbILC* (1988) Pt 2, 30, para 167, suggests that due diligence is 'essentially a defence' and thus 'the burden of proving it should lie with the state of origin', but the case law reviewed *supra*, Ch 3, section 4, does not bear this out.

But why make states liable for damage they have not caused? Even where a state is potentially responsible in international law, to whatever extent, it is far from clear that states should be the only or even the principal source of recourse for those injured by transboundary damage. Claiming compensation from a government for pollution caused by industry amounts in effect to a state subsidy and undermines the 'polluter pays' principle.[71] Allowing direct recourse against the enterprise causing the damage would do more to facilitate a 'polluter pays' approach to the allocation of transboundary costs than making states a guarantor for industry.[72] Moreover, only governments can bring international claims against another state. Finding a forum with jurisdiction will thus depend on the consent of another state, which may not be easy to obtain. In practice very few claims for transboundary damage have been handled in this way. It will usually be simpler, quicker, and economically more efficient to make those who cause pollution or other forms of damage pay, rather than states. From this perspective, state responsibility and the liability of states are and should be no more than residual sources of redress. These arguments favoured a second option—developing the law of civil liability.

(b) The International Law Commission's articles on liability

In an attempt to move beyond the limitations of the existing law on state responsibility, the ILC initially proposed to make states liable for significant transboundary harm caused by any activity covered by their draft liability articles.[73] The obligation to compensate other states would not cover unforeseeable risks, but would include unavoidable harm which the source state could not prevent by exercising due diligence.[74] At the same time the ILC's proposals did not place the source state in the same position as if it were at fault. Equitable compensation would instead be negotiated as part of a balance of interests between the parties, 'in accordance with the principle that the victim of harm should not be left to bear the entire loss'.[75]

These were relatively novel proposals, however, and they did not rest on any clear foundation in general international law. They proved too controversial for many states. Nevertheless, in 2001, largely at the behest of developing states, the UN General Assembly requested the ILC to resume work on liability, 'bearing in mind the interrelationship between prevention and liability, and taking into account the developments in international law and comments by Governments'.[76] This suggests a recognition by

[71] See 1992 Rio Declaration, Principle 16, *infra*, Ch 5.

[72] See *Vellore Citizens Welfare Forum v Union of India* (1996) 5 SCC 647, where the Indian Supreme Court relied on the principle to justify imposition of absolute liability on the polluter both for injury to private parties and for environmental reinstatement costs which the government would otherwise have borne.

[73] 1996 ILC draft Liability Article 5. For the full text of the 1996 draft see *Report of the Working Group on International Liability etc, ILC Report* (1996) GAOR A/51/10, Annex 1, 235. For a brief resumé see Boyle and Freestone (eds), *International Law and Sustainable Development* (Oxford, 1999) 73–85; de La Fayette, 6 *RECIEL* (1997) 321–33.

[74] 1996 draft Article 1.

[75] 1996 draft Article 21, on which see *ILC Report* (1996) Annex 1, 320.

[76] UNGA Res 56/82 (2001).

at least some governments that existing law on liability for transboundary damage remained insufficient and that some additional measures were necessary.

The most fundamental question confronted by the Commission was whether to continue to focus on extending the liability of states in international law along the lines envisaged in 1996. However meritorious the idea may be in theory, few governments, in whatever context, have shown any enthusiasm for accepting that no-fault liability for damage caused by activities within their jurisdiction should fall on states themselves.[77] Marking an important change of direction, the ILC did not return to that model of loss allocation. Thus, for essentially pragmatic rather than principled reasons, the Commission opted to focus on 'loss allocation among different actors involved in the operations of the hazardous activities',[78] rather than making states directly liable in international law. Having eschewed state liability as a solution, the ILC's subsequent work necessarily addressed the civil liability of operators. In most cases corporations or other private operators of a harmful activity would become strictly liable in national law for transboundary damage. In effect, therefore, the polluters would have to pay, not the states within whose territory they operate. To that extent the ILC recognized the reality that much, if not most, transboundary environmental damage is caused by and mainly affects private parties, rather than states as such.

States would still remain responsible for their own fault in international law, including their failure to provide for civil liability in the form envisaged by the Commission. Essentially, however, the Commission's proposals would build directly on the private law civil-liability models already adopted for oil, nuclear, and other environmental risks. There would still be strict liability, but it would not fall on states. The outlines of the Principles for Allocation of Loss finally adopted in 2006 are considered fully in Chapter 5.

2(5) INTERACTION OF CIVIL LIABILITY AND INTERSTATE CLAIMS: THE LOCAL REMEDIES RULE

In general international law, interstate claims involving responsibility for injury to aliens are normally conditional on the prior exhaustion of local remedies, which usually entails resort to the relevant national legal system as a preferred means of redress. Only if civil justice is effectively denied, or if no redress is available, will an international claim then be admissible.[79] The ILC's 2006 Principles for Allocation of Loss are 'without prejudice to the rules relating to state responsibility and any claim

[77] Special Rapporteur's *2nd Report*, UN Doc A/CN 4/540 (2003) para 22.

[78] *ILC Report* (2003) GAOR A/58/10, para 168. See Boyle, 17 *JEL* (2005) 3; Kiss and Shelton, in Ndiaye and Wolfrum, *Law of the Sea, Environmental Law and Settlement of Disputes*, 1138–51.

[79] *ELSI Case*, ICJ Reports (1989) 15, paras 50–63; ILC, 2001 State Responsibility Article 44(b). See Amerasinghe, *Local Remedies in International Law* (2nd edn, Cambridge, 2004); Trindade, *The Application of the Rule of Exhaustion of Local Remedies in International Law* (Cambridge, 1983); Okowa, *State Responsibility for Transboundary Air Pollution* (Oxford, 2000) 217–21.

that may lie under those rules'.[80] It seems clear that the Commission envisages civil liability and state responsibility as potentially complementary regimes. The preference of states and the ILC for non-discriminatory access to national remedies, civil liability and compensation schemes as a means of dealing with transboundary environmental nuisances is already well established.[81] The view that local remedies should be exhausted when adequate and available would leave interstate claims as a residual option to be exercised only when other remedies have been exhausted or do not exist.

However, it has been suggested that the local remedies rule is inapplicable to cases of transboundary environmental harm. The underlying idea is that the injured party must have assumed the risk of being subject to the jurisdiction of a foreign state:

> even where effective local remedies exist, it would be unreasonable and unfair to require an injured person to exhaust local remedies where his property has suffered environmental harm caused by pollution, radioactive fallout or a fallen space object emanating from a State in which his property is not situated . . .[82]

The Draft Articles on Diplomatic Protection thus exclude the local remedies rule where there is no 'relevant connection' between the injured party and the state responsible.[83] On this view, governments would remain free to make an interstate claim on behalf of anyone affected by transboundary damage without first exhausting local remedies. Particularly in cases where the damage is widespread, and the victims are numerous and poor, governmental action at interstate level may well be the only realistic option and should not be excluded. The procedures of the UN Compensation Commission ('UNCC') for bringing compensation claims against Iraq are the most recent example of governments espousing claims on behalf of a mass of individual victims.[84] Whether such claimants should be left to their local remedies would in that type of case be a matter for their own government to decide.

But in more typical cases of transboundary nuisances it is not obvious why the absence of a relevant connection with the respondent state should exclude the local remedies rule even where the injured victims would suffer no hardship in pursuing local remedies and it would be feasible to do so. This will especially be true where the victim has the choice of suing in the place where the injury has occurred or would occur, rather than in the state where the harmful activity is located. For reasons elaborated at some length in Chapter 5, states have clearly found it desirable to encourage resort to local remedies as a means of de-escalating such transboundary disputes, and the logic of this policy is implicit in Principles 10 and 16 of the Rio Declaration. The ILC accepts that the authority in support of its relevant connection requirement is limited and contradictory, and its conclusion is tentative.[85] In *Trail Smelter* there were no local

80 *ILC Report* (2006) GAOR A/61/10, 111, para 7.

81 See *infra*, Ch 5.

82 *ILC Report* (2006) GAOR A/61/10, 80–1, para 7.

83 2006 Draft Article 15(c).

84 See Kazazi, in Bowman and Boyle (eds), *Environmental Damage in International and Comparative Law*, 111 and generally, Rosenfeld, 1JIDS (2013), 159.

85 *ILC Report* (2006) GAOR A/61/10, 82, para 9.

remedies that could be exhausted in Canada because of the extraterritorial location of the damage and the narrowly territorial jurisdiction of Canadian courts: interstate arbitration was the only possibility.[86] Given this admittedly shaky foundation and the absence of any compelling justification, the Commission's blanket dismissal of the local remedies rule in transboundary pollution cases appears questionable.

2(6) REMEDIES FOR ENVIRONMENTAL DAMAGE

No attempt has yet been made, either in the ILC's articles on state responsibility, or in those on the prevention of transboundary harm, to develop remedies specifically adapted to environmental damage.[87] The remedies available for breach of environmental obligations are thus determined by general international law.[88] Where the responsibility of a state is established, an obligation arises first to discontinue the wrongful conduct, secondly to offer guarantees of non-repetition, and third to make 'full reparation' for the injury caused.[89] Article 34 of the ILC 2001 Articles on State Responsibility defines full reparation as 'restitution, compensation and satisfaction, either singly or in combination'. In principle, 'damage to the environment, and the consequent impairment or loss of the ability of the environment to provide goods and services, is compensable under international law', and may include 'indemnification for the impairment or loss of environmental goods and services in the period prior to recovery and payment for the restoration of the damaged environment.'[90]

Reparation is a flexible concept, however. As Brownlie observes: 'the interaction of substantive law and issues of reparation should be stressed'.[91] The appropriateness of particular forms of reparation, or of other responses, thus depends on the circumstances of individual cases. Recognizing this, the ILC commentary notes that: 'The most suitable remedy can only be determined in each instance with a view to achieving the most complete satisfaction of the injured state's interest in the 'wiping out' of

[86] Read, 1 *CYIL* (1963) 222. The ILC commentary appears not to appreciate this point. In the Chernobyl disaster there were also no local remedies because there was no liability under Soviet law. But in the Sandoz pollution disaster on the Rhine, and the *Handelskwekerij Case*, local remedies did exist and were used. See *infra*, Ch 5, section 3(2).

[87] See generally Gray, *Judicial Remedies in International Law* (Oxford, 1987); Mann, *Further Studies in International Law* (Oxford, 1990) Ch 4; Brownlie, *State Responsibility*, Ch 13; *id*, in Lowe and Fitzmaurice (eds), *Fifty Years of the International Court of Justice* (Cambridge, 1996) 557–66; Okowa, *State Responsibility for Transboundary Air Pollution in International Law* (Oxford, 2000) 203–21; Shelton, 96 *AJIL* (2002) 833.

[88] *Border Activities Case*, ICJ Reports (2018) paras 29–43.

[89] *Border Activities Case*, ICJ Reports (2018) para 30; *Diallo Case*, ICJ Reports (2010) 691, para 161; *Avena Case*, ICJ Reports (2004) 59, para 119; *Gabčíkovo-Nagymaros Case*, ICJ Reports (1997) 7, para 150; ILC 2001 State Responsibility Articles 30–1, 35–7 and commentary in Crawford, *The ILC's Articles etc*, 196–206, 211–34. See also Crawford, Pellet, Olleson (eds), *The International Law of Responsibility* (Oxford, 2010) Chs 38–42; Crawford, *State Responsibility* (Cambridge, 2013) 459–538.

[90] *Border Activities Case*, ICJ Reports (2018) para 42.

[91] *State Responsibility*, 234. See also Combacau and Alland, 16 *NYIL* (1985) 108, who argue that 'it is above all the consideration of "content" and the primary obligation in its widest meaning, which explains why a certain consequence is attached specifically and *ab initio* to its breach'.

all the injurious consequences of the wrongful act'.[92] In environmental disputes, states will primarily be concerned with preventing further harm or the risk of harm, securing better cooperation, or obtaining compensation for damage to people, property and natural resources, clean-up costs and restoration of the environment. The only consistent feature of much of the jurisprudence relating to environmental disputes is that it has usually reiterated the duty to consult or negotiate;[93] in a few cases tribunals have also indicated measures to be taken by the parties,[94] and in only two have they awarded compensation for transboundary damage.[95]

(a) Restitution and preventive remedies

Restitution is given the narrowest possible meaning by the ILC: 'to re-establish the situation which existed before the wrongful act was committed'.[96] It neither includes establishment of the situation that would have existed but for the wrong, nor does it require a transfer of any profit accruing to the wrongdoer because of the wrong. In an environmental context restoration of a damaged environment is the most obvious form of restitution. Parties to the 1992 CBD have an obligation to 'rehabilitate and restore degraded ecosystems and promote the recovery of threatened species.'[97] That has also been the outcome in claims before the UNCC against Iraq and in the *Border Activities* litigation.[98] The issue will primarily be one of fact: what has been lost and what can be done to restore it? It will of course be necessary to determine whether and how far restoration of the damaged environment or its equivalent is possible or is not otherwise disproportionately burdensome to the wrongdoer within the terms of the ILC's Article.[99] Restoration of the *status quo ante* will not necessarily be either adequate or appropriate to the wrong suffered in every case. But if restoration is possible and appropriate, compensation to cover the necessary work will then be the normal remedy.[100]

States also have an obligation to cease unlawful conduct and to guarantee non-repetition.[101] The underlying principle is respect for the rule of law.[102] In most cases,

92 II *YbILC* (1993) Pt 2, 63. See also *Chorzow Factory Case (Indemnity)* PCIJ Ser A No 17 (1928) 47–8; *Avena Case*, ICJ Reports (2004) 12, para 119; *Pulp Mills Case*, ICJ Reports (2010) 14, para 274.

93 *Lac Lanoux Arbitration*, 24 *ILR* (1957) 101; *Icelandic Fisheries Cases*, ICJ Reports (1974) 3 and 175; *Gabčíkovo-Nagymaros Case*, ICJ Reports (1997) 7, operative para (2)B; *MOX Plant Case (Provisional Measures)* ITLOS Reports (2001) para 82; *Land Reclamation (Provisional Measures)* ITLOS Reports (2003) para 92; *Pulp Mills Case*, ICJ Reports (2010) 14, paras 113–5, 146–50; *Chagos MPA Arbitration*, PCA (2015) paras 519, 534, 544.

94 See *Behring Sea Fur Seals Arbitration* (1898) 1 *Moore's Int Arb* 755; *Trail Smelter Arbitration*, 35 *AJIL* (1941) 684; *Land Reclamation (Provisional Measures)* ITLOS Reports (2003).

95 *Trail Smelter Arbitration*, 33 *AJIL* (1939) 182, and 35 *AJIL* (1941) 684; *Border Activities Case*, ICJ Reports (2018).

96 ILC 2001 State Responsibility Article 35. See Crawford, *The ILC's Articles etc*, 213–7.

97 Article 8(f).

98 *Border Activities Case*, ICJ Reports (2018) paras 42–53. On the UNCC see *infra*.

99 On disproportionate burden see *Pulp Mills Case*, ICJ Reports (2010) 14, paras 273–5, and *infra*, next section.

100 See next section.

101 ILC, 2001 State Responsibility Article 30.

102 Corten, in Crawford, Pellet, Olleson, *The Law of International Responsibility*, 545; Crawford, *State Responsibility*, 459.

courts simply declare that a state has or has not acted in accordance with its obligations, and refer to its duty to make reparation.[103] Legal restitution, that is an order for the repeal or alteration of some legislative, judicial, or administrative act, will be appropriate where there is an ongoing violation of a state's international obligations. On this basis the ICJ ordered the revocation of authorizations, permits or licences in the *Whaling Case* once it concluded that they had been issued in violation of the 1946 ICRW.[104]

A state may also be required to 'take effective steps' to ensure compliance with its obligations.[105] The *Trail Smelter Case* remains the best illustration of the power of courts and tribunals to prescribe measures to prevent repetition of environmental damage.[106] In that case Canada was ordered to implement regulations controlling the future operation of the smelter, and to compensate for any damage which recurred notwithstanding compliance. Although Canada had to take measures to protect the USfrom serious injury, its right to continue to operate the smelter was maintained. Thus, a balance of interests between the two parties was achieved through the tribunal's order, and indeed this formed the main object of the arbitration.[107]

In several environmental disputes the applicant has asked the court to order permanent cessation of a potentially harmful activity.[108] No such order has yet been made. In *Pulp Mills*, the ICJ rejected Argentina's argument that construction of the plant was illegal and that it should be pulled down. Its finding that Uruguay had not complied with Statute's procedural requirements was deemed sufficient satisfaction: there was 'no cause to order cessation' of the mill.[109] The Court emphasised that 'restitution must be appropriate to the injury suffered, taking into account the nature of the wrongful act having caused it.'[110] It noted that Uruguay had not breached any of its substantive obligations, and that 'ordering the dismantling of the mill would not, in the view of the Court, constitute an appropriate remedy for the breach of procedural obligations.'[111] This conclusion reflects the particular facts of the case; a stronger case might justify a different answer.[112]

[103] See e.g. *Gabčíkovo-Nagymaros Case*, ICJ Reports (1997) 7, operative paras (1) and (2); *Pulp Mills Case*, ICJ Reports (2010) 14, operative para (1); *Chagos MPA Case*, PCA (2015) para 547(B).

[104] ICJ Reports (2014) 226, para 245.

[105] *Bosnian Genocide Case*, ICJ Reports (2007) 43, operative para 8; *Tehran Hostages Case*, ICJ Reports (1980) 3, operative para 3.

[106] 35 *AJIL* (1941) 712ff. Gray, *Judicial Remedies in International Law*, 12 emphasizes that the *compromis* expressly empowered the tribunal to prescribe measures.

[107] Rubin, 50 *Oregon LR* (1971); Read, 1 *CYIL* (1963) 213; Boyle, 39 *ICLQ* (1990) 18–19.

[108] *Pulp Mills Case*, ICJ Reports (2010) 14; *Aerial Spraying Case*, ICJ application 2007.

[109] *Pulp Mills Case*, ICJ Reports (2010) 14, paras 267–80.

[110] *Ibid*, para 274. See also *Border Activities/San Juan River Cases*, ICJ Reports (2015) para 226.

[111] *Ibid*, para 275.

[112] See for example the agreement between Ecuador and Colombia terminating Colombia's aerial spraying of herbicides within the border area: *Aerial Spraying Case*, ICJ Order of 13 September 2013.

Where there has been a failure to notify or consult the only remedy identified by the ILC,[113] case law,[114] and state practice,[115] is for the applicant state to request the necessary information and initiate consultations. Thus, in the *Chagos MPA Case*, the arbitrators concluded that 'It is now open to the Parties to enter into the negotiations that the Tribunal would have expected prior to the proclamation of the MPA.'[116] They did not order the termination of the marine protected area declared by the UK. Similarly, the only remedy afforded by any international tribunal for failure to carry out an EIA or monitoring is to order appropriate studies to be carried out.[117] Where the measures taken to protect neighbouring states from environmental damage are inadequate, international tribunals have ordered additional measures to be taken.[118] In most such disputes, the parties are ordered to.[119] In the *Gabčíkovo-Nagymaros Case*, the Court concluded that '[i]n this case, the consequences of the wrongful acts of both Parties will be wiped out "as far as possible" if they resume their cooperation in the utilization of the shared water resources of the Danube' and it ordered them to do so.[120]

International tribunals generally also have power to make interim orders to protect the rights of the parties, or the marine environment, pending settlement of a dispute.[121] Provisional measures applications are dealt with urgently and expeditiously: where there is a risk of imminent and potentially irreparable transboundary environmental damage, such an application will be the most effective means of securing a remedy pending a negotiated settlement or a hearing on the merits.[122] In appropriate cases this may entail temporary cessation of the activity.[123] Moreover, as we saw in Chapter 3, interim orders to cooperate in protecting the marine environment have been granted even where there is no proof of imminent harm.[124] In the *Land Reclamation Case* the

113 ILC, 2001 Articles on Prevention of Transboundary Harm, Article 11; 1997 UN Watercourses Convention, Article 18.

114 *Lake Lanoux Arbitration*, 24 *ILR* (1957) 138 ('if a neighbouring State has not taken the initiative, the other State cannot be denied the right to insist on notification of works or concessions which are the object of a scheme'); *Chagos MPA Case*, PCA (2015) paras 519, 528–544. See *infra*, Ch 10.

115 See e.g. *Sudanese–Egyptian dispute regarding the Aswan High Dam* and *US–Mexico dispute regarding salinity of the Colorado River*, cited in *ILC Report* (1988) GAOR A/43/10, 131–33; see also Kirgis, *Prior Consultation in International Law: A Study in State Practice* (Charlottesville, 1983) 43, 66.

116 PCA (2015) para 544.

117 *Trail Smelter Arbitration*, 33 AJIL 182 (1939) 209; *Gabčíkovo-Nagymaros Case*, ICJ Reports (1997) 78, para 140; *Land Reclamation (Provisional Measures)* ITLOS Reports (2003) para 106

118 *Trail Smelter Arbitration*, 35 *AJIL* 684 (1941) 726; *Gabčíkovo-Nagymaros*, 82, para 155(2); *Land Reclamation Arbitration* (2005) operative para 2, Annex.

119 *Gabčíkovo-Nagymaros Case*, para 150; *MOX Plant (Provisional Measures)* para 82; *Land Reclamation (Provisional Measures)* para 92; *Land Reclamation Arbitration*, operative para 2 and Annex; *Southern Bluefin Tuna (Provisional Measures)* para 78 and operative para (e).

120 *Gabčíkovo-Nagymaros Case*, para 150. See also *Pulp Mills Case*, ICJ Reports (2010) 14, para 281.

121 ICJ Statute, Article 41; 1982 UNCLOS, Article 290; 1995 UN Fish Stocks Agreement, Article 31. See Rosenne, *Provisional Measures in International Law* (Oxford, 2005).

122 *Pulp Mills Case (Provisional Measures)* ICJ Reports (2006) 113, paras 72–5; *Southern Bluefin Tuna Cases (Provisional Measures)* ITLOS Reports (1999). See *supra*, Ch 3, section 5(4).

123 *Indus Waters Kishenganga Arbitration (Interim Measures)* PCA (2011) but contrast *Pulp Mills*, where an application for cessation was rejected.

124 *MOX Plant (Provisional Measures)* ITLOS Reports (2001); *Land Reclamation (Provisional Measures)* ITLOS Reports (2003). See *supra*, Ch 3, section 5(5).

parties were also required to carry out a study of possible impacts on the marine environment. Since interim orders are binding, they must be taken seriously.

(b) Compensation

Restitution is 'very frequently inadequate to ensure a complete reparation'.[125] In these circumstances, compensation will in many cases become 'the main and central remedy following an internationally wrongful act'.[126] Compensation for environmental damage to a state's territory is covered by a number of modern liability treaties,[127] and is the basis for some of the awards made by the UNCC in claims against Iraq.[128] It is also now the subject of one ICJ judgment.[129]

What is mainly in issue is whether claims can be made for environmental harm not quantifiable in terms of damage to people or property or economic loss. Although the precedents are few in number, international claims for environmental damage point to the availability of compensation for environmental restoration and clean-up costs; environmental monitoring, inspection and assessment; measures to mitigate or prevent further harm; loss of ecosystem services through deforestation, loss of vegetation, erosion and so on.[130] This list is broad enough to cover damage to ecosystems, biodiversity, and protected or wilderness areas.

In principle, compensation should fully restore the injured party's position, but it may not always be easy to determine the extent of any damage. The ICJ has held that 'the absence of adequate evidence as to the extent of material damage will not, in all situations, preclude an award of compensation for that damage.'[131] In such cases it has been willing to award equitable compensation.[132] Similarly, under the 1972 Space Objects Liability Convention (Article 12) compensation is determined in accordance with 'international law and the principles of justice and equity',[133] but must be sufficient to restore the party on whose behalf the claim is presented 'to the condition which would have existed if the damage had not occurred'. The negotiators of this treaty deliberately rejected any limits on liability, but in the analogous *Cosmos 954* claim Canada did not recover its full costs of $14 million, but claimed $6 million, and settled ex gratia for $3 million.[134]

The ILC recognizes that, in making awards of compensation, international arbitral tribunals and claims commissions have drawn on private law analogies, but it

[125] *YbILC* (1993) 1, Pt 2, 62. [126] *Ibid*, 63, 76.

[127] Convention on Civil Liability for Oil Pollution Damage, *infra*, Ch 9; 1996 Vienna Convention on Civil liability for Nuclear Damage, *infra*, Ch 7.

[128] See *infra*.

[129] *Border Activities Case*, ICJ Reports (2018) paras 44ff.

[130] See e.g. *Border Activities Case*, ICJ Reports (2018) paras 29–43; *Trail Smelter Arbitration*, 33 *AJIL* (1939) 182 & 35 *AJIL* (1941) 684; *Cosmos 954 Claim*, and UNCC practice, *infra*. For a comprehensive survey see Handl, 34 *IJMCL* (2019) 602.

[131] *Border Activities Case*, ICJ Reports (2018) para 35.

[132] *Diallo Case*, ICJ Reports (2012) 337, para 33. See also *Border Activities Case*, ICJ Reports (2018) para 35, where the Court also cites the *Trail Smelter Arbitration*.

[133] This formulation was deliberately adopted in preference to the *lex loci*. See Cheng, *Studies in International Space Law*, 332–41.

[134] See Schwartz and Berlin, 27 *McGill LJ* (1982) 676.

concludes that these precedents do not give us detailed general rules on the matter.[135] Its draft articles indicate two important limits on the right to claim compensation, however. First, compensation can only be appropriate where the damage has been caused by the wrongful act. The test applied by the ICJ is 'whether there is a sufficiently direct and certain causal nexus between the wrongful act . . . and the injury suffered by the Applicant.'[136] The Court accepts that in environmental cases the damage may have several causes, that the science establishing causation may be uncertain, and that the burden of proof may have to be applied flexibly.[137] The ILC dismisses the distinction between direct and indirect damage as ambiguous and of 'scant utility',[138] although its preferred alternative requirement of a 'clear and unbroken causal link' is scarcely less problematic. Whatever test is used, the obligation to compensate for damage is not unlimited, and is bounded by some inherent notion of remoteness or proximity. Thus regardless of whether international law in principle compensates for environmental damage, however defined, there will inevitably be some cases where compensation is denied on grounds of non-proximity or remoteness.

Secondly, only 'financially assessable damage' is compensable.[139] The term 'financially assessable' was adopted in the draft articles because the earlier reference to 'economically assessable' damage was thought inappropriate to cover, for example, the wrongful extinction of endangered wildlife of no 'economic' value,[140] although it did include damage to 'the State's territory in general, to its organization in a broad sense, its property at home and abroad . . .'.[141] This list begs the question whether all damage to a state's territory is assessable in monetary terms. The problem with environmental damage is precisely that it may not be. Although almost everything can be either restored or given a monetary value in some fashion, what is not clear are the limits, if any, to acceptable methods of valuation. The ICJ has held that 'first, international law does not prescribe any specific method of valuation for the purposes of compensation for environmental damage; secondly, it is necessary, in the view of the Court, to take into account the specific circumstances and characteristics of each case.'[142] The Court in the *Border Activities Case* referred to various methods of valuation cited by the parties, including those endorsed in UNEP Guidelines and decisions of the parties to the 1992 CBD , but it relied on them only where they offered 'a reasonable basis for valuation'.[143] Quite how the Court valued the losses is not clear from the judgment.

135 *YbILC* (1993) II, Pt 2, 68. See generally Barker in Crawford, Pellet, Olleson, *The Law of International Responsibility*, 599.

136 *Border Activities Case*, ICJ Reports (2018) para 32.

137 *Ibid*, paras 33–34.

138 *Ibid*, 68–9. Compare UNSC Resolution 687, which allows claims against Iraq only if the damage is direct.

139 ILC, 2001 State Responsibility Article 36.

140 *ILC Report* (2000) GAOR A/55/10, Ch IV, para 193. Compare 1998 draft Article 44, and commentary at *YbILC* (1993) II, Pt 2, 71.

141 *YbILC* (1993) II, Pt 2, 72.

142 *Border Activities Case*, ICJ Reports (2018) para 52.

143 *Ibid*, paras 44–53.

Would the attribution of notional or non-market-based valuations to depleted natural resources be covered under this formulation? Such valuations have been employed in US, Italian, and Russian law,[144] but have been rejected by the International Oil Pollution Compensation Fund. The Fund's view is that it cannot compensate for oil pollution damage assessed 'on the basis of an abstract quantification of damage calculated in accordance with theoretical models'.[145] If the rules of international law on compensation are as general and flexible as the ILC believes, then all of these approaches are probably acceptable in principle, even if in practice they are then narrowed for the purposes of specific treaty-based compensation schemes.

At the same time we should remember that the ILC's Draft Articles are a framework of general principles, not a precise prescription for every eventuality. Even if the availability of compensation is limited to 'financially assessable damage', there remains much scope for interpretation of that phrase in a manner which takes full account of the particular demands of environmental valuation. This suggests that we focus on methods of valuation, on overcoming the objection that something which is not necessarily 'property' and which may have no 'market value' has no economic worth. This is clearly not a task for lawyers alone: it requires at least the input of economists and others skilled in techniques of valuation.[146]

In this respect the UNCC's decisions dealing with environmental claims against Iraq provide the most relevant contemporary precedents. They are particularly innovative on questions of valuation, restoration and monitoring.[147] The Security Council held Iraq liable for 'any direct loss, [or] damage, including environmental damage and the depletion of natural resources . . . as a result of Iraq's unlawful invasion and occupation of Kuwait'.[148] As interpreted by the UNCC, Resolution 687 covers, inter alia, reimbursement of clean-up assistance costs, compensation for reasonable measures to assess and monitor damage to the environment and public health, and to clean up and restore the environment.[149] While rejecting many of the environmental claims for lack of evidence linking them with the invasion, the Commission allowed some substantial claims for reinstatement of the *status quo ante*, subject to the qualification that

[144] *Commonwealth of Puerto Rico v SS Zoe Colocotroni* 456 F Supp 1327 (1978) and 628 F 2d 652 (1980); *Antonio Gramsci* (No 2) and *Patmos* cases, IOPC Fund, *Annual Report* (1990) 23, 27. See Maffei, in Francioni and Scovazzi, *International Responsibility for Environmental Harm* (London, 1991) 381 and generally, Wetterstein (ed), *Harm to the Environment* (Oxford, 1997); Bowman and Boyle (eds), *Environmental Damage in International and Comparative Law* (Oxford, 2002).

[145] 1971 IOPC Fund Resolution No 3 (1980) reaffirmed by 1992 IOPC Fund Resolution No 3 (1996).

[146] See *Border Activities Case*, ICJ Reports (2018), where the ICJ had little difficulty assessing the value of environmental damage.

[147] See Sand, 35 *EPL* (2005) 244; Gautier, in Ndiaye and Wolfrum (eds), *Law of the Sea, Environmental Law and Settlement of Disputes* (Leiden, 2007) 177; Kazazi, *ibid*, 1109; Martin, in Kerbrat and Maljean Dubois (eds), *Le droit international face aux enjeux environnementaux* (Paris, 2010) 257; Payne and Sand (eds), *Gulf War Reparations and the UN Compensation Commission* (Oxford, 2011).

[148] UNSC Res 687 (1991).

[149] UNCC Gov Council, Decision 7, revised 16 March 1992, para 35; UNCC F4 Claims 2nd Decision (2002) paras 29 and 32–5.

the 'primary emphasis must be placed on restoring the environment to pre-invasion conditions, in terms of its overall ecological functioning, rather than on the removal of specific contaminants or restoration of the environment to a particular physical condition'.[150] Where restoration to a natural state was not possible or reasonable the cost of making equivalent provision was awarded.[151] The UNCC found no legal basis for excluding pure environmental damage that has no commercial value.[152] To that extent its approach is comparable to the International Oil Pollution Compensation ('IOPC') Fund's practice of allowing reasonable reinstatement measures aimed at accelerating natural recovery of environmental damage.

One of the panel of commissioners has summarized five elements of UNCC practice:

(i) precautionary monitoring to identify and assess long-term risks to public health and the environment;
(ii) reimbursement of mutual assistance costs in environmental emergencies;
(iii) the obligation for claimants to mitigate and contain damage to the environment;
(iv) valuation methods to ensure the remediation of lost ecological services; follow-up tracking to ensure the environmental effectiveness of remediation;
(v) making the disbursement of compensation awards conditional upon compliance with agreed environmental objectives and standards ('green conditionality').

In his view the multilateral UNCC process was better able to represent the general environmental concerns of the international community than the traditional bilateral perspective of state responsibility.[153] It could only do so, however, because the Security Council had found Iraq liable and created a mechanism for giving effect to that decision. This was an important procedural innovation. It is unlikely that an international court could have handled matters in the same way.[154]

2(7) STANDING TO BRING CLAIMS

Standing to bring international claims is in principle confined to 'injured states'.[155] What this means can be observed in the second phase of the *South West Africa Case*.[156] Liberia and Ethiopia, although original members of the League of Nations with certain

150 UNCC F4 Claims 3rd Decision (2003) paras 47–8.

151 UNCC F4 Claims 5th Decision (2006) para 82.

152 *Ibid*, para 57.

153 Sand, 35 *EPL* (2005) 244; *id*, 54 *JYIL* (2011) 151. See also Kazazi, in Bowman and Boyle (eds), *Environmental Damage in International and Comparative Law*, 111.

154 But see *Border Activities Case*, ICJ Reports (2018) where the court had no difficulty dealing with a bilateral inter-state claim for environmental damage.

155 ILC, 2001 State Responsibility Article 42. See generally, Crawford, *The ILC's Articles on State Responsibility*, 254–60; Gray, *Judicial Remedies in International Law*, 211–15; Charney, 10 *Mich JIL* (1989) 57.

156 ICJ Reports (1966) esp 20–3; *Brownlie's Principles of Public International Law* (8th edn, Oxford, 2012) 580–84.

rights under the mandates agreement, were held to have no legal right or interest in South Africa's compliance with its obligations towards the inhabitants of the territory. That was a matter for the League alone and individual members acquired no independent standing to bring violations before the ICJ. This was an unusual case, however, whose unsuccessful outcome is a consequence of a narrow analysis of the legal relationship between the League, its members and the mandatory power. Although the term 'injured state' is used by Article 42 of the ILC Articles on State Responsibility in broadly comparable terms, this will cause little difficulty in most interstate environmental disputes. A denial of high seas fishing rights, as in the *Icelandic Fisheries Cases*,[157] or high seas pollution affecting a coastal state, would clearly fall within the ILC's conception of an injured state, for example.

More problematic, however, are violations of international law affecting only the global commons, or areas of common concern, such as the ozone layer or global climate. As in the *Nuclear Tests Cases*,[158] such violations may not per se affect the rights of any individual state, but rather those of the community of states as a whole. The problem of standing in this context is thus particularly concerned with how community rights can be enforced, it at all, by unaffected states through interstate claims, or by some other form of public interest representation.

International law recognizes the possibility that certain obligations may be enforceable on behalf of the international community.[159] In the *Barcelona Traction Case*[160] the ICJ referred to obligations *erga omnes* in respect of which all states would enjoy standing to bring claims, and the normal nationality of claims rules would cease to apply. On that basis, in the *Obligation to Prosecute or Extradite Case* it accepted that any party could invoke the Court's jurisdiction under the 1984 Convention against Torture.[161] The ILC's approach allows states to enforce collective interests in terms broad enough to encompass the more significant global environmental responsibilities and to permit an *actio popularis* in certain circumstances. The 2001 Articles on State Responsibility envisage five categories of potential claimant: [162]

Article 42(a): An injured state may claim, i.e. when an obligation owed to that state is breached;

Article 42(b)(i): A specially affected state may claim if the obligation breached is owed to that state as part of a group of states, or to the international community as a whole;

Article 42(b)(ii): Any state may claim if the breach of obligation is of such a character that it affects the enjoyment of rights and obligations by all states concerned;

[157] ICJ Reports (1974) 3. [158] ICJ Reports (1974) 253, 457.

[159] See generally Crawford, *1st Rept*, UN Doc A/CN4/490/Add 1 (1998) paras 69–71; Tams, *Enforcing Obligations Erga Omnes in International Law* (Cambridge, 2005); Ragazzi, *The Concept of International Obligations Erga Omnes* (Oxford, 1997); Rosenne, in Anghie and Sturgess (eds), *Legal Visions of the 21st Century* (The Hague, 1998) 509; Simma, 250 *Recueil des Cours* (1994) 293–301.

[160] ICJ Reports (1970) 3. [161] ICJ Reports (2012) paras 68–70.

[162] See ILC commentary in Crawford, *The ILC's Articles on State Responsibility*, 254–60, 276–80.

Article 48(1)(a): Any state may claim if the obligation breached is established for the protection of the collective interests of a group of states, including the claimant state;

Article 48(1)(b): Any state may claim if the obligation breached is owed to the international community as a whole.

Essentially the first three categories of claimant are all 'injured states', i.e. those covered by Article 42. Here the claimant state will be affected by the breach and will necessarily be enforcing its own rights. Claims falling within the last two categories, i.e. those covered by Article 48, are genuinely public interest claims, enforcing *erga omnes* obligations. They can be initiated by any state within the terms of that article.

Article 48 takes account of the growing number of multilateral treaties and customary law concerned with the protection of the global environment or of areas of common interest or concern, such as the Conventions on World Heritage, Trade in Endangered Species, Ozone Depletion, Climate Change, Biological Diversity, Dumping at Sea, Whaling, or the Law of the Sea. These agreements cannot be dismissed as mere expressions of a principle of good neighbourliness. That they create obligations whose intended beneficiaries are the international community of states as a whole has been partially acknowledged by the new terminology of 'common concern of mankind' found in the 1992 Climate Change Convention and the 1992 CBD.[163] The ILC has acknowledged that all parties have a collective and individual interest in the enforcement of such treaties.[164] In these cases any state party should have standing to sue for breach or non-compliance: this was the assumption by all parties and the ICJ in the *Whaling Case*.[165] The same will be true of *erga omnes* customary obligations, including the duty to protect the marine environment or the environment of areas beyond national jurisdiction.[166]

However broadly the right to protect community interests is expressed, it does not follow that the full range of reparation will be available to third states acting for this purpose.[167] What is clear is that third states have the same right as injured states to seek cessation of any breaches of obligations owed to the international community as a whole.[168] Beyond that, the availability of reparation will depend on the circumstances of the breach, the extent to which the claimant's interests are affected, and the nature of the risk to community interests. It is, for example, unlikely that individual states will be

163 *Supra*, Ch 3, section 4(1).

164 See Crawford, *1st Report* (1998) UN Doc A/CN 4/460, para 100; Boyle and Harrison, (2013) 4 *JIDS* 254–5, and *infra*, section 4.

165 ICJ Reports (2014). Australia claimed to be upholding the collective interest of all parties to the ICRW: pleadings, CR 2013/18, 28, para 19 (Burmester). See *infra*, section 4(5).

166 See *South China Sea Arbitration*, PCA (2016) paras 939–93, where, however, the case rested on breach of Part XII of the 1982 UNCLOS.

167 Charney, 10 *Mich JIL* (1989) 57, and *id*, in Francioni and Scovazzi (eds), *International Responsibility for Environmental Harm*, but compare Abi-Saab, in Weiler et al, *International Crimes of State* (Berlin, 1989) 141.

168 ILC, 2001 State Responsibility Article 48(2); *Obligation to Prosecute or Extradite*, ICJ Reports (2012) paras 68–70.

entitled to demand reparation for material damage to the global environment beyond any clean-up or reinstatement costs which they may incur.[169] Any further satisfaction will probably be limited to acknowledging that there has been a breach. Account must also be taken of the risk of multiple claimants rendering settlement of a dispute more difficult or resulting in measures disproportionate to the violation or injury.

In practice the protection of community interests will in many cases involve no more than the right to make diplomatic protests. The possibility of third states taking unilateral action or countermeasures, such as refusal of access to Exclusive Economic Zone ('EEZ') fish stocks or to ports, or embargoes on trade, in order to induce compliance, is increasingly constrained by WTO treaty obligations.[170] Moreover the ILC Articles on State Responsibility specifically allow countermeasures only if taken by an injured state.[171] This would not preclude one state from taking countermeasures where all states are injured states within the terms of Article 48, but the ILC deliberately left open the question whether collective countermeasures can also be applied by non-injured states.[172]

There is one further way of looking at the protection of community interests under the ILC State Responsibility Articles, however. If the wrongful act is a 'serious breach' of a 'peremptory norm of general international law', other states will be under a duty not to recognize its legality and they must cooperate to bring the violation to an end.[173] The intention behind this provision is to allow for an exceptional response in the event of 'gross or systematic failure' to comply with obligations affecting the international community's most important interests. It has some precedent in international law.[174] In its original form the predecessor draft article was intended to apply to obligations for 'the safeguarding and preservation of the human environment such as those prohibiting massive pollution of the atmosphere or the seas'.[175] It is far from clear, however, whether any environmental obligations have been recognized as non-derogable peremptory norms by the international community as a whole in accordance with Article 53 of the 1969 VCLT. The issues are not susceptible to simplistic assumptions, but international courts have so far applied the concept of peremptory norms only to aggression, torture, and genocide.[176]

[169] Boyle, in Wetterstein (ed), *Harm to the Environment* (Oxford, 1997) Ch 7; Charney, in Francioni and Scovazzi (eds), *International Responsibility for Environmental Harm*.

[170] On WTO law, see *infra*, Ch 13. See also 1992 Rio Declaration, Principle 12. See generally Wolfrum, 272 *Recueil des Cours* (1998) 9, 59–77; Murase, 253 *Recueil des Cours* (1995) 283, 324ff.

[171] Article 49.

[172] Article 54. See Koskenniemi, 72 *BYIL* (2001) 337.

[173] Articles 40–1. These replace the concept of criminal responsibility previously found in Article 19 of the earlier text of the ILC's draft articles. See Crawford, *1st Rept*, (1998) UN Doc A/CN 4/490, Add 1–3; *ILC Report* (1998) GAOR A/53/10, Ch VII, paras 241–331; *ILC Report* (2000) GAOR A/55/10, Ch IV, paras 358–63, 374–83.

[174] See *Namibia Advisory Opinion*, ICJ Reports (1971) 16.

[175] See text of Article 19 in the ILC's 1996 draft articles.

[176] *Paramilitary Activities in Nicaragua Case*, ICJ Reports (1986) 14, paras 172–86; *Prosecutor v Furundzija*, 38 ILM (1999) 317 (ICTY); *Al-Adsani v United Kingdom*, (2002) 34 EHRR 11, paras 52–67; *Bosnian Genocide Case*, ICJ Reports (2007) 43, paras 31 and 161.

As we shall see in the next section, however, collective supervision of global environmental responsibilities by intergovernmental commissions, conferences of treaty parties, or international organizations will often be a more effective and realistic remedy than public interest claims and countermeasures by individual states.

2(8) CONCLUSIONS: THE UTILITY OF STATE RESPONSIBILITY

While potentially relevant to environmental disputes, reliance on state responsibility has serious deficiencies in this context. First, claims may be brought only by states; the provision of diplomatic protection is discretionary and the state entitled to claim is the sole judge of whether it should do so.[177] This decision may be made on grounds unrelated to the environmental issues in the individual case. Especially where the harm is to common spaces, or where states may be reluctant to create precedents affecting their own future conduct, there is less likelihood that a willing plaintiff will appear or press claims to the full. Moreover, the jurisdiction of international tribunals is rarely compulsory;[178] without agreement to resort to litigation or a claims settlement process, claims can only proceed by negotiation. Whatever method is used, the process will often be slow and expensive, and it gives the individual victim no control over the negotiation of any settlement.

Secondly, insofar as claims may be made only by states with standing, and the remedies available may be limited or inadequate, it is potentially more difficult to use international claims as a means of protecting the environment of common areas. This leads one writer to conclude that:

> In so far as the concept of responsibility to the international community as a whole is a reality, this is through the functioning of international organizations rather than any formal judicial procedure. International organizations provide a partial substitute for the lack of any general action on behalf of the world community and also for the lack of compulsory judicial settlement.[179]

Thirdly, although compensation for the costs of transboundary environmental damage may be recovered through international claims, making states liable is an inefficient means of allocating these costs. Uncertainty surrounding liability standards, whether states or private parties should be made liable, the type of environmental damage covered, and the role of equitable balancing, means that the outcome of any claim remains inherently unpredictable and points to the absence of a fully principled basis for determining who should bear transboundary costs.

The most important objection to state responsibility, however, is that it is an inadequate model for the enforcement of international standards of environmental

[177] *Barcelona Traction Case*, ICJ Reports (1970) 4, paras 78–9. Claims in respect of injury to individuals must also satisfy the nationality of claims rule: see *Nottebohm Case*, ICJ Reports (1955) 4. See ILC Draft Articles on Diplomatic Protection, *ILC Report* (2006) GAOR A/61/10, commentary to Articles 2 and 3.

[178] See *infra*, section 4.

[179] Gray, *Judicial Remedies in International Law*, 215, and see *infra*, section 3.

protection. Like tort law, it complements, but does not displace, the need for a system of regulatory supervision. It is this failing which explains the emphasis states have placed on the development of treaty regimes of environmental protection enforced by multilateral non-compliance procedures ('NCPs') or resort to transboundary legal proceedings, and the failure to develop or reform the law relating to state liability for environmental harm. Commentators have rightly discerned a 'corresponding decline in recourse to the law of state responsibility'.[180] Moreover, equal access to civil remedies and other civil-liability schemes offer a better means of allowing the recovery of transboundary environmental costs. For most forms of transboundary or marine pollution damage civil liability and insurance schemes now represent the primary recourse available to individual claimants and states.[181] Such schemes also emphasize the responsibility of individual polluters for the protection of the environment. In this respect state responsibility operates too indirectly and may appear to exempt those corporations or officials whose actions, policies, or decisions have led to harmful consequences. One writer concludes that: 'It is not surprising in such circumstances if states behave badly'.[182]

But it does not follow that state responsibility is of no continuing significance. First, without the more comprehensive codification of environmental standards, and the wider use of supervisory institutions, there may be no other basis for enforcing customary international law. Secondly, civil liability schemes, although valuable, have their own drawbacks and deficiencies which make it necessary to retain the option of recourse through international claims. This point is particularly clear with regard to major nuclear accidents, such as the Chernobyl disaster.[183] Lastly, non-compliance procedures, whatever their potential, do not always work as an effective substitute.

3 TREATY SUPERVISION AND COMPLIANCE

3(1) BREACH OF TREATY OR NON-COMPLIANCE?

In Chapter 2 we saw how multilateral environmental agreements have become an especially prominent means of developing international environmental law and regulating environmental risks and sustainable use of natural resources. How do states enforce or ensure compliance with this growing body of treaty law? If violations of a multilateral environmental treaty are revealed, what consequences could then follow? Several approaches are possible. Breach of treaty is a wrongful act entailing a duty to afford reparation in accordance with the law of state responsibility discussed above. It may additionally entitle the injured party to retaliate by taking proportionate

[180] Shelton, 96 *AJIL* (2002) 854. [181] See *infra*, Ch 5. [182] Allott, 29 *Harv IJL* (1988) 1.
[183] See *infra*, Ch 7.

countermeasures aimed at restoring equality between the parties,[184] or by terminating or suspending the treaty if the breach is 'material'. However, termination of a treaty on any ground is not easy to achieve unless all the parties agree. The terms of Article 60 of the 1969 VCLT require there to be either repudiation of the treaty or breach of a provision essential to its object and purpose; in practice this wording has resulted in courts almost never finding such a breach.[185] As one writer concludes: 'Article 60 simply does not work. It does not mean what it says and it does not say what it means.'[186]

The *Gabčíkovo-Nagymaros Case* illustrates the point. Hungary relied on repudiation by both parties, as well as necessity, fundamental change of circumstances, and impossibility of performance to justify its claim that the 1977 Treaty had terminated. All of these arguments were rejected on the facts. Although the ICJ accepted that important aspects of the treaty had not been complied with and that the scheme now in operation was not even an approximate application of the treaty, it referred to the possibility that reciprocal non-compliance might justify termination as 'a precedent with disturbing implications'.[187] Nevertheless, given the scale of construction work actually undertaken and the fact that a scheme of power generation had come into operation, even if not the one envisaged by the treaty, the Court's reluctance to contemplate a situation no longer regulated by any treaty is surely correct.

In the case of multilateral regulatory treaties, including those intended to protect the global or regional environment, breach is even more unlikely to justify termination. Not only does Article 60 make agreement of all the other parties a precondition, but termination is an inherently inappropriate response in most cases, however serious the breach. Thus, it would have served no purpose to conclude that Russia's non-compliance with the 1987 Montreal Protocol terminated its participation in that treaty.[188] What needs to be achieved in such situations is compliance with the terms of the treaty. From this perspective emphasis on the continued integrity of the treaty and the widest possible participation are the most important considerations. Demanding reparation for breach is also likely to be unhelpful in such cases because of the implication of wrongdoing. Breach of treaty retains its theoretically wrongful character, but for multilateral regulatory treaties its implications have more often been avoided than observed. Thus, in the case of environmental treaties, states have generally favoured softer procedures which make use of international institutions, treaty supervisory bodies or diplomatic methods to deal with non-compliance.

Academic studies have shown that deliberate non-compliance with environmental treaties is not the principal problem which treaty institutions face, for the simple

[184] On countermeasures see ILC, 2001 State Responsibility Articles 49–54 and *Air Services Arbitration* 54 *ILR* (1978) 304.

[185] 1969 VCLT, Article 60; *Chorzow Factory Case*, PCIJ Ser A, No 8/9 (1927) 21; *Namibia Advisory Opinion*, ICJ Reports (1971) 16; *ICAO Council Case*, ICJ Reports (1972) 67; *Gabčíkovo-Nagymaros Case*, ICJ Reports (1997) 7, paras 105–14; *Croatia/Slovenia Arbitration, Partial Award*, PCA (2016) paras 215–25, and see generally Rosenne, *Breach of Treaty* (Cambridge, 1985); Reuter, *An Introduction to the Law of Treaties* (London, 1989) 150ff.

[186] Klabbers, 8 *YbIEL* (1997) 36–40.

[187] At para 114. See Fitzmaurice, 11 *Leiden JIL* (1998) 321.

[188] See *infra*, Ch 6, section 3(3).

reason that states typically agree to measures that they believe can be complied with at little or no cost.[189] For the same reason, as the 1997 Kyoto Protocol shows, if the treaty is not strong enough, full compliance will not solve the problem it is intended to address.[190] Nevertheless, where problems do arise, intergovernmental bodies can provide both formal and informal methods for settling disputes and monitoring compliance. Their principal importance lies in facilitating multilateral solutions, usually within the COP, both to resolve questions of treaty interpretation and allegations of breach or non-compliance with the treaty.

Some scholars have characterized this approach as 'managerialist'—in the sense that active management of compliance is required rather than enforcement.[191] Others refer to it as 'dispute avoidance' because it seeks to minimize resort to arbitration or judicial settlement.[192] The NCPs considered below are an example, as is the power given to some treaty bodies to undertake inquiry or conciliation, but dispute avoidance in a wider sense is characteristic of many environmental treaties, even when no formal provision is made.

3(2) TREATY SUPERVISORY BODIES

The treaty supervisory bodies we consider in this section are useful insofar as they exercise a form of collective supervision, enabling individual parties to be held accountable to the other parties for non-compliance.[193] Accountability may thus extend to a wider community than the affected state and involve also the participation of NGO observers, although none of the environmental treaties goes as far as the 1944 Convention Establishing the International Labour Organization ('ILO'), under which employers and trade union organizations participate directly in the process of scrutiny.

Reliance on autonomous treaty bodies has been identified as part of a general trend away from the solution of problems by strictly judicial means and towards the resolution of conflicts through an equitable balancing of interests and ad hoc political compromise.[194] Used in this way such mechanisms become a forum for negotiation and mutual assistance, rather than adjudication of legal disputes. The underlying perception is that community pressure and the scrutiny of other states in

[189] See e.g. Victor, Raustiala and Skolnikoff (eds), *Implementation and Effectiveness of International Environmental Commitments* (Cambridge, Mass, 1998) 662.

[190] See *infra*, Ch 6, and Mitchell, in Bodansky, Brunnée, and Hey, *Oxford Handbook of International Environmental Law* (Oxford, 2007) 893.

[191] Chayes et al, in Brown Weiss and Jacobson (eds), *Engaging Countries: Strengthening Compliance with International Environmental Accords* (Cambridge, Mass, 2000) 39–62. But for an important critique of this approach see Brunnée, in Winter (ed), *Multilevel Governance of Global Environmental Change* (Cambridge, 2006) 387.

[192] UNEP, *Study on Dispute Avoidance and Dispute Settlement in International Environmental Law*, UNEP/GC 20/INF/16 (1999).

[193] On the nature of these bodies see Churchill and Ulfstein, 94 *AJIL* (2000) 623 and *supra* Ch 2, section 5.

[194] Simma, in Macdonald and Johnston (eds), *Structure and Process of International Law* (The Hague, 1983) 485; Rosenne, *Breach of Treaty* (Cambridge, 1985) 39–44; Gehring, 1 *YbIEL* (1990) 35.

an intergovernmental forum may be more effective in securing a higher level of compliance than more confrontational methods.[195] Moreover, it is possible for supervisory mechanisms to give a flexible interpretation to treaties of this kind and to apply to this process experience and knowledge of the issues concerned. The IWC, the Meeting of the Parties to the 1987 Montreal Protocol , and the consultative meeting of the 1972 London Convention afford particularly good examples of this form of conflict resolution.[196] The absence of any provision for institutional supervision is, by contrast, often a sign that a treaty is ineffective and leads to obsolescence. Older treaties in this category, such as the 1940 Western Hemisphere Convention, have for this reason aptly been described as 'sleeping treaties' and their impact on contemporary environmental protection is likely to be limited. As Lyster observes, 'simply by requiring its Parties to meet regularly to review its implementation, a treaty can ensure that it stays at the forefront of its parties' attention'.[197]

The key tasks which treaty supervisory bodies perform are those of information and data collection, receiving and reviewing reports on implementation by states, overseeing independent monitoring and inspection, and facilitating compliance with agreed standards of conduct. These obligations or standards will usually have a treaty basis, but the technique is also capable of application to rules of customary law or to soft law.[198] It is, for example, one method by which the equitable utilization of shared resources can be implemented,[199] or by which preferential or shared rights to common resources such as high seas fisheries can be allocated, as envisaged in the *Icelandic Fisheries Case* and the 1995 UN Fish Stocks Agreement.[200]

Another reason for resorting to treaty supervisory mechanisms is that compliance with the 1973/78 MARPOL Convention, the 1972 London Convention, or the 1973 CITES, to take three examples, cannot readily be secured by suspension or termination of the treaty in cases of material breach, as envisaged by Article 60 of the 1969 VCLT. As we saw earlier, termination for breach would primarily harm the international community, not the defaulting state, and would run counter to a policy of ensuring the widest possible participation in such agreements.[201] In such cases accountability

195 See generally Brown Weiss and Jacobson (eds), *Engaging Countries: Strengthening Compliance with International Environmental Accords*; Victor, Raustiala, and Skolnikoff (eds), *The Implementation and Effectiveness of International Environmental Commitments*; Handl, 5 *Colorado JIELP* (1994) 305; Beyerlin, 56 *ZAÖRV* (1996) 602; Kingsbury, 19 *Mich JIL* (1998) 345; Cameron, Werksman, and Roderick (eds), *Improving Compliance with International Environmental Law* (London 1996); Wolfrum, 272 *Recueil des Cours* (1998) 9; de Chazournes, 99 *RGDIP* (1995) 37.

196 On the IWC, see Birnie, 29 *NRJ* (1989) 903, and *infra*, Ch 12, section 4; on the LDC, see *infra*, Ch 8, section 4 and on the Montreal Protocol, *infra*, Ch 6, section 3.

197 Lyster, *International Wildlife Law* (Cambridge, 1985) 12.

198 Victor et al, *The Implementation and Effectiveness of International Environmental Law*, Ch 6; Shelton (ed), *Commitment and Compliance* (Oxford, 2000).

199 See *infra*, Ch 10.

200 See *infra*, Ch 12.

201 *Supra*, section 3(1) and see Fitzmaurice, in Treves et al (eds), *Non-Compliance Procedures and Mechanisms etc*, 467–74; Macdonald and Johnston (eds), *Structure and Process of International Law* (The Hague, 1983) 485; Rosenne, *Breach of Treaty*, 39–44.

through international institutions or treaty bodies may be the only practical remedy available.[202]

(a) Trusteeship

The most sophisticated example of an international supervisory regime is UN trusteeship.[203] The essence of this trust, like the concept of common heritage later employed by the 1982 UNCLOS, is that its performance is subject to international scrutiny and supervision. Although disputes could come before the PCIJ or the ICJ in certain circumstances,[204] judicial settlement has not been the primary method for ensuring compliance by administering powers with their treaty obligations. Instead, the Mandates Commission of the League, or the Trusteeship Council of the UN, were invested with supervisory functions,[205] creating a model of accountability to the international community, reinforced by the ultimate authority of the UN General Assembly to pronounce on the conduct of the mandatory power in case of non-compliance.[206] There are obvious parallels here with oversight of MEAs.[207] Not surprisingly, therefore, it has sometimes been suggested that the Trusteeship Council should assume a supervisory responsibility for the global commons, or more generally for the global environment.[208] The idea has made no headway in the face of political resistance to UN reform, but elements of international trusteeship can nevertheless be discerned in the environmental responsibilities of the ISA,[209] the GEF and the World Bank.[210] Apart from funding environmental protection projects, what these latter institutions have in common with trusteeship is that they monitor compliance with a range of MEAs as a condition of any loans or grants they make.[211]

(b) Autonomous treaty bodies

Autonomous treaty bodies offer a more basic model of institutional supervision.[212] The use of autonomous bodies for supervisory purposes is not new. It dates back to the Rhine Commission, established in 1815, with power to regulate navigation on the river, and to settle disputes.[213] Some of the techniques of political supervision and

[202] Handl, 5 *Tulane JICL* (1997) 35–7, and *supra*, section 2(5).

[203] Covenant of the League of Nations, Article 22; UN Charter, Chapter 12. See Redgwell, *International Trusts and Environmental Protection* (Manchester, 1999) 146–66.

[204] See *South West Africa Case*, ICJ Reports (1950) 128; *South West Africa Cases*, ICJ Reports (1962) 319 and (1966) 9.

[205] *South West Africa (Voting Procedure) Case*, ICJ Reports (1955) 121.

[206] *Namibia Advisory Opinion*, ICJ Reports (1971) 16.

[207] Redgwell, in Chambers and Green (eds), *Reforming International Environmental Governance: from Institutional Limits to Innovative Reforms* (Tokyo, 2005) 183.

[208] See Redgwell, *ibid*, 178–95; Palmer, 86 *AJIL* (1992) 259.

[209] See *supra*, Ch 2, section 5(3).

[210] Werksman, 6 *YbIEL* (1995) 27.

[211] *Supra*, Ch 2, section 4(7).

[212] See generally Churchill and Ulfstein, 94 *AJIL* (2000) 623.

[213] Congress of Vienna, Final Act, 9 June 1815, Article 32, Annex 16B. See also the 1856 Treaty of Paris which established the first Danube commission and Skubiszewski, 41 *BYIL* (1965) 168; Vitanyi, *The International Regime of River Navigation* (Alphen aan den Rijn, 1979) Chs 1–2.

control employed here have become more widely used since 1945, more especially in the field of human rights.[214] As we saw in Chapter 2, modern MEAs have also created an elaborate network of commissions and conferences or meetings of the parties. These are now the principal mechanisms for evaluating MEA effectiveness and supervising compliance. A provision for the parties 'to keep under continuous review and evaluation the effective implementation' of the treaty,[215] or some similar wording, is found in most modern environmental treaties. A variety of supervisory techniques can be used for this purpose.

3(3) SUPERVISORY TECHNIQUES

Effective supervision of the operation and implementation of treaty regimes depends on the availability of adequate information. This can be obtained in several ways.

(a) Reporting and monitoring

Most treaties require states to make periodic reports on matters affecting the treaty[216]. The extent of this obligation varies, but it will usually cover at least the measures taken by the parties towards implementing their obligations. Information must also usually be provided to enable the parties to assess how effectively the treaty is operating. The 1996 Mediterranean Protocol on Land-based Sources of Marine Pollution, for example, calls on the parties to communicate the results of monitoring of levels of marine pollution, as well as measures they have taken, results achieved, and difficulties encountered.[217] The 1989 Basel Convention requires an annual report on all aspects of transboundary trade and disposal of such substances, and on 'such other matters as the conference of the Parties shall deem relevant'.[218] Similarly, Article 8 of the 1973 CITES provides for the parties to maintain records of trade in listed species and to report on the number and type of permits granted. This information must be made available to the public. The 2001 POPS Convention also requires the parties to report on production, import, and export of listed chemicals; national inventories are made public and can be compared.[219] In some cases reporting requirements are designed to monitor how well the parties are enforcing a treaty. Thus the 1946 ICRW and the 1991 Antarctic Protocol oblige the parties to communicate reports submitted by national

[214] See Alston and Crawford (eds), *The Future of Human Rights Treaty Monitoring* (Cambridge, 2000).

[215] 1989 Basel Convention , Article 15; *infra,* Ch 8. See also 2003 Protocol on Pollutant Release Registers, Article 17(2); 2001 POPS Convention, Article 16; 2000 Biosafety Protocol, Article 35; 1998 Aarhus Convention, Article 10.

[216] See Bodansky in Alston and Crawford (eds), *The Future of UN Human Rights Treaty Monitoring,* Ch 17; Wolfrum, 272 *Recueil des Cours* (1998) 9, 36–43; Sachariew, 2 *YbIEL* (1991) 31; Wettestad, in Bodansky, Brunnée and Hey, *Handbook of IEL*, 975–94

[217] Article 13. See also 1996 Protocol to the 1972 London Convention, Article 9; 1992 Paris Convention for the Protection of the Marine Environment of the Northwest Atlantic, Article 22 and Annex IV, Article 2.

[218] Article 13.

[219] Article 15. See arguments of the parties in the *Pulp Mills Case*, ICJ Reports (2006).

inspectors concerning infractions, while the 1973/78 MARPOL Convention calls for reports from national authorities on action taken to deal with reported violations and on incidents involving harmful substances.[220]

This sort of information is meant to enable the parties to review and evaluate the treaty's impact. Where the treaty additionally requires the information to be made public, NGOs and other interested groups are also able to monitor progress. The obvious weakness is that much will depend on the diligence and accuracy of the reporting authorities, and the record of many states in this regard is poor. Despite this, many treaty COPs have found it possible to assess implementation and outcomes and, where necessary, NCPs can be employed to pressurize defaulting states into submitting the necessary data.[221]

(b) Fact-finding and research

Treaty institutions are not necessarily confined to a passive role as recipients of information. In many cases the power they enjoy to commission fact finding or research provides the essential scientific basis for adopting further measures and formulating policies of conservation and pollution control.[222] Some treaties also create scientific or technical committees as subsidiary bodies to provide expert advice. These committees, or the treaty secretariat, may offer a measure of independent verification or peer review of the information supplied by states, a point explicitly recognized in the 1978 Great Lakes Water Quality Agreement,[223] and in provision for expert review in the UNFCCC regime.[224] The value of information obtained independently of governments is obvious in the operation of fisheries conservation bodies and other highly contentious situations such as climate change. Thus it is important that these bodies should not be dependent on government scientists for expertise, but should be able to employ their own experts, or call on international scientific bodies such as the ICES or the SCAR.[225] The latter possibility is essential if small and modestly resourced institutions are to have access to high quality independent advice. The FAO and a variety of NGOs may also provide useful, though in the latter case not always detached, expertise.

(c) Inspection

The most assertive method of information-gathering and supervision allows international institutions to undertake inspections to verify compliance with international agreements and standards.[226] The strongest examples of inspection by international

[220] 1946 ICRW, Article IX(4); 1991 Antarctic Protocol, Articles 13 and 17; 1973/78 MARPOL Convention, Articles 6 and 8.

[221] On non-compliance see *infra*, section 3(4).

[222] See especially the use of the Intergovernmental Panel on Climate Change by the parties to the 1992 Climate Change Convention, *infra*, Ch 6.

[223] See *infra*, Ch 10, section 3(2).

[224] See, *infra*, Ch 6, section 4(5).

[225] *Supra*, Ch 2, section 6.

[226] See generally Oeter, 28 *NYIL* (1997) 101.

agencies are found in the arms-control field.[227] Here inspections are usually compulsory and reports are sent to the Security Council. The IAEA's inspection powers with regard to non-proliferation of nuclear weapons conform to this pattern. But the powers of inspection of this agency with regard to the safety of nuclear installations are not compulsory and may be employed only if requested by states.[228] This is the more usual pattern of environmental treaties, where provision for compulsory inspection by international institutions is exceptional. The main examples are concerned with the marine environment. The IWC has power to place observers on board whaling vessels to report back to the Commission. But these observers are nominated by member states willing to participate in the scheme on a mutual basis. In practice this means that observers from whaling nations are appointed to inspect each other's operations.[229] This falls well short of independent compulsory inspection. A few fisheries treaties have somewhat similar provision for mutual inspection, again reporting to the relevant Commission.[230] Only in the Antarctic treaty system have states accepted compulsory inspection as a means of informing the Consultative Meetings of possible violations of applicable treaties.[231] Thus there is clearly room for the wider adoption of inspection or expert review as a means of ensuring compliance with environmental treaties,[232] although this observation must also take account of the additional provision made by some treaties for national inspection and of the role of NGOs in bringing to light violations.

3(4) NON-COMPLIANCE PROCEDURES

NCPs are usually designed to secure compliance with the terms of a treaty or legally binding decision, although they are sometimes also applied to non-binding soft law.[233]

227 See e.g. 1990 Arms Control and Disarmament Agreement; 1968 Nuclear Non-Proliferation Treaty; Security Council Resolution 687 (1991) and Butler (ed), *Control Over Compliance with International Law* (Dordrecht, 1991) 31; Schoenbaum et al, *Trilateral Perspectives on International Legal Issues* (New York, 1998) Ch 11.

228 *Infra*, Ch 7.

229 Birnie, 29 *NRJ* (1989) 903; Lyster, *International Wildlife Law*, 31f.

230 1949 International Convention for North-West Atlantic Fisheries, Protocol on Joint Enforcement; 1978 Convention on Future Multilateral Cooperation in North-West Atlantic Fisheries, Article 18. Compare Article 21 of the 1995 UN Fish Stocks Agreement, which permits unilateral inspection of fishing vessels for law enforcement purposes.

231 The 1959 Antarctic Treaty, Article VII and the 1991 Antarctic Protocol , Article 13 provide for national inspectors, but the latter also makes provision for the meeting of the Consultative Parties to appoint observers to act on its behalf.

232 See generally Wolfrum, 272 *Recueil des Cours* (1998) 9, 43–8.

233 See generally Bodansky, *The Art and Craft of International Environmental Law* (London, 2010) Ch 11; Loibl, in Fitzmaurice, Ong, Merkouris (eds), *Research Handbook on International Environmental Law* (Cheltenham, 2010) Ch 20; Treves et al (eds), *Non-Compliance Procedures and Mechanisms and the Effectiveness of International Environmental Agreements* (The Hague, 2009); Mitchell, in Bodansky, Brunnée and Hey, *Oxford Handbook of IEL* (Oxford, 2007) 893–921; Beyerlin, Stoll and Wolfrum (eds), *Ensuring Compliance with Multilateral Environmental Agreements* (Leiden, 2006); Fitzmaurice and Redgwell, 31 *NYIL* (2000) 35; Shelton (ed), *Commitment and Compliance* (Oxford, 2000); Brown Weiss and Jacobson (eds), *Engaging Countries: Strengthening Compliance with International Accords* (Cambridge, Mass, 1998).

A number of environmental treaties have introduced formal NCPs for this purpose,[234] but even without such a formal procedure, non-compliance problems are likely to be handled in a similar way in many environmental regimes.[235] When used in a treaty context it is not entirely clear that 'non-compliance' differs in any material sense from 'breach' or 'non-application'.[236] What is at issue is a failure to meet the required legal standard set by the treaty and at this level the distinction is merely terminological. Some writers have also pointed to the importance of distinguishing between non-compliance and failure to take effective action to meet the objectives of a treaty, a situation which can arise even where the parties are in full compliance with its terms.[237] Non-compliance is thus a narrower concept which focuses only on commitments, rather than on broader questions affecting the further development and effectiveness of a regulatory regime.

As we saw earlier, most NCPs are best understood as a form of 'dispute avoidance' or 'alternative dispute resolution', in the sense that resort to binding third-party adjudication is avoided.[238] NCPs are unlike courts in several respects.[239] They are designed to facilitate forward-looking multilateral solutions to questions of treaty interpretation and non-compliance with the treaty. The consent of the respondent state need not be obtained before the process is initiated. Standing is not required to make a complaint: in most cases any party to the treaty or the treaty secretariat may do so; a party may even refer itself in order to secure assistance or more lenient treatment.[240] In some cases NGOs and members of the public can complain and participate in the process, or provide information to secretariats.[241] The process is thus potentially more inclusive than international litigation, an option only for states. It is, in effect, a public interest process, not a bilateral one, but one in which concern for due process and some degree of independence nevertheless remain important in order to ensure legitimacy.[242]

NCPs thus represent an important and potentially effective alternative to inter-state litigation. The fundamental assumption is that when governments voluntarily

[234] In addition to those discussed below, compliance procedures are also envisaged or established by 1989 Basel Convention , Article 19; 1992 OSPAR Convention, Article 23; 2000 Protocol on Biosafety, Article 34; 2001 POPS Convention, Article 17; 2003 Protocol on Pollutant Release and Transfer Registers, Article 22; 2013 Convention on Mercury, Article 15. UNEP adopted Guidelines on Compliance with MEAs in 2001. See generally UNEP, *Compliance Mechanisms Under Selected MEAs* (UNEP, 2007).

[235] Gehring, 1 *YbIEL* (1990) 54. See e.g. the 1973 CITES Convention, on which see Sand, 8 *EJIL* (1997) 29, and *infra*, Ch 11, section 3.

[236] See Fitzmaurice and Redgwell, 31 *NYIL* (2000) 35 and *supra*, section 3(1).

[237] Victor, Raustiala, and Skolnikoff (eds), *Implementation and Effectiveness*, 6–8.

[238] See Chinkin, in Evans (ed), *Remedies in International Law*, 128–34; Fitzmaurice and Redgwell, 31 *NYIL* (2000) 35; Adede, in Lang (ed), *Sustainable Development and International Law* (London, 1995) Ch 8.

[239] See Treves, in Treves et al, *Non-Compliance Procedures and Mechanisms* 499–518; Bodansky, *The Art and Craft of International Environmental Law*, 248.

[240] See e.g. 1987 Montreal Protocol, Annex IV (1998), Articles 1–4. Compare Article 15 of the 2013 Convention on Mercury, under which only the COP or the party involved may refer non-compliance to the Implementation and Compliance Committee.

[241] Notably the 1998 Aarhus Convention NCP, *infra*, section 3(4)(b) and see Epiney, in Beyerlin, Stoll, Wolfrum, *Ensuring Compliance with MEAs*, 319–352; Kravchenko, 18 *Colorado JIELP* (2007) 1.

[242] See in particular the 1998 Aarhus Convention NCP, *infra*.

undertake commitments they normally intend to comply.[243] They operate on the understanding that it is better to assist and encourage states than to penalize them for failing. The treaty parties will usually seek to shape consensus on the issue in dispute, and the process is intended to reinforce the stability, transparency, and legitimacy of the regime as a whole.[244]

The outcome of the procedure can be the provision of assistance or other inducements to encourage future compliance, but if necessary more compelling responses are also possible, ranging from the withholding of funds by the World Bank or the GEF to the suspension of treaty rights and privileges pending full compliance. Sanctions of this kind can be effective, particularly where they involve loss of the right to trade.[245]

Where, as in the case of climate change or ozone depletion, non-compliance affects all parties to the treaty, there is considerable merit in designing a process for securing compliance which is multilateral in character and allows all parties, as well as NGOs, to participate. Although it is possible to accommodate a multiplicity of participants in judicial proceedings, it is not easy to do so, and an adversarial procedure is not well suited to the resolution of the kind of non-compliance problems likely to arise under global environmental treaties.[246] Moreover, soft settlement typically facilitates more readily than judicial processes the necessary input of scientific and technical expertise required to deal with issues of compliance under agreements of this kind. Those are probably the major contributions of the processes of review developed from the 1987 Montreal Protocol.

(a) The Montreal Protocol as a model non-compliance procedure

Dispute avoidance is best exemplified by the NCP adopted by parties to the 1987 Montreal Protocol.[247] This procedure can be invoked by any party to the protocol, by the protocol secretariat, or by the party itself, wherever there are thought to be problems regarding compliance. The matter is then referred for investigation by an Implementation Committee consisting of ten parties elected on the basis of equitable geographical representation. The main task of the committee is to consider the submissions, information, and observations made to it with a view to securing an amicable solution of the matter on the basis of respect for the provisions of the Protocol.

243 Bilder in Shelton (ed), *Commitment and Compliance*, 66.

244 Chayes, in Brown Weiss and Jacobson (eds), *Engaging Countries etc*, 43; Brunnée, in Winter (ed), *Multilevel Governance of Global Environmental Change* (Cambridge, 2006) 387–408.

245 E.g. suspension of trade under the 1973 CITES, *infra*, Ch 11, section 3(4), and Sand, 8 *EJIL* (1997) 29. On the relationship with countermeasures and other responses to breach of treaty see Fitzmaurice and Redgwell, 31 *NYIL* (2000) 35.

246 See *infra*, next section.

247 Article 8, and Annex IV, as adopted at Copenhagen in 1992, and amended 1998. See *infra*, Ch 6, section 2(3); Lesniewska, in Fitzmaurice et al, *Research Handbook on International Environmental Law*, Ch 22; Jacur, in Treves et al (eds), *Non-Compliance Procedures and Mechanisms etc*, 11; Yoshida, *The International Legal Regime for the Protection of the Stratospheric Ozone Layer* (2nd edn, Leiden, 2019), Ch 5; and UNEP, *Report of the Implementation Committee for the Montreal Protocol, 20th Meeting*, UNEP/OzL Pro/Imp Com/20/4, paras 24–33.

This is very similar to the provision for negotiation of a friendly settlement under the 1950 ECHR.[248] The Implementation Committee can seek whatever information it needs through the secretariat; for this purpose it may also visit the territory of the party under investigation if invited to do so. A report is made to the full MOP, which decides what steps to call for in order to bring about full compliance. These can include the provision of appropriate financial, technical, or training assistance in order to help the party to comply. If these measures are insufficient, cautions can be issued, or, as a last resort, rights and privileges under the treaty can be suspended in accordance with the law of treaties.[249] The MOP will also decide on appropriate action when a developing state notifies the secretariat of its inability to implement the protocol through the failure of developed states to provide finance or technology.[250]

A comparable procedure has been adopted under the 1979 LRTAP Convention.[251] An Implementation Committee has responsibility for reviewing compliance by the parties with all the Convention's protocols under a common procedure.[252] As in other NCPs its task is to consider referrals 'with a view to securing a constructive solution'. The Executive Body (i.e. the parties) may decide on non-discriminatory measures to secure compliance, but the only measure specifically indicated is the provision of assistance. Its decisions require consensus and can thus be easily blocked. The 1992 Climate Change Convention provides an even softer 'multilateral consultative process' to resolve questions regarding implementation.[253] Conducted by a panel of experts, rather than by other member states, it remains non-judicial, non-confrontational, and advisory rather than supervisory. No sanctions of any kind can be imposed, not even suspension of rights and privileges; there is power only to recommend measures to facilitate cooperation and implementation and to clarify issues and promote understanding of the Convention.

(b) The Aarhus Convention Compliance Committee

Although in many respects similar to the Montreal Protocol NCP, the most innovative features of the 'non-confrontational, non-judicial and consultative' procedure established under Article 15 of the 1998 Aarhus Convention are that members of the public and NGOs may bring complaints before a non-compliance committee whose

248 1950 ECHR, Article 28 provided that the Commission on Human Rights 'shall place itself at the disposal of the parties concerned with a view to securing a friendly settlement of the matter on the basis of respect for human rights as defined in the Convention'.

249 Montreal Protocol, annex V, as adopted 1992. On suspension or termination of treaties see 1969 VCLT, especially Articles 44, 58, 60.

250 Montreal Protocol, Article 5(4)–(7) as revised 1990. The NCP cannot be invoked against a party who has made such a notification.

251 Szell, in Lang (ed), *Sustainable Development and International Law* (London, 1995) 97; Milano, in Treves et al (eds), *Non-Compliance Procedures and Mechanisms etc*, 169.

252 Executive Body, Decision 1997/2, in UNECE, *Report of the 15th Session of the Executive Body* (1997) Annex III. See also Article 11 of the POPS Protocol, Article 9 of the Heavy Metals Protocol, Article 9 of the Acidification Protocol, and Article 9 of the Gothenburg Protocol, *infra*, Ch 6, section 2(3).

253 Article 13, and see *infra*, Ch 6, section 4(5).

members are not only independent of the parties but may be nominated by NGOs.[254] In all these respects it is somewhat closer to human rights treaty-monitoring bodies such as the UN Human Rights Committee than to the Montreal Protocol NCP.[255] The process was strongly opposed by the US during negotiations,[256] but it has nevertheless been accepted throughout Europe and the former Soviet states. The committee hearing complaints has given rulings which interpret and clarify provisions of the convention and a body of case law is emerging.[257] There have been findings of non-compliance against several parties resulting in recommendations that the respondent states should change their law, develop better implementation, or engage in capacity-building and training.[258]

However, not all respondent governments have cooperated with the Compliance Committee or implemented its recommendations.[259] In theory it is then open to the MOP to suspend a non-complying party's treaty rights and privileges or take other appropriate measures to secure compliance.[260] Kravchenko concludes that 'independence, transparency, and NGO involvement in the Convention's novel compliance mechanism represent an ambitious effort to bring democracy and participation to the very heart of compliance itself'.[261] In all of these respects the Aarhus procedure is significantly stronger than any other currently in operation. Nevertheless, individual complainants would be well advised to appreciate that many of the same rights they enjoy under the 1998 Aarhus Convention can also be asserted under the 1950 ECHR, in a judicial forum, with an established record of compliance by states.[262]

(c) The Kyoto Protocol Compliance Committee

Although the 1997 Kyoto Protocol has now been replaced by the 2015 Paris Agreement, the Protocol's compliance procedures are unique among environmental agreements,

254 Aarhus Convention, Decision 1/7: Review of Compliance, *Report of 1st Mtg of Parties*, UN Doc ECE/MP PP/2/Add 8 (2004). See also Report of the Compliance Committee, UN Doc ECE/MP PP/2005/13 (2005) and generally Kravchenko, 18 *Colorado JIELP* (2007) 1; Koester, 2 *J Eur Env & Plng L* (2005) 31; Pitea, in Treves et al, *Non-Compliance Procedures and Mechanisms etc*, 221; Koester, ibid, 277. The compliance procedure adopted in 2007 under the 1999 UNECE Protocol on Water and Health is modelled directly on the Aarhus procedure. Other NCPs with independent members but with no public participation include the Compliance Committees of the Biosafety Protocol and the Kyoto Protocol.

255 See generally Alston and Crawford (eds), *The Future of UN Human Rights Treaty Monitoring* (Cambridge, 2000).

256 But compare procedures for individual enforcement under the 1993 North American Agreement on Environmental Cooperation, *infra*, Ch 5, section 2(6).

257 *Infra*, Ch 5.

258 The most extensive relates to Spain: Communication ACCC/C/2008/24. See also Communication ACCC/C/2008/32 concerning compliance by the European Union [locus standi before the ECJ].

259 Kravchenko, 18 *Colorado JIELP* (2007) 46–7. See in particular Decision V/9n on compliance by UK (ECE/MP.PP/2014/2/Add.1); Decision V/9b on compliance by Austria (ECE/MP.PP/2014/2/Add.1); Decision V/9k on compliance by Spain (ECE/MP.PP/2014/2/Add.1).

260 Decision 1/7: Review of Compliance, para 37. See Koester, in Ulfstein, Marauhn, and Zimmermann (eds), *Making Treaties Work: Human Rights, Environment and Arms Control* (Cambridge, 2007) Ch 8.

261 Kravchenko, 18 *Colorado JIELP* (2007) 49.

262 See *infra*, Ch 5, section 2(5).

and for that reason are worth examination. As we will see in Chapter 6, complying with the 1997 Kyoto Protocol is not necessarily easy or cheap. However willing states may have been when they became parties, there are substantial economic and political pressures to delay or compromise on commitments. The implementation mechanisms are complex, involving joint implementation, emissions trading between developed states, and a clean-development mechanism requiring reductions in emissions by developing states. In effect, parties have the right to transfer implementation of their commitments to other states. All these complicated arrangements have to be verified, and all parties have a mutual interest in trust and transparency.

The task of ensuring compliance with the 1997 Kyoto Protocol was thus thought to be particularly crucial to its success.[263] The procedure adopted under Article 18 reflects these concerns.[264] Its purpose is to 'facilitate, promote and enforce compliance' with commitments under the Protocol. It is the last of these objectives—enforcement—which gives it a distinctive character unique among environmental treaties. 'Questions of implementation' may be submitted by the party concerned, or by any other party. They are considered by a Compliance Committee, elected by the parties, whose members serve 'in their individual capacities'. There is no NGO participation on the Committee, but competent intergovernmental organizations and NGOs may submit relevant information. In practice, initiation of procedures before the Kyoto Compliance Committee has mainly resulted from the work of the expert review teams, whose 'in-depth review' of national inventories of greenhouse-gas emissions provides the initial evidence of non-compliance. The Committee then has a choice when deciding how to deal with non-compliance. Like other compliance committees, it can give advice and make recommendations on implementing the protocol, offer assistance, or arrange technology transfer and capacity building. These are the responsibility of the 'facilitative branch'. In practice, parties have in most cases resolved their problems during the expert review process, and the facilitation process has not been needed.[265]

Alternatively, the matter can be referred to the 'enforcement branch'. Members of this body must be lawyers, the party concerned will be entitled to a public hearing and due process, and decisions must be based on evidence, must be reasoned and made public. There can be an appeal to the COP if due process has been denied. The reason for adopting such a quasi-judicial process is that the enforcement branch has the power to impose real penalties on a non-complying party. Inter alia, emissions reductions may be increased and eligibility to participate in emissions trading or the

[263] See Werksman, 9 *YbIEL* (1998) 48; *id*, *Responding to Non-Compliance Under the Climate Change Regime* (OECD, 1998).

[264] 1997 Kyoto Protocol, Decision 27/CMP 1: Procedures and Mechanisms Relating to Compliance, *1st MoP*, FCCC/KP/CMP/2005/8/Add 3 (2006). See Brunnée, Doelle, Rajamani (eds), *Promoting Compliance in an Evolving Climate Regime* (Cambridge, 2012); Urbinati, in *Non-Compliance Procedures and Mechanisms etc*, 63; Fitzmaurice, 8 *Singapore YIL* (2004) 23; Stokke, Hovi, and Ulfstein (eds), *Implementing the Climate Regime: International Compliance* (London, 2005) 39ff.

[265] Brunnée, Doelle, Rajamani (eds), *Promoting Compliance*, 98.

clean-development mechanism may be withdrawn. In effect, treaty rights can be suspended in order to restore compliance with the Protocol. This is also possible under other non-compliance procedures,[266] but given the economic significance of the potential penalties in this case a more formal procedure was thought desirable.

At this point we can see that the idea of compliance procedures as non-confrontational and non-judicial has given way to a process that has more in common with the dispute settlement body of the WTO—an entirely deliberate parallel. It does not follow that in this form it will necessarily be more effective than 'softer' non-compliance procedures. The WTO Dispute Settlement Body has not succeeded in resolving every WTO dispute satisfactorily, if by that we mean ensuring compliance with WTO agreements. Nor is it obvious why a state that finds non-compliance with Kyoto advantageous should change its mind if its emissions reduction targets are further increased or its eligibility to meet them by trading emissions is taken away. Thus, Canada simply withdrew from the 1997 Kyoto Protocol when it found compliance burdensome. In practice, however, enforcement proceedings against other parties did result in compliance by the states concerned and eligibility to participate in mechanisms under Articles 6, 12, and 17 of the Protocol was restored.[267]

There are large theoretical questions here about the reasons for compliance and the right balance between incentives and penalties.[268]

4 SETTLEMENT OF INTERNATIONAL ENVIRONMENTAL DISPUTES

4(1) THE ROLE OF LITIGATION IN ENVIRONMENTAL DISPUTES

Litigation is an expensive and often uncertain option for any state seeking to settle a dispute, and negotiation, conciliation or resort to non-compliance procedures will often be preferable. International courts and arbitral tribunals have played only a limited role in the development of international environmental law, but the number of cases has grown steadily since the first edition of this book was published in 1991.[269] It has been observed that these cases 'are seldom, if ever brought purely to achieve legal objectives, and instead are often part of the "theatre" of environmental diplomacy.'[270]

266 See Montreal Protocol, *supra*.

267 See proceedings against Croatia, Romania, Slovakia, Lithuania and Ukraine in the period 2012–16. In 2019 Monaco and Kazakhstan were under investigation.

268 See Haas in Shelton, *Commitment and Compliance*, Ch 2; Bilder, ibid, Ch 3; Grubb, 16:6 *Climate Policy* (2016) 673–681.

269 See generally Boyle and Harrison, 4 *JIDS* (2013) 245; Stephens, *International Courts and Environmental Protection* (Cambridge, 2009); *id*, in Klein (ed), *Litigating International Law Disputes* (Cambridge, 2014) 284; Romano, in Bodansky, Brunnée and Hey, *Handbook of IEL*, Ch 45; Lowe and Fitzmaurice (eds), *Fifty Years of the International Court of Justice* (Cambridge, 1996) Ch 15.

270 Stephens, in Klein, *Litigating International Law Disputes* 291.

We start, therefore, with the caveat that states litigate for a variety of reasons, some of which may have little or nothing to do with the merits of the dispute. There are four main reasons for litigating an inter-state environmental dispute.

First, litigation can reinforce environmental diplomacy and assist in settling disputes. For example, in the *Aerial Spraying Case* the written proceedings helped identify and isolate the issues and eventually facilitated a negotiated settlement a few weeks before the scheduled ICJ hearing. Secondly, litigation gives weaker states some leverage over their bigger and more powerful neighbours.[271] Defending the rights of the weak against the strong is what a system of justice is supposed to do, and litigation in such cases succeeds often enough to make it a real option. Thirdly, some environmental cases come to court more for domestic reasons than because of any real prospect of success—in effect the international dispute is a façade for getting a government out of domestic political problems. This is perhaps the best way to understand *Pulp Mills, MOX Plant, Whaling in the Antarctic,* or the *Chagos MPA Cases.*[272] Fourthly, litigation may be the best or only option when the parties to a dispute need an authoritative ruling on the law, on the interpretation of a treaty, or on the underlying facts.[273] A judicial or arbitral decision may clarify the situation and facilitate a settlement, whether directly, or through further negotiation, or simply by legitimising the status quo.[274]

Despite its potential benefits, litigation is not an easy option. The first and foremost problem is the difficulty of finding an adequate jurisdictional basis for potentially complex environmental disputes. Only a minority of states currently accept the ICJ's compulsory jurisdiction,[275] often with extensive reservations. There is, for example, little point trying to sue the US in inter-state environmental disputes as it no longer accepts ICJ compulsory jurisdiction, nor is it a party to 1982 UNCLOS.[276] China, Russia, or France also do not accept ICJ compulsory jurisdiction. Even fewer states accept the compulsory jurisdiction of the ITLOS with respect to disputes arising under 1982 UNCLOS, although the default mechanism of Annex VII compulsory arbitration has been the basis for a growing list of cases that are in some degree environmental.[277]

International environmental law, as already noted in Chapter 1, is made up of multiple, overlapping, treaties, based on a framework of customary international law, interpreted and applied in conformity with general principles agreed by the

[271] See e.g. *South China Sea Arbitration (Philippines/China)*(2016); *Aerial Spraying Case (Ecuador/Colombia)*(2013).

[272] See Stephens in Klein (ed), *Litigating International Law Disputes* 287.

[273] See e.g. *Gabčíkovo-Nagymaros Dam Case*, ICJ Reports (1997) 7; *San Juan River/Border Activities Cases*, ICJ Reports (2015) 665.

[274] See Lowe, in Ndiaye and Wolfrum (eds), *Law of the Sea, Environmental Law and Settlement of Disputes* (Leiden, 2007) 235–47.

[275] Some 70 states had made declarations under Article 36(2) of the Statute at the time of writing.

[276] The US has accepted compulsory adjudication for disputes arising under the 1995 UN Fish Stocks Agreement, and a number of regional fisheries agreements.

[277] *MOX Plant*; *Southern Bluefin Tuna*; *Swordfish*; *Land Reclamation*; *Chagos Marine Protected Area*; *South China Sea*. Only the last two were decided on the merits.

international community. A case involving small island states affected by climate change, for example, might rely on the 1992 Climate Change Convention, the 2015 Paris Agreement, the 1982 UNCLOS, the 1992 CBD, the law of state responsibility, the customary obligation of due diligence, the precautionary principle, and even some human rights law.[278] Each of the applicable treaties will have its own dispute settlement provisions or none; of the treaties mentioned, only 1982 UNCLOS provides for compulsory dispute settlement by courts or tribunals. Relatively few environmental treaties do so, despite the recommendations of the WCED that greater use be made of compulsory dispute settlement.[279] Those that do will generally limit jurisdiction to disputes concerning interpretation or application of the treaty in which the dispute settlement clause is found, but there may then be uncertainty about the proper forum or the applicable law if the dispute straddles several treaties.[280]

Thus, it may not be possible to formulate a case on which any one court or tribunal could adjudicate all of the relevant legal issues. The outcome may be a cluster of separate cases,[281] or a case that is not really the one the applicant state would like to bring, but the one that it can bring. This is not a phenomenon unique to environmental disputes. It is inherent in a system of international dispute settlement based on the consent of the parties.[282]

Such jurisdictional fragmentation could of course be avoided where a state has given general consent to the settlement of disputes, whether by an optional clause declaration under Article 36(2) of the ICJ Statute, or under the Pact of Bogotá.[283] In the ideal world we might prefer an environmental dispute settlement treaty which provided for compulsory adjudication for all the relevant treaties, customary law and general principles applicable in relations between the parties to any environmental dispute. One model might be the WTO Dispute Settlement Body whose jurisdiction is to decide disputes concerning any of the WTO 'covered agreements' listed in annex I of the 1994 WTO Agreement.[284] But we do not have such a system for environmental disputes, and the result is that environmental cases viewed as a whole present a picture of jurisdictional complexity. What is most remarkable in these circumstances is that there are any cases at all.

A second, equally fundamental, constraint is that although international organizations, NGOs, and companies can all be party to an arbitration based on

278 Werksman, in Wannier and Gerrard (eds),, *Threatened Island Nations: Legal Implications of Rising Seas and a Changing Climate* (Cambridge, 2013); Wewerinke, *State Responsibility, Climate Change and Human Rights under International Law* (London, 2019).

279 The WCED, *Our Common Future* (OUP 1987) 334. See *infra*, section 4(5).

280 See *OSPAR Arbitration*, PCA (2003); *MOX Plant Arbitration*, PCA (2003); *Southern Bluefin Tuna Arbitration*, ICSID (2000) and generally Romano, in Bodansky, Brunnée, and Hey, *Handbook of IEL*, Ch 45.

281 E.g. the *Swordfish Case* before ITLOS and the WTO. See Nollkaemper, in Faure and Ying (eds), *China and International Environmental Liability* (Cheltenham, 2008) 11.

282 One obvious example in an entirely different context is the *Lockerbie Case* (1992) ICJ Reports 114.

283 The latter instrument has been invoked in several environmental disputes: see *San Juan River/Border Activities Case*, and the *Aerial Spraying Case*.

284 *Infra*, Ch 13.

international law,[285] only states can at present be parties to contentious proceedings before the ICJ, while only competent intergovernmental organizations (not states) may seek advisory opinions.[286] As Sir Robert Jennings has observed,[287] the ICJ's narrow jurisdiction *ratione personae* reflects a conception of participation in the international legal system that is almost a hundred years old, increasingly anomalous, and out of step with contemporary international society. Other international tribunals, including those concerned with human rights, commercial and investment disputes, international claims, or the EU, have adopted broader rules on access. In certain kinds of proceedings before the ITLOS the range of potential parties may include not only international organizations, NGOs, and private parties but also 'fishing entities', such as Taiwan.[288] This offers the possibility of creating a judicial process capable of accommodating conceptions of participation already apparent when we look at international environmental law-making, or at environmental institutions, or even at national environmental law. But such a process is not the one we currently have in the majority of environmental disputes.

Finally, as we saw earlier in this chapter, judicial proceedings and arbitration are less well adapted to the multilateral character of many environmental problems than supervision by meetings of the parties to treaty regimes, including non-compliance procedures.[289] Contentious litigation is inherently bilateral, and in inter-state arbitration it is rare to find any provision for third-party intervention.[290] Before the ICJ and the ITLOS third parties may intervene as of right only if the interpretation or application of a treaty to which they are party is in question.[291] This would entitle any party to a multilateral environmental treaty, such as the 1985 Ozone or 1992 Climate Change Conventions, to intervene and make representations in any litigation concerning those treaties.

Multilateral interests are not so well protected in disputes concerned with customary law, where there is merely a discretion to allow intervention when the legal rights of a third party are 'affected' by the decision in a case.[292] States are not permitted to intervene in such cases for the purpose of assisting a court to decide what the law is, nor can they use intervention as a means of initiating what is in effect a new dispute.[293] This narrow interpretation of Article 62 of the ICJ Statute may deny third parties the opportunity to intervene in cases where the respondent state is violating the rights of

[285] As under the PCA's 2001 Optional Rules for Arbitration of Disputes Relating to Natural Resources and/or the Environment.

[286] Statute, Articles 34, 65. [287] Jennings, 89 *AJIL* (1995) 493.

[288] Article 20(2) of the Statute of the ITLOS provides that: 'The Tribunal shall be open to entities other than States Parties in any case expressly provided for in Part XI [see Article 189] *or in any case submitted pursuant to any other agreement conferring jurisdiction on the Tribunal which is accepted by all the parties to that case.*'

[289] See *supra*, section 3.

[290] But see 1907 Hague Convention for the Pacific Settlement of International Disputes, Article 84.

[291] Statute of the ICJ, Article 63; Statute of the ITLOS, Article 32. New Zealand made use of this right in the *Whaling Case*: see Declaration of Intervention by New Zealand, Order of 6 February 2013.

[292] Statute of the ICJ, Article 62; Statute of the ITLOS, Article 31.

[293] *Land, Island and Maritime Frontier Case (Nicaragua Intervention)* ICJ Reports (1990) 92, paras 52–105; *Malta/Libya Continental Shelf Case (Italian Intervention)* ICJ Reports (1984) 3.

all states, or of the international community as a whole in the case of obligations *erga omnes*. It may be that the International Court would simply view such interventions as attempts to make representations on the law or to turn a bilateral dispute into a multi-party one.[294] It could plausibly be said that the decision in one case does not 'affect' the rights of non-parties to the dispute, who remain free to bring proceedings of their own. There is an obvious risk of states using intervention to bring claims over which the court would otherwise have no jurisdiction in original proceedings. Allowing multiple third parties with competing interests to intervene in litigation may also make it harder to settle a dispute, may deter states from going to court, and may thus undermine the UN Charter's concern for the peaceful resolution of interstate disputes by whatever means the parties choose.

4(2) CHOICE OF FORUM

General international law takes an eclectic approach to the methods and fora used to settle international disputes.[295] Article 33 of the UN Charter gives pre-eminence to the principle that disputes must be settled peacefully but leaves the choice of means to the parties. Despite its status as the 'principal judicial organ' of the UN, the ICJenjoys no priority as a forum for dispute settlement. The Court's jurisdiction, in common with all international judicial and arbitral tribunals, is based on the consent of the states parties to each dispute. It has no general jurisdiction to hear applications submitted unilaterally save to the extent provided for by Article 36 (2) of the Statute of the Court, or in other treaties such as the 1982 UNCLOS.

Nor is the ICJ necessarily the preferred forum under those treaties which do provide for compulsory binding settlement. As we shall see below, the 1991 Antarctic Protocol refers all disputes to arbitration, unless the parties agree otherwise, while the 1994 Agreement Establishing the WTO creates its own system of specialized panels, an appeal body, and arbitration, for the purpose of settling trade disputes, a number of which have involved environmental questions. Part XV of 1982 UNCLOS brings disputes concerning the marine environment and living resources of the high seas within compulsory jurisdiction,[296] but it allows the parties to choose various forums, including conciliation, several forms of arbitration, the ICJ, or the ITLOS.[297] If the parties cannot agree on a forum, arbitration is obligatory. Most UNCLOS cases have gone to arbitration.

294 For a detailed review of the case law see Chinkin, *Third Parties in International Law* (Oxford, 1993) Chs 7, 12; Crawford, *State Responsibility* (Cambridge, 2013) 656–65; Palchetti, 6 *Max Planck Yb UN Law* (2002) 139–181. See also Okowa's discussion of the attempt by four states to intervene in the 1995 *Nuclear Tests Case*, in Evans (ed), *Remedies in International Law*, 164–7. All four states were in effect making the same claim as New Zealand.

295 See generally Merrills, *International Dispute Settlement* (5th edn, Cambridge, 2014); Collier and Lowe, *The Settlement of Disputes in International Law* (Oxford, 1999).

296 See *infra*, section 4(5).

297 1982 UNCLOS, Articles 284, 287. See Boyle, 46 *ICLQ* (1997) 37; Klein, *Dispute Settlement in the UN Convention on the Law of the Sea* (Cambridge, 2005).

The creation of the ITLOS has widened the choice of forum for contentious cases and advisory opinions concerning the protection of the marine environment or the conservation of marine living resources.[298] There are possible risks in this, of a fragmentation of the international legal system, and of a diminution of the ICJ's authority and centrality as the principal judicial organ of the UN.[299] But there are also benefits, in the specific expertise of 21 judges with 'recognized competence' in the law of the sea, in a stronger and more responsive jurisprudence, and in the encouragement more states may feel when contemplating judicial settlement.[300] In general, the cases suggest that, with some limited exceptions, the different UNCLOS dispute settlement fora have applied the Convention consistently and coherently.[301] Fragmentation in the case law of international courts and tribunals is not an obvious problem.[302]

4(3) PUBLIC-INTEREST ENVIRONMENTAL LITIGATION

Public interest litigation for environmental purposes is well established in many advanced legal systems, although not universally. It serves the instrumental purpose of enforcing the law when no-one is specifically injured and there is a public interest in protecting the environment. Responsibility for taking action in the public interest may rest primarily or exclusively with public authorities: for example in EU law it is the European Commission's responsibility to ensure that member states comply with their environmental responsibilities,[303] and litigation by NGOs is discouraged by restrictive rules on standing.[304] At present the ISA is the only other international body with power to sue member states, and only within its restricted field of competence over exploitation of the deep seabed and protection of the marine environment from activities in the Area.[305] The Authority is also able to sue contractors directly, as well as being competent to issue emergency orders in order to prevent, contain and minimize serious harm to the marine environment.[306] However, many national legal systems facilitate public interest litigation by NGOs and private parties when public authorities have either failed to act or lack the power or resources to do so.[307] This more liberal version of the concept is promoted and facilitated by the 1998 Aarhus Convention

[298] See Rothwell, in Ndiaye and Wolfrum, *Law of the Sea, Environmental Law and Settlement of Disputes*, 1007–24.

[299] Oda, 244 *Recueil des Cours* (1993) II, 127–55; *id*, 44 *ICLQ* (1995) 863; Guillaume, 44 *ICLQ* (1995) 848.

[300] Charney, 90 *AJIL* (1996) 69; Boyle, 22 *IJMCL* (2007) 369. See generally Merrills, 54 *NILR* (2007) 361.

[301] See Boyle, 47 *RBDI* (2014) 182.

[302] See generally Webb, *International Judicial Integration and Fragmentation* (2013, Oxford), and *supra*, Ch 1, text at n 241.

[303] *Commission of the European Communities v Ireland* (2006) ECJ Case C-459/03.

[304] See *Stichting Greenpeace Council v EC Commission* (1998) ECR I-1651. But contrast the ECJ case law on access to national courts: see Müller, 23 *JEL* (2011) 505.

[305] 1982 UNCLOS, Article 187(b)(i).

[306] 1982 UNCLOS, Articles 165(2)(k) and 187(c)(ii).

[307] *Infra*, Ch 5, section 2(6).

insofar as NGOs are covered by the Convention's provisions on access to justice in national courts.[308]

As we saw earlier in this chapter, international law does not make general provision for an *actio popularis* by states. Only those environmental obligations which affect the international community as a whole have an *erga omnes* character potentially enforceable by any state; even then the consent of the respondent state is still essential for jurisdictional purposes in any international litigation.[309] In practice public interest environmental litigation involving states is most likely to arise under multilateral treaties.[310]

An alternative to interstate litigation, however, is to allow international organizations to seek advisory opinions on environmental questions that fall within their competence. The UN General Assembly and the Security Council may seek advisory opinions from the ICJ on any question of international law, while ECOSOC, the IMO, the WHO, the IAEA, and possibly UNEP may do so in respect of matters falling within their specific competence.[311] The ITLOS has a more limited power to give advisory opinions,[312] but its *Advisory Opinion on the Responsibilities of States with Respect to Activities in the Area* provides the most comprehensive treatment of international environmental law by any international court or tribunal.[313] An advisory opinion carries the same legal authority as a judgment in interstate proceedings, and provides a means of clarifying and developing the law, but without the facility for making binding orders. As the cases demonstrate, it is possible for states and relevant international organizations to make representations in advisory proceedings,[314] and to that extent a genuine multilateralism is possible.

It is sometimes argued that NGOs and other non-state actors should also have the power to represent the public interest by initiating or intervening in contentious interstate proceedings.[315] Such bodies and groups are already represented as observers in environmental treaty negotiations; their participation in any legal proceedings could be beneficial for the same reasons: provision of information and expertise, detachment from the interests of specific states, the ability to reflect civil society rather than the views of governments. Article 34 of its Statute gives the ICJ power to request or receive information from 'public international organizations' (such as the UN or its specialised agencies) in contentious cases, but this provision has been narrowly construed and does not extend to NGOs.[316] The ITLOS has allowed IUCN to participate

308 See 1998 Aarhus Convention, Articles 4(1)(a) 6 and 9; *infra*, Ch 5.

309 *East Timor Case*, ICJ Reports (1995) para 29 and *supra*, section 2(6).

310 See discussion of *Whaling in the Antarctic Case*, *infra*, section 4(5).

311 ICJ Statute, Articles 65–8. See *AOs on Nuclear Weapons*, ICJ Reports (1996) 66, 226.

312 See *Request for an Advisory Opinion Submitted by the Sub-Regional Fisheries Commission*, ITLOS Reports (2015) paras 53–61, and 1982 UNCLOS, Article 191.

313 ITLOS Seabed Disputes Chamber (2011); French, 26 *IJMCL* (2011) 525.

314 In the *AO on Sub-Regional Fisheries*, 22 states, three IGOs, two fisheries commissions, and IUCN made written and/or oral submissions.

315 See Shelton, 88 *AJIL* (1994) 611; Sands, 30 *Harv ILJ* (1989) 393.

316 ICJ Rules of Court, Article 69(4): the organisation must consist of states. See Boyle and Harrison, 4 *J Int Dispute Settlement* (2013) 264–6.

in advisory proceedings because it is formally an international organisation, but it declined to accept *amicus curiae* submissions from NGOs.[317] However, in the *Asbestos Case*, the WTO Appellate Body permitted NGOs to apply for leave to file a written brief, but all such applications were then rejected.[318] It is always open to states to adopt NGO submissions as part of their own case,[319] and there is no reason to believe this would not also be permissible before the ICJ or ITLOS.[320]

There are reasons to be cautious about broadening NGO access to international courts. NGOs are not in reality representative of civil society, but at best only of their own members. Their policies and priorities may be driven by factors other than a rational appreciation of true global environmental needs: it is notable, for example, that no NGO objected or sought to stop the destruction by China of important coral reefs in the South China Sea.[321] Some environmental NGOs engage in illegal activities.[322] Many of the wealthiest and most influential NGOs are American or European, and do not necessarily reflect Third World concerns or perspectives. For all these reasons it may be preferable to broaden the rights of other states or intergovernmental organizations to represent the public interest in international legal proceedings rather than extend that right to NGOs.[323]

4(4) AN INTERNATIONAL ENVIRONMENTAL COURT OR SPECIAL PROCEDURES FOR ENVIRONMENTAL CASES?

In 1993 the International Court established a special chamber for environmental cases under Article 26(1) of its Statute, composed of seven judges. Thirteen years later none of the ICJ's growing list of environmental cases had come before the chamber and it was abolished. States had shown no interest, for two main reasons. First, the chamber offered no obvious advantages over the full court; the judges of the chamber were not necessarily specialists in international environmental law, nor were the procedures any different. Secondly, it was not easy to identify what is an environmental case. Cases may raise environmental issues, whether legal or factual, but they rarely do so in isolation. The *Gabčíkovo-Nagymaros Case*, for example, is as much about the law of treaties, international watercourses, state responsibility, and state succession, as it is about environmental law. Much the same could be said about the *Pulp Mills* litigation

317 Compare the Tribunal's treatment of Greenpeace and WWF in its *AOs on Activities in the Area* and the *Sub-Regional Fisheries Commission*. See also ICJ Statute, Article 66, under which IUCN could also participate in ICJ advisory opinions.

318 *EC—Measures Affecting Asbestos* (2001) WT/DS135/AB/R paras 50–7. See also *US-Lead and Bismuth*, WTO AB (2000) WT/DS138/AB/R, paras 39–41.

319 *US—Import Prohibition of Certain Shrimp and Shrimp Products* (1998) WT/DS58/AB/R, paras 79–91.

320 ICJ practice Direction XII allows international NGOs to file amicus briefs which can then be used by states or IGOs in their pleadings, but they are not otherwise part of the case.

321 See *South China Sea Arbitration (Jurisdiction and Merits)* PCA (2016).

322 See e.g. the *Arctic Sunrise Case*, ITLOS Reports (2013).

323 See Boyle and Harrison, 4 *JIDS* (2013) 256–66.

and almost every other inter-state 'environmental' case. In these circumstances the parties need a generalist court, not a specialist one.[324]

Nor is the view that there should be a specialist environmental court, similar to the ITLOS, borne out by experience.[325] Specialist tribunals are most useful when they have a special body of law to apply, usually a treaty such as the 1950 ECHR, the 1982 UNCLOS or the GATT and related WTO agreements. There is a case for such bodies, not only because of their specialist expertise and procedures, but also because they relieve the ICJ of a burden of litigation it could not sustain. But as this book has shown, international environmental law is not a self-contained, codified system of this kind. Settling environmental disputes requires a wide-ranging grasp of international law as a whole; it is not a discrete specialism which can readily be detached for the purposes of litigation.

Moreover, although creating an environmental court might give environmental disputes more prominence, it does not follow that its judges could give the environment more prominence. The forum would be new, but the applicable law would be the same as before. Nor could it monopolize the field: other specialized tribunals such as the ECtHR, the ITLOS, or the WTO Appellate Body would still have to decide environmental issues in the course of their normal work. It is difficult to see how a specifically environmental court could avoid the risk of over-specialization and distorted focus for which the WTO disputes system has been criticized. These points help explain why the idea of creating an international environmental court for inter-state disputes has made no progress.[326] The present eclectic system handles these cases better than any narrowly specialised court is ever likely to.[327]

This does not mean that there is no role for specialized tribunals or procedures for environmental cases. During the UNCLOS negotiations it was recognized that no single forum would be appropriate for the whole range of issues likely to arise in disputes under that convention. Provision was therefore be made for specialist bodies, not necessarily composed of lawyers, to deal with the more technical matters.[328] Special arbitrators appointed under Annex VIII are selected for their expertise in fisheries, protection of the marine environment, scientific research, or navigation. Technical experts may also be appointed to sit with the ICJ, ITLOS, or an arbitral tribunal in accordance with Article 289. It is thus possible within the UNCLOS scheme to tailor the choice of tribunal to the characteristics of each dispute, and to bring in technical expertise where necessary. The Convention certainly cannot be characterized

[324] See Okowa, in Evans (ed), *Remedies in International Law,* Ch 10; Boyle and Harrison, 4 *JIDS* (2013) 247–50.

[325] See Lowe and Fitzmaurice (eds), *Fifty Years of the ICJ,* 302–8; Okowa, loc cit, 168–72; Hey, *Reflections on an International Environmental Court* (The Hague, 2000); but for a more positive view compare Postiglione, 23 *EPL* (1993) 73–8; Pauwelyn in Chambers and Green (eds), *Reforming International Environmental Governance.*

[326] The arguments and the literature are reviewed by Pedersen, 24 *JEL* (2012) 547.

[327] See Boyle and Harrison, 4 *JIDS* (2013) 245.

[328] See Adede, *The System for Settlement of Disputes under the UN Convention on the Law of the Sea* (Dordrecht, 1987) 242ff; Sohn, 10 *IJMCL* (1995) 205.

as favouring adjudication by lawyers. It shows how environmental disputes could be handled within the Convention's scheme even where they involve mainly technical, or a mix of legal and technical, issues. In such cases resort to special arbitration, or the appointment of experts to sit with judicial or arbitral tribunals, may be the most appropriate way of ensuring that appropriate expertise is applied to deciding the dispute.[329] In the *South China Sea Arbitration* three experts were appointed to assist the tribunal, inter alia on environmental matters.

A similar freedom to draw on technical expertise is available to states in environmental disputes not governed by 1982 UNCLOS.[330] The *Trail Smelter Arbitration* blends legal and technical expertise to produce an award that is competent and creative in both fields.[331] More recently the UNCC's awards on environmental damage have demonstrated the value of combining specialist legal and valuation expertise when assessing compensation.[332] The PCA has adopted rules intended to reflect the particular characteristics of environmental disputes by allowing, inter alia, for expedited procedures, participation of non-state entities, and assistance from scientific experts.[333]

The ICJ also possesses a general power either to sit with expert assessors or to request outside bodies to carry out an inquiry or give an expert opinion.[334] The Court has been criticized for not doing so in the *Gabčíkovo-Nagymaros Case*[335] although, given its conclusion that the parties should negotiate, technical expertise was evidently not considered relevant to the outcome of the case. In the *Pulp Mills Case* Judges Simma and Al-Khasawneh dissented on this question, arguing that 'the Court on its own is not in a position to assess and weigh complex scientific evidence of the type presented by the Parties.'[336] They advocated the appointment of experts by the Court under Article 50 of the ICJ Statute.[337] Judges Greenwood and Keith disagreed. In their view the Court's task was to make its own judgment on the evidence and neither they nor the majority had any difficulty doing so.[338] Given the nature of the evidence,[339] this seems the right approach in the circumstances of the case. Moreover, for a court to

329 See Anderson in Nordquist et al (eds), *Law, Science and Ocean Management* (Leiden, 2007) 505–18.

330 In the *Kishenganga Arbitration (Partial Award)* PCA (2013) one of the seven arbitrators in a river dispute was a scientist appointed for his expertise in hydrology.

331 33 *AJIL* (1939) 182, and 35 *AJIL* (1941) 684.

332 *Supra*, section 2(4).

333 2001 Optional Rules for Arbitration of Disputes Relating to Natural Resources or the Environment.

334 ICJ Statute, Articles 30, 50.

335 Okowa, in Evans (ed), *Remedies in International Law*, 167; Foster, *Science and the Precautionary Principle in International Courts and Tribunals* (CUP, 2011) 101–102; Riddell and Plant, *Evidence Before the International Court of Justice* (London, 2009) 334.

336 *Ibid*, para 4.

337 *Ibid*, para 8. The Court's use of Article 50 is examined by White, in Lowe and Fitzmaurice (eds), *Fifty Years of the ICJ*, Ch 28 but see also Foster, 5 JIDS (2014, 139.

338 See the judgment at para 168, and Judge Keith, sep op, paras 8–13, with whom Judge Greenwood agreed. See also *Border Activities/San Juan River Cases*, ICJ Reports (2015) 665, para 176.

339 Argentina did not contest the water quality monitoring data which showed that the plant's effluent emissions were within agreed limits set by the river commission (CARU).

rely on experts of its own risks handing the decision over to those experts, and it is far from clear that states—or the Court—would or should be willing to take that risk.[340]

The ICJ's conclusion in *Pulp Mills* was thus that 'it is the responsibility of the Court... ...to determine which facts must be considered relevant, to assess their probative value, and to draw conclusions from them as appropriate.'[341] The cross-examination of expert witnesses allows the court to test the probative value of their evidence.[342] The careful and competent treatment of the voluminous and complex scientific evidence in *Pulp Mills*, the *Whaling Case*, and the *South China Sea Arbitration* does not suggest that international courts and tribunals cannot be trusted with expert or scientific evidence: we are not dealing here with matters that properly educated persons of reasonable intelligence cannot grasp, even if they are lawyers.

What *Pulp Mills* does not clarify, however, is the standard of proof in environmental cases: the Court's judgment is confused on this point,[343] and at best it can only be said that the standard of proof may vary from case to case.[344] Judge Greenwood urged the Court to accept the balance of probabilities as the standard of proof because, inter alia, 'the nature of environmental disputes is such that the application of the higher standard of proof would have the effect of making it all but impossible for a State to discharge the burden of proof.'[345] It remains to be seen whether this view will prevail.[346]

Thus the lack of a specialized international environmental court appears to be no handicap to the settlement of environmental disputes. The wide choice of means available to the parties, and their inherent freedom to choose the most appropriate, provides ample scope for ensuring that disputes can be competently handled, that scientific expertise can be accommodated, and that the probative value of the evidence can be tested. Nor would the problems of facilitating multilateral participation in legal proceedings necessarily be solved by creating a specialist tribunal. In practice there seems no good reason why the present approach of locating environment-related cases within the existing system of international courts and tribunals should not continue to work, provided the system is used intelligently and appropriately.

340 Riddell and Plant, *Evidence Before the International Court of Justice* 334. But for the contrary argument see Payne, *Proc ASIL* (2015) 193.

341 *Pulp Mills Case*, ICJ Reports (2010) 14, para 168.

342 In the *Whaling Case* and the *Aerial Spraying Case* the ICJ required the parties' experts to submit brief written and oral statements which could then be subjected to cross-examination in court. The same procedure was followed in the *South China Sea Arbitration*, where the arbitrators questioned the experts extensively.

343 The Court found that Argentina had failed to provide 'clear,' 'convincing,' 'conclusive' or 'sufficient' evidence of any contravention of the agreed water quality standards or of other provisions of the Statute: see paras 225, 228, 254, 257, 259, 262, 264, 265.

344 Compare *Pulp Mills Case*, Sep Op Greenwood, paras 25–26 and *Oil Platforms Case*, ICJ Reports (2003) 234, Sep Op Higgins, paras 30–34, with the Court's judgment in *Pulp Mills* at paras 180, 225, 228, 254, 257, 259, 262, 264, and 265, and see further Boyle and Harrison, 4 *JIDS* (2013) 267–273, where the case law and literature are reviewed.

345 *Pulp Mills Case*, para 26.

346 See also *Border Activities Case*, ICJ Reports (2018) paras 33–5 where Judge Greenwood's point is implicitly acknowledged.

4(5) ADJUDICATION OF TREATY DISPUTES

Treaties may be interpreted and applied differently by different states, even when acting in good faith. In this context the inclusion of compulsory, binding, third-party dispute settlement procedures in multilateral treaty regimes can serve a variety of objectives.[347] The commonest is to provide a mechanism for authoritative 'interpretation or application' of the treaty. The phrase 'interpretation and application' covers not only questions concerning the meaning of a treaty but also issues of compliance and responsibility for breach of treaty.[348] It can involve *application* of other rules of international law only if the treaty so provides and the tribunal has jurisdiction.[349]

Provision for judicial settlement of treaty disputes can also give the parties a mechanism for dealing with non-compliance.[350] Judicial institutions can serve as the main guarantors of a treaty's integrity, undertaking not only the task of interpretation and the adjudication of alleged breach, but also determining the validity of reservations and derogations. As one former legal adviser explains:

> What is important—what is indeed crucial—is that there should always be in the background, as a necessary check upon the making of unjustified claims, or upon the denial of justified claims, automatically available procedures for the settlement of disputes.[351]

Despite these attractions, provision for compulsory judicial settlement or arbitration remains, as we saw above, relatively rare in environmental treaties. A few European treaties allow any party to refer disputes concerning 'interpretation or application' to binding arbitration,[352] as does the 1973/78 MARPOL Convention.[353] The 1972 London Convention provides for such cases to be referred unilaterally to binding arbitration or by agreement to the ICJ.[354] Many other environmental treaties have no dispute settlement clause at all or merely provide for negotiation, followed by arbitration or judicial settlement if all parties to the dispute agree.[355] One common provision is for

347 Sohn, 150 *Recueil des Cours* (1976) 195; Bilder, 144 *Recueil des Cours* (1975) 139; Chinkin, in Crawford and Rothwell (eds), *The Law of the Sea in the Asian Pacific Region* (Dordrecht, 1995) 237, and see generally Merrills, *International Dispute Settlement* (5th edn, Cambridge, 2014) Ch 12.

348 *Chorzow Factory Case (Jurisdiction)* PCIJ Sers A, No 9 (1927) 20–5. See also *German Interests in Polish Upper Silesia Case* (1925) PCIJ Sers A (1926) No 6, 24–5 and No 7, 17ff; *Interpretation of the Peace Treaties Case,* ICJ Reports (1950) 75; *Oil Platforms Case,* ICJ Reports (1996) 803.

349 *OSPAR Arbitration*, PCA (2003), at paras 101–5; *MOX Plant Arbitration,* PCA (2003) para 19. But *interpretation* by reference to other rules of international law is still a dispute about interpretation of the core treaty: see *South China Sea Arbitration (Jurisdiction)*, PCA (2015) paras 176–8.

350 See eg the *Whaling in the Antarctic Case*, ICJ Reports (2014) 226, discussed *infra*, this section, part (c).

351 Sinclair, *The Vienna Convention on the Law of Treaties*, (2nd edn, Manchester, 1984) 235.

352 1976 Rhine Chemicals Convention, Article 15; 1979 Berne Convention on the Conservation of European Wildlife and Natural Habitats, Article 18; 1992 Paris Convention for the Protection of the Marine Environment of the Northeast Atlantic, Article 32; 1999 Rhine Convention, Article 16.

353 Article 10.

354 1972 Convention, procedure agreed by the parties under Article XI; 1996 Protocol, Article 16.

355 1973 CITES, Article 28; 1980 Convention for the Conservation of Antarctic Marine Living Resources, Article 25; 1989 Basel Convention , Article 20; 1991 Espoo Convention , Article 15; 1992 Convention on the Transboundary Effects of Industrial Accidents, Article 21; 1992 Convention on the Protection and Use of Transboundary Watercourses and Lakes, Article 22; 1995 Agreement on the Conservation of African-Eurasian Migratory Water Birds, Article 12; 1998 Aarhus Convention, Article 16.

negotiation followed by compulsory non-binding conciliation if agreement cannot be reached on any other means of settlement.[356] Some treaties also allow a party to make an optional declaration accepting compulsory judicial settlement or arbitration, but this operates only against other states making a similar declaration. Like the optional clause in Article 36(2) of the ICJ Statute, this falls well short of a general system of compulsory binding settlement of disputes. Apart from disputes under the 1982 UNCLOS, the only recent environmental case to be brought under a compulsory adjudication clause in a treaty is the *Pulp Mills Case*, initiated by Argentina under Article 60 of the Statute of the River Uruguay.

This pattern is consistent with the view that international adjudication has too many disadvantages in an environmental context to be widely attractive to states as a primary means of multilateral treaty enforcement. The inclusion of non-compliance procedures in a growing number of environmental treaties emphasizes the importance of collective supervision by the parties in this context,[357] while relatively weak dispute settlement clauses indicate the continuing opposition of many states to compulsory adjudication. Although courts are not unmindful of the need for purposive construction, the parties to a treaty are usually best placed to decide for themselves what is appropriate, and can help the regime evolve by their decisions if there is consensus. This explains why it has been possible to reinterpret or amplify some treaties, such as the 1946 ICRW, in quite radical ways, without involving courts.[358]

(a) Dispute settlement under the 1982 UNCLOS Part XV

The 1982 UNCLOS is one of the very few treaties under which environmental disputes fall potentially within the compulsory jurisdiction of international tribunals,[359] although it remains open to the parties to make alternative arrangements which will then prevail over UNCLOS Part XV.[360] Articles 286-288 make provision for unilateral reference of disputes concerning interpretation or application of the Convention or related agreements to the ITLOS, the ICJ, or an arbitral tribunal—including disputes about XII of UNCLOS—the part that deals with protection and preservation of the marine environment.[361] Article 297(1) further extends compulsory jurisdiction 'to

[356] 1979 LRTAP Convention, Article 9; 1985 Ozone Convention, Article 11; 1992 Convention on Climate Change, Article 14; 1992 CBD, Article 27; 1994 Convention to Combat Desertification, Article 28; 1994 Protocol on the Further Reduction of Sulphur Emissions, Article 9.

[357] *Supra*, section 3.

[358] See Birnie, 12 *IJMCL* (1997) 307, 488; *Whaling in the Antarctic Case*, ICJ Reports (2014) 226, paras 78–83.

[359] 1982 UNCLOS, Articles 279–99, and Annexes VI–VII. See generally Freestone, Barnes and Ong (eds), *The Law of the Sea* (Oxford, 2006) Chs 20, 21; Klein, *Dispute Settlement in the UNCLOS* (Cambridge, 2005); Merrills, *International Dispute Settlement* (5th edn, Cambridge, 2014) Ch 8; Rayfuse, 36 *VUWLR* (2005) 683.

[360] Articles 281–2. See *South China Sea Arbitration (Jurisdiction and Admissibility)* PCA (2015) paras 212–229; 299–321.

[361] UNCLOS Article 285 and *South China Sea Arbitration (Jurisdiction and Admissibility)* PCA (2015) paras 174–8, 408. On the meaning of 'marine environment' see Ch 9, *infra*, section 2.

certain disputes involving the contravention of legal instruments beyond the four corners of the Convention itself and ensures that such disputes will not be dismissed as being insufficiently related to the interpretation and application of the Convention.'[362] This includes contravention of 'specified international rules and standards for the protection and preservation of the marine environment', including those established 'through a competent international organization or diplomatic conference.'[363] It follows that violations of IMO conventions will be fully within compulsory jurisdiction.[364] So are high seas fisheries disputes or disputes about illegal fishing in a coastal state's EEZ or territorial sea,[365] but disputes concerning coastal state management of EEZ living resources are specifically excluded from compulsory jurisdiction, even when the stocks concerned also straddle or migrate through the high seas.[366] Allegations of a failure by coastal states to ensure proper conservation and management of EEZ stocks must, however, be submitted to conciliation.[367] The ITLOS has power to prescribe binding provisional measures to protect the marine environment or living resources.[368] As we saw in Chapter 3 it has used this power quite liberally to set catch quotas, require environmental studies, and promote cooperation.[369]

These provisions are indicative of the importance of judicial supervision in controlling the exercise of jurisdiction and authority conferred by the 1982 UNCLOS on states, particularly coastal states, and on international institutions. They were a necessary part of a 'package deal' whose provisions represented a global consensus, from which only limited derogation would be permitted.[370] Compulsory third-party dispute settlement is thus an integral element in a Convention whose integrity and consistent application were among the primary interests of the many states involved in its negotiation. Judicial supervision can be seen in this context as an essential means of stabilizing a complex balance of rights and duties, while accommodating inevitable pressure for continued development of the law to fit new circumstances.[371] Few of these considerations apply with the same force to other environmental treaties, which in most cases are less concerned with the allocation and control of power than with facilitating cooperative solutions to common problems. In this context institutional supervision remains in general the more appropriate means of control and development.

[362] See *Chagos MPA Arbitration*, PCA (2015) paras 315–22.

[363] Article 297(1)(c). See also Article 297(1)(b) which affirms jurisdiction over violations of coastal state laws in conformity with the Convention and other rules of international law.

[364] *Chagos MPA Arbitration*, PCA (2015) para 316. The alternative view is that these rules are incorporated by reference in Articles 208–211 and are thus already covered by Article 288(1).

[365] Article 297(3)(a); *South China Sea Arbitration (Jurisdiction)*, PCA (2015) para 223. See also 1995 UN Fish Stocks Agreement, Articles 27–32.

[366] Article 297(3)(a); *Chagos MPA Arbitration*, PCA (2015) paras 297–304. See Boyle, 14 *IJMCL* (1999) 1.

[367] Article 297(3)(b).

[368] 1982 UNCLOS, Article 290; 1995 UN Fish Stocks Agreement, Article 31.

[369] See *supra*, Ch 3, section 7(6).

[370] See *infra*, Ch 9, section 2.

[371] Oxman, in Soons, *Implementation of the Law of the Sea Convention through International Institutions*, 650.

(b) The Protocol to the Antarctic Treaty on Environmental Protection

Apart from the 1982 UNCLOS and related treaties, the only other comprehensive scheme for the settlement of environmental disputes is found in the 1991 Protocol to the Antarctic Treaty.[372] No new court is created, but disputes concerning interpretation or application of certain articles of the protocol are subject to compulsory arbitration, once attempts at negotiation and conciliation have been exhausted.[373] Any party to the treaty may also make a declaration accepting as compulsory the jurisdiction of the ICJ and/or arbitration. The arbitral tribunal provided for in the schedule is composed of persons 'experienced in Antarctic affairs' with a 'thorough knowledge' of international law. The tribunal has power to 'indicate' provisional measures to preserve the respective rights of the parties to the dispute and to 'prescribe' provisional measures to prevent serious harm to the Antarctic environment or associated ecosystems. Only the latter are binding. Unusually in an arbitration, there is provision for a third party to intervene in the proceedings if it believes it has a legal interest, 'whether general or individual', which may be substantially affected by the award of the tribunal. This wording may be broad enough to allow any party to the protocol to intervene, as would be the case under Article 32 of the Statute of the ITLOS in cases involving interpretation or application of the UNCLOS.[374] The arbitral tribunal is required to apply the Antarctic Protocol, and other applicable rules and principles of international law not incompatible with it, but the parties may alternatively agree to let the tribunal decide *ex aequo et bono*. This is a sophisticated, but so far untested scheme, which draws substantially on Part XV of the 1982 UNCLOS.

(c) Standing to sue under MEAs

Although, as we saw earlier, not all MEAs create *erga omnes partes* rights enabling any party to sue in respect of breach by any other party,[375] the ICJ judgment in *Belgium v Senegal* provides clear authority for the proposition that all parties to *erga omnes* treaties have a collective and individual interest in their enforcement.[376] The Court noted that obligations under the 1984 Convention against Torture may be defined as 'obligations *erga omnes partes*' and it concluded that:

> 'The common interest in compliance with the relevant obligations under the Convention against Torture implies the entitlement of each State party to the Convention to make a

[372] See Articles 18–20 and Schedule, and see generally, Francioni and Scovazzi (eds), *International Law for Antarctica* (2nd edn, The Hague, 1996) 603–23.

[373] Notably Articles 7, (mining) 8 (EIA) 15 (emergency response) and the Annexes.

[374] Compare the narrower wording of Article 31 of the ITLOS Statute on intervention by interested parties.

[375] *Supra*, section 2(5).

[376] *Obligation to Prosecute or Extradite (Belgium v Senegal)* ICJ Reports (2012) 422, paras 68–70. See also Crawford, *ILC Articles on State Responsibility, Ist Report* (1998) UN Doc.A/CN.4/460, para 100; *SS Wimbledon*, PCIJ Ser A, No1 (1923) 20, and Gray, *Judicial Remedies in International Law*, 211ff, but compare Chinkin, *Third Parties in International Law* (Oxford, 1993) 282–3.

claim concerning the cessation of an alleged breach by another State party. If a special interest were required for that purpose, in many cases no State would be in the position to make such a claim.'[377]

The Court's focus on 'the common interest... of each State party' in ensuring compliance with *erga omnes* treaty obligations is what distinguishes this type of case from advisory opinions, and from treaties where the obligations are merely reciprocal in character.[378] In cases concerned with the global common interest any state party will have standing to invoke dispute settlement machinery without having to show that it is specially affected.[379]

The *Whaling Case* initiated by Australia against Japan is a good example of public interest litigation of this kind in an environmental context.[380] No Australian rights were in dispute and the case turned solely on interpretation of the object and purpose of the 1946 ICRW and whether Japanese special permit whaling was indeed carried out for scientific purposes.[381] As presented the case was about treaty compliance. In other treaties, this kind of issue might be referred to a non-compliance procedure for a decision by the parties collectively, but no such procedure exists within the ICRW regime. What this case tells us is that international courts and treaty non-compliance procedures can serve the same purposes, even if the processes and mechanisms by which they do so differ markedly.

That conclusion leaves open the possibility that States may choose to litigate bilaterally instead of pursuing an alternative multilateral non-compliance process. Should they be allowed to do so? Is there an argument for the judicial process deferring to the diplomatic, especially when the case is ostensibly one involving the public interest? There is an inherent tension between these very different concepts of dispute settlement.[382] Should we view litigation as an alternative means of promoting the public interest in treaty compliance—in effect another version of forum shopping? Or should one take precedence over and exclude resort to the other?

The arguments are finely balanced, and they depend in part on what the purpose of non-compliance procedures is thought to be. For those who see NCPs as a form of dispute avoidance, the underlying perception is that the scrutiny of other states in an intergovernmental forum may be more effective in securing a higher level of

377 *Obligation to Prosecute or Extradite*, paras 68–9. Some judges questioned the conclusions of the Court in this regard; see e.g. Judges Skotnikov and Xue.

378 WTO agreements, for example, create a network of essentially bilateral trade relations: see 1994 GATT, Article XXIII and Pauwelyn, *Conflict of Norms in Public International Law* (Cambridge, 2003) 315–24.

379 ILC, 2001 Articles on Sate Responsibility, commentary on Article 48, at paras (2) and (10).

380 See Cançado Trindade, Sep Op, *Whaling Case, Declaration of Intervention by New Zealand*, Order of 6 February 2013, at para 71: 'The [ICRW] concerns a matter of general or common interest, and is to be implemented collectively by States Parties, thus contributing to the public order of the oceans.' See also Gray, 109 *AJIL* (2015) 589.

381 *Whaling in the Antarctic Case*, ICJ Reports (2014).

382 See Klabbers, in Bodansky, Brunnée, Hey, *Oxford Handbook of IEL* 1000–7; Stephens, *International Courts and Environmental Protection*, 81–9.

compliance than more confrontational methods involving litigation.[383] Moreover, if, as in the *Whaling Case*, the underlying dispute is ultimately about the future evolution of a multilateral regulatory regime, rather than simply about compliance with the existing regime, it is not obvious that a judicial process involving only three of the treaty parties is the better way of addressing the question.[384] A multilateral negotiating process would ensure that all parties to the treaty agree on and are bound by any decision on what it means and how it should be applied in future. Given the public interest context of this discussion, it seems difficult to argue convincingly that litigation should be preferred over a more multilateral and inclusive process.[385] This suggests that international litigation should thus be a last resort, available for public interest purposes in respect of *erga omnes* treaty obligations only when no more appropriate process for providing an authoritative interpretation or ensuring compliance is available or is likely to succeed.[386]

4(6) DISPUTE SETTLEMENT BY TREATY SUPERVISORY BODIES

Formal settlement of environmental disputes may also fall within the competence of treaty bodies. The US–Canadian International Joint Commission (ICJ) is a leading example. Article 10 of the 1909 Boundary Waters Treaty permits it to act as an arbitrator, with the consent of both parties, but for reasons explained in Chapter 10 it has not found favour in this role. More use has been made of its power of conciliation under Article 9 of the Treaty, because this places no obligation on the parties to comply with its recommendations. It was asked to conciliate in the early stages of the *Trail Smelter* dispute, but without ultimate success. In the early 1980s the IJC also acted as mediator between British Columbia and the City of Seattle in the Skagit River dispute.[387]

Some dispute settlement powers have been given to the Commission for Environmental Cooperation ('CEC') established under the 1993 NAAEC as part of the NAFTA accords. This agreement is principally concerned with ensuring that each party 'effectively' enforces its own environmental laws through appropriate government action. There is limited provision for private access to remedies in each party's legal system, and NGOs or private individuals may also complain about inadequate law enforcement to the secretariat of the CEC, which has power to investigate and report, but no power to compel action.[388] Unresolved disputes concerning law enforcement

383 UNEP, *Study on Dispute Avoidance and Dispute Settlement in International Environmental Law*, UNEP/GC.20/INF/16 (1999).

384 Lowe, 61 *ICLQ* (2012) 209, 214–6. The Court's interpretation of Article 8 of the ICRW is binding on New Zealand, Australia and Japan, but not on other parties to the treaty: ICJ Statute, Articles 59 and 63(2).

385 But for the contrary argument, see Beyerlin and Marauhn, *International Environmental Law* (Oxford, 2011) 386–7.

386 A comparison with Article 281 of UNCLOS is relevant here.

387 Cooper, 24 *CYIL* (1986) 247, 285–90, who also notes the Commission's role as a mediator; Bilder, 70 *Michigan LR* (1972) 513ff.

388 Fitzmaurice, 52 *ICLQ* (2003) 334, and see *infra*, Ch 5.

may be taken up at interstate level, however. In such cases the CEC then has power to investigate, mediate or conciliate between the parties to see whether a mutually satisfactory solution can be agreed. If this proves impossible, and if trade or competition are affected, a dispute may go to arbitration. The arbitrators have power to approve remedial measures, to impose a substantial fine, or to suspend NAFTA benefits. This is a potentially powerful dispute settlement scheme, but it is principally aimed at Mexico; Canadian provinces are bound only if they agree on ratification. Moreover, while the Agreement's focus on disputes about enforcement of national law represents a novel but useful extension of international dispute settlement,[389] it also precludes it from operating as a mechanism for settling disputes about international environmental law.

A few agreements involve the relevant body in settling treaty disputes. Disputes arising out of the 1995 Mekong River Agreement may be referred to the Mekong River Commission,[390] while the 1994 ITTA provides that any dispute arising under the agreement shall be referred to the Council of the ITTO for a 'final and binding' decision.[391] This enables the Council to interpret the agreement definitively. The benefit of dealing with such disputes in this way is that it keeps control over interpretation and development of the treaty in the hands of the parties collectively, rather than surrendering it to an independent third party, or to the parties acting unilaterally.

4(7) DIPLOMATIC METHODS OF DISPUTE SETTLEMENT

Diplomatic methods of settlement facilitate negotiation of a dispute without resort to bilateral adjudication or multilateral non-compliance procedures. They have two principal advantages. First, and most importantly, the parties remain in control of the outcome. They can walk away at any time and, until agreement is reached in the form of a treaty, there will be no final or binding determination of rights or obligations. Secondly, there are the added benefits of cheapness, flexibility, privacy, and complete freedom to determine who is involved, what expertise is relevant, and the basis on which any solution will be sought. The solution need not be based on international law. In many of these respects diplomatic settlement has much in common with the concept of alternative dispute resolution in national legal systems,[392] although it differs in the important respect that interstate negotiation will not necessarily take place against a background of resort to compulsory adjudication should the parties fail to reach agreement.

389 Compare the approach to transborder law enforcement adopted in the 1974 Nordic Environmental Protection Convention. This convention allows public bodies as well as individuals to initiate legal action in neighbouring jurisdictions, and it provides for a commission to give 'an opinion' on the permissibility of environmentally harmful activities.

390 Articles 18(c), 24(f), 34, 35.

391 Article 31. Producing and consuming states have an equal number of votes in the Council and decisions which cannot be agreed by consensus are taken by majority vote.

392 Chinkin, in Evans (ed), *Remedies in International Law*, 123–40.

(a) Mediation and good offices

These methods of dispute settlement involve the assistance of a third party in facilitating negotiations.[393] The process is voluntary and works only if the parties want to reach agreement. A number of environmental treaties allow for the possibility of mediation or good offices.[394] The main virtue of both types of settlement process is that the parties are able to avoid taking adversarial roles, while the third party is not involved in a formal adjudication. Global or regional organizations may provide good offices, mediation, or conciliation for states involved in environmental disputes. The World Bank mediated a solution to the Indus River dispute, resulting in negotiation of the 1960 Indus Waters Treaty.[395] UNEP could offer its good offices or act as a mediator or conciliator, since its responsibilities include the power to provide 'at the request of all the parties concerned advisory services for the promotion of cooperation in the field of the environment', and the Executive Director can also bring problems to the attention of the Governing Council for its consideration

(b) Conciliation and inquiry

Conciliation and inquiry involve more than facilitating negotiations.[396] In the former a third party can be empowered to indicate possible solutions, which may include findings on matters of law and of fact. Commissions of inquiry will normally deal only with fact finding, a particularly important issue in many environmental disputes. The parties are not obliged to accept the findings or proposed solutions, however, nor do these necessarily represent an adjudication of the legal issues. Thus the conciliators appointed to settle a maritime boundary dispute between Norway and Iceland described their task in the following terms:

> [T]he Conciliation Commission shall not act as a court of law. Its function is to make recommendations to the two governments which in the unanimous opinion of the Commission will lead to acceptable and equitable solutions of the problems involved.[397]

Nevertheless, conciliation is often used in disputes where the main issues are legal, and conciliators are often lawyers. As the *Jan Mayen Conciliation* illustrates, legal precedents and state practice may be taken into account, but in this case they were only 'possible guidelines' for a solution. In a few cases, however, conciliators have been

393 Cooper, 24 *CYIL* (1986) 284; Barnes, in Dupuy (ed), *The Future of International Law of the Environment* (Dordrecht, 1985) 167.

394 E.g. the 1979 Berne Convention on the Conservation of European Wildlife and Natural Habitats, Article 18(1).

395 Cooper, 24 *CYIL* (1986) 285.

396 Merrills, *International Dispute Settlement*, Ch 4; Cooper, 24 *CYIL* (1986) 287, and see Bar-Yaacov, *The Handling of International Disputes by Means of Inquiry* (London, 1974). See UN Rules for the Conciliation of Disputes, UN Doc A/50/33 (1995).

397 *Jan Mayen Conciliation*, 20 *ILM* (1981) 797, 823. See also 1969 VCLT, Annex, para 6; Article 19, 2001 ILC Articles on Prevention of Transboundary Harm, *ILC Report* (2001) GAOR A/56/10; 1974 Nordic Convention for Protection of the Environment, Articles 11–12.

asked to do more than this, and to make recommendations on what the parties merit, rather than what they will accept.[398] Depending on the mandate in specific cases, conciliation can thus vary from a form of institutionalized negotiation to something akin to non-binding arbitration.

Conciliation is widely employed in dispute-settlement provisions in multilateral environmental treaties, including the 1982 UNCLOS.[399] It is also one of the roles of the US–Canadian International Joint Commission.[400] Comparatively few environmental treaties provide for an inquiry procedure, but the 1991 Espoo Convention is an important example.[401] The first such inquiry assessed the possible risks posed by river works on the Romania–Ukraine border.[402] There are also several instances of states resorting to scientific inquiry to establish the causes or consequences of environmental pollution or depletion of natural resources.[403]

As alternatives to judicial settlement or arbitration, the attractions of conciliation and inquiry are obvious: whatever the outcome of the proceedings, the parties remain free to negotiate a politically acceptable settlement of their differences without being bound to adhere strictly to treaty provisions or rules of international law. This means that conciliation awards are of limited value as legal precedents, and they may also have an adverse effect on the integrity of a treaty if they sanction what are in effect negotiated violations or departures from the formal rules. Compulsory conciliation in the context of a multilateral treaty dispute in effect becomes an extension of supervision by the COP and a reflection of the essentially political nature of this process with its emphasis on consensus and persuasion rather than adjudication or sanctions. We need then to recall the variety of functions dispute-settlement provisions may perform and avoid the temptation to see them always as an exercise in rule-based adjudication and enforcement. While the treaties in question remain binding, the parties are free to decide when, how, and how far to implement them. In this obvious sense they can be described as 'soft' rather than 'hard' law.[404] As Koskenniemi points out, 'Though procedure is far from irrelevant, it cannot be successfully used nor interestingly discussed without regard to the types of outcomes it is intended, or likely, to produce'.[405]

398 Merrills, *International Dispute Settlement*, Ch 4.

399 1982 UNCLOS, Annex V. See the *Conciliation between the Democratic Republic of Timor-Leste and the Commonwealth of Australia*, PCA (2018).

400 See *infra*, Ch 10.

401 Article 3. See also Article 19, 2001 ILC Articles on Prevention of Transboundary Harm, *ILC Report* (2001) GAOR A/56/10; 1974 Nordic Convention for Protection of the Environment, Articles 11–12.

402 See Espoo Inquiry Commission Report on the Danube-Black Sea Navigation Route (2006), *supra*, Ch 3, section 4(4).

403 See e.g. the *Trail Smelter Arbitration*, and the use of the IJC under Article 9 of the US–Canada Boundary Waters Treaty.

404 See Boyle, 48 *ICLQ* (1999) 909–12.

405 60 *Nordic JIL* (1991) 74.

5 CONCLUSIONS

In considering how the international legal system handles environmental disputes, the diversity of issues needs to be emphasized. Where the problem is one of compliance with agreed standards of global or regional environmental protection, treaty COPs and non-compliance committees afford multilateral forums appropriate to the protection of common interests. Such procedures will be stronger and more effective if they facilitate openness, informed scrutiny, and resort where necessary to judicial organs by way of review. They should not be seen as an inferior substitute for adjudication, but potentially as a more effective means of exercising a form of international trusteeship over the environment. They give substance to the ILC's conception of certain multilateral treaty obligations having an *erga omnes partes* character. Moreover, effective multilateral supervision also makes unilateral responses less likely and ensures greater consistency and continuity in the development of state practice.

Resort to international judicial machinery remains an alternative means of resolving environmental claims, but its utility should not be exaggerated, despite the increased environmental caseload of international courts and tribunals. International proceedings will rarely be the best way of settling claims for environmental injury; in this context greater reliance has rightly been placed on facilitating resort to national legal systems, considered in the next chapter, or on international claims procedures. At the same time, litigation has proved its utility as a means of challenging failure to carry out an EIA or to cooperate with neighbouring states in the management of transboundary environmental risks.[406] Like negotiating a new treaty, it can also have the politically satisfying effect of appearing to do something about the environment.

Moreover, international adjudication provides a form of third-party determination of rights over natural resources, or over common spaces,[407] but here too supervisory institutions will usually prove more attractive because of their various advantages, including flexibility, accessibility, and capacity for resolving matters multilaterally without necessarily following existing rules of international law. Finally, advisory opinions have shown how *erga omnes* environmental rules could be adjudicated in a relatively multilateral process outside the normal framework of bilateral contentious litigation.

The ILC's completed work on 'International Liability' remains a missed opportunity to place liability for environmental damage on a more satisfactory basis. It is thus doubtful whether the concept of state liability will assume greater significance than at present in the resolution of environmental disputes, although states will continue to be responsible for damage caused by a breach of their obligation of due diligence, or in breach of treaty, or by a prohibited act.

406 See *supra*, Ch 3, section 4.

407 As in the *Fisheries Jurisdiction Cases*, ICJ Reports (1974) 3 and 175; *Chagos MPA Arbitration*, PCA (2015); *South China Sea Arbitration*, PCA (2016).

In the next chapter we consider some alternative approaches to the implementation and enforcement of international environmental law which have begun to change the emphasis of the whole subject. Relying less on interstate claims, or on mechanisms of international supervision, the development of human-rights approaches to environmental protection and the economic logic of the polluter-pays principle have made claims by individuals an increasingly attractive means of dealing with domestic or transboundary environmental problems. But the diversity of the issues needs emphasis in this context also. National remedies are not necessarily alternatives to the system considered in this chapter, but are more often complementary to it, and only in certain respects more useful. The variety of approaches now available for the resolution of international environmental disputes does indicate the increasing sophistication of the international legal system. It is testimony to the fact that considerable efforts have been made over the past forty years to develop the law in this field by states parties to various treaties and by international organizations such as the OECD, the Council of Europe, the IMO, the IAEA, UNECE, UNEP and the PCA.

5

NON-STATE ACTORS: ENVIRONMENTAL RIGHTS, LIABILITY, AND CRIMES

1 INTRODUCTION

The two previous chapters were concerned with the law applicable in interstate relations. In this chapter we consider some of the environmental rights and obligations which attach to individuals, corporations, and NGOs in international law. The emergence of environmental rights marks perhaps the most significant shift in the focus of international environmental law over the past twenty-five years, more significant than the injection of environmental concerns into WTO law because it empowers individuals and reaches directly into the core of national policies on a wide range of issues. We explore first what potential there may be for using human-rights law to compel governments to address environmental conditions within their own territory. Is there or should there be a 'right' to a healthy, sustainable, or ecologically sound environment? Can the rights to life, private life, or property be useful in cases about air or water pollution, for example? Should international law promote public participation in environmental decision-making or public-interest law enforcement by environmental NGOs? What role if any could human rights law play in promoting sustainable development or combatting climate change? Secondly, we consider the rights and liabilities of non-state actors in a transboundary setting: is making corporate polluters liable to compensate their victims preferable to holding states responsible for transboundary pollution? Which national legal system is applicable in transboundary cases of this kind? Should states harmonize their national law on environmental liability or establish compensation schemes for environmental damage and provide other remedies for domestic or transboundary claimants? These are mainly questions of private international law and comparative law. Thirdly, we look briefly at other mechanisms for promoting corporate environmental accountability. Corporations have to comply with national law in the countries where they operate and are subject to the normal rules of civil liability for environmental damage, but are they bound to respect international environmental law in general? Should they be accountable for failing to meet internationally agreed standards and by what means? Last, we look at the role of international criminal law in enforcing environmental standards.

1(1) ENVIRONMENTAL RIGHTS

Why should environmental protection be treated as a human rights issue? There are several possible answers.[1] Most obviously, and in contrast to the rest of international environmental law, a human rights perspective directly addresses environmental impacts on the life, health, private life, and property of individual humans rather than on other states or the global environment. It may thus serve to secure higher standards of environmental quality, based on the obligation of states to take measures to control pollution affecting health and private life. It helps to promote transparency, democratic governance, and the rule of law in this context: governments become directly accountable for regulating and controlling environmental nuisances, including those caused by corporations, and for facilitating access to justice and enforcing environmental laws and judicial decisions. Lastly, the broadening of economic and social rights to embrace elements of the public interest in environmental protection has given new life to the idea that there is, or should be, in some form, a right to an ecologically sound and sustainable environment.

Advocates of environmental rights use this terminology to ascribe value or autonomous status to the interests and claims of humans, trees, animals, the environment, and so on.[2] By doing so, they seek to force lawmakers and institutions to take account of those interests, and to accord them a priority which they might not otherwise enjoy and to make them part of the context for interpreting legal rules. The entrenchment of such values within the legal system may extend to the appointment of representatives to speak or act on their behalf but, as an articulation of values, such rights do not cease to be significant merely because no judicial means can be found for their expression. Used in this sense, even future generations may have 'rights', as we saw in Chapter 3.

Critics point out that it is unnecessary to construct 'rights' of this kind to deal with problems of conflicting social and economic priorities.[3] The attempt to do so may lead to the false assumption that social changes are thereby effected, when

[1] See Merrills, in Bodansky, Brunnée, and Hey (eds), *Oxford Handbook of International Environmental Law* (Oxford, 2007) 663; Hayward, *Constitutional Environmental Rights* (Oxford, 2005); Giagnocavo and Goldstein, 35 *McGill LJ* (1990) 356–7; D'Amato and Chopra, 85 *AJIL* (1991) 21.

[2] For an influential account see C D stone, *Should Trees Have Standing? Law, Morality, and the Environment.* (Oxford, 2010), and on the arguments for animal rights see Sunstein and Nussbaum (eds), *Animal Rights* (Oxford, 2004)and *infra*, Ch 11, section 1(2).

[3] Giagnocavo and Goldstein, 35 *McGill LJ* (1990) 361; Emond, 22 *OsHLJ* (1985) 325; Elder, *ibid*, 285.

what is needed is a longer term focus on tackling global environmental problems and ensuring the sustainability of life on Earth, as we saw in Chapter 2. To argue that value should be ascribed to future generations, animals, rivers, or the environment in general, does not tell us what that value should be or how it should be weighed against other values or 'rights'. [4] It may assume, moreover, that such interests are incapable of protection unless represented independently of other interests, and that litigation rather than regulation offers the best means for doing so. The argument for environmental rights in this form shares the problems of expressing and implementing claims to other economic and social rights in legal form, with the added complication that the potential claimants may not yet exist, may be non-human, or inanimate.

Thus, the main danger of the environmental rights argument is that it may not necessarily lead to any greater protection for the environment than could be made available through better regulation, or better law enforcement. Moreover, it is a perspective on environmental protection in which human rights lawyers have shown remarkably little interest until recently and the literature is mainly written by environmentalists or generalist international lawyers.[5] But Stone's argument that creating rights is not the same as introducing more protective rules should be noted. He points out that 'rights' introduce a flexibility and open-endedness that no rule can capture.[6] Above all, they may trump other claims or values which do not have the status of rights.[7] Thus the environmental rights perspective is not one that can be ignored.

1(2) THE ROLE OF NATIONAL LAW

The argument for individual rights stands apart as the strongest of these environmental rights claims. The pragmatic point is that by addressing the rights and responsibilities of individuals directly, international law facilitates wider participation in processes of national governance and environmental decision-making and provides a more effective approach to the enforcement and implementation of environmental law, primarily through the use of national legal systems and the promotion of public interest litigation by individuals and NGOs. The importance of national law can be observed at three levels.

[4] See Gillespie, in Rajamani and Peel (eds), *The Oxford Handbook of International Environmental* (Oxford, 2021) and *infra*, Ch 11, section 1(2).

[5] See in particular Boer, *Environmental Law Dimensions of Human Rights* (Oxford, 2015); Anton and Shelton, *Environmental Protection and Human Rights* (Cambridge, 2011); Francioni, 21 *EJIL* (2010) 41; Merrills, in Bodansky, Brunnée and Hey (eds), *The Oxford Handbook of International Environmental Law* (Oxford, 2007) 663; Ebbesson, *ibid*, 681; Boyle, 18 *Fordham Environmental Law Review* (2007) 471; Boyle and Anderson (eds), *Human Rights Approaches to Environmental Protection* (Oxford, 1996). For two pioneering articles by human rights specialists see Loucaides, 75 *BYIL* (2004) 249; Desgagné, 89 *AJIL* (1995) 263.

[6] Stone, 45 *S Cal LR* (1972) 488.

[7] Merrills, in Bodansky, Brunnée, and Hey (eds), *Handbook of IEL*, 666.

First, national law is the medium through which states will usually implement their international obligations and regulate the conduct of their own nationals and companies both inside their borders and beyond. It both serves as the principal source of legal remedies for individual claimants and enables effect to be given to the notion of individual or corporate responsibility.[8] In this context, the obligation to provide 'effective access' to justice before national courts, referred to in Principle 10 of the 1992 Rio Declaration, has provided the basis for significant developments in environmental rights and liabilities at regional level and in the work of the ILC.[9] The use of criminal sanctions for environmentally harmful activities within a states' own territory is required by a few treaties, such as the 1973 CITES,[10] but otherwise is largely regulated by national law. Exceptionally, some environmental offences may be treated as crimes against international law over which all states have jurisdiction wherever they are committed.[11]

Secondly, national law may be used as a means of reallocating the costs of transboundary environmental harm.[12] Here it becomes an alternative to reliance on interstate claims, in contrast to which the main advantages are that individual claimants gain control over the proceedings and liability is placed directly on the polluter or enterprise causing environmental damage. The role of international law in this context is to ensure access to effective remedies by, inter alia, removing obstacles to transboundary litigation and harmonizing national liability laws.[13] More generally, making national remedies available is consistent with the view that there are significant advantages in avoiding resort to interstate remedies for the resolution of transboundary environmental disputes wherever possible.[14]

Finally, international law is in some jurisdictions and in certain circumstances directly applicable as national law. To that limited extent it may in theory be possible for claimants to rely on environmental treaties or customary law before national courts. In practice the leading study of the subject concluded that 'the role of national courts in implementing international environmental law has been rather limited to date'.[15] The only notable exception is that some human-rights treaties have become a significant basis for environmental claims and are usually applicable by national courts. The European and Inter-American Conventions on Human Rights are the most prominent examples.

[8] *Infra*, sections 3–5. [9] *Infra*, section 2. [10] *Infra*, section 6. [11] *Ibid.*

[12] *Infra*, section 3. [13] *Infra*, section 4.

[14] Levin, *Protecting the Human Environment* (New York, 1977) 31–8; Sand, in OECD, *Legal Aspects of Transfrontier Pollution* (Paris, 1977) 146; Bilder, 144 *Recueil des Cours* (1975) 224; Handl, 1 *YbIEL* (1990) 18ff.

[15] See Anderson and Galizzi (eds), *International Environmental Law in National Courts* (London, 2002) 9. But for an exceptional example see *Urgenda Foundation v The Netherlands*, Hague Dist Ct (2015) and Ct of Appeal (2018), which purports to give effect to the 1992 Climate Change Convention by ordering the Netherlands to reduce its greenhouse gas emissions. The case was under appeal at the time of writing.

2 HUMAN RIGHTS AND THE ENVIRONMENT

2(1) INTRODUCTION

In 1972 the UNCHE declared that 'Man has the fundamental right to freedom, equality and adequate conditions of life, *in an environment of a quality that permits a life of dignity and well-being*, and he bears a solemn responsibility to protect and improve the environment for present and future generations'.[16] This grand statement might have provided the basis for subsequent elaboration of a human right to environmental quality,[17] but its real-world impact has been noticeably modest. It was not repeated in the 1992 Rio Declaration, which merely makes human beings the 'central concern of sustainable development' and refers only to their being 'entitled to a healthy and productive life in harmony with nature'.[18] As Dinah Shelton noted at the time, the Rio Declaration's failure to give greater emphasis to human rights was indicative of uncertainty and debate about the proper place of human-rights law in the development of international environmental law.[19] There is still room for debate.[20]

The relationship between human rights and environmental protection is challenging for the agenda of human rights institutions, and for UNEP, because it straddles two competing bureaucratic hegemonies, but also because it poses some difficult questions about basic principles of human rights law and their relationship to economic development. We will explore these questions in later sections of this chapter. Environmental rights do not fit neatly into any single category or 'generation' of human rights. They can be viewed from at least three perspectives. First, existing civil and political rights, including the ICCPR, can provide some basis for environmental protection. The UN Human Rights Council ('UNHRC') distinguishes in this context between 'human rights vital to environmental policy-making' and 'human rights vulnerable to environmental harm.'[21] Procedurally, the former empower individuals by facilitating participation in environmental decision-making and access to justice. Substantively, the latter compel governments to meet minimum standards of protection for life, health, private life, and property, from environmental harm. Human rights bodies and courts can adjudicate on the rights concerned in response to complaints from individuals.

A second possibility is to treat a healthy or ecologically sustainable environment as an economic or social right, comparable to those whose progressive attainment is promoted by the 1966 ICESCR.[22] The main argument for this approach is that it

16 Principle 1, 1972 Stockholm Declaration.

17 See Sohn, 14 *Harv ILJ* (1973) 451–5.

18 Principle 1, 1992 Rio Declaration. But see also Principle 10, considered below.

19 Shelton, 3 *YbIEL* (1992) 75, 82ff.

20 See UNHRC, *Preliminary Rept of Independent Expert on human rights obligations relating to a safe, clean, healthy and sustainable environment*, A/HRC/22/43 (2012) [hereafter 'UNHRC *Preliminary Rept* (2012)']

21 See UNHRC *Preliminary Rept* (2012) 7–12.

22 See Riedel, Giacca, Golay (eds), *Economic, Social and Cultural Rights in International Law* (Oxford, 2014) Chs 1 and 10; Dennis and Stewart, 98 *AJIL* (2004) 462; Eide, Krause and Rosas (eds), *Economic, Social and Cultural Rights* (Dordrecht, 2001); Craven, *The International Covenant on Economic, Social, and Cultural Rights* (Oxford, 1995).

would privilege environmental quality as a value, giving it comparable status to other economic and social rights such as development, and priority over non rights-based objectives. Like other economic and social rights it would be programmatic and in most cases enforceable only through relatively weak international supervisory mechanisms.[23] At present no such right is explicitly included in the ICESCR.[24]

The third option would treat environmental quality as a collective or solidarity right, giving communities or peoples rather than individuals a right to determine how their environment and natural resources should be protected and managed.

The first approach is essentially anthropocentric insofar as it focuses on the harmful impact on individual humans, rather than on the environment itself: it amounts to a 'greening' of human-rights law, rather than a law of environmental rights.[25] The second approach comes closer to seeing the environment as a good in its own right, but nevertheless one that will always be vulnerable to trade-offs against other similarly privileged but competing objectives, including the right to economic development. The third approach is the most contested. Not all human-rights lawyers favour the recognition of third generation rights, arguing that they devalue the concept of human rights, and divert attention from the need to implement existing rights fully.[26] The concept hardly featured in the agenda of the 1993 UN World Conference on Human Rights, and in general it adds little to an understanding of the nature of environmental rights, which are not inherently collective in character. However, there are examples of collective rights which can have environmental implications, such as the protection of minority cultures and indigenous peoples,[27] or the right of all peoples freely to dispose of their natural resources, recognized in the 1966 ICCPR and ICESCR[28] and in the 1981 African Charter on Human and Peoples Rights.[29]

2(2) THE ENVIRONMENT IN HUMAN-RIGHTS TREATIES

Among human-rights treaties only the 1981 African Charter on Human and Peoples' Rights proclaims environmental rights in broadly qualitative terms.[30] It protects both the right of peoples to the 'best attainable standard of health' (Article 16) and

[23] Principally the UNCESCR, but also the CEDAW and the Committee on the Rights of the Child.

[24] See *infra*, section 2(4). [25] See *infra*, sections 2(5) and (6).

[26] Alston, 29 *NILR* (1982) 307; *id*, 78 *AJIL* (1984) 607; Brownlie, in Crawford (ed), *The Rights of Peoples* (Oxford, 1988) 1.

[27] See 1966 ICCPR, Article 27, under which minorities have the right to enjoy their own culture, including the exploitation of natural resources, and 1989 ILO Convention No 169 Concerning Indigenous and Tribal Peoples, Article 7(4) which provides that 'Governments shall take measures, in cooperation with the peoples concerned, to protect and preserve the environment of the territories they inhabit.'

[28] Common Article 1(2) and see also ICESCR, Article 25 and ICCPR, Article 47. For drafting history of Article 1(2) see Cassese, in Henkin (ed), *The International Bill of Rights: The Covenant on Civil and Political Rights* (New York, 1981) 32ff, and Rosas, in Eide, Krause, Rosas (eds), *Economic, Social and Cultural Rights*, Ch 6, 117, who notes that Article 1 'establishes minimum rules for the right of the entire population to economic and social rights against its own government.'

[29] Article 21. See *infra*.

[30] But see also the 2012 ASEAN Human Rights Declaration, Article 28. The Declaration is non-binding.

their right to 'a general satisfactory environment favourable to their development' (Article 24). The 1981 African Charter is the only human rights treaty to combine economic, social, civil and political rights and make them all justiciable before an international court. In the *Ogoniland Case* the African Commission held, inter alia, that Article 24 of the Charter imposes an obligation on the State to take reasonable measures 'to prevent pollution and ecological degradation, to promote conservation, and to secure ecologically sustainable development and use of natural resources'.[31] Specific actions required of States in fulfilment of Articles 16 and 24 include 'ordering or at least permitting independent scientific monitoring of threatened environments, requiring and publicising environmental and social impact studies prior to any major industrial development, undertaking appropriate monitoring and providing information to those communities exposed to hazardous materials and activities and providing meaningful opportunities for individuals to be heard and to participate in the development decisions affecting their communities'.[32]

The African Commission's final order is also the most far-reaching of any environmental rights case. It calls for a 'comprehensive clean-up of lands and rivers damaged by oil operations', the preparation of environmental and social impact assessments, and provision of information on health and environmental risks and 'meaningful access to regulatory and decision-making bodies'.[33] As Shelton observes, 'The result offers a blueprint for merging environmental protection, economic development, and guarantees of human rights'.[34] *Ogoniland* is a remarkable decision which goes further than any previous human-rights case in the substantive environmental obligations it places on states. No other treaty contains anything directly comparable, although Article 11 of the 1988 San Jose Protocol to the [Inter-]American Convention proclaims a right to live in a 'healthy environment',[35] and several decisions of the Inter-American Commission on Hunan Rights (IACHR) and Inter-American Court of Human Rights (IACtHR) have interpreted the rights to life, health, and property to afford protection from environmental destruction and unsustainable development.[36] These precedents go some way towards achieving the same outcome as Article 24 of the 1981 AfricanCharter.

The only other treaties to make specific provision for environmental rights are the 1998 Aarhus Convention and the 2018 Regional Agreement on Access to Information, Public Participation and Justice in Environmental Matters in Latin America and the Caribbean ('ECLAC Agreement'). The Preamble to the 1998 Aarhus Convention not only recalls Principle 1 of the Stockholm Declaration and recognizes that 'adequate

[31] *The Social and Economic Rights Action Center and the Center for Economic and Social Rights v Nigeria*, ACHPR, No 155/96 (2002) paras 52–53 ['*SERAC v Nigeria*']. See Shelton, 96 *AJIL* (2002) 937; Coomans, 52 *ICLQ* (2003) 749; Ebeku, 3 *African HR LJ* (2003) 149, at 163; Nwobike, 1 *African JLS* (2005) 129, at 139; Chenwi, in Knox and Pejan (eds), *The Human Right to a Healthy Environment* (Cambridge, 2018) Ch 4.

[32] Para 54. [33] Para 69. [34] Shelton, 96 *AJIL* (2002) 937, 942.

[35] See also *Advisory Opinion OC 23-17*, IACtHR (2017), which holds that the right to a healthy environment is a human right, and *Portillo Càceres v Paraguay*, UNHRC Comm No 2751/2016 (2019).

[36] See *Mayagna (Sumo) Awas Tingni Community v Nicaragua*, IACtHR Ser C, No 79 (2001); *Maya Indigenous Community of the Toledo District v Belize*, IACHR Case 12.053 (2004); *Yanomani Indians v Brazil*, IACHR Decision 7615 (1985). See *infra*, section 2(5).

protection of the environment is essential to human well-being and the enjoyment of basic human rights, including the right to life itself' but also asserts that 'every person has the right to live in an environment adequate to his or her health and well-being, and the duty, both individually and in association with others, to protect and improve the environment for the benefit of present and future generations'.[37] The 1998 Aarhus Convention and the 2018 ECLAC Agreement represent an important extension of environmental rights, but also of the corpus of human-rights law. First, they build upon the long-established human right of access to justice and on procedural elements that serve to protect the rights to life, health, and family life.[38] Secondly, they confer rights directly on individuals and not just on states. Unusually for an environmental treaty the most innovative features of the 'non-confrontational, non-judicial and consultative' procedure established under Article 15 of the 1998 Aarhus Convention are that members of the public and NGOs may bring complaints before a non-compliance committee whose members are not only independent of the parties but may be nominated by NGOs.[39]

However, as we will see below, the focus of both treaties is largely procedural in content, limited to public participation in environmental decision-making and access to justice and information.[40] As a conception of environmental rights they owe little to Stockholm Principle 1 and everything to Principle 10 of the 1992 Rio Declaration, which gives explicit support in mandatory language to the same category of procedural rights.[41] The 1998 Aarhus Convention is widely ratified in Europe and has influenced the jurisprudence of the ECtHR, whose decisions are considered below. The 1998 Aarhus Convention is also important because, unlike the 1950 ECHR, it gives particular emphasis to public interest activism by NGOs.[42] But as one critic has pointed out, while the Convention endorses the right to live in an adequate environment, it 'stops short, however, of providing the means for citizens directly to invoke this right'.[43]

Other human-rights treaties either make no explicit reference to the environment at all or do so only in relatively narrow terms, focused on human health,[44] which adds

[37] The UK made a declaration on signing the Convention that this provision is 'an aspiration', not a legal right. Article 4 of the 2018 ECLAC Agreement is more strongly worded.

[38] *Infra*, section 2(6).

[39] *Supra*, Ch 4, section 3. There is no comparable provision in the 2018 ECLAC Agreement.

[40] *Infra*, section 2(6). But see Article 4 of the 2018 ECLAC Agreement.

[41] See also UNCED, Agenda 21, Ch 23, esp 23.2, and see *infra*.

[42] Articles 4(1)(a), 6 and 9 are considered below.

[43] Hayward, *Constitutional Environmental Rights*, 180. The same could be said of the 2018 ECLAC Agreement.

[44] On health see 1988 Additional Protocol to the Inter-American Convention on Human Rights, Article 11; 1989 European Charter on Environment and Health; WCED Legal Principles, Article 1; 1989 Convention on the Rights of the Child, Article 24(2)(c); 1961 European Social Charter, Article 11, on which see Trindade, in Brown Weiss (ed), *Environmental Change and International Law*, 281–4 and references there cited. See generally Dupuy (ed), *The Right to Health as a Human Right* (Alphen aan den Rijn, 1979) 340; Willis, 9 *Georgetown IELR* (1996–7) 195; Toebes, *The Right to Health as a Human Right in International Law* (Oxford, 1999). UNGA Resolution 45/94 (1990) declared that 'all individuals are entitled to live in an environment adequate for their health and well-being'. For fuller discussion of other treaty provisions, see Churchill, in Boyle and Anderson (eds), *Human Approaches to Environmental Protection* Ch 5.

little or nothing to case law derived from the right to life. Insofar as most human-rights treaties have relevance to environmental rights it is mainly or exclusively through the growing body of jurisprudence in which the 'greening' of other rights has been pursued with increasing vigour.[45] The 1950 ECHR, adopted in 1950, says nothing about the environment. Nevertheless, like other such treaties, it is a 'living instrument', pursuant to which changing social values can be reflected in the jurisprudence. The ECtHRhas consistently held that 'the Convention . . . must be interpreted in the light of present-day conditions'.[46] With regard to environmental rights this is exactly what the Court has done. The rapid development of environmental jurisprudence in Europe has resulted in rejection of proposals for an environmental protocol to be added to the 1950 ECHR.[47] However, a *Manual on Human Rights and the Environment* adopted by the Council of Europe reviews the Court's decisions and sets out some general principles.[48] Nevertheless, it remains the case that 'The Convention is not designed to provide a general protection of the environment as such and does not expressly guarantee a right to a sound, quiet and healthy environment'.[49] Despite its evolutionary character, therefore, the European Convention falls short of guaranteeing a right to a decent or satisfactory environment if that concept is understood in broader, essentially qualitative, terms unrelated to impacts on specific humans.

2(3) ENVIRONMENTAL RIGHTS AND THE UN HUMAN RIGHTS INSTITUTIONS

Overall the record of the UN human rights institutions in addressing environmental impacts on human rights is mixed and scarcely compares to the more active and impressive work of regional human rights courts and national courts in many developing countries. An early attempt to adopt a declaration on human rights and the environment terminated in 1994 when an ambitious draft declaration failed to secure the backing of states.[50] The Office of the High Commissioner for Human Rights

45 *Infra*, section 2(5).

46 *Soering v UK* (1989) 11 EHRR 439, para 102 and *Öcalan v Turkey* (2003) 37 EHRR 10. The Inter-American Court of Human Rights takes the same approach to interpretation of the 1969 Inter-American Convention: see *Advisory Opinion on the Right to Information on Consular Assistance* (1999) IACtHR Series A, No 16, paras 114–5; *Advisory Opinion on the Interpretation of the American Declaration on the Rights and Duties of Man* (1989) IACtHR Series A, No 10, para 43; *Mayagna (Sumo) Awas Tingni Community v Nicaragua* (2001) IACtHR Ser C, No 79, paras 146–8.

47 Council of Europe: Committee of Experts for the Development of Human Rights, *Final Activity Rept on Human Rights and the Environment* (Strasbourg, 2005) 2–3. In 2010 the Committee of Ministers again decided not to add a right to a healthy and viable environment to the ECHR.

48 Council of Europe, *Manual on Human Rights and the Environment* (2nd edn, Strasbourg, 2012) ['Council of Europe Manual']. See *infra*, section 2(5), and Loucaides, 75 *BYIL* (2005) 249; Desgagné, (1995) 89 *AJIL* 263; Shelton, *Joint UNEP-OHCHR Expert Seminar on Human Rights and the Environment: Background Paper No 2* (Geneva, 2002).

49 Council of Europe Manual, 7. See also *Kyrtatos v Greece* [2003] ECHR 242, para 52, *infra*, section 2(5).

50 ECOSOC, *Draft Principles on Human Rights and the Environment*, Annex I, 6 July 1994. The text of the draft declaration is reproduced in Boyle and Anderson, 67–69. See Popovic, 27 *Columbia Human Rights Law Review* (1996) 487; Weeramantry, sep op, *Gabčíkovo-Nagymaros Case*, ICJ Reports (1997) 7.

('OHCHR') returned to the problem in 2009, emphasizing that 'While the universal human rights treaties do not refer to a specific right to a safe and healthy environment, the UN human rights treaty bodies all recognize the intrinsic link between the environment and the realization of a range of human rights, such as the right to life, to health, to food, to water, and to housing.'[51] Three theoretical approaches were subsequently identified.[52] The first sees the environment as a 'precondition to the enjoyment of human rights'. The second views human rights as 'tools to address environmental issues, both procedurally and substantively'. The third integrates human rights and the environment under the concept of sustainable development. The third approach is the one most clearly reflected in the current agenda of the UNHRC.

(a) UNHRC special rapporteurs on environmental issues

The UNHRC has appointed special rapporteurs to report on various environmental issues.[53] A number of these independent reports have covered environmental conditions in specific countries,[54] but the most significant is the long-standing appointment of a special rapporteur on illicit movement and dumping of toxic and dangerous products and wastes. The activity of the special rapporteur is confined to country visits and annual reports. One incumbent paints a discouraging picture of his impact:

> 'The Special Rapporteur remains discouraged by the lack of attention paid to the mandate. During consultations with Member States, the Special Rapporteur is often confronted with arguments that issues of toxic waste management are more appropriately discussed in environmental forums than at the Human Rights Council. . . . He calls on the Human Rights Council to take this issue more seriously. He is discouraged by the limited number of States willing to engage in constructive dialogue with him on the mandate during the interactive sessions at the Human Rights Council.'[55]

This report is revealing for what it says about the lack of priority given to the subject and the sense that it is not really perceived as a human rights issue at all.

(b) UNHRC Special Rapporteur on the enjoyment of a 'safe, clean, healthy and sustainable environment'

A special rapporteur was appointed by the UNHRC in 2012 to report on the substantive and procedural dimensions of human rights obligations relating to the enjoyment of a 'safe, clean, healthy and sustainable environment' and the role of various

51 OHCHR, *Rept on Climate Change and Human Rights*, UN Doc A/HRC/10/61 (2009) para 18 ('OHCHR 2009 Rept').

52 OHCHR, *Analytical Study on the Relationship between Human Rights and the Environment*, UN Doc A/HRC/19/34 (2011) paras 2, 6–9 ('OHCHR 2011 Rept').

53 For a full summary see OHCHR 2011 Rept, paras 41–55.

54 See e.g. UNHRC, *Rept of the Independent Expert on the Issue of Human Rights Obligations Related to Access to Safe Drinking Water and Sanitation, Addendum, Mission to Costa Rica*, UN Doc A/HRC/12/24/Add.1 (2009); UNHRC, *Rept of the SR on the Situation of Human Rights in the Democratic People's Republic of Korea*, UN Doc A/HRC/10/18 (2009).

55 UNHRC, *Rept of the SR on the Adverse Effects of the Illicit Movement and Dumping of Toxic and Dangerous Products and Wastes on the Enjoyment of Human Rights*, UN Doc A/HRC/9/22 (2008) para 34.

institutional mechanisms in implementing those obligations.[56] His reports articulate a largely uncontroversial account of what human rights law has contributed to environmental protection at the national and international level. The 'Framework Principles on Human Rights and the Environment' proposed in his final report lack the ambition of the 1994 draft principles, although he recommends that the Human Rights Council consider recognising a right to a healthy environment.[57] At the same time there is value in setting down those elements already reflected in the jurisprudence and in national law, and on which some degree of international consensus is achievable. The rapporteur has at least demonstrated that regional practice considered below has global significance, including the procedural rights enshrined in the 1998 Aarhus Convention, the obligation to assess environmental impacts and ensure a reasonable balance between economic development and environmental protection, the need to implement and enforce applicable environmental standards, and to protect vulnerable groups such as indigenous peoples.[58] UNHRC resolution 31/8 (2016) endorses most of these recommendations, including access to information, public participation, access to justice, and the enjoyment of a 'safe, clean, healthy and sustainable environment'.[59] It remains to be seen what becomes of his 2018 Report.

(c) Human rights and climate change

Climate change is a threat to life on Earth as we know it; everyone will be affected if attempts to control and mitigate its causes and effects do not succeed.[60] Thus, the fundamental challenge posed by climate change is not so much to particular human rights here and now, but to future generations and humanity itself.

Climate change is already regarded in international law as a 'common concern of humanity',[61] and thus as an issue in respect of which all states have legitimate concerns. The UNHRC is therefore right to take an interest in the matter.[62] Its first report noted, however, that '[w]hile climate change has obvious implications for the enjoyment of human rights, it is less obvious whether, and to what extent, such effects can be qualified as human rights violations in a strict legal sense'.[63] The report goes on to explain how the multiplicity of causes for environmental degradation and the difficulty

56 UNHRC, *Rept of the Independent Expert/Special Rapporteur on human rights obligations relating to a safe, clean, healthy and sustainable environment: Preliminary Rept*, UN Doc A/HRC/22/43 (2012); *Mapping Rept*, UN Doc A/HRC/25/53 (2013); *Compilation of Good Practices*, UN Doc A/HRC/28/61 (2015); *Note by Secretariat*, UN Doc A/HRC/31/53 (2015); *Final Rept*, UN Doc A/HRC/37/59 (2018).

57 UN Doc A/HRC/37/59 (2018).

58 See *Mapping Rept*, UN Doc A/HRC/25/53 (2013).

59 See generally Knox and Pejan (eds), *The Human Right to a Healthy Environment*, esp Chs 1 (Knox) and 11 (Limon).

60 See *infra*, Ch 6.

61 *Supra*, Ch 3, section 4(1).

62 UNHRC Resolution 10/4 (2009); id, *Rept of the Independent Expert/Special Rapporteur etc*, UN Doc A/HRC/31/52 (2016). See generally Boyle, 67 *ICLQ* (2018) 759; Knox and Pejan (eds), *The Human Right to a Healthy Environment*, esp Chs 11–13; Knox in Carlarne et al (eds), *The Oxford Handbook of International Climate Change Law* (Oxford, 2016), 213; Atapattu, *Human Rights Approaches to Climate Change: Challenges and Opportunities* (Abingdon, 2015); Humphreys (ed), *Human Rights and Climate Change* (Oxford, 2009); Knox, 33 *Harv ELR* (2009) 477.

63 OHCHR 2009 Rept, para 70.

of relating specific effects to historic emissions in particular countries make attributing responsibility to any one state problematic. But, for reasons considered below, this is only partly relevant.

Governments undoubtedly have a responsibility to protect anyone within their territory from the effects of pollution or other environmental changes that degrade the right to life, private life, property or other human rights, regardless of which states have caused the harm.[64] Human rights treaty bodies have addressed the implications of climate change mainly from this perspective, and they have stressed the obligation of states parties to protect vulnerable communities.[65] However, in the climate change context, where the impacts are global, the key question is whether greenhouse gases ('GHG') emitting states also have a legal responsibility to protect people in *other* states from the harmful impacts of those emissions on the global climate. Human rights treaties generally require a state party to secure the relevant rights and freedoms only for everyone within its own territory or subject to its jurisdiction. The question whether these treaties can have extra-territorial application is for that reason a difficult one.[66] It is also harder to contend that parties to the 1982 UNFCCC regime, including the major GHG emitters, have failed to strike the right balance between their own state's economic development and respect for human rights in other states if they have either complied with or are exempt from GHG emissions reduction targets agreed by the international community as a whole.[67] Thus, however serious the effects of climate change may be, it does not follow that any state has necessarily violated any particular human rights.

The UNHRC special rapporteur has taken a broader view, however, observing that 'whether or not climate change legally violates human rights norms is not the dispositive question.'[68] His report emphasises the global character of the threat climate change poses for the enjoyment of human rights, and focuses on the need for global cooperation to tackle climate change effectively in order to avert serious harm to those rights:

'. . .in addition to employing a human rights perspective to examine how individual States should address climate change at the national level, based on the obligation of each State to protect against the effects of climate change within its own jurisdiction, it is also appropriate to examine how States should address climate change in cooperation with one another.'[69]

[64] See the cases considered *infra*, section 2(5).

[65] The practice of the Committee on the Rights of the Child, CEDAW, and the ICESCR is reviewed in CIEL, *States' Human Rights Obligations in the Context of Climate Change* (Washington, 2018). In 2019 a group of eight Torres Strait Islanders submitted a claim to the UN Human Rights Committee alleging that Australia's contribution to emissions together with its failure to establish adequate adaptation measures violates their human rights.

[66] *Infra*, section 2(7).

[67] Greenhouse gas emissions reduction targets under Kyoto do not apply to developing countries, including China, India and Brazil. On the essentially voluntary character of the 2015 Paris Agreement see *infra*, Ch 6, section 4(4).

[68] UN Doc A/HRC/31/52 (2016) para 36.

[69] *Ibid*, para 45.

On this view of human rights law 'All states have a duty to work together to address climate change, but the particular responsibilities necessary and appropriate for each State will depend in part upon its situation.'[70]

The 2015 Paris Agreement says inter alia that states 'should, when taking action to address climate change, respect, promote and consider their respective obligations on human rights.'[71] As Rajamani observes, 'This recital carefully circumscribes the impact of an explicit reference to human rights in the Paris Agreement.'[72] Human rights law is neither incorporated into the 2015 Paris Agreement by this wording, nor does it explicitly constitute a standard by which the adequacy of efforts taken by the parties to implement the objectives of the 2015 Paris Agreement might be judged.[73]

The 2015 Paris Agreement also commits the parties for the first time to 'Holding the increase in the global average temperature to well below 2 °C.'[74] Building on this Agreement, the UN special rapporteur reiterates the obligation of states to assess climatic effects of activities within their jurisdiction; to control the activities of business and industry when these may cause climate change; to facilitate public participation in decision-making with respect to climate change; and to provide effective remedies for those adversely affected. His most important conclusion is that by itself the 2015 Paris Agreement will not prevent 'disastrous consequences for human rights' if states merely meet the commitments they have undertaken. It follows that '[f]rom a human rights perspective, then, it is necessary not only to implement the current intended contributions, but also to strengthen those contributions to meet the target set out in article 2 of the 2015 Paris Agreement.'[75] On this view States which do not implement their Paris commitments with respect to climate change will also fail to meet their commitment to cooperate in fulfilling human rights.[76] A focus on the right to life leads to a similar conclusion: 'States should adopt a proactive approach . . ., responding in a meaningful way to the best available science and to local concerns, be vigilant in the protection of vulnerable individuals and communities and integrate consideration of threats to the right to life into policies and measures relevant to climate mitigation.'[77]

A human rights perspective on climate change serves to reinforce political pressure from the more vulnerable developing states. Its utility is partly rhetorical, but it could be used more effectively by UN human rights bodies to focus attention on how states parties respond to the 2015 Paris Agreement. The Committee on Economic, Social

70 *Ibid*, para 46. See also Knox in Carlarne et al (eds), *The Oxford Handbook of International Climate Change Law* (Oxford, 2016) Ch 11.

71 Preamble. On efforts to include human rights in the agreement see Rajamani, 22 *JEL* (2010) 391; *id*, in Knox and Pejan (eds), *The Human Right to a Healthy Environment*, Ch 13.

72 Rajamani, in Knox and Pejan, *op cit*, Ch 13.

73 See Rajamani, *ibid*. But compare Duyck, 26 *YbIEL* (2015) 3; Savaresi in Duyck, Johl, and Jodoin (eds), *Routledge Handbook of Human Rights and Climate Governance* (Abingdon, 2017) Ch 3.

74 Article 2(1)(a), but 'in the context of sustainable development and efforts to eradicate poverty.' See *infra*, Ch 6.

75 *Ibid*, paras 72–84.

76 *Ibid*, but note the more nuanced wording of the Preamble, *supra*, n 70.

77 Cook, 3 *EHRLR* (2019) 274, relying inter alia on General Comment No 36, *infra*, text at n 160.

and Cultural Rights ('UNCESCR') has begun to address the failure of some states to reduce greenhouse gas emissions, preserve carbon sinks, and promote renewable energy.[78] It has also taken the view that the 1992 Convention on Climate Change and the 2015 Paris Agreement are relevant to interpreting the UNCESCR.[79] The debate on climate change and human rights thus broadens out into a focus on environmental quality and sustainability.[80]

2(4) A RIGHT TO A HEALTHY, SUSTAINABLE OR ECOLOGICALLY SOUND ENVIRONMENT?

The most far-reaching case for environmental rights comes in the form of claims to a healthy, sustainable or ecologically sound environment: to a substantive right involving the promotion of a certain level of environmental quality.[81] What constitutes such an environment is a value judgment, on which reasonable people will differ. As with sustainable development, policy choices abound: what weight should be given to natural resource exploitation over nature protection, to industrial development over air and water quality, to land-use development over conservation of forests and wetlands, to energy consumption over the risks of climate change, and so on? Here too, the questions posed are not readily justiciable before international courts. Litigating them would turn an essentially political judgment into a legal one. It would take power away from democratically accountable politicians and give it to courts or treaty bodies. Such indeterminacy is also a reason, it is argued, for not rushing to embrace new rights without considering their implications.[82] Nevertheless, the concept continues to enjoy support, most notably in over 100 national constitutions or human rights laws.[83] Research has shown that 'the incorporation of the right to a healthy environment in a country's constitution leads directly to two important legal outcomes: stronger environmental laws, and court decisions defending the right from violations.'[84] Indian courts in particular, have given the right to life and other provisions of the Constitution a very vigorous environmental interpretation.[85] The result has been a jurisprudence which, more than in any other country, uses human-rights law to

[78] ICESCR Concluding Observations on: Australia (2017); Russian Federation (2017); Canada (2016). See also CEDAW Concluding Observations on Norway (2017).

[79] Concluding Observations on Australia (2017).

[80] See Boyle, 23 *EJIL* (2012) 613, and *infra*, section 2(4).

[81] See generally Knox and Pejan (eds), *The Human Right to a Healthy Environment*.

[82] Alston, 78 *AJIL* (1984) 607; Handl, in Trindade (ed), *Human Rights, Sustainable Development and the Environment* (San Jose, 1992).

[83] See e.g. South African Constitution, s 24; Constitution of Brazil, Article 225; Turkish Constitution, Article 56; Russian Constitution, Article 42; Spanish Constitution, Article 45. Compare the reality revealed in *Fadeyeva v Russia* [2005] ECHR 376 and *Taskin v Turkey* [2006] 42 EHRR 50, and chapters by Boyd, Daly and May, in Knox and Pejan (eds), *The Human Right to a Healthy Environment*.

[84] Boyd, in Knox and Pejan (eds), *The Human Right to a Healthy Environment*, Ch 2; id, *The Environmental Rights Revolution: A Global Study of Constitutions, Human Rights, and the Environment* (Vancouver, 2012).

[85] On the use of 'directive principles' in Indian case law see Anderson and Galizzi (eds), *International Environmental Law in National Courts*, 150–1.

address questions of environmental quality.[86] Given the poor quality of India's environment, however, the highly activist jurisprudence is hardly surprising. Courts may be the answer in India, but better government may also be a better answer.[87]

(a) The current international law

Sohn argued that Principle 1 of the 1972 Stockholm Declaration created an individual human right to 'an environment of a quality that permits a life of dignity and well-being,'[88] but no treaty refers explicitly to environmental rights in these terms. When the concept is employed in a similarly broad and autonomous form, as in Article 24 of the 1981 African Charter on Human and Peoples' Rights, it appears as a collective right only: 'All peoples shall have the right to a generally satisfactory environment favourable to their development'. As the *Ogoniland Case* amply demonstrates, however, it is no less justiciable in legal proceedings.[89]

Despite their evolutionary character, other human rights treaties do not guarantee a right to a healthy, sustainable or ecologically sound environment if that concept is understood in qualitative terms unrelated to impacts on the rights of specific humans. As the ECtHR reiterated in *Kyrtatos*, 'neither Article 8 nor any of the other articles of the Convention are specifically designed to provide general protection of the environment as such . . .' [90] This case involved the illegal draining of a wetland. The court could find no violation of the applicants' right to private life or enjoyment of property arising out of the destruction of the area in question. Although they lived nearby, the applicants' rights were not affected. They were not entitled to live in any particular environment, or to have the surrounding environment indefinitely preserved. The applicants succeeded only insofar as the state's non-enforcement of a court judgment violated their Convention rights. The IACHR has similarly rejected as inadmissible a claim on behalf of all the citizens of Panama to protect a nature reserve from development.[91] Nor does the practice of the UN Human Rights Committee differ. In a case about genetically modified crops it held that 'no person may, in theoretical terms and by *actio popularis*, object to a law or practice which he holds to be at variance with the Covenant.'[92] None of these cases lends support to any conception of a free-standing individual right to any particular kind of environment. Reviewing the question in 2012, the UNHRC Special Rapporteur noted that 'no global agreement sets out an explicit right to a healthy (or satisfactory, safe or sustainable) environment. . . . . . . Nor have the later conferences on sustainable development in Johannesburg in 2002 and Rio de Janeiro in 2012 proclaimed a right to a healthy environment.'[93]

86 See *infra*, section 2(5).

87 For critiques of the activist role of judges see Dam and Tewary, 17 *JEL* (2005) 383; Razzaque, 18 *Fordham ELR* (2007) 587. Compare Desgagné, 89 *AJIL* (1995) 266–70.

88 14 *Harv ILJ* (1973) 455.

89 *Supra*, section 2(2).

90 *Kyrtatos v Greece* [2003] ECHR 242, para 52.

91 *Metropolitan Nature Reserve v Panama*, IACHR [2003] at 524, para 34.

92 *Brun v France* [2006] ICCPR Comm No. 1453/2006, para 6.3.

93 UN Doc A/HRC/22/43 (2012) para 14.

(b) Should there be a right to a healthy, sustainable or ecologically sound environment?

Should we then create such a right? There are obvious problems of definition and anthropocentricity, well-rehearsed in the literature.[94] First, there is little consensus on the most appropriate terminology. The UNHRC Sub-Commission which first considered the question in 1994 referred variously to the right to a 'healthy and flourishing environment' or to a 'satisfactory environment' in its report, and to the right to a 'secure, healthy and ecologically sound environment' in the draft principles.[95] Most recently, the UNHRC has used the phrase 'safe, clean, healthy and sustainable environment.'[96] What any of these mean is largely a subjective judgment but, as we saw in Chapter 2, that has not stopped the UN from endorsing sustainable development as the core principle of international environmental law and policy.

Secondly, it has been argued that by looking at the problem in moral isolation from other species such a human right may reinforce the assumption that the environment and nature exist only for human benefit and have no intrinsic worth in themselves. This is precisely the kind of non-ecocentric approach which ecological theorists have opposed because they believe it is insufficiently comprehensive and inconsistent with ecological reality and biological diversity.[97] At the same time, as we will see in Chapters 11-12, many environmental agreements do address the needs of ecological protection and biological diversity and there is no inherent reason why a human rights perspective should not also balance competing values and needs with respect to the natural world. Indeed, human rights law already recognises that environmental protection is a legitimate aim of public policy and law that may constrain or limit the exercise of the right to possessions and property or other human rights.[98]

Thirdly, there are deeper issues of legal architecture to be resolved. At the substantive level, a healthy, sustainable or ecologically sound environment should not be confused with the procedural innovations of the 1998 Aarhus Convention, or with the case law on the right to life, health or private life. To do so would make it little more than a portmanteau for the greening of existing civil and political rights. The ample jurisprudence reviewed in the next section of this chapter clearly shows this to be unnecessary and misconceived. To be meaningful, a right to a healthy, sustainable or ecologically sound environment has to address the environment as a public good, in

[94] See e.g. Handl, in Cançado Trindade (ed), *Human Rights, Sustainable Development and the Environment* 117; *id*, in Eide, Krause and Rosas (eds), *Economic, Social and Cultural Rights* (2nd edn, Dordrecht, 2001) 303; Boyle and Anderson, *Human Rights Approaches*, Chs 2–4. Contrast Shelton, 28 *Stanford JIL* (1991) 103.

[95] ECOSOC, *Human Rights and the Environment*, Final Rept (1994) UN Doc E/CN 4/Sub 2/1994/9, 59.

[96] UN HRC, *Rept of the Independent Expert/Special Rapporteur on human rights obligations relating to a safe, clean, healthy and sustainable environment: Preliminary Rept*, UN Doc A/HRC/22/43 (2012); UN HRC Resolution 31/8 (2016).

[97] See Eckersley, *Environmentalism and Political Theory* (London, 1992); Gillespie, *International Environmental Law, Policy and Ethics* (Oxford, 1997) Ch 1.

[98] *Infra*, this section, part (c).

which form it bears little resemblance to the accepted catalogue of civil and political rights,[99] a catalogue which for good reasons there is great reluctance to expand.[100]

Thus, a right to a healthy, sustainable or ecologically sound environment is arguably best envisaged, not as a civil and political right adjudicated by judges, but within the context of economic, social and cultural rights, where to some extent it already finds limited expression in Articles 11 (right to food) and 12 of the 1966 ICESCR. Article 12's narrow focus on 'environmental and industrial hygiene' is understandable, given that environmental issues were not high on the international agenda until the 1970s. Recognising this, the UNCESCR has tried to make the Covenant more relevant to the environment and sustainable development. General Comments 12, 14 and 15 have interpreted Articles 11 and 12 to include a sustainable food supply and access to sufficient, safe, and affordable water for domestic uses and sanitation.[101] They also cover the prevention and reduction of exposure to harmful substances including radiation and chemicals, or other detrimental environmental conditions that directly or indirectly impact upon human health. As these 'Comments' show, economic and social rights can be interpreted by reference inter alia to evolving environmental law.[102]

Economic and social rights are generally concerned with encouraging governments to pursue policies which create conditions of life enabling individuals or peoples to develop to their full potential. They are programmatic, entailing progressive realization in accordance with available resources, but nevertheless requiring states to 'ensure the satisfaction of, at the very least, minimum essential levels of each of the rights'.[103] Compliance is monitored by an independent committee which can only make general recommendations to states parties, rather than by litigating individual complaints through commissions and courts.[104] Critics point to the 'built-in defects' of this monitoring process, including poor reporting and excessive deference to states.[105] But the UNCESCR's interpretations of the 1966 Covenant have also had some impact on related areas of international law, including Article 10 of the 1997 UN Watercourses Convention, which gives priority to 'vital human needs' when allocating scarce water

99 See Francioni, 21 *EJIL* (2010) 41, 50; Rachovitsa, 66 *ICLQ* (2017) 557, 584.

100 Alston, 78 *AJIL* (1984) 607.

101 UNCESCR, *General Comment No.12: The Right to Adequate Food,* UN Doc E/C.12/1999/5 (1999); *General Comment No.14: The Right to the Highest Attainable Standard of Health,* UN Doc E/C.12/2000/4 (2000); *General Comment No. 15: The Right to Water,* UN Doc E/C.12/2002/11 (2003).

102 Chuffart and Viñuales in Riedel et al (eds), *Economic, Social and Cultural Rights in International Law,* 287–295. The ICJ has held that 'great weight' should be attributed to interpretations adopted by independent treaty supervisory bodies: see *Diallo Case,* ICJ Reports (2010) paras 66–67.

103 UNCESCR, General Comment No 3: The Nature of States' Parties Obligations (1990) interpreting Article 2 of the Covenant. See Craven, *The International Covenant on Economic, Social and Cultural Rights* (Oxford, 1995) Ch 3.

104 On an individual complaints mechanism for the ICESCR see Dennis and Stewart, 98 *AJIL* (2004) 462. The authors regard the idea as misguided.

105 Leckie, in Alston and Crawford (eds), *The Future of UN Human Rights Treaty Monitoring* (Cambridge, 2000) 129. See also 1966 ICESCR, Articles 16–21; UNCESCR, General Comment No 1: Reporting by States Parties (1989); Craven, *The International Covenant on Economic, Social and Cultural Rights*, Ch 2.

resources.[106] On this view, existing economic and social rights help guarantee some of the indispensable attributes of a healthy, sustainable or ecologically sound environment. What more would explicit recognition of such a right add to the 1966 ICESCR?

Arguably, it would add what is currently lacking from the corpus of UN economic and social rights, namely a broader and more explicit focus on environmental quality which could be balanced directly against the Covenant's economic and developmental priorities. Despite the efforts of the UN treaty organs to invest the 1996 ICESCR with greater environmental relevance, it still falls short of giving environmental quality recognition as a significant public interest. Lacking the status of a right means that environmental protection can be trumped by those values which do have that status, including economic development and natural resource exploitation.[107] This is an omission which needs to be addressed if the environment as a public good is to receive the weight it deserves in the balance of economic, social and cultural rights.

The key question therefore is what values we think a covenant on economic and social rights should recognize in the modern world. Is the environment—or the global environment—a sufficiently important public good to merit economic and social rights status comparable to economic development? For three reasons the answer to this question has to be yes. First, because global conventions on, inter alia, climate change, the marine environment and biological diversity demonstrate that these are matters of common concern for all states and are fundamental to any conception of a sustainable global environment.[108] Secondly, because the UN and international courts have repeatedly endorsed the promotion of sustainable development as the core principle of international environmental law for all states.[109] Thirdly, because as we saw in Chapter 3, although international law recognises that states have a right to sustainable development; they have no right to unsustainable development.[110] UN human rights law does not yet recognise a right to a sustainable or ecologically sound environment in these terms, but the UNHRC has moved closer to doing so.[111] This would reconceptualise in the language of economic and social rights the idea of a sustainable global environment as a common good or common concern of humanity.[112]

(c) Integrating sustainable economic development and human rights

Existing human rights law both supports and qualifies the principle of sustainable development. It may also be limited by it. Public participation in environmental decision-making, elaborated in Principle 10 of the Rio Declaration, can be seen as a

[106] See *Convention on the Law of the Non-Navigational Uses of International Watercourse: Rept of the Sixth Committee convening as the Working Group of the Whole*, Un Doc A/51/869 (1997).

[107] Merrills, in Bodansky, Brunnée, and Hey (eds), *Handbook of IEL*, 666.

[108] *Supra*, Ch 3, section 4(1).

[109] *Supra*, Ch 2, section 2(5).

[110] *Supra*, Ch 3, section 2.

[111] UNHRC Resolution 31/8 (2016) para 5(a) encourages States 'To adopt an effective normative framework for the enjoyment of a safe, clean, healthy and sustainable environment.'

[112] See Boyle, in Kaltenborn and Kuhn (eds), *Human Rights and Sustainable Development Goals* (Berlin, 2018).

means of legitimizing decisions about sustainable development, rather than simply an exercise in extending participatory democracy or improving environmental governance.[113] The incorporation of Aarhus-style procedural rights into general human rights law significantly advances this objective.[114] In this context the most important feature of *Taskin v Turkey* is that it envisages an informed process.[115] The IACHR,[116] the UN Human Rights Committee,[117] and the African Commission[118] have taken a similar approach to consultation in cases concerning logging, oil extraction, and mining on land belonging to indigenous or tribal peoples. All these cases are about the integration of environmental concerns in decisions about economic development.

Inevitably there will be cases where legitimate environmental objectives and the economic rights of particular individuals or groups come into conflict. Establishing wildlife reserves, regulating polluting activities, or controlling resource extraction, for example, may impair the use or value of property, hamper economic activity, or restrict the right of indigenous peoples to make traditional use of natural resources. In extreme cases environmental regulation may amount to a taking of property or an interference with private and family life, entitling the owner to compensation.[119]

Particularly in cases involving alleged interference by the state with peaceful enjoyment of possessions and property, the Strasbourg Court has consistently taken the view that environmental protection is a legitimate objective of public policy.[120] It has refused to give undue pre-eminence to property rights, despite their supposedly protected status under the 1st Protocol.[121] Regulation in the public interest is not inconsistent with the terms of the protocol, provided it is authorized by law and proportionate to a legitimate aim. Thus in *Apirana Mahuika and Ors v New Zealand* the UNHRC upheld the state's right to conserve and manage natural resources in the interests of future generations provided this did not amount to a denial of the applicant's rights.[122] States have been allowed a wide margin of appreciation to pursue environmental objectives provided the rights of individuals to private and family life or protection of possessions and property are balanced fairly against environmental benefits for the community as a whole.[123]

113 UNCED, *Agenda 21* (1992) Ch 23, especially para 23.2; OHCHR 2011 Rept, paras 2, 7–9.

114 See *infra*, section 2(6). 115 *Ibid*.

116 See *Maya Indigenous Community of the Toledo District v Belize*, Case 12.053, IACHR (2004) para 150.

117 See *Ilmari Lansman and Ors v Finland* (1996) ICCPR Comm No 511/1992, para 9.4, and *Lubicon Lake Band v Canada* (1990) ICCPR Comm No 167/1984, para 32.2.

118 *SERAC v Nigeria*, ACHPR (2002).

119 See *Sporrong and Lonnroth v Sweden* (1982) ECtHR Sers A/52.

120 See e.g. *Kristiana Ltd v Lithuania* [2018] ECHR 124; *Matos e Silva Lda v Portugal* (1996) IV ECtHR; *Jacobsson v Sweden* No 2 (1998) I ECtHR; *Katte Klitsche and de la Grange v Italy* (1994) ECtHR Sers A/293B; *Svidranova v Slovak Republic* (1998) ECtHR App No 35268/97; *Chassagnou v France* (1999) ECtHR.

121 *Pine Valley Developments Ltd v Ireland* (1991) ECtHR Sers A/222, paras 57–9; *Katsoulis and Ors v Greece* [2004] ECtHR 321. Contrast *Mateos e Silva Ltd v Portugal* [1996] IV ECtHR where restrictions on property were found to be unnecessary.

122 (2000) ICCPR Comm No 547/1992. See also *Fredin v Sweden* (1991) ECtHR Sers A/192, paras 41–51.

123 See Shelton, in de Wet and Vidmar (eds), *Hierarchy in International Law* (Oxford, 2012) Ch 8.

But economic development is also a legitimate objective of public policy and may in some cases impact on human rights. The best example is *Hatton v United Kingdom*. Here the applicants challenged the extension of night flights at Heathrow Airport.[124] In the ECtHR's view the UK had acted lawfully, had done its best to mitigate the impact on the private life of those affected and had maintained a fair balance between the economic benefit to the community as a whole and the rights of individuals who lived near the airport. The state would be failing in its duty to those affected if it did not regulate or mitigate environmental nuisances or environmental risk caused by airport development projects,[125] but it was required to do so only to the extent necessary to protect life, health, enjoyment of property, and family life from disproportionate interference. The Grand Chamber's approach affords considerably greater deference towards government economic policy than at first instance and leaves little room for the Court to substitute its own view of the extent to which the environment should be protected from development:[126] '[T]he Court reiterates the fundamentally subsidiary role of the Convention. The national authorities have direct democratic legitimation and are, as the Court has held on many occasions, in principle better placed than an international court to evaluate local needs and conditions.'[127] On this basis, decisions about where the public interest lies are for politicians, not for courts, save in the most extreme cases.[128]

Hatton[129] is self-evidently about sustainable development, although the terms of the discussion are limited to balancing the direct impact on the health and family life of the applicants against the benefits to the community at large. The decision in *Ogoniland*[130] can also be seen as a challenge to the sustainability of oil extraction in that part of Nigeria. Given the degree of environmental harm and lack of material benefits for the Ogoni people, it is not surprising that the African Commission does not treat this case simply as a failure to maintain a fair balance between public good and private rights. The decision gives some indication of how a right to a healthy, sustainable and ecologically sound environment could be used, but its exceptional basis in Articles 21 and 24 of the 1981 African Charter has to be recalled. It is unique in adjudicating for the first time on the right of peoples to dispose freely of their own natural resources and in ordering extensive environmental clean-up measures to be taken.[131] Moreover, the rights created by the 1981 African Charter are peoples' rights, not individual rights, so the recognition of a public interest in environmental protection and

124 *Hatton v UK* [2003] ECtHR (Grand Chamber).

125 See also *Öneryildiz v Turkey* [2005] 41 EHRR 20, para 107; *Taskin v Turkey* [2006] 42 EHRR 50, paras 116–7.

126 *Hatton v UK* [2003] ECtHR, paras 97–104.

127 *Ibid*, para 97.

128 But compare the views of the dissenting judges and of the 1st instance chamber, and see Hart and Wheeler, 16 *JEL* (2004) 132–9.

129 *Hatton v UK* [2003] ECtHR.

130 *SERAC v Nigeria* (2002) ACHPR, *supra*, section 2(2).

131 Although ICCPR Article 1(2) also recognises the right of peoples to 'freely dispose of their natural wealth and resources', it is not justiciable by the UN HR Committee under the procedure for individual complaints laid down in the Optional Protocol: see *Lubicon Lake Band v Canada*, ICCPR Comm No 167/1984(1990) para 32.1.

sustainable development is less of an innovation. It illustrates what could be achieved with economic and social rights.

Do we want human rights courts deciding where the appropriate balance between human rights and economic and environmental policy objectives should lie? *Ogoniland* was an extreme case of patently unsustainable development violating human rights. *Hatton* may suggest that, except at the extremes, human rights courts are not usually the best bodies to perform this balancing task, compared with national or international political institutions. Even if European human rights law did endorse the right to a healthy, sustainable and ecologically sound environment, in whatever form, it seems unlikely that the outcome of *Hatton* would differ. On any view, the balance would in principle be for governments to determine and, on the facts of that case, any court or tribunal would probably have upheld the government's approach.

2(5) GREENING EXISTING HUMAN RIGHTS

Even if no independent right to a healthy, sustainable or ecologically sound environment has yet become part of international law, it is clear that environmental rights can usefully be derived from other existing treaty rights, in particular the rights to life, private life, property, and access to justice under the 1966 ICCPR,[132] the 1950 ECHR,[133] and the 1969 Inter-American Convention on Human Rights.[134] In Asia there is now an ASEAN Charter of Human Rights, and national law in some Asian jurisdictions is very sophisticated in the application of human rights law in environmental cases.[135]

The virtue of looking at environmental protection through the impact of harmful activities on life, private life or property is that it focuses attention on what matters most to individuals: the detriment to internationally protected values from uncontrolled environmental harm. Both the right to life and the right to respect for private life and property entail more than a simple prohibition on government interference: governments have a positive duty to take appropriate action to secure these rights,[136] as we can see in many of the cases, where the problem lay in a failure to regulate the activities of corporations, or legislate on environmental matters, or enforce existing environmental law.[137] This approach avoids the need to define such notions as a healthy or sustainable environment, it falls well within the competence of human-rights courts,

132 Articles 6(1) 14(1) 17. There is no right to property in the 1966 Covenant.

133 Articles 2, 6(1) 8, and Article 1, Protocol 1.

134 Articles 4(1) 8(1) 11(2) 21. See also the 1948 American Declaration on the Rights of Man, Articles I, III, XXIII.

135 See Boer and Boyle, *Human Rights and the Environment*, Rept of the 13th Asia-Europe Informal Seminar on Human Rights (2014).

136 See UNHRC CCPR/C/GC/36, General Comment No 36 on Article 6 of the ICCPR (2018) para 62; Desgagné, 89 *AJIL* (1995) 263; Churchill, in Boyle and Anderson, *Human Rights Approaches*, 91; Ramcharan, 30 *NILR* (1983) 297, 306; Trindade in Weiss (ed), *Environmental Change and International Law*, 271–7; Cook, 3 *EHRLR* (2019) 274.

137 See cases cited in next subsection, and in section 2(6).

and involves little or no potential for conflict with international environmental institutions or treaty COPs.

The greening of human rights law is not only a European phenomenon, but extends across the IACtHR, the African Court on Human and Peoples' Rights ('AfCHPR'), and the 1996 ICCPR. Judge Higgins has drawn attention to the way human rights courts 'work consciously to coordinate their approaches.'[138] There is certainly evidence of a cross-fertilization of ideas between the different human rights systems: 'The converging case law....... has generated the common understanding, in the regional (European and inter-American) systems of human rights protection. . .'.[139] The right to life has been a particularly fruitful source of environmental jurisprudence in several national jurisdictions, especially India. Here the courts have not only closed down industries causing harm to health and safety but have held that 'the right to life includes the right to live with human dignity and all that goes along with it', including the right to live in a 'healthy environment with minimal disturbance of [the] ecological balance', and they have drawn an explicit link with environmental quality.[140] Indian courts have used the right to life and the environmental provisions of the constitution as a basis for attacking state inaction. Some remarkable decisions have compelled the protection of the Taj Mahal, the creation of an Environmental Protection Agency, the closure of factories, the provision of pollution-free air and water, and the restoration of the 'ecological balance'.[141] Although the interpretation of the right to life adopted by Indian courts is expansive, it does show the potential for existing human rights to take on environmental dimensions. In those countries where the failure of governmental action is a major source of environmental harm, human-rights law, both national and international, has significant potential for remedying deficiencies in regulation and enforcement.[142]

(a) Environmental nuisances

As in India, the starting point for any discussion of international human-rights law and the environment is that a sufficiently serious failure by the state to regulate or control environmental nuisances or to protect the environment may amount to an

[138] Higgins, 55 *ICLQ* (2006) 791, at 798. See also *Diallo Case*, ICJ Reports (2010) paras 64–68.

[139] Judge Cançado Trindade, sep op, in *Caesar v Trinidad and Tobago*, IACtHR (2005) Series C No. 123, paras 6–12, at para 7. See generally Rachovitsa, 66 *ICLQ* (2017) 557.

[140] *Mullin v Union Territory of Delhi* AIR 1981 SC 746; *Bandhua Mukti Morcha v Union of India* (1984) 3 SCC 161; *Rural Litigation & Entitlement Kendra v State of Uttar Pradesh* AIR 1985 SC 652 and AIR 1987 SC 359; *Charan Lal Sahu v Union of India* (1986) 2 SCC 176; *T Damodhar Rao v Municipal Corp of Hyderabad*, AIR 1987 AP 171; *Subhash Kumar v State of Bihar* AIR 1991 SC 420; *MC Mehta v Kamal Nath* (2000) 6 SCC 213. These and other decisions are collected in UNEP, *Compendium of Summaries of Judicial Decisions in Environment Related Cases* (Colombo, 1997). See Boyle and Anderson (eds), *Human Rights Approaches*, Ch 10; Razzaque, 'Human Rights and the Environment: the National Experience in South Asia and Africa', *Joint UNEP-OHCHR Expert Seminar on Human Rights and the Environment: Background Paper No 4*, 14–16 January 2002.

[141] Not all of these decisions are based on the right to life, however. See e.g. *MC Mehta v Union of India* (1997) 2 SCC 353; *Jaganath v Union of India* (1997) 2 SCC 87.

[142] See Boyd, in Knox and Pejan (eds), *The Human Right to a Healthy Environment*, Ch 2.

interference with individual rights.[143] The main focus of the human rights case law dealing with pollution has been the rights to life, private life, health, water, and property.[144] Cases such as *Guerra, Lopez Ostra, Öneryildiz, Taskin* and *Fadeyeva*, show how human rights law can be used to compel governments to regulate environmental risks, enforce environmental laws, or disclose environmental information. All of these cases have common features.

First, there is an industrial nuisance—a chemical plant, smelter, tannery, mine, or waste disposal site, for example. The nuisance may be no more than the risk of living with pollution at levels that reduce air or water quality below accepted standards for human health. In *Dubetska v Ukraine*, the applicants succeeded because they had been unnecessarily exposed to increased health risks.[145]

Secondly, there is a failure to take adequate preventive measures to control these known sources of serious risk to life, health, private life, or property.[146] In contrast, where the state has done all it could to avoid a serious risk to individuals, there will be no violation of the Convention.[147]

Thirdly, it is irrelevant that the state itself does not own or operate the plant or industry in question. As the Court said in *Fadeyeva*,[148] the state's responsibility in environmental cases 'may arise from a failure to regulate private industry'. The state thus has a duty 'to take reasonable and appropriate measures' to secure rights under the convention. In *Öneryildiz* it emphasized that 'The positive obligation to take all appropriate steps to safeguard life for the purposes of Article 2 entails above all a primary duty on the State to put in place a legislative and administrative framework designed to provide effective deterrence against threats to the right to life'.[149] The Court had no doubt that this obligation covered the licensing, setting up, operation, security, and supervision of dangerous activities, and required all those concerned to take 'practical measures to ensure the effective protection of citizens whose lives might be endangered by the inherent risks'.[150]

These practical measures include law enforcement: it is a characteristic feature of *Guerra, Lopez Ostra, Taskin*, and *Fadeyeva* that the industrial activities in question

143 Council of Europe Manual, Appendix II; Pedersen in Knox and Pejan, *The Human Right to a Healthy Environment*, Ch 5.

144 *Öçkan and others v Turkey* (46771/99) paras 14, 22, 50; *Atanasov v Bulgaria* (2010) ECtHR, para 75; *Dubetska and others v Ukraine* [2011] ECtHR, paras 106–8; *Lopez Ostra v Spain* [1994] 20 EHRR 277; *Guerra v Italy* [1998] 26 EHRR 357; *Fadeyeva v Russia* [2007] 45 EHRR 10; *Öneryildiz v Turkey* [2005] 41 EHRR 20; *Taskin v Turkey* [2006] 42 EHRR 50, paras 113–9; *Tatar v Romania* [2009] ECtHR, para 88; *Budayeva v Russia* [2008] ECtHR; *SERAC v Nigeria* (2002) ACHPR; *Maya Indigenous community of the Toledo District v Belize* [2004] IACHR Case 12.053.

145 Paras 106–8. See also *Fadeyeva v Russia* (2007) 45 EHRR 10.

146 See e.g *Jugheli v Georgia* [2017] ECtHR 660

147 See e.g *Hatton v UK* [2003] ECtHR, *supra*, section 2(4); *Hardy and Maile v UK* (2012) ECtHR; *LCB v UK* (1999) 27 EHRR 212.

148 Para 89.

149 Para 89. See also *Kolyadenko v Russia* (2012) ECtHR, paras 157–61.

150 *Ibid*, para 90. For a comparable case in which precautionary measures were ordered by the Inter-American Commission see *Community of San Mateo de Huanchor and its members v Peru* (2004) IACHR Case 504/03.

were either operating illegally or in violation of environmental laws and emissions standards. In *Lopez Ostra* and *Taskin* the national courts ordered the closure of the facility in question, but their decisions had been ignored or overruled by the political authorities. In effect, there is a right to have the law enforced and the judgments of national courts upheld: 'The Court would emphasize that the administrative authorities form one element of a State subject to the rule of law, and that their interests coincide with the need for the proper administration of justice. Where administrative authorities refuse or fail to comply, or even delay doing so, the guarantees enjoyed by a litigant during the judicial phase of the proceedings are rendered devoid of purpose'.[151] The IACtHR has taken the same view pursuant to Article 25 of the 1969 Inter-American Convention.[152]

We can draw certain obvious conclusions from these cases. First, states have a positive duty to take appropriate measures to prevent industrial pollution, climate change impacts, or other forms of environmental nuisance such as logging from seriously interfering with health or the enjoyment of private life or property.[153] For example in *Maya Indigenous Community of the Toledo District v Belize*, the Inter-American Commission found that 'the State failed to put into place adequate safeguards and mechanisms, to supervise, monitor and ensure that it had sufficient staff to oversee that the execution of the logging concessions would not cause further environmental damage to Maya lands and communities'.[154] This is not a responsibility which can be left to industry or other states to fulfil. Its extent will of course depend on the harmfulness of the activity and the foreseeability of the risk. Once the risk ought to have been foreseen as a result of an EIA or in some other way (e.g. an official report) then the state has a duty to take appropriate action: it cannot wait until the interference with health or private life has become a reality.[155] In assessing whether a risk is foreseeable the precautionary principle may be relevant in situations of potentially serious or irreversible harm.[156]

Secondly, although the ECtHR refers to the need to balance the rights of the individual with the needs of the community as a whole, in reality the state's failure to apply or enforce its own environmental laws in many of these cases left no room for such a defence. This breach of domestic law necessarily constitutes a violation of the Convention.[157] States cannot expect to persuade a court that the needs of the community can best be met in such cases by not enforcing the law. A fortiori, if a national

151 *Taskin v Turkey* [2006] 42 EHRR 50, paras 124–5.

152 See *Mayagna (Sumo) Awas Tingni Community v Nicaragua* (2001) IACtHR Ser C, No 79, paras 106–14.

153 *Lopez Ostra v Spain* (1994) 20 EHRR 277; *Guerra v Italy* (1998) 26 EHRR 357; *Fadeyeva v Russia* [2005] ECHR 376; *Öneryildiz v Turkey* [2004] ECHR 657; *Taskin v Turkey* [2006] 42 EHRR 50.

154 (2004) IACHR, Case 12.053, para 47.

155 *Taskin*, para 113; *Öneryildiz*, paras 100–1.

156 See *Tatar v Romania* (2009) ECtHR, paras 109–120 and *supra*, Ch 3, section 6.

157 See e.g. *Fadeyeva Russia* [2005] ECtHR 376, para 95. Contrast *Hardy and Maile v UK* (2012) ECtHR, paras 220 and 231, where the Court held there had been no 'manifest error of appreciation by the national authorities in striking a fair balance between the competing interests in the case.'

supreme court has weighed the rights involved and annulled a permit for a harmful activity on the ground that it does not serve the public interest, the ECtHR is not going to reverse this judgment in favour of a national government.[158] At the same time, if the state has acted lawfully in the public interest it may be entitled to interfere to some degree with human rights.[159]

Thirdly, the beneficiaries of this duty to regulate and control sources of environmental harm are not the community at large, still less the environment per se, but only those individuals whose rights will be affected by any failure to act. The duty is not one of protecting the environment, but of protecting humans from significantly harmful environmental impacts.[160]

Other human rights bodies have begun to move in the same direction.[161] The obvious potential is recognised in the UN Human Rights Committee's General Comment No 36, adopted in 2018, which concludes that 'Environmental degradation, climate change and unsustainable development constitute some of the most pressing and serious threats to the ability of present and future generations to enjoy the right to life. Obligations of States parties under international environmental law should thus inform the contents of article 6 of the [ICCPR], and the obligation of States parties to respect and ensure the right to life should also inform their relevant obligations under international environmental law.'[162] The decision of the UN Human Rights Committee in *Portillo Cáceres v Paraguay* relies on this Comment in a case involving agricultural use of pesticides.[163]

(b) Indigenous culture and the environment

The 2007 UN Declaration on the Rights of Indigenous Peoples recognises that 'Indigenous peoples have the right to the conservation and protection of the environment and the productive capacity of their lands or territories and resources.'[164] A small number of environmental cases have concerned interference with the rights of indigenous peoples or other minorities to enjoy their own culture under Article 27 of the 1996 ICCPR. In *Ilmari Lansman and Ors v Finland* the UNHRC held that 'measures whose impact amount to a denial of the right will not be compatible with the obligations under article 27. However, measures that have a certain limited impact on the way of life of persons belonging to a minority will not necessarily amount to a denial

158 *Taskin v Turkey* [2006] 42 EHRR 50, para 117.

159 See discussion of *Hatton v United Kingdom, supra*, section 2(4).

160 See *Kyrtatos v Greece* [2003] ECtHR 242, para 52, and *infra*, section 2(7).

161 For IACHR precedents see *Advisory Opinion on Human Rights and the Environment* (2017) IACtHR, and *Maya Indigenous Community of the Toledo District v Belize* (2004) IACHR, Case 12.053.

162 UNHRC CCPR/C/GC/36 (2018) para 62. See Cook, 3 *EHRLR* (2019) 274.

163 UNHRC Comm No 2751/2016 (2019). See Moli,G in 69 *ICLQ* (2020) 735.

164 Article 29, UNGA Res 61/295 (2007). See also 1989 ILO Convention No 169 Concerning Indigenous and Tribal Peoples, Article 7(4), and generally Anaya, *Indigenous Peoples in International Law* (Oxford, 2000).

of the right under article 27'.[165] The Committee concluded that Finland had taken adequate measures to minimize the impact of stone quarrying on reindeer herding.

In somewhat similar circumstances, the Inter-American Commission and Court of Human Rights have relied instead on a broad reading of the right to property in order to afford indigenous peoples protection from environmental destruction and unsustainable development and they go some way towards achieving the same outcome as Article 27 of the 1996 ICCPR or Article 24 of the 1981 African Charter. In the *Maya Indigenous Community of Toledo Case*,[166] the IACHR accepted that logging concessions threatened long-term and irreversible damage to the natural environment on which the petitioners' system of subsistence agriculture depended. Citing *Ogoniland*, the IACHR concluded that there had been violations of their right to property in ancestral lands. Its final order required Belize to repair the environmental damage and to take measures to demarcate and protect their land in consultation with the community. The Commission's decision notes the importance of economic development but reiterates that 'development activities must be accompanied by appropriate and effective measures to ensure that they do not proceed at the expense of the fundamental rights of persons who may be particularly and negatively affected, including indigenous communities and the environment upon which they depend for their physical, cultural and spiritual well-being'.[167] Despite the different rights at issue in these cases, they all show a similar willingness to use whatever treaty provisions are available in order to protect the natural environment—in effect the habitat—of vulnerable indigenous peoples confronted by serious interference with their traditional livelihood and surroundings.

2(6) PARTICIPATORY RIGHTS

The strongest argument for specifically environmental rights focuses not on environmental quality but on procedural rights, including access to environmental information, access to justice and participation in environmental decision-making.[168] This approach rests on the view that environmental protection and sustainable

[165] (1996) ICCPR Comm No 511/1992, paras 9.4. See also *Ominayak and Lubicon Lake Band v Canada* (1990) ICCPR Comm No 167/1984, para 32.2; *Apirana Mahuika and Ors v New Zealand* (2000) Comm No 547/1993.

[166] *Maya Indigenous community of the Toledo District v Belize* (2004) IACHR, Case 12.053. See also *Mayagna (Sumo) Awas Tingni Community v Nicaragua* (2001) IACtHR Sers C, No 79; *Yakye Axa Indigenous Community v Paraguay* (2005) IACtHR, Sers. C, No 125; *Kichwa Peoples of the Sarayaku Community v Ecuador* (2012) IACtHR Sers C, No 145.

[167] Para 150. The decision is based on the 1948 American Declaration of the Rights of Man, not on the 1969 Inter-American Convention.

[168] See Zillman, Lucas and Pring (eds), *Human Rights in Natural Resource Development* (Oxford, 2002) especially Ch 1; Ebbesson, in Bodansky, Brunnée and Hey (eds), *The Oxford Handbook of International Environmental Law* (Oxford, 2007) Ch 29; Francioni (ed), *Access to Justice as a Human Right* (Oxford, 2007) Chs 1, 5; Ebbesson and Okowa (eds), *Environmental Law and Justice in Context* (Cambridge, 2009) esp Chs 6–11; Duvic-Paoli, 23 *YbIEL* (2013) 80.

development cannot be left to governments alone but require and benefit from notions of civic participation and transparency in public affairs already reflected in existing civil and political rights.[169] At its broadest, it can be represented as the application to environmental matters of arguments for democratic governance as a human right.[170] At its narrowest it is an argument for improving the quality and transparency of governmental decisions and promoting more effective enforcement.[171] The public-interest role of non-governmental organizations is especially important in this respect.[172]

The argument for participatory rights assumes that governments which operate with openness, accountability, and civic participation are more likely to promote environmental justice, to balance the needs of present and future generations in the protection of the environment, to integrate environmental considerations in governmental decisions, and to implement and enforce existing environmental standards than are closed, totalitarian, or undemocratic societies governed in a heavily centralized fashion. Empirically this is not difficult to demonstrate, especially by reference to countries with a disastrous environmental record such as East European states pre-1991 or contemporary China. In the Soviet Union, awareness of the environmental costs of totalitarianism appears to have been a significant factor in that country's post-communist revolution and its initial support for policies of environmental openness adopted by the Conference on Security and Cooperation in Europe ('CSCE') and UNECE.[173] But cases such as *Ogoniland* or *Maya Indigenous Community* show that the same criticism can sometimes be made of democratic states, insofar as certain groups are ignored or excluded from participation in decision-making on the exploitation of natural resources. This is an important reason for emphasizing the special claims of these vulnerable groups to 'meaningful consultation'.[174]

Although the Rio Declaration contains no explicit human right to a decent environment, Principle 10 lends substantial support in mandatory language for participatory rights of a comprehensive kind. It provides:

> Environmental issues are best handled with the participation of all concerned citizens, at the relevant level. At the national level, each individual shall have appropriate access to

[169] 1948 Universal Declaration on Human Rights, Articles 19, 21; 1966 ICCPR, Articles 19, 25; 1969 IACHR, Article 23; but compare 1950 ECHR, Protocol No 1, Article 3 of which provides only for free elections. See Partsch, in Henkin (ed), *The International Bill of Rights* (New York, 1981) 241–5 and cf *Nicaragua Case*, ICJ Reports (1986) 14, 131–2, and 1990 Charter of Paris (CSCE) 30 *ILM* (1991) 193.

[170] See Mason, *Environmental Democracy* (London, 1999); Franck, 86 *AJIL* (1992) 46; Crawford, 64 *BYIL* (1993) 113; Fox, 17 *Yale JIL* (1992) 539; Steiner, 1 *Harv HRYb* (1988) 77; Ebbesson, 8 *YbIEL* (1997) 51; 1993 UN Conference on Human Rights, Vienna Declaration, para 8.

[171] See Preamble to the 1998 Aarhus Convention; ECLAC, *Access to information, participation and justice in environmental matters in Latin America and the Caribbean: towards achievement of the 2030 Agenda for Sustainable Development*, LC/TS.2017/83 (Santiago, 2018) 13–14.

[172] *Infra*, this section, part (c).

[173] See Charter of Paris (OSCE) *supra*, n 168; 1995 Sofia Ministerial Declaration (UNECE) 26 *EPL* 34.

[174] *Maya Indigenous Community Case*, paras 154–5. See 1992 Rio Declaration Principle 22; Agenda 21, Chapter 26 and 1989 ILO Convention No 169 Concerning Indigenous and Tribal Peoples in Independent Countries. See also Agenda 21, Ch 24 on the role of women, and generally Shelton, 3 *YbIEL* (1992) 82–9; Ebbesson, 8 *YbIEL* (1997) 70–73; Triggs, in Zillman, Lucas, and Pring, *Human Rights in Natural Resource Development*, Ch 3.

information concerning the environment that is held by public authorities, including information on hazardous materials and activities in their communities, and the opportunity to participate in decision-making processes. States shall facilitate and encourage public awareness and participation by making information widely available. Effective access to judicial and administrative proceedings, including redress and remedy, shall be provided.

Whether one describes such rights in terms of a generic right to a healthy or sustainable environment is largely a matter of terminology. What is important is the recognition that they would add significantly to the protection of the environment and sustainable development.[175]

What distinguishes Principle 10 from participatory rights in the ICCPR and regional human rights conventions is its greater specificity and environmental focus, and its emphasis both on participation in environmental decision-making, including access to information, and on effective access to justice. These features justify the proposition that there is a role for human-rights law in promoting procedures for protection of the environment, and a need for further development over and above those more general rights already protected in human-rights treaties.[176]

For example, Article 10 of the European Convention only guarantees freedom to receive and impart information. It creates neither a right of access to information nor a duty to communicate information.[177] Access to, or communication of, environmental information may nevertheless be required under general human-rights law but only insofar as necessary in order to give effect to rights to life, private life, or access to justice.[178] In contrast, the 1998 Aarhus Convention and the 2018 ECLAC Agreement recognize a broad duty to inform.[179] Crucially, information rights under these UN agreements are not dependent on showing that the person seeking environmental information is a victim of a violation of the right to life, private life, or property. Similarly, access-to-justice articles of human-rights treaties apply to environmental disputes only when civil rights and obligations are at stake,[180] and they do not facilitate NGO standing, public-interest litigation, or judicial review and appeal in respect of decisions which affect the environment but not the rights of individuals.

In addition to the 1998 Aarhus Convention and the 2018 ECLAC Agreement, considered in the next section, Rio Principle 10 is reflected in UNEP's Bali Guidelines,[181] and in various regional agreements. One of the most far-reaching is the 2003 UNECE

[175] See UNCED Agenda 21, Ch 23, especially 23.2; 2030 Agenda for Sustainable Development, Goal 16; ECLAC, *Access to information, etc in Latin America and the Caribbean*, 13–17.

[176] See ECOSOC, *Human Rights and the Environment: Preliminary Rept*, UN Doc E/CN 4/Sub 2/1991/8; Kane, 18 *Yale LJ* (1993) 389; Handl, in Trindade (ed), *Human Rights, Sustainable Development and the Environment*, 117; Ebbesson, 8 *YbIEL* (1997) 51.

[177] *Guerra v Italy* (1998) 26 EHRR 357, para 55.

[178] See Gavouneli, 13 *Tulane ELJ* (2000) 303, and see *infra*, section 2(5)(c).

[179] Articles 4 and 5 respectively.

[180] 1966 ICCPR, Article 14; 1969 ACHR, Article 8; 1950 ECHR, Article 6(1) on which see *Taskin v Turkey* [2006] 42 EHRR 50.

[181] 2010 Guidelines for the Development of National Legislation on Access to Information, Public Participation and Access to Justice in Environmental Matters. See Etemire, 28 *JEL* (2016) 393.

Protocol on Strategic Environmental Assessment, under which 'Each party shall ensure early, timely and effective opportunities for public participation, when all options are open, in the strategic environmental assessment of plans and programmes'.[182] The public for this purpose includes relevant NGOs.[183] Other relevant treaties include the 1991 Espoo Convention,[184] the 1992 OSPAR Convention,[185] the 1992 UNECE Convention on the Protection and use of Transboundary Watercourses,[186] the 1993 Council of Europe Convention on Civil Liability for Damage Resulting from Activities Dangerous to the Environment,[187] and the 1993 NAAEC.[188] The latter agreement seeks inter alia to promote transparency and public participation.[189] It allows individuals and NGOs to complain to the secretariat that a state party is failing to enforce its environmental legislation. The secretariat investigates and reports its findings to the Commission.[190] One study concludes that the NAAEC procedure is 'weak in terms of transparency, efficiency, and effective public participation.'[191]

(a) Participatory rights under the Aarhus Convention

The first comprehensive multilateral scheme for giving effect to Rio Principle 10 is the 1998 Aarhus Convention.[192] The Convention takes account of the UNECE Guidelines on Access to Environmental Information and Public Participation in Decision-making adopted at Sofia in 1995 and is another example of soft law transformed into hard law. As a UNECE convention its participants include EU states and most of the former Soviet states, but it is open to any state to participate. Kofi Annan, formerly Secretary General of the UN, has observed: 'Although regional in scope, the significance of the 1998 Aarhus Convention is global ... [I]t is the most ambitious venture in the area of "environmental democracy" so far undertaken under the auspices of the United Nations'.[193] In his view the Convention has the 'potential to serve as a global framework for strengthening citizens' environmental rights'.[194] The focus on participatory rights reflects the opposition of many OECD members to the broader environmental-rights

[182] Article 8(1), *supra,* Ch 3, section 7. [183] Article 2(8).

[184] Articles 2(6) 3(8). See *supra,* Ch 3, section 7.

[185] Article 9 provides only for access to information. See *Dispute Concerning Access to Information under the OSPAR Convention (Ireland v UK)* PCA (2003).

[186] Article 16 provides only for access to information.

[187] Articles 14–16. See *Explanatory Rept* in Council of Europe CDCJ (92) 50.

[188] See Fitzmaurice, 52 *ICLQ* (2003) 334. [189] Article 1.

[190] See Articles 14, 15; Di Mento and Doughman, 10 *Georgetown IELR* (1998) 651–743; Markell, 12 *Georgetown IELR* (2000) 545–74; Knox, 28 *ELQ* (2001) 53ff.

[191] Fitzmaurice, in Ebbesson and Okowa (eds), *Environmental Law and Justice in Context* (Cambridge, 2009) 211–227.

[192] See UNECE, *The Århus Convention: An Implementation Guide* (2nd edn, New York, 2014) which gives detailed guidance; Duvic-Paoli, 23 *YbIEL* (2013) 80; Koester, in Ulfstein, Marauhn, Zimmermann (eds), *Making Treaties Work: Human Rights, Environment and Arms Control* (Cambridge, 2007) 179; Ebbesson, in Bodansky, Brunnée and Hey, *Oxford Handbook of IEL*, Ch 29; Francioni (ed), *Access to Justice as a Human Right* (Oxford, 2007) Chs 1 & 5; Lee and Abbott, 66 *MLR* (2003) 80; Ebbesson, 8 *YbIEL* (1997) 51.

[193] Annan, 'Foreword', UNECE, *The Århus Convention: An Implementation Guide* (1st edn, New York, 2000) v.

[194] *Ibid.*

approach of the 1994 draft UN declaration. Parties to 1998 Aarhus guarantee rights of access to information, public participation in decision-making, and access to justice in environmental matters. They are required by Article 9 to make those rights enforceable by a national court or independent tribunal. There is also a non-compliance procedure to which NGOs and individuals can take complaints.[195]

Under Article 4 of the 1998 Aarhus Convention anyone ('the public') is entitled to environmental information covered by the Convention, including NGOs 'promoting environmental protection' in accordance with national law. Access is not dependent on being personally affected or having some right or interest in the matter. In this respect it reflects the many national laws on the subject, including US law and EU directives.[196] Nor is access limited to nationals of the state concerned: Article 3(9) the convention's non-discrimination article, ensures that in transboundary cases foreign nationals and NGOs have the same rights as anyone else.[197] 'Environmental information' is broadly defined by Article 2(3) and includes information concerning the physical elements of the environment, such as water and biological diversity, as well as information about activities, administrative measures, agreements, policies, legislation, plans, and programmes likely to affect the environment, human health, safety, or conditions of life. Cost benefit and other economic analyses and assumptions used in environmental decision-making are also included. There are also detailed provisions on collection and dissemination of environmental information (Article 5). In all of these respects the Convention goes further than the case law based on general human-rights law referred to earlier. However, Article 4 applies only to information held by public authorities. Very important information held by industry or subject to the convention's commercial and industrial exception is not covered, although a Protocol on Pollutant Release and Transfer Registers adopted in 2003 will require industry to collect and report information about pollution emissions which parties must then make publicly available.[198]

Unlike access to information, participatory rights under Article 6 of the 1998 Aarhus Convention are available only to 'the public concerned', but this is broadly defined in Article 2(5) as 'the public affected or likely to be affected by, or having an interest in, the environmental decision-making; for the purposes of this definition, non-governmental organizations promoting environmental protection and meeting any requirements under national law shall be deemed to have an interest'. This would again require that national, foreign, or international NGOs be allowed to participate in decisions on a non-discriminatory basis, subject only to any legal requirements consistent with the convention.[199] Article 6 applies to decisions regarding a wide range

[195] See *supra*, Ch 4, section 3. [196] See Gavouneli, 13 *Tulane ELJ* (2000) 303.

[197] UNECE, Compliance Committee, *Bystre Deep-water Navigation Canal—Findings and Recommendation with regard to compliance by Ukraine* (Comms ACCC/C/2004/01 and 03) ECE/MP PP/C 1/2005/2/Add 3 (14 March 2005) paras 26–8; UNECE, *The Århus Convention: An Implementation Guide* (2nd edn, 2014) 72, and see *infra*, this section part (c).

[198] Comparable national schemes exist in the US and EU. See generally Sand, 63 *ZAÖRV* (2003) 487.

[199] *Supra*, n 196.

of activities, including the oil, chemical, and nuclear industries, smelters, wood pulp mills, and waste-management sites, motorways and airports, and the release of genetically modified organisms.[200]

Article 6(6) focuses on the information to be made available to the public, including:

- a description of the site and the physical and technical characteristics of the proposed activity, including an estimate of the expected residues and emissions;
- a description of the significant effects of the proposed activity on the environment;
- a description of the measures envisaged to prevent and/or reduce the effects, including emissions;
- an outline of the main alternatives studied by the applicant.

As a comparison with Annex II of the 1991 Espoo Convention shows, these are all matters normally included in an EIA: in effect implementing Aarhus will thus require some kind of EIA process.[201] The *Taskin* decision of the ECtHR, considered below, takes a very similar approach and makes explicit reference to Rio Principle 10 and the 1998 Aarhus Convention.[202] However, in a complaint involving construction of a nuclear power plant in Slovakia, participation in the EIA process alone was held to be insufficient.[203] Article 6(4) requires 'early' participation 'when all options are open and effective participation can take place,' and this was interpreted by the Compliance Committee to require participation at the permitting stage when a decision could have been taken not to proceed with construction.

Finally, Article 9 also makes general provision for access to justice in order to challenge breaches of national law relating to the environment when either the applicant's rights are impaired or they have a 'sufficient interest'.[204] 'Sufficient interest' is not defined by the 1998 Aarhus Convention, it appears to be narrower than the 'public concerned' employed in Article 6, and the parties could not agree on how far it provides for public-interest litigation by NGOs.[205] In its first ruling, the Aarhus Compliance

[200] See Annex I. Article 6 is amended by Decision II/1 on Release of GMOs. See UNECE, *Rept of 2nd Meeting of Parties to the Århus Convention*, ECE/MP PP/2005/2/Add 2 (2005).

[201] See UNECE, *The Århus Convention: An Implementation Guide*, 147–52. Annex II of the Espoo Convention additionally includes an indication of predictive methods, underlying assumptions, relevant data, gaps in knowledge and uncertainties, as well as an outline of monitoring plans.

[202] *Taskin*, paras 98–99. The Court also relied upon Council of Europe Parliamentary Assembly Recommendation 1614 (2003) which declares that member states should 'safeguard the individual procedural rights to access to information, public participation in decision-making and access to justice in environmental matters set out in the Århus Convention' (Principle 9 (iii)). See also *Kichwa Peoples of the Sarayaku Community v Ecuador* (2012) IACtHR Sers C, No 145, paras 204–7.

[203] Compliance Committee, Findings and Recommendations with regard to Communication ACCC/C/2009/41 (2010) paras 64–70.

[204] For a fuller account see Redgwell, in Francioni (ed), *Access to Justice as a Human Right* (Oxford, 2007) 153, although, following decisions of the compliance committee, standing under Article 9 may be less restrictive than suggested there.

[205] UNECE, *The Århus Convention: An Implementation Guide*, 129.

Committee held that 'Although what constitutes a sufficient interest and impairment of a right shall be determined in accordance with national law, it must be decided with "the objective of giving the public concerned wide access to justice" within the scope of the Convention'.[206] While Article 9(2) preserves the stricter requirements of legal systems that confer standing only on those whose rights have been violated,[207] parties must nevertheless ensure that they 'take fully into account the objective of the Convention to guarantee access to justice'.[208] They are not required to establish an *actio popularis*, but they must not use national law 'as an excuse for introducing or maintaining so strict criteria that they effectively bar all or almost all environmental organizations from challenging acts or omissions that contravene national law relating to the environment'.[209] Access to such procedures 'should thus be the presumption, not the exception'.[210] Under Article 9(3) applicants entitled to participate in decision-making will also have the right to seek administrative or judicial review of the legality of the resulting decision. A general failure to enforce environmental law will also violate Article 9(3).[211] Article 9(4) also requires that adequate, fair, and effective remedies are provided.[212] This reflects the decisions in *Lopez Ostra* and *Guerra* referred to earlier.

The 1998 Aarhus Convention is an important achievement; strongly supported by participating governments and the EU, to whose institutions it expressly applies,[213] and it has helped shape national law and practice throughout Europe. Moreover, as we have seen above, the non-discriminatory application of rights of public participation and access to environmental justice under Article 3(9) will also include transboundary claimants, and may thus facilitate resolution of transboundary environmental disputes.[214] The 1998 Aarhus Convention is significantly broader than the 1991 Espoo Convention in two important respects, however: it is not limited to a transboundary context, and in accordance with Articles 7 and 8 it also applies, with some important qualifications, to plans, policies and legislation.[215] Ultimately, it is public participation at this level, rather than at the project level to which Article 6 applies, that has the greatest potential to promote—or to retard—environmental protection. Article 7 provides that 'To the extent appropriate, each Party shall endeavour to provide opportunities for public participation in the preparation of policies relating to the environment'. Like Article 8, which deals with legislation, this wording is somewhat weaker

206 *Bond Beter Leefmilieu Vlaanderen VZW: Findings and Recommendation with Regard to Compliance by Belgium*, Compliance Committee, UNECE/MP PP/C 1/2006/4/Add 2 (2006) para 33.

207 E.g. Germany: see Section 42(2) of the Administrative Courts Act and Decision of the Administrative Court of Cologne (25 January 2007) 13 K 2858/06, para 41.

208 1998 Aarhus Convention, Decision II/2, Para 16; *Bond Beter Leefmilieu Vlaanderen VZW*, para 36.

209 *Ibid*, para 35.

210 *Ibid*, para 36. See also Article 9(3).

211 *Gatina, Gatin, Konyushkova: Findings and Recommendation with Regard to Compliance by Kazakhstan*, Compliance Committee, UNECE/MP PP/C 1/2006/4/Add 1 (2006) paras 30–1.

212 On the right to adequate remedies see section 4 below.

213 Article 2(2)(d) implemented by Regulation (EC) No 1367/2006 on the application of the Århus Convention to Community institutions and bodies (OJ L 264, 25.9.2006, 13).

214 *Infra*, section 2(7).

215 See also the 2003 Protocol on Strategic Environmental Assessment.

than Article 6. Nevertheless, this has not stopped the Compliance Committee from finding at least one state in breach.[216] It has also provided a basis for further development of state practice,[217] and no other human-rights treaty goes this far.

(b) The 2018 ECLAC Regional Agreement on Access to Information, Public Participation and Justice in Environmental Matters in Latin America and the Caribbean

The 2018 ECLAC Agreement is the outcome of a long process of negotiation sponsored by the UN Economic Commission for Latin America and the Caribbean. It is intended to give fuller effect to Rio Principle 10 than existing laws in the region, and is modelled on the 1998 Aarhus Convention, but in certain respects it goes beyond these precedents. In particular, there are specific provisions on indigenous peoples and other vulnerable groups, on the protection of environmental rights defenders, and on environmental information held by private parties.[218] Parties must 'guarantee the right of every person to live in a healthy environment' and 'an enabling environment for the work of persons, associations, organizations or groups that promote environmental protection, by recognizing and protecting them.'[219]

(c) Participatory rights under human-rights treaties

An important question posed by developments in the case law of the ECtHR and IACtHR is the extent to which the participatory rights contained in the 1998 Aarhus Convention and Principle 10 of the Rio Declaration have become part of general human-rights law. UNEP's 2010 Guidelines represent an attempt to put some content into Principle 10,[220] but the major contribution has come from human rights case law.[221]

The most significant case is *Taskin v Turkey*, about the licensing of a mine, in which the ECtHR held that 'whilst Article 8 [of the European Convention] contains no explicit procedural requirements, the decision-making process leading to measures of interference must be fair and such as to afford due respect to the interests of the individual as safeguarded by Article 8'.[222] The Court put the matter like this: 'Where a State must determine complex issues of environmental and economic policy, the decision-making process must first involve appropriate investigations and studies in order to allow them to predict and evaluate in advance the effects of those activities which might damage the environment and infringe individuals' rights and to enable them

216 *Dalma Orchards: Armenia*, Compliance Committee, UNECE/MP PP/C 1/2006/2/Add 1 (2006).

217 In the Almaty Guidelines adopted in 2005 the parties endorsed public participation in the decision-making of international bodies concerned with environmental protection: UNECE, *Rept of 2nd Meeting of Parties to the Århus Convention*, ECE/MP PP/2005/2/Add 5 (2005) paras 28–39.

218 Articles 5(4), 6(9)–(13) and 9.

219 Articles 4(1) and (6).

220 2010 Guidelines for the Development of National Legislation on Access to Information, Public Participation and Access to Justice in Environmental Matters.

221 On the IACHR see *Advisory Opinion on Environment and Human Rights*, IACtHR (2017).

222 *Taskin v Turkey* [2006] 42 EHRR 50, para 118.

to strike a fair balance between the various conflicting interests at stake'.[223] The words 'environmental impact assessment' are not used, but in many cases that is exactly what will be necessary to give effect to the evaluation process envisaged here. This passage and the Court's emphasis on taking into account the views of affected individuals strongly suggests that their participation in the decision-making process will be essential for compliance with Article 8. Similarly, the right to 'meaningful consultation' is upheld by the Inter-American Commission in the *Maya Indigenous Community of Toledo Case*,[224] by the African Commission in the *Ogoniland Case*,[225] and by the UN Human Rights Committee.[226]

In *Öneryildiz v Turkey* the ECtHR placed 'particular emphasis' on the public's right to information about dangerous activities which posed a threat to life.[227] Where governments engage in or permit dangerous activities with unknown consequences for health or private life, such as nuclear tests, there is a duty to establish an 'effective and accessible' procedure for allowing those involved to obtain relevant information.[228] In appropriate cases there is a duty to inform, not simply a right of access. In *Guerra*, Italy's failure to provide 'essential information' about the severity and nature of toxic emissions from a chemical plant was held to constitute a breach of the right to private life.[229] The judgment notes that the applicants were 'particularly exposed to danger' in the event of an accident at the factory, and there had been a violation of Italian legislation requiring that information concerning hazardous activities be made public. Finally, the *Taskin* judgment stipulates that 'the individuals concerned must also be able to appeal to the courts against any decision, act or omission where they consider that their interests or their comments have not been given sufficient weight in the decision-making process'.[230]

All of these decisions would also be covered by the terms of the 1998 Aarhus Convention but where the threat is to the environment, rather than to individuals, only the 1998 Aarhus Convention will apply. Moreover, the 1950 ECHR right of participation in decision-making is plainly not available to everyone, nor does it apply to decisions concerning the environment in general. Only those whose convention rights are in some way affected will benefit from this protection. This is significantly

223 *Taskin v Turkey* [2006] 42 EHRR 50, para 119.

224 Paras 154–5. The Commission relies, inter alia, on the right to life and the right to private life, in addition to finding consultation a 'fundamental component of the State's obligations in giving effect to the communal property right of the Maya people in the lands that they have traditionally used and occupied'.

225 *SERAC v Nigeria* (2002) ACHPR Comm 155/96.

226 *Ilmari Lansman and Ors v Finland* (1996) ICCPR Comm No 511/1992, para 9.5, which stresses the need 'to ensure the effective participation of members of minority communities in decisions which affect them', and *Apirana Mahuika and Ors v New Zealand* (2000) ICCPR Comm No 547/1993, para 9.8. See also ILO Convention No 169 Concerning Indigenous and Tribal Peoples.

227 Para 90.

228 *McGinley and Egan v United Kingdom* [1998] III ECtHR, paras 97, 101; *LCB v UK* (1999) 27 EHRR 212; *Brânduse v Romania* (2009) ECtHR; *Di Sarno v Italy* (2012) ECtHR 108 ('Article 8 may be relied on even in the absence of any evidence of a serious danger to people's health'); *Hardy and Maile v UK* (2012) ECtHR, paras 245–6.

229 Para 60.

230 *Ibid.*

narrower than under Article 6 of the 1998 Aarhus Convention. If Aarhus can be viewed as promoting public interest participation, the ECHR case law remains firmly grounded in individual rights. It is likely to prove harder to influence the outcome of any balancing of interests from this perspective.

Nevertheless, if *Hatton* shows a reluctance on the part of the ECtHR to grapple with the merits of a decision interfering with individual rights, *Taskin* convincingly demonstrates an unequivocal willingness to address the proper procedures for taking decisions relating to the environment in human-rights terms. This is a profound extension of the scope of Article 8 of the European Convention. It goes some way towards translating into European human-rights law the procedural requirements set out in Principle 10 of the Rio Declaration and elaborated in European environmental-treaty law, despite the fact that Turkey was not a party to the 1998 Aarhus Convention at the time.

(d) NGOs and participatory rights

Not only do environmental NGOs use access to information and lobbying to raise awareness of environmental concerns, but research has shown that they tend to have high success rates in enforcement actions and public interest litigation.[231] As we noted earlier, the 1998 Aarhus Convention is also important because, unlike human rights treaties, it provides for public interest activism by NGOs,[232] insofar as claimants with a 'sufficient interest' are empowered to engage in public interest litigation even when their own rights or the rights of victims of a violation are not in issue. Article 9 of Aarhus thus appears to go beyond the requirements of the 1950 ECHR. So does Article 6, which extends public participation rights to anyone having an 'interest' in the decision, including NGOs.[233]

The contrast between the broader public interest approach of the 1998 Aarhus Convention and the narrower human rights focus on the rights of victims of a violation is evident in the case-law.[234] This is a significant difference, with implications for any debate about an autonomous right to a healthy, sustainable, or ecologically sound environment. Moreover, the broader approach taken by Aarhus is followed in later European agreements.[235] This begs the question whether the ECtHR caselaw should follow the public interest precedent set by Aarhus, as it has in so many other

231 See de Sadeleer/Roller/Dross, *Access to Justice in Environmental Matters*, Final Rept, Doc ENVA.3/ETU/2002/0030, Part I, section 3.

232 Articles 4(1)(a) 6 and 9. See Pedersen, (2008) 21 *Georgetown IELR* 73.

233 Article 6 participation rights are available to 'the public concerned', defined by Article 2(5) as 'the public affected or likely to be affected by, or having an interest in, the environmental decision-making; for the purposes of this definition, non-governmental organizations promoting environmental protection and meeting any requirements under national law shall be deemed to have an interest.'

234 See *Kyrtatos v Greece* [2003] ECtHR 242, para 52; *Metropolitan Nature Reserve v Panama* [2003] IACHR, Case 11.533, at 524, para 34; *Brun v France* [2006] ICCPR Comm No. 1453/2006, para 6.3. See section 2(4) where these cases are further considered.

235 2003 UNECE Protocol on Strategic Environmental Assessment, Article 8(1).

respects?[236] Answering the question in the negative would merely affirm the existing position that human rights law does not have anything to say about protection of the environment as such. Answering it in the affirmative would go some way towards opening the door for a broader conception of the relationship between human rights and the environment.

The real test of Rio Principle 10's significance lies less in international treaties, however, than in national law.[237] It is here that most of the important applications of the principle have taken place. In particular, public interest litigation has become an important feature of access to environmental justice, whether in the form of class actions, or liberal rules of standing, or allowing intervention by NGOs. Decisions of courts in common-law countries have generally granted *locus standi* in administrative-review proceedings to environmental groups and NGOs on a liberal basis, although such groups must usually demonstrate some interest in the issue beyond a mere concern for the environment.[238] Influenced by the 1998 Aarhus Convention, certain civil-law jurisdictions also allow an *actio popularis* in environmental cases,[239] although standing before the European Court of Justice ('ECJ') remains very restrictive.[240] Nor is this more liberal trend confined to developed states. India,[241] Pakistan,[242] Bangladesh,[243] the Philippines,[244] Malaysia[245] and several Latin American jurisdictions[246] have also

236 See Schall, 20 *JEL* (2008) 417.

237 For a study of the partial implementation of Principle 10 see ECLAC, *Access to Information, Participation and Justice in Environmental matters in Latin America and the Caribbean* (Santiago, 2018).

238 For the US position see *Sierra Club v Morton* 405 US 727 (1972); *Lujan v Defenders of Wildlife* 504 US 555 (1992); *Friends of the Earth v Laidlaw*, 120 SCt 693 (2000) and Miller, 12 *JEL* (2000) 370. On New Zealand see *Environmental Defence Society v South Pacific Aluminium* (No 3) (1981) 1 NZLR 216. On UK law see *R v Secretary of State for Foreign and Commonwealth Affairs ex parte World Development Movement* [1995[1 All ER 611 and *AXA General Insurance Ltd v Lord Advocate* [2011] UKSC 46.

239 See especially the liberal approach adopted in the Italy: *Comitato Communa Bellis e Sanctuario v Commune di Ostiglia* (2006) Consiglio di Stato No 5760/2006 and in France: Conseil d'Etat, Decision of 26 April 1985 '*Ville de Tarbes*'. NGO standing in Germany is limited to s 61(2) of the 2002 Nature Conservation Act: see Federal Administrative Court (19 March 2003) 22 *Neue Zeitschrift für Verwaltungsrecht* (2003) 1120. For the Netherlands see *Urgenda Foundation v The Netherlands*, Hague Dist Ct (2015) paras 4.4–10 (English translation). See also de Sadeleer/Roller/Dross, *Access to Justice in Environmental Matters*, Final Rept, Doc ENVA 3/ETU/2002/0030, Part II, 76ff. Part I of this study surveys access to environmental justice in Western Europe.

240 See *Stichting Greenpeace Council v EC Commission* (1998) ECR I-1651; 3 *CMLR* (1998) 1; Gérard, 10 *JEL* (1998) 331; Davies, in Zillman/Lucas/Pring (eds), *Human Rights in Natural Resources Development*, 176.

241 E.g. *Bandhua Mukti Morcha v Union of India*, AIR 1984 SC 802; *Rural Litigation and Entitlement Kendra v State of Uttar Pradesh*, AIR 1985 SC 652; id, AIR 1987 SC 359; id, AIR 1988 SC 2187; *T Damodhar Rao v Municipal Corporation of Hyderabad*, AIR 1987 AP 171; *MC Mehta v Union of India* (1987) 1 SCC 395; id, (1987) 4 SCC 463; id, (1988) 1 SCC 471; id, (1997) 2 SCC 353.

242 *Shehla Zia v WAPDA*, PLD 1994 SC 416. See Lau, in, Boyle and Anderson (eds), *Human Rights Approaches to Environmental Protection*, Ch 14, who notes the Islamic-law basis for expanded public-interest litigation, expressed by Pakistan's Supreme Court and the four provincial High Courts in the 1991 Quetta Declaration.

243 *Farooque v Govt of Bangladesh* (1997) 49 DLR (AD) 1.

244 *Minors Oposa v Secretary of the Department of Environment and Natural Resources*, 33 *ILM* (1994) 173.

245 See *Ketua Pengarah Jabatan Sekitar and Anor v Kajing Tubek and Ors* [1997] 3 *MLJ* 23, but cf Harding, in Boyle and Anderson (eds), *Human Rights Approaches*, Ch 11.

246 For a comprehensive study see ECLAC, *Access to Information, Participation and Justice in Environmental matters in Latin America and the Caribbean* (Santiago, 2018).

embraced public-interest litigation on environmental issues. Judicial activism can be overdone, however, and some studies have questioned whether government by judges is equitable or environmentally effective.[247]

The main advantage of focusing on procedural rights is that it enables individuals and NGOs to enforce domestic environmental law and may help them shape domestic environmental policy. Public-interest litigation may also diminish problems of anthropocentricity to the extent that rights can be exercised on behalf of the environment or of its non-human components, and not solely for human benefit. They can also be employed in the interests of future generations.[248] A further advantage of such litigation is that it can serve as a means of making public bodies accountable for their actions under international law. It has enabled environmental groups in the US to seek review of governmental decisions affecting the Conventions on Trade in Endangered Species and Whaling,[249] while in India international environmental law, including treaties and the Rio Declaration, has been relied on in public-interest cases.[250] The extent to which public international law and treaties can be invoked or enforced by national courts varies across jurisdictions, however, and is beyond the scope of this book.[251]

It should not be overlooked, moreover, that governments also have a role as public-interest plaintiffs. Following the Bhopal disaster in India, the government assumed *parens patriae* power to negotiate a mass settlement of claims against Union Carbide.[252] In Australia, the Commonwealth government has relied on its treaty-making power in actions concerning non-compliance by state governments with the World Heritage Convention.[253] The European Commission is similarly empowered to bring proceedings against member states for non-compliance with directives implementing treaties to which the EU is a party.[254] Indeed, where the EU has legislative competence to

247 See Rajamani, 19 *JEL* (2007) 293.

248 See Philippines Supreme Court decision in *Minors Oposa v Secretary of the Department of Environment and Natural Resources*, 33 *ILM* (1994) 173; *Rural Litigation and Entitlement Kendra v State of Uttar Pradesh* AIR (1987) SC 359.

249 *Defenders of Wildlife Inc v Endangered Species Authority*, 659 F 2d 168 (1981); *Japanese Whaling Association v American Cetacean Society*, 478 US 221 (1986); Gibson, 14 *ELQ* (1987) 485.

250 *T Damodhar Rao v Municipal Corporation of Hyderabad* AIR 1987 AP 171; *People United for Better Living in Calcutta v West Bengal*, AIR 1993 Cal 215; *Indian Council for Environmental Action v Union of India* (1996) 3 SCC 212; *Vellore Citizens Welfare Forum v Union of India* (1996) 5 SCC 647; *Jagannath v Union of India* (1997) 2 SCC 87. See Anderson and Galizzi (eds), *International Environmental Law in National Courts*, Ch 8.

251 Anderson and Galizzi (eds), *International Environmental Law in National Courts*. See also UNEP's 2010 Bali Guidelines for the Development of National Legislation on Access to Information, Public Participation and Access to Justice in Environmental Matters.

252 See Bhopal Gas Leak Disaster (Processing of Claims) Act, 1985, and *Charan Lal Sahu* v *Union of India*, AIR 1990 SC 1480.

253 *Commonwealth of Australia v State of Tasmania* (1983) 46 ALR 625; *Richardson v Tasmanian Forestry Commission* (1988) 77 ALR 237; *Queensland v The Commonwealth of Australia* (1989) 167 CLR 232; Tsamenyi and Bedding, 2 *JEL* (1990) 117.

254 See *EC v France* (1990) ECR I-4337 (violation of CITES); *EC v France* (2004) Case C-239/03 (violation of Athens Protocol for Protection of the Mediterranean). Where treaty provisions have direct effect individuals can also sue: see e.g. *Syndicat Professionel etc v EDF* (2004) Case C-213/03 (Athens Protocol).

implement international environmental commitments, it is no longer possible for the member states to bring international judicial or arbitral proceedings *inter se*. They must either invite the Commission to use its enforcement powers or initiate proceedings against the other member state before the ECJ.[255]

2(7) EXTRATERRITORIAL APPLICATION OF HUMAN-RIGHTS TREATIES IN ENVIRONMENTAL CASES

The extraterritorial application of human rights law has normally arisen only where the State exercises jurisdiction or control over persons or territory abroad.[256] These precedents bear little resemblance to transboundary pollution, where the State only exercises jurisdiction over harmful activities located within its own territory. However, there are counter arguments.[257]

First, where it is possible to take effective measures to prevent or mitigate transboundary harm to human rights then the argument that the state has no obligation to do so merely because the harm is extraterritorial is not a compelling one. On the contrary, in keeping with the principle of non-discrimination,[258] the environmental impact of activities in one country on the right to life, private life or property in other countries should be taken into account and given due weight in the decision-making process.[259] There is no principled basis for suggesting that the outcome of cases such as *Hatton*[260] should depend on whether those affected by excessive noise or air pollution are in the same country, or in other countries. It seems consistent with the case-law and the 'living instrument' conception of human rights treaties to conclude that a State party must balance the rights of persons in other States against its own economic

[255] *Commission v Ireland* [*'MOX Plant Case'*] ECR [2006] I-4635, and see Churchill and Scott, 22 *IJMCL* (2007) 303.

[256] *AO on Legal Consequences of the Construction of a Wall in the Occupied Palestinian Territory*, ICJ Reports (2004) 136, paras 109, 112; *Application of the International Convention on the Elimination of All Forms of Racial Discrimination (Provisional Measures)*, ICJ Reports (2008) 386, para 109; *Ecuador v Colombia (Admissibility)* [2010] IACHR Rept No.112/10, paras 89–100; *Alejandre, Costa, de la Pena y Morales v Republica de Cuba* [1999] IACHR Rept No. 86/99, para23; *Coard v United States* [1999] IACHR Rept 109/99, para 37; *Al-Skeini v United Kingdom* [2011] ECtHR, paras 130–42; *Öcalan v Turkey* [2005] 41 EHRR 985, para 91; *Ilascu v Moldova and Russia* [2005] 40 EHRR 46, paras 310–19, 376–94; *Issa et al. v Turkey* [2004] 41 EHRR 567, para 71; *Cyprus v Turkey* [2002] 35 EHRR 30, para 78. See also General Comment No 31 adopted by the UN Committee for Human Rights, UN Doc HRI/GEN/1/Rev7, 192 at 194ff, para 10, and generally Milanovic, *Extraterritorial Application of Human Rights Treaties* (Oxford, 2011); Loucaides, *European Human Rights LR* (2006) 391; Gondek, 52 *Neths ILR* (2005) 349; Scheinin, in Coomans and Kamminga (eds), *Extraterritorial Application of Human Rights Treaties* (Antwerp, 2004) 73; Meron, 89 *AJIL* (1995) 78.

[257] For a fuller treatment see Boyle, 23 *EJIL* (2012) 613; Augenstein, in Morgera (ed), *The External Environmental Policy of the EU* (Cambridge, 2012) 278–84.

[258] *Infra*, section 3(2).

[259] As they would have to be in transboundary environmental impact assessments: see 1991 Espoo Convention, Article 3(8).

[260] *Hatton v UK* [2003] ECtHR (Grand Chamber).

benefit, and must adopt and enforce environmental protection laws for their benefit, as well as for the protection of its own population.[261]

Secondly, while it is less plausible to say that the polluting state 'controls' the territory of the state affected by pollution,[262] it is entirely plausible to conclude that victims of transboundary pollution fall within the 'jurisdiction' of the polluting state—in the most straightforward sense of legal jurisdiction. In this context the State is most likely to violate the human rights of those affected extraterritorially if it does not permit them equal access to environmental information and participation in EIA and permitting procedures, or if it denies access to adequate and effective remedies within its own legal system.[263] The jurisdiction of national courts to hear cases involving transboundary harm to extraterritorial plaintiffs is well-established in private international law and in environmental liability conventions.[264] There is little point requiring that national remedies be made available to transboundary claimants if they cannot also resort to international or regional human rights law when necessary to compel the polluting state to enforce its own court orders or laws, or to assess and take adequate account of the extraterritorially harmful effects of activities which it authorises and regulates. Thus, transboundary claimants should be entitled to equal access to environmental information, participation in EIA and other authorisation procedures, and access to justice in the national courts of the state in which the harmful activity is located. In Europe those rights for transboundary claimants are already recognised by the 1998 Aarhus Convention. Article 3(9) requires that 'the public shall have access to information, have the possibility to participate in decision-making and have access to justice in environmental matters *without discrimination as to citizenship, nationality or domicile* and, in the case of a legal person, without discrimination as to where it has its registered seat or an effective centre of its activities.'[265]

In an important *Advisory Opinion* delivered in 2017 the IACtHR concluded that in cases of transboundary harm 'a person is subject to the jurisdiction of the State of origin if there is a causal connection between the incident that took place on its territory and the violation of the human rights of persons outside its territory.'[266] The Court's Opinion refers in particular to the obligation to conduct an EIA, to facilitate

261 ILA, Committee on Transnational Enforcement of Environmental Law, Final Rept, Rule 2, and commentary, *Rept of 72nd Conference* (Toronto, 2006); OECD Council Recommendations and Knox (2002) 96 *AJIL* 291.

262 But significant transboundary pollution is arguably a violation of the permanent sovereignty of a state (and its people) over their own natural resources, and in a serious case might amount to a de facto expropriation: see the Preamble to the 2001 ILC Draft Articles on Prevention of Transboundary Harm from Hazardous Activities, ILC Rept (2001), GAOR A/56/10, and *SERAC v Nigeria*, ACHPR (2002) para 55.

263 See Principle 6(1), ILC Draft principles on the allocation of loss in the case of transboundary harm arising out of hazardous activities, ILC Rept (2006), GAOR A/61/10, paras 51–67. See also 1998 Aarhus Convention, Articles 3(9) and 9(4).

264 *Infra*, section 3.

265 See UNECE, *The Århus Convention-An Implementation Guide* (New York, 2014).

266 *Advisory Opinion on Environment and Human Rights*, IACtHR (2017) paras 103 and 104 (h); translation from Official Summary, para II(h).

access to information, public participation, and access to justice.[267] At the very least this suggests that transboundary claimants in Latin America now have the same rights as under the 1998 Aarhus Convention. Quite how broad the Court's Opinion is intended to be remains to be seen, but it takes the 1969 Inter-American Convention some way towards the position adopted by Ecuador in the *Aerial Spraying* case of saying that a state has an obligation to protect the human rights of those affected by transboundary pollution for which that state is responsible.[268] There is, however, a contrast here with the 2018 ECLAC Agreement, Article 2(d) of which defines 'public' to mean natural or legal persons who are 'nationals or that are subject to the national jurisdiction of the State Party.' This allows no scope for transboundary claimants.

2(8) CONCLUSIONS

The environmental caseload of human rights courts and treaty bodies indicates the importance of the topic in mainstream human rights law. The case law shows that human rights treaties guarantee everything a right to a *healthy* environment would normally be thought to cover if by that we mean human health. Through evolutionary interpretation they also guarantee in various ways the rights of access to environmental information, public participation in decision-making, and access to justice. The European, African, and Inter-American precedents are relevant to the interpretation of comparable rights in global human-rights conventions, and Principle 10 of the Rio Declaration would also sustain reading into the UN Covenants the procedural requirements found in the 1998 Aarhus Convention. The UNHRC special rapporteur has reached the same conclusion.[269]

The role of human rights law in democratising national decision-making processes and making them more rational, open and legitimate will become more, not less, significant when implementing international law on sustainable development, protection of biodiversity, and mitigation of climate change. Public participation, as foreseen in UNCED Agenda 21, is thus a central element in sustainable development and the High Commissioner for Human Rights is right to say so. The incorporation of Aarhus-style procedural rights into general human rights law significantly advances this objective. So do the strong provisions on public and NGO participation adopted by European states in the 2003 Protocol on Strategic Environmental Assessment.[270] They take the notion of public interest participation further even than the 1998 Aarhus Convention. This approach is appropriate if what constitutes sustainable development and an acceptable environment is essentially a matter for each society to determine according to its own values and choices, albeit within the confines of internationally agreed rules and policies and subject to some degree of international oversight. In that sense, the inclusion of Principle 10 in the Rio Declaration, combined with a 'greening' of existing

267 *Ibid*, para 103.
268 See Memorial and Reply of Ecuador, ICJ (2013).
269 *Supra*, section 2(3)(a).
270 *Supra*, section 2(6)(c).

human-rights law, is arguably of greater significance than the omission of an explicit right to a sustainable or ecologically sound environment.

Articulating a right to a sustainable or ecologically sound environment within the context of economic, social and cultural rights is not inherently problematic. Doing so would give greater weight to the public interest in protecting the global environment, promoting sustainable development, and mitigating climate change. This could be achieved within a process of 'constructive dialogue' with governments rather than through litigation in courts, in a manner which fully respects the wide margin of appreciation that states are entitled to exercise when balancing economic, environmental and social policy objectives. It would thereby legitimise the role of the UNCESCR in this context, without damaging the fabric of human rights law. It would build on existing precedents under the ICESCR, and reflect international policy on sustainable development endorsed at Rio in 1992, in subsequent international conferences, and in the 2015 Paris Agreement. The policies of individual states on energy use, reduction of greenhouse gas emissions, land use and deforestation could be scrutinised against the evidence of their global impact on human rights and the environment. The further elaboration of procedural rights, based on the 1998 Aarhus Convention, would facilitate implementation of such an approach, and give greater prominence globally to the role of NGOs in public interest litigation and advocacy. These two developments go hand in hand. In contrast, international human rights courts would remain limited to the protection of individual civil and political rights. They are ill-suited to broader forms of public interest environmental litigation for which other bodies, including national courts acting within their own constitutional mandate, are better equipped.

3 TRANSBOUNDARY ENVIRONMENTAL LITIGATION

3(1) INTRODUCTION

The problems of resorting to public international law to deal with transboundary environmental disputes have been explored in previous chapters: the lack of a forum with universal compulsory jurisdiction, the need to show a breach of due diligence by the state, and the reluctance of states to deal with environmental disputes in this way. These problems have not so far been significantly mitigated by the International Law Commission either in its work on state responsibility or international liability.

It is against this background that we can now examine the somewhat greater progress in opening up national legal systems to transboundary environmental litigation, particularly in Europe and North America, but also through civil liability conventions covering ultra-hazardous activities, such as oil transportation or nuclear power. There are three good reasons for encouraging resort to private-law remedies in transboundary environmental disputes. First, it de-escalates disputes 'to their ordinary neighbourhood level',[271] where they can be resolved using national law, and avoids turning them into interstate controversies based on problematic concepts of state responsibility in international law. Secondly, by allowing direct recourse against the enterprise causing the damage, it facilitates implementation of a 'polluter pays' approach to the allocation of environmental costs. A policy of internalizing the true economic costs of pollution is endorsed in Principle 16 of the Rio Declaration and by the OECD.[272] Thirdly, it empowers individuals by enabling the private plaintiff to act without the intervention of a government, and to that extent facilitates further development of a rights-based approach to environmental issues. This is consistent in general terms with the policy, considered earlier in this chapter, of promoting environmental rights through '[e]ffective access to judicial and administrative proceedings, including redress and remedy' in accordance with Principle 10 of the Rio Declaration. Moreover, a policy of encouraging resort to transboundary civil litigation and remedies recognizes the reality that many, if not most, transboundary environmental problems are mainly caused by and affect private parties, rather than states as such. In this context transboundary litigation not only provides an effective mechanism for dealing with transboundary harm, but may also offer the possibility of securing redress from multinationals whose operations in developing countries are sometimes difficult to control through local law.

Encouraging the solution of transboundary problems through national law also has disadvantages, which must be recognized. There may be no remedy, or no effective remedy, if the applicable legal system is favourable to the activities of polluters. No common legal standards will necessarily govern the availability of remedies in different states unless there is parallel progress in harmonizing environmental standards and liability for damage. Even where adequate laws exist, problems of jurisdiction, the availability of remedies and enforcement in transboundary cases may limit the usefulness of this form of litigation. Public and private international law can have a role in securing access to justice by removing some or all of these disadvantages and by ensuring that adequate national remedies are available to plaintiffs in transboundary cases. These objectives can be achieved in a variety of ways, but will usually involve addressing some or all of the following elements:

- non-discriminatory treatment of transboundary plaintiffs and equal access to available national procedures and remedies;
- resolving problems of private international law, particularly jurisdiction and choice of law in transboundary cases;
- harmonization of national laws dealing with liability for environmental damage.

[271] Sand, *Lessons learned in Global Environmental Governance* (New York, 1990) 31. For a succinct survey of the problems of transboundary litigation in environmental disputes see McCaffrey, in Von Bar (ed), *Internationales Umwelthaftungsrecht I* (Köln, 1995) 81.

[272] OECD, Council Recommendations C (72)128; C (74)223; C (89) 88 and C (90) 177. On the polluter pays principle, see *infra*, section 4(4).

3(2) EQUAL ACCESS TO NATIONAL REMEDIES

(a) The principle

Equality of access to transboundary remedies and procedures is based on the principle of non-discrimination: where domestic remedies are already available to deal with internal pollution or environmental problems, international or regional law can be used to ensure that the benefit of these remedies and procedures is extended to transboundary claimants. As defined by the OECD,[273] equal access and non-discrimination should ensure that any person who has suffered transboundary environmental damage or who is exposed to a significant risk of such damage obtains at least equivalent treatment to that afforded to individuals in the country of origin. This includes the provision of and access to information concerning transboundary environmental risks; participation in hearings, preliminary enquiries and the opportunity to make objections; and resort to administrative and judicial procedures in order to prevent pollution, secure its abatement, or obtain compensation—in other words, access to justice.[274] These rights of equal access are to be accorded not only to individuals affected by the risk of transboundary injury but also to foreign NGOs and public authorities, insofar as comparable entities possess such rights in the country of origin of the pollution.

The principle of non-discrimination as defined by the OECD also entails giving equivalent treatment to the domestic and transboundary effects of polluting activities, and requires that polluters causing transboundary pollution should be subject to legal standards no less severe than would apply to pollution with domestic effects only. In effect, transboundary pollution should not, under this principle, exceed levels that would be considered acceptable if occurring within the country of origin. To a limited extent Canadian and US legislation accepts the OECD's non-discrimination standard. Section 115 of the US Clean Air Act[275] permits the administrator of the US Environmental Protection Agency to direct US state governments to take stronger air-pollution abatement measures where an 'international agency' or the Secretary of State believes that pollution emanating from these states is endangering health and welfare in a foreign country. This provision was invoked by the EPA in 1980 on the basis of a report of the International Joint Commission concerning air pollution of the Great Lakes. However, the discretionary nature of the legislation meant that it was not a reliable mechanism for ensuring that Canadian interests received equal, or any, consideration in the control of US air pollution.[276] The Canadian Clean Air Act is intended

273 OECD Council Recommendations C74 (224); C (76) 55; C (77) 28, in OECD, *OECD and the Environment* (Paris, 1986). See generally McCaffrey, 1 *EPL* (1975) 1; Smets, 9 *EPL* (1982) 110; Willheim, 7 *AYIL* (1976) 174.

274 *Supra*, section 2(6) and see generally Francioni, *Access to Justice as a Human Right*, Ch 1.

275 42 USC 7415. See Schmandt, Clarkson, and Roderick, *Acid Rain and Friendly Neighbors* (Durham, NC, 1988) 226f.

276 *New York v Thomas*, 802 F 2d 1443, reversing 613 F Suppl 1472 (1985); *HM Queen in Right of Ontario* v *US*, 912 F 2d 1525 (1990). The US finally responded to Canadian complaints by amending the federal Clean Air Act in 1990.

to provide reciprocal protection for the US. Article 2 of the 1974 Nordic Convention also requires parties to equate domestic and transboundary nuisances when considering the permissibility of environmentally harmful activities.[277] As we noted earlier, human-rights law points in the same direction when balancing the interests of the community at large against the impact on the rights of particular individuals.

(b) Non-discrimination and equal access in international law

Although non-discrimination was included in the legal principles on environmental protection proposed by the WCED, this body concluded that it was still an 'emerging principle of international law', at least in the context of transboundary environmental claims.[278] International policy declarations, including the Stockholm and Rio Declarations, do not explicitly refer to equal access, nor do they demonstrate clear support for the principle of non-discrimination. However, given the ILC's consistent endorsement of the non-discrimination principle in a transboundary environmental context, and other precedents considered below, it can probably be assumed that it already reflects existing international law.[279] Article 15 of the ILC's 2001 Articles on Prevention of Transboundary Harm prohibits discrimination based on nationality, residence, or place of injury in granting access to judicial or other procedures, or compensation, in cases of significant transboundary harm.[280] Article 32 of the 1997 UN Watercourses Convention is comparable.[281] Both allow victims of transboundary pollution or damage to have direct recourse to local remedies in the state where the source of the harm is located. The rule as formulated by the ILC is residual. States are thus free to deal with questions of transboundary justice in some other way if they agree.[282] As we shall see below, an altogether different approach has been adopted in regional and global treaties dealing with liability for damage, including accidents involving oil tankers and nuclear installations.

[277] *Infra*, this section, part (c). It also makes provision for reciprocal access by administrative agencies to regulatory or licensing procedures.

[278] Munro and Lammers, *Environmental Protection and Sustainable Development* (London, 1986) 88. See *supra*, Ch 3, section 5(7).

[279] Smets, *Rev Eur Droit de l'Env* (2000) 3. In *Juridical Situation and Rights of Undocumented Migrants* (17 September 2003) I/A Court HR, OC-18/03, para 83, the IACHR held that 'the fundamental principle of equality and non-discrimination constitutes a part of general international law .... [it] has entered the realm of jus cogens.'

[280] See also the ILC's 2006 Principles on Allocation of Loss, Principle 8(2) *infra*, section 4(3).

[281] The inclusion of this article was questioned by several states, including India, Russia and Tanzania: see McCaffrey, 92 *AJIL* (1998) 97, 104. See also 1909 US–Canada Boundary Waters Treaty, Article 2, but compare *Soucheray and Ors v US Corps of Engineers*, 483 F Supp 352, denying relief on the ground that no action lay in respect of IJC decisions under this treaty; ILA, Montreal Rules on Water Pollution in an International Drainage Basin, 1982, Article 8; id, Helsinki Rules on Private Law Remedies for Transboundary Damage in International Watercourses, 1996, Articles 1–3, and *infra*, Ch 10.

[282] ILC Rept (2001) Prevention of Transboundary Harm, commentary to Article 15, para (4).

Discriminatory restrictions on transboundary access to justice may also violate the right to a fair trial under Article 6(1) of the 1950 ECHR,[283] or under Article 14 of the 1966 ICCPR, which specifically states: 'All persons shall be equal before the courts and tribunals'.

Insofar as it is possible to review the state practice on such a disparate topic, it is not easy to point to any clear picture. There are rules in some national legal systems which are difficult to reconcile with equality of access, such as the principle of *forum non conveniens*, the denial of jurisdiction in actions affecting foreign land, or the refusal to allow transboundary access to administrative proceedings on the ground that national legislation does not have extraterritorial application. At the same time there is significant regional support for equality of access to justice, and some undoubted examples of its application.

(c) Regional provision for equal access to remedies

It is mainly at regional level, in Europe and North America, that equal access and non-discrimination have received significant support. The OECD and the UNECE are the principal international organizations to have elaborated the content of the principle in detail and to have relied on it as an important element in the development of international environmental policy and law. Although the OECD's recommendations and decisions in this respect are not binding, they have had some influence on arrangements among certain member states, most notably in the 1974 Nordic Convention for the Protection of the Environment,[284] and in conventions adopted by the UNECE. Its 1991 Espoo Convention requires that members of the public in the affected state be given the equivalent opportunity to participate in relevant environmental impact assessment procedures available to the public in the party of origin.[285] The 1992 Convention on the Transboundary Effects of Industrial Accidents 'underlines' the principle of non-discrimination, reiterates the Espoo Convention's provision for equivalent access to procedures, and affords reciprocal access to justice.[286] Last, but most importantly, as we saw earlier, Article 3(9) of the 1998 Aarhus Convention requires the parties to afford access to information, justice, and decision-making without discrimination as to citizenship, domicile or place of registration or business. Because of this convention's extensive impact on the provision of domestic remedies and procedures, this article is potentially the most significant legal basis for claims of equal access in transboundary cases in UNECE states. In particular, it may ensure that cases are not dismissed on grounds of *forum non conveniens*, and may also limit denial of jurisdiction on grounds of extraterritoriality.

283 See *Lubbe v Cape plc* [2000] 1 WLR 1545, *supra*.

284 Kiss, 20 *AFDI* (1978) 808; Broms, in Flinterman, Kwiatkowska, and Lammers (eds), *Transboundary Air Pollution* (Dordrecht, 1986) 141; Phillips, *ibid*, 153; Ebbeson, in Hollo and Marttinen (eds), *North European Environmental Law* (Helsinki, 1995) 41. Only one case is recorded: *Saugbruksforeningen Case, Norsk Retstidende* (1992) 1618. Public-interest litigants do not have standing in Sweden but do in Norway. See Ebbeson, *loc cit*.

285 Article 2(6). See Ch 3 section 7.

286 Preamble and Article 9.

EU law does not explicitly provide for equal access, but the Regulation on Jurisdiction and the Recognition and Enforcement of Judgments in Civil and Commercial Matters ('Brussels I *bis* Reg')[287] has the effect of securing access to justice for transboundary litigants, and of precluding reliance on exclusionary doctrines such as *forum non conveniens* and non-recognition of foreign judgments. It will be considered further below. In North America the Commission established by the 1993 NAAEC has power to make recommendations on reciprocal access to courts and administrative agencies, but the agreement otherwise contains no non-discrimination clause.[288] It is possible that Article 6, which provides for 'interested persons' to have access to legal remedies for violation of environmental laws, may also apply to transboundary litigants. Ontario has made use of provisions in the US Clean Air Act allowing citizen suits for violation of Federal environmental standards while the Trans-Alaska Pipeline Act explicitly permits transboundary plaintiffs to do so.[289] A model Uniform Transboundary Pollution Reciprocal Access Act is also intended to remove jurisdictional limits on actions for transboundary damage, but it has been not been adopted in either Washington state or British Columbia, the two jurisdictions involved in the *Trail Smelter* dispute.[290]

The effect of these developments is that in North America and Europe transboundary legal proceedings have become a feasible, though still uncommon, method for recovering damages for air and water pollution injury affecting plaintiffs in other states. A good example is the litigation resulting from the Sandoz chemical spillage in the Rhine, which was successfully handled without any resort to interstate claims or international proceedings.[291] There is less information on the treatment of transboundary plaintiffs in other regions of the world, and especially in developing countries. However, the Pulp Mills dispute has shown that Argentine citizens enjoy equal

[287] The current version is Regulation 1215/2012, OJL 351/1 ('Brussels I *bis* Reg'), regulating proceedings instituted in the courts of EU Member States on or after 10 January 2015.

[288] 1993 NAAEC, Article 10(9). Canada, Mexico, and the US are parties to the agreement. See Knox, in Markell and Knox (eds), *Greening NAFTA: The North American Commission for Environmental Cooperation* (Stanford, 2003) Ch 5.

[289] See *Her Majesty the Queen in Right of Ontario v US Environmental Protection Agency*, 912 F 2d 1525(1990); Ontario's application for review of EPA action was refused: its standing to bring the action was not challenged or considered. See also Clean Air Act, 42 USC § 7415 and 7604; Clean Water Act, 33 USC § 1365(a) and (g); although these acts make no reference to transboundary plaintiffs, in *Pfizer Inc v Govt of India*, 434 US 308 (1978) the Supreme Court held that a foreign state is a 'person' for the purpose of entitlement to sue under anti-trust law. The Trans Alaska Pipeline Authorization Act, 43 USC § 1635(c)(1) allows 'any person or entity, public or private, *including those resident in Canada*' (emphasis added) to invoke the Act's liability provisions. See generally Hsu and Parrish, 48 *VJIL* (2007) 1.

[290] Adopted 1982 and implemented in Colorado, Connecticut, Manitoba, Michigan, Montana, New Jersey, Nova Scotia, Ontario, Oregon, Prince Edward Island, South Dakota, and Wisconsin. Text in *Uniform Laws Annotated*, vol 9B. See Rosencrantz, 15 *EPL* (1985) 105; Bernasconi, *Hague YIL* (1999) 35, 105–6; McCaffrey, in Von Bar (ed), *Internationales Umwelthaftungsrecht I*, 81, 85–6.

[291] See D'Oliviera, in Francioni and Scovazzi (eds), *International Responsibility for Environmental Harm* (Dordrecht, 1991) 429; *Michie v Great Lakes Steel Division* 495 F 2d 213 (1974); Ianni, *CYIL* (1973) 258; this case simply assumed without discussion that Canadian plaintiffs could bring a tort action for transboundary air pollution in the US.

access to remedies and procedures under Uruguayan law in respect of possible transboundary harm.[292] A protocol to the 1991 MERCOSUR Convention also provides for equal access to judicial procedures throughout the member states.[293]

(d) Implementation of a policy of equal access

Impediments to equal access primarily involve procedural and jurisdictional obstacles. One example is a rule found in some legal systems which denies jurisdiction over actions involving foreign land. In some cases it applies only to actions concerning title or trespass to land, but in others it includes extraterritorial effects of activities within the territory of the forum.[294] There is no obvious reason in principle why a forum in which activities causing transboundary damage are situated should refuse jurisdiction merely because the effects are extraterritorial, but it is this rule which explains why the *Trail Smelter Case* was referred not to the Canadian courts but to international arbitration.[295] The US–Canadian Uniform Transboundary Reciprocal Access Act was intended to remove this problem.[296] In *Aguinda v Texaco Inc*,[297] a US case involving oil spills and environmental damage in Ecuador, it was held that the local action rule is inapplicable under US Federal law where the case does not involve title to land or trespass, but may be relevant if the action relates closely to a specific piece of land. The problem is not significant in transboundary tort cases in Europe due in part to the jurisdictional provisions of the EU Regulation on Jurisdiction and the Recognition and Enforcement of Judgments, considered below, but it remains an obstacle in common-law jurisdictions outside Europe.

A more significant obstacle to equal access for the transboundary litigant in US law is the discretionary power of courts to dismiss cases on the ground that a foreign forum is a more appropriate venue for trial. Thus, even if it can be established that a national court does have jurisdiction, it does not follow that it will necessarily exercise it. The principle of *forum non conveniens*[298] allows the court to look at all the relevant factors in order to decide which legal system is better placed to decide the case. In the Bhopal litigation,[299] the US courts declined to hear Indian claims against Union Carbide because, in their view, the Indian courts were a more appropriate forum.

[292] See 1988 General Code of Procedure.

[293] 1992 Las Leñas Protocol on Jurisdictional Cooperation and Assistance, Ch III, Article 3.

[294] See e.g. *British South Africa Company v Compania de Moçambique* [1893] AC 602; *Hesperides Hotels Ltd v Muftizade* [1979] AC 508; *Albert v Frazer Companies Ltd* [1937] 1 DLR 39; *Dagi v Broken Hill Proprietary Co Ltd* (1997) 1 Victoria Reps 428. UK courts now have jurisdiction over torts affecting immovable property outside the UK under s 30 of the 1982 Civil Jurisdiction and Judgments Act. See generally Bernasconi, *Hague YIL* (1999) 102–6; OECD, *Legal Aspects of Transfrontier Pollution*, 98–102; McCaffrey, 3 *CWILJ* (1973) 191.

[295] Read, 1 *CYIL* (1963) 222. [296] *Supra*, n 289. [297] 850 F Supp 282 (1994).

[298] *Piper Aircraft Co v Reyno* 454 US 235 (1981); *Spiliada Maritime Corp v Cansulex Ltd* [1987] AC 460; *Connelly v RTZ Corp plc* [1998] AC 854. See Fawcett, *Declining Jurisdiction in Private International Law* (Oxford, 1995); Robertson, 103 *LQR* (1987) 398; id, 29 *Texas ILJ* (1994) 353; Weintraub, 29 *Texas ILJ* (1994) 321; Brand, 37 *Texas ILJ* (2002) 467.

[299] *In re Union Carbide Corporation Gas Plant Disaster at Bhopal* 634 F Supp 842 (1986); 809 F 2d 195 (1987); Muchlinski, 50 *MLR* (1987) 545.

The plaintiffs were Indian, most of the evidence was in India, the applicable law was likely to be Indian, and India had the stronger interest in setting appropriate standards of care. It was not, the court held, a matter of determining the most favourable forum for the plaintiff, but of balancing the public and private interests. The US courts had no public interest in trying cases brought against US corporations for their activities abroad. In effect, the judgment ensured that the plaintiffs' claims would never come before a court in either country, and left Union Carbide free to negotiate a very favourable settlement with the Indian government.

In *Aguinda,*[300] a US district court was persuaded that Ecuador was the more appropriate forum, on grounds similar to those relied on in *Union Carbide*. The *forum non conveniens* doctrine as applied in these cases thus discriminates against foreign plaintiffs while at the same time protecting the forum's own companies from liability for their actions abroad.[301] This may not matter as between developed countries, but when the plaintiffs are from developing countries it may in some cases amount to a denial of justice if no effective local redress is available, or if the plaintiffs are prevented by intimidation, corruption, civil war, or cost from resorting to local courts. Moreover, as we saw earlier, because of its inherently discriminatory character, dismissal on grounds of *forum non conveniens* may be incompatible with a number of UNECE treaties, most notably the 1998 Aarhus Convention. In some circumstances it is also arguably a breach of the right to a fair hearing of a civil claim guaranteed by a number of human-rights conventions, including Article 6 of the 1950 ECHR.[302]

Not all jurisdictions are as hostile to the human-rights and denial of justice issues as US courts appear to be. When persuaded that justice so requires, the UK's highest court has declined to dismiss actions on *forum non conveniens* grounds, for example where no legal aid or financial assistance would be available to enable a suit to be brought abroad.[303] In other common law jurisdictions the test for dismissal may also be stricter than in the US. Whereas American courts apply a US public-interest test, Australian courts require an abuse of process and will dismiss an action only if the defendant can show that Australia is clearly an inappropriate forum on this ground. Thus, in circumstances similar to Bhopal, indigenous peoples harmed by Australian mining operations in New Guinea, and denied access to justice there, were able to bring proceedings in Australia.[304] On the other hand American case law does provide

300 *Aguinda v Texaco Inc* 945 F Supp 625 (1996). The case was reinstated on appeal in 1998.

301 Bookman, 67 *Stanford LR* (2015) 1081; Prince, 47 *ICLQ* (1998) 573; Robertson, 103 *LQR* (1987) 398.

302 See also 1966 ICCPR, Article 14. The point was argued before but not decided by the UK House of Lords in *Lubbe v Cape plc* [2000] 1 WLR 1545. See *Axen v Federal Republic of Germany* (1983) ECtHR Ser A, No 72; *Dombo Beheer v Netherlands* (1993) ECtHR Ser A, No 274 and Fawcett, (2007) 56 *ICLQ* 1, 39–41.

303 *Connelly v RTZ Corp plc* [1998] AC 854; *Lubbe v Cape plc* [2000] 1 WLR 1545. See Muchlinski, 50 *ICLQ* (2001) 1; Ward, 12 *YbIEL* (2001) 105.

304 *Dagi v Broken Hill Proprietary Co Ltd* (1997) 1 Victoria Reps 428; see Prince, 47 *ICLQ* (1998) 573. On the 'clearly inappropriate forum' test see *Voth v Manildra Flour Mills* (1990) 171 CLR 538. In *Lubbe v Cape plc* [2000] 1 WLR 1545, the UK House of Lords rejected the view that public policy questions of the kind considered decisive in the Bhopal litigation had any role to play. See in particular the judgment of Lord Hope, Muchlinski, 50 *ICLQ* (2001) 1 and Ward, 12 *YbIEL* (2001) 105.

some limit on excessive jurisdictional claims over extraterritorial events with little or no connection to the forum and relieves judges of the burden of hearing sometimes complex cases that would be better heard locally.[305]

Forum non conveniens is unknown in civil-law systems, which exercise a more restrained jurisdiction than under common law, and it is incompatible with EU law on civil jurisdiction.[306] Courts in an EU member state thus have jurisdiction over companies domiciled in that state even for torts or delicts committed abroad; such proceedings may, however, still fail at the jurisdictional stage if the applicant cannot show an arguable case that the parent company exercised a sufficient degree of control over its overseas subsidiaries to be liable for any pollution or environmental damage they may have caused.[307]

(e) The limitations of equal access

The evident advantages of opening up local remedies to foreign parties as a means of settling transboundary disputes must be set against certain weaknesses or disadvantages inherent in what is a relatively limited form of access to justice. These problems need to be appreciated to understand why it is necessary to go beyond equal access if a satisfactory regional or international approach is sought:

- Equal access guarantees no substantive standard of environmental protection, and no procedural rights of any kind save to the extent that these are already available for domestic claimants.
- Equal access does not solve the problems of choice of law which arise in transboundary litigation.
- Equal access to a foreign forum may be disadvantageous on various grounds of inconvenience, language, unfamiliarity, and the plaintiff may be better off suing in his own domestic jurisdiction.

Why then, should the plaintiff be forced to sue abroad? The answer to this is that equal access to the polluting jurisdiction does not preclude access to any other forum: it leaves open the issue of jurisdiction and choice of forum in private international law, just as it does not resolve the question of choice of law. It is to these issues that we can now turn.

3(3) PRIVATE INTERNATIONAL LAW ISSUES IN TRANSBOUNDARY ENVIRONMENTAL LITIGATION

(a) Choice of law

Given that a claim for transboundary environmental damage may involve events, impacts, and persons in several countries, and possibly on the high seas, the question which legal system should determine liability and other issues is a real and important one.

305 See Muchlinski, 50 *ICLQ* (2001) 1.

306 *Owusu v Jackson* (2005) ECJ C-281/02;

307 Compare *Lungowe v Vedanta Resources Plc* [2017] EWCA Civ 1528, with *Okpabi v Royal Dutch Shell Plc* [2018] EWCA Civ 191.

One study in 1992 showed that as regards choice of law in transboundary environmental claims there was 'no discernible consensus'.[308] Things have changed in Europe, but otherwise the situation elsewhere remains much the same.

There are various possibilities, each of which is adopted in a number of legal systems:

i) The forum applies the law of the place where the harmful activity is located. This allows the legal consequences to be regulated by the jurisdiction within whose territory the activity takes place and gives legal effect to administrative licensing or statutory authorization by that state.
ii) The forum applies the law of the place where the injury occurred. This solution is one of those now adopted by EU law,[309] and is consistent with the application of Dutch law by the Dutch Court of Appeal in the *Handelskwekerij* litigation,[310] which arose out of pollution of the Rhine by a French company. However, applying the law of the place of injury may make it more difficult to integrate with administrative or statutory authorization by the state where the harmful activity is located.[311]
iii) The forum applies the law of the place in which the defendant company is domiciled or has its principal place of business. Some common-law countries are more likely to apply their own law if the defendant is domiciled or has its business there.
iv) The forum applies whichever is the more favourable law for the plaintiff, the so-called 'ubiquity' principle. This approach is adopted in German, Swiss, and Portuguese law, and it has also been adopted for environmental damage in EU law.[312]

Each of these choices has advantages and disadvantages, and no attempt will be made here to assess which represents the best approach. But the problem with a diversity of choice of law rules, and the lack of any global consensus, is that they add to the unpredictability, complexity, and expense of transboundary litigation, and are in that sense obstacles to better transboundary access to environmental justice. Moreover, it does not follow that a court will apply the same choice of law to all aspects of the case before it. US courts have often applied US law to determine the liability of American

[308] Kreuzer, 44 *Rev Espanola DI* (1992) 57. See also Hague Conference on Private International Law, *Note on the Law Applicable to Civil Liability for Environmental Damage* (1992); Beaumont, *Juridical Review* (1995) 28; Bernasconi, *Hague YIL* (1999) 74–88; Von Bar, 268 *Recueil des Cours* (1997) 303; ILA, *70th Conference Rept* (2004) 896.

[309] EU Regulation No 864/2007 on Non-Contractual Obligations (Rome II) Article 4.

[310] *Handelskwekerij GJ Bier and Stichting Reinwater v Mines de Potasse d'Alsace*, Repted in 19 *NYIL* (1988) 496.

[311] For an example of the problems see *Pakootas v Teck Cominco Metals Ltd* 452 F 3d 1066 (2006) ['*Trail Smelter II*'].

[312] Rome II Regulation, Article 7; Swiss Private International Law Act, 1987, Article 138. On Germany and Portugal see Kreuzer, 44 *Rev Espanola DI* (1992) 64–5. The Hague Conference on Private International Law considered whether to negotiate a convention to harmonize choice of law in transboundary environmental suits: see Bernasconi, *Hague YIL* (1999) 35; Beaumont, *Juridical Review* (1995) 28; Von Bar (ed), *Internationales Umwelthaftungsrecht I* (Köln, 1995).

defendants but then applied the plaintiff's legal system when it comes to assessing the compensation due. This is what happened in the *Amoco Cadiz Case*,[313] denying US damages to French plaintiffs.

Other possible approaches include giving the plaintiff a choice of forum, or undertaking measures to harmonize substantive liability in national law.

(b) Jurisdiction and 'forum shopping'

Transboundary environmental damage cases may involve elements in several countries. For that reason, private international law will often afford victims of transboundary harm a choice of forum in which to sue. The general principle most widely accepted is that proceedings may be brought (i) in the courts of the place where damage occurs (i.e. the transboundary victim's own state) or (ii) in the place where harmful activity is located, or (iii) in the place where the defendant is domiciled.[314] There is no consensus on whether jurisdiction is mandatory in these circumstances or may nevertheless be declined, and no agreement has been possible in negotiations on a global jurisdiction convention.

Jurisdiction will generally exist in the courts of the defendant's residence, domicile or place of business.[315] There may, however, be exceptions to this general rule. As we saw above when discussing equality of access to justice, in some legal systems extra-territorial environmental damage is excluded from the jurisdiction of courts outside the state where the injury occurs, while in others the principle of *forum non conveniens* is resorted to as a means of declining jurisdiction over actions brought by foreigners.

Jurisdiction will usually also exist in the place where the injury occurs, as for example in *Aguinda v Texaco* and in the Bhopal case, where there was no doubt that Ecuador and India respectively had territorial jurisdiction. Similarly, in the *Trail Smelter II* litigation, US courts held a Canadian company potentially liable under US legislation for transboundary damage caused by water pollution emanating from a smelter in Canada.[316] By virtue of international liability conventions pollution incidents at sea also fall under the jurisdiction of the courts of the states where the damage occurs.[317] The same is true under EU law, which in matters relating to tort or delict gives special jurisdiction to the courts of the place 'where the harmful event occurred or may occur'.[318] But it cannot be assumed that this is always the general rule. In US

313 *In re Oil Spill by Amoco Cadiz* 954 F 2d 1279 (1992). See generally Lowenfeld, *International Litigation and the Quest for Reasonableness* (Oxford, 1996) 86–90.

314 See respectively *Handelskwekerij GJ Bier v Mines de Potasse d'Alsace*, Case 21/76 [1976] II ECJ Reports, 1735; *Re Union Carbide Corporation* 634 F Supp 842 (1986); *In re Oil Spill by Amoco Cadiz* 954 F 2d 1279 (1992). All three jurisdictional bases are recognized by Articles 4 and 7 of the Brussels I *bis* Regulation, by the 2003 Kiev Protocol on Civil Liability and Compensation, Article 13, and by the 1993 Convention on Civil Liability for Damage to the Environment, Article 19. See generally 2006 ILA Conference Rept, Committee on Transnational Enforcement of Environmental Law, 664–5.

315 E.g. Brussels I *bis* Regulation, Article 4. See generally McLachlan and Nygh (eds), *Transnational Tort Litigation* (Oxford, 1996) esp Chs 1, 4, 12.

316 *Pakootas v Teck Cominco Metals Ltd* 452 F 3d 1066 (2006). See generally Hsu and Parrish, 48 *VJIL* (2007) 1.

317 See *infra*, Ch 9.

318 Brussels I *bis* Regulation, Article 7.

law there is some doubt as to whether it is constitutional to assert jurisdiction when injury in the US is merely fortuitous, and there are no other significant connecting factors, such as the place of business. If product liability cases are an apt analogy, which is far from certain, it would be necessary to show some 'purposeful direction' of transboundary pollutants, for example by locating a smelter or nuclear plant close to a border.[319]

A plaintiff who litigates where the damage occurs, rather than where the defendant is located, may also have to overcome the defence of sovereign immunity, if the enterprise responsible for the damage is part of a foreign state rather than a separate commercial entity. Some states now deny immunity from suit where the tort is deemed to have taken place within their own territory, or where it is not committed 'in the exercise of sovereign authority'.[320] The latter point could be relied on to exclude immunity for most state operated industrial activities on the ground that they are *iure gestionis*, which is the view taken by German and Austrian courts when the Soviet Union was sued in respect of the Chernobyl disaster.[321] Article 12 of the 2004 UN Convention on State Immunity, which deals with liability for loss or damage, would thus become relevant only if the activity causing transboundary harm is potentially entitled to immunity as an exercise of sovereign authority.[322] However, Article 12 would not apply to most cases of transboundary environmental harm because the 'author of the act or omission' would not normally be present in the forum state when the harm was caused. It follows that sovereign immunity is unlikely to be a serious obstacle to transboundary tort litigation in cases of environmental damage.[323]

One important consequence of the variety of jurisdictional rules applicable to transboundary tort cases is that the courts of several countries may have concurrent jurisdiction. In this situation, and subject to the exercise of any discretion to dismiss on *forum non conveniens* grounds, the plaintiff will have a choice of jurisdiction in which to proceed: in effect to go 'forum shopping'. Giving the plaintiff the choice of where to sue recognizes that a transboundary environmental tort will generally if not invariably involve elements located within at least two jurisdictions.

In the EU and European Economic Area such a choice is provided by Article 7 of the Brussels I *bis* Regulation, which, as we have seen, allows an action in tort to be brought 'in the courts of the place where the harmful event occurred or may occur'.

319 See *Ohio v Wyandotte Chemicals Corp* 401 US 493 (1971); *Asahi Metal Co. Ltd v Superior Court* 480 US 102 (1987); Juenger, in McLachlan and Nygh, *Transnational Tort Litigation*, 201ff, and McLachlan, *ibid*,17.

320 See for example UK State Immunity Act, 1978, ss 3(3)(c), 5; US Foreign Sovereigns Immunity Act, 28 USCA s 1605. See also 2004 UN Convention on State Immunity and Fox and Webb, *The Law of State Immunity* (3rd edn, Oxford, 2015) Ch 7.

321 ILA, *65th Conference Rept* (1992) Second Rept on State Immunity, 11; Fox and Webb, *The Law of State Immunity* 481–2. Note however that the nuclear liability conventions require immunities to be waived: see *infra*, Ch 7.

322 E.g. because it involved use of armed forces: see *Jurisdictional Immunities Case*, ICJ Reports (2012) paras 78–9.

323 Fox and Webb, *The Law of State Immunity*, 481–2, are confused on this point.

As interpreted by the ECJ in the case of *Handelskwekerij GJ Bier v Mines de Potasse d'Alsace*[324] this means both the place where the harmful effects are felt, and where the harmful activity is located, enabling Dutch tomato growers to proceed in the Dutch courts against a mining company whose polluting activities in France caused damage to their crops. The same article would also have allowed them to opt for suit in France, where the mine was located, or under Article 4 in the defendant's domicile, also France. The German Environmental Liability Act of 1990 also gives the plaintiff a choice of forum in transboundary pollution cases.[325]

At this point it is not proposed to consider how the plaintiff chooses the forum in which to sue, but merely to confine our attention to the advantages and disadvantages of forum shopping as an element in a regional or international system of transboundary environmental justice. Its virtues in an environmental context are fairly obvious: the plaintiff decides which system offers the most advantageous procedural and substantive rules and remedies, and thereby maximizes the chances of recovery. But the problems are also obvious: making this choice is no easy task, it adds to the complexity and expense of the case and is further complicated if the question of choice of law to be applied in each jurisdiction is also uncertain.

Moreover, there are certain advantages and disadvantages inherent in particular jurisdictional preferences. The forum in which the harmful activity is located is the one best able to handle multiple suits against a single defendant; courts in this position can more easily obtain evidence of fault and discovery of documents, grant and enforce preventive remedies, and apply limits on liability and insurance requirements. Against this, as observed earlier, are the problems of unfamiliarity, language, etc of proceeding in a foreign forum.

The forum in which the damage is suffered is best placed to assess that harm, and that is why the 1969 Convention on Civil Liability for Oil Pollution Damage opted for this choice.[326] But it is then harder to enforce remedies against a foreign defendant, to obtain evidence, and to handle multiple suits rationally if the damage affects several states. The possibility in Europe of a single transboundary pollution incident giving rise to suits in a variety of jurisdictions points to the impracticability of this kind of forum shopping for any business attempting to order its affairs to comply with its legal responsibilities: it will never be able to predict with certainty where it may be sued or by what laws it will be judged. This is not an approach which benefits access to environmental justice. Moreover, a foreign defendant may have no assets within the jurisdiction of the court or, in the case of ships or nuclear installations, the defendant's main or only asset may have been lost in the accident giving rise to the proceedings. Although a judgment or injunction may be recognized and enforced in other

324 Case 21/76, II *ECR* (1976) 1735. See also *Shevill v Presse Alliance SA* [1995] 2 WLR 499 in which the same interpretation of Article 5 was applied to a transboundary defamation case.

325 Hoffman, 38 *NILR* (1991) 27. So do the 1962 Nuclear Ships Convention, and the 1977 Convention on Civil Liability for Oil Pollution Damage Resulting from Sea-bed Exploration or Exploitation of Submarine Mineral Resources, neither of which is in force.

326 *Infra*, Ch 9.

countries, this can only be guaranteed where there are appropriate treaty provisions in force.[327]

A better variant of the *Handelskwekerij* approach is found in the 1993 Council of Europe Convention on Civil Liability for Damage Resulting from Activities Dangerous to the Environment, considered further below. This convention gives the plaintiff a choice of jurisdiction but avoids problems of choice of law by providing for harmonization of national laws on a basis of strict liability and by defining what forms of damage are actionable. Thus, consideration of the forms of transboundary justice becomes ultimately inseparable from the substance of the law. This leads us to consider the role of harmonization of national law on liability for environmental damage.

4 HARMONIZATION OF ENVIRONMENTAL LIABILITY

4(1) INTRODUCTION

Harmonization of national law on environmental liability, both at the substantive and procedural levels, serves three principal roles. First, it provides a common minimum standard for all legal systems. To that extent it is another means for ensuring the provision of 'effective access to judicial and administrative proceedings, including redress and remedy' required by Principle 10 of the Rio Declaration and considered in previous sections of this chapter. Secondly, harmonization has an important role in any scheme for transboundary access to justice. It can mitigate the conflict of laws problems referred to above and contributes to the creation of shared expectations on a regional basis. If the principal criteria for assessing progress towards environmental justice are the reduction of unpredictability, complexity, and cost, balancing the interests of plaintiffs in the widest possible choice of law and jurisdiction against the interests of defendants in ordering their affairs in an environmentally responsible manner, then greater harmonization, at least at regional level, remains a desirable goal. Thirdly, it can help promote implementation of the polluter-pays principle referred to in Principle 16 of the Rio Declaration and considered below.

Transboundary litigation will only be fully effective in environmental cases if common minimum standards apply regardless of where the proceedings are brought. The issues which need to be addressed in this context include the following:

- Liability: is it based on fault, strict liability or absolute liability?
- Remedies: to what extent are compensation for environmental damage, restoration costs, and injunctive relief available?

[327] But the international and supranational instruments are now extensive: see Brussels I *bis* Regulation; 1993 Convention on Civil Liability for Damage Resulting From Activities Dangerous to the Environment, Article 23; 1992 Convention on Civil Liability for Oil Pollution Damage, Article 10; 1997 Vienna Convention on Civil Liability for Nuclear Damage, Article 12. On the position where there is no treaty see Lowenfeld, *International Litigation and the Quest for Reasonableness* (Oxford, 1996) Ch 6, and on Europe see Kennet, *The Enforcement of Judgments in Europe* (Oxford, 2000).

- Recognition and enforcement of judgments: can the defendant's assets be reached and his activities controlled outside the territory of the forum?
- Compensation funds: are these necessary to allow adequate recovery in cases of serious loss?

Several examples of harmonization of civil liability already exist, including conventions dealing with pollution damage from ships and nuclear accidents. Although there are differences in detail, their main elements are (in most cases) a common scheme of strict liability for all parties, liability channelled to the owner or operator, limited in amount and supported by compulsory insurance and compensation funds. These conventions are examined in more detail in Chapters 7 and 9, but they have the merits of clarity, predictability, and relative simplicity for the plaintiff. No problems of forum-shopping or choice of law arise, the schemes are operational, and they provide an assurance that any compensation awarded will be recovered. They are important precedents for the sort of provision necessary to make such risks internationally acceptable, although they raise questions about the distribution of loss. None of the schemes follows the polluter-pays principle in full. Instead the burden of major losses is borne partly by the operator, partly by the industry or state concerned, and beyond that it falls on the innocent victim, or must be recovered in interstate claims. It is in these circumstances that state responsibility retains an important subsidiary role, as we saw in Chapter 4. Although compensation limits have not always been realistic, civil liability conventions of this kind afford litigants significant benefits when compared with equal access to national remedies.[328]

Principle 13 of the Rio Declaration calls on states to develop national law regarding liability and compensation for pollution victims and other environmental damage, and also requires them to cooperate 'in a more expeditious and determined manner' to develop international law in this respect. Some progress has been made in implementing Principle 13. The conventions on oil pollution damage and nuclear accidents have been strengthened,[329] and new treaties or protocols on liability for hazardous and noxious substances, wastes, and bunker fuel oil have been adopted.[330] There is a liability annex to the 1991 Antarctic Protocol,[331] and attempts have been made to reach international agreement on civil liability for other potential hazards, including the adoption of draft principles by the ILC in 2006, considered below.[332] One key issue is the extent to which there can be liability for environmental damage not otherwise

328 For an overview, see Boyle, 17 *JEL* (2005) 3; Xue, *Transboundary Damage in International Law* (Cambridge, 2003) Ch 2.

329 See *infra*, Chs 7, 9.

330 1996 Convention on Liability and Compensation for the Carriage of Hazardous and Noxious Substances by Sea, *infra*, Ch 9; 1999 Protocol on Liability and Compensation for Damage Resulting from the Transboundary Movements of Hazardous Wastes, *infra*, Ch 8; 2001 Convention on Civil Liability for Bunker Oil Pollution Damage, *infra*, Ch 9.

331 Annex VI, adopted in 2005. See Bederman and Keskar, 19 *Emory Int LR* (2005) 1383; de La Fayette, in Triggs and Riddell (eds), *Antarctica: Legal and Environmental Changes* (London, 2007) 109.

332 On GMOs see 2000 Biosafety Protocol, Article 27.

included under categories of property loss or personal injury. Here Articles 2(7)–(10) of the 1993 Lugano Convention on Civil Liability provide a useful model, and these provisions build on those already found in a number of other liability conventions.[333]

Sceptics rightly question whether liability treaties have had much impact on industry or contribute to improving environmental standards.[334] Lack of participation is a problem with many of the newer liability schemes; at best it casts serious doubt on their acceptability or relevance, and on the wisdom of negotiating any more of them.[335] The prospect of possibly extensive changes to national civil law is one reason for this hesitation; the selective application of strict liability in some areas but not others is another, insofar as it challenges fundamental concepts of national law and is incompatible with a principled approach to civil liability as a whole. This is an area in which some serious rethinking is overdue.[336]

4(2) THE 1993 LUGANO CONVENTION

The Council of Europe's Convention on Civil Liability for Damage Resulting from Activities Dangerous to the Environment[337] is the only treaty which provides for comprehensive harmonization of environmental liability, in Europe, or elsewhere. It envisages strict liability for dangerous activities and substances, placed on the operator of the activity in question. Liability is not limited in amount and thus reflects the polluter-pays principle more closely than other treaties under which the loss is spread. 'Damage' is widely defined and covers impairment of the environment, as well as injury to persons and property. For this purpose, the 'environment' includes natural resources, cultural heritage areas, and 'characteristic aspects of the landscape'. However, apart from loss of profit, recovery of compensation for environmental impairment is limited to the costs of 'reasonable measures of prevention and reinstatement actually undertaken or to be undertaken'. Reinstatement includes the introduction 'where reasonable' of the equivalent of destroyed or damaged elements of the environment, for example where exact restoration is impossible. Possible defences

333 Other conventions which also cover liability for environmental damage include 1989 Convention on Civil Liability for Damage Caused During Carriage of Dangerous Goods by Road etc, Article 1(10); 1992 Convention on Civil Liability for Oil Pollution Damage, Article 6; 1996 Convention on Liability and Compensation for Damage in Connection with the Carriage of Hazardous and Noxious Substances by Sea; 1997 Protocol to the Vienna Convention on Civil Liability for Nuclear Damage, Article 2(2) (4); 1999 Protocol on Liability and Compensation for Damage Resulting from Transboundary Movements of Hazardous Waste; 2001 Convention on Civil Liability for Bunker Oil Pollution Damage; 2003 Protocol on Civil Liability and Compensation for Damage Caused by the Transboundary Effects of Industrial Accidents on Transboundary Waters; 2005 Annex VI to the Protocol to the Antarctic Treaty on Environmental Protection, Article 6(1). See de La Fayette, in Bowman and Boyle, *Environmental Damage in International and Comparative Law* (Oxford, 2002) Ch 9; and *infra*, Chs 7, 9.

334 See Brunnée, 53 *ICLQ* (2004) 351; Bergkamp, *Liability and the Environment: Private and Public Law Aspects of Civil Liability for Environmental Harm in an International Context* (The Hague, 2001).

335 Churchill, 12 *YbIEL* (2001) 3.

336 See Sachs, 55 *UCLALR* (2008) 837.

337 See *Explanatory Rept* in Council of Europe CDCJ (92) 50; Bianchi, 6 *JEL* (1994) 21, 26–32.

to liability include war, hostilities, exceptional and irresistible natural phenomena, and act of a third party. Administrative authorization is not a defence, but 'tolerable' pollution is not actionable. The liability of the operator is assured by compulsory insurance. Jurisdiction is based on the provisions of the EU Regulation on Jurisdiction and Judgments. This is a sophisticated scheme, but it has attracted few ratifications, and without EU participation it has no prospect of entry into force. The Lugano Convention provided an obvious model for the ILC to draw upon in its attempts to codify principles of liability (considered below) but the main risk, had the Commission tried to follow this approach, was that it would prove over-prescriptive and result in an outcome unwelcome to many states. If such a solution is unappealing even in Europe what chance of success would it have elsewhere?

4(3) ILC PRINCIPLES ON ALLOCATION OF LOSS FOR TRANSBOUNDARY DAMAGE

Draft principles on liability and compensation for environmental damage were finally adopted by the ILC in 2006 after many years of deliberation.[338] Rather than making states directly liable in international law as originally envisaged,[339] the Commission's final text provides for states to make the polluter liable to transboundary victims in national law. The principles apply only to damage occurring on the territory of another state or in some other place under its jurisdiction or control.[340] In contrast to the Lugano Convention they do not as such require or envisage a general harmonization of national law relating to environmental damage, but in practice that will necessarily be the outcome to some extent.

At the heart of its scheme is an international standard of liability which affects not only compensation for damage but also the procedures and remedies through which it is to be obtained. Principle 6(1) sets out the core principle of prompt, adequate and effective compensation:

"States shall provide their domestic judicial and administrative bodies with the necessary jurisdiction and competence and ensure that these bodies have prompt, adequate and effective remedies available in the event of transboundary damage caused by hazardous activities located within their territory or otherwise under their jurisdiction or control."

Underlying this formulation is the understanding that non-discriminatory access to national remedies may not be enough to satisfy an international standard of access to justice.[341] The Commission refers to the *Trail Smelter Arbitration* as authority, noting

338 ILC Rept (2006) GAOR A/61/10, paras 51–67. For preparatory work see ILC Rept (2004) GAOR A/59/10, paras 158–76; ILC Rept (2003) GAOR A/58/10, paras 154–231; ILC Rept (2002) GAOR A/57/10, paras 430–57; Special Rapporteur Rao's 1st Rept (2003) A/CN 4/531; 2nd Rept (2004) A/CN 4/540; 3rd Rept (2006) A/CN 4/566.

339 *Supra*, Ch 4, section 2.

340 Principle 2.

341 Compare ILA, *67th Conference Rept* (1996) 401–15, International Watercourses, Article 2(1): 'States, individually or jointly, shall ensure the availability of *prompt, adequate and effective* administrative and judicial remedies for persons in another State who suffer or may suffer damage...' (emphasis added).

that 'the basic principle established in that case entailed a duty of a State to ensure payment of prompt and adequate compensation for any transboundary damage'.[342] Moreover, in requiring 'effective redress', 'adequate and effective remedies', or 'prompt and adequate compensation or other relief', Principle 10 of the Rio Declaration, Article 9(4) of the 1998 Aarhus Convention, and Article 235(2) of the 1982 UNCLOS all suggest that there are international standards of compensation and remedy for victims of environmental damage. As we saw earlier, the failure of a state to provide adequate redress to its own citizens for pollution or other forms of damage may in sufficiently serious cases also violate the rights to life, health, private life, property, and freedom to dispose of natural resources under international human-rights agreements.[343] An alternative foundation would draw from precedents on the taking of property in international law, making an obvious analogy with damage by pollution.[344] These precedents all show that Principle 6(1) builds on existing law. This element of the ILC scheme could represent its most significant contribution to the progressive development of the subject. The rest of the scheme then goes on to set out a model for transboundary liability drawn from existing civil liability conventions. These elements are essentially optional and open to implementation in a variety of ways.

Three important points about allocation of loss stand out when comparing the ILC Principles to existing civil liability and compensation schemes. First, strict liability is the universally accepted standard,[345] albeit with minor variations in the permitted defences. The ILC commentary accepts the argument that hazardous activities carry inherent risks and that it would be unjust and inappropriate to require proof of fault when accidents happen. It notes the adoption of strict liability in treaties and in national law, and on this point refers to its own draft as 'a measure of progressive development of international law'.[346] Secondly, as the examples of the 2001 Bunker Fuel Convention and the 1999 Protocol on Liability for Transboundary Waste show, channelling liability to a single owner or operator is not always a realistic option, and the choice of 'owner/operator liability' without more would represent in some cases too simplistic a solution without a broader definition of these terms.[347] Significantly, while the ILC scheme

342 ILC Rept (2004) GAOR A/59/10, International Liability, commentary to Principle 4, para 11. See also commentary to Principle 6, para 7.

343 *SERAC v Nigeria* (2002) ACHPR para 69; *Maya Indigenous Community of the Toledo District v Belize* (2004) IACHR, Case 12.053; *Fadeyeva v Russia* [2005] ECHR 376; *Taskin v Turkey* [2006] 42 EHRR 50, para 119. See above.

344 See for example *Sporrong and Lonnroth v Sweden* (1983) 5 EHRR 617, where planning blight was held to constitute a taking of property without compensation, contrary to Article 1, Protocol 1 of the European Convention on Human Rights. The 'prompt, adequate and effective' standard of compensation for expropriation is not universally accepted, however. See Amerasinghe, 41 *ICLQ* (1992) 22.

345 See ILC Principle 4. But the 2003 Kiev Protocol retains additional fault-based liability as provided for by national law. See also 1992 CLC, Articles 3, 5(2); 1993 Lugano Convention, Article 8(b) and 1999 Protocol on Liability for Transboundary Waste.

346 ILC Rept (2004) commentary to Principle 4, paras 15–17.

347 The 2001 Bunker Fuel Convention makes the shipowner, charterer, manager and operator jointly and severally liable. Under the 1999 Transboundary Waste Protocol generators, exporters, importers and disposers are all potentially liable at different stages of the wastes' journey to its eventual destination.

chooses to focus liability on operators, it also allows for alternatives. The 'operator' of the harmful activity should be primarily liable, not the state, but 'where appropriate' liability may be imposed on some other person or entity.[348] In practice the Commission's draft seems to assume that there may be more than one operator and, by implication, that liability may be joint and several. Thirdly, while most liability schemes spread the burden of loss through additional compensation funds,[349] each scheme has its own unique funding arrangements. There is no common pattern. In some cases, states carry the ultimate burden of residual compensation funding, as well as a residual liability in the event of operator insolvency; in others the costs are borne wholly by industry. This makes them difficult models from which to derive any general scheme of loss allocation that might secure universal agreement beyond the proposition that some such provision should be made. It may also suggest that different contexts require different solutions. Again, the ILC scheme allows for such diversity. In 'appropriate cases' additional compensation funding should be provided by industry, or if necessary by States.[350]

The Commission's text also replicates the definition of 'environmental damage' in the more modern liability treaties and is consistent with the practice of the UNCC and developments in national law.[351] Thus draft Principle 2(a) expressly includes damage to cultural property, the costs of reasonable measures of reinstatement of the environment, and reasonable response measures. In one respect the ILC Principles are potentially more progressive, however, because Principle 2(a)(iii) envisages liability for environmental damage per se, unrelated to the cost of response or restoration measures.[352] While some national laws already allow recovery of compensation for pure environmental damage, no previous liability agreement has gone this far.[353] The Commission says nothing on the question of valuation of such damage, although it notes that damages awarded do not have a punitive function. It defines 'victim' as the person or state that suffers damage, but its commentary notes that the term can include groups of local authorities, NGOs, or public trustees.[354]

While the 2006 ILC Principles as a whole cannot be viewed as an exercise in codifying customary international law, they show how the Commission has made use of

348 ILC Principle 4.

349 The 1993 Lugano Convention and the 2003 Kiev Protocol are notable exceptions.

350 ILC Principle 7.

351 ILC Rept (2004) commentary to Principle 2, paras 1–21. For fuller analysis see Bowman and Boyle (eds), *Environmental Damage in International and Comparative Law.*

352 ILC Rept (2004) commentary to Principle 2, para 12; ILC Rept (2006) commentary to Principle 2, paras (13)–(15). See also Special Rapporteur's 2nd Rept, para 31.

353 Compare 2004 Protocol to Amend the Paris Convention on Third Party Liability in the Field of Nuclear Energy, Article IB; 1992 Convention on Civil Liability for Oil Pollution Damage, Article 1(6); de La Fayette, 20 *IJMCL* (2005) 167, 202–5, and see generally Bowman and Boyle, *Environmental Damage in International and Comparative Law,* 213–322.

354 ILC Rept (2004) commentary to Principle 3, paras 3–6; ILC Rept (2006) commentary to Principle 2, paras (11)–(14) (29)–(30). The focus on 'victims' reflects Principle 13 of the 1992 Rio Declaration on Environment and Development. Compare the 2005 Antarctic Liability Annex under which states parties may sue the operator for the cost of environmental response and clean-up measures, but not for environmental damage per se. For comprehensive analysis of valuation of environmental damage and standing to sue see Brans, *Liability for Damage to Public Natural Resources* (The Hague, 2001).

general principles of law as 'an indication of policy and principle'.[355] The draft successfully reflects the modern development of civil-liability treaties, without in any way compromising or altering those which presently exist, or the right of victims to sue in their own state.[356] This is a notable achievement, but it may also be a double-edged attribute. On the one hand it is prudent to build on what states themselves have already negotiated. On the other, the reluctance of states to ratify those same treaties may indicate a less than wholehearted commitment to the idea of shifting the focus away from state responsibility for transboundary harm in favour of civil liability and individual access to justice. Given the unwillingness of states to extend their own liability on a non-fault basis, it is difficult to see what other choice the Commission could have made.

4(4) LIABILITY AND THE POLLUTER PAYS PRINCIPLE

The 'polluter-pays' principle is essentially an economic policy for allocating the costs of pollution or environmental damage borne by public authorities, but it also has implications for the development of international and national law on liability for damage. As defined by the OECD in a series of recommendations starting in the 1970s,[357] the principle entailed that the polluter should bear the expense of carrying out measures decided by public authorities to ensure that the environment is in an 'acceptable state' and that 'the cost of these measures should be reflected in the cost of goods and services which cause pollution in production and or in consumption'. The purpose of the OECD policy and recommendations on the subject was thus to internalize the economic costs of pollution control, clean-up and protection measures, and to ensure that governments did not distort international trade and investment by subsidizing these environmental costs.

It was not until the UNCED Conference that the polluter-pays principle for the first time secured international support as an environmental policy. Principle 16 of the Rio Declaration provides, in somewhat qualified terms, that:

> National authorities should endeavour to promote the internalisation of environmental costs and the use of economic instruments, taking into account the approach that the polluter should, in principle, bear the cost of pollution, with due regard to the public interest and without distorting international trade and investment.[358]

[355] See *South West Africa Advisory Opinion*, ICJ Reports (1950) 128, sep op McNair, 148.

[356] See Principles 6(3), 7.

[357] OECD, Recommendations C (72) 128 (1972); C (74) 223 (1974) reprinted in OECD, *OECD and the Environment*, (Paris, 1986) and C (89) 88 (1988) reprinted in 28 *ILM* (1989) 1320. See generally OECD, *The Polluter Pays Principle*, OCDE/GD(92)81 (1992); Smets, 97 *RGDIP* (1993) 339; id, in Campiglio, Pineschi, Siniscalco, and Treves (eds), *The Environment After Rio* (London, 1994) 131; de Sadeleer, *Environmental Principles: From Political Slogans to Legal Rules* (Oxford, 2002) 21–59.

[358] See generally Atapattu, *Emerging Principles of IEL* (Ardsley, 2006) Ch 6; Schwarz, in Viñuales (ed), *The Rio Declaration on Environment and Development* (Oxford, 2015) 429–50. The principle is defined in broadly similar terms in the 1992 Paris Convention, the 1992 Helsinki Convention on Transboundary Watercourses, the 1995 Barcelona Convention, and the 1996 Protocol to the 1972 London Convention. See also 1991 European Energy Charter, Article 19(1). Other treaties merely refer to the polluter pays principle without attempting to define it.

Given this wording, it cannot be said that the polluter-pays principle is intended to be legally binding: Principle 16 lacks the normative character of a rule of law.[359] Moreover, while some treaties require parties to 'apply the polluter pays principle',[360] others use the softer language of guidance.[361] Thus it is significant that the Preambles to the 1990 Oil Pollution Preparedness and Response Convention, the 1992 UNECE Convention on the Transboundary Effects of Industrial Accidents, and the 2003 Kiev Protocol on Liability for Pollution of Transboundary Waters and Lakes describe the 'polluter pays' principle only as a 'general principle of international environmental law'.

As such the principle only appears in a limited range of post-Rio treaties dealing with pollution of international watercourses, marine pollution, transboundary industrial accidents, and energy. Although it has been used more broadly in national environmental policy and legislation,[362] it is impossible to point to any general pattern of state practice. Implementation has largely been left to national rather than international action. As a result, both the choice of methods—taxation, charges, liability laws—and the degree of implementation, have been very variable, and few states have been fully consistent in their policy.[363] The most that can be said is that states, intergovernmental regulatory institutions and courts can and should take account of the principle in the development of environmental law and policy, but they are in no sense bound by international law to 'make polluters pay'. Moreover, reference to the public interest in Principle 16 leaves ample room for exceptions and thus for continued governmental subsidy. As adopted at Rio, the polluter-pays principle is neither absolute nor obligatory.

How then could the polluter-pays principle be used and developed in its more limited incarnation as a guiding principle? This is a more difficult question than it might first appear. Taxation is a relatively crude way to recoup the external costs of environmentally harmful activities. Charges to meet the cost of preventing, reducing, or restoring environmental damage can be more accurately targeted, but their impact in deterring environmentally harmful activities will vary. As experience with charging for disposal of oily residues from ships shows, charges can be counter-productive if

359 See *North Sea Continental Shelf Case*, ICJ Reports (1969) 3, para 72. Cf *Rhine Chlorides Convention Arbitral Award* (France/Netherlands) PCA (2004) para 103: '. .... le Tribunal ne pense pas que ce principe fasse partie du droit international général.'

360 1992 Paris Convention for the Protection of the Marine Environment of the NE Atlantic, Article 2(2)(b); 1992 Helsinki Convention on the Protection of the Marine Environment of the Baltic Sea Area, Article 3(4); 1994 Danube River Protection Convention, Article 2(4); 1995 Barcelona Convention for the Protection of the Marine Environment and the Coastal Region of the Mediterranean, Article 4.

361 1990 Convention on Oil Pollution Preparedness, Response and Cooperation, Preamble; 1992 Helsinki Convention on the Protection and Use of Transboundary Watercourses and Lakes, Article 2(5); 1996 Protocol to the 1972 London Convention, Article 3; 1999 Convention on the Protection of the Rhine, Article 4.

362 See e.g. Article 191(2) of the EU Treaty, which provides that 'Union policy on the environment .... shall be based on the precautionary principle and on the principles that preventive action should be taken, that environmental damage should as a priority be rectified at source and that the polluter should pay'.

363 On environmental taxes and trade see *infra*, Ch 13.

they make the polluter more likely to evade environmental protection measures in order to cut costs. The US practice of attempting to internalize environmental costs by making the polluter rather than public agencies directly responsible for conducting the clean-up and restoration after accidents such as the *Exxon Valdez* may also be counter-productive if the result is a dilatory and inadequate response. Charges and taxes cannot easily be targeted at accidental damage, nor can they be applied to transboundary polluters. In this sort of case there may be no practical alternative to state-organised action, with the taxpayer recovering the costs through liability laws and compensation schemes.

Thus full implementation of a polluter-pays approach may entail consideration of civil liability and compensation, especially if accidental damage to the environment is to be included.[364] The commentary on the ILC's 2006 draft principles on allocation of loss notes that: 'The Commission considers the polluter-pays principle as an essential component in underpinning the present draft principles to ensure that victims that suffer harm as a result of an incident involving a hazardous activity are able to obtain prompt and adequate compensation'.[365] Individual civil-liability actions are limited by the need to identify specific polluters, although this problem can be eased by the willingness of courts to impose joint liability on multiple tortfeasors, for example in cases of air pollution damage.[366] The extent to which civil liability then makes the polluter pay for environmental damage will depend on a variety of factors. If liability is based on negligence, not only does this have to be proved, but harm which is neither reasonably foreseeable nor avoidable will not be compensated and the victim or the taxpayer, not the polluter, will bear the loss. Strict liability is a better approximation of the polluter-pays principle, but not if limited in amount, as in internationally agreed schemes involving oil tankers or nuclear installations.[367] The limit for environmental damage in Antarctica is a mere 3 million SDRs: rather less than the sum paid by the USSR to Canada for clean-up costs after the Cosmos 954 satellite crashed in the Arctic.[368] Moreover, a narrow definition of damage may exclude environmental losses which cannot easily be quantified in monetary terms, such as wildlife, or which affect the quality of the environment without causing actual physical damage. An illustration of this problem is the case of *Merlin v BNFL*[369] where a house was rendered radioactive but the operator of the installation responsible was absolved from liability because there had been no damage to property within the terms of the statute, despite the

364 See OECD, *The Polluter Pays Principle*, but cf Smets, 97 *RGDIP* (1993) 339.

365 ILC Rept (2006) International Liability, commentary to the Preamble, at para (2). See also the commentary to Principle 3 where the ILC's view is set out more fully.

366 *Michie v Great Lakes Steel Division* 495 F 2d 213 (1974); Ianni, 11 *CYIL* (1973) 258.

367 See 1992 Conventions on Civil Liability for Oil Pollution Damage and on the Establishment of an International Fund for Compensation for Oil Pollution Damage, *infra*, Ch 9; 1960 Paris Convention on Third Party Liability in the Field of Nuclear Energy and 1997 Vienna Convention on Civil Liability for Nuclear Damage, *infra*, Ch 7.

368 Annex VI to the Antarctic Environmental Protocol, Article 9. See *supra*, Ch 4.

369 [1990] 2 QB 557. But compare *Blue Circle Industries Plc v Ministry of Defence* [1998] 3 All ER 385.

building's loss of market value. A significant amount of environmental injury is likely to remain uncompensated under civil liability in English law, and the same is true of some other legal systems, though not uniformly.[370] To this extent the polluter remains free to off-load certain environmental costs even under a strict liability regime.

A more fundamental problem with broader use of the polluter-pays principle is that it does not indicate who is the polluter and cannot as such determine liability.[371] The OECD and the ILC treat the operator of a hazardous installation as the 'polluter' in cases of accidental damage.[372] On this view the operator of an oil tanker is the polluter and should be responsible if the ship sinks. But it can equally be said that the cargo causes the damage and that the cargo owner is in that sense the polluter. Sensibly, the present internationally agreed scheme of liability and compensation for oil pollution treats both the ship's owner and the cargo owner as sharing responsibility, while excluding the liability of any other potential defendant in order to facilitate recovery by plaintiffs.[373] In this case what matters is *how* the responsibility is shared, and how the compensation is funded: asking who the polluter is will not answer these questions, nor will it do so in other complex transactions such as the carriage of hazardous wastes, a point fully recognized by the ILC draft principles on allocation of loss.[374]

An altogether different problem arises in the case of nuclear accidents. Here it is usually clear who the polluter is—the operator of the nuclear installation—but the adoption of a strict polluter-pays approach to liability is not economically feasible and would not be in the public interest. In the event of a serious accident, the scale of absolute and unlimited liability would be uninsurable and quickly bankrupt even the largest utility company. Unless the losses are to fall mainly on the innocent victims, some other approach to allocating them must be found, almost certainly by involving other states which use nuclear power. Thus, in Western Europe the uninsured risks are borne first by the state in which the installation is located and then above a certain level by a compensation fund to which participating governments contribute in proportion to their installed nuclear capacity and GNP.[375] In this case the basic concept is not one of making the polluter pay but of an equitable sharing of the risk, with a large element of state subsidy. An even more extensive departure from the polluter-pays principle has emerged with regard to Eastern European nuclear installations. The costs of remedial measures are so high, and the local economies so weak, that Western

[370] See also s 1 of the German Environmental Liability Act, 1990 which confines liability to cases of 'death, personal injury or property damage'. Cf the more generous approach to environmental compensation under the 1990 US Oil Pollution Act, s 1006(d)(1) and under US tort law, on which see *Commonwealth of Puerto Rico* v *SS Zoe Colocotroni* 628 F 2d 652 (1980). See also 2006 ILC Loss Allocation Principles, *infra*, section 4(3).

[371] Smets, 97 *RGDIP* (1993) 339, 357.

[372] See Rec C (89) 88 (1989) and OECD, *The Polluter Pays Principle*.

[373] See *infra*, Ch 9, section 6.

[374] See *infra*, section 4; 1999 Protocol on Liability and Compensation for the Transboundary Movement of Hazardous Wastes, *infra*, Ch 8, section 4, and the 1996 Convention on Liability and Compensation for the Carriage of Hazardous and Noxious Substances by Sea, *infra*, Ch 9, section 6(2).

[375] 1960 Paris Convention on Third Party Liability in the Field of Nuclear Energy and 1963 Brussels Supplementary Agreement, on which see *infra*, Ch 7.

European governments, who represent one large group of potential victims of any accident, have funded the work needed to improve safety standards. The same approach has reluctantly been adopted by the Dutch and other riparians on the Rhine in order to persuade the French to reduce pollution from their potassium mines.[376] Here, it is in effect the victim who pays.

Thus, the polluter-pays principle and the general policy of internalizing environmental costs cannot be treated as a rigid rule of universal application, nor are the means used to implement it going to be the same in all cases. A great deal of flexibility will be inevitable, taking full account of differences in the nature of the risk and the economic feasibility of full internalization of environmental costs in industries whose capacity to bear them will vary. As one author comments, 'The main difficulty with the full internalisation policy is that it cannot be implemented in practice unless some agreement is reached on the respective rights of the polluters and the victims'.[377] No doubt considerations of this kind account for the heavily qualified nature of Principle 16 of the Rio Declaration. Whatever its legal status, or its relationship to sustainable development, the polluter-pays principle cannot supply guidance on the content of national or international liability without further definition.

5 CORPORATE ENVIRONMENTAL ACCOUNTABILITY

Corporations are entitled to the protection of human-rights treaties and can also sue and be sued before national courts in the same way as individuals. As we have seen in the previous section, they may be held liable for transboundary environmental damage in the courts of the state where they are domiciled, the state where they conduct business, or the state where their activities cause environmental damage.[378] In reality, multinational corporations not infrequently escape effective accountability for their activities in developing states, especially where regulation is weak, enforcement lax, the judicial system ineffective, the government corrupt or inadequate. Moreover, attempts to sue multinationals in their home state may also encounter obstacles, such as the *forum non conveniens* defence, which effectively protects US corporations from suit in US courts for their overseas activities.[379] But even where none of these problems exist, in order to encourage and protect foreign investment, developing states may have to conclude

[376] 1976 Convention for the Protection of the Rhine from Pollution by Chlorides, on which see *infra*, Ch 10. For a general survey of this approach to the funding of environmental measures see OECD Environment Committee, *The Use of International Financial Transfers in Resolving Transfrontier and Global Pollution Problems*, ENV/EC (90) 25 (1990).

[377] Smets, in Campliglio, Pinsechi, Siniscalco, and Treves (eds), *The Environment After Rio* (London, 1994) 131.

[378] See generally Muchlinski, *Multinational Enterprises and the Law* (2nd edn, Oxford, 2007); Sornarajah, *The International Law of Foreign Investment* (Cambridge, 2004).

[379] *Supra*, section 3(2)(d).

bilateral investment treaties ('BITs') which restrict their ability to regulate foreign investors, who can if necessary resort to binding arbitration in case of breach.[380] Regulatory measures which purport to protect the environment have in a few cases been treated by arbitrators as expropriation of property—a 'regulatory taking'.[381] Some of the later BITs are intended to avoid such outcomes provided the regulatory measures are non-discriminatory.[382] In other cases changes in national law may amount to a denial of 'fair and equitable treatment' if there has been a failure to respect legitimate expectations, a lack of transparency or disregard for due process.[383] Faced with these constraints some governments may shy away from trying too hard to protect the environment.

There are several possible responses to these problems. One is to rely on human-rights litigation. The *Ogoniland Case* is a striking reminder that unregulated foreign investment which contributes little to the welfare of the local population may amount to a denial of human rights for which the host government is responsible. In such cases a BIT could not prevent changes in local law or policy necessary to give effect to fundamental human-rights obligations. As a straightforward matter of treaty law a BIT would have to be interpreted and applied consistently with any applicable human-rights treaties.[384] While this strategy may help protect the population from investment-led environmental damage, it will not protect the environment itself in situations falling short of a human-rights abuse. Attempts to hold corporations liable for breaches of international law have generally not worked, even in the US, where the Alien Tort Claims Act has not been invoked successfully in environmental claims for extra-territorial torts.[385] Corporations are not directly bound by environmental treaties or by customary international law,[386] and as we saw earlier, national courts have not been notably receptive to arguments based on international law in environmental cases.[387]

380 See Viñuales, *Foreign Investment and the Environment in International Law* (Cambridge, 2012); Pavoni, in Dupuy, Francioni, Petersmann (eds), *Human Rights and International Investment Law and Arbitration* (Oxford, 2009) Ch 22; Fauchald, 17 *YbIEL* (2006) 3; Muchlinski, 55 *ICLQ* (2006) 527; Waelde and Kolo, 50 *ICLQ* (2001) 811.

381 E.g. *Metalclad Corporation v United Mexican States*, ICSID Award (2000) but compare *SD Myers Inc v Canada*, UNCITRAL Partial Award (2000); *Methanex Corporation v United States of America*, UNCITRAL Final Award (2005); *Plama Consortium Ltd v Bulgaria*, ICSID Award (2008). Cf the ECHR cases on environmental restrictions on property cited *supra*, section 2(4)(c).

382 See Baughen, 18 *JEL* (2006) 207, 227.

383 Again compare *Metalclad Corporation v United Mexican States*, ICSID No ARB(AF)/97/1 (2000); with *Maffezini v Kingdom of Spain*, ICSID Award (2000); *CME Czech Republic BV v The Czech Republic*, UNCITRAL Partial Award (2001); *Plama Consortium Ltd v Bulgaria*, ICSID Award (2008).

384 1969 Vienna Convention on the Law of Treaties, Article 31(3). See generally Dupuy, in Dupuy et al (eds), *Human Rights in International Investment Arbitration*, 45; Simma, 60 *ICLQ* (2011) 573, 584–91, and case law cited there.

385 See *Kiobel v Royal Dutch Petroleum Co*, 569 US 108 (2013). Moreover, following *Sosa v Alvarez-Machain*, 124 S Ct 2739 (2004) ATCA is unlikely to cover violations of modern international environmental law. However, see also *Doe VIII v Exxon Mobil Corporation*, USCA (2011).

386 For an incisive study of the problems see Nollkaemper, in Winter (ed), *Multilevel Governance of Global Environmental Change* (Cambridge, 2006) 179–99. See also *Jesner v Arab Bank*, 138 S Ct 1386 (2018).

387 Anderson and Galizzi, *International Environmental Law in National Courts*, 9.

The UNHRC has tried to address some of these problems through its Guiding Principles on Business and Human Rights.[388] The 'Protect, Respect and Remedy Framework'[389] does not presuppose that international human rights obligations apply to corporations directly.[390] It focuses instead on the adverse impact of corporate activity on human rights and corporate complicity in breaches of human rights law by government. There are three pillars. First the State's continuing duty to protect human rights against abuses by business.[391] Secondly, the responsibility of corporations to respect human rights through the use of due diligence.[392] Thirdly, individual access to remedy: governments must ensure that where human rights are harmed by business activities there is adequate accountability and effective redress, whether judicial or non-judicial.[393] Although the UN Framework uses the language of human rights, what it has in mind are activities that cause death or injury, or lead to ill health, or pollute water supplies, or harm subsistence farming, or reduce food crops, or cause displacement of communities from their homes and villages, or endanger the welfare of indigenous peoples and their access to natural resources. These are all civil wrongs which should in principle be actionable under local law in any court with jurisdiction over the respondent. This is not an exhaustive list, but it illustrates the types of harm caused by corporate activity in developing countries that the UN Framework seeks to mitigate. Much of this harm is environmental.

While the 'Protect, Respect and Remedy' Framework addresses *what* states and businesses need to do to ensure respect for human rights, the Guiding Principles adopted in 2011 seek to move from concept to practice by indicating *how* to implement the Framework. [394] The Principles apply to all States and all business enterprises, both transnational and others, 'regardless of their size, sector, location, ownership and structure.'[395] A monitoring group will report annually to the UNHRC and the UNGA.[396]

An alternative strategy focuses on promoting corporate social responsibility, in which compliance with agreed environmental standards is monitored through

[388] UNHRC, 'Guiding Principles on Business and Human Rights: Implementing the United Nations "Protect, Respect and Remedy" Framework', UN Doc A/HRC/17/31, 21 March 2011, paras 73–74, 77. See Aaranson and Highham, *Re-Righting Business: John Ruggie and the Struggle to Develop International Human Rights Standards for Transnational Firms* (World Trade Institute, 2011).

[389] UNHRC, *Rept of the Special Representative of the S-G on the issue of human rights and transnational corporations and other business enterprises* (the 'Ruggie Rept'), UN Doc A/HRC/8/5, 7 April 2008.

[390] But some national courts have held that corporations are responsible for human rights breaches: see *In re Greenpeace Southeast Asia and Others* Case No. CHR-NI-2016-0001(2015), Philippines human rights commission

[391] *Ibid*, paras 27–50. [392] *Ibid*, paras 50–72.

[393] *Ibid*, paras 81–102. See also European Commission, *Human Rights and the Environment Applicable to European Enterprises Operating Outside the EU: A Study of the Legal Framework*, (Brussels, 2010). The proposals made in the study have not been implemented.

[394] Ruggie, Guiding Principles on Business and Human Rights: Implementing the United Nations 'Protect, Respect and Remedy' Framework, UN Doc A/HRC/17/31 (2011) ('Guiding Principles').

[395] UN Guiding Principles, 6 (general principles).

[396] UN Doc A/HRC/RES/17/4 (6th July 2011).

transparent reporting, NGO activism, and shareholder accountability.[397] The earliest and most significant standards adopted for this purpose are the OECD's Guidelines for Multinational Enterprises.[398] These have the support of the main capital exporting states, whose responsibility it is to ensure that companies comply. While not legally binding on companies, the OECD Guidelines represent a standard of public interest which may affect decisions of national courts and improve corporate performance.[399] Non-compliance complaints can be investigated by 'National Contact Points' (NCP).[400] The OECD also has a procedure for investigating complaints, although it is generally perceived as ineffective by NGOs and UNCTAD.[401] In extreme cases, involving illegal exploitation of natural resources in areas of conflict, the Security Council has used the OECD Guidelines as a basis for monitoring the conduct of multinational corporations and requiring governments to take action against companies found in breach.[402] However, governments have not generally been good at doing so. Human Rights Watch reported that 'The NCP procedure for dealing with these complaints in all relevant countries has been slow and ineffective. Most government representatives have chosen to use the most narrow, and sometimes unjustified, interpretations of the guidelines'.[403] The Security Council could if necessary apply UN sanctions under Chapter 7 of the UN Charter, but it has not so far chosen to do so.

Another method of promoting environmental accountability is through the work of the multilateral investment banks. The World Bank's corporate investment arm, the International Finance Corporation, applies a 'Policy on Environmental and Social Sustainability',[404] which requires compliance with various environmental standards. As we saw in Chapter 2, these standards include many of the major MEAs, as well as applicable national law. The World Bank Inspection Panel and the IFC ombudsman have power to investigate complaints from member governments, NGOs or individuals alleging a failure by the Bank to apply these standards.[405] Moreover, compliance may become an issue in interstate litigation. In the *Pulp Mills Case* compatibility with IFC standards by Botnia, the investor company, was one of the issues in dispute between Uruguay and Argentina.

Following several unsuccessful attempts by the UN to adopt its own global standards, a 'Global Compact' was promulgated by the Secretary General in 1999 with the object of securing business support for established UN principles, including

397 The literature is extensive. See generally Zerk, *Multinationals and Corporate Social Responsibility* (Oxford, 2019); Morgera, *Corporate Accountability in International Environmental Law* (2nd edn, Oxford, 2019); Ong, 12 *EJIL* (2001) 685.

398 For the current text see OECD, *The OECD Guidelines for Multinational Enterprises: Text, Commentary and Clarifications* (Paris, 2011). See Tully, 50 *ICLQ* (2001) 394.

399 Muchlinski, 50 *ICLQ* (2001) 24; *Morgera, Corporate Accountability*, 228–47.

400 *ibid.*

401 Morgera, *Corporate Accountability*, 231–5.

402 UNSC 1457 (2003) 1499 (2003).

403 Human Rights Watch, *The Curse of Gold* (New York, 2005) Ch IX.

404 IFC, *Performance Standards on Environmental and Social Sustainability* (2012) *supra*, Ch 2, section 4(7).

405 See *supra*, Ch 2.

sustainability.[406] It is difficult to evaluate the Compact's real-world impact, and the UN's own assessment is mixed: '. . . a clear gap remains between commitment to sustainability and evidence of implementation. . . . . There is still a very long way to go before the Global Compact principles around sustainable business become the universal norm.'[407]

Thus, while international environmental law does not apply directly to corporations, it is not irrelevant to their activities, as the examples discussed above show. At the same time, it is clear that international efforts to promote corporate environmental accountability are underdeveloped and frequently ineffective against powerful multinationals. Proposals to adopt a binding treaty on business and human rights have not so far made any progress.[408] The best method for controlling these companies remains the well-established one habitually deployed by developed states: effective regulation via national law and enforcement agencies. If that does not work, sue them. An alternative approach may entail application of international criminal law, considered further in the following section.

6 ENVIRONMENTAL CRIMES

The notion that individuals and corporations bear a responsibility towards the environment is not new. The Stockholm Declaration referred in Principle 1 to man's 'solemn responsibility' to protect and improve the environment. Subsequent formulations have preferred to emphasize the individual character of this obligation. Thus the World Charter for Nature talks of the duty of 'each person' to act in accordance with its terms.[409] The 1994 Draft Principles on Human Rights and the Environment state: 'All persons . . . have the duty to protect and preserve the environment'.[410] Moreover, a number of constitutions, including Article 51A of the Indian Constitution, refer to the individual's duty to protect and improve the natural environment or some similar concept.[411] None of the international instruments creates legally binding obligations for individuals or corporations as such. But they do provide a justification for using criminal responsibility as a means of enforcing international environmental law. The importance of criminal responsibility is that it provides added incentive to refrain

406 See *UN Guide to the Global Compact*; Morgera, *Corporate Accountability*, Ch 12.

407 UN Global Compact, *Impact: Transforming Business, Changing the World* (2015).

408 See UNHRC, *Report on the first session of the open-ended intergovernmental working group on transnational corporations and other business enterprises with respect to human rights, with the mandate of elaborating an international legally binding instrument*, UN Doc A/HRC/31/50 (2016), and Choudhury, 67 *ICLQ* (2018) 961.

409 Principle 24. See *infra*, Ch 11.

410 Para 21, *supra*, n 49.

411 See also Yemen, Article 16; Papua-New Guinea, Article 5; Peru, Article 123; Poland, Article 71; Sri Lanka, Article 28; Vanuatu, Article 7.

from harmful conduct by emphasizing its culpable character, and, in many cases, by allowing more stringent enforcement measures or penalties to be imposed.[412] Its use can be observed in the requirements of treaty enforcement in national law, in instances of extraterritorial jurisdiction, and in the concept of environmental crimes against international law.

6(1) ENFORCEMENT THROUGH CRIMINAL LAW

The implementation of most environmental treaties will usually require legislative and enforcement measures to be taken by governments. In general, these are part of the obligation of due diligence which states are called on to perform. How a state gives effect to this obligation will depend on what is required by the treaty in question, but in many cases the choice of means is left to the state's discretion.[413] Whether it relies on the criminal law to regulate individual or corporate conduct will then depend on the legal system in question. Other possible options include civil remedies, administrative or fiscal measures, and voluntary restraints.[414] But there are some situations for which states have agreed that conduct is sufficiently objectionable that criminal penalties are required. This is typically the case in treaties covering trade in hazardous wastes, marine pollution, and illegal trade in endangered species.[415] Criminal penalties are normally also employed to deal with illegal fishing.[416] In some of these cases the involvement of transnational organised crime makes international cooperation on law enforcement essential.[417]

In 1998 the Council of Europe adopted a Convention for the Protection of the Environment through Criminal Law.[418] The purpose of this agreement is to further a 'common criminal policy aimed at protection of the environment'. It is based on the belief that there is an important role for criminal law in this respect, and that serious violations of environmental law should be criminalized and made subject to adequate penalties. Article 2 requires the parties to criminalize polluting discharges; disposal, treatment, storage, export and import of hazardous waste; the operation of

412 See generally Richardson, Ogus, and Burrows, *Policing Pollution* (Oxford, 1982) 15–17.

413 The distinction between obligations of conduct and obligations of result is relevant here. See in particular II *YbILC* (1977) Pt 2, 11–30.

414 For a review of differing national approaches to the enforcement of environmental law see Macrory, *Regulatory Justice: Making Sanctions Effective: Final Rept* (2006); Mushal, 19 *JEL* (2007) 201; Faure and Svatikova, 24 *JEL* (2012) 253.

415 1989 Basel Convention, Article 4(3)–(4); 1991 Bamako Convention on the Ban of the Import into Africa, etc, of Hazardous Wastes, Article 9(2); 1973/78 MARPOL Convention, Article 4(2) (4); 1972 London Convention, Article 6(2); Paris Convention for the Prevention of Marine Pollution from Land-based Sources, Article 12(1); 1987 Protocol for the Prevention of Pollution of the South Pacific by Dumping, Article 12(2); 1982 UNCLOS, Articles 217(8) 230; 1973 CITES Convention, Article 8(1).

416 Subject to limitations set out in 1982 UNCLOS, Article 73.

417 See 2000 UN Convention against Transnational Organized Crime.

418 See Explanatory Report [1998] COETSER 5; Ercmann, 65 *Rev Int de Droit Pénal* (1994) 1199. On European practice see Ringelmann, 5 *Eur J of Crime, Crim L & Crim Just* (1997) 393, and for an international survey see Repts collected in 65 *Rev Int de Droit Pénal* (1994) 653–921. The Convention is not in force.

dangerous plant; and nuclear hazards, when these are unlawful, intentional, and reach a threshold of substantial injury. Article 3 allows this obligation to be extended to the same acts when committed negligently, and Article 4 applies to a wider range of unlawful activities, including interfering with protected areas and protected species of flora and fauna, without requiring any harm. The convention confers jurisdiction only on the state on whose territory, ships, or aircraft the offence is committed, and it provides for sanctions to take into account the seriousness of the offence. Imprisonment, fines, confiscation of assets, and measures of reinstatement of the environment are envisaged. This agreement's very general character suggests that it is unlikely to influence the practice of many states, even in Europe; most of the potential parties already employ criminal sanctions in many of the cases covered by the convention, while it can scarcely be said that it offers a minimum standard for criminal law, or criminal penalties. Twenty years after adoption it has few parties and is not in force.

6(2) EXTRATERRITORIAL CRIMINAL JURISDICTION

Jurisdiction in this context means the authority of a state under international law to prescribe and enforce laws. It is primarily an attribute of the sovereignty of states over their own territory, or over their own nationals.[419] Jurisdiction based on nationality is not confined to individuals, but applies also to companies, ships, aircraft, and spacecraft. The state retains jurisdiction over its nationals even when they are abroad or on the high seas; it is on this basis that flag states remain responsible for regulating pollution or fishing from ships on the high seas or in the maritime zones of other states.[420] Nationality is also in practice the only generally accepted basis for regulating persons and activities in Antarctica or on the deep seabed.[421] Although in principle there is nothing to stop states regulating their nationals when operating in other states, in practice most states will confine such cases of concurrent jurisdiction to serious criminal offences.[422]

In addition to these general principles of jurisdiction in customary law, international law also recognizes certain forms of extraterritorial jurisdiction based on the so-called protective principle. This is particularly important in the law of the sea. It provides the justification for the extension of coastal state jurisdiction within the exclusive economic zone for the purposes of protecting the marine environment and conserving living resources. The content of this jurisdiction is carefully defined by

419 See generally Bowett, in McDonald and Johnston, *The Structure and Process of International Law* (Dordrecht, 1983) 555; *Brownlie's Principles of International Law* (8th edn, Oxford, 2014) Ch 21.

420 See *infra*, Ch 9.

421 1959 Antarctic Treaty, Article 8; Triggs (ed), *The Antarctic Treaty Regime* (Cambridge, 1987) 88; 1982 UNCLOS, Article 209; *AO on Responsibilities and Obligations of States Sponsoring Persons and Entities with Respect to Activities in the Area*, ITLOS (2011) paras 77–8.

422 States are not entitled to *enforce* their laws on the territory of another state, however. On the more complex problems of jurisdiction over companies and their subsidiaries, see Muchlinski, *Multinational Enterprises and the Law*, Ch 5.

treaty and customary law, and it is not unlimited. Moreover, the power to enforce coastal state laws within the EEZ is more restricted than the power to prescribe. These limitations are more fully considered in later chapters.[423] The important point, however, is that this extended jurisdiction enhances the enforcement machinery in these two areas of environmental law. In both cases the main argument in favour of extra-territorial criminal jurisdiction has been the failure or inability of the flag state to police the high seas effectively. A similar argument underlies the possible extension of the concept of universal jurisdiction to cover certain environmental offences.

6(3) UNIVERSAL JURISDICTION AND CRIMES AGAINST INTERNATIONAL LAW

Universal jurisdiction entitles a state to prosecute an offence even in the absence of any connection based on nationality, territory, or the protective principle.[424] Piracy is the clearest example in customary international of this form of jurisdiction, which rests on the assumption that the crimes in question are contrary to international public order. Thus it is the interest of every state in suppressing such offences which justifies their status as crimes which all states may prosecute.[425] The basis of the ILC's 'Code of Offences Against the Peace and Security of Mankind', and of conventions dealing with torture and hijacking, is to ensure that every state in whose territory the alleged offender is present shall either try or extradite, and in contemporary international law this is in effect what is now meant by 'universal jurisdiction'.[426] Moreover, in 1998 a Statute establishing a permanent International Criminal Court was adopted. This court has concurrent jurisdiction to try war crimes, crimes against humanity, genocide and aggression, making these offences truly universal crimes under international law.[427]

It is the ILC's version of the universality principle with which the concept of port-state jurisdiction found in Article 218 of the 1982 UNCLOS is broadly comparable. The crucial feature of this article is that it gives the state in whose port a foreign vessel is present the right to prosecute for pollution offences committed on the high seas or in the maritime zones of other states, subject to a right of pre-emption by the flag state. Although this article represented progressive development when first adopted, today it is widely regarded as accepted law.[428]

423 See *infra*, Chs 9, 12.

424 Bowett, in McDonald and Johnston, *The Structure and Process of International Law*, 563ff.

425 *Lotus Case*, PCIJ Ser A, No 10 (1927) 70. It is of course necessary for states to adopt appropriate national legislation to give effect to their right of prosecution.

426 See 1996 Code of Offences, Articles 8, 9, and commentary in ILC Rept (1996) GAOR A/51/10, 42–55; *Questions relating to the Obligation to Prosecute or Extradite*, ICJ Reports (2012) 422, paras 87–95. See generally McCormack and Simpson, 5 *Crim L Forum* (1994) 1.

427 Statute of the International Criminal Court, Article 5. See Charney, 93 *AJIL* (1999) 452.

428 See *infra*, Ch 9. No comparable attempt has been made to extend jurisdiction over high seas fishing offences. Cf Articles 21 and 23 of the 1995 Agreement on Straddling Fish Stocks, which allow for boarding and inspection on the high seas and in port, but in either case reserve the right of prosecution to the flag state.

A limited category of environmental crimes subject to universal jurisdiction is included in the ILC's 1996 Code of Offences, and in the 1998 Statute of the International Criminal Court. The ILC initially took an expansive view: its 1986 formulation referred to 'any serious breach of an international obligation of essential importance for the safeguarding and preservation of the human environment' and it treated the offence as a crime against humanity.[429] Thereafter the scope and character of the offence was progressively narrowed. The 1991 draft covered only those who wilfully caused or ordered 'widespread, long-term and severe damage to the natural environment'.[430] The article finally adopted in 1996 retains the same very high threshold of intentional harm committed 'in a systematic manner or on a large scale,' but moves the offence into the narrower category of crimes against the peace and security of mankind.[431]

The effect of this re-classification and re-drafting is that the offence can be committed only during an armed conflict, only when the methods and means of warfare are 'not justified by military necessity', and only when the intended environmental damage 'gravely prejudices the health or survival of the population'. As defined by the Commission, the offence is far removed from its original form and has lost its autonomous character. Moreover, although it reflects some of the contemporary concern arising out of Iraq's environmental warfare against Kuwait in 1991, the final ILC text 'has been emasculated to such an extent that its conditions of applicability will almost never be met'.[432] Although the 1977 Additional Protocol I to the Geneva Conventions includes provisions on protection of the environment in time of armed conflict, which some writers see as representing customary law, it does not place these articles in the category whose grave breach constitutes a war crime.[433] Similarly, the ILC's commentary on the Code of Offences sought to 'avoid giving the impression that this type of conduct necessarily constitutes a war crime under existing international law'.[434]

The Commission's basic approach is retained in the Statute of the International Criminal Court but in a less emasculated form. The requirement that environmental damage must be the *intentional result* of an attack that gravely prejudices the population is dropped. There remain five essential elements of the war crime defined by Article 8 of the Statute. The attack itself must be intentional; it must be known that damage to the environment will be caused; the damage must be widespread, long-term, and severe; it must also be excessive in relation to the overall military advantage; and the crime must have been committed as part of a plan or policy *or* on a large scale.[435] Article 8 of the 1998 Statute can thus be regarded only as a step towards broadening the category of universal crimes under international law.

429 Article 12(4) II *YbILC* (1986) Pt 1, 86.

430 Article 14(6) ILC Rept (1989) GAOR A/44/10, 168f; Article 26, ILC Rept (1991) GAOR A/46/10. See also draft Article 22(2)(d).

431 Article 20(g) ILC Rept (1996) GAOR A/51/10, 110–20.

432 Tomuschat, 26 *EPL* (1996) 242. See *supra*, Ch 3, section 10.

433 Additional Protocol I Relating to the Victims of International Armed Conflicts, Articles 35, 55, 56, 85, and *supra*, Ch 3, section 10.

434 ILC Rept (1996) 120.

435 Articles 8(1) and 8(2)(a)(iv).

Nevertheless, the inclusion of environmental offences in the ICC Statute may prove to be significant. There is a case for treating very serious and deliberate environmental harm as a universal crime, since the public interest of all states is affected, and more effective enforcement is facilitated if individual states or the ICC are empowered to prosecute in order to protect the global common interest.[436] It might be said that the same argument applies equally strongly in peacetime, but the case for a broader offence, within the category of crimes against humanity rather than war crimes, has not so far been accepted by the international community or the ILC, nor has the proposed crime of 'ecocide', a concept so broad and uncertain in scope that it could not easily meet the requirements of human rights law.[437] This does not preclude further incremental developments in universal jurisdiction tied to more specific forms of conduct, such as illegal trade in hazardous waste or the dumping of radioactive waste. In this respect Article 218 of the 1982 UNCLOS remains an important precedent.

7 CONCLUSIONS

This chapter points first to the increasing importance of environmental rights perspectives in national and international environmental law. At a procedural level, strengthening individual participatory rights in national law has become an instrument for legitimizing national policies aimed at sustainable development, with implications principally for public-interest litigation, standing, and access to justice. At a substantive level, though less well developed internationally, environmental quality has become a human-rights issue, offering an approach to environmental protection very different from the inter-state regulatory system explored in the previous two chapters. Such developments may not necessarily make the task of reconciling developmental and environmental objectives any easier, since human-rights law can be used to obstruct greater environmental protection as well as to advance it.

Secondly, as studies for the Hague Conference have shown, unless greater harmonization of substantive environmental law can be achieved, the need for more coherence in the private international law aspects of transnational environmental litigation becomes more apparent. The increasing international emphasis on free movement of goods, capital, and investment has not yet been matched by a willingness to address the accountability of multinational corporations for environmental and human-rights abuses in developing countries. Nevertheless, cases such as *Lubbe v Cape* show how national conflict-of-laws rules which have hitherto shielded business are beginning to be affected by human rights and access-to-justice issues in novel and important ways that have implications for future environmental litigation.

436 In 2016, the Prosecutor of the ICC announced that the investigation of crimes within its jurisdiction that were 'committed by or result in the destruction of the environment, the illegal exploitation of natural resources, or the illegal dispossession of land' will be given priority.

437 See 1967 ICCPR, Article 15.

The development of environmental liability law called for in so many international agreements and declarations remains largely an aspiration, save in the discrete areas of marine pollution and nuclear accidents. The great caution shown by states on this question, both in Europe and elsewhere, suggests that most liability treaties will continue to gather dust. Finally, the evolution of international environmental criminal law appears equally tentative, confined at present largely to war crimes and jurisdiction over offences at sea. Despite these qualifications, we can see from this chapter that the Stockholm and Rio Declarations have significantly promoted individual environmental rights and prompted efforts to address the responsibilities of individuals and corporations for environmentally harmful consequences of their activities.

6

CLIMATE CHANGE AND ATMOSPHERIC POLLUTION

1 INTRODUCTION

The present chapter* looks inter alia at how international law has been used or could be used to help tackle the most significant environmental challenge of our time—global climate change. Few topics provide a better illustration of the importance of a globally inclusive regulatory regime focused on preventive and precautionary approaches to environmental harm—or of the problems of negotiating one on such a complex subject. In this context the 'framework treaty'[1] has provided the key regulatory tool. The 1992 UNFCCC is not the first such treaty to address atmospheric pollution, however, and it is best approached with two earlier models in mind: the 1979 LRTAP Convention and the 1985 Ozone Convention. Although both were initially little more than empty frameworks for further negotiation, they have evolved progressively to the point where they now represent two of the leading examples of international regulation providing a basis for real solutions to global and regional environmental problems.[2] Progress in this context has been made without sacrificing economic growth.[3]

Solutions to global climate change have not been so easily forthcoming. In principle, the same legal tools could be used to regulate greenhouse gas emissions and construct an international regime for tackling climate change but the intimate connection with economic growth has made international agreement on effective solutions especially hard to achieve. The sceptical stance of the US vis-à-vis the 1997 Kyoto Protocol and the 2015 Paris Agreement is an obvious example of this problem. Emerging economies have been similarly reluctant to engage in international agreements which might

*We are grateful to Professor Lavanya Rajamani of Oxford University and Navraj Ghaleigh of Edinburgh University for their contributions to revising this chapter.

[1] *Supra*, Ch 1, section 2(1). [2] *Infra*, sections 2, 3.

[3] UNECE, *Towards Cleaner Air: Scientific Assessment Report* (Oslo, 2016).

compromise economic performance, reflecting their sense of where historical responsibility lies. Tackling climate change is thus more a political and economic challenge than a legal one.[4] The efforts of the international regulatory regime to address these challenges by recourse to novel 'market based' mechanisms and differential treatment are discussed below, as is the post-Kyoto scheme for reducing greenhouse gas emissions through 'nationally determined contributions'. In the end it is likely to be technology that enables us to grapple with the causes of climate change, not law, but law can drive technological change, as it has with ozone depletion and acid rain.

1(1) DEGRADATION OF THE GLOBAL ATMOSPHERE

Climate change and depletion of the ozone layer are the two principal threats to the global atmosphere.[5] They are to some extent interlinked because some ozone-depleting substances also contribute to global warming (the so-called 'greenhouse effect'). During the 1980s evidence emerged linking the release of (CFCs, halons, and other chlorine-based substances with the gradual destruction of the ozone layer. This layer, located in the stratosphere but still well within the earth's atmosphere, is important because it filters sunlight and protects the earth from ultraviolet radiation. Loss of the atmospheric shield would have serious implications for human health, agriculture, and fisheries productivity over a long period, and could leave future generations a legacy of irreversible harm.[6]

Global climate change has largely been caused by increased anthropogenic emissions of GHGs over the past two centuries, but these emissions have greatly increased over the past thirty years and are still increasing.[7] The IPCC concludes that evidence of changes in the climate system is now unequivocal, with GHG concentrations increasing, the atmosphere and oceans warming at an accelerating rate, glaciers and polar ice melting, and sea levels rising.[8] The greenhouse effect is caused by atmospheric gases (principally carbon dioxide, methane and water vapour) regulating the sun's energy and—until now—making the earth habitable. In its absence, the earth's temperature would be about -18°C. Carbon dioxide was present in the pre-industrial (1750) atmosphere at a concentration of 280 parts per million (ppm). Its rise to 407 ppm

4 See for a good general account Nordhaus, *The Climate Casino* (New Haven, 2013).

5 For a comparison of the ozone depletion and climate change legal regimes, see Sunstein, 31 *Harv ELR* (2007) 1.

6 WMO, *Atmospheric Ozone 1985* (Geneva 1986); EPA, *An Assessment of the Risks of Stratospheric Modification* (Washington, DC, 1987). For the current position see WMO, *Scientific Assessment of Ozone Depletion* (Geneva, 2018).

7 IPCC, 'Summary for Policy Makers' in *Climate Change 2007: The Physical Science Basis: Contribution of Working Group 1 to the Fourth Assessment Report* (Cambridge, 2007). Hereafter 'IPCC 2007'. See also the later IPCC reports referred to below.

8 See generally, IPCC, *Climate Change 2013: The Physical Science Basis: Working Group I Contribution to the Fifth Assessment Report of the Intergovernmental Panel on Climate Change* (Cambridge, 2013). Hereafter 'IPCC 2013'. See also IPCC, *Special Report on the Ocean and Cryosphere in a Changing Climate* (2019); *State of the Climate in 2018*, Special Supplement to the *Bulletin of the American Meteorological Society* Vol 100, No 9 September 2019, hereafter '*State of the Climate 2018*.' On the IPCC see *infra*, this section.

by 2018 is substantially a function of increased fossil fuel combustion, notably through coal-fired power stations and transport. Other human activities, such as deforestation, also contribute to global climate change, as do emissions of methane from agricultural sources and the loss of soil carbon due to excessive ploughing and intensive agriculture. Atmospheric methane (with a global warming potential approximately 70 times greater than CO2) has more than doubled in concentration. In addition to such 'forcings' (human-induced changes in GHG concentrations), 'feedbacks' are also important—internal climate processes that may amplify the climate's response to certain conditions. For example, a warmer atmosphere holds more moisture which in turn causes further warming. In 2018 the level of GHGs in the atmosphere was higher than it had been for 800,000 years, with a warming influence almost 43 per cent higher than in 1990; only 2015, 2016 and 2017 had been hotter since records began.[9] On present trends it will not be possible to keep the increase in global temperatures below the 2°C allowed for in the 2015 Paris Agreement.[10]

The effects of global climate change are likely to be felt world-wide, but with differential impacts. Stronger hurricanes in the Caribbean are one consequence; drought and desertification in Africa are another. Some countries might benefit from a change to a more temperate climate but accelerating sea level rise may cause some low-lying island states to disappear altogether. Predicted rises in global temperatures would potentially have world-wide effects on forests, agriculture, water supplies, natural ecosystems, and population distribution.[11] The oceans have to some extent mitigated climate change, with 30 per cent of the anthropogenic CO2 emissions being absorbed, but this results in the sea becoming increasingly acidic and warmer; in 2019 ocean heating was at record levels.[12] Acidification and warming of the oceans cannot easily be reversed and they are, in that sense, a persistent form of marine pollution.[13] Their toxic effects include depleted fish stocks, coral bleaching and loss of marine biodiversity and ecosystems.

Science has a key role in determining the causes and likely consequences of climate change. The IPCC was established in 1988 by UNEP and the WMO 'anticipating the critical role that scientific consensus would play in building the political will to respond to climate change'.[14] Established to review the scientific evidence and make recommendations, the IPCC's reports are recognized as the definitive source of information. Despite some criticism from climate change sceptics, the IPCC's climate modelling has proved remarkably accurate; at worst it may be too conservative about the effects and timescales.[15] The Assessment Reports of 2007 and 2013 firmly

[9] *State of the Climate in 2018*.

[10] IPCC, *Global warming of 1.5°C: Summary for Policymakers* (Geneva, 2018); UNEP, *The Emissions Gap Report* (Nairobi, 2019) and see *infra*, section 4(8).

[11] IPCC, *Climate Change 2014: Impacts, Adaptation, and Vulnerability* (Cambridge, 2014).

[12] Cheng et al, 37 *Advances in Atmospheric Sciences* (2020) 137–42.

[13] IPCC, *Climate Change 2014: Synthesis Report* (Cambridge, 2014) 62, and see *infra* Ch 9.

[14] *Ibid*. See Ghaleigh in Carlarne, Gray and Tarasofsky (eds), *The Oxford Handbook of International Climate Change Law* (Oxford, 2016), Ch 3.

[15] See Hausfather et al, 47 *Geophysical Research Letters* (2019)

contradict suggestions that climate change is a natural, not an anthropogenic, phenomenon, finding that the observable rise in global average temperature since the mid-20th century is 'very likely' (that is, more than 90 per cent certain) to result from increased anthropogenic GHG emissions. If continued without any abatement at all such emissions could result in an average temperature change of up to 6.4°C by 2099.[16] The effect of anything approaching rise in temperature would be catastrophic. In addition, the IPCC predicts an average sea-level rise due to thermal expansion and melting of ice of up to 65 cm by the year 2100, with the probability of reduced precipitation in Africa, Southern Europe, Amazonia, and central North America due to temperature increases.

The IPCC accepts that there are 'unknowns' in the timing, magnitude, and regional patterns of climate change due to the complexity of the subject but there is otherwise no uncertainty about the anthropogenic causes or likely effects of climate change. Insofar as there is a consensus on tackling climate change it is largely a product of the IPCC's work; nonetheless, neither the 1997 Kyoto Protocol nor the 2015 Paris Agreement contain measures as far-reaching as the IPCC's findings would suggest are necessary.[17] Whether the Paris Agreement of 2015 can achieve more will be considered below. In contrast the 1987 Montreal Protocol's success can be explained by the relative absence of political controversy surrounding ozone depletion and the willingness of all parties to take the measures necessary to achieve the objectives of the 1985 Ozone Convention.

1(2) THE LEGAL STATUS OF THE ATMOSPHERE

The atmosphere is not a distinct category in international law. Because it consists of a fluctuating and dynamic air mass, it cannot be equated with airspace which, above land, is simply a spatial dimension subject to the sovereignty of the subjacent states.[18] But this overlap with territorial sovereignty also means that the atmosphere cannot be treated as an area of common property beyond the jurisdiction of any state, comparable in this sense to the high seas.[19] The alternative possibility of regarding it as a shared resource is relevant in situations of bilateral or regional transboundary air pollution, affecting other states or adjacent regional seas. UNEP has referred to 'airsheds' as examples of shared natural resources,[20] and this status is consistent with regional approaches to the control and regulation of transboundary air pollution adopted in the 1979 LRTAP Convention, and in regional seas agreements limiting air pollution of the North Sea, the Baltic, and the Mediterranean.[21]

[16] IPCC, *5th Assessment Report: Climate Change 2013: The Physical Science Basis: Summary for Policy Makers* (Cambridge, 2013).

[17] On Kyoto see Andressen and Skjaerseth, in Brunnée, Bodansky and Hey (eds), *Handbook of International Environmental Law* (1st ed, Oxford, 2007) 183–200; Bodansky, Brunnée and Rajamani (eds), *International Climate Change Law* (Oxford, 2017) Ch 6, and on Paris see *infra*.

[18] 1944 Chicago Convention on International Civil Aviation.

[19] 1958 Geneva Convention on the High Seas, Articles 1–2; 1982 UNCLOS, Articles 87, 89.

[20] *Report of the Executive Director*, UNEP/GC/44 (1975) para 86; *supra*, Ch 3, section 5(1).

[21] Handl, 26 *NRJ* (1986) 405.

The shared-resources concept is much less useful in relation to global atmospheric problems such as ozone depletion or climate change. What is needed here is a concept which recognizes the unity of the global atmosphere and the common interest of all states in its protection. The traditional category of common property is inadequate for this purpose. The same objection applies to the use of 'common heritage' in this context, with the additional difficulty that this concept has so far been applied only to mineral resources of the deep seabed and outer space.[22] The atmosphere is clearly not outer space, despite the difficulty of defining the boundaries of that area. Moreover, Article 135 of the 1982 UNCLOS provides that the status of the seabed does not affect superjacent airspace, and thus offers no support for any wider use of the common heritage concept. Significantly, common heritage was not employed in the 1985 Ozone Convention,[23] or in the 1992 UNFCC. The 1985 Ozone Convention defines the 'ozone layer' as 'the layer of atmospheric ozone above the planetary boundary layer'.[24] This does not mean that the ozone layer is either legally or physically part of outer space. It remains part of the atmosphere, and falls partly into areas of common property, and partly into areas of national sovereignty. One purpose of the convention's definition is to indicate that it is concerned with stratospheric ozone,[25] and not with low-level ozone, an air pollutant regulated by a protocol to the 1979 LRTAP Convention. More importantly, however, the definition treats the whole stratospheric ozone layer as a global unity, without reference to legal concepts of sovereignty, shared resources, or common property. It points to the emergence of a distinct status for the global atmosphere, which makes it appropriate to view the ozone layer as an area of common interest, regardless of who enjoys sovereignty over the airspace which it occupies.[26]

The same conclusion can also be drawn from UN General Assembly resolution 43/53 which declares that global climate change is 'the common concern of mankind'.[27] This phraseology was the outcome of a political compromise over Malta's initial proposal to treat the global climate as the common heritage of mankind. It has subsequently been followed in the Noordwijk Declaration of the Conference on Atmospheric Pollution and Climate Change,[28] by UNEP,[29] and in the Preamble to the 1992 Climate Change Convention. What it suggests is that the global climate has a status comparable to the ozone layer, and that the totality of the global atmosphere can now properly be regarded as the 'common concern of mankind'. By approaching the issues from this global perspective, the UN has recognized both the artificiality of territorial boundaries in this context, and the inadequacy of treating ozone depletion

22 See *supra*, Ch 3, section 3(1)(d). 23 See *infra*, section 3(2). 24 Article 1(1).

25 The stratosphere begins between 5 and 10 miles from the earth's surface and reaches a height of approximately 30 miles. Powered aircraft typically operate to heights of 10 miles, and exceptionally to about 20 miles.

26 International Meeting of Legal and Policy Experts, 1989, Ottawa, Canada, 19 *EPL* (1989) 78.

27 See Boyle, in Churchill and Freestone (eds), *International Law and Global Climate Change*; Soltau, in Carlarne et al (eds), *International Climate Change Law*, Ch 10.

28 19 *EPL* (1989) 220. 29 UNEP/GC 15/36 (1989).

and global climate change in the same way as transboundary air pollution, for which regional or bilateral solutions remain appropriate.

As we saw in Chapter 4, the status of 'common concern' is primarily significant in indicating the common legal interest of all states in protecting the global atmosphere, whether directly injured or not, and in enforcing rules concerning its protection.[30] While a UN General Assembly resolution alone may not be sufficient to confer this status, the 1985 Ozone Convention and the 1992 UNFCCC unquestionably do so.[31]

1(3) CUSTOMARY LAW AND GLOBAL ENVIRONMENTAL RESPONSIBILITY

The argument that the due diligence obligation considered in Chapter 3 applies to the protection of the global atmosphere is not difficult to make. Principle 21 of the Stockholm Declaration already forms the basis for the 1979 LRTAP Convention, the 1985 Ozone Convention, and the 1992 UNFCCC. Although the global atmosphere is not an area 'beyond the limits of national jurisdiction', and thus does not quite fit the precise terms of Principle 21 or of Rio Principle 2,[32] it should by analogy fall within the protection afforded by international law to common areas such as the high seas. This conclusion is implicit in the 1985 Ozone Convention, and in the designation of climate change as a matter of 'common concern' in the 1992 Climate Change Convention.[33]

Moreover, international claims concerning the conduct of atmospheric nuclear tests provide some precedent for the inference that, like the high seas, the global atmosphere must be used with reasonable regard for the rights of other states, including the protection of their environment and human health. As we will see in Chapter 9, such tests are arguably unreasonable and contrary to international law. UNEP Principles concerning weather modification for peaceful purposes recommend that these should also be carried out only after an assessment of their environmental consequences and in a manner 'designed to ensure that they do not cause damage to the environment of other states or of areas beyond the limits of national jurisdiction'.[34]

That conclusion begs the question what general international law has to say about climate change or ozone depletion apart from the relevant treaty regimes. The general obligation of States to take measures to prevent, reduce and control transboundary pollution and pollution of the marine environment was elaborated in the 2010 *Pulp Mills Case* and in the 2011 ITLOS *Advisory Opinion on Activities in the Area*. If this obligation can apply to nuclear fall-out there seems no reason not to apply it to emissions of GHGs or ozone depleting substances.[35] Both cause pollution of other states, the oceans and the global environment. But it is more than likely that whatever general obligation

30 *Supra*, Ch 4, section 2(7); Kirgis, 84 *AJIL* (1990) 585, but cf Brunnée, 49 *ZAöRV* (1989) 791.

31 *Supra*, Ch 3, section 3(1).

32 *Supra*, Ch 3, section 4(2).

33 See also UNGA Resolution 44/207 (1989) para 4, and UNEP Principles of Co-operation in Weather Modification (1980).

34 UNEP Principles of Co-operation in Weather Modification (1980).

35 Mayer, 5 *Climate Law* (2015) 1 and *supra*, Ch 3, sections 5 and 9.

states may have to deal with climate change will be fulfilled by complying with the 1992 UNFCCC, the 1997 Kyoto Protocol and the 2015 Paris Agreement. These represent, together with the 1985 Ozone Convention and its 1987 Montreal Protocol, the agreed standard of due diligence for the parties with respect to protection of the global atmosphere.[36] In this context due diligence inevitably represents a compromise between what is possible and what is economically acceptable—a compromise fatally reflected in the 1992 UNFCCC and 1997 Kyoto Protocol. Reformulating that problem in terms of the precautionary approach does not change things. The 1992 UNFCCC already acknowledges the applicability of the precautionary approach,[37] but that has not resulted in States going any faster or any further. They can legitimately say that what has been agreed represents their adoption of a precautionary approach. Is any international court likely to disagree? At best, an international court might be persuaded to interpret contested provisions of the 2015 Paris Agreement or the 1992 UNFCCC, or their interrelationship with the 1982 UNCLOS or other relevant treaties, and exhort the parties to cooperate in good faith, as the ICJ did in the *Gabčíkovo-Nagymaros Case*.[38] But to expect an international court to come up with a better climate change regime based on customary international law than states themselves have negotiated is to ask for a radically new approach to international law-making in general and to international environmental law in particular.

Thus, without dismissing the relevance of customary law as a starting point for negotiation of controls on greenhouse gas emissions or ozone depleting substances, it seems clear that, as in the case of long-range transboundary air pollution, further development of the law on a multilateral basis can only come through agreement and not through inter-state litigation.[39]

1(4) INTERNATIONAL POLICY AND THE REGULATION OF THE ATMOSPHERE

The foregoing considerations indicate something of the legal and scientific complexity surrounding the protection of the atmosphere and its various components. No single approach or legal regime is likely to be appropriate or possible. Moreover, the control of transboundary air pollution, ozone depletion, and climate change have posed difficult choices for many states in matters of economic and industrial policy.

For these reasons, attempts to negotiate international controls have made relatively slow progress, and for many states the preferable policy, at least initially, has been to delay action pending clearer scientific evidence and proof of harm. This explains the initial emphasis in the recommendations of the 1972 Stockholm Conference on the

36 See *supra*, Ch 3, section 5, and Carlarne et al, *International Climate Change Law*, Ch 2.

37 UNFCCC, Art. 3(3). See Wiener in Carlarne et al (eds), *International Climate Change Law*, Ch 8.

38 ICJ Reports (1997) 7. See Sands 28 *JEL* (2016) 19; Boyle 34 *IJMCL* 458 (2019).

39 See generally Carlarne et al, *International Climate Change Law*, Chs 1, 2, and 5; Bodansky, Brunnée and Rajamani, *International Climate Change Law*, Ch 2; Boyle, 63 *GYIL* 305 (2020).

need for monitoring programmes and more scientific research.[40] The same pattern has been repeated with regard to long-range transboundary air pollution, ozone depletion, and climate change. Only gradually have states been persuaded of the need for a precautionary approach to the risk of irreversible atmospheric harm. Although a precautionary approach is apparent in the negotiations for the 1985 Ozone Convention and its later protocol and amendments,[41] the need for precautionary action to deal with the risk of climate change remains only weakly recognized in the 1992 Climate Change Convention, the 1997 Kyoto Protocol, and the 2015 Paris Agreement.[42] Despite full compliance by all parties Kyoto alone could not meet or even come close to the 'ultimate objective' of stabilising GHG concentrations 'at a level that would prevent dangerous anthropogenic interference with the climate system.'[43] Whether the 2015 Paris Agreement can do so remains to be seen.

A second reason for the slow pace of international negotiations has been the need to ensure global participation. Fundamental questions of economic equity between developed and developing states are raised by ozone depletion and climate change, both of which are substantially the result of policies pursued principally by the developed, industrialized states. That was the reason for building common but differentiated responsibility into the obligations of developed and developing states under both regimes. Yet, in both cases, without serious constraints on the industrialised developing states no control strategy will work. Even with full US participation in the 2015 Paris Agreement, the developed economies cannot by themselves do all that would be necessary to contain the global temperature rise to 2° C. The developing economies—and above all China, which is now the world's biggest GHG emitter—will have to carry some of the burden. From this perspective common but differentiated responsibility as articulated in the 1992 UNFCCC and adopted in the 1997 Kyoto Protocol is not a viable basis for saving the climate.[44] To these equitable considerations must also be added the competing claims of future generations to inter-generational equity.[45]

A third important consideration in evaluating legal developments relevant to the protection of the atmosphere is the realization that transboundary air pollution, ozone depletion, and climate change are problems whose solution goes to the heart of a policy of sustainable development. This is recognized in Agenda 21 of the 1992 Rio Conference, in the 2002 Johannesburg Declaration on Sustainable Development, and in the 2015 SDGs, all of which support a range of measures to promote energy

[40] Recommendations 70, 71, 73, 77, 79, 81, and 83, UN Doc A/CONF/48/14/Rev. 1 (1972).

[41] Freestone, in Churchill and Freestone (eds), *International Law and Global Climate Change*, Ch 2, and see *infra*, section 3(2).

[42] *Infra*, section 4. [43] *Infra*, section 4(7).

[44] On common but differentiated responsibility see *supra*, Ch 3, section 4(3), and Rajamani, 65 *ICLQ* (2016) 493.

[45] Redgwell, in Churchill and Freestone (eds), *International Law and Global Climate Change*, Ch 3; Franck, *Fairness in International Law* (Oxford, 1995) Ch 12; Shue, *Climate Justice: Vulnerability and Protection* (Oxford, 2014) and *supra*, Ch 3, section 2(2)(b).

efficiency, energy conservation, and the use of environmentally sound and renewable energy sources in order to reduce harmful atmospheric emissions.[46] It should not be assumed that the most appropriate or effective means of implementing these policies are necessarily to be afforded by international law or international regulation. Rather, international law is one element in a broader strategy, whose success may depend at least in part on the willingness of states to commit themselves to and to implement economic and trade policies focused on sustainable use of energy. Their record in this respect has improved since the early 1980s, but it is still very far from convincing.[47]

2 TRANSBOUNDARY AIR POLLUTION

2(1) INTRODUCTION

WHO reports show that air pollution is today one of the world's most significant threats to human health.[48] Much of this is domestic pollution, but its principal sources are no different from the forms of transboundary air pollution regulated by international agreements in Europe and North America. They include the sulphur dioxide (SO2) and nitrogen oxides (NOx) produced by the combustion of fossil fuels for power generation and industrial use, to which must be added the increasing volume of particulates and volatile organic compounds from vehicles, and low-level ozone. Both SO2 and NOx are emitted naturally into the atmosphere, for example from volcanoes, but these represent only a small proportion of the global total.[49] Transboundary air pollution first emerged as a significant problem in North America and Europe, and it is here that regional regulation is the most advanced, and where the problems are now less serious. Agenda 21 pointed out that much less attention has been paid to transboundary air pollution in developing countries.[50] Thirty-five years later this remains true. In Asia and Africa industrialization and traffic growth are producing air pollution problems similar to or in some cases far worse than those of Europe and North America. Transboundary air pollution has also been caused on a substantial scale by the deliberate burning of Kuwaiti oil wells in 1991, the extensive forest fires in Borneo in 1997 and the Brazilian Amazon in 2019, and the annual burning of Indonesian forests.[51]

46 *Supra*, Ch 2, section 2. 47 *Infra*, section 4(7).

48 See data in HEI/IHME, *State of Global Air* (Boston, 2017). See also WHO Air Quality Standards, 2005.

49 See generally UNECE, *Towards Cleaner Air: Scientific Assessment Report* (Oslo, 2016); id, *Air Pollution Studies*, Nos 1–12 (1984–96).

50 *Report of the UNCED* (1992), Agenda 21, Ch 9. On ASEAN action to deal with transboundary air pollution see *infra*, section 2(5).

51 There is no reason in principle why states should not incur international responsibility for transboundary harm caused by forest fires, provided there has been some failure to act diligently on the part of the state concerned, for example by not controlling deliberate burning. See Tan, 48 *ICLQ* (1999) 826, and *id*, in Jayakumar et al (eds), *Transboundary Pollution*, Ch 12.

Once in the atmosphere, the distribution and deposition of pollution is a function of prevailing winds and weather patterns. The Programme for Monitoring and Evaluation of Long-range Transmission of Air Pollutants in Europe ('EMEP') has succeeded in quantifying the depositions in each country that can be attributed to emissions in any other, and has shown that the problem in Europe is not simply a bilateral one between adjacent states, but a regional one, in which most states contribute their own share of pollution, but some emerge as substantial net importers.[52] Greater transboundary effects are generated by reactions of sulphur, nitrogen, and other substances with water vapour in the atmosphere, where they form acidic compounds, deposited as acid rain, or create other pollutants such as ozone gas (O3). Sulphur deposition has been blamed for acidity of soil, lakes, and rivers and for reduced crop growth, death or degradation of forests, and the disappearance of fish and wildlife. It appears to accelerate the decomposition of buildings, poses health risks, and increases the release of toxic metals, either directly, or through leaching from soil or corrosion of plumbing. Ozone pollution of the lower atmosphere is thought also to harm crops and forests, either alone, or in combination with acid rain.[53]

Some air pollution is intercontinental and, as we will see in Chapter 8, this discovery has been a factor underlying the adoption of conventions controlling production and consumption of persistent organic pollutants and mercury.[54] Moreover, research conducted by GESAMP and in the North Sea and North American Great Lakes has shown that land-based air pollution of the marine environment is also significant, and in the case of metals and nutrients more so than for inputs from rivers, particularly to the open oceans.[55]

State practice in bilateral disputes involving the US, Canada, Norway, Sweden, the UK, Germany, and France suggests that the basic rule of customary international codified by Principle 2 of the Rio Declaration is applicable to transboundary air pollution.[56] On the other hand, it did not provide a solution to regional problems of air pollution or acid rain either in North America or Europe. Although those states which are net importers of pollution, such as the Nordic countries or Canada, have from time to time invoked Principle 21 of the Stockholm Declaration or *Trail Smelter*,[57] the preferred approach of all parties has been to negotiate agreed emissions standards with polluting states on a basis which takes account of the interests of both sides, while leaving aside the question of compensation for long-term damage previously inflicted.

[52] For an up-to-date assessment see UNECE, *Towards Cleaner Air: Scientific Assessment Report* (Oslo, 2016).

[53] See generally UNECE, *Air Pollution Studies*, Nos 1–12 (1984–96).

[54] See UNECE, *Towards Cleaner Air*.

[55] *Infra*, Chs 8, 9

[56] See generally Wetstone and Rosencranz, *Acid Rain in Europe and North America* (Washington, DC, 1983); Flinterman, Kwiatkowska, and Lammers (eds), *Transboundary Air Pollution* (Dordrecht, 1986) 121ff; Schmandt, Clarkson, and Roderick (eds), *Acid Rain and Friendly Neighbours* (Durham, NC, 1988); Pallemaerts, *Hague YIL* (1988) 189; McCormick, *Acid Earth* (London, 1997); Okowa, *State Responsibility for Transboundary Air Pollution in International Law* (Oxford, 2000).

[57] *Supra*, Ch 3, section 5.

In the 1979 LRTAP Convention equitable considerations have thus played an important part in tackling transboundary air pollution; where there is no applicable treaty it remains correct to observe that 'it will be customary international legal principles and rules which will principally shape the parties' respective starting positions and guide states in their negotiations'.[58] Customary international law was relied on successfully in the *Aerial Spraying Case* to secure a settlement of a long-standing air pollution dispute.[59] Effective solutions to the broader problem of long-range transboundary air pollution at a regional level can only be provided by cooperative regimes of international regulation, however. This is where the 1979 LRTAP Convention provides an important precedent.

2(2) 1979 GENEVA CONVENTION ON LONG-RANGE TRANSBOUNDARY AIR POLLUTION

This Convention remains the only major regional multilateral agreement devoted to the regulation and control of transboundary air pollution.[60] It treats the European air mass as a shared resource and the problem as one requiring coordination of pollution-control measures and common emission standards. In this sense it is comparable to the more advanced international watercourse agreements or treaties on land-based sources of marine pollution.[61] Its purpose is thus to prevent, reduce, and control transboundary air pollution, both from new and existing sources, and it contains no provision on liability for air pollution damage, whether under international law or through civil proceedings.[62]

The treaty came into force in 1983, and now has over fifty parties in Europe, North America, and Central Asia, including all the major polluter states. The text of the 1979 LRTAP Convention was weaker than the net importers of pollutants would have liked, but only through compromise of essential interests on both sides could such widespread adherence have been achieved.[63] However, as a framework treaty, it has for forty years provided the basis for the elaboration of further regulatory protocols which have made it one of the most successful and highly developed of the older environmental regimes.

'Long-range transboundary air pollution' is defined as pollution having effects at such a distance that 'it is not generally possible to distinguish the contributions of individual emission sources or groups of sources'.[64] Thus it is not aimed at *Trail Smelter*

58 Handl, 26 *NRJ* (1986) 423, 467.

59 See *Aerial Herbicide Spraying Case (Ecuador v Colombia)*, ICJ, Order of 13 September (2013); 2013 Agreement on Aerial Eradication of Illicit Crops by Colombia near the Ecuadorian Border (Colombia-Ecuador). The case is discussed by Boyle in Jayakumar et al (eds), *Transboundary Pollution*, Ch 9.

60 Gundling, in Flinterman, Kwiatkowska, and Lammers (eds), *Transboundary Air Pollution*, 19; Rosencranz, 75 *AJIL* (1981) 975; Fraenkel, 30 *Harv ILJ* (1989) 447; Okowa, *State Responsibility for Transboundary Air Pollution in International Law*, 24–59.

61 *Infra*, Chs 8, 10.

62 On responsibility for transboundary air pollution see *supra*, Ch 4, section 2(3).

63 Wetstone and Rosencranz, *Acid Rain in Europe and North America*, 140–4.

64 Article 1(b)

or *Aerial Spraying* type cases, but at regional problems of acid rain and other widely dispersed pollutants. Nor is it confined to effects harmful to human health or property. A much broader definition of 'pollution' is used, comparable to those found in marine pollution treaties, which includes harm to living resources, ecosystems, interference with amenities, and legitimate uses of the environment.[65] Amelioration of a wide range of potential environmental harm is thus the treaty's basic objective.

No concrete commitments to specific reductions in air pollution are contained in the treaty itself. Instead, the parties agreed broad principles and objectives for pollution-control policy, in language often so weak that one commentary described the treaty as no more than a 'symbolic victory' intended to reassure both the polluters and the victims.[66] Thus there is only an obligation to 'endeavour to limit' and 'as far as possible, gradually reduce and prevent' air pollution.[67] To achieve this, parties undertake to develop the best policies, strategies, and control measures, but these must be compatible with 'balanced development', and use the 'best available technology' which is 'economically feasible'.[68] A great deal of latitude was thus left to individual states to determine what level of effort they would put into pollution control and what cost they would be willing to pay in overall economic development. For major polluters in 1979, such as the UK, the US and West Germany, this elastic obligation was the condition for their acceptance of the treaty.

The 1979 LRTAP Convention also contains provisions on notification and consultation in cases of significant risk of transboundary pollution. These are only loosely comparable to the customary rule requiring consultation regarding shared resources or environmental risk.[69] Only 'major' changes in policy or industrial development likely to cause 'significant' changes in long-range air pollution must be notified to other states.[70] Otherwise, consultations need only be held at the request of parties 'actually affected by or exposed to a significant risk of long-range transboundary air pollution'.[71] However, the 1991 Espoo Convention has provided a stronger regime of assessment and consultation covering proposals to operate refineries, power stations, smelters, and other large-scale 'combustion installations' since its entry into force.[72] This convention requires the party initiating a proposed activity to take the initiative in providing notification to those likely to be affected, a position much closer to more recent treaty and ILC formulations than is found in the 1979 Geneva Convention.

Despite its evident weaknesses in 1979, the LRTAP Convention's real value is that it has provided a successful framework for cooperation in the development of further

[65] Article 1(a). See *supra*, Ch 3, section 9.

[66] Wetstone and Rosencranz, *Acid Rain in Europe and North America*, 145; Gundlling, in Flinterman, Kwiatkowska, and Lammers (eds), *Transboundary Air Pollution*, 21–3.

[67] Article 2. [68] Article 6. This article is directed 'in particular' at new or rebuilt installations.

[69] *Supra*, Ch 3, section 8.

[70] Article 8(b). Rosencranz, 75 *AJIL* (1981) 977 argues that 'few if any cases are likely to arise to trigger this article' because the threshold is so high.

[71] Article 5. [72] *Supra*, Ch 3, section 7. See also 1991 US–Canada Air Quality Agreement.

protocols covering all the main sources of transboundary air pollution. Articles 3, 4, 5, and 8 commit the parties to exchange information, conduct research, and consult on policies, strategies, and measures for combating and reducing air pollution. The 1999 Gothenburg Protocol to Abate Acidification, Eutrophication, and Ground-level Ozone ('Gothenburg Protocol') further refines these provisions and adds an innovative 'public awareness' requirement for emissions and deposition of the key air pollutants.[73] The convention is thus both a basis for continuing study of the problem, and for taking further coordinated action to deal with it, including a non-compliance procedure.[74] In this sense the weakness of its obligations as agreed in 1979 is deceptive. Given consensus among the parties, adoption of stronger and more effective measures has been possible within this framework. For this reason the creation of institutions is, as in other treaty regimes, of particular importance. The Executive Body's main task is to keep under review the implementation of the convention and the effectiveness of national policies.[75] Its success is best measured by the protocols which have been negotiated setting specific targets for reduction of emissions.

2(3) PROTOCOLS TO THE 1979 CONVENTION

The first SO2 protocol required the parties to reduce emissions or their transboundary fluxes by 30 per cent by 1993.[76] By then most parties were comfortable with a more sophisticated approach to the problem.[77] The second sulphur protocol, adopted in 1994,[78] was much more radical. Not only did it address the problem from a more realistic scientific perspective, it was also more effective in requiring the parties to reduce their total emissions, not merely their transboundary fluxes of SO2. It acknowledged the need for precautionary measures to prevent transboundary air pollution from continuing to cause damage to forests, natural resources, and the sensitive Arctic environment. Based on a 'critical loads' approach, its objective was to reduce sulphur deposition below the level at which long-term damage would be caused to ecosystems. Critical loads are the maximum amount of acidifying deposition an ecosystem can tolerate in the long term. These loads are based on mapping of actual SO2 deposition and sources. Instead of the single flat rate reduction for all parties used in the first

73 1999 Gothenburg Protocol, Article 8.

74 *Supra*, Ch 4, section 3(4)(a), and 1999 Gothenburg Protocol, Article 9.

75 Article 10. See also Article 10 of the 1999 Gothenburg Protocol. The 'Executive Body' consists of the parties to the Convention.

76 1985 Protocol on the Reduction of Sulphur Emissions. See Fraenkel, 30 *Harv ILJ* (1989) 470.

77 The US was not a party to the protocol. The 1991 Agreement Between the Government of the United States and the Government of Canada on Air Quality regulated air pollution in North America. On the effectiveness of this agreement see UNECE, *Towards Cleaner Air: Scientific Assessment Report* (Oslo, 2016). See now the 1999 Gothenburg Protocol to which both states are party, discussed *infra*.

78 1994 Protocol on Further Reduction of Sulphur Emissions. See Churchill, Kütting and Warren, 7 *JEL* (1995) 169; McCormick, *Acid Earth*, 73f; Jhaveri, Gupta, Ott, *The LRTAP Convention/2nd Sulphur Protocol: Possible Lessons for the Climate Convention* (FIELD, 1998).

protocol, the newer one set differentiated emissions targets for each party. Unlike the first sulphur protocol, whose 30 per cent figure was essentially arbitrary, the second sulphur protocol's critical loads approach was the product of a high degree of scientific knowledge, and to that extent a precautionary approach was no longer necessary. Nevertheless, the Protocol's differentiated commitments were fairer to all parties because they were based on calculations of actual sources and effects and required reductions only to the extent that they were needed.

The second sulphur protocol was replaced in 2019 when the amended Gothenburg Protocol adopted in 1999 came into force.[79] This protocol builds on the second sulphur protocol, but it sets critical loads and national emission ceilings not only for sulphur (SO2), but also for nitrogen oxides (NOx), volatile organic compounds (VOCs) and ammonia (NH3). Emissions must not exceed limits specified in the annexes. Revisions adopted in 2012 make the Gothenburg Protocol the first to set emission reduction commitments for fine particulate matter, including the climate pollutant black carbon (or soot). Reducing particulate matter (including black carbon) is a significant step in reducing air pollution, while also benefitting the global climate. Although the US stayed out of the earlier protocols, in 2017 it ratified the 1999 Gothenburg Protocol, thus bringing it (and Canada) within the critical loads and emissions control regime for SO2, NOx, VOCs and ammonia, albeit on different terms from parties in Europe and Central Asia. The regulatory regime established by the 1999 Gothenburg Protocol is complex, but it shows how far the parties have been able to move in forty years. There is a remarkable contrast here with the climate change regime. Both are sustained by science, but the air pollution science has been taken more seriously by politicians.

Finally, two protocols concluded in 1998 deal with airborne deposition of persistent organic pollutants (mainly pesticides and industrial chemicals), and heavy metals.[80] The first of these bans production and use of some substances, severely restricts the use of others, and requires destruction and disposal to be carried out in an environmentally sound manner compatible with the Basel Convention. The second phases out leaded petrol, reduces other emissions of lead, cadmium, and mercury from industry, incinerators, and power stations to below 1990 levels, and specifies use of best available technology. Additional substances can be added to either protocol by amendment of the annexes.[81] Some parties to the 1998 protocols voluntarily entered into additional commitments.

2(4) IMPLEMENTATION AND ASSESSMENT

Transboundary air pollution in Europe has undoubtedly fallen substantially, and especially SO2 pollution. By 1994 the 30 per cent target for reducing sulphur emissions had been met by all parties, and exceeded by nineteen of them, reducing total

[79] 1999 Gothenburg Protocol. See UNECE, *17th Rept of the Executive Body*, ECE/EB AIR/68 (1999), amended by decisions 2012/1 and 2012/2. It also replaced the 1988 NOx Protocol and the 1991 VOC Protocol.

[80] See Executive Body, *Rept of the Special Session*, ECE/EB AIR/55 and ECE/EB AIR/57 (1998).

[81] Criteria and procedures for doing so are set out in Executive Body Decisions 1998/1 and 1998/2.

emissions by 52 per cent. Even non-parties such as the UK and Poland had also exceeded the 30 per cent target. NOx emissions had either stabilized as required, or had reduced, giving a net fall of 9 per cent, although those parties who had promised a 30 per cent fall remained a long way short of this target, and further reductions would be difficult to achieve. One study concluded that 'deposition in excess of critical loads of acidification has been greatly reduced in Europe due to emission reductions' and that 'Recovery from acidification damage is particularly evident in the chemistry of acidified lakes and streams and in the reduction of corrosion for many materials.'[82] The most recent study confirms this assessment and concludes that 'economic growth and trends in air pollution have been progressively decoupled.'[83] There have also been large-scale reductions in US and Canadian air pollution following introduction of clean air legislation in the 1970s, despite substantial economic growth.[84] To that extent the problem of acid rain has substantially abated.

However, NOx emissions remain problematic, 'exceeding the critical loads of eutrophication in large areas in Europe and increase[ing] the risk of harmful effects, for example, the loss of biodiversity'.[85] Ozone and particulate levels in European and North American cities continue to exceed WHO guidelines.[86] Reports from the Implementation Committee show that there have been problems of non-compliance by some parties with the NOx and VOC protocols. Overall, although the picture is one of substantial compliance with the sulphur protocols, and the elimination of acid rain and lead in petrol, air pollution from other sources remains a serious threat to human health, even in Europe. The 1999 Gothenburg Protocol is a significant development in that respect, but it did not come fully into force until 2019; the key question is whether it will be fully implemented and what effect that will have on the remaining problems.

What is less clear is how far all the improvements which have come about can be attributed directly to implementation of the protocols. Any explanation of the reduction in sulphur emissions which has undoubtedly occurred must take account of evidence that this was significantly due to industrial changes in Russia and Eastern Europe after 1991, and to the increased use of gas or nuclear power for power generation in countries such as the UK and France, rather than to implementation of the Convention regime.[87] Nevertheless, in their reports to the Executive Body, the parties have concurred in viewing the Convention's impact on air pollution control and air-quality management as a positive one. Largely through increased knowledge, better

82 Working Group on Effects, *Convention on Long-range Transboundary Air Pollution: Review and assessment of air pollution effects and their recorded trends* (UK Natural Environment Research Council, 2004).

83 UNECE, *Towards Cleaner Air: Scientific Assessment Report* (Oslo, 2016).

84 *Ibid.*

85 Working Group on Effects, *supra*, n 82; see also UNECE, *Towards Cleaner Air etc* (Oslo, 2016).

86 *Ibid.*

87 Sand, in Helm (ed), *Energy: Production, Consumption, and Consequences* (Washington, 1990) 246; Wettestad, 7 *Global Env Change* (1997) 235. See also *National Strategies and Policies for Air Pollution Abatement*, UN Doc ECE/EB AIR/65 (1999).

technology, and the building of mutual confidence, the 1979 LRTAP treaty regime has helped to alter perceptions, to harmonise policies in participating states, and to reverse some of the earlier trends.[88]

2(5) AIR POLLUTION IN ASIA

Air pollution in Asia is a growing problem, visible to anyone who travels there. Much of this is domestic in origin, but some is transboundary. ASEAN already has a number of agreements and other instruments which cover air pollution, including the 1995 Co-operation Plan on Transboundary Pollution,[89] the 1997 Regional Haze Action Plan,[90] and the 2002 Agreement on Transboundary Haze Pollution.[91] The 2002 agreement has similarities to the 1979 Geneva Convention: it sets out objectives for reducing air pollution, it creates a conference of the parties with power to take further measures and adopt protocols, it provides for further research. Here is the basis for coordinated action within ASEAN: what it lacks are the protocols and programmes that would give it some bite.[92] That there is simply no substance to this regime is clearly shown by the dramatic difference to air pollution levels made by the COVID 19 pandemic shutdown in Asia.

3 PROTECTING THE OZONE LAYER

3(1) 1985 OZONE CONVENTION

UNEP initiated negotiation of a treaty to protect the ozone layer in 1981.[93] As with the 1979 LRTAP Convention, the interests of several groups had to be reconciled. These included developing countries, such as India, China, and Brazil, which were primarily concerned that restraints on the use of ozone-depleting substances might inhibit their industrial development, or that alternative technologies might not be available to them. The US, which had earlier acted unilaterally to reduce domestic production and consumption of CFCs, did not wish to remain at a disadvantage while others went on using them, and its position was strongly in favour of an international

[88] See in particular Wettestad, *Acid Lessons? Assessing and Explaining LRTAP Implementation and Effectiveness* (IIASA Working Paper, 1996); Jhaveri, Gupta, and Ott, *The LRTAP Convention/Second Sulphur Protocol: Possible Lessons for the Climate Convention* (FIELD, 1998).

[89] 1995 ASEAN Cooperation Plan on Transboundary Pollution.

[90] 1997 ASEAN Regional Haze Action Plan (ARHAP).

[91] 2002 ASEAN Agreement on Transboundary Haze Pollution; see also 1998 Malé Declaration on Control and Prevention of Air Pollution and its Likely Transboundary Effects for South Asia.

[92] See Tan and Syarif's chapters in Jayakumar et al (eds), *Transboundary Pollution*.

[93] For text and commentary on successive drafts see Ad Hoc Working Group on the Ozone Convention, UNEP/WG 69/8; UNEP/WG 78/2; UNEP/WG 78/4; UNEP/WG 78/10; UNEP/WG 94/3; UNEP/WG 94/4 and Add 1 and 2; UNEP/WG 94/8; UNEP/WG 94/11.

control regime. The EC represented the largest group of producers and was reluctant to commit itself to measures that might prove costly to implement. Moreover, some EC states resisted controls on the grounds that harmful effects had not been proven, and that the risk remained long-term and speculative. Unlike air pollution, however, no regime would be likely to work unless it was global, since the impact of ozone-depleting substances is the same wherever or however they originate, and would affect all states. Thus, as many parties as possible would have to be persuaded to join and there would have to be strong disincentives to deter relocation of CFC production to non-parties.[94]

Again following the pattern of the 1979 LRTAP Convention, the 1985 Ozone Convention made reference in its Preamble to Principle 21 of the 1972 Stockholm Declaration, but imposes few concrete obligations.[95] The weakness of its provisions indicated compromise between demands for more research and a commitment to firm action. Parties would have to take 'appropriate measures', including the adoption of legislation and administrative controls, to protect human health and the environment 'against adverse effects resulting or likely to result from human activities which modify or are likely to modify the ozone layer'.[96] The nature of these measures was not defined, but the parties had to cooperate in harmonizing policies and in formulating 'agreed measures, procedures and standards for the implementation of this Convention'. Nor did the convention specify any particular substances to which these measures must relate; it merely listed in an annex substances 'thought' to have the potential to modify the ozone layer.

The only measures which the convention required the parties to take concern assessment of the causes and effects of ozone depletion, the transmission of information, and the exchange of information and technology.[97] These provisions laid the basis for ensuring adequate monitoring and research, and for making substitute technologies and substances available to all, including developing countries. But Article 4, which dealt with the acquisition of alternative technology, was most unsatisfactory from the perspective of developing countries, since it merely required states to cooperate, in accordance with their own laws, regulations, and practices, in the development and transfer of technology and knowledge. This was significantly weaker than transfer of technology provisions in the 1982 UNCLOS,[98] and essentially left the matter to each state's discretion. Article 4 proved inadequate to satisfy the concerns of developing states that CFC substitutes might not be available to them, or would be prohibitively expensive, and the issue was reopened in later negotiations.

94 Ad Hoc Working Group, 2nd Session, 1982, 10 *EPL* (1983) 34; UNEP Working Group on CFCs, 16 *EPL* (1986) 139.

95 See generally Yoshida, *The International Legal Regime for the Protection of the Stratospheric Ozone Layer* (2nd edn, Leiden, 2019); Anderson and Sarma (eds), *Protecting the Ozone Layer* (London, 2002); Benedick, *Ozone Diplomacy* (2nd edn, London, 1998).

96 Article 2.

97 Articles 2(2)(a), 4, 5.

98 Cf 1982 UNCLOS, Article 144 and Annex III, Article 5.

Institutions created by the Convention comprised a regular Conference of the Parties (COP) and a secretariat. Like the Executive Body of the 1979 LRTAP Convention, the COP reviews implementation of the convention, receiving for that purpose reports from the parties and establishing the necessary programmes and policies. It is responsible for adopting new protocols and annexes, and for amending the convention. There is provision for dispute settlement in Article II.

Thus, like the 1979 LRTAP Convention, the 1985 Convention is largely an empty framework, requiring further action by the parties, who proved unable in 1985 to agree on proposals for more specific control measures.[99] Nevertheless, it is an important precedent with wider significance in environmental law. First, it is explicitly concerned with protection of the global environment, and defines adverse effects to mean 'changes in the physical environment or biota, including changes in climate, which have significant deleterious effects on human health or on the composition, resilience and productivity of natural and managed ecosystems, or on materials useful to mankind'.[100] This definition both recognizes the impact of ozone depletion on climate change, and adopts an ecosystem approach in terms which suggest that the natural environment has a significance independent of its immediate utility to man. Secondly, the 1985 Ozone Convention is one of the first to perceive the need for preventive action in advance of firm proof of actual harm, and in that sense it is indicative of the emergence of a more 'precautionary' approach than had been typical for earlier pollution conventions, including the 1979 LRTAP Convention.[101]

3(2) 1987 MONTREAL PROTOCOL

The 1987 Montreal Protocol[102] represents a much more significant agreement than the 1985 Ozone Convention. First, it sets firm targets for reducing and eliminating consumption and production of a range of ozone-depleting substances. These were supported particularly strongly by the US, which referred to the need to err on the side of caution and to recall the well-being of future generations, and by the Executive Director of UNEP, whose efforts ensured that a consensus emerged among the scientific experts on predicting the rate of ozone depletion and the regulatory measures needed to protect human health and the environment. Following scientific evidence that the standards adopted in 1987 would not be effective in reducing ozone depletion, however, additional substances were included by the amendments adopted in 1990 and 1992 and the timetable for complete elimination was revised and brought forward to 1996.[103] These changes were made possible by the development of new technology

[99] UNEP, Ad Hoc Working Group on the Ozone Convention, UNEP/WG 94/9. [100] Article 1(2).

[101] Preamble, and see Benedick, *Ozone Diplomacy*, 45, and *supra*, Ch 3, section 6.

[102] Ad Hoc Working Group of Legal and Technical Experts, First Session, UNEP/WG 151/L 4 (1986); *id*, Second Session, UNEP/WG 167/2 (1987); *id*, Third Session, UNEP/WG 172/2 (1987). See Benedick, *Ozone Diplomacy*.

[103] For amendments and adjustments see UNEP, *Handbook of Substances that Deplete the Ozone Layer* (10th edn, Nairobi, 2016) and subsequent updates. Decisions of the parties will also be found there.

and alternative substances, although in some cases these substitutes may still have an ozone-depleting potential; others are GHGs. Limited allowance was made for increases in production of ozone-depleting substances to meet domestic needs and to facilitate industrial rationalization. Control of consumption and production was necessary in order to protect the interests of producers and importers by deterring price inflation or over-production in the interim period until the eventual phase-out of these gases.[104]

Secondly, acknowledging the inequity of equal treatment for all, and the very small contribution to ozone depletion made by developing states, the protocol makes special provision for their needs. It was essential to encourage participation by these states, given their potential for increased production of CFCs, and the likelihood that this would simply nullify the actions of developed states. Although the 1987 text of the protocol would have allowed them a possibly substantial increase in production and consumption for domestic needs,[105] this option did not prove sufficiently attractive to prompt India and China to ratify, and would in any case have reduced its effectiveness. The accelerated timetable set for eventual phase-out by the subsequent revisions required a different approach to the position of developing states. Allowance was still made in the revised Article 5 for a ten-year delay in compliance with the control measures by this group, whose obligation to phase out production and consumption thus began to take effect only in 1999, but the protocol revision adopted new financial and technical incentives to encourage such states to switch as quickly as possible to alternative substances and technologies.[106] Article 10 established a multilateral fund whose purpose was to facilitate technical cooperation and technology transfer so that developing states did not have to rely on Article 5 to protect their interests.[107] The revised protocol required each party to take 'every practicable step' to ensure that substitutes and technology would expeditiously be transferred under 'fair and most favourable conditions' to developing states.[108] Although this provision by no means overcame the reluctance of chemical companies in the developed world to transfer technology,[109] and did not compel them to do so, the obligation of developing countries to comply with the protocol's control measures 'will depend upon' the effective implementation of these provisions on financial cooperation and transfer of technology. Moreover, if these provisions did not work effectively, developing states could refer the matter to a meeting of the parties, which would decide on appropriate action. Put shortly,

104 Explanatory Note by the Executive Director of UNEP, Montreal, 1987.

105 Article 5. See Rosencranz and Scott, 20 *EPL* (1990) 201.

106 Benedick, *Ozone Diplomacy*, Chs 12, 13, 16.

107 For an optimistic report of its success, see *10th Meeting of the Parties,* UNEP/OZL.Pro. 10/9 (1998) para 83f. The Multilateral Fund is administered by the World Bank, UNEP and UNDP. See UNEP, *Handbook of Substances etc*; Benedick, *Ozone Diplomacy*, 252–68; Keohane and Levy, *Institutions for Environmental Aid* (Boston, 1996) 89–126. The GEF also provides funding.

108 Article 10A.

109 Rosencranz and Scott, 20 *EPL* (1990) 201. Lawrence, 2 *JEL* (1990) concludes that reluctance to transfer CFC substitute technology was based primarily on financial rather than legal considerations.

developing states were given the power to put pressure on developed states to ensure that they were given the necessary means to meet the protocol's target for elimination of ozone-depleting substances. This was one of a number of innovative measures adopted in the 1990 revision to ensure compliance and effective implementation.

Thirdly, the protocol attempted to deal with the problem of non-parties by banning trade with these states in controlled substances or products containing such substances.[110] To take only one example, Korea was thus forced to participate if it wished to continue to export cars and fridges.[111] The parties also had to discourage the export of CFC production technology. During the 1987 negotiations the question of compatibility of this article with the GATT was raised.[112] Since the measures proposed were neither arbitrary nor unjustifiable and did not discriminate against non-parties as such, but could only be applied against those not following the protocol's control measures, it was concluded that Article 4 would be in accordance with Article 20(b) of the GATT concerning protection of human, animal, or plant life, or health, although the final judgement in the event of a bilateral dispute would rest with the WTO. There were already precedents for controls on trade with non-parties in the 1973 CITES, and under resolutions of the parties to the 1946 ICRW.[113]

3(3) REVISION AND COMPLIANCE

The institutional provisions of the 1987 protocol merit special note, since they are the key to its flexible development and enforcement. The powers enjoyed by the meeting of the parties to this protocol are unusual among environmental treaties. First, provided efforts to reach a consensus have been exhausted, certain decisions taken by a two-thirds majority ('adjustments') will bind all parties to the protocol, including those who voted against them.[114] To maintain the equitable balance between developed and developing states these decisions must be supported by separate majorities of both groups. In this way further adjustments and reductions in the production and consumption of controlled substances may be adopted and will enter into force within six months. The same rule applies to decisions concerning the financial mechanism and under Article 5. Objecting states retain the option of withdrawing from the protocol on one year's notice.[115] Other amendments to the protocol, including the addition of new controlled substances, must be made in accordance with Article 9 of the 1985 Ozone Convention, and will be effective only in respect of parties who ratify or accept them. This has not in reality hampered the ability of the COP to add further chemicals, and to keep others under review. The fifth and most recent amendment, adopted in 2016, will cut production and consumption of hydrofluorocarbons by 85 per cent.[116]

[110] Article 4, as revised 1990 and 1997.

[111] Andersen and Sarma, *Protecting the Ozone Layer*, 353.

[112] Ad Hoc Working Group, 2nd Session, 22; *id*, 3rd Session, 18. See *infra*, Ch 14.

[113] *Infra*, Chs 11 and 12.

[114] Article 2(9) as revised 1990. See *supra*, Ch 2, section 5.

[115] Article 19, but see 1990 revision.

[116] *Annex I of the report of the Twenty-Eighth Meeting of the Parties*. The amendment entered into force on 1 January 2019.

Secondly, Article 8 of the 1987 Protocol provides for a formal non-compliance procedure, the first multilateral environmental agreement to do so.[117] This procedure, which is described in Chapter 4, has been invoked on several occasions by parties who are in difficulty, including Russia, Belarus, Ukraine and other states from Eastern Europe and the former Soviet Union. Various measures have been recommended by the meeting of the parties to deal with these problems of non-compliance, including the provision of technical assistance, GEF funding, and the issuing of cautions.[118] Further funding from the GEF and the World Bank has been made conditional on the meeting of the parties certifying that compliance by these states is satisfactory. The same procedure has offered a useful means to ensure that parties provide the data required by Article 7 of the protocol concerning production, imports, and exports of controlled substances. Developing states have also been threatened with loss of Article 5 status for failure to report data. By 2017 the Implementation Committee was reporting no ongoing instances of non-reporting, apart from Kazakhstan and Ukraine, which had problems with data collection.[119]

Thus, although the non-compliance procedure is an example of 'soft enforcement', it is not without teeth, and it has enabled the parties to give serious and sustained attention to their responsibility for reviewing implementation of the protocol. The absence from the protocol of any other dispute settlement provision emphasises the importance of collective supervision and control, through multilateral negotiation and cooperation with the parties, rather than adjudication or arbitration.

3(4) ASSESSING THE MONTREAL PROTOCOL

One measure of the protocol's success is that it has 191 parties, including the EU, USA, Russia, China, India, and Brazil, the last three having joined following the adoption of the London amendments in 1990.[120] These amendments, together with the availability of significant financial assistance through the GEF and the multilateral fund, helped to ensure a very high participation from developing states. So did

117 Protocol Annex IV, as adopted at Copenhagen in 1992. Minor revisions were agreed in 1998: see *Rept of 10th MOP, Annex II*, UNEP/OzL Pro 10/9 (1998) and *Rept of Ad Hoc Group of Legal and Technical Experts*, UNEP/OzL Pro/WG 4/1/3 (1998). See UNEP, *Rept of the Implementation Committee for the Montreal Protocol, 20th Meeting*, UNEP/OzL Pro/ImpCom/20/4, paras 24–33; Yoshida, *The International Legal Regime for the Protection of the Stratospheric Ozone Layer* (2nd edn, Leiden, 2019), Ch 5; Usuki, 43 *Jap Ann IL* (2000) 19. See also Koskenniemi, 3 *YbIEL* (1992) 123, and *supra*, Ch 4, section 3.

118 See generally, Victor, Raustiala and Skolnikoff (eds), *The Implementation and Effectiveness of International Environmental Commitments* (Cambridge, Mass,1998) Chs 3, 4; Werksman, 36 *ZAöRV* (1996) 750; Benedick, *Ozone Diplomacy*, Ch 17.

119 *Rept of the Montreal Protocol Implementation Committee*, 58th meeting, UNEP/OzL.Pro/ImpCom/58/4 (2017).

120 See generally UNEP, *Rept of the Working Group of the Parties*, 17th Meeting (1998) UNEP/OzL Pro/WG 1/17/3; *id*, *Rept of the Implementation Committee* (1998) UNEP/OzL Pro/ImpCom/20/4; *id*, *Rept of the Working Group on Countries with Economies in Transition* (1995); *id*, *Rept of 10th Meeting of Parties*, UNEP/OzL Pro 10/9 (1998).

trade restraints: the number of Article 5 parties doubled once these came into force. Thus good progress has been made in securing the level of global adherence necessary for the protocol to work.

A second measure of success is evidenced by the dynamic and flexible way in which the regime has operated. Controls on ozone-depleting substances have been strengthened at successive meetings of the parties; new substances have been added; the supervisory institutions have evolved. Without the protocol and successive adjustments, ozone depletion would be ten times greater than currently.[121]

Thirdly, the level of compliance in developed states appears to have been high, with most phasing out the major ozone-depleting substances by 1996 as required by the accelerated timetable set by the protocol amendments. Problems submitted to the non-compliance procedure have largely been dealt with successfully, albeit at the price of some delay in implementation by states in Eastern Europe. Continued Russian production and export of controlled substances to other CIS states had been a persistent problem, but by 1998 this had been phased out with assistance from the GEF and the World Bank. The Implementation Committee was also reporting large falls in the total consumption of the main ozone-depleting substances. Once the protocol began to take effect, a black market developed, threatening to undermine the entire regime. By 1998, however, a new export/import licensing system to combat smuggling was in operation[122] and rocketing prices for CFCs suggested that illegal trade was being cut. The obligation of Article 5 parties to phase out production and consumption only began to take effect in 1999, so that by 1996 the world's main CFC producers, apart from Russia, were India and China. Thereafter data showed that consumption in a majority of developing countries had begun to fall significantly, and some parties, including China, had accelerated the phase out.[123] However, in 2019 it became apparent that significant emissions of ozone depleting substances were still occurring in China.[124] It remains unclear what the reason for this might be.

Finally, whereas scientific assessments showed that in its original 1987 form the Montreal Protocol would not have halted an accelerating level of ozone-depleting substances in the stratosphere, subsequent revisions were predicted to result in a gradually diminishing level after the year 2000, when increases attributable to past emissions were due to stabilize.[125] Provided the protocol is fully adhered to, global ozone losses and the Antarctic ozone hole should have recovered by around 2050. Other problems could affect the success of the protocol, including new ozone-depleting substances which it does not cover, but which are the subject of research and ongoing review. Although the protocol has encouraged resort to substitute substances and technologies, some of these

[121] Andersen and Sarma, *Protecting the Ozone Layer*, 346.

[122] Adopted as Article 4B of the Protocol in Decision IX/8 (1997). On the problem of illegal trade see Benedick, *Ozone Diplomacy*, 273–6; Brack, *International Trade and the Montreal Protocol* (London, 1996) 99–114.

[123] UNEP, *Rept. of 10th Meeting of Parties*, UNEP/OzL.Pro.10/9 (1998) paras 72ff.

[124] Rigby, Park et al, 569 *Nature* (2019) 546–550.

[125] WMO, *Scientific Assessment of Ozone Depletion* (Geneva, 2018).

are GHGs included in the 1997 Kyoto Protocol.[126] There is an evident need for coordination of these two regimes, but this has now been addressed by the 2016 amendment. Faced with the relatively straightforward task of eliminating production and consumption of ozone-depleting substances, the 1985 Ozone Convention and the 1987 Montreal Protocol have been a success.

4 THE CLIMATE CHANGE REGIME

4(1) INTRODUCTION

Climate change is *par excellence* a global problem—the 'common concern' of humanity to use the language of the 1992 UNFCCC)—potentially affecting all States, and for which global solutions are essential.[127] Regulating climate change has always been difficult because of the complexity of the issues and the diversity of the interests at stake.[128] This is not because the science is difficult or uncertain: it is not. We know that greenhouse gas emissions have already raised average global temperatures by some 0.7⁰C, and that on current trends they will most likely exceed 2⁰C.[129] That will inevitably cause damage on a significant scale, especially to countries that are already low-lying or arid. Since 78 per cent of global greenhouse gas emissions are generated by the G20 (the world's largest economies) it is largely their policies which will determine the outcome.[130] Industrialised States want to keep the costs of adaptation down and the timescales long. Many have serious problems convincing electorates and legislatures that more needs to be done, although in this respect Europe is arguably further advanced than its main competitors. It has certainly been more willing to make commitments on greenhouse gas (GHG) emissions reductions than the other big GHG emitters.[131] Many of the states most likely to be seriously affected by climate change are poorly resourced developing countries that rely heavily on larger states, the UN and the World Bank to come up with the money and resources they need to mitigate the worst effects. Despite initial success in influencing the Rio negotiations, they have had only limited leverage over the main players in subsequent negotiations.[132]

126 E.g. HFCs, included in Annex A of the Kyoto Protocol, and now covered by the 2016 amendment of the Montreal Protocol.

127 See *inter alia* Dryzek, Norgaard and Schlosberg (eds), *Oxford Handbook of Climate Change and Society* (Oxford, 2011); Carlarne, Gray and Tarasofsky, *Oxford Handbook of International Climate Change Law* (Oxford, 2016); Bodansky, Brunnée and Rajamani, *International Climate Change Law* (Oxford, 2017); Luterbacher and Sprinz, *Global Climate Policy* (Cambridge, Mass, 2018); Mayer, *The International Law on Climate Change* (Cambridge, 2018).

128 *Infra*, section 4(2). 129 *Supra*, section 1.

130 UNEP, *Emissions Gap Report 2019: Executive Summary*, vi.

131 In 2009 the EU Council agreed a unilateral emissions reduction target of 20 per cent by 2020, calculated from a 1990 baseline.

132 On Rio see Mintzer and Leonard, *Negotiating Climate Change* (Cambridge, 1994), and on subsequent negotiations see Luterbacher and Sprinz, *Global Climate Policy*, and *infra*, sections 4(3) and (4).

The UNFCCC adopted in 1992 initiated a process for negotiating further measures to reduce greenhouse gas emissions and sustain carbon sinks. As we saw in section 1 of this chapter that process has failed to meet its core objective of ensuring 'stabilization of greenhouse gas concentrations in the atmosphere at a level that would prevent dangerous anthropogenic interference with the climate system.'[133] The most fundamental weakness of the model of global climate regulation created by the 1992 UNFCCC is that it depends on the ability of the parties to reach agreement on further measures that are strong enough to have an impact within the necessary timescale. This cannot be taken for granted. The failure of the Copenhagen and Madrid negotiations in 2009 and 2019 shows that securing consensus in this diverse context requires compromises that may be unobtainable or may result in a text that is weaker or more ambiguous than many states are prepared to accept.[134]

Moreover, while the 1997 Kyoto Protocol dictated significant reductions in greenhouse gas emissions for some developed States based on 1990 levels, the protocol as a whole fell well short of what was needed to achieve a meaningful effect on atmospheric concentrations of GHGs.[135] Not only did the emissions limits imposed on developed state parties lack sufficient ambition,[136] but developing states were relieved of any obligation to constrain their own greenhouse gas emissions, however significant they might become. Thus, the rapidly rising CO2 emissions generated by China and India were unregulated by Kyoto. A key issue in the post-Kyoto climate negotiations was whether to start again with a new set of basic assumptions about who must take responsibility for reducing greenhouse gas emissions in future. The importance of the Paris Agreement adopted in 2015 is that it moves away from mandatory GHG emissions reductions by developed states in favour of requiring all parties to specify some level of nationally determined contribution to holding the increase in global temperature to 'well below' 2°C.[137]

The climate regime established by the 1992 UNFCCC is evolutionary in character but it is not the whole picture. Controlling climate change requires coordination of policies and measures by a range of international institutions inside and outside the UN system. Some GHGs are regulated by the 1987 Montreal Protocol rather than by the 1992 UNFCCC.[138] The use of sub-seabed depositories for carbon capture and storage must be compatible with the 1982 UNCLOS and the 1972 London Convention. That requires cooperation by the parties to those treaties.[139] Controlling greenhouse gas emissions from shipping requires regulatory action by the IMO if it is to be globally effective.[140] Moreover, greenhouse gas emissions also cause marine pollution and affect

[133] UNFCCC, Article 2. [134] Rajamani (2009) 58 *ICLQ* 803; id (2010) 59 *ICLQ* 824.

[135] *Infra*, section 4(3).

[136] Resulting in some cases in substantial overcompliance with GHG emissions limits: see Grubb, 16 *Climate Policy* (2016) 673, and *infra*, section 4(3).

[137] *Infra*, section 4(5) [138] *Supra*, section 3. [139] *Infra*, Ch 8, section 4.

[140] *Inpra*, Ch 9, section 4(3).

the marine environment. Pollution standards adopted within the 1992 UNFCCC regime may therefore constitute 'internationally agreed rules and standards' for the purposes of Part XII of the 1982 UNCLOS.[141] There is thus a close relationship between the climate regime and applicable law within the 1982 UNCLOS regime. As we note in Chapters 5 and 13 there are also important interactions with international human rights law and WTO law, and with other parts of international law.[142]

4(2) DEVELOPMENT OF THE UN FRAMEWORK CONVENTION ON CLIMATE CHANGE

Negotiating a climate change convention proved to be a much more difficult task than reaching agreement on the protection of the ozone layer.[143] The task of phasing out production and consumption of ozone-depleting substances was relatively simple compared to that of containing climate change, where the complexity of the issues and the economic implications were much greater. Whereas industrial processes that deplete the ozone layer are relatively discrete, controlling greenhouse gas emissions goes to the heart of energy, transport, agricultural, and industrial policy in all developed states and increasingly in developing ones too. Moreover, the role of carbon sinks means that deforestation, protection of natural habitats and ecosystems, sea-level rise, and sovereignty over natural resources are also important elements of the problem, within the broader context of sustainable development. Thus, the sectoral approach, which has traditionally dominated international regulation of the environment, is inappropriate to the interconnected and global character of climate change.

Following the adoption of numerous declarations at regional conferences calling for measures to reduce the emissions of CO2 and other GHGs, the elements of a climate change convention were first considered by a meeting of experts in Ottawa in 1989, and by the IPCC in 1990.[144] Negotiations were then initiated in 1990 by UN General Assembly resolution 45/212, and concluded in 1992 with the adoption at the Rio Conference of the 1992 UNFCCC.

141 *Infra*, Ch 9, section 2, and Boyle, 34 *IJMCL* (2019) 458.

142 On the implications of climate change for other areas of international law see Rayfuse and Scott (eds), *International Law in the Era of Climate Change* (London, 2012).

143 See Churchill and Freestone (eds), *International Law and Global Climate Change* (Bath, 1991); Barrett, *Convention on Climate Change: Economic Aspects of the Negotiations* (OECD, 1992); Bodansky, 3 *YbIEL* (1992) 60 and 18 *Yale JIL* (1993) 451; Nilsson and Pitt, *Protecting the Atmosphere: The Climate Change Convention and its Context* (London, 1994); Mintzer and Leonard (eds), *Negotiating Climate Change: The Inside Story of the Rio Convention*; Bodansky, Brunnée and Rajamani (eds), *International Climate Change Law*, Ch 5; Mayer, *The International Law on Climate Change*, Ch 3.

144 Statement of Legal and Policy Experts on Protection of the Atmosphere, Ottawa, 1989; IPCC Working Group III: Formulation of Response Strategies; Legal and Institutional Mechanisms, 1990. These and the series of conference declarations setting out the negotiating policy of various groups of states are reproduced in Churchill and Freestone (eds), *International Law and Global Climate Change*, 280ff.

Negotiated by consensus, and intended to attract universal participation, the 1992 UNFCCC reflects deep differences of opinion among the participating states about the measures needed and the allocation of responsibility for addressing the problem.[145] Not only was it necessary to acknowledge the differential needs and responsibilities of developed and developing states, but within each of these groups there were few common positions. Members of the Alliance of Small Island States, such as Nauru and Vanuatu, which might disappear in the event of sea level rise, were in favour of a strong convention. Their interests were far removed from those of OPEC oil producers such as Saudi Arabia and Kuwait, whose income and economies could seriously suffer if consumption of fossil fuels by developed states were to be reduced. Neither of these groups had much in common with the larger developing states such as China, Brazil, and India, which did not want to hinder their own economic growth and were keen for developed states to take the lead. Nor did the developed OECD economies share a common view on the measures that might be needed to tackle climate change. In particular, the US was not prepared to commit itself to specific emissions reductions or timetables and its opposition resulted in a convention that was significantly weaker than the commitments already undertaken voluntarily by a number of OECD states.[146] These divisions among major groups participating in the negotiations must be recalled when assessing and interpreting the Convention.

Like the 1985 Ozone Convention, the 1992 UNFCCC is neither a comprehensive 'law of the atmosphere', nor a fully formed and detailed regulatory regime, but merely a framework for reaching further agreement on policies and specific measures.[147] Although the commitments undertaken by the parties are similarly weak, the 1992 Convention differs significantly from the 1985 Ozone Convention in two important respects. First, it specifies objectives and principles to guide implementation of the Convention and further development of related legal instruments by the parties. Secondly, for the first time in any treaty, it makes the concept of 'common but differentiated responsibilities and respective capabilities' the explicit basis for the different commitments of developed and developing states parties, and for developed country leadership. The same differentiation underpins the Kyoto Protocol.

[145] For documentation on the negotiating history of the Convention see *Reports of the Intergovernmental Negotiating Committee for a Framework Convention on Climate Change*, UN Doc A/AC 237/6 (1st session); -/9 (2nd session); -/L 9 (3rd session); -/18 (5th session). The mandate of the INC is in UNGA Resolutions 44/207 (1989); 45/212 (1990); 46/169 (1991); and 47/195 (1992). See also UNEP Governing Council decisions 14/20 (1987); 15/36 (1989); SS II/3 (1990).

[146] Countries that had previously committed themselves voluntarily to stabilise or reduce CO2 emissions included Australia, Belgium, Canada, France, Germany, Italy, Japan, the Netherlands, New Zealand, the Nordic states, Switzerland, and the UK.

[147] See generally Freestone, in Carlarne, Gray and Tarasofsky (eds), *The Oxford Handbook of International Climate Change Law* (Oxford, 2016) Ch 5. On early proposals for a comprehensive 'law of the atmosphere' see Bodansky, 18 *Yale JIL* (1993) 451. On more recent ones see the work of the ILC on climate change.

4(3) OBJECTIVES, PRINCIPLES, AND COMMITMENTS

The objective of the Convention and of related instruments is not to reverse greenhouse gas emissions but to *stabilize* them 'at a level that would prevent dangerous anthropogenic interference with the climate system'. The Convention does not specify what that level might be, nor does Article 2 envisage that it should be achieved immediately, merely that it should be 'within a time frame sufficient to allow ecosystems to adapt naturally to climate change, to ensure that food production is not threatened and to enable economic development to proceed in a sustainable manner'. The wording of Article 2 suggests that the parties envisage some degree of climate change as inevitable, and that they are prepared to tolerate it provided it happens slowly enough to allow natural adaptation.[148] Article 2 must now be read together with the 2015 Paris Agreement, which is more specific on long-term objectives.[149]

Article 3 sets out the principles the parties shall be 'guided by' in their efforts to achieve the objective of Article 2. The principles listed in Article 3 reflect the contours of global environmental responsibility elaborated in the Rio Declaration and Agenda 21.[150] Thus they include reference to inter-generational equity, common but differentiated responsibility, the precautionary principle or approach, and the right of all parties to promote sustainable development, as well as the need to promote 'a supportive and open international economic system'. Article 3 also tries to flesh out some of the policy factors which should be taken into account by the parties, such as policies and measures to be comprehensive and cover all relevant 'sources, sinks and reservoirs' of GHGs. These policies and measures should be cost-effective in the sense that they ensure 'global benefits at the lowest possible cost'[151]—a consideration that looms large in the architecture of the Kyoto Protocol. Developed country parties are expected to 'take the lead' in combating climate change and its adverse effects,[152] while 'full consideration' must be given to the specific needs of vulnerable developing states and those which would bear a disproportionate or abnormal burden under the Convention.[153]

Article 3 takes a novel approach to environmental protection, but in the context of a dynamic and evolutionary regulatory regime such as the 1992 UNFCCC it has the merit of providing some predictability regarding the parameters within which the parties are required to work towards the objective of the Convention. In particular, it guides parties entering subsequent protocol negotiations or when

148 See Oppenheimer and Petsonk, 73 *Climatic Change* (2005) 195.

149 *Infra*, section 4(4).

150 *Supra*, Ch 3, section 4.

151 Article 3(3).

152 Article 3(1).

153 Article 3(2). See also Article 4(8) UNFCCC which refers inter alia to the needs and concerns of '[c]ountries whose economies are highly dependent on income generated from the production, processing and export, and /or on consumption of fossil fuels and associated energy-intensive products'. Demands from OPEC countries for special treatment in the form of compensation for loss of oil income were made at the Kyoto negotiations but rejected. Article 2(3) of the Protocol only recognizes the need to minimize the impact of implementing protocol commitments on countries listed in Article 4(8) UNFCCC.

the COP takes decisions under the various articles empowering it to do so. Given their explicit role as guidance, these 'principles' are not necessarily binding rules which must be complied with; their softer legal status is also indicated by the use of the word 'should' throughout this article.[154] However, Article 3 is not without legal effect. At the very least it is relevant to interpretation and implementation of the Convention as well as creating expectations that affect the negotiation of further instruments, such as the non-compliance procedure; it was reiterated in the mandate for negotiation of the 1997 Kyoto Protocol and is referred to in the Protocol itself.[155]

Article 4, which deals with the commitments undertaken by parties to the Convention, is based on the principle of common but differentiated responsibility.[156] Thus, although obligations in Article 4(1) are subject to 'specific national and regional development priorities, objectives and circumstances', they are nevertheless common to all parties, whereas the more onerous commitments in Article 4(2) apply only to developed states and the so-called 'economies in transition' of Eastern Europe (collectively referred to as Annex I parties). Articles 4(3)–(10) also make extensive provision for solidarity assistance to developing states in the form of funding and technology transfer. The implicit assumption is that developed states that historically contributed most of the greenhouse gas emissions should contribute most to tackling the problem, both by providing resources and by 'taking the lead' in adopting control measures. Article 4(7) underlines the leadership role to be played by developed countries: it makes the commitments of developing countries conditional on developed countries meeting their solidarity commitments. Although there is no explicit recognition of 'historical responsibility' in the text of the Convention, the Preamble acknowledges that historic emissions came mostly from developed countries, that developing country emissions were still relatively low, and that they would grow to meet their social and development needs.

Article 4(1) requires all parties to prepare national inventories of greenhouse gas emissions and sinks (such as forests); undertake national and regional programmes to mitigate climate change; promote scientific and technical cooperation; promote sustainable management of forests, oceans, and ecosystems; prepare for adaptation to the impact of climate change; and integrate climate-change considerations in social, economic, and environmental policies. This article encourages parties to take climate change into consideration and formulate policies on the subject but it does not compel them to adhere to any specific international standards for controlling it.

154 Mann, in Lang (ed), *Sustainable Development and International Law* (London, 1995) 67ff notes that the legal effect of Article 3 was deliberately minimized in the final draft.

155 See Preamble to the 1997 Protocol. Article 31(2) of the 1969 VCLT also suggests that Article 3 of the Convention is part of the context for interpreting the Protocol.

156 Mayer, *The International Law on Climate Change*, Ch 6 and *supra*, Ch 3, section 4(3).

The additional commitments undertaken by developed states in Article 4(2) consist principally of an obligation to adopt national policies and measures on the mitigation of climate change by limiting emission of GHGs and protecting and enhancing greenhouse gas sinks and reservoirs. In deciding what these policies and measures should be individual Annex I parties are free to take account inter alia of their different starting points, resources, economies and 'other individual circumstances, as well as the need for equitable and appropriate contributions by each of these Parties to the global effort'. No uniformity of approach is required, and economies in transition are additionally allowed a 'certain degree of flexibility' in implementing their commitments under this article. Information concerning the policies and projected emissions of each Annex I party must be communicated to the Conference of the Parties.

There is reference in Articles 4(2)(a) and (b) to the 'aim' of returning emissions to 1990 levels 'by the end of the present decade' (i.e. by 2000). Although the timescale envisaged here is more precise than in Article 2, the wording of these sub-articles creates neither a strong nor clear commitment, although this shortcoming is balanced by the provision for early review of their adequacy by the COP at its first meeting, and at regular intervals thereafter.[157] As it transpired, Annex I countries were collectively below their 1990 levels in 2000, but only because the economies of many 'economies in transition' had collapsed in the early 1990s. Individually the emissions of almost all the developed countries that were not economies in transition were significantly above their 1990 levels in 2000. In any case, at the time the Convention was negotiated, the parties recognized that it would be necessary to strengthen commitments in the light of new scientific information and further assessments of the problem. Following an IPCC report that, even with stabilization of greenhouse gas emissions at current levels, atmospheric concentrations would continue to rise for the next two centuries, the first COP, held at Berlin in 1995,[158] accepted that these commitments were inadequate, and provided a stronger mandate (commonly known as the 'Berlin Mandate') for negotiating new, more rigorous obligations for developed states under what became the 1997 Kyoto Protocol. As we shall see, however, the 2015 Paris Agreement reflects a reversion to Article 4(2)'s bottom-up approach to control of GHG emissions, applied to all parties.[159]

4(4) THE KYOTO PROTOCOL

(a) Commitments

The Berlin Mandate specified that the new Protocol would cover commitments beyond 2000, would elaborate stronger policies and measures for developed parties, and would set quantified objectives for emissions limitation and removal by sinks

157 Article 4(2)(d).

158 For decisions see *Report of the Conference of the Parties on its First Session* UN Doc UNFCCC/CP/1995/7/Add 1, on which see Oberthür and Ott, 25 *EPL* (1995) 144.

159 *Infra*, section 4(4).

within a specific timescale.[160] It was agreed, however, that no new commitments would be applied to developing states. The Kyoto Protocol adopted in 1997 met these objectives.[161]

The key feature of the protocol is its establishment, for the first time, of quantitative restrictions on emissions from developed industrialized economies. These states—listed in Annex B of the Protocol[162]—are required to limit emissions of the six GHGs listed in Annex A. Crucially, however, and in contrast to the 1987 Montreal Protocol, those constraints focus only on emissions within the developed country concerned; they ignore emissions from developing countries, including those generated by goods exported to Annex B parties, nor do they constrain production or export of fossil fuels by any party.

The quantified emissions limitation and reduction commitments contained in Article 3(1) sought to ensure that overall emissions from Annex B states are reduced to at least 5 per cent below 1990 levels within the period 2008 to 2012. Article 3(1) set different limits for each party, reflecting their differing ability to reduce emissions, access to clean technology, use of energy and so on. In most cases (including the EU, USA, and Japan) a reduction of between 5 per cent and 8 per cent is specified, but New Zealand, Russia, and Ukraine had only to stabilize emissions, while Norway, Australia, and Iceland were permitted to increase by amounts ranging from 1 per cent to 10 per cent.

Whilst reductions of 5 per cent or so may seem low, this figure is deceptive. Choice of 1990 as the main base year means that percentage reductions of up to 30 per cent or more of emissions would have to be made by those states whose greenhouse gas emissions were significantly higher in 2008-2012 compared to 1990. The US is in this category: in 2000 a cut of some 36 per cent would have been needed to reduce its emissions to 1990 levels. In certain circumstances economies in transition, including Russia and Ukraine, could opt for a base year earlier than 1990[163] in order to enable them to *increase* emissions because their economies had contracted so sharply since then. Developing states were not included in Annex B so no emissions limits applied to them and they were not required to do more than meet their existing commitments under Article 4(1) of the Convention.[164] China and India were thus free to greatly increase GHG emissions over the next two decades.

160 Decision 1/CP1 (1995).

161 See Oberthür and Ott, *The Kyoto Protocol* (Berlin, 1999); Yamin, 7 *RECIEL* (1998) 113; Freestone and Streck (eds), *Legal Aspects of Implementing the Kyoto Protocol* (Oxford, 2005); Carlarne, Gray and Tarasofsky (eds), *The Oxford Handbook of International Climate Change Law*, Chs 5 and 16; Mayer, *The International Law on Climate Change*, Ch 3. For drafting history see Depledge, *Tracing the Origins of the Kyoto Protocol: An Article by Article History*, UN Doc UNFCCC/TP/2000/2 (New York, 2000); *Repts of the Ad Hoc Group on the Berlin Mandate* (1995–7) UN Doc UNFCCC/AGBM/1995/2–1997/8 (8 sessions); COP, Chairman's Draft UN Doc UNFCCC/CP/1997/CRP.2 and *Rept of the COP* (3rd session, 1998) UN Doc UNFCCC/CP/1997/7, part V.

162 The list of parties in Annex B Kyoto Protocol is substantially similar to that in Annex I of the UNFCCC.

163 Ibid, Article 3(5). Annex I parties may use 1995 as a base year for gases listed in Article 3(8).

164 Ibid, Article 10.

The Protocol committed Annex B developed state parties to take action on a range of matters additional to those already covered by the Convention, including energy efficiency, promotion of renewable energy, reduction and phasing out of subsidies that contravene the objectives of the Convention, and control of emissions from ships and aircraft.[165] Land-use changes or forestry activities undertaken since 1990, which resulted in the removal of GHGs (known as 'carbon sinks'), could be offset against emissions to meet the net figures set by the Protocol, but there was no obligation to conserve carbon sinks.[166] Kyoto would not hinder Brazil from developing the Amazon rainforest.

The 1997 Kyoto Protocol was an advance on the 1992 UNFCCC, insofar as it provided for more specific remedial and precautionary action to address climate change. At the time of adoption it represented the best that could be achieved but it addressed emissions reductions only at the margins, focusing on 'modest reductions from current levels on the part of major emitters rather than setting overall emissions levels and confronting the question of how to allocate emissions permits on a global scale.'[167] There was no attempt to establish a carbon (or GHG) budget for the atmosphere as a whole The protocol thus represented only a first step in the development of a stronger regime. It entered into force in 2005; among the major GHG emitters only the US failed to become a party. Only European states and Australia have entered into a second phase of emissions reductions commitments under an amendment to the protocol.[168]

(b) The impact of the Kyoto Protocol on greenhouse gas emissions

The first commitment period established by Kyoto expired in 2012, so it is possible to gauge its overall impact. The EU met not only its Kyoto obligations, but also its own voluntary commitment to achieve a 20 per cent reduction by 2020.[169] Other Annex I parties also met their Kyoto targets, in some cases by a significant margin.[170] Even the US, although not a party to Kyoto, markedly reduced its GHG emissions over the same period.[171] However, since Kyoto targets are focused on GHG emissions rather than on consumption, this is a somewhat illusory achievement. It is more than offset by increased GHG emissions in those developing countries from which the EU and US now import manufactured goods, most of all China. On that basis EU and US

165 Ibid, Article 2. 166 Ibid, Article 3(3).

167 Young, in Dryzek et al, *Oxford Handbook of Climate Change and Society*, 628.

168 The 2012 Doha Amendment. The amendment had still not entered into force in December 2019.

169 EEA Technical Report No 2/2011, *European Union greenhouse gas inventory 1990–2009 and inventory report 2011: Submission to the UNFCCC Secretariat* (Copenhagen, EEA, 2011).

170 Grubb, 16 *Climate Policy* (2016) 673–681. However, Canada withdrew from the protocol in order to avoid non-compliance.

171 However its emissions were still higher than in 1990: see Quéré CL et al, 10 *Earth System Science Data* (2018) 2141, and the *Global Carbon Atlas* http://www.globalcarbonatlas.org/en/content/welcome-carbon-atlas.

consumption emissions are estimated to have risen by over 40 per cent since 1990, corresponding to the rapid acceleration in Chinese production.[172] China is not only the biggest emitter but has by far the fastest growth in emissions. Its 2017 CO2 emissions were up by over 400 per cent on 1990 levels.[173] However, on a *per capita* basis, Chinese emissions ere still less than one-third of the US, while European and Japanese per capita emissions were just under half those of the US.

Most importantly, there has been no overall reduction in the rate of increase in atmospheric CO2 or global mean temperature. Limiting global temperature increase to 1.5° C or even 2° C is not achievable on this basis. Given the conclusions of successive IPCC Assessment Reports we can see that Kyoto alone could not meet the 'ultimate objective' of stabilising GHG concentrations 'at a level that would prevent dangerous anthropogenic interference with the climate system.'[174] China, India and other major developing economies such as Brazil and the oil producing states plainly have to carry more of the burden. That conclusion is central to understanding the rather different approach taken by the Paris Agreement in 2015.

(c) Market-based mechanisms

Three market-based mechanisms intended to facilitate emissions reductions—the Clean Development Mechanism (Article 12), Joint Implementation (Article 6), and Emissions Trading (Article 17)—are the most striking aspect of the Kyoto Protocol.[175] Not only were these viewed by the US and other developed state parties as an essential means of meeting their commitments in a cost-effective manner,[176] but some of them also provide a means by which developing states may restrain growth in their own emissions, and achieve sustainable development. Recent assessments of the 1997 Kyoto Protocol show that the flexibility mechanisms 'have proved pivotal to enabling compliance – without them, Japan and several others would have had to follow the Canadian route.'[177]

The possibility that some developed states might find it economically advantageous to meet their commitments jointly, and that developing states might also benefit from such assistance, was envisaged in Articles 4(2)(a) and 4(5) of the 1992 UNFCCC and in a decision of the first COP, although the commitments of each party would not thereby be modified.[178] Such ideas were more fully articulated in the 1997 Kyoto Protocol. Before examining the three mechanisms it is necessary to consider their conceptual underpinnings.

[172] Brinkley and Less, *Carbon Omissions—Consumption-based accounting for international carbon emissions* (London, Policy Exchange, 2010).

[173] *Global Carbon Atlas, supra*, n 171.

[174] UNFCCC, Article 2, and *supra*, section 1.

[175] See generally Freestone and Streck (eds), *Legal Aspects of Implementing the Kyoto Protocol.*

[176] Although not initially by the EU—see Damro and Mendez, 12 *Environmental Politics* (2003) 2, 71–94.

[177] Grubb, 16 *Climate Policy* (2016) 677.

[178] See Decision 5/CP1 (1995) and generally Missfeldt, 7 *RECIEL* (1998) 128; Barrett, in Cameron, Werksman, Roderick (eds), *Improving Compliance with International Environmental Law* (London, 1996) 229.

(i) Economic background

The Kyoto's Protocol's use of market-based instruments to generate emission reductions is commonly described as innovative or radical.[179] Whilst this may be true in the context of international environmental regulation, its pedigree in both theory and practice is venerable. Those familiar with Law and Economics theory will recognize in techniques such as carbon trading the legacy of Pigovian and Coasian economics. The former identified the social benefits of compelling companies to pay for the costs of their own pollution,[180] whilst the latter's *The Problem of Social Cost* demonstrated how allocating property rights and allowing trade yields pareto efficient results.[181] These insights laid the foundations for market mechanisms, such as emissions trading, as an alternative to traditional command-and-control methods, based on its claim to deliver environmental outcomes at the least cost. Each of the three Kyoto market-based mechanisms seeks to draw on the logic of the Coasian privatization of the commons and trading the resultant property rights with a view to achieving emission reductions in the most cost-effective manner, in the optimal global location.

The rationale of mechanisms such as emissions-trading is that a regulator sets a cap on aggregate emissions, distributes the right to emit to regulated facilities (with their emission allowances totalling less than the aggregate emissions), and permits the market to determine the emission price and degree of abatement at individual facilities. If the regulator allows regulated facilities to transfer their emission allowances, the distribution of emission reductions among facilities will be equal to the marginal cost of emission reductions among facilities.[182] If the marginal cost of emission reductions varies among facilities, total costs can be lowered by reallocating greater effort to the facility that can lower emissions at a lower cost. Thus, when marginal cost is equal among facilities, total costs are lowest and the environmental target is reached.

Market mechanisms were first used as environmental tools in the USA in the 1990s in the form of Title IV of the Clean Air (Amendment) Act 1990. A response to SO2 generated acid rain, the Act allocated a fixed number of allowances to the electricity industry, with firms being required to surrender allowances for tons of SO2 emitted, with transfers and banking being permitted.[183] The success of the scheme in terms of costs but also as a driver of abatement innovation exceeded expectations. As a consequence, emissions trading gained favour domestically and most significantly at the multilateral level, where it formed a key negotiating strategy for the Clinton administration in negotiations leading to Kyoto.[184]

179 See Freestone and Streck (eds), *Legal Aspects of Implementing the Kyoto Protocol*, Ch 1.

180 See Pigou, *The Economics of Welfare* (London, 1920).

181 See Coase, 3 *Journal of Law and Economics* (1960) 1. See also Kramer, 'A Coda to Coase', in *In the Realm of Legal and Moral Philosophy: Critical Encounters* (Basingstoke, 1998) and Pearce, 27 *Annual Review of Energy and Environment* (2002) 57.

182 'Marginal cost' is the additional cost to achieve an additional unit of emissions at any facility.

183 See Streck and Gehring, 35 *Environmental Law Reporter* (2005) 10,219.

184 See MacKenzie, *The Political Economy of Carbon Trading*, 29 *London Review of Books* (2007) 29–31, and Damro and Mendez, 12 *Environmental Politics* (2003) 2.

(ii) Clean Development Mechanism

The Clean Development Mechanism ('CDM') has been the most widely used of the three mechanisms;[185] it is the only one available to developing states. The CDM enables Annex I parties to finance activities that reduce anthropogenic emissions in non-Annex I parties.[186] The resultant Certified Emission Reductions ('CERs') can be used by the Annex I party to help meet its emissions targets under the 1997 Kyoto Protocol. Host parties benefit from projects that contribute to sustainable development, facilitating transfer of technology and capacity building. Typical projects include renewable energy, fuel switching, and the capture of the most damaging of GHGs such as methane and hydrofluorocarbon ('HFCs'). However, emissions reductions generated by the CDM must remain 'supplemental' to 'significant' domestic action taken by the Annex I party.[187]

The main drawback of the CDM is the complex approval process involving, inter alia, a 'Designated National Authority' of the host party and registration by the CDM Executive Board.[188] It must be shown that GHG emissions after project implementation are lower than would have occurred in the most plausible alternative scenario.[189] Having been generated, verified, and certified, an equivalent quantity of CERs are issued to parties and project participants.[190]

This very simplified account indicates the complex nature of the CDM project cycle. Whilst rigorous procedural safeguards are necessary, the attendant transaction costs are high. Similarly, the centrality of the Designated National Authority to the process can operate as a bureaucratic barrier. In many non-Annex I parties, such an entity may not exist, causing delay at best, at worst a non-functioning system. It is notable that the distribution of registered CDM projects is heavily skewed towards the more developed non-Annex I parties such as China, which accounts for nearly 50 per cent, and India, which accounts for over 20 per cent of registered projects, with all of Africa accounting for less than 3 per cent of registered projects.[191] There have been efforts to remedy this geographical imbalance in the distribution of projects, including by the EU, which from 2013 only allowed new CERs from projects based in least-developed countries to enter the EU emissions trading system (EUETS).[192] Although the CDM formed a significant share of the carbon market in its early days, following uncertainty over the future of the 1997 Kyoto Protocol, there has been a rapid decline in its use.[193]

185 Grubb, 16 *Climate Policy* (2016) 677.

186 Article 12, UNFCCC. See Freestone and Streck (eds), *Legal Aspects of Implementing the Kyoto Protocol*, Chs 9–13.

187 Article 12(3) and 15/CP7. Reporting obligations are imposed by Articles 5, 7, 8 of the Kyoto Protocol.

188 3/CMP 1, Annex, para 36: 'Registration is the formal acceptance by the Executive Board of a validated project as a CDM project activity. Registration is the prerequisite for the verification, certification and issuance of CERs relating to that project activity.'

189 See 1997 Protocol, Article 12(5) and 3/CMP 1, Annex, para 43.

190 3/CMP 1, Annex, para 66; KP Article 12(8).

191 https://cdm.UNFCCC.int/Statistics/Public/CDMinsights/index.html, accessed on June 20, 2019.

192 European Commission, Climate Action, *The EU Emissions Trading System (EU ETS)*.

193 Bodansky, Brunnée and Rajamani, *International Climate Change Law* (Oxford, 2017), Ch 6.

(iii) Joint implementation

Under joint implementation (JI),[194] one Annex I party may implement an emission-reducing project or a project that enhances removals by sinks in another Annex I party and by doing so generate emission reduction units (ERUs) that will count towards meeting its own Kyoto target, as defined by Article 6. As with the CDM, joint implementation aims to offer Parties a flexible and cost-efficient means of fulfilling a part of their Kyoto commitments, while the host party benefits from foreign investment and technology transfer. A JI project must provide a reduction in emissions by sources, or an enhancement of removals by sinks, that is additional to what would otherwise have occurred and projects. The Marrakesh Accords established an Article 6 Supervisory Committee to verify ERUs generated through joint implementation projects,[195] but post-Kyoto there is now only limited international oversight and transparency of the former JI activities, and this has led to concerns about their environmental integrity.[196] However, in comparison with the CDM, activity under this mechanism is modest.

(iv) International emission trading

Article 17 provides a framework for Annex I parties to 'participate in emissions trading for the purposes of fulfilling their commitments' provided that such trading is 'supplemental to domestic actions for the purpose of meeting quantified emission limitation and reduction commitments'.[197] Parties that may otherwise not meet their commitments are thereby able to trade units in the form of assigned amount units,[198] certified emission reductions,[199] emission reduction units,[200] and removal units.[201] The Marrakesh Accords set out detailed modalities for the accounting and verification of assigned amounts, and established national registries, and an independent international transaction log, maintained by the FCCC secretariat, to verify the validity of transactions[202] and to prevent double counting.[203]

Although not created under the legal authority of the 1997 Kyoto Protocol, the EU ETS[204] is the keystone in the EU's complex attempts to comply with its commitments.

194 See Freestone and Streck (eds), *Legal Aspects of Implementing the Kyoto Protocol*, Chs 6–8.

195 Ibid, para 3.

196 UNFCCC, Joint Implementation, *Concept note: Input from the Joint Implementation Supervisory Committee to CMP 12, Version 01.0* (March 3, 2016) UN Doc JI-JISC38-AA-A05.

197 Freestone and Streck (eds), *Legal Aspects of Implementing the Kyoto Protocol*, Chs 22–9; Grubb, 7 *RECIEL* (1998) 140; Oberthür and Ott, *The Kyoto Protocol*, 187–205.

198 AAUs are units issued by Parties to the Kyoto Protocol into their national registry up to their assigned amount.

199 CERs are the tradeable units of the CDM. CERs are defined in 3/CMP 1, Annex, paragraph 1(b) as 'a unit representing one tonne of carbon dioxide-equivalent sequestered or abated . . . CERs are issued to project participants in CDM projects pursuant to Article 12 of the Kyoto Protocol and the CDM modalities and procedures'.

200 ERUs are units converted from either AAUs or removal unit RMU and issued to project participants in Joint Implementation project activities.

201 RMUs are issued by Parties to the Kyoto Protocol in respect of net removals by sinks from activities covered by Article 3(3) and Article 3(4) (in the land use, land use change and forestry sector).

202 13/CMP 1, Annex, para 38. Registries are set up under 3/CMP 1 and 13/CMP 1.

203 13/CMP 1.

204 Directive 2003/87/EC. See Freestone and Streck (eds), *Legal Aspects of Implementing the Kyoto Protocol*, Ch 23.

Perhaps ironically, given its initial resistance to the market-based instrument of emissions trading in favour of more command-and-control regulatory and taxation schemes, the scheme has become the single largest carbon market in the world, accounting for over three-quarters of international carbon trading.[205] Whilst the EU ETS has undoubtedly greatly contributed to the EU's ability to influence policy-making at the national and international levels, it should not be judged an unqualified success. In its first phase (2005–2007) EU Member State governments granted emission allowances for free. Combined with overly generous National Allocation Plans, the first phase came badly unstuck in May 2006 when the market crashed, losing over 70 per cent of its value. However, through successive phases (2008–2012, and 2013–2020), the caps on emissions allowances have been progressively reduced, with free allowances gradually limited to new installations and to those sectors at the most risk of relocating outside the EU.

4(5) THE PARIS AGREEMENT

(a) The long approach to the Paris Agreement

The 1997 Kyoto Protocol, for all its innovative features, attracted less and less political support over time. The US rejected it in 2001, arguing that it excluded China and India from GHG mitigation targets and would cause serious harm to the US economy.[206] Canada withdrew from the Kyoto Protocol in 2012 and several developed countries, including Japan and Russia, have refused to participate in the second commitment period. For all these reasons the future of the 1997 Kyoto Protocol and its market mechanisms is uncertain. In any case, the disenchantment many developed states had begun to demonstrate for the Protocol suggested that it was unlikely to be environmentally effective.

The climate change regime thus turned its attention to extending GHG mitigation actions and commitments to developing countries and the US. These negotiations took many twists and turns, in particular since the legal form of any successor agreement and the role of common but differentiated responsibility in that agreement were deeply disputed. In 2009 some measure of agreement was reached between the major GHG emitters and many vulnerable nations. The Copenhagen Accord required UNFCCC Annex I parties to commit to emissions targets, and non-Annex I parties to undertake mitigation actions. The Accord also established the Green Climate Fund, and developed countries committed to mobilizing USD 100 billion per year by 2020 for climate action.[207] However, the Accord was rejected by members of the Bolivarian Alliance—Bolivia, Cuba, Ecuador, Nicaragua, Venezuela—as well as Sudan and Tuvalu, both for procedural irregularities in its negotiation, as well as substantive inadequacies.[208] As COP decisions require consensus for adoption,

205 European Commission, Climate Action, *The EU Emissions Trading System (EU ETS)*.

206 The White House, Office of the Press Secretary, *Text of a Letter from the President to Senators Hagel, Helms, Craig, and Roberts* (March 13, 2001).

207 Decision 2/CP15, Annex.

208 See for further details Rajamani, 59 *ICLQ* (2010) 824; Bodansky, 104 *AJIL* (2010) 230.

parties could only resolve to 'take[s] note' of the Copenhagen Accord.[209] Yet a year later, at the 2010 Cancun conference, many of the key compromises contained in the Accord were incorporated into COP decisions, otherwise known as the Cancun Agreements.[210] The Copenhagen Accord/Cancun agreements represented a paradigm shift in the climate change regime as they opened the door for self-selected GHG mitigation targets and actions, a move away from the multilaterally negotiated GHG mitigation targets of the Kyoto Protocol.[211] This resulted in greater symmetry, albeit not uniformity, between developed and developing countries on GHG mitigation targets and actions, and in doing so began the gradual process of diluting the deeply contentious Kyoto-style differentiation. Although negotiated only by 28 heads of state and government, 141 countries subsequently accepted the Accord, while only 8 countries expressly rejected it.[212]

At the 2011 Durban conference parties launched a negotiating process for a 'Protocol, another legal instrument or agreed outcome with legal force under the Convention, applicable to all'.[213] This carefully worded negotiating mandate provided an insight into the key issues that were to test the negotiating process in the years that followed. First, whether it should be a binding instrument or not, and the legal nature of the obligations it should contain, were disputed. Secondly, the extent of differentiation in the GHG mitigation commitments for developing countries was controversial. The phrase 'applicable to all' was intended to signal that the new instrument would represent a step change from the 1997 Kyoto Protocol in this respect. However, as many developing countries noted, the phrase 'applicable to all' suggests universality not uniformity of application, thus this issue remained contentious. The term 'under the Convention' similarly revealed a dispute over the interpretation of the principle of common but differentiated responsibilities and respective capabilities, as well as the extent to which the balance of responsibilities between developed and developing countries in the 1992 UNFCCC should be replicated in any new agreement. These issues proved key in the four-year negotiating process that followed, and the resulting 2015 Paris Agreement reflects finely balanced compromises on each of them.

(b) Key features of the Paris Agreement

(i) Objective

The 2015 Paris Agreement[214] identifies the goal of '[h]olding the increase in the global average temperature to well below 2°C above pre-industrial levels and pursuing efforts to

[209] 2/CP15. [210] Decision 1/CP16. [211] 2/CP15, 6, paras 4–5.

[212] UNFCCC, *Information provided by Parties to the Convention relating to the Copenhagen Accord.*

[213] Decision 1/CP17.

[214] See generally Mayer, *The International Law on Climate Change*, Ch 3; Klein, Carazo, Doelle, Bulmer, Higham (eds), *The Paris Agreement on Climate Change* (Oxford, 2017); Bodansky, 110 *AJIL* (2017) 288; Rajamani, 65 *ICLQ* (2016) 493

limit the temperature increase to 1.5°C above pre-industrial levels. . .'.[215] This temperature goal concretizes the much looser 1992 UNFCCC objective of 'prevent[ing] dangerous anthropogenic interference with the climate system' by setting out, in terms of avoided temperature rise, the limits of what is 'dangerous'.[216]

(ii) Central obligations

The primary vehicle identified in the 2015 Paris Agreement to achieve this aspirational goal is nationally determined contributions ('NDCs') from parties. Article 4(2) obliges parties ('Each Party shall') to 'prepare, communicate and maintain' NDCs. This is only a procedural obligation, not a quantified emission limitation and reduction commitment as such. It is, however, subject to a good faith expectation that parties 'intend to achieve' their NDCs. Thus the 2015 Paris Agreement does not dictate to parties what their NDCs should be, or how they should implement them, rather it requires them to follow a series of discrete procedures designed to illuminate how they arrive at their self-selected contributions, what these contributions are, and what steps are being taken to implement and achieve them.[217] The 2015 Paris Agreement does, however, contain a substantive obligation in relation to NDCs. The second sentence of Article 4(2) reads, 'Parties shall pursue domestic mitigation measures, with the aim of achieving the objectives of such contributions.' Parties are obliged to pursue domestic measures, a substantive obligation, but only with the 'aim' of achieving the objectives of the NDCs. This is an obligation of conduct in that parties are not obliged to meet the objectives, targets, or goals identified in their NDCs, only to exercise best efforts to do so. This obligation is essentially one of 'due diligence,' and within the context of general international law it would have to be interpreted from that perspective.[218]

There is an implicit recognition in the 2015 Paris Agreement that self-selected NDCs may not add up to what is necessary to meet the temperature goal of the Agreement. Thus, the Agreement contains an 'ambition cycle' intended to provide a forward 'direction of travel' for the regime, and to trigger progressively more ambitious NDCs. The elements of the 'ambition cycle' include five-yearly national contributions; each contribution a progression on the last and reflecting that state's highest possible ambition; information accompanying contributions to enhance their clarity, transparency, and understanding; biennial reports tracking progress in achieving contributions; five-yearly global stock-takes to assess collective progress towards the goals of the 2015 Paris Agreement; and a facilitative implementation and compliance mechanism to encourage parties to comply with their obligations and hold them accountable.[219]

215 Paris Agreement, Article 2(1). On the legal significance of the temperature goal see further Rajamani and Werksman, 376 *Philosophical Transactions of the Royal Society* (2018) 1.

216 Article 2.

217 For a fuller discussion of the legal character of provisions in the Paris Agreement, see Bodansky, Brunnée and Rajamani, *International Climate Change Law*, Ch 7; and Rajamani, *Innovation and Experimentation in the International Climate Change Regime*, Recueil des Cours (forthcoming 2020), Ch III.

218 See also Article 4(3); Voigt, 3 *Questions of International Law* (2016) 17, and *supra*, Ch 3, section 5.

219 Paris Agreement, Articles 4(2), 4(3), 4(8), 4(9), 13, 14, and 15.

(iii) Differentiation

Although these core procedural obligations are 'applicable to all', the 2015 Paris Agreement does differentiate in favour of developing countries, albeit in a more nuanced form than the Kyoto Protocol. Different elements of the 2015 Paris Agreement reflect different forms of differentiation. In the context of GHG mitigation commitments the 2015 Paris Agreement embraces 'self-differentiation.' Since parties' contributions are self-selected and tailored to national circumstances, in practice these may well be different from each other. But the autonomy parties enjoy is gently circumscribed through normative expectations in relation to their contributions—expectations that each successive contribution will reflect a progression and that party's highest possible ambition,[220] and that developed countries should continue taking the lead.[221]

With respect to finance, the 2015 Paris Agreement contains a more conventional form of differentiation, requiring developed countries to take the lead in providing and mobilizing finance.[222] On transparency the Paris Agreement provides for flexibilities tailored to capacities.[223] The 2015 Paris Agreement, deliberately so, contains no references to the Annexes of the Convention or the 1997 Kyoto Protocol, suggesting that the categorical form of differentiation—categories of parties matched to categories of commitments –prevalent in the earlier climate change regime has given way to a more nuanced and dynamic form of differentiation. This is reflected in the 2015 Paris Agreement's articulation of the principle of common but differentiated responsibilities and respective capabilities that contains the US-China brokered qualification, 'in light of different national circumstances.'[224]

(iv) Human rights

The Preamble to the 2015 Paris Agreement acknowledges that climate change is a common concern of humankind, and that '*Parties should, when taking action to address climate change, respect, promote and consider their respective obligations on human rights, the right to health, the rights of indigenous peoples, local communities, migrants, children, persons with disabilities and people in vulnerable situations and the right to development, as well as gender equality, empowerment of women and intergenerational equity*'. Despite much effort to achieve more during the negotiations, this is all the agreement says on the subject of human rights.[225] That does not mean that human rights are irrelevant to climate change: on the contrary, as we saw in Chapter 5, human rights law and institutions have the potential to influence the success or otherwise of the 2015 Paris Agreement.

220 Ibid, Article 4(3). 221 Ibid, Article 4(4). 222 Ibid, Article 9. 223 Ibid, Article 13.

224 Ibid, Article 2(2); The White House, Office of the Press Secretary, *US-China Joint Announcement on Climate Change, Beijing, China, 12 November 2014*, para 2.

225 See Boyle, 67 *ICLQ* (2018) 759; Rajamani, 22 *JEL* (2010) 391; Duyck, 26 *YbIEL* (2015) 3, and *supra*, Ch 5, section 2(3)(c).

(v) The Paris Rulebook

The Paris Rulebook comprises various modalities, procedures, and guidelines that elaborate the parties' obligations under the 2015 Paris Agreement, and flesh out the Agreement's procedures and mechanisms, including the global stock-take, and the implementation and compliance mechanism.[226]

The Rulebook seeks to circumscribe the discretion parties have in the 2015 Paris Agreement, as well as to instil accountability for the implementation and achievement of NDCs. In the absence of substantive obligations of result for NDCs, these detailed procedural rules make progress in implementing and achieving NDCs more transparent. However, the Rulebook is deferential, as is the 2015 Paris Agreement, to 'national determination'. Thus, for instance, parties are required to provide the listed information only 'as applicable' to their NDC.[227] A list of qualitative or quantitative indicators that a party 'could include, as appropriate'[228] to track progress towards implementation and achievement of their NDCs is optional.[229]

4(6) SUPERVISION AND COMPLIANCE

The supervisory role of the parties under the 1992 UNFCCC, 1997 Kyoto Protocol and 2015 Paris Agreement is among the most elaborate in any environmental treaty and includes a number of significant innovations. The COP serves as the principal supervisory institution; it is required to meet regularly and to keep the adequacy, implementation, and effectiveness of both instruments under review.[230] For this purpose it receives advice from subsidiary bodies for science and technology (SBSTA), and implementation (SBI).[231] The former assesses the state of scientific knowledge relating to climate change and the effects of implementation measures. The latter assists in the 'assessment and review of the effective implementation' of the Convention and the Protocol and considers reports from parties under Article 12 of the Convention and Article 7 of the Protocol concerning implementation and projected emissions. It is this body which has also been responsible for developing detailed guidelines on issues such as transfer of technology, and the financial mechanism. Both subsidiary bodies are composed of experts acting as governmental representatives. Together, the COP and its subsidiary bodies provide the essential political and technical oversight and management of the whole climate change regime.

[226] The full set of decisions agreed to at the UNFCCC 24th COP, characterized as the 'Paris Rulebook', is available at https://UNFCCC.int/process-and-meetings/the-paris-agreement/paris-agreement-work-programme/katowice-climate-package. See Rajamani and Bodansky, 68 *ICLQ* (2019) 1023.

[227] Decision 4/CMA 1, para 7.

[228] Decision 18/CMA 1, Annex, para 66.

[229] Ibid, Annex, para 65.

[230] UNFCCC, Article 7; 1997 Protocol, Article 13; Paris Agreement, Article 16; See Werksman, 9 *YbIEL* (1998) 48.

[231] UNFCCC, Articles 9, 10; 1997 Protocol, Article 15; Paris Agreement, Article 18. However, the IPCC remains the principal source of authoritative and independent scientific and technical advice.

One of the innovative features of the regime, however, is that before national reports are considered by the relevant subsidiary body and the COP an in-depth review is conducted by a team of experts.[232] These reviews are coordinated by the secretariat and the experts who conduct them are selected from nominees of governments and international organizations. The purpose of the review is to provide 'a thorough and comprehensive technical assessment' of all aspects of implementation by any party, and to identify and report on any problems or other factors influencing the fulfilment of commitments. The teams generally visit each party to discuss the report. Their findings are circulated to all parties.

The 2015 Paris Agreement establishes a similar 'technical expert review' for the transparency reports that parties are required to submit.[233] These reports track the targets, policies, and measures contained in parties' NDCs as well as the domestic mitigation measures that parties are taking to meet these targets.[234] The information submitted by parties is reviewed through the technical expert review.[235]

Review by experts serves two useful functions. First, it helps ensure that reporting by parties is adequate, accurate, and consistent. Secondly, it introduces an important and desirable element of quasi-independent expertise to the process of scrutiny. In effect, review teams have the ability to report on the performance of individual states in implementing the Convention, Protocol and Agreement, and to point out any inadequacy in their reporting. Early in-depth reviews showed that the EC, Japan and the US would not meet 1990 emissions levels in 2000.[236] The secretariat is required to draw such findings to the attention of the COP. It is then up to the COP to take the necessary decisions. The closest analogy to this process is the use of expert assessment teams by the IAEA when invited to review the safety of nuclear installations, but the process established here is probably stronger than anything so far adopted by that organisation.[237] It represents an attempt to provide for a significant measure of transparency and international verification of national reporting.

What happens, however, if such reviews show that a party is failing to fulfil its commitments? There are several options. The Convention makes provision for a 'multilateral consultative process' to resolve questions regarding implementation.[238] It is intended to be an even softer form of dispute avoidance than non-compliance procedures: conducted by a panel of experts, it is non-judicial in character, non-confrontational, and advisory rather than supervisory. No sanctions can be imposed; there is power only to recommend measures to facilitate cooperation and implementation and to clarify issues and promote understanding of the Convention. Parties may bring questions concerning their own implementation or that of other parties to

232 The mechanism was first established by Decision 20/CP1 (1995) and subsequently incorporated in Article 8 of the 1997 Protocol. See UN Doc UNFCCC/CP/13 (1996) and Werksman, 9 *YbIEL* (1998) 48.

233 18/CMA 1, Annex, Ch I.E, para 10(b).

234 Ibid, Annex, Ch III.B and Ch III.D.

235 2015 Paris Agreement, Article 13(11).

236 Werksman, 9 *YbIEL* (1998) 66.

237 *Infra*, Ch 7.

238 UNFCCC, Article 13; 1997 Protocol, Article 16. For details of the process approved by the 4th COP see *6th Rept of the Ad Hoc Working Group on Article 13* (1998) UN Doc UNFCCC/AG13/1998/2, Annex II.

the Multilateral Consultative Committee; the COP may also do so. This process represents a further move away from formal binding third-party dispute settlement in favour of procedures that facilitate compliance but cannot compel it. Given the lack of real commitments in the Convention this is not a serious weakness in that context. However, reliance on the deterrent effect of inspection and publicity is not a guarantee of compliance with commitments on a matter as economically fundamental as GHG emissions. Given the possibilities for evasion and abuse it had been argued that, unlike ozone depletion, 'purely facilitative approaches to non-compliance may not answer parties' concerns about the need to ensure that all parties pull their weight and that the protocol's market mechanisms provide confidence to investors'.[239] Thus to police the market mechanisms the 1997 Kyoto Protocol established a compliance mechanism, with the ability to impose penal consequences for non-compliance. The unusually complex process adopted in 2006, and involving facilitative and enforcement procedures, is considered further in Chapter 4.

The 2015 Paris Agreement, with its emphasis on procedural obligations, and greater deference to national determination, contains a facilitative implementation and compliance mechanism, one that is designed to be 'expert-based and facilitative' in nature and function in a manner that is 'transparent, non-adversarial and non-punitive'.[240] The Paris Rulebook lays down detailed modalities and procedures for the operationalization of the implementation and compliance committee.[241] These rules identify ways of initiating the committee's consideration of an implementation and/or compliance issue, outline the process that the committee is to follow in considering such issues, and describe the outputs of the committee's process and the measures it can take.[242] These measures and outputs, in keeping with the facilitative nature of the mechanism, are soft responses involving 'dialogue', assistance and recommendations.[243] The most stringent of these measures is a 'finding of fact'.[244]

Another option in cases of non-compliance is to resort to dispute settlement as provided for in Article 14 of the Convention, Article 19 of the Protocol, and Article 24 of the Agreement. However, negotiation and non-binding conciliation are the only compulsory procedures envisaged here, unless both parties to the dispute have declared their acceptance of ICJ jurisdiction or arbitration. Moreover, even for parties who do accept adjudication or arbitration, these articles are probably not adequate for dealing with the questions likely to be thrown up by joint implementation or clean development projects and emissions trading, all of which may also involve private parties and private law. Neither procedure is multilateral in character and any judgment would be binding only on the parties to the litigation, not on the other parties to the 1992 UNFCCC, the 1997 Protocol or the 2015 Paris Agreement.[245]

239 Werksman, 9 *YbIEL* (1998) 100.

240 Paris Agreement, Article 15(3).

241 Decision 20/CMA 1, Annex. See generally Zihua, Voigt and Werksman, 9 *Climate Law* (2019) 65.

242 20/CMA 1, Annex.

243 Ibid, para 30(a).

244 Ibid, para 30(e).

245 *Supra*, Ch 4, section 4.

There is also the possibility of litigating compliance with the 2015 Paris Agreement under Part XV of the 1982 UNCLOS insofar as greenhouse gas emissions cause marine pollution; such a dispute would be within the Convention's provision for compulsory dispute settlement.[246] National courts also have a role to play in securing compliance in some jurisdictions.[247]

Finally, collective or unilateral trade measures could be used against parties whose nationally determined contributions result in carbon 'leakage' from more stringent controls on greenhouse gas emissions elsewhere.[248] As we will see in Chapter 13, the *Shrimp-Turtle* case before the WTO Appellate Body provides a template, if necessary, for carefully focused trade measures designed to put pressure on states that are not supporting or implementing internationally agreed commitments to protect the global environment, including states whose policies on climate change do not show the degree of ambition required by the 2015 Paris Agreement.[249]

4(7) ENVIRONMENTAL IMPACT ASSESSMENT AND CLIMATE CHANGE

Should the potential greenhouse gas emissions of large industrial or energy projects be the subject of an EIA if they are likely to contribute to global warming and cause damage in other states? In principle there seems no reason why not. Some states do include climate change impacts in their EIA process where appropriate.[250] EIA in international law is normally required for planned 'activities' or 'projects' that are likely to cause significant transboundary harm.[251] However, the 1991 Espoo Convention defines transboundary impact as 'any impact, *not exclusively of a global nature*, within an area under the jurisdiction of a party. . . . '[252] Does this exclude GHG emissions which make a significant contribution to global warming from the obligation to do an EIA? Possibly, but in addition to their impact on global temperatures, GHG emissions are especially likely to cause transboundary harm in states that are low-lying and vulnerable to sea-level rise, acidification of the oceans, and loss of marine productivity.

246 See Boyle, 34 *IJMCL* (2019) 458, and *supra*, Ch 4, section 4.

247 See *Urgenda v The Netherlands*, Hoge Raad (2019); Peel and Osofsky, *Climate Change Litigation: Regulatory Pathways to Cleaner Energy* (Cambridge, 2015); id, 'Climate Change Litigation', 16 *Annual Review of Law and Social Science* (2020). See also *In re Greenpeace Southeast Asia and Others* Case No. CHR-NI-2016-0001 (2015).

248 See Mehling et al, 113 *AJIL* (2019) 433.

249 Se *infra*, Ch 13, section 2.

250 E.g. Canada, on which see Craik, *The International Law of EIA* (Cambridge, 2008), 212–216. The current state practice is comprehensively reviewed in Mayer, 68 *ICLQ* (2019) 271, who argues that customary international law requires possible climate impacts to be assessed.

251 1991 Espoo Convention, Article 2(3); 1987 UNEP Goals and Principles of Environmental Impact Assessment, Principle 1; ILC, 2001 Articles on Transboundary Harm, Articles 1, 2(a), 7; *Pulp Mills on the River Uruguay Case* (2010) ICJ Reports, paras 204–5, and see *supra*, Ch 3, section 7.

252 1991 Convention on EIA, Article 1(viii). The 2003 Protocol on Strategic Environmental Assessment contains no comparable limitation: see Article 10.

Here the impact is arguably not 'exclusively of a global nature' but specific to those particular states.[253] In any event, Article 206 of the 1982 UNCLOS requires parties to assess the potential for 'significant and harmful changes to the marine environment' of activities under their jurisdiction or control. Article 206 has been construed broadly, including 'activities with an impact on the environment in an area beyond the limits of national jurisdiction.'[254]

Whatever the 1991 Espoo Convention may say, there seems no reason to read the 1982 UNCLOS as excluding GHG emitting activities from the obligation to carry out an EIA for potential impacts on the marine environment.[255] EIA of this kind embraces the licensing or approval of industrial, energy and transport undertakings, *inter alia*,[256] but would not necessarily cover plans or policies of a more general kind—whether to use coal or oil for power generation, for example. However, Article 4(1)(f) of the 1992 UNFCCC adopts a broader perspective, requiring parties to take climate change into account when formulating 'social, economic and environmental policies and actions.' In effect this is a reference to 'strategic environmental assessment' (SEA).[257] It envisages, inter alia, impact assessments 'determined nationally' and on the wording of Article 4 it could include energy policy.

4(8) LOSS AND DAMAGE

None of the climate agreements makes specific provision for civil liability or state responsibility for loss or damage caused by climate change, whether in the past or in future. Agreement was reached in 2013 on the creation of a mechanism to deal with loss and damage.[258] Article 8 of the 2015 Paris Agreement reaffirms that mechanism in terms which are far removed from any assertion or acceptance of state responsibility for past or future damage resulting from climate change.[259] The law on responsibility for transboundary harm potentially applies in the context of climate change,[260] but such a claim would raise large questions about causation, knowledge of risk, joint liability, and the inter-relationship with the 1992 UNFCCC regime, including the loss and damage mechanism agreed in 2013. As we saw in Chapter 4, states

[253] In 2010 Micronesia made representations to the Czech Republic concerning an EIA for a lignite power station: see Rayfuse and Scott, *International Law in the Era of Climate Change*, 336–7.

[254] See *Advisory Opinion on Activities in the Area*, 2011 ITLOS Seabed Disputes Chamber, paras 145–50.

[255] For a review of other precedents see CBD, *Background on the Development of Voluntary Guidelines for the Consideration of Biodiversity in Environmental Impact Assessments and Strategic Environmental Assessments in Marine and Coastal Areas*, UNEP/CBD/SBSTTA/16/INF/16, 11 April 2012.

[256] See the activities listed in the 1991 Convention on EIA, Annex 1.

[257] On which see *supra*, Ch 3, section 7.

[258] Decision 2/CP.19 (2013) Warsaw international mechanism for loss and damage associated with climate change impacts, UNFCCC/CP/2013/10/Add.1.

[259] UNFCCC Decision 1/CP.21, para 51, states that 'Article 8 of the Agreement does not involve or provide a basis for any liability or compensation.' See generally Klein et al, *The Paris Agreement on Climate Change*, 224–238.

[260] *Supra*, Ch 4, section 2.

are responsible for loss and damage only if caused by a breach of obligation; proving that any particular state was in breach of its treaty obligations with respect to climate change and therefore responsible for causing historic damage would not be easy.[261] Customary international law would not be relevant since in this context the *lex specialis* is the one set out in the 1992 regime except for the tiny number of non-parties. On any of these grounds a claim for compensation for damage predating the 2015 Paris Agreement would almost certainly fail.

The governments of Nauru, Tuvalu, Kiribati, Fiji, and Papua-New Guinea made declarations on signature or ratification stating that the 1992 UNFCCC did not constitute a renunciation of any rights under international law concerning state responsibility for adverse effects of climate change or a derogation from the principles of general international law. They made similar declarations on signature or ratification of the 1997 Kyoto Protocol and the 2015 Paris Agreement. Insofar as these declarations seek to pre-empt the applicable law they risk being treated as reservations contrary to Article 24 of the 1992 UNFCCC. A claim at some point in the future for further damage resulting from failure to deliver on Paris or UNFCCC commitments would potentially have greater traction,[262] and in the case of damage to the marine environment or coastal states would be subject to compulsory jurisdiction under Part XV of the 1982 UNCLOS.[263]

4(9) ASSESSMENT OF THE CLIMATE CHANGE REGIME

In the last decade, climate change has assumed a prominence in public discourse that is unprecedented in international environmental law. The range of actors—state and non-state; governmental and non-governmental; commercial and otherwise; national, sub-national and supra-national—engaged in tackling climate change is commensurate with the scale of the challenge. The following assessment seeks to illustrate the complexity of the international climate change regime as it has evolved.

(a) The UNFCCC

At the time of its adoption in 1992 the Climate Change Convention was criticized for containing 'only the vaguest of commitments regarding stabilization and no commitment at all on reductions'.[264] Understandably, the US' position was that 'there is nothing in any of the language which constitutes a commitment to any specific level of emissions at any time'. It was noted also that 'Many of the Convention's provisions do not attempt to resolve differences so much as paper them over', and that there was no provision for international monitoring or fact finding.[265] Nor does the Convention acknowledge responsibility on the part of industrialized states to compensate other

261 *Supra*, Ch 4, section 2, and see also Faure and Nollkaemper (2007) 26 *Stanford Env LJ* (2007) 123.

262 See Boyle, 34 *IJMCL* (2019) 458.

263 See 1982 UNCLOS, Articles 235 and 286, and *supra*, Ch 4, section 4(5)(a).

264 Bodansky, 18 *Yale JIL* (1993) 451.

265 Ibid.

states for the harm caused by greenhouse gas emissions beyond a vague commitment to assist vulnerable developing country parties to meet the costs of adaptation.[266]

Whilst valid criticisms in 1992, much has since changed. Even in 1992 the Climate Change Convention contained more substance than the 1985 Ozone Convention or the 1979 LRTAP Convention. Like those agreements, the test of success lies not in the commitments made in the Convention itself but in its subsequent evolution. Most importantly the Convention did achieve an equitable balance acceptable to the great majority of developed and developing states,[267] and as of June 2019 it has 197 parties. The adoption of the Kyoto Protocol in 1997 demonstrated that agreement on stronger emissions limits and earlier timetables was possible, despite the difficulty of maintaining meaningful consensus. Similarly, the adoption of the 2015 Paris Agreement 'under the Convention'[268] testifies to the 1992 UNFCCC's ability to adapt to changing political imperatives and evolve in a different direction.

(b) The Kyoto Protocol

The 1997 Kyoto Protocol, with its stark differentiation between developed and developing countries, represents a particular interpretation of the principle of common but differentiated responsibilities and respective capabilities, and model of developed country leadership. As a model it was justified by the pattern of historical GHG emissions, as well as differing capacities and resources, but less suited to emerging trends in GHG emissions across the world. Historically, cumulative emissions from developed countries are about 2.3 times that of developing countries.[269] Yet, developing country annual emissions are now 60 per cent of the total global CO_2 emissions[270] and emissions from large developing countries are projected to keep rising.[271] The 2018 World Energy Outlook ('WEO') predicts a doubling of electricity demand from developing countries,[272] with corresponding increases in CO_2 emissions. In 2005, China surpassed the US as the world's largest annual emitter of CO_2;[273] in 2017, its share of global emissions was 27 per cent, compared to 13 per cent for the US and 9 per cent for the EU.[274] Per capita emissions for most developing countries, remain low however, and equity concerns remain salient. India's per capita CO_2 emissions at 1.8 tonnes,

[266] Article 4(4), and *supra*, section 4(7).

[267] Bodansky, 18 *Yale JIL* (1993) 451. See generally Redgwell, in Churchill and Freestone (eds), *International Law and Global Climate Change*, 41; Franck, *Fairness and International Law and Institutions*, Ch 12.

[268] Paris Agreement, Article 2 chapeau.

[269] CO_2 emissions from UNFCCC Annex I countries from 1850 to 2014 are 957,536 $MtCO_2$ and from non-Annex I are 421,357 $MtCO_2$. For data for Cumulative Total CO_2 Emissions Excluding Land-Use Change and Forestry from 1850 to 2014 see World Resources Institute (WRI), *CAIT Climate Data Explorer*, 2017.

[270] Total CO_2 emissions from Annex I countries for 2014 are 12,927 $MtCO_2$ and from non-Annex I are 20,288 $MtCO_2$. See ibid.

[271] See IPCC, Working Group III contribution to AR5, *Climate Change 2014: Mitigation of Climate Change*, 125–30, and UNEP, *Emissions Gap Report 2019: Executive Summary*, iv-vi.

[272] International Energy Agency, *World Energy Outlook 2018*, Executive Summary, 3.

[273] Based on data from the WRI, *CAIT Climate Data Explorer*, 2017.

[274] Olivier and Peters, *Trends in Global CO_2 and Total Greenhouse Gas Emissions: 2018 Report* (2018), 4.

and even China's at 7.7 tonnes, for instance, are significantly below the US average of 15.7 tonnes.[275] Nevertheless, given increasing emissions from developing countries in Asia, their participation in mitigation efforts is key to the long-term effectiveness of the climate regime. The 1997 Kyoto Protocol's first commitment period running from 2008-2012 covered 24 per cent of 2010 global emissions,[276] while its second commitment period running from 2013 to 2020, with several developed countries opting out, covers less than 11 per cent of 2014 global emissions,[277] even assuming the relevant amendment enters into force. The 2015 Paris Agreement seeks to fill this gap in the climate change regime by ensuring universal participation in GHG mitigation efforts.

There is no formal decision on the future of the 1997 Kyoto Protocol beyond the second commitment period. However, the near universal support for the 2015 Paris Agreement—its scope, coverage and breadth, its architecture, and its distinctive approach to differentiation—signals a lack of appetite among developed countries for extending the 1997 Kyoto Protocol beyond 2020. Indeed, the eight-year duration of the second commitment period was chosen so as to end when the 2015 Paris Agreement's NDCs were expected to take effect, and thus to avoid a commitment gap.[278]

(c) The Paris Agreement

The 2015 Paris Agreement marks a decisive turn in the climate change regime from prescriptive internationally negotiated targets for developed countries to self-selected national contributions by all countries; from substantive obligations to mitigate GHGs to procedural obligations to report on efforts to mitigation GHGs; from obligations of result that require states to achieve prescribed GHG emissions targets to obligations of conduct that require states to make best efforts to achieve their self-selected contributions; and from stark differentiation in favour of developing countries to nuanced differentiation, along with enhanced discretion for all.[279] This turn in the climate change regime brings with it considerable challenges in implementation, compliance and effectiveness. The self-selected NDCs submitted under the 2015 Paris Agreement cover 99 per cent of global emissions, but these fall well short of 2°C or 1.5°C trajectories.[280] Indeed, on current commitments, UNEP predicts global warming of about 3.5°C by 2100, or a tripling of the current level of warming as assessed by the IPCC in 2018.[281] To avert this, the 2015 Paris Agreement's 'ambition cycle' will have to trigger ever more ambitious NDCs from parties: 'By 2030, emissions would need to be 25 per cent to 55

275 Ibid, 25, 30.

276 Shishlov, Morel and Bellassen, 16 *Climate Policy* (2016) 768.

277 Australia, New Zealand, the EU, Iceland, Norway, and Switzerland accounted for less than 11 per cent of 2014 global GHG emissions, excluding LULUCF, in the second commitment period. See WRI, *CAIT Climate Data Explorer*, 2017.

278 Bodansky, Brunnée and Rajamani, *International Climate Change Law*, Ch 6.

279 Rajamani, *Innovation and Experimentation in the International Climate Change Regime*, Ch V.

280 UNFCCC, *Aggregate effect of the intended nationally determined contributions: an update—Synthesis report by the secretariat* (2016), UN Doc UNFCCC/CP/2016/2, 12, figure 2.

281 UNEP, *The Emissions Gap Report 2019*, 27.

per cent lower than in 2018 to put the world on the least-cost pathway to global warming to below 2°C and 1.5°C respectively.'[282]

The 2015 Paris Agreement relies, more than earlier instruments, on a productive interplay: between the facilitative international regime and strong national policies and actions; between binding procedural obligations and normative expectations, good faith, and due diligence; and, between state and non- and sub-state actors and processes; between hard-edged binding obligations and notably softer wording.[283] Although the 2015 Paris Agreement entered into force in record time,[284] some states have become notably sceptical. The US announced its withdrawal in 2016, while Brazil withdrew an offer to host the next UN climate conference. The pace of deforestation in the Amazon greatly increased in 2019. Whether the complex set of inter-locking factors, incentives and processes—of which the 2015 Paris Agreement's commitments and processes are only a part—will trigger more ambitious action, and deliver a stable climate, remains to be seen. But at the time of writing in 2019 there were some easy targets that would make a significant difference to the outcome if adopted, including an immediate ban on new oil drilling and new coal fired power stations and the early phasing out of existing coal and oil fired power stations.[285] What do we value more? An unsustainable economy based on fossil fuel production and consumption? Or a sustainable global climate?

5 CONCLUSIONS

This chapter has illustrated several points of general significance. First, although customary international law remains important in providing a basis for solutions to problems of atmospheric protection, the negotiation of global treaty regimes is essential if detailed and comprehensive international regulation is required. Secondly, progress has been made in refining the operation of international regulatory and supervisory regimes, of which the institutional machinery established by the 1985 Ozone Convention and the 1987 Montreal Protocol are now among the most significant examples.[286] Thirdly, whatever the legal status of the precautionary principle or approach, its influence on the evolution of international regimes is apparent in the examples covered by this chapter. But the significance of this conclusion should not be exaggerated. Endorsing the principle does not answer the question what measures are to be taken, or by whom, and it is clear that substantial problems of global and regional economic equity have to be addressed if the necessary action is to be undertaken by a sufficiently large number of relevant states. This conclusion only serves to

[282] Ibid, *Executive Summary*, v.

[283] See further, Rajamani, 28 *JEL* (2016) 337.

[284] The Paris Agreement entered into force on 4 November 2016.

[285] See UNEP, *Emissions Gap Report 2019: Executive Summary*, xi.

[286] *Supra*, Ch 2, section 5.

emphasize that the use of legal controls and the machinery of international justice cannot of themselves ensure the attainment of environmental goals endorsed by international policymakers, given the substantial changes in energy policy, industrial activity, and technology which are needed, and the economic implications this may have for developed and developing states. It is thus not surprising that the fairness of the climate regime in particular remains deeply contested: but it also needs to be grasped that fairness or equity will not save the climate.[287] What matters is whether strong enough measures are taken by all parties.

No other topic covered by this book presents the problems of inter and intragenerational equity and global governance in such stark contours. Climate change potentially affects all elements of the global environment, including land use and food supply, sustainable water resources, preservation of biodiversity, sea levels and the marine environment, the polar ice caps, the survival of tropical forests, and human health. Unchecked, it may change the world as we know it irreversibly. Tackling it represents probably the greatest challenge the UN system has ever faced.

[287] See further, Vanderheiden, *Atmospheric Justice: A Political Theory of Climate Change* (Oxford, 2008); Kanbur and Shue (eds), *Climate Justice: Integrating Economics and Philosophy* (Oxford, 2018).

7

NUCLEAR ENERGY AND THE ENVIRONMENT

1 INTRODUCTION

As the Chernobyl reactor accident in 1986 showed, nuclear power creates risks for all states, whether or not they choose to use this form of energy. Every state, and the global environment, is potentially affected by the possibility of radioactive contamination, the spread of toxic substances derived from nuclear energy, and the long-term health hazards consequent on exposure to radiation.[1] In catastrophic cases the level of injury to individual states and the global environment may be severe. International law is capable of moderating these ultra-hazardous risks by assuring stronger regulation, more effective multilateral oversight, and enhanced provision for liability and compensation in cases of transboundary damage. Such a policy entails limitations on the freedom of states to conduct hazardous activities within their own territory which they have sometimes been reluctant to endorse, but it represents a price which may have to be paid if nuclear energy is to remain internationally acceptable.

At the same time, nuclear power offers a carbon-free alternative to fossil fuels in the generation of electricity. As with oil tankers, the varying age and quality of the technology in use and the way it is managed may greatly affect the level of risk to human health and the environment. The nuclear industry and the oil tanker industry are vulnerable to their weakest performers, usually those with the oldest technology or the least well-regulated and supervised by national authorities. Collectively both

[1] See IAEA, *Summary Report on the Post Accident Review Meeting on the Chernobyl Accident* (Vienna, 1986); UKAEA, *The Chernobyl Accident and its Consequences* (London, 1987); NEA/OECD, *The Radiological Impact of the Chernobyl Accident in OECD Countries* (Paris, 1988); *Report of the United Nations Scientific Committee on the Effects of Atomic Radiation*, GAOR 37th Session (New York, 1982) and 41st Session (New York, 1986); IAEA/INFCIRC 383 (1990); and INFCIRC 510 (1996). See also *Report of the President's Commission on the Accident at Three Mile Island* (Washington DC, 1979).

industries have a strong vested interest in the assurance of safety and the elimination of major accidents. In both cases the terms on which such ultra-hazardous technology will be tolerated have been determined multilaterally, through international organizations, rather than by the users alone. Nuclear power and maritime transport of oil are thus the leading examples of international regulation of a whole industry on safety and environmental grounds by an intergovernmental agency. International regulation and oversight are necessary but have not been wholly sufficient in either case; both have noticeably been strengthened and improved in response to disasters.

Whether the nuclear power industry has now attained acceptable levels of risk to international society cannot be answered in the abstract or solely by reference to regulatory standards and technical capabilities, but must take into account public perceptions of risk, as well as the alternatives and the competing risks, such as climate change. For all governments these are inevitably difficult policy choices in which there are few electoral advantages. The Fukushima reactor accident in 2011 has not made that choice any easier, since it shows that even in a technologically advanced and sophisticated society like Japan serious nuclear accidents can still happen. Renewable energy arguably offers a safer, more reliable, and more economical source of energy.

1(1) INTERNATIONAL NUCLEAR POLICY

In the early days of nuclear energy it was widely believed that the benefits outweighed the risks and could be shared by all.[2] This optimistic view was reflected in international policy. The IAEA was created in 1956 with the object of encouraging and facilitating the spread of nuclear power.[3] Nuclear energy, it was assumed, would contribute to 'peace, health and prosperity' throughout the world.[4] The prevalent belief then was that the health and environmental risks could be managed successfully by governments and the IAEA through cooperation on safety matters. Successive declarations of international bodies maintained this belief in the dissemination of nuclear energy. In 1977 the UN General Assembly reaffirmed the importance of nuclear energy for economic and social development and proclaimed the right of all states to use it and to have access to the technology.[5] The success of this early exercise in technology transfer can be measured today in over 450 nuclear power plants operating in thirty countries.

There were fewer illusions about nuclear weapons. Non-proliferation beyond the five permanent members of the Security Council quickly became an international

[2] Agreed Declaration on Atomic Energy, Washington, 1945, 1 *UNTS* 123 (US, Canada, UK); UNGA Res 1(1) (1945); President Eisenhower's 'Atoms for Peace Address', GAOR 8th Session, 470th meeting, paras 79–126; Szasz, *The Law and Practices of the IAEA* (Vienna, 1970) Chs 1, 2; McKnight, *Atomic Safeguards* (New York, 1971) Ch 1.

[3] IAEA Statute, Articles III(1)–(4) as amended (1961).

[4] IAEA Statute, Article III.

[5] UNGA Res 32/50 (1977). See also UNGA Res 36/78 (1981) and GAOR, 41st Session, 1987, *Report of the Preparatory Committee for the UN Conference for the Promotion of Industrial Co-operation in the Peaceful Uses of Nuclear Energy.*

arms-control policy, although not accepted by all. Thus, a second role for the IAEA was to ensure that nuclear power was used for peaceful purposes only.[6] In 1968, the policy of non-proliferation and the powers of the IAEA were strengthened by the Nuclear Non-Proliferation Treaty ('NPT').[7] Three nuclear powers and a large majority of UN members acknowledged 'the devastation that would be visited upon all mankind by a nuclear war', and agreed further measures intended to prevent the spread of nuclear weapons. Although the treaty reaffirmed the belief that nuclear technology, including weapons technology, had beneficial peaceful applications which should be available to all, the linkage between non-proliferation and the peaceful uses of nuclear power has remained controversial for some states, such as India, and hindered agreement on further nuclear cooperation.[8]

The 1968 Treaty did nothing to reduce the arsenals of existing nuclear weapons powers. At first the testing of those arsenals proceeded freely, without objection, even in the South Pacific where it was mainly carried out. In the 1950s the main reservations about these tests concerned disruption of local populations and interference with high seas freedoms.[9] The existence of a threat to health and the environment was recognized, however, by three nuclear powers, in the 1963 Partial Test Ban Treaty which banned nuclear weapons tests in the atmosphere, outer space, and under water.[10] But testing by France and China continued, prompting condemnation at the Stockholm Conference in 1972[11] and at the UN.[12]

Australia and New Zealand failed in their attempts to have the ICJ declare further French atmospheric and underground tests illegal.[13] Their experience, reinforced by mounting evidence of the long-term effects of earlier tests in Australia and elsewhere,[14]

[6] Statute, Articles II, III. See Lamm, *The Utilization of Nuclear Energy and International Law* (Budapest, 1984); Potter, *Nuclear Power and Non-Proliferation* (Cambridge, Mass, 1982); Willrich, *International Safeguards and Nuclear Industry* (Baltimore, 1973). The 1957 Euratom Treaty provides for safeguards against diversion among European member states.

[7] See Handl, 19 *Tulane JICL* (2010) 1; Goldblat, 256 *Recueil des Cours* (1995) 9–192; Müller, Fischer, Kötter (eds), *Nuclear Non-Proliferation and Global Order* (Oxford, 1994); Fischer, *The Non-Proliferation of Nuclear Weapons* (New York, 1971); Willrich, *Non-Proliferation Treaty* (Charlottesville, 1968).

[8] UN, *Rept of the Prepcom for the UN Conference for the Promotion of International Co-operation in the Peaceful Uses of Nuclear Energy*, GAOR, 37th Session, 1983 and 40th Session, 1986. See Bosch and Reisman, in de Chazournes and Sands (eds), *International Law, the ICJ and Nuclear Weapons* (Cambridge, 1999) 375, 473. In 2019 the only nuclear-armed non-parties were India, Pakistan, North Korea and Israel.

[9] McDougal and Schlei, 64 *Yale LJ* (1995) 648; Margolis, *ibid*, 629.

[10] 1963 Treaty Banning Nuclear Weapons Tests in the Atmosphere, in Outer Space and Under Water.

[11] A/CONF 48/14/Rev. 1; Res 3(1) (1972).

[12] UNGA Res 3078 XXVIII (1973). Similar resolutions had been passed annually since 1955.

[13] *Nuclear Tests Cases (Australia v France)* ICJ Reports (1973) 99 (Interim measures); ICJ Reports (1974) 253 (Jurisdiction); *(New Zealand v France)* ICJ Reports (1973) 135 (Interim Measures); ICJ Reports (1974) 457 (Jurisdiction); Prott, 7 *Sydney LR* (1976) 433; Dugard, 16 *VJIL* (1976) 463; New Zealand Ministry of Foreign Affairs, *French Nuclear Testing in the Pacific* (Wellington, 1973); Dupuy, 20 *GYIL* (1977) 375; MacDonald and Hough, *ibid*, 337; Kos, 14 *VUWLR* (1984) 357.

[14] See *Rept of the UN SCEAR* (1972) GAOR 27th Session, Suppl No 25 and (1982) GAOR, 37th Session, Suppl No 45.

prompted the creation in 1985 of a South Pacific Nuclear Free Zone.[15] The prohibition among the parties of nuclear tests, or the dumping of radioactive waste at sea, within this zone, indicated the growing strength of regional and international opposition to such activities on environmental grounds. That opposition contributed to the adoption of a Comprehensive Test Ban Treaty in 1996. If it ever enters into force this agreement will prohibit all nuclear tests and institute a strong scheme of international verification, but it remains unratified by China, India, Israel, Iran, Pakistan, and the United States. All five permanent members of the Security Council have nevertheless ceased nuclear weapons testing.[16] At the same time the ICJ has held that the threat or use of nuclear weapons is not per se unlawful under customary international law, but in terms which place severe limits on their use.[17] In addition to other constraints, the Court reiterated both the obligation to protect the natural environment against the widespread, long-term and severe damage that nuclear weapons would cause, and the need to meet standards of necessity and proportionality in pursuing otherwise legitimate military objectives. Implicitly the ICJ also recognized the inter-generational implications of the use of nuclear weapons, but it stopped short of expressly acknowledging rights for future generations.

1(2) NUCLEAR POWER: THE EMERGENCE OF ENVIRONMENTAL CONCERN

It was the popularity of nuclear power as an answer to the oil crisis of the 1970s which ultimately brought long-term health and environmental consequences to the forefront of international concern. The Stockholm Conference in 1972 had called for a registry of emissions of radioactivity and international cooperation on radioactive waste disposal and reprocessing.[18] It recognized that the latter was a growing problem, caused by the increasing use of nuclear power, but offered no clear policy. Oceanic dumping of nuclear waste was partially banned in 1972, suspended entirely in 1983, and banned outright by the 1996 Protocol revising the 1972 London Convention, leaving disposal on land or reprocessing as the only viable options.[19] But nuclear reactor accidents at Three Mile Island in the US and Chernobyl in the Soviet Union showed how serious were the risks for health, agriculture, and the environment posed by nuclear power.[20]

15 1985 South Pacific Nuclear Free Zone Treaty. See also 1995 South Pacific Regional Convention on Hazardous Wastes (Waigani Convention). Other nuclear weapons-free zones have been created in Latin America (1967 Tlateloco Treaty for the Prohibition of Nuclear Weapons in Latin America) Africa (1996 African Nuclear Free Zone Treaty) and Asia (1996 ASEAN Nuclear Free Zone Treaty) on which see Goldblat, 256 *Recueil des Cours* (1995) 108–38.

16 *Infra*, section 3.

17 *AO on the Threat or Use of Nuclear Weapons*, ICJ Reports (1996) 226. See de Chazournes and Sands (eds), *International Law, the ICJ and Nuclear Weapons*; Mahmoudi, 66 *Nordic JIL* (1997) 77; Nystuen et al (eds), *Nuclear Weapons under International Law* (Cambridge, 2015), and *supra*, Ch 3, section 5.

18 A/Conf 48/14/Rev 1, Rec 75, *Action Plan for the Human Environment.*

19 *Infra,* Ch 8, section 3. Problems arising from the illegal transboundary movement and disposal of nuclear waste are also considered in Ch 8.

20 *Supra*, n 1.

Spreading contamination over a wide area of Eastern and Western Europe, the accident at Chernobyl in 1986, like the sinking of the *Torrey Canyon* oil tanker in 1967, revealed the limitations of international policy for containing catastrophic risks, and some of the true costs of nuclear power.

Chernobyl cast doubt on the adequacy of national and international regulation of nuclear facilities. It showed how limited were the powers of the IAEA,[21] and how little agreement existed on questions of liability and state responsibility. It gave new importance to the interest of neighbouring states in the siting of nuclear power plants, the opportunities for consultation on issues of safety, and the right to prompt notification of potentially harmful accidents. It demonstrated too, that the fundamentally benign view of nuclear power adopted in the 1950s now required modification, with new emphasis on stronger international control of safety matters.[22] For the first time, an international body, the Council of Europe, was prepared to describe nuclear energy as 'potentially dangerous', to recommend a moratorium on construction of new facilities, and the closure of those that did not meet international standards.[23] Some states, mainly in Western Europe, abandoned plans to build new reactors. More did so following the Fukushima reactor accident in 2011. Within the IAEA, however, the predominant belief remains that, through stronger international cooperation and more modern technology, the risks of nuclear energy can be contained and made environmentally acceptable, thereby reducing reliance on fossil fuels, and helping to counter global warming.[24] One of the beneficial effects of Chernobyl has been the development and strengthening of the international regulatory regime for the safe use of nuclear energy.[25] The accident at Fukushima has shown once again, however, that international regulation alone cannot guarantee safety if national regulators and the companies which operate nuclear power plants mismanage or fail to re-assess periodically the risks inherent in the technology.[26] Fukushima was predicted; precautionary action was not taken.[27] That failure has proved extremely costly for Japan.[28]

[21] Barkenbus, 41 *Int Org* (1987) 483; Cameron et al (eds), *Nuclear Energy Law After Chernobyl* (London, 1988); 159ff, 179ff; Handl, 92 *RGDIP* (1988) 5; Sands, *Chernobyl: Law and Communication* (Cambridge, 1988).

[22] See IAEA General Conference, Special Session, 1986, IAEA/GC (SPL 1)/4 and GC(SPL 1)/15/Rev 1, at 25 *ILM* (1986) 1387ff; OECD Nuclear Energy Agency, 15th Report, *NEA Activities in 1986*, 29ff; European Community, *20th General Report* (1986) paras 759–62; WCED, *Our Common Future* (Oxford, 1987) 181ff.

[23] Parliamentary Assembly Rec 1068 (1988).

[24] 1996 Moscow Declaration on Nuclear Safety and Security, IAEA/INFCIRC/509 (1996) and see IAEA's statement on the environmental benefits of nuclear power at the Kyoto meeting of the parties to the UNFCCC, IAEA/PR97/40 (1997).

[25] For an overview see IAEA, *International Nuclear Law in the Post-Chernobyl Period* (Vienna, 2006).

[26] See National Diet of Japan, *The Official Report of the Fukushima Nuclear Accident Independent Investigation Commission* (Tokyo, 2012); IAEA, *The Fukushima Daiichi Accident* (Vienna, 2015); NEA/OECD, *The Fukushima Daiichi Nuclear Power Plant Accident: OECD/NEA Nuclear Safety Response and Lessons Learnt* (Paris, 2013); Burns, 11 *Washington U Glob Studs LR* (2012) 739; id, 101 *NLB* (2018) 7.

[27] See the IAEA report, previous note.

[28] See Nadesan, *Fukushima and the Privatization of Risk* (Basingstoke, 2013). The *Financial Times*, 26 March 2016, reported that the disaster has cost Japanese taxpayers in excess of $100 billion.

2 THE INTERNATIONAL REGULATION OF NUCLEAR ENERGY

Like oil tankers, nuclear installations are potentially hazardous undertakings whose risk to health, safety, and the environment is best met by regulation. Because the consequences of failure to regulate adequately may cause injury or pollution damage to other states and the global environment, international regulation—the setting of common standards, supervised by international institutions—offers the best means of ensuring a generally accepted minimum level of environmental protection. The benefits of this approach accrue to the international community, which gains protection from unilaterally chosen levels of risk, but the burdens fall on national governments, which lose the freedom to determine for themselves the most appropriate balance of safety and development in their own territories.[29]

For oil tankers, the choice of international regulation was made in the 1970s. The minimum duties of flag states in matters of environmental protection were laid down in detail in international conventions and given additional legal force by the 1982 UNCLOS.[30] A relatively strong scheme of enforcement exists. For nuclear power it was not until the adoption of Conventions on Nuclear Safety and the Safety of Spent Fuel and Radioactive Waste Management in 1994 and 1997 that minimum standards of environmental protection from nuclear risks could be comparably assured. These treaties have codified much of the customary international law relating to nuclear activities and have given greater legal force to IAEA safety principles and standards. Both treaties represent an important stage in the evolution of international regulation and supervision of nuclear power and its waste products. Nevertheless, the primary responsibility for ensuring the safety of nuclear power remains with national governments. The Fukushima accident has exposed some serious weaknesses in that system,[31] which can only be as good as its weakest link.

2(1) IAEA AND THE REGULATION OF NUCLEAR RISKS

The IAEA[32] was the product of compromise following failure to agree on US proposals for international management of all nuclear power by an international body.[33] Its main tasks were confined to encouraging and facilitating the development and

[29] See generally Burns, 101 *NLB* (2018) 7; Handl, in Jayakumar et al (eds), *Transboundary Pollution: Evolving Issues of International Law and Policy* (Cheltenham, 2015) Ch 8; Pelzer, 91 *Nuclear Law Bull* (2013) 43; Handl, 92 *RGDIP* (1988) 50; OECD, *International Nuclear Law in the Post-Chernobyl Period* (Paris, 2006).

[30] 1982 UNCLOS Articles 211, 217–8, 220; *infra*, Ch 9.

[31] For a comprehensive overview see Handl, in Jayakumar et al (eds), *Transboundary Pollution*, Ch 8; Pelzer, 91 *Nuclear Law Bull* (2013) 43.

[32] Tonhauser and Wetherall, 56 *Jap YIL* (2013) 283.

[33] Szasz, *The Law and Practices of the IAEA*, Ch 1; Potter, *Nuclear Power and Non- Proliferation*, Ch 2; McKnight, *Atomic Safeguards*, Ch 1.

dissemination of nuclear power,[34] and ensuring through non-proliferation safeguards that it was used for peaceful purposes only.[35] Setting standards for health and safety in collaboration with other international agencies was very much an incidental or secondary responsibility.[36]

The Chernobyl accident resulted in a significant alteration of the Agency's priorities. The IAEA provided the main forum for consideration of measures made necessary by the accident and member states endorsed the importance of the Agency's role in safety and radiological protection matters.[37] Among the recommendations of a review group were that the Agency should promote better exchanges of information among states on safety and accident experience, develop additional safety guidelines, and enhance its capacity to perform safety evaluations and inspections on request.[38] The Convention on Assistance in cases of Nuclear Emergency also gives it the new task of coordinating assistance and responding to requests for help, while the Nuclear Safety and Radioactive Waste Conventions adopted in 1994 and 1997 have enhanced its importance as the principal international regulatory body for civil nuclear power. Thus despite its very different objectives in 1956, the Agency has developed a significant nuclear safety role. Rather like the IMO after the *Torrey Canyon* disaster, it has acquired a new environmental perspective as perhaps the one positive result of Chernobyl.

(a) Powers over health and safety

Article III.A.6 of the IAEA Statute authorizes the Agency to adopt 'standards' of safety for the purposes of protecting health and minimizing danger to life and property from exposure to radiation, in collaboration with other UN agencies, such as WHO, FAO, ILO, or the OECD. The term 'standards' includes regulations, rules, requirements, codes of practice and guides. Those adopted by the IAEA have taken a variety of forms depending on their function, but three basic categories can be distinguished.[39] 'Safety fundamentals' provide a statement of basic objectives, concepts and principles for ensuring safety in general terms.[40] 'Safety requirements' lay down detailed regulatory standards which must be satisfied in order to ensure the safety of specific types of installation or activity. 'Safety guides' are recommendations, based on international experience, and usually deal with ways and means to ensure the observance of safety requirements.

[34] Statute, Article III(1)–(4). In practice the development of the international nuclear industry has relied more heavily on assistance from other states than on the IAEA. See Szasz, *The Law and Practices of the IAEA*, Ch 2; McKnight, *Atomic Safeguards*, Ch 2.

[35] Statute, Article III(5).

[36] Statute, Article III(6); Szasz, *The Law and Practices of the IAEA*, Ch 22.

[37] IAEA, 30th Conference, Special Session, GC/SPL 1/Res 1. See also statement of the Group of Seven on the implications of the Chernobyl Accident, 15 *ILM* (1986) 1005. See Handl, 92 *RGDIP* (1988) 50; Blix, 18 *EPL* (1988) 142.

[38] IAEA, *Summary Report on the Post Accident Review Meeting on the Chernobyl Accident* (Vienna, 1986).

[39] For a fuller account see IAEA, *Measures to Strengthen International Co-operation in Nuclear Radiation and Waste Safety*, IAEA/GC(41)/INF/8, Pt B, and IAEA/GC(43)/INF/8 (1999).

[40] See IAEA Safety Series SF-1, *Fundamental Safety Principles: Safety Fundamentals* (Vienna, 2006).

IAEA standards cover such subjects as radiation protection, transport and handling of radioactive materials, radioactive-waste disposal, and safety of nuclear installations. They are regularly updated in the light of current technical advice from the Agency's own independent specialist advisory bodies and the International Commission for Radiological Protection, whose recommendations seek to limit the incidence of radiation-induced cancers and genetic disorders to an 'acceptable' level. The Board of Governors first approved radiation protection requirements in 1962 and has revised periodically thereafter.[41] Agency regulations on safe transport of nuclear material were adopted first in 1961, and a Code of Practice on the International Transboundary Movement of Radioactive Waste was added in 1990 in order to exclude such material from the 1989 Basel Convention.[42] In 1974 the IAEA initiated the Nuclear Safety Standards Programme ('NUSS') establishing basic international minimum safety standards and guiding principles regulating the design, construction, siting, and operation of nuclear power plants.[43] According to the director general these establish 'the objectives and basic requirements that must be met to ensure adequate safety in the operation of nuclear power plants'.[44] The important point is thus that the Agency has competence over a wide range of safety and health issues relating to all aspects of the use of nuclear energy: what it lacked until 1994 was the ability to give any of these standards obligatory force.

(b) The legal effect of IAEA health and safety standards

Nothing in the Statute confers any binding force on IAEA health and safety standards, or requires member states to comply with them.[45] While, under the statute, the same is true of non-proliferation safeguards, in practice the IAEA enjoys much stronger power in that field as a result of the 1968 NPT and regional agreements. The effect of the 1968 NPT is to make obligatory the acceptance of non-proliferation safeguards through bilateral agreements with the Agency, and to allow periodic compulsory Agency inspection for the purpose of verification.[46] Compliance with the overall scheme of non-proliferation safeguards is monitored by the UN General Assembly and Security Council.

No comparable attempt has been made to require universal adherence to health and safety standards.[47] Safeguards agreements and safeguards inspections relate only to

[41] See IAEA, *Radiation Protection and Safety of Radiation Sources: International Basic Safety Standards* (Vienna, 2014)(approved jointly by IAEA, FAO, ILO, WHO, OECD/NEA, and the Pan American Health Organization).

[42] See IAEA Safety Series SSR-6, *Regulations on Safe Transport for Radioactive Materials* (Vienna, 2012); Code of Practice on the International Transboundary Movement of Radioactive Waste, IAEA/INFCIRC/386 (1990) and 1989 Basel Convention, Article 1(3) on which see *supra*, Ch 8.

[43] IAEA GC(XXXII)/Res/489 first approved texts of five NUSS codes in 1988. For current standards see IAEA, *Long-term Structure of the IAEA Safety Standards and Current Status* (Vienna, 2017).

[44] 30 *IAEA Bulletin* (1988) 58.

[45] Szasz, *The Law and Practices of the IAEA*, 679ff.

[46] Article III, NPT Treaty.

[47] Barkenbus, 41 *Int Org* (1989); Szasz, *The Law and Practices of the IAEA*, Ch 22; Cameron et al, *Nuclear Energy Law after Chernobyl*, 4ff.

non-proliferation; they give the IAEA no power over health and safety.[48] Only where the Agency supplies materials, facilities, or services to states does the statute give it the power to ensure, through project agreements, that acceptable health, safety, and design standards are adopted.[49] In such cases, but only in such cases, it also has the right to examine the design of equipment and facilities to ensure compatibility with its standards, and the right to send inspectors to verify compliance.[50] If these are not met, further assistance may be terminated and membership of the Agency withdrawn.[51] Considerable latitude is normally allowed, however, provided national practices meet the minimum criterion of offering an 'adequate' means of controlling hazards and ensuring effective compliance.[52]

These powers over safety relate only to materials or facilities supplied by[53] or through[54] the IAEA; states cannot be required to place their other facilities or materials under its standards merely because they seek its assistance, although they may do so voluntarily.[55] Where assistance is supplied under bilateral agreement without IAEA involvement, even these limited powers are lost, and the practice in such cases has been to provide only for safety consultations with the supplier state.[56]

It is clear therefore that as a general rule the IAEA Statute confers no binding force on any of the Safety Standards adopted by the IAEA. Nevertheless, despite their non-binding character, IAEA health and safety standards have been a significant contribution to controlling the risks of nuclear energy. Governments are consulted during the formulation stage[57] and drafting is carried out in cooperation with specialist bodies, such as ICRP.[58] The Agency's standards thus reflect a large measure of expert and technical consensus, and it is for this reason, rather than their legal status, that they have

[48] IAEA/INFCIRC/153, paras 46, 71–3; Szasz, *The Law and Practices of the IAEA*, 662f. See e.g. Safeguards Agreement between the Agency, Israel, and the US, 1975, TIAS 8051 and others listed, Ruster and Simma, *International Protection of the Environment* (hereafter 'Ruster and Simma') xiii, 6468ff. IAEA/INFCIRC/153, para 28 defines the objective of NPT safeguards as 'the timely detection of diversion of significant quantities of nuclear material from peaceful nuclear activities to the manufacture of nuclear weapons or of other explosive devices or for purposes unknown, and deterrence of such diversion by the risk of early detection'.

[49] Articles III(6) XI, XII. The Agency does not in fact receive or supply materials as envisaged in Article IX; it now arranges for others to do so.

[50] Statute, Article XII; Inspectors Doc/IAEA/GC(V)/INF 39, Annex, paras 9, 11.

[51] Statute, Article XII. [52] INFCIRC/18/Rev 1, paras 2, 4.

[53] See e.g. agreements listed in Ruster and Simma xii, xxvii.

[54] See e.g. trilateral agreements between IAEA, the US, and Argentina, 30 UST 1539; Indonesia, 32 UST 361; Malaysia, 32 UST 2610.

[55] Statute, Articles III(6) XII A; IAEA/INFCIRC/18/Rev 1, para 25.

[56] See e.g. US–Brazil Agreement, 1972, 23 UST 2478; US Thailand Agreement, 1974, TIAS 7850; FRG–Brazil Agreement, 1975, Ruster and Simma, xiii, 6472ff, and others listed at 6415–29.

[57] Szasz, *The Law and Practices of the IAEA*, 672f; IAEA, *Experience and Trends in Nuclear Law* (Vienna, 1972).

[58] The ICRP is a private association of scientific experts, comparable to ICES or SCAR: see Smith, 30 *IAEA Bulletin* (1988) 42. For IAEA cooperation with other international bodies, see Szasz, *The Law and Practices of the IAEA*, Ch 12; IAEA, *Measures to Strengthen International Co-operation in Nuclear Radiation and Waste Safety*, GC(43)/INF/8/(1999).

been influential and serve as important guidelines for most states in regulating their nuclear facilities. They have resulted in an appreciable degree of harmonization.[59]

Given their undoubted influence on the regulation of nuclear risks at national level, can IAEA standards then be regarded as 'soft law'? One problem with this view is that IAEA standards are not necessarily adopted by the Agency's General Conference, in which all member states are represented, but by the Board of Governors.[60] They may thus lack the evidence of international support which approval by the IMO Assembly confers on non-binding IMO resolutions under Article 16 of the 1948 IMO Convention. In such cases it is more difficult to describe IAEA standards as 'soft law', or to regard them as representing a standard of due diligence for states to meet as a matter of customary law. But approval by the General Conference of some of the more important standards gives them a politically more authoritative status which can be translated more easily into soft law.[61] A second problem is that IAEA standards are themselves divided into those written in mandatory form, using the word 'shall', and those using the more recommendatory 'should'. Use of the mandatory form, coupled with endorsement by the General Conference does suggest a higher level of commitment than mere recommendations or guidelines.[62]

However limited the legal status of IAEA standards adopted under the IAEA Statute may be, there is no doubt that other treaties do give binding force to certain IAEA standards for parties to the relevant agreements. Immediately following the Chernobyl disaster IAEA's soft law guidelines for early notification of nuclear accidents were transformed into a now widely ratified treaty.[63] More recently, the 1994 Convention on Nuclear Safety and the 1997 Joint Convention on the Safety of Spent Fuel and Radioactive Waste Management ('Joint Convention')[64] have incorporated the main elements of the IAEA's fundamental safety standards for nuclear installations, radioactive-waste management, and radiation protection, and most of its Code of Practice on the Transboundary Movement of Radioactive Waste. The 'Fundamental Safety Principles', adopted in 2006, apply to all nuclear facilities and activities.[65] Moreover, those remaining IAEA standards which retain a soft law status may still be relevant when determining how the basic obligations of states parties to these agreements are to be implemented. Under the 1997 Joint Convention there is also an obligation to take account, inter alia, of relevant IAEA standards in national law. As we shall see in the next section, these various agreements have significantly strengthened the legal force of IAEA standards and, in conjunction with non-binding common safety

59 Szasz, *The Law and Practices of the IAEA*, 673, 682ff; Cameron et al (eds), *Nuclear Energy Law after Chernobyl*, 4, 159ff.

60 Szasz, *The Law and Practices of the IAEA*, 669ff.

61 See e.g. IAEA/GC (XXXII)/Res/489 (1988) approving the NUSS code.

62 See e.g. IAEA Safety Series No 111-S, *Establishing a National System for Radioactive Waste Management* (Vienna, 1995) and compare the more recommendatory wording of the 1990 Code of Practice on International Transboundary Movement of Radioactive Waste, *infra*.

63 See *infra*, section 3(2). 64 See *infra*, section 2(2). 65 *Supra*, n 40.

standards, have created a stronger legal framework for the international regulation of nuclear risks.[66] Whether that framework is strong enough remains to be seen.

(c) IAEA as an international inspectorate and review body

The IAEA has only a limited power to act as an international nuclear safety inspectorate under its Statute. Compulsory inspections are possible only where an assistance agreement with the Agency is in force, and in practice this power is rarely used.[67] However, the Agency can, if requested, also provide safety advice and a review of safety practices for any nuclear installation or waste disposal site. An important recommendation acted on in response to the Chernobyl accident was that the IAEA should enhance its capability for providing such services and that states should make more use of them.[68] Different aspects of nuclear safety are now covered by a range of IAEA review programmes. Of these the most prominent is the OSART programme for reviewing safety at nuclear reactors.[69] This facility has become quite widely used by states; over 150 reviews have been carried out since the programme started in 1982.

IAEA safety inspections are valuable to governments because of their independence and the reassurance they provide. Assessments of Soviet and Russian dumping in the Kara and Barents Seas and in the North Pacific concluded that the radiological risks are small,[70] despite the international concern aroused by the discovery that this form of disposal had occurred. Nevertheless, if unsafe practices are found, the Agency can only recommend, not enforce changes. Thus, when it inspected Bulgaria's only reactor in 1991 and found it in very poor condition, with various safety-related deficiencies, the Agency urged the Bulgarian government to take immediate measures, but it could not compel closure. Similarly, an IAEA inspection of the Chernobyl plant in 1994 disclosed continuing serious deficiencies and a failure to meet international safety standards. Although the Agency cannot ensure compliance with international safety standards, making safety audits of this kind an accepted practice does provide a means for distinguishing good from bad safety performers, and brings international pressure to bear on the latter. In the case of Chernobyl it has also helped generate an international campaign to provide finance and assistance with upgrading.

While the Chernobyl accident showed the usefulness of the IAEA in coordinating responses to serious accidents and in acting as a forum for considering further measures, it also exposed its weakness as a safety inspectorate.[71] Because they take place only in response to a request, the Agency's procedures by themselves cannot ensure

66 IAEA, *Nuclear Safety Review 1997*, GC(41)/INF/8.

67 Statute, Article 12; Szasz, *The Law and Practices of the IAEA*, 696.

68 IAEA, *Summary Report of the Post Accident Review Meeting on the Chernobyl Accident* (Vienna, 1986).

69 OSART stands for Operational Safety Review Team. IAEA/GC(XXXII)/Res/459 invites member states to use OSART on a voluntary basis. Other types of safety review include ASSET, the Assessment of Safety Significant Events Team, and IRRT, the International Regulatory Review Team. For fuller details see IAEA, *Nuclear Safety Review 1997*, GC(41)/INF/8, Annex C-5.

70 *Ibid.* 71 Barkenbus, 41 *Int Org* (1987) 487ff; Handl, 92 *RGDIP* (1988) 18.

systematic assessment of the safety of nuclear installations, nor are they reinforced by any safety reporting obligations under the Statute. IAEA member states thus had no basis on which to review and monitor each other's practices. Without such reporting, there was no means, prior to adoption of the 1994 Convention on Nuclear Safety, of assessing whether agreed international safety standards had been met. Now that binding minimum international standards for nuclear installations and radioactive waste have been laid down by treaty,[72] obligatory reporting has at last been introduced. How far this may provide a basis for more systematic review by the parties of national safety standards is considered below. However, it remains the case that IAEA has no general power of compulsory inspection, and no power to close down a nuclear installation, however unsafe.[73] Fukushima has not altered that position.

2(2) INTERNATIONAL AGREEMENTS ON NUCLEAR SAFETY

At a special review conference held following the Chernobyl accident, IAEA member states affirmed their individual responsibility for ensuring nuclear and radiation safety, security, and environmental compatibility, while acknowledging the central role of the IAEA in encouraging and facilitating cooperation on these matters.[74] At the same time they also considered the possibility of adopting mandatory international minimum safety standards for reactors as a means of strengthening international regulation of nuclear energy. No agreement could be reached for a variety of reasons. There were practical problems: reconciling different national standards, modifying existing installations, added financial and administrative burdens. There were also significant political and policy obstacles: establishing mandatory international standards would require some surrender of national sovereignty in this field and assumes that uniform standards for all reactor types are possible and would indeed enhance overall safety. This crucial assumption is not universally accepted, even after the Chernobyl and Fukushima accidents.[75]

The realization that Chernobyl-type reactors would remain in widespread use in Eastern Europe, and that they could not easily be upgraded by the states in which they were located, prompted further discussions, including an international conference on the safety of nuclear power. Following this, in 1991, the General Conference of the IAEA, representing all member states, invited the Agency to prepare an outline of a

72 See next section.

73 On the closure of unsafe installations see 1994 Nuclear Safety Convention, Article 6, considered *infra*.

74 IAEA, 30th Conference, Special Session, 1986, 16 *EPL* (1986) 138. UNGA Res 41/36 (1986) called for the highest standards of safety in the design and operation of nuclear plants. See also 1996 Moscow Declaration on Nuclear Safety and Security, IAEA/INFCIRC/509.

75 See in particular Pelzer, 91 *Nuclear Law Bull* (2013) 43 at 76, but contrast Handl, in Jayakumar et al (eds), *Transboundary Pollution* (Cheltenham, 2015) Ch 8. See also Burns, 101 NLB (2018) 15–17; Reyners and Lellouche, in Cameron et al (eds), *Nuclear Energy Law after Chernobyl*, 16f, 164f, 182f; Handl, 92 *RGDIP* (1988) 5, 7ff; and Kamminga, 44 *ICLQ* (1995) 872.

nuclear safety convention, and to develop a common basis on which to judge whether the safety of existing reactors built to earlier standards is acceptable.[76] Two years later the General Conference also requested the Agency to prepare a convention on the safety of radioactive-waste management.[77] These decisions led to the adoption of the Nuclear Safety Convention in 1994 and the Joint Convention in 1997. Neither convention was negotiated as a consensus 'package deal'; unlike almost every other global environmental agreement reservations are not prohibited. Although the 1994 Nuclear Safety Convention was adopted by consensus, the 1997Joint Convention was opposed by Pakistan and New Zealand and several articles were also adopted by majority vote, in some cases against strong opposition.[78]

These two conventions are similar in their relatively conservative approach to the regulation of nuclear risks. Their most important feature is that for the first time they give binding treaty status to some of the IAEA's most fundamental standards of nuclear safety law affecting most aspects of civil nuclear reactors, radioactive-waste management, and spent fuel disposal and reprocessing. Turning soft law into hard law does not necessarily mean that the law itself has changed, for, though formally non-binding, some of these IAEA standards reflected existing customary law on matters such as the diligent regulation of transboundary risks or the requirement of prior informed consent for transboundary waste disposal. Nevertheless, incorporation of these basic principles in treaty form does reinforce their status, and more especially so in those Eastern European states where the problems of nuclear safety have been most acute, such as Russia, Bulgaria, and Slovakia.

However, by rejecting proposals for more elaborate framework conventions and making no provision for the adoption of further regulatory protocols,[79] or for the parties to adopt further regulatory measures or even to make recommendations for further measures,[80] responsibility for the future development of international nuclear safety standards remains in the hands of IAEA member states acting outside the framework of the two nuclear safety conventions. Some commentators have strongly criticised this deference to national sovereignty,[81] but as Handl observes, 'the Conventions' perceived deficiencies are the result of a carefully considered legislative choice driven by negotiating states' insistence that nuclear safety remain a national responsibility. . .'[82] Much depends on how each convention is interpreted, however,

[76] IAEA, GC(XXXV)/RES/553 (1991). [77] IAEA, GC(XXXVII)/RES/615 (1993).

[78] Article 3(1) was adopted by 60–3, with 7 abstentions; Article 27 (1)(ii) by 57–5, with 2 abstentions. However, a proposed New Zealand amendment to Article 27(1)(ii) had earlier been defeated by 28–25 with 19 abstentions, and a Turkish amendment by 29–13 with 30 abstentions.

[79] de La Fayette, 5 *JEL* (1993) 31.

[80] 1994 Nuclear Safety Convention, Article 20; Joint Convention, Article 30. It is of course open to the member states of IAEA to adopt further measures or make recommendations.

[81] See Boustany, 61 *Nuclear Law Bull* (1998) 39; Barkenbus and Forsberg, 20 *Ann Rev of Energy and the Environment* (1995) 179.

[82] Handl, in Jayakumar et al (eds), *Transboundary Pollution*, 200. See also Burns, 101 *NLB* (2018) 15–17 who surveys the literature.

including the phrase 'appropriate steps'.[83] These and other inherently evolutionary terms require compliance with whatever safety standards parties to the Convention chose to regard as 'appropriate'. It is thus open to them to further internationalise the law on nuclear safety, should they wish to do so. The impact of the 1994 Nuclear Safety Convention and the 1997 Joint Convention on international nuclear law, and on the powers of the IAEA, could potentially be more dynamic than appears at first sight.[84] In practice, this evolution has not yet come about. The Fukushima accident set in motion a review process which has led to some strengthening of the guidance issued under the Convention on Nuclear Safety, and improvements in the Article 20 review process. The COP also adopted the Vienna Declaration on Nuclear Safety,[85] but proposals for amendment of the 1994 Nuclear Safety Convention were not pursued.[86] It has largely fallen to national regulators to act upon the lessons learned.

Both conventions rely on a process of reporting and peer review by the COP to ensure their effectiveness.[87] This process is considered below.

(a) The Nuclear Safety Convention

The 1994 Nuclear Safety Convention's objectives are to maintain a high level of nuclear safety in civil nuclear power plants and related facilities, to protect individuals, society and the environment from harmful radiation, and to prevent or mitigate accidents[88].[89] It seeks to pursue these objectives by enhancing national measures and international cooperation, rather than by fully internationalizing the regulation and supervision of the nuclear industry. Instead, it reaffirms that 'responsibility for nuclear safety rests with the state having jurisdiction over a nuclear installation', and requires each party to establish and maintain a national legislative and regulatory framework for the safety of nuclear installations, including a system of licensing, independent inspection, and enforcement of applicable regulations.[90] It entails, in the words of the Preamble, 'a commitment to the application of fundamental safety principles for nuclear installations rather than of detailed safety standards'. Almost all states, including all the civil nuclear states are parties.

The principal obligations embodied in the Convention are based largely on the IAEA's own safety fundamentals for nuclear installations. They also represent, according to the director general of the IAEA, 'an international consensus on the basic

83 1994 Nuclear Safety Convention, Article 29; Joint Convention, Article 38, and see Handl, 72 *Nuclear Law Bull* (2003) 7.

84 Handl, in Jayakumar et al (eds), *Transboundary Pollution*, 200–1.

85 For the text see 2015 Diplomatic Conference, CNS/DC/2015/2/Rev.1.

86 See generally Handl, in Jayakumar et al (eds), *Transboundary Pollution*, Ch 8; Johnson, 91 *Nuclear Law Bull* (2013) 7.

87 Handl, 72 *Nuclear Law Bull* (2003) 7.

88 See Jankowitsch-Prevor in OECD, *International Nuclear Law in the Post Chernobyl Period* (Paris, 2006); Kamminga, 44 *ICLQ* (1995) 872; de La Fayette, 5 *JEL* (1993) 31; Reyners, 99 *RGDIP* (1995) 605.

89 Preamble and Article 1. For *travaux préparatoires* see IAEA, *Convention on Nuclear Safety* (IAEA Legal Series No 16, Vienna, 1994).

90 Articles 7–9.

concepts underlying the regulation and management of safety and the operation of nuclear installations'.[91] Parties are thus required to take 'appropriate steps' to ensure that safety at nuclear installations is given 'due' priority, that levels of trained staff are adequate, that quality assurance programmes are established, that comprehensive and systematic safety assessments are carried out periodically, that radiation exposure is as low as reasonably achievable, and that emergency plans are prepared.[92] Further articles specify appropriate steps with regard to the siting, design, construction, and operation of civil nuclear installations.[93] What is 'appropriate' in all these different instances will have to be assessed in the circumstances of each case, and may change as safety standards evolve. As well as emphasising that the Convention does not commit states to the application of *detailed safety standards*, the Preamble also refers to 'internationally formulated safety guidelines which are updated from time to time and so can provide *guidance* on contemporary means of achieving a high level of safety'. The IAEA itself takes the view that its own safety standards represent 'a consistent, reliable means of ensuring the effective fulfilment of obligations of States under the Conventions'.[94]

Thus the Convention takes a significant step towards defining the obligations of states operating nuclear installations, but only in fairly general terms. Insofar as it gives effect to IAEA 'safety fundamentals' it can be seen as an elaboration of the general rule of customary international law regarding diligent regulation and control of potentially harmful activities in accordance with Principle 2 of the Rio Declaration and other precedents, rather in the same way that Articles 206–12 of the 1982 UNCLOS elaborate the same general rule in regard to protection of the marine environment.[95] Where the 1994 Nuclear Safety Convention differs from 1982 UNCLOS is that it does not directly incorporate all the more detailed safety standards for nuclear power adopted by the IAEA in the way that 1982 UNCLOS incorporates and renders directly binding on parties the 'generally accepted international rules and standards' of the 1973/78 MARPOL annexes and other internationally agreed instruments.[96]

Article 6 attempts to deal with the problem of unsafe existing nuclear reactors by requiring the party concerned to ensure that 'all reasonably practicable improvements' are made as a matter of urgency to upgrade safety. Where that is not possible the reactor must be shut down 'as soon as practically possible'. This does not necessarily mean immediately, however: account may be taken of the availability of alternative energy sources, as well as the 'social, environmental and economic impact'. The practical effect of this latitude is that East European Chernobyl-style reactors have remained in operation until economic alternatives can be found, but reports on progress in upgrading or closure are subject to review by the meeting of the parties

[91] IAEA, *Convention on Nuclear Safety*, Legal Series No 16, at 65, para 16.

[92] Articles 10–16. [93] Articles 17–19.

[94] El Baradei, Foreword, IAEA Safety Series SF-1, *Fundamental Safety Principles: Safety Fundamentals* (Vienna, 2006).

[95] *Infra*, Ch 7. [96] *Ibid.*

in accordance with Articles 5 and 20. Decisions on the future of such reactors are thus not left entirely to the discretion of the state concerned.[97] Given the importance of nuclear power to Eastern Europe, Article 6 represents an inevitable compromise, whose success has depended on the availability of appropriate technical assistance from other states and the IAEA.

The IAEA's own commentary on the Convention notes that 'It is not designed to ensure fulfilment of obligations by parties through control and sanction', but will function by a process of 'peer review'. Article 20 provides for the parties to meet periodically to review reports on measures they have taken to implement their international safety obligations. Article 20(3) also specifies that each party 'shall have a reasonable opportunity to discuss the reports submitted by other Contracting Parties and to seek clarification. . .' The purpose of these review meetings is to allow experts 'to identify problems, concerns, uncertainties, or omissions in national reports, focusing on the most significant problems or concerns';[98] they are not meant to enable parties to review the safety of individual installations, but to learn from each other through 'a constructive exchange of views' after a 'thorough examination of national reports'. The expectation is that technical cooperation measures may then be identified with a view to resolving any safety problems.

The institution of a system of periodic reviews marks a new phase of collective oversight of nuclear safety. Review meetings have covered a wide range of topics, including security questions, safety culture, and the structure and functioning of national regulatory bodies—some concern has been expressed about their independence from political control.[99] The post-Fukushima review meetings again identified improving national regulators' independence, safety culture, transparency and openness as one of the challenges to be addressed.[100] This is not explicitly a non-compliance procedure, nor does the Convention contemplate any machinery for independent verification of national reports, but the right to seek clarification and to comment on reports does provide an opportunity for scrutiny.

The 1994 Nuclear Safety Convention's peer review system compares unfavourably with most of the more recent global environmental agreements. One critical commentator described it as 'rudimentary', but noted that it may develop a momentum of its own, as other environmental agreements have done.[101] The Convention is open to participation by non-nuclear states, who should have a strong interest in ensuring effective oversight, but there is no evidence that this has in fact happened.[102] In practice not all parties submit reports or participate actively in review meetings; the

97 See concerns expressed in *1st Review Meeting of the Parties* (1999) IAEA/GOV/INF/1999/11-GC(43)11, Annex II. But cf Kamminga, 44 *ICLQ* (1995) 872.

98 Annex to the Final Act, para 3. See also *1st Review Meeting of the Parties* (1999) Annex II, para 4; IAEA, *Guidelines under the INSC Regarding the Review Process* (1998) IAEA/INFCIRC/571 and 572. The guidelines were revised post-Fukushima: see IAEA Doc. INFCIRC/571/Rev.5 (2012) and IAEA Doc. INFCIRC/572/Rev.3 (2011).

99 See *Summary Rept of the 3rd Review Meeting* (2005).

100 See *Summary Rept of the 7th Review Meeting* (2017).

101 See Kamminga, 44 *ICLQ* (1995) 872.

102 The *Rept of the 7th Review Meeting* (2017) notes that only a few non-nuclear states commented on the challenges the meeting was meant to discuss.

reviews lack focus on critical safety issues and are essentially a paperwork exercise, not an inspection of actual facilities; and the process is not entirely transparent.[103] Intergovernmental organizations, but not NGOs, may be invited to send observers to meetings of the parties. Although a summary of discussions and conclusions must be made public, individual countries will not be named and the content of peer reviews must remain confidential.[104] This makes it hard to assess whether the system has any impact on specific states.

The Fukushima accident highlighted the inadequacy of the system, and an IAEA Ministerial Conference called for it to be strengthened.[105] Proposals made by Switzerland to enhance the transparency and effectiveness of the review process were not adopted, however, and only modest changes to the guidelines were agreed by the Conference of the Parties.[106]

The 1994 Nuclear Safety Convention's potential impact in mitigating the risks of nuclear power should not be viewed in isolation from the safety-related work of the IAEA as a whole, but as we saw earlier, a state's nuclear facilities may be inspected by the IAEA only with the state's consent. The Convention does nothing to change that. As Handl observes, 'In the absence of mandatory in-country international safety reviews, there is simply no guarantee that national practices might not end up compromising global safety.'[107]

(b) The Joint Convention on the Safety of Spent Fuel and Radioactive Waste Management

This agreement[108], adopted by IAEA member states in 1997, follows the model of the 1994 Nuclear Safety Convention, and it has the same objectives of ensuring high safety standards and prevention of accidents.[109] Article 1 also recognizes the intergenerational implications of nuclear-waste disposal, and these are further addressed in the convention's specific obligations. In accordance with Article 3 the convention applies both to radioactive-waste disposal and spent-fuel management,[110] but with two notable exceptions which make it less than comprehensive. First, due to Indian and Pakistani opposition, reprocessing of spent fuel, and spent fuel held for reprocessing,

103 See Handl, in Jayakumar et al (eds), *Transboundary Pollution*, 206.

104 See Articles 24–5, 27, and *Guidelines under the INSC Regarding the Review Process.*

105 IAEA Doc INFCIRC/821 (2011) para 12.

106 For details see Handl, in Jayakumar et al (eds), *Transboundary Pollution*, 207–8 and Johnson, 91 *Nuclear Law Bull* (2013) 12–13.

107 *Ibid*, 207.

108 See Cameron, in Horbach (ed), *Contemporary Developments in Nuclear Energy Law* (The Hague, 1999) 117; de Kageneck and Pinel, 47 *ICLQ* (1998) 409

109 For summary records of the Diplomatic Conference held in 1997 and other *travaux préparatoires* see IAEA GOV/INF/821-GC(41)/INF/12 (1997).

110 The 1997 Joint Convention will in some cases overlap with the 1994 Nuclear Safety Convention: the latter applies to radioactive waste or spent fuel held 'on the same site' and 'directly related to the operation of [a] nuclear power plant': Article 2(i). Once a nuclear plant ceases to be a 'nuclear installation' it moves out of the 1994 Nuclear Safety Convention and into the Joint Convention: NSC, Article 2(i).

are included only if the relevant contracting party so declares. However, the three main reprocessing states, France, Japan, and the UK all made voluntary declarations of inclusion during the negotiation of the Convention.[111] Second, spent fuel or waste from military installations are included only if transferred to permanent civilian control, or if the relevant party so declares. No declarations on this matter were made at the conference.

The main provisions of the convention are similar to those found in the 1994 Nuclear Safety Convention. They set out general safety requirements for the management of spent fuel and radioactive waste, the design, siting, and operation of related facilities, and the establishment of a regulatory framework and independent regulatory body.[112] These obligations are based mainly on the IAEA's 1995 Principles of Radioactive Waste Management,[113] which thus become the second of the IAEA's fundamental safety standards to acquire a new binding treaty status. The 1997 Joint Convention also has exactly the same kind of control regime as the 1994 Nuclear Safety Convention, although the national reporting requirements are more detailed and potentially onerous.[114] Some elements of the 1997 Joint Convention go beyond what is required by the earlier convention, however.

In keeping with agreements relating to other types of hazardous waste,[115] and with Article 19(viii) of the 1994 Nuclear Safety Convention, generation of radioactive waste must be kept to a minimum, but parties must also must aim to avoid imposing 'undue burdens' on future generations, including burdens that are greater than permitted for present generations. Although still heavily qualified, this appears to be the strongest provision on intergenerational equity in any environmental treaty.[116] More specifically, consistently with Antarctica's status as a world park, storage or disposal of nuclear waste or spent fuel on the continent is wholly prohibited by Article 27(1). This reiteration of Article 5 of the 1959 Antarctic Treaty has the effect of making the latter provision applicable to third states who are parties to the Joint Convention.

Compared to the 1994 Nuclear Safety Convention, the 1997 Joint Convention gives greater effect to IAEA or OECD/NEA soft law in setting minimum standards for national regulation. Not only must national law provide 'effective' protection for individuals, society and the environment, it must also give 'due regard to internationally endorsed criteria and standards'.[117] This formulation does not make IAEA or OECD/NEA soft law binding on parties to the 1997 Joint Convention, but it strengthens the view that nuclear soft law is particularly relevant in deciding whether states have taken the 'appropriate steps' required by the principal provisions of the convention.

[111] *Summary Record of the 4th Plenary Meeting*, RWSC/DC/SR 4, paras 93–5, in IAEA/GOV/INF/821-GC(41)/INF/12(1997).

[112] Articles 4–26.

[113] IAEA Safety Series No 111-F (1995). See also IAEA Safety Series No 111-S, *Establishing a National System for Radioactive Waste Management* (1995).

[114] Articles 29–37.

[115] See *infra*, Ch 8.

[116] Articles 4(v)–(vi) 5(vi)–(vii). On intergenerational equity see *supra*, Ch 3.

[117] Articles 4(iv) 11(iv). These will include IAEA radiation protection standards.

Moreover, whereas the 1994 Nuclear Safety Convention provides only that radiation exposure shall not exceed prescribed *national* dose limits,[118] Article 24 of the 1997 Joint Convention requires national radiation limits to have 'due regard to internationally endorsed standards on radiation protection'. Article 24 also requires parties to the 1997 Joint Convention to implement 'appropriate corrective measures' to control or mitigate accidental releases of radioactivity; there is no comparable obligation in the 1994 Nuclear Safety Convention, despite the greater risk of accidents.[119]

Article 27 also gives binding force for the first time to the main provisions of the IAEA's 1990 Code of Practice on the International Transboundary Movement of Radioactive Waste,[120] a soft law instrument whose provisions were based on the 1989 Basel Convention.[121] Waste or spent fuel may only be exported if the state of destination has the requisite capacity to handle such materials in a manner consistent with the convention and if it has given its prior informed consent. If these conditions are not met, reimport of the material must be allowed. However, disputes among the negotiating states about freedom of navigation at sea resulted in a provision on the rights of transit states which differs from the Code of Practice.[122] Instead of affording transit states the same right of prior informed consent as enjoyed by the state of intended disposal, and as provided for in the 1990 Code of Practice, Article 27(1) of the 1997 Joint Convention merely stipulates that 'transboundary movement through States of *transit* shall be subject to those international obligations which are relevant to the particular modes of transport utilised', without making clear what those obligations are. What appears from the conference records is that, in the view of the bare majority of states who supported the text as finally adopted, international law does not require prior notice and consent for transit through the territorial waters or exclusive economic zone of another state.[123]

2(3) OTHER INTERNATIONAL REGULATORY BODIES

(a) Euratom

The Euratom Treaty was signed by EC member states in 1957 for the purpose of creating a nuclear common market.[124] It continues to provide the basis of EU competence in this field. The treaty's objectives include the application of uniform safety

118 Article 15.

119 See *infra*, section 3(3)(b).

120 IAEA GC (XXXIV)/939 (1990). The 1990 Code is a good example of IAEA soft law at its weakest: most provisions are written in non-mandatory terms, using the word 'should'.

121 See *infra*, Ch 8. The 1989 Basel Convention applies to nuclear waste unless specifically covered by other international instruments: see Article 1(3).

122 See *Summary Records of the 4th Plenary Meeting*, RWSC/DC/SR 4 and SR.5, paras 119–139, and 1–40.

123 For fuller discussion see *infra*, Ch 8.

124 1957 Euratom Treaty, Article 2 and Ch IX; IAEA, *Nuclear Law for a Developing World* (Vienna, 1969) 39ff; Grunwald, in Cameron et al (eds), *Nuclear Energy Law after Chernobyl*, 33.

standards to protect the health of workers and the general public against radiation.[125] Other provisions are intended to ensure non-diversion of nuclear materials for military purposes.[126] Safety is thus only one aspect of EU nuclear responsibilities. Unlike the IAEA Statute, however, the Euratom Treaty requires member states to implement safety directives and to ensure that they are enforced.[127] Radioactivity levels must be controlled by member states and are monitored by the European Commission through national reporting.[128] Following the Chernobyl accident the Commission temporarily restricted the import of affected foodstuffs, and it has since adopted regulations allowing it to specify permitted levels of radiation contamination in food.[129] The main protection against nuclear risks which the Euratom Treaty offer other states is the right of the EU to be consulted or to inspect in certain circumstances. Article 34 of the treaty obliges states to consult the Commission when they propose to conduct particularly dangerous nuclear experiments in their territories, and to obtain its consent if these are liable to affect other member states. Article 37 requires notification to be given to the Commission when radioactive substances may contaminate other states, for example by disposal at sea or into rivers.[130] Although the Commission may only comment on the proposal, the process nevertheless involves independent expert review, and the findings would provide some indication of likely problems, if any.

The Article 37 procedure has been used, inter alia, to review nuclear fuel reprocessing facilities at Sellafield and the findings were relied on by the UK in the MOX plant litigation. Other states have no right to participate in the review; however, following the Fukushima accident, the EU adopted a revised nuclear safety directive instituting a system of mandatory peer review carried out jointly by the member states or in 'close co-ordination' with the Commission.[131] Finally, EU law requires nuclear states to give urgent notice to their neighbours of any accident which involves exposure of the population to radiation and to give information on how to minimize the consequences of the accident or of measures taken to deal with it.[132]

(b) OECD

Some 85 per cent of all civil nuclear installations are in OECD member states, and the OECD's Nuclear Energy Agency ('NEA') has become an important forum for

125 Articles 2(b) 30, 31. See *European Parliament v Council* [1991] ECR I-4529 (*'Chernobyl II'*).

126 Article 2(e) and Ch VII.

127 Articles 33, 38.

128 Articles 35, 36 Euratom Treaty. In 1989, the Commission decided to exercise its power of inspection of environmental radioactivity monitoring facilities under Article 35 Euratom in order to ensure their proper functioning and efficiency.

129 Council Regs 3954/87, 2218/89, 2219/89; Commission Reg (Euratom) 770/90.

130 In ECJ Case 187/87 (1988) *Land Sarre v Minister for Industry, Posts and Telecommunications*, 1 *CMLR* (1989) 529, the ECJ determined that article 37 required notification to be given before *authorization* of any discharge.

131 Council Directive 2014/87/Euratom.

132 Council Decision 87/600/Euratom; Council Directive 89/618/Euratom; Council Directive 96/29/Euratom, Articles 50, 51(5). See generally, Cameron et al (eds), *Nuclear Energy Law after Chernobyl*, 40ff.

cooperation at various levels, including the harmonization and development of national nuclear law on a consensus basis.[133] The aims of this organization are similar to those of the IAEA, without its safeguards role. They include encouraging the adoption of common standards dealing with public health and the prevention of accidents.[134] Standards on such matters as radiation protection and waste management have been developed in collaboration with the IAEA and other bodies, but once again there is no power to compel compliance. The OECD has also been responsible for negotiation of conventions on third-party liability.[135]

(c) ILO

ILO has sponsored a widely supported Convention (ILO Convention No 115, 1960) on protecting workers against radiation and it issues various non-binding recommendations on the subject.

2(4) THE EFFECTIVENESS OF INTERNATIONAL REGULATION

There have undoubtedly been improvements in the international regulation of nuclear safety since the Chernobyl accident. Legally binding treaty commitments and improved opportunities for international supervision and inspection have reduced the freedom of governments to determine their own balance of safety and economic interest. In 1999 an intergovernmental conference concluded that considerable progress had been made in improving national regulation and the independence and competence of nuclear regulatory authorities in Eastern Europe, although it noted the continuing need to improve technical capabilities and ensure adequate resources for national regulators.[136] These developments lend some substance to the commitment made by governments in the 1996 Moscow Declaration on Nuclear Safety and Security to give 'absolute priority' to using nuclear power consistently with fundamental principles of nuclear safety. Since then Fukushima has rather undermined the claim made in the Declaration that nuclear power can provide an environmentally safe alternative to fossil fuels.[137] That accident shows that even a technologically sophisticated state heavily reliant on nuclear power cannot be relied upon to give 'absolute priority' to nuclear safety or IAEA safety standards.

[133] See Strohl, in IAEA, *Licensing and Regulatory Control of Nuclear Installations* (Vienna, 1975) 135; Cameron et al (eds), *Nuclear Energy Law after Chernobyl*, 6ff; Reyners, 32 *European Yearbook* (1984) 1.

[134] ENEA Statute, Article 1.

[135] 1960 Convention on Third Party Liability in the Field of Nuclear Energy, with 2004 Protocol, *infra*, section 5.

[136] International Conference on Strengthening Nuclear Safety in Eastern Europe, IAEA/GC(43)INF/6 (1999).

[137] But for the view that it can do so see NEA/OECD, *Five Years after the Fukushima Daiichi Accident: Nuclear Safety Improvements and Lessons Learnt* (Paris, 2016).

3 CONTROL OF TRANSBOUNDARY NUCLEAR RISKS

3(1) INTERNATIONAL OBLIGATIONS

The 1994 Nuclear Safety Convention and the 1997 Joint Convention are the first global treaties to commit states to control the risks of nuclear energy for environmental objectives. Nevertheless, there is ample evidence that states had already recognized the existence of an obligation to minimize nuclear risks and to prevent injury to other states, or radioactive pollution of the global environment.[138] Nuclear powered merchant ships[139] and satellites[140] must comply with internationally agreed standards of safety and radiation protection, and the same principle is accepted for the transboundary transport of radioactive substances.[141] Only the military uses of nuclear power fall outside these rules, which show that in contrast to their practice concerning nuclear power plants, states have been more willing to accept obligatory standards of international regulation for nuclear risks when these occur in common spaces. Thus the problem of defining the content of an obligation of due diligence, posed by the uncertain legal status of IAEA standards, is confined mainly to the operation of nuclear power stations within national borders.

Moreover, the dumping of radioactive waste at sea, or its discharge into the marine environment through land-based or airborne sources is now largely prohibited. Insofar as it was formerly permitted on the high seas, dumping had to comply with international regulations and the requirements of relevant treaty regimes, and is now banned on precautionary grounds.[142] Further prohibitions on radioactive-waste disposal exist in the Antarctic,[143] in Asia and the Pacific,[144] and in Africa.[145] It was argued in Chapter 3 that what constitutes 'pollution' varies according to context, so these precedents are particularly important in showing that the emission of radioactive substances into the environment of common spaces is presumed to constitute

138 IAEA/GC(SPL 1)Res/1 (1989); Okowa, *State Responsibility for Transboundary Air Pollution in International Law* (Oxford, 2000) Ch 4; Kirgis, 66 *AJIL* (1972) 290. In the dispute over nuclear testing in the Pacific, France accepted 'its duty to ensure that every condition was met and every precaution taken to prevent injury to the population and the fauna and flora of the world' (note to New Zealand of 19 Feb 1973, in *French Nuclear Testing in the Pacific*).

139 1974 Safety of Life at Sea Convention, Annex, Ch 8, and Attachment 3.

140 UNGA Res 47/68 (1992); 1967 Treaty on Principles Governing the Activities of States in the Exploration and Use of Outer Space.

141 1997 Joint Convention, *supra*, section 2; 1989 Basel Convention, *supra*, Ch 8; 1990 Code of Practice on the International Transboundary Movement of Radioactive Waste, *ibid*.

142 See *infra*, Ch 8.

143 1959 Antarctic Treaty, Article 5; Recommendation VIII-12, 8th Antarctic Treaty Consultative Meeting, 1975; 1997 Joint Convention, Article 27(1).

144 1986 Noumea Convention for the Protection of the Natural Resources and Environment of the South Pacific, Article II; 1989 Protocol for the Protection of the South East Pacific Against Radioactive Pollution; 1995 Waigani Convention on Hazardous Wastes in the South Pacific; 1996 ASEAN Treaty on the SE Asia Nuclear-Weapon Free Zone, Article 3.

145 1991 Bamako Convention, *infra*, Ch 8; 1996 African Nuclear Free Zone Treaty, Article 7.

prohibited pollution irrespective of any threshold of material injury or interference with amenities or resources.[146] The only possible exception is that below a certain level of radioactivity some proof of harm may be needed.[147]

With regard to nuclear explosions the same conclusion is indicated by the 1963 Nuclear Test Ban Treaty. This treaty prohibits weapons test explosions in the atmosphere, outer space, at sea, in Antarctica, or in any circumstances where radioactive debris spreads beyond the territory of the testing state. Its effect is that tests must be conducted underground and cause no escape of pollution. Not all nuclear powers are parties to this treaty, however,[148] and its status in customary law has been disputed. In the *Nuclear Tests* case,[149] the ICJ declined to decide whether atmospheric tests carried out by France violated customary international law, but it did hold that France had by its public statements unilaterally committed itself to conduct no more tests of this kind. Since 1980 all Chinese tests have in practice also complied with the 1963 Treaty.[150] Regional agreements prohibit all nuclear weapons testing in the territory of Latin American, South Pacific, South-east Asian, and African states parties.[151] Only North Korea continues to test nuclear weapons; it does so in defiance of Security Council resolutions.[152]

Given the weight of international opposition expressed in these agreements to all forms of deliberate radioactive pollution of common spaces, and the tacit compliance of non-parties with the 1963 Treaty since 1980, the case for a prohibition of nuclear testing founded on customary law, but excluding underground tests, is now strong.[153] This conclusion does not extend beyond deliberate nuclear tests or peaceful explosions, however. It does not mean that accidental radioactive explosions, such as the Chernobyl reactor accident, per se represent a violation of international law without showing a failure of due diligence,[154] nor does it imply that the actual use of nuclear

[146] Kirgis, 66 *AJIL* 1972) and *supra*, Ch 3, section 9.

[147] E.g. in the case of land-based discharges of low-level radioactive waste,

[148] North Korea, France and China are the main nuclear states to remain outside the 1963 treaty, but France is a party to the 1996 Comprehensive Test Ban Treaty (CTBT). China, India, Iran, Israel, Pakistan, North Korea, and the US are not parties to the CTBT.

[149] ICJ Reports (1974) 253, paras 47–53; Gros, 279ff; Petren, 305ff; de Castro, 389ff; Barwick, 427ff.

[150] China announced in 1986 that it did not intend to conduct further atmospheric tests. Its last atmospheric test took place in 1980. See SIPRI, *Yearbook* (Oxford, 1987) 45–52. Subsequent North Korean, Indian, and Pakistani tests have all taken place underground.

[151] 1967 Tlateloco Treaty for the Prohibition of Nuclear Weapons in Latin America and the Caribbean, Article 1; 1985 South Pacific Nuclear Free Zone Treaty, Article 6; 1996 ASEAN Nuclear Weapon-Free Zone Treaty, Article 3; 1996 African Nuclear Weapon-Free Zone Treaty, Article 5. The Tlateloco Treaty permits nuclear explosions for peaceful purposes.

[152] See UNSC Resolutions 2094; 2270; 2321; 2375.

[153] Lammers, *Pollution of International Watercourses* (Dordrecht, 1984) 319–27; Kirgis, 66 *AJIL* (1972) 295f, but cf Margolis, 64 *Yale LJ* (1955) 648 and McDougal and Schlei, *ibid*, 629, who support only a standard of reasonableness but disagree about its implications for the permissibility of nuclear tests. Singh and McWhinney, *Nuclear Weapons and Contemporary International Law* (2nd edn, Dordrecht, 1989) 230–3, conclude that the number of adherents indicates that the 1963 Treaty is now accepted as customary law. Okowa, *State Responsibility for Transboundary Air Pollution in International Law*, 99–110, concludes that atmospheric testing is not unlawful.

[154] Boyle, 60 *BYIL* (1989) 272–4, 290–6; *id*, in Butler (ed), *Perestroika and International Law* (Dordrecht, 1990) 203. See *supra*, Ch 3.

weapons is forbidden by international law. Although some writers argue that this is the case, their views are based on the indiscriminate character of nuclear weapons and other humanitarian considerations.[155] While recognizing the importance of these considerations in its *Advisory Opinion on Nuclear Weapons*, the International Court did not find the threat or use of nuclear weapons in all circumstances illegal, but it did recognize the customary status of explicit treaty limitations on methods of warfare which cause widespread, long-term, and severe damage to the natural environment.[156] However, the use of nuclear weapons is prohibited entirely in Latin America, Africa, South-east Asia, and the Pacific.[157] The 1977 Additional Protocol also prohibits attacks on nuclear power stations not used in support of military operations.[158]

The *Nuclear Tests Cases*[159] raised the question whether the deposit of radioactive particles on the territory of another state, or on the high seas, constitutes serious harm or an interference with high seas freedoms. The peculiar difficulty which radioactive fallout poses is that injury may not be immediate or apparent, and the claimants in the *Nuclear Tests Cases* did not allege that they had suffered actual harm, but based the main part of their claim on a violation of their territorial sovereignty. The development of international standards of radiation exposure, based on evidence of long-term effects, provides an obvious method for establishing an agreed threshold of harm which takes account of the absence of immediate injury.[160] Inconsistent practices among those affected were revealed by the Chernobyl accident, and the work of the ICRP, IAEA, WHO, and FAO has in their respective fields subsequently concentrated on elaborating common guidelines. Thus it is now easier than it was in 1974 to determine when serious radiation injury or harm has occurred, and this should no longer constitute an obstacle to international claims.

Consistently, the precedents considered here point to the conclusion that Principle 2 of the Rio Declaration, and other authoritative statements of the obligation to control sources of environmental harm are applicable to nuclear risks.[161] States do have an international responsibility based in customary law for the safe conduct of their nuclear activities, notwithstanding that they may take place entirely within their own borders.

155 See Pogany (ed), *Nuclear Weapons and International Law* (Aldershot, 1987); de Chazournes and Sands (eds), *International Law, the ICJ and Nuclear Weapons*, 131–448.

156 ICJ Reports (1996) 226; 1977 Additional Protocol 1 to the Geneva Red Cross Conventions, Articles 35, 55, and see de Chazournes and Sands (eds), *International Law, the ICJ and Nuclear Weapons*.

157 1985 South Pacific NFZ Treaty; 1967 Tlateloco Treaty; 1996 African and ASEAN Nuclear Weapon-Free Zone Treaties.

158 1977 Additional Protocol I, *ibid*. Article 56. See also the condemnation of Israel's attack on an Iraqi nuclear reactor: UNSC Res 487 (1981); IAEA Board of Governors, Res S/14532 (1981) in 20 *ILM* (1981) 963 but note the US attack on Iraqi nuclear facilities during the 1991 Kuwait conflict.

159 *Supra*, n 13.

160 Handl, 92 *RGDIP* (1988) 55; Sands, *Chernobyl*, 15.

161 *Supra*, Ch 3, section 5, and Okowa, *State Responsibility for Transboundary Air Pollution in International Law*, 110–30.

3(2) NUCLEAR INSTALLATIONS: NOTIFICATION AND CONSULTATION

Neighbouring states do not have a veto on the siting of nuclear installations near borders.[162] However, Article 17(iv) of the 1994 Nuclear Safety Convention requires a nuclear installation state to consult other parties 'in the vicinity of a proposed nuclear installation, insofar as they are likely to be affected by that installation and, upon request providing the necessary information to such Contracting Parties, in order to enable them to evaluate and make their own assessment of the likely safety impact on their own territory of the nuclear installation.'[163] This is at present the strongest acknowledgement that there may be some limits on the freedom of states to locate nuclear installations near a border, but there are indications that it reflects state practice in this respect. The evidence of bilateral agreements among European states, confirms that principles of notification and consultation intended to minimize transboundary risks have been applied to planned nuclear installations, although most of these treaties are limited to installations within 30km, 'or in the vicinity' of, an international border.[164] All require a full exchange of information on the proposed installation, so that other states may review the decision-making process and data and offer appropriate comments on safety and health protection. In most cases permanent commissions are established to consider matters of joint interest affecting public health.[165]

Specific examples of state practice on transboundary consultation include Ireland's representations in 1996 to a public inquiry in the UK, successfully opposing on safety grounds the licensing of a deep storage facility at Sellafield, bordering the Irish Sea.[166] In 1997 a proposal to dispose of Taiwanese nuclear waste at border sites in North Korea was similarly shelved after South Korean protests over safety. Border siting remains a contentious issue, however,[167] notably with respect to nuclear plants close to Lithuania's border.[168]

In contrast, port visits by nuclear-powered vessels have entailed the prior negotiation of bilateral agreements and are subject to the consent of the port state.[169] Where

162 *Supra*, Ch 3, section 8. See also Lenaerts, in Cameron et al (eds), *Nuclear Energy Law After Chernobyl*, 73ff; but compare Handl, in Jayakumar et al (eds), *Transboundary Pollution*, 207–19.

163 See to the same effect Articles 6 and 13 of the Joint Convention, and see also 1991 Espoo Convention, Articles 3, 5, 6; *supra*, Ch 3, section 8(2).

164 E.g. 1980 Agreement between Spain and Portugal on Co-operation in Matters Affecting the Safety of Nuclear Installations in the Vicinity of the Frontier, Ruster and Simma, xxvii, 420; 1977 Netherlands–FRG Memorandum on Exchange of Information and Consultation in Border Areas, *ibid*, 275; 1977 Denmark–FRG Agreement Regulating the Exchange of Information on the Construction of Nuclear Installations along the Border, 17 *ILM* (1978) 274.

165 E.g. 1966 Belgium–France Convention on Radiological Protection with regard to the Installations of the Ardennes Nuclear Power Station, 988 *UNTS* 288; 1982 Switzerland–FRG Agreement on Mutual Information on Construction and Operation of Nuclear Installations in Border Areas, II *Bundesgesetzblatt* (1983) 734 and agreements listed *supra*, n 149 between Spain–Portugal and Netherlands–FRG.

166 *Supra*, Ch 3, fn 570.

167 See Handl, in Jayakumar et al (eds), *Transboundary Pollution*, 211 and fn 95.

168 See Lithuania, *6th National Report to the Convention on Nuclear Safety* (2013) 102–3.

169 Boulanger, in IAEA, *Experience and Trends in Nuclear Law*, 125; Haselgrove, *ibid*. In part the insistence on prior agreement reflects the failure of nuclear ship operators to ratify the 1962 Brussels Convention on the Liability of Operators of Nuclear Ships, *infra*, section 5.

such vessels are merely in transit through the territorial sea of another state, however, the right of innocent passage applies, and no obligation of prior notice or consent appears to arise.[170] Such ships may be required to carry documents and observe special precautionary measures established by the 1974 SOLAS Convention.[171] However, the passage of nuclear cargoes in the territorial sea remains controversial, and not all coastal states accept the position stated here.[172]

Lastly, both the use of nuclear power sources in outer space, and the conduct of nuclear explosions for peaceful purposes appear to require prior notification to the relevant international organization and must be preceded by a safety assessment. Information on radioactive fallout must be communicated, and in case of unplanned satellite re-entry, sub-orbital states are to be consulted.[173]

These precedents all point first to the conclusion that states are not debarred by international law from acquiring and using nuclear technology simply because it poses a risk of injury to other states or to the environment. Subject only to compliance with the required standards of diligent control and procedural obligations considered above, 'each state is free to act within the limits of its sovereignty',[174] and to act on its own assessment of the risk. But there must also be such an assessment: nuclear installations fall squarely within the threshold of transboundary risk for the purposes of environmental impact assessment.[175]

Second, leaving aside the exceptional rules applied to nuclear ships, the evidence of state practice examined here is consistent with the view that states must notify and consult their neighbours in cases of significant transboundary risk, with a view to ensuring reasonable regard for the rights and legitimate interests of other states. As we saw in Chapter 3, the application of this rule to transboundary risks, including the risks posed by nuclear installations, is required by customary international law and other precedents.[176] Although in its 2001 Articles on Prevention of Transboundary Harm the ILC requires the negotiation in these cases of an equitable balance of interests,[177] state practice continues to favour the more limited rule indicated here.[178]

170 1982 UNCLOS, Articles 17–19, 21–4; 1989 Basel Convention, Article 4(12); 1997 Joint Convention, Article 27(3); 1985 South Pacific Nuclear Free Zone Treaty, Article 5; 1996 African NWFZ Treaty, Article 2(2); 1996 ASEAN NWFZ Treaty, Article 7, and infpra, Ch 9, but contrast the 1996 Izmir Protocol on Transboundary Movements of Hazardous Waste in the Mediterranean, Article 6(4) which requires prior notice of passage.

171 1982 UNCLOS, Article 23.

172 For a fuller discussion see Handl, in Jayakumar et al (eds), *Transboundary Pollution*, 229–31; Caron and Schreiber (eds), *The Oceans in the Nuclear Age: Legacies and Risks* (Leiden, 2010).

173 UNGA Res 47/68 (1992); Tlateloco Treaty, Article 18, but cf Article 34, Euratom Treaty, *supra*, section 2.

174 ICJ Reports (1973) 131, per Judge Ignacio Pinto, and *supra*, Ch 3, sections 5–8.

175 The 1991 Espoo Convention applies to nuclear installations: see *supra*, Ch 3, section 7.

176 *Supra*, Ch 3, section 8.

177 Articles 9(2)10, on which see *supra*, Ch 3, section 8(2).

178 See especially the 1991 Espoo Convention, Articles 3, 5, 6, and *supra*, Ch 3, section 8(2) but compare Handl, in Jayakumar et al (eds), *Transboundary Pollution*, 209–19.

The narrowness of this obligation as it has been applied in state practice should be observed, however, particularly in its application to nuclear power. The Chernobyl reactor was not in a border area, and states have not consulted in such cases, save, as we shall see, in cases of emergency.[179] In contrast, it is significant that the ILC's 2001 articles extend the requirement of consultation to all activities creating significant transboundary risk wherever located.[180] The need for improved transboundary consultation over the siting of new nuclear plants remains unresolved post-Fukushima.[181] Moreover, it is questionable whether for nuclear installations transboundary consultation is enough to ensure that neighbouring states and the environment are adequately protected from unilaterally determined nuclear risks. What is lacking in such cases is a rule comparable to that applied in certain cases of dumping at sea, requiring prior consultation and approval of the relevant international organization.[182] This solution seems preferable to one making nuclear activities dependent on the agreement of neighbouring states, but avoids the excessive unilateralism of the present law.

3(3) COOPERATION AND ASSISTANCE IN CASES OF NUCLEAR EMERGENCY

(a) Notification

The existence of a general obligation to notify other states and cooperate in cases where they are at risk from nuclear accidents or incidents is confirmed both by regional practice in Western Europe, and by international conventions. Most of the European treaties contain provisions for the timely supply of information in cases of emergency and require radioactivity monitoring systems to be established to alert governments of the danger.[183] A small number also require cooperation in response to such an emergency. Following the Chernobyl accident, the Soviet Union was

179 See *infra*, section 3(3). However, Appendix III of the 1991 Convention on Transboundary EIA requires the parties also to consider 'more remote proposed activities which could give rise to significant transboundary effects far removed from the site of the development'.

180 *Supra*, Ch 3, section 8.

181 See *Summary Rept, 5th Review Meeting, Convention on Nuclear Safety* (2011) paras 38–9.

182 *Infra*, Ch 8, section 3.

183 Agreement between Spain and Portugal, *supra*, n 164; Belgium–France Convention, *supra*, n 165; 1979 Agreement between France and Switzerland Concerning Exchange of Information in Case of Accidents, *Ruster and Simma*, xxvii, 382; 1983, UK–France Exchange of Notes Concerning Exchanges of Information, 60 *UKTS*, Cmnd 9041; 1978 Agreement between Switzerland and FRG Concerning Radiological Disaster Relief, *Ruster and Simma*, xxvii, 337; 1981 Agreement between France–FRG on Mutual Information in the event of Radiological Incidents, I *Bundesgesetzblatt*, 885; 1983 Agreement between France and Luxemburg on Exchange of Information in Case of Radiological Emergencies, 34 *NLB* (1984) 42. A further series of such agreements have been prompted by the Chernobyl accident; 1987 Agreement between Belgium and the Netherlands on Co-operation in Nuclear Safety, 41 *NLB* (1988) 42; 1987 Norway–Sweden Agreement on Exchange of Information and Early Notification Relating to Nuclear Facilities, 17 *EPL* (1987) 41; 1987 UK–Norway Agreement on Early Notification, Cmnd. 371; 1987 Finland–USSR Agreement on Early Notification of a Nuclear Accident, 39 *NLB* (1987) 4; 1987 FRG–GDR Radiation Protection Agreement, 40 *NLB* (1987) 44; 1987 Denmark–Poland Agreement on Exchange of Information, 41 *NLB* (1988) 49, and similar agreements with the FRG, USSR, UK, and Finland. These are all intended to give effect to the provisions of the 1986 IAEA Notification Convention.

criticized for failing to give adequate and timely information to other states likely to be affected by the disaster. Implicit in this criticism was a belief that such notification should reasonably be expected.[184] In addition to the practice of a growing number of states supporting such an obligation, the IAEA had developed guidelines on reporting of incidents and information exchange in 1985,[185] but these were non-binding.

One result of Chernobyl was the opening for signature of the 1986 Convention on Early Notification of a Nuclear Accident.[186] This imposes on parties a duty to notify other states likely to be affected by transboundary releases of 'radiological safety significance'. Information on the occurrence and on means of minimizing its radiological consequences must be supplied, to enable other states to take all possible precautionary measures. The Convention specifies in detail what information is to be given, and requires states to respond promptly to requests for further relevant information. It is less clear, however, at what point a release acquires radiological safety significance; this provision deliberately avoids objective definition, and thus leaves substantial discretion to states where incidents occur. The effectiveness of the Convention is also dependent on states possessing a basic radiological monitoring and assessment capability. Unlike bilateral treaties in Europe, the Convention does not require states to acquire this capability; where it is lacking, it is difficult to see how they will be able to respond effectively.[187]

Due to superpower opposition, the Convention does not cover nuclear accidents involving military facilities, such as nuclear submarines, but the Soviet Union gave notice when two such vessels ran into difficulty, and the UK has undertaken to do so.[188] Since the Convention applies only to 'transboundary releases', it would seem that accidents whose consequences do not extend beyond national borders, or which occur wholly on the high seas are also excluded.[189]

Although the Convention is open to criticism for the apparent looseness of its terminology, and the range of excluded occurrences, it does justify the conclusion that the timely notification of nuclear accidents likely to affect other states is a customary obligation.[190] Japan provided information about the Fukushima accident in accordance with Article 3 of the Early Notification Convention.[191]

184 Group of Seven, Statement on the Implications of the Chernobyl Nuclear Accident, 25 *ILM* (1986) 1005; IAEA General Conference, Special Session, 1986, IAEA GC (SPL 1)/Res/1.

185 IAEA/INFCIRC/321, Guidelines on Reportable Events, 1985.

186 See generally Cameron et al (eds), *Nuclear Energy Law After Chernobyl*, 19ff; Adede, *The IAEA Notification and Assistance Conventions* (Dordrecht, 1987); Handl, 92 *RGDIP* (1988) 24ff.

187 Rosen, *IAEA Bulletin* (1987) 34f.

188 25 *ILM* (1986) 1369. The UK declaration specifically includes voluntary notification of military accidents; others refer to 'all' or 'any' accidents.

189 Cameron et al (eds), *Nuclear Energy Law After Chernobyl*, 24.

190 See also 1974 SOLAS Convention, Regulation 12; UNGA Res 47/68 (1992) Principle 5.

191 IAEA, *Activities in Response to the Fukushima Accident*, GOV/INF/2011/8, n 1.

(b) Assistance

Assistance in cases of nuclear emergency is also the subject of an IAEA Convention, which allows states to call for international help to protect 'life, property and the environment' from the effects of radioactive releases.[192] The IAEA is given a coordinating role, and an obligation to respond to a request by making available appropriate resources.[193] No explicit obligation to render assistance is placed on other states, however, even where an installation within their territory is the cause of harm, nor is there any provision for joint contingency planning comparable to that found in many maritime treaties.

Thus, in general, the Convention facilitates, but does not require a response to, nuclear accidents or emergencies. It main achievement is to give assisting states and their personnel immunity from legal proceedings brought by the requesting state, and an indemnity for proceedings brought by others. These provisions are open to reservation, however.[194]

Like the small number of bilateral treaties which provide in more general terms for emergency assistance,[195] the IAEA Convention leaves responsibility for making the request and taking or directing appropriate action in its territory with the state which needs help.[196] It creates no duty either to seek assistance, or to control the emergency. A failure to do so may of course incur state responsibility if it results in harm to others, under general principles discussed below. But unlike maritime casualties, where states also have a recognized right of intervention or self-help to protect their own coasts,[197] there is no generally accepted basis in international law for intervention by neighbouring states seeking to avert the consequences of a nuclear catastrophe, such as Chernobyl. Any attempt to take unilateral preventive action within another state, or to render unrequested assistance in these circumstances would in principle appear to be a violation of the source state's sovereignty.[198] At most, necessity might be pleaded in defence of any state undertaking such intervention in circumstances of grave and imminent peril.[199] By leaving the requesting state the decisive role, the

[192] 1986 Convention on Assistance in the Case of a Nuclear Accident or Radiological Emergency; see also IAEA/INFCIRC/310, Guidelines for Mutual Emergency Assistance Arrangements. See generally Cameron et al (eds), *Nuclear Energy Law After Chernobyl*, 26ff; Adede, *The IAEA Notification and Assistance Conventions*.

[193] On IAEA assistance to Japan during the Fukushima accident see IAEA, *Activities in Response to the Fukushima Accident*, GOV/INF/2011/8.

[194] Articles 8, 10. Four states have excluded Article 8; two have excluded Article 10.

[195] E.g. 1963 Nordic Mutual Emergency Assistance Agreement in Connection with Radiation Accidents, 525 *UNTS* 76; 1966 Belgium–France Convention, *supra*, n 164; 1981 Belgium–France Agreement on Mutual Assistance in the Event of Catastrophic and Serious Accident, 34 *NLB* (1984) 42; 1977 France–FRG Agreement on Mutual Assistance in the Event of Catastrophic and Grave Disasters, II *Bundesgesetzblatt* (1980) 33; 1980 FRG–Belgium Agreement on Mutual Emergency Assistance, *ibid.* (1982) 1006.

[196] Article 3.

[197] 1969 Convention on Intervention in Case of Maritime Casualties; 1982 UNCLOS, Article 221, *infra*, Ch 9.

[198] Cf the Security Council's condemnation of Israel's attack on an Iraqi Nuclear reactor: UNSC Res 487 (1981); see also IAEA Board of Governors Resolution S/14532; *Corfu Channel Case*, ICJ Reports (1949) 32–6; *Case Concerning Diplomatic and Consular Staff in Tehran*, ICJ Reports (1980) 43, but see Bilder, 14 *Vand JTL* (1981).

[199] ILC, 2001 Articles on State Responsibility, Article 25, on which see *Gabčíkovo-Nagymaros Case*, ICJ Reports (1997) 7, paras 49–58.

IAEA Convention does nothing to disturb this position. Assistance, as provided for in the instruments referred to here is thus sharply different from intervention or self-protection. In short, it is not obligatory, it need not be sought, and it cannot be given without consent. The Assistance Convention was not invoked by Japan during the Fukushima accident.[200]

4 STATE RESPONSIBILITY FOR NUCLEAR DAMAGE

4(1) STRICT OR ABSOLUTE RESPONSIBILITY

The ultra-hazardous character of nuclear installations, in the sense that damage caused by accidents may be widespread, serious, and long-lasting, was for some writers the basis for asserting that state responsibility in such cases will be strict or absolute.[201] That position, and its application to nuclear energy, is the focus of attention in this section, although it is questionable whether the ultra-hazardous category is wide enough to cover all nuclear activities, including those, such as discharge of radioactive waste into the sea, whose effects are cumulatively harmful rather than immediately catastrophic.[202]

The main argument advanced by these writers rests on inferences drawn from the use of strict or absolute liability as a general principle in national legal systems and civil liability treaties concerned with nuclear accidents.[203] The tendency of the treaties, however, is to avoid direct implication of the source state in responsibility for damage and to emphasize the liability in national law of the operator or company which caused the damage.[204] The possibility of state responsibility is not precluded, but the scheme of these civil-liability treaties involves states only as guarantors of the operators' strict liability, or in providing additional compensation funds. Moreover, the burden of this residual responsibility is either spread equitably across a group of nuclear states or left in part to lie where it falls through limitation of liability. In neither case does the polluting state bear responsibility for the whole loss.[205] The extent of its liability is further limited by the narrow definition of nuclear damage used in the older treaties.[206]

These factors make the nuclear liability conventions weak precedents for any particular theory or standard of state responsibility for harm; they seem inconsistent

200 IAEA, *Activities in Response to the Fukushima Accident*, GOV/INF/2011/8, n 1.

201 Jenks, 117 *Recueil des Cours* (1966) 105; Smith, *State Responsibility and the Marine Environment* (Oxford, 1987) 112–15; Handl, 16 *NYIL* (1985) 68ff; Hardy, 36 *BYIL* (1960) 237; Goldie, 16 *NYIL* (1985) 204ff; *contra*, Okowa, *State Responsibility for Transboundary Air Pollution in International Law*, 110–130, and see *supra*, Ch 4, section 2.

202 Jenks, 117 *Recueil des Cours* (1966) 122, views *Trail Smelter* as a case of liability for ultra-hazardous operations. This is very much broader than most interpretations, however.

203 See esp Goldie, 14 *ICLQ* (1965) 1189, and *supra*, Ch 4, section 2.

204 See *infra*, section 5.

205 *Ibid*. Compare the 1972 Convention on International Liability for Damage Caused by Space Objects which places no limit on liability.

206 But for revised formulations see *infra*, section 5(7).

with the view that states are absolutely or strictly responsible in international law for damage emanating from their territory even in cases of ultra-hazardous activities.[207] As with national laws employing standards of strict or absolute liability contingent on compulsory insurance and limitation of liability, it is difficult to treat complex schemes of loss distribution as indicating a standard of responsibility for states themselves in the less highly developed circumstances of international law.

A second argument concerning the standard of liability is based, as we saw in Chapter 4, on the concept of objective responsibility for breach of obligation. When applied to accidental injury emanating from nuclear installations, this concept focuses on the conduct of the state in failing to meet its obligation of diligent control and is distinguishable from fault only in eliminating subjective elements of intention or recklessness. Responsibility in such cases is neither strict nor absolute since it cannot be established by proof of damage alone. But where nuclear damage is the result of some internationally prohibited activity, such as the dumping of radioactive waste at sea, or atmospheric nuclear tests, objective responsibility results not from a failure of due diligence, but simply from the harm caused in deliberate violation of international law. This is much closer to a standard of strict or absolute responsibility, and offers a sounder basis for such concepts than any inferences from national law or civil-liability conventions.[208] While the evidence of state practice reviewed below does not unequivocally support this analysis, some of the claims in question predate the present consensus on prohibition of deliberate radioactive pollution, and cannot be taken as a wholly reliable guide to the present law.

4(2) STATE CLAIMS

State claims or settlements involving damage caused by nuclear activities provide little support for any one standard of responsibility. Rather, they demonstrate the lack of international consensus on this point. In 1955 the US paid compensation to Japanese fishermen injured by one of its nuclear tests, but disclaimed any admission of legal responsibility.[209] Japan and New Zealand reserved the right in diplomatic protests to hold the US and France responsible for any loss or damage inflicted by further tests in the Pacific,[210] but made no claims. Canada asserted in 1979 that the standard of

[207] Miatello, in Spinedi and Simma (eds), *UN Codification of State Responsibility* (New York, 1987) 306ff; Handl, 92 *RGDIP* (1988) 35ff. *Contra*, Smith, *State Responsibility and the Marine Environment*, 114ff. Poor ratification of all but the Paris Convention is another factor lessening the significance of these conventions: see *infra*, section 5(8).

[208] On objective responsibility see Ch 4, section 2. On the prohibition of deliberate pollution see *supra*, section 3.

[209] Settlement of Japanese Claims for Personal and Property Damage Resulting from Nuclear Tests in Marshall Islands (1955) 1 *UST* 1, *TIAS* 3160, 4 Whiteman, *Digest* 553; Margolis, 64 *Yale LJ* (1955) 629; McDougal and Schlei, *ibid*, 648.

[210] Whiteman, *Digest* 585f; *Nuclear Tests* Cases, ICJ Pleadings (1978) II, 22–30; Australian notes on the subject made no reference to compensation but did assert that the tests should be terminated: *ibid*, I, 2ff. In an exchange of notes dated 10 December 1993 Australia accepted an *ex gratia* payment of £20million from the UK in settlement of all claims relating to UK nuclear tests that took place on Australian territory in the 1950s and 60s.

absolute responsibility for space objects, including those using nuclear power and causing the deposit of radioactive material, had become a general principle of international law, and it relied on this in a successful claim for compensation from the Soviet Union following the crash of Cosmos 954. But this claim was supported by the 1972 Space Objects Liability Convention, to which both states were party;[211] the very different approach of the nuclear-liability conventions undermines the relevance of this precedent in other cases of accidental harm.

Responses to the Chernobyl disaster provide the most telling evidence of state practice so far. This accident caused widespread harm to agricultural produce and livestock in Europe and affected wildlife, in some cases severely.[212] Clean-up costs were incurred and compensation was paid by several governments to their own citizens for produce which was destroyed as a precautionary measure, or which was rendered unusable. Evidence of long-term health risks shows increased levels of various cancers and other illnesses within the population exposed.[213]

Despite this provable loss, no claims were made against the Soviet Union by any affected state, although the possibility was considered by some governments.[214] Uncertainty over the basis for such a claim, reluctance to establish a precedent with possible future implications for states which themselves operate nuclear power plants, and the absence of any appropriate treaty binding on the Soviet Union are the main reasons for this silence.[215] It was also unclear whether liability would extend to damage to the environment, or to the costs of precautionary measures taken by governments. The Soviet Union made no voluntary offer of compensation, and questioned the necessity of precautionary measures taken by its neighbours, maintaining that they suffered little or no damage.[216] The failure to demand or to offer compensation in this case shows the difficulty of reconciling doctrinal support for any standard of strict or absolute responsibility with the evidence of state practice, limited as it is. It points to the conclusion that responsibility for a failure of due diligence, that is for causing avoidable loss only, provides a more convincing interpretation of the actual practice of states and the present state of customary law in cases of accidental environmental damage.[217] The question then would be what constitutes a failure of due diligence in cases involving nuclear accidents? Here the most obvious answer would be that the 1994 Convention on Nuclear Safety and related IAEA soft law provide prima facie

[211] *Claim for Damage Caused by Cosmos 954*, 18 *ILM* (1979) 902; 1972 Convention on International Liability for Damage Caused by Space Objects. The USSR denied the applicability of the 1972 Convention to the damage which had occurred.

[212] *Supra*, n 1.

[213] WHO, *Health Effects of the Chernobyl Accident and Special Health Care Programmes: Report of the UN Chernobyl Forum Health Expert Group* (Geneva, 2006).

[214] West Germany, Sweden, and the UK reserved their position.

[215] Sands, *Chernobyl*, 27.

[216] USSR Proposed Programme for Establishing an International Regime for the Safe Development of Nuclear Energy, 1986, repr in Sands, *Chernobyl* 227.

[217] See *supra*, Ch 4, section 2, and Okowa, *State Responsibility for Transboundary Air Pollution in International Law*, 110–30.

evidence of the standard of conduct required from nuclear states. If there is no departure from this standard of care there is no responsibility on the part of the state.

4(3) REFORMING THE LAW OF STATE RESPONSIBILITY FOR NUCLEAR INJURY

As we saw in chapter 4, the desirability of securing international agreement on appropriate principles of state responsibility for harm resulting from nuclear accidents was acknowledged as one of the lessons of Chernobyl.[218] In 1990 the IAEA established a Standing Committee on Liability for Nuclear Damage to undertake a comprehensive review of this problem, including revision of the existing 1963 Vienna Convention on Civil Liability for Nuclear Damage ('Vienna Convention').[219] Initially the ILC's articles on 'International Liability' attracted some attention as a possible model for new provisions based on the strict liability of the state where the nuclear installation is located, and proposals were made by a number of states.[220] Opposition from the leading nuclear powers made this an untenable option, and the revised Vienna Convention does not address the question of the liability of states in international law, apart from acknowledging that the rights and obligations of the parties under general international law remain unaffected by the Convention. However, the parties did agree to adopt a new publicly funded compensation scheme, based on the earlier European scheme established in 1963, under which the state in which the installation is situated provides limited additional funding, and thereafter other states parties also contribute up to a ceiling.[221] Nuclear states cannot be compelled to participate in this scheme, however, and some, including Russia, have not.

Despite the undoubted improvements made since 1990 to the global scheme for civil liability and compensation, recourse to state responsibility will remain necessary if affected states are to be fully compensated in the event of a serious accident causing damage in excess of the limits for liability and compensation under the Vienna Convention. Moreover, civil liability and compensation schemes do not apply to military installations. For these reasons, the two systems of public and private liability remain complementary rather than alternative elements in the overall legal regime for nuclear accidents. The more convincing proposals for reform which were not adopted would have incorporated elements from both systems, possibly in a unified claims process modelled in part on the precedent set by the UN Compensation Commission for claims arising out of Iraq's invasion of Kuwait.[222]

[218] USSR Proposed Programme, *supra*, n 215; Handl, 92 *RGDIP* (1988) 5; *id*, in NEA/OECD, *Nuclear Accidents: Liabilities and Guarantees: Proceedings of the NEA/OECD Symposium* (Paris, 1992).

[219] See IAEA, *Reports of the Standing Committee on Liability for Nuclear Damage*, 1st -17th sessions (1990–97).

[220] See IAEA/Gov/INF/509 and Politi, in Francioni and Scovazzi (eds), *International Responsibility for Environmental Harm* (Dordrecht, 1991) 473; Handl, 92 *RGDIP* (1988) 5. Poland's proposal for a supplementary scheme of state liability is in IAEA/SCNL/11/3 (1996).

[221] See 1997 Convention on Supplementary Compensation for Nuclear Damage, *infra*, next section.

[222] Handl, 92 *RGDIP* (1988) 5. On the UNCC see *supra*, Ch 4, section 2(6).

Without further agreement on whether state responsibility for nuclear damage is strict or requires a failure of diligence, on a forum in which claims can be brought, and on how the burden of reparation should be allocated among public and private actors, it is difficult to conclude that state responsibility at present affords a realistic prospect of redress in the event of international claims arising out of accidental nuclear damage. There is no doubt that in most cases reliance on the revised civil liability and compensation schemes provided by the 1997 Protocol to the Vienna Convention and the 2004 Protocol to the Paris Convention would be preferable if they were widely ratified and applicable law in the key nuclear states. This is especially the case now that non-party claims are possible.[223] Unfortunately the 2004 Protocol was still not in force in 2019 and the 1997 Protocol had only 13 parties, none of them significant nuclear states. It follows that compensation for a serious nuclear accident may still depend on inter-state claims and the law of state responsibility for breach of obligation.

5 CIVIL LIABILITY FOR NUCLEAR DAMAGE

Civil liability proceedings are the preferred method employed by the majority of nuclear states for reallocating the costs of transboundary nuclear accidents. In a few cases, bilateral arrangements simply apply the principle of equal access and non-discrimination to nuclear risks, and a number of national legal systems also facilitate transboundary proceedings, including forum shopping.[224] The limited utility of equal access has persuaded most nuclear states to adopt a more sophisticated model. This is provided by four international conventions which create a special regime of civil liability.[225] Nuclear incidents within Western Europe are covered by the OECD Paris Convention of 1960,[226] to which all Western European nuclear states are party. The Vienna Convention of 1963[227] offers a comparable scheme for global participation that now includes Russia and all of Eastern Europe, and a variety of states elsewhere in the world, but not four major nuclear states: China, Japan, Canada, and the US are all non-parties.

223 *Infra*, section 5(6).

224 1974 Nordic Convention on the Protection of the Environment, Article 1; 1976 Nuclear Liability Rules (US–Canada); 1986 Agreement on Third Party Liability in the Nuclear Field (Switzerland-FRG). On equal access and forum shopping see *supra*, Ch 5.

225 See generally, Lee, 12 *JEL* (2000) 317; Miatello, in Spinedi and Simma (eds), *United Nations Codification of State Responsibility* (New York, 1987) 287; IAEA, *Nuclear Law for a Developing World*, 109–82; Hardy, 36 *BYIL* (1960) 223; Cigoj, 14 *ICLQ* (1965) 809; Reyners, in IAEA, *Licensing and Regulatory Control of Nuclear Installations*, 243; IAEA, *Experience and Trends in Nuclear Law*, 69ff; Arrangio Ruiz, 107 *Recueil des cours* (1962) 575ff; Fornassier, 10 *AFDI* (1964) 303; Cameron et al, *Nuclear Energy Law*.

226 Amended by 1964 and 1982 Additional Protocols both in force, and 2004 Protocol, not yet in force. See Berman and Hydeman, 55 *AJIL* (1961) 966; Arrangio-Ruiz, 107 *Recueil des Cours*, 582ff, and explanatory memorandum, 8 *European Yearbook* (1960) 225.

227 See IAEA, *Civil Liability for Nuclear Damage, Official Records* (Vienna, 1964).

A Joint Protocol links the Paris and Vienna conventions and allows claims to be made under either.[228] A 1997 protocol revising the Vienna Convention was meant to encourage participation by Eastern European nuclear states whose Soviet-era reactors continue to pose a higher risk of serious accidents with transboundary effects, but it has only partly succeeded and Russia and Ukraine are not parties.[229] Finally, two more treaties deal with nuclear ships[230] and maritime carriage of nuclear materials,[231] but neither is widely ratified.

All four treaties seek to harmonize important aspects of liability for nuclear accidents and incidents in national laws, without requiring complete uniformity in every respect. They create a common scheme for loss distribution among the victims, making the operator liable but reinforced by state-funded compensation schemes. These aspects distinguish the scheme from equal access to national remedies adopted by OECD, and make it more beneficial to litigants, who are given the assurance of compensation without proof of fault. At the same time, the scheme is also intended to give the nuclear industry protection from unlimited, unpredictable liability involving multiple actions against suppliers, builders, designers, carriers, operators, and states as potential defendants.[232] Although this kind of protection is now difficult to justify in the case of the highly developed nuclear industry in Western Europe, North America, or Japan, it remains an essential element of international efforts to provide help to the East European nuclear industry.[233]

The nuclear liability conventions thus reflect on the one hand an early recognition of the need for a stronger system of loss distribution, appropriate to the serious risks of nuclear accidents, and on the other a desire to encourage the infant nuclear industry. Both points again distinguish nuclear liability from transboundary air or water pollution, where equal access has generally remained the limit of state practice in civil liability matters.[234] While this special nuclear regime does not go so far as the Convention on Liability for Damage Caused by Space Objects,[235] in that liability is not

[228] 1988 Joint Protocol Relating to the Application of the Vienna Convention and the Paris Convention. See also Paris Convention, Article 2, as amended 2004.

[229] See IAEA, *Reports of the Standing Committee on Liability for Nuclear Damage,* 1st-17th sessions (1990–97). The final report of the committee is in IAEA/Gov/2924. The 1997 Liability Protocol had 14 parties in 2019 but only 7 from Eastern Europe.

[230] 1962 Brussels Convention on the Liability of Operators of Nuclear Ships; Hardy, 12 *ICLQ* (1963) 778; Konz, 57 *AJIL* (1963) 100; Szasz, 2 *JMLC* (1970) 541; Colliard, 8 *AFDI* (1962) 41; Cigoj, 14 *ICLQ* (1965) 809. The Convention is not in force. None of the states which license nuclear ships is a party.

[231] 1971 Brussels Convention Relating to Civil Liability in the Field of Maritime Carriage of Nuclear Material, IAEA, *International Conventions on Civil Liability for Nuclear Damage*, 55; Strohl, in IAEA, *Experience and Trends in Nuclear Law*, 89.

[232] Preamble to the Paris Convention, IAEA, *Conference on Civil Liability*, 66f; Berman and Hydeman, 55 *AJIL* (1961); Konz, 57 *AJIL* (1963) 105; Cameron et al (eds), *Nuclear Energy Law After Chernobyl*, 98f.

[233] See also the 2003 Framework Agreement on a Multilateral Nuclear Environmental Programme in the Russian Federation which indemnifies nuclear suppliers upgrading Russian nuclear reactors.

[234] *Supra*, Ch 5, section 4. But compare the 2004 Kiev Protocol on Civil Liability and Compensation for Damage Caused by the Transboundary Effects of Industrial Accidents on Transboundary Waters.

[235] *Supra*, Ch 4, section 2.

placed directly on the state, the influence of the nuclear example can be seen in later treaties dealing with liability for oil pollution from ships.[236]

5(1) THE SCHEME OF THE CONVENTIONS

Although there are variations, the overall scheme of the four conventions is based on the same five elements, as reflected in the protocols of 1997 (Vienna Convention) and 2004 (Paris Convention):[237]

(i) Liability is absolute and requires only proof that the damage was caused by a nuclear incident. No proof of fault or negligence is required as a condition of liability. Certain exceptions such as armed conflict, civil war, or negligence of the victim are allowed.[238] However, damage caused by terrorist acts is not an exception.

(ii) Liability is channelled exclusively to the operator of the nuclear installation or ship which causes the damage, and all other potential defendants are protected.[239] Operators are liable only in accordance with the relevant convention. In certain cases a carrier or handler of nuclear material may be treated as an operator, and several operators may be jointly liable.[240]

(iii) Limitations may be placed on the total amount and duration of liability but this is not obligatory except in the case of ships.[241]

(iv) Payment up to the prescribed limit of liability is supported by compulsory insurance or security held by the operator and guaranteed by the state of installation or registry.[242] For accidents covered by the Paris and Vienna Conventions, additional public funds are provided under supplementary conventions.[243]

(v) Rules determine which state or states have jurisdiction over claims and all other recourse to civil proceedings elsewhere is precluded.[244]

236 1969 International Convention on Civil Liability for Oil Pollution Damage with 1984 Protocol; *infra*, Ch 9.

237 Subsequent references are to the conventions as revised in 1997 and 2004. At the time of writing the 1997 Protocol had entered into force; the 2004 Protocol had not.

238 Vienna Convention, Article IV; Paris Convention Articles 3, 9; Brussels Convention on Nuclear Ships, Articles II, VIII. The 1997 and 2004 Protocols delete the previous 'grave natural disaster' exception.

239 Vienna Convention, Article II; Paris Convention, Articles 3, 6; Brussels Convention on Nuclear Ships, Article II. The Convention Relating to Maritime Carriage, Article I, channels liability to operators who would be liable under the Paris or Vienna Conventions, or under national laws which are at least as favourable to those suffering damage.

240 Vienna Convention, Article II(2); Paris Convention, Article 4(d)

241 Vienna Convention, Articles V, VI, as amended 1997; Paris Convention, Articles 7, 8, as amended 2004; Brussels Convention on Nuclear Ships, Articles III, V.

242 Vienna Convention, Article VII, as amended 1997; Brussels Convention on Nuclear Ships, Article III; Paris Convention, Article 10, as amended 2004.

243 1963 Convention Supplementary to the Paris Convention with Additional Protocols of 1964, 1982, and 2004; 1997 Vienna Convention on Supplementary Compensation for Nuclear Damage.

244 Vienna Convention, Article XI; Paris Convention, Article 13 as amended 2004; Brussels Convention on Nuclear Ships, Article X.

This scheme draws partly on the example of early national nuclear legislation, notably the US Price-Anderson Act of 1957.[245] In most cases, the treaties leave states some discretion to modify their basic elements, however. National laws may thus adopt different limitation periods or insurance and liability ceilings.[246] Some states have used this power to set much higher liability ceilings; a few, such as the Federal Republic of Germany, have opted for unlimited liability in certain circumstances.

Although fewer variations are allowed under the Brussels Convention on Nuclear Ships, none of the treaties requires complete uniformity of implementation. Rather, as the IAEA commentary on the Vienna Convention explains, the principal objectives are to enumerate minimum international standards which will be flexible and adaptable to a variety of legal, social, and economic systems, while also designating which state will have exclusive legislative and jurisdictional competence.[247]

The Conventions cover most, but not all, potential sources of nuclear damage. The Paris and Vienna Conventions apply to 'nuclear installations', a term broadly defined to include reactors, reprocessing, manufacturing, and storage facilities, where nuclear fuel, nuclear material, and radioactive products or waste are used or produced.[248] They also apply to the transport of nuclear material or the handling of nuclear waste.[249] The revised Paris Convention has been extended to cover installations 'in the course of being decommissioned.'[250] The Brussels Convention covers nuclear-powered ships, their fuel and incidental waste, but not the carriage of nuclear material by sea.[251] This latter is subject to other conventional regimes.[252] Most uses and by-products of civil nuclear power will thus fall under one or other of these headings, and only nuclear tests, military installations, nuclear weapons, and peaceful nuclear explosions are excluded.[253]

5(2) WHY LIABILITY WITHOUT FAULT?

The combination of no-fault liability with a ceiling on damages, supported by insurance and state indemnity, made civil liability for nuclear risks unusual when the conventions were first adopted, although they have since become the pattern for later

[245] Atomic Energy Damages Act 1957, 42 USC 2011–284, as amended. See Cameron et al (eds), *Nuclear Energy Law After Chernobyl*, Chs 9, 10; and Tomain, *Nuclear Power Transformation* (Bloomington, 1987) Chs 1, 8. The Act imposes a liability ceiling, requires compulsory insurance, and provides for Federal indemnity payments; it does not make operators exclusively liable, however, and it leaves the standard of liability to be settled by each state.

[246] Vienna Convention, Article V, as amended 1997; Paris Convention, Articles 7, 8, as amended 2004. Germany and Austria had already reserved the right to make liability absolute.

[247] IAEA, *Conference on Civil Liability*, 67.

[248] Vienna Convention, Article I, as amended 1997; Paris Convention, Article 1, as amended 2004.

[249] Vienna Convention, Article II; Paris Convention, Article 4.

[250] Article 1, as amended 2004.

[251] Article XIII.

[252] i.e. the Paris or Vienna Conventions, or other conventions governing maritime cargoes, to the extent that these are not displaced in favour of the Paris and Vienna Conventions by the Convention on Maritime Carriage of Nuclear Material, 1972. See Strohl, in IAEA, *Experience and Trends in Nuclear Law* (Vienna, 1972) 89.

[253] Article 3 of the 1997 Protocol specifically excludes 'nuclear installations used for non-peaceful purposes'.

liability schemes.[254] An OECD study notes that these elements are found in national laws and are not new, but:

'The originality of the system of nuclear liability lies rather in the fact that for the first time these various notions have been systematically applied to a whole industry and have been broadly accepted internationally'.[255]

The choice of no-fault liability was justified on several grounds: it would relieve courts of the difficulty of setting appropriate standards of reasonable care, and plaintiffs of the difficulty of proving breach of those standards, in a relatively new, complex, and highly technical industrial process; the risk of very serious and widespread damage, despite its low probability, placed nuclear power in the ultra-hazardous category; it would be unjust and inappropriate to make plaintiffs shoulder a heavy burden of proof in respect of such an industry whose risks are only acceptable because of its social utility as a source of energy.[256] Thus the arguments are broadly comparable to those used in the case of the state responsibility.

Whether liability is described as absolute, or merely strict, is a matter of degree.[257] The more exculpating factors are recognized the less appropriate it becomes to use the term absolute. Liability is then strict in the limited sense that fault or negligence are not required; in effect the burden of proof is moved to the defendant. On this spectrum, the nuclear liability conventions fall some way between liability for oil pollution damage, where liability is strict rather than absolute,[258] and liability for space objects, where the launch state is exonerated from absolute liability only when the damage on Earth results from the intention or gross negligence of a claimant state or persons it represents.[259]

The imposition of strict or absolute liability for nuclear incidents is supported by a substantial body of national legislation, including some states not parties to the conventions themselves.[260] Reference to national tort laws or civil codes may also

254 *Supra*, Ch 5, section 4.

255 OECD Environment Committee, *Compensation for Nuclear Damage*, 20 *NLB* (1977) 50.

256 *Conference on Civil Liability*, 76; Cigoj, 14 *ICLQ* (1965) 831ff; OECD Environment Committee, *Compensation for Nuclear Damage*, 52. See generally, Goldie, 14 *ICLQ* (1965) 1189; Kelson, 13 *Harv ILJ* (1972) 151; Jenks, 117 *Recueil des Cours* (1966) 99.

257 Goldie, 14 *ICLQ* (1965) 1215; and *id*, 16 *NYIL* (1985) 317. Some writers use these terms interchangeably, however, while others prefer to substitute the term 'responsibility for risk': see e.g. de Arechaga, 159 *Recueil des Cours* (1978) 271ff. These authors are, however, discussing primarily the responsibility of states in international law, not civil liability.

258 *Infra*, Ch 9., section 8(3).

259 1972 Convention on International Liability for Damage Caused by Space Objects, Article VI; Cheng, *Studies in International Space Law* (Oxford, 1997) 326–7.

260 See NEA, *Nuclear Legislation: Third Party Liability* (Paris, 1976). Non-parties with strict liability laws include Canada, Nuclear Liability and Compensation Act, 2015; Japan, Acts Nos 147&148 of 1961 amended by Act No 19 of 2009; Brazil, Act No 6453/1977; Switzerland, Federal Nuclear Energy Liability Act 1983, all available in *Nuclear Legislation in OECD and NEA Countries* at https://www.oecd-nea.org/law/legislation/. US Federal Law, 42 USC 2210, does not specifically impose strict liability but allows for a waiver of defences and of questions of negligence, contributory negligence, and assumption of risk in indemnity cases. In *Duke Power Co v Environmental Study Group*, 438 US 59 (1978) this was held to establish the right to compensation without proof of fault. In cases not covered by Federal Law, strict liability is a matter for state law: see *Silkwood v Kerr McGee Corp*, 464 US 238 (1984); Stason, 12 *Vand LR* (1958) 93.

supply evidence of a general principle of strict or absolute liability for dangerous or unusual activities, but such principles do not invariably cover nuclear installations.[261] One important benefit of the nuclear conventions is thus to clarify and harmonize the standard of liability in national law.

5(3) THE CHANNELLING OF LIABILITY

The channelling of all liability to the operator of nuclear installations or nuclear ships has the advantages of simplifying the plaintiff's choice of defendant and establishing a clear line of responsibility,[262] since one who is not an operator may not be held liable for incidents falling within the terms of the conventions.[263] The possibility of transferring liability to a carrier of nuclear material[264] or a handler of radioactive waste[265] does not materially diminish this concentration of liability, although it provides for an alternative and more extended definition of the term 'operator', and recognizes that there may be a need for special treatment in such cases.[266] Several operators may also be held jointly and severally liable for the same nuclear incident,[267] and the conventions provide rules for determining when liability for materials in transport passes from one operator to another, and when operators become or cease to be liable for material imported or exported.[268]

The choice of the operator as the focus of liability, rather than any other potential defendant, is based on the assumption that the operator of an installation or a ship is usually in the best position to exercise effective responsibility for it, and to secure adequate insurance.[269] This assumption is not universally shared; German, Greek, and Austrian

261 Goldie, 14 *ICLQ* (1965) 1247; Kelson, 13 *Harv ILJ* (1972) 197; Hardy, 36 *BYIL* (1960) 223. It is doubtful whether in the UK publicly operated nuclear installations would at common law be subject to strict liability, either under *Rylands v Fletcher* (1868) LR 3 HL 330 (see *Dunne v NW Gas Board* [1964] 2 QB 806) or nuisance (see *Allen v Gulf Oil* [1981] 1 All ER 353) but liability for nuclear installations is now based on the Nuclear Installations Act 1965.

262 *Conference on Civil Liability*, 72; Hardy, 36 *BYIL* (1960) 247ff; Cigoj, 14 *ICLQ* (1965) 822ff.

263 Vienna Convention, Article II(5) but see also Articles II(2) and IV(5). Paris Convention Article 6(b); Brussels Convention on Nuclear Ships, Article II(2).

264 Vienna Convention, Article II(2); Paris Convention Article 4(d).

265 Vienna Convention, Article II(2); there is no comparable provision in the Paris Convention. See also Brussels Convention on Nuclear Ships, Article II(4).

266 Vienna Convention, Article II(1); Paris Convention, Article 4; Hardy, 36 *BYIL* (1960) 247f; *Conference on Civil Liability*, 74.

267 Vienna Convention, Article II(3) (4); Paris Convention, Article 5(d); Brussels Convention on Nuclear Ships, Article VII; *Conference on Civil Liability*, 75.

268 Vienna Convention, Article II(1); Paris Convention, Articles 4(a) (b); *Conference on Civil Liability*, 73.

269 Hardy, 36 *BYIL* (1960) 247; Cigoj, 14 *ICLQ* (1965) 823; Konz, 57 *AJIL* (1963) 105; Strohl, in IAEA, *Experience and Trends in Nuclear Law*, 89. But cf the 1969 Convention on Civil Liability for Oil Pollution Damage, *infra*, Ch 9., which places liability on the owner of the ship, rather than the operator. However, this Convention allows a right of recourse against operators or others who cause damage intentionally *or recklessly*.

reservations to the Paris Convention allow for persons other than the operator to be held additionally liable.[270] The main argument for this extension is that it strengthens the incentive for all concerned, including manufacturers and suppliers, to behave responsibly.

To some extent the nuclear conventions accept this point, by allowing a liable operator a right of recourse against those who cause nuclear damage intentionally.[271] This is a narrow exception, however, which still leaves the operator solely responsible for the negligence or carelessness of others,[272] unless broader indemnities can be voluntarily negotiated. For most European states, this arrangement has proved acceptable, since operators will be adequately protected by insurance. The criticism that denying wider recourse dilutes the incentive for others to behave responsibly[273] can be met in two ways; states are free to employ criminal law or civil penalties,[274] and the efficient control of construction and operational standards for nuclear installations is arguably a sufficient safety policy.[275]

It is important to note that it makes no difference that the operator of a nuclear installation or ship will in many cases be a state, or state entity. The civil liability conventions ensure that states or their organs are precluded from invoking jurisdictional immunities, except in relation to the execution of judgments.[276] Thus, apart from this exception, states sued under the Conventions will be subject to the same liability, and enjoy the same defences, as other categories of defendants.

5(4) ALLOCATION OF LOSS

The scale of potential damage a serious nuclear accident could cause is likely to be well beyond the capacity of individual operators of nuclear installations to bear.[277] All the nuclear conventions allow each state party to limit the operator's liability. The option of doing so is intended primarily to make insurance easier to obtain.

270 Legislation in Austria and Germany has, however, remained within the terms of the Paris Convention on this point. For the position in the US, see Cameron et al (eds), *Nuclear Energy Law After Chernobyl*, Ch 9.

271 Vienna Convention, Article X; Paris Convention Article 6(f); Brussels Convention on Nuclear Ships, Article II(6).

272 Cf the broader right of recourse allowed under that 1969 Convention on Civil Liability for Oil Pollution Damage, *infra*, Ch 9., section 6(2).

273 Pelzer, 12 *NLB* (1973) 46.

274 *Conference on Civil Liability*, 83; this argument has been the focus of debate in the US: see Cameron et al (eds), *Nuclear Energy Law After Chernobyl*, 146f.

275 OECD, Environment Committee, *Compensation for Nuclear Damage*, 20 *NLB* (1977) 76.

276 Vienna Convention, Article XIV; Paris Convention, Article 13(e); Brussels Convention on Nuclear Ships, Article X(3). The exclusion of jurisdictional immunities was opposed by Soviet bloc representatives at the Vienna Conference, and the inclusion of this provision is one reason for their failure to sign the Convention.

277 The Three Mile Island accident is thought to have cost US $1 billion; $52 million was paid out by insurers: Cameron et al (eds), *Nuclear Energy Law After Chernobyl*, 151ff. Estimates of the possible cost of a core meltdown in the US reach $15 billion: US GAO report, *Nuclear News*, Sept. 1986. The Chernobyl accident may have caused damage in the USSR totalling $3 billion, including $1.2 billion in compensation payments: Shapar and Reyners, *The Nuclear Third Party Liability Regime in Western Europe: The Test of Chernobyl* (OECD, Paris, 1987).

Without it, insurers might be reluctant to cover such potentially enormous risks, or to do so fully.[278] Compulsory insurance is what guarantees the operator's liability.[279] If insurance funds prove insufficient for this purpose, the state must step in and provide them. This is a unique feature of the nuclear conventions; it acknowledges the residual responsibility of states to compensate for damage caused by nuclear activities where the operator is unable to do so or is itself a state.[280] In return for this guarantee of compensation for plaintiffs, it also protects the industry itself from a burden of ruinous liability.[281] Since much will depend on the views of individual insurance markets, and their ability to pool risks internationally, the conventions set only minimum limits and allow states to fix higher ones, or to have no limit at all.[282]

Although all the nuclear conventions focus liability on the operator as the source of damage or pollution, two Supplementary Compensation Conventions acknowledge that this approach is insufficient and involve states in meeting substantial losses in excess of the operator's capacity to cover them through insurance. It cannot be said that any of the nuclear liability conventions fully implements the 'polluter pays' principle or recognizes the unlimited and unconditional liability of states within whose border nuclear accidents occur. What they do recognize, if imperfectly, is that the scale of possible damage has to be widely and equitably borne if nuclear power is to be internationally acceptable. This conclusion further weakens the already tenuous case for treating any of these agreements as evidence for the strict or absolute liability of the source state in international law for the full measure of any damage its nuclear activities may cause.

(a) The Paris Convention Scheme

The scheme adopted in the liability conventions is not intended to cover all loss in full, for by permitting limitation of the operator's liability it necessarily envisages wider distribution of uninsured loss. Partly because the Paris Convention operator liability limit of around €20 million[283] has always been low compared to the probable cost of a serious accident, this Convention is supplemented by a long-established

[278] *Conference on Civil Liability*, 78; Hardy, 36 *BYIL* (1960) 240ff; Cameron et al (eds), *Nuclear Energy Law After Chernobyl*, 109

[279] Vienna Convention, Article VII, as amended 1997; Paris Convention, Article 10; Brussels Convention on Nuclear ships, Article III.

[280] Vienna Convention, Article VII; Brussels Supplementary Convention, Article 3(b)(i). See Miatello, in Spinedi and Simma, *United Nations Codification of State Responsibility*, 297–9, 302–5. There is no comparable arrangement under the 1969 Convention on Civil Liability for Oil Pollution Damage.

[281] *Conference on Civil Liability*, 78.

[282] Vienna Convention, Article V; Paris Convention, Article 7; *Conference on Civil Liability*, 78. Note that the Brussels Convention on Nuclear Ships, Article III, sets a single obligatory limit, following the practice of maritime liability conventions. The Federal German Atomic Energy Act, 1985, was the first to abolish liability ceilings in a Paris Convention state, although for internal claims only. See Pfaffelhuber and Kuchuk, 25 *NLB* (1980) 70. Switzerland and Japan also have unlimited liability. See Shapar and Reyners, *Nuclear Third-Party Liability*, for comparative tables of national liability limits, and Deprimoz, 32 *NLB* (1983) 33.

[283] Article 7 establishes a normal minimum level of 15 million SDRs, equivalent to approximately 20 million Euros.

system of state-funded compensation at a level greatly above the minimum liability limits.[284] The European scheme thus spreads the burden of serious losses more broadly, first to the installation state and then across the community of Western European states as a whole. The important question is whether the overall scheme is adequate and strikes the right balance between state-funded compensation, industry protection, and victim protection. In practice, until revised in 2004, the Paris Convention and the Brussels Supplementary Convention placed the main burden of compensation on governments. The scale of this redistribution can be seen in the figures. Beyond the operator's basic liability a further 175 million SDRs would be drawn from the contracting party in whose territory the nuclear installation is situated and an additional 125 million from all other contracting parties.[285] If the 2004 Protocols ever come into force[286], however, the operator's liability will rise massively to a minimum of €700 million—roughly thirty-five times the present limit—and additional state-funded compensation will take the total available to €1500 million. Moreover, the formula whereby all states parties contribute compensation funds to the common pool has been altered so that 65 per cent of the contribution is based on installed nuclear power and only 35 per cent on GNP, rather than 50 per cent as before. This will make the new scheme a little more attractive to non-nuclear states, although Ireland and Luxemburg remain non-parties at the time of writing. Thus the main burden of funding nuclear damage will shift significantly to nuclear operators (and their insurers) and the total available will offer greater potential for meeting the cost of a significant nuclear accident.

Despite these improvements, however, a really serious accident on the scale of Chernobyl could still result in uncompensated damage beyond the limits of the Paris/Brussels scheme. In this remote possibility, that part of the loss will then lie where it falls, although claims under the general international law of state responsibility remain possible in respect of the uncompensated loss.[287]

Compensation amounts under the revised Paris and Brussels Conventions (2004)

	Before revision	After revision
First tier Operator's liability insurance	SDR 15 million or national limit	€700 million minimum
Second tierInstallation state public funds	Difference between the first tier and SDR 175 million	Difference between first tier and €1200 million

[284] 1963 Brussels Supplementary Convention on Third Party Liability in the Field of Nuclear Energy, as amended by a Protocol of 1982. See Lagorce, in IAEA, *Nuclear Law for a Developing World* (Vienna, 1969) 143; Fornasier, 8 *AFDI* (1962) 762.

[285] 1982 Protocol. 100 million SDRs is worth approximately 140 million Euros.

[286] In 2019 neither protocol was in force.

[287] *Supra*, section 4.

Continued

	Before revision	After revision
Third tier	SDR 125 million	€300 million
All parties contribute according to GNP and installed reactor power (Article 12)	---------------------	---------------------
	TOTAL SDR 315 million = €440 million	*TOTAL €1500 million*

(b) The Vienna Convention Scheme

The Paris Convention scheme for limited liability plus supplementary state-funded compensation provided the model on which revision of the Vienna Convention in 1997 is based.[288] Greatly increased sums are now available to victims of nuclear accidents under this revised scheme which came into force for some states in 2003. First, in all but special cases,[289] the operator's liability under the Vienna Convention has risen to a minimum of 300 million SDRs[290] (approximately US$400 million at 1999 values). Under a new Convention on Supplementary Compensation,[291] the installation state will provide a further 300 million SDRs, and thereafter all other parties also contribute according to a formula under which non-nuclear states contribute less, and the poorest nothing at all, in return for simplified access to compensation at levels that could now exceed $1,000,000,000.[292] Losses beyond that limit can only be recovered in international claims against the state concerned.

In order to make the benefits of the 1997 Supplementary Convention as widely available as possible—to create a genuinely global liability and compensation regime—participation is not confined to parties to the Vienna Convention, but is also open to Paris Convention states (although none have become parties) and to states not party to either convention if their law conforms to the same basic principles of liability for nuclear accidents.[293] Some important nuclear states have taken advantage of this opportunity, including the United States, Canada, Japan and India. For all these states the advantages of participation in the 1997 Protocol are twofold: they gain access to compensation in the event of a serious accident affecting them, as well as the assurance

[288] See IAEA, *Reports of the Standing Committee on Liability for Nuclear Damage,* 1st –17th sessions (1990–97) and for commentary see IAEA, *International Law Series No 3* (Vienna, 2007).

[289] Under Article 5 of the Vienna Convention, as amended 1997, the lowest possible liability which may be set by installation states 'having regard to the nature of the nuclear installation or the nuclear substances involved and to the likely consequences of an incident' is 5 million SDRs. This is not intended to be an appropriate limit for a nuclear reactor.

[290] Vienna Convention, Article V, as amended 1997. A 15-year transitional period is allowed.

[291] See Mc Rae, 95 *NLB* (2015) 7.

[292] 1997 Supplementary Convention, Articles III(1) IV.

[293] 1997 Supplementary Convention, Articles XVIII, XIX. The requirements which must be met by non-parties to the Paris and Vienna Conventions are set out in an annex.

that their own liabilities will be shared across all participating states.[294] Those with least to gain are the non-nuclear states such as Ireland who are not parties to the Paris or Vienna Conventions, because they would have to contribute to the general compensation pool, albeit at a much-reduced level. However, to cater for such cases the convention does make provision for non-party claims.[295]

There is one important limitation on participation in the 1997 Supplementary Convention: it is only open to those states that are also parties to the 1994 Nuclear Safety Convention.[296] Few states would wish to commit themselves to contribute to a compensation fund if the accident risks in some participating states are much higher than in others. This requirement was meant to encourage Eastern European states to meet IAEA fundamental safety requirements[297] if they wish to have access to the protection of the Supplementary Convention. It would have been a significant achievement had Eastern Europe participated as hoped, and they are all now parties to the 1994 Nuclear Safety Convention, but by 2019 only Montenegro and Romania had ratified the Supplementary Convention. It follows that for Russia, Ukraine, and several other Eastern Europe states liability and compensation will still be governed by the old pre-Chernobyl rules of the unreformed 1963 Vienna Convention to which they remain parties.[298] Thus the reality is that hopes of a reformed and truly global nuclear liability regime remain just that—hopes.

5(5) BRINGING CLAIMS UNDER THE CONVENTIONS

The nuclear conventions simplify the jurisdictional issues which would otherwise arise under national law in bringing transboundary civil actions. First, they determine which state has jurisdiction over claims against operators or their insurers. In the case of nuclear installations, the location of the nuclear incident causing the damage, or exceptionally, of the installation itself, is normally the deciding factor.[299] The object of this extended definition, and the reason jurisdiction does not simply follow the location of the installation, is to cater for incidents caused by material in transit. Cases of multiple jurisdiction are to be dealt with by agreement of the parties under the Vienna Convention[300] or by a tribunal under the Paris Convention.[301] This tribunal would decide which court was 'most closely related to the case in question'. However, acknowledging the concerns of coastal states over the risk of pollution damage arising from maritime transport of nuclear cargoes, the 2004 revision of the Paris Convention gives the courts of the coastal state exclusive jurisdiction over claims arising out of incidents in the exclusive economic zone.[302] This conforms to the jurisdictional provisions of the 1992 Convention on Civil Liability for Oil pollution Damage.[303] In the case of nuclear ships, however, both the licensing state and the state or states where the damage occurs have jurisdiction.[304]

294 See Mc Rae, 95 *NLB* (2015) 10–14.
295 *Infra*, section 5(6).
296 Articles XVIII, XIX.
297 *Supra*, section 2.
298 *Supra*, section 5, first paragraph.
299 Vienna Convention, Article XI, as amended, 1997; Paris Convention Article 13.
300 Article XI(3).
301 Article 13(c).
302 Article 13(b).
303 *Infra*, Ch 9.
304 Brussels Convention on Nuclear Ships, Article X.

Second, judgments given by courts competent in accordance with the conventions must be recognized and enforced in other member states, with certain limited exceptions which do not allow reconsideration of the merits of the case.[305] This facility is now of limited practical importance within most of Europe, since judgments will normally be recognized under EU law,[306] but elsewhere it is an important further guarantee of access to compensation funds in transboundary cases.

Lastly, actions brought pursuant to all these conventions must commence within the appropriate limitation period, which in most cases is now thirty years from the date of the nuclear incident, unless national law or the conventions provide differently.[307]

Major international accidents at Chernobyl and Bhopal, as well as the damage done to Kuwait in 1991, have shown the need for claims procedure capable of handling the large number of potential actions which may arise out of a serious accident. The 1997 revisions to the Vienna Convention do not create any special procedure for this purpose, but for the first time they do permit states to bring actions on behalf of their own nationals, domiciles or residents who suffer damage.[308]

5(6) NON-PARTY CLAIMS

The major argument against allowing non-party claims is that with limited funds to call on, adding more claimants will reduce the share available for those in contracting states, without reciprocal benefits. Extension to non-parties may be advantageous, however, if it permits operators to limit their liability to non-party claimants and it may facilitate transport of nuclear materials across non-party territories.[309] A provision on non-parties was deleted from the 1963 text of the Vienna Convention after opposition to the notion that they might benefit.[310] No consistent practice was followed by contracting parties to the 1960 Paris Convention, but several did allow non-party claims to be made.[311] With some qualifications, both the revised Vienna Convention and the Paris Convention now extend the benefit of their provisions on operator

[305] Vienna Convention, Article XII, as amended, 1977; Paris Convention, Article 13(d); Brussels Convention on Nuclear Ships, Article XI(4).

[306] EU Regulation No 1215/2012 on jurisdiction and the recognition and enforcement of judgments in civil and commercial matters.

[307] Vienna Convention, Article VI, as amended 1997; Paris Convention, Article 8, as amended 2004. See FRG, Atomic Energy Act 1985, s 32; UK, Nuclear Installations Act 1965; Switzerland, Federal Nuclear Energy Liability Act 1983.

[308] Vienna Convention, as amended 1997, Article XIA. In the Bhopal accident, the Indian Government passed legislation permitting it to take over the claims brought by the injured victims: *supra*, Ch 5, n 249. See also the claims procedure adopted for the UN Compensation Commission, *supra*, Ch 4, section 2(6)(b).

[309] *Conference on Civil Liability*, 184, para 55.

[310] *Ibid*, Committee of the Whole, 183f; Plenary, 121ff.

[311] Germany, Atomic Energy Act 1985, s 24(4); Denmark, Compensation for Nuclear Damage Act 2014; Finland, Nuclear Liability Act 1972; Netherlands, Act on Liability for Damage Caused by Nuclear Incidents 1979 as amended; Sweden, Nuclear Liability Act 1968; UK, Nuclear Installations Act 1965, as amended by Nuclear Installations (Liability for Damage) Order 2016.

liability to claimants who suffer damage in the territory of a non-contracting state, or to incidents which arise there,[312] but non-party claimants are denied recourse to additional public funds provided under the two Supplementary Conventions unless the other parties agree.[313] Non-parties with nuclear installations on their territory who do not afford reciprocal benefits are also excluded from the liability conventions.[314] Both conventions provide jurisdictional rules for incidents occurring outside the territory of a party,[315] but these provisions are intended to resolve conflicts, not to extend the application of either instrument.

None of these changes are helpful in the case of accidents like Chernobyl, since the issue there involved the liability of a non-party operator rather than extension of benefits to non-party claimants. Non-party operators cannot be held liable under any of the conventions, and jurisdiction will in such cases be determined by ordinary rules of national law, with all the difficulties referred to earlier. Participation in the conventions by nuclear states—the source of potential defendants—is for this reason the best way of gauging international acceptance of the civil liability regime.

5(7) NUCLEAR DAMAGE AND THE ENVIRONMENT

A common feature of the nuclear conventions before 1997 had been their relatively narrow definition of 'damage'. Like the *Trail Smelter* case their focus was on loss of life, personal injury, or loss or damage to property.[316] The Brussels and Vienna Conventions allowed parties to extend this definition, but the legislation of OECD states closely followed the provisions of the Paris Convention.[317] What was clearly missing was a broader environmental or ecological perspective.

Following the model for a new definition of damage in the 1992 Convention on Civil Liability for Oil Pollution Damage,[318] the revised Paris and Vienna Conventions have now been extended to include the costs of preventive measures and reinstatement of the environment, as well as loss of income.[319] This definition affords a more realistic approach to damage if the true costs of nuclear incidents are to be borne by the nuclear industry. Such additional environmental costs might also be recoverable against states in international law, following the outcome of the Canadian claim for clean-up costs arising out of the Cosmos 954 crash.[320]

312 Paris Convention, Article 2, as amended 2004; Vienna Convention as amended 2004, Article 1A.

313 Vienna Supplementary Convention, Article V(1); Brussels Supplementary Convention as amended, Article 2(a) but see also Article 15 which allows extension to non-parties by agreement. But non-parties to the liability conventions may also participate in the Supplementary Compensation Conventions.

314 Paris Convention, Article 2, as amended 2004; Vienna Convention as amended 2004, Article 1A.

315 Vienna Convention, Article XI(2); Paris Convention Article 13(b).

316 Vienna Convention, Article 1(1)(K); Paris Convention, Article 3(a); Brussels Convention on Nuclear Ships, Article 1(7); Noltz, *NLB* (1987) 87, and *supra*, Ch 3, section 5.

317 See OECD, *Nuclear Legislation: Third Party Liability* (Paris, 1976).

318 *Infra*, Ch 9., section 8.

319 Vienna Convention, Article 1(1)(K) as revised, 1997; Paris Convention, Article 1, as revised 2004.

320 See *supra*, Ch 4, section 2.

6 CONCLUSIONS

Despite their longevity, no significant claim has ever been brought under either of the principal nuclear liability conventions, in itself something of a demonstration of the safety of nuclear reactors in the countries which are parties to the relevant conventions. The positive features of the nuclear conventions as models for other environmental liability regimes are self-evident: they facilitate individual access to legal remedies, they eliminate or minimize difficult issues of proof and liability, and they offer a scheme which ensures the availability of compensation funding regardless of the solvency of the defendant. They also provide a precedent for treating ultra-hazardous but socially acceptable activities as risks which require exceptional provision for wider loss distribution, based only in part on the absolute or strict liability of the polluter.

Given the pattern of participation by nuclear states, the Paris and Vienna Conventions' practical significance is mainly confined to Europe and Latin America. The most immediate consequence of the Chernobyl accident has been the growth in parties to the Vienna Convention on Civil Liability, which now include all of Eastern Europe and most of Latin America. Not only has this made upgrading East European reactors less of a liability risk for contractors and those providing assistance, it has also ensured that Western and Eastern Europe are covered by comparable and linked liability regimes. This is important since Europe has the world's largest concentration of nuclear facilities and the highest likelihood of transboundary consequences arising from nuclear incidents. At the same time it is notable that the 2004 revisions to the Paris Convention were still not in force in 2019 and that the 1997 revisions to the Vienna Convention, although in force, had not been widely ratified. For those few states who are parties to the 1997 Vienna Supplementary Compensation Convention (including Canada, India, Japan and the US) the compensation regime now affords better redress in the event of a serious accident, but it remains remarkable that they have not been joined by all the other parties to the Vienna Convention,.

As we have seen, the option of resorting to an international claim against a nuclear state is potentially useful only if the respondent state has failed to exercise its regulatory responsibilities diligently. However, in providing evidence of an internationally agreed standard of due diligence, the 1994 Nuclear Safety Convention does make it easier to identify with more precision what those responsibilities are, and thus potentially provides the basis for a claim in general international law should legal proceedings ever prove necessary.

The evidence considered here does not show that nuclear activities involving significant transboundary risk are prohibited by international law, nor does it indicate that they may take place only on equitable terms agreed with states likely to be affected. Instead, the international community has generally accepted the lawfulness of civil nuclear activities, provided they are regulated to a high standard, adequately monitored by independent national regulatory authorities, and subject to peer review by IAEA member states, with liability regimes in place that afford some assurance of redress for transboundary victims in the event of an accident. These are, in effect, the conditions under which the inherent risk imposed on international society by nuclear states is rendered acceptable. This suggests that any state which cannot or will not adequately regulate its nuclear industry to international standards or make satisfactory arrangements for compensating its non-nuclear neighbours in the event of serious accident should not be permitted the freedom to pursue nuclear activities. The assertion that all states have the right of access to nuclear technology must be seen in this light.

8

INTERNATIONAL REGULATION OF TOXIC AND PERSISTENT POLLUTANTS AND WASTE

1 INTRODUCTION

1(1) THE PROBLEM

Toxic and persistent substances such as chemicals, plastics, industrial wastes, or agricultural pesticides create environmental risks which are international in several senses.[1] First, the release of persistent and potentially toxic substances into the environment may have long-term and cumulative effects on human and animal health over a wide area, including the marine environment. Studies have shown how over many decades persistent organic pollutants such as mercury have been transported to the Arctic,[2] where marine life and animals show significantly higher levels of bio-accumulation than at lower latitudes. These pollutants originate in the industrial areas of Europe, Asia, and North America, but migrate northwards under the influence of winds and oceanic currents. Similarly, 'plastics, including microplastics, in the marine environment are a rapidly increasing problem due to their large and still increasing use combined with the inadequate management and disposal of plastic waste'.[3] While in some cases the release of these toxic or persistent substances into the environment

* We are grateful to Professor James Harrison, University of Edinburgh, for his contribution to revising this chapter.

[1] UNGAOR, 44th Session, *Rept of the Secretary General on Illegal Traffic in Toxic and Dangerous Products and Wastes*, UN Doc A/44/362 (1989); Pallemaerts, *Toxics and Transnational Law* (Oxford, 2002) Ch 1, and *infra*, Ch 9, introduction.

[2] See *infra*, section 2(4).

[3] UNEA Resolution 1/6 (2014) para 4, and *supra*, Ch 9, n 7.

is caused by disposal as waste, or through air- or waterborne emissions, ultimately this problem can only be addressed by minimizing the generation of toxic or persistent substances in industrial products and processes and for agricultural purposes.

Secondly, international trade in wastes and chemicals poses a potential risk of accidental pollution of the marine environment and of transit states. Importing states are also at risk where trade takes place without their knowledge or consent, or where, as in the case of some developing states, they possess inadequate management and scientific facilities, or limited understanding of the risks involved. Many developing countries thus continue to use pesticides and other chemicals long banned or restricted in more developed states. Trade in these circumstances may be a consequence of lower standards of regulation or of a willingness to accept for use or disposal substances banned or regulated elsewhere. Taking advantage of these lower standards involves a transfer of environmental costs from manufacturers in developed industrialized economies to the peoples and environment of developing states who may be least able to bear them. It may also result in significant effects on the rights to life or health, or on other human rights of populations in areas where waste is disposed of or recycled.[4]

Trade in hazardous wastes will be advantageous, however, if it removes for reprocessing or safe disposal substances which could not be dealt with in an environmentally sound manner in the country of origin, or which would otherwise be disposed of at sea. The bulk of this trade does not involve developing states, and a general policy of eliminating it among industrialized nations would be environmentally and economically inefficient and hamper attempts to reduce marine pollution from dumping or land-based sources. Elimination of trade among developed countries would also put further pressure on developing states in Africa, Latin America, and the Caribbean who are already the main recipients of illegal traffic in toxic waste for disposal. The disappearance of landfill sites in industrialized countries, escalating disposal costs, and the difficulty of obtaining approval for incineration facilities have all contributed to a growing demand for waste disposal in the developing world. It is mainly to counter this problem that international regulation of transboundary movements of hazardous waste proved necessary in the 1980s. More recently, however, the disposal of redundant ships, electronic equipment and other potentially valuable wastes has created recycling opportunities for developing states and brought about a shift in policy.

1(2) INTERNATIONAL POLICY

As we will see, the 1972 London Convention, the 1989 Basel Convention, the 1998 Rotterdam Convention on Prior Informed Consent, the 2001 POPs Convention, the 2013 Convention on Mercury, and, in somewhat weaker form, the regional

[4] See UNHRC, *Rept of the Special Rapporteur on the adverse effects of the illicit dumping of toxic and dangerous products and wastes*, UN Doc A/HRC/7/21 (2008) and *infra*, section 4(7).

agreements on land-based sources of marine pollution, share a common philosophy indicative of the trend of contemporary international policy.[5] In general, these agreements have endorsed a precautionary approach which, inter alia, favours reducing the generation of toxic and hazardous or persistent waste through cleaner production technology and processes, eliminating the most harmful chemicals and other materials from production and use, and controlling trade in other categories of hazardous or persistent wastes and substances. International policy can thus be summarized as an attempt to balance environmental protection and economic development.

Agenda 21 of the 1992 Rio Conference set out three priorities. First, it endorsed environmentally sound management, giving priority to waste reduction.[6] Secondly, it proposed international action on land-based sources of pollution.[7] Thirdly, it called for better risk assessment of chemicals and the phasing out or banning of chemicals 'that pose an unreasonable and otherwise unmanageable risk to the environment or human health and those that are toxic, persistent and bio-accumulative and whose use cannot be adequately controlled'.[8] The Johannesburg Plan of Implementation reiterated these policy objectives and it set the goal 'to achieve, by 2020, that chemicals are used and produced in ways that lead to the minimization of significant adverse effects on human health and the environment, using transparent, science-based risk assessment procedures and science-based risk management procedures, taking into account the precautionary approach.'[9] This goal forms the backdrop to much of the work being done by UNEP, and the FAO, IMO, WHO, and the MEAs mentioned above. These decisions point towards an increasing integration of policy, focused on 'environmentally sound management of chemicals and all wastes throughout their life cycle' and a substantial reduction of waste generation 'through prevention, reduction, recycling and reuse'.[10] States have adopted the so-called Strategic Approach to International Chemicals Management, which includes a set of instruments, including a Global Plan of Action on International Chemicals Management overseen by an international conference that meets periodically in order to assess progress in implementing the agreed policy measures.[11] Yet, it remains true that '[t]here is at present no single, overarching international institutional framework for addressing environmental and public health risks from hazardous substances and activities.'[12] Although UN policy has begun

[5] See generally Pallemaerts, *Toxics and Transnational Law*; Wirth, in Bodansky, Brunnée, and Hey (eds), *Oxford Handbook of International Environmental Law* (Oxford, 2007) Ch 17; Kummer Peiry, in Fitzmaurice, Ong and Merkouris (eds), *Research Handbook on International Environmental Law* (Cheltenham, 2010) Ch 29.

[6] *Agenda 21*, Ch 20. See also UNEP, GC Decision SS 11/4 B (1990) 20 *EPL* (1990) 157 and OECD Council Recommendation C(90) 164 on integrated pollution prevention and control, 21 *EPL* (1991) 90.

[7] *Agenda 21*, Ch 17, on which see , Ch 9, section 1(2).

[8] *Agenda 21*, Ch 19.

[9] Johannesburg Plan of Implementation (2002) para 23. See also *The Future We Want* (2012) para 213, and *supra*, Ch 2, sections 2(3) and (4).

[10] 2030 Agenda for Sustainable Development, SDG 12.4 and 12.5, *supra*, Ch 2, section 2(5).

[11] See Perrez, 15 *RECIEL* (2006) 245–257.

[12] Wirth, in Bodansky, Brunnée, and Hey (eds), *Handbook of IEL*, 421.

to address the environmental risks posed by plastics, here too the regulatory and institutional framework 'remains fragmented and elusive.'[13]

2 INTERNATIONAL REGULATION OF TOXIC AND PERSISTENT POLLUTANTS

2(1) INTRODUCTION

If pollution is principally a harmful change in the chemical composition of air, water, and soil, then it could be said that much of international environmental law involves the regulation of chemicals. That is certainly true of air pollution resulting in acid rain, or ozone depletion resulting from the migration of CFCs and other chemicals into the upper atmosphere. We considered these problems in Chapter 6. International regulation of land-based sources of marine pollution, dumping at sea, and international trade in hazardous waste also addresses emission and disposal of chemicals, together with heavy metals, radioactive substances, plastic and biological matter. These subjects are dealt with in later sections of this chapter. In this section we look at international regulation specifically aimed at toxic chemicals and persistent pollutants, including the 1998 Rotterdam Convention on Prior Informed Consent, the 2001 POPs Convention, and the 2013 Convention on Mercury. There is plainly a need to coordinate measures adopted in each of these different but overlapping fields. Cooperation between the 1989 Basel Convention, the 2001 POPs Convention, and the 1998 Rotterdam Convention on Prior Informed Consent is thus essential.[14]

2(2) TRADE IN CHEMICALS: THE ROTTERDAM CONVENTION ON PRIOR INFORMED CONSENT

International trade in chemicals and pesticides is regulated in several ways. Transport of chemicals by sea is regulated by the IMO and is covered by Annexes II and III of the 1973/7 MARPOL Convention.[15] Trade in waste containing toxic chemicals is subject to the prior informed consent and environmentally sound disposal requirements of the 1989 Basel Convention[16], as well as several regional seas protocols.[17] Together with

[13] Schäli, *The Mitigation of Marine Plastic Pollution in International Law: Facts, Policy and Legal Implications* (PhD submitted to the University of Bern, 2020). See also UNEP, *Combating Marine Plastic Litter and Microplastics: An Assessment of the Effectiveness of Relevant International, Regional and Subregional Governance Strategies and Approaches*, UNEP/EA.3/INF/5 99 (2018) and UNEA Resolutions 4/6 and 4/9 (2019).

[14] See UNEP, *Rept of Ad hoc Joint WG on Enhancing Cooperation and Coordination*, UNEP/FAO/CHW/RC/POPs/WG 2/18 (2008). In 1995 FAO, ILO, OECD, UNEP, UNIDO, and WHO also created an Inter-organization Programme for the Sound Management of Chemicals: see 34 *ILM* (1995) 1311.

[15] See *infra*, Ch 9, section 4. [16] See *infra*, section 4.

[17] E.g. 1996 Izmir Protocol on the Prevention of Pollution of the Mediterranean Sea by Transboundary Hazardous Wastes and their Disposal ('Mediterranean Protocol'); 1998 Tehran Protocol on the Control of Marine Transboundary Movements and Disposal of Hazardous Wastes and Other Wastes.

guidelines on trade in chemicals and pesticides adopted by UNEP and the FAO,[18] the 1989 Basel Convention provided a model for the 1998 Rotterdam Convention on Prior Informed Consent, adopted in 1998.[19] This Convention applies only to international trade in 'banned or severely restricted chemicals' and 'severely hazardous pesticides' judged to pose a risk to human health or the environment.[20] It does not prohibit trade, but creates a procedure designed to ensure prior informed consent by the state of import. The 1998 Convention covers two situations.

First, where the state of export has banned or severely restricted use of a chemical in its territory, it must give prior notification of any export to other states and provide the required information. It is for the state of import to determine its response in accordance with its rights under the 1998 Convention (Article 12). This is an important provision that seeks to prevent companies based in developed countries continuing to export hazardous chemicals and pesticides that have been banned in their home country to developing countries, which may be unaware of the risks.

Secondly, the 1998 Convention regulates trade in particular chemicals and pesticides listed in Annex III. Upon listing, each party must notify the Convention secretariat whether it wishes to ban, limit, or permit import of the listed substances. Trade may continue with those states that indicate their willingness to permit imports, whereas exporting states must take measures to ensure that exporters within their jurisdiction comply with any limits or bans on trade that have been notified (Article 11). States that ban imports must also prohibit production for domestic consumption (Article 10(9)) in order to comply with WTO rules on non-discrimination.[21]

At the time of writing thirty-two pesticides and fourteen industrial chemicals have been included in Annex III. The process to add further substances to the Annex is complex and 'a major challenge.'[22] Once the Secretariat has received notification of regulatory action from states in at least two regions regarding a particular chemical,[23] it must inform the Chemical Review Committee, whose task is to make a recommendation on listing to the COP. It follows from this procedure that a chemical widely banned in Europe could not be considered for listing unless a state in another region supported the proposal. A slightly different procedure exists for severely hazardous pesticides which can be proposed for listing by a developing country or a country with an economy in transition if use within its territory is causing problems.[24] Criteria set out in Annexes II and IV require the Review Committee to make a scientific assessment of the proposing

[18] FAO, International Code of Conduct on the Distribution and Use of Pesticides (rev'd 2002); UNEP, London Guidelines for the Exchange of Information on Chemicals in International Trade (rev'd 1989). See Pallemaerts, *Toxics in Transnational Law*, 441–556; Victor, Raustiala and Skolnikoff (eds), *The Implementation and Effectiveness of International Environmental Commitments* (Cambridge, Mass, 1998) Ch 6.

[19] See Pallemaerts, *Toxics in Transnational Law*, 557–94.

[20] Article 3. For definitions of these terms see Article 2.

[21] On the WTO aspects of the negotiation see Pallemaerts, *Toxics in Transnational Law*, 584–94.

[22] VanderZwaag, 33 *Houston JIL* (2010–11) 605, 617.

[23] Article 5(5). There are 7 regions: see *Rept of 1st COP*, decision RC-1/2 (2002).

[24] Article 6(1).

state's risk evaluation and the need for PIC controls to be applied.[25] Among other factors, they must take into account whether the risk exists 'only in a limited geographical area or in other limited circumstances'. This emphasizes again the need for a chemical to pose problems beyond a single region. The final decision whether to amend the list is a political judgement taken by the COP.[26] Such decisions require consensus, which gives every state a veto, but once adopted they enter into force for all parties without the need for further ratification and with no right to opt out.[27] This is an unusual procedure, about which some states had expressed concern during negotiations, and it was not adopted in the 2001 POPs Convention, which follows the more common majority vote/opt-out procedure also employed by the 1987 Montreal Protocol for adding additional ozone-depleting substances. This has meant that listing of additional chemicals in Annex III is far from automatic and there have been examples where a recommendation to list a chemical banned in several regions and supported by the Review Committee was not adopted despite meeting all the necessary criteria because of objections from a small number of states in the COP.[28] The ability of any state to block the listing of additional chemicals or pesticides, however harmful they are shown to be, is plainly open to abuse and seems to be an obvious weakness of the regime. At the seventh COP, in 2015, it was agreed to investigate options for improving the effectiveness of the process,[29] although any change that required an amendment to the treaty would require consent of all the relevant states.[30]

It is noteworthy that the 1998 Rotterdam Convention on Prior Informed Consent makes no reference to the precautionary principle. While this omission may in practice have made no difference to the unsuccessful attempts at listing, the 2001 POPs Convention does not make the same mistake.[31] It is also notable that, unlike the 1989 Basel Convention, the 1998 Convention makes no provision for illegal traffic nor does it require the state of export to accept re-importation of illegally exported chemicals. This is a particularly unfortunate omission since the UNEP Governing Council had drawn attention to illegal traffic in the decision initiating the negotiations.[32] Although Article 17 requires a non-compliance procedure to be negotiated 'as soon as practicable', it took until 2019 for a new Annex VII on compliance to be adopted, demonstrating the problem with putting off such decisions until the entry into force of an instrument.[33] There is thus considerable room for further evolution in a dysfunctional convention whose already modest terms reflect the influence of a powerful international chemical industry and the resistance

[25] Articles 5(6), 6(5). [26] Article 7(2). [27] Article 22(5).

[28] See e.g. the protracted debate over the listing of chrysotile asbestos in *Rept of the COP to the Rotterdam Convention on the work of its seventh session*, 4–15 May 2015, Document UNEP/FAO/RC/COP.7/21, paras 87–98.

[29] See COP Decision RC-7/5.

[30] 1998 Rotterdam Convention on Prior Informed Consent, Article 21(5). [31] See next section.

[32] UNEP GC, Decision 18/12 (1995). See also UNCED, *Agenda 21*, Ch 19, paras 19.66–8 and UNGA Res 44/226 (1989) both of which refer to 'illegal traffic in toxic and dangerous products and wastes'.

[33] See Decision RC-9/7 (2019), with the Compliance Committee expected to be established in 2021. Contrast the approach of the Minamata Convention, discussed below.

of a number of industrialized states. It is not surprising that the procedures of the older UNEP and FAO voluntary schemes are regarded as more environmentally friendly.[34] Nevertheless, the Convention makes an interesting link between action that is taken at the domestic level and the triggering of international obligations and, despite its 'immensely cumbersome and complicated'[35] procedures, states have managed to agree on the addition of new chemicals, demonstrating that the system can work in practice. The only industrialized state not a party to the 1998 Convention is the US.

2(3) PERSISTENT ORGANIC POLLUTANTS: THE POPS CONVENTION

A small group of chemicals have become the subject of specific international regulation because of their persistent, toxic, and bio-accumulative character. Known generically as persistent organic pollutants ('POPs') these chemicals are now recognized as posing long-term hazards to human and animal health over a wide area, often far from where they originate. Some are produced for industrial or agricultural use, such as PCBs and DDT. Others, mainly dioxins and furans, are emitted incidentally by industrial processes. All can end up in the food chain. Like CFCs, the most appropriate policy for all of them is to phase out production and consumption, while allowing for essential uses and encouraging a switch to less harmful substitutes and processes. These are the principal objectives of the POPs Convention, adopted in 2001.[36] At the time of writing the Convention was in force with 184 parties, the US again being the prominent exception amongst the main industrialized states.[37] The treaty has five distinct features.

First, the 2001 POPs Convention expressly proclaims a precautionary approach to the protection of human health and the environment (Article 1). On that basis, and following the model of the 1987 Montreal Protocol and the 1998 UNECE POPs Protocol,[38] states are required to prohibit or eliminate the production and use of nine chemicals listed in Annex A, and to restrict production and use of DDT as indicated in Annex B (Article 3). Specific exemptions allow continued import and use of some of these substances for a limited period, provided that each state making use of this facility is identified on a public register held by the secretariat (Article 4). This system of country-specific exceptions was designed to allow for special needs of particular countries to be identified, subject to periodic review by the parties. A state wishing to renew an exception must justify its request to the other parties. This appears to imply that the parties may reject the application if they are not satisfied by the reasons given.

[34] Pallemaerts, *Toxics in Transnational Law*, 578. [35] Kummer, 8 *RECIEL* (1999) 323–330, 329.

[36] For a discussion of the negotiation, see Lallas, 95 *AJIL* (2001) 692, 695; 19 *UCLA J Env L&P* (2000/1) 83, 114–46.

[37] On the US position see Fuller and McGarrity, 28 *Wm & Mary Env L & Pol Rev* (2003) 1.

[38] 1998 POPs Protocol to the 1979 Convention on Long-range Transboundary Air Pollution, *supra*, Ch 6.

If that is correct then it gives the POPs Convention a control mechanism which effectively reverses the burden of proof and leaves no possibility of retaining an exemption by opting out of COP decisions. This resembles the prior-justification procedure once used to control dumping of waste at sea under the 1972 Oslo Dumping Convention. Once all exemptions have expired no further requests may be made and use of that chemical is then banned outright.[39]

Secondly, measures must be taken to deal with existing stocks of POPs and the processes which emit them. Stockpiles of substances listed in Annexes A and B are to be identified, managed, and disposed of in a 'safe, efficient and environmentally sound manner'. (Article 6) Ultimate disposal will entail destruction of their persistent organic content. Anthropogenic releases of POPs listed in Annex C must be minimized and eventually eliminated 'where feasible' through action plans, substitute materials and processes, and other practical measures that can 'expeditiously achieve a 'realistic and meaningful level of release reduction or source elimination'.[40] For this purpose parties must 'promote' the use of BAT and best environmental practices ('BEP') defined in Article 5 of the Convention and through decisions of the COP, for existing sources and they must require new sources to use them within four years from entry into force. This aspect of the Convention represents a considered compromise between those who sought complete elimination and other states that regarded this as unrealistic in the short term.[41] Initial proposals to set targets and a timetable for reducing and eliminating emissions were not pursued, and Article 5 emerged as an obligation of conduct (to take the specified measures)—rather than one of result (reducing/eliminating emissions). It was the subject of litigation in the *Pulp Mills Case* where Uruguay argued that the technology it proposed to use met the required BAT standard.[42]

Thirdly, again following the model of the 1987 Montreal Protocol, trade is restricted. Export and import of listed chemicals or wastes is banned unless intended for permitted use or for environmentally sound disposal (Article 3(2)). Export to non-parties is allowed only if they also comply with the principal requirements of the Convention.[43] None of these trade restrictions poses any problem of compatibility with WTO rules: they are non-discriminatory, have protection of human and animal health as their principal aim, and cannot be characterized as a 'disguised restriction on international trade'.[44]

Fourthly, although the 2001 POPs Convention is not a framework convention in the normal sense, further annexes can be added and it is open to the parties to list additional chemicals in the annexes. This option has been used to increase the scope of chemicals covered by the Convention; 14 substances have been listed since 2009. Like the 1998 Rotterdam Convention on Prior Informed Consent, proposals to add other chemicals are assessed by experts in a Review Committee whose processes are designed to allow transparency and informed recommendations based on a 'risk

[39] Article 4(9). [40] Article 5(b). [41] Lallas, 95 *AJIL* (2001) 702.
[42] ICJ Reports (2010), paras 220, 228. [43] See Article 3(2)(b).
[44] 1994 GATT, Article XX. See *infra*, Ch 13.

profile' which identifies the likelihood of 'significant adverse human health and/or environmental effects such that global action is warranted'.[45] Here too the precautionary principle reappears: 'Lack of full scientific certainty shall not prevent the proposal from proceeding'.[46] Nevertheless, the committee has been criticized for allowing lack of full scientific certainty to delay action, frustrating the effective implementation of the precautionary approach.[47] Furthermore, the final decision is a made by the COP. This decision should also be taken 'in a precautionary manner', suggesting that, unlike the 1998 Rotterdam Convention on Prior Informed Consent, uncertainty will be resolved in favour of listing,[48] but it will rely upon the political will of the parties to make this a reality. Unlike the 1998 Rotterdam Convention on Prior Informed Consent, listing decisions can be made by a three-quarter majority vote if there is no consensus, so it is easier to list new substances.[49] Nevertheless, it remains open to any state to opt out within a year if it does not wish to be bound.[50]

Another reflection of the precautionary approach is found in Articles 3(3) and (4) which call upon parties to take measures, through established regulatory and assessment schemes for new chemicals, to prevent the production and use of new pesticides or new industrial chemicals which exhibit the characteristics of POPs. Yet, this obligation does not go as far as requiring states to set up regulatory and assessment schemes for new chemicals where they do not already exist and there are no minimum standards by which states must comply; states are merely required to 'take into account' the POPs criteria in the Convention.

Fifthly, while there is no express reference to 'common but differentiated responsibility' in the Convention, it shares the main elements of this concept with the 1987 Montreal Protocol. Most importantly there are commitments by developed states to make technology, technical assistance, and funding available to developing states parties.[51] It is recognized that 'the extent to which developing country Parties will effectively implement their commitments' will depend on the developed countries fulfilling their side of this bargain.[52] Moreover, while sustainable economic development and poverty eradication are acknowledged to be the 'first and overriding priorities' of developing states, Article 13 appears to envisage a balance between these considerations and 'the need for protection of human health and the environment'. The 'specific needs and special situation' of the least developed states and small island states are also to be taken fully into account. Unlike the 1987 Montreal Protocol, however, there are no special timescales for developing-state elimination of listed chemicals, but developing states are more likely to rely on the exemptions for continued use of certain POPs.

[45] Article 8. See Annexes D, E, F for details of information required to make this judgement.

[46] Article 8(7)(a). [47] Ditz and Tuncak, 23 *RECIEL* (2014) 181–194, 187. [48] Article 8(9).

[49] At the seventh meeting of the COP in 2015, a vote was taken on the listing of pentachlorophenal: see Rept of the 7th Meeting, UNEP/POPs/COP.7/36, paras 145–149.

[50] Article 22(3). See also Article 25(4) which allows a party to substitute an opt-in procedure at the time of ratification.

[51] Articles 12, 13. [52] Article 13(4).

All of these provisions suggest that developing country elimination of POPs will proceed more slowly than elsewhere unless other parties show adequate solidarity. It is particularly important therefore that a financial mechanism administered by the GEF is created for the purpose of assisting developing countries to implement the Convention (Article 13(6)). The COP is empowered to give guidance to the GEF mechanism on policy and programme priorities and to review the effectiveness of the Convention and the financial mechanism at periodic intervals.[53] In practice, there has been a gap between the required funding identified by the COP and the funding provided and this problem is only likely to increase as the scope of the Convention expands.[54] In this regard, a review of the financial mechanism has identified a need for the COP to provide more explicit guidance on funding priorities for the GEF, although the same report also points out that the GEF has not always followed COP guidance in the past.[55]

Finally, there are requirements for all parties to report on national implementation (Article 15). By 2019 the parties had still been unable to agree on a non-compliance procedure and it has been observed that 'the treaty's stringent obligations and growing mandate, and the difficulties parties have had in accessing funds to support implementation, mean that establishment of the non-compliance procedures would contradict the interests of many States.'[56]

2(4) THE MINAMATA CONVENTION ON MERCURY

The Convention on Mercury, adopted in 2013, addresses a single substance, mercury, and related compounds, which have been known to cause significant health and environmental threats for decades.[57] A global treaty was deemed to be necessary due to the problems associated with long-range transport and bioaccumulation. The Preamble to the Convention recognizes that 'mercury is a chemical of global concern' but it makes a special mention of 'the particular vulnerabilities of Arctic ecosystems and indigenous communities because of the bio-magnification of mercury and contamination of traditional foods.' The risks in this region are increased, but nevertheless require global action to tackle them.

Many of the substantive provisions of the 2013 Convention on Mercury draw upon previous treaties in this field. In relation to mercury-added products and processes in which mercury compounds are used the Convention utilizes a listing procedure modelled upon the 2001 POPs Convention, which requires states to phase out specific products or processes by a set date, subject to country-specific exemptions registered with the Secretariat (Articles 4-6). One way in which the 2013 Convention

53 Articles 13(6) 13(7) 16.

54 *Third Review of the Financial Mechanism—Note by the Secretariat*, UNEP/POPs/COP.6/23 (2012) 6.

55 *Id*, 4–5.

56 See Templeton and Kohler, 23 *RECIEL* (2014) 211–220, 219.

57 See Eriksen and Perrez, 23 *RECIEL* (2014) 195–210, 206; VanderZwaag, *China Oceans LR* (2015) 208; Smith, in Sancin and Dine (eds), *International Environmental Law: Contemporary Concerns and Challenges in 2014* (Ljubljana, 2014) 715.

on Mercury goes beyond the 2001 POPs Convention is that exemptions may only be extended once for a five-year period, essentially meaning that all of the products and processes will be phased out within ten years of the entry into force of the Convention. The Convention is more lenient when it comes to emissions to the atmosphere, however, and it simply requires states to control and 'where feasible' reduce emissions from the point sources listed in Annex D (Article 8(1)). For new sources of emissions states must use BAT and BEP (Article 8(4)) defined in a similar way to the 2001 POPs Convention.

A significant achievement of the 2013 Convention on Mercury is the regulation of the sources of mercury. Essentially, new primary mercury mining is banned and parties are only permitted to continue existing mining operations for fifteen years after the entry into force of the Convention (Article 3). Special provisions apply to artisanal and small-scale gold mining (Article 7). Finally, the Convention deals with waste, the interim storage of mercury, and contaminated sites (Articles 10-12), making explicit reference to the 1989 Basel Convention, albeit with the caveat that the relevant definitions from the latter treaty cannot be applied to non-parties to the 1989 Basel Convention; this provision is largely aimed at the US, which would not have been able to accept the treaty with a reference to another treaty to which it is not a party. The Convention does not refer to the precautionary approach, presumably because the harmful effects of mercury are widely known and there is no relevant scientific uncertainty.[58]

Unlike the Rotterdam and POPs Conventions, the 2013 Convention on Mercury establishes an implementation and compliance committee (Article 15). Given the impasse in agreeing compliance procedures under the other chemical treaties, the 2013 Convention on Mercury has been held up as 'groundbreaking and very progressive.'[59] However, the remit of the Committee is much more limited than comparable institutions under other treaties, which raises doubts over whether effectiveness has been sacrificed for the sake of agreement.[60] Unlike e.g. the 1997 Kyoto Protocol, the 2013 Convention on Mercury compliance mechanism is solely 'facilitative in nature' meaning that states will not be penalised if they are found to be in non-compliance. Templeton and Kohler note that 'facilitative measures are not without drawbacks.'[61] Moreover, the Committee is limited to considering issues on the basis of written reports from a state about its own compliance, national reports submitted by states under the Convention, or situations referred to it by the COP. The ability of the secretariat or another individual contracting party to independently trigger the non-compliance procedure is notably absent. Compliance will also be assisted by the existence of a 'two-track' mechanism[62] that includes a GEF Trust Fund and a 'specific international programme to support capacity-building and technical assistance.' (Article 13(6)) The financial provisions are notable for emphasizing that all parties, within their

58 Eriksen and Perrez, 23 *RECIEL* (2014) 195, 201.

59 Eriksen and Perrez, 23 *RECIEL* (2014) 195, 208. 60 *Ibid*, 215. 61 *Ibid*. 62 *Ibid*, 216.

capabilities, should contribute to these mechanisms, thus moving away from the more rigid developed/developing country dichotomy that is found in other treaties.

The 2013 Convention entered into force in 2017; it is notable, particularly in light of its attitude to other chemicals treaties, that the US was the first country to ratify. During negotiations the US made sure the treaty did not go beyond its existing domestic law.

Taken together, the existing treaties on chemicals and hazardous waste offer a degree of protection to human health and the environment, but they do not cover all known threats or risks. Other heavy metals, such as lead and cadmium,[63] as well as electric and electronic materials, are good examples of gaps in the international legal framework.[64] In the early negotiations for a legally binding instrument on mercury, some states had suggested the adoption of a framework convention that could be amended in future to add other chemicals of concern, although this approach was not pursued due to heavy resistance from the US, Canada and Japan amongst others. The problem-by-problem approach has been criticized by some commentators due to the increased costs and the need for large numbers of meetings.[65] Some efforts have been made to increase synergies between the existing treaties, such as holding joint COP meetings,[66] but new instruments will still be needed if gaps in the international legal regime are to be filled.[67] In the meantime, efforts to coordinate national approaches take place through various non-binding initiatives such as the International Conference on Chemicals Management, the Strategic Approach to International Chemicals Management,[68] or voluntary partnerships led by UNEP.

3 POLLUTION OF THE MARINE ENVIRONMENT FROM LAND-BASED SOURCES

3(1) INTRODUCTION

As we explain in the next chapter, only since adoption of the 1982 UNCLOS has there been general recognition of an obligation to protect the marine environment from pollution originating from land-based sources.[69] Regional treaties amplify

63 See Decision I/5 of the UNEP Environmental Assembly (2014) para 25.

64 See e.g. Kummer Peiry, in Fitzmaurice, Ong and Merkouris (eds), *Research Handbook on IEL*, 174.

65 See e.g. Kummer Peiry, *ibid*, 174.

66 See Rotterdam COP Decision RC-4/11; Stockholm COP Decision SC-4/34; Basel COP Decision BC-IX/10. See also Minamata Convention, Article 24(4).

67 See UNEP, *Global Chemical Outlook* (2013) 183. The report identifies strong industry resistance as a reason for the lack of progress on lead and cadmium.

68 See e.g. Perez, 15 *RECIEL* (2006) 245–257.

69 See generally Harrison, *Saving the Oceans through Law* (Oxford, 2017) Ch 4; Vanderzwaag, and Powers, 23 *IJMCL* (2008) 423; Hassan, *Protecting the Marine Environment from Land- based Sources of Pollution* (Farnham, 2006); Mensah, in Boyle and Freestone (eds), *International Law and Sustainable Development* (Oxford, 1999) Ch 13; Williams and Davis, 29 *O&CM* (1995) 207; Boyle, 16 *Marine Policy* (1992) 20–35.

and implement the general provisions of Part XII of 1982 UNCLOS.[70] Article 207 of UNCLOS does no more than establish a general framework for the regulation of land-based sources of marine pollution.[71] It requires states to take measures, including the adoption of laws and regulations, to prevent, reduce, and control pollution from land-based sources. The definition of 'land-based sources' includes 'rivers, estuaries, pipelines and outfall structures', to which regional treaties usually add pollution from coastal establishments, and sometimes also from airborne sources.[72] The 1996 Mediterranean Protocol on Transboundary Movement of Hazardous Waste and 1999 Caribbean LBS Protocol cover 'activities' as well as sources, while the 1992 OSPAR Convention for the Protection of the Marine Environment of the NE Atlantic ('OSPAR Convention') and Helsinki Convention refer to pollution from 'point or diffuse inputs from all sources on land', whether these are waterborne, airborne, or come directly from the coast. It is clear that these definitions are meant to be fully comprehensive of all possible inputs to the sea. However, seabed installations are generally dealt with separately by all of the relevant treaties, including the 1982 UNCLOS, and for that reason are not considered here.[73]

Unlike the 1982 UNCLOS articles dealing with pollution from ships, dumping, or seabed installations, Article 207 does not require adherence to any minimum international standards established by international organizations. States must, however, take account of 'internationally agreed rules, standards and recommended practices and procedures'.[74] The international rules and standards found in the 2001 POPs Convention and the 2013 Convention on Mercury would fall within Article 207,[75] but there are currently no international rules or standards controlling plastic that

[70] 1978 Kuwait Convention on Protection of the Marine Environment from Pollution, Articles 3, 6; 1981 Abidjan Convention for the Protection and Development of the Marine and Coastal Environment of the West and Central African Region, Articles 4, 7; 1982 Jeddah Convention for the Conservation of the Red Sea and Gulf of Aden, Articles 1, 6; 1983 Cartagena Convention for the Protection and Development of the Marine Environment of the Wider Caribbean, Articles 4, 7; 1985 Nairobi Convention for the Marine and Coastal Environment of the East African Region, Articles 1, 7; 1986 Noumea Convention for the Protection of the Natural Resources and Environment of the South Pacific Region, Articles 5, 7; 1992 OSPAR Convention, Article 2; 1992 Helsinki Convention for the Protection of the Marine Environment of the Baltic Sea Area, Article 3; 1992 Convention on the Protection of the Black Sea Against Pollution, Articles 5, 7; 1995 Barcelona Convention for the Protection of the Marine Environment and Coastal Region of the Mediterranean, Articles 4, 8.

[71] For the drafting history of Article 207, see Nordquist (ed), *United Nations Convention on the Law of the Sea: A Commentary*, iv (Dordrecht, 1991) 125–34.

[72] See for example 1983 Quito Protocol, Article 2; 1981 Abidjan Convention, Article 7; 1983 Cartagena Convention, Article 7; 1985 Nairobi Convention, Article 7; 1986 Noumea Convention, Article 7; 1974 Nordic Convention for the Protection of the Environment, Article 1; 1990 Kuwait Protocol for the Protection of the Marine Environment against Pollution from Land-based Sources, Article 1; 1992 Protocol on Protection of the Black Sea Marine Environment against Pollution from Land-based Sources, Article 1; 1996 Protocol for the Protection of the Mediterranean Sea against Pollution from Land-based Sources and Activities, Article 1; 1999 Caribbean Protocol, Article 1.

[73] See next chapter.

[74] Articles 207(1) (5). See also 3rd UNCLOS, *Official Records*, ii (1974) 317, para 20 (Canada) 328 (China) and cf Kenyan draft articles A/CONF 62/C 3/42 (1974) and 10-power draft, A/CONF 62/C 3/L 6 (1974) ibid, iii, 245, 249.

[75] See previous section, and Harrison, *Saving the Oceans through Law*, Ch 4.

might do so.[76] National laws must also minimize 'to the fullest extent possible' the release of toxic, harmful, noxious, or persistent substances, but it is for each state to determine what measures to take and whether action should be global, regional, bilateral, or national. Again, the POPs and Mercury Conventions would be relevant when applying this article. It is otherwise for each state to determine which substances require regulation and control; the essential point is that it is not discharges of waste which are the object of this obligation, but only discharges which result in 'pollution' as defined by Article 1(1)(4). As we saw in Chapter 3, this term provides only the most general guidance, and precludes useful generalization. Its effect is to give states a further discretion in their implementation of Article 207. This partly explains the significant variations in what different regional treaties prohibit or control, despite their almost identical definition of pollution,[77] and shows how contingent on the circumstances of each sea interpretation of this term proves to be in practice. Thus, one of the objects of regional treaties is to identify which substances will be treated as causing 'pollution' and in what circumstances.[78] One result is that the input of plastics to the marine environment is better regulated and controlled in some regions than in others.[79]

Articles 122 and 123 of the Convention, which deal with enclosed and semi-enclosed seas, merely reaffirm the general position that states must cooperate in measures of environmental protection. They do not alter the conclusion that, with regard to the control of land-based pollution, states have a wide discretion concerning the action they must take. At most, these articles may sustain a stronger obligation to cooperate in negotiating common pollution standards than is implied for oceanic areas by Article 207 alone.[80] Major regional agreements on land-based marine pollution are not limited to enclosed or semi-enclosed seas, nor do institutional arrangements treat enclosed and semi-enclosed seas differently from other oceanic areas.[81] Thus, although it provides the convention's only significant legal basis for protecting the marine environment from land-based pollution, Article 207 is drafted in terms which give no specific

[76] UNEP, *Combating Marine Plastic Litter and Microplastics: An Assessment of the Effectiveness of Relevant International, Regional and Subregional Governance Strategies and Approaches*, UNEP/EA.3/INF/5 99 (2018).

[77] Based on Article 1(1)(4) of UNCLOS. Some of the newer treaties refer to 'marine ecosystems' rather than 'marine life'. See 1992 OSPAR Convention, Article 1(d); 1992 Helsinki Convention, Article 2(1); 1995 Barcelona Convention, Article 2; 1999 Caribbean Protocol, Article 1(3); 1992 Black Sea Convention, Article 2(1); 1983 Quito Protocol, Article III; 1982 Jeddah Convention, Article 1(3); 1985 Nairobi Convention, Article 2(b); 1978 Kuwait Convention, Article 1(a); 1986 Noumea Convention, Article 2(f).

[78] Compare 1996 Mediterranean Protocol, Annex 1; 1992 Helsinki Convention, Annex 1; 1992 OSPAR Convention, Annex 1, and see *infra*.

[79] *Supra*, n 76.

[80] Vukas, in Vidas (ed), *Protecting the Polar Marine Environment* (Cambridge, 2000) Ch 2; Fitzmaurice, in Barrett and Barnes (eds), *The Law of the Sea: UNCLOS as a Living Treaty* (London, 2016) 293–325.

[81] See *infra*, and c.f. UNEP, Principles of Conduct in the Field of the Environment Concerning Natural Resources Shared by Two or More States, *supra*, Ch 3. The Executive Director of UNEP has referred to enclosed and semi-enclosed seas as examples of shared resources, UNEP Doc GC/44, (1975) para 86.

content to the underlying obligation of due diligence found in customary law. Like the comparable provision dealing with atmospheric pollution (Article 212) it lacks both the more precise content of the articles concerned with pollution from dumping or from ships, or any comparable means for its direct enforcement.[82]

The reasons for this are that states were generally unwilling to adopt a stronger text during the 1982 UNCLOS negotiations. They wished to preserve for themselves as much freedom of action as possible in balancing environmental protection measures against the needs of their own economies, where land-based activities generate much of the most harmful pollution. For this reason, Article 207(4) explicitly allows account to be taken of 'characteristic regional features, the economic capacity of developing states and their need for economic development'.[83]

This phraseology leaves little doubt that states did not wish to commit themselves to the same level of international control as is imposed on other sources of marine pollution. The social and economic costs of such measures were seen as unacceptably high, and the preferred solution was thus a weaker level of international regulation, a greater latitude for giving preference to other national priorities, and resort to regional co-operation as the primary level at which international action should occur. The largely hortatory character of this policy is evident in the wording of Article 207(3)–(4) which provide that states shall 'endeavour' to harmonize their policies at the appropriate regional level and to establish global and regional rules. Article 123 is similarly elusive with regard to enclosed or semi-enclosed seas, requiring states only to 'endeavour' to coordinate the implementation of their rights and duties with respect to protection of the marine environment. These formulations are without significant normative content. They tend to demonstrate that, as it stands, Article 207 does not require states to take strong or effective measures.

At the time it was drafted, Article 207 did correspond to the practice of states, regionally and nationally. When compared to the most advanced regional regimes in operation some forty years later, it is less clear that it still does so. International practice has introduced a more stringent approach to the regulation of land-based sources, particularly at the regional level, although there is still significant diversity across different regions.

3(2) REGIONAL ADOPTION OF COMMON STANDARDS

As we have seen elsewhere, the main environmental benefit of common standards of pollution prevention is that they ensure a coordinated approach in areas of common interest such as enclosed or semi-enclosed seas.[84] In the case of industrial pollution an important further benefit is the economic advantage derived from a reduction in

[82] Cf *infra*, section 3(6) *and* Ch 9.

[83] See also 1996 Mediterranean Protocol, Article 7(2); 1983 Quito Protocol, Article 6, and 3rd UNCLOS, *Official Records, supra*, n 71.

[84] See generally Harrison, *Saving the Oceans through Law*, Ch 4

unfair competition. The counter-arguments applied to land-based sources of pollution are also important, however. Strict regulation of this form of pollution has substantial economic, social, and political implications for industrial economies and developing states alike. Those wishing to protect their freedom to decide for themselves how to develop sustainably may rely on assertions of national autonomy in the use of territory and permanent sovereignty over natural resources in order to limit the possibilities for international regulation, oversight, and enforcement. Moreover, geographical and ecological considerations point to substantial differences in the absorbtive capacity of different seas. Although land-based pollution affects most coastal areas, shallow, enclosed or semi-enclosed, seas such as the Baltic, North Sea, or Mediterranean are especially sensitive,[85] and need greater protection than open oceanic areas. All of these considerations may point to the doubtful utility of seeking detailed international regulation of land-based sources of pollution and help explain the relatively weak framework approach adopted by the 1982 UNCLOS and the UNEP regional-seas programme. Not surprisingly, where they have been willing to cooperate, states have preferred regional or sub-regional arrangements, believing that they offer greater flexibility in accommodating the economic, geopolitical, and ecological needs of particular seas and their adjacent states and provide a better basis for common standards of regulation. But the main consequence of this regionalization of the problem has been the legitimation of weak standards and weak supervisory institutions. States have not always addressed the regional problems with the seriousness merited by scientific reports.

(a) UNEP's Regional Seas Programme

UNEP's regional seas treaties all require states to endeavour to control land-based pollution. These general provisions are no more specific than Article 207 of the 1982 UNCLOS and merely repeat the duty to take 'appropriate measures', but they do offer a framework for the negotiation of regional controls, particularly in developing states. Despite its relative success in mobilizing cooperation on other matters and involving a large number of states, the coverage of the Regional Seas Programme has only slowly increased over the years. At the time of writing, protocols on land-based sources of marine pollution had been adopted in the Mediterranean, South-East Pacific, Persian Gulf, Black Sea, the Red Sea, the Caribbean, and for the Western and Eastern coasts of Africa. The content of the instruments varies depending upon when they were adopted.

The 1983 Quito Protocol covering the South-East Pacific illustrates weaknesses typical of most of the older generation of land-based pollution agreements, including in many respects the 1992 Black Sea Protocol.[86] The 1983 Quito Protocol requires the parties only to 'endeavour' to adopt measures to prevent, reduce and control marine pollution from specifically listed substances; those on the black list are generally

85 On the specific problems of these seas see OSPAR, *Quality Status Reports for the North-East Atlantic* (London, 2000 and 2010); Helsinki Commission, *Fourth Periodic Assessment of the State of the Marine Environment of the Baltic Sea Area* (Helsinki, 2001).

86 But on steps to modernize the Black Sea regime see Vinogradov, 22 *IJMCL* (2007) 585 and *supra*, Ch 9, section 3(2)(c).

distinguished by toxicity, persistence, or bioaccumulation and the aim is to eliminate discharges; those on the grey list must be controlled so that the amount and location of discharge are compatible with protection of the marine environment, but emissions need only be progressively reduced. However, discharge of blacklisted substances is not immediately prohibited; instead it is for the parties individually or jointly to decide on timetables, priorities, and measures, taking into account capacity to adapt existing facilities, the economic capacity of the parties and their development needs. Similar language continues to be found in the revised 1996 Mediterranean Protocol,[87] and in the 1999 Caribbean Protocol.[88] It is a common feature of the UNEP LBS protocols to acknowledge the differentiated responsibility of developing state parties. In practice this allows a great deal of leeway for developing states to act in accordance with their own priorities and capabilities, and in that respect nothing has changed in agreements negotiated or revised since UNCED.

There is greater emphasis on environmental impact assessment and monitoring in post-UNCED agreements,[89] and the black- and grey-listing of harmful substances has been abandoned in favour of a less rigid approach which encourages use of 'best available' or 'most appropriate' technology. Moreover, some of the more recent instruments, such as the revised 1996 Mediterranean LBS Protocol, the 2010 Nairobi LBS Protocol[90] and 2012 Abidjan LBS Protocol[91] make reference to the precautionary principle and the polluter-pays principle, thus reflecting the influence of UNCED and Agenda 21 on this area of law. Other reflections of this influence include provisions relating to access to information, education, awareness, publication and access to justice in the 2010 Nairobi LBS Protocol and the 2012 Abidjan LBS Protocol.[92] Despite this evolution in the legal framework, the challenge will be to ensure effective implementation, which will require significant investment and will in part depend upon financial and technical support from outside the region.[93]

(b) European agreements on land-based sources of marine pollution

The oldest and most developed regional agreements regulating land-based sources of marine pollution are those applicable to the North-East Atlantic[94] and the Baltic.[95] Both have been renegotiated since UNCED, and the revised Paris (OSPAR) and Helsinki

[87] See Article 7. [88] See Article 3. [89] See next section.

[90] 2010 Protocol for the Protection of the Marine and Coastal Environment of the Western Indian Ocean from Land-Based Sources and Activities.

[91] 2012 Protocol concerning the Cooperation in the Protection and Development of the Marine and Coastal Environment from Land-Based Sources and the Activities in the Western, Central and Southern Africa Region.

[92] Abidjan LBS Protocol, Article 6. See also Nairobi LBS Protocol, Article 15.

[93] The Protocols contain provisions on financial support; see Abidjan LBS Protocol, Articles 18 and 21; Nairobi LBS Protocol, Articles 17 and 20. In 2019 neither protocol was in force.

[94] 1992 Paris Convention, replacing 1974 Paris Convention. See Hey, IJlstra, Nollkaemper, 8 *IJMCL* (1993) 1; Juste, 97 *RGDIP* (1993) 365; Hilf, 55 *ZAÖRV* (1995) 580; Pallemaerts, 13 *IJMCL* (1998) 421; de La Fayette, 14 *IJMCL* (1999) 247.

[95] 1992 Helsinki Convention, replacing 1974 Convention. See Fitzmaurice, *International Legal Problems of the Environmental Protection of the Baltic Sea* (Dordrecht, 1992); Ehlers, 8 *IJMCL* (1993) 191; Jenisch, 11 *IJMCL* (1996) 47; Fitzmaurice et al, 13 *IJMCL* (1998) 379–420; Pallemaerts, ibid, 421; Ebbesson, 43 *GYIL* (2000) 38.

Conventions entered into force in 1998 and 2000 respectively. They have many of the characteristic features of other regional regulatory regimes and are comparable in many respects to the Rhine Protection Convention or the Great Lakes Water Quality Agreement reviewed in Chapter 10. The OSPAR and Helsinki Commissions function as regional supervisory institutions. An important feature, however, has been the interplay with other more overtly political bodies, notably the International North Sea Conference, the Organization for Security and Co-operation in Europe, and the EU. These bodies have at various times helped set the political agenda for policy and regulatory action by the OSPAR and Helsinki Commissions.

Although both agreements affirm the duty of parties to prevent and eliminate land-based marine pollution, like the UNEP Regional Seas Treaties they do not as such prescribe detailed standards for doing so. Only the Helsinki Convention actually bans the discharge of any substances.[96] Otherwise, national authorities remain responsible for setting pollution control standards, as well as for the grant of permits and inspection. However, parties are required to follow priorities listed in annexes to both treaties and to use (or to take into account) 'best available technology' and 'best environmental practice'. What these terms mean is only partially answered by the treaties themselves and requires further elaboration by the parties.[97] Coordination of treaty implementation thus depends partly on adherence to licensing criteria indicated in the treaties, and partly on the success of the regional supervisory bodies in negotiating common standards, guidelines and timetables.

Agreement on these matters has not always been easy to reach, and remains far from comprehensive.[98] A further problem common to all the European treaties on marine pollution is that standards once adopted only have the status of recommendations (as in the 1992 Helsinki Convention),[99] or if binding (as under the 1992 Paris Convention) do not apply to states which opt out by timely objection.[100] Enforcement of agreed standards remains the responsibility of national authorities alone; there is no provision for independent inspection, or for prior approval of permits by intergovernmental bodies, but parties must institute their own system for regular monitoring and inspection to ensure compliance with national authorizations and regulations. Moreover, there are requirements under both regimes for the parties to report to the regional commission, although only the OSPAR Commission has the power to assess compliance.[101]

[96] Annex 1, Part 2: principally DDT and PCBs.

[97] See criteria in Annex II of the 1992 Helsinki Convention and for OSPAR practice see Pallemaerts, 13 *IJMCL* (1998) 440–6.

[98] See Pallemaerts, ibid, and *infra*.

[99] See Fitzmaurice, *International Legal Problems of the Environmental Protection of the Baltic Sea*, 72–82. On non-binding recommendations under OSPAR see Nollkaemper, 13 *IJMCL* (1998) 355, and generally in *The Legal Regime for Transboundary Water Pollution: Between Discretion and Constraint* (Dordrecht, 1993) Ch 5.

[100] 1992 Paris Convention, Article 13.

[101] 1992 Helsinki Convention, Article 16; 1992 OSPAR Convention, Articles 22–23.

(c) The North Sea and the Mediterranean

Two examples, the North Sea and the Mediterranean, indicate the essential point common to all four schemes: that even these developed regimes are only as good as the parties allow them to be.

The North Sea states are a relatively cohesive and homogeneous group with a strong political commitment to environmental protection. Initially, cooperation took place through the International North Sea Conference (INSC),[102] whose calls for stricter regulation and substantial reductions in pollution led to new measures using technology to reduce the need for polluting emissions.[103] Today, cooperation largely takes place through the OSPAR Commission and the EU. The OSPAR Commission's area of responsibility includes the North Sea and it has adopted common standards for emission of various harmful substances.[104] EU directives have harmonized some standards for North Sea member states and the European Marine Strategy Framework Directive has been particularly important in driving forward the environmental agenda by requiring states in the region to maintain or achieve good environmental status in the marine environment by the year 2020 at the latest.[105] This objective is now reflected in the North-East Atlantic Environment Strategy, adopted by the OSPAR Commission in 2010 and setting the agenda for the organization for the following ten years.[106] The Strategy expressly calls for the continuous reduction of discharges, emissions and losses of hazardous substances, to be achieved through integrated management of human activities in order to reduce impacts on the marine environment. The OSPAR Commission has the ability to adopt binding decisions, but it has preferred to issue recommendations in relation to land-based sources, underlining states' general desire for flexibility. Some commentators have criticized the reforms as 'disappointingly general', failing to set quantitative targets and deadlines, not transforming INSC commitments into binding law, and for a 'loss of focus and normative force'.[107]

The 1992 Convention has, however, made provision for a non-compliance process, for NGO access to Commission proceedings, for limited public access to information,

[102] 1st INSC, Bremen Declaration, 1984, 14 *EPL* (1985) 32; 2nd INSC, London Declaration, 1987, 27 *ILM* (1988) 835; 3rd INSC, Hague Declaration, 1990, IMO Doc MEPC/29/INF 26; 4th INSC, Esbjerg Declaration (1995). See Ehlers, 5 *IJECL* (1990) 3; Hayward, ibid, 91; Pallemaerts, 7 *IJMCL* (1992) 126; id, 13 *IJMCL* (1998) 421. On the legal status of North Sea Conference Declarations see Nollkaemper, 13 *IJMCL* (1998) 355.

[103] Hayward, 5 *IJECL* (1990) 94–6; Wettestad and Andresen, *The Effectiveness of International Resource Cooperation* (Lysaker, 1991) 56–73; de La Fayette, 14 *IJMCL* (1999) 247; Pallemaerts, 13 *IJMCL* (1998) 421; Sadowski, in, Ringbom (ed), *Competing Norms in the Law of Marine Environmental Protection* (London, 1997) Ch 6; Skaerseth, *North Sea Cooperation* (Manchester, 2000).

[104] Article 31 provides that decisions, recommendations and agreements adopted under the 1974 Paris Convention continue to be applicable under the new Convention unless incompatible with it or expressly terminated by the parties. For a list of measures so terminated see OSPAR Decision 98/1. For a review of PARCOM practice see Pallemaerts, 13 *IJMCL* (1998) 421.

[105] Directive 2008/56/EC (2008) establishing a Marine Strategy Framework.

[106] OSPAR Agreement 2010–3, expressly recalling the Marine Strategy Framework Directive and noting the need to ensure 'maximum synergy wherever possible.'

[107] See also Hey, IJlstra, and Nollkaemper, 8 *IJMCL* (1993) 1.

and for protection of marine ecosystems and biodiversity.[108] Decisions and recommendations adopted by the OSPAR Commission 'represent a more comprehensive and integrated approach to the prevention of marine pollution from land-based activities than the earlier piecemeal approach',[109] and to this extent UNCED objectives have been taken into account. Indeed, the actions of the Commission must be seen in the broader context of its efforts to promote good environmental status by regulating other polluting activities and its efforts to identify marine species and ecosystems that require special protective measures.[110] Achieving these objectives, however, requires not only coordinated national action, but cooperation with other international organizations responsible for related issues, for example the Rhine, Meuse, Scheldt, and Elbe Commissions in relation to watercourses.[111]

The Mediterranean region is larger, and shows greater economic, social, and political diversity than the North Sea. Explicit recognition of the needs of developing states on the southern and eastern shores of this region has made it more difficult to achieve agreement on common standards.[112] Land-based pollution in this area is regulated by the 1996 Syracuse Protocol to the Barcelona Convention, which replaces the earlier Athens Protocol.[113] The revised protocol was intended as a response to UNCED, the 1994 Tunis Declaration on Sustainable Development in the Mediterranean, and the 1995 Washington Declaration and Global Plan of Action. Its geographical scope is broadened to cover the entire hydrologic basin of the Mediterranean Sea. The parties undertake generally to 'eliminate' pollution from land-based sources and are specifically required to give priority to phasing out inputs of substances that are toxic, persistent, and liable to bio-accumulate. In doing so they must take account of factors listed in the protocol or its annexes, including, inter alia, best available techniques and practices, and clean technology, 'where appropriate'.[114] They are also expected to formulate and adopt common guidelines and standards on such matters as effluent treatment, water quality, and discharge concentrations. However, they must take into account not only local conditions and existing pollution, but also the economic capacity of the parties and their development needs.[115] The obligation to eliminate

108 Articles 9, 11, 22, 23, and Annex V (1998) and *infra*, Ch 9. There is no provision for public participation but see 1998 Aarhus Convention, *supra*, Ch 5.

109 Pallemaerts, 13 *IJMCL* (1998) 446.

110 See e.g. OSPAR List of Threatened and/or Declining Species and Habitats, OSPAR Agreement 2008-06; OSPAR Recommendation 2010/5 on the assessment of environmental impacts on threatened and/or declining species; OSPAR Recommendation 2010/2 amending OSPAR Recommendation 2003/3 on a Network of Marine Protected Areas.

111 See *infra*, Ch 10.

112 Article 7.

113 See Raftopoulos, in Vidas and Schei (eds), *The World Ocean in Globalisation* (Leiden, 2011) 507; Pallemaerts, *Toxics and Transnational Law*, Ch 6; Scovazzi (ed), *Marine Specially Protected Areas: the General Aspects of the Mediterranean Regional System* (The Hague, 1999) Ch 7; Raftopoulos, *The Barcelona Convention and its Protocols* (London, 1993).

114 Article 5. Criteria for the definition of BAT and BEP are listed in Annex IV and are taken from the 1992 Paris Convention.

115 Article 7.

and phase out pollution must therefore be read with these substantial qualifications in mind. The Preamble suggests that this obligation must also be read with the precautionary principle in mind, but the only article on this is found in the revised Convention, not in the Protocol. The Convention's general provisions on sustainable development, the polluter-pays principle, integrated coastal-zone management, protection of areas of ecological importance, and conservation of natural resources remain relevant.[116] A non-compliance procedure included in the Convention is applicable to the Protocol,[117] and it has been revised to strengthen the process.[118] Finally, there is provision for monitoring and reporting on the effectiveness of measures taken. The Mediterranean Action Plan provides guidance on concrete measures and timetables.[119] It is these measures and their oversight by the compliance committee and other institutions associated with the Mediterranean regional seas framework that have driven the agenda for land-based sources in the region.

The 1996 Protocol has been described as a compromise between environmentalist NGOs and the chemical industry, allowing binding measures and timetables to be adopted, while postponing phase-out of emissions until agreement can be reached.[120] The Protocol is clearly stronger than its predecessor, and since entry into force in 2008 the parties have adopted numerous action plans and binding decisions implementing its provisions.[121] As in the North Sea and Baltic the role of the EU is especially important.[122]

3(3) MONITORING, EIA AND AVOIDANCE OF RISK TO THE MARINE ENVIRONMENT

Regulation is only part of the answer to the problem of protecting the marine environment from land-based sources of pollution. Two procedural obligations are widely recognized in this context: prior environmental impact assessment, and monitoring of the environmental effects of any discharges.[123] These obligations assume particular importance in those regional seas where no agreement on coordinated regulatory

116 Article 4. 117 1995 Barcelona Convention, Article 27.

118 Decision IG 17/2: Procedures and mechanisms on compliance under the Barcelona Convention and its Protocols. See also Decision IG 21/1; Decision IG.22/15.

119 1996 Protocol, Article 15.

120 Article 15 and Scovazzi, *Marine Specially Protected Areas*, Ch 7.

121 See e.g. Decision IG.22/08 on National Action Plans; Decisions IG.22/10 and IG.21/07 on Marine Litter Management; and Decisions IG.20/08.1 and 3; IG.19/08 and 09 reducing or phasing out inputs of mercury, DDT and various other chemicals.

122 See Directive 2008/56/EC (2008): Marine Strategy Framework Directive.

123 1982 UNCLOS, Articles 204–6; 1978 Kuwait Convention, Articles 10, 11; 1981 Abidjan Convention, Articles 13, 14; 1983 Cartagena Convention, Articles 12, 13; 1982 Jeddah Convention, Articles 10, 11; 1985 Nairobi Convention, Articles 13, 14; 1986 Noumea Convention, Articles 16, 17; 1981 Lima Convention, Articles 8, 9; 1983 Quito Protocol, Articles 8, 9; 1990 Kuwait LBS Protocol, Articles 7, 8; 1992 OSPAR Convention, Annex I, Article 2; 1992 Helsinki Convention, Articles 3(5) 7; 1995 Barcelona Convention, Articles 4(3) 12; 1996 Mediterranean LBS Protocol, Article 8; 1999 Caribbean LBS Protocol, Articles 6, 7.

standards exists, since in these cases they afford the only mechanism for limiting unilateral decisions which disregard impacts on the quality of the marine environment.

As we saw in Chapter 3, prior environmental impact assessment facilitates informed decisions. By enabling the risk of pollution or other forms of harm to the environment to be identified in advance, it may give the state an opportunity to take measures which will prevent or mitigate this risk.[124] The view that such assessments are required for potentially harmful impacts on the marine environment is reinforced by the 1982 UNCLOS and regional agreements. Article 206 of the 1982 Convention provides:

> When states have reasonable grounds for believing that planned activities under their jurisdiction or control may cause substantial pollution of or significant and harmful changes to the marine environment, they shall as far as practicable assess the potential effects of such activities on the marine environment and shall communicate reports of the results of such assessments [to the competent international organizations].

The evidential standard for showing the 'reasonable grounds' required for the application of Article 206 is unlikely to be an onerous one, and there is some latitude when determining whether 'reasonable grounds' exist.[125] Some of the regional treaties refer only to 'major projects',[126] and case law and state practice suggest that large scale dredging, the laying of oil and gas pipelines on the seabed, seabed mining operations and oil and gas drilling will all typically require an EIA.[127] While 'the incidence of environmental impact assessment procedures......in marine areas beyond national jurisdiction is relatively low',[128] there is no reason in principle why Article 206 should not apply in an appropriate case, as it does in relation to deep seabed mining.[129]

Like all of the regional seas treaties, Article 206 is silent on the question of what is required in an EIA, so the general law will apply in default of any applicable regional agreement.[130] In Europe the 1991 Espoo Convention provides the most detailed EIA regime for this area, including the marine environment.[131] The 1992 CBD has adopted

124 UNEP Montreal Guidelines, Article 12; 1986 Noumea Convention, Article 16(2); 1983 Cartagena Convention, Article 12(2).

125 See *South China Sea Arbitration*, PCA (2016) paras 947–48, 987–91, and *supra*, Ch 3, section 7. For a fuller analysis of Article 206 see Elferink, 27 *IJMCL* (2012) 449; Warner, *ibid*, 481.

126 1985 Nairobi Convention, Article 13; 1983 Cartagena Convention, Article 12; 1986 Noumea Convention, Article 16. Compare 1981 Abidjan Convention, Article 13; 1983 Kuwait Convention, Article 11; 1981 Lima Convention, Article 8; 1995 Barcelona Convention, Article 4; 1999 Caribbean LBS Protocol, Article 7, which apply to 'any planned activity'. Article 7 of the 1992 Helsinki Convention applies only where an EIA 'is required by international law or supra-national regulations'.

127 *South China Sea Arbitration*, PCA (2016) paras 987–991; *Land Reclamation Case*, ITLOS (2003) paras 74, 99; *AO on Activities in the Area*, ITLOS (2011) paras 146–50; Koivurova and Polonen, 25 *IJMCL* (2010) 151.

128 Warner, *Protecting the Oceans Beyond National Jurisdiction* (Leiden, 2009) 51.

129 *AO on Activities in the Area*, ITLOS Reports (2011) paras 146–50; Recommendations for the Assessment of Possible Environmental Impacts Arising from Exploration for Polymetallic Nodules in the Area, ISBA/16/LTC/7 (2010). See generally Elferink, 27 *IJMCL* (2012) 449.

130 *South China Sea Arbitration* PCA (2016) paras 987–991; *Border Activities/San Juan River Cases*, ICJ Reports (2015) 665, paras 104, 157; and *supra*, Ch 3, section 7(5). See also Koivurova and Polonen, 25 *IJMCL* (2010) 151; Elferink, 27 *IJMCL* (2012) 449.

131 *Supra*, Ch 3, section 7(5).

guidelines on integrating marine biodiversity into the EIA process; though 'voluntary', failure to apply them could constitute a breach of Article 206 or other applicable treaty provisions.[132] Failure to follow national law on EIA is also likely to be a breach of Article 206, while failure to notify the 'competent international organizations' could be treated as evidence that no EIA has been carried out.[133]

Neither the 1982 UNCLOS nor UNEP's regional seas treaties require notification and prior consultation with other states likely to be affected by land-based sources of marine pollution or seabed operations. But such an obligation is recognized by the 1992 Paris Convention,[134] the 1983 Quito Protocol,[135] and by a few treaties dealing with offshore operations.[136] Moreover, we will see in Chapter 9 that 'the duty to co-operate is a fundamental principle in the prevention of pollution of the marine environment under Part XII of the Convention and general international law'.[137]

The more difficult question is how to apply these elements of 'good neighbourliness' to cases where harm to the marine environment rather than to other states is foreseen. Without exception, all the treaties call for states to monitor pollution and make reports to other parties through regional institutions.[138] This reflects consistent support for Article 204 of the 1982 UNCLOS. In contrast to situations where other states are at risk, and regional commissions may recommend solutions to parties in dispute,[139] only the 1989 Kuwait Protocol calls for consultation with other contracting states where the marine environment as such is at risk, not merely other states.[140] But as the *South China Sea Arbitration* clearly shows, protection of the marine environment is an *erga omnes* obligation and any party to 1982 UNCLOS is entitled to bring proceedings under the Convention's provisions on compulsory jurisdiction.[141] In that context China's manifest failure to cooperate was found to be a violation of Articles 197 and 123 of 1982 UNCLOS.[142]

132 2015 CBD *Voluntary guidelines for the consideration of biodiversity in environmental impact assessments (EIAs) and strategic environmental assessments (SEAs) in marine areas* (2015), and for background, see note by the Executive Secretary, UNEP/CBD/SBSTTA/16/INF/16 (2012). On the role of soft law in implementing treaty provisions see *supra*, Ch 1.

133 *South China Sea Arbitration*, PCA (2016) paras 987–991.

134 Article 21.

135 Article 12.

136 1986 Canada–Denmark Agreement for Cooperation Relating to the Marine Environment, Article 4; 1989 Kuwait Protocol on Marine Pollution from Exploration and Exploitation of the Continental Shelf, Article IV; 1994 Protocol for the Protection of the Mediterranean Sea Against Pollution Resulting from the Exploration and Exploitation of the Continental Shelf and Sea-bed, Article 26; and see also UNEP GC 9/5/Add 5/Article III, Aspects Concerning the Environment Related to Offshore Drilling and Mining Within the limits of National Jurisdiction, 1981, Part E.

137 *MOX Plant Case*, ITLOS Reports (2001), para 82; *Land Reclamation Case*, ITLOS Reports (2003), para 92; *South China Sea Arbitration*, PCA (2016) paras 946, 985–6.

138 See 1982 UNCLOS, Articles 204, 205, and regional treaties, *supra*.

139 1992 Paris Convention, Article 21; 1983 Quito Protocol, Article 12; 1996 Mediterranean LBS Protocol, Article 12, which allow solutions to be recommended to parties in dispute.

140 Article IV.

141 The specific point was not addressed by the arbitral tribunal but is implicit in its findings at paras 939–93; see generally *supra*, Ch 4, section 2(6).

142 See paras 985–6.

These provisions on prior assessment and monitoring reflect the 1982 UNCLOS, but they do not compare favourably with the stronger regimes of prior consent or prior assessment and consultation through international organizations found in the 1972 London Convention, the 1989 Basel Convention, or the 2001 POPs Convention. They do not fully reflect more recent endorsement of the 'precautionary principle' but are much closer to the procedures adopted in international watercourse agreements. This tends to confirm the earlier conclusion that controls on all sources of land-based pollution remain relatively underdeveloped, but generally consistent with customary principles.

3(4) RELATIONSHIP WITH THE LAW OF INTERNATIONAL WATERCOURSES

As we will see in Chapter 10, international watercourses are not only a source of transboundary pollution, but a major contributor to marine pollution. The development of regional regimes to regulate watercourse environments has many similarities to those now controlling land-based sources of pollution.[143] Nevertheless there are differences between the two categories, and coordination gives rise to certain problems. First, it is doubtful whether the concept of equitable utilization has a role in regulating the marine environment, in contrast to the law of international watercourses.[144] Although the obligation to protect the marine environment is not absolute, and allows a significant balancing of interests at various levels, this is not the same as saying that states need only prevent pollution which is inequitable or unreasonable, nor does it imply that abuse of rights is the conceptual basis for pollution control. None of the treaties, including the 1982 UNCLOS and those dealing with enclosed or semi-enclosed seas, supports reliance on equitable utilization or abuse of rights in this way. Secondly, equitable utilization is mainly concerned with reconciling the interests of riparians, not those of coastal states or of the international community. A system which looks only at riparian interests in individual rivers will fail to offer a basis for common regional standards of environmental protection focused on the needs of particular regional seas. Moreover, equitable utilization is defective in giving too little weight to environmental considerations among a range of other relevant circumstances.[145] Even when implemented by institutional arrangements, as in the Rhine, these are likely to represent the wrong states with the wrong perspective: that of riparian rights.

For all these reasons, the regional treaties on prevention of marine pollution from land-based sources offer a more appropriate and efficient approach to the problem of protecting the marine environment. Their institutional structure more readily

143 See Pallemaerts, *Toxics and Transnational Law*, Ch 7.

144 Boyle, 14 *Marine Policy* (1990) 151. Cf the now discarded ILC draft Article 17(2) on 'International Watercourses', and commentary, *Rept of the ILC*, 43rd Session (1988) UN Doc A/43/10, 6972 and compare 1997 UN Watercourses Convention, Article 23. The latter makes no reference to equitable utilization: see *Rept of the* (1990) UN Doc A/45/10, 169, and *supra*, Ch 10.

145 See *infra*, Ch 10.

accommodates a balance of interests between the needs of the source states, and the capacity of the marine environment to absorb polluting inputs, since states with a direct interest in use of the sea will be involved. One method of integrating the protection of international watercourses into this system is to create institutional links between watercourse and regional seas commissions, including representation of landlocked riparians and non-riparian coastal states in the appropriate regional bodies. The role played by the International North Sea Conference in securing Swiss participation, and in persuading the Rhine Commission to adopt protection of the marine environment as an objective, offers an example of this approach.[146] However, such links by themselves are insufficient; what must be emphasized is that the obligations of all states with regard to land-based pollution of the marine environment should be fully applied to international watercourses. European and Mediterranean practice follows this principle explicitly or implicitly.[147] In these cases primary responsibility for agreed measures remains with the relevant international watercourse commission, but riparians assume a responsibility for protecting the marine environment and a duty in customary law towards coastal states and other users of the adjacent seas.[148]

3(5) A GLOBAL REGIME FOR LAND-BASED SOURCES?

The regional nature of the treaty regimes on land-based sources, the scope for national discretion in the administration of permits, the recognition of a double standard for developing countries, and the absence in some cases of regional agreement on specific standards sharply differentiate control of land-based pollution from the international regulation of pollution from ships, or from dumping. Apart from the obligation to eliminate a flexible category of more harmful substances, regional agreements provide insufficient evidence of uniformity of practice to constitute an international or global standard and suggest that the customary obligation to prevent marine pollution from land-based sources has remained essentially general in character, with little objective content. Its implementation remains dependent primarily on national action, regional cooperation, and further agreement. The slow progress of such cooperation indicates the continuing importance of industrial and economic factors in this sphere and the desire of states to balance those considerations against the needs of environmental protection.

[146] 9th Ministerial Conference of the International Commission for the Protection of the Rhine, 1988. See Nollkaemper, 5 *IJECL* (1990) 125. Switzerland is not a party to the Paris Convention, but it is a party to the 1999 Rhine Convention, on which see *infra*, Ch 10.

[147] 1996 Mediterranean Protocol, Article 11(1); 1992 Helsinki Convention, Article 6(4); 1992 OSPAR Convention, Annex 1, Article 2. At its 3rd meeting, the OSPAR Commission resolved that 'there was no doubt that the scope of the Convention included "such discharges into watercourses as affect the maritime area" and the setting of limit values for those discharges', PARCOM III/10/1. On the Black Sea see Vinogradov, 22 *IJMCL* (2007) 585.

[148] Nollkaemper, 5 *IJECL* (1990) 123; Rémond-Gouilloud, in Johnston, *The Environmental Law of the Sea*, 236; 1997 UN Watercourses Convention, Article 23; 1994 Danube Convention, Preamble and Article 2; 1999 Rhine Convention, Article 3(5) and commentary, *infra*, Ch 10.

The preference of states for regional agreements to control land-based sources of pollution has meant that no global treaty comparable to the 1972 London Convention exists. In advance of the 1992 Rio Conference, several proposals were made for a new global instrument intended to strengthen the existing law on land-based sources of marine pollution and provide better institutional arrangements for coordinating regional action.[149] Agenda 21, Chapter 17 called on states to consider updating, strengthening, and extending the earlier 1985 Montreal Guidelines on Land-Based Sources of Marine Pollution, and UNEP was invited to convene a conference. The outcome was the adoption in 1995 of the Washington Declaration on the Protection of the Marine Environment from Land-based Activities ('Washington Declaration'),[150] together with a Global Programme of Action ('GPA').[151] The Declaration reaffirmed the importance of integrated coastal zone and catchment area management, and the need for 'sustained and effective action' to deal with all land-based impacts on the marine environment. The GPA also emphasized the need for adequate funding for implementation and access to clean technology by developing states.[152] The process was not intended to replace existing mechanisms, with implementation largely to be carried out by states acting domestically, or through regional seas bodies or other competent organizations. The GPA has brought a new focus on sewage inputs, destruction of habitats, and development of integrated coastal area and river basin management.[153] However, the UN's 2015 SDGs continue to call for further action: '(1) By 2025, [to] prevent and significantly reduce marine pollution of all kinds, in particular from land-based activities, including marine debris and nutrient pollution; (2) By 2020, sustainably manage and protect marine and coastal ecosystems to avoid significant adverse impacts, including by strengthening their resilience, and take action for their restoration in order to achieve healthy and productive oceans; (3) Minimize and address the impacts of ocean acidification, including through enhanced scientific cooperation at all levels.'[154] A review of the GPA in 2018 again concluded that 'a more responsive and effective governance and institutional structure' is required.[155] UNEP's review of the law relating to plastic in the marine environment reached the same conclusion.[156]

149 See *Rept of 13th Consultative Meeting*, IMO/LDC 13/15 (1990) Annex 4; Resolution LDC 40/13 (1990) and *Rept of the Intergovernmental Meeting of Experts on Land-based Sources of Marine Pollution*, UN Doc/A/CONF 151/PC/71, 3; UNEP proposals for a global convention, ibid, 10, and UNEP decision SS 11/6 (1990) calling for strengthened institutions, legal and other measures at regional and global level.

150 UNEP (OCA)/MED IG 6/5, in 6 *YbIEL* (1995) 883. See Harrison, *Saving the Oceans through Law*, Ch 4; Mensah, in Boyle and Freestone (eds), *International Law and Sustainable Development* (Oxford, 1999) Ch 13. For *travaux préparatoires* see reports of the Intergovernmental Meetings of Experts held at Halifax, 1991; Nairobi, 1993; Rekjavik, 1995.

151 On implementation of the GPA see UNEP, *The Global Programme of Action for the Protection of the Marine Environment from Land-Based Activities: A 20-year Perspective on a Unique Programme to Advance the Ocean Agenda*, UNEP/GPA/IGR.4/INF/3 (2018).

152 On the role of the GEF see Freestone, Barnes and Ong (eds), *The Law of the Sea*, Ch 16.

153 See 2001 Montreal Declaration on the Protection of the Marine Environment from Land- based Activities; 2012 Manila Declaration on Furthering Implementation of the Global Programme of Action for the Protection of the Marine Environment from Land-based Activities.

154 See SDG 14 and targets, UNGA Res 70/1 (2015).

155 UNEP, *The GPA etc: A 20-year Perspective*, para 223.

156 *Supra*, n 76.

Like the North Sea Declarations, the 1995 Washington Declaration and GPA provide some evidence of a political commitment to stronger action and an indication of agreed priorities. As we saw earlier, all these declarations may have had some influence on the further development of regional treaties and regimes. Nevertheless, the 1995 Washington Declaration and GPA fall well short of the initial proposals for a binding global treaty which several governments and NGOs had supported. The reasons for this are easy to identify. Developing countries did not see the need for stronger action. There was a widespread belief that the problems were regional rather than global and that differences between regions made a common global approach difficult. Many countries continued to prefer action at national, sub-regional or regional level, and viewed stronger global regulation as an interference in internal matters.

For all these reasons it has been argued that 'the objective of a global legal instrument has turned out to be both unrealistic and indeed unnecessary'.[157] It is also true that higher standards of pollution control would not flow from a global treaty that merely reflected existing priorities, and that intergovernmental supervision of stronger political commitments in the GPA does not necessarily require a treaty basis. A more sceptical view is that once again economic and industrial priorities prevailed, making harmonization more difficult, and delaying a more significant transformation of the applicable international law.[158] In these respects the contrast with the evolution of international law relating to dumping is striking. There is nothing in the 1995 Washington Declaration or its subsequent history to suggest that it has in any way changed international law relating to pollution of the sea from land-based activities. That the UN's 2015 SDGs have to reiterate the problem speaks volumes.

4 DUMPING AT SEA

4(1) THE PERMISSIBILITY OF DUMPING

With limited exceptions, the dumping of harmful waste at sea is now illegal[159]. In 1972, the Stockholm Conference called for an international regime to regulate dumping,[160] and the 1972 London Convention was duly concluded in the same year. It was later supplemented by regional treaties, considered below. These precedents formed the basis for Articles 210 and 216 of the 1982 UNCLOS which require states to regulate and control pollution of the marine environment caused by dumping at sea, but do not prohibit it. Thus, despite its global status, the 1972 London Convention is not a complete code for the

157 Mensah, in Boyle and Freestone (eds), *International Law and Sustainable Development*, 312.

158 Nollkaemper, 27 *ODIL* (1996) 153.

159 Harrison, *Saving the Oceans through Law* (Oxford, 2017) Ch 5; Churchill and Lowe, *The Law of the Sea* (3rd edn, Manchester, 1999) 363ff; Letalik, in Johnston (ed), *The Environmental Law of the Sea*, 217ff; de La Fayette, 13 *IJMCL* (1998) 515; Redgwell, in Freestone, Barnes and Ong (eds), *The Law of the Sea* (Oxford, 2006) Ch 10.

160 Recommendation 86(c) Action Plan for the Human Environment.

regulation of dumping; it must be read in conjunction with the jurisdiction conferred on coastal and flag states under other UNCLOS and customary international law.

A review of long-term strategy for the 1972 London Convention was initiated by the 13th Consultative Meeting.[161] In 1993 extensive revisions were made,[162] and in 1996 the 1972 Convention was replaced entirely by a new 1996 Protocol which has since entered into force for most of the industrialised world except Russia and the US.[163] The revisions and the new protocol effectively put an end to dumping of potentially hazardous waste at sea or the export of such waste for dumping by non-parties. The global dumping regime has thus become one of the strongest applications of a precautionary approach to environmental risk. In effect, the 1972 London Convention has become a non-dumping convention whose only real challenge is to ensure that compliance is more fully monitored and effectively controlled.[164]

The existence and widespread ratification of a convention applicable to all marine areas outside internal waters means that dumping is the subject of a global regime, not primarily a regional one. Regional agreements were mainly of significance in imposing higher standards in enclosed or semi-enclosed seas in advance of the more general prohibition agreed in 1996. As indicated by Article 210 of the 1982 UNCLOS, this global regime is based on attainment of international minimum standards by all states, which limits their national discretion and makes no allowance for double standards or economic development.[165] Although the number of ratifications of the 1996 Protocol is still less than half that for the 1972 Convention, it is has been argued that it is to the Protocol that Article 210 of the 1982 UNCLOS refers.[166] In this respect, the legal regime of dumping is closer to the regulation of pollution from ships than to pollution from land-based sources. Only a limited range of largely harmless matter may now be dumped under permit.[167] This is a much more stringent application of the precautionary principle than is found in most regional controls on land-based pollution. Finally, dumping is subject to supervision by an international forum, the London Convention Consultative Meeting, in addition to regional bodies.[168]

161 *Rept of 13th Consultative Meeting*, IMO/LDC 13/15 (1990).

162 Birnie, 12 *IJMCL* (1997) 488, 514–31; Res LC 49(16); Res LC 50(16) Res LC 51(16) (1993) amending Annex 1. See also 1997 Waste Assessment Guidelines, which modify the application of Annex III.

163 For drafting history see *Rept of 18th Consultative Meeting* (1996) para 5.

164 de La Fayette, 13 *IJMCL* (1998) 515.

165 1982 UNCLOS, Article 210(6). For an account of the drafting of Article 210, see Nordquist, *Commentary*, iv, 15,568.

166 de La Fayette, 13 *IJMCL* (1998) 516; Redgwell, in Freestone, Barnes and Ong (eds), *The Law of the Sea*, 184–6. But for a more cautious view see Harrison, *Saving the Oceans through Law*, 110, and Hong and Lee, 55 *Marine Policy* (2015) 47.

167 E.g. dredged material, sewage sludge, organic material, ships, platforms and other structures: see 1972 Convention, Annexes I and II as revised 1993; 1996 Protocol, Annex 1; 1992 OSPAR Convention, Annex II, Article 3; 1995 Barcelona Protocol, Article 4 (but sewage may not be dumped). Under the 1992 Helsinki Convention only dredged material may be dumped: see Article II and Annex V. Following the *Brent Spar* controversy, OSPAR Decision 98/3 (1998) prohibits parties from dumping disused offshore installations in the NE Atlantic and North Sea: see Kirk, 46 *ICLQ* (1997) 957; id, 48 *ICLQ* (1999) 458; de La Fayette, 13 *IJMCL* (1998) 522–6. The 1992 Helsinki Convention does not permit dumping of such installations in the Baltic.

168 See *infra*.

4(2) WHY PROHIBIT DUMPING?

The major argument against dumping at sea is that it allows a small number of industrialized states acting for their own benefit to impose pollution risks on many others, perhaps extending into future generations.[169] While prior assessment of the risks involved, and of the suitability of sites, will minimize the possibility of future harm, it cannot eliminate scientific uncertainty or risk entirely. Like nuclear power or the carriage of oil by sea, the main issue is thus not solely the availability of less-harmful alternatives; rather, the acceptability of dumping depends significantly on the degree of risk, if any, which the international community is willing to accept without any countervailing benefit for potentially affected states. Treaty commitments have moved away from the view implicit in the original text of the 1972 London Convention that dumping at sea is permissible unless proven harmful. Following endorsement of the precautionary approach by the parties in 1992, leading to revision of the Convention in 1993 and explicit incorporation in Article 3(1) of the 1996 Protocol, as well as in regional treaties, the position now is that dumping is permissible only if there are no alternatives and it can be proven harmless to the environment, a significant reversal of the burden of proof.[170] Thus, the proposition that dumping remains in principle a legitimate use of the oceans, notwithstanding the possibility of disposal on land, and the possible risk to other states, is now untenable in the light of recent state practice and treaty commitments. In this context it is not inappropriate to draw conclusions concerning the development of customary law from the practice of parties to the 1972 London Convention and the various regional agreements. Those parties include nearly all the industrialized nations and a comparable number of developing states. There is no evidence, unusually, of any non-party dumping significant wastes at sea, or asserting a freedom to do so beyond that implied by the 1982 UNCLOS and the various global and regional instruments.

4(3) WHAT IS 'DUMPING'?

Dumping is defined by the 1972 London Convention and the 1982 UNCLOS as the 'deliberate disposal at sea of wastes or other matter'.[171] It includes disposal of redundant ships, aircraft, or oil and gas platforms, including abandonment or toppling of these and other man-made structures at sea.[172] Discharges occurring in the normal

[169] Boehmer-Christiansen, 10 *Marine Policy* (1986) 131; Bewers and Garrett, 11 *Marine Policy* (1987) 121f.

[170] LDC Res 44 (14); 1972 Convention, Annex I as revised 1993; 1996 Protocol, Articles 3(1) 4(1)(2) and Annex 2; 1997 Waste Assessment Guidelines; 1992 OSPAR Convention, Article 4; 1992 Helsinki Convention, Article 3 (2). See Hey, *The Precautionary Approach and the LDC*, published as LDC 14/4 (1991); de La Fayette, 13 *IJMCL* (1998) 515; Kirk, 46 *ICLQ* (1997) 957, and *supra*, Ch 3.

[171] 1972 Convention, Article 3(1); 1982 UNCLOS, Article 1(5); 1992 Helsinki Convention, Article 2(4); 1976 and 1995 Barcelona Protocol, Article 3. Compare 1972 Oslo Convention, Article 19 and 1996 Protocol to the 1972 London Convention, Article 1(4)(1) which define dumping as deliberate disposal '*into* the sea', and 1992 OSPAR Convention, Article 1(f) which defines it as disposal 'in the maritime area' (emphasis added).

[172] 1972 Convention, Article 1(1) as interpreted by the Parties in *Rept of the 13th Consultative Meeting*, LDC 13/15, para 7.4; 1996 Protocol, Article 1(4); 1992 OSPAR Convention, Article 1(f); 1992 Helsinki Convention, Article 2(4); 1992 Black Sea Convention, Article 2; 1995 Barcelona Protocol, Article 4(2)(d).

operation of ships or platforms do not constitute dumping, nor, a fortiori, do accidental spillages. Incineration at sea is explicitly covered by the 1993 revisions and the 1996 Protocol, as is disposal 'in the sea-bed or subsoil', but only if accessed by vessels or structures 'at sea'.[173] However, amendments to Annex I adopted in 2006 permit permanent carbon sequestration under the seabed in accordance with guidelines adopted by the parties. This will facilitate a possible method for reducing atmospheric CO_2 emissions from power stations and other industrial sources.[174] Further amendments were adopted in 2009 to facilitate transboundary movement of carbon dioxide for the purposes of storage in the seabed.[175] Given that this required a change to the text of the 1996 Protocol, as opposed to a modification of the annexes, this amendment will only enter into force once it has been positively accepted by contracting parties.[176] States have been urged to work towards ratification of the amendments in order to support the development of related climate change mitigation technology.

4(4) RADIOACTIVE WASTE DUMPING

The need to find a safe medium for disposal of radioactive waste material is one of the more intractable problems of nuclear power.[177] Disposal in Antarctica is forbidden by treaty;[178] disposal or reprocessing on land carries risks for the health of present and future generations. One response, initially adopted by several nuclear states including the UK, US, and Japan, was to dump radioactive waste at sea. The 1972 London Convention for that reason prohibited the dumping only of high-level radioactive matter defined by IAEA as unsuitable for this form of disposal, and it permitted the dumping of low-level waste to be conducted subject to IAEA guidelines.[179] Some states regarded the IAEA standards as being unacceptably low, however, and applied their own more stringent rules. Regional practice was overwhelmingly opposed to radioactive dumping, particularly in enclosed or semi-enclosed seas.[180] Growing

173 Article 1(4)(1). This definition appears exclude tunneling from shore. See also 1986 Noumea Protocol, Article 10.

174 See Resolution LP.1(1) (2006); Scott, 18 *Georgetown IELR* (2005) 57.

175 Resolution LP.3(4) on the Amendment to Article 6 of the London Protocol.

176 See Langlet, (2015) 30 *IJMCL* 395–417. In 2020 the amendment was not in force.

177 Hey, 40 *NILR* (1993) 405; Welsch, 28 *GYIL* (1985)322; Curtis, 14 *ODIL* (1984) 383; Mani, 24 *Indian JIL* (1984) 235; Van Dyke, 12 *Marine Policy* (1988) 82; Boehmer- Christiansen, 10 *Marine Policy* (1986) 119; Bewers and Garrett, 11 *Marine Policy* (1987) 121, review the scientific studies.

178 1959 Antarctic Treaty, Article 5; Recommendation VIII-12, 8th Antarctic Treaty Consultative Meeting, 1975; 1991 Antarctic Protocol, Annex III, Article 2.

179 Annex 1, para 6; Annex II, para (d). The IAEA's definition and recommendations appear in IAEA Doc INFCIRC/205/Add 1 (1975) and INFCIRC/205/Add 1/Rev 1 (1978); see now IAEA, Safety Series No 78, *Definition and Recommendations for the Convention on the Prevention of Marine Pollution, etc* (Vienna, 1986) adopted 1986 at the 10th Consultative Meeting of the LDC.

180 1992 Helsinki Convention, Article 11; 1986 Noumea Convention, Article 10, (Article 11 also prohibits storage of radioactive wastes or matter in the Convention area); 1989 Protocol for the Protection of the South-East Pacific Against Radioactive Pollution; 1992 Black Sea Protocol, Article 2 and Annex 1; 1992 OSPAR Convention, Annex II, Article 3(3); 1995 Barcelona Protocol for the Prevention of Pollution by Dumping, Annex 1.

opposition among a majority of 1972 London Convention parties and pressure from NGOs led to a moratorium on all radioactive dumping at sea, pending further study.[181] In 1993 Annex I was amended, and the moratorium became binding on all parties, save for Russia, which eventually withdrew its objections in 2005.[182] All radioactive waste dumping is now prohibited under the 1996 Protocol.

4(5) GEOENGINEERING AND THE DUMPING REGIME

The 1972 London Convention and 1996 Protocol extend not only to dumping, but also to the 'placement of matter' that is contrary to the aims of the treaties.[183] The precise meaning of this phrase has been contested and its application has in practice been determined on a case-by-case basis. This flexibility has allowed the dumping regime to be extended to address emerging issues concerning potential threats to the marine environment. In this regard, a significant decision was made at the 2008 Consultative MOP to the 1996 Protocol, which confirmed that 'the scope of the London Convention and Protocol includes ocean fertilization activities.'[184] This decision was aimed at controversial proposals to add iron, or other nutrients such as urea or phosphorus, to seawater in order to stimulate the uptake of carbon by natural organisms such as phytoplankton. Whilst ocean fertilization may have the potential to reduce the amount of carbon dioxide in the atmosphere, thereby contributing to the mitigation of climate change, it is also feared that there may be significant repercussions on the marine environment.[185] The 2008 Resolution brings the regulation of ocean fertilization under the remit of the dumping regime and any proposal would therefore at least require a licensing by relevant states before it could go ahead. An Assessment Framework for Scientific Research involving Ocean Fertilization, requiring prior risk assessment and monitoring of activities by the competent authorities, was adopted in 2010 in order to promote harmonization of national policies in this respect.[186] For parties to the 1996 London Protocol, the practice would be completely prohibited by the stricter approach to dumping regulation under that instrument. To allow research on the potential impacts of ocean fertilization, an amendment to the 1996 Protocol was agreed in 2013, which establishes a new regime for the authorization of geoengineering activities falling under the auspices of the Protocol. The amendment introduces a new article into the Protocol according to which 'contracting parties shall not allow the placement of matter into the sea from vessels, aircraft, platforms or other man-made structures at sea for marine geoengineering activities

[181] LDC Resolution 14(7) 1983 and Resolution LDC 21(9) 1985. See Bewers and Garrett, 11 *Marine Policy* (1987) and Forster, 16 *EPL* (1986) 7.

[182] Resolution LC 51 (16); 1996 Protocol, Annex I. See de La Fayette, 13 *IJMCL* (1998) 515; IMO, *Rept of 21st Consultative Meeting*, LC 21/13 (1999) para 6.

[183] 1972 Convention, Article 3(1)(c); 1996 Protocol, Article 1(4)(2)(2).

[184] Resolution LC-LP.1(2008) on the Regulation of Ocean Fertilization, para 1.

[185] See inter alia CBD COP Decision IX/16C, 30 May 2008. See also CBD COP Decision X/33, paras 8(w) and (x).

[186] Resolution LC-LP.2(2010) on the Assessment Framework for Scientific Research involving Ocean Fertilization.

listed in annex 4, unless the listing provides that the activity or the subcategory of an activity may be authorized under a permit.'[187] At present, only iron fertilization is listed in Annex 4, although it will be possible to add further activities in the future. Once this amendment enters into force the dumping regime will become the primary instrument for the regulation of ocean fertilization. This choice of institutional framework means that states have prioritized a precautionary approach to the issue and developments will be subject to scrutiny of the regular meetings of the parties.

4(6) LICENSING AND ENFORCEMENT

The essence of the 1972 London Convention and of the regional agreements is that permitted matter may not be dumped at sea without a prior permit issued by the relevant national authorities.[188] Both the 1996 Protocol and the Waste Assessment Guidelines adopted in 1997 by the parties to the 1972 Convention emphasize that the use of waste prevention techniques, the 'practical availability of other means of disposal', 'environmentally friendly alternatives', and the need for a 'comparative risk assessment involving both dumping and the alternatives' must be taken into account.[189] The guidelines state categorically that a permit to dump 'shall be refused' if there are opportunities to re-use, recycle or treat the waste without 'undue risks to human health or the environment or disproportionate costs'. Uncertainties in assessing impacts on the marine environment must be considered and the precautionary approach applied. The final judgement on the grant of permits rests with the national licensing authority. Moreover, since the object of the London Convention is to set minimum standards of acceptable national regulation, it is open to licensing authorities to adopt additional criteria, or more stringent regulations, or to prohibit dumping altogether.[190] Primary responsibility for issuing permits rests with the state where the waste is loaded, regardless of the nationality of the ship or aircraft, or where the dumping is to take place. Vessels of parties to the Convention cannot escape this provision by loading in non-party states; in this case the flag state is required to act as a licensing authority.[191] Moreover, since flag states will retain concurrent jurisdiction over their vessels,[192] they will have a right independent of the London Convention to regulate dumping notwithstanding the grant of a permit elsewhere.

187 London Dumping Protocol, Article 6bis, introduced by Resolution LP.4(8)(2013) Annex.

188 1996 Protocol, Article 4; 1992 OSPAR Convention, Annex II, Article 4; 1992 Helsinki Convention, Annex V; 1992 Black Sea Protocol on Dumping, Articles 3, 4; 1995 Barcelona Protocol on Dumping, Articles 5, 6; 1986 Noumea Protocol on Dumping, Articles 5, 6.

189 1996 Protocol, Article 4(1)(2) and Annex 2; 1997 Guidelines for the Assessment of Wastes or Other Matter that May be Considered for Dumping. The 1997 Guidelines are largely identical to Annex 2 of the 1996 Protocol and in effect amend Annex III of the 1972 Convention. See de La Fayette, 13 *IJMCL* (1998) 521.

190 1996 Protocol, Articles 3(4) 4(2); 1982 UNCLOS, Article 210(1) and (6) and Commentary in UN, *Pollution by Dumping: Legislative History* (New York, 1985) 21.

191 1996 Protocol, Article 9(2); 1992 Helsinki Convention, Article 11; 1992 Black Sea Protocol, Annex V; 1995 Barcelona Protocol on Dumping, Article 10(2); 1986 Noumea Protocol on Dumping, Article 11(2). The 1992 OSPAR Convention refers only to 'the appropriate national authority' without definition.

192 *The Lotus Case*, PCIJ Ser A, No 10 (1927); 1982 UNCLOS, Article 211(2); 1996 Protocol, Article 10(1) and *supra*, Ch 9, section 4(2).

It is also clear that no dumping may take place within the internal waters or territorial sea of another state without its consent; since no claim to innocent passage will be involved where dumping is under way, the coastal state will necessarily enjoy full jurisdiction over ships engaged in this activity.[193] Article 210(5) of the 1982 UNCLOS extends this principle of prior consent to dumping in the exclusive economic zone and on the continental shelf, in respect of which coastal states enjoy sovereign rights.[194] Coastal states thus have jurisdiction to issue licences, and to regulate or prohibit all dumping within 200 miles of their coast (and to the outer limit of the shelf beyond 200 miles in accordance with Article 76) after consulting other states which may be affected. Thus the main significance of the 1982 Convention with regard to dumping is that it gives coastal states a regulatory jurisdiction that was not expressly provided for in the London Convention, and which, as in the case of flag state regulation, may be invoked notwithstanding the grant of a permit elsewhere. This conclusion is further strengthened by the 1989 Basel Convention which requires prior consent to be obtained from importing states before dumping at sea within their jurisdiction.[195]

Jurisdiction to enforce laws relating to dumping follows the same pattern. Each party must take measures with respect to vessels or aircraft registered in its territory or flying its flag, or loading matter which is to be dumped, or believed to be engaged in dumping 'under its jurisdiction'.[196] The latter phrase can now be taken as a reference to dumping inside territorial waters, the territorial sea, exclusive economic zone, or continental shelf, as provided for in Article 216 of the 1982 UNCLOS.[197] Both conventions are imperative in requiring states to enforce laws on dumping.[198]

There is little doubt that these provisions reflect customary law, including the evolution of the exclusive economic zone and extension of coastal state jurisdiction, concurrent with that of the flag state. However, they leave open the question of high seas enforcement. Since port state enforcement jurisdiction is confined to cases of actual loading, it will not cover high seas dumping.[199] Beyond the EEZ, or in cases where the coastal state does not claim jurisdiction, only the flag state will have jurisdiction to enforce dumping regulations and, as we saw in Chapter 7, this may often be an ineffective remedy.

[193] 1982 UNCLOS, Articles 18, 19(2)(h) 210(5) and *supra*, Ch 9. Note that the application of the 1996 Protocol to internal waters is restricted by Article 7.

[194] 1982 UNCLOS, Articles 56; 77.

[195] See *infra*, section 5.

[196] 1996 Protocol, Article 10(1); 1992 OSPAR Convention, Article 10(1); 1992 Black Sea Protocol, Article 8; 1995 Barcelona Protocol on Dumping, Article 11; 1986 Noumea Protocol on Dumping, Article 12. Cf 1992 Helsinki Convention, Article 11, which does not extend coastal state powers beyond the outer limit of the territorial sea.

[197] Article 216(1)(a); UN, *Pollution By Dumping*, 15–17, 29.

[198] cf Article 216(2) of the 1982 UNCLOS, however: 'No state shall be obliged by virtue of this article to institute proceedings when another state has already instituted proceedings in accordance with this article.'

[199] 1982 UNCLOS, Article 216(1)(c); 1996 Protocol, Article 10(1). 1982 UNCLOS Article 218, which confers port state jurisdiction over high seas pollution 'discharges' from ships, would not appear to apply to 'dumping'. See *supra*, Ch 9. However, 1996 Protocol, Article 10(3) and 1992 OSPAR Convention, Article 10(2) envisage cooperation and reporting procedures for high seas dumping.

4(7) REGIONAL TREATIES AND DUMPING

Both the 1972 London Convention and the 1982 UNCLOS accept the possibility of regional arrangements for the control of dumping.[200] Article 8 of the London Convention refers in particular to parties 'with common interests to protect in the marine environment in a given geographical area', and allows them to take account of characteristic regional features. Regional agreements may set higher standards, but must be consistent with the global requirements of the London Convention. Regional agreements or protocols apply in the North-East Atlantic and North Sea, the Baltic, the Mediterranean, the Black Sea, and the South Pacific, areas which are mostly enclosed or semi-enclosed seas and in which dumping may cause special problems.[201] As we have already seen, most of the applicable treaties and protocols are fully consistent with the revised London Convention and the 1996 Protocol. The 1991 African Convention on Transboundary Movement of Hazardous Waste ('African Convention') also prohibits all dumping of hazardous waste at sea by the parties and within the parties' maritime zones.[202]

In all other respects the regional treaties are modelled closely on the London Convention, including their licensing, enforcement, and supervision arrangements. By adding an additional level of institutional supervision they provide a more immediate focus for ensuring compliance, but it seems clear that unlike the control of land-based pollution of the sea, one of the factors which has made the control of dumping effective is the interplay of global and regional rules and institutions. This does suggest that however strong the case for regional arrangements to cater for special circumstances, these are best located within a clear global framework of minimum standards of sufficient stringency, reinforced by the wider community pressure which a body such as the Consultative Meeting of the parties to the London Convention can provide.

4(8) ASSESSING THE LONDON DUMPING CONVENTION

The 1972 London Convention is generally regarded as one of the more successful regulatory treaties of the 1970s. A report prepared by the IMO in 1991[203] attributed reductions in dumping at sea to the efforts of contracting parties to find alternative disposal methods, to recycle wastes, and to use cleaner technology, and it concluded that the Convention had provided an effective instrument for the protection of the marine environment. Since then decisions taken by the parties with regard to incineration and radioactive and industrial waste have strengthened this trend towards

200 London Convention, Article 8; 1996 Protocol, Article 12; 1982 UNCLOS, Article 210(4).

201 1995 Barcelona Protocol for the Prevention of Pollution of the Mediterranean Sea by Dumping from Ships and Aircraft; 1986 Noumea Protocol for the Prevention of Pollution by Dumping; 1992 OSPAR Convention; 1992 Black Sea Convention.

202 Article 4(2). See also 1995 South Pacific Convention on Hazardous Wastes, Article 4(3) although this merely reaffirms commitments under other treaties.

203 UNCED Prepcom, UN Doc A/CONF 151/PC/31 (1991).

elimination of dumping at sea as a method of waste disposal. Another measure of the Convention's relative success is the number of regional agreements which now supplement its global provisions.

In Chapter 2 we noted that one of the main reasons for the Convention's evolution in this way has been the range and diversity of parties participating in regular consultative meetings. The Consultative Meeting has been notably successful in generating international consensus on the development of policy for dumping at sea. It has facilitated the adoption of increasingly stringent standards and enabled a wider community of states not engaged in this activity to apply pressure on those who are involved to moderate or abandon practices which posed a risk to the marine environment. It has also provided a forum for resolving disputed issues, such as sub-seabed disposal of radioactive waste. Only about forty parties regularly participate in consultative meetings, but among these there is an approximate balance of industrialized and developing states. It cannot be said that the Convention is of interest only to industrialized nations, and even some of these, such as the Scandinavian states, have long been opposed to dumping as a method of waste disposal. Although membership is thus far from universal, the Convention is plainly not controlled by pro-dumping states, nor is there evidence that significant dumping is practised by non-parties. Moreover, the involvement of NGOs has been an important feature of the Consultative Meetings, enabling environmental and industry groups to lobby members and provide expert advice for the delegations of several states. Greenpeace and ACOPS have been particularly active and effective in pressing for development of the Convention and in bringing to the attention of parties evidence of violations, such as the alleged dumping of radioactive waste by the USSR disclosed at the 14th Consultative Meeting in 1991.[204] As this example shows, the Consultative Meetings were able to exercise some control over compliance under the 1972 London Convention, despite the absence of a formal non-compliance procedure, but the 1996 Protocol now provides for one.[205] In practice, therefore, the Convention has largely achieved its objective of establishing a global framework for international action.

5 INTERNATIONAL TRADE IN WASTES

5(1) THE PERMISSIBILITY OF TRADE IN HAZARDOUS WASTES AND SUBSTANCES

The transboundary impact of trade in hazardous waste for disposal underlies the regime of shared responsibility found in the 1989 Basel Convention and regional

[204] See *Rept of the 21st Consultative Meeting*, paras 6.15–6.22, and Stokke, in Victor et al (eds), *Implementation and Effectiveness of International Environmental Commitments* (Cambridge, Mass, 1998) Ch 11.

[205] Article 11. A compliance procedure was adopted in 2007. See *Rept of the 29th Consultative Meeting*, LC 29/17 (2007) para 5 and Annex 7.

conventions dealing with this subject.[206] Unlike state practice in the case of nuclear installations, air pollution, or international watercourses, where the polluting state's freedom of action is limited only by its obligations of due diligence, notification and prior consultation, the 1989 Basel Convention firmly asserts the sovereignty of the receiving state to determine what impacts on its territory it will accept. Above all, the principle of prior informed consent on which it is based points to an important difference in approach. It cannot now be assumed that waste disposal in other states is permissible unless shown to be harmful. Instead, a strong form of the precautionary approach obliges the export state to demonstrate that the wastes will be managed in an 'environmentally sound manner'.

Prior to the 1992 Rio Conference, international policy declarations disclosed differing views on the permissibility of trade in hazardous waste. Industrialized economies represented in OECD accepted that production of hazardous wastes should be minimized as far as possible, that disposal should take place within member states where consistent with environmentally sound management, and that trade in wastes should be reduced and should take place on a basis of prior notification and environmentally sound management. Nevertheless, developed states did not seek to eliminate transboundary disposal entirely.[207] Regional groupings of developing states, in contrast, condemned all trade involving export of waste from developed to developing countries for disposal in their territories.[208] Their belief was that regulation would merely legitimise an unacceptable practice. Among the strongest exponents of this view was the Organization of African Unity ('OAU'), which declared dumping of nuclear and industrial wastes a crime against the African people, and called on African states not to accept waste from industrialized countries. OAU policy is reflected in the 1991 African Convention, which prohibits imports into Africa from non-parties and regulates trade in waste among African states.[209] Regional treaties covering the Mediterranean and the South Pacific also prohibit export of hazardous waste to developing state parties and small island state parties respectively, and ban imports by those states.[210] In addition, the fourth Lomé Convention, concluded in 1989, committed the EC to prohibit exports of radioactive or hazardous waste to any African, Caribbean, or Pacific Island states parties, and prohibited those states from importing such waste from the EC or from anywhere else.[211]

206 Kummer, *International Management of Hazardous Wastes: The Basel Convention and Related Legal Rules* (Oxford, 1995); Louka, *Overcoming Barriers to International Waste Trade* (Dordrecht, 1995); Bitar, *Les Mouvements Transfrontières de Déchets Dangereux Selon la Convention de Bâle* (Paris, 1997); Handl and Lutz, 30 *Harv ILJ* (1989) 351; Hackett, 5 *AUJILP* (1990) 291; Bothe, 33 *GYIL* (1990) 422; Desai, 37 *Indian JIL* (1997) 43.

207 See Kummer, *International Management of Hazardous Wastes*, 113–71.

208 ACP/EEC Joint Assembly, Madrid, 1988; ECOWAS, 11th Summit, Lomé, 1988; Final Document of the First Meeting of States of the Zone of Peace and Cooperation in the South Atlantic, Rio, 1988; Organization of African Unity, Resolution CM/Res 1153, 28 *ILM* (1989) 567.

209 See Kummer, *International Management of Hazardous Wastes*, 99–103; Biggs, 5 *Colorado JIELP* (1994) 333; Eze, 15 *Afr J Int'l & Comp L* (2007) 208. See also the comparable 1992 Central American Agreement on the Transboundary Movement of Hazardous Wastes, Article 3(1).

210 1996 Mediterranean Protocol. For a survey of regional agreements see UNEP/CHW 4/Inf 12 (1998).

211 Article 39, and Annexes VIII–X, 29 *ILM* (1990) 783. See Kummer, *International Management of Hazardous Wastes*, 107–12.

Like OECD, UNEP policy in promoting a global agreement initially preferred effective control of the waste trade rather than prohibition. Its 1985 Cairo Guidelines[212] acknowledged the need to respect international law applicable to protection of the environment and sought to ensure environmentally sound management of wastes. They formed the basis for the main international regulatory regime, the 1989 Basel Convention. Although unable to secure a trade ban, African states participated in the Basel negotiations, and their proposals on specific points were accepted.[213] The 1989 Basel Convention quickly attracted widespread support and the US remains the only significant non-party.

The Rio Conference did not support a ban on waste trade with developing countries. Nevertheless, Principle 14 called on all states to discourage or prevent transboundary transfer of substances hazardous to health or the environment. In 1994, developing countries, supported by Greenpeace, persuaded the second COP to the 1989 Basel Convention to ban the export from OECD countries of hazardous waste destined for disposal or recycling in non-OECD countries. This decision was formally incorporated in the Convention by amendment the following year,[214] but it entered into force only in 2019, after extensive efforts to promote ratification.[215] The ban applies only to an agreed list of hazardous wastes,[216] but it makes no distinction between disposal of waste and reuse or recycling, nor does it distinguish between developing states which possess adequate waste disposal or recycling facilities and those which do not. This is part of the problem: some developing states see economic opportunities in recycling valuable wastes, such as redundant ships and electronic equipment. For that reason they no longer favour a complete ban on waste trade,[217] but staying out of the 1989 Basel Convention is not an option, since Article 4(5) bans waste trade with non-parties.

However, despite the ban, not all trade in waste involving developing countries is prohibited. Under the 1989 Basel Convention, the 1991 African Convention, and the 1995 Convention to Ban the importation into Forum Island Countries of Hazardous and Radioactive Wastes and to Control the Transboundary Movement of Hazardous wastes within the South Pacific Region ('South Pacific Convention', also known as the Waigani Convention), trade in waste among developing states parties is not prohibited,

212 Cairo Guidelines and Principles of Environmentally Sound Management of Hazardous Wastes, 1985, UNEP/WG 122/3; 16 *EPL* (1986) 5, 31, approved by UNEP/GC 14/30 (1987).

213 UNEP, *Proposals and Position of the African States During Negotiations on the Basel Convention* (1989); Dakar Ministerial Conference on Hazardous Wastes, 1989.

214 Decision II/12, *Rept of 2nd COP*, UNEP/CHW 2/30 (1994); Decision III/1, *Rept of 3rd COP*, UNEP/CHW 3/35 (1995) inserting new preambular paragraph 7bis, new Article 4A, and new Annex VII. Only Russia expressly refused to accept the ban, but the US was also opposed, although not a Basel party. For background see Kitt, 7 *Georgetown IELR* (1995) 485.

215 See Basel Convention COP Decision 12/1, Rep of the 12th COP, UNEP/CHW.12/27 (2015) paras 44–46, and decision BC-10/3.

216 See Decision IV/9, adding new annexes VIII and IX, *Rept of 4th COP*, UNEP/CHW 4/35 (1998).

217 Kummer-Peiry. The Basel Convention on Control of Transboundary Movements of Hazardous Wastes and their Disposal, 107 *Proc ASIL* (2013) 434–5.

nor is export from these states to developed states parties. Moreover, Article 11 of the 1989 Basel Convention permits parties to conclude regional agreements with other parties *or non-parties*, provided these agreements 'do not derogate from the environmentally sound management of hazardous wastes and other wastes as required by this Convention'. If they meet this standard, and comply with the notice requirements of Article 11(2), developing state parties will still be able to import waste from developed states, although some may be debarred from doing so under regional agreements. It might also be argued that a developing state which accepts the ban amendment thereby accepts that it may not meet the standard of environmentally sound management with regard to waste from OECD states and, if so, that it will be in breach of its obligations under the Convention if it accepts such imports, even if trade takes place under an Article 11 agreement.[218]

In the absence of a wider consensus among exporting and importing states, it cannot be said that a policy of ending all trade in hazardous wastes has prevailed at a global level, nor that all waste exports to developing countries are illegal. What has been achieved is a compromise that places three important and far-reaching restrictions on this trade. First, as the 1991 African Convention indicates, it is clear that all states have the sovereign right to ban imports individually or regionally and that this right is recognized in the 1989 Basel Convention and by OECD states.[219] The 1989 Basel Convention further strengthens this right to prohibit trade in waste by providing for import bans to be notified to other parties through the secretariat; no state may then permit transboundary movement of wastes to a party prohibiting their import nor, save by special agreement, is transport for disposal by non-parties permitted.[220]

Secondly, transboundary movement is permitted only in circumstances where the state of export does not have the capacity or facilities to dispose of the wastes in an environmentally sound manner itself, unless intended for recycling. To this end, the 1989 Basel Convention is based on a philosophy of minimizing the generation of hazardous waste and promoting disposal at source. The African, South Pacific, and Mediterranean Conventions place additional emphasis on the use of clean production methods 'which avoid or eliminate the generation of hazardous wastes'. They represent the strongest indication of the growing international emphasis on waste disposal at source and the adoption of a precautionary approach to pollution control.[221]

218 See Crawford and Sands, *The Availability of Article 11 Agreements in the Context of the Basel Convention's Export Ban on Recyclables* (ICME, Ontario, 1997) 22. See also de La Fayette, 6 *YbIEL* (1995) 703 and Kummer, *International Management of Hazardous Wastes*, Ch 3.

219 1989 Basel Convention, Preamble, and Declaration annexed to the Final Act of the Basel Conference, 1989. See also OECD Decision C(83) 180, Preamble; 1991 African Convention, Article 4(1). Some 107 states were reported to have banned waste imports by 1995.

220 Articles 4(1) (2)(e) (5) 7, 11, 13. See also OECD Decision C(83) 180, Principle 8; Decision C(86) 64, para I, and 1991 African Convention, Article 4(3)(11).

221 1989 Basel Convention, Preamble and Articles 4(2)(a)(b)(d) 4(5) (9); 1985 Cairo Guidelines, Principle 2; 1991 African Convention, Preamble, and Articles 1(5) and 4(3); 1995 South Pacific Convention, Article 4(4); 1996 Mediterranean Protocol, Articles 5, 6; OECD Recommendation C(76) 155, Annex, Para 3; UNGA Res 43/212 (1988) 19 *EPL* (1989) 29; OECD Decision C(90) 178, and Recommendation C(90) 164.

Lastly, the Basel and regional conventions demonstrate widespread agreement that trade which does take place requires the prior informed consent of transit and import states,[222] that illegal trade must be prevented, that illegally exported waste should be accepted for reimport by the state of origin,[223] and that conditions of management, transport, and ultimate disposal must be environmentally sound, and compatible with the protection of health, the environment, and the prevention of pollution.[224]

These principles probably already represent customary law, since they are supported in part by state practice, by the sovereign right of states to control activities in their own territory, and by the responsibility of exporting states for activities within their jurisdiction which harm other states or the global environment.[225] By also placing on importing states an obligation of environmentally sound management,[226] the 1989 Basel Convention recognizes that they too have a responsibility in international law for the protection of their own environment, peoples, and future generations, and it makes their management of imported waste a matter of legitimate international concern. Uniquely, the 1989 Basel Convention is thus based on a system of environmental responsibility shared among all states involved in each transaction.

5(2) THE SCOPE OF THE BASEL CONVENTION

The 1989 Basel Convention is concerned only with household and hazardous waste disposed of or intended for disposal or recycling.[227] 'Disposal' is defined in broad terms.[228] It includes landfill, release into watercourses, the sea, or seabed, incineration, permanent storage, or recycling. One consequence is that the 1989 Basel Convention will apply to waste exported for dumping in coastal state maritime zones where, as we have seen, Article 210(5) of the 1982 UNCLOS already requires coastal state consent.[229] Wastes are 'hazardous' only when listed in the Convention's annexes, or if defined as such by national law and notified to the Convention's Secretariat.[230] In 2019 the annexes were amended to include certain categories of plastic waste that are difficult to recycle.[231] Radioactive wastes are excluded because they are covered by

[222] 1989 Basel Convention, Article 6; 1991 African Convention, Articles 4, 6, 7; 1995 South Pacific Convention, Article 6; 1996 Mediterranean Protocol, Article 6(3). See also OECD Decision C(86) 64, para I; Council Regulation COM (90) 415 Final; UNGA Res 43/212 (1988).

[223] 1989 Basel Convention, Article 9; 1991 African Convention, Article 9; South Pacific Convention, Articles 8, 9; Mediterranean Protocol, Articles 7, 9. See also OECD Decision C(83) 180, Principle 9; UNGA Res. 43/212 (1988).

[224] 1989 Basel Convention, Preamble and Articles 4(2)(c)–(e) (g) 7, 8; 1991 African Convention, Article 4. See also OECD Decision C(83) 180.

[225] Handl and Lutz, 30 *Harv ILJ* (1989) 359–60; Kummer, *International Management of Hazardous Wastes*, Ch 7; UNGA Res 43/212 (1988); 1985 Cairo Guidelines, Principle 2.

[226] Article 4.

[227] Articles 1, 2(1); 4A and Annexes I, II, VII and VIII. But it does not cover trade in waste for recycling in OECD state parties: see Article 4A.

[228] Article 2(4) and Annex IV. [229] See *supra*, section 4.

[230] Article 3. Cf the African Convention, Article 2, which is broader than the Basel definition.

[231] COP decision BC 14/12 (2019), 'Amendments to Annexes II, VIII and IX to the Basel Convention' UNEP/CHW.14/12.

other arrangements.[232] So are wastes derived from the 'normal operations of a ship', thus enabling oil or chemical cargo residues to be discharged to a port reception facility if in accordance with the 1973/78 MARPOL Convention.[233] Unlike the 1972 London Convention, there are no categories of hazardous waste which may not be exported. OECD's definition follows the same pattern but allows for bilateral or unilateral departure from the basic classification.[234] The 1989 Basel Convention acknowledges no such freedom but instead sets an obligatory minimum standard for states.[235]

Trade in hazardous substances not intended for disposal or recycling is not regulated by the 1989 Basel Convention, although the 1991 African Convention does apply where substances have been banned, refused registration, or voluntarily withdrawn in the country of manufacture for health and environmental reasons. With this exception the main legal constraints on trade in hazardous substances are those supplied by customary law, non-binding instruments such as UNEP's Guidelines for the Exchange of Information on Chemicals in International Trade or the FAO's Code of Conduct on the Distribution and Use of Pesticides, and the 1998 Rotterdam Convention on Prior Informed Consent.[236] Like the earlier guidelines, the latter convention provides further evidence that international law recognizes the shared responsibility of importing and exporting states for the protection of health and the environment, and an obligation of good neighbourliness.

5(3) THE REQUIREMENT OF PRIOR INFORMED CONSENT

Only rarely does international law require the prior consent of other states before environmentally harmful activities may be undertaken. As we saw in Chapter 3 the *Lac Lanoux Case* expressly rejects such a rule for the use of shared resources, nor does it normally apply to pollution of common spaces. In these cases, prior informed consultation at most is called for.[237] Unusually, the essence of the control system established by the 1989 Basel Convention is the need for prior, informed, written consent from transit states and the state of import.[238] Only in the case of transit states which are parties to the Convention can this requirement be waived in favour of tacit acquiescence.[239] Information must be supplied which is sufficient to enable the nature and effects on health and the environment of the proposed movement to be assessed.[240]

There are two ways in which the requirement of prior informed consent is enforced. The first is by making the state of export accept the return of illegal waste where practicable or, where the importer is at fault, imposing on the state of import a duty to ensure safe disposal of the waste.[241] There is some evidence that state practice already

232 See *sufra*, Ch 7. The African and South Pacific Conventions do cover nuclear waste.

233 Article 1(4). On MARPOL see *infra*, Ch 9. The Basel Convention COP has, however, called for guidance on how to improve the sea-land interface, building upon work carried out by the IMO in this respect; see Basel Convention COP Decision 12/16 (2015).

234 Decision C(88) 90, 28 *ILM* (1989) 257.

235 Article 1(1).

236 *Supra*, section 2(2).

237 See *supra*, Ch 3, section 8 and *infra*, Ch 10.

238 Articles 4(1)(c) 4(2)(f) 6(1)–(2) 6(10) 7.

239 Article 6(4).

240 Articles 4(2)(f) 6(1) and Annex V.

241 1989 Basel Convention, Article 9; 1991 African Convention, Article 9; 1996 Mediterranean Protocol, Article 7; 1995 South PacificConvention, Article 8.

favours the return of illegally exported waste to the state of origin, as in the case of the *Karin B*, whose cargo Italy was obliged to take back.[242] The second method employed by the 1989 Basel Convention is to ensure that states punish illegal traffic as a criminal offence.[243] It is possible that this provision might justify an extraterritorial protective jurisdiction over foreign nationals engaged in the illegal export of hazardous waste to a country which has prohibited its import.[244] This would provide an additional enforcement mechanism where the exporting state's procedures are lax or inadequate. One difficulty with these otherwise salutary enforcement rules is the possibility that they may result in illegal dumping at sea; the phasing out of dumping at sea will resolve this difficulty, however.[245] Another problem is the qualified nature of the duty to reimport: 'impracticability' is a vague and subjective notion which the exporting state itself is left to interpret. Once again the 1991 African Convention is stronger: Article 9 simply compels the exporting state to ensure that illegal waste is taken back within thirty days, without reference to practicality.

The requirement of prior consent, as we have seen, is simply an expression of the sovereignty of a state over the use of its territory and resources. It is this which differentiates transboundary disposal of wastes from the use of common spaces or shared resources. Where transit takes place through maritime areas, however, no such basis in territorial sovereignty exists. In the exclusive economic zone, foreign vessels enjoy high seas freedom of navigation.[246] In the territorial sea, although subject to coastal state sovereignty, they have a right of innocent passage.[247] Ships carrying dangerous or noxious substances in the territorial sea may be confined to the use of designated sea lanes and are required to carry documents and observe special precautionary measures established by international agreement, but they do not lose their rights of passage, and may not be discriminated against.[248] Article 4(12) of the 1989 Basel Convention appears to leave these navigational rights in the EEZ and territorial sea unaffected. In general, maritime states have interpreted this to mean that prior notice or consent for the passage of vessels carrying hazardous wastes or substances is not required, but not all coastal states accept this view.[249] As with oil tankers, the more convincing conclusion is that the passage of ships carrying dangerous cargoes

[242] UK House of Lords, *2nd Rept of the Environment Committee on Toxic Waste*, i (1988–9) para 253; Handl and Lutz, 30 *Harv ILJ* (1989) 360; Weinstein, 9 *IJMCL* (1994) 135.

[243] Articles 4(3)–(4) 9(5). See also 1991 African Convention, Article 4(1); 1996 Mediterranean Protocol, Article 9(2); 1995 South Pacific Convention, Article 9(2).

[244] *The Lotus Case*, PCIJ Ser A, No 10 (1927) 28.

[245] *Supra*, section 4.

[246] 1982 UNCLOS, Article 58.

[247] 1982 UNCLOS, Articles 2, 17–21; *Corfu Channel Case*, ICJ Reports (1949) 3.

[248] 1982 UNCLOS, Articles 22–5. Documentation and special precautionary measures are required by the 1973/78 MARPOL Convention for oil, noxious liquids, and chemicals in bulk.

[249] See e.g. the British declaration on the 1989 Basel Convention, 39 *ICLQ* (190) 944, but *contra*, Haiti *Note Verbale* of 18 Feb 1988, 11 *LOSB* (1988) 13, and Article 6(4) of the 1996 Mediterranean Protocol. Article 4(4)(c) of the African Convention recognizes 'the exercise by ships and aircraft of all states of navigation rights and freedoms as provided for in international law and as reflected in relevant international instruments'. Article 2(5) of the 1995 South Pacific Convention preserves rights and obligations under 1982 UNCLOS.

may be regulated by coastal states according to international standards, but these vessels cannot unilaterally be excluded from exercising their rights of navigation, despite the risk they pose.[250] However, in appropriate circumstances the designation of Particularly Sensitive Sea Areas, areas to be avoided, traffic lanes and compulsory pilotage schemes, *inter alia*, will allow passage to be controlled.[251]

5(4) ENVIRONMENTALLY SOUND MANAGEMENT

The primary obligation imposed by the 1989 Basel Convention is to manage the transboundary movement of waste in an environmentally sound manner. This obligation applies to exporting, transit, and importing states alike,[252] and also to trade with non-parties, which may only be conducted under an agreement providing for management no less environmentally sound than is required by the Convention.[253] The crucial point is that states must not permit export or import of waste if they believe that it will not be handled in an environmentally sound manner.[254] Developing states do not escape this responsibility for sound management of imported waste; if they cannot meet it, they must either seek assistance, relying on the Convention's provisions for international cooperation, or prohibit the import.[255] Nor can the exporting state escape its obligations by transferring responsibility to the state of transit or import; wherever the waste is sent the exporting state retains a responsibility for ensuring its proper management at all stages until final disposal, and must permit reimport if necessary.[256]

What is meant by 'environmentally sound management' is defined in the Convention only in general terms: 'taking all practicable steps to ensure that hazardous waste or other wastes are managed in a manner which will protect human health and the environment against the adverse effects which may result from such wastes'.[257] Much more detail is given in guidelines progressively adopted by the parties.[258] These explain what

[250] 1982 UNCLOS, Articles 21(2) 211; but see Pineschi, in Francioni and Scovazzi (eds), *International Responsibility for Environmental Harm* (Dordrecht, 1991) 299.

[251] See *supra*, Ch 9, section 5(3).

[252] Article 4.

[253] Articles 4(5) and 7 as qualified by Article 11. Article 6 of the 1996 Protocol to the 1972 London Convention prohibits export of waste for dumping at sea by non-parties.

[254] Articles 4(2)(e) (g) and 4(8); 1991 African Convention, Article 4(3)(n).

[255] Articles 4(2)(g) and 10; Handl and Lutz, 30 *Harv ILJ* (1989) 363.

[256] Articles 4(10) and 8; 1991 African Convention, Articles 4(3)(o) and 8.

[257] Article 2(8); 1991 African Convention, Article 1(10).

[258] See in particular Basel Declaration on Environmentally Sound Management, Decision V/1, *Rept of 5th COP*, UNEP/CHW 5/29 (1999) Annex II; Decision II/13 on Technical Guidelines for the Environmentally Sound Management of Waste, *Rept of 2nd COP*, UNEP/CHW 2/30 (1994); Decision VI/20 on Technical Guidelines for the Environmentally Sound Management of Biomedical and Health-care Wastes; Decision VI/21 on Technical Guidelines for the Identification and Environmentally Sound Management of Plastic Wastes; Decision VI/24 on Technical Guidelines for the Environmentally Sound Management of the Full and Partial Dismantling of Ships, *Rept of 6th COP*, UNEP/CHW 6/40 (2003) Decision 12/3 on Technical Guidelines for the Environmentally Sound Management of Wastes consisting of, or contaminated with, Persistent Organic Pollutants, *Rept of 12th COP*, UNEP/CHW.12/27 (2015); Decision 12/4 on Technical Guidelines for the Environmentally Sound Management of Wastes consisting of, or contaminated with, Mercury, *Rept of 12th COP*, UNEP/CHW.12/27 (2015). See also UNEP's 1985 Cairo Guidelines.

the parties mean by 'environmentally sound management' and are intended to be a point of reference for the development of national waste-management strategies. The principal aims of the Convention are reiterated, including waste prevention and minimization, least transboundary movement, recycling, self-sufficiency and proximity of disposal. Criteria to be used in assessing the soundness of waste-management standards include the following: whether the regulatory and enforcement infrastructure can ensure compliance, whether waste sites are authorized and of adequate standard to deal with the waste in question, whether operators of waste sites are adequately trained, whether sites are monitored, and whether waste generation is minimized through best practice and clean production methods. What is environmentally sound in the country of import may also depend on the level of technology and pollution control available in the exporting country: the implication is that it is unlikely to be environmentally sound to import waste from states with higher standards of waste disposal.[259] Additional guidance is provided for wastes identified as requiring priority attention.

Although these guidelines are not obligatory, their adoption by the parties gives them persuasive force as a basic standard for states to meet in fulfilling their obligations under the 1989 Basel Convention. As such they have a legal significance comparable to IAEA guidelines for the disposal of radioactive waste and they can easily be updated. The Guidelines have been supplemented by a Framework for the Environmentally Sound Management of Hazardous Wastes and Other Wastes adopted at the 11th COP in 2013. The Framework is intended to provide a practical guide on what countries should do at the national level in order to overcome the challenges of implementing environmentally sound management of waste.[260] The Framework is part of a broader technical assistance programme to support states in the implementation of international rules relating to the management of hazardous substances. This element of the international regime is considered vital to ensuring the effectiveness of the Convention and cooperation between the secretariats of the 1989 Basel Convention and related treaties (POPs and Rotterdam Conventions).

International standards for the carriage of dangerous goods also govern some aspects of the transport of hazardous waste.[261] In some cases, such as annexes to the 1973/78 MARPOL Convention and the International Maritime Dangerous Goods ('IMDG') Code, these are already legally binding, but the 1989 Basel Convention goes further by requiring that packaging, labelling, and transport should conform to generally accepted rules and standards and take account of internationally recognized practices, whether or not these are otherwise obligatory.[262] This is a strong indication

[259] 1994 Technical Guidelines, para 9(b). See also the amendments to the Convention adopted in 1995, *supra*.

[260] Basel COP Decision 11/1, *Rept of 11th COP*, UNEP/CHW.11/24 (2013).

[261] E.g. 1973/78 MARPOL Convention, Annexes II, III; IMO International Maritime Dangerous Goods Code (IMDG); 1944 Convention on International Civil Aviation, Annex 18; 1957 European Agreement Concerning the International Carriage of Dangerous Goods by Road; 1985 Convention and Regulation on the International Carriage of Dangerous Goods by Rail.

[262] Article 4(7)(b); 1991 African Convention, Article 4(3)(m).

that transport failing to comply with international standards cannot be regarded as environmentally sound management.

In substance, this obligation is no more than a reformulation of the standard of due diligence which has generally been employed to describe international obligations for the control of environmentally harmful activities or substances.[263] Like the 1982 UNCLOS, the 1989 Basel Convention identifies the detailed content of this standard by reference to other instruments, and allows for further development. In this sense its provisions on environmentally sound management are a starting point only, not a complete code in themselves.

5(5) IMPLEMENTATION AND SUPERVISORY INSTITUTIONS

Further development of the 1989 Basel Convention regime is the responsibility of the COP established for this purpose. It has power to adopt decisions, amendments and protocols, and to undertake any additional action required to further the objectives of the Conventions.[264] The obligatory provision of information from parties regarding transboundary movements, their effects on health and the environment, and any accidents during transport or disposal,[265] gives the Conference a basis on which to review the effectiveness of the Convention and the policies of states. In most respects the 1989 Basel Convention's provision for international supervision thus follows the typical pattern adopted in many environmental treaties.[266] Unusually, the COP has pioneered direct participation by industry as a means of securing agreement on how to handle end-of-life electronic equipment such as mobile phones and computers.

Although several additional functions are given to the secretariat, including assistance in identifying illegal traffic,[267] the role of this body in verifying alleged breaches of obligation under Article 19 of the Convention is confined to relaying 'all relevant information' to the parties. This allows it only a limited monitoring function which falls well short of some proposals made at the Basel Conference to give the secretariat stronger verification powers.[268] Neither the secretariat nor other parties are given any power of independent inspection, an omission which limits the potential effectiveness of the Convention's control and supervision regime. However, a procedure adopted in 2003 allows possible non-compliance to be referred by the party in difficulty, or by another party, or by the secretariat.[269] In common with most non-compliance procedures, a committee nominated by the parties has the power to offer advice or make recommendations to facilitate implementation and compliance. Cautions may only be issued by the COP. Although there is no express provision for suspension of

263 *Supra*, Ch 3, section 5. 264 Article 15. 265 Article 13. 266 *Supra*, Ch 2, section 5.

267 Article 16.

268 See Kummer, 41 *ICLQ* (1992) 530 and proposal by Nigeria, UNEP/WG 191/CRP 14. Cf Article 13 of the 1996 Mediterranean Protocol.

269 Decision VI/12, *Rept of 6th COP*, UNEP/CHW 6/40 (2003). See UNEP, *The Basel Convention Mechanism for Promoting Implementation and Compliance: Celebrating a Decade of Assistance to Parties* (Geneva, 2011).

trade rights, in an appropriately serious case such a response would be consistent both with the law of treaties and practice in other trade-related MEAs, such as the 1973 CITES.[270] The alternative is to resort to dispute settlement machinery, but this requires the agreement of the parties concerned.[271]

5(6) STATE RESPONSIBILITY AND CIVIL LIABILITY

A major defect of the 1989 Basel Convention at the time of its adoption was the absence of any agreement on principles of liability and compensation for damage resulting from transboundary movements of waste. The Convention does require the parties to cooperate in adopting a protocol on this question, and it recognizes that states are liable in international law for the non-fulfilment of their environmental obligations.[272] Potential recourse to customary principles of state responsibility for environmental damage is a necessary element of any regime of environmental protection but, as in the case of nuclear damage, it must be combined with an effective scheme of transboundary civil liability if compensation is to be a realistic remedy in cases of illegal traffic where recourse is sought against the exporter. Negotiations began in 1990 to identify the elements of such a protocol, including an international fund from which compensation payments could be made to claimants bringing legal proceedings in national courts.[273]

The Protocol on Liability and Compensation,[274] adopted by the parties in 1999, shares many of the essential features of other liability treaties but differs in certain important respects. It applies only to damage resulting from the transboundary movement and disposal of waste. No single operator is liable at all stages, nor is the generator always liable. Instead, generators, exporters, importers, and disposers are all potentially liable at different stages of the waste's journey to its eventual destination. In general, during export and transit the person who notifies the states concerned of a proposed transboundary movement of waste will be liable (this will be either the generator or the exporter of the waste); then the ultimate disposer of the waste assumes liability once possession is transferred. In this case, the shipper and the importer will not be liable. Where the waste is classified as hazardous only in the state of import, then the importer will also be liable until the disposer takes possession. There are additional rules covering who is liable when no notification is given, or when waste has to be returned to the state of origin.

270 *Supra*, Ch 4, section 3. 271 Article 20, Annex VI.

272 Article 12 and Preamble.

273 *2nd Rept of the ad hoc Working Group of Legal and Technical Experts*, UNEP/CHW/WG 1/2/L1 (1991) and corr 1. See generally Kummer, *International Management of Hazardous Wastes*, Ch 6; Handl and Lutz, 30 *Harv ILJ* (1989) 359; Murphy, 88 *AJIL* (1994) 24. Muchlinski, *The Right to Development and the Industrialisation of Less Developed Countries: The Case of Compensation for Major Industrial Accidents* (Commonwealth Secretariat, London, 1989) offers a valuable critique of the issues from the point of view of less developed countries.

274 See *Rept of 5th COP*, UNEP/CHW 5/29 (1999) Annex III; Soares and Vargas, 12 *YbIEL* (2001) 69.

Liability under the Protocol is strict, subject to a limited range of defences. Additional fault-based liability is placed on any person whose failure to comply with laws implementing the 1989 Basel Convention or whose wrongful, intentional, reckless, or negligent acts or omissions have caused the damage. Where several parties are liable, which is clearly possible, liability is joint and several. There is a right of recourse against any other person liable under the Protocol, or under a contract, or under the law of the competent court. There are no limits on the amount recoverable for fault-based liability. Other liability limits are determined by national law, but the Protocol sets a minimum level in accordance with a formula based on the amount of the waste (Annex B) and insurance or other financial guarantee is compulsory. Supplementary compensation covering environmental damage is provided on an interim basis from a fund established by the COP.[275] It is available only to developing state parties or economies in transition. This limitation is not a feature of other compensation schemes. Another difference is that the fund is financed by voluntary contributions from the parties to the Convention. There is no requirement for industry to contribute.

A number of states and NGOs voiced serious criticisms of the Protocol.[276] African states criticized the failure to provide an adequate and permanent compensation fund. Australia, Canada, and NGOs were concerned that parties to Article 11 agreements could opt for alternative liability arrangements, thereby creating confusion and protracted litigation as to which liability regime is applicable. They also believed that channelling liability to the exporter/notifier, rather than to the person in operational control (i.e. the waste generator) did not properly reflect the polluter pays principle. Waste generators would be able to pass on the burden of liability to exporters, and would have less incentive to monitor disposal standards themselves. Leaving national law to determine maximum liability limits would also create further uncertainty and inconsistency, while the minimum limits based on waste tonnage would in some cases be too low, in others too high, depending on the nature of the waste. In their view, shared by others, these deficiencies were likely to delay ratification, and indeed the Protocol had not yet entered into force by the end of 2020.

Regional agreements also make some provision for civil liability. In Europe, the 1993 Lugano Convention on Civil Liability would apply insofar as waste disposal or recycling involve production, handling, storage, use, or discharge of dangerous substances.[277] This agreement is not in force. The 1991 African Convention and the 1996 Mediterranean Protocol call on the parties to develop liability rules, but no results have been forthcoming under either treaty. The 1986 US–Canada and US–Mexico Agreements allow for compulsory insurance as a condition of entry, and in the latter case also require the authorities where practicable to secure compensation through existing national law.[278]

275 Decision V/32, *Rept of 5th COP*, UNEP/CHW 5/29 (1999) and Decision VI/14, *Rept of 6th COP*, UNEP/CHW 6/40 (2003). Compare the 1992 Convention on the Establishment of an International Fund for Compensation for Oil Pollution Damage, *supra*, Ch 9.

276 *Rept of the 5th COP*, UNEP/CHW 5/29 (1999) paras 83–9; 30 *EPL* (2000) 43.

277 *Supra*, Ch 5.

278 Articles 9 and 14 respectively. For US law see the 1980 Comprehensive Environmental Response, Compensation and Liability Act, which creates a 'superfund' for clean-up costs and imposes strict liability on anyone with a legal interest in the waste disposal site.

5(7) AN ASSESSMENT OF THE BASEL CONVENTION

The most serious criticisms of the 1989 Basel Convention are that it legitimizes trade which cannot adequately be monitored or controlled, and leaves developing states vulnerable to unsafe disposal practices.[279] The entry into force of the ban on waste exports from OECD to non-OECD countries goes some way towards addressing the second problem. Moreover, the Convention leaves open the possibility of import bans on a national or regional basis, and provides an effective mechanism for publicizing these or other restrictions. The 1991 African Convention indicates how regional measures to give stronger protection to third world countries remain a viable option under the 1989 Basel Convention. This is undoubtedly a more realistic means of safeguarding these countries than a complete international ban on all trade in hazardous waste.[280]

Developing countries remain particularly vulnerable to illegal waste trade, however. This is probably the biggest problem facing the 1989 Basel Convention. Indeed it is sufficiently serious to be characterized by the UN Human Rights Commission as a form of 'environmental racism' and a serious threat to the rights to life and health in Africa and developing nations elsewhere.[281] The Commission acknowledged that the 1995 amendment banning the export of hazardous wastes from OECD to non-OECD countries should lead to a major reduction in such trade, but it pointed to the difficulties faced by developing countries in implementing the Convention effectively within their territories, and the need for stronger action by developed states to prevent illegal traffic. Fraud, corruption, and the use of 'shell companies' all undermine efforts to control a trade which has significant connections with organized crime. So does uncertainty about the boundary between the 1973/78 MARPOL and 1989 Basel Conventions, a problem illuminated by the serious health effects of waste offloaded from an oil tanker in Abidjan.[282] In this case prosecutions and a large mass-damages action have resulted. The parties to the 1989 Basel Convention have called for stronger measures to deal with illegal traffic, including appropriate sanctions or penalties, and cooperation through Interpol and the World Customs Organization.[283] However, apart from seeking to assist developing countries to enhance their capacity to control illegal trade, there is little the Convention organs can do about it: jurisdiction over criminal activity remains a matter for individual parties. When detected, illegal exports can be returned to

[279] See Handl, in Canadian Council on International Law, *Proceedings of the 18th Annual Conference* (1989) 367.

[280] *Ibid*, 371.

[281] Resolution 1997/9, UN Doc E/CN 4/RES/1997/9 (1997). The Commission appointed a special rapporteur to investigate the issue. See UN Commission on Human Rights, 57th session, *Rept on Adverse Effects of the Illicit Movement and Dumping of Toxic and Dangerous Products and Wastes on the Enjoyment of Human Rights*, UN Doc E/CN 4/2001/55 (2001) and subsequent reports.

[282] *Supra*, Ch 9, and UNEP, *Rept of 1st meeting of the Expanded Bureau of the 8th meeting of the Conference of the Parties to the Basel Convention* (2007) UNEP/SBC/BUREAU/8/1/7, section III.

[283] Decision IV/12, *Rept of 4th COP*, UNEP/CHW 4/35 (1998).

the state of export. This does happen, but it is not always easy to identify the export state nor is it necessarily practical to secure return of the waste. Although it gives export states some incentive to control illegal traffic, the duty to re-import is not by itself sufficient to ensure effective suppression.

Other aspects of the 1989 Basel Convention also require consideration if it is to succeed in reducing the risks of unregulated waste disposal. Although progress has been made in defining in more detail what 'environmentally sound management' consists of, the Convention's implementation remains dependent on assumptions that importing states have the expertise and technology required to handle this trade, if they choose to do so, and that exporting states are realistically in a position to assess the capabilities of importers. A regime of shared responsibility may be desirable, but it is not clear that importing states will necessarily have the ability to protect themselves, nor that exporting states will in practice do this for them. The obvious risk is that both exporting and importing states may take an essentially subjective view of what constitutes 'environmentally sound management' and of the risks involved in transboundary waste movements. The argument that informed public scrutiny is likely to be the most effective way of policing transboundary waste movements is a cogent one,[284] but this implies a level of transparency and public access to decision-making which the 1989 Basel Convention does very little to require or promote.[285]

The Convention offers a model for regulating other problems of transboundary trade, whether in hazardous chemicals or technologies, and it affords evidence of the development of customary principles which may govern these activities. As we have seen, some of its main principles are already applied by analogy to international trade in chemicals. The Bhopal chemical plant accident indicates some of the legal complexities affecting trade in hazardous technology, however, particularly in questions of liability and the obligations of importing states.[286] Thirty years later these have not been resolved. Yet it is difficult to resist the conclusion that here too the principle of prior informed consent, and the assurance of environmentally sound management, would have an important potential role in any dispute.

6 CONCLUSIONS

The importance of adequate institutional machinery for supervising implementation of environmental protection treaties and ensuring their continued development is clearly illustrated in this chapter. The relative success of the 1972 London Convention

284 Handl and Lutz, 30 *Harv ILJ* (1989) 373.

285 But see *supra*, Ch 5, section 2(6).

286 See generally Muchlinksi, 50 *MLR* (1987) 545; Anderson, in Butler (ed), *Control Over Compliance with International Law* (Dordrecht, 1991) 83; Francioni, in Francioni and Scovazzi, *International Responsibility for Environmental Harm*, 275.

and the 1989 Basel Convention in evolving to meet new priorities, the slower progress of regional institutions dealing with land-based marine pollution, and the severe limitations of the 1998 Rotterdam Convention on Prior Informed Consent, indicate both the strengths and weaknesses of international regulation. Continuing problems of illegal traffic in hazardous waste and chemicals also show that an international regime is only as strong as the capacity of national administrations to implement and enforce it. The lack of adequate compliance machinery is only part of the reason for the difficulty of enforcing the 1989 Basel Convention.

Nevertheless, the evidence of state practice and international conventions considered here support the propositions expressed by Articles 192 and 194 of the 1982 UNCLOS that states are obliged by international law to protect the marine environment by taking diligent measures to prevent, reduce, and control pollution of common areas. The trend towards phasing out most forms of dumping, both globally and regionally, suggests that the dumping of potentially toxic waste at sea is now unlawful. Moreover, the acceptance, both in state practice and in international conventions, of the principle of prior informed consent as a condition for the disposal of toxic wastes and substances in the territory or maritime zones of other states supports the view that this has become a requirement of general international law. Growing support for a precautionary approach to protection of the environment is apparent in the development of clean technology requirements, in the prohibition of dumping, in the stronger regulation of land-based disposal to the marine environment, and in the requirement of prior environmental impact assessment for waste-disposal activities affecting other states and the sea. The 2001 POPs Convention also indicates the influence of the precautionary principle in international regulatory regimes, although the 1998 Rotterdam Convention on Prior Informed Consent plainly does not. However, the evidence supports the view expressed in Chapter 3 that it is premature to treat the precautionary principle as a rule of customary international law, or to draw firm conclusions regarding its specific content.

It must also be concluded that the generality and weakness of the provisions of the 1982 UNCLOS and of regional conventions in dealing with land-based sources of pollution have both undermined their effectiveness and contributed to their failure to give more concrete content to the obligation to protect and preserve the marine environment. While a global convention might lead to improved institutional supervision of measures to deal with this source of pollution, effective action requires a level of political commitment and international consensus, supported by necessary economic and technical assistance and cooperation that has so far been absent. Renewed attempts to deal more successfully with these problems, and to integrate the prevention of land-based marine pollution into a much broader framework of sustainable development of coastal zones and ocean resources, have resulted from the 1992 Rio Conference and from subsequent follow-up conferences.[287] What has emerged is a

[287] See in particular the 2015 SDGs, para 14, *supra*, Ch 2, section 2.

more integrated and precautionary approach to marine resource management which encompasses pollution control, ecosystem protection, the impact of climate change, and an enhanced role for international and regional institutions, and which no longer assumes that the oceans are an 'infinite sink or receptacle for wastes and an endless supply of free and open access resources'.[288] Nearly three decades after UNCED it still remains to be seen whether this appreciation of the limitations of earlier international law and institutional arrangements for the management of land-based activities and their impact on the oceans will lead to more radical and effective measures of international and regional cooperation to protect the oceans.

288 UNEP, *Rept of the Meeting of Government–Designated Experts*, UNEP (OCA)/WG 14/L1/Add 2 (1991) and, for a recent review, UNEP, *The Global Programme of Action for the Protection of the Marine Environment from Land-Based Activities: A 20-year Perspective on a Unique Programme to Advance the Ocean Agenda*, UNEP/GPA/IGR.4/INF/3 (2018).

9

PREVENTION OF MARINE POLLUTION

1 INTRODUCTION

The oceans are the world's largest expanse of common space. They have been freely used for maritime commerce, exploitation of living resources, extraction of oil and gas, and as a disposal area for the waste products of industry, agriculture, domestic life, and war. The pressure of international competition for living resources led to the conclusion of the first multilateral treaties on seals, fisheries, and whaling in the early twentieth century.[1] Since then over-fishing and degradation of marine ecosystems have intensified. The subsequent history and development of international law relating to conservation of marine living resources and biodiversity is considered in Chapter 12, but in this chapter and the next we focus on threats to the health of the marine environment as a whole, and in particular on marine pollution.

The emergence of marine pollution as a problem of international concern was evident as early as 1926, when a draft convention on pollution from ships was drawn up at a conference in Washington, but not opened for signature. By the late 1960s awareness of the impact of pollution and human populations on coastal environments had become widespread. The *Torrey Canyon* disaster in 1967 contaminated large areas of coastline by oil and exemplified the risk posed by the transport of polluting

* We are grateful to Professor James Harrison, University of Edinburgh, for his contribution to revising this chapter.

[1] 1911 Fur Seals Convention; 1923 Northern Pacific Halibut Convention; 1930 Pacific Salmon Fisheries Convention; 1931 Whaling Convention.

substances at sea. The discovery that mercury emissions from a factory at Minamata in Japan had poisoned fish and endangered the health of coastal communities showed that comprehensive control of all potential pollution sources was required. Scientific studies conducted in the 1970s and 80s identified significant pollution of the sea by oil, persistent organic compounds, chemicals, nuclear waste, and the effluent of urban, industrial society.[2] For all these reasons protection of the marine environment from pollution and sustainable use of its living resources have been significant issues in the modernization of the law of the sea brought about by the 1982 UNCLOS and subsequent agreements.

Because of the considerable attention devoted to the control of oil pollution from ships and dumping of waste at sea, these are today a much-reduced component of marine pollution. Even the major oil tanker accidents contribute less than the amount of oil believed to seep into the oceans naturally.[3] Blowouts at oil wells such as *Deepwater Horizon* can cause serious pollution,[4] but such accidents are rare. The major challenges facing the marine environment today come not from shipping or oil wells but from land-based activities and climate change.[5] Sewage, industrial waste, and agricultural run-off are the most common types of pollutant which enter coastal waters from land, mostly through rivers. Some of these pollutants are directly toxic to marine life and humans or spread disease. Others contribute to eutrophication and oxygen depletion, resulting in loss of marine biodiversity and altering sensitive ecosystems.[6] Research has also shown that more than 8 million tons of plastic are entering the oceans annually.[7] High concentrations of microplastics have been found even in remote areas, and in marine living resources, including coral reefs. Further harmful impacts on the marine ecosystem are caused by the incidental transport of invasive species in ships' ballast water and their discharge many thousands of miles from their natural habitat. Thus, effective pollution control is important not only for the general health of the marine environment but also for its impact on the conservation of fish stocks, endangered species and marine ecosystems.

Climate change has also begun to harm marine ecosystems. The surface ocean absorbs around one quarter of the carbon dioxide emitted to the atmosphere, at increasingly rapid rates,[8] resulting in acidification with harmful impacts on marine life. It also absorbs over 90 per cent of the excess heat generated by global warming,

2 GESAMP, *The State of the Marine Environment* (UNEP, 1990) and see *infra*, Ch 8.

3 GESAMP, *Reports and Studies No 75: Estimates of oil entering the marine environment from sea-based activities* (London, 2007).

4 See *infra*, section 5(3).

5 UN, *Rept of S-G: Oceans and Law of the Sea*, GAOR/A/72/70 (2017); GESAMP, *Reports and Studies No 71: Protecting the oceans from land-based activities etc* (UN, 2001); GESAMP, *Reports and Studies No 91: Pollution in the Open Oceans 2009–2013* (London, 2015); IMO, *Third Greenhouse Gas Study* (London, 2015).

6 UNEP/GPA, *The State of the Marine Environment* (Nairobi, 2006).

7 GESAMP, *Reports and Studies No 93: Sources, fate and effects of microplastics in the marine environment: part two of a global assessment* (London, 2016).

8 CBD, *Technical Series no 46: Scientific Synthesis of the Impacts of Ocean Acidification on Marine Biodiversity* (Montreal, 2009) 9.

resulting in higher ocean temperatures, melting ice shelves in the polar seas, loss of coral reefs and other vulnerable marine species, alterations in the distribution of marine species, and ultimately sea level rise.[9] All of this constitutes marine pollution as defined by Article 1(1)(4) of the 1982 UNCLOS.[10]

Although 'there is no longer room for complacency in our approach to protection and management of the open oceans',[11] it is the biologically productive coastal waters that remain the most seriously affected by environmental changes and where international action is most urgent. Regional agreements concerned with enclosed or semi-enclosed seas have attempted to coordinate environmental measures in these areas.[12] Since 1992, they have been strengthened and extended in response to Agenda 21 of the Rio Conference, with renewed emphasis on sustainable development, a precautionary approach, and integrated coastal-zone management. There is evidence that this has begun to reverse the deterioration of some regional seas. In the north-east Atlantic, for example, the OSPAR Commission concluded in 2000 that 'The trends towards worsening pollution have been reversed, and in a substantial number of significant cases the source of the pollution has been stopped.'[13] Nevertheless, ten years later, problems remained in many coastal areas, while biodiversity, seabirds and other marine species continued to decline, as ocean temperatures, sea levels, and acidification all increased.[14] Other regional seas have fared less well: the Gulf of Mexico now has the largest biologically dead zone of any semi-enclosed sea.[15] Since 1950 the areas of dead ocean where there is little or no oxygen have quadrupled in size, and even more in coastal areas.[16]

1(1) THE 1982 UN CONVENTION ON THE LAW OF THE SEA

The 1982 UNCLOS was intended to provide:

> a legal order for the seas and oceans which will facilitate international communication, and will promote the peaceful uses of the seas and oceans, the equitable and efficient utilization of their resources, the conservation of their living resources, and the study, protection and preservation of the marine environment.[17]

It thus attempts for the first time to establish a global framework for the rational exploitation and conservation of the sea's resources and the protection of the marine environment, while also recognizing the continued importance of freedom of navigation and other traditional freedoms of the seas.

[9] IOC/UNESCO, Building Stewardship for the Ocean, *ICES Journal of Marine Science* (4 June 2009) 1–4; FAO, *Climate Change Implications for Fisheries and Aquaculture* (Rome, 2008); IPCC, *Special Report on the Ocean and Cryosphere in a Changing Climate* (2019). See generally, Allsopp *et al*, *State of the World's Oceans* (Dordrecht, 2009) Ch 5.

[10] *Supra*, Ch 3, section 9, and see Boyle, 34 *IJMCL* (2019) 458.

[11] GESAMP, *Reports and Studies No 91: Pollution in the Open Oceans 2009–2013* (London, 2015).

[12] See *infra*, Ch 8.

[13] OSPAR, *Quality Status Report 2000* (London, 2000) 102.

[14] OSPAR, *Quality Status Report 2010* (London, 2010) 'Key findings.'

[15] UNEP/GPA, *The State of the Marine Environment*, 21.

[16] Breitburg et al, 359 *Science* 46 (5 Jan 2018).

[17] Preamble.

The process of developing international law on the marine environment was given substantial impetus by the 1972 UNCHE and the 1992 Rio Conference on Environment and Development. Recommendations of the Stockholm Conference led directly to the adoption of the 1972 London and Oslo Dumping Conventions, the 1973/78 MARPOL Convention and the 1974 Helsinki Convention for the Protection of the Marine Environment of the Baltic Sea Area ('Helsinki Convention'). These precedents formed the basis for UNEP's Regional Seas Agreements and Part XII of the 1982 UNCLOS.[18] The 1982 Convention was intended to be comprehensive in scope and universal in participation. In these respects it has been largely successful. On many issues it has also been treated as customary law by courts, international organizations, and non-parties.[19]

Part XII of the 1982 UNCLOS thus effected a number of fundamental changes in the international relating to the marine environment.[20] Perhaps the most important in this chapter is that pollution is no longer an implicit freedom of the seas. States are required to control all sources of marine pollution, and more generally to protect and preserve the marine environment as a whole, not simply the environment of other states. In this respect Part XII and the provisions of Part XI on the deep seabed reflect the parallel development of general international environmental law.[21] A second change involves the balance of power between flag states, more concerned with freedom of navigation and fishing, and coastal states, more concerned with effective regulation and control, although many states fall into both categories and thus faced complex policy choices in negotiating the 1982 UNCLOS. In this legal regime, flag states, coastal states, port states, international organizations, and intergovernmental commissions each have important roles, powers, and responsibilities,[22] which combine to produce one of the more successful and complex international environmental regimes.

Negotiated by consensus as an interlocking package deal,[23] the Convention's provisions form an integral whole, protected from derogation by compulsory settlement of disputes, a prohibition on reservations, and a ban on incompatible *inter se* agreements.[24] Within these limits, it is capable of further evolution,[25] whether through amendment,[26] the incorporation by reference of other generally accepted international

18 UN Doc A/CONF 48/14/Rev 1, Action Plan, Recommendations 86–94, and see also Intergovernmental Working Group on Marine Pollution, UN Doc A/CONF 48/8, para 197, repr as Annex III to the Conference Report. See Ch 2, *supra*.

19 See e.g. *Territorial and Maritime Dispute (Nicaragua/Colombia)*, ICJ Reports (2012) 624, paras 114–118; 138–9; 177; 182, and Roach, 45 *ODIL* (2014) 239.

20 See generally Harrison, *Making the Law of the Sea* (Cambridge, 2011).

21 See especially *AO on Activities in the Area*, ITLOS (2011); *South China Sea Arbitration*, PCA (2016) and *supra*, Ch 3.

22 See in particular *AO on Fisheries*, ITLOS (2015) and *infra*, section 4.

23 UN, *Convention on the Law of the Sea* (New York, 1997) 'Introduction', 1–4. See also Caminos and Molitor, 79 *AJIL* (1985) 871; Buzan, 75 *AJIL* (1981) 324; Allott, 77 *AJIL* (1983) 1.

24 Articles 279–99, 309, 311(3). See Boyle, 54 *ICLQ* (2005) 563.

25 See Barrett and Barnes (eds) *The Law of the Sea* (BIICL, 2016) Ch 1.

26 Articles 312–14. However, no such amendments have yet been adopted.

rules and standards,[27] the adoption of additional global and regional implementing agreements and soft law,[28] or interpretation by reference to subsequent practice and other rules of international law in accordance with Article 31 of the 1969 VCLT.[29] Multilateral negotiating processes, both at the UN and in other international organizations and conferences, continue to play a central role in the development of the law of the sea. The IMO provides the principal forum for further law-making with respect to pollution from ships, while the FAO oversees the further development of fisheries law. Both organizations are considered in more detail in Chapter 2. Regulation of the oceans affects many other interests, however, and has continued to generate proposals for further development from various bodies, including the COP to the 1992 CBD,[30] the UN General Assembly,[31] and the Informal Consultative Process on Law of the Sea.[32] The law relating to the marine environment cannot be understood without reference in particular to the recommendations of the Rio Conference, considered below, and the 1992CBD, whose impact on conservation of marine living resources is considered in Chapter 12.

1(2) AGENDA 21 AND THE MARINE ENVIRONMENT

The 1982 UNCLOS is referred to in Agenda 21[33] of the 1992 Rio Conference Report as providing 'the international basis upon which to pursue the protection and sustainable development of the marine and coastal environment and its resources'.[34] Nevertheless, Chapter 17 of Agenda 21 introduces several new elements not found in the 1982 UNCLOS, including an emphasis on integrated and precautionary approaches to protection of the marine and coastal environment. The focus is no longer principally on the control of sources of marine pollution, but more broadly on the prevention of environmental 'degradation' and the protection of marine ecosystems. For the first time protection of the exclusive economic zone is linked with sustainable development of coastal areas and sustainable use of marine living resources. Although Agenda 21 cannot amend the 1982 UNCLOS, and is not binding on states, it can be taken into

[27] See especially Articles 21(2) 119, 207–12. In most cases these global standards are derived from IMO regulatory conventions. See *infra*, section 4.

[28] See e.g. the 1995 UN Fish Stocks Agreement, and related codes of conduct and international plans of action, *infra*, Ch12.

[29] See in particular *South China Sea Arbitration*, PCA (2016), and *supra*, Ch 1, section 2.

[30] See *infra*, Ch 12.

[31] E.g. the 1995 UN Fish Stocks Agreement and the annual UNGA resolutions on fisheries and law of the sea.

[32] See de La Fayette, in Freestone, Barnes, and Ong (eds) *The Law of the Sea* (Oxford, 2006) Ch 4.

[33] See generally Treves, in Campiglio et al (eds) *The Environment After Rio* (London, 1993) 161; Nollkaemper, *Marine Policy* (1993) 537; Cicin-Sain and Knecht, 24 *ODIL* (1993) 323; Beyerlin, 55 *ZAÖRV* (1995) 544; Birnie, in Norton et al (eds) *The Changing World of International Law in the 21st Century* (The Hague, 1998) 3; Falk and Elver, in Vidas and Østreng (eds) *Order for the Oceans at the Turn of the Century* (The Hague, 1999) 145; Yankov, in Boyle and Freestone (eds) *International Law and Sustainable Development* (Oxford, 1999) 271; Tanaka, 19 *IJMCL* (2004) 483

[34] Agenda 21, Ch 17, para 17.1.

account when interpreting or implementing the Convention and it has had the effect of legitimizing and encouraging legal developments based on these changed perspectives.[35] Agenda 21 thus illustrates how 'a more conceptually sophisticated' focus on protection of the marine environment has evolved out of Part XII of UNCLOS.[36] As one writer observes: 'It is hard to conceive of the development of modern law of the sea and the emerging international law of the environment in ocean-related matters outside the close association and interplay between the 1982 UNCLOS and Agenda 21'.[37]

This broader perspective has been reinforced by subsequent state practice, regional agreements, and case law.[38] The 20 year review of the Agenda 21 reaffirmed 'the importance of the conservation and sustainable use of the oceans and seas and of their resources for sustainable development' and committed states 'to effectively apply an ecosystem approach and the precautionary approach in the management, in accordance with international law, of activities having an impact on the marine environment'.[39] The UN's 2015 SDGs reflect similar concerns.[40] SDG 14 addresses conservation and sustainable use of the oceans and marine resources. In aiming to reduce marine pollution 'of all kinds', land-based sources and ocean acidification are specifically identified as priorities. So is ending overfishing, illegal, unreported and unregulated fishing and destructive fishing practices.[41]

How these developments have further changed the law can be seen in the rewriting of regional seas agreements, revision of the 1972 London Convention, extension of treaty schemes on liability for pollution damage, and the adoption in 1995 of a Declaration and Global Programme of Action on Protection of the Marine Environment from Land-based Activities.[42] A precautionary approach to the protection of marine ecosystems and biological diversity is now addressed in various ways, but in particular through the 1992 CBD and the 1995UN Fish Stocks Agreement. These issues are further explored in Chapter 12.The broader Rio objective of integrating protection of the marine and coastal areas, living resources, and associated ecosystems is not straightforward, however.[43] First, what are the landward limits of 'the coastal zone'? It has been described as 'the interface where the land meets the ocean', including reefs, deltas, wetlands, beaches, coastal plains, and so on, but the limits 'are often arbitrarily defined' and differ from state to state.[44] Even the 2008 Mediterranean Protocol on Integrated Coastal Zone Management noticeably leaves it to individual states to define the coastal zone to which the protocol applies.[45] Most regional protocols on land-based sources of marine pollution protect internal waters (i.e. those on the landward

35 See *infra*, Ch 8, section 3, and *South China Sea Arbitration*, PCA (2016) discussed *infra*, Ch 12.

36 Falk and Elver, in Vidas and Østreng (eds) *Order for the Oceans*, 153.

37 Yankov, in Boyle and Freestone (eds) *International Law and Sustainable Development*, 272.

38 *Infra*, and see especially *South China Sea Arbitration*, PCA (2016) paras 939–49; 956–66; 970; 983–93.

39 *The Future We Want*, UNGA Res 66/288 (2012) annex, para 158.

40 UNGA Resolution 70/1 (2015) annex.

41 See the full list of targets identified for SDG 14.

42 See *infra*, Ch 8.

43 See generally Tanaka, 19 *IJMCL* (2004) 483.

44 1993 Noordwijk Guidelines for Integrated Coastal Zone Management (World Bank).

45 2008 Protocol, Article 3.

side of the territorial sea baseline such as bays, deltas, and estuaries) up to the freshwater limit, which would cover some of the areas just listed; those which create specially protected wildlife areas usually extend further to include related land areas, such as wetlands and beaches. The most extensive, the revised 1996 Mediterranean Protocol on Pollution from Land-based Sources and Activities includes not only the Mediterranean Sea, internal waters, brackish waters, coastal marshes, lagoons, and related ground waters, but also 'the entire watershed area within the territories of the Contracting Parties, draining into the Mediterranean Sea Area'.[46] While this definition acknowledges the theory that the 'coastal zone' should extend to the watersheds of all rivers flowing into the sea, in practice so much land is then included that the concept is likely to be unacceptable to some states for the same reason that the drainage basin has been resisted in the law of international watercourses.[47]

Second, what are the seaward limits? Integrated management of marine ecosystems and coastal areas is not easy to reconcile with the unaltered 1982 UNCLOS division of the oceans into zones of exclusive national jurisdiction out to 200 miles from the coast or within an extended continental shelf thereafter.[48] In ecosystem terms, such national or jurisdictional boundaries are inherently arbitrary and neither the territorial sea nor the exclusive economic zone reflects a rational basis for integrated management of marine ecosystems, whatever their economic and jurisdictional benefits to coastal states. The failure of US efforts in the UNCED negotiations and in the ICJ to secure recognition of the alternative concept of the 'large marine ecosystem' merely serves to re-emphasise that despite post-Rio evolution, ecosystem management in ocean areas is a policy tool, not a legally precise concept,[49] and that effective inter-state cross-boundary cooperation at global and regional level remains essential to the sustainable management of large marine ecosystems.

Third, even where, as in Antarctica, national jurisdictional claims are in abeyance, and the landmass and surrounding ocean are treated for regulatory purposes as a common area, cooperative application of integrated ecosystem management has not been easy.[50] There is no internationally agreed definition of a concept which is scientifically complex and inherently difficult to define even at the national level. One study

[46] 1996 Protocol, Articles 2, 3; Scovazzi (ed), *Marine Specially Protected Areas*, 85. The 1990 Kingston Protocol on Specially Protected Areas and Wildlife, Article 1(c) includes related watersheds and terrestrial areas; see also Black Sea Protocol on Land-based Activities, Article 3; East African Protocol on Land-based Activities, Article 2.

[47] See *infra*, Ch 10.

[48] See Tanaka, 19 *IJMCL* (2004) 483; Mossop, in Toledo and Tassin (eds) *Biodiversity Beyond National Jurisdiction: A Navigating Guide through the New Implementing Agreement to UNCLOS* (Belo Horizonte, 2017).

[49] See Wang, 35 *ODIL* (2004) 41; Juda, 30 *ODIL* (1999) 89; Alexander, *Marine Policy* (1993) 186; Cicin-Sain and Knecht, 24 *ODIL* (1993) 339; Treves, in Campiglio et al, *The Environment After Rio*; Redgwell, in Boyle and Freestone (eds) *International Law and Sustainable Development*, Ch 9. The ICJ has consistently rejected attempts to redraw maritime boundaries in accordance with environmental or ecosystem considerations: see *Gulf of Maine Case*, ICJ Reports (1984) 246 and *Jan Mayen Case*, ICJ Reports (1993) 38. On ecosystems generally see *infra*, Ch 11, and on ecosystem approaches to fisheries management see *infra*, Ch 12, section 2(3)(c).

[50] See 1991 Protocol to the Antarctic Treaty on the Environment, and Redgwell, in Boyle and Freestone (eds) *International Law and Sustainable Development*, Ch 9.

concludes that 'the diversity of contexts – natural as well as social – renders the articulation of predetermined measures both unrealistic and unhelpful.'[51]

Achieving integrated management of the marine environment is even more difficult in areas beyond national jurisdiction where freedom of the high seas and exclusive flag state jurisdiction predominate. Regardless of their legal basis, any measures for the protection of the high seas must be accepted by all relevant flag states if they are to be effective.[52] The UN General Assembly has repeatedly highlighted the need for international institutions to cooperate and coordinate their policies, but it lacks the power to mandate such action.[53] Moreover, as Harrison observes, 'the focus of many institutions on a limited activity may lead them to discount the cumulative or interactive effects that arise from human activities at sea.'[54] There are limited examples of inter-sectoral cooperation at present;[55] a proposed 1982 UNCLOS implementing agreement on the conservation of marine biological diversity beyond national jurisdiction could establish a global framework for more integrated management of the marine environment,[56] but by the end of 2020 negotiations were still ongoing. Many of these issues are considered further in the next chapter and in Chapter 12.

2 UNCLOS PART XII

The emergence of an obligation to protect the marine environment is evidenced by Part XII[57] of the 1982 UNCLOS, by case law,[58] and by multilateral agreements. These include the 1972 London Convention, the 1973/8 MARPOL Convention, which deals with pollution from ships, and a variety of regional treaties requiring states to control land-based sources of marine pollution, dumping, and seabed operations.[59] The degree of acceptance of these various treaties and the consensus expressed by states in negotiating the environmental provisions of the 1982 UNCLOS suggest

51 Langlet and Rayfuse (eds) *The Ecosystem Approach in Ocean Planning and Governance* (Leiden, 2019) 447, but see also *infra*, Ch 12, section 2(3)(c).

52 CBD, Article 22; Wolfrum and Matz Luck, 4 *Max Planck YBUNL* (2000) 445–480.

53 See UNGA Res 60/30 (2006) and Harrison, in Rayfuse (ed), *Research Handbook on International Marine Environmental Protection Law* (Cheltenham, 2015) 76–77.

54 Harrison, *Saving the Oceans through Law*, 275. See e.g. UN S-G, *Oceans and the Law of the Sea*, UN Doc A/71/74 (2016) para 74.

55 See Harrison, *op cit*, Ch 10.

56 UNGA Resolution 69/292 (2015). See Tladi 30 *IJMCL* (2015) 654; Ardron et al 49 *Marine Policy* (2014) 98–108, 104–5; Scott, 27 *IJMCL* (2012) 849; Drankier, 27 *IJMCL* (2012) 291; de La Fayette, 24 *IJMCL* (2009) 221.

57 See generally Harrison, *Saving the Oceans Through Law* (Oxford, 2017); Beurier, *Droit international de l'environnement* (Paris, 2017) Ch 7, Pt II; Rothwell and Stephens, *The International Law of the Sea* (2nd edn, Oxford, 2016) Ch 15; Tanaka, The *International Law of the Sea* (3rd edn, Cambridge, 2019) Ch 8; Churchill and Lowe, *The Law of the Sea* (3rd edn, Manchester, 1999) Ch 15;Vidas and Østreng (eds), *Order for the Oceans at the Turn of the Century* (The Hague, 1999); O'Connell, *The International Law of the Sea* (Oxford, 1984) ii, Ch 25.

58 *Chagos Marine Protected Area Arbitration*, PCA (2015); *South China Sea Arbitration*, PCA (2016) and see also *AO on Activities in the Area*, ITLOS Reports (2011).

59 On regional treaties see *infra*, section 3.

that its articles on the marine environment are supported by a strong measure of *opinio juris* and represent an agreed codification of existing rules and principles which have become part of general international law.[60] There is thus nothing essentially novel in the proposition first articulated in Article 192 of the 1982 UNCLOS that 'states have the obligation to protect and preserve the marine environment', although this may not have been the case when the article was first proposed in 1975. Moreover, this obligation is more strongly expressed than in Principle 2 of the Rio Declaration, insofar as Article 193 reaffirms the sovereign right of states to exploit their natural resources but only 'in accordance with their duty to protect and preserve the marine environment'.

The content of this obligation is elaborated in more detail by Article 194 and subsequent provisions.[61] It is evident from the 1982 UNCLOS that 'the obligations in Part XII apply to all States with respect to the marine environment in all maritime areas, both inside the national jurisdiction of States and beyond it. Accordingly, questions of sovereignty are irrelevant to the application of Part XII of the Convention.'[62] This formulation goes beyond the older customary rule on transboundary harm in two key respects. First, it reflects the extension to global common areas first contemplated by Principle 21 of the Stockholm Declaration.[63] Second, it also requires states to protect their own marine environment. This was one of the points at issue in the *South China Sea Case*, where China's dredging and construction activities affected both its own claimed internal waters and territorial sea, as well as the wider environment of the whole South China Sea.

The 'marine environment' for this purpose includes 'rare and fragile ecosystems as well as the habitat of depleted, threatened, or endangered species and other forms of marine life.'[64] The ITLOS has confirmed in more general terms that 'living resources and marine life are part of the marine environment.'[65] A similar conclusion was reached by the arbitral tribunal in the *Chagos Arbitration* when it held that 'Article 194 is . . . not limited to measures aimed strictly at controlling pollution and extends to measures focused primarily on conservation and the preservation of ecosystems.'[66] In that case the ecosystems in question were coral reefs. The obligations of states to protect the marine environment are thus not confined to the protection of economic interests, private property, or the human use of the sea, and the Convention's definition of 'pollution' appears to confirm that point with its reference to 'marine life'.[67] This conclusion is consistent with the provisions of modern treaties dealing with the

[60] Ch 17 of Rio Agenda 21 refers to 'International law, *as reflected in the provisions of the United Nations Convention on the Law of the Sea*' (emphasis added). On the drafting history of Articles 192–5 see Nordquist (ed), *United Nations Convention on the Law of the Sea: A Commentary*, iv (Dordrecht, 1991) 36ff.

[61] *South China Sea Arbitration*, PCA (2016) para 941.

[62] *Ibid*, para 940. [63] *Supra*, Ch 3, section 5.

[64] Article 194(5); *South China Sea Arbitration*, PCA (2016) para 945.

[65] *AO on Fisheries*, ITLOS Reports (2015) para 216.

[66] *Chagos Marine Protected Area Arbitration*, PCA (2015) para 538. See also *South China Sea Arbitration*, PCA (2016) para 945.

[67] Article 1(1)(4) *supra*, Ch 3, section 9.

wider environmental impact of marine pollution, including the 1992 Protocol to the 1969 Convention on Civil Liability for Oil Pollution Damage and the 1989 Salvage Convention,[68] both of which cover environmental damage, and with regional treaties and protocols concerned with especially sensitive ecological areas.[69]

Part XII represents another important advance over the 1958 Geneva Conventions in formulating the obligation of environmental protection in terms which are comprehensive of all sources of marine pollution.[70] Thus it applies to ships, land-based activities, seabed operations, dumping, and atmospheric pollution, and provides a framework for treaties both global and regional on each of these topics. In this respect the comprehensive scope of the 1982 Convention follows the pattern established by the 1974 Helsinki Convention, and subsequently adopted in UNEP's regional-seas treaties. Part XII is also in principle applicable to climate change, insofar as acidification and warming of the oceans fall within the definition of marine pollution. However, this conclusion serves only to bring the 1997 Kyoto Protocol and the 2015 Paris Agreement within the scope of 'generally accepted international rules and standards' referred to in Part XII; it adds nothing of substance to the climate change regime.[71]

Moreover, as we saw in Chapter 3, 'the duty to cooperate is a fundamental principle in the prevention of pollution of the marine environment under Part XII of the Convention and general international law. . . . . .'.[72] The Convention thus requires states to carry out environmental impact assessment and monitoring, to maintain contingency plans against marine pollution, and to notify other states of imminent damage.[73] In all these respects later treaties and developments in general international law have amplified the Convention's provisions.[74]

The Convention must also be interpreted and applied taking other developments in general international law into account.[75] The definition of pollution in Article 1, the general obligation to take measures to prevent, reduce and control pollution and to protect ecosystems and habitats of marine life under Article 194, the obligation to do an environmental impact assessment in Article 206, and the responsibility of States for protection and preservation of the marine environment under Article 235 are all potentially affected by the more liberal approach to proof of environmental risk

68 *Infra*, sections 5 and 6.

69 1985 Nairobi Protocol Concerning Protected Areas and Wild Flora and Fauna in Eastern Africa; 1990 Kingston Protocol Concerning Specially Protected Areas and Wildlife of the Wider Caribbean; 1996 Barcelona Protocol Concerning Specially Protected Areas and Biological Diversity in the Mediterranean.

70 Articles 194, 207–212.

71 See Boyle, 34 *IJMCL* (2019) 458; Redgwell, ibid, 440; Harrison, *Saving the Oceans Through Law*, Ch 9.

72 *South China Sea Arbitration*, PCA (2016) paras 946, 985; *MOX Plant Case (Provisional Measures)* ITLOS Reports (2001), para 82; *Land Reclamation Case (Provisional Measures)* ITLOS Reports (2003) para 92. See also Articles 123, 197, 199–202 and *Southern Bluefin Tuna Cases (Provisional Measures)* ITLOS Reports (1999) para 78.

73 Articles 198, 199, 204–206.

74 *Supra*, Ch 3, sections 5–8.

75 1969 VCLT, Article 31; *supra*, Ch 1, section 2.

envisaged by Rio Principle 15,[76] and by the 1992 CBD.[77] Although the *South China Sea* arbitral tribunal does not use the words 'biological diversity' in its award, the potential loss of biodiversity in the South China Sea was the key element of the damage to the marine environment predicted by the expert evidence and accepted by the tribunal. To that extent it is clear that the 1982 UNCLOS Part XII protects marine biodiversity.

But perhaps the most significant feature of Part XII is the way the concept of due diligence is handled. As with other treaties it makes reference to the need to take 'all measures necessary' to prevent and control pollution damage to other states, but moderates this requirement by allowing use of the 'best practicable means at their disposal and in accordance with their capabilities' where the risk is to the marine environment in general, rather than to other states. This wording implies some degree of flexibility and discretion, particularly for developing countries, whose interests received particular attention in the drafting of this part of the Convention.[78] The significance of this point can be seen more clearly in Articles 207 and 212, dealing with the control of land-based and atmospheric sources of pollution, where reference is made to economic capacity, development needs, and 'characteristic regional features'. State practice in this regard is examined in Chapter 8 and confirms the view that the Convention's treatment of both issues largely defers to the priorities set regionally or by individual states.

These unhelpful generalities are absent, however, in the provisions dealing with pollution from ships, dumping, and seabed operations, and it is here that the Convention does establish some important and concrete principles. The essential point is that in these cases states must give effect to or apply rules and standards no less onerous than 'generally recognized international rules and standards'.[79] Although precise phraseology varies in detail, and not all writers are agreed on the correct interpretation, Articles 208, 210, and 211 of the Convention have the effect of incorporating into the primary obligation to prevent pollution the evolving standards set, inter alia, by the 1972 London Convention, the 1973/78 MARPOL Convention annexes, relevant IAEA guidelines, IMO codes, and other soft law instruments agreed and adopted by a preponderance of maritime states. States parties to the 1982 UNCLOS will thus be

[76] *Southern Bluefin Tuna Cases*, ITLOS (1999) paras 77–79; *AO on Activities in the Area*, ITLOS (2011) paras 125–35.

[77] See *South China Sea Arbitration*, PCA (2016) paras 945 and 983.

[78] Nordquist and Park (eds), *Report of the US Delegation to the UN Convention 3rd UNCLOS* (Honolulu, 1983) 47–51, 74, 89; Kindt, 20 *VJIL* (1979) 313; Nordquist (ed), *UNCLOS Commentary*, iv, 64.

[79] On the variety of meanings attributed to the phrase 'generally accepted international rules and standards', see Vukas, in Soons (ed), *Implementation of the Law of the Sea Convention Through International Institutions* (Honolulu, 1990) 405; Bernhardt, 20 *VJIL* (1980) 265; Van Reenen, 12 *NYIL* (1981) 3; Vignes, 25 *AFDI* (1979) 712; Molenaar, *Coastal State Jurisdiction over Vessel-Source Pollution* (The Hague, 1998) Ch 5; Birnie, in Ringbom (ed), *Competing Norms in the Law of Marine Environmental Protection* (The Hague, 1997) 31; Harrison, *Making the Law of the Sea* (Cambridge, 2011) 171–179. For the status of other IMO and ILO conventions as 'generally accepted international standards' for the purposes of Article 211 of the 1982 UNCLOS, see Valenzuela, in Soons (ed), *Implementation of the Law of the Sea Convention etc* 187, and more cautiously, Oxman, 24 *NYUJILP* (1991–2) 109.

compelled as a matter of 1982 UNCLOS treaty law to adopt the basic standards set inter alia by the annexes to the London and MARPOL Conventions, and other IMO Conventions, even if they are not parties to them.[80] Ships flagged in non-parties to the 1982 UNCLOS would similarly be subject to the same standards due to their widespread adoption and the general compliance of non-parties in coastal state and port enforcement measures.[81]

Understood in these terms, the 1982 Convention is important because of its endorsement of an evolutionary system of international regulation. Thus it delegates to the IMO the task of defining and updating the detailed content of the obligation of due diligence as formulated in Article 194 with respect to pollution from ships and dumping at sea. For other sources of pollution, including land-based and airborne, regional groupings of states perform the same task, though with much greater room for flexible solutions tailored to the needs of each region.

3 REGIONAL SEAS

3(1) UNCLOS AND REGIONAL RULES

Although the 1982 Convention, like the law of the sea itself, is primarily concerned with a global system of international law governing all aspects of the use of the oceans, the Convention's reference at various points to regional rules,[82] regional programmes, regional cooperation, and so forth does indicate that we are not dealing with a single legal regime of universal application but with one which allows for significant regional variations.[83] There is specific provision for regional cooperation in enclosed and semi-enclosed seas,[84] and in respect of marine living resources.[85] Failure to cooperate as required by these provisions is a breach of treaty.[86]

Part XII of the 1982 UNCLOS also makes reference to regional rules and standards in various contexts, including elaboration of regional rules and standards for the

80 Boyle, 79 *AJIL* (1985) 347, and see *South China Sea Arbitration* PCA (2016) para 1082, where the tribunal held that the IMO COLREGS Convention bound both Parties 'by virtue of Article 94 of the Convention.'

81 By 2020, 155 states representing 98.86% of world shipping tonnage were parties to Annexes I and II of MARPOL; 87 states were parties to the 1972 London Convention, on which see *infra*, Ch 8. On coastal state and port enforcement see *infra*, section 4.

82 Harrison, *Saving the Oceans through Law*, Ch 10, 281–9; Oral, *Regional Co-operation and Protection of the Marine Environment under International Law* (Brill, 2013); Treves in Nordquist, Moore, Mahmoudi (eds), *The Stockholm Declaration and the Law of the Marine Environment* (Dordrecht, 2003) 137; Boyle, in Vidas (ed), *Protecting the Polar Marine Environment* (Cambridge, 2000) Ch 1; Vallega, 24 *O&C Man* (1994) 17; Knecht, 24 *O&C Man* (1994) 39; Johnston, *Regionalisation of the Law of the Sea* (Cambridge, 1978); Boczek, 16 *CWRJIL* (1984) 39.

83 On universalism and regionalism see generally Crawford, in UN, *International Law on the Eve of the Twenty-First Century: Views from the International Law Commission* (New York, 1997) 99–121.

84 Articles 122–3.

85 Articles 63–7, 117–8.

86 *South China Sea Arbitration* PCA (2016) paras 984–6, 993.

protection of the marine environment.[87] Article 237 preserves the freedom of states to make further 'special conventions and agreements' relating to the protection and preservation of the marine environment, provided these are 'concluded in furtherance of the general principles and objectives of this Convention'. The same article preserves obligations under existing agreements on the marine environment but requires them to be 'carried out in a manner consistent with the general principles and objectives' of the Convention. UNEP's regional seas agreements, FAO's regional fisheries agreements, and regional schemes for port state control are thus an important contribution to implementing the 1982 UNCLOS and meeting the goals of sustainability and integrated ecosystem management set out in Chapter 17 of Rio Agenda 21 and in the 2002 Johannesburg Declaration and Plan of Implementation.

Nowhere does the 1982 UNCLOS specify what is meant by 'regional', although the term is clearly something less than 'global'. The best interpretation is that a region is defined by the context in which the issue arises. Article 122 offers one approach in its reference to enclosed or semi-enclosed seas,[88] defined as 'a gulf, basin or sea surrounded by two or more states and connected to another sea or the ocean by a narrow inlet or consisting entirely or primarily of the territorial seas and exclusive economic zones of two or more coastal states'. A number of treaties concerned with protection of the marine environment are regional in this sense, notably those relating to the Mediterranean, the Baltic, the Red Sea, the Black Sea, and Persian Gulf.[89] So is the South China Sea, but here there is no functioning regime for regional environmental protection or resource management.[90] What makes these areas special is their relative ecological sensitivity and separation from the marine environment of adjacent oceans. They represent in varying degrees 'problem sheds' or areas within which protection of the marine environment requires regional coordination if control measures are to be effective.[91] These considerations are of particular significance in the control of land-based sources of pollution, and as we shall see in the next chapter, the 1982 Convention's articles largely assume that this source will be controlled nationally or regionally, rather than by global rules.[92] This partly accounts for the generality of the Convention's provisions on the subject, although some progress has subsequently been made in strengthening regional action.

[87] Article 197 and see *South China Sea Arbitration* PCA (2016) paras 946, 987. See also Articles 199–201, 235.

[88] See Vukas, in Vidas (ed), *Protecting the Polar marine Environment*, Ch 2; Vallega, 24 *O&C Man* (1994) 17.

[89] 1995 Barcelona Convention for the Protection of the Marine Environment and Coastal Region of the Mediterranean; 1992 Helsinki Convention for the Protection of the Marine Environment of the Baltic Sea Area; 1982 Jeddah Convention for the Conservation of the Red Sea and the Gulf of Aden Environment; 1992 Bucharest Convention on the Protection of the Black Sea against Pollution; 1978 Kuwait Convention for Cooperation on the Protection of the Marine Environment from Pollution.

[90] *South China Sea Arbitration* (2016) PCA, paras 946–7. See Chircop, 41 *ODIL* (2010) 334.

[91] Okidi, 4 *ODIL* (1971) 1; Schachter and Serwer, 65 *AJIL* (1971) 84.

[92] But contrast *South China Sea Arbitration* (2016) PCA, paras 984–6, 993.

A 'region' does not have to be composed on this ecological basis, however. Political considerations, common interests, or geographical proximity are other factors influencing the conclusion of regional treaties.[93] Some of the UNEP regional seas treaties relate to coastal areas where the only factor connecting participants is their location on a common coastline, rather than any identity of interest or shared ecological problems. The conventions dealing with the south-east Pacific and north-east Pacific coasts of Latin America and the Atlantic and Indian Ocean coasts of Africa fall into this category.[94] Others, in the south Pacific or the Caribbean, are largely defined by the proximity and shared interests of a number of island states.[95] For UNEP, defining a region is largely a question of policy: what is the most sensible geographical and political area within which to address the interrelated problems of marine and terrestrial environmental protection? As one author points out, 'development of the basic regional concept has not been stimulated by scientific thought but by the decision-making context and practice of the UN system'.[96] From this perspective it does not matter how a region is defined so long as it works. What does seem to be important is that there should be close correspondence between the 'political' region and the 'geographical' region: that is undoubtedly one of the central lessons of UNEP's regional-seas programme.[97]

Leaving aside their composition, the more important question concerns the role which it is appropriate for regional regulation of the marine environment to play. There are several possible answers to this question. At one level, regional arrangements are simply a means of implementing policies which are necessary in the interests of a specific community of states and which can best be tackled on a regional basis. Cooperation in cases of pollution emergencies, or in the exploitation of fish stocks are good examples, because the range of states affected is relatively limited. In other cases, such as enclosed or semi-enclosed seas or Arctic waters, physical characteristics may dictate the regional application of more onerous standards of environmental protection than would suffice for open oceanic areas. This factor is the main justification for special regional rules governing the discharge of pollution from ships or the dumping of waste at sea. The need to cater for such special cases is recognized in the 1982 UNCLOS,[98] although it is important to observe that for pollution from ships or dumping the Convention insists that regional rules should be no less effective than more

93 Alexander, 71 *AJIL* (1977) 84; id, 2 *ODIL* (1974) 151; id, 11 *Ocean YB* (1994) 1; Hayward, 8 *Marine Policy* (1984) 106; Boczek, 16 *CWRJIL* (1984) 39; Vallega, 24 *O&C Man* (1994) 17.

94 1981 Lima Convention for the Protection of the Marine Environment and Coastal Area of the SE Pacific; 1981 Abidjan Convention for Cooperation in the Protection and Development of the Marine and Coastal Environment of West and Central Africa; 1985 Nairobi Convention for the Protection, Management, and Development of the Marine and Coastal Environment of East Africa; 2002 Convention for Cooperation in the Protection and Sustainable Development of the Marine and Coastal Environment of the Northeast Pacific.

95 1983 Cartagena Convention for the Protection and Development of the Marine Environment of the Wider Caribbean; 1986 Noumea Convention for the Protection of the Natural Resources and Environment of the South Pacific Region.

96 Vallega, 24 *O&C Man* (1994) 26.

97 *Ibid.*

98 1982 UNCLOS, Articles 211(6) and 234, and see *infra*, Ch 8.

generally accepted international rules, and that regional treaties cannot be taken as an opportunity for falling below those rules. By facilitating some regional flexibility, however, regional arrangements do help accommodate the special needs and varying circumstances of a range of seas with diverse ecological and oceanographic characteristics within the general international law of the sea.

A second reason for resort to regional arrangements is that they may facilitate cooperation in negotiating stronger (or more precautionary) environmental standards and supervising compliance. This is particularly true in the North Sea, the Baltic, and the Mediterranean, where intergovernmental supervisory institutions have been established;[99] there are other regions, however, where no effective multilateral commissions exist, or where the role played by institutions remains limited to a symbolic presence.[100]

Third, regional treaties can be seen as a means of giving effect to the framework provisions of the 1982 Convention, and as evidence of the implementation and adoption of that Convention's main principles at regional level. Their conformity in most respects with the 1982 UNCLOS is an indication of their legislative function in international law, and of the present legal status of the 1982 Convention's provisions on protection of the marine environment.[101]

Lastly, regional regimes may offer a more appropriate basis for the integrated ecosystem and coastal zone management called for by Rio Agenda 21. This approach, which takes account of the need to conserve marine biodiversity and fisheries, is reflected inter alia in the 1992 OSPAR Convention,[102] in the 1995/6 revisions of the Mediterranean Convention regime,[103] and in the 1991 Antarctic Protocol.[104] It is a significant innovation. Not only is it now harder to draw a clear dividing line between the marine environment and the land environment, as we saw above, but a state may also be considered to form part of a marine region even if it has no sea-coast, provided its adjacent land area falls sufficiently within the ambit of the 'coastal zone' to require environmental management as a single entity. Thus although they have no coastline on the Arctic Ocean, Sweden and Finland may nevertheless be 'Arctic states' for the purpose of integrated management.[105] This is scarcely surprising, given that the greatest

[99] See esp Hey, 17 *IJMCL* (2002) 325; Papanicolopulu, in Rothwell et al (eds), *The Oxford Handbook of the Law of the Sea* (Oxford, 2015) 621.

[100] See *infra*, Ch 8.

[101] Some regional agreements do pose problems of conformity with UNCLOS, however: see 1981 Lima Convention, Article 1 (area of application).

[102] Hey, 17 *IJMCL* (2002) 325.

[103] Vallega, 29 *O&C Man* (1995) 251; id, 31 *O&C Man* (1996) 192 and *infra*, next section.

[104] 1991 Protocol, Articles 2 and 3(1) of which commit parties to 'the comprehensive protection of the Antarctic environment and dependent and associated ecosystems'. For this purpose the cold-water marine ecosystem surrounding Antarctica, known as the 'convergence', would appear to be included. See Boyle, in Vidas (ed), *Protecting the Polar Marine Environment*, Ch 1; Vidas, *ibid*, Ch 4; Redgwell, in Boyle and Freestone (eds), *International Law and Sustainable Development* (Oxford, 1999) Ch 9.

[105] Similarly, Switzerland now participates in the International North Sea Conference: see *infra*, Ch 8. The 1996 Ottawa Declaration establishing the Arctic Council does not define the 'Arctic'. See Molenaar, 27 *IJMCL* (2012) 553; Rothwell, 6 *YbIEL* (1995) 65; Vanderzwaag, in Vidas and Østreng (eds), *Order for the Oceans*, 231.

impact on the marine environment comes not from the uses of the sea considered in this chapter, but from land-based activities considered in the next chapter. As we have seen, however, such an interpretation of what is meant by 'coastal zone' may prove in practice too extensive to be readily acceptable to all states.

3(2) REGIONAL SEAS AGREEMENTS

Some twenty treaties can be identified which are 'regional' in the various senses described above and which relate to the protection of the marine environment.[106] These fall into two main groups; first, those concerned with enclosed or semi-enclosed seas in the northern hemisphere where the major problems are those of industrial pollution and land-based activities, and second, a group of UNEP-sponsored treaties which establish a broadly uniform pattern of principles for a majority of developing countries, mainly in the southern hemisphere. The number of states now involved in these regional seas treaties, and in other UNEP regional seas programmes, is such that they cannot be dismissed as special cases; they represent a substantial body of practice of more general significance for the law of the marine environment as a whole. Most have been supplemented, replaced, amended, or reinterpreted to reflect post-UNCED objectives and principles; in this respect they illustrate both the flexibility of framework or umbrella treaties as regulatory instruments and the continuing evolutionary character of the law of the sea notwithstanding codification in the 1982 UNCLOS.

(a) The North Sea and north-east Atlantic

The North Sea has a longer history of regional environmental cooperation than any other semi-enclosed sea. Initially regulated by a series of overlapping agreements adopted piecemeal, it remains outside UNEP's Regional Seas Programme, and still lacks an over-arching framework treaty.[107] However, the series of International North Sea Conferences ('INSC')[108] which first met in 1984, has provided an important political forum in which to define and coordinate increasingly stringent environmental objectives. The declarations of these Conferences are not legally binding treaties, but the principle of good faith does entail an expectation that implementation will be promoted at national and regional level. Some of the Conference undertakings have been translated into action through relevant regional treaty bodies, in particular the OSPAR Commission. This body supervises implementation of the most important regional agreement, the 1992 OSPAR Convention[109] which extends to the

[106] *Supra*, nn 89, 94–5.

[107] See Saetevik, *Environmental Cooperation Among North Sea States* (London, 1986); IJlstra, 3 *IJECL* (1988) 181; papers collected in 5 *IJECL* (1990); Pallemaerts, 7 *IJECL* (1992) 1; Sadowski, in Ringbom (ed), *Competing Norms in the Law of Marine Environmental Protection*, 109; Skjaerseth, in Victor et al (eds), *The Implementation and Effectiveness of International Commitments* (Cambridge, Mass, 1998) 327; *id, North Sea Cooperation* (Manchester, 2000); Hey, 17 *IJMCL* (2002) 325.

[108] See *infra*, Ch 8.

[109] Hey, IJlstra and Nollkaemper, 8 *IJMCL* (1993) 1; Hilf, 55 *ZAÖRV* (1995) 580; de la Fayette, 14 *IJMCL* (1999) 247, and see *infra*, Ch 8.

north-east Atlantic, the North Sea and adjacent Arctic waters. The 1992 Convention replaces and updates two earlier treaties regulating pollution of the sea from land-based and offshore sources, and dumping.[110] It also empowers the parties to tackle other issues affecting sustainable protection of the marine environment by adopting new annexes or taking binding decisions. The first such measure was an annex on Protection and Conservation of Ecosystems and Biological Diversity. A series of decisions and recommendations has enabled the Convention to evolve in ways that reflect more fully the commitments undertaken in Agenda 21.[111] In particular the OSPAR Commission has broadened the scope of the precautionary principle, endorsed an ecosystem approach to marine conservation, and developed detailed standards for the BAT and BEP required by the 1992 OSPAR Convention.[112] It has collaborated with the Northeast Atlantic Fisheries Commission and relevant coastal states to create an innovative system of marine protected areas covering the high seas and seabed near the Azores.[113]

(b) The Baltic

The 1974 Helsinki Convention was the first regional seas treaty to cover control of marine pollution from all sources. It had an important influence on the formulation of the marine pollution provisions of the 1982 UNCLOS, and of UNEP's regional seas treaties. It was replaced in 1992 by a more comprehensive agreement whose objective is to promote restoration and preservation of the ecological balance of the Baltic Sea and coastal ecosystems 'influenced by the Baltic Sea'.[114] Thus it not only deals with pollution but also requires parties to conserve natural habitats, biological diversity and ecological processes, and ensure sustainable use of natural resources.[115] The new treaty incorporates many of the pertinent Rio principles, including the precautionary principle and the polluter-pays principle. An action plan was adopted in 2007 with the objective of restoring the Baltic marine environment by 2021. The Helsinki Commission has adopted guidelines or recommendations on a wide range of specific issues.[116]

[110] 1972 Oslo Dumping Convention, and 1974 Paris Convention for the Prevention of Marine Pollution from Land-based Sources: see *infra*, Ch 8.

[111] See 1998 Sintra Statement, Decision 98/2 on Disposal of Disused Offshore Installations, and others listed on the website of the OSPAR Commission.

[112] See inter alia Statement on the Ecosystem Approach to the Management of Human Activities, 1st Joint Min. Meeting of the Helsinki and OSPAR Commissions, Bremen, 2003.

[113] Ribeiro, 25 *IJMCL* (2010) 183; *id*, in Ribeiro (ed), *30 Years After the Signature of UNCLOS*, 179, and Scovazzi, *ibid* 210.

[114] See Fitzmaurice, in Barrett and Barnes (eds), *The Law of the Sea* (BIICL, 2016) Ch 11; Ehlers, 8 *IJMCL* (1993) 191; Jenisch, 11 *IJMCL* (1996) 47; Platzoder and Verlaan, *The Baltic Sea: New Developments in National Policies and International Cooperation* (The Hague, 1997); Greene, in Victor et al, *The Implementation and Effectiveness of International Environmental Commitments*, 177; Fitzmaurice, 13 *IJMCL* (1998) 379; Ebbesson, 43 *GYIL* (2000) 38; Brusendorff and Ehlers, 17 *IJMCL* (2002) 351.

[115] See inter alia Statement on the Ecosystem Approach to the Management of Human Activities, 1st Joint Min. Meeting of the Helsinki and OSPAR Commissions, Bremen, 2003.

[116] See the Helsinki Commission's website.

(c) The Mediterranean and the Black Sea

Adopted in 1976, the Barcelona Convention for the Protection of the Mediterranean Sea Against Pollution is the oldest UNEP regional seas agreement, while the Convention on the Protection of the Black Sea Against Pollution is the newest. The Barcelona Convention is unusual in having to accommodate not only the interests of developed northern hemisphere industrialized economies but also the less-developed countries on its southern and eastern shores, and it is the only one to recognize the need for different standards according to the economic capacity of the parties and their need for development.[117] In 1995 the Barcelona Convention also became the first to be comprehensively amended, expanded and re-named in line with Agenda 21.[118]

Unlike earlier regional agreements in the Baltic and North Sea, the Barcelona Convention is a framework treaty, laying down only general rules that have been supplemented by more detailed protocols and action plans.[119] This technique was followed by all subsequent UNEP regional-seas agreements; it has enabled new topics to be addressed without amending the basic treaty, and allows for differences in participation and the geographical scope of each protocol, while retaining common supervisory institutions. Current Mediterranean Sea protocols cover specially protected areas and biodiversity, emergency cooperation, dumping, land-based pollution, seabed pollution, transboundary movement of hazardous waste, and integrated coastal zone management.[120]

The Black Sea Convention takes little explicit account of Agenda 21 and differs from the original Barcelona Convention model only in protecting fisheries and marine living resources from harmful effects. It is otherwise limited to general obligations to control all sources of pollution, although protocols adopted at the same time do establish further rules on land-based sources and dumping. However, in 1993 a ministerial Declaration on Protection of the Black Sea committed the parties to take appropriate measures to implement Agenda 21, Chapter 17 principles and objectives.[121] This declaration does at least illustrate how the parties are free to reinterpret and develop treaties whose texts were not drafted with Agenda 21 in mind.

117 1996 Protocol on Pollution from Land-based Sources and Activities, Article 7. See *infra*, Ch 8.

118 1995 Convention for the Protection of the Marine Environment and the Coastal Region of the Mediterranean. The revised convention entered into force in 2004.

119 See generally Scovazzi (ed), *Mediterranean Specially Protected Areas: the General Aspects and the Mediterranean Regional System* (The Hague, 1999) Ch 7; Raftopoulos, in Vidas and Schei (eds), *The World Ocean in Globalisation* (Leiden, 2011) 507; Gavouneli, 23 *IJMCL* (2008) 477; Vallega, 19 *Marine Policy* (1995) 47; id, 31 *O&C Man* (1996) 199; id, 29 *O&C Man* (1996) 251; Scovazzi, 10 *IJMCL* (1995) 543; Raftopoulos, 7 *IJECL* (1992) 27; Chircop, 23 *ODIL* (1992) 17; Juste, in Miles and Treves (eds), *The Law of the Sea: New Worlds, New Discoveries* (Honolulu, 1992); Haas, *Saving the Mediterranean* (New York, 1991).

120 For the text of protocols and action plans see the UNEP website.

121 See also the 1993 Black Sea Environment Programme and 2002 Strategic Action Plan. See also Vinogradov, 22 *IJMCL* (2007) 585.

(d) Other UNEP regional seas programmes

UNEP's regional-seas programme[122], initiated in 1974, facilitates cooperation and the provision of assistance in protecting the marine environment where expertise and facilities may be lacking. It now covers fourteen areas where there is some level of cooperation.

Following the pattern established by the Barcelona Convention, most of the regional seas programmes are supported by framework conventions and action plans. Their geographical scope extends to the territorial sea and exclusive economic zones of participating states. All are comprehensive in their inclusion of sources of marine pollution, but the extent to which further protocols have been adopted varies. Most now give some form of protection to marine living resources and coastal ecosystems, usually by permitting the creation of specially protected areas.[123] In those areas designated under the Caribbean Protocol both the passage of ships and activities that could harm endangered species, their habitats or ecosystems are controlled. Other regional seas protocols address dumping in the South Pacific, the Black Sea, and the Mediterranean. Most of the regional programmes include arrangements for combatting major incidents of marine pollution, and the regional treaties all have protocols on this subject. Land-based pollution is regulated by protocols in the Caribbean, the Persian Gulf, the South-East Pacific, the Red Sea, Eastern Africa, and Western and Central Africa, in addition to the Mediterranean and Black Sea.[124] A further development is the adoption of protocols on transboundary movement of hazardous wastes and pollution from continental shelf operations in the Mediterranean and the Persian Gulf.[125] The latter are particularly important given the lack of any globally agreed standards for the prevention of pollution from seabed operations.[126]

The past decade has seen a large amount of activity under the regional seas programme and the number of protocols has increased, although some are yet to enter into force or lack full participation. Implementation is the key challenge for many developing states parties, and it is for this reason that some authors have noted that the regional seas programme has been 'ineffective.'[127] Indeed, UNEP itself has identified institutional reform as a key challenge for the future of the regional seas

[122] UNEP, *Setting a Course for Regional Seas* (Nairobi, 2014); UNEP, *A Strategy for the Seas: the Regional Seas Programme, Past Present and* Future (Nairobi, 1983); Oral, in Rayfuse (ed), *Research Handbook on International Marine Environmental Law* (Cheltenham, 2015); Vallega, 24 *O&C Man* (1994) 17; Verlaan and Khan, 31 *O&C Man* (1996) 83; Haas, 9 *Ocean Yb* (1991) 188; Akiwumi and Melvasalo, 22 *Marine Policy* (1998) 229.

[123] 1985 Eastern African Protocol Concerning Protected Areas and Wild Fauna and Flora; 1986 Noumea Convention, Article 14; 1989 SE Pacific Protocol for the Conservation and Management of Protected Marine and Coastal Areas; 1990 Kingston Protocol Concerning Specially Protected Areas and Wildlife; for the Mediterranean and Black Sea, see previous section. See Scovazzi (ed), *Marine Specially Protected Areas*, Ch 2.

[124] 1983 SE Pacific Protocol; 1990 Kuwait Protocol; 1999 Caribbean Protocol; 1995 Red Sea Protocol; 2010 Eastern African Protocol; 2012 Western and Central African Protocol.

[125] 1996 Mediterranean Protocol; 1998 Kuwait Protocol.

[126] See *infra*, section 4(3).

[127] Louka, *International Environmental Law* (Cambridge, 2006) 153. See also Rochette and Billé, 28 *IJMCL* 433 (2013)

programme.[128] In general the more successful programmes appear to be those with a strong institutional framework and the political will to ensure the continued evolution and implementation of action plans. Overall, there has clearly been a change in emphasis from pollution control to sustainable management of the marine environment and its resources, in line with objectives outlined in Agenda 21. All of this builds on elements already found in the 1982 UNCLOS, evidencing the shift from use-oriented to resource-oriented approaches, which it has been said, is the essence of the new law of the sea.[129]

4 MARINE POLLUTION FROM SHIPS

4(1) THE NATURE OF THE PROBLEM

Without the shipping industry[130] much of the world's principal source of energy—oil—could not be moved from where it is extracted to where it is refined and marketed. Many other commodities are also moved in bulk by sea, including chemicals, wood pulp, and vegetable oil, to name only a few of the substances which have ended up on beaches after shipwrecks. Nor would international trade as currently understood be possible without container ships. The shipping industry is large, many of the ships are huge, and none are unsinkable. Over the past thirty years the industry has very substantially restructured. Most ships were once registered in and therefore regulated by a small number of advanced industrial economies with a long maritime tradition—principally the UK. Today, almost half the world's merchant fleet is still owned by European companies, the rest mostly by Japanese, Chinese, American, Russian, Korean, and Indian operators.[131] But many of these ships, and especially those involved in international trade, are now registered not where they are owned but in a growing list of 'flag of convenience' states. The advantage of 'flagging-out' for the owners or operators of ships is that they pay less tax, they can employ cheaper crew, and regulation may be less stringent or less efficiently applied than it would be under more established flag states. Flag-of-convenience states have little or no connection with the shipping industry apart from offering the facility of an open register. Many

128 UNEP, *Global Strategic Directions for the Regional Seas Programmes 2008–2012*, UNEP (DEPI)/RS.9/6, 31 October 2007, paras 12 and 14; UNEP, *Setting a Course for Regional Seas* (UNEP, 2014) 31.

129 Haas, 9 *Ocean Yb* (1991) 211.

130 See Harrison, *Saving the Oceans through Law* (Oxford, 2017) Ch 6; Beurier, *Droit international de l'environnement* (Paris, 2017) Ch 7, Pt II; Tan, *Vessel-Source Marine Pollution* (Cambridge, 2006); Molenaar, *Coastal State Jurisdiction over Vessel-Source Pollution* (The Hague, 1998); Brown, *The International Law of the Sea* (Aldershot, 1994) I, Ch 15; Mitchell, *International Oil Pollution at Sea* (Cambridge, Mass, 1994); Bodansky, 18 *ELQ* (1991) 719; Abecassis and Jarashow, *Oil Pollution from Ships* (2nd edn, London, 1985); M'Gonigle and Zacher, *Pollution, Politics and International Law: Tankers at Sea* (London, 1979).

131 See Tan, *Vessel-Source Marine Pollution*, 63–4 for details.

of the newer ones are developing countries without a significant maritime tradition or infrastructure, such as St Kitts or Mongolia, but some such as Panama, Liberia, and Honduras have a long history as open registries. Other developing countries, including India and China, have also built up a substantial industry of their own, but this is unusual and Saudi Arabia, Singapore, Taiwan, and Malaysia are the only other developing states among the leading ship-owning nations.

These changes in the shipping industry are important for two reasons.[132] First, as we saw in Chapter 2, the main international regulatory body for shipping— the IMO—is dominated by the largest flag states, and these are now mostly flag-of-convenience developing countries, some of which have only a limited interest in the quality and operating standards of the ships for which they are responsible in international law. Second, these same states will inevitably find it harder to regulate, inspect and enforce the law against ships which, while flying their flag, will rarely if ever enter any of their ports. In order to fulfil their regulatory responsibilities, the maritime administrations of these states therefore have to rely on the so-called 'classification societies' which historically have provided ship inspection and certification services for governments and insurance companies.[133] Some of these societies are very good, but some are sufficiently bad that governments have begun to prosecute or sue them for negligence when poorly maintained oil tankers break up at sea.[134] Flag states and ship operators have considerable freedom in selecting where to go for these services, and there is little to prevent them choosing the most convenient rather than the best. In this environment, substandard ships that are older, or poorly maintained, or with inadequately trained crews, are an inevitable outcome. It is these ships which pose the biggest threat to the marine environment of coastal states. Flag state enforcement will typically be poor or non-existent, even when infractions are reported by coastal states. Of course all ships have to call at ports and, as we will see, it is here that serious inspections, detentions and enforcement can be deployed to mitigate the risk. The most effective port state controls are now in Europe, North America, and Japan, which import most of the world's oil and other hazardous commodities. But in other regions of the world substandard ships are less likely to be bothered.

Pollution from ships is generally of two kinds: operational and accidental. Operational pollution is a function of the manner in which ships operate. Oil tankers, for example, traditionally washed their oil tanks and disposed of oily residue at sea, causing significant volumes of pollution. Other ships also discharge oily wastes from engine rooms and cause significant pollution from sewage discharges and rubbish disposal at sea. Ballast water may contain cargo residues or alien species which when transported to other areas can cause serious ecosystem damage. The objective of international regulation in this context has been as far as possible to eliminate the need for such discharges, through technical solutions and the provision of shore facilities for the reception of waste and cargo residues.

[132] *Ibid*, 47–62. [133] *Ibid*, 43–7.

[134] See IOPC Funds, *Annual Report* (2004) 77 (*Erika*) and 102 (*Prestige*). See also the *Annual Reports* of the Paris and Tokyo MOUs where the record of individual classification societies is analysed.

The second, more dramatic, form of marine pollution emanates from marine casualties. The sinking of large oil tankers such as the *Torrey Canyon, Amoco Cadiz, Exxon Valdez, Nakhodka, Erika*, or *Prestige* exemplifies the scale and potential severity of such accidents, whose seriousness derives mainly from the volume of oil or other pollutants released in one place. They harm coastal communities, fisheries, wildlife, and local ecology. In some areas, such as the Arctic or Antarctic, climatic conditions exacerbate both the long-term effects and the difficulty of dealing with this kind of pollution. The purpose of regulation here is to minimize the risk and give coastal states adequate means of protecting themselves and securing compensation.

Neither problem should be exaggerated; as we saw in Chapter 8, the major sources of marine pollution are on land, not afloat. But, like nuclear installations, oil tankers and other vessels carrying hazardous and noxious cargoes represent a form of ultra-hazardous risk for all coastal states, which it is the object of international law to moderate and control. A dominant theme of the UNCLOS III conference was the failure of the traditional structure of jurisdiction over ships and maritime areas to protect the interests of those coastal states whose proximity to shipping routes made them particularly vulnerable. On the one hand the duty of the flag state to adopt and enforce appropriate regulations was too imperfectly defined and observed. On the other, the power of the coastal state to regulate shipping and activities off its coast was too limited. The 1973/78 MARPOL Convention and the 1982 UNCLOS address these problems by extending the enforcement powers of coastal and port states, at the expense of the flag state's exclusive authority, and by redefining and strengthening the latter's obligations towards the protection of the marine environment. The result is a relatively complex structure of authority over maritime activities, which tries to reconcile the effective enforcement of environmental regulations with the primary concern of maritime states in freedom of navigation.[135] How far this balancing act has been successful will be considered below: it has certainly led to improvements, but it has not eliminated vessel-source pollution.

4(2) FLAG STATE JURISDICTION OVER VESSEL POLLUTION

The primary basis for the regulation of ships is the jurisdiction enjoyed by the state in which the vessel is registered or whose flag it is entitled to flag ('the flag state'). Although Article 91 of the 1982 UNCLOS refers to the need for a genuine link between the state of nationality and the ship, this ambiguous provision was not intended to eliminate 'flags of convenience', where registration, rather than ownership, management, nationality of the crew, or the ship's operational base, is the only substantial connection. In the *MV Saiga Case* the ITLOS held that 'the purpose of the provisions of the Convention on the need for a genuine link between a ship and its flag State is to secure more effective implementation of the duties of the flag State, and not to establish criteria by reference to which the validity of the registration of ships in a flag

[135] Boyle, 79 *AJIL* (1985) 347; Bernhardt, 20 *VJIL* (1979) 265 and see generally Allott, 77 *AJIL* (1983) 1.

State may be challenged by other States'.[136] Thus, however tenuous the link, it is the flag state which is responsible for regulating safety at sea and the prevention of collisions, the manning of ships and the competence of their crews, and for setting standards of construction, design, equipment, and seaworthiness.[137] These responsibilities include taking the measures to prevent pollution referred to below.

Moreover, in customary law, only the flag state has jurisdiction to enforce regulations applicable to vessels on the high seas. In the *Lotus Case*,[138] the Permanent Court of International Justice referred to the principle that no state may exercise jurisdiction over foreign vessels on the high seas, but by this it meant only that foreign vessels could not be arrested or detained while on the high seas, not that regulations could not be enforced by other states once the ship had voluntarily entered port. As we shall see, this case forms the basis for port state jurisdiction over high seas pollution offences referred to in Article 218 of the UNCLOS. Even when the ship is within the territorial jurisdiction of other states, however, the flag state does not lose its jurisdiction; regardless of where it is operating, a ship must therefore comply with the laws of its own flag.

The 1982 UNCLOS makes radical changes in the exclusive character of flag state enforcement jurisdiction but leaves intact the central principle of earlier law that the flag state has responsibility for the regulation and control of pollution from its ships. This duty is redefined, however, in terms requiring greater uniformity in the content of the applicable regulations. These must now 'at least have the same effect' as the 1973/78 MARPOL Convention, which as we will see shortly represents 'generally accepted international rules and standards' in this context.[139] Since flag states retain a discretion under this wording to set more onerous standards, the effect of Article 211 of the 1982 UNCLOS is to make MARPOL annexes, and other relevant international standards referred to below an obligatory minimum.

Article 217 reinforces this conclusion by requiring flag states to take measures necessary for the implementation and effective enforcement of international rules and standards. These measures must include the certification and inspection procedures instituted by MARPOL and SOLAS, and must be sufficient to ensure that vessels are prohibited from sailing until they can comply with the relevant regulations. The remaining provisions of Article 217 reiterate the obligation of flag states to investigate violations and bring appropriate proceedings, and to act on the request of other states where a violation is reported. In substance, therefore, a flag state bound by Article 217 is required to do all that the 1973/78 MARPOL Convention already demands. There is thus nothing novel in principle in the treatment of flag state regulation in the 1982 UNCLOS: it fully accords with customary and conventional law,[140] although as with

136 *MV Saiga (No 2) (Merits)* ITLOS Reports (1999) paras 62–88, at para 83. However, whether a state has conferred the right to fly its flag is a question of fact: see *'Grand Prince' Case (Belize v France)* ITLOS Reports (2001) paras 89–94.

137 1982 UNCLOS, Articles 94; 211(2); *Virginia G Case*, ITLOS Reports (2014) paras 110–17. See generally Churchill and Lowe, *The Law of the Sea*, Ch 13; O'Connell, *The International Law of the Sea*, ii, Ch 20.

138 PCIJ (1927) Ser A, No 10, 169.

139 1982 UNCLOS, Articles 211(2); 217.

140 Boyle, 79 *AJIL* (1985) 363ff; Popp, *CYIL* (1980) 3; Bernhardt, 20 *VJIL* (1979) 265.

other provisions of the Convention these articles are part of a broader package deal and are not necessarily applicable in every respect to ships of non-parties.

The 1982 UNCLOS thus gives the flag state ample power to regulate marine pollution from vessels and other aspects of the operation of ships likely to pose a risk to the environment, such as seaworthiness standards. Moreover, it requires them to do so effectively, even if they may in practice have to act in cooperation with coastal and port states. Both the content of this duty, and the manner in which it is enforced, have been the subject of more specific international agreements negotiated mainly through the IMO, which is usually the 'competent international organization' referred to in this context by the 1982 UNCLOS.[141]

The purpose of these IMO agreements is to provide internationally recognized common standards for flag states and coastal states to follow in regulating the safety of shipping and the protection of the environment. They include the 1966 International Convention on Load Lines, the 1972 Convention on the International Regulations for Preventing Collisions at Sea (COLREGS) and the 1974 SOLAS, all of which are intended to minimize the risk of maritime accidents by regulating navigation, construction, and seaworthiness standards. ILO Convention No 147 Concerning Minimum Standards in Merchant Ships and the 1978/2010 IMO Convention on Standards of Training, Certification, and Watch-keeping lay down additional standards for competency, hours of work, and crewing of vessels.[142] A 1978 Protocol to the 1974 SOLAS Convention makes the use of certain additional safety features mandatory for oil tankers and other large vessels, both for safety of navigation and pollution prevention purposes. An important SOLAS amendment which came into force in 1998 makes compliance with the IMO's Code on International Safety Management ('ISM Code') mandatory, inter alia, for all oil and chemical tankers.[143] Ships can only be certified by the flag state if the operating company (this may be the owner, charterer, or manager) has in place safety and environmental policies, instructions and procedures in accordance with the Code. In effect an operator's licence, the certification required by the ISM Code, has been described as 'the most revolutionary change adopted by the IMO in its 40 years of existence'. The underlying assumption is that operating companies are best able to ensure that ships meet adequate operational standards. Like airlines, shipping companies whose vessels do not meet the required standards will be unable to operate. Some 78 per cent of ships were thought to comply at the time of entry into force, although nearly twenty years later, some deficiencies continue to exist.[144] Most of these agreements are

141 IMO, *Implications of the United Nations Convention on the Law of the Sea for the International Maritime Organization*, Document LEG/Misc.7 (2012) 7.

142 See generally Blanco-Bazan, in Couper and Gold (eds), *The Marine Environment and Sustainable Development*, (Honolulu, 1993) 448; Valenzuela, in Soons (ed), *Implementation of the LOSC through International Institutions*, 187; Churchill and Lowe, *The Law of the Sea*, Ch 13; Molenaar, *Coastal State Jurisdiction over Vessel-Source Pollution*, 60ff.

143 See 1974 SOLAS Convention, Chapter IX, as amended 1994; IMO Res A 848 (20) 1997 and A 913(22) 1999; Valenzuela, in Vidas and Østreng (eds), *Order for the Oceans*, 502–4.

144 In 2014, 1801 deficiencies related to the ISM were identified by states participating in the Paris MOU region; Paris MOU Annual Report 2014, 46. Other MOU regions also continue to report high levels of deficiencies in this regard.

very widely ratified and adopted by maritime states, and they can be readily amended and updated by the IMO.[145] Although in most cases their primary purpose is to ensure better safety standards, they are also an essential means of reducing the threat to the marine environment posed by maritime accidents or the discharge of pollutants and invasive species. To that extent they constitute a form of international regulation of the environmental risks of transporting oil and other substances by sea, with the IMO acting as the main regulatory and supervisory institution.

The IMO has also adopted regulatory standards that are directly aimed at the prevention of pollution from ships. The 1954 London Convention for the Prevention of Pollution of the Sea by Oil, and its successor the 1973/78 MARPOL Convention both address operational pollution and the risk of accidents. Several more recent treaties have been adopted to address particular hazards posed by shipping. The 2001 Anti-Fouling Substances Convention[146] regulates the use of paints and other substances applied to a ship's hull, but which can also cause harmful effects to marine organisms. The 2004 Ballast Water Convention[147] attempts to control the global spread of invasive species in ship's ballast water. Both of these latter treaties expressly mandate a precautionary approach to shipping regulation and they require parties to proactively identify potential risks through scientific research and monitoring,[148] or to adopt measures that have been verified as causing no harm to the marine environment.[149]

The 1973/78 MARPOL Convention is perhaps the most important of these instruments because it provides a long-established and reasonably successful regulatory model whose real-world impact can be measured. Indeed, the more recent treaties use the same regulatory techniques as MARPOL and will be enforced by flag states and port states on the same basis. For that reason they will not be examined in detail here.[150]

4(3) THE 1973/78 MARPOL CONVENTION

This Convention, first adopted in 1973, was substantially amended in 1978 to facilitate entry into force.[151] The Convention's principal articles mainly deal with jurisdiction and powers of enforcement and inspection; the more detailed anti-pollution regulations are contained in annexes which can be adopted and amended by the Marine Environment Protection Committee of the IMO, subject to acceptance by at least

145 *Supra*, Ch 2, section 4.

146 Hereafter 'AFS Convention'. In April 2020, it had 81 parties representing 96% of global tonnage

147 Hereafter 'BWM Convention.' In April 2020 it had 83 parties representing 81% of tonnage.

148 AFS Convention, Article 8.

149 BWM Convention, Article 2(7) and Regulation D-2.

150 For a detailed analysis of the BWM Convention, see Tsimplis, 19 *IJMCL* (2004) 411. For a discussion of the AFS Convention, see Tan, *Vessel-Source Marine Pollution* and de la Fayette, 16 *IJMCL* 155 (2001).

151 See generally M'Gonigle and Zacher, *Pollution, Politics and International Law*, 107ff; Tan, *Vessel-Source Marine Pollution*, 107–75; O'Connell, *The International Law of the Sea*, ii, 1003; Abecassis and Jarashow, *Oil Pollution from Ships*, Ch 3; IMO, *Focus on IMO: MARPOL—25 Years* (London, 1998).

two-thirds of parties constituting not less than 50 per cent gross tonnage of the world merchant fleet.[152] However, as more ships flag out to developing country open registers, the 50 per cent tonnage requirement is becoming harder to achieve, and Annex VI on air pollution, adopted in 1997, did not enter into force until 2005.

(a) The MARPOL annexes

Unlike the 1954 London Convention, MARPOL annexes are not confined to oil pollution, but also regulate other types of ship-based pollution, including chemicals and other noxious liquids, garbage, sewage, and air pollution. All parties are bound by Annexes I and II, which regulate the carriage of oil and chemicals respectively. Other annexes are optional and participation varies but is still substantial. The parties to MARPOL in 2020 comprised almost 99% per cent of merchant tonnage, which puts Annexes I and II in the category of 'generally accepted international rules and standards' prescribed by Article 211 of the 1982 UNCLOS as the minimum content of the flag state's duty to exercise diligent control of its vessels in the prevention of marine pollution. The same could be said for optional Annexes III–VI, whose tonnage participation rates in 2020 were 98 per cent, 96 per cent, 98 per cent, and 96 per cent respectively. As we have seen, there are also grounds for treating MARPOL regulations as a standard enforceable against vessels of all states, whether or not they have ratified the 1973/78 MARPOL Convention.[153] At the same time, it must be remembered that, under Article 16 of this Convention, states parties are not bound by amendments they have not accepted, so there may be different regulations in force simultaneously for different flag states. This undoubtedly complicates the question of what rules a non-party to MARPOL must apply under Article 211.

The 1973/78 MARPOL Convention's approach to the regulation of oil pollution is broadly similar to the 1954 Convention in relying mainly on technical measures to limit the need for oil or chemical discharges at sea. Thus, it controls the location of discharges, by defining prohibited areas and excluding coastal zones; it controls the quantity of pollution, by limiting the rate of discharge; it controls the need for discharges, by setting equipment standards intended to reduce the volume of waste oil, or to separate oil from ballast water, and by calling on governments to provide port discharge facilities. Similar regulatory techniques are applied in the other MARPOL Annexes to minimize pollution from packaged goods, sewage, garbage and air pollution.

The annexes also specify construction standards in considerable detail. Later regulations do not normally apply to existing ships, because to do so might require substantial reconstruction, but they were nevertheless amended in 1992 to phase out older single-hull oil tankers and again in 2001 and 2003 to advance the deadline following the *Erika* and *Prestige* disasters.[154] These older vessels had become an unacceptable risk for coastal states and a liability for the industry, but the IMO's action was precipitated

152 *Supra*, Ch 2, section 4(4). 153 *Supra*, section 2(2).

154 Annex I, regulations 13F and G, or 20 and 21 in the revised Annex. The final phase-out date for all categories was 2010. See Tan, *Vessel-Source Marine Pollution*, 139–54.

by an imminent EU ban.[155] In general terms, MARPOL regulations take advantage of modern technology and operating methods to eliminate all but minimal levels of operational discharges, to ensure that these have the least impact on coastal states, and to emphasize port discharge for residues which cannot otherwise be disposed of. The most harmful Annex II residues will normally have to be off-loaded to a certified port discharge facility. The discharge at sea of oily waste and some chemical residues is still permitted in limited volumes, but only if it takes place en route, more than fifty miles from land and not in special areas where virtually all discharges are prohibited.[156] The special areas listed in the convention include the Mediterranean, the Black Sea, the Baltic, the Red Sea, and the Persian Gulf—all enclosed or semi-enclosed seas, where, as we saw earlier, more stringent standards are necessary. The more open waters of the Gulf of Aden, the Gulf of Oman, the North Sea and North West European waters, the Caribbean, South African waters, and the Antarctic Ocean, have subsequently been added to this list.

In two respects the 1973/78 MARPOL Convention differs significantly from the 1954 London Convention. First, it is designed to allow additional annexes, or amended annexes, to be easily and quickly adopted by the IMO. Annexes I and II have been amended frequently in response to new technology and growing environmental awareness, and were further revised and simplified in 2004, partly in order to take account of the precautionary approach. Most recently, a MARPOL annex was amended to include the regulation of greenhouse gas emissions from international shipping.[157] This is a major development as it represents the contribution of the shipping industry to global efforts to mitigate climate change in accordance with Article 3 of the 1997 Kyoto Protocol.[158] Ships constructed after the entry into force of the regulations will be required to meet specific energy efficiency targets phased in, and gradually increased, from 2015. However, the long lifespan of ships means that it will be some time before we see a reduction in the greenhouse gas emissions of the shipping sector.

Second, a more effective scheme of enforcement was adopted in response to pressure from coastal states dissatisfied with the observance of the 1954 Convention. This scheme, reviewed in the following sections, involves the cooperation of coastal states, port states, and flag states in a system of certification, inspection, and reporting whose purposes are to make the operation of defective vessels difficult or impossible and to facilitate the performance by flag states of their primary jurisdiction to prosecute and enforce applicable laws. Better enforcement has made the 1973/78 MARPOL Convention a major advance on the 1954 Convention and provides evidence of the impact independent inspection can have in securing compliance with environmental protection treaties.

155 See *infra*, section 4(3). 156 Annex I, regulations 9 and 10; Annex II, regulations 3–6.

157 See Part IV of Annex VI, and IMO Res MEPC 304/72 (2018).

158 Harrison, *Ocean Yearbook* (2013) 359, 369; Kopela, 24 *YbIEL* (2014) 70–101.

(b) Certification and inspection under the MARPOL Convention

The flag state has two main responsibilities in ensuring that its vessels comply with the technical standards set by MARPOL. It must inspect the vessel at periodic intervals, and it must issue an 'international oil pollution prevention certificate'.[159] This certificate provides prima facie evidence that the ship complies with the requirements of MARPOL: it 'shall be accepted by the other parties and regarded for all purposes covered by the present Convention as having the same validity as a certificate issued by them,[160] but the Convention does not leave the question of compliance to the flag state alone. A novel provision, subsequently adopted in other IMO Conventions, allows ships required to hold a certificate to be inspected by any party in whose ports they are present ('port states').[161]

This form of port state control is not to be confused with the extended port state jurisdiction provided for in Article 218 of the 1982 UNCLOS, since it involves no extraterritorial competence to legislate or enforce treaty-based or customary rules of law beyond the port state's own waters. MARPOL relies instead on the undoubted jurisdiction possessed by states to regulate conditions of entry to or passage through their internal waters, including ports.[162] In this sense the practice, while novel in its application to pollution, is not a departure from existing principles of maritime jurisdiction referred to earlier.

Inspection under Article 5 of the 1973/78 MARPOL Convention may be carried out to confirm possession of a valid certificate, or to determine the condition of the ship where there are 'clear grounds' for believing that it does not correspond 'substantially' with the certificate. Since 1996 a new MARPOL regulation has also allowed port state inspection 'where there are clear grounds for believing that the master or crew are not familiar with essential shipboard procedures relating to the prevention of pollution'.[163] Where non-compliance with a MARPOL certificate is revealed, port states must not allow such ships to sail unless they can do so without presenting an unreasonable threat of harm to the marine environment. Their most effective sanction is therefore to restrain the vessel in port until it can be repaired to a suitable standard or directed to a repair yard. In less serious cases, the ship must be reported to the flag state for appropriate action or prosecuted for any violation of the port state's own law which arises from non-compliance with the convention.[164] The port state must not unduly delay ships, however.[165]

159 Annex I, regulations 4, 5. A comparable requirement applies to chemical tankers and ballast water.

160 Article 5(1).

161 Article 5.

162 Churchill and Lowe, *The International Law of the Sea*, Ch 3; Molenaar, 38 *ODIL* (2007) 225, but cf qualifications noted by Valenzuela, in Soons, *Implementation of the LOSC through International Institutions*, 200ff. On possible limits to port state jurisdiction see Molenaar, in Ringbom (ed), *Competing Norms in the Law of Marine Environmental Protection*, 201.

163 Regulation 8A, Annexes I, II, III, V. See Valenzuela, in Vidas and Østreng (eds), *Order for the Oceans*, 500.

164 Articles 4, 5(3) and SOLAS. On US experience with prosecutions for violations of MARPOL see Udell, in Vidas (ed), *Law, Technology and Science for Oceans in Globalisation* (Leiden, 2010) 269.

165 Article 7.

Port state inspection may also be used to supply evidence of a violation of the Convention's discharge regulations. This facility may be crucial to the enforcement of these regulations. The problem facing the flag state is that without cooperation from port states in furnishing evidence it may be unable to mount successful prosecutions. With this in mind, Article 6 of MARPOL therefore permits inspection by port states for this purpose and does not limit the power to situations where there are 'clear grounds' for suspicion, as in Article 5. A report must be made to flag states when a discharge violation is indicated, and flag states must then bring proceedings if satisfied that the evidence is sufficient. It is also open to any party, including a coastal state, to request inspection by the port state if there is sufficient evidence that the ship has discharged harmful substances 'in any place'. This would include high seas violations as well as violations in the maritime zones of other states. But, although port states do prosecute pollution violations occurring in their own internal waters or territorial sea, and Article 220(1) of the 1982 UNCLOS confirms their power to do so, MARPOL confers on them no extraterritorial jurisdiction to prosecute violations which occur elsewhere.[166]

An efficient scheme of port state inspection and control is in many respects a more practical means of deterring substandard vessels than flag state enforcement of international rules and standards, since such vessels will more often come within the reach of port states, where arrest or detention will provide a costly deterrent. It also reduces the need for coastal states to interfere with passing traffic, while facilitating prosecution of those ships which offend within coastal zones. Moreover it has the merit that it can be applied to the vessels of non-parties to MARPOL or SOLAS as a condition of port entry. Article 5(4) of MARPOL supports this view by requiring port states to ensure that no more-favourable treatment is given to the ships of non-parties. State practice under port state inspection schemes now in force in most of the major shipping regions indicates that non-parties have generally acquiesced in this application to their vessels of MARPOL and SOLAS standards.[167] Article (3) of the 1982 UNCLOS requires port states to give due publicity to port entry conditions, and to communicate them to the IMO, but it too assumes their right to determine these conditions for themselves. The conclusion that non-party flag states are effectively bound by MARPOL and SOLAS in this manner further strengthens the earlier argument for treating these conventions as indicative of the flag state's obligations in customary law. It does mean that states have little to gain by staying outside either Convention.[168]

Since the impact of port state inspection will tend to be reflected in traffic patterns, with substandard vessels favouring the more lenient ports, these inspection schemes will not work effectively unless they operate systematically and consistently. Where,

166 But cf 1982 UNCLOS, Article 218, *infra*.

167 Molenaar, *Coastal State Jurisdiction*, 172–3. Handl, in Ringbom (ed), *Competing Norms*, 223, rejects the argument that port state application of IMO conventions to non-party vessels violates the *pacta tertiis* rule.

168 See Valenzuela, in Soons, *Implementation of the LOSC through International Institutions*, 205ff.

as in Europe, ports in a variety of jurisdictions are potentially available, coordination is essential. Under the Paris Memorandum of Understanding ('MOU') on Port State Control, port authorities in the EU states, Canada, Norway, Iceland, and Russia co-operate in a programme of vessel inspection which aims to ensure that each participating administration inspects vessels in accordance with agreed criteria relating to the risk profile of the vessel and the inspection capacity of individual states.[169] Under the new scheme, high-risk vessels, such as oil and chemical tankers, or older ships, should be inspected every time they enter port, whereas vessels considered to pose a lower threat will be inspected less frequently. The participating countries managed to inspect 18,430 vessels in 2014. This was a smaller number than under the old regime, but more importantly, it was reported that 'fewer ships have been inspected more than once, thereby reducing the inspection burden.'[170] Indeed, the changes were primarily designed to promote a more effective way of selecting which vessels should be inspected and to reward compliance. The new inspection regime has also resulted in a lower number of deficiencies and detentions.[171] However, it is possible that this is a result of substandard shipping avoiding European ports altogether and the problem may simply have been pushed elsewhere.

Several other MOUs have also moved towards a new inspection regime based upon the risk profile of vessels, including the 1993 Tokyo MOU on the Asia-Pacific Region (from January 2014) and the 2000 Black Sea MOU (from January 2016).There is already evidence that this has similarly resulted in decreasing the total number of under-performing vessels identified.[172] Inspection schemes operating in Latin America, the Asia-Pacific Region, the Red Sea, the Caribbean, the Mediterranean, the Indian Ocean, Western and Southern Africa, continue, however, to set numerical targets for inspections and it is clear that there is much less capacity in these regions to establish a regime as effective as the one operating in Northern Europe.[173] Even within a regional scheme, there may be wide variation in inspection and detention rates. Effective port-state control requires a commitment of expertise and technical resources which can no more be guaranteed when inspections are carried out by port states rather than by flag states. Even in Europe port state control is far from perfect. This suggests that extension of port state control to other regions will not necessarily solve the problem of substandard shipping.

169 See Keselj, 30 *ODIL* (1999) 127; Schiferli, 11 *Ocean YB* (1994) 202; Kasoulides, *Port-State Control and Jurisdiction: Evolution of the Port-State Control Regime* (Dordrecht, 1993); Anderson, in Boyle and Freestone (eds), *Sustainable Development and International Law*, 325; Valenzuela, in Vidas and Østreng (eds), *Order for the Oceans*, 485. On the legal status of MOUs see Aust, 35 *ICLQ* (1986) 787.

170 Paris MOU Annual Report 2014, 18.

171 *Ibid*, 7.

172 Tokyo MOU Annual Report 2014, 2.

173 See 1992 Vinã del Mar Agreement on port state control in Latin America (20% of foreign vessels visiting port); 1996 Caribbean MOU (15% of foreign vessels visiting port); 1997 Mediterranean MOU; 1998 Indian Ocean MOU (10% of foreign vessels visiting port); 1999 Abuja MOU (15% of foreign vessels visiting port); 2004 Riyadh MOU (10% of foreign vessels visiting port). See Ringbom (ed), *Competing Norms in the Law of Marine Environmental Protection*, 138.

Nevertheless, all of the regional schemes provide good evidence of state practice on several points which are relevant to interpretation of Articles 211, 218, and 219 of the 1982 UNCLOS. First, they are limited to ensuring compliance with treaties that are in force, and to which the state undertaking the inspection is a party, but it is not a requirement that the flag state of the vessel should also be a party. Second, except where no valid certificate is produced (for example because the vessel is from a non-party to MARPOL or SOLAS) full inspection is allowed only if there are 'clear grounds' for believing that the vessel, or its equipment or crew, are substandard.[174] Third, there must be no discrimination between flags, but targeting priority inspections towards vessels from flags with a poor record is acceptable. In such cases 'clear grounds' for full inspection are deemed to exist. Finally, there is power in cases of serious deficiency to detain vessels or to ban them from ports in the region.

(c) Jurisdiction under the MARPOL Convention

Negotiation of the 1973/78 MARPOL Convention coincided with increasing pressure from coastal states for extension of their pollution control jurisdiction beyond the narrow three-mile territorial sea which then prevailed for most states. It was clear that this controversial question would be an important topic for consideration in the UNCLOS III negotiations. For this reason MARPOL itself relies, like the 1954 Convention, primarily on regulation and prosecution by flag states, but it leaves open the possibility of extending the jurisdiction of coastal and port states by providing in Article 4(2) that 'Any violation of the requirements of the present Convention within the jurisdiction of any party to the Convention *shall* be prohibited and sanctions *shall* be established therefore under the law of that Party'. This can be read as a recognition of the customary rule that coastal states may regulate pollution within their own internal waters and territorial sea, although it arguably goes further by turning a power to regulate into a duty to do so. But Article 9(3) at the same time makes clear that the term 'jurisdiction' in the Convention 'shall be construed in the light of international law in force at the time of application or interpretation of the present Convention'. Thus it must now be read in the light of subsequent developments, including the emergence of coastal state pollution jurisdiction in the exclusive economic zone, considered below. The important point here is simply that MARPOL itself does not prevent the extension of jurisdiction beyond the territorial sea, but neither does it authorize or compel such action.

The Convention does try to strengthen flag state enforcement in a number of ways, however. Regardless of where they occur, violations must be prohibited, proceedings must be brought if there is sufficient evidence, and penalties must be adequate in severity. It is not open to the flag state to adopt a more lenient attitude simply because the offence is committed on the high seas or in the waters of some distant state: these are precisely the situations where its duty to act effectively requires emphasis. In order to facilitate flag state prosecution of such offences, all parties are required to report

174 On what constitute clear grounds see Paris MOU, Section 4.1.

incidents at sea involving harmful substances, and the flag state must then act appropriately when informed of suspected violations.[175] Moreover, as we saw earlier, evidential problems can be overcome if port state inspections identify substandard vessels or discharge violations. Thus MARPOL does go some way towards promoting more effective enforcement by flag states, but it does not entirely remove the practical problems which in many cases have made port state control the more realistic method of ensuring higher levels of compliance.

(d) Assessing the impact of MARPOL

All of the Annexes to MARPOL[176] have now entered into force and they have received widespread support, with all of them covering at least 96 per cent of the global tonnage. In this respect, MARPOL has been successful in meeting the objective, set out in the Preamble, of 'establishing rules not limited to oil pollution having a universal purport.' Furthermore, the standards contained in MARPOL, as well as many of the other regulatory treaties falling under the competence of the IMO, have been regularly updated in order to ensure their continuing effectiveness. The tacit amendment procedures have meant that such changes enter into force with minimal delay. Yet, acceptance of the rules and implementation of the rules are two different things and it is therefore necessary to consider the impact of MARPOL in practice.

As we saw in Chapter 4, the implementation and effectiveness of most modern environmental treaties is monitored in some form by treaty supervisory institutions. States must report, non-compliance procedures exist to deal with complaints or difficulties, and funding and technical assistance may be available to help developing countries. The 1973/78 MARPOL Convention and other IMO regulatory conventions are unusual in lacking many of these features. Although flag states are required to report to the IMO on action they have taken with regard to ships found to have violated MARPOL standards, and on a list of matters relevant to implementation of the Convention, their record of doing so is generally poor, and largely confined to developed states whose own tonnage is now a diminishing proportion of the whole.[177] Even if it does have information, the IMO has no process for dealing effectively with noncompliance issues, such as the persistent failure of some states to provide the port discharge facilities required by Annexes I and II of MARPOL. In 1992 it established a Flag State Implementation Committee (FSIC) with responsibility for 'the identification of measures necessary to ensure effective and consistent global implementation of IMO instruments' by flag states.[178] One outcome has been the development of a Member State Audit Scheme, which became mandatory from January 2016.[179] The audit scheme

[175] Article 4.

[176] See Tan, *Vessel-Source Marine Pollution*, 230–85; Sasamura, in Couper and Gold (eds), *The Marine Environment and Sustainable Development* (Honolulu, 1993) 306; Mitchell, *Intentional Oil Pollution at Sea* (Cambridge, Mass, 1994); Peet, 7 *IJECL* (1992) 277.

[177] See Articles 4(3) 6(4) 11, and Mitchell, *Intentional Oil Pollution*, Ch 4.

[178] See Roach, in Nordquist and Moore (eds), *Current Maritime Issues and the IMO* (The Hague, 1999) 151; de La Fayette, 16 *IJMCL* (2001) 215–26.

[179] IMO Assembly Resolutions A.1067(28) and A.1070(28).

will require all states to undergo independent scrutiny by technical experts selected by the IMO Secretary General in order to determine whether they have taken the necessary steps to comply with their obligations under, inter alia, the 1973/78 MARPOL Convention and 1974 SOLAS Conventions. However, the audit scheme cannot be compared to a compliance mechanism, as the results of audits will remain confidential, unless the audited state consents to their publication. It follows that the scheme is largely a tool to assist states to identify problems and to take action themselves. Audited states will be encouraged to develop action plans to follow up on the audit results, but there will be no means by which IMO Members can oversee compliance under this scheme. Nevertheless, anonymised reports on what issues have been identified through audit may help the newly branded Committee on the Implementation of IMO Instruments to identify priorities for action, offering an opportunity for the organization to move away from a reactive mode of regulation to one that may be able to do more to preempt problems.[180]

Evidence of port state inspections undertaken around the world demonstrates that overall detention rates are going down, and that a large percentage of deficiencies and detentions are attributable to a small number of flags of convenience. The Paris MOU operates a blacklist of the flag states which are responsible for the worst performing vessels. In 2019, the black list included Sierra Leone, Mongolia, Saint Kitts and Nevis, Belize, Comoros, Palau, the Cook Islands, Togo, Moldova and Tanzania.[181] Several of these flag states are also found on the black lists of other regional MOUs.[182] It cannot be assumed that the problem is simply one of flags of convenience or developing state registers, however. A number of states in both categories, including Liberia and the Bahamas, have established good records. Strangely, while the worst performers in Latin American ports also include flag of convenience vessels from Cyprus and Malta, ships from Belize, Honduras, Panama, and St Vincent apparently perform much better there than in Europe or the United States.[183] The continuing detention of vessels from black-listed states suggests that substandard vessels are not completely deterred from returning to Paris or Tokyo MOU ports, and that shipping companies are not deterred from flagging out to substandard registers.[184]

At the same time, MOU figures show that deficiency and detention rates for oil and chemical tankers are below the average for all ships.[185] By far the largest category of substandard vessels are the less environmentally hazardous general cargo and bulk carriers.[186] What does appear tenable is the conclusion that MARPOL and

180 See Harrison, *Saving the Oceans through Law*, 143–5.

181 Paris MOU, *Annual Report* (2019) 31.

182 See Tokyo MOU, Annual Report (2019) 34 listing Tanzania, Togo, Mongolia, Sierra Leone, DPR Korea, St Kitts and Nevis, Barbados, Palau, Niue, Federated States of Micronesia.

183 Viña del Mar MOU, *Annual Report* (1998). Figures for the Tokyo MOU and the US Coastguard are closer to those for Europe; see Tan, *Vessel-Source Marine Pollution*, 250–1.

184 See in particular Tan, *Vessel Source Marine-Pollution*, 239–85.

185 40% of oil tanker inspections in 2014 revealed some deficiencies, but only 1.4% resulted in detention. The average rate of detentions for all ships was 3.2.% (Paris MOU). The 2014 oil tanker detention rate under the Tokyo MOU was 2.05% against an average for all ships of 4.35%.

186 Paris MOU, *Annual Report* (2014); Tokyo MOU, *Annual Report* (2014).

SOLAS, in conjunction with enhanced port state control, have been substantially more effective than the 1954 London Convention in ensuring that oil and chemical tankers operating in the northern hemisphere conform to higher construction and equipment standards for pollution control and maritime safety.[187] It is of course this conclusion which is of most significance for protection of the marine and coastal environment, rather than the deficiency or detention rates for all ships. If MARPOL and SOLAS have undoubtedly affected the way oil and chemical tankers are built and equipped, how has it affected the way they are operated? This is a more difficult question. GESAMP reports have consistently noted a decline in operational discharges and oil spillages at sea from tankers, concluding that the entry into force of MARPOL 'had a substantial positive impact' in reducing operational pollution from all types of vessel.[188] GESAMP's assessment for the period 1988–97 showed some 457,000 tonnes of oil entering the sea annually from ships, or 70 per cent of the total from all human activities.[189] Of this total, 205,000 tonnes annually were estimated to come from operational sources (but only 4 per cent from oil tankers) and 164,000 tonnes from accidents at sea, mainly involving oil tankers. The decline in operational discharges from oil tankers may suggest improvements in coastal states complying with their duty to provide port reception facilities over this period,[190] but that merely shifts the problem of treatment and disposal of sometimes very hazardous wastes onto land. In one of the most serious incidents of its kind, hazardous MARPOL slops were denied offloading at Rotterdam, which could not handle them, but eventually discharged to a port reception facility in West Africa and then dumped in the surrounding city.[191] It can at least be said that the MARPOL prohibition on discharge at sea was effective in this case but that merely points up the absence of any comparable regulation of discharge on land. Provided the discharge is to a certified port reception facility, no international law is broken.[192]

Illegal discharges can only be controlled if detected and if action is then taken. In practice this requires either port state inspection relying on oil discharge records as evidence, or a level of surveillance and monitoring of vessels at sea which is only likely to be attainable by developed coastal states with appropriate resources in aircraft and naval or coastguard patrols. Moreover, the failure of many coastal states to adopt extended enforcement jurisdiction in their EEZ has meant that prosecutions for

187 See Kasoulides, *Port State Control and Jurisdiction*; Mitchell, *Intentional Oil Pollution*, 135ff; EC, *Common Policy on Safe Seas* (Brussels, 1993) 39ff, paras 61–8.

188 GESAMP, *The State of the Marine Environment* (Nairobi, 1990); id, *Reports and Studies No 50: Impact of Oil and Related Chemicals on the Marine Environment* (London, 1993); GESAMP, *Reports and Studies No 75: Estimates of oil entering the marine environment from sea-based activities* (IMO, 2007).

189 The remainder came from offshore installations (3%) coastal installations (17.8%) and small craft (8.2%).

190 Annex I, Reg 12.

191 UNEP, Rept of 1st meeting of the Expanded Bureau of the 8th meeting of the Conference of the Parties to the Basel Convention (2007) UNEP/SBC/BUREAU/8/1/7, section III.

192 MARPOL discharges are excluded from the Basel Convention. See Article 1(4). The problems with port reception facilities are fully explored in Mitchell, *Intentional Oil Pollution*, Ch 6; Tan, *Vessel Source Marine Pollution*, 251–73.

discharges in waters beyond the territorial sea remain largely the responsibility of flag states. Reports communicated to the IMO concerning the application of MARPOL have given no reliable indication of the record of flag state prosecutions, nor of the Convention's success in reducing high seas pollution, since only a minority of mainly developed states have submitted reports as required. These do show extensive referral of violations by port and coastal states, but subsequent flag state action is reported in less than a quarter of such cases. One reason for this is that differing legal standards for exchange and admissibility of evidence continue to make successful prosecution of polluters difficult, and when fines are imposed, the average tends to be low,[193] despite the emphasis in MARPOL itself that penalties 'shall be adequate in severity to discourage violations.'[194] These factors indicate that prosecution of ships is unlikely to be a significant factor in any reduction of oil in the sea.

Quantifying MARPOL's impact is not straightforward, and the data do not point to any clear conclusion, except that operational pollution from tankers appears to have declined, while discharges from other types of vessel remain a problem. Major tanker disasters have continued to occur however, some of which indicate weaknesses in the proficiency of crews and the seaworthiness and construction standards of older vessels. The *Exxon Valdez, Aegean Sea, Haven, Braer, Sea Empress, Evoikos, Nakhodka, Erika*, and *Prestige* have all been the subject of large compensation claims.[195] With the exception of the *Exxon Valdez* all were registered in flag of convenience states: Greece, Liberia, Cyprus, Malta, and the Bahamas. These states account for only a small proportion of the hundred or more tanker incidents dealt with by the IOPC Fund, but their ships appear to have larger pollution spills than Japanese and Korean vessels, which account for more than half the total number of claims. Once single-hull tankers are all phased out the number of severe accidents may decline, but double hulls are not as easy to repair or inspect, and we will not know whether the policy has succeeded until these ships are twenty or thirty years old.[196]

5 COASTAL AND PORT STATE ENVIRONMENTAL JURISDICTION

5(1) IN INTERNAL WATERS AND THE TERRITORIAL SEA

In most respects the 1982 UNCLOS does not alter or extend the coastal state's rights in internal waters or the territorial sea.[197] In this context its purpose is simply to clarify and define the limits of those rights. The territorial sea regime envisaged by the Convention is thus a compromise: it offers coastal states power to regulate pollution,

[193] Paris Memorandum, *Annual Report* (1990) 20; Kasoulides, in Soons (ed), *Implementation*, 432; Mitchell, *Intentional Oil Pollution*, Chs 5, 7; Peet, 7 *IJECL* (1992) 277.

[194] MARPOL, Article 4(4).

[195] See *infra*, section 8(3).

[196] Frank, 20 *IJMCL* (2005) 1.

[197] But see UNCLOS Article 218, *infra*, section 5(3).

while preserving the right of innocent passage for all ships and international control of construction, design, equipment, and manning standards.[198] What the Convention does change is the maximum breadth of the territorial sea, which it extends from three to twelve miles, a decision overwhelmingly adopted in state practice. By itself, however, this extension was not enough to satisfy the needs or claims of coastal states. The more important decision, therefore, was to go beyond the territorial sea by giving coastal states exclusive rights over natural resources and jurisdiction to control pollution and marine scientific research in a new 200 mile 'exclusive economic zone' created by the 1982 UNCLOS.

(a) Environmental jurisdiction in internal waters and the territorial sea

The coastal state's jurisdiction to regulate the marine environment depends on its sovereignty or sovereign rights over maritime zones contiguous to its coasts. Until the 1970s these zones were for the most part of limited extent. In internal waters, such as ports, the coastal state is free to apply national laws and determine conditions of entry for foreign vessels.[199] After the *Exxon Valdez* accident the United States became the first to ban all single-hull oil tankers from its ports without waiting for agreement in the IMO.[200] The most obvious argument in favour of the lawfulness of this response to a major environmental disaster is that it falls within the customary jurisdiction of a port state to regulate matters affecting the peace and good order of the port because of the risk of accidents and consequential pollution. No state is known to have objected to the US action; it represents a clear precedent for a similar ban by the EU following the sinking of the *Prestige* oil tanker.[201] Legislation of this kind remains an unusual assertion of jurisdiction, however; for most states the interests of comity with other nations and freedom of navigation have until now dictated greater restraint in the unilateral regulation of foreign ships.[202]

In the territorial sea, the coastal state also enjoys sovereignty, and with it the power to apply national law.[203] The coastal state's right to regulate environmental protection in territorial waters has been assumed or asserted in national legislation and in treaties on such matters as oil drilling, dumping or pollution from ships. This right includes three important powers: the designation of environmentally protected or

[198] Boyle, 79 *AJIL* (1985) 347. See M'Gonigle and Zacher, *Pollution, Politics, and International Law*, 244–5 and Tan, *Vessel-Source Marine Pollution*, 176–229 for critical analysis of this part of the 1982 Convention.

[199] *Nicaragua Case*, ICJ Reports (1986) paras 212–13; Churchill and Lowe, *The Law of the Sea*, 61; de La Fayette, 11 *IJMCL* (1996) 15–16.

[200] 1990 Oil Pollution Act. See critical analysis by Valenzuela, in Soons, *Implementation of the LOSC through International Institutions*, 212 ff.

[201] EC Regulation 417/2002, amended by Reg 1726/2003. See Boyle, 21 *IJMCL* (2006) 15; Frank, 20 *IJMCL* (2005) 1.

[202] See generally Churchill and Lowe, *The Law of the Sea*, Ch 3; O'Connell, *The International Law of the Sea*, Ch 22.

[203] 1982 UNCLOS, Article 2; Churchill and Lowe, *The Law of the Sea*, Ch 4; O'Connell, *The International Law of the Sea*, Chs 19, 24.

particularly sensitive sea areas,[204] the designation and control of navigation routes for safety and environmental purposes,[205] and the prohibition of pollution discharges.[206]

In each of these respects the coastal state enjoys a substantial measure of national discretion: it is, for example, free to set stricter pollution discharge standards for ships than the international standards required by the 1973/78 MARPOL Convention. But unlike the earlier 1958 Territorial Sea Convention, or MARPOL, which are both silent on the point, the 1982 UNCLOS expressly excludes from the coastal state's jurisdiction the right to regulate construction, design, equipment, and manning standards for ships, unless giving effect to international rules and standards, which for this purpose means primarily the 1973/78 MARPOL Convention, and the 1974 SOLAS Convention.[207] The reason for this exclusion is self-evident: a coastal state must not use its jurisdiction to hamper the right of innocent passage through the territorial sea or suspend the right in straits used for international navigation.[208] This right is enjoyed by the vessels of all nations, and it is an essential safeguard for freedom of maritime navigation. Foreign vessels do not thereby acquire exemption from coastal state laws, but these laws must be in conformity with international law, and must not have the practical effect of denying passage.[209]

(b) Control of vessel pollution in the territorial sea

What then can a coastal state legitimately do when a foreign vessel is found violating international pollution regulations in the territorial sea, or when it poses a risk of accidental pollution or environmental harm? What the coastal state cannot do is to close its territorial waters to foreign ships in innocent passage, even where their cargo presents a significant environmental risk, as in the case of oil tankers.[210] Passage in these circumstances does not cease to be innocent, and must be afforded without discrimination. At most, the coastal state will be entitled to take certain precautionary measures

204 See *infra*.

205 1982 UNCLOS, Article 22, which requires states to take into account IMO recommendations, but does not require IMO approval. Mandatory vessel traffic management (VTS) in the territorial sea and Mandatory Ship Reporting (MSR) are provided for under SOLAS 1974, Ch V; traffic separation schemes (TSS) under the 1972 Collision Regulations Convention. See also IMO Resolutions A 857(20); A 851(20); A 572(14) as amended by MSC 165(78); A 927(22) and generally Roberts, 20 *IJMCL* (2005) 135; Plant, in Ringbom (ed), *Competing Norms in the Law of Marine Environmental Protection*, 11; IJlstra, in Soons, *Implementation of the LOSC through International Institutions*, 216; Warren and Wallace, 9 *IJMCL* (1994) 523.

206 1972 London Convention, Article 4(3); 1973/78 MARPOL Convention, Article 4(2); 1982 UNCLOS, Article 21(1)(f).

207 1982 UNCLOS, Article 21(2); Article 211(4). See especially the opposing views of Canada and Bulgaria on this question, 3rd UNCLOS, 6 *Official Records*, 109, 112.

208 *Corfu Channel Case*, ICJ Reports (1949) 1; 1958 Territorial Sea Convention, Articles, 14–16; 1982 UNCLOS, Articles 17–19, 24–5; Churchill and Lowe, *The Law of the Sea*, 81ff, and see generally Ngantcha, *The Right of Innocent Passage and the Evolution of The International Law of the Sea* (London, 1990). On regulating passage in straits, see 1982 UNCLOS, Article 41; Oxman, 10 *IJMCL* (1995) 467; Oral, in Barrett and Barnes, *Law of the Sea* (BIICL, 2016) Ch 10, and generally, Caminos and Cogliati-Bantz, *The Legal Regime of Straits* (Cambridge, 2014).

209 1958 Territorial Sea Convention, Article 17; 1982 UNCLOS, Article 21(4).

210 1982 UNCLOS, Article 24(1).

to minimize the risk: it may, for example, require ships carrying nuclear materials or other inherently dangerous or noxious substances, such as oil or hazardous waste, to carry documentation, observe special precautionary measures approved by the IMO or established by international agreements such as MARPOL, or confine their passage to specified sea lanes in the interests of safety, the efficiency of traffic, and the protection of the environment.[211] Following the *Braer* disaster off the Shetland Islands in 1993, the IMO also amended the SOLAS Convention to allow coastal states to require ships to report their presence to coastal authorities when entering designated zones, including environmentally sensitive areas.[212]

The application of these principles can be observed in state practice concerning environmentally sensitive areas covered by special areas protocols,[213] or Particularly Sensitive Sea Areas ('PSSAs') designated by the IMO.[214] A PSSA is 'an area that needs special protection through action by the IMO because of its significance for recognized ecological, socio-economic, or scientific attributes where such attributes may be vulnerable to damage by international shipping activities'.[215] PSSAs designated by the IMO include the Great Barrier Reef, the Florida Keys, the Wadden Sea, the Canary Islands, the Sabana-Camagüey Archipelago, the Torres Strait, the Baltic Sea, the Strait of Bonifacio, Saba Bank, the Galapagos Archipelago, the Papahanaumouakea National Marine Monument in Hawaii, and Western European waters. They 'may be regarded as fulfilling general obligations in the LOS Convention and in a number of treaties designed to protect the marine environment and/or biodiversity'.[216] In such cases the passage of ships through the territorial sea may be regulated in order to minimize the risk of adverse environmental effects or serious pollution but, here too, the important point is that while ships may be required to avoid certain areas, the right of innocent passage is not lost.[217] Mandatory ship reporting is a common element of such schemes, but additional measures may also be taken with IMO approval. Thus in 1990, Australia obtained IMO designation of the Great Barrier Reef as a PSSA within an extended territorial sea and imposed

211 1982 UNCLOS, Articles 22(2) and 23. On hazardous waste shipments see 1989 Basel Convention on the Control of Transboundary Movements of Hazardous Wastes, Article 4(12) and 1991 Bamako Convention, Article 4(4)(c) *infra*, Ch 8, section 4, but see *contra* Haiti, *Note Verbale* of 18 Feb 1988, in 11 *LOSB* (1988) 13 and Pineschi, in Francioni and Scovazzi (eds), *International Responsibility for Environmental Harm* (Dordrecht, 1991) 299.

212 1974 SOLAS, Chapter V, Regulation 8–1. See Plant, in Ringbom (ed), *Competing Norms*, 11.

213 Mediterranean, Caribbean and East African protected areas protocols, *supra*, section 3.

214 See IMO Res A 927(22) and materials collected in 9 *IJMCL* (1994). See also Roberts, *Marine Environmental Protection and Biodiversity Conservation: The Application and Future Development of the IMO's Particularly Sensitive Sea Area Concept* (Berlin, 2006); Kachel, *Particularly Sensitive Sea Areas: The IMO's Role in Protecting Vulnerable Marine Areas* (Berlin, 2008); Churchill, in Caddell and Thomas (eds), *Shipping, Law and the Marine Environment in the 21st Century* (Witney, 2013) 73.

215 IMO Res A 982(24) annex, para 1.2.

216 de La Fayette, 16 *IJMCL* (2001) 155, 186.

217 1982 Geneva Protocol Concerning Mediterranean Specially Protected Areas, Article 7(e); 1990 Kingston Protocol Concerning Specially Protected Areas, etc, of the Wider Caribbean, Article 5(2)(c); and see IMO, Working Group on Guidelines for Particularly Sensitive Sea Areas, MEPC 29 and 30 (1990). Cf, however, Canada's 1972 Arctic Waters Pollution Act, and 1982 UNCLOS, Article 234.

compulsory pilotage requirements.[218] The United States also designated the Florida Keys as an 'area to be avoided' and prohibited the operation of tankers in these waters under the 1972 Marine Protection, Research, and Sanctuaries Act, again with the approval of the IMO. However, as adopted by the IMO in Resolution A 927(22) the PSSA concept does not expand the powers of coastal states in the territorial sea; it merely coordinates a range of available powers under the 1982 UNCLOS, 1974 SOLAS Convention, and 1972 COLREGS Convention, inter alia. PSSAs can extend into the exclusive economic zone—the North Sea/Western European PSSA is an example—but with more limited effects.[219]

(c) Arrest of ships for pollution in the territorial sea

Although the practical exercise of a right to arrest ships in passage poses serious dangers to navigation, and is rarely used as a means of enforcing anti-pollution regulations, both the 1972 London Convention and the 1973/78 MARPOL Convention require coastal states to apply and enforce their provisions against all vessels in the territorial sea. This right is recognized in the 1982 UNCLOS, subject to that Convention's provisions on innocent passage and the existence of clear grounds for suspecting a violation.[220] However, the mere violation of regulations will not necessarily deprive the vessel of its right of innocent passage or justify arrest. Innocent passage was defined by the 1958 Territorial Sea Convention as passage which is 'not prejudicial to the peace, good order or security' of the coastal state. This vague terminology appeared to allow coastal states ample room for subjective judgments of the question of innocence, and it is arguably not an accurate reflection of the treatment of innocent passage in the *Corfu Channel Case*.[221] That decision implied a rather more objective test, now reflected in Article 19 of the 1982 UNCLOS. This provision was not intended to change the law but to clarify it in terms affording less scope for potentially abusive interference with shipping.

The significant point is that only pollution which is 'wilful and serious' and contrary to the Convention will deprive a vessel in passage of its innocent character, which necessarily excludes accidental pollution from having this effect. Moreover, while operational pollution is invariably deliberate, it is less often serious, and may sometimes be justified by weather or distress. Under this formulation, therefore, it will rarely be the case that ships causing operational pollution will cease to be in innocent passage. Nor would it permit single-hull tankers to be banned from the territorial sea, since a mere violation of construction standards will not be enough to deprive a ship of its right to innocent passage. Only when they lose this right can their entry into territorial waters be denied or terminated by eviction or arrest. In most cases the preferable solution will be to rely on port states for enforcement purpose.[222]

218 MEPC 45/30 (1990) and MEPC 133/53 (2005) which extends the scheme to the Torres Strait. See Okkesen et al, 9 *IJMCL* (1994) 507.

219 See *infra*, section 4(3)(b).

220 1972 London Convention, Article 7; 1973/78 MARPOL Convention, Article 4(2); 1982 UNCLOS, Article 220(2).

221 *Corfu Channel Case*, ICJ Reports (1949) 1.

222 See *infra*, section 5(3).

5(2) ENVIRONMENTAL JURISDICTION IN THE EEZ

The EEZ, which extends up to 200 nautical miles from the territorial sea baseline, confers on coastal states sovereign rights over living and mineral resources, and jurisdiction with regard to the protection and preservation of the marine environment.[223] In the *Libya-Malta Continental Shelf Case* the ICJ found that: 'the institution of the EEZ with its rule on entitlement by reason of distance is shown by the practice of states to have become part of customary law'.[224]

The central feature of the EEZ regime is that it preserves for all states high seas freedom of navigation within the zone, rather than the more restrictive territorial sea right of innocent passage.[225] Coastal states acquire the power to regulate pollution from seabed installations and dumping within the EEZ, and to protect ecosystems and biodiversity, but their regulatory jurisdiction over vessels is limited to the application of international rules for enforcement purposes only.[226] Essentially this is a power to apply MARPOL regulations (Article 211(5)). Only a small number of coastal states have legislation implementing Article 211(5);[227] others, such as the United States, have asserted jurisdiction in their EEZ only for certain purposes, such as fisheries conservation or dumping, but have not legislated to control pollution from ships beyond the territorial sea. Some states have made no EEZ claims (e.g. in the Mediterranean) but a few of these have nevertheless legislated on all or most of the matters covered by EEZ jurisdictional powers. A few others have EEZ pollution legislation which could be interpreted as exceeding what the 1982 UNCLOS allows, notably on passage for ships carrying nuclear or hazardous waste, or which fails to reflect the carefully balanced qualifications and limitations laid down in the UNCLOS articles.[228]

The effect of this new regime is less radical than some coastal states had sought. That it does no more than permit them to apply MARPOL and other relevant instruments is evident from the wording of article 211(5), which refers only to coastal state laws 'conforming to and giving effect to generally accepted international rules and standards' for the prevention, reduction, and control of vessel-source pollution.[229] In this context MARPOL regulations and other international standards adopted by the IMO thus represent the normal limit of coastal state competence and act as a necessary restraint

223 1982 UNCLOS, Article 56; *3rd UNCLOS, Official Records*, ii, 317–20; M'Gonigle and Zacher, *Pollution, Politics and International Law*, Ch 6; Nordquist, *UNCLOS Commentary*, iv, 180ff. See Orrego-Vicuna, *The Exclusive Economic Zone: Regime and Legal Nature Under International Law* (Cambridge, 1989); Kwiatkowska, *The 200-Mile EEZ in the New Law of the Sea* (Dordrecht, 1989); Attard, *The Exclusive Economic Zone* (Oxford, 1987).

224 ICJ Reports (1985) 13, para 34.

225 1982 UNCLOS, Articles 56(2) 58.

226 Articles 208, 210, 211(5)–(6).

227 Churchill and Lowe, *The Law of the Sea*, 352, list Russia, Bulgaria, Romania, Malaysia, Sweden, Antigua, St.Kitts, St.Lucia, and the Ukraine.

228 See Churchill and Lowe, *The Law of the Sea*, 351–3; Molenaar, *Coastal State Jurisdiction over Vessel Source Pollution*, 363–82. For a listing of national EEZ claims and legislation see Kwiatkowska, 9 *IJMCL* (1994) 199, 337; id, 10 *IJMCL* (1995) 53.

229 On the meaning of this phrase, see Molenaar, *Coastal State Jurisdiction over Vessel Source Pollution*, Ch 10.

where there is evident potential for excessive interference with shipping. Coastal states have acquired little real discretion about the kind of anti-pollution legislation they may apply in the EEZ. In particular, as in the territorial sea, they are denied the power to set their own construction, design, equipment, and manning standards for vessels or to refuse passage. Following the *Prestige* disaster, unilateral action by some European states to ban single-hull oil tankers from their EEZs encountered strong opposition and could not easily be reconciled with the 1982 UNCLOS, or with the new PSSA subsequently adopted for Western Europe.[230] Mandatory reporting or routeing schemes also require IMO approval if they extend to the EEZ and must be supported by scientific and technical evidence.[231] Nor does the designation of special areas or PSSAs by the IMO confer any power on coastal states to act unilaterally in setting construction or equipment standards for ships entering the EEZ, although it may allow the imposition of higher standards relating to pollution discharges or to control navigation.[232]

The solitary exception to the Convention's preference for the application of international regulations in the EEZ is found in Article 234. This article was a concession to Canadian and Russian interests in the protection of the Arctic Ocean. It applies to ice-covered areas within the limits of the EEZ, and allows coastal states a broad discretion, free from IMO supervision, to adopt national standards for pollution control, provided only that these have due regard for navigation and are non-discriminatory. It remains uncertain whether this Article goes as far as Canada's 1970 Arctic Waters Pollution Act in authorizing limitations on navigation.[233] Article 234 assumes ice-cover in the EEZ; if the Arctic becomes ice-free for part of the year this special regime may cease to apply.[234]

In general, the 1982 UNCLOS can best be seen as serving the interests of maritime states within the EEZ although the extension of jurisdiction does give a wider area of control to coastal states if they choose to use it. In the exercise of jurisdiction within the EEZ, coastal states must have due regard for the rights and duties of other states, including the right of freedom of navigation. This freedom is largely protected by ensuring uniformity of applicable pollution standards, and by preserving the ability of maritime states to influence the formulation of those standards within the IMO. Although the international regulations adopted through that body represent an expression of compromise and common interest among the various groups represented there, including environmental NGOs and industry associations, there is little doubt

[230] Frank, 20 *IJMCL* (2005) 9–10. See generally Laly-Chevalier, 50 *AFDI* (2004) 581.

[231] 1974 SOLAS, Regulation V/8 and V/8–1. See Plant, in Ringbom (ed), *Competing Norms in the Law of Marine Environmental Protection*, 11; Roberts, 20 *IJMCL* (2005) 135.

[232] For a fuller analysis of UNCLOS Article 211(6) and its relationship to PSSAs and MARPOL special areas, see Frank, 20 *IJMCL* (2005) 28–38; de La Fayette, 16 *IJMCL* (2001)155, 190–2. de La Fayette emphasises the importance of PSSAs in providing additional powers within the EEZ, with IMO approval.

[233] McRae and Goundrey, 16 *UBCLR* (1982) 197; Pharand, 7 *Dalhousie LJ* (1983) 315; Johnson and Zacher, *Canadian Foreign Policy and the Law of the Sea* (Vancouver, 1977) Ch 3. Canada has subsequently redrawn its territorial sea baselines to extend its jurisdiction over the waters of its northern archipelago, and it has also claimed a 200-mile EEZ.

[234] But see to the contrary Dremliuga, 48 *ODIL* (2017) 128.

that maritime states have tended to predominate.[235] However, the continued growth of flags of convenience since 1982 makes the identification of 'maritime states' an increasingly difficult task. Thus, it should not be assumed that states with a low registered tonnage, such as the United States, do not have a substantial interest in maritime navigation, or that their influence in IMO can be disregarded. Nevertheless, the essential point remains that the Convention's articles on the regulation of vessel pollution by coastal states are primarily important as a basis for enforcement of MARPOL and other international standards, and do not authorize 'creeping jurisdiction' over the high seas.

5(3) ENFORCEMENT JURISDICTION BEYOND THE TERRITORIAL SEA

It was eventually accepted during the the 1982 UNCLOS negotiations that the problem of non-compliance by ships with international regulations could not be remedied by flag state enforcement alone, and that the port state control provisions of MARPOL were not in themselves a sufficient alternative.[236] The main question was whether to allow coastal states full authority to arrest and prosecute vessels for pollution offences within the EEZ, a solution consistent with the extension of their prescriptive jurisdiction, or whether to concentrate instead on the increased use of port state jurisdiction as the main complement to the flag state's authority. The advantage of the former was that it would give those states which suffered most from substandard ships or illegal discharges the opportunity to protect themselves directly, rather than by relying on flag states. The disadvantages were the threat to freedom of navigation, and as in the territorial sea, the practical dangers of interfering with ships at sea. Moreover, coastal-state enforcement afforded no remedy for high seas pollution offences outside the EEZ. From this perspective, port state jurisdiction to prosecute violations emerged as the more attractive alternative, since it presented no danger to navigation and afforded better facilities for investigation and the collection of evidence concerning offences, regardless of where they had taken place.[237]

(7) Enforcement of pollution regulations in the EEZ

The regime for coastal state enforcement in the EEZ, once more, is a compromise between the two extremes. Coastal states are not given full jurisdiction to enforce international regulations against ships in passage in the EEZ. They can do so if the vessel

235 See especially McGonigle and Zacher, *Pollution, Politics and International Law*, Chs 3, 7; Hayashi, 16 *IJMCL* (2001) 501; de La Fayette, 16 *IJMCL* (2001) 215–20; Gaskell, 18 *IJMCL* (2003) 172–4; Tan, *Vessel-Source Marine Pollution*, 29–74.

236 Ryngaert and Ringbom (eds), *Port State Jurisdiction: Challenges and Potential*, 31 *IJMCL* Special Issue (2016) 395; Marten, *Port State Jurisdiction and the Regulation of International Merchant Shipping* (Heidelberg, 2014); Molenaar, *Coastal State Jurisdiction over Vessel Source Pollution*, 382–99; *id*, in Freestone, Barnes and Ong (eds), *The Law of the Sea*, Ch 11; Kasoulides, *Port-state Control and Jurisdiction*.

237 Lowe, 12 *San Diego LR* (1975) 624; Bernhardt, 20 *Vand JTL* (1979) 265; Kasoulides, in Soons, *Implementation of the LOSC through International Institutions*; ILA, *Report of the 56th Conference* (1974) 400–8.

voluntarily enters port,[238] but otherwise their powers in the EEZ itself are graduated according to the likely harm. Only when there is 'clear objective evidence' of a violation of applicable international regulations resulting in a discharge of pollution which causes or threatens to cause 'major damage' to the coastal state are arrest and prosecution permitted. Even then, a ship has a right to prompt release upon payment of a reasonable bond or other financial security,[239] and the ship may in this case only be detained if necessary to prevent an unreasonable threat of damage to the marine environment.[240] In contrast, where the violation has resulted only in a 'substantial discharge' causing or threatening 'significant pollution', the vessel may be inspected for 'matters relating to the violation'—that is, in effect, for evidence of the illegal discharge, provided this is justified by the circumstances, including information already given by the ship.[241] Where none of these conditions exist, the coastal state is confined to seeking information concerning the ship's identity and its next port of call.[242] The port state may then be asked to take appropriate action.

Although these graduated enforcement powers in the EEZ leave coastal states considerable latitude in determining what action is justified in individual cases, and may for that reason lead to uncertainty and inconsistency in their use, they do amount to rather less than the competence enjoyed by coastal states in the territorial sea, and in less serious cases they still leave enforcement to flag states, or as we shall see, to port states. In this form the jurisdiction of coastal states remains a limited one for protective purposes only, but this is consistent with the nature of their rights in the EEZ. In practice, few states have resorted to the exercise of these powers in full and it is doubtful whether in this respect Article 220 of the 1982 UNCLOS has had any significant effect.[243]

(b) Port state enforcement of pollution regulations

In contrast to the limited jurisdiction of coastal states, the more radical development is that Article 218 gives port states express power to investigate and prosecute pollution discharge violations wherever they have taken place. This power covers both high-seas offences, and violations within the coastal zones of another state, although in the latter case the port state may only act in response to a request from the state concerned. Apart from this limitation, the port state's jurisdiction under this article is independent, in the sense that no request from the flag state is necessary, but the flag state does enjoy a right of pre-emption, considered below.

The obvious advantage of Article 218 is that it may ensure prompt prosecution of polluters where the coastal state is unable or incompetent to act, or where the vessel is unlikely to come within the flag state's authority. In effect this article recognizes

[238] Article 220(1). This power applies only to violations which have occurred 'within the territorial sea or the exclusive economic zone of *that* state'.

[239] Article 226(1)(b). [240] Article 226(1)(c). [241] Article 220(5)–(6).

[242] Article 220(3).

[243] For the drafting history of Article 220, see Nordquist (ed), *UNCLOS Commentary*, iv, 281ff. For national legislation, see Molenaar, *Coastal State Jurisdiction over Vessel Source Pollution*, 389–98.

the inability or ineffectiveness of flag states when dealing with pollution incidents on the high seas, and gives the port state the power to act in the public interest, independently of any effects on its own waters or of any jurisdictional connection based on nationality, territory, or protection. In that sense, Article 218 creates a form of universal jurisdiction, concurrent with that of the flag state, and in some cases, with the coastal state.[244]

It is, however, a novel development in the law of the sea to confer jurisdiction on port states in this way. Although the *Lotus Case* did permit Turkey to prosecute a foreign vessel in a Turkish port for an offence which had occurred on the high seas, that decision owed much to the erroneous equation of ships with floating territory, and the court's specific conclusion regarding collisions has since been reversed by treaty.[245] Thus it cannot convincingly be asserted that the exercise of port state jurisdiction over high seas pollution offences contemplated by Article 218(1) is based on pre-UNCLOS customary law. Only two states and the EU are known to have implemented Article 218 (1);[246] port state practice otherwise appears to remain within the more limited regime provided by MARPOL and the regional schemes considered earlier. However, given the extensive and largely unopposed way in which port state control and jurisdiction in general have developed since 1982, and the consensus surrounding the 1982 UNCLOS provisions, it may be that no state would now deny that Article 218 has become customary law.[247]

One result of Article 218 is that flag states no longer enjoy exclusive jurisdiction over all high seas offences, although this is not concurrent jurisdiction in the ordinary sense, where either party is entitled to prosecute. Except in cases of major damage to the coastal state, the flag state under the 1982 Convention has in all cases a right of pre-emption[248] which enables it to insist on taking control of any prosecution. It must continue the proceedings, and it loses the right if it repeatedly disregards its obligation of effective enforcement of international regulations. Nevertheless, in most cases it remains the flag state which will determine whether proceedings by coastal states or port states are to be allowed.

(c) Safeguards and limitations

Finally, in exercising any of these enforcement powers, coastal and port states must observe certain safeguards whose purpose is to prevent excessive exercise

244 See *supra*, Ch 5, section 6 for further discussion, and Nordquist (ed), *UNCLOS Commentary*, iv, 258ff.

245 PCIJ (1927) Ser A, No 10, 169 and cf 1952 Brussels Convention for the Unification of Certain Rules Relating to Penal Jurisdiction; 1958 High Seas Convention, Article II; 1982 UNCLOS, Article 97.

246 Belize, Maritime Areas Act 1992, s 24(4); UK, Merchant Shipping (Prevention of Oil Pollution) Regulations, 1996, regs 34–9, SI 1996 No 2154; EC Directive 95/21 (1995) Article 3(1)(e) on which see Ringbom, *The EU Maritime Safety Policy and International Law* (The Hague, 2008) Ch 5.

247 Compare the cautious views of Kwiatkowska, *The 200 Mile EEZ*, 184 and Churchill and Lowe, *Law of the Sea*, 352–3, with the more positive conclusion of Anderson, in Boyle and Freestone (eds), *International Law and Sustainable Development*, 343. See generally McDorman, 28 *JMLC* (1997) 305.

248 Article 228. See Kwiatkowska, *The 200-Mile EEZ*, 184; Nordquist, *UNCLOS Commentary*, iv, 348ff.

of their authority.[249] In particular they must not act in a discriminatory fashion. Monetary penalties only may be imposed for violations, except in the case of wilful and serious pollution of the territorial sea. Military or government-owned vessels in non-commercial service continue to enjoy immunity from the jurisdiction of port and coastal states in all circumstances, although states must ensure that these vessels act in a manner consistent with the Convention's provisions on the environment 'so far as is reasonable and practicable',[250] and should presumably discipline officers responsible for pollution offences, including collisions.

5(4) POLLUTION OF THE CONTINENTAL SHELF

Within 200 miles from the coast the EEZ and continental shelf overlap; beyond 200 miles the regime of the continental shelf applies to the seabed within national jurisdiction, while the water column remains high seas.[251] Unlike the EEZ the continental shelf exists *ipso facto* and does not have to be claimed.[252] The coastal state will thus have responsibility for protecting the marine environment of its own shelf pursuant to Articles 192, 194, 208 and 214 of the 1982 UNCLOS. Environmentally the relevance of the continental shelf regime is threefold.

First, the coastal state has exclusive sovereign rights over the natural resources of the shelf, including oil and gas.[253] It is the coastal state which must protect the marine environment from pollution caused by oil and gas drilling and pipelines.[254] The *Deepwater Horizon* incident in the Gulf of Mexico highlighted the potentially devastating effects of a major blowout on an oil rig, sparking renewed interest in the negotiation of international instruments to address this source of pollution.[255] The inadequacy of the US

[249] Articles 223–33; Nordquist, *UNCLOS Commentary*, iv, 320ff.

[250] Article 235; 1926 Brussels Convention for the Unification of Rules Concerning the Immunity of State-Owned Ships.

[251] UNCLOS, Articles 76, 78. See generally Mossop, *The Continental Shelf Beyond 200 Nautical Miles* (Oxford, 2019).

[252] UNCLOS, Article 77(3); *North Sea Continental Shelf Case*, ICJ Reports (1969) 3, paras 19, 42–43.

[253] UNCLOS, Articles 77, 81.

[254] UNCLOS, Articles 208, 214; Harrison, *Saving the Oceans Through Law*, Ch 8. All UNEP agreements acknowledge an obligation to control pollution from this source: see especially 1994 Protocol for the Protection of the Mediterranean Sea against Pollution Resulting from Exploration and Exploitation of the Continental Shelf ('Madrid Protocol'); 1992 Helsinki Convention, Article 12 and Annex VI; 1992 OSPAR Convention, Article 5 and Annex III; 1990 Kuwait Protocol Concerning Marine Pollution Resulting from Exploration and Exploitation of the Continental Shelf; 1973/78 MARPOL Convention, Article 2(4) and Annex 1, Reg 21; 1981 UNEP Conclusions of a Study of Legal Aspects of the Environment Relating to Offshore Mineral Exploitation and Drilling, UNEP/GC 9/5/Add 5/Annex III, *7 EPL* (1981) 50; Gavounelli, *Pollution from Offshore Installations* (Dordrecht, 1995); Vinogradov and Wagner, in Gao (ed), *Environment Regulation of Oil and Gas* (The Hague, 1998) Ch 3; Lyons, in Warner and Kay (eds), *Routledge Handbook of Maritime Regulation and Enforcement* (Abingdon, 2015) 193–211.

[255] See Vinodogradov, 44 *ODIL* (2013) 335–362; Liu, in Rayfuse (ed), *Research Handbook on International Marine Environmental Law*, 190–205; Redgwell, in Barrett and Barnes (eds), *The Law of the Sea* (BIICL, 2016) Ch 6.

regulatory system illustrates clearly the effects of deregulation and the lack of any international minimum standards.[256]

Second, the coastal state has jurisdiction over dumping on the seabed out to the limits of the continental shelf.[257]

Third, the coastal state has responsibility for protecting sedentary species which fall within its continental shelf jurisdiction, both within 200 miles of the coast and beyond. This is an important point because coral reefs are a sedentary species (when living) and they form the single most vital part of the entire marine ecosystem. Protection and preservation of the marine environment under Part XII thus also affects the continental shelf regime set out in Part VI of the 1982 UNCLOS.[258]

6 POLLUTION OF THE HIGH SEAS AND DEEP SEABED

Beyond 200 miles the high seas are no longer within the jurisdiction of the coastal state for ecological purposes. They are a common area in which fishing and pollution are regulated only by the flag state of the vessel concerned.[259] Articles 192 and 194 continue to apply to the marine environment as a whole, however, and flag states will have to ensure that their vessels comply with international rules and standards on pollution from ships and dumping in accordance with Articles 210 and 211.[260] As we saw in Chapter 3, the deep seabed and its mineral resources are the 'common heritage of mankind' and may not be appropriated by any state.[261] Mineral exploitation is administered by the International Seabed Authority (ISA), which grants licences to mining corporations and regulates their activities. It has responsibility for protecting the marine environment, including marine living resources, from any harmful effects of seabed mineral activities which it licences.[262] Article 209 requires states which sponsor seabed mining companies to regulate pollution from their activities no less effectively than the international rules and standards adopted by the ISA.

The question whether the ISA also has power—or should be given the power—to regulate the exploitation and conservation of the biodiversity and marine genetic resources found on the deep seabed remains unresolved, and in 2020 was still the subject

256 For details see US Congress, *Report from the National Commission on the BP Deepwater Horizon Oil Spill and Offshore Drilling* (Washington, 2011).

257 1982 UNCLOS, Article 210(5) and see *infra*, Ch 8, section 4(6).

258 See *infra*, Ch 12, section 2.

259 On the limited situations in which arrest of fishing vessels by other states may be permitted on the high seas see *infra*, Ch 12.

260 *Supra*, section 4.

261 *Supra*, Ch 3, section 3(1)(d).

262 1982 UNCLOS, Article 145; ISBA Regulations on Prospecting and Exploration for Polymetallic Nodules, Doc ISBA/19/C/17 (2013); Cobalt-rich Ferromanganese Crusts, ISBA/18/A/11 (2012); Polymetallic Sulphides, ISBA/16/A/12/rev 1 (2010); ISBA Clarion-Clipperton Environmental Management Plan; *AO on Activities in the Area*, ITLOS (2011) and generally Harrison, *Making the Law of the Sea* (Cambridge, 2011) Ch 5; Jaeckel, 30 *IJMCL* (2015) 93.

of ongoing negotiations.[263] The problem is complex, because the marine ecosystem does not reflect the distinction between the seabed and water column adopted in the 1982 UNCLOS. For environmental purposes the seabed and water column require integrated treatment.[264] Given how little we know about the deep-sea ecosystem and the long-lasting effects of any resource extraction at such extreme depths, there is a good case for applying a precautionary approach to seabed mining.[265] The more difficult question is what doing so might mean: at the very least it involves closing ecologically sensitive areas to exploration and exploitation because the potential damage may be irrecoverable.[266]

7 POLLUTION INCIDENTS AND EMERGENCIES AT SEA

7(1) INTERNATIONAL COOPERATION AND ASSISTANCE

International cooperation[267] to deal with pollution incidents or emergencies at sea is primarily a matter of prudent self-interest, but international law does impose certain obligations on states confronted with such risks. Both customary law and Article 198 of the 1982 UNCLOS indicate that once they are aware of imminent or actual pollution of the marine environment, states must give immediate notification to others likely to be affected.[268] This requirement is also reiterated in most regional-seas agreements.[269] In addition, regional agreements, and the 1982 UNCLOS require states to cooperate, in accordance with their capabilities, in eliminating the effects of such pollution, in preventing or minimizing the damage, and in developing contingency plans.[270]

263 *Infra*, Ch 12, section 2(2)(d).

264 See Mossop, in Toledo and Tassin (eds), *Guide to the Navigation of Marine Biodiversity Beyond National Jurisdiction* (Belo Horizonte, 2017); Drankier et al, 27 *IJMCL* (2012) 375.

265 See ISBA regulations cited *supra*, n 261, and *AO on Activities in the Area*, ITLOS (2011) paras 122, 125–35.

266 See Rayfuse, 27 *IJMCL* (2012) 773, 777–80.

267 See generally Kiss, 23 *GYIL* (1980) 231; Abecassis and Jarashow, *Oil Pollution from Ships*, Ch 7; IMO/UNEP, *Meeting on Regional Arrangements for Cooperation in Combating Major Incidents of Marine Pollution* (London, 1985); de Rouw, in Couper and Gold, *The Marine Environment*.

268 *Supra*, Ch 3, section 8.

269 See e.g. 1976 Barcelona Convention, Article 9(2); 1983 Cartagena Convention, Article 11(2); 1978 Kuwait Convention, Article 9(b); 1983 Bonn Agreement for Cooperation in Dealing with Pollution of the North Sea by Oil and Other Harmful Substances, Article 5. See also 1990 International Convention on Oil Pollution Preparedness, Response and Cooperation, Article 5(1).

270 1982 UNCLOS, Article 199; 1983 Bonn Agreement; 1971 Copenhagen Agreement Concerning Cooperation in Measures to Deal with Pollution of the Sea by Oil; 1974 Helsinki Convention, Annex VI; 1976 Barcelona Protocol Concerning Cases of Emergency; 1978 Kuwait Protocol Concerning Cases of Emergency; 1981 Abidjan Protocol Concerning Cases of Emergency; 1981 Lima Protocol on Regional Cooperation Cases of Emergency; 1982 Jeddah Protocol Concerning Cases of Emergency; 1983 Cartagena Protocol Concerning Cooperation in Combating Oil Spills; 1987 Noumea Protocol Concerning Emergencies; 1985 Nairobi Protocol Concerning Cases of Emergency, 1990 Lisbon Agreement of Cooperation for the Protection of the North-East Atlantic Against Pollution. See also bilateral arrangements between the UK and France, UK and Norway, Denmark and Germany, and Caribbean Island states, listed by IMO/UNEP *supra*, n 266, at para 2.10. Other bilateral agreements apply between the US and Canada and the US and Mexico.

Article 7 of the 1990 Convention on Oil Pollution Preparedness, Response, and Cooperation ('OPPRC Convention') a global instrument adopted by the IMO following the *Exxon Valdez* disaster in Alaska, further commits parties to respond to requests for assistance from states likely to be affected by oil pollution. The IMO must be informed of major incidents,[271] and under Article 12, it is given responsibility for coordinating and facilitating cooperation on various matters, including the provision on request of technical assistance and advice for states faced with major oil pollution incidents. Parties may also seek the IMO's assistance in arranging financial support for response costs.[272] A Protocol adopted in 2000 extends the principles of the 1990 Convention to pollution incidents involving hazardous and noxious substances.[273]

The IMO's role under the OPPRC Convention and the 2000 Protocol on Preparedness, Response and Co-operation to Pollution Incidents by Hazardous and Noxious Substances ('HNS Protocol') is comparable to that played by the IAEA under the Convention on Assistance in Cases of Nuclear Emergency.[274] Although not then in force, the 1990 Convention provided the basis for the IMO coordination of technical support and financial assistance for governments dealing with serious marine pollution during the conflict in the Persian Gulf in January 1991.[275] Further coordination is provided regionally by centres established with the assistance of the IMO and UNEP.[276] In the North Sea, the 1983 Bonn Agreement divides that area into zones for which states are individually or in some cases jointly responsible, but other parties remain obliged to use their best endeavours to provide assistance if requested. Although these agreements generally allocate the costs of cooperative action to the state requesting assistance, or to those which act on their own initiative, this is usually without prejudice to rights to recover these costs from third parties under national or international law.[277]

7(2) CONTROLLING POLLUTION EMERGENCIES AT SEA

(a) General obligations

Quite apart from their obligation to cooperate, states may also be required to respond to pollution emergencies individually, in cases where the incident falls within their jurisdiction or control. Failure to do so may then amount to a breach of the state's obligations in customary law to control sources of pollution, even if the emergency itself

271 Article 5(3). 272 Article 7(2).

273 Defined by reference to those listed in IMO Conventions and Codes. 274 See *infra*, Ch 9.

275 UNCED, Prepcom, UN Doc A/CONF 151/PC/72(1991).

276 E.g. the Regional Marine Pollution Emergency Response Centre in Malta, the Marine Emergency Mutual Aid Centre in Bahrain, and the Regional Coordination Unit, in Jamaica. See IMO/UNEP, *Regional Meeting, supra*.

277 1983 Bonn Agreement, Article 9; 1990 Oil Pollution Preparedness, Response, and Cooperation Convention, Annex.

is not attributable to state action or inaction.[278] This assumption is consistent with the 1982 UNCLOS, which requires states to ensure that pollution arising from 'incidents or activities' under their jurisdiction or control does not spread beyond areas where they exercise sovereign rights, or is not transferred to other areas.[279] Moreover, Article 194 specifically mandates measures to prevent accidents and deal with emergencies emanating from all sources of marine pollution.

The 1990 OPPRC Convention and the HNS Protocol apply these basic principles to pollution incidents caused by ships, offshore installations, and port-handling facilities which threaten the marine environment or the coastline or related interests of individual states.[280] The parties must take all appropriate measures to prepare for and respond to such incidents. In particular, a national system capable of responding promptly and effectively must be established, including the designation of a competent national authority and a national contingency plan. Information concerning these arrangements must be provided to other states. Parties are also required to ensure that offshore oil operations within their jurisdiction, and port-handling facilities, are conducted in accordance with emergency procedures approved by the competent national authority. These provisions are somewhat stronger than those generally found in a number of regional or bilateral schemes.[281]

Although the primary responsibility for responding effectively will thus fall in most cases on the relevant coastal states, flag states also have a responsibility for ensuring that their vessels are adequately prepared to deal with emergencies. Article 3 of the 1990 Convention requires the parties to ensure that vessels flying their flag have on board an oil pollution emergency plan in accordance with the IMO provisions. For this purpose the Convention provides that vessels are subject to port state inspection under existing international arrangements referred to earlier.

(b) Coastal state powers of intervention

It is unrealistic to expect flag states themselves to maintain the capacity to respond to accidents involving their vessels wherever they occur, and apart from the provisions of Article 3, the 1990 Convention does not attempt to make them do so. The right of coastal states to intervene beyond their territorial sea in cases of maritime casualties involving foreign vessels that are likely to cause pollution damage is, therefore, an important safeguard for these states in protecting themselves from the risks posed by oil tankers and other ships carrying toxic or hazardous substances in passage near their shores.[282] Although as we have seen, in principle, vessels exercising high seas freedoms are subject only to the jurisdiction of the flag state, an exceptional right of coastal state

[278] See e.g. *Corfu Channel Case*, ICJ Reports (1949) 3 and *supra*, Ch 3, section 4.

[279] Articles 194(2) 195.

[280] De Rouw, in Couper and Gold (eds), *The Marine Environment* (Honolulu, 1991).

[281] Compare 1978 Kuwait Convention, Article 9 and protocol; 1982 Jeddah Protocol; 1981 Abidjan Protocol; 1981 Lima Protocol; 1976 Barcelona Protocol; 1983 Cartagena Protocol.

[282] Abecassis and Jarashow, *Oil Pollution from Ships*, Ch 6.

intervention in cases of a threatened pollution emergency at sea can be derived from the principle of necessity.[283] Following doubts raised about British intervention in the *Torrey Canyon* tanker disaster the rights of coastal states were clarified by the 1969 Convention on Intervention on the High Seas in Cases of Oil Pollution Casualties.[284] This Convention was extended to other forms of marine pollution from ships by a 1973 Protocol.

There can be little doubt today that a right of intervention beyond the territorial sea has become part of customary law. Apart from the widespread ratification and implementation of the 1969 Convention itself, Article 221 of the 1982 UNCLOS and Article 9 of the 1989 International Convention on Salvage respectively assume the right of coastal states to take measures under customary and conventional international law or under generally recognized principles of international law,[285] despite important differences in the wording of these provisions. The 1969 Convention permits parties to take:

> Such measures on the high seas as may be necessary to prevent, mitigate or eliminate grave and imminent danger to their coastline or related interests from pollution or threat of pollution of the sea by oil, following upon a maritime casualty or acts related to such a casualty which may reasonably be expected to result in major harmful consequences.[286]

This article places significant limitations on the coastal state's right of intervention beyond the territorial sea. First, it applies only to cases of maritime casualties, defined as:

> collision of ships, stranding or other incident of navigation, or other occurrence on board a ship or external to it resulting in material damage or imminent threat of material damage to a ship or cargo.[287]

This definition would not cover operational pollution, however serious, or dumping at sea, even if illegal. Moreover, no measures may be taken against warships or government ships under the Convention, although in such cases a defence of necessity might nevertheless be relied upon.

Second, the references to 'grave and imminent' danger of pollution resulting in 'major harmful consequences' were intended to establish a high threshold of probability and of harm, so as to avoid the danger of precipitate action by coastal states

283 ILC 2001 Articles on State Responsibility, Article 25; *Gabčíkovo-Nagymaros Case*, ICJ Reports (1997)7, paras 51–52.

284 O'Connell, *The International Law of the Sea*, ii, 1006; Abecassis and Jarashow, *Oil Pollution from Ships*, 116, paras 6–14.

285 Churchill and Lowe, *The Law of the Sea*, 355; de Rouw, in Couper and Gold (eds), *The Marine Environment*. A Soviet proposal to incorporate an explicit right of intervention in the 1982 UNCLOS was not accepted: see UN Doc A/CONF 62/C.3/L25, 3rd UNCLOS, 4 *Official Records* (1975) 212. The Soviet delegation interpreted the words 'pursuant to international law, both customary and conventional' in Article 221 as giving states not parties to the 1969 Convention the right to intervene 'within the limits defined by that Convention': 3rd UNCLOS, 9 *Official Records*, 162, para 52. See also Nordquist, *UNCLOS Commentary*, iv, 303ff.

286 Article 1(1). A British proposal to apply the 1969 Intervention Convention to the territorial sea was rejected as unnecessary and undesirable by the Brussels Conference: see Abecassis and Jarashow, *Oil Pollution from Ships*, 121f. Churchill and Lowe, loc cit, argue that 'on the high seas' includes intervention in the EEZ.

287 Article 2(1).

causing undue interference with shipping beyond the territorial sea.[288] Following the *Amoco Cadiz* accident, however, some states, including France, argued strongly that the wording of 1969 Convention was too restrictive, and that intervention should be permitted at an earlier stage.[289] Although the 1969 Convention remains unchanged, the text of Article 221 of the 1982 UNCLOS was altered during negotiations to omit any reference to 'grave and imminent danger', and it now assumes a right of intervention when there is merely 'actual or threatened damage' which may 'reasonably be expected' to result in 'major harmful consequences' to the coastal state's interests.[290] Under the 1969 Convention these harmful consequences include direct effects on coastal activities such as fishing, tourist attractions, public health, and the well-being of the area concerned, 'including conservation of living marine resources and of wildlife'.[291] This is broad enough to justify action necessary to protect the coastal environment.

Third, the measures which coastal states are entitled to take are not specified by the 1969 Convention, but depend on what is necessary for their protection, and must be proportionate to the risk and nature of the likely damage.[292] In the *Torrey Canyon* disaster military aircraft were used to destroy the vessel and set fire to the oil; such extreme action will rarely now be regarded as necessary or useful and is unlikely in most cases to be justified given present experience in handling shipping casualties. The more appropriate response will usually involve the assistance of tugs and salvage services. The main significance of the right of intervention is thus that it allows coastal authorities to override the ship's master's discretion in seeking salvage assistance, and may enable them to direct damaged vessels away from their shores. This may not always be the right response: in some cases it would be better to allow damaged vessels to enter port or head for sheltered areas where their cargo can safely be offloaded. There is some evidence that in directing the *Prestige* away from their shores Spain and Portugal made the eventual pollution disaster inevitable and worsened its effects. The IMO has adopted guidance designed to provide a framework to assist coastal states to make a decision on whether to offer a place of refuge to a floundering vessel.[293] While coastal states may ultimately be within their rights to deny a safe refuge to such vessels even

[288] The non-application of the 1969 Convention to the territorial sea has left states free to set more liberal conditions for intervention there: see e.g, UK Merchant Shipping Act, 1995, sections 55, 137–141 which allow intervention if 'urgently needed' to deal with a shipping accident which will or may cause pollution 'on a large scale' in the UK or its waters, but with exceptions, adaptations or modifications for foreign ships outside UK waters.

[289] See Lucchini, 24 *AFDI* (1978) 721; Nordquist (ed), *UNCLOS Commentary*, iv, 313.

[290] Cf Article 222, ICNT, and see 3rd UNCLOS, 8 *Official Records*, 152; 10 ibid, 100. Note, however, the view of the Soviet delegation at UNCLOS that the proposed text of Article 221 'should not be held to give the coastal state more extensive rights of intervention in cases of maritime casualty than the rights of intervention it already enjoyed under the terms of the International Convention Relating to Intervention on the High Seas', quoted in Nordquist (ed), *UNCLOS Commentary*, iv, 313. Kwiatkowska, 22 *ODIL* (1991) 173 notes that a right of intervention based on the wording of Article 221 has been adopted by Bulgaria, Romania, Malaysia, New Zealand, and Russia.

[291] Article 2(4). [292] Article 5.

[293] IMO Resolution A.949(23) (2003); see also Chircop, 33 *ODIL* (2002) 207; Van Hooydonk, *CMI Yearbook* (2003) 329; Morrison, *Places of Refuge for Ships in Distress: Problems and Methods of Resolution* (Leiden, 2008); Blanco-Bazan, in Ribeiro (ed), *30 Years After the Signature of UNCLOS*, 71ff.

in distress, it needs to be recalled that Article 195 of the 1982 UNCLOS specifically prohibits states from acting 'to transfer, directly or indirectly, damage or hazards from one area to another'. In such circumstances the appropriateness of any action a coastal state may take will depend on what is necessary to protect all those who may potentially be affected.[294] The 1969 Intervention Convention also seeks to limit excessive coastal-state action by requiring it to consult and notify the flag state and report measures to the IMO.[295] The final right of decision remains with the coastal state, however. Damage caused by measures taken in excess of the Convention must be compensated, and disputes are subject to compulsory conciliation and arbitration.[296]

(c) Notification by vessels and offshore installations

Coastal states can only intervene effectively if informed of impending disasters in a timely manner, whether by surveillance, by other states, or by the masters of vessels, including those in distress. A number of treaties, including the 1990 Convention on Oil Pollution Preparedness, Response, and Cooperation, provide for states to request or require masters of ships and aircraft to report casualties and pollution observed at sea;[297] as we saw earlier, there is also provision for states themselves to report known pollution hazards to other states. The 1990 Convention also applies to offshore installations.

A serious weakness of the 1969 Intervention Convention was its failure to deal with the crucial issue of notification by the master of the vessel involved in the maritime emergency. Subsequent treaties have not been wholly successful in remedying this omission. The 1973/78 MARPOL Convention requires masters of vessels involved in pollution incidents to report without delay, but does not say to whom.[298] The 1982 UNCLOS merely provides that international rules and standards should include those relating to prompt notification to coastal states, but seems to assume that no such rules yet exist.[299] A more satisfactory formulation is found in Article 4 of the Oil Pollution Response Convention, under which the flag state is responsible for requiring masters to report without delay to 'the nearest coastal state' any event on their ship involving the discharge or probable discharge of oil. The HNS Protocol applies the same rule to the wide variety of other toxic substances now likely to be involved in maritime accidents and emergencies.

An alternative and possibly more effective approach would concentrate on the power of coastal states to regulate the provision of information by ships concerning pollution

294 Frank, 20 *IJMCL* (2005) 1, 53–62. 295 Article 3. 296 Articles 6, 8.

297 See also 1983 Bonn Agreement. Protocols in UNEP Regional Conventions invariably take the stronger form. See e.g. Barcelona Protocol, Article 8.

298 Article 8 and Protocol 1. See also IMO Res A 851(20). The provisions of UNEP Regional Seas Protocols will also apply. In some cases these assume that reports will go to the flag state and be communicated from there: see e.g. Barcelona Protocol, Article 8.

299 Article 211(7). Protocol 1 of the 1973/78 MARPOL Convention could constitute such 'international rules and standards'.

incidents in their EEZ or territorial sea. Coastal state interests are sufficiently strongly involved to justify such action to reinforce flag state control. Article 211(5) of the 1982 UNCLOS may provide the legal basis for coastal state regulation based on Protocol 1 of the 1973/78 MARPOL Convention, although none of the regional agreements appears to adopt this approach. Mandatory reporting by vessels may also be required under the 1974 SOLAS Convention.[300]

(d) Salvage

The basis on which most maritime salvage services have traditionally operated is the 'no cure no pay' principle. This provides salvors with no reward for work carried out benefiting the coastal state and reducing the liability of the vessel owner for pollution damage if the vessel itself is lost. Coastal state intervention may exacerbate this problem if it renders salvage of the vessel more difficult. The 1969 Intervention Convention allows coastal states to override the master's discretion in calling for salvage assistance and empowers them, as we have seen, to take necessary measures to protect the coastal environment, but it provides no incentive for salvors themselves to assist in this task. Following measures already taken by Lloyds to revise salvage contracts, a new convention dealing, inter alia, with the environmental aspects of salvage was adopted by the IMO in 1989.[301]

The 1989 International Convention on Salvage is mainly concerned with private-law matters, and the rights of coastal states to intervene remain unaffected, although Article 11 requires them to take account of the need to ensure the efficient and successful performance of salvage operations, and thus may affect decisions on matters such as access to ports. The Convention applies to judicial or arbitral proceedings brought in a state party and which relate to salvage operations, but it also covers salvage operations conducted by or under the control of public authorities.[302] It does not cover warships or government non-commercial ships entitled to immunity, nor does it apply to offshore installations.[303]

There are two main features of the Convention. Salvors are entitled to 'special compensation' for salvage operations, in respect of a vessel or its cargo, which have prevented or minimized damage to the environment, and they have a duty of care to carry out salvage operations in such a way as to prevent or minimize this damage.[304] Thus the Convention does not apply to environmental protection unrelated to the salvage of a vessel or its cargo, but it has the important effects that protection of the environment is regarded as a 'useful result' even if the vessel itself is lost, and also that expenses are recoverable in excess of the limit for salvage of the vessel or cargo alone.[305]

300 Regulation V/8, adopted 1994, in force 1996.

301 Redgwell, 14 *Marine Policy* (1990) 142; Gold, 20 *JMLC* (1989) 487; Kerr, ibid, 505.

302 Articles 2, 5.

303 Articles 3, 4.

304 Articles 8, 14. 'Damage to the environment is defined in Article 1(d) to mean substantial physical damage to human health or to marine life or resources in coastal or inland waters or areas adjacent thereto caused by pollution, contamination, fire, explosion or similar major incidents.'

305 Cf. Article 13 which limits the reward for salvage of the vessel or property to the salved value thereof.

Salvors thus have a continued incentive and obligation to mitigate environmental damage even after the vessel is saved, or after it sinks. The salvor is correspondingly penalized by loss or reduction of its reward if through negligence or misconduct damage to the environment is not averted or minimized.[306] However, consistently with the traditional 'no cure no pay' principle the salvor will remain uncompensated for efforts, however great, which lead to no useful result, whether because the vessel is lost, or because damage to the environment cannot be reduced or averted. This Convention came into force in 1986.

7(3) POLLUTION RESPONSE IN THE INTERNATIONAL SEABED AREA

Pollution emergencies arising from mining operations beyond national jurisdiction are subject to a complex regime, involving individual contractors and the International Seabed Authority as the body responsible for promoting the protection of the marine environment in the Area. The Regulations adopted by the Authority all contain rules relating to pollution emergencies that threaten significant harm to the marine environment.[307] These Regulations are binding not only on Member States of the Authority, but also on contractors carrying out mining operations in the Area.

Prior to commencing operations, contractors are required to submit a contingency plan to the Secretary-General stating what measures will be taken in the case of an environmental emergency.[308] This contractor must also provide assurances that it has adequate and appropriate equipment to deal with pollution incidents and it should conduct periodic emergency response exercises.[309] If its activities do cause or are likely to cause serious harm to the marine environment, a contractor is required to immediately notify the Secretary-General of the Authority, as well as warning other contractors and shipping operating in the vicinity.[310] The Regulations go into some detail in prescribing what information must be included in the notification, such as the coordinates of the area affected, a description of any action being taken by the contractor to prevent, contain or minimize any harm to the marine environment, and any supplementary information reasonably requested by the Secretary-General.[311] Whilst this makes clear that it is in the first place up to the contractor to decide what action to take in order minimize any harm, the Secretary-General is required to 'monitor developments' and the organs of the Authority are also empowered to issue emergency orders as may be reasonably necessary to prevent, contain and minimize serious harm to the marine environment.[312] Such emergency orders should give directions to the contractors and they may include orders for the suspension or adjustment of operations. If the contractor itself does not take sufficient action, the Authority may ultimately step in and take 'such practical measures as are necessary to prevent, contain and minimize any such serious harm to the marine environment.'[313] In accordance with the polluter

[306] Articles 14(5) 18. [307] See UNCLOS, Article 162(w).
[308] Nodules Regulations, Annex 4, section 6.1. [309] *Ibid.* [310] *Ibid.*
[311] *Ibid*, section 6.2. [312] Nodules Regulations, Reg. 32(6). [313] Ibid.

pays principle, the contractor must reimburse the Authority for any expenses incurred in taking measures to respond to a pollution emergency.[314]

On paper, it would appear that this regime ensures that prompt and effective action can be taken to minimize environmental damage to the fragile ecosystems found in the deep seas. Two caveats must be made, however. Firstly, mining operations in the Area are in their infancy and it thus remains to be seen how the Authority will operationalize its oversight mandate and exercise control over contractors in practice. Secondly, the approach of granting extensive powers to an international organization to oversee response measures on behalf of the international community cannot easily be transferred to other contexts. In this respect the pollution response regime outlined in the Liability Annex to the Antarctic Environment Protocol is very different: it places responsibility on operators without any institutional oversight.[315]

8 RESPONSIBILITY AND LIABILITY FOR MARINE POLLUTION DAMAGE

8(1) STATE RESPONSIBILITY

Article 235(1) of the 1982 UNCLOS affirms the orthodox proposition that 'states are responsible for the fulfilment of their international obligations concerning the protection and preservation of the marine environment' and goes on to add that 'They shall be liable in accordance with international law'. There is no reason to doubt that this responsibility extends to flag states in respect of their vessels, and to coastal states in respect of activities which they permit within their jurisdiction or control.[316] A number of authors have argued that in respect to ultra-hazardous activities at sea, such as the operation of large oil tankers, the liability of the flag state is strict, and the same view may be taken regarding offshore oil installations because of the serious risks these pose for other states.[317] As we saw in Chapter 4 the evidence in support of a standard of strict liability for states is not strong. Moreover it has not been applied by the 1982 UNCLOS to state responsibility for deep seabed operations. Instead, Article 139 of the Convention provides that in respect of damage resulting from deep seabed operations, states are liable only for a failure to carry out their responsibilities, and shall not be liable for damage caused by national operators 'if the state party has taken all necessary and appropriate measures to secure effective compliance' with the requirements of the Convention. This clearly points to a

[314] Nodules Regulations, Annex 4, section 6.4.

[315] 2005 Annex VI, Article 5; Bederman and Keskar, 19 *Emory Int LR* (2005) 1383.

[316] *AO on Fisheries*, ITLOS Reports (2015) para 138; Smith, *State Responsibility and the Marine Environment* (Oxford, 1988) Chs 10–12 and *supra*, Ch 4.

[317] See e.g, Smith, op cit, 114–18, 160–3, 210–13; and Handl, 74 *AJIL* (1980) 547, where the state practice and literature are reviewed.

due diligence standard of liability for sponsoring states, as confirmed by the Seabed Disputes Chamber in its 2011 *Advisory Opinion*.[318]

A second reason for doubting academic views on the alleged strict liability of states for damage to the marine environment is that there is almost no state practice from which to draw conclusions. In a few cases, flag states have paid compensation for pollution from oil tankers, and some writers treat this as supporting a principle of strict or absolute liability comparable to the position asserted by Canada in the Cosmos 954 claim.[319] These are exceptional examples, however; in general, pollution from ships has not been the subject of interstate claims, even in cases as serious as the *Amoco Cadiz* or the *Prestige*, but has instead been dealt with under national law or civil liability and compensation schemes considered below. The same is true of most oil spills from offshore installations. In one of the most serious of these, the IXTOC I blowout, Mexico refused to accept any responsibility for injury caused in the United States, and the matter was ultimately resolved in civil claims.[320] This is consistent with the approach adopted in UNEP's 'Study of Legal Aspects' of offshore mineral exploration and drilling,[321] and with bilateral and regional arrangements elsewhere,[322] all of which assume or require that operators will be made liable in civil law. Although in 1986 the parties to the 1972 London Convention called for the development of 'procedures for the assessment of liability in accordance with the principles of international law regarding state responsibility for damage to the environment of other states or to any other area of the environment resulting from dumping',[323] no progress has been made, and the question of state responsibility for dumping remains unresolved, under this Convention and under all of the regional agreements.

Thus, although at a theoretical level, it is correct to conclude that 'the international legal order currently possesses a perfectly adequate foundation for an equitable and effective regime of state responsibility for marine environmental injury',[324] the failure of states to resort to this foundation is its most conspicuous feature. Alternative approaches based instead on the liability of the polluter have proved more appealing in practice, and for all of the reasons already observed in Chapter 5, these are probably also preferable in principle.

318 *AO on Activities in the Area*, ITLOS Reports (2011) para 204.

319 *Supra*, Ch 4, section 2.

320 IXTOC 1 Agreement, 22 *ILM* (1983) 580; Smith, *State Responsibility and the Marine Environment*, 117.

321 UNEP/GC 9/5/Add 5/App III (1981).

322 1977 International Convention on Civil Liability for Oil Pollution Damage from the Exploration for or Exploitation of Submarine Mineral Resources (No ratifications); 1983 Canada-Denmark Agreement for Cooperation Relating to the Marine Environment, Article 8, 23 *ILM* (1983) 269; 1974 Offshore Pollution Liability Agreement, 13 *ILM* (1974) 1409 (since updated); 1994 Madrid Protocol for the Protection of the Mediterranean Sea against Pollution from the Continental Shelf, Article 27. See also 1990 Kuwait Protocol on Pollution from land-based sources, Article 13, and generally Schoenbaum, 24 *JEL* (2012) 395.

323 Resolution LDC 21(9) 1986; Kasoulides, 26 *San Diego LR* (1989) 497. See also 1996 Protocol, Article 15.

324 Smith, *State Responsibility and the Marine Environment*, 255.

8(2) THE POLLUTER PAYS PRINCIPLE

The question of who should be responsible for compensating damage to the environment is also dealt with by the polluter pays principle, as examined in Chapter 5. As we saw there, the principle is primarily intended to ensure that the costs of dealing with pollution are not borne by public authorities but are directed to the polluter. The Preamble to the 1990 Oil Pollution Response Convention describes the polluter-pays principle as a 'general principle of international environmental law', and a number of regional seas treaties adopted or revised since the Rio Conference call on states to apply it more generally to the costs of marine pollution and environmental damage caused by ships, land-based activities and dumping.[325]

Despite this general endorsement of the polluter pays principle, there is little evidence that it has influenced state practice or resulted in more comprehensive schemes of liability for damage to the marine environment at global or regional level. Parties to the revised 1972 London Convention continue to 'undertake to develop procedures regarding liability' for marine pollution damage, as do the parties to several regional seas agreements, but no progress has been made in this regard over many years.[326] The only significant extension of maritime liability which might be linked to the polluter pays principle is the 1992 revision of the Oil Pollution Liability and Fund Conventions, the adoption of a Convention on Liability and Compensation for the Carriage of Hazardous and Noxious Substances by Sea in 1996 and the Convention on Civil Liability for Bunker Oil Pollution Damage in 2001.[327]

These treaties illustrate two of the limitations of the polluter pays concept. First, the question who is the polluter is not self-evident in a complex industry such as shipping. In one sense the operator of an oil or chemical tanker is the polluter and should be responsible if the ship sinks. But it can equally be said that the cargo causes the damage and the cargo owner is the real polluter. Alternatively, it might be argued that the shipowner is most directly responsible for seaworthiness, has the strongest interest in insuring the vessel, and should therefore be treated as the polluter. Then again, ships sink and cause pollution for various reasons. Sometimes a third party such as a harbour pilot or a navigation authority is at fault. Who among all these possibilities should be made liable for the damage is a policy choice, not one capable of being answered by the polluter-pays concept. Sensibly, the present internationally agreed scheme of liability and compensation for pollution from ships treats both

[325] 1992 Paris Convention, Article 2(2)(b); 1992 Helsinki Convention, Article 3(4); 1995 Barcelona Convention, Article 4(3)(b); 2010 Amended Nairobi Convention, Article 4(5).

[326] This provision follows 1982 UNCLOS, Article 235(3). See 1996 Protocol on the Prevention of Marine Pollution by Dumping, Article 15; 1995 Barcelona Convention, Article 16; 1986 Noumea Convention, Article 20; 1983 Caribbean Convention, Article 14; 1982 Jeddah Convention, Article 13; 1981 Abidjan Convention, Article 15; 1978 Kuwait Convention, Article 13. Cf 1981 Lima Convention, Article 11, which instead reiterates UNCLOS Article 235(2). Attempts to conclude a liability protocol to the Barcelona Convention foundered in 1997: see UNEP (OCA)/MED WG 117/3 (1997). See generally Lefeber, in Vidas and Østreng (eds) *Order for the Oceans*, 507.

[327] See next section.

the shipowner and the cargo owner as sharing responsibility, while excluding to a large extent the liability of any other potential defendant in order to facilitate easy recovery by plaintiffs.

A second problem is that it is not necessarily realistic to expect the 'polluter' to pay in full for all the damage caused. This is especially so in the shipping industry, where insurance is the main source of a shipowner's liability funding. All of the maritime liability treaties limit this liability, as well as the compensation from industry funds, and also exclude certain kinds of loss. This has significant implications when it comes to making the polluter pay for environmental damage. When compensation is limited, there may not be enough to meet all claims for death, injury, property loss, economic loss, and environmental harm. Some of these losses may have to be prioritized, or paid pro rata, or excluded altogether. Again, this is a policy choice; as implemented in the present series of maritime liability and compensation treaties the main conclusion is that not all environmental loss is covered.

The most notable exclusion is environmental damage on the high seas beyond the exclusive economic zone. The point is exemplified by Article 3 of the 1992 Oil Pollution Fund Convention, which is expressly confined to pollution damage in the territory, territorial sea, EEZ, or within 200 miles of the state concerned, and to 'preventive measures, wherever taken, to prevent or minimize *such* damage'.[328] The 1989 Salvage Convention is similarly limited; although it provides 'special compensation' for salvage which prevents or minimizes 'damage to the environment', this phrase is defined to mean 'substantial physical damage to human health or to marine life or resources in coastal or inland waters or areas adjacent thereto'.[329] This does not include salvage on the high seas if no state is likely to benefit from the actions taken.

There is no inherent reason why liability and compensation schemes of this kind could not apply to damage to common spaces and resources. The point, however, is whether it makes sense to deal with the problem in this way. There is a strong case for doing so in regard to clean-up costs, if only because this may prevent damage affecting other states or the marine environment. There may also be a case for measures to restore the marine environment to its natural state. But suppose the spill cannot be cleaned up, and no harm to other states ensues, and restoration will take place naturally or is not possible? The role, if any, of damages in this context cannot be compensatory, since there is no measurable loss to anyone, nor can it be restorative.[330] Rather, it becomes punitive. Punishment in these circumstances is better left to criminal prosecution for violation of MARPOL or SOLAS regulations, if any.[331]

328 Emphasis added. See also 1992 Convention on Civil Liability for Oil Pollution Damage, Article 2.

329 Articles 1(d) 8, 14.

330 See UNCC practice, *supra*, Ch 4, section 2(4).

331 See Boyle, in Wetterstein (ed), *Harm to the Environment* (Oxford, 1997) 95ff, but cf Leigh, 14 *Australian YIL* (1993) 143–5.

8(3) CIVIL LIABILITY FOR OIL POLLUTION FROM SHIPS

The problems of jurisdiction, choice of law, standard of liability, and enforcement of judgments which typically affect transboundary claims for pollution damage[332] are amplified in the case of ships and can result in protracted and unsatisfactory litigation when maritime accidents cause serious pollution. The *Torrey Canyon* disaster of 1967 showed the need for international agreement on a regime of civil liability for such accidents and prompted the IMO to call an international conference in 1969.[333] Resolving the difficulties confronting coastal states in securing adequate compensation was not simply a matter of removing jurisdictional obstacles, harmonizing liability, and ensuring the polluter would pay, however. Rather more important was the question how the loss should be distributed, given the long-standing tradition of permitting shipowners to limit their liability in maritime claims and the argument that in the case of oil, the cargo owners might reasonably be expected to share in the burden.

The 1969 Convention on Civil Liability for Oil Pollution Damage ('CLC'), in conjunction with the 1971 Convention on the Establishment of an International Fund for Compensation for Oil Pollution Damage, represent one approach to the establishment of a more satisfactory regime for oil pollution liability.[334] This scheme was partially based on the earlier nuclear liability conventions, which are considered in detail in Chapter 7 and to which reference should be made. The oil pollution conventions enable claims for 'pollution damage' to be brought in the courts of the state party where the damage occurs, regardless of where the ship[335] causing the damage is registered. Like port state enforcement of the 1973/78 MARPOL Convention, the vessel does not have to be from a state party to the Liability Convention: the coastal state has jurisdiction because that is where the damage occurs. The 1969 and 1971 Conventions were amended by Protocols adopted in 1992, the principal effects of which are to raise liability and compensation limits, to include pollution damage in the EEZ as well as in the territory and territorial sea of a party to the Conventions, and to include the cost of preventive measures for the first time.[336] In this section attention will focus primarily on the differences between the amended oil pollution and nuclear liability regimes.

332 *Supra*, Ch 5, section 3.

333 IMCO, *Official Records of the International Legal Conference on Marine Pollution Damage* (London, 1969) and see Keaton, 21 *CLP* (1968) 94; Brown, ibid, 113.

334 See Abecassis and Jarashow, *Oil Pollution from Ships*, Chs 10, 11; de La Rue (ed), *Liability for Damage to the Marine Environment* (London, 1993); Gauci, *Oil Pollution at Sea: Civil Liability and Compensation for Damage* (Chichester, 1997); de La Rue and Anderson, *Shipping and the Environment* (London, 1998); Tan, *Vessel-Source Marine Pollution*, 286–342.

335 'Ship' means 'any seagoing vessel . . . constructed or adapted for the carriage of oil in bulk as cargo': 1992 Oil Pollution Convention, Article 1(1). See also IOPC Fund *Annual Report* (1999) para 9.

336 Liability limits have been raised again under amendments adopted in 2000. References are to articles in the 1969 and 1971 Conventions *as amended in 1992 and 2000* unless otherwise stated. The 1971 Fund Convention ceased to have effect in 2002 and the 1971 Fund was formally wound up in December 2014, having resolved all outstanding cases. The 1969 and 1992 Liability Conventions will coexist until all parties denounce the earlier text.

The most important difference concerns the allocation of liability and the distribution of compensation costs. The 1992 Oil Pollution Liability Convention channels liability not to the ship's operator, nor to the cargo owner, but to the shipowner, who may be sued only in accordance with the Convention, and who is required to carry insurance for this purpose. Under Article 3 no claim for compensation may be made against the ship's manager, operator, charterer, crew, pilot, salvor, or their servants or agents, unless the damage resulted from their personal act or omission 'committed with intent to cause such damage, or recklessly and with knowledge that such damage would probably result'.[337] While this provision will preclude strict liability or negligence claims for pollution damage against any of these third parties, they may remain liable to victims if the conditions of the exception to Article 3 can be proven. Such suits are rare, but the *Erika* case demonstrates that they are possible, with the French courts holding that the representative of the registered owner, the president of the management company, the classification society that had certified the vessel, and the charterer, could all be sued by victims of the 1999 oil spill because they fell within the exception in Article 3 of the CLC by virtue of their reckless action in relation to the vessel.[338] In any case, the CLC does not prevent the ship owner from bringing an action against third parties in accordance with national law in order to recompense any losses incurred by the owner.

The owner's liability under Article 3 is strict, rather than absolute, in the sense that although no fault or negligence need be shown, no liability arises where the owner can prove that the loss resulted from war, hostilities, insurrection, civil war, or natural phenomena, such as hurricanes, of an 'exceptional, inevitable and irresistible character', or was wholly caused intentionally by a third party or by the negligence of those responsible for navigation aids.[339]

The owner is entitled to limit liability[340] according to a formula related to the tonnage of the ship, and to an overall total. The limit was far exceeded by claims arising out of the *Nakhodka* spill, when a total of US$220 million was paid out by the fund. One purpose of the 1992 Protocols and the amendments adopted in 2000 was therefore to raise these limits substantially. The owner's liability for damage rises to a maximum of 89.7 million SDRs (c US$139 million) for the very largest tankers;[341] thereafter, the

[337] Compare the 1969 text of the Liability Convention, which did not bar claims against the operator of the *Amoco Cadiz* in US courts (rather than suing the owner in France under the CLC Convention). See Abecassis and Jarashow, *Oil Pollution from Ships*, 555, and Eskenazi, 24 *JMLC* (1993) 371. Under the 1992 version of Article 3, proceedings against a ship operator would no longer be possible, nor would claims against the ship's pilot found responsible for the *Sea Empress* disaster.

[338] 'Erika', 64 *Droit Maritime Français* 985 (Cour de Cassation) 25 September 2012, 992; see discussion in Jacobsson, 20 *JIML* (2014) 18–29, 27.

[339] Article 3(2). See also Article 3(3).

[340] Article 5. The 1969 Convention removes this right in case of 'actual fault' by the owner; the 1992 text does so only where the damage is caused intentionally or recklessly. On limitation of liability in maritime law see Popp, 24 *JMLC* (1993) 335.

[341] I.e. more than 140,000 tons: Liability Convention, Article 5(1). Smaller ships are liable on a graduated scale: a 50,000-ton tanker would be liable to a maximum of about US$42 million. Under the Small Tanker Oil Pollution Indemnification Agreement (STOPIA) the major P & I clubs have agreed to reimburse the International Fund up to a higher limit for incidents involving small tankers insured with them and entered into their pooling arrangements; see Harrison, 5 *Int J of Law in Context* (2009) 379.

International Oil Pollution Compensation Fund ('IOPC Fund') is liable to compensate for any damage in excess of the owner's liability,[342] up to a total of 203 million SDRs (c US$315 million, including whatever is obtained from the owner). The creation of a supplementary fund in 2003 took the limit to 750 million SDRs or about US$1165 million.

Unlike the nuclear conventions, contributions to the IOPC Fund come not from states, but from a levy on oil importers, mainly the oil companies whose cargoes the vessels are likely to be carrying.[343] The combined effect of the Oil Pollution Liability and Fund Conventions is thus that, in the more serious cases, the owners of the ship and the owners of the cargo are jointly treated as 'the polluter' and share equitably the cost of accidental pollution damage arising during transport. As with nuclear accidents, the capacity of the insurance market has been a factor in determining the limit of the owner's liability,[344] although unlimited liability in the United States has not prevented shipowners from securing insurance cover. In addition to raising the limit of this liability under the CLC, another important change made by the 1992 Protocols is to abolish the shipowner's right to have recourse to the Fund in order to relieve a portion of their liability. Under Article 5 of the 1971 Fund Convention this was permitted even where the total damage did not exceed the limit set by the 1969 Liability Convention. Shipowners will now have to bear the costs of any oil spill up to the full limit of their liability, and only for additional losses thereafter will the Fund's resources be called on. One calculation indicates that under the 1992 Protocols the shipowner's average share of the amount payable for pollution damage will rise from 47 to 68 per cent.[345] This should give insurers a stronger incentive to monitor the quality of the ships they insure.

But the Fund Convention also has an additional, wider, purpose of providing compensation even where no liability for damage arises under the Liability Convention, or where the shipowner's liability is not met by compulsory insurance, leaving him financially incapable of meeting his obligations.[346] In these respects the Fund provides a form of security for claimants which governments provide under the nuclear liability conventions. However, the IOPC Fund is exonerated from liability where the pollution damage results from an act of war, hostilities, civil war or insurrection, or where the oil is discharged from a warship or government-owned ship entitled to immunity, or where the claimant cannot prove that the damage resulted from 'an incident involving one or more ships'.[347] The importance of the last provision is that where the source of the oil is unidentified, no compensation is obtainable. Thus there remain certain situations in which the innocent victim will be without any effective recourse. It should also be observed that parties to the Liability Convention are not obliged to become parties to the Fund Convention, but most have done so.[348]

342 Fund Convention, Article 4(1)(c). These figures apply to incidents after 1 November 2003. The Fund's early practice is reviewed by Brown, in Butler (ed), *International Shipping*, 275; for details of more recent awards and claims see *Annual Report of the IOPC Funds* (London, 2006).

343 But under Article 14 governments may assume this responsibility.

344 Abecassis and Jarashow, *Oil Pollution from Ships*, 215.

345 *Ibid*, 241.

346 Article 4(1)(a)–(b).

347 Article 4(2).

348 In April 2020, there were 141 parties to the 1992 Civil Liability Convention and 118 parties to the 1992 Fund Convention.

8(4) ENVIRONMENTAL DAMAGE

Article 1(6) of the 1992 Liability Convention makes clear that compensation for impairment of the environment is recoverable, but the relatively narrow terms in which it does so should be noted.[349] Compensation is limited to 'the costs of reasonable measures of reinstatement actually undertaken or to be undertaken'. This would not be broad enough to cover the loss of marine organisms included in the *Zoe Colocotroni Case*,[350] or the notional formula for water pollution damage used by the Soviet court in the *Antonio Gramsci Case*,[351] and accords with the view of the IOPC Fund Assembly that pollution damage assessment 'is not to be made on the basis of an abstract quantification of damage calculated in accordance with theoretical models'.[352] This definition also allows recovery for loss of profit arising out of impairment of the environment, for example in the case of losses suffered by fishermen or hotel owners, but such claims had already been allowed by the IOPC Fund. It also includes pollution damage in the coastal state's EEZ, or in an area up to 200 miles from its territorial sea baselines. The Protocol's environmental perspective is clearly preferable to the very limited definition of damage found in the 1969 and 1971 Conventions, but it still stops short of using liability to penalize those whose harm to the environment cannot be reinstated or quantified in terms of property loss or loss of profits, or which the government concerned does not wish to reinstate, or which occurs on the high seas.[353] To this extent the true environmental costs of oil transportation by sea continue to be borne by the community as a whole, and not by the polluter. A cogent argument can be made that the limited terms on which the CLC/Fund regime compensates for environmental damage no longer reflects either national or international law.[354]

8(5) AN ASSESSMENT OF THE OIL POLLUTION LIABILITY AND COMPENSATION SCHEME

The Liability and Fund Conventions have generally worked well in the large majority of over one hundred incidents resulting in claims to the IOPC Fund. Almost all of these claims have been met promptly and in full, often without resort to litigation. Claims allowed have included clean-up costs, preventive measures, and lost income for fishermen, fish processors, and the tourist industry. Some have also involved

349 de La Fayette, 20 *IJMCL* (2005) 167; Abecassis and Jarashow, *Oil Pollution from Ships*, 237, 277; Jacobson and Trotz, 17 *JMLC* (1986) 467; Wetterstein, *LMCLQ* (1994) 230.

350 *Commonwealth of Puerto Rico v SS Zoe Colocotroni*, 456 F Suppl 1327 (1978); 628 F 2d 652 (1980).

351 See Brown, in Butler, *International Shipping*, 282ff; Bianchi, in Wetterstein (eds) *Harm to the Environment*, 113ff.

352 IOPC Fund Resolution No 3 on Pollution Damage (October, 1980). See also the claims made in respect of the *Antonio Gramsci* (No 2) and the *Patmos*, reported in IOPC Fund, *Annual Report* (1990) 23, 27, and the *Haven*, id, *Annual Report* (1999) para 10.2. In all three cases the Fund rejected claims for unquantified environmental damage. See Maffei, in Francioni and Scovazzi (eds) *International Responsibility for Environmental Harm*, 381.

353 Boyle, in Wetterstein (ed), *Harm to the Environment*, 83.

354 See Handl, 34 *IJMCL* (2019) 602.

environmental restoration costs, such as mangrove swamps. Over one hundred states have become parties to the 1992 Protocols, representing some 92–95 per cent of relevant tonnage. Some significant oil-importing states have declined to do so, however, including the United States, mainly because the liability limits were still thought by Congress to be too low. Prompted by the *Exxon Valdez* disaster in Alaska, the US Oil Pollution Act of 1990 introduced limits on liability under US law greatly in excess even of the 1992 Protocols, and allowed unlimited liability in a wider range of situations, including gross negligence, wilful misconduct, and violation of applicable Federal regulations.[355] This must be seen against total clean-up costs for the *Exxon Valdez* incident estimated at US$2,500 million, but it has the effect of precluding US ratification of the Fund and Liability Conventions. The 1992 Protocols would not guarantee full compensation for such damage. Moreover even the smaller claims made in respect of the loss of the *Erika* and the *Prestige* exceeded the maximum then available from the 1992 Fund.[356] When this happens, payment of individual claims is not only reduced but delayed until contested claims are resolved, either by negotiation or in court, and governments may have to forego some of their clean-up and environmental-restoration claims.[357] The implications of this for the inclusion of environmental damage in a scheme intended principally to compensate individuals for property and economic loss are obvious, and have prompted the question: 'What is the use of comprehensive liability if it can be subject to considerable limitations?'[358] We can see immediately why the liability and compensation limits were further raised in 2000, and a Supplementary Fund established.[359] It seems likely that this will sustain the Fund's capacity to meet the cost of future large-scale pollution disasters, and the ability to respond in this way is some indication of the importance attached to the scheme by the industries which benefit from it.

Like the nuclear liability and compensation conventions, the oil pollution scheme is a precedent for other forms of hazardous activity and an alternative to reliance on state responsibility for environmental damage.[360] As with other such schemes, limitation of liability and equitable sharing of the costs remain controversial, but it is of course precisely those features which make the Oil Pollution Liability and Fund Conventions broadly acceptable to the shipping industry and which ensure that the oil industry cannot offload all of the incidental cost of moving its products by sea. Nevertheless, when substandard vessels—such as the *Erika* and the *Prestige*—can cause such

355 The Act also leaves individual US states free to adopt their own higher liability standards. See Ruhl and Jewell, 8 *OGTLR* (1990) 234; *eid*, 9 *OGTLR* (1990) 304; George and de La Rue, 11 *OGTLR* (1990) 363; Noyes, 7 *IJECL* (1992) 43.

356 IOPC Funds, *Annual Report* (2004) 45.

357 See IOPC Funds, *Annual Report* (2004) for details of incidents involving the *Haven*, the *Braer*, the *Nakhodkha*, the *Aegean Sea*, the *Prestige*, and the *Erika*.

358 Wetterstein, *LMCLQ* (1994) 230, 243. On the question how far general economic loss should be compensated see ibid, 14 *Ann Droit Mar & Oceanique* (1996) 37.

359 Membership of the Supplementary Fund is currently limited to states in the North-East Atlantic, the Baltic, the Northern Mediterranean, as well as Australia, South Korea, Japan, and Canada.

360 *Supra*, Ch 4, section 2.

enormous losses, it is worth asking whether limits on the shipowner's liability can still be justified, and whether the cargo receivers should not also be required to contribute rather more for the privilege of transporting oil in defective ships. Proposals of this kind were considered at the IMO but rejected after opposition from some flag states.[361] Another option pursued by Spain following the *Prestige* disaster was to sue the classification society for negligently failing to detect corrosion and other structural defects. In this instance the claim was ultimately dismissed on the basis that the classification society did not owe a duty of care to the victims of oil pollution under the applicable law.[362] Nevertheless, liability of classification societies remains a much-debated issue[363] and it is ultimately a question of national law.[364]

As an alternative to civil claims, accidents involving defective ships may lead to other proceedings. Clear evidence of significant wrong-doing may result in criminal prosecution of those involved. In the case of the *Erika*, France successfully prosecuted the owner, the management company, the classification society and the cargo owner. The court imposed fines on all the defendants totalling 900 million euros, and awarded damages of 192 million euros.[365] Criminal actions clearly require a higher level of proof than civil claims.[366] Nevertheless, given the persistence of substandard ships, the renewed focus on criminal sanctions in European law may be an inevitable response to the limitations of civil liability and the IOPC Fund.[367] The *Erika* disaster also illustrates that polluters may have to pay for the disposal of waste produced by them. In a judgment rendered against Total, the ECJ interpreted the European Waste Framework Directive as applying to oil that had been washed up on shore following the incident.[368] Whilst this decision extends the options for public authorities to recover clean-up costs, it also threatens the balance established by the Civil Liability and Fund Conventions.[369]

8(6) LIABILITY FOR OTHER FORMS OF POLLUTION FROM SHIPS

The Liability and Fund Conventions[370] cover only oil from oil tankers or ships that are 'constructed or adapted for the carriage of oil in bulk as cargo.'[371] They do not constitute a universal regime for all types of cargo, or for all types of ship. Oil pollution from other

361 See IOPC Funds *Annual Report* (2004) 34–5.

362 See *Kingdom of Spain v American Bureau of Shipping*, US Court of Appeals for the Second Circuit (2012), 2012 *American Maritime Cases* 2113.

363 See Gahlen, *Civil Liability for Accidents at Sea* (Berlin, 2015) 118–126.

364 Approaches vary from jurisdiction to jurisdiction; see de Bruyne, 45 *JMLC* (2014) 181–232.

365 See judgment of the Cour de Cassation.

366 See Mukherjee, in Ndiaye and Wolfrum (eds) *Law of the Sea, Environmental Law and Settlement of Disputes* (Brill, 2007) 463–496.

367 Directive 2005/35/EC applies only to reckless discharges or intentional damage. At present it does not apply to accidents. See *Intertanko Case* (2007) ECJ C-308/06.

368 *Commune de Mesquer v Total*, ECJ Case C-188/07 (2008).

369 See Gahlen, *Civil Liability for Accidents at Sea*, 162; Somers and Gonsaeles, 41 *JMLC* (2010) 57–83.

370 See generally de La Fayette, 20 *IJMCL* (2005) 167.

371 1992 CLC, Article I(1).

types of ships thus falls outside of the regime. The 2001 Bunkers Convention was developed to address part of this gap, providing for the liability of owners of ships, other than oil tankers, for pollution caused by spills of bunker fuel.[372] This treaty, which entered into force in November 2008, follows the model of the Oil Pollution Liability Convention by imposing strict liability for oil pollution damage on ship owners.[373] The definition of ship owner is, however, broader than under the Oil Pollution Liability Convention, as it permits the possibility of legal action against a range of actors, including the bareboat charterer, manager or operator of the ship, alongside the registered owner.[374] These actors are jointly and severally liable,[375] so the victim of bunker pollution may have a choice of whom to sue. Another key difference with the 1992 Convention is that the Bunkers Convention does not impose a new limit of liability on ship owners, but rather it permits liability to be limited in accordance with relevant national law or international treaties.[376] As such, there is no separate fund for bunker fuel pollution and victims will have to make claims against a general limitation fund, competing with other potential claims.[377] Furthermore, there is no second tier of compensation if the limits of liability of the ship owner are reached. One feature of the Oil Pollution Liability Convention that has been maintained is the requirement for compulsory insurance for vessels of more than 1000 gross tonnes. This obligation is placed on the registered owner, 'who will for this reason probably be the first target of oil pollution victims.'[378]

Other treaties have sought to extend civil liability to other sources of pollution. A 1971 Convention extends the liability of an operator of a nuclear installation to the maritime carriage of nuclear material; in most situations a shipowner will not be liable.[379] A protocol to the 1989 Basel Convention provides a separate and slightly different regime of liability and compensation for the transboundary movement of hazardous waste.[380] A more significant development is the adoption by the IMO in 1996 of a Convention on Liability and Compensation for the Carriage of Hazardous and Noxious Substances by Sea.[381] The HNS Convention applies to a range of noxious, dangerous, or hazardous liquids, gases, substances and bulk chemicals as defined in Annex II of the 1973/78 MARPOL Convention and in other international codes. It does not apply to oil pollution damage as defined in the Oil Pollution Liability Convention, but oils listed in Annex I of MARPOL are nevertheless included. Due to a very slow uptake by states, the HNS Convention was amended by a protocol adopted in 2010 and it is this amended instrument that is discussed below. Ten years later both the Convention and the Protocol had still not entered into force.

372 See generally Wu, 33 *JMLC* (2002) 553; Tsimplis, *LMCLQ* (2005) 83; Zhu, *Compulsory Insurance and Compensation for Bunker Oil Pollution Damage* (Berlin, 2007).

373 Bunkers Convention, Article 3.

374 Bunkers Convention, Article 1(3).

375 Bunkers Convention, Article 3(2).

376 Bunkers Convention, Article 6.

377 See Gahlen, *Civil Liability for Accidents at Sea*, 188.

378 *Ibid*, 179.

379 *Infra*, Ch 9, section 5.

380 *Infra*, Ch 8.

381 See Wetterstein, *LMCLQ* (1994) 230; de la Rue and Anderson, *Shipping and the Environment*, Ch 7. An attempt to adopt a convention at the IMO in 1984 was not successful. See Resolution 1, IMO LEG/CONF 6/64/Add 1, and Draft Convention, IMO LEG/CONF 6/3.

The legal regime created by the HNS Convention is similar to the 1992 version of the Oil Pollution Liability and Fund Conventions in almost all respects, albeit that both ship owner liability and cargo owner liability are dealt with in a single instrument. The strict liability of the shipowner is channelled and limited in the same way as the Oil Pollution Liability Convention, although the HNS regime introduces an additional exception from liability when it can be demonstrated that the shipowner had not been informed of the hazardous and noxious nature of the substances being shipped.[382] The 2010 amendments also differentiate the limits of a shipowner's liability depending on whether the substances were carried in bulk or in packaged form. The reason for this distinction is that only cargo owners of substances shipped in bulk contribute to the second tier of compensation and they were concerned that they would be cross-subsidizing shipments of other substances.[383] Given the range of substances covered by the regime, the HNS Fund is unsurprisingly a more complex institution than its oil-focused counterpart. The HNS Fund will oversee four accounts from which compensation may be paid: a general account, an oil account, a liquefied natural gas account and a liquefied petroleum gas account.[384] Each account will only provide compensation for incidents involving substances that have contributed to that account. Contributions to the HNS Fund come from the receivers of HNS cargoes, or from governments on their behalf.

Like the Oil Pollution Convention, the HNS Convention covers reinstatement of environmental damage occurring in the territory, territorial waters or exclusive economic zone of any party. An Australian proposal to include high seas environmental damage was not accepted, but the agreed text of Article 3 does apply to damage (including preventive measures) anywhere at sea, provided it is not 'damage by contamination of the environment'.[385] This text should enable fishers to claim for economic losses if high seas fish stocks are poisoned,[386] and it would also cover precautionary high seas clean up intended to protect potentially affected states, but it would seem to rule out environmental reinstatement of the high seas, insofar as that might be possible, or any claim to notional damages for pure environmental loss, wherever suffered. It is not clear that the 2010 amendments have completely overcome doubts raised about the compensation scheme for HNS products, however, and it has failed to attract any ratifications since the Protocol was adopted.

9 CONCLUSIONS

This chapter has demonstrated the extent to which an international legal regime for the control of marine pollution from ships has developed since 1972, and the degree to which it has proved effective. Although in certain respects there remain significant

382 HNS Convention, Article 7(2)(d). 383 *Ibid*, 156.

384 HNS Convention (as amended by 2010 Protocol) Article 16. 385 Article 3(c).

386 This was also an Australian proposal: see IMO LEG 65/3/4 (1991).

problems in enforcing international pollution regulations at sea, and in controlling the risks of serious accidents, there is evidence that relevant international and regional conventions, most notably the 1973/78 MARPOL Convention, have led to improved protection of the marine environment. There is also some reason to conclude that international regulation of serious environmental risks has proved more successful with regard to ships than for other comparably hazardous undertakings. The regulatory system based on MARPOL and on other conventions such as the 1974 SOLAS has worked reasonably well under the supervision of the IMO, which has shown the flexibility and responsiveness necessary to keep pace with new developments, and has successfully provided a forum in which competing interests can be balanced. Moreover, the system of enforcement employed against delinquent vessels has overcome some of the earlier problems of exclusive reliance on flag state control, although it is clear that further improvements remain necessary.

The 1982 UNCLOS has proved largely uncontroversial in its approach to prevention of marine pollution. An acceptable balance of interests between maritime states and coastal states appears to have been achieved. It has largely put an end to unilateral claims and 'creeping jurisdiction' over the high seas.[387] But it is more doubtful whether the Convention's carefully structured extension of coastal and port state jurisdiction has, in reality, had much impact on the control and reduction of pollution from ships, although the EEZ regime does have significant implications for dumping at sea and the conservation of living resources. The Convention has also been less satisfactory in dealing with other sources of marine pollution, in particular land-based sources, as the following chapter makes clear. Perhaps the most positive element of Part XII of the Convention is its elevation of international conventions such as MARPOL to the status of international standards within a global regime applicable to all states. The Convention's impact in this respect will largely have been achieved despite the continued non-participation of the United States and a small number of other states.

Widespread ratification and entry into force of the 1982 UNCLOS is important, however. Its more novel provisions on matters such as port state jurisdiction over high seas pollution offences and international management and regulation of deep seabed mining have come into effect. Most importantly, the dispute settlement machinery has operated to restrain unilateral or regional claims to jurisdiction over shipping or natural resources and to protect the 'package deal' on which the Convention is based.[388] It is true that UNCED has shown the Convention's articles on straddling and highly migratory fish stocks, on land-based sources of marine pollution, and on protection of the marine biodiversity to be insufficient.[389] Yet it is also clear that the Convention has not prevented the law of the sea from continuing to evolve, by

[387] Churchill, 48 *GYIL* (2005) 81; Franckx, 48 *GYIL* (2005) 117.

[388] See the *South China Sea Arbitration*, PCA (2015) (Jurisdiction) and (2016) (Jurisdiction and merits), and *supra*, Ch 4, section 4(5)(a).

[389] See *infra*, Chs 8 and 12.

agreement and through litigation, in a way that is responsive to these environmental concerns.[390] From that perspective, as these chapters have shown, the importance of UNCED for the marine environment can be seen in the substantial rewriting of regional fisheries law by the 1995 UN Fish Stocks Agreement; in the revision of the regional seas treaties and protocols to take account of Agenda 21; in the prohibition of dumping under the 1996 Protocol to the 1972 London Convention; in the revision and extension of maritime environmental liability and compensation schemes; and in the more modest developments relating to land-based sources of marine pollution. While it is still correct to observe that the 1982 UNCLOS has generally been more successful in addressing specific sources of pollution such as ships or dumping than in establishing a comprehensive and integrated 'system for sustainable development', it has shown its value as a foundation for the continued development of marine environmental law in a coherent form.[391] That is a notable success.

[390] See Boyle, 54 *ICLQ* (2005) 563; Birnie, 12 *IJMCL* (1997) 307, and *infra*, Chs 8, 12.

[391] See in particular the *South China Sea Arbitration*, PCA (2016).

10

INTERNATIONAL WATERCOURSES: ENVIRONMENTAL PROTECTION AND SUSTAINABLE USE

1 INTRODUCTION

Fresh water is a finite resource; the more we pollute it the less there is to use.[1] A sustainable supply of fresh water is not merely fundamental to environmental protection, biodiversity, and so on, but to life itself. Access to clean water was a priority issue in the UN's Millennium Development Goals ('MDGs') and by 2015 the number of people without access to safe drinking water had halved.[2] But even without taking climate change into account, water supply remains inadequate in much of equatorial Africa and Central Asia; desertification is exacerbated by over-extraction of underground water supplies; irrigation, which accounts for 80 per cent of water consumption in many developing countries, is wasteful, causes salinity and renders soil ultimately unusable for agriculture; untreated sewage and nitrate fertilizers widely used in agriculture pollute water supplies.[3] Across the globe population growth and increased living standards are reflected in demand for water at increasing levels that cannot be met indefinitely.[4] Faced with large-scale diversion, extraction, or loss of unpolluted water supplies, many

[1] The scientific literature is summarised by de Chazournes, *Fresh Water in International Law* (Oxford, 2013) 3–5 and McCaffrey, in Jayakumar, Koh, Beckman and Phan (eds), *Transboundary Pollution: Evolving Issues of International Law and Policy* (Cheltenham, 2015) Ch 4.

[2] WHO and UNICEF Joint Monitoring Programme, *Progress on Drinking Water and Sanitation, 2015 Update and MDG Assessment* (Geneva, 2015).

[3] See *Proceedings of the 10th Stockholm Water Symposium*, 13–16 August, 2001 and the 2006 *UN World Water Development Report* (UNESCO).

[4] *Comprehensive Assessment of the Freshwater Resources of the World*, UN Doc E/CN.17/1997/9 (1997).

rivers and lakes no longer support a natural ecosystem, leading to loss of wetlands, swamps, and other natural habitats for wildlife. Some major watercourses, such as the Aral Sea, are at risk of disappearing. Others, including the Yangtse, suffer periodic interruptions due to reduced rainfall. Added to these problems of poor management and inadequate governance are the effects of climate change on freshwater supply, with melting of mountain glaciers in all continents and changing rainfall patterns already posing a real threat to the continued flow of major rivers.[5]

Historically, international water law was not particularly concerned with environmental problems. Its principal focus, evident in the ILA's codification of 1966 (The Helsinki Rules) and in the older literature, was mainly on the allocation of water between upstream and downstream states, and only incidentally were environmental or sustainability concerns served. As we shall see later in this chapter, both the 1992 UNECE Convention on the Protection and Use of Transboundary Watercourses and Lakes[6] ('1992 UNECE Watercourses Convention') and the 1997 UN Watercourses Convention have sought to modernise the law. Serious efforts have been made globally and regionally to address earlier shortcomings and to give international water law a broader ecological perspective within a legal framework more attuned to sustainable use and water shortage than hitherto.[7] The ICJ has contributed to this development of the law in its three decisions on the subject,[8] arguably going further than the 1997 UN Watercourses Convention in certain respects.[9] There has thus been a significant 'greening' of the subject, both globally and regionally.

1(1) THE SCOPE OF INTERNATIONAL WATERCOURSE LAW

The term 'international watercourse' is used in this chapter primarily as a convenient designation for rivers, lakes, or groundwater sources shared by two or more states. Such watercourses will normally either form or straddle an international boundary,

[5] IPCC, *Climate Change and Water: Technical Paper VI* (IPCC, 2008).

[6] The Convention entered into force on 6 October 1996. In 2019 it had 43 parties and two protocols, on Water and Health, and Civil Liability. For background material see *Rept of the Working Party on Water Problems*, 5th Special Session, ENVWA/WP 3/CRP 9 (1991); draft convention, ENVWA/WP 3/R 19/Rev1 (1991); *Rept of the 1st Meeting of Parties*, ECE/MP WAT/2 (1997). See Tanzi, *The UNECE Convention on the Protection and Use of Transboundary Watercourses and International Lakes* (Brill, 2015); Nollkaemper, *The Legal Regime for Transboundary Water Pollution: Between Discretion and Constraint* (Dordrecht, 1993). For a comparison of the UNECE Convention and the UN Convention see UNECE, *The Economic Commission for Europe Water Convention and the UN Watercourses Convention* (UN, 2015).

[7] See also the treaties covered in section 3, *infra*, and generally de Chazournes, *Fresh Water in International Law* (Oxford, 2013); McCaffrey, *Law of International Watercourses*; Benvenisti, *Sharing Transboundary Resources* (Cambridge, 2002).

[8] See *Gabčíkovo-Nagymaros Dam Case*, ICJ Reports (1997) 7; *Pulp Mills on the River Uruguay Case*, ICJ Reports (2010) 14; *Border Activities/San Juan River Cases*, ICJ Reports (2015) 665 and see also *Indus Waters Kishenganga Arbitration (India/Pakistan)* PCA (2013).

[9] See in particular Benvenisti, *Sharing Transboundary Resources*, Ch 7; Stephens, in Klein (ed), *Litigating International Law Disputes* (CUP 2014) 297–9; Boyle, 8 *YbIEL* (1997) 13–20. All three see *Gabčíkovo* as a particularly formative decision.

or in the case of rivers, they may flow through a succession of states.[10] They may also be wholly or partly underground.[11] A problem of geographical definition then arises. How much of such a watercourse system is it proper for international law to address? The possibilities range from simply that portion which crosses or defines a boundary, to the entire watershed or river basin, with its associated lakes, tributaries, groundwater systems, and connecting waterways wherever they are located. Modern bilateral and regional treaties have tended to adopt the basin approach, because it is the most efficient means of achieving control of pollution and water utilization.[12] Examples of such arrangements are widespread in Africa,[13] but also include the Amazon, the Plate, and the Mekong.[14] In Europe the basin concept has been used in controlling pollution of the Rhine, Danube, Elbe, Meuse, and Scheldt rivers[15] and, in North America, of the Great Lakes.[16] It has been favoured by declarations of international conferences, including the Stockholm and Rio Conferences,[17] and the UN Water Conference held at Mar Del Plata in 1977,[18] and it forms the basis of codification undertaken by the Institut de Droit International[19] and by the International Law Association's Helsinki and Berlin Rules.[20]

Older treaties are more likely to follow the narrower definition found in the Final Act of Congress of Vienna, which focused on international rivers separating or traversing the territory of two or more states and declared them open for navigation by all riparians.[21] The 1992 UNECE Watercourses Convention provides the contemporary

[10] See McCaffrey, *Law of International Watercourses*, Ch 2.

[11] See ILC Articles on Transboundary Aquifers, Article 4, GAOR, 63rd Session, Supp 10 (2008); McCaffrey, *Law of International Watercourses*, Ch 14.

[12] Kearney, II *YbILC* (1976) Pt 1, 184ff.

[13] Examples include the 1999 Protocol on Lake Victoria; 2000 Protocol on Shared Watercourse Systems in the Southern African Development Community; the 1972 Senegal River Basin Treaty; 1987 Zambezi River System Agreement; 1963 Act Regarding Navigation and Economic Co-operation between States of the Niger Basin; 1964 Convention and Statute Relating to the Development of the Chad Basin. See McCaffrey, *3rd Rept on International Watercourses, etc*, UN Doc A/CN 4/406 (1987) 18; Godana, *Africa's Shared Water Resources: Legal and Institutional Aspects of the Nile, Niger and Senegal River Systems* (London, 1985).

[14] See 1978 Treaty on Amazonian Cooperation; 1969 Treaty on the River Plate Basin; 1995 Agreement for Sustainable Development of the Mekong River Basin.

[15] 1976 Convention on the Protection of the Rhine against Chemical Pollution; 1999 Convention for the Protection of the Rhine; 1990 Convention for the Protection of the Elbe, Article 1; 1990 Agreement on Co-operation on Management of the Water Resources in the Danube Basin; 1994 Convention on Co-operation for Protection and Sustainable Use of the Danube River, Articles 1(b) 3; 1994 Agreement on the Protection of the Rivers Meuse and Scheldt, Articles 1, 3.

[16] 1978 Great Lakes Water Quality Agreement, amended 1983 and 2012. See Utton and Teclaff, *Transboundary Resources Law* (Boulder, 1987) 27ff.

[17] 1972 UNCHE, Action Plan for the Human Environment, Rec 1, UN Doc A/Conf 48/14/Rev1; 1992 UNCED, Agenda 21, Ch 18.9, UN Doc A/Conf 151/26/Rev1.

[18] *Rept of the UN Water Conference*, Mar Del Plata, 14–25 Mar 1977. See generally II *YbILC* (1986) Pt 1, 325ff.

[19] 49 *Ann Inst DDI* (1961) Pt II, 381; 58 *Ann Inst DDI* (1979) Pt II, 197; Salmon, ibid, 193–263.

[20] ILA Helsinki Rules (1996) Article II; ILA Berlin Rules (2004) Article 3.

[21] See *ILC Report*, II *YbILC* (1979) Pt 1, 153f; 1909 US–Canada Boundary Waters Treaty, *repr* 146 *Recueil des Cours* (1975) 307.

framework for regulation and management of European rivers;[22] superficially it adopts essentially the same narrow definition of 'transboundary waters'.[23] It requires only these waters, rather than the river basin or watershed, to be managed and conserved in an ecologically sound and rational way and used reasonably and equitably.[24] At the same time, however, parties are required to control transboundary impacts, including pollution, to ensure conservation and restoration of ecosystems, and to cooperate in protecting the environment not just of transboundary waters but also of 'the environment influenced by such waters, including the marine environment'.[25] In practice this comes close to a basin approach; it will be necessary for states to control pollution of the wider drainage basin or watercourse system in order to produce the desired result in boundary areas.

The 1992 UNECE Watercourses Convention is the first regional framework convention dealing with international watercourses.[26] Treaties negotiated under it are less circumspect in their geographical scope: the 1994 Danube Convention applies to the Danube River basin and catchment area and it is not limited to control of transboundary impacts; the 1994 Agreements on the Meuse and Scheldt require the parties to take measures across the whole drainage area of these rivers, while the 1999 Rhine Convention applies to the Rhine, ground water and ecosystems interacting with the Rhine, and its catchment area, insofar as it contributes to pollution or flooding of the Rhine. Moreover, in 1997, parties to the 1992 UNECE Watercourses Conventionadopted the Helsinki Declaration,[27] in which they recognized the need for integrated management of all freshwater sources and committed themselves 'to apply, as appropriate, the principles of the Convention when drawing up, revising, implementing and enforcing' national laws and regulations on the management of internal as well as transboundary water resources. It is evident that the 1992 Convention has in practice resulted in the adoption of a basin-wide approach among its parties.

Some upstream states resisted the drainage basin concept during the ILC negotiations and the term does not appear in the 1997 UN Watercourses Convention.[28] However, 'international watercourse' is defined broadly to mean 'a system of surface waters and groundwaters constituting by virtue of their physical relationship a unitary whole and normally flowing into a common terminus'.[29] It applies regardless of

22 UNECE Europe includes Central Asia: Kazakhstan, Turkmenistan and Uzbekistan are parties. An amendment adopted in 2003 but not yet in force opens up the convention to global participation.

23 Article 1(1). 24 Article 2. 25 Articles 2, 3.

26 See also 2000 Protocol on Shared Watercourse Systems in the Southern Africa Development Community, and 2012 Great Lakes Water Quality Agreement, *infra*, section 3(3).

27 *Rept of the 1st Meeting of Parties*, ECE/MP WAT/2 (1997), annex. See also the Protocol on Water and Health adopted in 1999. Article 5(j) calls for integrated management of 'the whole of a catchment area', including natural ecosystems, groundwaters, and coastal waters.

28 Schwebel, II *YbILC* (1979) Pt 1, 153ff; Evensen, ibid, (1984) Pt 1, 104f; McCaffrey, ibid, (1986) Pt 1, 101, para 16.

29 1997 UN Convention, Articles 1 and 2. See II *YbILC* (1986) Pt 2, 62, para 236, and *ILC Report* (1991) 154–61, where objections to the term 'watercourse system' are noted.

the size of the river or the volume of water flow.[30] The Convention also applies to the uses of international watercourses and their waters (other than navigation), and to 'measures of protection, preservation and management related to the uses of those watercourses and their waters.'[31] For this purpose it includes an obligation to protect watercourse ecosystems.[32] The ILC commentary observes that 'the present articles would apply to uses not only of waters actually contained in the watercourse, but also those diverted therefrom.'[33]

Thus defined, the 1997 UN Convention applies to much more than the waters which mark or cross a boundary. As McCaffrey notes, 'the drainage basin is functionally equivalent – at least hydrologically – to that of the watercourse system.'[34]

1(2) WATER RESOURCES: PRINCIPLES OF ALLOCATION

One approach to the admissibility of watercourse pollution is to treat it as an aspect of the allocation of water resources. Before considering specific issues relating to pollution and environmental protection it is therefore necessary to establish the basis on which water resources will be allocated among those states with a claim to their use. Four theories are commonly advanced:[35] territorial sovereignty, territorial integrity, equitable utilization, and common management.

(a) Territorial sovereignty

One view is that states enjoy absolute sovereignty over water within their territory and are free to do as they please with those waters, including extracting as much as necessary, or altering their quality, regardless of the effect this has on the use or supply of water in downstream or contiguous states. This theory is often known as the Harmon doctrine, after the US Attorney General who asserted the absolute right of the US to divert the Rio Grande.[36] Modern commentators mostly dismiss the doctrine.[37] Apart from its bias in favour of upstream states, it has little support in state practice and does not represent international law. Even the US quickly retreated from the full Harmon doctrine in

[30] The commentary to Article 2 thus refers to 'streams' as examples of a watercourse: II *YbILC* (1994) Pt.2, 90. See for an example *Waters of the Silala Case (Chile v Bolivia)* ICJ Application (2016).

[31] Article 1. The term 'preservation' was adopted by the UN 6th Committee in preference to the ILC's use of 'conservation', on the understanding that preservation included 'conservation': see UN, *Rept of the 6th Committee convening as the Working Group of the Whole*, GAOR A/51/869, 11th April 1997, para 8.

[32] See *infra*, section 2.

[33] ILC Report, II *YbILC* (1994) Pt.2, 89, para (2).

[34] McCaffrey, *Law of International Watercourses*, 37.

[35] McCaffrey, *Law of International Watercourses*, Ch 5; Bourne, 6 *UBCLR* (1971) 115; Caflisch, 219 *Recueil des Cours* (1989) 48ff.

[36] 'The fact that the Rio Grande lacks sufficient water to permit its use by the inhabitants of both countries does not entitle Mexico to impose restrictions on the US which would hamper the development of the latter's territory or deprive its inhabitants of an advantage with which nature had endowed it and which is situated entirely within its territory. To admit such a principle would be completely contrary to the principle that the US exercises full sovereignty over its national territory', 21 *Ops Atty Gen* (1895) 274, 283.

[37] See e.g. McCaffrey, *Law of International Watercourses*, 108–126.

treaties with Mexico and Canada which are more consistent with the principle of equitable utilization.[38] India at one time asserted 'full freedom . . . to draw off such waters as it needed' from the Indus, but the treaty which concluded this dispute is generally regarded as effecting an equitable apportionment of the waters.[39] India's argument was again rejected in the *Indus Waters Kishenganga Arbitration*, which held that in customary international law the right of an upstream state to abstract water 'cannot be absolute', and that it must ensure a minimum flow of water in order to avoid environmental damage to the downstream state and to protect other existing uses.[40] The Harmon doctrine has never had much currency in Europe because of its fundamental inconsistency with the freedom of navigation which characterized major European rivers after 1815.[41]

(b) Territorial integrity

Equally questionable is the obverse of the Harmon doctrine, the principle of absolute territorial integrity or riparian rights. This theory would give the lower riparian the right to a full flow of water of natural quality. Interference with the natural flow by the upstream state would thus require the consent of the lower riparian. Egypt has in the past interpreted the Nile treaties in this way.[42] In this form the doctrine appears devoid of more than limited support in state practice, jurisprudence, or the writings of commentators.[43] It is sometimes confused with the idea that states may acquire servitudes in the use of rivers, and with the principle that states may not use or permit the use of their territory in such a manner as to cause harm to other states. But these are separate principles: neither or them necessarily benefits only downstream or contiguous states, nor can it safely be assumed that they confer rights amounting to absolute territorial integrity.

(c) Equitable utilization

The most widely endorsed theory treats international watercourses as shared resources, subject to equitable utilization by all the riparian states.[44] On this view no single state has absolute sovereignty over the watercourse. This proposition requires some clarification, however. The view that international watercourses are 'shared resources' was initially adopted by the ILC, and enjoys some support,[45] but the concept itself encountered significant opposition among states on account of its alleged novelty and

38 McCaffrey, *Law of International Watercourses*, 102–110. At II *YbILC* (1986) Pt 1, 105–9, he concludes: 'viewed in the context of US diplomatic and treaty practice, the "Harmon Doctrine" is not, and probably never has been actually followed by the state that formulated it'.

39 McCaffrey, II *YbILC* (1986) Pt 1, 109f; id, *Law of International Watercourses*, 288–98.

40 *Indus Waters Kishenganga Arbitration*, PCA (2013) paras 436–447.

41 Cohen, 146 *Recueil des Cours* (1975) Ch 1, contrasts European and N American experience: transboundary navigation was less important in the latter case.

42 McCaffrey, *Law of International Watercourses*, 128–9; 258–72.

43 McCaffrey, *Law of International Watercourses*, 126–135.

44 McCaffrey, *Law of International Watercourses*, Ch 10; Bourne, 6 *UBCLR* (1971) 120; Arechaga, 159 *Recueil des Cours* (1978) 192ff.

45 *Rept of the Executive Director of UNEP*, UNEP/GC/44, para 86; *Lac Lanoux Arbitration*, 24 *ILR* (1957) 119; *Gabčíkovo-Nagymaros Case*, ICJ Reports (1997) 7, paras 147, 152.

uncertain legal implications.[46] Specific reference to 'shared resources' was deleted from ILC draft articles in 1984,[47] in the belief that nothing of substance was thereby lost and that what mattered was the elaboration of obligations and rights attaching to watercourses which are in practice shared.[48] Among these obligations is the principle of equitable utilization.

Equitable utilization rests on a foundation of shared sovereignty, and is not to be confused with equal division.[49] Instead it will generally entail a balance of interests which accommodates the needs and uses of each state. This basic principle enjoys substantial support in judicial decisions, state practice, and international codifications. It was expressly applied by the ICJ in *Gabčíkovo-Nagymaros* and *Pulp Mills*. In *Gabčíkovo* Slovakia was found to be inequitably diverting too much of the flow of water.[50] In *Pulp Mills* Argentina was inequitably appropriating too much of the river's capacity for unregulated pollutants.[51] The principle of equitable utilization is implicitly followed in the *Lac Lanoux Arbitration*, where the tribunal recognized that, in carrying out diversion works entirely within its own territory, France nevertheless had an obligation to consult Spain, the other riparian, and to safeguard her rights in the watercourse.[52] This does not mean that any use of an international watercourse affecting other states requires their consent, but it does indicate that the sovereignty of a state over rivers within its borders is qualified by a recognition of the equal rights of other states to make equitable use of the water.

Settlements of river disputes in North America and the Indian subcontinent by states which had previously asserted a different position tend to confirm this conclusion.[53] These and other examples of state practice listed in the work of the ILC have persuaded successive rapporteurs to endorse equitable utilization as an established principle of international law.[54] Article 5(1) of the 1997 UN Watercourses Convention thus provides:

> Watercourse states shall in their respective territories utilize an international watercourse in an equitable and reasonable manner . . .

The same principle has also been adopted in other codifications,[55] in the 1992 UNECE Watercourses Convention,[56] and in other regional agreements.[57]

[46] *Supra*, Ch 3, section 3(1).

[47] Evensen, II *YbILC* (1984) Pt 1, 110, para 48.

[48] McCaffrey, II *YbILC* (1986) Pt 1, 103, para 74: 'It therefore appears that, while the reformulation of article 6 has resulted in the loss of a new and developing concept [shared natural resources], it has produced greater legal certainty, and, when viewed in connection with other draft articles, has not resulted in the elimination of any fundamental principles from the draft as a whole.'

[49] *Territorial Jurisdiction of the International Commission of the River Oder Case*, PCIJ Ser A No 23 (1929); *Diversion of Water from the Meuse Case*, PCIJ Ser A/B No 70 (1937).

[50] ICJ Reports (1997) 7, paras 78, 85, 147, 150.

[51] ICJ Reports (2010) 14, paras 177, 266.

[52] 24 *ILR* (1957) 101; Lester, 57 *AJIL* (1963) 828. See *infra*, section 2.

[53] McCaffrey, *Law of International Watercourses*, 102–110; 128–9.

[54] McCaffrey, II *YbILC* (1986) Pt 1, 103–5, 110ff; Schwebel, ibid, (1982) Pt 1, 75ff.

[55] ILA Berlin Rules, Article 12; ILA Helsinki Rules, Article IV.

[56] Article 2(2) requires states to ensure that transboundary waters are used in a 'reasonable and equitable way'.

[57] See in particular the Protocol on Shared Watercourses in the Southern Africa Development Community, *infra*, section 3.

What constitutes 'reasonable and equitable' utilization is not capable of precise definition. As in other contexts, whether the equitable delimitation of maritime boundaries, or the allocation and regulation of shared fishing stocks, the issue turns on a balancing of relevant factors and must be responsive to the circumstances of individual cases.[58] Article 6 of the 1997 UN Watercourses Convention identifies factors relevant to determining what is equitable and reasonable utilization in that context.[59] These factors include:

(a) geographic, hydrographic, hydrological, climatic, ecological, and other factors of a natural character
(b) the social and economic needs of the watercourse states concerned
(c) the population dependent on the watercourse in each state
(d) the effects of the use or uses of the watercourse in one watercourse state on other watercourse states
(e) existing and potential uses of the international watercourse
(f) conservation, protection, development, and economy of use of the water resources of the watercourse and the costs of measures taken to that effect
(g) the availability of alternatives, of corresponding value, to a particular planned or existing use.

This list is not meant to be exhaustive; consideration must be given to all the interests likely to be affected by the proposed use of the watercourse.[60] Both the benefits and the negative consequences of a particular use are to be taken into account.[61]

Moreover, a listing of factors says nothing about the priority or weight given to each one, or how conflicts are to be reconciled. These remain matters calling for comparative judgement in individual cases,[62] and for this reason, uncertainty in application is the main difficulty affecting the principle of reasonable and equitable use in the context of international watercourses. Given the complexity of the balancing process and the likelihood that the needs of states may change, the optimal solution will usually be some form of common management designed to achieve equitable use of the watercourse system on an ongoing basis.[63] Thus equitable utilization leads naturally to the fourth theory, that of common management.

58 *North Sea Continental Shelf Cases*, ICJ Reports (1969) 50, para 93; *Icelandic Fisheries Cases*, ICJ Reports (1974) 3; and 1982 UNCLOS, Articles 69, 70, 74, 83, and *supra*, Ch 3.

59 Compare ILA Berlin Rules (2004) Article 13; ILA Helsinki Rules (1966) Article V, and *Rept of the African-Asian legal Consultative Committee*, summarized in II *YbILC* (1982) Pt 1, 87, paras 94–8. For a comprehensive discussion see Fuentes, 67 *BYIL* (1996) 337.

60 *Lac Lanoux Arbitration*, 138f, 'Account must be taken of all interests, of whatsoever nature, which are liable to be affected by the works undertaken, even if they do not correspond to a right'; see also ILA Helsinki Rules, Commentary, 488, and 1997 UN Watercourses Convention, Article 6(1) (3).

61 UNGA, 51st Session, *Rept of the 6th Committee Working Group*, GAOR A/51/869 (1997) para 8.

62 1997 UN Watercourses Convention, Article 6(3); *ILC Report* (1994) 235; ILA, Helsinki Rules, Commentary, 489.

63 Schwebel, II *YbILC* (1982) Pt 1, 76, para 70; McCaffrey, II *YbILC* (1986) Pt 1, 132, para 177.

(d) Common management

Common management combines the idea that watercourse basins are most efficiently managed as an integrated whole and the need to find effective institutional machinery to secure cooperation on environmental, social, and economic objectives.[64] It represents a community-of-interest approach which goes beyond the allocation of equitable rights, however, and opens up the possibility of integrating development and international regulation of the watercourse environment.[65] As we have seen, modern state practice prefers the basin or hydrologic-system approach to watercourse management.[66] This is usually accompanied by the creation of international institutions in which all riparian states cooperate in formulating and implementing policies for the development and use of a watercourse. Examples of such arrangements are the Lake Chad Basin Commission,[67] the River Niger Commission,[68] the Permanent Joint Technical Commission for Nile Waters,[69] the Zambezi Intergovernmental Monitoring and Co-ordinating Committee,[70] the Intergovernmental Co-ordinating Committee of the River Plate Basin,[71] the Amazonian Cooperation Council,[72] and the Danube River Protection Commission.[73] The US–Canadian International Joint Commission[74] is an example of common management applied to a more limited watercourse area. These institutions vary in their detailed form and the scope of their responsibilities. Some are not involved in environmental management;[75] in other cases, such as the International Commission for the Protection of the Rhine,[76] or the Moselle Commission,[77] this is their only purpose. As in the case of fisheries or wildlife conservation commissions their success is dependent on the degree of cooperation they can engender.[78]

Common management institutions have become the basis for environmental regulation and sustainable development of a number of international watercourses.[79] Progressive development of this approach has long been endorsed by international

[64] Schwebel, ibid, (1982) Pt 1, 76, para 70; Fitzmaurice, 14 *YbIEL* (2003) 3.

[65] See generally McCaffrey, *Law of International Watercourses*, 147–70; Benvenisti, *Sharing Transboundary Resources*, Ch 7; Toope and Brunnée, 91 *AJIL* (1997) 26; Benvenisti, 90 *AJIL* (1996) 384. Scanlon and Iza, 14 *YbIEL* (2003) 81 develop the concept of 'environmental flows' for this purpose.

[66] *Supra*, section 1(1).

[67] 1964 Convention and Statute Relating to the Development of the Chad Basin.

[68] 1963 Act Regarding Navigation and Economic Co-operation between the States of the Niger Basin.

[69] 1959 Agreement Between the UAR and the Republic of the Sudan for the Full Utilization of Nile Waters, and 1960 Protocol Establishing Permanent Joint Technical Committee, in UN, *Legislative Texts and Treaty Provisions Concerning the Utilization of International Rivers for Purposes Other than Navigation*, UN Doc ST/LEG/Ser B/12, 143ff.

[70] Agreement on the Action Plan for the Environmentally Sound Management of the Common Zambezi River System. See *infra*, section 3.

[71] 1969 Treaty on the River Plate Basin; 1973 Treaty on the River Plate and its Maritime Limits.

[72] 1978 Treaty for Amazonian Cooperation.

[73] 1994 Convention on Cooperation for the Protection and Sustainable Use of the Danube River.

[74] 1909 Boundary Waters Treaty.

[75] E.g. the Nile Commission.

[76] *Infra*, section 3.

[77] 1961 Protocol Concerning the Constitution of an International Commission for the Protection of the Moselle Against Pollution.

[78] See *supra*, Ch 2, section 5.

[79] See *infra*, section 3.

political institutions,[80] and adopted by codification bodies. Both the Stockholm Declaration on the Human Environment[81] and the UN Water Conference Mar Del Plata Action Plan[82] called on states to establish such commissions where appropriate for coordinated development, including environmental protection. The 1992 UNECE Watercourses Convention and the 1997 UN Watercourses Convention include provision for common management institutions, but in notably different terms. The UNECE Convention is the stronger, requiring riparian states both to conclude bilateral or multilateral agreements or arrangements to prevent, reduce, and control transboundary pollution or other impacts, and to establish joint bodies, whose tasks are defined in some detail. States are entitled to participate in these arrangements 'on the basis of equality and reciprocity', although coastal states may join only at the invitation of riparians.[83] Not only is this blueprint for future regional management of European watercourses obligatory for parties to the Convention, but existing arrangements must also be modified to ensure consistency with its 'basic principles'.

In contrast, under the provisions of the 1997 UN Watercourses Convention the parties need only 'consider' the creation of joint mechanisms or commissions as a means of giving effect to their duty of cooperation and consultation regarding optimal utilization and management of an international watercourse.[84] Moreover, unlike the 1992 UNECE Watercourses Convention or the 1995 UN Fish Stocks Agreement,[85] the 1997 Convention does not alter existing watercourse agreements, such as those governing the Nile or the Amazon, nor does it necessarily require that future watercourse agreements be consistent with its basic principles.[86] On the contrary, under Article 3, parties to later agreements may 'apply and adjust' the provisions of the Convention to the characteristics and uses of specific watercourses. The 1997 Convention is thus an optional framework code or 'guideline' whose provisions are not only subject to

80 See e.g. UN Committee on Natural Resources, UN Doc E/C 7/2 Add 6, 1–7; Economic Commission for Europe, Committee on Water Problems 1971, UN Doc E/ECE/Water/9, annex II; Council of Europe Rec 436 (1965). For a useful survey of lessons learned, see 1998 Berlin Recommendations on Transboundary Water management (UNECE).

81 1972 Stockholm Action Plan for the Human Environment, UN Doc A/Conf 48/14/Rev 1, Rec 51.

82 *Rept of the UN Water Conference*, Mar del Plata, 1977.

83 See generally Article 9. An earlier reference to participation on an 'equitable' basis was changed in the final text in favour of 'equality' of participation: see UNECE, *2nd Draft Convention*, ENVWA/WP.3/R.19/Rev1 (1991) 5. Watercourse Agreements concluded in accordance with the 1992 Convention include the 1999 Convention for the Protection of the Rhine; the 1994 Convention on Co-operation for the Protection and Sustainable Use of the Danube River; and the 1994 Agreements on the Protection of the Rivers Meuse and Scheldt.

84 See Articles 8, 24. McCaffrey, 92 *AJIL* (1998) 104, criticizes Article 24 as 'too modest'. Cf Vinogradov, 3 *Colorado JIELP* (1991) 238, and see Schwebel, 3rd *Rept*, II *YBILC*, Pt 1 (1982) 65; McCaffrey, 6th *Rept*, II *YBILC*, Pt 1 (1990) 42–52; *ILC Report*, II *YBILC*, Pt 2 (1991) 73–4.

85 *Supra*, Ch 2, section 5.

86 Article 3. Parties may 'consider' harmonizing existing agreements with the Convention's basic principles. See McCaffrey, 92 *AJIL* (1998) 98. Contrast Article 311(2) (3) of the 1982 UNCLOS. Ethiopia, France and Turkey voted against adoption of Article 3.

reservation, but may be departed from ad hoc by any of the parties.[87] While this may facilitate or even encourage common management of international water resources, the Convention does not require it. However, every watercourse state is entitled to participate in watercourse negotiations or agreements on terms set out in Article 4 of the Convention,[88] and also to participate 'in an equitable and reasonable manner' in the use, development and protection of the watercourse in accordance with Article 5(2). McCaffrey notes that while the idea behind Article 5(2) is well developed in many river basins, its codification by the ILC is novel.[89] However, in the *Gabčíkovo-Nagymaros Case* the ICJ viewed Article 5(2) as reflecting 'in an optimal way' the concept of common utilization of shared resources and noted that re-establishment of a joint management regime by the parties to the dispute would accord with its terms.[90]

Although cooperation in joint management institutions is not obligatory as a matter of general international law, the foregoing treaties and declarations do recognize that it is a necessary and desirable principle, aptly described by the ILC's special rapporteur as a 'principle of progressive international law'.[91] Examples of state practice in the functioning of such institutions are considered further below.[92]

2 PROTECTION OF WATERCOURSE ECOSYSTEMS

2(1) POLLUTION AND PERMISSIBLE USES OF WATERCOURSES

River pollution generally originates from industrial effluent, agricultural run-off, or domestic sewage discharge.[93] Apart from specific treaty regimes, there is little contemporary support for the view that such polluting uses are per se impermissible. Few modern treaties endorse an absolute prohibition on detrimental alteration of water quality.[94] Instead, the modern trend is to require states to regulate and control river pollution, prohibiting only certain forms of pollutant discharge, and distinguishing

[87] See Article 3(3) and agreed statements of understanding in UNGA, 51st Session, *Rept of the 6th Committee Working Group*, GAOR A/51/869 (1997) para 8, in 36 *ILM* (1997) 719. Reservations are not prohibited. On the 1997 Convention see generally McCaffrey, *The Law of International Watercourses*, Ch 9.

[88] In this respect the 1997 Convention follows the strong precedent set by the 1995 UN Fish Stocks Agreement, *supra*, Ch 2, section 5. Note however that the entitlement is limited to negotiations or agreements that affect the *entire* watercourse. For negotiations affecting only part of the watercourse see Article 4(2) and McCaffrey, 92 *AJIL* (1998) 98–9.

[89] 92 *AJIL* (1998) 100.

[90] ICJ Reports (1997) 7, para 147.

[91] II *YbILC* (1984) Pt 1, 112, para 59.

[92] See *infra*, section 3.

[93] See generally McCaffrey, in Jayakumar et al, *Transboundary Pollution*, Ch 4; McIntyre, *Environmental Protection of International Watercourses under International Law* (Farnham, 2007); Nollkaemper, *The Legal Regime for Transboundary Water Pollution* (London, 1993); Lammers, *Pollution of International Watercourses* (The Hague, 1984); Colliard, in OECD, *Legal Aspects of Transfrontier Pollution* (Paris, 1977).

[94] For a full list see Fuentes, 69 *BYIL* (1998) 146–50.

between new and existing sources.[95] Moreover, the contemporary focus is not simply on pollution per se, but on broader issues of protecting ecosystems and the environment.[96]

Early European practice frequently prohibited industrial or agricultural pollution harmful to river fisheries or domestic use of water.[97] Only as the balance of demands on river utilization changed did this strict approach give way to a more varied pattern. For major industrial rivers, such as the Rhine, the later treaties show clearly a greater tolerance of polluting uses.[98]

North American practice followed a similar trend. A prohibition of pollution of boundary waters applied only when human health or property were injured.[99] Despite the explicit priority given to domestic and sanitary uses by the 1909 Boundary Waters Treaty, industrial and agricultural pollution of the Great Lakes became established, until a new regulatory regime was agreed in 1972.[100] Until 1973 the US maintained that it was not required to deliver to Mexico water of any particular quality from the Colorado River, provided its polluting use of the river for irrigation was reasonable.[101] Nor do treaties elsewhere typically prohibit polluting uses. The 1960 Indus River Treaty limited industrial use and required measures to prevent undue pollution affecting other interests, but the implication that polluting uses are entitled to consideration consistent with equitable utilization is clear.[102]

95 See *infra*, section 2(3). Few watercourse treaties define the term pollution, however. Differing definitions are offered by the ILA's Helsinki Rules, Article 9, the IDI's 1979 Resolution on the Pollution of Rivers and Lakes, Article 1, and the 1997 UN International Watercourses Convention, Article 21(1). See also 1978 Great Lakes Water Quality Agreement Article 1(J); and the UNECE Guidelines on Responsibility and Liability Regarding Transboundary Water Pollution, Article 1(1)(b).

96 See *infra*, sections 2(3) and (4).

97 1869 Convention Between the Grand Duchy of Baden and Switzerland Concerning Fishing in the Rhine, Ruster and Simma, ix, 4695; 1887 Convention Establishing Uniform Provisions on Fishing in the Rhine and its Tributaries, Article 10, ibid, x, 4730; 1893 Convention Decreeing Uniform Regulations for Fishing in Lake Constance, Article 12, ibid, x, 4759; 1923 Agreement between Italy and Austria Concerning Economic Relations in Border Regions, Article 14, ibid, xi, 5504; 1922 Provisions relating to the Belgian–German Frontier, part III, Article 2, ibid, xi, 5495; 1882 Convention between Italy and Switzerland Concerning Fishing in Frontier Waters, ibid, 5413; 1906 Convention between Switzerland and Italy Establishing Uniform Regulations Concerning Fishing in Border Waterways, Article 12, ibid, xi, 5440; for more recent examples, see 1957 Agreement Concerning Fishing in Frontier Waters (Yugoslavia–Hungary) Article 5, ibid, ix, 4572; 1971 Frontier Rivers Agreement (Finland-Sweden) Ch 1, Articles 3, 4, Ch 6, Article 1, ibid, x, 5092. See generally Colliard, in OECD, *Legal Aspects of Transfrontier Pollution.*

98 1892 Convention between Luxemburg and Prussia Regulating Fisheries in Boundary Waters, para 11, Ruster and Simma, ix, 4753; 1922 Agreement Relating to Frontier Watercourses, Article 45 (Denmark-Germany) ibid, 5473; 1958 Convention Concerning Fishing in the Waters of the Danube, Article 7, UN, *Legislative Texts,* 427; 1912 Agreement on the Exploitation of Border Rivers for Industrial Purposes (Spain–Portugal) Ruster and Simma, xi, 5449; 1956 Convention on the Regulation of the Upper Rhine (France–FRG) UN, *Legislative Texts,* 660.

99 1909 US–Canada Boundary Waters Treaty, Article IV. See Zacklin and Caflisch, *International Rivers and Lakes* (1981, The Hague) Ch 1; Bourne, 28 *NILR* (1981) 188; Fuentes, 69 *BYIL* (1998) 150–5.

100 See *infra*, section 3.

101 See 1944 Colorado River Treaty, and cf 1973 Agreement on Permanent and Definitive Solution of the International Problem of the Salinity of the Colorado River; Brownell and Eaton, 69 *AJIL* (1975) 255.

102 Article 4.

State practice regarding land-based sources of pollution points to the prohibition of discharges of certain toxic substances, especially if these are persistent or highly radioactive.[103] But so long as no such substances are involved, the main conclusion must be that most polluting or environmentally harmful uses of international rivers are wrongful only if they infringe the rights of other states or the limits specifically prescribed by particular river treaties.[104] Other riparians do, however, have a number of claims on the quality of a watercourse. These include the right to equitable utilization, to protection from sources of serious transboundary harm, and to procedural rights of information exchange, consultation, and negotiation.[105]

Moreover, these rights must now be set in the context of the emergence of obligations to protect and preserve the ecosystems of international watercourses,[106] and to regulate and control sources of river pollution which contribute to pollution of the marine environment.[107] This approach to pollution control is important because it moves the issue away from exclusive concentration on the rights of riparians and acknowledges the broader international significance of watercourse environments; it places more emphasis on environmental protection, and illustrates in particular how equitable utilization, the most widely accepted principle of watercourse law, is perhaps the least useful for the development of environmental law.

2(2) ENVIRONMENTAL HARM AND EQUITABLE UTILIZATION

The relationship between equitable utilization of an international watercourse on the one hand and the control of pollution and protection of the environment on the other has been among the more controversial problems affecting the codification of international law relating to freshwater resources. From the perspective of equitable utilization, water quality and environmental protection are relevant factors to take into account when balancing the interests of the riparians involved, although they will not necessarily outweigh competing development needs such as industrial use or irrigation.[108] In the *Gabčíkovo-Nagymaros Case*,[109] the ICJ held that Slovakia, 'by unilaterally assuming control of a shared resource, and thereby depriving Hungary of its right to an equitable and reasonable share of the natural resources of the Danube—with continuing effects on the ecology of the riparian area of the Szigetköz—failed to respect the proportionality which is required by international law'. In this case, the environmental effects of large-scale water diversion had a significant impact on the overall equitable balance.

[103] See *supra*, Ch 8.

[104] See *Pulp Mills Case*, ICJ Reports (2010) 14; Fuentes, 69 *BYIL* (1998) 162–3; and *infra*, sections 2(3) & (4).

[105] Other approaches, such as abuse of rights or good neighbourliness are sometimes referred to in the literature but there is no evidence that these reflect international practice or afford additional bases for resolving pollution disputes: Lester, 57 *AJIL* (1963) 833ff; Sette Camara, 186 *Recueil des Cours* (1984) 164 ff.

[106] 1997 UN Watercourses Convention, Articles 20–21; *infra*, section 2(4).

[107] See *infra*, Ch 8.

[108] See ILA, Berlin Rules, Article 13; Helsinki Rules, Articles IV and X, *Rept of 52nd Conference* (1966) 484, 496–7; Montreal Rules on Pollution, Article 1, *Rept of 60th Conference* (1982) 531–5; Seoul Complementary Rules, Article 1, *Rept of 62nd Conference* (1986) 232.

[109] ICJ Reports (1997) 7, para 85.

The most contested view is that pollution, or environmental damage, will only be impermissible if, but only if, another state is thereby deprived of its claim to equitable utilization of the waters.[110] Advocates of this position argue that in determining the permissibility of pollution or other environmentally harmful uses, equitable utilization must take precedence over competing principles, including any obligation to prevent potential harm to other states. This approach, it is said, ensures that upstream states are not prevented from developing new uses for their watercourses in ways that might adversely affect established uses in downstream states. If this is correct, then 'an equitable use by one state could cause "appreciable" or "significant" harm to another state using the same watercourse, yet not entail a legal "injury" or be otherwise wrongful'.[111] If, alternatively, 'A watercourse state's right to utilize an international watercourse in an equitable and reasonable manner finds its limit in the duty of that state not to cause appreciable harm to other watercourse states',[112] then dams or irrigation projects that would reduce the flow of water could be constructed only with the consent of affected states.

Upstream states were generally most in favour of equitable utilization as the controlling principle during negotiation of the UN Watercourses Convention; downstream states were naturally more concerned to secure a greater and more predictable level of protection than would result from equitable balancing.[113] These competing views were reflected in the long-standing debate within the ILC over the drafting and relative priority of Articles 5 and 7 of the Convention, dealing respectively with equitable utilization and the prevention of harm to other states.[114]

There are four problems with giving equitable utilization priority over obligations to prevent harm, including environmental harm. First, the apparent conflict between these principles is unreal and often based on a misunderstanding of the obligation to prevent harm in international law.[115] This is not an absolute obligation—international law simply does not prohibit all transboundary harm, even through the medium of a river. For that reason, as explained in Chapter 3, it is misleading to suggest, as many commentators on international watercourse law do, that there is a 'no harm principle' in international law. As we saw in Chapter 3, what international law requires is that states take adequate steps to control and regulate sources of transboundary harm within their territory or subject to their jurisdiction. Thus formulated, the obligation is one of conduct, of due diligence, rather than an outright prohibition.[116] If this is correct—and

110 See e.g. Bourne, 3 *CYIL* (1965) 187; Handl, 13 *CYIL* (1975) 156; id, 14 *RBDI* (1978) 40.

111 McCaffrey, II *YbILC* (1986) Pt 1, 133ff. See also Schwebel, ibid, (1982) Pt 1, 103, draft Article 8(1) and Handl, 13 *CYIL* (1975) 180.

112 *ILC Report* (1988) GAOR A/43/10, 84.

113 Crook and McCaffrey, 91 *AJIL* (1997) 374; Rahman, 19 *Fordham ILJ* (1995) 24.

114 See McCaffrey, 17 *Denver JILP (1989)* 505–10; Handl, 3 *Colorado JIELP* (1992) 123; Bourne, 35 *CYIL* (1997) 222. For the final ILC commentary on the issue see II *YbILC* (1994) Pt 2, 96–105. Only four states voted against Articles 5–7 as finally adopted: China, France, Turkey, and Tanzania.

115 McCaffrey, 4th Rept, UN Doc A/CN 4/412/Add 2 (1988); Fuentes, 69 *BYIL* (1998) 135–45. But cf Handl, 3 *Colorado JIELP* (1992) 123.

116 II *YbILC* (1994) Pt2, 103, 124. Redgwell, in Jayakumar et al, *Transboundary Pollution*, 13–16 summarises the key point, and see generally *supra*, Ch 3, section 5.

the state practice, treaties and case law overwhelmingly show that it is[117]—then there is no real need to determine whether equitable utilization takes precedence or not. A state which fails to do its best to control avoidable harm to another state cannot easily maintain that it is acting equitably or reasonably, whichever principle prevails. Neither does an obligation to do its best to minimize unnecessary or avoidable harm to other states impede the reasonable and equitable development of a watercourse or the use of its waters in whatever way a state chooses. Unavoidable harm to a downstream state is not unlawful unless it is inequitable.[118]

Secondly, the evidence for applying equitable balancing to obligations of pollution control or environmental protection of international watercourses is weak. None of the treaties which regulate these matters does so.[119] Nor do the *Pulp Mills* or the *Border Activities/San Juan River Cases*.[120] The *Lac Lanoux Case* held only that a diversion of the waters which caused no injury to Spain and which was accompanied by a full opportunity for consultation did not require her consent or violate any international obligation.[121] Handl's argument that the case confirms recourse to a balancing of interests as a means of determining responsibility for pollution injury rests on slender inference from Spanish interpretation of the relevant treaty.[122] Indeed, by accepting that 'only a limited amount of damage' might be caused to other states, Spain's argument rather points in the opposite direction.[123] Reliance on *Trail Smelter*[124] to support a balance of interests is similarly unconvincing, because this interpretation confuses responsibility for harm with the availability of injunctive relief under a *compromis*.[125] This factor also makes analogous decisions of federal courts questionable precedents on the role of equity in water pollution cases.[126] On the contrary, the US decisions relied on in *Trail Smelter*, and the *Trail Smelter Case* itself, insist that states have no right to cause serious injury by pollution, not that they have no right to cause inequitable or unreasonable injury.[127]

Thirdly, Article 5 of the 1997 Convention itself indicates that the equitable and reasonable use of a watercourse must be consistent both with sustainable use and with the 'adequate protection of the watercourse'. The ILC commentary notes that this provision is meant to cover, inter alia, conservation, water flow, and control of pollution, drought and salinity, and that it 'may limit to some degree the uses that might be made of the waters'. Equitable use is thus not an unfettered right.[128]

Finally, the view that ecological factors can only constrain inequitable uses of an international watercourse allows insufficient weight to be given to the principle of sustainable development. As we saw in Chapter 3, sustainable development entails the integration of environmental protection and economic development. Integration is

[117] Ibid. [118] See *supra*, Ch 3, section 5(6). [119] See *infra*, section 2(3).
[120] *Supra*, Ch 3, section 5(6). [121] 24 *ILR* (1957) 101, 111–12, 123–4. See Lester, 57 *AJIL* (1963) 838ff.
[122] Handl, 13 *CYIL* (1975) 180f. Cf Handl, 26 *NRJ* (1986) 405, 421f, however.
[123] At 124. [124] 33 *AJIL* (1939) 184 and 35 *AJIL* (1941) 684.
[125] But cf Dickstein, 12 *Columbia JTL* (1973) 493ff.
[126] Lammers, *Pollution of International Watercourses*, 486ff. [127] Handl, 26 *NRJ* (1986) 421f.
[128] II *YbILC* (1994) Pt 2, 97. On sustainable use see *infra*, section 2(5).

not simply a matter of equitable balancing between competing factors, however; it is a process which involves continuing obligations of environmental impact assessment, monitoring, and preventive action which cannot be disregarded merely because the proposed use is equitable. This much appears to have been recognized by the ICJ in the *Gabčíkovo-Nagymaros Case*.[129]

Among international codifications, only the 1966 ILA Helsinki Rules explicitly require states to prevent pollution injury 'consistent with the principle of equitable utilization'.[130] This provision purports to rely mainly on *Trail Smelter* and other authorities considered here; not surprisingly it has been strongly criticized.[131] The 1997 UN Watercourses Convention and the 2002 ILA Berlin Articles adopt a different approach. First, Article 6 of the UN Watercourses Convention includes ecological factors and protection and conservation of the watercourse as relevant factors when determining whether a use is equitable. This is uncontroversial, as reflected in the ICJ's judgment in *Gabčíkovo*. Secondly, Article 7(1) codifies a general obligation to take all appropriate measures when utilizing an international watercourse to prevent significant harm to other watercourse states, but in terms which recognize this as an obligation of due diligence, not an absolute prohibition of all harm.[132] The current ICJ case law reflects the same view of customary international law.[133] Thirdly, Articles 20 and 21 explicitly require watercourse states to protect and preserve international watercourse ecosystems and to prevent, reduce and control pollution of a watercourse causing significant harm to other states, their environment, their use of the waters, or the living resources of the watercourse.[134]

The only plausible reading of Articles 7(1), 20, and 21 is that these obligations of due diligence are not themselves subject to equitable balancing but must be complied with independently of any claim of equitable utilization.[135] Bourne summarizes the point clearly:

> if a state is acting within its rights as defined in Articles 5 and 6, it is under a duty to prevent, eliminate, or mitigate harm to other watercourse states by all appropriate, presumably

129 ICJ Reports (1997) para 140, and see *infra*, section 2(5).

130 Article 10(1). The commentary notes, at 499: 'the international duty stated in this article regarding abatement or the taking of reasonable measures is not an absolute one. This duty, therefore, does not apply to a state whose use of the waters is consistent with the equitable utilization of the drainage basin.' See also 1982 ILA Montreal Rules on Transfrontier Pollution, Article 1, and the 1973 Draft Declaration of the Asian-African Legal Consultative Committee, II *YbILC* (1974) Pt 2, 338.

131 Dickstein, 12 *Columbia JTL* (1973) 495ff; Handl, 26 *NRJ* (1986) 421ff.

132 See McCaffrey and Sinjela, 92 *AJIL* (1998) 100; Bourne, 35 *CYIL* (1997) 223–5, and *supra*, Ch 3, section 5(5). An explicit requirement to 'exercise due diligence' in the ILC's 1994 draft of Article 7 was altered to read 'take all appropriate measures' in the 1997 Convention text, but no change in meaning results. Compare the ILC's 1991 draft Article 7, which read: 'Watercourse states shall utilize an international watercourse in such a way as not to cause appreciable harm to other watercourse states.' For a cogent explanation of the background and implications of this change see Benvenisti, *Sharing Transboundary Resources*, 161–8.

133 *Gabčíkovo-Nagymaros Case*, ICJ Reports (1997) 7; *Pulp Mills Case*, ICJ Reports (2010) 14; *Border Activities/San Juan River Cases*, ICJ Reports (2015).

134 See next section.

135 Salman, 41 *NRJ* (2001) 981, at 1007–10 argues otherwise but his treatment is tendentious and unsupported by the cases and the literature that he cites. It is also inconsistent with *Pulp Mills* and the *Border Activities/San Juan River Cases*.

reasonable measures; in short it must act without malice and with due diligence—a proposition that is not disputed.[136]

However, where *despite taking all appropriate measures* significant harm nevertheless results, Article 7(2) then, but only then, requires the parties to negotiate an equitable solution. At this point, equity does take over in defining the rights of the parties. As McCaffrey points out, Article 7(2) acknowledges that harm may in some cases have to be tolerated; he concludes that 'The facts and circumstances of each case, rather than any *a priori* rule, will ultimately be the key determinants of the rights and obligations of the parties.'[137] This approach is largely consistent with the ILC's draft Articles on the Prevention of Transboundary Harm: it accepts that unavoidable harm is not per se wrongful or prohibited, but that a failure to mitigate or compensate for it may be inequitable.[138] Precisely what the rights of watercourse states are in this situation cannot be stated with precision, beyond saying that they must negotiate and that the factors listed in Article 6 of the 1997 UN Watercourses Convention will be relevant. At the same time, the Convention as a whole suggests that the general requirement to exercise due diligence to prevent avoidable harm to the environment of other states applies to the use of international watercourses in the same way that it applies to other activities within a state's jurisdiction or control. Again, none of the ICJ case law suggests otherwise.

Equitable balancing is thus applicable to pollution and environmental protection of international watercourses in two situations only: where the harm is less than 'significant', or where it is significant but unavoidable by the exercise of due diligence. In carrying out this balancing process, two points are particularly relevant to pollution and environmental issues. First, where potential uses conflict, such as industrial waste disposal and fishing, no priority can be assumed. While some treaties do establish a priority, there is no settled practice and each river must be considered individually.[139] Article 10 of the 1997 UN Watercourses Convention recognizes this point by providing that no category of use has inherent preference over any others. Subject to giving 'special regard' to 'vital human needs' and exercising due diligence, as required by Articles 20 and 21, protection of the river environment and its living resources must compete with other equitable claims.[140]

Secondly, there is no automatic preference for established uses. An inflexible rule protecting such uses would in effect allow the creation of servitudes. These have not generally found favour with states.[141] Instead, commentators and the views of

136 Bourne, 35 *CYIL* (1997) 225.

137 McCaffrey and Sinjela, 92 *AJIL* (1998) 101–2. See also Bourne, 35 *CYIL* (1997) 223–5.

138 *Supra*, Ch 3, section 4(1). Note also the agreed statement of understanding adopted with regard to Article 7(2): 'In the event such steps as are required by article 7(2) do not eliminate the harm, such steps as are required by article 7(2) shall then be taken to mitigate the harm': UNGA, 51st Session, *Rept of the 6th Committee Working Group*, GAOR A/51/869 (1997) para 8.

139 See e.g. 1909 Boundary Waters Treaty, Article VIII; 1960 Indus Waters Treaty, Articles 3, 4; 1976 Rhine Chemicals Convention, Article 1.

140 *Infra*, section 2(6).

141 Lester, 57 *AJIL* (1963) 834ff.

codification bodies suggest that an equitable balance of interests may in an appropriately strong case allow for the displacement or limitation of earlier established uses. At most these earlier uses enjoy a weighty claim to qualified preference.[142] European and North American practice referred to earlier seems consistent with this conclusion, which the *Lac Lanoux Case* implicitly supports.[143]

Equitable utilization is useful as a means of introducing environmental factors into the allocation of shared watercourse resources, but as a basis for comprehensive environmental protection of those watercourses it is a principle of only modest utility. Not only is it unpredictable in application, through its stress on the individuality of each river and the multiplicity of relevant factors, but it tends to neglect the broader environmental context of rivers as part of a hydrologic cycle affecting terrestrial ecosystems and the health of the oceans.[144] Moreover, the common regional standards of water quality necessary in that context are less likely to find a place in equitable arrangements balancing only the needs of riparians. As Handl observes, 'it is entirely conceivable that ecological factors, to the extent they are of actual or potential concern to other riparian states, might after all be insufficiently taken into account or altogether disregarded in a solution that primarily promotes the interests—and at that perhaps those of a socio-economic nature at the cost of ecological ones—of the directly involved states'.[145]

As we have seen, equitable utilization is generally workable on a multilateral basis only if supported by appropriate institutions and coordinated policies. Thus, only as part of the trend to common management and international regulation of transboundary watercourses does it have a role in resolving environmental disputes.[146]

2(3) PREVENTION OF TRANSBOUNDARY POLLUTION AND ENVIRONMENTAL HARM

The proposition that states are under a customary obligation to take appropriate measures to prevent or minimize significant transboundary harm through their use of an international watercourse is now well established in the case law, including the *Gabčíkovo-Nagymaros, Pulp Mills, Indus Waters Kishenganga* and the *Border Activities/San Juan River Cases*.[147] Article 7 of the 1997 UN Watercourses Convention states the general principle, which successive rapporteurs and the ILC have regarded as a codification of established customary law for all forms of damage to other states.[148] In defining the threshold at which this obligation operates, the ILC initially preferred the term 'appreciable harm', meaning more than perceptible, but less than 'serious'

142 ILA Helsinki Rules, Articles V(d) VII, VIII, and commentary at 493.

143 Bourne, 3 *CYIL* (1965) 187, 234–53. See also the position taken by Chile in the *Waters of the Silala Case*.

144 See *infra*, Ch 8.

145 Handl, 13 *CYIL* (1975) 191f.

146 A point recognized by Article 5(2) of the 1997 UN Convention.

147 *Supra*, Ch 3, section 5.

148 Schwebel, II *YbILC* (1992) Pt 1, 91, para 111; Evensen, ibid, (1983) Pt 1, 172; McCaffrey, ibid, (1986) Pt 1, 133; *ILC Report*, GAOR A/43/10 (1988) 88ff. See generally McCaffrey, *Law of International Watercourses*, Ch 11.

or 'substantial'.[149] What it envisaged was harm of some consequence, for example to health, industry, agriculture, or the environment. Subsequent adoption of 'significant' harm as the appropriate threshold in Articles 7 and 21(2) of the 1997 Convention is largely a cosmetic change.[150] The general principle clearly includes pollution or environmental damage, as Article 21(2) goes on to provide:

> Watercourse states shall, individually, and where appropriate, jointly, prevent, reduce and control pollution of an international watercourse that may cause significant harm to other watercourse states or to their environment, including harm to human health or safety, to the use of the waters for any beneficial purpose or to the living resources of the watercourse . . . [151]

In its commentary, the ILC noted that the obligation to 'prevent' in Article 21 relates to new pollution of international watercourses, and 'includes the duty to exercise due diligence to prevent the threat of such harm.'[152] The obligation to 'reduce' and 'control' applies to existing pollution.[153] Article 21 is based on Article 194 of the 1982 UNCLOS and other precedents considered in Chapter 3.[154] The number of watercourse treaties which expressly or implicitly incorporate such an obligation has grown steadily.[155] The *Pulp Mills Case*[156] and the *Border Activities/San Juan River Cases*[157] provide further confirmation of the Commission's view that Article 21(2)'s antecedents are well grounded in state practice.[158]

[149] II *YbILC* (1982) Pt 1, 98, paras 130–41; *ILC Report* (1988) GAOR A/43/10, 85–6.

[150] See *supra*, Ch 3, section 4.

[151] For commentary, see ILC Report (1990) GAOR A/45/10, 159. For earlier versions, see Evensen, *2nd Rept*, I *YbILC* (1984) Pt 1, 118–20, Articles 20–3; Schwebel, *3rd Rept*, II *YbILC* (1982) Pt 1, 144, Article 10, ILC Report (1988) GAOR A/43/10, 57, Article 16(2).

[152] ILC Report, II *YbILC* (1994) Pt 2, 122, para (4). See also *Rept of the 6th Committee*, GAOR A/51/869 (1997) para 8, commentary on articles 21, 22 and 23: 'As reflected in the commentary of the International Law Commission, these articles impose a due diligence standard on watercourse states.'

[153] ILC Report, II *YbILC* (1994) Pt 2, 122, para (4).

[154] ILC Report (1990) GAOR A/45/10, 159ff.

[155] See e.g. 1909 Boundary Waters Treaty (US–Canada) Articles II, IV; 1960 Indus Waters Treaty (India–Pakistan) Article 4; 1922 Agreement Relating to Frontier Watercourses (Germany–Denmark); 1960 Convention on the Protection of Lake Constance Against Pollution; 1950 Treaty Concerning the Regime of the Soviet Hungarian Frontier, Article 17; 1960 Treaty Concerning the Course of the Common Frontier (Germany–Netherlands) Article 58; 1976 Convention on the Protection of the Rhine Against Chemical Pollution; 1990 Agreement Concerning Co-operation on Management of Water Resources of the Danube Basin (EC–Austria); Article 3; 1992 UNECE Watercourses Convention, Article 2; 1994 Agreements on Protection of the Rivers Meuse and Scheldt, Article 3,; 1994 Convention on Co-operation for the Protection and Sustainable Use of the Danube River, Articles 5–6; 1994 Agreement on the Protection and Utilization of Transboundary Waters (China–Mongolia) Articles 4, 6; 1995 Mekong River Agreement, Article 7; 1995 Israel–Jordan Peace Treaty, Article 6 and Annexes II, IV; 2000 Protocol on Shared Watercourse Systems in the Southern African Development Community, Article 4(2)(b); 1999 Convention on the Protection of the Rhine, Article 5. See Fuentes, 69 *BYIL* (1998) 145ff; Nollkaemper, *The Legal Regime for Transboundary Water Pollution: Between Discretion and Constraint* (Dordrecht, 1993).

[156] ICJ Reports (2010) 14. See *supra*, Ch 3, section 5.

[157] ICJ Reports (2015).

[158] ILC Report (1988) GAOR A/43/10, 60, para 148 (draft Article 16(2)).

One ILC rapporteur, McCaffrey, dealt with the choice between a standard of due diligence and more stringent obligations of pollution prevention in international watercourses. Although the latter interpretation is implicit in the view of some members of the Commission who continued to favour a regime of strict liability for watercourse pollution, the rapporteur could find little or no evidence of state practice recognizing strict liability for damage which was non-accidental or did not result from a dangerous activity.[159] In his view, this indicated that the standard required of the state was generally one of due diligence, implicit in the *Trail Smelter* arbitration and supported by state practice. This standard afforded the appropriate flexibility and allowed for adaptation to different situations, including the level of development of the state concerned.

McCaffrey's due diligence interpretation is explicit throughout Articles 7, 21(2), and 23 of the 1997 UN Watercourses Convention. Most of the more modern treaties support his view, although others which prohibit environmental harm, or pollution, or specified pollutants, may sustain a stricter interpretation.[160] Thus, although the context and formulation of individual treaties is important and may lead to a different conclusion, the evidence does tend to favour the rapporteur's interpretation of a general duty of due diligence in the regulation and control of transboundary water pollution. Moreover, use of the formula 'prevent, reduce and control' in Article 21 also supports the conclusion that there is no absolute obligation of prevention. In this respect the ILC commentary notes that the practice of states 'indicates a general willingness to tolerate even significant pollution harm, provided that the watercourse state of origin is making its best efforts to reduce the pollution to a mutually acceptable level'.[161] As we saw in chapter 3, the modern case law amply confirms the correctness of McCaffrey's conclusion.[162] The obligation of due diligence requires, inter alia, regulation and administrative control of potentially harmful activities, vigilance in enforcement, adoption of a precautionary approach in situations of scientific uncertainty, and environmental impact assessment, notification and consultation with other States whenever activities pose a risk of significant transboundary harm.[163]

Cooperation between riparians in the elaboration and supervision of detailed standards of pollution control and prevention through international river commissions is, as in other contexts, an important means of giving concrete content to this general

159 *ILC Report* (1988) GAOR A/43/10, 64f.

160 See e.g. Articles 7 and 8 of the 1995 Mekong River Basin Agreement, which require parties to make every effort to 'avoid, minimise and mitigate' harmful effects to the environment, but also call for cessation of uses causing substantial damage, and compensation therefor. In effect this latter provision amounts to a prohibition of such harmful uses.

161 II *YbILC* (1994) Pt 2, 122, para 4, and *ILC Report* (1990) GAOR A/45/10, 161. See also 1992 UNECE Watercourses Convention, Articles 2(2) 3, and *supra*, Ch 3. The same point is evident in Article 5(4)(b) of the 1999 Rhine Convention, which commits the parties only to a gradual reduction in discharges of hazardous substances, but compare 1995 Mekong Agreement, previous note.

162 *Supra*, Ch 3, section 5(5).

163 *Pulp Mills Case*, ICJ Reports (2010) 14, paras 197, 204 and 223; *AO with Respect to Activities in the Area*, ITLOS (2011) paras 110–120, 131–35; 145–9; *Border Activities/San Juan River Cases*, ICJ Reports (2015) paras 104, 153, 168. See *supra*, Ch 3, section 5(5)

obligation of due diligence. Article 21(3) summarizes the practices which are common in most of the modern watercourse treaties: it calls for mutually agreed measures such as establishing lists of prohibited and controlled substances, water quality objectives and criteria, and techniques and practices to deal with point and diffuse sources of pollution.[164] This is what defeated Argentina in the *Pulp Mills Case*: the parties had agreed water quality standards for the River Uruguay and Argentina could not show that effluent from the pulp mill exceeded them. By definition there was no pollution of the river from this source and no breach of the applicable treaty.

The 1992 UNECE Watercourses Convention is more explicit than the 1997 UN Watercourses Convention in certain respects, including specifying that pollution prevention measures shall if possible be taken at source, and be 'guided by' the precautionary principle, the polluter-pays principle, and the needs of future generations. Article 3 requires the development of limits on pollution discharges based on 'best available technology' or 'best environmental practices', emissions reduction through use of non-waste technology, and application of an 'ecosystems approach' to sustainable water resources management. There are additional requirements of environmental impact assessment and monitoring of transboundary impacts. Whether these requirements are stronger than the 1997 UN Convention is doubtful: they are largely reflected in the standard of due diligence applied as general international law by the ICJ in *Pulp Mills*.[165] The UNECE Convention has provided the framework for subsequent negotiation of environmental protection agreements for European rivers, including the 1999 Rhine Convention and the 1994 Danube Convention.[166]

As we saw in Chapter 3, it is difficult to make confident assertions concerning the general applicability of the precautionary principle or approach. From that perspective, the failure of the 1997 UN Convention to refer to precaution is unhelpful, but not necessarily significant. The ILC's view that the precautionary approach is implicit in Articles 20 and 21 of the 1997 UN Watercourses Convention[167] derives support from its inclusion in the 1992 UNECE Watercourses Convention and subsequent European watercourse agreements, although only in its weakest form as guidance to the parties.[168] The precautionary principle or approach is also found in newer agreements on land-based sources of marine pollution, such as the 1992 Paris Convention, which applies to most Western European rivers,[169] and in the 2012 Great Lakes Water Quality Agreement, which covers a significant part of North America.[170] But, as *Pulp Mills* and other cases show, the precautionary approach may affect the interpretation and application of a treaty even if not specifically referred to.[171]

164 See generally, Nollkaemper, *Transboundary Water Pollution*. In this respect the Convention also reflects practice in regional treaties on land-based sources of marine pollution. See *supra*, Ch 8.

165 *Supra*, Ch 3, section 5(5).

166 156 See 1999 Rhine Convention, Articles 3–5; 1994 Danube Convention, Articles 5, 6, 7, and Annex 1; 1994 Agreements on the Meuse and Scheldt, Article 3.

167 II *YbILC* (1994) Pt 2, 120, para 9, and 122, para 4.

168 1992 UNECE Watercourses Convention, Article 2(5); 1999 Rhine Convention, Article 4; 1994 Agreements on the Meuse and Scheldt, Article 3; 1994 Danube Convention, Article 2(4).

169 *Supra*, Ch 9.

170 *Infra*, section 3.

171 *Supra*, Ch 3, section 6.

It is now generally accepted that states have a duty to protect the marine environment, and in particular to control land-based sources of marine pollution. These sources include pollution from rivers. Article 23 of the 1997 UN Watercourses Convention recognizes this point. Corresponding closely to Article 207 of the 1982 UNCLOS, which deals generally with land-based pollution, Article 23 sets no specific standard of conduct beyond an obligation to take all necessary measures to protect estuaries and the marine environment, 'taking into account generally accepted international rules and standards'. The regional-seas treaties considered in Chapter 8 support the underlying implication of the ILC's codification that the basis of pollution control in international rivers is no longer to be found mainly in customary obligations concerning equitable utilization or harm prevention, but in regional regimes employing common standards of environmental protection for river pollution, and in the requirements of international cooperation. As we saw in Chapter 8, there remain problems of coordinating the operation of watercourse and regional seas commissions in a manner which achieves the ILC's objective.

2(4) PROTECTION OF WATERCOURSE ECOSYSTEMS

The environmental obligations of watercourse states are not limited to protecting other states or the marine environment from pollution.[172] As we saw in the previous section, Articles 20 and 22 of the 1997 UN Convention also provide for the protection and preservation of the ecosystems of international watercourses. Moreover, ecosystem protection is at the core of the environmental concerns in all of the modern case law.[173] It is one of the reasons for establishing a minimum flow requirement in the *Indus Waters Kishenganga Case*, while in *Pulp Mills* and the *Certain Activities/ San Juan River Cases* wetlands designated as protected areas under the 1971 Ramsar Convention were potentially at risk.[174]

Articles 20 and 22 are modelled respectively on Articles 192 and 196 of the 1982 UNCLOS. The ILC commentary treats Article 20 as a specific application of the more general rule in Article 5 concerning optimal and sustainable use of an international watercourse 'consistent with the adequate protection thereof,' and it concludes that '[t]here is ample precedent for the obligation contained in Article 20 in the practice of States and the work of international organizations'.[175] The draft article was accepted

172 Moynihan, in Razzaque and Morgera (eds), *Biodiversity and Nature Protection Law* (Cheltenham, 2016); Toope and Brunnée, 91 *AJIL* (1997) 26; Bourne, 35 *CYIL* (1997) 215; Fuentes, 69 *BYIL* (1998) 119; McCaffrey, *The Law of International Watercourses*, Ch 12; Benvenisti, *Sharing Transboundary Resources*, which despite its title is mainly about ecosystem management. On ecosystems see *infra*, Ch 11.

173 E.g. *Pulp Mills Case*, ICJ Reports (2010) 14, paras 188, 214.

174 See McCaffrey, in Jayakumar et al, *Transboundary Pollution*, 100–112. In *Gabčíkovo* Hungary's case turned in part on a report identifying a risk to the Danube's ecosystem. On the 1971 Ramsar Convention see *infra*, Ch 11, section 3(1).

175 II *YbILC* (1994) Pt 2, 119. See also *ILC Report*, GAOR A/45/10 (1990) 147, 169; *Pulp Mills Case*, ICJ Reports (2010) 14, paras 75–143; 170–5.

without opposition in 1997. Article 22 deals with the introduction of new or alien species detrimental to the ecosystem, and according to the ILC it is necessary because 'pollution' does not include biological alterations. There are few precedents for it in other watercourse treaties.[176]

In both articles the obligation to 'protect' or 'preserve' the ecosystem from harm or the threat of harm once again requires the exercise of due diligence. 'Preservation' applies particularly to 'freshwater ecosystems that are in a pristine or unspoiled condition'; according to the ILC, these must be maintained 'as much as possible in their natural state'.[177] The Commission also suggests that Article 20 provides an 'essential basis for sustainable development' and gives priority to maintaining the viability of aquatic ecosystems as life support systems. However, this preservationist interpretation not only goes beyond any concept of equitable balancing, it is inconsistent with the ICJ's more cautious approach to sustainable development in the context of the previously pristine Danube.[178] Where the ILC seeks preservation from development, the ICJ opts merely for integration of environmental protection and economic development.

Reflecting its earlier desire to avoid reference to shared natural resources or drainage basins, the Commission justifies its focus on the watercourse 'ecosystem', rather than the watercourse 'environment', by pointing to the latter's potential inclusion of surrounding land areas. Thus the 'watercourse ecosystem' is not intended to cover areas beyond the watercourse itself.[179] This narrow conception of ecosystem protection is not widely shared,[180] and it has been criticized as a missed opportunity to develop what in policy terms can be seen as a desirable basis for water management.[181] However, the ILC commentary goes on to define an ecosystem as 'an ecological unit consisting of living and non-living components that are interdependent and function as a community' and thus comes close to recognizing that interdependence cannot be confined to the watercourse alone; a major watercourse system or basin will cover a multiplicity of 'ecosystems' existing—or coexisting—at various levels of interdependence within and beyond the physical confines of the watercourse itself.[182] Thus defined, an 'ecosystem' is indistinguishable from 'the environment' as used in

[176] But see 2000 Protocol on Shared Watercourse Systems in the Southern African Development Community, Article 4(2)(c). For ILC Commentary see II *YbILC* (1994) Pt 2, 122.

[177] II *YbILC* (1994) Pt 2, 119. See also *South China Sea Arbitration*, PCA (2016) para 941, where the tribunal interpreted UNCLOS Article 192: 'This "general obligation" extends both to "protection" of the marine environment from future damage and "preservation" in the sense of maintaining or improving its present condition.'

[178] See *Gabčíkovo-Nagymaros Case*, ICJ Reports (1997) 7, *supra*, Ch 3, section 2. See also *Pulp Mills Case (Interim Measures)*, ICJ Reports (2006) 113. For a different view of Article 20 see *infra*, and see also Bourne, 35 *CYIL* (1997) 215.

[179] II *YbILC* (1994) Pt 2, 118.

[180] Compare Article 2 of the 1999 Rhine Convention, which applies to 'aquatic *and terrestrial* ecosystems which interact or could again interact with the Rhine', and 1995 Mekong Agreement, Articles 3 and 7, requires the parties to protect inter alia the 'ecological balance' of the Mekong River basin. For other examples see *infra*, this section. Contrast the narrower approach taken by the ICJ in *Border Activities/San Juan River Cases*, ICJ Reports 2015, paras 209–13, which focuses on fish, invertebrates and algae in the river.

[181] Toope and Brunnée, 91 *AJIL* (1997) 26. But cf Fuentes, 69 *BYIL* (1998) 119.

[182] II *YbILC* (1994) Pt 2, 118.

Article 21, which according to the Commission includes 'flora and fauna dependent on the watercourse'. It is doubtful if the Commission's careful choice of terminology really does confine the potential scope of this obligation in a meaningful way. Any attempt to protect a river 'ecosystem' cannot avoid affecting the surrounding land areas or their 'environment'.

A final problem which Article 20 throws up but fails to answer is the question of whose ecosystem it protects. Is the article aimed at protecting watercourse ecosystems in downstream states from harm caused by upstream states? Or is it also, or only, aimed at requiring an upstream state to protect its own watercourse ecosystem? Only if it does both is it consistent with a full ecosystem approach.[183] The subsequent articles of Part IV of the 1997 UN Watercourses Convention are all concerned with harm to other states or the marine environment and can be said to codify existing customary law on these matters. This may suggest that Article 20 is merely a chapeau to these articles and must accordingly be construed narrowly, thereby eliminating from its scope any ecosystem damage that remains purely internal in character. If this is correct, then the ecosystem approach endorsed by the Convention is further narrowed.[184] However, the ILC commentary clearly views watercourse ecosystem protection as a specific application of a more general obligation to protect ecosystems, regardless of any transboundary impact.[185] This view does make sense, since it recognizes the ecological unity of the watercourse and the artificiality of international boundaries when ecosystem management is imperative. Article 20 may thus imply that the legal obligations attaching to the use and management of an international watercourse are no longer determined solely by its transboundary aspects, but also apply to internal environmental protection. That would make ecosystem protection within one state a matter of common concern for all the riparians.[186]

It is thus apparent that the 1997 UN Watercourses Convention is ambiguous, and possibly even confused, in the scope and depth of its commitment to watercourse ecosystem protection. Not surprisingly, Article 20 has been criticized both for going beyond customary law and for not being ambitious enough in developing the law on an ecosystem basis.[187] It is also true that whatever its merits, comprehensive ecosystem protection remains an underdeveloped concept in general international law, and that it is not yet possible to conclude that states have a general duty to protect and preserve ecosystems in all areas under their sovereignty.[188] Do regional treaties and practice

[183] Toope and Brunnée, 91 *AJIL* (1997) 26.

[184] Toope and Brunnée, 91 *AJIL* (1997) 26, 51.

[185] II *YbILC* (1994) Pt 2, 120. McCaffrey, *Law of International Watercourses*, 458–60, takes the same view, and concludes that 'unlike Article 21, the obligation is not triggered by significant harm to another watercourse state or the threat thereof'.

[186] Compare *South China Sea Arbitration (Final Award)* PCA (2016) paras 939–41, where the tribunal found China in breach of Article 194(5) of UNCLOS, even though relevant ecosystems were largely within Chinese internal or territorial waters.

[187] Compare Fuentes, 69 *BYIL* (1998) 119, and Toope and Brunnée, 91 *AJIL* (1997) 26. Bourne, 35 *CYIL* (1997) 215, appears to see the article as an expression of the principle of equitable use, and thus of existing customary law.

[188] See *infra*, Ch 11. But for a detailed treatment see Benvenisti, *Sharing Transboundary Resources*, Ch 5.

lend stronger support to the narrower proposition that there is a developing obligation with regard to watercourse ecosystems?

It has been argued that the 1992 UNECE Watercourses Convention makes a more significant commitment to watercourse ecosystem protection than the 1997 UN Watercourses Convention.[189] Article 2(2) specifically requires parties to 'ensure conservation and, where necessary, restoration of ecosystems', and Article 3 calls for measures to promote sustainable water resource management and 'the application of the ecosystems approach'. Both provisions are placed within articles expressly aimed at preventing or controlling transboundary impact and all the subsequent monitoring and control provisions focus on transboundary rather than internal impacts. This may indicate no greater commitment to comprehensive ecosystem protection than the UN Convention. However, the 1997 UNECE Helsinki Declaration[190] committed the parties to regulating internal waters in accordance with appropriate provisions of the UNECE Convention in order to ensure consistency with the management of transboundary waters. The parties also adopted a programme of integrated management of water and related ecosystems. Moreover, treaties governing the Rhine, the Danube, the Meuse, and the Scheldt, all of which were negotiated in accordance with the 1992 UNECE Watercourses Convention, show a similarly broad commitment to ecosystem protection. They do not deal only with transboundary impacts, nor do they adopt a narrow definition of the relevant ecosystem.[191] Modern watercourse agreements between developing states follow a comparable pattern. The 1995 Mekong Agreement is the most comprehensive. It requires the parties to protect the environment, natural resources, aquatic life, and 'ecological balance' of the Mekong River basin, and to avoid or minimize harmful effects.[192]

These agreements support the ILC's conclusion that ecosystem protection is a developing element in the law and practice of states relating to international watercourses, and they suggest that Article 20 of the 1997 UN Watercourses Convention should not be interpreted too narrowly or limited to the control of transboundary harm. It is also noteworthy that in no case are obligations of ecosystem protection or preservation subject to equitable balancing; this does not mean, however, that they necessarily take precedence over watercourse development, or that ecosystems must be preserved from all development. The overriding objective of sustainable development is acknowledged, especially in developing country agreements.[193] In effect therefore, a balance is required, integrating economic and social development on the one hand and ecosystem

[189] Toope and Brunnée, 91 *AJIL* (1997) 26. On the 1992 Convention see *supra*, n 6.

[190] 1st Meeting of the Parties, *supra*, n 6.

[191] 1994 Danube Convention, Article 2(3) (5); 1994 Agreements on the Protection of the Meuse and Scheldt, Article 3; 1999 Rhine Convention, Articles 2, 3, 5. See also 1990 Elbe Convention which requires parties to cooperate to achieve a healthy diversity of river species and as natural an ecosystem as possible.

[192] Articles 3, 7. See also 1994 China–Mongolia Treaty on Joint Watercourses, Article 4; 1994 Israel–Jordan Peace Treaty, Annex IV; 2000 Southern African Protocol, Articles 4(2((a) & (c).

[193] See e.g. 2000 Protocol on Shared Watercourses on the SADC; 1995 Mekong River Treaty; 1999 Rhine Convention; 1994 Agreements on the Rivers Meuse and Scheldt. And see 1992 Dublin Statement on Water and Sustainable Development; 1998 Declaration of the UN Conference on Water and Sustainable Development, UN Doc E/CN 17/1998/16, Annex 9/4 (1998).

and environmental protection on the other, and it is in this sense that the ILC's references to protection and preservation of ecosystems probably should be understood.[194]

2(5) THE RELEVANCE OF OTHER ENVIRONMENTAL AGREEMENTS

As we saw in Chapter 1 it is important to ensure a coherent relationship between environmental agreements and with the rest of international law. A notable feature of the modern case law on international watercourses is the willingness to interpret older river treaties in accordance with modern international environmental law, even when the applicable treaty contains no specific reference to the protection of the 'environment' or the preservation of 'ecosystems'.[195] Like the agreements in those cases, the wording of Articles 20 and 21 of the 1997 UN Watercourses Convention allows evolutionary interpretation in accordance with international law.[196] At the very least the references to protection and preservation of 'ecosystems' and the 'environment' will include conservation of biological diversity, protection and preservation of wetlands of international importance, and of endangered species.[197] Moreover, as we saw in Chapter 8, the now extensive system of regional treaties on land-based sources of pollution supplies some of the same ecosystem protection for otherwise non-international watercourses.

The 1992 CBD and the 1971 Ramsar Convention also place important ecological obligations on states affecting both international and non-international watercourses,[198] so the totality of the applicable law extends well beyond specific watercourse agreements or the UN or UNECE Watercourse Conventions. These considerations are recognized in a few watercourse treaties.[199] Once watercourse ecosystem protection and sustainable use of water resources are embraced by international law, a sharp division between international and non-international watercourses becomes much more difficult to maintain.

2(6) SUSTAINABILITY AND CONSERVATION OF WATER RESOURCES

(a) Sustainable development and water resources law

As the *Gabčíkovo-Nagymaros* and *Pulp Mills Cases* show, international watercourse development is constrained in part by the limits of equitable use, in part by evolving environmental obligations, and in part by considerations of sustainable development.[200] In *Pulp Mills* the ICJ noted that 'the present case highlights the importance of

194 See *infra*, section 2(6).

195 See in particular the *Indus Waters Kishenganga Arbitration (Partial Award)* PCA (2013); *Pulp Mills Case*, ICJ Reports (2010) 14; *Gabčíkovo-Nagymaros Case*, ICJ Reports (1997) 7. See McCaffrey, in Jayakumar et al, *Transboundary Pollution*, 100–110.

196 1969 VCLT, Article 31(3)(c) on which see *supra*, Ch 1, section 2(3)(a).

197 See *South China Sea Arbitration (Final Award)* PCA (2016) paras 945, 954–60, and see also 1971 Ramsar Convention, *infra*, Ch 11, section 3(1), where the same points are reflected in the text.

198 See de Chazournes, *Fresh Water in International Law*, 131–146; Moynihan in Razzaque and Morgera (eds), *Biodiversity and Nature Protection Law*, and *infra*, Ch 11.

199 See 1990 Elbe Convention, Article 1(2); 1999 Rhine Convention, Article 3(1).

200 *Supra*, Ch 3, section 2(1).

the need to ensure environmental protection of shared natural resources while allowing for sustainable economic development'.[201] In Chapter 3 it was argued that sustainable development is best viewed as an objective or consideration to guide national or international policies or decisions on resource use, rather than as substantive standard appropriate for judicial review and determination. The implications of sustainable development are thus primarily procedural. What is required is a process which integrates both development objectives and environmental protection, and which takes account of future as well as present needs. The balance which emerges from this process is necessarily a value judgement in which neither the environment nor the needs of the future will necessarily prevail. However, it is a judgement which affects not only boundary or transboundary watercourses but all water resources within all states. Unlike equitable utilization, sustainable development is thus not a principle to be applied only in the context of transboundary impacts on other watercourse states, but a principle of general or universal application. A watercourse development may be equitable as between two riparians but it will not necessarily be sustainable if it does not integrate environmental, developmental, and intergenerational considerations in the manner envisaged by the Rio Declaration.

This is not to say that third states are entitled to challenge unsustainable watercourse developments which do not directly affect them, but watercourse states will be entitled to insist on a management process which affords a proper place to sustainable development. This is recognized explicitly in Article 24 of the 1997 UN Watercourses Conventions and it is one of the implicit lessons of the *Gabčíkovo-Nagymaros Case*.[202] It is this perspective which is perhaps the most remarkable feature of watercourse treaties concluded since 1990, and which has begun to alter the existing law on water resources in quite subtle ways, as it has also done for fisheries law.[203] We can see that most of the new watercourse agreements now recognize in some form the importance of sustainable development, sustainable use, or sustainable management as an aim or objective.[204] Environmental protection obligations in these agreements are no longer confined to pollution control and transboundary damage, but require a more comprehensive integration of ecological considerations affecting a watercourse, including impacts on biological diversity, ecosystems, and the marine environment.[205] Water resources must be conserved and used

[201] ICJ Reports (2006) 113, para 80.

[202] At paras 140–2. See also *Pulp Mills Case*, ICJ Reports (2006) 113 and ICJ Reports (2010) 14, para 77.

[203] On fisheries law see Boyle and Freestone (eds), *International Law and Sustainable Development* (Oxford, 1999) especially Chs 6–8, and *infra*, Ch 12.

[204] 1988 Agreement on the Zambezi River, Preamble; 1992 UNECE Watercourses Convention, Preamble, Articles 2, 3; 1994 Danube Convention, Preamble, Article 2; 1994 Conventions on the Meuse and Scheldt, Article 3; 1995 Mekong River Basin Agreement, Article 1; 1995 SADC Protocol on Shared Watercourses, Preamble, Article 2, with 2000 Revised Protocol, Article 2; 1999 Rhine Convention, Preamble, Articles 3, 4; 1997 UN Watercourses Convention, Preamble, Articles 5, 6, 24; 1999 Rhine Convention, Preamble, Articles 3, 4; 1999 UNECE Protocol on Water and Health, Articles 1, 4. See also 1992 UNCED, *Agenda 21*, Ch 18; 1992 Dublin Statement on Water and Sustainable Development; 1998 Declaration of the UN Conference on Water and Sustainable Development, UN Doc E/CN 17/1998/16, Annex.

[205] See previous sections.

sustainably. In many cases the precautionary principle is to be applied by governments and watercourse commissions when taking decisions or adopting policies concerning watercourse management.[206] Nor is this emphasis on sustainability confined to rivers in the developed world: it is equally evident in treaties such as the 1987 Agreement on the Action Plan for the Environmentally Sound Management of the Common Zambezi River System, the 1995 and 2000 Protocols on Shared Watercourse Systems in the Southern African Development Community, or the 1995 Agreement on Cooperation for the Sustainable Development of the Mekong River Basin.[207]

Moreover, although as we saw earlier the 1997 UN Watercourses Convention does not alter existing treaties,[208] the *Gabčíkovo-Nagymaros* and *Pulp Mills Cases* illustrate how older watercourse treaties may be affected by the objective of sustainable development and the need to integrate environmental and economic considerations in an inter-generational perspective. The ICJ found in *Gabčíkovo* that although a bilateral treaty dating from 1977 continues to govern the operation of the dam, it does so not in static isolation but in dynamic conjunction with other rules and principles of international law relating to international watercourses, sustainable development, and environmental protection.[209] In effect the Court interpreted the 1977 treaty by reference to these newer rules, while at the same time drawing heavily on the principal obligations codified in the 1997 UN Watercourses Convention. It was this approach which enabled the Court to hold that, notwithstanding the 1977 Treaty's silence on the subject, the monitoring of environmental effects is a continuing obligation for the parties under general international law, and that new norms of international law, including those relevant to sustainable development, have to be taken into account for continuing activities as well as for new developments. The Court took the same approach to a 1975 treaty in *Pulp Mills,* reading into it, inter alia, an obligation to conduct an EIA, as required by customary international law.[210]

This approach has similar implications for the interpretation of other older watercourse treaties, such as those governing the Nile or the Indus.[211] In addition, it shows that watercourse agreements are neither self-contained regimes,[212] nor do they freeze the applicable law at the date of the conclusion of the relevant treaty. A watercourse treaty governs what it governs—if, for example, it makes no provision for environmental impact assessment or monitoring of future projects, there is no evident reason why the general law on EIA and monitoring should not apply, unless of course the treaty expressly or impliedly excludes it.[213] Problems remain in determining the

206 1992 UNECE Watercourses Convention, Article 2; 1994 Danube Convention, Article 2(4); 1994 Conventions on the Meuse and Scheldt, Article 2(3); 1999 Rhine Convention, Article 4; 1999 UNECE Protocol on Water and Health, Article 5(a) 2012 Great Lakes Water Quality Agreement, Article 2(4).

207 See *infra*, section 3.

208 Article 3; see *supra*, section 1(2)(d).

209 At paras 112, 140.

210 See *supra*, Ch 3, section 7.

211 See *Indus Waters Kishenganga Arbitration (Partial Award)* PCA (2013) paras 447–452.

212 On self-contained regimes see *Case Concerning Diplomatic and Consular Staff in Tehran,* ICJ Reports (1980) 3, and Simma, 16 *NYIL* (1985) 111.

213 See *Border Activities/San Juan Rivers Cases,* ICJ Reports (2015) 665, and *supra*, Ch 3, section 7.

precise relationship between such a treaty and general law, but the Court's conclusion that the law governing a complex and ongoing project of this kind cannot be viewed in static terms is surely correct.

(b) Sustainable utilization and the right to water

The obligation of states to utilize their natural resources sustainably was considered in Chapter 3. As we saw there, it has become a prominent element in post-1992 treaties concerned with tropical timber and straddling and highly migratory fish stocks. Article 5 of the 1997 UN Watercourses Convention also refers to attaining 'optimal and sustainable utilization'[214] of international watercourses, while the 1992 UNECE Watercourses Convention requires parties to reduce transboundary impacts by ensuring 'sustainable water-resources management'.[215] Similarly, the 1995 Mekong River Basin Agreement calls for cooperation in 'sustainable development, utilization, management and conservation of water', and it goes on to lay down rules to maintain minimum water flows during dry periods.[216] There is enough evidence here to show that sustainable utilization is at least an evolving element of international watercourses law, and an essential element if the objectives of sustainable development and international policy are to be fully realized.[217]

It is relatively easy to see what the concept of sustainable use means when applied to tropical timber or fish: use should be non-exhaustive, that is the resource should as far as possible be conserved so that it is available indefinitely.[218] Conservation in this sense is not a new element in international watercourses law. Fuentes points out that it was relevant to establishing an equitable regime for the Indus River in 1942 and 1960. She concludes that intentional or negligent wastefulness demonstrates the absence of any real need for the water.[219] Article 5 of the ILA's 1966 Helsinki Rules reflects this by listing 'the avoidance of unnecessary waste' as an equitable factor. Article 6 of the 1997 UN Watercourses Convention prefers 'conservation, protection, development and economy of use...... and the costs of measures taken to that effect'. This formulation allows for lack of means as a justification.

In some cases wasteful use is more than merely an element in an equitable balance. The 1992 UNECE Watercourses Conventionrequires states to take all appropriate measures to ensure the conservation of transboundary waters,[220] while the Mekong Agreement calls for cooperation in this respect. Pollution is arguably one form of

214 On the principle of 'optimal utilization', see Hafner, 45 *Austrian JPIL* (1993) 45. Cf ILA Berlin Rules, Article 7, which requires states to take 'all appropriate measures to manage waters sustainably'. This is not limited to international waters.

215 Article 3. See also 1994 Danube Convention, Article 2; 1999 Rhine Convention, Article 3(1) but this agreement does not refer to sustainable use as such.

216 Articles 1, 6.

217 See in particular 2002 World Summit on Sustainable Development, *Plan of Implementation*, UN Doc A/CONF 199/20, 6, paras 23–8 and Epiney, 63 *ZAÖRV* (2003) 377.

218 See *supra*, Ch 3, section 3(2).

219 69 *BYIL* (1998) 179–85.

220 Article 2. See also 1994 Danube Convention, Article 2.

'unnecessary' waste of water, and the development of stronger controls on harmful emissions will also contribute to conservation of water resources.

More often the problem affecting international watercourses is not wasteful or exhaustive use but priority between competing uses, and the question is not whether a use is sustainable, but sustainable for what purpose? As Article 10 of the 1997 UN Watercourses Convention indicates, '[i]n the absence of agreement or custom to the contrary, no use of an international watercourse enjoys inherent priority over other uses'. At the same time the article goes on to accord special regard in any equitable balance to 'vital human needs', suggesting at least an inchoate priority, though without specifying whether these needs are limited to drinking water and sanitation, or also include economic and agricultural needs.[221] Sustaining human life and health as a priority for water resource allocation in situations of scarcity can be supported by reference to international human-rights law, especially the right to life, the right freely to dispose of natural resources, and the right to water itself.[222]

The UN Committee on Economic, Social and Cultural Rights has concluded that states are required to ensure an adequate and accessible supply of water for drinking, sanitation, and nutrition, based on Articles 11 and 12 of the 1966 UN Covenant.[223] These at least would appear to be vital human needs, and a conflicting use is arguably neither sustainable nor equitable if it prevents them from being met.[224] There is little doubt that the UN Watercourses Convention and other watercourses treaties would be interpreted and applied taking these human rights into account.[225] Thus, whatever the legal status of sustainable use as a legal principle, it is clear from these various precedents that, where access to clean water and sanitation is inadequate for human health, applicable human rights standards may be violated.[226] Procedural rights for individuals and NGOs—access to justice and information, and public participation in decision-making affecting access to water—will also be applicable.[227] Inter alia this has implications for privatization of public water supplies and foreign investment in water.[228]

221 The 6th committee commentary indicates that 'In determining "vital human needs" special attention is to be paid to providing sufficient water to sustain human life, including both drinking water and water required for the production of food in order to prevent starvation.' *Rept of the 6th Committee Working Group*, GAOR A/51/869 (1997).

222 See generally de Chazournes, *Fresh Water in International Law*, Ch 5; McCaffrey, 5 *Georgetown IELR* (1992) 1; Benvenisti, 90 *AJIL* (1996) 406ff; Tully, 14 *YbIEL* (2003) 101; Fitzmaurice, 18 *Fordham ELR* (2007) 537; Arden, 65 *ICLQ* (2016) 771, and *supra*, Ch 5, section 2(4).

223 UNCESCR, General Comment No 15: The Right to Water, UN Doc E/C 12/2002/11 (2003); WHO, *The Right to Water* (Geneva, 2003). See also UNGA Res 64/292 (2010) and UNHRC Res 15/L.14 (2010) both of which affirm a right to water and sanitation.

224 See 1999 UNECE Protocol on Water and Health. The Protocol takes priority over other less stringent agreements: Article 4 (9).

225 VCLT, article 31(3)(c).

226 See in particular *Xàkmok Kàisek Indigenous Community v Paraguay*, IACtHR (2010); UNESCR, General Comment No 15, para 44(a); de Chazournes, *Fresh Water in International Law*, Ch 5.

227 See 1999 UNECE Protocol on Water and Health; Barral, 67 *ICLQ* (2018) 931, and *supra*, Ch 5, section 2(6).

228 See Viñuales, 21 *Georgetown ELR* (2008–9) 733.

2(7) TRANSBOUNDARY ENVIRONMENTAL COOPERATION

(a) Notification, consultation, and negotiation in cases of environmental risk

Much of the law on this topic has been addressed by the ILC in its 2001 Articles on the Prevention of Transboundary Harm, and by the ICJ in the *Gabčíkovo-Nagymaros* and *Pulp Mills Cases*. There is no need to repeat here the analysis of these and other precedents given in section 8 of Chapter 3.[229] All that remains to be said is that the same procedural requirements apply to activities affecting the uses of international watercourses. That conclusion is amply supported by the 1997 UN Watercourses Convention,[230] case law,[231] and commentators.[232] In this context procedural requirements are particularly important as a means of giving effect to the principle of equitable utilization and for avoiding disputes among riparians over the benefits and burdens of river development.[233]

The inclusion of articles on transboundary notification and consultation in the 1997 UN Watercourses Convention was opposed by only three states, all upstream: Ethiopia, Rwanda and Turkey. As McCaffrey observes, acceptance by most delegations of the basic obligation to provide prior notification is itself important: 'it provides further evidence that the international community as whole emphatically rejects the notion that a state has unfettered discretion to do as it wishes with the portion of an international watercourse within its territory'.[234]

These procedural requirements are generally regarded as applicable where the proposed use of a watercourse creates a risk of significant harm or adverse effects in another state.[235] Moreover, although many older treaties are concerned only with works which affect navigation or the flow or course of a river, the same procedural norms have been applied to the adverse effects of river pollution or the risk of environmental harm.[236] Treaties expressly requiring prior consultation in such cases include the Convention on the Protection of Lake Constance,[237] the 1994 Danube Convention,[238] and the 1974

229 But for an overview see Rieu-Clarke, 24 *YbIEL* (2014) 102.

230 Articles 8–9, 11–19. For commentary see *YbILC* (1994) Pt 2, 105–8; *ILC Report* (1988) GAOR A/43/10, 114ff.

231 *Lac Lanoux Arbitration*, 24 *ILR* (1957) 101; *Gabčíkovo-Nagymaros Case*, ICJ Reports (1997) 7; *Pulp Mills Case*, ICJ Reports (2010) 14. See *supra*, Ch 3, section 8.

232 Kirgis, *Prior Consultation in International Law* (Charlottesville, Va, 1983) Ch 2, reviews the state practice in detail. See generally Leb, *Cooperation in the Law of Transboundary Water Resources* (Cambridge, 2013); McCaffrey, *Law of International Watercourses*, Ch 13; Salman and de Chazournes (eds), *International Watercourses: Enhancing Cooperation and Managing Conflict* (World Bank, 1998).

233 McCaffrey, *2nd Rept*, II *YbILC* (1986) Pt 1, 139.

234 92 *AJIL* (1998) 103.

235 1997 UN Watercourses Convention, Article 12; ILA Berlin Rules, Articles 57, 60; ILA Helsinki Rules, Article XXIX; IDI Salzburg Rules, Articles 4, 5.

236 Kirgis, *Prior Consultation*, 40, 86.

237 1960 Convention on the Protection of Lake Constance Against Pollution, Article 1(3) and see also 1966 Treaty Regulating the Withdrawal of Water from Lake Constance; Kirgis, *Prior Consultation*, 24 observes: 'These two treaties set up a comprehensive prior consultation system for Lake Constance, without requiring prior consent.'

238 Articles 10(f) 11. See also 1990 Agreement Concerning Co-operation on Management of Water Resources in the Danube Basin.

Nordic Convention on the Protection of the Environment.[239] In other treaties, such as the 1973 Agreement between the US and Mexico,[240] references to consultation in case of possible 'adverse effects' or 'transboundary impacts' will also cover pollution or environmental harm, unless as in the case of the 1960 Indus Waters Treaty, their terms are too specific to include consultation in such situations.[241] This conclusion is implicitly supported by the 1997 UN Watercourses Convention, which does not distinguish between consultation in cases of environmental harm or other possible adverse effects. Furthermore, the growing practice of information exchange and consultation, through international river commissions, on the establishment of pollution emission standards, toxic discharges, and measures threatening increased pollution points to an obligation covering these matters even where there is no treaty requirement to consult.[242] Treaties relating to land-based sources of pollution provide further evidence of the importance of this form of institutional consultation machinery in relation to river pollution.[243]

As in other respects, regional patterns may be significant, and Europe and North America offer the most developed examples of cooperation in matters of notification and consultation. But although practice with regard to environmental risks for international watercourses elsewhere is less extensive, there is no evidence of any substantial departure from the general principles under discussion here.[244] Nor has any distinction been drawn in an environmental context between contiguous and successive rivers or lakes.[245] Only a few states, such as Brazil, have previously opposed explicit consultation obligations for successive watercourses, and the normative significance of such practice is questionable.[246]

239 *Supra*, Ch 5, section 3. See also 1994 Israel–Jordan Peace Treaty, Annex II, Article 5.

240 1973 US–Mexico Agreement on the Permanent and Definitive Solution to the International Problem of the Salinity of the Colorado River, Article 6, on which see Kirgis, *Prior Consultation*, 66; 1960 Netherlands–FRG Frontier Treaty, Articles 60–2; Kiss and Lambrechts, 15 *AFDI* (1969) 726ff.

241 This treaty requires consultation only in respect of engineering or hydro-electric works causing interference with waters: Kirgis, *Prior Consultation*, notes: 'the Treaty neither expressly nor by implication requires consultation before new potential pollutants are introduced into the waters', at 44–5.

242 1997 UN Watercourses Convention, Article 21(3). See also 1992 UNECE Watercourses Convention, Articles 9–13; 1994 Danube Convention, Article 12; 1964 Statute Relating to Development of the Chad Basin, Article 5; 1962 Convention Concerning the Protection of the Waters of Lake Geneva Against Pollution, on which see Kiss and Lambrechts, 15 *AFDI* (1969) 732–3; Kirgis, *Prior Consultation*, 25; the same point applies to the Rhine, Moselle, and Saar Commissions and to the 1909 US–Canada Boundary Waters Treaty (Article 9); see Kirgis, op.cit, 28, who notes other examples.

243 See *supra*, Ch 8.

244 See e.g. 1964 Agreement Concerning the Niger River Commission, Article 12; 1964 Statute Relating to Development of the Chad Basin, Articles 5, 6; 1968 African Convention on the Conservation of Nature and Natural Resources, Articles 5(2) 14(3); 1971 Act of Santiago Concerning Hydrologic Basins; 1971 Buenos Aires Declaration on Water Resources; 1971 Act of Buenos Aires on Hydrologic Basins; 1995 Mekong River Basin Agreement; 2000 Protocol on Shared Watercourse Systems in the Southern African Development Community; Kirgis, *Prior Consultation*, 77; Bourne, 22 *UTLJ* (1972) 172.

245 Kirgis, op cit, 26.

246 Brazilian opposition to prior consultation requirements is summarized by Kirgis, op.cit, 72ff. The text of a bilateral agreement of 29 September 1972 between Argentina and Brazil that settled their dispute over consultations with respect to the Parana River was later adopted by the General Assembly as Resolution 2995 (1972). Brazil did not vote against part III of the 1997 UN Watercourses Convention.

While the general principle is beyond serious argument, its application may pose difficulties in particular cases. One of the most difficult questions remains that of deciding who determines when the circumstances require prior notification and consultation. The principle of good faith imports some limit of reasonableness in unilateral assessments by the proposing state, and in the *Lac Lanoux* arbitration, the tribunal observed:

> A state wishing to do that which will affect an international watercourse cannot decide whether another state's interests will be affected; the other state is sole judge of that and has the right to information on the proposals.[247]

Thus the decision is not one for the proposing state alone to take once the possibility of adverse effects is foreseen.[248] The affected state is itself entitled to initiate the process of notification and consultation, if the proposing state does not act.[249]

There is scope for abuse in this formulation, however, which prompted the ILC to prefer a broader, additional, requirement of notification, consultation and negotiation wherever there are 'possible effects' of whatever kind, including beneficial ones.[250] This is complemented by a more general provision for cooperation in the exchange of information relating to the state of the watercourse.[251] Although the 1933 Montevideo Declaration and the 1992 UNECE Watercourses Convention[252] are among a few instruments supporting notification and consultation in situations unqualified by reference to possible adverse effects, some commentators have questioned whether such an extensive obligation represents established law.[253] The most that can be said is that a state must notify and consult wherever a possible conflict of interest exists.

The purpose of prior notification is of course to provide adequate information on which consultation can if necessary take place. An obligation to notify is widely accepted in watercourse treaties and international declarations.[254] It has been treated as customary law by successive rapporteurs of the ILC.[255] However, the regime elaborated in Articles 12 to 19 of the 1997 UN Convention is in certain respects

247 24 *ILR* (1957) 101, 119.

248 Kirgis, *Prior Consultation*, 41 argues: 'Any reasonable doubt must be resolved in favour of notification.'

249 1997 UN Convention, Article 18.

250 1997 UN Convention, Article 11; cf Article 12, and see McCaffrey, 17 *Denver JILP* (1989) 505, 511f; Handl, 3 *Colorado JIELP* (1992) 127–9, and for commentary, II *YbILC* (1994) Pt 2, 111.

251 Article 10; see *infra*, section 2(7)(b).

252 Articles 10, 13. See also 1999 Rhine Convention, Article 5; 1994 Danube Convention, Articles 10(f) 11, 12.

253 See Bourne 22 *UTLJ* (1972) 173ff; Kirgis, *Prior Consultation*, 41, n 146, observes that the *Lac Lanoux* arbitration leaves this question undecided.

254 See *ILC Report* (1988) GAOR A/43/10, 117–24; McCaffrey, *3rd Rept*, II *YbILC* (1987) Pt 1, 28–35, and e.g. 1923 Convention Relating to the Development of Hydraulic Power Affecting More Than One State; 1960 Convention on the Protection of Lake Constance; 1960 Indus Waters Treaty; 1975 Statute of the River Uruguay, Articles 7–12; 1990 Danube Basin Agreement; 1995 Mekong River Basin Agreement.

255 *ILC Report* (1988) 115–26; 1984 draft articles 11, 12; Evensen, *2nd Rept*, II *YbILC* (1984) Pt 1, 114 and *1st Rept*, ibid, (1983) Pt 1, 174–6. See also ILA Helsinki Rules, Article XXIX, and IDI Salzburg Resolution, 1961, Article 5.

a special one.[256] Notification must be timely, allow six months for reply, and contain sufficient information for evaluation of the proposal, including the results of any environmental impact assessment undertaken. The ILC's reports provide substantial evidence of the adoption of these principles in agreements among riparian states, although in certain respects the 1997 UN Watercourses Conventionarticles go beyond international practice, for example in stipulating six months as a reasonable maximum period for reply.[257]

Where notification confirms the existence of a conflict of interests, or where affected states request it, consultation and negotiation are required.[258] The *Lac Lanoux Arbitration* shows how the process of prior consultation and negotiation has been interpreted by an international tribunal, not only as a treaty stipulation, specific to relations between France and Spain,[259] but more generally as a principle of customary law.[260] The tribunal found that: 'The conflicting interests aroused by the industrial use of international rivers must be reconciled by mutual concessions embodied in comprehensive agreements'.[261] Consultation and negotiation in good faith are required, not as a mere formality, but as a genuine attempt to conclude an agreement. Each state is obliged to give a reasonable place to the interests of others in the solution finally adopted, even if negotiations for this purpose are unsuccessful, 'though owing to the intransigence of its partner'.[262] But subject to compliance with these procedural obligations, other states have no veto over the development of a river.[263]

In most respects the 1997 UN Watercourses Convention closely follows the principles laid down in the *Lac Lanoux* arbitration, the *Icelandic Fisheries Case*,[264] and the *North Sea Continental Shelf Cases*[265] concerning the conduct of consultations and negotiations.[266] Where the implementation of planned measures would be inconsistent with Articles 5 or 7 of the Convention, because it entails inequitable utilization of the watercourse or would cause appreciable harm to other states, an 'equitable resolution' is called for on the basis of 'reasonable regard' for each party's rights and legitimate

256 Compare the less detailed provisions in the ILC's 2001 Articles on Prevention of Transboundary Harm, *supra*, Ch 3, section 8.

257 *ILC Report* (1988) 125ff. Article 15 requires the notified state to respond as early as possible *within* the six-month period. Cf Evensen, *1st Rept*, 175, where six months is proposed only as a reasonable *minimum* period for reply, and Article 3(1) of the 1990 Danube Basin Agreement, which provides for consultations within 3 months of notification.

258 1997 UNWC, Articles 17(1) and 18(2).

259 1866 Treaty of Bayonne and Additional Act.

260 24 *ILR* (1957) 101, 129f. See Bourne, 22 *UTLJ* (1972) 197: 'This decision of course was based on the terms of the treaty. Nevertheless, it does intimate that there is a general principle of customary international law requiring states to take the interests of co-basin states into consideration and thus necessarily leads to the obligation to give notice, to consult and to negotiate.' Kirgis, *Prior Consultation*, 39, views the case as supporting a customary obligation to engage in 'meaningful preliminary negotiations'.

261 24 *ILR* (1957) 101, 119.

262 *Ibid*, 101, 141, and see 119, 128.

263 *Ibid*, 101, 128–38. Some treaties do, however, require prior *consent* of the affected riparians before works can be undertaken: this practice is reviewed by Kirgis, *Prior Consultation*, 40, who concludes that it is mainly European but does not apply to pollution or environmental harm.

264 ICJ Reports (1974) 3, paras 71, 78.

265 ICJ Reports (1969) 3, paras 85, 87.

266 See *ILC Report* (1988) 131–3; Kirgis, *Prior Consultation*, 362ff.

interests.[267] Although reliance on equitable solutions in cases of transboundary harm has been criticized earlier, the Commission's conclusion that international law requires states to notify and negotiate as a means of reconciling conflicting rights and interests is clearly consistent with the recognition of equitable utilization as the main basis for allocation of rights and interests in shared water resources. Nothing in the subsequent ICJ case law contradicts the requirements elaborated in articles 11 to 18 of the 1997 UN Watercourses Convention.[268]

The 1997 UN Watercourses Convention also indicates some of the consequences of a failure to notify or negotiate with affected states. This will first be a breach of obligations and may render the state responsible for harm caused by the omission.[269] Another possible consequence is the loss of any claim to priority,[270] but this is rejected by Bourne as unsupported by authority.[271] As we have seen, the 1997 Convention allows the potentially affected state to request information and negotiation, if it has reasonable grounds for the request.[272] This approach is consistent with the view of the *Lac Lanoux* tribunal that 'if the neighbouring state has not taken the initiative, the other state cannot be denied the right to insist on notification of works or concessions which are the object of a Scheme',[273] and it accords with state practice in several disputed cases.[274]

Failure to respond to notification, or to an offer of consultation, may indicate waiver or tacit consent (acquiescence) to any proposed works.[275] The 1997 Convention provides that although the proposing state may proceed with its plans in the absence of any response, it remains subject to obligations of equitable utilization and the prevention of significant harm.[276] The implication here is that whatever tacit consent arises from a failure to reply or participate in negotiations does not extend to a breach of the proposing state's primary obligations. This conclusion is consistent with the view that the threshold for inferring waiver is high, and that a mere failure to assert a claim does not of itself amount to acquiescence.[277]

267 UNWC, Articles 15, 17.

268 See discussion of *Gabčíkovo-Nagymaros, Pulp Mills* and *Border Activities/San Juan River Cases, supra*, Ch 3, section 8.

269 Bourne, 22 *UTLJ* (1972).

270 ILA Helsinki Rules, Article XXIX(4).

271 22 *UTLJ* (1972) 190.

272 UNWC, Article 18, and see *ILC Report* (1988) 134–6. See also Danube Basin Agreement, Article 3.

273 24 *ILR* (1957) 101, 138.

274 See e.g. the Sudanese-Egyptian dispute regarding consultation over the Aswan High Dam and the US–Mexico dispute regarding salinity of the Colorado River, noted in *ILC Report* (1988) 131–3; Kirgis, *Prior Consultation*, 43, 66.

275 2001 ILC Articles on State Responsibility, Article 45; Crawford, *State Responsibility* (Cambridge, 2013) 558–60.

276 UNWC, Article 16. See *ILC Report* (1988) 129ff.

277 See *Phosphate Lands in Nauru Case*, ICJ Reports (1992) 240, paras 12–21, and commentary to Article 45 in *ILC Report* (2001) GAOR A/56/10, 43–365, reproduced in Crawford (ed), *The ILC's Articles on State Responsibility* (Cambridge, 2002).

The ILC took the view that during the period for reply, consultation, and negotiation, good faith requires that implementation of any plans be postponed, but not indefinitely, and this is reflected in the Convention.[278] Prolonging negotiations unilaterally will itself be inconsistent with good faith, and to counter this possibility, the 1997 Convention adopts a six-month limit during which to resolve the dispute.[279] State practice undoubtedly favours postponement, but the evidence suggests that this is often much more protracted than the Commission envisages.[280]

(b) Information exchange

The regular exchange of data and information on the state of the watercourse, and on the impact of present and planned uses can also be regarded as part of a general obligation to cooperate.[281] The ILA's 1966 Helsinki Rules recommend such an exchange, while the 2004 Berlin Rules and Article 9 of the 1997 UN Convention require it.[282] The ILC's rapporteur has pointed to the large number of agreements, declarations, and resolutions which provide for exchanges of information.[283] The practice of river commissions dealing with pollution has facilitated and encouraged exchange information on pollution of drainage basin waters.[284]

Bourne, reviewing the state practice, concluded that a general obligation to exchange information about watercourses had not yet crystallized into international law,[285] but in view of the ILC's more recent evidence, this is too cautious. Information exchange is simply an attribute of the obligation to cooperate set out in Article 8 of the 1997 UN Convention. Moreover the importance of regular exchanges of information in fulfilling the obligations of equitable utilization of a shared resource and preventing harm to other states or the environment can be emphasized in support of Article 9.[286]

(c) Emergency cooperation

The general principle that states must notify each other and cooperate in cases of emergency to avert harm to other states applies also to international watercourses.

278 1997 Convention, Articles 14, 17(3); *ILC Report* (1988) 127ff, 130ff.

279 Article 17(3). Cf Article 6 of the 1961 IDI Salzburg Resolution which allows for negotiations 'within a reasonable time' and see Bourne, 10 *CYIL* (1972) 231f.

280 E.g. the *Lac Lanoux* negotiations, which began in 1917, and the proposal eventually considered by the tribunal was put forward in 1950. The case was referred to arbitration in 1956. Negotiations between Sudan and Egypt over the Aswan Dam took five years: see Garretson et al, *The Law of International Drainage Basins*, 274f. See *ILC Report* (1988) 131–3; Kirgis, *Prior Consultation*, 73 observes that Brazil's objections to prior consultation may be attributable to the likelihood of delays in its economic development. For examples of treaties which support postponement, see 1964 Chad Basin Statute, and 1960 Convention on the Protection of Lake Constance, Article 1.

281 Leb, *Cooperation in the Law of Transboundary Water Resources*, Ch 4.

282 Helsinki Rules, Article XXIX(1); Berlin Rules, Article 56.

283 *4th Rept* (1988) UN Doc A/CN 4/412, paras 15–27; *ILC Report* (1988) 106–14.

284 See e.g. 1976 Rhine Chemicals Convention, Articles 2, 8, 12; 1992 UNECE Watercourses Convention, Articles 6, 13; 1994 Danube Convention, Article 12; 1999 Rhine Convention, Article 5(1).

285 22 *UTLJ* (1972) 206. Leb, *Cooperation in the Law of Transboundary Water Resources*, 115–8 is less cautious.

286 McCaffrey, *3rd Rept* (1987) paras 29–38; *4th Rept* (1988) paras 12–14, 27.

Bourne views it as part of a state's duty of reasonable care in the supervision of its territory;[287] McCaffrey treats it as part of the duty of equitable utilization.[288] Most of the treaties are concerned more with natural disasters, such as floods,[289] but a few require notification to other states and relevant international organizations in cases of accidental discharge of toxic or polluting substances likely to affect other states or water quality.[290] Switzerland was criticized by its neighbours in 1986 for its failure to offer timely warning under Article 11 of the 1976 Rhine Chemicals Convention agreement when fire at the Sandoz Chemical plant caused toxic pollution of the Rhine.[291] Article 28 of the 1997 UN Watercourses Convention takes the broader approach and requires expeditious notification of any emergency posing an 'imminent threat' of serious harm to other states, whether from natural causes or human conduct, 'such as industrial accidents'. However, both the wording and the antecedents of this article strongly suggest an intention to cover pollution or environmental emergencies.[292]

The 1997 UN Watercourses Convention extends the obligations of a riparian beyond mere notification in cases of emergency, and requires it to take action to prevent, mitigate, or neutralize the danger to other watercourse states.[293] This is in keeping with precedents in other fields, such as the law of the sea, and with the obligation of due diligence on which the decision in the *Corfu Channel Case*[294] is based, but it is as yet reflected in only a few watercourse treaties such as the 1961 Columbia River Basin Treaty.[295]

3 REGIONAL COOPERATION AND ENVIRONMENTAL REGULATION

The management of international watercourses through regional cooperation provides the most comprehensive basis for environmental protection and pollution control. Individual river commissions differ in their exact functions, in their powers, and in their success at persuading member governments to adopt and implement effective environmental measures. Nevertheless they share certain common characteristics.[296] First, as we saw in Chapter 2, with some exceptions, they offer an intergovernmental

287 22 *UTLJ* (1972) 186ff. 288 *4th Rept* (1988) para 27. 289 Bourne, 22 *UTLJ* (1972) 182.

290 2012 Great Lakes Water Quality Agreement, Article 6; 1999 Convention on the Protection of the Rhine, Article 5(6); 1976 Rhine Chemicals Convention, Article 11; 1976 Convention on the Protection of the Rhine Against Pollution by Chlorides, Articles 4, 11.

291 Rest, 30 *GYIL* (1987) 160, 162, 165.

292 Compare the ILC's 1991 draft Article 25(2) which applied explicitly to 'pollution or environmental emergency'. See also *ILC Report* (1988) para 180; McCaffrey, *4th Rept*, (1988) para 27; Evensen, *1st Rept* (1983) para 176.

293 Articles 27–28. 294 ICJ Reports (1949) 4; *supra*, Ch 3, section 5.

295 Article 18(3). See also the 1990 UNECE Code of Conduct on Accidental Pollution of Transboundary Inland Waters, E/ECE/1225.

296 See generally, de Chazournes, *Fresh Water in International Law*, Ch 6; Godana, *Africa's Shared Water Resources*, Ch 6; Kiss and Lambrechts, 15 *AFDI* (1969) 718; Benvenisti, *Sharing Transboundary Resources*, Ch 6.

forum for notification, consultation, and negotiation to take place, for coordinating responses to emergency situations, for data and information on environmental matters and water quality to be collected and disseminated, and for the coordination of policy and research.[297]

Secondly, international river commissions facilitate cooperation, *inter alia*, on pollution control and the maintenance or restoration of water quality through the adoption, implementation, and periodic review of common environmental standards appropriate for their particular river basin.[298] Not all river commissions have this regulatory role, but the growing number which do is evidence of their significance in controlling watercourse pollution.[299] In essence they give specific content to the obligation to prevent transboundary pollution and environmental harm and protect and preserve ecosystems.[300]

Moreover these river commissions are complemented by a series of multilateral treaties which establish institutions and standards for the regulation of marine pollution from land-based sources, including national and international rivers.[301] Thus in north-western Europe, the 1974 Paris Convention and its successor 1992 Convention have become the main basis for regional control of river pollution, together with measures adopted by the EU. From this perspective the relative weakness of earlier international commissions established to protect European rivers such as the Rhine, Moselle, and Saar from pollution is less significant than it might appear,[302] and the treatment of land-based sources of marine pollution in Chapter 8 should be read in conjunction with the points made here.

The effectiveness of a river commission is primarily dependent on negotiating agreed solutions to shared problems within the area covered by the relevant treaty. These points are well illustrated by consideration of some of the more significant commissions in Europe, North America, and Africa.

297 Leb, *Cooperation in the Law of Transboundary Water Resources*, Ch 4.

298 See especially 1992 UNECE Watercourses Convention, Article 9, and Leb, *Cooperation in the Law of Transboundary Water Resources*, Ch 5.

299 See 1964 Finland–USSR Agreement Concerning Frontier Watercourses; 1962 Convention Concerning the Protection of the Waters of Lake Geneva Against Pollution; 1961 Protocol Establishing an International Commission for the Protection of the Saar Against Pollution; 1961 Protocol Concerning the Constitution of an International Commission for the Protection of the Moselle Against Pollution, 1963 Agreement Concerning the International Commission for the Protection of the Rhine Against Pollution; 1975 Statute of the River Uruguay, Article 56; 1976 Rhine Chlorides and Chemicals Conventions; 1971 Finland–Sweden Frontier Rivers Agreement; 1909 US–Canada Boundary Waters Treaty; 1978 & 2012 US–Canada Great Lakes Water Quality Agreements; 1973 Argentina–Uruguay Treaty Concerning the River Plate; 1964 Statute Relating to the Development of the Chad Basin; 1987 Agreement on the Action Plan for the Environmentally Sound Management of the Common Zambezi River System; 1990 Magdeburg Convention on the International Commission for the Protection of the Elbe; 1994 Danube Convention; 1999 Rhine Convention.

300 See e.g. the role of the River Uruguay Commission ('CARU') in the *Pulp Mills Case*, ICJ Reports (2010) 14.

301 See *supra*, Ch 8, section 3.

302 See generally Nollkaemper, *The Legal Regime for Transboundary Water Pollution* (Dordrecht, 1992); Pallemaerts, *Toxics in Transnational Law* (Oxford, 2002) Chs 4–7.

3(1) THE INTERNATIONAL COMMISSION FOR THE PROTECTION OF THE RHINE

This commission was established in 1950 and reorganized in 1963 and 1999.[303] Its functions were initially to arrange for research into Rhine pollution, and to make proposals and prepare guidelines for protection of the river from pollution.[304] However, these required the unanimous agreement of the parties.[305] Beyond collaboration through the commission, no other obligations of pollution control were created. Despite serious problems of chemical and salt pollution in the river, Lammers, reviewing the work of the commission in its first twenty years concluded that 'the Rhine Commission has not been able to achieve any result of significance'.[306] Investigations had been carried out, but inability to reach agreement on specific measures had blocked progress.

Not until 1976 was it possible to negotiate, through the Commission, framework conventions on chemicals and chlorides pollution. Under the 1976 Rhine Chemicals Convention, the parties committed themselves to progressive elimination or strict regulation of specified groups of pollutants.[307] Emissions were controlled by a system of prior authorization by governments, and emission standards and timetables for eliminating the more serious pollutants were proposed by the Commission. Standards for other pollutants were determined nationally.[308] The Rhine Commission was also given responsibility for coordinating national programmes, receiving reports from governments, evaluating results, and proposing further measures. It thus performed monitoring, regulatory, and supervisory functions in respect of member states fulfilment of their obligations, but effective implementation continued to depend on further agreement on emission standards and the coordination of national measures.[309] The development of EU emission and water-quality standards for most of the Rhine's riparians has gone some way towards achieving this.[310]

Both the 1963 Rhine Commission Agreement and the 1976 Rhine Chemicals Convention were replaced by the 1999 Convention on the Protection of the Rhine.[311] Adopted in accordance with the 1992 UNECE Watercourses Convention, to which all the Rhine states are party, the new Rhine Convention for the first time provides a comprehensive approach to environmental protection which is no longer limited to the control of chemical pollution. Instead, its explicit objective is the sustainable development of the Rhine ecosystem.[312] The pre-existing approach to pollution control is largely

303 See now 1999 Convention for the Protection of the Rhine. The Rhine Protection Commission should not be confused with the General Commission for the Rhine established by the Congress of Vienna in 1815.

304 1963 Rhine Commission Agreement, Article 2.

305 Ibid, Article 6.

306 See Lammers, *Pollution of International Watercourses*, 175.

307 1976 Convention on the Protection of the Rhine Against Chemical Pollution, Article 1, and Annexes I, II; Lammers, *Pollution of International Watercourses*, 187; Pallemaerts, *Toxics in Transnational Law*, 206–28.

308 Cf Articles 3–5 (Annex 1 substances) and Article 6 (Annex II substances).

309 See Lammers, *Pollution of International Watercourses*, 189–90.

310 See Nollkaemper, *The Legal Regime for Transboundary Water Pollution*, Ch 3.

311 In force for all the Rhine states and the EU in 2003. See Pallemaerts, *Toxics in Transnational Law*, 229–32.

312 Article 3.

maintained and strengthened,[313] but the parties are now committed, inter alia, to the pursuit of environmentally sound and rational management of water; protecting species diversity; conserving, restoring, and improving natural habitats, flood plains, and river-beds and banks; taking account of ecological factors when developing the waterway; and helping to restore the North Sea. In pursuing these aims, the parties are to be guided by the precautionary and preventive principles, the polluter-pays principle and sustainable development. They are to afford priority to 'rectification at source', apply 'best environmental practice', and avoid increasing or transferring damage. To some degree these provisions in Articles 3 and 4 of the 1999 Convention consolidate developments and decisions that had already taken place, notably under the Rhine Action Programme, adopted in 1987 following the Sandoz accident.[314] Decisions and recommendations adopted under the earlier treaties will remain in force under the new regime.

The 1999 Convention also gives the Rhine Commission stronger powers to take binding decisions and enhances the transparency of its work. In particular, decisions on measures adopted by unanimity must be implemented by all member states in a manner and to a timetable stipulated by the Commission.[315] Inability to implement must be reported; on that basis, or following further consultations among the parties, the Commission may decide on measures to assist implementation.[316] In effect, this provision creates a form of non-compliance procedure. Observers, including relevant NGOs, may make reports or be consulted as specialists and can participate in Commission meetings if invited.[317] The Commission also has a duty to consult affected NGOs before decisions are taken, and to publicise reports on the state of the Rhine and the results of its work.[318]

The 1976 Rhine Chlorides Convention[319] is intended to reduce French chloride discharges into the river, and to prevent any increase in discharges by other parties. After a long delay, occasioned by France, the treaty entered into force in 1985. The Rhine Commission's functions under this treaty include receiving national reports, making proposals for further limitations, and monitoring compliance with chloride levels set by the Convention.[320] This treaty sets an unusual precedent in distributing across all riparians, including injured downstream states, the costs of measures taken by France to control chloride pollution.[321] In most watercourse treaties these costs fall on the polluting state. What the Chlorides Convention represents is an attempt to produce an equitable solution of the dispute between France and the Netherlands

313 See Articles 5(4) 8(1). The parties are also required to implement the EU's Water Framework Directive, 2000/60/EC.

314 8th Ministerial Conference of the Rhine States, 1987. See Nollkaemper, *The Legal Regime for Transboundary Water Pollution*, Ch 3, esp 100, 127; Pallemaerts, *Toxics in Transnational Law*, 216–26.

315 Articles 5(5) 10, 11.

316 Article 11(3) (4).

317 Article 14.

318 Articles 14(3) 8(4).

319 1976 Convention on the Protection of the Rhine Against Pollution by Chlorides, as amended by Additional Protocol, 1991. See Lammers, *Pollution of International Watercourses*, 183ff; Bernauer, in Keohane (ed), *Institutions for Environmental Aid* (Cambridge, Mass, 1996).

320 Articles 2, 3, 6, 9. For detailed regulations see 1991 Additional Protocol.

321 Lammers, *Pollution of International Watercourses*, 176ff. France and Germany pay 30% each; the Netherlands, 34%; Switzerland, 6%; 1991 Additional Protocol, Article 4. See also *Rhine Chlorides Convention: Arbitral Award of 12 March 2004* (France/Netherlands) PCA.

in which neither side pressed its legal rights to the full. However, one detailed study shows that while the Convention has been implemented, it has played little part in reducing chloride pollution or in mitigating environmental impact: these have instead come about mainly through industrial re-structuring.[322]

The Rhine treaties provide for compulsory unilateral arbitration[323] as a remedy for breach of obligation by states parties, but no such claims have been made, even when, as in the Sandoz accident, there is evidence of a possible breach of obligation.[324] Instead, damage occurring in downstream states has been the subject of civil actions in national courts or before the ECJ. These cases illustrate the value of EU law in affording a choice of venue for claims brought directly against polluters in private law, and a preference for local remedies over international claims even for clean-up costs incurred by riparian governments.[325]

Historically, the original regime for protecting the environment of the Rhine could be criticized mainly for dealing inadequately with pollutants and for the slow pace of progress towards broader environmental protection. As Lammers points out, it was easier to secure commitments to prevent new or increased pollution than to reduce existing pollution.[326] But the present institutional structure now compares favourably with other such bodies and the 1999 Convention has the significant merit of applying to the Rhine Basin and ecosystem, not just to the Rhine itself.

Moreover, following inclusion in the Rhine Action programme of a commitment to protect water quality in the North Sea, operation of the Rhine Commission has increasingly been coordinated with the OSPAR Commission and the International North Sea Conference.[327] Thus, the Rhine offers an example of significant progress in the regional management of international watercourse pollution and environmental protection and is the first to take account of the marine environment.

3(2) THE US–CANADIAN INTERNATIONAL JOINT COMMISSION

The International Joint Commission was established by the 1909 Boundary Waters Treaty with jurisdiction over all rivers and lakes along which the US–Canadian border passes.[328]

322 Bernauer, in Keohane (ed), *Institutions for Environmental Aid*.

323 1999 Rhine Convention, Article 16; Chlorides Convention, Article 12(3); Chemicals Convention, Article 15.

324 D'Oliviera, in Francioni and Scovazzi (eds), *International Responsibility for Environmental Harm* (Dordrecht, 1991) 429.

325 *Handelskwekerij Bier v Mines de Potasse d'Alsace*, II *ECR* (1976) 1735, allowing proceedings in the place of injury or in the place of discharge. See *supra*, Ch 5, section 3. See also Lammers, *Pollution of International Watercourses*, 196–206.

326 *Pollution of International Watercourses*, 192f. For other criticisms see Nollkaemper, *The Legal Regime for Transboundary Water Pollution*, Ch 3.

327 On the OSPAR Commission and the INSC, see *supra*, Ch 8.

328 Text in Cohen, 146 *Recueil des Cours* (1975) 221; see also Heasley and Macfarlane (eds), *Border flows: a century of the Canadian-American water relationship*, (Calgary, 2016); Bourne, 28 *NILR* (1981) 188; Le Marquand, 33 *NRJ* (1993) 59; Schmandt, Clarkson, and Roderick (eds), *Acid Rain and Friendly Neighbors* (2nd edn, Durham, NC, 1988) Ch 8; Graham, in Zacklin and Caflisch, *International Rivers and Lakes*, 3; Bilder, 70 *Michigan LR* (1972) 469.

This is not fully a 'basin treaty', since for most purposes 'boundary waters' excludes tributaries or rivers flowing across the boundary,[329] but it does cover the Great Lakes, and transboundary pollution.[330]

Uniquely, and unlike the Rhine Commission, the IJC does not resemble an intergovernmental conference. Rather, it is more like an administrative agency, composed not of representatives of the parties, but of independent experts who function quasi-judicially through public hearings and whose decisions are rendered by majority vote.[331] Its unity, its independence of both governments, and the binding character of its decisions are its most important and unusual characteristics.[332]

The importance of these features is that the Commission's approval is required before either state may permit the use, obstruction, or diversion of waters affecting the natural level or flow.[333] Although for these purposes each state enjoys 'equal and similar rights', the Commission's decisions apportion those rights according to criteria which protect existing uses and give preference to domestic and sanitary purposes, navigation, power, and irrigation in that order.[334] Thus its primary function is to make binding determinations regarding the equitable utilization of the flow of the waters.

But these powers apply only within a narrow field of uses; they do not address questions of water quality and are therefore of limited environmental relevance. The Boundary Waters Treaty prohibits pollution of boundary waters and waters flowing across the boundary,[335] but only if it causes injury to health or property, and the parties have in practice treated this provision as a basis for compromise and balancing of interests, not as an absolute prohibition.[336] Moreover, the Commission's role under the treaty in pollution disputes is essentially one of conciliation and inquiry: it makes findings of fact and recommendations on matters referred to it by either party.[337] These findings and recommendations are not binding, and the terms of reference are carefully controlled by the parties. Thus its independence in investigating pollution matters is strictly limited in scope, and may even hamper its usefulness as a bargaining forum.[338]

On a few occasions since 1945 environmental problems have been referred to the Commission, and this has enabled it to fulfil some of the monitoring and policy-formation functions of other more recently established bodies. Its most significant achievement has been a report on the Great Lakes, resulting in the negotiation of an

329 Preliminary article.

330 Article IV, dealing with pollution, applies to 'waters flowing across the boundary'.

331 Boundary Waters Treaty, Articles 7, 8, 12; Cohen, 146 *Recueil des Cours*, 257ff. and 267ff.

332 Cohen, 146 *Recueil des Cours*, 257; Bilder, 70 *Michigan LR* (1972) 518ff.

333 Boundary Waters Treaty, Articles 3, 4.

334 Boundary Waters Treaty, Article 8; Cohen, 146 *Recueil des Cours*, 254–6.

335 Article IV. 336 Bilder, 70 *Michigan LR* (1972) 511–17.

337 Article IX; Cooper, 24 *CYIL* (1986) 247, 285–90, who also notes the Commission's role as a mediator; Bilder, 70 *Michigan LR* (1972) 513ff. An unratified treaty drafted in 1920 would have given the Commission power to investigate violations of Article IV of its own motion and required parties to take proceedings against the persons responsible. Ruster and Simma, xi, 5704; Bilder, loc cit, 490f.

338 Bilder, 70 *Michigan LR* (1972) 520f.

agreement on Great Lakes Water Quality in 1972.[339] As an ILC study notes: 'This report and full response by Governments dramatically illustrates the increasingly important role that the Commission is playing in dealing with environmental questions along the Canada–US boundary.'[340] Generally the Commission has had a record of making politically acceptable recommendations and a good reputation for fact finding; its flexibility has been a major asset.[341] It has not found favour in its other role as an arbitral body however,[342] mainly because it lacks appropriate expertise. The *Trail Smelter* and *Gut Dam* arbitrations[343] were conducted by ad hoc tribunals; in all other cases direct negotiation has been the parties' preferred method of dispute settlement.[344]

The 2012 Great Lakes Water Quality Agreement replaced the earlier agreements of 1972 and 1978.[345] Because the 2012 agreement, like its predecessor, adopts an ecosystem approach, its geographical coverage is broader than the 1909 Boundary Waters Treaty. Its purpose is to restore and maintain water quality in the Great Lakes and to eliminate or reduce environmental threats (Article 2). Inter alia the parties are to be guided by an ecosystem approach, the polluter pays principle, the precautionary approach, public engagement, sustainability, science-based management, and zero discharge of chemicals of mutual concern. The objectives listed in Article 3 envisage waters safe to drink; free of pollutants harmful to health, wildlife or aquatic organisms; free of nutrients, invasive species and contaminated groundwater; and which support wetlands and the habitats of native species. These objectives are kept under review by the parties and the IJC (Article 5), which makes appropriate recommendations (Article 7). The agreement is comprehensive in character, more demanding than its predecessors, and comparable to treaties on land-based sources of marine pollution.[346] Its provisions reflect forty-five years of progress in restoring the health of lakes that had once been close to death.

The IJC retains the additional powers and responsibilities it was given in 1972 and 1978 to collect data, conduct research and investigations, make recommendations to the parties, and report on the effectiveness of measures taken under the Agreement (Article 7). For these purposes it has its own scientific and water quality advisory boards. Unusually it also has authority to verify independently the data and information supplied by the parties. Thus it now performs most of the characteristic roles of

[339] Ibid, 489ff. Schmandt, Clarkson, and Roderick, *Acid Rain*, 194–7. The Agreement was replaced in 1978, and again in 2012.

[340] II *YbILC* (1974) Pt 2, 355.

[341] Schmandt, Clarkson, and Roderick, *Acid Rain and Friendly Neighbors*, 191–4; Bilder, 70 *Michigan LR* (1972) 520f.

[342] 1909 Boundary Waters Treaty, Article X.

[343] 8 *ILM* (1969) 118.

[344] Cooper, 24 *CYIL* (1986) 247.

[345] On the 1972 Agreement, see Cohen 146 *Recueil des Cours*, 278ff; Kiss and Lambrechts, 20 *AFDI* (1974) 797. On the 1978 Agreement, see Rasmussen, *Boston CICLJ* (1979) 499; Toope and Brunnée, 91 *AJIL* (1997) 26, 52–8. On the 2012 Agreement see Heasley and Macfarlane (eds), *Border flows: a century of the Canadian-American water relationship, Ch 1*. Jetoo and Krantzberg, 11 *Int Jo of Sustainability in Economic, Social, and Cultural Context* (2015) 1.

[346] See *supra*, Ch 8.

other pollution commissions, save that of acting as a forum for intergovernmental negotiation. The parties are, however, required to consult and review the Commission's periodic reports and consider appropriate action (Article 5), so it may act as a useful catalyst for negotiation.

Recognition of the need for an ecosystem approach combined with comprehensive environmental policies based on adequate research and monitoring are the most significant features of the Great Lakes Water Quality Agreements.[347] The IJC's role is important in providing the necessary independent review and enabling policy to evolve in an adaptable and informed way. In all of these respects the 1978 and 2012 Agreements are among the more advanced watercourse agreements. However, it is noteworthy that the parties have not extended this comprehensive approach to other elements of their transboundary watercourse system.[348] North American practice thus falls short of cooperation to protect the ecosystem of their shared watercourse system,[349] but, in respect at least of the Great Lakes, it offers a strong example of such cooperation.

3(3) SHARED WATERCOURSES IN THE SOUTHERN AFRICA DEVELOPMENT COMMUNITY

The 2000 Protocol on Shared Watercourse Systems in the Southern Africa Development Community ('SADC Protocol')[350] represents one of the more ambitious approaches to environmental protection of river basins in the developing world. It is untypical of earlier treaties in Africa, whose main concern was river development, but exemplifies the potential of common management in addressing environmental problems.[351] It is modelled closely on the 1997 UN Watercourses Convention.

The SADC Protocol attempts to address sustainable development of Southern Africa's watercourses on a regional basis. Its objectives include promoting sustainable utilization and environmentally sound development of shared water resources, and harmonization of national water law and policy.[352] Article 3 sets out basic principles which the parties agree to apply to the region's watercourses. It affirms the sovereign rights of each riparian over utilization of watercourses within its territory, commits the parties to sustainable development, and to respect and apply existing international law relating to utilization and management of their shared watercourses. The Protocol

347 Schmandt, Clarkson, and Roderick, *Acid Rain and Friendly Neighbors*, 203; Toope and Brunnée, 91 *AJIL* (1997) 26.

348 Cf 1961 Columbia River Basin Treaty.

349 1997 UN Watercourses Convention, Article 20, *supra*, section 2(4).

350 The protocol agreed in 2000 replaced an earlier one adopted in 1995. See Malzbender and Earle, in Loures and Rieu-Clarke (eds), *The UN Watercourses Convention in Force: Strengthening International Law for Transboundary Water Management* (London, 2013).

351 See also 1999 Protocol on Lake Victoria; 1987 Agreement on the Action Plan for the Environmentally Sound Management of the Common Zambezi River System; Godana, *Africa's Shared Water Resources*.

352 Article 2.

adopts the wording of the 1997 UN Watercourses Convention on sustainable and equitable use, protection of ecosystems and prevention of pollution.[353] It thus becomes the first regional agreement to apply the provisions of that convention.

Full implementation requires the creation of intergovernmental commissions, management boards, and monitoring units for each of the shared drainage basins in the region.[354] Shared watercourse agreements are to be negotiated.[355] The 2002 Incomati River Basin Agreement is the first to be adopted.

As in Europe, the value of a framework convention of this kind is twofold. First, it identifies basic principles on which the parties can agree regardless of the adoption of further agreements covering specific watercourses. Secondly, it provides a flexible basis for the development of institutions and the harmonization of law and policy for each regional watercourse. Its value in this context will depend entirely on the successful negotiation and implementation of more detailed agreements or institutional arrangements for individual watercourses. Once again it also illustrates the influence which the 1992 Rio Declaration and the commitment to sustainable development have had on international law relating to freshwater resources.

4 CONCLUSIONS

The law of international watercourses has for most of its history been concerned with the allocation and use of a natural resource of international significance, not with its conservation or environmental protection. The point was made in Chapter 3, however, that requirements of conservation and sustainable use are of increasing importance in regard to these resources, and the evidence of this chapter indicates how far such obligations now affect the management of international water resources.

While it can be asserted with some confidence that states are no longer free to pollute or otherwise destroy the ecology of a shared watercourse to the detriment of their neighbours or of the marine environment, definitive conclusions concerning the law in this area are more difficult to draw. There is first the major problem of the diversity of watercourse systems and the regional and bilateral arrangements governing their use. From this body of treaty law and state practice only the most general of inferences can usefully be made. With regard to pollution control and environmental protection the difficulties of generalization are exacerbated by the relatively sparse and recent character of the precedents and practice which can be relied on.

Secondly, although the 1997 UN Watercourses Convention can be said in many respects to reflect existing customary international law, it remains in certain respects controversial. In particular, the relationship between equitable utilization, which is a right as well as a duty, and the obligation of harm prevention, is a continuing source

[353] Articles 3–4. [354] Article 5. [355] Article 6.

of difficulty. This is of less significance for pollution control, where the general obligations of states to control this form of harm are fairly well accepted, than for other uses of a watercourse.

These difficulties, and other objections to the 1997 Convention expressed by some governments and writers, should not be exaggerated. It must be stressed that international watercourses are not the subject of a separate and wholly self-contained body of law, but are also governed by rules and principles, and in some cases also by international agreements, of more general significance. As we have seen, the law of the sea may be particularly relevant where pollution affects the marine environment. But it is not simply pollution which is the main problem but a broader question of ecological protection. Many international and national watercourses are also important habitats for wildlife and migratory species, such as salmon, and these may be seriously affected by the building of dams, or the re-routing of rivers and draining of wetlands. Thus, conservation treaties and related rules of international law governing living resources, including fisheries, are of particular importance in this context, and reference should be made to later chapters where these matters are considered.

The importance of viewing an international watercourse not merely as a shared natural resource to be exploited, but as a complete ecosystem whose development has diverse effects of an international character also emphasizes the limited utility of the principle of equitable utilization. Although correctly seen as the main principle of international watercourse law, this principle cannot sustain more than a modest role mainly confined to allocating riparian rights. It affords an insufficient basis for measures of more comprehensive environmental protection. Nor does it ensure the integration of ecological, developmental and inter-generational considerations which is central to sustainable development as the overriding objective of contemporary water resources policy.

Such measures can only usefully be negotiated multilaterally, with their implementation subject at least to intergovernmental supervision and control, as we saw in Chapter 2. In this respect, the development of cooperative regimes for the common management of international watercourses has not yet been sufficiently comprehensive or effective. Environmental protection arrangements in Europe and North America are incomplete, apply only to certain rivers, and have only slowly been implemented. Many African watercourse treaties are sophisticated in content, but of little practical importance due to their limited implementation, and some rivers, most notably the Nile, are still managed on the basis of outdated regimes agreed many years ago. The record of states in the cooperative management of watercourse resources is thus an inadequate one, despite the general international endorsement of this approach in principle.

11

CONSERVATION OF NATURE, ECOSYSTEMS, AND BIODIVERSITY

1 INTRODUCTION

1(1) THE PROBLEM

Humanity's survival on earth depends on the conservation of nature—of the world's natural resources comprising the soil, water, the atmosphere, and forests, plants, and life forms that these sustain.[1] While the number of known species is about 1.75 million,[2] far more are as yet uncatalogued, with estimates of the total number of species in existence ranging from 10 million to 100 million, including the insects[3] and smaller organisms. Of the 52,500 species of vertebrates known to be extant only some 4,630 are mammals, 9,750 are birds, 8002 reptiles and 4,950 amphibians, whereas a minimum of 70,000 species of molluscs have been identified.[4] As we will see below, these proportions are not reflected in the degree of international regulation—nor in the

[1] See eg the Millenium Ecosystem Assessment, *Ecosystems and Human Well-Being: Biodiversity Synthesis* (2005), 49: 'Humans are fully dependent on Earth's ecosystems and the services that they provide, such as food, clean water, disease regulation, climate regulation, spiritual fulfillment, and aesthetic enjoyment.'

[2] Groombridge and Jenkins, *World Atlas of Biodiversity Earth's Living Resources in the 21st Century* (UNEP-WCM, University of California Press, 2002)16; see generally Wilson's classic study, *The Diversity of Life* (London, 1992) and ibid., *The Future of Life* (London, 2002).

[3] Over 40% of (known) insect species are threatened with extinction: Sánchez-Bayo and Wyckhuys (2019) 232 *Biological Conservation* 8. The main drivers of insect species decline, in order of importance, are habitat loss owing to intensive agriculture, agro-chemical pollutants, invasive species and climate change. Paradoxically, agriculture—and all ecosystems—depend on insect pollinators: see eg CBD COP Decision XIV/6 (2018) on 'Conservation and sustainable use of pollinators'.

[4] *World Atlas of Biodiversity*, 18, Table 2.1.

legal literature—where the charismatic pull of mega-fauna such as elephants, pandas, whales, dolphins, and pinnipeds, can be observed.[5]

The amount of biological diversity now extant is thought to be at its maximum and further speciation is unlikely to occur. In this respect diversity should be regarded as a non-renewable resource: when threatened by large-scale degradation or destruction, whether from natural or human activities, this diversity is irreplaceable. If such a disaster occurs, modern technology cannot reproduce the subtle differences between varieties that have evolved over millions of years, or their interactions with different ecosystems. As Swanson puts it, biodiversity, defined in 1992 CBD article 2[6] as 'the variability among living organisms from all sources, including inter alia, terrestrial, marine and other aquatic ecosystems and the ecological complexes of which they are part' including diversity 'within species, between species and of ecosystems', 'is valuable precisely because it is the output of [a] four billion-year-old evolutionary process, not for the sake of the variety itself'.[7] It is valuable for the evolutionary range of its variety and because it therefore has a fine-tuned resilience to physical conditions, as well as the power to adapt and thus provide a buffer against future assaults on life supporting systems. Yet humans have depleted this range of natural resources, including species, and replaced them by limited cultivation and domestication of a few selected species,[8] thus reducing diversity and expanding their own niche by increasing the populations of their own and these chosen species, without much regard for ensuring that these developments are compatible with maintaining diversity and thus sustainable in the long term.

Humanity's 'ecological footprint' now exceeds the biological capacity of the earth, and continues to do so by an ever wider margin.[9] There is now widespread scientific consensus that biodiversity is being lost, and that pressures on biodiversity are increasing. At the start of this millennium, UNEP's Global Environmental Outlook report[10] to the WSSD in 2002, and the Millenium Ecosystem Assessment in 2005,[11] provided stark reminders of the continuing rate of species extinction and ecosystem degradation, largely as a product of human activities, notwithstanding the extent of international regulation. The latter, a global inventory of natural resources compiled by 1300 scientists from 95 countries, concluded that about 60 per cent of the planet's ecosystems are being degraded or used unsustainably. This conclusion was reinforced

5 Bowman, Davies and Redgwell, *Lyster's International Wildlife Law* (2010) Ch 1.

6 See further part 5 below.

7 Swanson, *Global Action for Biodiversity* (London, 1997) 9.

8 Almost all species loss has occurred since human agriculture developed thousands of years ago: Ceballos, Ehrlich and Raven, 117:24 *Proceedings of the National Academy of Sciences of the United States of America* (2020) 13596–602.

9 See UN, draft 5th edition of the *Global Biodiversity Outlook* (2020). Bowman in Bowman, Davies and Goodwin (eds), *Research Handbook on Biodiversity and Law* (Edward Elgar, 2016) 3.

10 It revealed that some 11,046 species of flora and fauna were known to be facing a high risk of extinction: UNEP, *Global Environmental Outlook-3 (Geo-3)* (2002).

11 Millenium Ecosystem Assessment, *Ecosystems and Human Well-Being: Biodiversity Synthesis* (2005).

by the 2010 *Global Biodiversity Outlook*[12] acknowledging that the 2010 target, set in 2002, to achieve a significant reduction in the rate of biodiversity loss had not been met.[13] The 2014 *Global Biodiversity Outlook* paints a similarly gloomy picture, with the average rate of extinction for birds, mammals and amphibians still increasing; genetic diversity of domesticated livestock eroding, with more than one-fifth of breeds at risk of extinction; and the wild relatives of domesticated crop species increasingly threatened by habitat fragmentation and climate change.[14]

Most recently, a 2019 UN Report concluded that nature is now declining globally at rates unprecedented in human history and that the rate of species extinctions is accelerating, with around 1 million animal and plant species now threatened with extinction, many within decades.[15] The direct driver[16] of biodiversity loss is human activity resulting in habitat change, overexploitation, pollution, the introduction of invasive species, and climate change,[17] with grave impacts of such loss on humanity around the world now likely.[18] Indirect drivers include economic activity, demographic change, socio-political factors, cultural and religious factors, and scientific and technological change. Species extinction, 'the most fundamental and irreversible human impact on nature', has also increased globally.[19] The Report concludes:

> Past and ongoing rapid declines in biodiversity, ecosystem functions and many of nature's contributions to people mean that most international societal and environmental goals [[20]] . . . will not be achieved based on current trajectories. These declines will also undermine other goals, such as those specified in the Paris Agreement adopted under the United Nations Framework Convention on Climate Change and the 2050 Vision for Biodiversity. The negative trends in biodiversity and ecosystem functions are projected to continue or worsen in many future scenarios in response to indirect drivers such as rapid human population growth, unsustainable production and consumption and associated technological development.[21]

12 The 'flagship publication' of the CBD, this is a periodic report that summarises the latest data and trends in global biodiversity and progress towards achieving the targets and objectives of the Convention. Four reports have been published to date, with a fifth due in 2020 to coincide with the end of the current Strategic Plan/UN Decade for Biodiversity 2011–2020.

13 CBD, *Global Biodiversity Outlook 3* (2010), 9; see further part 6 below.

14 CBD, *Global Biodiversity Outlook 4—A mid-term assessment of progress towards the implementation of the Strategic Plan for Biodiversity 2011–2020* (2014), 14; on the state of the oceans, see also GRID-Arendal and UNEP, *World Ocean Assessment Overview* (2016) and *infra* Ch 12.

15 Intergovernmental Science-Policy Platform on Biodiversity and Ecosystem Services (IPBES), *Global Assessment Report on Biodiversity and Ecosystem Services—Summary for policymakers* IPBES/7/10/Add.1, 29 May 2019, 4. See also 'Progress on [SD]Goal 15' (rates of extinction).

16 Millenium Ecosystem Assessment, *Ecosystems and Human Well-Being: Biodiversity Synthesis* (2005), 49.

17 *Global Biodiversity Outlook 3*, 9; *Global Biodiversity Outlook 4*, 9; *Biodiversity and Ecosystem Services*, 5.

18 *Biodiversity and Ecosystem Services*, n 14. One such grave impact is the COVID-19 pandemic, which has been linked with human encroachment on habitat and wildlife trade: see eg Ceballas et al., n 8.

19 From 0.82 in 1993 to 0.73 in 2019 (on the IUCN Red List where 1 indicates no threat of extinction to any species, and 0 indicates that all species are extinct): 'Progress of Goal 15 in 2019' <https://sustainabledevelopment.un.org/sdg15>; see also n 8 above.

20 Such as those embodied in the 2030 Agenda for Sustainable Development and the Aichi Biodiversity Targets, discussed further below.

21 *Biodiversity and Ecosystem Services*, 6–7.

Whether this means that imminent disaster threatens the planet is not a view shared by all; some take the view that, though deeply troubling, the current state of biodiversity conservation is not irredeemable[22] or that the market economy can best resolve the threats.[23] What is clear is that there is considerable cause for concern and a need to adopt a precautionary approach[24] both to identification of serious threats to biodiversity and the measures now required to counter these, bearing in mind that in some sense we are responsible for the survival of nature, not just to present and future generations, but also to other existing and potential species. These needs and responsibilities have been recognized, inter alia, by the UN General Assembly which first designated an International Year of Biodiversity in 2010, followed by the UN Decade 2011-2020.[25]

As is clearly evident, biodiversity loss is more than an environmental problem alone and is increasingly treated as such. Explicit recognition of the need to reduce marine and terrestrial biodiversity loss is, for example, a key element of SDGs 14 and 15[26] adopted in 2015. This embrace of biodiversity loss and its reduction as part of the 2002 MDGs, and now these 2015 SDGs, is indicative of a wider acknowledgement of the various anthropogenic pressures on biodiversity and of the importance of maintaining 'the earth's fundamental support systems' by the international community as a whole.[27] However, in a common refrain, the SDGs likewise have not reached their 2020 targets as 'land degradation continues, biodiversity loss is occurring at an alarming rate, and invasive species and the illicit poaching and trafficking of wildlife continue to thwart efforts to protect and restore vital ecosystems and species.'[28]

Against this backdrop, this chapter identifies how international law seeks to ensure the protection and conservation and sustainable use[29] of nature, its ecosystems and biodiversity, and the effectiveness of measures developed to conserve land-based living resources, forests, and deserts. The instrument at the heart of biodiversity conservation and sustainable use is the 1992 CBD, which both provides a framework for international action and offers support to developing countries to enable them to bear the additional burdens involved. It is part of a web of biodiversity-related treaties for

[22] While the 2019 *Global Assessment Report on Biodiversity and Ecosystem Services* notes that negative trends in nature will continue to 2050 and beyond in all of the policy scenarios it explores, an exception is those that include transformative changes across economic, social, political and technological factors: ibid., 5. 'Transformative' is defined as 'a fundamental, system-wide reorganization across technological, economic and social factors, including paradigms, goals and values'.

[23] Eg Lomborg, *The Skeptical Environmentalist* (Cambridge, 2001) and Rogers, 76 *Int Affairs* (2000), 315–23, esp 323.

[24] Discussed *supra*, Ch 3, section 6.

[25] UNGA Resolution A/Res/65/161, 11 March 2011.

[26] See for example SDG 15.5: 'Take urgent and significant action to reduce the degradation of natural habitats, halt the loss of biodiversity and, by 2020, protect and prevent the extinction of threatened species.'

[27] Bowman *Biodiversity Handbook* 22.

[28] 'Progress of Goal 15 in 2019' <https://sustainabledevelopment.un.org/sdg15>.

[29] For an overview see *supra*, Ch 3, section 3.

the conservation of migratory and land-based species and habitat, considered in this chapter, and of marine living resources considered in the following chapter.[30]

1(2) THE ROLE OF LAW IN NATURE PROTECTION

Although there have been national laws protecting terrestrial and marine living resources since comparatively early times, the perception that species and nature require conservation under international law is of comparatively recent origin. It was not until over-exploitation of living resources, especially those hunted by two or more states, began to lead to failures of stocks or herds of particular species so severe that they might be in danger of extinction that serious interest was taken in the need to develop legal obligations and principles for their protection and conservation. The first approaches to this problem were simplistic; as territorial states had sovereignty over their territory, they were assumed to have exclusive rights to all the natural resources found there, living and non-living, and this was extended to the territorial sea and airspace. Once found in areas subject to sovereignty, no other state could have access to these resources nor play a role in their management without the express consent of the territorial sovereign. Natural resources found in areas beyond national jurisdiction, for example, on the high seas or the seabed below it or in the airspace above it, and indeed the air itself were regarded as common property and a doctrine of freedom of access for all states was applied.[31] It was only following increasing evidence of the serious adverse effects of over-exploitation of certain species, particularly at sea,[32] that development of more sophisticated legal regimes focused on conservation and sustainable use began, mainly, though not exclusively, in the second half of the twentieth century.

Indeed, conservation of birds has been regulated since the turn of the last century,[33] while whales were regulated ad hoc by one or two states from 1597 onwards.[34] National control of the taking of such migratory species was recognized to be insufficient to conserve them since it could not be enforced on foreign territory or on foreign vessels outside national jurisdiction at sea. Similar 'policing' issues arose for fisheries, and were addressed in one of the earliest fisheries treaties, the 1882 Convention for Regulating the Police of the North Sea Fisheries (Overfishing Convention).[35]

[30] Both terrestrial and marine species and habitat protection are also sometimes considered under the rubric of 'international wildlife law' which 'is concerned with 'conserving and avoiding the extinction of species of wild animals and plants': Wiersema, in Rajamani and Peel (eds), *The Oxford Handbook of International Environmental Law* (Oxford, 2nd ed, 2020); see also *Lyster's International Wildlife Law* passim.

[31] As discussed *supra*, Ch 3, section 3.

[32] And see *infra*, Ch 12.

[33] See the 1902 Convention to Protect Birds Useful to Agriculture 102 *BFSP* 969, concluded by European states to protect avian predators of insects and other pest species harmful to crop yields. It was preceded by a bilateral agreement between Austria-Hungary and Italy: 1875 Declaration for the Protection of Birds Useful to Agriculture 4 *IPE* 1561; and by the colonial era 1900 Convention for the Preservation of Wild Animals, Birds and Fish in Africa 94 *BFSP* 715. All have since been replaced by later treaties: see Bowman, 11 *JEL* (1999) 88–92.

[34] See the examples of whaling regulations in Birnie, *International Regulation of Whaling* (Dobbs Ferry, NY, 1985), I, 102–4.

[35] See also the 1885 Convention for the Uniform Regulation of Fishing in the Rhine. Reprinted respectively in Marine Mammal Commission, *Compendium of Selected Treaties*, 2nd Update, 475, and *Ruster and Simma*, xxv, 200.

A significant number of wildlife treaties now exist at the global, regional, and bilateral levels. Some protect a single species, such as polar bears or vicuña,[36] or a group of species, such as whales or migratory birds,[37] initially from excessive exploitation and, increasingly, for habitat protection. Others adopt a regional approach to conservation, for example, in the Western Hemisphere (North and South America), Africa, Europe, South-east Asia, the South Pacific, and Antarctica.[38] There are in addition many bilateral treaties, especially for protection of birds and seals.[39] In addition to the species-specific treaties, there are a number of treaties for global wildlife regulation. Four, referred to by Lyster in the first major monograph on international wildlife law as the 'Big Four',[40] remain of particular significance and importance to the global regime for protection of wildlife, both marine and terrestrial, namely the 1971 Ramsar Convention; the 1972 World Heritage Convention; the 1973 CITES; and the 1979 Convention on the Conservation of Migratory Species of Wild Animals ('CMS'). To these must now be added instruments concerned with plant protection,[41] the 1951 International Plant Protection Convention ('IPPC') and the 2001 International Treaty on Plant Genetic Resources for Food and Agriculture ('ITPGRFA'), and of course the 1992 CBD) itself. All of these MEAs form the main subject-matter of this chapter.

While the importance of protecting natural ecosystems as such had begun to be more widely perceived well before 1992, the conclusion of the 1992 CBD at UNCED filled a 'biodiversity gap', regulating the interaction of species and of habitat, and ecosystems,[42] in a holistic rather than piecemeal manner.[43] Since UNCED further conventions and principles have been adopted for protecting such wide-ranging habitats as deserts,[44] forests,[45] and mountain areas.[46] Collectively, these are of particular

36 1973 Agreement on the Conservation of Polar Bears; 1979 Andean Convention for the Conservation and Management of Vicuña.

37 1946 International Convention for the Regulation of Whaling; 1995 Agreement on Conservation of African–Eurasian Migratory Water Birds.

38 See eg the 1940 Convention on Nature Protection and Wildlife Preservation in the Western Hemisphere; 1968 African Convention, to be replaced by the 2003 revision when it enters into force; 1979 Convention on the Conservation of European Wildlife and Natural Habitats (Berne Convention); 1985 ASEAN Agreement on the Conservation of Nature and Natural Resources (not in force); 1976 Apia Convention on Conservation of Nature in the South Pacific; 1980 Convention on the Conservation of Antarctic Marine Living Resources, each of which is discussed in *Lyster's International Wildlife Law*.

39 Eg 1916 US–UK Convention for the Protection of Migratory Birds, 12 *TIAS* 375; 1936 US–Mexico Convention for the Protection of Migratory Birds and Game Mammals, 178 *LNTS* 309, supplemented by Agreement of 1972, 837 *UNTS* 125.

40 S Lyster, *International Wildlife Law* (1985).

41 As Amos laments, 'Despite being the ecological foundations of all life on Earth, plants receive little attention in law': Amos, *International Conservation Law: The Protection of Plants in Theory and Practice* (Routledge, 2020). See further section 3(5) below.

42 On the CBD's ecosystem approach, see *infra* section 5.

43 The 1980 CCAMLR was the first major treaty to adopt an ecosystem approach whereby the effects of exploitation of one species on all other species and on the ecosystem as a whole must be taken into account in taking measures. However, it is applicable only to the Southern Ocean, and at the time of the adoption of the CBD in 1992, had not been successfully operationalised. On subsequent development of CCAMLR, and of the ecosystem approach of the 1991 Environmental Protocol to the Antarctic Treaty, see *infra* section 5.

44 *Infra*, section 4(1). 45 *Infra*, section 4(2). 46 *Infra*, section 4(3).

significance as fulfilling the aims of the 1992 CBD[47] and each is considered in more detail later in this chapter.[48] The Madrid Protocol added to the Antarctic Treaty in 1991 also provides a vehicle for application of the 1992 CBD's holistic ecological approach as it aims to provide comprehensive environmental protection to the whole Antarctic area and its living resources, terrestrial and marine, and is considered further below.

Regulation has tended to reflect strongly anthropocentric values of 'usefulness' to human beings—self-interest to humanity being the oldest justification for conservation[49]—and any humane considerations such as less harmful methods of killing[50] were counterbalanced by the exceptions for eradication of species considered harmful ('nuisibles') to human interests.[51] Living species were also not treated very differently from other resources, and as a result living resources were long regarded as being as 'mineable' as minerals.[52] Indeed, even today living resources are frequently included within the general description of 'natural resources',[53] though as sustainable living creatures—especially those that migrate—they are very different from static non-renewable minerals. while the 1992 CBD refers to 'biological resources', including 'genetic resources, organisms or parts thereof, populations, or any other biotic components of ecosystems with actual or potential use or value for humanity',[54] this comes under the heading of 'Sustainable Use of Biological Diversity', requiring its parties to 'integrate consideration of the conservation and sustainable use of biological resources into national decision-making'.[55] The implications of this definition and the obligations of conservation and sustainable use are discussed below.

Legal developments have also been influenced by changing philosophical perceptions of nature and living creatures.[56] Early philosophers, such as Plato, made no

[47] Together with the International Whaling Commission, these comprise the members of the Liaison Group of the Biodiversity-Related Conventions, established to enhance coherence and cooperation in implementation, and coordinated by the CBD Secretariat: see eg CBD Decisions VII/26, IX/27 and X/20.

[48] *Infra*, sections 3–6.

[49] And still predominant, as the opening to this chapter attests; see further discussion in Gillespie, n 61.

[50] See eg the 1875 Declaration which prohibited the use of poison and narcotics to catch birds; the 1902 Convention prohibited devices for the mass killing of birds (Article III). Such prohibitions are found in later instruments: see eg the 1968 African Convention, Article VII(2) and the 1973 Agreement on the Conservation of Polar Bears, Article IV. However, much stronger animal welfare, biodiversity and ecosystem concerns are evident in more modern treaties: see eg Annex II to the 1991 Protocol on Environmental Protection to the Antarctic Treaty on Conservation of Antarctic Fauna and Flora, Articles 1 and 3.

[51] The 1902 Convention allowed killing birds harmful to hunting, fishing, or local agriculture (Article IX) with list 2 comprising 'oiseaux nuisibles'; see also the 1900 Convention Article 2 (13) and (15), and Table 5.

[52] Holt, 9 *Marine Policy* (1985), 192–213.

[53] As in the 1947 GATT article, on which see eg the Shrimp-Turtle Case, discussed *infra*, Ch 13, section 1.2

[54] Article 2. See also 'marine genetic resources' in *infra* Ch 12.

[55] Article 10; on the legal status of natural resources see *supra*, Ch 3, section 5. With respect to the components of biodiversity, however, the 2004 Addis Ababa Principles and Guidelines for the Sustainable Use of Biodiversity, adopted by COP Decision VII/12, call for the 'more efficient, ethical and humane use' of such components. See further below, section 5.

[56] See further *supra*, Ch 3.

attempt to distinguish individual animals or accord them rights.[57] They viewed their special attributes as representative of the whole species; it was not considered that the taking of individuals from that species damaged the species as a whole.[58] This belief was reinforced by the view that, unlike humans, animals could not be subject to duties.[59] Even when science and philosophy combined in the Middle Ages in the doctrine of 'natural philosophy' each discipline continued to embrace the generalized concept of 'species' rather than concentrating on individual specimens. These concepts were underpinned by the Roman law doctrine that animals *ferae naturae* did not belong to any person and could, therefore, be captured by anyone when found in international areas, such as the high seas and the airspace above them. Species which could not be corralled and domesticated, such as fish, marine mammals, and birds outside national territory, were thus regarded as common property resources.[60]

Perceptions have changed significantly, however.[61] First of all, the common property doctrine[62] has being overlaid with concepts of 'common heritage', 'common interest', and 'common concern'. The underlying concepts of common property and related concepts affecting the legal status of natural resources and common spaces have already been outlined in Chapter 3.[63] As we saw there, new concepts such as 'common heritage' and 'common concern'[64] have, in the case of the former, been confined to certain mineral resources and not applied to shared natural resources and in case of the latter, have as yet been included only in hortatory preambles to treaties, including the 1992 Climate Change Convention and 1992 CBD and the 2001 FAO Treaty on Plant Genetic Resources, and in some of the growing numbers of codes, declarations, and strategies for conservation. Moreover, since 'international law continues to struggle with "collective" or "community" aspirations', these treaty regimes at least have 'the potential to turn pragmatic cooperation into genuine normative communities' and

57 On contemporary arguments for animal rights see Sunstein and Nussbaum (eds), *Animal Rights* (Oxford, 2004).

58 Clark, *The Moral Status of Animals* (Oxford, 1977), 64–5; he provides a bibliography of relevant early works.

59 Linzey, *Animal Rights* (London, 1976); ibid, 12 *Jnl of Legal Education* (1964–5), 185ff; Singer and Regan (eds), *Animal Rights and Legal Obligations* (New York, 1976); Tribe, 83 *Yale LJ* (1976), 1315ff; Sunstein and Nussbaum (eds), *Animal Rights* (Oxford, 2004).

60 See Fulton, *The Sovereignty of the Seas* (Edinburgh, 1911), v–vii; Grotius, *The Freedom of the Sea or the Right Which Belongs to the Dutch to Take Part in the East India Trade*, trans Magoffin and Scott (New York, 1916); and see Behring Sea Fur seals arbitration, *infra*, Ch 12, section 4.

61 Gillespie in Rajamani and Peel (eds), *The Oxford Handbook of International Environmental*; ibid., *International Environmental Law, Politics and Ethics* (Oxford, 2nd edn, 2014) *passim*, and the extensive bibliography provided at 151–90; *Lyster's International Wildlife Law*, Ch 3; Sarkar, *Biodiversity and Environmental Philosophy* (Cambridge, 2005); Light and Rolston (eds), *Environmental Ethics: An Anthology* (Oxford, 2003).

62 For the impact of the Bonn Convention, CITES and the Protocol on Environmental Protection to the Antarctic Treaty, on the concept of wild animals and plants as property susceptible of ownership, see Sprankling, *The International Law of Property* (Oxford, 2014) 79–81.

63 *Supra*, Ch 3, section 5(1)–(4); see also Brunnée, in Bodansky, Brunnee, and Hey (eds), *The Oxford Handbook of International Environmental Law*, Ch 23.

64 *Supra*, Ch 3, section 3(1)(a–c).

offer 'promising settings in which to mediate between "individual State interest" and "the global concerns of humanity as a whole"'.[65]

Additionally, there is increasing public concern for the protection of animals and for their welfare, as species valuable for their own sake, with special emphasis on endangered species, habitats, and rational management.[66] Some support for humane considerations, and of the moral considerability of animals, may be found in the provisions of 1973 CITES, for example,[67] which are aimed at securing the welfare of animals introduced into international trade.[68] Whether there is a discrete body of international law protecting animals at the national and international levels is a more difficult question,[69] though increasing attention is being paid to the close relationship between legislation protecting animal welfare and its role in conserving animals and, incidentally biodiversity, as we shall see.[70] Animal welfare issues are thus relevant to the development of international and national law protecting biodiversity, but they are not a dominant concern.[71] Indeed, at the international level some controversy still surrounds the introduction of welfare protection in general, and humane treatment in particular. For example: in 1999 the parties to the 1946 ICRW, under pressure from those few states still whaling, changed the name of its long-standing 'Working Group on Humane Killing' to 'Working Group on Killing Methods and Associated Welfare Issues';[72] and the failure of the International Standards Organization's Draft Humane Trapping Standards to attract consensus has been attributed to the difficulty of defining the term 'humane'.[73] To date, it is only at the regional level, through the Council of Europe—which as early as 1961 declared that the humane treatment of animals is 'one of the hallmarks of Western civilization'—that a series of conventions has been

[65] Brunnée, in Bodansky, Brunnée, and Hey (eds), *The Oxford Handbook of International Environmental Law*, 572, drawing on the language of the separate opinion of Judge Weeramantry in the *Case Concerning the Gabčíkovo-Nagymaros Project (Hungary v Slovakia)* [1997] ICJ Reports 7; see also ibid., in Benvenisti and Nolte (eds), *Community Interests Across International Law* (OUP, 2018).

[66] Eg Wilkins (ed), *Animal Welfare in Europe: European Legislation and Concerns* (The Hague, 1997); Austen and Richards (eds), *International Animal Welfare Law* (The Hague, 2000) (texts of relevant international, regional, and European instruments); *Lyster's International Wildlife Law* Ch 20; Cao and White (eds), *Animal Law and Welfare—International Perspectives* (Springer, 2016); Scholtz (ed), *Animal Welfare and International Environmental Law* (Edward Elgar, 2019).

[67] Also in support are the Preambles of the ASEAN, Bern, and Western Hemisphere Conventions, and non-binding goal-setting instruments including the World Charter for Nature and the World Conservation Strategy, establishing their underlying philosophy and object and purpose.

[68] Eg Article 3(2)(c). See Bowman, 1 *JIWLP* (1998) 9–63; Harrop and Bowles, ibid, 64–94.

[69] Though recent publications are facilitating such research: eg Wilkins (ed), *Animal Welfare in Europe: European Legislation and Concerns* (The Hague, 1997) *passim* and 20(1) *JIWLP* (2017) passim (international law and wildlife wellbeing). Austen and Richards (eds), *International Animal Welfare Law* (The Hague, 2000), collect the texts of relevant international, regional, and European instruments.

[70] On this, see also Bowman, 1 *JIWLP* (1998) 9–63.

[71] For discussion of whether welfare considerations are emerging as a general principle of international law, see *Lyster's International Wildlife Law*, Ch 20.

[72] IWC, *Chairman's Report of the 51st Annual Meeting*, 24–8, May 1999, 6–10; the Working Group was established in 1982 and has had workshops on killing methods every 3–5 years since 1992, most recently in 2006. See, generally, Harrop 6 *JIWLP* (2003) 79 and *Lyster's International Wildlife Law*, Ch 20.

[73] See 1998 ISO/DIS 10990–5.

concluded specifically, rather than incidentally, protecting animals from suffering. Each is based on the principle that 'for his own well-being, man may, and sometimes must, make use of animals, but that he has a moral obligation to ensure, within reasonable limits, that the animal's health and welfare is in each case not unnecessarily put at risk.'[74] The EU has adopted decisions which make these conventions binding in all EU member states.[75]

A further factor is renewed attention on the concept of animal rights[76] and, while it is not possible here to examine in detail the arguments regarding the moral considerability of animals, suffice to note that there is a growing literature and drafts of an international Declaration of Animal Rights,[77] as well as of a convention,[78] have been under consideration for some years at the non-governmental level. The draft declaration is without legal status but has served to focus attention on gaps in the law by laying down in detail certain principles relating to animal protection. No specific legislative response has followed on the question whether killing animals is wrong or whether all or only some animals are to be regarded as sharing sufficient human characteristics to have individual rights attributed to them and to be legally protected from so-called 'speciesism', as humans are protected from racism.[79]

There is also a tension between the different perspectives of animal rights and welfare advocates,[80] who consider that all species should be protected for ethical and

74 Five conventions have been concluded in total: the 1968 Convention for the Protection of Animals During International Transport, *ETS* No 65, (with 1979 Additional Protocol, *ETS* No 103; Convention revised and updated in 2003, *ETS No* 193); the 1976 Convention for the Protection of Animals kept for Farming Purposes, *ETS* No. 87 (with 1992 Additional Protocol *ETS* No 145); the 1979 Convention for the Protection of Animals used for Slaughter, *ETS* No 102; the 1986 Convention for the Protection of Vertebrate Animals used for Experimental and other Scientific Purposes, *ETS* No 123 (with 1998 Additional Protocol *ETS* No 170); and the 1987 Convention for the Protection of Pet Animals, *ETS* No 125. See also Pavan, *A European Cultural Revolution: The Council of Europe's Charter on Invertebrates*, Council of Europe (Strasbourg, 1986).

75 See Camm and Bowles, 12 *JEL* (2000) 197–205. Concern for animal welfare is also embedded in Article 13 TFEU: 'In formulating and implementing the Union's agriculture, fisheries, transport, internal market, research and technological development and space policies, the Union and the Member States shall, since animals are sentient beings, pay full regard to the welfare requirements of animals, while respecting the legislative or administrative provisions and customs of the Member States relating in particular to religious rites, cultural traditions and regional heritage.'

76 See Sunstein and Nussbaum (eds), *Animal Rights* (Oxford, 2004); Clark, *The Moral Status of Animals* (Oxford, 1977), 64–5.

77 Universal Declaration of the Rights of Animals, proclaimed on 15 Oct 1978 by the International League of Animal Rights. Its Preamble recognizes that 'all animals have rights'; Article 1 provides that 'All animals are born with an equal claim on life and the same rights to existence'; Article 2 that 'Man as an animal species shall not arrogate to himself the rights to exterminate or inhumanly exploit other animals'; Article 3 that 'All Animals shall have the right to the attention, care and protection of man'; texts in Allen, 28 *NY Law School LR* (1983) 414–5, n 259. Several members of the Council of Europe had relevant laws by the 1970s: see Taylor, 1 *Animal Reg Stud* (1977) 73; the US has extensive legislation, Allen, op cit, 422–5.

78 See Favre in Cao and White (eds), *Animal Law and Welfare* Ch 5.

79 For general discussion see Redgwell in Boyle and Anderson (eds), *Human Rights Approaches to Environmental Protection* (Clarendon, 1996).

80 On the notion of 'rights' in this context see *supra*, Ch 5, section 1(1) and Stone, 45 *S Cal LR* (1972) 450, 488. Outhwaite identifies three regulatory paradigms: animal health, animal welfare, and conservation: 29 *JEL* (2017) 322.

humanitarian reasons however adverse their effect on humans or on populations or individuals of other species,[81] and of environmentalists who urge that particular species should be protected for ecological reasons, that is, as part of an ecosystem, which includes the animals, plants, and micro-organisms together with the non-living components of their environment.[82] This difference in views is reflected in the progress of both national and international law and the number and nature of the instruments adopted.

1(3) REGULATORY TECHNIQUES

There are a number of common regulatory techniques adopted in wildlife treaties. First, as in pollution treaties, easily amended annexes allow for a flexible system of listing, enabling new species to be added quickly if required (and where there is sufficient agreement).[83] Conservation of habitats is also an integral part of effective wildlife conservation and several of the major conventions specifically provide for habitat protection. Designation of national parks, nature reserves and protected areas is one means of giving special protection to endangered wildlife and ecologically important areas, onshore and offshore. Provision of financial assistance is another important management tool, since both the taking of necessary conservation measures and the non-exploitation of wildlife have economic consequences, especially for developing states. Each technique will be considered in turn.

(i) Listing and permitting

Listing is generally combined with a system of permits, each state party being required to implement the necessary legislation. As we saw in chapter 2, provision for a regular forum within which the parties can meet, discuss, exchange information and otherwise inform, and negotiate—whether it be an ad hoc commission established by the Convention, regular conferences of the parties, or an existing international organization—allows the parties to fine-tune the requisite conservation measures in accordance with scientific advice and political support, taking account of the economic and social and the impact on development. As with other

[81] See Linder, 12 *Harv ELR* (1988) 175ff; Regan, *The Case for Animal Rights* (New York, 1983); Singer, *Practical Ethics* (New York, 1979); ibid, *In Defence of Animals* (Washington DC, 1985); Bowman, in Bowman and Redgwell (eds), *International Law and the Conservation of Biological Diversity* (London, 1996) 5–32, Cheyne, 12 *JEL* (2000) 293–316; Harrop, ibid, 333–60; McIntyre (ed), *Mind in the Waters* (New York, 1974); Tribe, 83 *Yale LJ* (1974) 1315; Reed, 12 *Idaho LR* (1976) 153; Sagoff, 84 *Yale LJ* (1974) 33; Allen, 28 *NY Law School LR* (1983) 377–429; Stone, 45 *Scal LR* (1972), 450; Winters, 21 *SDLR* (1984), 911–40; Hersovice, *Second Nature: The Animal Rights Controversy* (Toronto, 1985) 42–55; Gillespie, *International Environmental Law, Politics and Ethics* (Oxford, 1997) *passim* and 141–4.

[82] There may also be a distinction in terms of the object of regulation, with wild animals the focus of conservation, albeit that such regulation evolved 'in terms of utility and the avoidance of over-exploitation': Outhwaite, 29 *JEL* (2017), 322.

[83] *Supra*, Ch 2, section 5(2)(d).

MEAs, supervision by the parties remains the key to ensuring the effectiveness and further evolution of all of these regulatory regimes.[84]

The 1968 African Convention on the Conservation of Nature and Natural Resources ('1968 African Convention')[85]—but not its 2003 revision—lists natural resources according to the degree of protection required: those threatened with extinction are banned from hunting unless this is required in the national interest or for scientific purposes; the others can be hunted only under special authority. These provisions can be applied to unlisted species to preserve particular national fauna. Measures taken must be scientifically based and reconciled with customary rights.

The 1979 CMS also provides for listing of threatened species in appendices according to the degree of threat.[86] The need for conservation measures depends on whether a species has a favourable or unfavourable 'conservation status', namely, the sum of the influences acting on it that may affect its long-term distribution and abundance (Article 1(1)(c)). Species are listed, on the basis of reliable scientific evidence, in one of two appendices according to their degree of endangerment. Parties that are 'Range States' of that species, that is states exercising jurisdiction over any part of the range of a migratory species that is listed as having an unfavourable conservation status, or whose flag vessels take it beyond national jurisdictional limits, must conclude international agreements to conserve them (Article 2).[87]

The 1979 Bern Convention on the Conservation of European Wildlife and Natural Habitats[88] also lists endangered species on two appendices according to the degree of threat (Article 7) and requires parties to take such measures as closed seasons, prohibition of taking (as required), and prohibition of indiscriminate means of capture, though exceptions can be permitted. Parties are also required to take appropriate measures to conserve the habitat of species listed on the appendices and there are special provisions for migratory species. Its Standing Committee of member states of the Council of Europe can make recommendations on all these matters and has done so.

The listing system is also used to protect wetlands (as defined therein) in the 1971 Ramsar Convention.[89] Each party must designate suitable wetlands in its territory for inclusion in a List of Wetlands of International Importance (Article 2), maintained by a Bureau established under the Convention. The choice is made on the basis of their international significance in terms of ecology, botany, zoology, limnology, or hydrology. The wetlands remain subject to national sovereignty but parties must promote their conservation in conformity with the international obligations laid down in the Convention. Conferences meet regularly: they can give advice on, amongst other things, conservation, wise use, and management. The parties have been increasingly

84 On fisheries agreements see *infra*, Ch 12 and on other agreements see infra, this chapter.

85 See *Lyster's International Wildlife Law* 278–304; ibid, 29 *NRJ* (1989) 979–1000; De Klemm, 29 *NRJ* (1989) 935–78.

86 See *Lyster's International Wildlife Law*, 129–55.

87 See *infra*, section 3(3).

88 See *Lyster's International Wildlife Law* Ch 10; Lasén Díaz, 19 *RECIEL* (2010) 185–96.

89 See *infra*, section 3(1).

active on all these issues, as illustrated later in this chapter, even though their obligations are expressed in general terms only.

Under the 1972 World Heritage Convention,[90] areas that are listed constitute a world heritage for whose protection it is the duty of the international community as a whole to cooperate (Articles 6 and 11), but remain under the sovereignty of the state in which it is located (Article 2). The World Heritage Committee maintains a list of those areas considered to be of outstanding universal value in terms of criteria established by it. Thus it is not all natural heritage which is to be protected, conserved, and transmitted to future generations and which will be eligible for inscription on the World Heritage List.

Under 1973 CITES,[91] species whose survival is threatened by international trade therein or in specimens thereof or which may become so unless trade is regulated, are listed on appendices, which can be amended at the biennial conferences of its parties. As the example of the African elephant discussed further below illustrates, listing (and delisting) decisions can become highly politicized. Export and import of those threatened with extinction (listed on Appendix 1) requires prior issue and presentation of an export and import permit; these are issued only if certain conditions are met (Article III). Re-export similarly requires a prior permit. The advice of both the national Scientific and Management Authorities, established under the Convention, must be sought on questions such as whether export will be detrimental to the species' survival, whether or not the specimen was obtained in breach of state laws, and whether the method of shipment minimizes risk of injury, damage to health, or cruel treatment, etc, of animals concerned. The export-import permit system is the crux of this Convention but, as we will see below, exemptions are permitted. Whether or not the 1973 CITES system is the best approach to conserving wildlife and biodiversity is considered in section 3(4) below.

(ii) Protection of habitat

Conservation of species' habitats is an integral part of their effective conservation.[92] Several of the major wildlife conventions now specifically provide for habitat protection. Amongst these is the 1968 African Convention which provided for the creation of 'special reserves' set aside for conservation of wildlife and protection of its habitat (Article III), within which killing and human settlement is controlled, and also for 'partial reserves' or 'sanctuaries' set aside to protect particularly threatened animal or plant species (especially those listed) and the biotypes necessary for their survival. It also requires maintenance and extension of existing conservation areas and possible creation of new ones to protect representative ecosystems and those peculiar to a territory and that parties establish protective zones round these areas for control of detrimental activities (Article X, 1968). The 2003 revision provides similarly for 'conservation areas' to conserve representative ecosystems or areas with a high degree

[90] See *infra*, section 3(2). [91] See *infra*, section 3(4).

[92] On fisheries conservation measures, see *infra* Ch 12.

of biological diversity, and ensure conservation of species, including those threatened or of special scientific or aesthetic value (Article XII). Buffer zones are also to be established where activities outside a conservation are detrimental to the purposes for conservation within the conservation area (Article XII(4)). The definition and management objectives for different categories of conservation area—strict nature reserve, wilderness area, national park, natural monument, habitat/species management area, protected landscape/seascape, and managed resource protection area—are set forth in Annex 2. These categories clearly reflect the influence of other instruments, including the 1992 CBD and the 1972 World Heritage Convention.

The 1971 Ramsar Convention is concerned with protecting 'the fundamental ecological functions of wetlands as regulators of water regimes and as habitats supporting a characteristic flora and fauna, especially waterfowl'. The 1972 World Heritage Convention defines 'natural heritage' to include 'areas which constitute the habitat of threatened species of animals of outstanding universal value from the point of view of science or conservation' (Article 2). The 2019 Operational Guidelines state that nominated natural heritage properties must contain, inter alia, 'the most important and significant natural habitats for *in-situ* conservation of biological diversity, including those containing threatened species of Outstanding Universal Value from the point of view of science or conservation'.[93] The 1979 CMS defines habitat as 'any area in the range of a migratory species which contains suitable living conditions for that species'. Range states of the Appendix I species must try to conserve and restore habitats important to removing these species from danger of extinction (Article III(4)(a)) and agreements concluded by range states must provide for conservation and restoration of habitats important in maintaining a favourable conservation status (Article V(5)(e)). The 1979 Bern Convention's stated titular and preambular aims include conservation of natural habitats, as also do its general provisions. This is a major purpose of the Convention. Several articles lay down obligations on parties to promote policies, enact legislation, and take other measures for this purpose (Articles 3, 4, and 12). The 1940 Western Hemisphere Convention's aim is also to protect representatives of species in their natural habitat.[94]

Despite these provisions in major conventions, however, the record of states parties in implementing habitat protection measures is generally considered less good than than in their implementation of permit systems. States often limit habitat protection to national parks or nature reserves or do not extend it to certain species. These limitations are discussed further below.

(iii) Protected areas

National parks and nature reserves are a means of giving special protection to endangered wildlife and ecologically important areas. Antarctica is the largest and most important nature reserve specifically so designated and protected by treaty. In addition

[93] *Operational Guidelines for the Implementation of the World Heritage Convention* 2019, para 77.

[94] Referred to as a 'sleeping treaty' in the first edition of *Lyster's International Wildlife Law* (1985).

to a ban on all mineral extraction, the 1991 Antarctic Protocol provides, inter alia, for measures to conserve flora and fauna.[95] The largest marine reserve in the world has also been designated in the Antarctic, in the Ross Sea.[96] As noted above, both the 1940 Western Hemisphere Convention and the 1968 African Convention, with its 2003 revision, also encourage the creation of national parks, nature reserves, nature monuments, and strict wilderness reserves, all of which are defined and for which various protective measures are laid down.[97] In situ conservation including the designation of protected areas is one of the core regulatory tools under the 1992 CBD. Article 2 defines protected area as 'a geographically defined area which is designated or regulated and managed to achieve specific management objectives' and in 2010 the parties to the 1992 CBD agreed an ambitious target of ensuring that within a decade at least 17 per cent of terrestrial and inland water areas and 10 per cent of coastal and marine areas, especially areas of particular importance for biodiversity and ecosystem services, are conserved through effectively and equitably managed, ecologically representative and well-connected systems of protected areas and other effective area-based conservation measures.[98] As we will see below, setting such ambitious targets is one thing, achieving them has been quite another.

Considerable work on protected areas and their management has been undertaken by IUCN.[99] It defines protected area as 'a clearly defined geographical space, recognized, dedicated and managed, through legal or other effective means, to achieve the long-term conservation of nature with associated ecosystem services and cultural values.' Six categories of protected area are employed, classified according to the level of protection required, from Ia 'strict nature reserve', 'a strictly protected areas set aside to protect biodiversity and also possibly geological/geomorphical features, where human visitation, use and impacts are strictly controlled and limited to ensure protection of the conservation values' to VI, a protected area with sustainable use of natural resources, which are 'generally large, with most of the area in a natural condition, where a proportion is under sustainable natural resource management and where low-level non-industrial use of natural resources compatible with nature conservation is seen as one of the main aims of the area'. The significance of IUCN's protected areas classification system and management approach is its influence on State practice. For example, the UK's Overseas Territories[100] now constitute the world's largest system

[95] Article II and Annex 2. [96] See *infra* Ch 12.

[97] 1968 African Convention, Articles 3, 10; 1940 Convention on Nature Protection and Wildlife Preservation, Article II. See *Lyster's International Wildlife Law*, Chs 8 (Western Hemisphere), 9 (African Convention).

[98] CBD, COP 10 (2010) Decision X/2, Aichi Target 11. This target was endorsed at the Rio+20 Summit in 2012: UNGA, *The Future We Want*, para 177. See also UNGA Res 66/231 (2011).

[99] See the current *Guidelines for applying protected area management categories* available at: https://www.iucn.org/theme/protected-areas/about/protected-area-categories.

[100] The CBD has been extended to some OTs (British Virgin Islands; Cayman Islands; Gibraltar; St Helen; Ascension; and Tristan da Cunha) and two Crown Dependencies (Isle of Man and Jersey) with its reporting obligations under the CBD including them: see, for example, Annex 4 of the UK's 5th National Report to the CBD (2014), 56–68 (Ascension) available at https://www.cbd.int/doc/world/gb/gb-nr-05-en.pdf.

of national MPAs with 14 OTs holding 94 per cent of the UK's biodiversity,[101] contributing to the UK achieving the 10 per cent marine protected area objective under the 1992 CBD. Many of the OT MPA designations refer to IUCN's protected areas categories. For example, in 2016 Pitcairn's EEZ was declared an IUCN 'Category I fully protected, no-take MPA'[102] while St Helena has declared an IUCN Category VI (Sustainable Use) MPA.[103]

(iv) Provision of financial assistance and capacity building

A persistent theme throughout this chapter is the need for adequate financing of wildlife treaties.[104] For example, Article XXVIII of the revised 2003 African Convention recognises the 'central importance of financing to the achievement of the purposes of the Convention' and calls on each State Party 'taking into account its capability' to 'make every effort to ensure that adequate financial resources are available for the implementation of the Convention'. Funding is central to effectiveness, whether it is the cost of the bodies supporting the treaty system, of implementation, or of participation at meetings of the parties. Most of the agreements considered here contain a funding mechanism, generally based on contributions set in accordance with UN 'tariffs'. Additional contributions may be forthcoming from specially designated funds, such as the trust fund arrangements under the World Heritage, CMS and Ramsar Conventions. The 1992 CBD is in a different position as the 'beneficiary' of the GEF, which also administers the financial mechanism related to the implementation of the 2000 Cartagena Biosafety Protocol ('Cartagena Protocol') (and Supplementary Protocol), and the Nagoya Protocol Implementation Fund. The Biodiversity Liaison Group has expressed the view that the GEF should provide support for all biodiversity-related conventions.[105] To a limited extent it now does so: particularly pertinent for habitat conservation is the GEF's Small Grant Programme ('SGP') which, in partnership with the UN Foundation ('UNF'), provides funding for 'Community Management of Protected Areas for Conservation' ('COMPACT') including designated World Heritage sites, Ramsar sites and biosphere reserves.[106] External support has also been obtained from the GEF for a major capacity-building initiative for critical sites along AEWA flyways.[107]

Funding is thus piecemeal, and in some cases dependent on external donations and partnering arrangements. Indeed, attracting additional, external sources of financial support is of increasing importance for wildlife treaties. Trust funds and other forms of

101 Papastavridis and Redgwell (forthcoming, 2021).

102 See Pitcairn Islands Marine Protected Area Ordinance 2016, 12 September 2016, available at http://government.pn/Laws/2016-09-13%20Pitcairn%20Islands%20Marine%20Protected%20Area%20Ordinance%202016.pdf

103 See Blue Belt Overseas Territory Work Plan: St Helena (15 October 2018), p 2, available at https://assets.publishing.service.gov.uk/government/uploads/system/uploads/attachment_data/file/757648/Blue_Belt_work_plan_-_St_Helena.pdf

104 See also Boisson de Chazournes in Bodansky et al, Ch 41.

105 BLG-3, para. 9.

106 See further www.sgp.undp.org

107 The 'Wings Over Wetlands' project (WOW): see www.wingsoverwetlands.org.

ad hoc financing are now an important source of revenue, above and beyond 'regular' contributions. This has been particularly evident in fund-raising for emergency response to threats to wildlife and habitat such as the 'Rapid Response Facility' under the 1972 World Heritage Convention and the Great Apes Survival Project ('GRASP'), a public/private partnership launched in 2001 and led by UNESCO and UNEP. It now involves 23 range states, several donor nations, thirty non-governmental organisations, and four wildlife treaties (the 1972 World Heritage Convention, the 1992 CBD, 1979 CMS and 1973 CITES).[108] Another significant source of external funding is the UNF mentioned above[109] which has funded, inter alia, the International Corporate Wetlands Restoration Partnership, a joint initiative with the Nature Conservancy and the Gillette Company designed to leverage private financial contributions to match existing international mechanisms under conventions such as Ramsar and the 1972 World Heritage Convention.[110]

International financial institutions also have a role to play in facilitating wildlife conservation, especially bearing in mind the role of the World Bank as the trustee of the GEF which it administers jointly with UNDP and UNEP. Implementation facilitation also occurs through the ordinary loan arrangements of the World Bank, which have 'mainstreamed' the environment and which peg project compliance measures to international standards, including international agreements for the conservation of wildlife.[111] Other international institutions have a role to play in capacity-building, such as the Commonwealth Secretariat and its involvement in financing legal expertise in the drafting of maritime legislation for the implementation of the 1982 UNCLOS in Africa and the Caribbean region in particular.

International wildlife law has also responded to the problem of lack of scientific knowledge and expertise impeding national action. The Global Taxonomic Initiative under the 1992 CBD aims at closing the developing country knowledge gap in respect of biological diversity through species identification. It is also designed to plug general scientific knowledge gaps which exist regarding the nature and extent of biological diversity; the Global Register of Migratory Species under the 1979 CMS is further example of capacity-building of general scientific knowledge. In addition, the clearing house mechanisms established under a number of wildlife agreements are a web-based system to facilitate the exchange of knowledge and expertise through the Parties themselves, including examples of implementing legislation.

Ultimately, the question is one of the allocation of scarce national resources in the face of competing national demands and pressure for eg agricultural and urban

[108] www.grasp.org

[109] An independent public charity under US law founded in 1998 after Ted Turner's gift of $1 billion to the United Nations. It encourages public/private partnerships.

[110] See www.icwrp.org.

[111] See, inter alia, Environmental Assessment Sourcebook Updates No. 10, March 1996 (International Agreements on Environment and Natural Resources: Relevance and Application in Environmental Assessment) and No. 20, October 1997 (Biodiversity and Environmental Assessment). See also No. 28, June 2002 (Wetlands and Environment Assessment). Full text is available at www.worldbank.org

development, deforestation and mining. Ultimately, as we saw in Ch 2, conservation of vital natural capital goes to the heart of national and international policy on sustainable development. The political will to ensure effective implementation of existing and future wildlife obligations is a crucial factor. This may be influenced by external pressures, such as regular meetings of the COP and compliance review, and by internal pressures generated by civil society and the role of major groups in the sustainable development process, which was acknowledged at Rio in Agenda 21. But as Helm argues, 'It is not hard to make the case that the process of destruction [of natural capital] has gone too far, and that renewable natural capital as a whole is already well below the optimal level. . .The state of core ecosystem services, from climate to fresh water and soils, is already a serious cause for concern.'[112]

(v) Reporting, Monitoring and Compliance Review

The first generation of international wildlife treaties rarely provided for any degree of monitoring or oversight of national implementation. Increasingly, however, modern wildlife treaties provide for a comprehensive feedback loop, from implementation to monitoring to reporting to international review to non-compliance mechanisms. This underscores the evolutionary nature of many wildlife treaty instruments and the dynamic effect of decision-making by the conference of the parties, as well as the impact of the work of treaty subsidiary bodies and secretariats. Perhaps the most striking example of monitoring and reporting obligations giving rise to new prescriptions is the evolution of the 1979 CMS, a major framework agreement with a number of 'daughter' agreements addressed to specific species, one of which ('EUROBATS') is already 'second generation'.[113]

Under most international wildlife agreements, States Party not only have the obligation to implement but also an express obligation to report upon such implementation. Through reporting, it is possible to obtain a snapshot of overall implementation and enforcement patterns. Such reporting obligations might include supplying the text of implementing laws and measures (eg 1979 CMS); transmission of specimens of the documentation employed when implementing the permitting or certification system required (eg 1973 CITES); supplying the results of monitoring environmental conditions (eg 1991 Environmental Protocol to the AT); and publication of records kept, and of the results of monitoring, as well as the compilation of official reports, or summaries thereof, reflecting application and enforcement of the treaty (eg 1973 CITES). A number of wildlife treaties have had, and continue to have, problems with non-submission of reports[114] and inaccuracies in them, sometimes deliberately so.[115] Non-state actors can play an important role here, as a source of additional information

112 Helm, *Natural Capital: Valuing the Planet*, 63. See *supra*, Ch 2.

113 And the Siberian Crane MoU substantially revised: see further *infra* section 3(3).

114 See, for example, compliance review of non-reporting under CITES, discussed in section 3(4) below.

115 Such as deliberate Russian misreporting of whaling effort: Chayes and Handler Chayes, *The New Sovereignty; Compliance with International Regulatory Agreements* (Harvard University Press, 1995),155.

on national implementation, e.g. the Wildlife Trade Monitoring Record ('TRAFFIC') under 1973 CITES and BirdLife International under Ramsar.

The link between reporting, implementation and compliance has also given rise to a relatively new phenomenon in the context of national implementation of international wildlife obligations, and that is compliance review. This type of review occurs through scrutiny of implementation performance by a standing (or implementation or compliance) committee (eg the 1991 Alps Convention and Protocols, the 'files' procedure of the Bern Convention, and the role of the WHC World Heritage Committee under the 1972 World Heritage Convention) and/or by the COP (e.g. 1973 CITES). Some more recent instruments make provision for the future establishment of an implementation review procedure, such as the compliance mechanism envisaged and then subsequently established under the 2000 Cartagena Protocol to the 1992 CBD. Typically, compliance procedures are designed to ensure a return to compliance through a range of techniques, including the possibility of facilitative and/or coercive measures (eg access to facilitative financing, or the suspension of trading privileges, if any).[116]

A number of obstacles to effective implementation may arise, and come to be highlighted under treaty-based non-compliance or other procedures. Under 1973 CITES, 1971 Ramsar, and the 1979 CMS, for example, a number of non-compliance cases have arisen from an inability of states effectively to carry out their reporting obligations. For developing country parties, this is often a consequence of lack of financial resources and of technical expertise. Harmonising of reporting obligations, as has occurred under Ramsar, is one method for streamlining the reporting burden and enhancing compliance. Lack of scientific knowledge and expertise is another issue, evident for example in the implementation of the 1992 CBD, where especially developing country parties are hampered by inadequate scientific knowledge of the full extent of biodiversity contained within their borders. This is exacerbated by the fact that much of the taxonomic research is carried out by developed countries, a fact recognised and sought to be redressed by the treaty bodies through the Global Taxonomic Initiative referred to above. In situ conservation obligations under the 1992 CBD may require the designation of protected areas, with the need consequently to enforce such designation, an issue also under a number of other wildlife treaties. 1973 CITES is dependent on the issuance of certificates and careful monitoring of points of entry for illegally traded flora and fauna, as indeed is the 2000 Cartagena Protocol to the 1992 CBD regulating the transboundary movement of living modified organisms. In general, there are six types of obstacles to national implementation, which may operate individually or collectively: (i) financial; (ii) technical; (iii) scientific; (iv) legal and administrative; (v) political; and (vi) textual (i.e. the treaty text itself may be insufficiently clear and precise to give rise to precise obligations for national implementation).[117] In recognition of these barriers to implementation, implementation facilitation is now a key feature of contemporary wildlife treaty arrangements.

116 See further on compliance *supra*, chapter 4.

117 See, generally, Redgwell in Bodansky, Brunnée and Hey (eds), *The Oxford Handbook of International Environmental Law* (Oxford, 2008).

2 SIGNIFICANCE AND EFFECTIVENESS OF THE MAJOR GLOBAL WILDLIFE CONVENTIONS

It is virtually impossible to assess the effectiveness of the wildlife conservation regime from a cross-sectoral perspective, or to evaluate the effect on conservation of one species of all the measures that have been—or might be—applied to it under the full range of conventions, and particularly in the context of the broad requirements of the 1992 CBD. It is somewhat easier to evaluate the relative effectiveness of the techniques provided under particular conventions, although even here it is not possible to give an overview of all state practice in implementation of a convention; some global conventions are less well ratified than others, as in the case of the 1979 CMS, and this *per se* reduces their effectiveness. The requirements of the 1992 CBD now necessitate a broader approach to coordination and cooperation among all the relevant sectoral conventions at all levels, as recognized in the practice of its treaty institutions considered in this chapter.[118]

It has always to be borne in mind that a range of concepts, principles, and measures, specific and non-specific, can be invoked to protect wildlife. Some are undoubtedly more effective than others. Adoption in 1972 of the Stockholm Declaration, Recommendations, and Action Plan greatly accelerated the conclusion of wildlife conventions over the following decade. UNCED in 1992 added the CBD and placed existing wildlife conventions within the framework of sustainable development. There is thus considerable state practice under the major conventions in the form of resolutions, amendments to the relevant appendices, and states' acceptance or rejection of these. Reviewing all the developments within these conventions, and even more so the relevant national laws implementing them, is too large a task for a work of the present kind. Fuller treatment is found in Lyster's seminal work *International Wildlife Law*, the first edition of which outlined progress up to 1984 under twenty-seven treaties, while the second edition in 2010 adds to this tally.[119] In this section, we shall again confine our review mainly to Lyster's 'big four' treaties, which remain the centrepiece of wildlife law and were listed at the outset of this chapter—the 1971 Ramsar Convention; the 1972 World Heritage Convention; the 1979 CMS, and the 1973 CITES. By virtue of their relevance to the conservation strategies outlined in this chapter, especially those now set by the 1992 CBD, these treaties continue to influence development of the international law on conservation of wildlife. To this analysis two further instruments are added, concerned with plant protection *per se*, the 1951 IPPC and the

118 At every one of its meetings, the 1992 CBD's COP has reaffirmed the importance it attaches to cooperation and coordination between it and other relevant conventions, institutions, and processes: See *CBD Handbook*, Sec IV and Guide to Article 26.

119 Lyster, *International Wildlife Law* (Cambridge, 1985) and Bowman, Davies and Redgwell, *Lyster's International Wildlife Law* (2nd edn, Cambridge, 2010).

2001 ITPGRFA.[120] Together with the1992 CBD, also discussed in detail below, these comprise a legally separate but inter-linked and evolving web of biodiversity-related treaties.[121]

2(1) 1971 CONVENTION ON WETLANDS OF INTERNATIONAL IMPORTANCE ESPECIALLY AS WATERFOWL HABITAT (RAMSAR CONVENTION)

The Ramsar Convention is the only global environmental treaty addressed to a particular ecosystem, the conservation and wise use of wetlands primarily as habitat for wild birds.[122] It is also the first wildlife convention, the Whaling Convention apart, to aim at global participation.[123] There are currently 171 contracting parties,[124] with over 2,388 sites designated for the List of Wetlands of International Importance covering a total surface area of nearly 254 million hectares (an area larger than Mexico). To place these figures in historical context, in 1992 there were only 65 contracting parties with 549 wetlands listed. Compared with the other biodiversity-related conventions, participation, especially by developing States, was low until the establishment of a facilitative funding mechanism and the additional spur of the 1992 CBD itself.

The total area of wetlands 'from tundra to tropics' is estimated within the range of 4-6 per cent (up to 570 million hectares) of the earth's land surface.[125] The first site to be designated under the 1971 Ramsar Convention was the Cobourg Peninsula in Australia, in 1974, and the largest sites are Ngiri-Tumba-Maindombe in the Democratic Republic of Congo and Queen Maud Gulf in Canada, each of which covers over six million hectares, while others are as small as one hectare.[126] Many parties have exceeded the minimum legal requirement of one site designation, though both distribution and size of areas covered requires further enlargement to achieve

[120] Apart from early pioneers such as de Klemm, *Wild Plant Conservation and the Law* (IUCN Environmental Policy and Law Paper No 24, Gland, 1990) there had until recently been little attention paid to plant conservation in international law. See Amos, *International Conservation Law: The Protection of Plants in Theory and Practice* (CRC Press, 2020).

[121] The CBD collaborates with these six other biodiversity-related conventions through the Biodiversity Liaison Group which it established in 2002. Linkages between the conventions are facilitated by the InforMEA initiative of UN Environment https://www.informea.org.

[122] *Lyster's International Wildlife Law* (2010), Ch 13; Navid, 29 *NRJ* (1989) 1001; 20 *IUCN Bull* 4–6 (1989); Special Report: Wetlands; Bowman, 42 *Neths ILR* (1995) 1; Bowman, 66 *ICLQ* (1995) 540; id, 11 *JEL* (1999) 87, 281; Owen, 13 *JEL* (2001) 21ff; Matthews, *The Ramsar Convention on Wetlands: Its History and Development* (Ramsar Convention Bureau, 1993); Shine and de Klemm, *Wetlands, Water and the Law* (IUCN Environmental Policy and Law Paper No 38, Gland, 1999); Farrier and Tucker, 12 *JEL* (2000) 21.

[123] For bilateral and regional approaches, see *Lyster's International Wildlife Law* Part III 'Regional wildlife regulation'.

[124] Earlier wildlife treaties– Ramsar, WHC and CITES—are open to States only, in contrast with the 1979 CMS (Art XV) and the CBD (Art 34) which provide for participation by REIOs.

[125] Mitsch and Gosselink, *Wetlands* (5th ed, Hoboken, 2015); UNEP-World Conservation Monitoring Centre has suggested an estimate of about 570 million hectares (5.7 million km2); roughly 6% of the Earth's land surface: see also Ramsar Handbook I, 10.

[126] E.g. Ile Alcatraz (Guinea) and Hosnie's Spring on Christmas Island (Australia).

conservation purposes not only under the 1971 Ramsar Convention, which 'takes the lead on wetlands biodiversity',[127] but also to fulfil the 1992 CBD's requirements considered in the final section of this chapter. Parties with the most sites are the UK (170) and Mexico (142) though Bolivia has the largest area (14.8 million hectares).[128]

For the conservation and wise use of wetlands, and to fulfil the 1992 CBD's requirements for *in situ* conservation of biodiversity, it is not enough merely to list sites. The list must include the most important wetland types, including those supporting endangered species or threatened ecological communities, and effective conservation and management measures must be taken within them.[129] According to the 1971 Ramsar Convention's 2018 Global Wetland Outlook[130]—the first global report specifically on the status of wetlands and the services they provide—wetlands are lost three times faster than natural forests with an estimated 87 per cent of wetland resources lost since 1700.[131] While the total wetlands remaining today are estimated to exceed the size of Canada, as with the state of biological diversity conservation more broadly, the message is one of accelerated decline, with 35 per cent of wetlands sites with available information lost since 1970 and a quarter of wetlands plants and animals at risk of extinction.[132] The achievements under the 1971 Ramsar Convention must be viewed in this light.

Much has nevertheless been accomplished under a convention of initially rather unpromising beginnings and subject to internal[133] and external[134] criticism. It is still an extraordinarily brief instrument of only 13 articles which was also notably 'institution-light' at the outset.[135] NGOs played an important role in developing the 1971 Ramsar Convention and a continuing partnership with NGOs provides vital technical and financial support.[136] The general nature of its provisions has given rise to problems of interpretation, albeit that its rather weak obligations are buttressed by stronger procedural obligations such as reporting.[137] The soft language is a reflection of

127 See e.g. Ramsar Resolution 5.1 (1993). In turn, the CBD COP has recognised the Ramsar Convention's lead implementation role for wetlands for the CBD (Decision III/21, para 7) and approved joint work plans for collaborative activities, the most recent being the 5th joint work programme (2011–2020). In 1996 a Memorandum of Cooperation was concluded between the CBD and Ramsar Convention Secretariats, renewed in 2011.

128 See www.ramsar.org

129 See discussion of the criteria for identifying wetlands of international importance below.

130 Patterned on the more well-established Global Biodiversity Outlook, above.

131 Dudley (ed), *Global Wetland Outlook: State of the World's Wetlands and their Services to People* (Ramsar Convention Secretariat, 2018) 3.

132 Ibid; see also Finlayson et al, 39 *Wetlands* (2019) 1.

133 At the very first COP a list of key deficiencies in the Convention were identified and listed: see Recommendation 1.8.

134 See e.g. World Conservation Strategy (1980), section 15, para 5.

135 The Convention established a COP (Article 6) and secretariat ('bureau'—Article 8). A standing committee and a scientific review panel have since been added.

136 Five NGOs have been designated as 'International Organization Partners': BirdLife International, IUCN, International Water Management Institute, Wetlands International, and WWF International.

137 Wiersema, in Peel and Rajamani (eds), *The Oxford Handbook of International Environmental Law* (2nd edn, Oxford, 2021) Ch 32, 15.

sovereignty concerns, with Article 2(3) expressly providing that 'inclusion of a wetland in the List does not prejudice the exclusive sovereign rights of the Contracting Party in whose territory the wetland is situated'.[138] However, over time its provisions have been subject to extensive elaboration through Resolutions or Recommendations[139] issued by the regular meetings of the COP[140] and by two extraordinary meetings of the Parties.[141]

(a) Listing, conservation and 'wise use' of wetland sites

The most important obligations are to: (i) record internationally significant wetlands on its List of Wetlands of International Importance;[142] (ii) 'promote' their conservation and, as far as possible, the 'wise use' of all wetlands within their territory, including by establishing nature reserves in wetlands;[143] and (iii) cooperate with respect to transboundary wetlands, shared water systems, and shared species.[144] These are the oft-quoted 'three pillars' of the Convention. What the Convention does not do is to prohibit or regulate the taking of wetland species but, as discussed below, wetland use must not adversely affect its ecological character, thus affording indirect protection to species and ecological communities through protection of their critical habitat. There is an important interlinkage here with the 1979 Bonn Convention on Migratory Species ('Bonn Convention') considered below, insofar as wetlands are a vital habitat for migratory birds and many other migratory species. Conservation and restoration of habitat is also an obligation under that convention.[145]

The chief mechanism under the 1971 Ramsar Convention is the listing of sites for protection under national law. Each contracting party is required to designate 'suitable wetlands' within its territory for inclusion on the List of Wetlands of International Importance, the 'flagship' of the Convention.[146] Unlike the 1972 World Heritage Convention, which operates a screening procedure for sites nominated for inscription on the World Heritage List, Ramsar allows unilateral designation of sites for listing. Indeed, a State is not considered a full party to the Convention unless and until a site has been designated[147] (again in contrast with the 1972 World Heritage Convention).

[138] See also Art 3 CBD; on the balancing between sovereignty and community interest in Art 6 WHC, see further below section 3(2).

[139] Article 6(2)(f). Examples include Resolution 5.1 (1993) on the *Framework for the implementation of the Ramsar Convention* which amplified conservation obligations and Resolution 5.5 (1993) establishing the Scientific and Technical Review Panel (STRP). Since 1999 all measures adopted have been resolutions, though there appears little legal difference between them: see further *Lyster's International Wildlife Law* 430–1.

[140] The COPhas met 12 times since 1980, the most recent being COP13 (2018) in Dubai, with COP14 (2021) timed to coincide with the fiftieth anniversary of the conclusion of the Convention.

[141] In 1982, adopting the Paris Protocol inserting an amendment clause into the Convention (Article 10*bis*) and adopting versions in all six official UN languages, and in 1987, adopting the institution-building Regina Amendments to Articles 6 and 7, defining the powers of the COP, establishing the inter-sessional Standing Committee, the Ramsar Bureau (permanent secretariat) and a budget.

[142] Article 2. [143] Article 3(1) and Article 4(1).

[144] Article 5; see also Resolution VII.19 *Guidelines for international cooperation under the Ramsar Convention* (May 1999) allowing for joint designation of wetlands across borders ('Transboundary Ramsar Sites').

[145] 1980 CMS, Articles III(4) and V(5)(e), and see *infra*, section 3(3)(a). [146] Article 2(1).

[147] Article 2(4) and Article 9.

So long as the proposed site fulfils one of the Criteria for Identifying Wetlands of International Importance[148] and has been designated by the appropriate national authority it will be added to the List which is maintained by the Ramsar Secretariat. The Criteria have evolved over time and reflect concerns both regarding ecosystem and species protection and biodiversity conservation.[149] Some sites may have been protected under national law before listing but listing them becomes a means of raising their profile and securing national action when they are threatened;[150] other states list sites not yet protected. Many sites at the time of listing are already within nature reserves; some become so after listing but only a few states take measures restricting activities *outside* these areas to protect them from harm.[151]

Conservation obligations are set out in Articles 3 and 4. In Article 3(1) the parties are required to 'formulate and implement their national planning so as to promote the conservation of wetlands included in the List, and as far as possible the wise use of wetlands in their territory'.[152] At the very least Article 3(1) involves an obligation not to cause harm to listed sites, if possible.[153] Moreover, the first half of Article 3(1) is not limited to protection of listed sites within the territory of the Contracting Party (unlike the obligation of wise use), but reflects 'some form of collective responsibility for [all] such sites'; 'designation as sites of international importance means that they are 'resources of "common concern" to the international community as a whole'.[154] Other parties thus have a general right to seek to uphold compliance with the 1971 Ramsar Convention; it is in effect an *erga omnes* regime.[155] Article 4 requires parties, inter alia, to 'promote' the conservation of the 'wetlands and waterfowl', establish nature reserves and wardens, and 'endeavour' to increase waterfowl populations.

What does the Convention mean by 'wise use' and how does it differ, if at all, from sustainable use or optimal use? The Convention does not define the term, but the

148 Elaboration of the 'international significance' criterion in Article 2(2) is set out in Appendix D of the *Strategic Framework and guidelines for the future development of the List of Wetlands of International Importance of the Convention on Wetlands*, 2012 revision, adopted by Resolution XI.8, most recently revised (Appendix E2 on peatlands, an important carbon sink) by Resolution XIII.12.

149 Over half of the sites designated are under Group A (criterion 1: sites containing representative, rare or unique wetlands types) and Group B (criteria 2–4: sites of international importance for conserving biological diversity, based on species and ecological communities).

150 For example, the Convention has been identified in national reports as instrumental in the abandonment of: a proposed rubbish disposal site near one of the last remaining mudflat systems in Nagoya, Japan; plans to build a new airport near the Cliffe Marshes Ramsar site in the UK; and a proposed tourist development near the Ramsar site on the Caribbean island of Bonaire. See *An Introduction to the Convention on Wetlands* (Ramsar Convention Secretariat, 2016) 13; further examples are cited in *Lyster's International Wildlife Law* ch 13.

151 In contrast, see the reference to buffer zones in the WHC Operational Guidelines below.

152 Article 2. However, only 73 parties have a 'National Wetland Policy or equivalent' with a further 18 reporting 'elements of such a policy': 2018 *Global Wetland Outlook*, 62.

153 *Lyster's International Wildlife Law* 424.

154 *Lyster's International Wildlife Law* 420, cited with approval in the Separate Opinion of Judge Dugard in *Border Activities/San Juan River Cases*, ICJ Reports (2015) 665, para 41. On the implications of 'common concern' see *supra*, Ch 3, section 4(1).

155 On *erga omnes* obligations see Ch 4, *supra*, section 2(7).

parties have done so: 'wise use of wetlands' is 'the maintenance of their ecological character, achieved through the implementation of ecosystem approaches,[156] within the context of sustainable development'.[157] This 'slightly delphic allusion to "ecosystem approaches", is intended to reflect the practice of the 1992 CBD, with Ramsar resolutions appearing to treat 'conservation' and 'wise use' as 'a sort of composite concept' without clear distinction between them.[158] This is not to suggest that use—or development—is an objective for every wetland, since 'wise use' of wetlands clearly demands 'the maintenance of their ecological character'.[159] In this context sustainability may entail the limitation or avoidance of use or development.[160] Wise use is thus not significantly different, if at all, from sustainable use.

Article 3(2) requires that parties obtain and pass 'without delay' any information about actual or likely human-induced changes to the ecological character of 'any wetland in its territory' to the Ramsar Secretariat.[161] The obligation to report on threats and changes in the ecological character implies taking action to address such threats.[162] The importance of NGOs is underscored by the practice of the Ramsar Secretariat in treating notifications of changes in ecological character by a third party (e.g. a national or local NGO) as an Article 3(2) notification, subject to verification with the relevant Contracting Party.[163] This can be an important buttress given that a third of Contracting Parties do not have in place national mechanisms for reporting human-induced adverse changes to their Ramsar sites.[164] COP resolutions have repeatedly called on parties with sites at risk 'to take swift and effective action' to prevent or remedy changes in ecological character.[165] Though not all parties provide this information, many have reported conservation measures taken to avoid disturbance of listed sites.[166] Analysis of state practice, however, concludes that the number of sites reported at risk is 'an implausibly low figure' given results of other reporting mechanisms under the Convention revealing the 'widespread poor and deteriorating status of Ramsar sites'.[167]

[156] See further *supra*, Ch 3 and section (6) below.

[157] 'Conceptual Framework for the Wise Use of Wetlands and the Maintenance of their Ecological Character': Resolution IX.1, Annex A (2005). The Ramsar Convention Secretariat produces *Handbooks for the Wise Use of Wetlands* containing official scientific, technical and policy guidance for the parties on the three pillars of the Convention, with illustrative materials and case studies, now in its 5th edition (2016) with 21 *Handbooks*.

[158] *Lyster's International Wildlife Law*, Ch 13, n 80, citing Resolution VIII.14, para 11, as a particularly good example.

[159] Ibid.

[160] See discussion of sustainable use, *supra*, Ch 3, section 3(2).

[161] Elaborated in *Ramsar Handbook* 17 (5th edn) and see Davidson et al, 71 *Marine & Freshwater Research* (2020a) 117.

[162] This is reflected in national wetland and biodiversity laws which often rely on 'avoid-mitigate-compensate' as part of the permitting process for a development activity with a precautionary emphasis on 'avoid': *Global Wetland Outlook* 62; Gardiner et al, *Avoiding, mitigating and compensating for loss and degradation of wetlands in national laws and policies* (Ramsar Scientific and Technical Briefing Note no. 3, 2012).

[163] *Ramsar Handbook* 1, 50; Davidson et al, 71 *Marine & Freshwater Research* (2020a) 119.

[164] Davidson et al, ibid, 120.

[165] Starting from Recommendation 4.8: see e.g. Resolution VIII.8, para 20; Resolution IX.15, para 20.

[166] *Lyster's International Wildlife Law*, 423.

[167] Davidson et al (2020a), 120; ibid, (2020b) 71 *Marine & Freshwater Research* 127; and *Global Wetland Outlook* 6.

While the Convention is clearly important for the protection of wetlands within national borders (unlike the law of international watercourses), it is also relevant to transboundary wetlands or those that form part of an international watercourse. Article 5 requires parties to consult about implementation of the Convention generally, but especially in the case of transboundary wetlands or shared watercourses. In the *Border Activities/San Juan River Cases* Judge Dugard found that Article 3(2), read with Article 5, required Nicaragua to carry out an EIA and consult Costa Rica when planning an activity—dredging the San Juan river—that potentially affected conservation of wetlands in both countries.[168] The Court disagreed, holding instead that Article 3(2) was limited to notifying the Ramsar Secretariat about ecological changes,[169] while Article 5 embodied only a general obligation to consult 'about implementing obligations arising under the Convention,' not a specific obligation to consult Costa Rica with respect to the dredging of the river.[170] But the Court also found that Nicaragua's roadworks had not changed the ecological character of the wetlands; had they done so in a manner that could impact on Costa Rica the general obligations of transboundary environmental impact assessment, notification, consultation and prevention or remediation considered in Chapter 3 would then have applied.[171] What the judgment reveals is that the 1971 Ramsar Convention, like other environmental treaties, cannot be read as a complete codification of international law relating to shared wetlands.

(b) Implementation and compliance

Once designated, Ramsar sites are to be protected under national law but, as we have seen, they also acquire conservation significance for the international community as a whole. Thus, while, it is estimated that nearly half of Ramsar listed sites do not have a management plan,[172] the requirement to submit triennial reports on the implementation of the treaty to the contracting parties provides an opportunity for review of national implementation by other parties. Failure to promote conservation and wise use may lead to inclusion on the 'Montreux Record of Ramsar sites requiring priority attention' which highlights threats to designated sites.[173] The ultimate sanction is delisting because of the irremediable loss of the values which led to Ramsar listing in the first instance. This has never occurred; nor have any sites been deleted owing to 'urgent national interests' as provided for in the Convention.[174]

Sites requiring priority attention may not formally be added to the Montreux Record without the consent of the State concerned. There are currently 49 sites which

168 ICJ Reports (2015) 665, Sep Op, para 44. 169 Ibid, para 172. 170 Ibid, para 110.

171 *Supra*, Ch 3, sections 5–8, and see also Ch 10, *supra*, on the law of international watercourses.

172 'According to the Ramsar Sites Information Service, 48% of the current 2,315 designated Ramsar Sites (1,120) have a management plan, and it is reported as effectively implemented at 37% (860) of the Sites.' *Rept of the Sec-Gen on the Implementation of the Convention*, COP13 Doc.11.1(2018) para 36.

173 See Resolutions 5.4 (1993) and VIII.8 (2002).

174 Article 2(5). Parties have invoked the 'urgent national interest' clause to *restrict* the boundaries of a Ramsar site on three occasions only: Belgium in the 1980s, Australia in 1997 (though not ultimately implemented), and Germany in 2000. Further guidance on implementation of Article 2(5) is found in Resolution VIII.20 (2002).

have been added to the Montreux Record with consent.[175] Failure to conserve wetlands may result, inter alia, from lack of capacity. Thus, a Small Grants Fund for Wetland Conservation and Wise Use was also established in 1990 with the express purpose of facilitating compliance, along with other forms of technical assistance. The Ramsar Advisory Mission (formerly 'the Monitoring Procedure') was established as a technical assistance mechanism to provide advice to states on problems or threats which have caused Montreux listing to be contemplated. Site visits are an integral part of this mechanism and, as with the Montreux listing procedure itself, are conditional upon the agreement of the contracting party concerned. As of November 2019, the Ramsar Advisory mechanism had been applied on 93 occasions, most recently in Russia (Kurgalsky Peninsula). For sites covered by both Ramsar and the 1972 World Heritage Convention such visits may be requested and carried out jointly, as for example, when Ichkeul National Park in Tunisia was listed on both the Montreux Record and the 1972 World Heritage Convention Heritage in Danger List.[176]

Conservation efforts may be assisted by listing on the Montreux Record with consequent access to technical assistance and facilitative financing under the Convention and elsewhere: for example, the listing of the Azraq Oasis in Jordan assisted in obtaining funding from the Global Environmental Facility and of the Austrian Donau-March-Thaya-Auen in obtaining European Commission funding. However, a 2018 analysis of Ramsar Advisory Mission Reports identifies a lack of consistency over time and between regions in the way in which missions are prepared, conducted and reports finalised, and weak attention to follow-up, reducing their impact within and beyond Ramsar. It recommends comprehensive revision and updating of the 'extremely brief guidelines on operation' of the procedure established in 1990 and unchanged since, with improved communication regarding the technical assistance purpose of the mechanism to dispel 'misperceptions or misrepresentations of the [Ramsar Advisory Mission] as a negative procedure'.[177] Statistical analysis of the Record indicates that voluntary placing of the sites on the Record by Contracting Parties has been 'little used' and has progressively decreased since 1990—and this in the face of the accelerating degradation of wetlands.[178]

(c) Assessment of the Ramsar Convention

Successive Conferences of the Parties have strengthened the 1971 Ramsar Convention's administrative procedures, established a permanent Secretariat, a Standing Committee, and a financial regime of contributions based on the UN scale. These changes and the

[175] For the complete list see <http://www.ramsar.org>.

[176] In fact, the Park is one of a few sites which are protected by listing under three agreements: Ramsar (1980), WHC (1979), and Biosphere Reserve (1977). Details of listings can be found on the Ramsar website: <http://www.ramsar.org>. It was removed from the WHC Danger list in 2006, and from the Montreux Record in 2016, owing to improvements in the ecological character of the site. While designated, it received significant financial and technical support from both conventions in making these improvements.

[177] Jones and Pritchard, *STRP Task 4.2 Comprehensive review and analysis of Ramsar Advisory Mission (RAM) reports*, Final Consultancy Report (2018); see also Pritchard, *Changes in ecological character of wetland sites: a review of Ramsar guidance and mechanisms* (Ramsar Convention Secretariat, 2014).

[178] Davidson et al, 71 *Marine & Freshwater Research* (2020a) 121.

increased authority accorded to the Conference and its productive use of Resolutions have all enhanced the effectiveness of the Convention and encouraged cooperation between its Secretariat and those of other conventions, especially the 1979 CMS and the 1992 CBD. An agreement with the World Heritage Secretariat has enabled their scientific and technical bodies to exchange information, cooperate and coordinate activities aimed at achieving the 1992 CBD goals. There are now over 30 sites jointly designated under the 1971 Ramsar and 1972 World Heritage Conventions.[179]

A Strategic plan adopted by the parties in 2015 acknowledges the problems affecting wetlands, and sets out a programme to reverse the global decline.[180] The Secretary-General's Report in 2018 noted, however, that although the site network continues to grow, effective planning and integrated management of Ramsar Sites shows no real progress; threats continue to increase; progress on restoration is declining; assistance from the UN and other global or regional bodies is also declining.[181] The report concluded once again that the parties need to improve implementation of the Convention and effective management of Ramsar sites. Adoption of a precautionary approach, omitted from the substantive articles of the 1992 CBD and the 1971 Ramsar Conventions, remains stalled. Recommendations were made in 1993 that activities affecting wetlands should be governed by the precautionary principle and that, when comprehensive understanding of the ecological constraints is lacking, they should be prohibited.[182] Current guidance adopted by the Ramsar parties still does not reflect that approach.[183]

Whilst the 1971 Ramsar Convention parties have clearly developed the 'wise use' concept, an essentially pragmatic approach to listing is not conducive to the holistic approach of the 1992 CBD.[184] Ramsar is restricted by its focus on 'wetlands', divorced from their wider catchment areas, a perspective challenged by scientists and not adopted in the 1992 CBD.[185] In reality 'wise use' requires regulation and management of related biological resources whether inside or outside protected areas.[186] The 1971 Ramsar Convention is essentially sectoral and its approach is not well tuned to the holistic, broadly ecoystem approach required to implement the 1992 CBD. To some degree it shows how an older MEA can adapt and evolve towards sustainable developmental goals, but as the current deteriorating state of wetlands attests, while the 1971 Ramsar Convention may have 'come of age',[187] implementing it effectively requires further attention from states parties.

179 Apart from joint designation, there is the issue of overlapping designations. A 2016 report identified 263 areas with multiple designations: see Clamote Rodrigues and Schaaf, *Managing MIDAS: Harmonising the Management of Multi-Internationally Designated Areas: Ramsar Sites, World Heritage sites, Biosphere Reserves and UNESCO Global Geoparks* (IUCN, 2016). They identify 97 Ramsar Sites which are also inscribed wholly or partially in 70 World Heritage sites. On countering fragmentation of habitats under key international wildlife treaties, see generally, Trouwborst in Bowman, Davies and Goodwin (eds), *Research Handbook on Biodiversity and Law* (Cheltenham, 2016) Ch 8.

180 Ramsar Strategic Plan 2016–2024: Resolution XII.2 (2015).

181 Ibid.

182 Resolution RES C 5.6 (Annex), 5th COP (1993), Intro, para 6.

183 Resolution IX.1, Annex A (2005).

184 For an early assessment see Bowman, 66 *ICLQ* (1995) 560.

185 See *infra*, section 6(2). But compare UN Watercourses Convention, Article 20, which takes the same restricted approach to watercourse ecosystems, *supra*, Ch 10, section 2(4).

186 CBD Article 8(c)–(d).

187 Bowman (1995) 42 *Neths ILR* 1.

2(2) THE 1972 WORLD HERITAGE CONVENTION

The World Heritage Convention was adopted under UNESCO auspices, mere months after the 1972 Stockholm Conference. The purpose of the 1972 World Heritage Convention is the identification, protection, conservation, presentation, and transmission to future generations of cultural and natural heritage of outstanding universal value.[188] The 1972 World Heritage Convention is thus unusual in its express linkage of nature conservation and preservation of cultural properties, seeking to achieve a balance between the two. Protection of designated natural and cultural heritage is conferred by inscription on the World Heritage List of natural and cultural sites satisfying the inscription criteria under the Convention. As such it has one important characteristic in common with the 1971 Ramsar Convention, with which it has concluded a Memorandum of Understanding: it works on the basis of maintaining a list of protected sites ('properties' under the Convention). At present there are 1,121 properties on the list, 869 cultural, 213 natural, and 39 mixed properties in 167 States parties.[189] However, unlike under the 1971 Ramsar Convention, it is not necessary to have a site listed to become a full participating party to the Convention.[190] The World Heritage Fund provides an incentive for developing states to list sites, and with 193 States parties it enjoys participation by virtually all states vital to global conservation of outstanding natural sites. Owing inter alia to the basis upon which properties are inscribed onto the World Heritage List, outstanding universal value and representativeness take precedence over geographic distribution: 47 per cent of listed properties are located in Europe and North America, and only 8 per cent in Arab States and 9 per cent in Africa.[191]

(a) The listing process

The effectiveness of the Convention is dependent upon States parties offering up properties for designation since UNESCO has no independent listing power. Listing applications must include details of how the property is managed and protected under national legislation; as under the 1971 Ramsar Convention, subsequent protection is thus a task for national law. The Convention makes clear that *international* protection of the world's cultural and natural heritage is limited to 'the establishment of a system of international cooperation and assistance designed to support States parties to the convention in their efforts to conserve and identify that heritage' (Article 7). Independent evaluation of properties proposed by States for inscription on the List is carried out by a technical advisory body, which for natural heritage is IUCN. Article 2

[188] *Lyster's International Wildlife Law*, Ch 14; Atherton and Atherton, 69 *ALJ* (1995) 631ff; Churchill, in Bowman and Redgwell (eds), *International Law and the Conservation of Biodiversity* (London, 1996) 83; Francioni and Lenzerini (eds), *The 1972 World Heritage Convention: A Commentary* (Oxford, 2008).

[189] Of this total, 39 are transboundary properties shared by two or more States, such as the Mount Nimba Strict Nature Reserve (Côte d'Ivoire and Guinea) and Waterton-Glacier (Canada-US).

[190] For a full list by country and property, see http://whc.unesco.org.

[191] These are the geographic regions employed by UNESCO.

of the Convention defines natural heritage to include natural features, geological and physiological formations and precisely delineated areas 'which constitute the habitat of threatened species of animals and plants of outstanding universal value from the point of view of science or conservation', and natural sites.[192] The criteria for inscription on the List are set forth in *Operational Guidelines* which are revised regularly by one of the Convention bodies, the World Heritage Convention, in order to reflect changes in the implementation of the Convention.[193] IUCN conducts the original review of natural sites, though the sites are nominated by the state party in whose territory they are located; IUCN retains a role under the *Operational Guidelines* in evaluating the natural heritage nominations which are submitted to it by the Secretariat. A precise listing procedure has been laid down: a small Bureau of Committe members, consisting of twenty-one states, overviews proposals on the basis of the *Operational Guidelines* and distributes its recommendations to all states parties. Listing thus takes time.[194]

The Guidelines laid down for listing natural properties narrow the choice to physical areas of outstanding universal value, though these can include marine as well as terrestrial sites.[195] The Convention is thus useful to conservation of wildlife only in protecting certain habitats (mostly in national parks[196]). A species itself, however extraordinary, cannot be listed, in contrast with the CMS and the 1973 CITES. One of the criteria for the assessment of outstanding universal value set forth in the Guidelines explicitly acknowledges the contribution of the Convention to biodiversity conservation and preventing species extinction, enabling a property to be listed if it 'contains the most important and significant natural habitats for in-situ conservation of biological diversity, including those containing threatened species of Outstanding Universal Value from the point of view of science or conservation'.[197] The property has to fulfil 'conditions of integrity' which ensure that it is large enough to comprehend the essential components of the support system it represents and that it is sustainable. Outstanding universal value and conditions of integrity are linked with protection and management of properties with the requirement for adequate long-term legislative, regulatory, institutional, and/or traditional protection and management to ensure their safeguarding.[198]

192 For commentary on Article 2, see Redgwell in Francioni and Lenzerini, *The 1972 World Heritage Convention*, 63.

193 Currently, Operational Guidelines for the Implementation of the *World Heritage Convention*, WHC.19/01, 10 July 2019.

194 Hales, 4 *Parks* (1980) 1–3; see also Francioni and Lenzerini, *The 1972 World Heritage Convention* Ch 2 and 2019 Operational Guidelines, para 61.

195 UNESCO's 2001 Convention on the Underwater Cultural Heritage does not apply to natural heritage (Article 1(1)).

196 The most common legal management tool for World Heritage natural sites is national park or other protected area designation under national law, which may have preceded nomination for inscription: *Implementation of the Convention in the light of twenty-five years' practice*, WHC-96/CONF 201/15 (1996) 8, para 3.1; see also 2019 Operational Guidelines, para 102.

197 Ibid, para 77(x).

198 Ibid, para 97. The purpose of management is 'to ensure the effective protection of the nominated site for present and future generations': para 109.

Sustainable use is acknowledged and properties may support a variety of uses if compatible with their outstanding universal value; but for some properties 'human use would not be appropriate'.[199] Given the diverse character of World Heritage properties there is clearly no 'one size fits all' approach to this issue, nor do the Guidelines contain an explicit list of incompatible activities. However, the World Heritage Committee (WHC) has repeatedly taken the view that mineral, oil and gas exploration or development is incompatible with World Heritage status and has in particular cases exhorted States to cancel petroleum permits.[200] The adverse effects of mining, oil or gas, or quarry activities on World Heritage properties have been catalogued,[201] with the overwhelming majority affecting natural or mixed properties.

Individual nominations must now be drawn from the state's 'tentative list'—essentially an inventory of natural and cultural heritage suitably for inclusion on the List—to be reviewed and resubmitted every decade or so.[202] This forms a benchmark against which to measure the inclusiveness of the List. However, an IUCN report to the Convention highlights a continuing cultural bias in the tentative lists and their poor technical quality, thus diminishing their value as a planning and evaluation tool.[203] Nonetheless, a 1997 review of wetland and marine protected areas concluded that the 1972 World Heritage Convention protects sites with a broader range of biome values than under the 1971 Ramsar Convention because of the role of the WHC.[204]

Listing is decided by the WHC. Though properties must be selected on their own merits, considerations of balance with cultural properties and cost and availability of funds for protection are likely to have some influence; political difficulties can intervene if title to the territory concerned is disputed. However, the increasing number of sites of outstanding natural heritage now listed, including marine sites, does represent an important contribution to the network of conventions relevant to biodiversity conservation, and the Secretariat of the 1992 CBD has participated in a project to harmonize the reporting requirements of this Convention, as well as those of the 1973 CITES, Ramsar, and CMS Conventions and has developed joint work

[199] Ibid, para 119.

[200] See generally Decision 37.COM 7 (Part III); and on Virunga National Park in the DRC e.g. Decision 38 COM 7A.37, Decision 39.COM 7A.4; Decision 40.COM 7A.41 (exhortation to cancel petroleum permits). The most recent (2019) Decision 43 COM 7A.11 expresses a newer concern about proposals to alter the boundaries of the Park for the purpose of permitting petroleum activities, which is contrary to the requirements of the Operational Guidelines (para 165). For the impact of petroleum see also the delisting of the Arabian Oryx Sanctuary in Oman, and the removal of the Belize Barrier Reef System from the Danger List in 2018 after improved management, including a permanent moratorium on offshore petroleum activities.

[201] According to the World Heritage State of Conservation Information System, from 1984–2015, there were 411 reports on 79 World Heritage properties in 47 States Parties concerning mining, oil or gas, or quarrying issues. See further 'World Heritage and Extractive Industries' at https://whc.unesco.org/en/extractive-industries/

[202] Ibid, paras 62, 65.

[203] See WHC-07/31 Com/9, 23 May 2007. IUCN also prepared independent lists, with regional and biome studies to enhance knowledge of natural heritage of outstanding universal value, and in 1996 launched a Natural Heritage Programme to support development of a global strategy for natural heritage sites.

[204] Thorsell, Levy and Sigaty, *A Global Overview of Wetland and Marine Protected Areas on the World Heritage List* (Gland, 1997) 1.

programmes.[205] Today an estimated 50 per cent of global natural heritage of outstanding universal value is on the List, a significant achievement.[206] But the cultural 'bias' of the List persists. For some time the Convention has sought to encourage parties to nominate natural as well as cultural sites to address concerns regarding the representativeness of the World Heritage List, with indifferent success.[207] The 2019 additions to the List contained twenty-four new cultural properties, only four natural properties, and one mixed property.

(b) Conservation obligations

Obligations concerning conservation are spelt out in Articles 4 and 5 of the Convention. Parties must do all they can to ensure identification, protection, and transmission of the natural heritage, including its biodiversity, to future generations,[208] using to the utmost their own resources and, when appropriate and obtainable, international financial, scientific, and technical aid and cooperation. They must adopt protective policies, set up management services for conservation, carry out relevant research to remove threats, take other appropriate measures, and institute training. The *Operational Guidelines* encourage the adoption of many modern environmental management methods such as: defined boundaries reflecting the spatial requirements of habitat and species and to prevent human encroachment; buffer zones; active management including planning, monitoring, evaluation and feedback; robust environmental impact assessment requirements; and key stakeholder involvement.[209]

In a rare case before domestic courts, Articles 4 and 5 were judicially considered by the High Court of Australia in the case of *Commonwealth of Australia v The State of Tasmania*[210] in 1983. The Court (with the Chief Justice dissenting) held that these provisions imposed a legal duty on Australia, a party to the Convention, to protect its listed wilderness parks in Tasmania, despite the generality of the expressions used in these articles and the degree of discretion left to states concerning the precise measure to be taken; Australia must act in good faith to do all it could to achieve the objectives of these articles. As no other such national cases seem to have arisen, it is impossible to say whether other states' courts would hold likewise. These obligations, under the Convention, extend also to non-listed sites that are 'natural heritage' within the Convention's definitions and situated in the territory of the state party concerned.

Finally, in another provision which accords with the 1992 CBD's requirements and should encourage them to respect ecological as well as aesthetic values, states parties must educate their populations to appreciate and enjoy the sites and submit, through

205 *Handbook of the CBD*, Sec. IV, Guide to Decisions, cooperation with other biodiversity-related conventions processes and organizations, Notes on COP's consideration of cooperation with these, Dec. IV/15, para. 2. On the relationship between the WHC and other conventions protecting natural heritage, see Redgwell, in Francioni and Lenzerini, *The 1972 World Heritage Convention*, 377.

206 See further whc.unesco.org.

207 Redgwell in Francioni and Lenzerini, op cit 81–2.

208 See Redgwell, in Yusuf (ed), *Standard-setting in UNESCO: Normative Action in Education, Science and Culture* vol I (Leiden, 2007) 267.

209 2019 Operational Guidelines, part II.F paras 96–119.

210 46 *ALR* (1983) 625.

the Committee, biennial reports to the General Conference of UNESCO on the relevant legislative and administrative measures they have taken. Protection of sites thus becomes a matter of national pride; there is considerable evidence that this is so, but it can also attract additional visits and cause environmental degradation, requiring further protective measures.[211]

(c) Compliance

In addition to stipulating the criteria for listing, published in the *Operational Guidelines*, the WHC is also responsible for establishing the 'List of World Heritage in Danger', the latter designation signalling that major operations are necessary for conservation of the property and for which assistance has been requested under the Convention. Threats to the outstanding universal value of World Heritage properties are the familiar human-induced impacts ranging from incompatible development projects to poaching and armed conflict, as well as threats from 'sudden ecological and geological events' such as tsunami and earthquakes, and 'management and institutional frameworks' such as gaps in the legal framework and governance deficiencies.[212] Unlike Ramsar, listing does not require the consent of the State concerned[213] though considerable emphasis is placed on cooperation with them. 'Requested assistance' is broadly interpreted and may be requested by any Committee member, or the Secretariat, and 'assistance' includes expressions of concern by the Committee and inscription on the List of World Heritage in Danger itself.[214] Under this List, the property must be threatened by 'serious and specific danger' (Article 11(4)) which under the Guidelines may be ascertained or potential danger. For ascertained danger, it must be 'specific and proven imminent danger', for example, that there is a threat of a serious decline in the population of an endangered species or 'severe deterioration of the natural beauty or scientific value of the property', or it is under 'major threats which could have deleterious effects on its inherent characteristics', such as a development project.[215] Threats must be correctable by human action. At present there are 53 properties (36 cultural and 17 natural) in 33 State Parties on the World Heritage in Danger List, with Syria (6 properties) and the DRC and Libya (5 properties each) reflecting the disproportionate presence of Arab (40 per cent) and African states (30 per cent). In certain circumstances, properties that have so deteriorated as to lose the characteristics qualifying them for inclusion in the list of threatened sites may be removed from the list; this is the ultimate consequence of a State's failure to fulfil its obligations under the Convention. Unlike the 1971 Ramsar Convention, there have been deletions from the World Heritage List. This happened for the first time in 2007 with the removal of

[211] See, for example, the ongoing management issues for the World Heritage site of Chitwan National Park, one of the most popular tourist sites in Nepal, *infra* n 219.

[212] See the 2008 'List of Factors Affecting Properties' identifying 14 primary factors and numerous secondary factors based on analysis of the 'state of conservation reports' by the Parties.

[213] For discussion of early tussles between the Committee and Australia over the possible danger listing of Kakadu National Park, see further Redgwell in Francioni and Lenzerini, op cit, ch 2.

[214] 2019 Guidelines, para 177.

[215] Ibid, para 180.

the Oman Arabian Oryx Sanctuary from the List after numbers of this endangered species tumbled to a mere four viable breeding pairs and the sanctuary was reduced 90 per cent in size, a downgrading the WHC considered to be incompatible with the values for which the natural heritage site was inscribed in 1994. The second occasion was in 2009 with the removal from the List of the cultural landscape,[216] the Dresden Elbe Valley in Germany, owing to the construction of a bridge over the river Elbe.

Danger listing may be perceived either as a form of 'name and shame' or as a means of highlighting for the international community difficulties in conserving heritage values and seeking assistance in addressing them. Indeed, as under the 1971 Ramsar Convention, there has been a concerted effort to underscore the implications and benefits of Danger Listing and remove the perceived stigma.[217] Whatever the perception, the clear expectation upon danger listing is that steps will be taken by the State party concerned to reduce and/or eliminate the danger posed to world cultural and natural heritage, often in consultation with the key stakeholders in the site and in the activities related to it, and with access to technical and financial assistance. Improvements in conservation will lead to removal from the Danger List, as has occurred for 40 properties up to 2019.[218] Success may also come in averting threats before Danger Listing becomes necessary.[219] This has been facilitated by the evolution of 'reactive monitoring' under the Convention, which supplements the periodic (every six years) reporting by the Contracting Parties required under Article 29 of the Convention on the legislative and administrative measures adopted for the application of the Convention and the state of conservation of inscribed properties.[220] This ad hoc form of institutional oversight is now formalised in the *Operational Guidelines*, and is the most comprehensive monitoring system of any of the site-based biodiversity-related conventions.[221] It comprises reporting by the Secretariat, other sectors of UNESCO and the Advisory

216 In 1992, the World Heritage Convention became the first convention to recognise and protect cultural landscapes, with 114 properties now inscribed on the World Heritage List under the cultural landscape criteria: see, generally, N. Mitchell, G. Rössler and P.-M. Tricaud, *World Heritage Cultural Landscapes: A Handbook for Conservation and Management*, World Heritage Papers 26 (2009). On regional landscape protection under the Council of Europe's European Landscape Convention, see *infra* section 4(3)..

217 See Decision 40 COM 7 para 27. An example of the benefits is the Florida Everglades, inscribed in 1979 and on the Danger List from 1993 to 2007 and again from 2010 to the present, owing to the impact of pollution, encroaching human development, and high levels of tourism. Danger Listing has provided an important stimulus to significant Federal and State allocations of financial and human resources to assist with conservation and restoration measures.

218 Recent natural heritage examples are Comoé National Park in Côte d'Ivoire and Simien National Park in Ethiopia in 2017, and Belize Barrier Reef Reserve System in 2018.

219 Frequently highlighted examples include: the cancellation of a river diversion project owing to adverse impacts on the Royal Chitwan National Park in Nepal, one of the last remaining refuges of the Bengal tiger and one-horned Asiatic rhinoceros; relocation of an aluminium plant which would have affected the archaeological site of Delphi in Greece; and refusal of permission to extend to commercial scale saltworks in El Vizcaino Bay in Mexico, the last pristine reproduction lagoon for the Pacific grey whale.

220 2019 Operational Guidelines, Ch IV.A (reactive monitoring) and Ch V (periodic reporting). Further 'success stories' are cited in UNESCO Reactive Monitoring Review Team, *Strengthening the Effectiveness of the World Heritage Monitoring Process* (Final Report, 31 August 2019) 16–17.

221 Reactive Monitoring Review Team, para 18.

Bodies to the Convention on the state of World Heritage properties that are under threat, in cooperation with the State Parties concerned upon whom the obligation to protect cultural and natural properties continues primarily to rest.[222] A range of steps may result, from no action or the provision of technical assistance, to inscription on the Danger List or removal entirely from the List (with prior notice to the State Party concerned).[223]

(d) Assessment of the World Heritage Convention

The 1972 World Heritage Convention both overlaps with and goes beyond the 1971 Ramsar Convention in conserving habitats. It lays more stringent and specific obligations on parties to take conservation measures and its provisions for financial assistance have provided the model for Ramsar and other conventions which have subsequently followed its example. For sites listed can provide protection but the limitations on listing, and the problem of securing ongoing protection and integrity of inscribed sites, prevent it from being the major instrument of habitat protection.

2(3) THE 1979 CONVENTION ON THE CONSERVATION OF MIGRATORY SPECIES OF WILD ANIMALS (CMS)

The 1979 CMS is not quite a pygmy amongst the giants of the 'big four' species and habitat treaties considered here, but it has had the lowest profile.[224] This is in part due to its relatively slow start;[225] however, today there are 130 parties,[226] of whom about half are developing countries, with near universal membership in Africa and Europe. It conserves habitat, inter alia, as well as aiming to protect during their migration terrestrial, marine and avian species from a variety of threats. These threats include reduction of habitat in breeding areas, excessive hunting along migration routes (corridors, swimways and flyways), and degradation of feeding grounds.[227] Reversing the trends of species and biodiversity loss and maintaining and restoring 'ecological connectivity' is a key objective of the 1979 CMS[228] and a significant contribution to the post-2020 Global Biodiversity Framework.[229] With its cross-cutting themes of

222 2019 Operational Guidelines, para 169. 223 Ibid, para 176.

224 *Lyster's International Wildlife Law*, Ch 16; Lyster, 29 *NRJ* (1989) 979; Osterwoldt, ibid, 1017; Johnson, in Soons (ed), *Implementation of the Law of the Sea Convention Through International Institutions* (Honolulu, 1990) 363; Glowka, 3 *JIWLP* (2000) 205; Anastassiadis, 30 *EPL* (2000) 49ff; Caddell, 16 *Colorado JIELP* (2005) 113.

225 At COP2 (1988) 'the air of despondency over its future was palpable': *Lyster's International Wildlife Law* 582.

226 The EU is a party (alongside its member States) as the CMS is open to REIOs: see Article XV.

227 Vagg discusses eleven specific threats and challenges: invasive species; by-catch; habitat loss; turbines; oil spills; 3; wildlife watching; avian influenza; electrocution; unsustainable hunting and poaching; and wildlife crime: Vagg, *CMS Family Guide: The Encyclopedia of the Convention on the Conservation of Migratory Species of Wild Animals* (UNEP/CMS Secretariat, 4th edn, 2015).

228 See e.g. CMS COP Resolution 10.3 on the Role of Ecological Networks in the Conservation of Migratory Species; and, generally, CMS Resolution 11.02 (Rev. COP12), Annex 1 'Strategic Plan for Migratory Species 2015-2023' (2014).

229 'Ecological Connectivity in the post-2020 Global Biodiversity Framework' CMS Notification 2019/021 (2019).

wildlife species and habitat protection throughout species' migratory range, the 1979 CMS has a particular contribution to make to transboundary biodiversity conservation.[230] 1979 CMS Resolutions frequently reiterate that 'the Convention on Biological Diversity (CBD) decision VI/20 recognized CMS as the lead partner in the conservation and sustainable use of migratory species over their entire range.'[231] Further synergies are evident in the recognition that the application by the CMS parties of the CBD's Addis Ababa Principles on Sustainable Use[232] 'could contribute to reducing many of the causes of loss of migratory species (e.g., by-catch, unsustainable harvesting, overexploitation, unsustainable hunting and other negative impacts) and lead to better conservation of habitats for migratory species.'[233]

As with Ramsar, however, the 1979 CMS had inauspicious beginnings, with few parties and little initial progress after its entry into force in 1983. However, over time participation has significantly increased and from COP6 in Capetown (1999) there has been a marked uptick in progress under the Convention[234] such that by COP 11 in Quito (2014) a major review and consolidation of COP Resolutions and Recommendations was launched.[235] The 1979 CMS remains relatively institution-light, with a Scientific Council in addition to the Standing Committee and Secretariat, though supplemented by working groups on specific issues. There is also the CMS Small Grants Programme (SGP), established at COP4 (1994) aimed as a 'grassroots tool' to assist implementation in developing countries in particular. A small Secretariat, provided initially by UNEP, is located in Bonn but has experienced chronic underfunding owing to the continuing failure of many parties to pay their contributions and expenses, which has long limited its staffing, convening of meetings of its Standing Committee, and scope for action, a point returned to below.

(a) Listing and conservation techniques

As the *Behring Sea Fur Seals Arbitration* showed,[236] conservation of migratory species which range across national boundaries necessarily requires concerted action by all states that exercise jurisdiction over any part of the migratory range of that species. They are a classic illustration of a shared natural resource.[237] Cooperation between

230 Ong in Fitzmaurice, Ong and Merkouris, *Research Handbook on International Environmental Law* 519, 532.

231 See e.g. CMS Resolution 12.14 (2017).

232 For further discussion of the Principles, see further below, section (6).

233 CMS Resolution 8.1 (2005) on 'Sustainable Use', which also 'recognises that sustainable use (both consumptive and non-consumptive) may provide incentives for conservation and restoration because of the social, cultural and economic benefits that people could derive from that use and that, in turn, sustainable use cannot be achieved without effective conservation measures.'

234 Anastassiadis, 30 *EPL* (2000) 49.

235 'Recommendations' were abolished, obsolete Resolutions repealed, and a new category of 'Decisions' was created for time bound requests of specific action from the Parties or Convention bodies. For the complete list of existing regulations which were amended at COP 12 (2017) see Vagg, *CMS Family Guide* 'Current Resolutions of the COP (2/3)'.

236 *Infra*, Ch 12, section 4(1).

237 See 1978 UNEP Principles on Conservation and Harmonious Utilization of Natural Resources Shared by Two or More States and *supra*, Ch 3, section 3(1)(b).

range states is thus a key feature of the 1979 CMS,[238] as it is in the 1982 UNCLOS[239] and the 1946 International Convention on the Regulation of Whaling,[240] both of which also regulate migratory species.

Two principal conservation techniques are employed under the 1979 Bonn Convention. First, 'endangered' species are listed on Appendix I; the taking of these animals is prohibited except for scientific purposes or traditional subsistence uses.[241] Range States 'shall endeavour' to conserve and restore important habitats, prevent activities or remove obstacles that 'seriously impede' migration, and control other factors endangering the species.[242] 'Endangered' means that the species is 'in danger of extinction throughout all or a significant portion of its range'.[243] The term has been further interpreted by the COP as meaning 'facing a very high risk of extinction in the wild in the near future' with the 1979 CMS definition intended generally to correspond with the IUCN Red List Criteria.[244] 'Taking' of such species is defined as 'hunting, fishing, capturing, harassing, deliberate killing, or attempting to engage in such conduct.'[245] The prohibition on taking is the only mandatory obligation imposed on range states by Article III ('shall prohibit'); other obligations are modified by phrases such as 'shall endeavour' and 'to the extent feasible and appropriate'.[246] The obligations with respect to listed species are supplemented by COP Resolutions addressing reduction and elimination of adverse impacts—e.g. anthropogenic noise—and additional habitat protection.[247]

Definitions of 'range' and 'range states' are laid down in the Convention and a list of range states is maintained by the Secretariat; parties inform it when they consider themselves to be a range state for migratory species listed in the appendices; this includes submitting information on vessels registered under their flag engaged in taking these species (which could include birds) outside national jurisdictional limits and plans for such activities concerning relevant species (Article VI). The 1979 CMS thus provides a framework within which Range States can cooperate in undertaking scientific research, restoring habitats, and removing impediments ('activities or obstacles'[248]) to

238 Article II. 239 Article 64, on which see *infra*, Ch 12, section 2(3)(a).

240 *Infra*, Ch 12, section 4(2).

241 Article III(1–3) and (5). Taking is also allowed for 'propagation or survival of the species', and in 'extraordinary circumstances.' In 2017 a 'National Legislation Programme' was launched, alongside the Review Mechanism discussed below, to secure long-term compliance with the obligations in Article III(4) (a) and (b) and (5).

242 Article III(4). 243 Article I(e).

244 CMS Resolution 11.33 (Rev. CP 12), para 1; *Guidelines*, para 4. 245 Article I(1)(i).

246 See Article III(4); similar wording is contained in Article IV: 'shall endeavour' (Article IV(3)); 'encouraged to take action' (Article III(4)).

247 E.g. CMS Resolution 12.14 'Adverse Impacts of Anthropogenic Noise on Cetaceans and Other Migratory Species' (2017) and CMS Resolution 13.X 'By-Catch Mitigation Measures for Marine Mammals in National Fishing Operations'; and CMS Resolution 12.13 'Important Marine Mammal Areas' (2017).

248 Roads, fences, power lines, and renewable energy installations such as wind turbines, are examples. On the impact of the latter, see eg CMS Resolution 7.5 'Wind Turbines and Migratory Species' (2002) and, more generally on reconciling selected energy sector developments with conservation of migratory species, CMS COP11 Resolution 11.27 'Renewable Energy and Migratory Species' (2014) and COP13 'Renewable Energy Technologies and Migratory Species: Guidelines for Sustainable Deployment' UNEP/CMS/COP13/CRP26.4.2.1 (2020).

the migration of Appendix I listed migratory species. At present, there are 183 migratory species listed in Appendix I.[249]

Secondly, the Convention provides for the conclusion of formal conservation 'AGREEMENTS' (including Memoranda of Understanding ('MOUs')) between Range States for the conservation and management of migratory species listed in Appendix II. These are species which have 'unfavourable conservation status' and require international agreement for their conservation and management, or 'which would benefit significantly from international cooperation' (Article IV). Under the Convention, 'conservation status of a migratory species' means 'the sum of the influences acting on the migratory species that may affect its long-term distribution and abundance' (Article I(1)(b)). 'Favourable' conservation status requires population dynamics which indicate that the species is 'maintaining itself on a long-term basis as a viable component of its ecosystems', that it is not likely to be reduced in the long-term, that there is sufficient habitat, and that abundance approaches historic levels (Article I(1)(c)). The focus here is on long-term sustainability; any taking of Appendix II species must be viewed from that perspective.

The form of the AGREEMENT for Appendix II species must provide for conservation, restoration of habitats important to favourable conservation status (as necessary and feasible), and protection from disturbance of that habitat, including, inter alia, introduction or control of exotic species detrimental to it (Article V). If required, the AGREEMENT should institute appropriate machinery to execute its aims, monitor its effectiveness, and prepare the necessary reports to the Conference of the Parties. To date, seven AGREEMENTS[250] and 19 MOUs[251] have been concluded covering inter alia cetaceans and sharks, seals, turtles, elephants, gorillas, various bird species, deer and antelopes, and which form the 'CMS Family' of instruments legally autonomous from the CMS but linked with it.[252] The 1979 CMS thus has a framework character, encouraging Range States to conclude regional or global AGREEMENTS (or MOUs) in respect of Appendix II species, and upon the conclusion of which the success of the 1979 CMS depends.

249 At CMS COP13 (Gandhinagar, 2020) ten new species were added: seven to Appendix I (the Asian Elephant, Jaguar, Great Indian Bustard, Bengal Florican, Little Bustard, Antipodean Albatross and the Oceanic White-tip Shark) and three to Appendix II (the Urial, Smooth Hammerhead Shark and the Tope Shark).

250 Agreement on the Conservation of Albatrosses and Petrels (ACAP); Agreement on the Conservation of Cetaceans of the Black Sea, Mediterranean Sea and Contiguous Atlantic Area (ACCOBAMS); Agreement on the Conservation of African-Eurasian Migratory Waterbirds (AEWA); Agreement on the Conservation of Small Cetaceans of the Baltic, North East Atlantic, Irish and North Seas (ASCOBANS); Agreement on the Conservation of Populations of European Bats (EUROBATS); Agreement on the Conservation of Gorillas and their Habitat (Gorilla Agreement); and Agreement on the Conservation of Seals in the Wadden Sea (Wadden Sea Seals).

251 For the full list see <https://cms.int/en/cms-instruments/mou. There are also four special species initiatives, involving cooperation with range States and other bodies (eg CITES): the African Carnivores Initiative, the Central Asian Flyway, Central Asian Mammals Initiative, and Sahelo-Saharan Megafauna.

252 See e.g. 'Enhancing Synergies and Common Services among CMS Family Instruments' UNEP/CMS/Resolution 11.3 (2014); Vagg, *CMS Family Guide: The Encyclopedia of the Convention on the Conservation of Migratory Species of Wild Animals* (UNEP/CMS Secretariat, 4th edn, 2015).

There is plainly a considerable difference in the method of protecting species under these two appendices: specific obligations are laid down for Appendix I species, whereas AGREEMENTS (or MOUs) are required for Appendix II species. However, the 1979 CMS explicitly allows stricter domestic conservation measures for Appendix I and II species and for conservation of migratory species not listed in either appendix (Article XII(3)). Moreover, both appendices adopt a precautionary approach to listing: 'in case of uncertainty regarding the status of a species, the Parties shall act in the best interest of the conservation of the species concerned and, when considering proposals to amend Appendix I or II, adopt measures that are proportionate to the anticipated risks to the species'.[253] Although some States take the view that reservations undermine the Convention,[254] reservations may be made to amendments to an Appendix (i.e. listing) within 90 days of the amendment taking effect.[255] Removal from the List is only possible where 'reliable evidence, including the best scientific evidence available' indicates that the migratory species is no longer endangered, and not likely to become endangered again with the loss of Appendix I status.[256] This represents a strong version of the precautionary approach to conservation, requiring proof that the population is no longer in danger and can sustain de-listing.[257] Indeed, the pattern of amendments to both Appendices has been one of adding species to its protection, including 'uplisting' from Appendix II to Appendix I.[258]

Examples of particular species may, if warranted, be found on both Appendix I and on Appendix II (Article IV(2)). For example, the blue, humpback, right, and bowhead whales and the Mediterranean monk seal are listed on Appendix I, while white whales and certain populations of common, grey, and monk seals, porpoises, and the sea cow (dugong) are listed in Appendix II.[259] AGREEMENTS have since been concluded dealing, inter alia, with seals and small cetaceans.[260] In practice it is also possible for dual-listing of species under the 1979 CMS and other international agreements, including the 1946 International Convention for the Regulation of Whaling.[261] Whether CMS Appendix I-listed species would be jeopardised without parallel protection under CITES Appendix I was unresolved at COP13 (2020) and is to be revisited at COP14 (2023).[262] There is further overlap and diffusion of responsibility with the 1971

253 CMS Resolution 11.33 (Rev. CP 12), para 3.

254 For example, at COP13 (2020) Israel highlighted that reservations undermine the goals and effectiveness of the Convention and proposed, unsuccessfully, the inclusion of language to that effect: 18:83 *ENB* (2020) 13.

255 Article XI(6). See UNEP/CMS/COP13/Doc 27.4 (29 November 2019).

256 Article III(3).

257 *Supra*, Ch 3, section 6. This may be contrasted with de-listing under the Ramsar and World Heritage Conventions, where de-listing is contemplated not as a sign of a conservation success, but rather as a consequence of the loss of the international importance of a wetland or the outstanding universal value of world heritage.

258 For discussion of whether this leads to reluctance to list large carnivores on Appendix II owing to potential 'uplisting' to Appendix I, see Lewis and Trouwborst *Front.Ecol.Evol.* 18 December 2019.

259 For the complete List see <https://www.cms.int/en/species>

260 See n 272 below.

261 See *infra*, Ch 12, section 4.

262 There is consultation between CITES and the CMS Secretariat and Scientific Council regarding proposals to list species on CITES Appendix I: see e.g. CITES CoP16 Doc. 77 Annex 4 (2013) and CMS Notification 2016/018.

Ramsar Convention and the 1979 Berne Convention on the Conservation of European Wildlife ('Berne Convention') and ad hoc conventions on particular species such as whales, seals, birds, turtles, polar bears, and vicuña. Rights and obligations under other treaties are not affected by the 1979 CMS:[263] in case of conflict, other treaties, including UNCLOS and the ICRW, will prevail.

In addition to AGREEMENTS under Article IV(3) there are also 'agreements' under Article IV(4). Both are intended to cover the whole migratory range and be open to all range states whether or not parties to the Convention (Article V(2)), but an Article IV(4) agreement is meant to cover 'any population or any geographically separate part of the population of any species or lower taxon of wild animals, members of which periodically cross one or more national jurisdictional boundaries.' These broad terms allow inclusion of species not listed in Appendix II or even falling within the definition of 'migratory' given in the Convention. The aim is to protect species that would benefit from international cooperation but whose circumstances either do not fulfil the criteria for listing on Appendix II or have not yet been listed.[264] The flexibility afforded by Article IV(4) 'arguably [is] the most innovative and productive feature of the 1979 CMS system to date.'[265]

(b) Institutional supervision

The COP is the 'decision-making organ' of the Convention, supported by a secretariat and a Scientific Council.[266] It is the responsibility of the COP to review progress on conservation, make recommendations to the parties and decide on any additional measures that should be taken (Article VII). As we have seen it is the COP which decides on listing and de-listing, advised by the Scientific Council. The COP determines the Scientific Council's functions, which may include 'making *recommendations*'[267] on species to be included in the appendices, together with an indication of their range and on the specific measures to be included in the AGREEMENTS. NGOs 'technically qualified in protection, conservation and management of migratory species' may be granted observer status (Article VII(9)).

One of the key tasks of the COP has been to interpret and develop the Convention, many of whose terms are ambiguous, including the definition of 'migratory species' in Article 1, which refers, inter alia, to species that 'cyclically and predictably' cross boundaries. The COP at its second meeting adopted guidelines for application of the term 'migratory species', indicating that 'cyclically' relates to a cycle of any nature, such as astronomical (circadian, annual, etc), life, or climatic cycles, and of any frequency,

263 Article XII(1–2). See also Johnson, in Soons (ed), *Implementation of the Law of the Sea Through International Institutions* (Honolulu, 1990) 363.

264 See CMS Resolution 12.8 'Implementation of Article IV and V of the Convention' with Annex 'Criteria for Assessing Proposals for New Agreements' (2017), repealing earlier Resolutions (eg Resolution 11.12).

265 *Lyster's International Wildlife Law* 583. Thus, for example, China and Russia participate in the conservation arrangements for the Siberian Crane, pursuant to an MOU, though neither is a party to the CMS; and NGOs may participate in these non-treaty arrangements, such as the International Council for Game and Wildlife Conservation with respect to the MOU concerning the slender-billed curlew.

266 Articles VII-IX.

267 Article VII(5), emphasis added.

and that 'predictably' implies that a phenomenon can be expected to recur in a given set of circumstances, though not necessarily regularly in time.[268] This removed some of the ambiguity inherent in the original definition. Progress on these definitional problems has encouraged wider participation in the Convention; practical application by conclusion of AGREEMENTS is the best clarifier of its inadequacies.

It appeared at an earlier stage that some states were inhibited from concluding AGREEMENTS because they considered them a form of treaty, requiring parliamentary or other official approval for adoption—a complex problem in federal states—which might have to be sought annually as AGREEMENTS proliferated.[269] The Second COP agreed that a less formal agreement, such as a Memorandum of Understanding, could be concluded between governmental administrations, as a preliminary to a more formal agreement.[270]

From the third COP, cooperative mechanisms have been gradually strengthened to improve the pathways to listing on Appendix I and to the conclusion of AGREEMENTS, as well as to ensure the effective conservation of species already listed in Appendices I and II. Now termed 'concerted actions', it is the collective responsibility of the Parties to take 'priority conservation measures, projects, or [to undertake] institutional arrangements' which are designed to: (i) improve the conservation status of the selected species or group of species under Appendix I and Appendix II; or (ii) support the conclusion of an AGREEMENT by enabling conservation measures to be progressed in the meantime; or (iii) represent an alternative to such an instrument.[271] Proposals for concerted action are submitted by the Parties, the Secretariat, or other relevant stakeholders, to the CMS Scientific Council for evaluation and transmission with recommendations to the COP. In 2020, for the first time, a proposal for concerted action (for the Baltic porpoise) was submitted by NGOs alone[272] and adopted by the COP. In total, new and extended Concerted Actions were agreed for 14 species for the triennium 2021-23[273] as well as consideration of progress reports

[268] These terms are regularly reviewed, with COP13 (2020) further defining 'cyclically' for example ('relates to a cycle of any nature') and 'predictably' ('implies that a phenomenon can be anticipated to recur in a given set of circumstances, though not necessarily regularly in time'): UNEP/CMS/COP13/CRP27.2.

[269] As an example of the early internal domestic legislative and other problems inhibiting conclusion of Agreements, see Osterwoldt, 29 *NRJ* (1989) 1035–48, on the difficulties facing Germany, Denmark, and the Netherlands, whose different perceptions concerning the 'taking' of seals under the CMS inhibited conclusion of an agreement for conservation of the harbour seals in the Wadden Sea.

[270] Lyster, 29 *NRJ* (1989) 992–3; on MOUs see Aust, 35 *ICLQ* (1986) 787.

[271] Consolidated in UNEP/CMS/Resolution 12.28 (2017) and Annex 1 'Guidelines to the Implementation of the Concerted Actions Process'.

[272] Humane Society International, ORCA, Whale and Dolphin Conservation, and Coalition Clean Baltic, all supporting ASCOBANS and the Baltic Sea Harbour Porpoise Action Plan. The species is listed as critically endangered under the IUCN Red List and by HELCOM under the regional seas arrangement for the Baltic, the 1992 Helsinki Convention on the Protection of the Marine Environment of the Baltic Sea Area.

[273] For the nut-cracking chimpanzees of West Africa; Asian elephant; Giraffe; Sahelo-Saharan megafauna (species of oryx, gazelle and sheep); Irawaddy dophin; South Asian River dolphin; harbour porpoise in the Baltic and Iberian peninsula; common guitarfish, largetooth and smalltooth sawfish; common guitarfish and bottlenose wedgefish; Great Indian bustard; and Antipodean albatross: see UNEP/CMS/COP13/Doc 28.2.1- Doc 28.2.12).

on the implementation of existing concerted actions.[274] Consultation with all Range States for the species concerned is encouraged, but not mandatory, despite objections to amendments on the basis of non-consultation.[275]

(c) Implementation and compliance

The potential of the 1979 CMS for comprehensive protection of migratory species is far from fully realized; neither of the techniques it provides has yet been fully or effectively used. Recognising the need to improve implementation and strengthen compliance with the Convention, the contracting parties adopted (COP 12, Manila, 2017) a review mechanism intended as '[a] supportive, non-adversarial and facilitative' process to provide support for Parties experiencing difficulties with implementation of the Convention.[276] No reports had been received by the Secretariat by the time of COP13 in 2020. It is thus not yet possible to evaluate the success of this process in contributing to the effectiveness of the 1979 CMS, other than to make two observations. The first is that the 1979 CMS has joined the ranks of most major multilateral environmental agreements in establishing a process for facilitating implementation, recognising that compliance with Convention obligations and the effectiveness of implementation measures are critical to the conservation and management of migratory species.[277] The second is that while the basis for review by the Standing Committee is wide—it may be 'triggered' not only by self-reporting, but by other Parties, the CMS institutions (Secretariat or Standing Committee) and by '[a]ny body or agency technically qualified in protection, conservation and management of migratory species', e.g. an accredited NGO—the possibility for the submissions of the party concerned to remain confidential has obvious implications for the transparency of the process.[278] In keeping with the facilitative nature of the review process, the response of the Standing Committee when an 'implementation matter' has been identified is first and foremost to give the Party concerned 'every opportunity to correct them within a reasonable time frame', failing which further measures ranging from further advice and assistance, technical and verification missions, to a warning and request an implementation action are available. There is no equivalent of the Montreux Record (Ramsar) or Danger List (World Heritage Convention)—though each in turn emphasizes their facilitative nature[279]—though reporting by the Standing Committee to the COP of actions taken could come to serve a similar purpose.

(d) Assessing the CMS

Though the increase in the number of parties and AGREEMENTS is encouraging, the success of the 1979 CMS depends not only on the existence and use of these techniques but on participation in the Convention by all states that are range states of threatened

274 UNEP/CMS/COP13/Doc 28.1.1-Docs 28.1.8.

275 See e.g. Australia at COP13 (2020).

276 Specifically, Articles III.4, III.5, III.7 and VI.2: UNEP/CMS Resolution 12.9 and Decisions 12.6–12.9 (2017). Two agreements within the CMS Family already had review mechanisms, AEWA and ACCOBAMS.

277 As acknowledged in the Preamble to UNEP/CMS/Resolution 11.7 (2014), indents 2 and 4.

278 UNEP/CMS/Resolution 12.9 (2017), part B.

279 See above sections 2(1)(b) and 2(2)(c).

species, which in practice means that near universal membership is required. Neither the US nor Canada are party to the Convention, arguing that existing conservation measures or those planned in their countries would not be benefitted by 1979 CMS participation.[280] This, coupled with the fact that not all threatened migratory species have been listed, adds to its limitations. Moreover, non-ratification of the Convention by any of the range states of some of the species listed on Appendix I means that the Convention's provisions for their protection are at best hampered, and at worst, nugatory. Of the major non-participants, China, Russia, the Democratic Republic of Korea and the Republic of Korea, Japan, and the US are all range states for over twenty-five Appendix I species, thus imperilling their full protection. Such weaknesses have rendered the 1979 CMS less effective than it might be.

Moreover, a preliminary review of the status of CMS listed species presented at COP13 (2020)[281] reveals alarming declines in populations of most listed species, with the conservation status of 87 per cent of species listed on Appendix I and 56 per cent of the species listed on Appendix II of 'global concern.' Population trends are decreasing for 73 per cent of Appendix I species and 48 per cent for Appendix II. While fish are the more rapidly declining taxa, more than 90 per cent of CMS-listed species are impacted by biological resource use,[282] and three out of four Appendix 1 species are impacted by intentional use,[283] with about 20 per cent subject to forms of persecution and control.[284] That stable or increasing population trends have been observed for only 14 per cent of Appendix I species and 18 per cent of Appendix II is scant comfort.

Underfunding also remains an acute issue for the 1979 CMS.[285] Its flagship *Status of the World's Migratory Species* report, first mandated by the COP in 2014, is still not finalised owing to lack of funds.[286] As shown by other biodiversity treaties, these 'status of' reports are highly influential in publicising the work of the treaty and the challenges confronting it. Yet the Parties have proved resistant to measures proposed to improve the situation. For example, if three years or more in arrears, a Contracting

280 Osterwoldt, 29 *NRJ* (1989) 1028. Threatened species in these countries are mainly migratory birds covered by the 1916 Convention between the USA and Great Britain for the Protection of Migratory Birds.

281 UNEP/CMS/COP13/Doc.24.

282 'Defined in the IUCN – CMP Unified Classification of Direct Threats as "Threats from consumptive use of 'wild' biological resources including both deliberate and unintentional harvesting effects; also persecution or control of specific species"': UNEP/CMS Press Release, 'CMS to Present Preliminary Review of the Conservation Status of Migratory Species' 19 February 2020.

283 'With reference to the IUCN classification of threats, this includes hunting and collecting terrestrial animals and fishing and harvesting aquatic resources at both small and large scales, when the species being assessed is the target.' Ibid.

284 'Examples of persecution/control include wolf control, pest control, persecution of snakes because of superstition, beach protection with sharks nets, sharks and seals killed because they eat commercial fish species, etc.' Ibid.

285 As of COP13 in 2020, EUR 1 million remained unpaid, a quarter of the total operating budget. In contrast, NGO activity is estimated to contribute USD 20 million annually to CMS-related migratory species work globally: 18:83 *ENB* (2020) 1, 15.

286 Only a preliminary review was available at COP13, with no funds committed to it in the budget so funding will only come from voluntary sources.

Party might be prevented from submitting listing proposals[287]—a measure clearly counterproductive to achieving the 1979 CMS's objectives, yet so too is chronic underfunding on this scale.

On a more positive note, synergies with other conventions such as the 1971 Ramsar Convention, the 1973 CITES, and the 1992 CBD, are regularly highlighted and further cooperation encouraged, along with new AGREEMENTS. With respect to the former, the current Strategic Plan for the CMS[288] confirms that its primary goal is to ensure the favourable conservation status of migratory species, thereby contributing to global sustainability; it has harmonised its work with that of the 1992 CBD and the 2020 target of significantly reducing the rate of biodiversity loss. Thus, however slowly, the 1979 CMS seems at least to be pointing in the right direction.

2(4) 1973 CONVENTION ON INTERNATIONAL TRADE IN ENDANGERED SPECIES

(a) Objectives

Unlike the other treaties considered here, the direct purpose of the 1973 CITES is not the protection of animal and plant species or habitat *per se*. Rather, its objective is to control or prohibit international trade in species or their products where those species are in danger of extinction owing to unsustainable demand.[289] As such, it is one of the MEAs to employ trade-related environmental mechanisms as a regulatory tool and is further considered in Chapter 13. While loss of habitat through human encroachment (land clearance, agriculture and industry) poses the greatest threat to wildlife and to the conservation of biological diversity,[290] commercial exploitation and trade contribute to species decline. Roughly 5,800 animal species 'from leeches to lions' and 30,000 plant species 'from pine trees to pitcher plants' are now covered in the 183 States presently parties to the 1973 CITES. It includes whole groups of species, such as primates, cetaceans, corals, cacti and orchids, while in some cases only a subspecies or geographically separate populations of species (eg the population of just one country) are listed.[291] The 1973 CITES is not designed directly to conserve migratory or other species in their habitats nor to protect them from other threats to their existence such

287 18:83 *ENB* (2020) 1, 15. One of the conditions of access to the CMS Small Grants Programme is not to be more than three years in arrears with payments of assessed contributions to the CMS budget by the deadline for submission of proposals: see the Revised Guidelines for the Operation of the SGP, UNEP/CMS/Conf.10.43.

288 Strategic Plan 2015–2023, para 12.

289 From a copious literature see, inter alia, Wijnstekers (former Secretary-General of CITES), *The Evolution of CITES* (11th edn, Cambridge, 2018)1006; *Lyster's, International Wildlife Law*, Ch 15; Hutton and Dickson (eds), *Endangered Species, Threatened Convention: The Past, Present and Future of CITES* (London, 2000); Favre, *International Trade in Endangered Species* (The Hague, 1989); Harland, *Killing Game* (Westport, 1994); Lyster, 29 *NRJ* (1989), 979; De Klemm, ibid, 953; Sand, 8 *EJIL* (1997) 29, esp 52–3; Ruiz Muller, *IUCN Newsletter* (1997) 1; Hepworth, 1 *JIWLP* (1998) 412; Ong, 10 *JEL* (1998) 291–316; Baker, 2 *JIWLP* (1999) 1; Bowman, 2 *JIWLP* (1999) 9– 63.

290 See Maxwell et al, 536 *Nature* (2016) 43.

291 See <https://www.cites.org/eng/disc/species.php>.

as pollution, over-exploitation, or by-catches, but as it covers not only species of animals but also of plants, it does play a role in preserving component parts of the habitat of some species and thus to the conservation of biodiversity.

This contribution is reflected in the 1973 CITES 'vision statement' to 2020, which is to '[c]onserve biodiversity and contribute to its sustainable use by ensuring that no species of wild fauna or flora becomes or remains subject to unsustainable exploitation through international trade, thereby contributing to the significant reduction of the rate of biodiversity loss and making a significant contribution towards achieving the relevant *Aichi Biodiversity Targets*.'[292] This vision statement neatly encapsulates the controversy surrounding CITES, which on the one hand is described as 'perhaps the most successful of all international treaties concerned with wildlife conservation'[293] and, despite its limited scope, as 'the cornerstone of international wildlife law,'[294] yet criticized on the other for its implicit legitimization of wildlife trade, albeit regulated under the Convention.[295] These tensions between its role in conservation (prohibiting trade in species threatened with extinction) and trade (controlled trade in species not yet threatened with extinction but might become so) have endured since the conclusion of the 1973 CITES. They are evident most particularly in debates regarding listing on the Appendices, and on whether to permit trade which supports conservation objectives, as the trade in elephant ivory discussed below illustrates. The Preamble to the 1973 CITES also evidences an intergenerational concern ('wild fauna and flora in their many beautiful and varied forms are an irreplaceable part of the natural system of the earth which must be protected for this and generations to come') and recognises the aesthetic, scientific, cultural, recreational and economic value of wildlife (third recital). Animal welfare concerns are evident in Articles III, IV and V, which require minimization of the risk to living specimens of injury, damage to health or cruel treatment.[296]

(b) Controlling trade

Whatever these controversies, there is no doubt that many species are declining not only because of loss of habitat but also because of increased exploitation.[297] A major

292 CITES Strategic Vision 2008–2020, Conf. 16.3 (Rev. CoP17) 3. On the Aichi Biodiversity Targets, see further below section 6. See also SDG 15.17 which requires states to '[t]ake urgent action to end poaching and trafficking of protected species of flora and fauna and address both demand and supply of illegal wildlife products'; CITES Strategic Vision 2021–2030 (Conf. 18.3 (2019)) also emphasizes CITES contribution to the post 2020 Global Biodiversity Framework and to achieving the 2030 Agenda for Sustainable Development through 'legal and sustainable' international trade in fauna and flora.

293 See e.g. Ong in Fitzmaurice, Ong and Merkouris (eds), *Research Handbook on International Environmental Law* (Cheltenham, 2010), Ch 24, 525.

294 Wiersema in Peel and Rajamani, *Oxford Handbook of International Environmental Law* Ch 32.

295 As Trouwborst et al identify, 'ideological differences between the Parties as to the weight to be given to strict protection versus sustainable use are also an increasing challenge for the Convention': 67 BIOSCIENCE 784(2017).

296 On conservation and animal welfare concerns, see above, section 1(2).

297 Wildlife trade has been identified as the second biggest threat to biodiversity, after habitat loss, with a recent study finding 958 species listed by IUCN as in danger of extinction were so owing to international trade: Frank and Wilcove, 363 *Science* (2019) 686.

contributory factor to this is trade, an especially serious threat since the ease of modern transport has facilitated the shipping of live animals and plants and their products all over the world. This trade is very lucrative; millions of live animals and birds are transported to meet the demands of the pet trade, ornamental plants are in great demand, and fur skins, shells, leather, timber, and artefacts made from these products are all traded in on a large scale, as also was ivory until recently.[298] 'Trade' includes 'export, re-export, import and introduction from the sea,'[299] and thus also covers the taking or capture of marine living resources on the high seas or deep seabed.[300]

The technique of controlling import and export of such species and products is also found in some regional and other conventions,[301] but the innovatory aspect of the 1973 CITES is that it has established an elaborate but workable operational system in which a national export/import permit system is combined with a national institutional system on a global scale.[302] It consists of regulating by means of a permit system international trade in species that are listed on its three appendices according to whether, and to what extent, they are threatened by international trade. For species listed on Appendix I—those that are threatened with extinction—sustainable trade is not considered possible. There were 450 species on the Appendix I list when the Convention entered into force; today there are over 800 species with a greater variety of wildlife, and around 300 species of endangered plants are represented.[303] For those species international commercial trade between parties has been effectively prohibited. Here the problem is not trade, but poaching, illegal trafficking and the involvement of transnational organised crime.[304] While Article VIII(1) requires parties to enforce the Convention, inter alia by penalizing illegal trade and possession of illegal specimens, addressing these problems requires improved national criminal enforcement and international criminal cooperation.[305]

For species or populations listed on Appendix II CITES focuses on the promotion of sustainable trade in order to control exploitation. Appendix II is by far the largest of the three appendices, and the majority of the species listed on it are plants.[306] International

298 See the CITES trade database: https://trade.cites.org

299 Article I(c).

300 Article I(e): 'introduction from the sea' means 'transportation into a State of specimens or any species which were taken in the marine environment not under the jurisdiction of any State'. This does not cover exploitation in the EEZs of coastal states.

301 See *Lyster's International Wildlife Law*, Ch 15 and *infra*, Ch 13.

302 The system is analogous to prior informed consent/advanced informed agreement regimes: Ong in Fitzmaurice et al, *Research Handbook on International Environmental Law* 526; and see section 2(4) below.

303 Included in this list, inter alia, are all apes, lemurs, the giant panda, many South American monkeys, great whales, cheetahs, leopards, tigers, Asian and African elephants, all rhinoceroses, many birds of prey, cranes, pheasants, all sea turtles, some crocodiles and lizards, giant salamanders and some mussels, orchids (8 species), and cacti.

304 See UNGA Res 69/314 (2015). For recent global assessment of the state of wildlife crime—including trends since its first report in 2016—see UNODC, *World Wildlife Crime Report 2020: Trafficking in protected species* (UNODC, Vienna, May 2020).

305 Ibid, and *supra*, Ch 5, section 6(1).

306 This list is much larger than Appendix I, with over 30,000 species. Included in this list are primates, cats, otters, whales, dolphins and porpoises, seahorses, birds of prey, all species of flamingo, tortoises, crocodiles and orchids (around 30,000 species), mahogany, fur seals, the black stork, birds of paradise, the coelacanth, some snails, birdwing butterflies, and black corals.

trade is permitted in these species provided it is controlled and monitored so that the species does not become endangered. Proper documentation issued by the exporting state is required, including a determination by the Scientific Authority that export will not be detrimental to the survival of that species. In making that determination Parties should 'make use of the *Principles and Guidelines for the Sustainable Use of Biodiversity*, also taking into account scientific, trade and enforcement considerations determined by national circumstances, as well as the recommendations of the Animals and Plants Committees.'[307] The biggest gap in the coverage of the 1973 CITES is that for political reasons no commercially exploited fish species appear on any appendix however endangered or over-fished they may be.[308]

To ensure that threatened species are not traded under the pretext that they are a different species, Article II(2)(b) allows so-called 'look alike' species to be added to Appendix II, even if not threatened. These are 'specimens' of species, defined in Article I(b)(i) as an animal or plant, whether alive or dead, including (for Appendix I and II species) 'any readily recognizable part or derivative thereof'. Such parts include ivory, horns, and skins but, as the term 'readily recognizable' is not defined in the 1973 CITES, it is left to each state to compile its own list or deal with this problem ad hoc since it is essential to effective enforcement that customs officials should be enabled to identify such items. Thus the 1973 CITES presents another example of a treaty in relation to which many developing states need training and advice if they are to comply with its demands effectively.

Finally, Appendix III includes all species the parties identify as being subject to regulation in their own jurisdiction for purposes of preventing or restricting exploitation and needing other parties' cooperation to control trade.

(c) The listing process

The parties themselves, at their biennial meetings, review the working of the the 1973 CITES and discuss possible changes to the appendices, including removal of particular species from the list or from Appendix I to Appendix II—so-called 'downlisting.' In common with many of the pre-UNCED treaties, the precautionary principle is not found in the text of the 1973 CITES but has subsequently been adopted by COP resolution and applies to the listing and de-listing process.[309]

For Appendices I and II, amendment (listing or delisting) occurs by a vote of the parties requiring a two-thirds majority of those present and voting, though once adopted the decision is binding on all Contracting Parties unless there are reservations.[310] While general reservations are not permitted under the 1973 CITES, reservations are

307 Resolution Conf 13.2 (Rev CoP14), adopting the Addis Ababa Principles and Guidelines of the CBD, on which see *infra*, section 6.

308 See *infra*, Ch 12, section 1(2)

309 Resolution Conf. 9.24 (Rev. CoP17), Criteria for amendment of Appendices I and II, Annex 4 Precautionary measures.

310 Article XV.

permitted to the amendments to the Appendices within a limited period following adoption, thus rendering the reserving State a non-party to CITES with respect to trade in the species concerned.[311] The majority of reservations under all three appendices are with respect to birds and mammals. For example, Japan, Iceland and Norway have entered reservations against the listing under Appendix I of various cetacea, and Saudi Arabia has done so regarding various birds of prey.

(d) Implementation

In common with the other treaties examined here, the effectiveness of the 1973 CITES is dependent on national implementation. CITES requires that each party establish at least one Management Authority and Scientific Authority, responsible for ensuring that the required conditions for the issue of permits (laid down respectively in Articles III, IV, and V for each Appendix) have been complied with.[312] It sets conditions for export, re-export, and import permits.[313] Article III prohibits the export of specimens of Appendix I species without the prior grant and submission of an export permit. An export permit is issued only if the Management Authority is satisfied not only that the species has been legally obtained but that, if they are to be exported alive, conditions for their transportation conform to the standards laid down in the Convention and only if the Scientific Authority is satisfied that export will not be detrimental to the species' survival. Each transhipment requires an individual permit. Re-export of Appendix I species is banned unless a re-export certificate is issued for which similar prerequisites apply. An export permit cannot be issued for Appendix I species unless an import permit has already been issued; this latter is not a prerequisite for export of Appendix II species. It is this requirement of an import permit and, in the case of live specimens, proof that the intended recipient has the necessary equipment to accommodate and care for them, that represents the most effective enforcement technique for Appendix I species.[314] The further requirement that the relevant Management Authority must also be satisfied that the specimen will be used primarily for non-commercial purposes effectively limits trade among parties to specimens used only for scientific and educational purposes or, in certain circumstances, for hunting trophies, subject to modifications introduced at the Gaborone Conference in favour of small, exceptional quotas of specimens of species otherwise prohibited from import.[315]

Because import permits *are not* required for Appendix II species a large trade takes place, which has been a matter of concern to the COP over many years. It has accordingly made recommendations to ensure that trade conforms to the the 1973 CITES requirement that export will not be in such quantities as to be detrimental to the species' survival.[316] Each state party is then responsible through exercise of its customs controls, inter alia, for ensuring that listed species and specimens imported and exported are covered by the appropriate permits.

[311] As provided for in Articles XV(3) and XXIII. The current list is available at cites.org.

[312] Article IX.

[313] Articles III–VII.

[314] Article III(3).

[315] *Lyster's International Wildlife Law*, Ch 15.

[316] Article IV(2).

(e) Compliance

The 1973 CITES' compliance review process is based on infractions reports by the Secretariat to the COP with the effective sanction for non-compliance being temporary suspension of trade in specimens of CITES-listed species with the non-complying party.[317] Presently there are 25 (developing) States subject to one or more recommendations to suspend trade in certain species owing to 'significant trade' in contravention of the 1973 CITES, many within the last five years, though the longest 'temporary' suspensions have applied for 25 years to Madagascar and the Solomon Islands. A recommendation to suspend all trade, or all commercial trade, may be made where non-compliance affects implementation of the 1973 CITES as a whole, namely, the failure to: provide timely annual reports (eg Afghanistan, Djibouti, Grenada); enact the appropriate national legislation (eg Djibouti, Liberia, Somalia); ensure effective compliance and enforcement (eg Guinea). Recommendations can cover non-parties (Haiti, for significant trade in the Queen conch, since 2003). In practice this has been a potent tool for ensuring proper national implementation of the 1973 CITES' obligations to enact legislation, develop work plans, control legal/illegal trade, and/or improve the basis for government decision-making.[318] It has also encouraged participation in the 1973 CITES, with some accessions by States previously subject to trade suspensions while non-parties (Bahrain, Iraq, and Tajikistan).

(f) Institutional supervision

The COP is empowered inter alia to consider and adopt amendments to the appendices, review progress in restoration and conservation of species, and make recommendations for improving the effectiveness of the Convention.[319] The CITES Secretariat is responsible inter alia for monitoring the overall operation of the Treaty, preparing reports and making recommendations on implementation to the COP.[320] It receives and responds to information obtained through reports of parties, including information about non-compliance or other adverse effects of trade in listed specimens.[321] Only the COP and the Secretariat are explicitly envisaged under the Convention, but very swiftly a Standing Committee (facilitating work between biennial meetings of the COP) was established (1979) followed by a Plant Committee (1983) and an Animals Committee (1987) to provide scientific advice and guidance.[322]

The Conferences of the Parties have dealt over the years with many of the interpretational and operational problems posed by the Convention.[323] Measures adopted include criteria for the listing and de-listing of species on the appendices established

317 Article XIII. See generally Reeve, *Policing International Trade in Endangered Species: The CITES Treaty and Compliance* (London, 2002); Wijnstekers, *The Evolution of CITES*, Ch 16.

318 Yeater and Vasquez, 10(3) *RECIEL* (2002) 271.

319 Article XI. 320 Article XII. 321 Articles XII(d) and (e); XIII.

322 See in particular Resolution Conf. 11.1 (Rev. CoP 18.2) on the establishment of committees; and Annex 2 (terms of reference of the Animals Committee and the Plant Committee).

323 For a full list of Resolutions currently in effect (from COP18, 2019), see https://www.cites.org/eng/res/index.php

at the first meeting of the Parties and regularly updated since;[324] measures concerning shipment of live animals in order to ensure their safe handling and welfare in transit and on arrival;[325] detailed restrictions on import of hunting trophies have been adopted and revised;[326] standardised conference-approved documentation, including model permits and use special security paper or serially numbered adhesive security stamps;[327] and clarification of key terms as already noted above.[328]

As might be expected, much of the controversy surrounding the 1973 CITES has focused on listing (and de-listing) in the Appendices, with the listing of the African elephant particularly contentious. The African elephant was moved to Appendix I in 1990, since poaching and sale of ivory had caused severe decline in some elephant populations. This decision prohibited all trade in elephant ivory and led to a dramatic fall in sales, but the adverse socio-economic consequences led to a partial relaxation in an attempt to seek a compromise between wildlife protection and human development.[329] Elephant populations in Botswana, Namibia, South Africa, and Zimbabwe (which, under good management, were reputed to have recovered) were moved to Appendix II, with one-off sales of existing ivory stocks permitted, in 1997 and 2007, in order to generate income for further conservation measures. [330] The argument for down-listing and allowing managed trade was that it would give local people an incentive to conserve and manage elephant populations, because they would benefit from doing so.[331] It has been suggested that the 1973 CITES membership influenced Zimbabwe to adhere to the ban on trade whilst working to change the regime to its advantage.[332] The decision to move these elephant populations to Appendix II remains controversial, since it is impossible to distinguish ivory so obtained from ivory taken from illegally poached specimens. At the same time a complete ban on trade in ivory neither encouraged nor rewarded wise conservation, which may require culling as herds recover, or local respect for the law. But allowing some trade has not stopped poaching and illegal trafficking of ivory, and as we saw earlier the focus of current attention is now on improving law enforcement and international criminal cooperation.[333]

324 *Proc 1st COP*, Conf 1.2, 33, known henceforth as 'the Bern Criteria'; for the current revision see Resolution Conf. 9.24 (Rev. CoP17).

325 *Proc 6th COP*, Doc 6.19; Resolution 6.2.4. On CITES contribution to animal welfare, see Bowman, 1 *JIWLP* (1998) 9–63.

326 *Proc 2nd COP*, Conf 2.11, 48; most recently Conf. 17.9.

327 *Proc 3rd COP*, Confs 3.6, 3.7, 46–52.

328 Other examples include 'primarily commercial purposes' which COP5 clarified means 'All uses whose non-commercial aspects do not clearly predominate' (it being for the importer to establish this) and that 'commercial' included any such transaction even if not wholly commercial: *Proc 5th COP*, Doc 5.10.

329 See Rolfes, in *Endangered Species, Threatened Convention* 74–8, 86; Barbier, et al, *Elephants, Economics and Ivory* (London, 1990); and Glennon 84 *AJIL* (1990) 1.

330 On the regulation of ivory trade see Resolution Conf 10.10 (Rev CoP14). See further, Mofson, in Hatton and Dickson (eds),*Threatened Convention: The Past, Present and Future of CITES* (London, 2000) 107–22; and *Lyster's International Wildlife Law*, Ch 16.

331 See, in particular, Harland, *Killing Game* (Westport, 1994), and see *infra*.

332 Mofson, loc cit, 114. She recounts one Zimbabwean official stating that it was 'better to work on CITES from within. It doesn't end with elephants; once you are an outsider you have no input or involvement. We realize we will benefit from staying in . . . and . . . we are hosting the next COP'.

333 See UNGA Res 69/314 (2015) and *supra*, section 3(4)(b).

Cooperation between NGOs and the secretariat is crucial to the success of the 1973 CITES,[334] particularly in monitoring trade. Data for purposes of monitoring trade are collected by the Wildlife Trade Monitoring Unit located in the UK. It receives information from governments and IUCN/WWF's TRAFFIC offices in various states. This, backed by information supplied by other NGOs, enables the CITES Secretariat to identify problems and take responsive measures. Annual reports from member states back up this process. As information accrues, the assumption is that the effectiveness of the 1973 CITES is correspondingly enhanced. Nonetheless, smuggling is widespread, particularly through Taiwan, which because of the ambivalence surrounding its territorial status is not a party to the 1973 CITES. China's poor record of enforcement is also a major problem.[335]

(g) Assessing CITES

Empirically it is difficult to know how much the existence of the 1973 CITES has made a difference to illegal wildlife trade,[336] and views are divided on its effectiveness.[337] While regulated trade may help with species conservation and assist local communities to benefit from their sustainable utilization, achieving it is fraught with uncertainties in ascertaining a sustainable level of exploitation for particular species,[338] and whether demand can be sufficiently controlled to avoid over-exploitation and increased killing.[339] Sustainable utilization of certain species– eg charismatic megafauna—may be opposed even if trade in other animals and plants is not, or there may be ethical objections to any trade in any species. This is indeed 'an area riven both by uncertainty and fundamental value disagreements'. [340]

Critics also point to over-zealous listing of specimens not seriously endangered,[341] to the 1973 CITES' weakness in allowing major exemptions, which provide loopholes for illegal trade, and to the practical difficulties of enforcement, which enables trade in large numbers of species listed on all appendices to escape detection since enforcement is left to individual states parties, whose domestic wildlife laws, scrutiny, and controls vary greatly in scope and enforcement.[342] The Secretariat thus arranges

[334] As provided for in Article XII(I).

[335] See Mushkat, 34 *Env L & P* (2010) 493, and see also *South China Sea Arbitration*, discussed *infra*, Ch 12, section 2(3)(d).

[336] Wiersema, in Peel and Rajamani, *Oxford Handbook of International Environmental Law* 9.

[337] Contrast for example *Lyster's, International Wildlife Law*, Ch 16 and Favre, *Convention on Trade in Endangered Species* (Dordrecht, 1990). Baker sees much room for improvement on compliance: see Baker, 2 *JIWLP* (1999) 1; see also Wandesforde-Smith, 19 *JIWLP* (2016) 365 and in reply Wiersema, 20 *JIWLP* (2017) 207; Bowman, 22 *RECIEL* (2013) 228.

[338] Although listing decisions are intended to be based on science, it has frequently been observed that many voting decisions and CITES COPS are 'extremely political': Wiersema, in Peel and Rajamani, *Oxford Handbook of International Environmental Law* 10.

[339] Wiersema, ibid; Shonfield, 15 *CWILJ* (1985) 127–58.

[340] Wiersema, ibid.

[341] E.g. the Antarctic minke whale, which has never been endangered, on which see *infra*, Ch 12, section 4.

[342] See e.g. Conf 17.6 'Prohibiting, preventing, detecting and countering corruption, which facilitates activities conducted in violation of the Convention' (2016).

enforcement seminars for customs officers and Interpol,[343] facilitates cooperation between them, offers training to Management Authorities, and maintains a collection of slides depicting forged documents. Some parties provide funds for technical assistance. Allowing trade with non-parties whose documentation substantially conforms to CITES[344] has also presented problems. TRAFFIC, however, is an effective part of a network cooperating with the IUCN in monitoring international trade in wildlife and plants. It reports on the data gathered and provides analyses of wildlife trade statistics. Publicizing this trade in itself provides one of the most effective controls on it.

The Convention has been shown to have other weaknesses. The non-binding nature of Conference resolutions and the fundamental weakness of the reservations system, which, since it exempts parties formally entering objections to a listing from being bound by it, in effect puts such parties in a position equivalent to non-parties with whom trade is permitted, and undermines the aims of the Treaty regime. Like most wildlife conventions, Article XXIII of the 1973 CITES permits reservations to conservation measures in order to maximize participation and protect national interests. Reservations can be lodged, on adhering to the Convention, to listings on Appendices I and II or within ninety days of their adoption by the Conference, and subsequently at any time in written form, without specification of reasons, a procedure that results in that party being treated as a non-party in relation to the species concerned.[345] Exhortations by successive conferences that parties should refrain from use of these procedures has had little effect. Compilation by the Secretariat of lists of non-parties whose scientific assessment of whether proposed trade 'substantially conforms' to the 1973 CITES requirements are found by it not to meet the required standards for issue of permits has been more effective.

It has long been suggested that a limit could be placed on the number of reservations a party may enter; their duration could be limited and all reservations could be periodically reviewed.[346] But in its current unreformed state Article XXIII has in particular allowed some key fishing states to block attempts at listing any of the growing number of endangered high seas fish species.[347] Trade in unsustainably caught fish is one of the major threats to the marine environment; without support from the 1973 CITES, the 1982 UNCLOS and the 1995 UN Fish Stocks Agreement are undermined.[348] There is a real contrast here with marine mammals, nearly all of which have benefitted from a CITES listing that has given teeth to the moratorium on commercial whaling introduced in 1982, allowing many whale stocks slowly to recover.[349] Moreover in the *South China Sea Arbitration* the the 1973 CITES listing of giant clams and sea turtles allowed arbitrators to conclude that China had violated its obligation

343 See, generally, UNGA 69/314 *Tackling illicit traffic in wildlife* (2015); and Interpol, *Global Wildlife Enforcement* (2019).

344 Article X. 345 Article XV(3). See Steward, 14 *Cornell ILJ* (1981) 424.

346 Steward, 14 *Cornell ILJ* (1981) *passim*.

347 See Guggisberg, *The Use of CITES for Commercially Exploited Fish Species* (Heidelberg, 2015), and *infra*, Ch 12, section 1(2). Contrast Article 10 of the UNFSA, *infra*, Ch 12, section 3(3)(d).

348 Guggisberg, ibid. 349 See *infra*, Ch 12, section 4.

to protect the marine environment under Part XII of the 1982 UNCLOS.[350] Here the interplay of both treaties proved crucial to the case.

These weaknesses are not insurmountable; parties have the power to resolve the textual ambiguities and to use enforcement powers effectively, if so minded. Amendment procedures are also available, both for the the 1973 CITES substantive articles and its appendices.[351] Even early critics conceded that the 1973 CITES provides 'a highly practical mechanism incorporating a structure designed to deal with a complex international situation'[352] which attempts to balance legitimate trade interests in renewable resources with the need to protect endangered species.[353] A real challenge to the 1973 CITES now comes from the changed framework of perceptions concerning use of wildlife in the 21st century. A golden thread weaving through the Strategic Vision for the Convention up to 2030 is conservation and sustainable use: that the 1973 CITES parties act 'in the best interest of the conservation of species, working to ensure their use is legal and sustainable'.[354] Goal 4 explicitly recognizes 'the important contribution of CITES to the 2030 Agenda for Sustainable Development' and locates the 1973 CITES at the intersection between trade, the environment and development, a theme we return to in chapter 13. In echoes of early nineties concerns regarding development 'trumping' environment, much now depends on the 1973 CITES' effective implementation in order to achieve a better balance between progressive socio-economic development and the conservation of wildlife for future generations.[355]

3 PLANT PROTECTION[356]

While even simple dictionary definitions of 'the environment' include plants,[357] they have historically received little attention in law[358] save for where of importance for humans, particularly for agriculture.[359] Today, however, their importance as 'the ecological foundations of all life on Earth' is widely recognized: as the vision statement for the 1992 CBD's *Global Strategy for Plant Conservation* expresses it, 'Without plants there is no life.'[360] The need to protect flora as well as fauna is now found recognized in a wide range of instruments, such as the 1964 Agreed Measures for the Conservation of Antarctic Fauna and Flora, subsequently incorporated as Annex II of the 1991

350 See *infra*, Ch 12, section 2(3)(d). 351 Articles XV–XVII. 352 Shonfield, 15 *CWILJ* (1985) 127.

353 Steward, 14 *Cornell ILJ* (1981) 429. 354 Conf 18.3, Annex, 3.

355 Ong, 10 *JEL* (1998) 291–314.

356 Forests, a key plant biome, are considered *infra* section 4(2).

357 See also the definition of 'wildlife law' *supra*, n 30.

358 As noted above, apart from early pioneers such as de Klemm, there had until recently been little attention paid to plant conservation in international law: see Amos, *International Conservation Law* (2020).

359 See n 33 above.

360 CBD Decision X/17, Consolidated update of the Global Strategy for Plant Conservation 2011–2020. The Strategy considers plants in the terrestrial, inland water and marine environments and applies to the three primary levels of biodiversity, namely, plant genetic diversity, plant species and communities and their associated habitats and ecosystems. See further *infra* section 5.

Environmental Protocol to the 1959 Antarctic Treaty,[361] Article III of the 1968 African Convention,[362] and Article 2 of the 1972 WHC.[363] As the common ordering of 'fauna' first reflects, the tendency is however for animals in general, and charismatic megafauna in particular, to predominate.[364] Moreover, as the 1968 African Convention example illustrates, flora and fauna are often subject to the same provisions[365] encouraging an ecologically inappropriate 'one size fits all' approach to conservation.[366] Threats to conservation status may be similarly intermingled, eg a quarter of wetlands plants and animals are at risk of extinction.[367]

Even where distinction is made, such as under the 1979 Bern Convention, it does not carry this through to habitat protection.[368] In other respects, however, this Convention marks a departure in its approach to the conservation of wild flora and fauna and their natural habitats, including migratory species.[369] Appendix I is reserved exclusively for plants, and presently contains over 700 species. Whilst reservations are permitted against listed species, very few relate to plants in Annex I.[370] Another example is the 1973 CITES, which established a Plant Committee (1983) before an Animals Committee (1987), to provide scientific advice and guidance to the COP and other Convention bodies.[371] As noted above, the threat to plants posed by illegal trade is

361 Annex II 'Conservation of Antarctic Fauna and Flora'. Article 1(c) EP defines 'native plant' as 'any terrestrial or freshwater vegetation, including bryophytes, lichens, fungi and algae, at any stage of its life cycle (including seeds, and other propagules), indigenous to the Antarctic Treaty area'. See generally Redgwell, 43 *ICLQ* 599 (1994).

362 Eg Article III of the 1968 African Convention defines 'natural resources' to include 'flora and fauna', and defines 'specimen' as 'an individual example of wild animal or wild plant or part of a wild plant'.

363 Which defines natural heritage to include delineated areas 'which constitute the habitat of threatened species of animals and plants of outstanding universal value from the point of view of science or conservation'. For commentary on Article 2, see Redgwell in Francioni and Lenzerini, *The 1972 World Heritage Convention*, 63.

364 This is reflected in the scientific literature: on taxonomic bias in biodiversity data and societal preferences, see Troudet et al., 7(1) *Scientific reports* (2017) 9132. As they observe, 'focusing on a few, often charismatic, species, prevents reaching global conclusions and developing efficient conservation plans' and that 'Rare, small or uncharismatic creatures do play pivotal functions in ecosystems'. Moreover, as noted above, Wilson estimates that 'less than 1% of known species have been carefully studied': Wilson, 289 *Science* 2279 (2000).

365 See also eg ASEAN, Arts 3–5; Western Hemisphere Convention, Art V. Under Annex II of the 1991 EP, Article 3 addresses 'protection of native fauna and flora', with Annex A listing protected species, of which there is only one, the Ross seal. Annex B of the EP lists permitted imports under Art 4, with both domestic and laboratory plants permitted to be imported into Antarctica.

366 Amos, *International Conservation Law* 73.

367 Ibid; see also Finlayson et al, 39 *Wetlands* (2019) 1.

368 Contrast protection of species (Art 5 flora; Arts 6–7 fauna) with Art 4 (protection of habitats of wild flora and fauna species).

369 Reflecting the emphasis on transboundary cooperation in conservation efforts, the 51 parties to this Council of Europe Convention include several African States—Burkina Faso, Morocco, Senegal and Tunisia—which participate by invitation of the Committee of Ministers: see further *Lyster's International Wildlife Law* 297.

370 See *supra*, section 2(1).

371 See in particular Resolution Conf. 11.1 (Rev. CoP 18.2) on the establishment of committees; and Annex 2 (terms of reference of the Animals Committee and the Plant Committee).

reflected in the fact that there are nearly 30,000 species of plants listed on CITES three appendices,[372] and around 5,800 species of animals.

There are key ecological differences between animals and plants which need to be reflected in legal regulation, such as the more restricted capacity of plants to adapt to climate change impacts especially on a short time scale[373] and the importance of ecological representativeness, over size and number, of protected areas.[374] As we will see below in the discussion of the 1992 CBD, protected areas designation is a key tool for the in situ conservation of biological diversity, but the ecological representativeness of sites, of particular importance for the conservation of plants, needs to be improved.[375]

While our examination of plants is woven into broader discussion of species, habitat and ecosystem protection, two instruments specifically addressed to plants have been concluded which are of importance in the trade context in particular. These are the 1951 IPPC, revised in 1997, and the 2001 ITPGRFA, replacing the non-binding 1983 International Undertaking on Plant Genetic Resources.[376] The 1983 Undertaking was a significant initiative as it aimed to ensure that plant genetic resources should be explored, preserved, evaluated, and made available for plant breeding and scientific purposes.[377] This nascent regime did not, however, represent a comprehensive global approach to protection of the earth's biodiversity and did little to protect resources found wholly within a state's national jurisdictional limits.[378] In 2001 the Undertaking was replaced by a treaty,[379] the 2001 ITPGRFA, which contains provisions on plant genetic resources and benefit sharing which are closely linked with the 1992 CBD, and the 2010 Nagoya Protocol in particular, and is considered further below.

The 1951 IPPC, as its name suggests, is concerned with the protection of plants, both wild and cultivated, from the threat of pests and diseases, and with minimizing the adverse trade effects of phytosanitary measures.[380] It has been amended twice, most recently in 2007 to reflect more contemporary phytosanitary concepts and its role in relation to the SPS Agreement. The 1951 IPPC also builds on and cooperates

372 *Supra*, section 3(4).

373 On the global scale, climate change is expected to lead to changes in the timing of biological events, such as flowering and the relationship between plant and pollinator. And the effects will not be evenly felt: while, for example, mosses are highly adaptable as they 'enjoy easy dispersal, through light windborne spores, and can rapidly colonize suitable new habitat' trees by contrast migrate at a much slower rate.

374 GBO-4, 82–5. Representativeness is also a criterion for designation under the WHC: see *supra*, section 3(2).

375 Juffe-Bignoli et al., *Protected Plant Report 2014: Tracking progress towards global targets for protected areas* (UNEP-WCMC, 2014) 40.

376 See de Klemm (1990); Amos (2020).

377 Resolution 8/83 adopted by the 22nd FAO Conference on 23 November 1983 as amended by 'interpretations' adopted in 1989 and 1991. On this see Rose, in Bowman and Redgwell (eds), *International Law and Biodiversity* (The Hague, 1996) 150.

378 See eg the 1991 modification which, in a common refrain, continues to recognize plant genetic resources as the 'heritage of mankind' but subject to the sovereignty of the state with property rights exercisable over them.

379 For background see Louka, *International Environmental Law: Fairness, Effectiveness, and World Order* (Cambridge, 2006), Ch 7.

380 On which see further *infra* ch 13 section 4(1).

with a significant network of regional organisations for plant protection.[381] Like the 2001 ITPGRFA, there are close links with the 1992 CBD, particularly with respect to the impact of alien invasive species on biodiversity.[382] Decisions of the CBD COP[383] have stressed the need for cooperation with and participation in other treaty instruments addressed to invasive alien species such as the 1951 IPPC and called on them to 'note' the lack of international standards pertaining to non-pest invasive alien species.[384] The international standards-setting function of the IPPC's Commission on Phytosanitary Measures[385] has been recognized in the WTO SPS Agreement[386] and IPCC standards have been cited as the relevant international standards in WTO disputes, eg *Japan—Measures Affecting the Importation of Apples.*[387] The Committee on Sanitary and Phytosanitary Measures is required to cooperate with, inter alia, the IPPC Secretariat 'with the objective of securing the best available scientific and technical advice for the administration of th[e SPS] Agreement and in order to ensure that unnecessary duplication of effort is avoided'.[388]

4 DESERTS, FORESTS AND LANDSCAPE

As noted in chapter 2, it was hoped that the Rio process would bring about not only a convention conserving biodiversity but also conventions on desertification and forests. From 1974 onwards, the UN, UNEP, and various conferences of concerned international organizations and bodies had drawn attention to the increasingly serious economic consequences of the expansion of arid lands[389] and destruction of forests, especially tropical forests. Various recommendations emerged from these and were

381 There are 10 Regional Plant Protection Organisations established by treaty, comprising the IPPC network e.g. the 1951 International Convention for the Establishment of the European and Mediterranean Plant Protection Organization; the 1954 Phytosanitary Convention for African South of the Sahara; the 1956 Plant Protection Agreement for the Asia and Pacific Region; the 1959 Agreement Concerning Co-operation in the Quarantine of Plants and Their Protection Against Pests and Diseases; and the 1993 Agreement for the Establishment of Near East Plant Protection Organization. See further www.ippc.int/

382 See eg Commission on Plant Measures (CPM) recommendation *LMOs, biosecurity and alien invasive species* (R-01) (2001).

383 See Decisions VIII/27 (2006) and IX/4 (2008).

384 Decision IX/4 (2008).

385 Arts X and XI IPPC.

386 International standards, guidelines and recommendations on plant health: see Annex A(3)(c) SPS Agreement.

387 Cited as embodying the relevant international standards were eg the 1996 Guidelines for Pest Risk Analysis, International Standard for Phytosanitary Measures No.2 and the 2001 Pest Risk Analysis for Quarantine Pests, International Standard for Phytosanitary Measures No.11: *Japan—Measures Affecting the Importation of Apples* WT/DS245/AB/R, 75, para 205.

388 Article 12.3 SPS Agreement.

389 The Sahelian drought 1968–1973 focused international attention on this issue, leading inter alia to UNGA Res 3337 (XXIX) 1974 on international cooperation to combat desertification followed by UNGA Res 3511 (XXX) 1975 instructing UNEP and UNDP to convene a UN Conference on desertification, which produced a (largely ineffective) Plan of Action: see Tolba, *The United Nations Conference on Desertification: A Review*, 6; 1978 UNEP adopted an Action Plan on Drought and Desertification: UNEP/GC.6/11, 24 May 1979.

promoted, inter alia, by UNEP, UNESCO, and the FAO,[390] but action lagged until the spread and severity of desertification and rate of destruction of forests led to intensified demands for action. This was inhibited, however, by the insistence of the states concerned that the issues involved fell wholly within their national sovereignty.[391]

Thus, although some progress was made on definitional aspects, the goal of concluding conventions on these topics was not attained at UNCED in 1992, though Agenda 21 did define and draw attention to desertification, and a non-binding statement of principles relating to forests was adopted. While action on desertification swiftly followed with the adoption in 1994 of the Desertification Convention, there is still no global forests treaty, with responsibility for forests fragmented across institutions and regions. Both forests and deserts comprise terrestrial ecosystems which are addressed in SDG 15, 'Life on Land', which aims to 'protect, restore and promote sustainable use of terrestrial ecosystems, sustainably manage forests, combat desertification, and halt and reverse land degradation and halt biodiversity loss'.[392]

4(1) THE CONVENTION TO COMBAT DESERTIFICATION

Following the recommendation made in Agenda 21, the UN General Assembly initiated negotiation of a convention focusing particularly on states experiencing serious drought in Africa.[393] States were, however, anxious to avoid conflict and overlap with existing conventions, such as those on climate change and biodiversity. Problems also arose concerning the conclusion and status of specific regional instruments which it was agreed should be an integral part of the convention. A UN Convention to Combat Desertification ('UNCCD') was eventually concluded in 1994,[394] with four annexes covering Africa, Latin America and the Caribbean, Asia, and the Northern Mediterranean, with a fifth annex added subsequently in 2001 covering the Central and East European region. The 1994 UNCCD entered into force in 1996 and currently has 197 parties.[395] It thus enjoys the most widespread participation of any of the instruments considered here, but this high level of participation has not translated into effective prevention of desertification under the 1994 UNCCD, not least because the Convention is weak on specific commitments.

As in the case of the 1992 CBD, reference is made in the 1994 UNCCD Preamble to many of the Rio Declaration's goal-setting principles, such as sustainable development

[390] On the role of these bodies in environmental governance, see further *supra*, Ch 2 section 3.1.

[391] See eg example of the Amazonian rain forest at n 414.

[392] See *supra*, Ch 2.

[393] UNGA Res 47/188 (1992). This was the first to do so: Article IV of the 1968 African Convention and Article VI of the 2003 African Convention, for example, address the issue only obliquely. Dry and subhumid lands biodiversity is also one of the thematic areas under the CBD.

[394] For reports on the difficulties experienced in negotiation, see 23 *EPL* (1993) 202–3; 24 *EPL* (1994) 36. See generally Bekhechi, 101 *RGDIP* (1997) 101; (2003) 12:2 *RECIEL* passim; Johnson, Mayrand, and Paquin (eds), *Governing Global Desertification: Linking Environmental Degradation, Poverty and Participation* (Ashgate, 2006).

[395] With 29 parties, including the EU, outside of any regional implementation grouping.

and accounting for the interests of future generations.[396] It recognizes human beings as being at the centre of concerns to combat desertification and mitigate drought but does not explicitly adopt the 'common concern' language found in the 1992 CBD and the 1992 Climate Change Convention. Nonetheless the Preamble recognises the 'urgent concern of the international community' about the adverse impacts of desertification and drought which is reflected in the text and, as the problems are stated to be of 'global dimensions in that they affect all regions of the world', it is also acknowledged that 'joint action of the international community is needed to combat' them.[397] Mindful of the relationship between desertification and other global environmental problems, the parties also 'bear in mind' the contribution that combating desertification will have to achieving their objectives under the UNFCCC[398] and 1992 CBDs.[399] Stress is laid on the need to resolve the economic and social problems of the areas concerned, the prevalence of developing states in the areas,[400] and the need for sustainable economic growth. The parties reaffirm Rio Declaration Principle 2 concerning the right to pursue their own developmental as well as environmental policies. The human-centred and sustainable development approach of the 1994 UNCCD has subsequently been reflected in the key role it plays in the implementation of the 'land-degradation neutrality (LDN)' goal of SDG 15.3,[401] which aims '[b]y 2030, [to] combat desertification, restore degraded land and soil, including land affected by desertification, drought and floods, and strive to achieve a land degradation-neutral world'. Although non-binding—as are the voluntary LDN goals under the 1994 UNCCD—some have optimistically viewed this LDN goal as 'a promising new strategy with the potential to revitalize the international agenda to fight desertification/land degradation and drought'.[402] The timeline for the current strategic framework under the 1994 UNCCD (2018-2030) dovetails with that for the SDGs.

Desertification is defined in Article 1 UNCCD as meaning 'land degradation in arid, semi-arid and dry humid areas resulting from various factors, including climatic variations and human activities'. Such areas cover about 46.2 per cent of the global

396 Its 'dual focus on poverty and the environment makes it a sustainable development convention': Johnson et al. (eds), *Governing Global Desertification*, 1.

397 For analysis of this preambular language, see French, 'in Bowman, Davies and Goodwin (eds), *Research Handbook on Biodiversity and Law* (Edward Elgar, 2016), 345–6.

398 The multiplier effect of climate change and human activities is confirmed in the most recent IPCC report: 'Desertification and changing climate are projected to cause reductions in crop and livestock productivity (high confidence), modify the composition of plant species and reduce biological diversity across drylands (medium confidence). Rising CO2 levels will favour more rapid expansion of some invasive plant species in some regions.' *Climate Change and Land: An IPCC Special Report on climate change, desertification, land degradation, sustainable land management, food security, and greenhouse gas fluxes in terrestrial ecosystem* (2019).

399 In 1998 a Memorandum of Cooperation was concluded between the Secretariats of the CBD and UNCCD, and the CBD's SBSTTA has recommended improving synergies between the CBD and UNCCD regarding the former's thematic work on dry and sub-humid lands biodiversity: see eg CBD SBSTTA 8 Recommendation VIII/4 (2003).

400 Thus potentially 'tempering' recognition of the global nature of the problem with 'a decidedly regional perspective': French in Bowman et al., *Research Handbook on Biodiversity and LawaHanhAN* 346.

401 See 1994 UNCCD COP12, Decision 3 (2015).

402 Minelli, Erlewein and Castillo, *International Yearbook of Soil Law and Policy 2016* (2017) 85.

land area and are home to 3 billion people.[403] Combating desertification includes activities aimed at (i) prevention or reduction of land degradation, (ii) rehabilitation of partly degraded land, and (iii) reclamation of desertified land. As is the case with all of the instruments considered here, but of particular import for the 1994 UNCCD with its bottom up approach,[404] national implementation plays a crucial role in combating the problem of desertification, and there is the accompanying need for 'new and additional funding' and access to technology, without which States—especially the least developing—will find it difficult to comply. Much of the development of implementing measures requires transfer of technology and financial support, invoked in other articles, so far as the many developing countries in the desertified areas are concerned. They also note that it will be necessary to base strategies on rigorous scientific knowledge if they are to be effective, and stress the urgent need to improve 'the effectiveness and coordination of international cooperation'.

One of the key instruments for the implementation of the Convention is the development of national, subregional and regional action programmes which are being developed by country parties affected by desertification and land degradation in Africa, Asia, Latin America, the Caribbean, the Northern Mediterranean and Central and Eastern Europe. Developed country parties have the obligation to support affected countries through the provision of additional financial resources and by facilitating access to technology, knowledge, and know-how (Articles 6 and 20). As noted in Chapter 2, the GEF is the designated funding mechanism for 1994 UNCCD.

Oversight of implementation is provided by a Committee for Review of Implementation of the Convention (CRIC) which, within the current framework of the 2018-2030 strategic plan,[405] considers progress in implementation of the 1994 UNCCD's five strategic objectives, namely: (1) to improve the condition of affected ecosystems, combat desertification/land degradation, promote sustainable land management and contribute to land degradation neutrality; (2) to improve the living conditions of affected populations; (3) to mitigate, adapt to, and manage the effects of drought in order to enhance resilience of vulnerable populations and ecosystems; (4) to generate global environmental benefits through effective implementation of the 1994 UNCCD; and (5) to mobilize substantial and additional financial and non-financial resources to support the implementation of the Convention by building effective partnerships at global and national level.[406] Reporting is one mechanism for enhancing transparency and oversight, and the 1994 UNCCD is no exception.

403 *Climate Change and Land: An IPCC Special Report on climate change, desertification, land degradation, sustainable land management, food security, and greenhouse gas fluxes in terrestrial ecosystem* (2019), ch 3, 7.

404 See Tal and Cohen, 31 *Harvard Environmental Law Review* (2007) 163.

405 The first decanal strategic plan did not commence until 2008, not least because the early years of the Convention were preoccupied with 'process, institutions and budgets': Bassett and Talafré, 12:2 *RECIEL* (2003) 133.

406 For the most recent report, see UNCCD/CRIC(17)/9, 3 April 2019.

However, reporting on progress has been patchy[407] even with COP13 moving to reporting every four years. Though the Convention has now been in force for over a quarter century, political support remains weak notwithstanding the large number of parties. Despite the great need to combat the problems of desertification and aridity and their socio-economic consequences, the Convention has failed to engender the urgent and positive action required. In this it has so far been following in the footsteps of its predecessor, the non-binding Plan of Action (1978). However, given the linkages between desertification, land degradation and drought (DLDD) and loss of animal habitat and the spread of diseases (including COVID-19) from animals to humans, the contribution of the 1994 UNCCD to improved land management may now garner heightened attention.[408]

4(2) THE FOREST PRINCIPLES AND RELATED INSTRUMENTS

Forests[409] have value as an exploitable reservoir of timber and fuel, as a source of food, as a habitat rich in wildlife, and as a major reservoir of biodiversity.[410] In addition they act as sinks for absorption of carbon, with deforestation a contributor to global climate change.[411] Where such deforestation occurs as the result of deliberate forest burning for agriculture, it is also a significant cause of transboundary air pollution.[412] Despite the high profile given to deforestation, little has been done to control this problem internationally. The instruments adopted to date are weak with forest governance highly fragmented and even contested between institutions.[413] As discussed

407 The first reporting process under the UNCCD 2018–2030 Strategic Framework officially concluded on 31 August 2018. In total, 141 reports out of 196 were submitted, of which 138 provided data suitable for the preliminary analyses.

408 *UNCCD and the COVID-19 crisis: land-based solutions for healthy people and a sustainable planet* (UNCCD, 2020), 3.

409 On these see Schally, 4 *YbIEL* (1993) 30–50; Szekeley, in Campiglio et al (ed), *The Environment after Rio* (The Hague, 1994) 65–9; Tarasofsky, *The International Forest Regime: Legal and Policy Issues* (Bonn, 1995); König, in Wolfrum (ed), *Enforcing International Environmental Standards* (Heidelberg, 1996) 337–71; Canadian Council on International Law, *Global Forests and International Environmental Law* (The Hague, 1996); Yamin, 9 *YbIEL* (1998) 316–19; Saint-Laurent, in Dodds (ed), *The Way Forward* (London, 1999) 65; Sand, 1 *Int Envtl Agmts: Politics, Law and Economics* (2001) 33, 41; Mackenzie, 21 *RECIEL* (2012) 114; Eikermann, *Forests in International Law: Is There Really a Need for an International Forest Convention?* (Heidelberg, 2015).

410 As noted in the recent UN Strategic Plan for Forests, they 'are among the world's most productive land-based ecosystems and are essential to life on Earth': ECOSOC Res 2017/4, 7 July 2017, annex I, para 1.; see also the Millenium Ecosystem Assessment, ch 21 'Forests and Woodland Systems'.

411 Metz et al (eds), *Climate Change 2007: Mitigation. Contribution of Working Group III to the Fourth Assessment Report of the Intergovernmental Panel on Climate Change* (Cambridge, 2007), ch 9; *supra*, Ch 6(3).

412 *Supra*, Ch 6, section 2(2).

413 Including the UN Forum on Forests, a subsidiary body of ECOSOC; FAO's Committee on Forestry (COFO); and UNCTAD's International Tropical Timber Organization: see *supra* Ch 2, section 3(2). No fewer than 15 'global international organizations, institutions and secretariats' are identified as having 'substantial programmes on forests' including the CBD, UNCCD, CITES, and UNFCCC: see Collaborative Partnership on Forests, *CFP Strategic Vision Towards 2030*, CITES Plant Committee PC25 Inf. 1, 17 and 20–23 July 2020, 2.

in chapter 5, contributing to this state of affairs is opposition to international governance owing to sovereignty concerns—in consequence of which international aid and cooperation can be rebuffed as a trespass on sovereignty[414]—and the implications for thc rights of indigenous peoples.

Attempts to negotiate at Rio an International Convention on Conservation and Development of Forests,[415] as proposed by the UN in 1990, were blocked by the irreconcilable concerns of developed and developing states, led especially by Brazil and Malaysia. Instead, the curiously entitled 'Non-legally Binding Authoritative Statement of Forest Principles' was adopted which 'falls 100 per cent short' of providing even the most elementary basis for the protection of the world's forests.[416] The failure of the negotiations at UNCED was partly attributable to the fact that developed states did not propose to submit their own boreal forests to criteria for sustainable utilization and the European Community attempted to trade developed states' agreement to a desertification convention as a quid pro quo for developing states' acceptance of a forest treaty.[417] The resulting polarization and sensitivity over sovereignty issues still inhibits conclusion of a comprehensive global convention despite the accelerating destruction of tropical forests.

Where economic interests coincide, however, agreement can be reached. In 2006 a new ITTA was concluded. This 2006 Agreement, though paying greater attention to sustainable development, is still effectively little more than a commodity-market adjustment among consumer and producer states, with a commitment to increase international trade in tropical timber from sustainably managed and legally harvested forests. Indeed, the contrasting fortunes of an international treaty on forest conservation and biodiversity, and the concluded ITTA, underscore the 'public/private' divide in forest governance, and the tensions between views of forest ecosystem services as a public good or as a fixed natural resource supplying timber and other forest products of economic value rather than a richly diverse ecosystem to be conserved for the benefit humanity.[418]

In contrast with the successful completion of a new ITTA, the UN Forum on Forests has since 2000 sought to spromote the International Agreement on Forests, but without success. Non-binding instruments remain prevalent, though no more effective. The 2016 UN Forest Instrument[419] renamed 'non-legally binding instrument

414 See for example in 2019 Brazilian President Bolsonaro initially rejected a G7 offer of c $20 million in aid to Amazonian countries to combat forest fires in the Amazonian rainforest, and a reforestation plan, on sovereignty grounds amongst others: *BBC News*, 27 August 2019. Located primarily in Brazil, the Amazonian rainforest is the world's largest rainforest, home to 10% of known global biodiversity, and a significant carbon sink.

415 Eikermann, *Forests in International Law* 43.

416 Szekely in L Campiglio et al (eds), *The Environment After Rio* (London, 1994), 65.

417 Since then, however, the EU has promulgated a coordinated forest strategy to secure recognition of European forests' diversity, 29 EPL (1999) 48–69.

418 Eikermann, *Forests in International Law* 190, suggests their status as a 'hybrid good'.

419 UNGA Res 70/199, 16 February 2016. Para 2(a) reiterates its voluntary, non-legally binding character. For the first iteration see UNGA Res 62/98, 17 December 2007.

on all types of forests', sets a number of objectives to be achieved by 2030.[420] In 2017 the UN General Assembly adopted the first 'UN Strategic Plan for Forests 2017-2030'[421] which is designed to further progress in achieving the SDGs and the Aichi Biodiversity Targets under the 1992 CBD. As noted above,[422] while no binding forest instrument has emerged, what these developments have underscored is an acceptance that sustainable management is a core principle applicable to forests. Additionally, forests have also been addressed under the climate regime, both as a carbon sink and the through attempts to manage the effects of deforestation in releasing sequestered carbon,[423] and forest biodiversity is one of the 1992 CBD's thematic areas.[424] Some forests are also protected to some extent by listing under the 1972 World Heritage Convention[425] and a number of regional treaties contain general provisions on rational or sustainable use of tropical forests.[426] Of the latter, only the 1985 ASEAN Convention requires a serious commitment to forest protection in a broader environmental context, but it is not in force.[427]

4(3) PROTECTION OF LANDSCAPE

While landscape protection[428] in national law may be traced back to at least the early 19th century, international legal protection is relatively recent.[429] Some of the tools we have already discussed, such as protected area designation[430] and cultural landscape designation under the 1972 World Heritage Convention,[431] may also serve to protect landscape. Additionally, particular landscapes have been the subject of individualized attention, eg the 1991 Alpine Convention.[432] However, the first treaty exclusively

420 ECOSOC Res 2015/33, 22 July 2015, 'International arrangement on forests beyond 2015', adopted on the recommendation of the 11th session of the United Nations Forum on Forests: E/CN.18/2015/L.2/Rev.1, 18 May 2015. This arrangement 'is composed of the United Nations Forum on Forests and its member States, the secretariat of the Forum, the Collaborative Partnership on Forests, the Global Forest Financing Facilitation Network and the Trust Fund for the United Nations Forum on Forests': ibid, para 1(b).

421 UNGA Res 71/285, 1 May 2017, adopts the strategic plan for forests 2017–2030 contained in annex I to ECOSOC Res 2017/4, 7 July 2017.

422 *Supra*, Ch 2 section 3(2).

423 See *supra*, Ch 10 for discussion of REDD.

424 See section 6 below.

425 *Supra*, section 3(2) and *Commonwealth of Australia v State of Tasmania*, 46 ALR (1983) 625; see also IUCN, *A Global Overview of Forest Protected Areas on the World Heritage List* (Gland, 1997).

426 See the 1993 Central American Convention on Management and Conservation of Natural Forest Ecosystems and Forest Plantation Development and the 1978 Treaty for Amazonian Cooperation, 17 *ILM* (1978) 1045. Article 4 of the latter affirms the exclusive sovereignty of each state over its own forests, but does promote cooperation. The 1989 Declaration of San Francisco adopted by the parties, inter alia, recognizes the importance of the Amazonian ecosystem for biodiversity, the need for joint preservation policies and the rational use of forest resources.

427 The Treaty was drafted by IUCN. See eg Article 6.

428 See generally A Streker, *Landscape Protection in International Law* (OUP, 2018).

429 Ibid, ch 3.

430 Eg 'Protected landscape' is one of IUCN's protected areas categories.

431 Cultural landscape protection was introduced in 1992.

432 In particular, the 1994 Protocol Concerning Environmental Protection and Landscape Management; see also the 2003 Framework Convention on the Protection and Sustainable Development of the Carpathians (Art 4).

to address landscape protection is the Council of Europe (CE)'s 2000 European Landscape Convention, concluded in 2000 and which came into force on 1 March 2004 and now has 40 ratifications.[433]

The Preamble invokes, in an unusual context, many of the UNCED principles discussed in chapter 2, records the CE's aim of 'safeguarding and realising the ideals and principles which are their common heritage', and notes the 'important public interest role of landscape' which is a 'basic component of the European natural cultural heritage'. It notes the accelerating transformation of landscapes resulting from a number of impacts of modern developments, many economically based. It aims to preserve the high-quality landscapes as 'key elements of individual and social well-being', using measures that 'entail rights and responsibilities for everyone'. 'Landscape' for its purposes amorphously means 'an area, as perceived by people, whose character is the result of the action and interaction of natural and/or human factors'. Thus 'everyday, outstanding and damaged landscapes are all come within its scope'.[434] In a departure from the approach of the WHC, for example, no listing approach is adopted (a 'List of Landscapes of European Significance' did not make it to the final text) nor established criteria nor categories. Rather, a participative approach to landscape designation is emphasized, underscored by the preambular reference to the 1998 Aarhus Convention.[435] In 2008 the parties adopted Guidelines for the Implementation of the Convention to assist the development of national landscape policy[436] and created the Steering Committee for Culture, Heritage and Landscape, reflecting the acknowledgement 'that it would be easier to achieve the objectives of the Convention if the representatives of contracting parties had the possibility of meeting regularly to devise joint-coordinated programmes and of jointly monitoring the application of the convention'.[437] However, it has proven difficult to select areas for effective protection given the vast number of potential sites which are likely to fall within the broad definition employed under the Convention and in an instrument that lacks 'legal bite'. While it

433 European Landscape Convention and Explanatory Report, Council of Europe, Strasbourg, 2000; IUCN, *Landscape conservation law: present trends and perspectives in international and comparative law* (2000); Streker, ch 6. Once the 2016 Protocol of amendment enters into force, the renamed 'Council of Europe Landscape Convention' will be open (by invitation) to participation by non-European member states (Art 14 (1)).

434 ELC Explanatory Report, para 45.

435 The forms of participation are elaborated upon in the Appendix to Recommendation CM/Rec (2019) 8 of the Committee of Ministers to member States with a view to the implementation of the European Landscape Convention of the Council of Europe—Landscape and democracy: public participation, adopted by the Committee of Ministers on 16 October 2019.

436 Recommendation CM/Rec (2008) 3 of the Committee of Ministers to member states on the guidelines for the implementation of the European Landscape Convention, adopted by the Committee of Ministers on 6 February 2008; see further Recommendation CM/Rec (2019) 7 of the Committee of Ministers to member States with a view to the implementation of the European Landscape Convention of the Council of Europe, adopted by the Committee of Ministers on 16 October 2019.

437 ELC Explanatory Report, para 65.

is attributed with helping to change attitudes towards the interaction of human beings and their environment,[438] it has not contributed substantially to legal protection of landscapes.

5 REGIONAL CONVENTIONS[439]

Most regional conventions cover a variety of species. The Preamble to the 1940 Western Hemisphere Convention expresses the intention of the American Republics to protect 'representatives of all species and genera of their native flora and fauna, including migratory birds, in sufficient numbers and over areas extensive enough to assure them from becoming extinct through any agency within man's control'. These species are then listed in an amendable Annex. Unfortunately, however, its nineteen parties have not been active in these respects at the international level, hence Lyster's eponymous reference to it as a 'sleeping treaty'.[440] The 1968 African Convention ensures in Article VII, the 'conservation, wise use and development of faunal resources' which it lists in an annex. It requires parties to maintain a variety of existing conservation areas and consider the need for others to protect ecosystems important to conservation of species. These obligations are repeated, and elaborated upon in Articles X–XII of the 2003 African Convention, a revision of the 1968 Convention which is not yet in force.[441] It replaces 'faunal resources' with 'natural resources', which is defined to include flora and fauna, and also refers to 'threatened species' of flora and fauna. Such species are not listed in the annexes, which do contain further elaboration of the definition and management objectives of conservation areas, definition of critically endangered, endangered, and vulnerable species, and lists the prohibited means of taking. The 1979 Berne Convention aims, in Article 1, to conserve those wild fauna in Europe which are listed in amendable appendices. The Convention is not limited to members of the Council of Europe but is also open to non-members that participated in its elaboration, the European Community, and any other states invited to sign. The 1980 CCAMLR extends to all Antarctic marine living resources, including birds (Article 1). The parties to the 1985 ASEAN Agreement aim at 'ensuring the survival and promoting the conservation of all species under their jurisdiction and control'

438 See, for example, contributions to the 10-year assessment of the Convention: *Proceedings of the Council of Europe Celebration of the 10th Anniversary of the European Landscape Convention* (Council of Europe, 2012). See also *Council of Europe European Landscape Convention: Contribution to human rights, democracy and sustainable development* (Council of Europe, 2018).

439 See esp Churchill, in Bowman and Redgwell (eds), *International Law and the Conservation of Biodiversity*, 71–90, esp 73–7, 80–5; Bowman, in Anke, Tegner, and Basse (eds), *Effectiveness of International Nature Conservation Agreements* (Copenhagen, 1997) 105–54; Gehring, 1 *YbIEL* (1990) 35ff; *Lyster's International Wildlife Law* Part III 'Regional Wildlife Regulation'.

440 Lyster, *International Wildlife Law* (1st edn, Cambridge, 1985). The second edition notes, however, that the Convention has likely had a catalytic effect on national legislative efforts, especially in the establishment of protected areas: ibid, Ch 8.

441 See further Mekouar, 34/1 *EPL*, 43, and *Lyster's International Wildlife Law*, Ch 9.

(Article 3) but only endangered species are listed in an appendix. As early as 1950 an International Convention for Protection of Birds[442] stated that 'all birds should in principle be protected', and that endangered and migratory species require special protection. The 1995 Agreement on the Conservation of African–Eurasian Migratory Water Birds covers a much larger area, encompassing not only the whole of Europe and Africa, but also Arabia and part of the Arctic. It requires parties to conserve all such birds, defined as those that are 'ecologically dependent on wetlands for at least part of their annual cycle', and it gives 'special attention' to endangered species.[443] As already indicated, there are also international conventions protecting single species in specific regions, for example, the 1973 Agreement on the Conservation of Polar Bears and the 1974 Convention for the Conservation and Management of the Vicuña. More recently, the parties to the 1993 North American Agreement on Environmental Cooperation concluded, under the auspices of the Commission on Environmental Cooperation, a Monarch Butterfly Sister Protected Area Network and a Northern American Monarch Conservation Plan, to protect the habitat of this migratory, though not yet endangered, species.

The preambular articulation of international community interest or inter-generational interest in protection of living resources is generally coupled not with the institution of international management bodies with independent powers but with expression of the duty of states parties to cooperate and establish machinery through which they can do so.[444] This is evidenced in all the conventions cited so far, the 1992 CBD being no exception, confining recognition of 'the common concern of mankind' to its Preamble and merely expressing therein also 'determination' to 'conserve and use' biodiversity for 'the benefit of present and future generations', without concession to their 'interest'. Of particular relevance in this respect also are the regional conventions, even those not identifying 'common interest' or 'concern' as such. The Preamble to the 1979 Berne Convention merely expresses the need for greater 'unity' and co-operation among members. No international authority is established; action is left to each contracting party, though the Convention does institute a Standing Committee of the Parties and secretariat functions are fulfilled by the Council of Europe itself.

Another regional convention, the 1980 CCAMLR[445] was the first international instrument to adopt an expressly ecosystem approach to the conservation of marine living resources in the Southern Ocean, defined in Article I as 'the complex of relationships of Antarctic marine living resources with each other and their physical

[442] Open only to European States; now, superseded by the EC Birds Directive 1979; see Birnie, in Bowman and Redgwell (eds), *International Law and the Conservation of Biodiversity* (London, 1996) 221–5.

[443] This Agreement is concluded under Article IV of the 1979 Bonn Convention.

[444] *Report of United Nations Conference on the Human Environment*, 1972, 12.

[445] For background and assessment, see *Lyster's International Wildlife Law*, Ch 11, section 3; Redgwell, in Boyle and Freestone eds, *International Law and Sustainable Development* (Oxford, 1999); Howard, 38 *ICLQ* (1989) 104. For recent challenges in applying an ecosystem approach under CCAMLR, see Rayfuse, 45 *ELQ* (2018) 53.

environment'.[446] Article II applies it to resource conservation and management[447] and thus adopts a more advanced conservation strategy than the maximum sustainable yield of other living resource agreements.[448] The 1980 CCAMLR was adopted before a major Antarctic fishery emerged, thus evidencing a general precautionary approach to the conservation of marine living resources which later proved inspirational for the precautionary methodology developed under the 1992 CBD.[449] However, the application of an ecosystem approach has not been without its difficulties[450] and at the time of the adoption of the CBD in 1992 it had not yet been successfully operationalized under CCAMLR. Though this picture has improved, one of the lessons from the 1980 CCAMLR is that ecosystem management is not a panacea; all the frailties of mono-species management, including problems of implementation and enforcement, remain. Thus, in addition to ecosystem monitoring and management measures,[451] the 1980 CCAMLR has also adopted 'conventional' fisheries control measures ranging from catch limits to methods of harvesting and inspection and compliance measures.[452]

The 1968 African Convention also failed to provide any new international machinery for cooperation in disbursement of what it refers to as 'mankind's capital' of living resources—not even a regular meeting of the conference of the parties. This failing will be remedied when the revised 2003 version of the Convention enters into force, since it provides for a secretariat and for regular meetings of the COP and empowers the COP to establish further subsidiary bodies of a scientific and technical nature in particular (Article XXVI). But this falls far short of institutional management of the 'natural resources' regulated by the Convention. The 1985 ASEAN Agreement expresses the desire to take both individual and joint conservatory actions, recognizes that international cooperation is essential to attain many of these goals and that the Agreement is essential to achieving these purposes, but again no supra-national authority is established. The Agreement has never entered into force, though this has not prevented a degree of environmental cooperation within ASEAN including a non-binding 2003 Declaration on Heritage Parks which notes the *in situ* conservation requirements of the 1992 CBD and an Agreement for Regulation of Wildlife Trade to bring it into line with the 1973 CITES.

446 An ecosystem approach was adopted for the whole of the Antarctic Treaty Area under the 1991 Environmental Protocol to the 1959 Antarctic Treaty, which categorizes Antarctica 'and dependent and associated ecosystems' as 'a nature reserve, devoted to peace and science' (Article 2). See further Redgwell 43 *ICLQ* (1994) 599.

447 See in particular Article II(3)(b) which refers, inter alia, to maintaining the 'ecological relationship between harvested, dependent and related populations of Antarctic marine living-resources'.

448 On approaches to fisheries conservation, see further *infra* Ch 12.

449 Report of the Executive Secretary, Conservation and Sustainable Use of Marine and Coastal Diversity, UNEP/CBD/SBSTTA/3/4, 12 May 1997, para 39.

450 Indeed, it took eleven years from the entry into force of 1980 CCAMLR for precautionary catch limits to be adopted for krill, the fishing of which by Japanese and (then) Soviet fishers had been one of the drivers for its conclusion: *Lyster's International Wildlife Law* 359–60; Howard, 38 *ICLQ* (1989) 111.

451 As noted in Ch 12, in 2016 CCAMLR declared the world's largest high seas MPA in the Ross Sea.

452 See further *Lyster's International Wildlife Law* 363–4.

There exists also a large number of bilateral cooperative agreements on conservation of nature,[453] a few of which recognize, in terms similar to the multilateral conventions, the international value of the resources concerned. A good example is the 1987 US–Canadian Agreement on the Conservation of the Porcupine Caribou Herd, which recognized that it is 'a unique and irreplaceable natural resource of great value which each generation should maintain and make use of so as to conserve them for future generations'.[454] It also recognizes the traditional harvesting rights of indigenous peoples and acknowledges the need to establish cooperative bilateral mechanisms to coordinate the parties' conservatory activities but adds that it should be implemented by existing rather than new management structures.

Clearly, regional bodies, though important, cannot protect highly migratory species that migrate globally or traverse the waters or territories of several regions or frontiers that border two or more regions. There is a need for overarching global conventions to protect such species and for coordination between the institutions and measures established to administer and operate the regional conventions. A regional approach, though valuable within the region, is not sufficient to solve the problems addressed by the global conventions discussed here, although insofar as species reside in particular regional areas for part of their lifecycle, they can be effectively protected by local measures as long as they are at least as effective as those required under the global conventions.

6 CONSERVATION OF BIOLOGICAL DIVERSITY AND BIOSAFETY

6(1) INTRODUCTION

Notwithstanding the extent of species and habitat protection outlined above, until the conclusion of the CBD in 1992, no global instrument regulated the interaction of species and habitat, and of ecosystems, in a holistic way.[455] As we have seen, previous strategies and instruments were concerned with ensuring, on an ad hoc basis, the 'rational' or 'wise' use of common property or shared resources,[456] with the protection of

[453] An interesting example of the interplay between bilateral, trilateral, and multilateral endeavours is the regulation of the polar bear. The Memorandum on Implementation of the Agreement between the USA and the USSR on Cooperation in the Field of Environmental Protection, which includes conservation of rare and endangered species of animals and plants, general wildlife conservation, and management, facilitated conclusion of the multilateral 1973 Polar Bears Agreement. This multilateral agreement has in turn been enhanced by the conclusion in 2000 between the USA and the Russian Federation, after eight years of negotiations, of the Agreement on the Conservation and Management of the Alaska–Chukotka Polar Bear Population: see 97 *AJIL* (2003) 192–3.

[454] UST, *TIAS* 11259.

[455] For contributions placing the CBD in its broader context, see Bowman and Redgwell, *Conservation of Biological Diversity* (1996). Trouwborst refers to this fragmentation as the challenge of 'connectivity conservation' in Bowman et al, *Handbook on Biodiversity* 219.

[456] On fish and marine mammals, see *infra*, Ch 12.

migratory species and their habitats, and of outstanding natural heritage sites under the 1972 World Heritage Convention, or with preventing over-exploitation of certain species of wild fauna and flora through control of international trade under the 1973 CITES. Regional treaties, on the other hand, have addressed conservation of the ecosystems of particular areas such as Antarctica,[457] certain regions in south-east Asia, the Caribbean and the western Indian Ocean. These have all contributed considerably to protection of biodiversity, and continue to do so, but in a piecemeal fashion.

UNEP perceived this 'biodiversity gap' and initiated negotiations in 1989 designed to conclude a Convention on Biological Diversity (the 1992 CBD) in time for signature at UNCED in Rio.[458] However, although the need for such a convention was by then widely recognized, achieving agreement was another matter and numerous difficulties were encountered in concluding negotiation of the CBD in time for signature at Rio.[459] This was duly accomplished, and the Convention entered swiftly into force a mere 18 months later. Today it has nearly universal participation with 196 parties.[460]

Significant developing country participation was crucial to the effectiveness of the Convention given that the most biologically rich parts of the planet are located within developing equatorial States. Participation is facilitated through funding (the GEF is the funding mechanism for the 1992 CBD) and differentiation of implementation obligations through 'according to respective capabilities' language. The Convention also provides a framework for national regulation of access to biological resources ('bioprospecting') on mutually agreed terms and benefit-sharing where such resources are exploited for commercial benefit.[461] The role of indigenous peoples' knowledge and the application of traditional intellectual property rights principles remain areas of controversy under the Convention though without impairing developing country participation. The key outlier is the US, which during negotiations expressed concerns particularly regarding the intellectual property and technology transfer provisions of

457 Despite its innovative approach to ecosystem management, nowhere in the 1980 CCAMLR is there reference to 'biological diversity'. The same is true of UNCLOS, which was concluded a decade before the Rio instruments brought biological diversity and other concepts such as sustainable development to the fore: see further *infra* Ch 1 and Ch 12; for discussion of modern environmental concepts in UNCLOS, see Churchill in Rayfuse (ed), *Research Handbook on International Marine Environmental Law* (Cheltenham, 2015), Ch 1.

458 UNEP/GC/Res 15/34, 1989.

459 See further eg Burhenne-Guilmin and Casey-Lefkowitz, 3 *YbIEL* (1992) 43; McConnell, *The 1992 CBD: A Negotiating History* (The Hague, 1996); Koester, 27 *EPL* (1997) 175; Svensson, in Sjøstedt et al (eds), *International Environmental Negotiations: Process, Issues and Context* (Stockholm, 1993) 164–91; Boyle, in Bowman and Redgwell (eds), *International Law and the Conservation of Biological Diversity* (The Hague, 1996) 33. On the Convention generally, see Hermitte, XXXVIII *AFDI* (1992) 844; Convention on Biological Diversity Handbook (CBD Secretariat, 3rd edn, 2005) hereafter *CBD Handbook*; Klemm and Shine, *Biological Diversity Conservation and Law: Legal Mechanisms for Conserving Species and Ecosystems*, IUCN Environmental Policy & Law Paper Series No 29 (Gland, 1993); Redgwell, in Koufa (ed), *Protection of the Environment for the New Millenium, Thesaurus Acroasium*, Volume XXXI (Thessaloniki, 2002) 355–96; 6:3 (1997) and 11:1 (2002) *RECIEL passim*.

460 A number of Parties made individual or joint declarations concerning various aspects of the Convention either on its adoption or on signing or ratifying or both (excluding declarations made pursuant to Article 27 regarding dispute settlement): for text see Sec VIII, *CBD Handbook* and https://treaties.un.org/

461 Elaborated upon in the 2010 Nagoya Protocol: see further section 6(9) below.

the Convention (Articles 15 and 16) which, it argued, 'Threatened to retard biotechnology and undermine the protection of ideas'.[462] In the event, President Clinton's administration signed the Convention but the US has not ratified it,[463] and is now the only State not to have done so.

Securing consensus resulted in a text with many ambiguities and omissions, much bland language and qualified commitments.[464] Both its Preambular recitals and its substantive articles are expressed in broad terms, the requirements of which are often further weakened by additional qualifications. These include such phrases as 'as appropriate', 'as far as possible', 'practicable in accordance with particular conditions and capabilities', 'taking into account special needs', 'likely to', 'grave and imminent', 'significant', and such limited requirements as to 'endeavour', 'encourage', 'promote', and 'minimize'.[465] Omitted substantive provisions on which no agreement could be reached included the precautionary principle, referred to only in the Preamble discussed below; responsibility for damage to biodiversity, whether in national or international areas;[466] and a compilation of global lists of protected areas and species,[467] as, inter alia, in the 1972 World Heritage Convention, and, for their particular purposes, the 1979 Bonn and Berne Conventions and the 1973 CITES. These lists are left to the parties' national measures and any hopes that these might subsequently be added in a further Protocol or Protocols to the 1992 CBD have proved forlorn ones. The final agreement reached was on a text notably different from the fifth draft produced by the INC,[468] and the trade-offs involved have been illuminatingly described by participants in the process. [469]

A marked feature of the 1992 CBD is that its provisions are mostly expressed as overall goals, rather than precisely defined obligations.[470] As with any treaty provisions using hortatory language, the risk which arises is that any resulting targets eg addressing biodiversity loss will be ineffective because they are too vague to be

[462] Statement by US President Bush, to the UNCED, 12 June 1992; see Coughlin, 31 *Col JTL* (1993) 337.

[463] The CBD was submitted to the US Senate on 20 November 1993 and is one of 37 treaties not to receive Senate advice and consent to ratification (the 1983 Gaborone amendment to CITES; UNCLOS and its 1994 Implementing Agreement; the Rotterdam Convention on Prior Infomred Consent and Stockholm POPS Conventions; and the Agreement on the Conservation of Albatrosses and Petrels, are other environmental examples): US Department of State, 'Treaties Pending before Senate', 22 October 2019.

[464] For criticism, see e.g. Boyle: 'There is much sense in the US objections to the weakness and unsatisfactory nature of the Treaty text', in Bowman and Redgwell (eds), *International Law and the Conservation of Biological Diversity*, 48.

[465] For detailed analysis of the Preamble and each article see Glowka et al, *Guide to CBD* and *CBD Handbook*.

[466] A provision only rarely found in international environmental treaties: see, generally, *supra*, Ch 4. On liability under the 2000 Cartagena Protocol, see further below.

[467] As urged particularly by France: see further Hermitte, 38 *AFDI* (1992) 844–70.

[468] UNEP/Bio Div/N7-ING 5/2 (1992). UNEP acted as Secretariat for the negotiating process.

[469] See eg Koester, head of the Danish delegation at all the CBD negotiation meetings who notes, inter alia, the role played by UNEP's then Executive Director Tolba in facilitating the final agreement: Koester, 27 *EPL* (1997) 175, 181.

[470] De Klemm, 26 *EPL* (1996) 247, 252.

implemented and not underpinned by legally binding obligations for states.[471] It is also a 'framework' convention,[472] ie one that lays down various guiding principles at the international level which states parties are required to take into account in developing national law and policy to implement its objectives, but to which can also be added subsequent *ad hoc* protocols on related issues laying down more specific and detailed requirements and standards. The 1992 CBD specifically provides in Article 28 that parties must cooperate in formulating protocols for adoption at the COP. To date two Protocols have been adopted: the 2000 Cartagena Protocol, trailed in Article 19(3) of the Convention; and the 2010 Nagoya Protocol on Access and Benefit Sharing. Each is discussed further below.

6(2) OBJECTIVES OF THE BIODIVERSITY CONVENTION

The 1992 CBD defines biodiversity broadly to encompass the variability among living organisms from all sources, including, *inter alia*, terrestrial, marine, and other aquatic ecosystems and the ecological complexes of which they are part. Article 1 sets out as the Convention's three main objectives: (a) the conservation of biodiversity, (b) the sustainable use of its components, and (c) the fair and equitable sharing of the benefits arising from the utilization of genetic resources. [473] Balancing these three objectives is the ecosystem approach, defined as 'a strategy for the integrated management of land, water and living resources that promotes conservation and sustainable use in an equitable way'.[474] This approach has been adopted by the COP as the framework for the analysis and implementation of the objectives of the Convention;[475] ecosystem resilience has the added benefit of playing an important role in climate change mitigation and adaptation,[476] a topic of increasing importance under the Convention.[477]

Articles 6–20 of the Convention then seek to translate these objectives into binding commitments in substantive provisions, which include key provisions on, inter alia, measures for conservation and sustainable use of biological diversity[478] and, in more guarded language, of its components,[479] both *in situ*[480] and *ex situ*;[481] incentives for the

471 See Harrop and Pritchard, 21 *Glob Env Change* (2011) 474; on 'soft' treaty language, see *supra*, Ch 1.

472 Along with eg the Ozone and Climate Change Conventions discussed *supra*, Ch 6.

473 See Chandler, 3 *Col JILP* (1993) 141.

474 See CBD COP Decision VII/11 *Ecosystem approach* (2004), Annex 1, para 1. Interactions among organisms and their environment, and recognition that humans, and their cultural diversity, form part of some ecosystems is an integral part of the approach: ibid., para 2.

475 Decisions II/8; SBSTTA Recommendation V/10. See also the 'Jakarta Mandate' on Marine and Coastal Biological Diversity adopted by the COP in 1997, *infra*, Ch 12.

476 Aichi Target 15; see further C Epple et al., *Managing ecosystems in the context of climate change mitigation: A review of current knowledge and recommendations to support ecosystem-based mitigation actions that look beyond terrestrial forests* (Technical Series No.86. Secretariat of the Convention on Biological Diversity, Montreal, 2016).

477 Climate responses as various as biofuel production and forms of geoengineering such as ocean fertilization have been the subject of CBD COP decisions related to their biodiversity impacts: see e.g. Decision X/37 and Decisions X/33 and XIII/4 respectively.

478 Article 6. 479 Article 10. 480 Article 8. 481 Article 9.

conservation and sustainable use of biological diversity;[482] research and training;[483] public awareness and education;[484] assessing the impacts of projects upon biological diversity;[485] regulating access to genetic resources;[486] access to and transfer of technology;[487] and the provision of financial resources for national activities intended to achieve the Convention's objectives.[488]

The Convention clearly illustrates the extent to which biological diversity is an issue that cuts across all the issues addressed above, and in the following chapter, with respect to terrestrial and marine species and habitat conservation and protection, inter alia.[489] Both its Preambular assertions and substantive articles are relevant, for example, to combating deforestation and desertification, planning and management of land resources, managing fragile ecosystems on land and at sea, promoting sustainable utilization of all living resources and, as its parties have observed, it 'ushers in a new era' concerning access to genetic resources governed by the Convention.[490]

6(3) JURISDICTIONAL SCOPE

The Convention applies to biodiversity from all sources, viz terrestrial, marine, and other aquatic sources. It also distinguishes, in Article 4, between its application to the components of biodiversity found within the territory of a state party, which they must protect, and processes and activities carried out under their jurisdiction or control regardless of where their effects occur, which they must at least identify and monitor, both within their territories and beyond the limits of national jurisdiction. So far as rights within their own territories are concerned Article 3 reiterates Principle 21 of the 1972 Stockholm Declaration but omits the developmental aspects introduced by the Rio Principle 2 formulation of this right.[491] Thus it merely recognizes the sovereign right of states to exploit their own resources, i.e. within their own territory, pursuant to their own environmental policies, subject to ensuring that activities within their jurisdiction or control do not cause harm to other states or areas beyond their national jurisdictional limits. The legal implications of this 'responsibility' are unclear since no guidelines are provided, again reflecting the disagreements during the negotiations between developed and developing states.[492]

The view of the developed states who did not want a generalized declaration of principles is evidenced by the interpretive declaration made by the UK stating that this 'Principle' was intended to apply only to the 1992 CBD.[493] This has resulted in a

[482] Article 11. [483] Article 12. [484] Article 13. [485] Article 14.

[486] Article 15. [487] Article 16. [488] Article 20.

[489] This breadth is further illustrated by CBD's seven thematic work programmes comprising: marine and coastal biodiversity; mountain biodiversity; agricultural biodiversity; forest biodiversity; inland waters biodiversity; dry and sub-humid lands biodiversity; and island biodiversity.

[490] *Statement from the Conference of the Parties to the Convention on Biological Diversity to the Commission on Sustainable Development at its third session*, Annex to Decision 1/8, paras. 9–10.

[491] See *supra*, Ch 3, section 2. [492] Ibid.

[493] The UK made a Declaration to the effect that Article 3 sets out a guiding principle to be taken into account in the implementation of the Convention, i.e. that it does not create a general principle of international law.

somewhat perfunctory treatment of the transboundary issue since customary international law, as well as several international agreements, at least require notification and consultation between states.[494] Moreover, the concept of permanent sovereignty has not prevented resource conservation within a state's territory from being treated as a question of common concern for all states, requiring, as a minimum, a duty to cooperate for the benefit of the international community.[495] Article 5 does require states to cooperate, directly or through international organizations concerning areas beyond national jurisdiction[496] and other matters of mutual interest for conservation and sustainable use of biological diversity, but this is too general a provision to clarify issues concerning liability for transboundary harm in the absence of any relevant guidance from other provisions or direct invocation of the precautionary principle.

These lacunae do not mean that states can disregard the possible consequences of their actions since Article 14 requires parties, albeit only 'as far as possible and appropriate', to 'introduce appropriate procedures' requiring environmental impact assessment of proposed projects 'likely to have significant adverse impacts on biological diversity with a view to avoiding or minimizing such effects', and 'to introduce appropriate arrangements to ensure that the environmental consequences of its programmes and policies that are likely to have significant adverse impacts on biological diversity are duly taken into account'.[497] Though this provision is weakened by use of vague terms such as 'likely to', it does apply to assessments within national boundaries, not solely, as does the 1991 EIA Convention, to transboundary effects. This reinforces the point made earlier that in certain contexts—and conservation of biological diversity is one of them—it might also be arguable that the management of a state's own domestic environment is a matter of international concern independently of any transboundary effects.[498] This may be linked to Article 14 in that it has been cited as an indication 'that the duty to conduct EIAs may extend to activities that have impacts that are confined to the State of origin's territory, but have consequences for issues of common concern'.[499]

However, Article 14 does not specify the kinds of activities to be assessed nor the documentation required.[500] Further, in the *Border Activities/San Juan River Cases* the ICJ, while largely endorsing its general approach to EIA articulated in *Pulp Mills*[501] held

494 *Supra*, Ch 3, section 5.

495 Handl, 1 *YbIEL* (1990) 32; *supra*, Ch 3, section 3(1)(a).

496 On the legal regime applicable to marine biodiversity, including genetic resources and their 'bioprospecting' in areas beyond national jurisdiction, see Ch 12.

497 Article 14(1)(b).

498 *Supra*, Ch 3, section 7.

499 Craik, in Viñuales (ed), *The Rio Declaration on Environment and Development* (Oxford, 2015) 459, making it clear that this is a qualified obligation owing to the 'as far as possible and as appropriate' language.

500 Nor have these been significantly developed through subsequent COP decisions: see eg Decision VIII/28 'Voluntary Guidelines on Biodiversity-Inclusive Impact Assessment'. Contrast with the more detailed approach of the 1991 UNECE Convention on Environmental Impact Assessment in a Transboundary Context discussed *supra*, Ch 3, section 7.

501 See para 162, confirmed in operative para 229(6) of the judgment, finding that Costa Rica had not complied with its obligation under general international law to conduct an EIA of the road construction, before turning briefly at paras 163–4 to consider Nicaragua's submission that EIA was required by Article 14 of the CBD.

that 1992 CBD Article 14 'does not create an obligation to carry out an environmental impact assessment before undertaking an activity that may have significant adverse effects on biological diversity',[502] arriving at this conclusion without recourse to anything other than the text of Article 14.[503] The submissions of the parties further underscore the extent to which, in the absence of specific direction in the 1992 CBD, there is scope for opinions to differ on whether this general threshold for an EIA has been met.[504] Consequently, 'truly global' commitments to EIA, as under the 1992 CBD, may require new assessment methodologies, thus far expressed in voluntary implementation guidelines.[505] By leaving much detail to the individual judgement of states parties, as well as requiring them to act only 'as far as possible and appropriate' to assess whether or not particular projects and programmes are 'likely to have a significant adverse impact', the parties may well escape any form of EIA, particularly when the possible risks may be long-term and difficult to predict. The notification and consultation provisions of the 1992 CBD are likewise weak, save for where there is 'imminent or grave danger or damage' to the biodiversity of other States and/or areas beyond national jurisdiction, with the obligation immediately to notify potentially affected States of such danger or damage and 'initiate action to prevent or minimize such danger or damage'.[506]

6(4) PROVISIONS OF THE CONVENTION RELEVANT TO ACHIEVEMENT OF ITS OBJECTIVES: THE PREAMBLE

As noted above, many of the contentious issues in negotiated the 1992 CBD were avoided rather than resolved by relegating them to opaque language in the Preamble. Such recitals, however vaguely expressed, are nonetheless important as a guide to the parties' intentions in adopting particular measures,[507] as these examples illustrate.

(a) Intrinsic and other values of biodiversity

The Preamble's first recital begins by recognizing, without further explanation, 'the intrinsic value of biological diversity'[508], as well as a range of other values—ecological,

[502] Also considered at length were requirements of notification and consultation, though without any express reference to the CBD.

[503] See *supra,* section 3 for discussion of the Ramsar Convention.

[504] *Certain Activities* para 163 et seq. Nicaragua submitted that Costa Rica had failed to carry out the EIA required under the Convention, while it responded that (a) it had in place the appropriate procedures required under Article 14 with respect to 'projects that are likely to have a significant adverse effect on biological diversity' and (b) in any event, the road construction did not reach this threshold.

[505] Craik in Viñuales (ed), *The Rio Declaration* 463; see CBD COP Decision VIII/28 on Voluntary Guidelines on Biodiversity-Inclusive Environmental Impact Assessment UNEP/CBD/COP/DEC/VIII/28, 15 June 2006, and for background to the Decision, CBD Technical Series No. 26 (2006).

[506] Respectively, Article 14 (c) and (d); contrast with the 2000 Cartagena Protocol below.

[507] 'The interpretational conclusions to be drawn from the Preamble are as binding upon the parties as those from any other part of the treaty': Fitzmaurice, 33 *BYIL* (1957) 200, 229.

[508] Tinker, 28 *Vand JTL* (1995) 778, 800, notes the difficulties of valuing biodiversity as the value of genes, species, and ecosystems is little understood; there are both direct and indirect values, mere existence values, as yet unknown uses and store house values; i.e. preserving stocks of genes and micro-organisms that might permit organisms and ecosystems to recover. See also *Lyster's International Wildlife Law,* Ch 3; Fosci and West in Bowman et al (eds), *Research Handbook on Biodiversity and Law* 55.

genetic, social economic, scientific, educational, cultural, recreational, and aesthetic. It does not mention the problem of attributing value to genetically modified organisms ('GMOs').[509] The other Preambular recitals refer to biodiversity, however, solely as a 'resource'. The substantive articles define 'biological resources' as including 'genetic resources organisms or parts thereof, populations or any other biotic component of ecosystems *with actual or potential use or value to humanity*', a more anthropocentric approach. The Preamble reinforces this in noting that conservation and sustainable use of biodiversity is critical for meeting the food, health, and other needs of the growing world population.

(b) Needs of developing countries

The Preamble recognizes 'the special needs of developing countries' for 'new and additional financial resources' and for 'appropriate' access to relevant technologies. It is widely perceived that these must certainly be provided for if there is to be a substantial increase in the world's ability to address biodiversity loss. Several articles of the Convention address these concerns.[510] The Preamble also notes in this regard the (unspecified) 'special conditions' of the least developed countries and of small island states,[511] both of which groups' special interests are otherwise unacknowledged in the Convention's substantive articles, although the overriding priority of economic and social development and eradication of poverty for developing countries is recognized. Several of the latter, however, do provide for financial aid and transfer of technology, including biotechnology, but not to the extent that developing countries had hoped for, as we shall see. In general, however, since the Preamble does not create obligations, it is notably more ecocentric than the substantive articles, which reflect more anthropocentric concerns.

(c) The legal status of biodiversity: implications of common concern

This highly contentious issue has been resolved by 'affirming' in the Preamble only that 'the conservation of biodiversity is a common concern of humankind'. Although this is also the solution adopted in the UNFCCC,[512] the precise scope of this formulation of value remains obscure, as was no doubt the intention. As we saw in Chapter 3, at the very least it does provide some general basis for international action, giving all states an interest in, and the right to conserve, biodiversity and for the parties to the Convention, and even non-parties, to observe and comment upon the progress of others in fulfilling their respective obligations and responsibilities for this purpose, both within their own national jurisdiction and beyond it, as discussed below. The meetings

509 On this see, Tew, Kate, and Laird, 76 *Int Affairs* (2000) 241–65, who underline the different perceptions that value can have on access and benefit sharing arrangements.

510 Especially on access and benefit sharing, and on finance and technology, discussed below.

511 Susceptible to inundation from sea-level rise, inter alia: compare the recognition of particular vulnerabilities to the adverse effects of climate change of low-lying and other small island countries in the Preamble to the UNFCCC.

512 *Supra*, Ch 6(3).

of the COP, at which non-party states and various international organizations (as well as governmental and non-governmental bodies qualified in relevant fields) can have observer status,[513] provides a forum in which criticism can be voiced and common problems and solutions discussed. Much depends on effective use of these processes if the Convention is to achieve its aims, on which the picture is mixed as we see below. Acknowledging biological diversity as a common concern also makes it clear that biological resources are neither shared resources nor common property available for appropriation and use by all, as are migratory species of animals or fish which cross national boundaries or are found in the high seas, the conservation problems concerning which are discussed above and in Chapter 12.

(d) The precautionary approach and inter-generational equity

The Preamble and Article 2 on 'Use of Terms' contain the only references in the Convention to these important conservation principles, whose legal significance was considered above.[514] However, the Preamble does not refer to these two principles in the terms used in the Rio Declaration. Whereas the latter states that 'the right to *development* must be fulfilled so as to equitably meet the developmental *and* environmental needs of present and future generations',[515] the Convention's Preamble merely expresses, and only in its last recital, the parties 'determination' 'to conserve and sustainably use biological diversity for the *benefit* of present and future generations', omitting the reference to development and thus giving it a more environmental perspective. This rather weakly expressed inter-generational perspective is only partially reinforced by the definition of 'sustainable use' set forth in Article 2, requiring use of biological diversity in a way that maintains its potential 'to meet *the needs and aspirations* of present and future generations'.[516]

Second, while the Rio Declaration calls for a 'precautionary approach', expressly stating that 'when there are threats of serious or irreversible damage, lack of full scientific certainty shall not be used as a reason for postponing cost effective measures to prevent environmental degradation',[517] the Convention's Preamble merely notes that 'where there is a threat of *significant reduction or loss* of biodiversity, lack of full scientific certainty should not be used as a reason for postponing measures *to avoid or minimize* such threat'. In both cases the formulation is significantly weaker than in the Rio Declaration, though the failure to cite the precautionary principle explicitly is to some extent offset by the Convention's provisions on environmental impact assessment discussed below. Moreover, the substantive articles of the Convention are also ambiguous, as we shall see. The Preamble thus provides little encouragement for application of the Rio principles to biodiversity conservation, though it is possible for any related agreements to apply these Rio principles more effectively, as is illustrated above,[518] so as to

513 Article 23(5). 514 See esp Ch 3. 515 Emphasis added. 516 Emphasis added.

517 Principle 15, on which see *supra*, Ch 3, section 6.

518 See eg Agreements on the conservation of migratory species (Conservation of the African-Eurasian Migratory Waterbirds; Conservation of Cetaceans of the Black Sea, Mediterranean, and contiguous Atlantic Areas; and Conservation of Albatrosses and Petrels) in section 3 above.

further the aims of sustainable use of biological resources. Most significantly, the risk posed to the environment and to human health from GMOs is reflected in emphasis on precaution in the 2000 Cartagena Protocol, discussed further below.[519]

6(5) OBLIGATIONS UNDER THE CBD

(a) Conservation of biological diversity and biological resources

While the 1992 CBD differentiates between the conservation of biological diversity on the one hand and the sustainable use of its components on the other,[520] the language employed leaves no doubt that it permits the use of biological resources only in a manner which 'avoid[s] or minimize[s] adverse effects on biological diversity.'[521] Conservation of biological diversity and biological resources is thus the prime objective of the Convention. The requirements in this regard are broad: Parties must adopt national strategies, plans or programmes for their conservation and sustainable use and integrate these and sustainable use into their national sectoral or cross-sectoral plans, programmes, and policies (Article 6), and monitor identified components of biodiversity, and identify processes and categories of activities impacting adversely upon it (Article 7). Adopting and reporting on national biodiversity strategies and action plans (NBSAPs) is a key implementation element of the Convention.[522]

But the most significant obligations placed on Parties concern *in situ*, and to a lesser extent, *ex situ* conservation, addressed in Articles 8 and 9 respectively. '*In situ* conservation' means 'the conservation of ecosystems and natural habitats and the maintenance and recovery of viable populations of species in their natural surroundings, and in the case of domesticated or cultivated species in the surroundings where they have developed their distinctive properties'. '*In situ* conditions' refers to the situation 'where genetic resources exist within ecosystems and natural habitats, and, in the case of domesticated or cultivated species, in the surroundings where they have developed their distinctive properties'. '*Ex situ* conservation' means, according to Article 2, 'conservation of components of biological diversity outside their natural habitats' (i.e. removing specimens or parts thereof from the wild and keeping them in a viable conditions elsewhere; generally in zoos, aquaria, and wildlife parks). Article 9 makes it clear that *ex situ* conservation of the components of biological diversity is predominantly to be used for the purpose of complementing *in situ* measures, and preferably to be taken in the country of origin of such components. The interpretation and application of both *in situ* and *ex situ* conservation obligations rests significantly on scientific advice concerning the viability of species and habitats and, in common with many of the MEAs considered here, the 1992 CBD established the a Subsidiary Body on Scientific, Technical and Technological Advice ('SBSTTA') for this purpose.

519 Arts 10(6) and 11(8); see also art 5(7) of the SPS Agreement, discussed *infra* Ch 13.

520 Article 1.

521 Article 10(b).

522 See COP Decisions IX/8 and X/2, and Aichi Biodiversity Target 17.

Article 8 lists the wide range of measures required to protect the diffuse elements which collectively constitute the essential elements of *in situ* biodiversity. Many of these measures draw on the regulatory techniques described above and which are found conservation treaties pre-dating the 1992 CBD, though in some cases with a more modern twist in their implementation under the 1992 CBD. They include (a) establishing a system of protected areas; (b) regulation and management of biological resources important for the conservation and sustainable use of biological diversity both inside and outside protected areas; (c) protection of ecosystems and natural habitats and maintenance of viable populations of species in 'natural surroundings'; (d) environmentally sound and sustainable development in areas adjacent to protected areas ('buffer zones'); (e) rehabilitation and restoration of degraded areas and recovery of species; (f) control of use and release of modified living organisms when they are likely to have adverse environmental impacts;[523] (g) prevent the introduction of, and control or eradicate invasive alien species; (h) respect, preserve and maintain indigenous and local communities' knowledge, innovations and practices and encourage equitable sharing of benefits arising from utilization thereof; (i) protection of threatened species and populations; (j) regulation or management of processes and activities which threaten biodiversity.[524] Although some of these are conservation measures with a considerable pedigree, the 1992 CBD addresses some of their shortcomings, such as the requirement for protected areas to be consistent with the ecosystem approach of the 1992 CBD, and include buffer zones.

Article 9 contains a much briefer list of *ex situ* conservation obligations. Though *ex situ* conservation in the past has been regarded as a cul de sac and thus most conservation effort has concentrated on habitat protection as the main device for maintaining species, the view that *ex situ* and *in situ* measures are complementary is now widely accepted but their relative importance is irrelevant; rather what matters is the optimum blend of measures to deal with individual management problems. For example, in the case of endangered species, blanket prohibitions on taking all wild specimens can be unhelpful when there is a need to remove specimens from the wild for captive breeding in order to preserve and restore them. A number of existing national regional and international instruments provide exceptions for these purposes.[525]

In both the cases of *in situ* and *ex situ* conservation, parties are required (under Articles 8(m) and 9(e) respectively) to cooperate in providing financial and other support for the conservation measures listed, especially to developing countries. In the case of the latter, they must also cooperate in establishing and maintaining *ex situ* conservation facilities in developing countries mindful, inter alia, of the general obligation to prefer the country of origin for such measures.

[523] See further below section 6(9) for discussion of the 2000 Cartagena Protocol.

[524] On invasive alien species, and indigenous and local communities, see further below.

[525] See eg the survey in Warren, in Bowman and Redgwell (eds), *International Law and the Conservation of Biological Diversity*, 135–42.

(b) Sustainable use

Sustainable use means using the components of biodiversity 'in a way and at a rate that does not lead to the long-term decline of biological diversity'[526] and in so doing 'meet the needs and aspirations of present and future generations'.[527] Some of the basic features of sustainable use include: monitoring of use; management on a flexible basis attuned to the goals of observing biological unity, adopting a holistic ecosystem approach; restoring areas of depleted biodiversity; adoption of both an integrated and a precautionary approach; ensuring inter-generational equity; and basing measures on scientific research. Certainly the various strategies outlined earlier in this chapter have identified these requirements but at present it is not clear to what extent state practice on these aspects has developed the concept of sustainable use beyond its formulation as a guiding principle into a legally binding obligation and if so what its content is. The main purpose of using this term in the Convention was indeed to allow a variety of flexible approaches so long as their goal is achieved. Nonetheless, Article 6 of the Convention does require parties to develop national strategies, plans, or programmes for conservation and rational use, or adapt existing ones to reflect the Convention's requirements and integrate conservation and sustainable use into relevant sectoral or cross-sectoral plans, programmes, and policies (though only to the extent of their capabilities), whilst Article 7 specifically requires identification of components of biodiversity 'important' for conservation and use, which are indicated, in very general categories, on the list provided in Annex I.[528] These must also be monitored, with particular regard to those requiring 'urgent' conservation measures and those offering the 'greatest potential for sustainable use'. Finally, parties are required to identify processes and categories of activities which have, or are likely to have 'significant adverse impacts' on conservation and sustainable use of biodiversity, monitor their effects and 'maintain and organize' by 'any mechanism', the data derived therefrom. These provisions of the Convention have been amplified by the fourteen 'interdependent practical principles' set forth in the Addis Ababa Principles and Guidelines for the Sustainable Use of Biodiversity which were adopted at the seventh COP to the CBD in 2004.[529] These apply to both consumptive and non-consumptive uses of biodiversity components and take into account requirements related to: (i) policies, laws, and regulations; (ii) management of biological diversity; (iii) socio-economic conditions; and (iv) information, research and education.[530]

526 On the background of the concept and the ambiguities inherent in the term, see Johnston, in Bowman and Redgwell (eds), *International Law and the Conservation of Biological Diversity*, 51– 69, and see further, *supra*, Ch 3, section 3(2).

527 Article 2.

528 These relate to specified ecosystems and habitats; species and communities; described genomes and genes which are either important or threatened. On the absence of a list of globally important species and habitat, see above section 6(1).

529 See Decision VII/12 (2004), Annex II; following an implementation review, this was supplemented by Decision X/32 (2010). Decision VII/12 was adopted at the same COP, and linked with, the Decision on Ecosystem Management, Decision VII/11 (2004).

530 Guidelines, para 4.

(c) Alien species

Various problems are posed by the introduction of 'alien,' 'exotic', or 'non-indigenous species' into the environment.[531] For example, a European Environment Agency study identified harm to biodiversity ranging from competition with or predation of native species; transmission of disease or harm to native organisms; and hybridization of native and alien species.[532] Invasive alien species now occur in all taxonomic groups, including animals, plants, fungi and microorganisms, and can affect all types of ecosystems. Despite recognition of the ecological damage caused by such introductions, the pursuant loss of biological diversity and the potential for severe economic and developmental losses, such introductions are increasing. Amongst other things, international trade has enhanced the pathways for their introduction, unintentionally through ballast water, raw wood products and packaging materials, and intentionally through imports for the pet and ornaments trade, for example.[533] New infrastructure projects can have devastating ecological consequences: the Suez Canal is estimated to have introduced over 300 tropical species to the Mediterranean causing major changes to indigenous flora and fauna.[534] There are also dangers in manipulating nature by transplanting specimens bred in captivity into *in situ* locations or introducing some species from the wild, into such locations, whether accidentally or deliberately.

International concern relating to introductions of invasive alien species has been evidenced for some years by inclusion of reference to the problem in a growing number of instruments at international and regional levels and concerns expressed in several international organizations.[535] Several sets of recommendations, guidelines, codes of conduct, and the like have now been promulgated by, inter alia, the FAO and IMO, as well as the Council of Europe.[536] But there is an inconsistency in treatment of the problems involved, particularly in relation to the specifics of implementation and key issues such as control or elimination after release, or the questions of responsibility for

[531] Ibid; Glowka and De Klemm, 26 *EPL* (1996) 247–54; Perrault and Muffett, 11 *RECIEL* (2001) 211; Rayfuse, in Bodansky, Brunnee, and Hey (eds), *The Oxford Handbook of International Environmental Law*, 385–7; Davies in Bowman et al (eds), *Research Handbook on Biodiversity and Law* 184. For debates on what is 'invasive' and 'alien' see further Riley, 22 *GIELR* (2009–2010) 157.

[532] European Environment Agency, *The Impacts of Invasive Alien Species in Europe* (EEA, 2012) 10.

[533] Rayfuse, ibid, 386. Thus, for example, CBD COP7 called on Parties to consider risks of invasive species introduction when reviewing international, bilateral and regional arrangements, such as trade arrangements, and called on the CBD Executive Secretary to collaborate with the WTO Secretariat: see Decision VII/13, paragraph 5(d)–(e).

[534] Shine, Williams and Gundling, *A Guide to Designing Legal and Institutional Frameworks on Alien Invasive Species* (IUCN, Gland, 2000) 7; see also McNeeley et al (eds), *a Global Strategy for Invasive Species* (IUCN, 2001).

[535] Glowka and De Klemm, 26 *EPL* (1996) 247; Perrault and Muffett, 11 *RECIEL* (2001) 211. See also the range of instruments and institutions identified in the CBD SBSTTA's in-depth review of ongoing work on alien species that threaten ecosystems, habitats or species.

[536] Ibid; see also Rayfuse, in Bodansky, Brunnee, and Hey (eds), *The Oxford Handbook of International Environmental Law*, 385–7; for assessment of EU regulation of IAS, see Davies in Bowman et al (eds), *Research Handbook on Biodiversity and Law* 184.

damage resulting from such introductions, remain unaddressed.[537] However, international regulation of invasive alien species has been piecemeal and inconsistent, lacking common definitions and approaches: alien invasive species are included in instruments regulating pests[538] and have been addressed in instruments addressed to particular pathways through which invasive alien species may be introduced. For example, Chapter 17 of Agenda 21 acknowledged the need to develop rules on ballast water discharges, and in 2004 an IMO Convention for the Control and Management of Ships' Ballast Water and Sediments was concluded which calls on States to prevent, minimize, and ultimately eliminate the transfer of harmful aquatic organisms and pathogens through such ballast and sediments.[539]

Article 8(h) of the 1992 CBD calls on parties to 'prevent the introduction of, control or eradicate those alien species which threaten ecosystems, habitats or species', without offering guidance on the criteria for determining the occurrence of a 'threat'. Invasive alien species are a cross-cutting issue under the Convention, with other articles also relevant, notably Article 7 requiring parties, particularly for purposes of Articles 8–10, to identify and monitor the components of biodiversity and to identify processes and categories of activities which have or are likely to have significant adverse impacts on conservation and use of biological diversity and monitor their effects through sampling and other techniques.

Although there have been calls for the conclusion of a Protocol on invasive species,[540] the response of the COP has been to develop, through SBSTTA, guiding principles for the prevention, introduction, and mitigation of impacts of alien species and to establish, again through SBSTTA, an Ad Hoc Technical Expert Group on Gaps and Inconsistencies in the International Regulatory Framework in Relation to Invasive Species. COP6 adopted 'Guiding Principles', annexed to its decision on alien species,[541] to be applied 'as appropriate' in the context of activities aimed at implementing Article 8(h). These principles call for measures of prevention and mitigation, including control and eradication, and require that such measures 'should, as appropriate' be based on precautionary and ecosystem approaches.[542] The COP has also requested the Global Invasive Species Programme,[543] in developing a programme to deal with such

537 In their survey of existing instruments, Glowka and De Klemm note that similar differences in coverage arise in relation to national laws on the subject: *supra*, n 535, 249–50.

538 See the 1951 IPPC, revised 1997, *supra*, section 3(5), and the 1959 Agreement Concerning Cooperation in the Quarantine of Plants and Their Protection against Pests and Diseases.

539 See *supra*, Ch 13.

540 Glowka and De Klemm, 26 *EPL* (1996) 247; see CBD COP Decision V/8, paragraph 16, which calls for consideration of the possibility of developing an international instrument.

541 Decision VI/23 (2000). The Guidelines had been adopted on an interim basis from COP5, Decision V/8.

542 Australia objected to the wording of the precautionary approach contained in Guiding Principles 1 and 10, and entered a formal objection to the wording and to the consensus adoption of the text in the light of such objection: see UNEP/CBD/COP/6/20, paras 294–324.

543 Established in 1997 to assist with implementation of Article 8(h) CBD, the four founding partners are CABI (Commonwealth Agriculture Bureaux (CAB) International), IUCN, the Nature Conservancy, and the South African National Biodiversity Institute: see eg JA McNeely et al (eds), *Global Strategy on Invasive Alien Species* (IUCN, Gland, 2001); R Wittenberg and MJW Cock (eds), *Invasive Alien Species: A Toolkit of Best Prevention and Management Practices* (CABI, Wallingford, 2001); and www.gisp.org.

species, to ensure consistency with the Article 8(h) provisions and relevant provisions of other articles, including Article 15 on access to genetic resources.[544] Convention parties have been encouraged to develop, inter alia, country-driven projects at all levels (national, regional, subregional, and international) to address this issue and have requested the financial mechanism established pursuant to the Convention to provide adequate support for these.[545] Gaps in the international regulatory framework were considered by the ad hoc technical experts group established in 2004 with recent COP decisions[546] stressing the need for cooperation with and participation in other treaty instruments addressed to invasive alien species such as the 1951 IPPC and the Ballast Water Convention noted above. Rather than seek to plug the gap itself, in 2008 the COP called on other bodies, including the WTO, the World Organization for Animal Health, and the FAO, to 'note' the lack of international standards pertaining to non-pest invasive alien species.[547] The various pathways for introduction are recognized in the request to the CBD's Executive Secretary to collaborate with the IMO, the International Civil Aviation Organization ('ICAO'), and the CITES secretariat, to address regulatory gaps but also to reduce duplication of effort. The 2004 Guidelines continue to provide the framework for national implementation of Article 8(h) under the Convention, with parties encouraged to submit 'case studies, lessons learned and best practice' in their implementation of the Guidelines with respect to risk assessment, monitoring and surveillance, management of pathways, and on restoration and rehabilitation, with SBSTTA playing a further technical role in the identification and dissemination of best practice.[548]

(d) Role of indigenous people's rights in relation to biodiversity

Increasing recognition of the interrelationship between the natural environment, sustainable development, and the well-being of indigenous peoples[549]—for whom the natural environment is, in essence their habitat[550]—is evident in general international law and in the 1992 CBD. ILO Convention 169 Concerning Indigenous and Tribal Peoples in Independent Countries recognizes the right of indigenous peoples to be consulted and to participate in national and regional development plans and strategies, for their cultures and relationship to the environment to be respected, their rights to natural resources in their lands safeguarded, and to participate also in use, management, and conservation of these resources.[551] While significant as the only

544 See Decision V/8. 545 See, for example, Decision III/9 and Decision IV/1.6.

546 See Decisions VIII/27 (2006) and IX/4 (2008). 547 Decision IX/4 (2008). 548 Ibid.

549 See Shelton, 5 *YbIEL* (1994) 77; Woodliffe, in Bowman and Redgwell (eds), *International Law and the Conservation of Biological Diversity*, Ch 13; on indigenous rights and the environment, see also Ch 5 *supra*, section 2(5)(b). Akwé: Kon Voluntary Guidelines for the Conduct of Cultural, Environmental and Social Impact Assessments regarding Developments Proposed to Take Place on, or which are Likely to Impact on, Sacred Sites and on Lands and Waters Traditionally Occupied or used by Indigenous and Local Communities (Decision VII/16).

550 See human rights case law discussed *supra*, Ch 5.

551 Sutherland, 27 *EPL* (1997) 13–30, 16; see also Triggs, in Zillman, Lucas, and Pring (eds), *Human Rights in Natural Resource Development* (Oxford, 2002).

treaty in force that specifically addresses indigenous peoples' rights and interests, it has not been widely ratified by countries with indigenous populations.[552] Until the Rio Conference, developed states had also been reluctant to accept the value, now recognized in Agenda 21, of 'holistic, traditional scientific knowledge of their lands, natural resources and environment'.[553] Further recognition of rights and standards in this field came in 2007, after nearly twenty-five years of contentious negotiations, with the adoption[554] by the United Nations General Assembly of a Declaration on the Rights of Indigenous Peoples,[555] including those relevant to environment and development. The Preamble recognizes 'that respect for indigenous knowledge, cultures and traditional practices contributes to sustainable and equitable development and proper management of the environment' while Article 25 confirms the right of indigenous peoples 'to maintain and strengthen their distinctive spiritual with their traditionally owned or otherwise occupied and used lands, territories, waters and coastal seas and other resources and to uphold their responsibilities to future generations in this regard'. Article 29 acknowledges that indigenous peoples 'have the right to the conservation and protection of the environment and the productive capacity of their lands or territories and resources' and links this to a state obligation to provide assistance programmes for such conservation and protection.[556] While no doubt influential in terms of its reflection of the aspirations of indigenous peoples, the Declaration is not binding, with some developed states with indigenous populations voting against the resolution and a number of other states expressing reservations owing to the Declaration's provisions on, inter alia, land and resources.[557]

While recognizing 'the close and traditional dependence of many indigenous local communities embodying traditional lifestyles on biological resources', the Preamble and Article 8(j) of the 1992 CBD notably avoid the use of either the terms 'rights' or 'peoples'. Moreover, the Convention does not define 'indigenous communities', there is no cross-referencing to any definitions provided in ILO or other conventions,[558] and the 1992 CBD COP merely 'took note' of the 2007 UN Declaration.[559] The ambiguous language of the Preamble and Article 8(j) arises from the fact that international law on indigenous peoples and protection of the environment of indigenous peoples remains controversial.[560] Unsurprisingly, as we discuss below, the 2010 Nagoya Protocol adopts

552 For two Latin American studies see Aguilar Fabra and Fernandes, in Boyle and Anderson (eds), *Human Rights Approaches to Environmental Protection* (Oxford, 1996), Chs 13–14.

553 Agenda 21, Ch 26.1.

554 UNGA Res 61/295, adopted on 13 September 2007, by 143 votes in favour, 4 against (Australia, Canada, New Zealand, and the US) and 11 abstentions (Azerbaijan, Bangladesh, Bhutan, Burundi, Colombia, Georgia, Kenya, Nigeria, Russian Federation, Samoa, and Ukraine). For explanation of the voting see A/61/PV 107.

555 The Declaration was drafted by the Working Group on Indigenous Populations of the UN Sub-Commission on the Prevention of Discrimination and Protection of Minorities, within the context of the UN's 1994–2004 Decade of the World's Indigenous Peoples.

556 See also Article 29(2) which prohibits the storage or disposal of hazardous materials on lands or territories of indigenous peoples without their 'free, prior and informed consent'.

557 See n 554 above.

558 See eg ILO Convention No 169 (1989).

559 Decision IX/13 (2008).

560 For an overview of progress in this field see Sutherland, 27 *EPL* (1997) 13–30.

a similarly cautious approach to the issue, with no reference to ILO Convention 169 and only preambular reference to the Declaration.

The Convention Preamble recognizes only 'the desirability' of 'sharing equitably' the benefits arising from use of traditional knowledge. Article 8(j) goes little further. It provides that each party shall 'as far as possible and appropriate' and subject to its national legislation, 'respect, preserve and maintain knowledge, innovations and practices of indigenous and local communities embodying traditional lifestyles relevant for the conservation and sustainable use of biological diversity and promote their wider application with the approval and involvement of the holders of such knowledge, innovations and practices and encourage the equitable sharing of the benefits arising from the utilization of such knowledge, innovations and practices'.[561] The Convention says nothing about the important role played by indigenous communities and local people in the *in situ* management of wildlife and habitats. However, at COP14 in 2018 an 'indicative, non-exhaustive list of elements of methodological guidance for identifying, monitoring and assessing the contribution of indigenous peoples and local communities to the achievement of the objectives of the Strategic Plan for Biodiversity 2011-2020 and the Aichi Biodiversity Targets' was elaborated.[562]

The CBD's COP established an Ad Hoc Working Group to address implementation of Article 8(j)[563] which, inter alia, participated in the negotiation of the 2010 Nagoya Protocol. Through its work voluntary guidelines have been adopted for: (i) the conduct of cultural, environmental, and social impact assessment of development planned for, or likely to impact on, sacred sites and lands and waters traditionally occupied or used by indigenous and local communities;[564] (ii) ethical conduct to ensure respect for the cultural and intellectual heritage of indigenous and local communities relevant for the conservation and sustainable use of biological diversity;[565] and (iii) on the repatriation of traditional knowledge.[566] Within the Working Group, the Parties involved are merely 'encouraged' to include in their delegations representatives of concerned indigenous and local communities with lifestyles relevant to conservation and sustainable use of biological diversity. It seems unlikely that the COP will provide the vehicle for further clarification of the contentious issue of indigenous and local communities rights; rather it is endeavouring to ensure that, to the extent permitted by the parties, it

561 Further development of an international regime on access and benefit sharing which is relevant to traditional knowledge, innovations and practices associated with genetic resources, and in developing fair and equitable sharing of benefits arising from their utilization, has occurred with conclusion of the 2010 Nagoya Protocol, discussed further below.

562 Decision 14/16; see also Decision XIII/20.

563 Article 8(j) is a cross-cutting issue under the Convention. Thus decisions pertinent to indigenous and local communities have also been taken pursuant to Articles 10(c), 15, 16, 17(2), 18(4), and 19, as well as under thematic work programmes relating to marine and coastal, agricultural, inland water and forest biodiversity, and biodiversity of dry and sub-humid lands.

564 Adopted at COP7..

565 The Tkarihwaié:ri Code of Ethical Conduct to Ensure Respect for the Cultural and Intellectual Heritage of Indigenous and Local Communities, Decision X/42.

566 The Rutzolijirisaxik Voluntary Guidelines for the Repatriation of Traditional Knowledge Relevant for the Conservation and Sustainable Use of Biological Diversity, Decision 14/12.

will provide the forum[567] within which such communities can participate and thus influence the parties when developing policies, guidelines or protocols impinging upon their interests, including their lands and resources, contributing their own unique perspective and knowledge.

(e) Living modified organisms and biosafety

Article 8(g) requires parties to establish or maintain means to regulate risks arising from biotechnology, taking into account those associated with use and release of living modified organisms ('LMOs'), which are likely to have adverse environmental impacts that could affect conservation and sustainable use of biotechnology, taking into account also the risks to human health.[568] This obligation is not geographically limited under the Convention, so it applies not only to components of biological diversity within the limits of national jurisdiction, but also to processes and activities, regardless of where they occur, which are carried out under its jurisdiction and control. This article is closely related to Article 19 concerning the handling of biotechnology and its benefits. The responsibility for taking measures falls on the parties. The Convention does not define 'LMOs' but it was understood that it includes GMOs, provided these are alive.[569] There are two distinct kinds of LMOs. The first category includes organisms whose genetic material has been modified by traditional or conventional techniques such as plant breeding or artificial insemination; the second includes organisms whose genetic material has been modified more directly, e.g. through recombitant DNA technology; these are the ones generally referred to as GMOs.[570] The extent to which LMOs developed from modern biotechnological techniques to present environmental and health risks is controversial. Determining the likelihood of risk requires scientific input and a precautionary approach based on assessment, consequent regulation, and either management or control of the risks. A major factor in US reluctance to ratify the Convention was its fear that this provision might inhibit the application and commercialization of biotechnologies, fail to protect intellectual property rights, and reduce royalty payments, especially to pharmaceutical companies which need biological resources as raw materials for development of drugs.

Although the Convention offers no guidance, there exists a considerable number of policy guidelines developed through the FAO, the OECD, the United Nations Industrial Development Organization ('UNIDO'), and the WHO which could form a basis for developing future regulation. Implementing effective programmes involves not only issues of law and economics, but of biological science. Thus many developing countries are likely to need help on all these aspects as well as financial and technical assistance. It also involves fulfilment of obligations under Article 19(4) to provide information on available use, safety, and environmental impact information when a

567 There is also close cooperation between the CBD and the United Nations Permanent Forum on Indigenous Issues.

568 On trade-related aspects see *infra*, Ch 13.

569 See 22 *EPL* (1992) 205, 206. This excludes, for example, synthetic biology,

570 Glowka, et al, *A Guide to the CBD*, 45–6.

specific LMO is exported to another party. Article 19 relates to handling of biotechnology generally and distribution of its benefits. Article 19(3) requires parties to consider the need for a protocol setting out procedures on safe transfer, handling, and use of LMOs that may have an adverse effect on conservation and sustainable use of biodiversity, including in particular provision for advanced informed agreement.[571]

The first COP of the CBD parties in 1994 initiated consideration of a protocol.[572] Negotiations focused on such issues as objectives, definitions, scope, application of the Advanced Informed Agreement Notification procedures, relation to agreements other than the protocol, aspects of risk, relevant national authorities, capacity building, illegal traffic, liability and redress, and the financial mechanisms and resources. Disagreement on most of these and other issues was such that concern was expressed that if an insufficiently precautionary approach was adopted to the little understood impacts of LMOs on biodiversity-rich countries, the resultant instrument would be no more than a mechanism for information exchange. Safety, not trade, should be its main objective on this view, based on the precautionary principle—otherwise the importing countries would bear an unfair burden.[573] The inability to reach agreement reflected the clash between the trade interests of the US (which, though not a party to the 1992 CBD, participated in the negotiation of the Protocol) and other GMO crop exporters and the environmental concerns of others, as well as the treatment of commodities and domestic regimes in contrast to international regulatory regimes; the US insisting that WTO rules must prevail over any biosafety agreement.[574] Such significant disagreements prevented adoption at Cartagena in 1999 but a resumed session in Montreal in 2000 achieved consensus, with the Protocol duly adopted on 29 January 2000 and opened for signature on 15 May 2000.[575] It entered into force on 11 September 2003 and presently has 170 parties. Its provisions are considered in more detail in section 6(8) below, while its compatibility with WTO law is discussed in Chapter 13.

6(6) INCENTIVES TO PARTICIPATION AND COMPLIANCE

A marked feature of the Convention is the incentives it offers to developed and developing states to participate, to implement it, and to cooperate in balancing their different interests. Inclusion of provisions safeguarding access to genetic resources was an essential element so far as developed states were concerned. Sharing the financial burden and other burdens of conserving resources by enhancing access to funding, technology, information, training, education and scientific research, enabling them to conserve and sustainably exploit their biological resources, were key objectives of the

[571] McGraw, 11 *RECIEL* (2002) 19, refers to criticisms of this choice as reflecting an absence of 'sound science'—why not a Protocol on traditional knowledge or on alien species, for example?

[572] 28 *EPL* (1998) 268–73. [573] Ibid, 273.

[574] Some of these issues are addressed in the *EC—Biotech Case* in the WTO, and considered in Chapter 13 below. On the background to the Protocol see 29 *EPL* (1999) 84–5, and Draft Text Submitted by the Chair, ibid, 138.

[575] See Stoll, 10 *YbIEL* (1999) 82; Quereshi, 49 *ICLQ* (2000) 535 and *infra*, Ch 13.

developing states, as we have seen.[576] Compromises were arrived at on all these goals in the interests of consensus.

(a) Fair and equitable sharing of benefits

Fair and equitable sharing of resources is the second of the Convention's main objectives and its effective implementation is key to its success.[577] Whilst again confirming, in Article 15(1), states' sovereign rights to natural resources and their authority to determine access to genetic resources, parties are required by Article 15(7) to take measures aimed at sharing in a fair and equitable way, not only the results of research and development, but the benefits arising from commercial and other uses of these resources with the party providing them, upon mutually agreed terms. For good or for ill, this leaves the balancing to further negotiation. Provider parties are also required to create conditions facilitating access by other parties for environmentally sound uses (as no criteria are provided for 'soundness' the provider party is left to apply its own) and must also minimize restrictions on access which would defeat the Convention's aims. Other paragraphs address the benefits deriving from actual use of the genetic resources, which might include participation in scientific research based on these (Article 15(b)) as well as those referred to in Article 5(7). More specific benefits are referred to in other articles, including Articles 16(3), 19(1), and 19(2), concerning various uses of relevant technology. The failure of provider parties to fulfil their part of the bargain in allowing access, and of parties seeking access to offer sufficient quid pro quo in terms of inducements such as technology transfer, participation in the scientific research involved, and other forms of genuine benefit sharing, were the main catalyst for negotiation of the 2010 Nagoya Protocol.

The COP has confirmed that human genetic resources are not included within the Convention's scope[578] and concentrated on collecting and sharing information on all national and regional approaches to regulatory access to genetic resources and disseminating this. It has thus asked parties to supply the relevant information on their national legal, policy, and administrative measures in order to produce a survey, and appointed a regionally balanced expert panel to work on development of a common understanding of basic concepts and options for access and benefit-sharing on mutually agreed terms, including guiding principles, guidelines and codes of best practice for access and benefit sharing. These might address requirements for prior informed consent in provider countries; a clearly established mechanism for giving consent; mutually agreed terms on benefit sharing, intellectual-property rights, and technology transfer; reference to country of origin in patent applications; efficient permitting and regulatory procedures; and incentive measures to encourage the conclusion

576 See further Ansari and Jamal, 88 *Indian JIL* (2000) 134; Nayar and Ong, in Bowman and Redgwell (eds), *International Law and the Conservation of Biological Diversity*, Ch 12.

577 See Morgera in L Krämer and E Orlando (eds), *Principles of Environmental Law* Elgar Encyclopedia of Environmental Law Vol VI (Cheltenham, 2018) 323.

578 *CBD Handbook*, Sec IV, Decision II/11, para 2, ref Article 2, use of terms.

of contractual partnerships. By analogy with UNEP's and the IMO's practice, it was feasible that some form of 'soft law' guidelines or codes might emerge from these initiatives in the long-term. Indeed, in 2002 the Bonn Guidelines were adopted as an attempt to streamline access and benefit-sharing procedures, but served only further to burden the parties with a daunting checklist of procedures and requirements.[579] As we discuss below, these were followed almost immediately with calls to negotiate what became the 2010 Nagoya Protocol. For the handful of States not party to the 2010 Nagoya Protocol, the 1992 CBD and these interpretative guidelines will continue to govern this issue.

(b) Financial incentives

It was accepted at the start of negotiations that developing countries would require substantial assistance to enable them to implement the Convention and that the financial burden would have to be shared among all parties.[580] For example, Agenda 21 estimated that in the period 1993–2000 about US$3.5 billion would be needed annually to fund required conservatory activities; others put this at US$17 billion. Article 20 places different responsibilities on all parties and on developed-state parties. Thus all parties must, but only 'in accordance with (their) capabilities', 'undertake' to provide 'financial support' and 'incentives' for implementation of the Convention,[581] subject to Article 11's qualifications concerning adoption of 'economically and socially sound measures'[582]—a phrasing described as 'subtle and deceptive',[583] since it allows for wide choice. What is really required are more specific and direct incentives and disincentives, with avoidance of so-called 'perverse' incentives which can have undesirable effects.

For the first time in any global environmental treaty, Article 20(2) lays down a clear obligation on the parties, not just an 'undertaking', to provide 'new and additional financial resources to enable developing state parties to meet the agreed full incremental costs to them of the implementing measures which fulfil the obligations of this Convention'. However, this provision, vital to the Convention's success, includes several ambiguities. The qualification that the source of funds be new and additional necessitates establishment of new funding mechanisms which are not part of existing development assistance and do not undermine existing sources. Both the costs of conservation measures adopted by developing states and of measures to build up their administrations and develop necessary technology can be recovered by them, but this is not an unfettered right; such costs have to be 'agreed' upon between the developing country concerned and the financial mechanisms established under Article 21; moreover the measures taken must aim to achieve the Convention's obligations. In effect these new finances represent the inducement required to persuade developing countries to conserve their genetic resources. This is underlined by the condition included

579 For assessment see Etty, 2006 YBIEL 506 (2007).

580 See, Johnston, in Bowman and Redgwell (eds), *International Law and the Conservation of Biological Diversity*, 271–88.

581 Article 20(1).

582 On the wide variety of tools available see Glowka et al, *A Guide to the CBD*, 63–4.

583 On its limitations see ibid, 63.

in Article 20(4) which determines that 'the extent to which developing country parties will effectively implement their commitments under this Convention will depend on the effective implementation by developed country parties of their commitments under this Convention related to financial resources and transfer of technology'. The close linkage of performance to 'conservation obligations with provision of funding' is apparent but developing states use of any funds provided is, under Article 21(2), subject to monitoring and evaluation on a regular basis; both the COP and the funding mechanism (GEF) play a role in this[584] since the latter has to ensure that measures for which funding is sought conform to policies, strategies, and priorities determined by the former.[585] In effect this modifies Article 3, since developing states are thus only free to decide their own environmental polices if they do not apply for funding.[586] In 1997 the COP and the GEF adopted a Memorandum of Understanding between them to give effect to Article 21(1) of the Convention and paragraph 26 of the GEF Instrument, which provides that the COP assesses the amount of replenishment funds, on the basis of guidance given by the COP itself. It also covers cooperation between the Convention and the GEF.[587] It has been suggested that whether or not developing states observe this system, which means that their own policies become integrated into general international policy on utilization and conservation, will depend on whether the benefits of international funding exceed the benefits of utilization of the relevant resources or areas deriving from policies formulated solely at the national level.[588] Thus the Convention could become the source of funding provided the activities in issue at least do provide for management or protection of biological diversity. In this way this incentive is aimed at compensating the developing states concerned for losses deriving from reorientation of their current economic uses of such biological resources as rain forests.

(c) Access to and transfer of technology

Articles 16–19 deal with transfer of technology in several different senses. First, the parties undertake in Article 16(1) to provide or facilitate access and transfer to other parties of technologies 'that are relevant to the conservation and sustainable use of biological diversity or make use of genetic resources and do not cause significant damage to the environment'. Second, parties must take measures 'with the aim that' parties which provide genetic resources have access to and transfer of technology which

584 On the role of the restructured GEF see *supra*, Ch 2, section 4(4). The GEF has established *Operational Criteria for Enabling Activities: Biodiversity* (Washington, 2000), which have been revised on several occasions to take account of guidance from the COP.

585 As required under Article 21(2), comprehensive guidance was issued at COP1 and at each subsequent COP this guidance has been refined and augmented. In addition there is a regular triennial review of the effectiveness of the financial mechanism.

586 Wolfrum (ed), *Enforcing Environmental Standards: Economic Mechanisms as Viable Means* (Berlin, 1996) 39–93.

587 For the text, see *CBD Handbook*.

588 Wolfrum (ed), *Enforcing Environmental Standards: Economic Mechanisms as Viable Means* (Berlin, 1996).

makes use of those resources.[589] Third, parties must take measures to provide for the 'effective' participation in biotechnology research of those providing genetic resources, and to 'promote and advance priority access on a fair and equitable basis' to the results and benefits of biotechnologies based on the provision of genetic resources.[590] Transfer of technology provisions in earlier treaties, such as UNCLOS, have usually been controversial, on several grounds. There is first the reluctance of governments to compel companies and private parties to transfer technologies that may not be commercially available; second there have been objections to the terms on which any transfer will take place, particularly if this is not at market prices; and, third, there is the question of intellectual property rights which may be lost if transfer is required. The 1992 CBD attempts to deal with some of these issues.

Transfers under Article 16(1) must be on 'fair and most favourable terms', and in other cases on 'mutually agreed' terms. Governments are specifically required by Article 16(4) to ensure that the private sector facilitates access to, and joint development and transfer of, technology. These provisions are likely to be easiest to implement in the case of countries providing access to genetic resources since they will again be in a position to bargain for the benefits they will receive, but for some governments, such as the US, the suggestion of compulsion placed on industry is undoubtedly objectionable and has, inter alia, inhibited its ratification of the Convention. Intellectual property issues are important because the transfer of patented technology is specifically envisaged.[591]

Article 16(2) provides that access and transfer 'shall be provided on terms which recognize and are consistent with the adequate and effective protection of intellectual-property rights', while Article 16(5) calls for the parties to cooperate to ensure that intellectual-property rights 'are supportive of and do not run counter to' the objectives of the Convention. This appears to be an attempt to satisfy both sides; intellectual property rights are to be respected but only insofar as they assist rather than hinder implementation of the Convention.

However, behind these references there remain unresolved questions about the scope of intellectual property rights and whether they benefit the providers of genetic resources or only those who make use of them. Natural genetic resources, or genetically altered organisms which result from experimentation, are not necessarily always patentable or a source of legally protectable rights. Discovery of a new species of fish, for example, could not be patented; like most natural resources it is simply a commodity which can be bought and sold by anyone. Patentable rights may arise either in respect of a new process for isolating and developing substances, or for new uses for existing substances or possibly in respect of a substance which had no previous

589 Article 16(3).

590 Article 19(1), (2). See Coughlin, 31 *Col JTL* (1993), 337, for examples of access agreements which provide for technology transfer.

591 There is a large literature on the problems arising; see Walden, in Bowman and Redgwell (eds), *International Law and the Conservation of Biological Diversity*, 171–89; Footer, 10 *YbIEL* (1999) 48; Asebey and Kempenaar, 28 *Vand JTL* (1995) 703; Kushan, ibid, 755 and Winter, 2 *JEL* (1992) 167. See also *infra*, Ch 13.

known existence. The extent to which these principles enable the products of biotechnology to be protected will vary, and remains controversial in national patent systems. Much depends on how far intellectual property itself is prepared to go in protecting the products of biotechnology and the original natural genetic resource. For the US it is clear that the risk of losing protection for genetic engineering is thought to be too high to support the Convention; though clearly this is not a problem which has deterred other developed states from ratifying the Convention. The COP has taken some decisions aimed at resolving some of these problems, including encouraging cooperation with WIPO and the WTO.[592]

6(7) INSTITUTIONAL SUPERVISORY BODIES AND COMPLIANCE PROCEDURES

(a) Compliance procedures

The Convention makes no provision for enforcement in the sense of establishing an international inspection or observer system; indeed that would be an impossibility for a Convention of this kind which provides a broad framework of 'soft' obligations and requires much enactment of national legislation for its efficacy.[593] As the majority of the areas and species concerned are found within national jurisdiction, enforcement *strictu sensu* is, therefore, a matter for national authorities. But, as the conservation of biodiversity is categorized as 'a common concern of humankind', the extent to which its contracting parties, and even non-parties, fulfil this obligation is potentially subject to international overview and complaints. The effectiveness of this criticism depends largely on the institutional structures available for voicing it both inside the Convention's structure and in the wider international community.

At the international level, as already observed, the Convention establishes numerous incentives aimed at inducing compliance. At the national level it adopts a similar approach. Article 11 requires that each contracting party shall 'as far as possible and appropriate', 'adopt economically and socially sound measures that act as incentives for the conservation and sustainable use of components of biological diversity'. It does not provide guidance concerning what these incentives might or should be. The COP, however, having affirmed that implementation of incentive measures, in a broad social, cultural, and economic context, is of central importance to the realization of the three objectives of the Convention, resolved that such measures would be included ('as appropriate') on the COP's agenda and integrated into the sectoral and thematic items under its medium-term work programme. It also encouraged parties to review their existing legislation and economic policies, identify and promote incentives for conservation and sustainable use, stressing the importance of taking appropriate action on incentives that threaten biological diversity. It encouraged parties to incorporate market and

592 E.g. Decisions III/7 and Annex. See also *infra*, Ch 13.

593 See generally *supra*, Ch 4 and Bothe, in Wolfrum (ed), *Enforcing Environmental Standards: Economic Mechanisms as Viable Means* (Berlin, 1996) 13–38, esp conclusions at 38.

non-market values of biological diversity into policies, programmes, national accounting systems, and investment strategy (such plans, etc, being required in Article 6).[594]

Otherwise, the COP relies on promotion of other methods advocated in the Convention such as development of training and capacity-building programmes (Article 12); public education and awareness (Article 13); impact assessment (Article 14); exchange of information (Article 17); and cooperation, which is referred to in several articles. It invites parties to 'share their experiences on these incentive measures with and make available case studies to the Secretariat' with a view to the Secretariat providing guidance to the parties on designing and implementing incentive measures.

Reporting procedures for complaints with overview and comment from treaty bodies is a feature of some of the other environmental conventions referred to above, but not yet under the 1992 CBD (but see the 2000 Cartagena Protocol, below). However, it does require each party to present to the COP reports on measures taken by it to implement the Convention and their effectiveness in meeting the objectives of the Convention.[595] This provides an opportunity for the COP, and since 2012, the Subsidiary Body on Implementation it established, to overview these reports, to comment on any weaknesses or failures of parties in this respect.[596]

Responsibility for overviewing compliance with the Convention's requirements in areas beyond national jurisdiction will generally fall within the competence, if any, of appropriate international and regional bodies; Article 5 requires parties to cooperate 'as far as possible and appropriate' with other parties, directly or through competent international organizations, in respect of these areas on matters of mutual interest, and presumably compliance is such a matter. Whilst Article 22 asserts that the Convention does not affect parties' rights (and obligations) deriving from other international agreements to which they are party, unless their exercise would damage or threaten biodiversity, it also requires that parties implement the Convention, so far as it relates to the marine environment, 'consistently' with states' rights and obligations under the law of the sea. This raises interesting possibilities concerning application of the Law of the Sea Convention's provisions on enforcement, compliance, and dispute settlement to biodiversity issues.[597]

(b) Institutional structure

The Convention's governing body is the COP established under Article 22[598]. Its key function is to keep the Convention's implementation under review.[599] This and other functions are set out in Article 23. As well as reviewing scientific and other sources

594 Herkenrath 11 *RECIEL* (2002) 29.   595 Article 26.

596 Decision XII/26. The SBI replaced an Ad Hoc Open Ended Working Group on Review of Implementation of the Convention, and to date has met twice (2016 and 2018). The four functions and core areas of work of the SBI comprise: (a) review of progress in implementation; (b) strategic actions to enhance implementation; (c) strengthening means of implementation; and (d) operations of the Convention and the Protocols.

597 On LOSC, see , Chs 7 and on marine biodiversity, Ch 12.

598 On the limitations of these arrangements see the *CBD Handbook*, xvi–xx and *passim*.

599 Decision IV/10 A, para 5(b).

of advice,[600] it can adopt protocols[601] and amendments to the Convention and its annexes[602] and consider further annexes.[603] It can also establish such subsidiary bodies as are deemed necessary to implement the Convention,[604] and contact (through the Secretariat) executive bodies of conventions dealing with 1992 CBD matters in order to establish 'appropriate forms' of cooperation with them.[605] It is not, however, given any explicit independent role of monitoring or inspection but, as already mentioned, has in practice 'encouraged' initiatives relating to this. The Secretariat, established under Article 24, can inter alia perform any function assigned to it by any protocol,[606] report to the COP,[607] coordinate with other relevant international[608] bodies, enter into relevant contractual arrangements,[609] as well as performing any other functions assigned to it by the COP.[610] UNEP was designated to fulfil the Secretariat function. Unfortunately despite the parties now numbering 196, only a small number attend the COPs. In addition to these bodies, the Convention established a Subsidiary Body on Scientific, Technical and Technological Advice[611] and a Clearing House Mechanism ('CHM')[612] to promote and facilitate technical and scientific cooperation. Over time the COP has also established other subsidiary organs to provide advice on biosafety (Open Ended Working Group on Biosafety), access and benefit sharing (Expert Panel on Access and Benefit Sharing), on indigenous knowledge (Open Ended Ad Hoc Working Group on Article 8(j)) and on protected areas (Ad Hoc Open-ended Working Group on Protect Areas).[613]

(c) Dispute settlement

Article 27 addresses disputes concerning 'interpretation and application' of the Convention and its protocols[614] and Annex II sets out arbitration procedures, but the only compulsory method of settlement is negotiation. All else, including resort to arbitration or the ICJ, is optional, although states may declare acceptance of one or both of these methods as compulsory. This is the typical clause found in most environmental treaties; it offers little or no assurance that unresolved matters of interpretation, or alleged excess of power by the COP or the financial mechanism can be settled by any third-party process.[615]

(d) Liability and responsibility

The perfunctory treatment of transboundary issues in the 1992 CBD has already been noted above, with Article 14(1) doing little more than restate the customary law obligation to notify of transboundary harm.[616] There is little remaining in the final text

600 Article 23(4)(b). 601 Article 23(4)(c). 602 Article 23(4)(e). 603 Article 23(4)(f).
604 Article 23(g). 605 Article 23(4)(h). 606 Article 24(a). 607 Article 24(i)(b).
608 Article 24(c). 609 Article 24(d). 610 Article 24(e). 611 Article 25.
612 Article 18(3). 613 Decisions II/5, IV/8, IV/9, and VII/28 respectively.

614 E.g. Article 27 extends to the 2000 Cartagena Protocol with the crucial distinction that the Protocol contemplates in Article 34 thereof, and indeed has established, a compliance mechanism which is 'without prejudice' to the operation of Article 27. See section 6(8)(e) below and, generally, Fitzmaurice and Redgwell, XXXI *NYIL* (2000) 35.

615 Cf the *ICAO Council Case*, *ICJ Rep* (1972) 6, 56–60, and see generally *supra*, Ch 4.

616 See Ch 4, *supra*, and, more generally, Okowa 71 *BYbIL* (1996) 275.

of the 1992 CBD relating to responsibility[617] and liability issues, a contentious issue during negotiations, with Article 14(2) merely calling on the parties to 'examine . . . the issue of liability and redress, including restoration and compensation, for damage to biodiversity except where such liability is purely an internal matter'. As we discuss immediately below, liability provisions are contained in the 2000 Cartagena Protocol.

6(8) THE 2000 CARTAGENA PROTOCOL

(a) Regulation of biosafety under the Protocol: Advanced Informed Agreement

As we noted above, the 1992 CBD expressly recognized the need to develop further international regulation of the transfer and use of LMOs which may have adverse effect on the conservation and sustainable use of biodiversity, and the 2000 Cartagena Protocol was duly concluded in 2000.[618] It defines 'living modified organism' as 'any living organism that possesses a novel combination of genetic material obtained through the use of modern biotechnology' (Article 3(f)). In fact the Protocol addresses two general categories of LMO: (i) those intended for release into the environment (e.g. seeds for cultivation or animal breeding stock); and (ii) those intended for use in food or feed, or for processing (e.g. corn, cotton, and soy). The latter are of particular concern to the US as the chief exporter of genetically modified crops. In the event the Protocol distinguishes between these categories, subjecting organisms intended for direct use as food or feed, or for processing, to a less onerous regime (Article 11) than that applicable to LMOs intended for direct release into the environment (Articles 7–10).

A marked feature of the Protocol is its overtly precautionary approach, with Article 1 making express reference to the precautionary approach contained in Principle 15 of the 1992 Rio Declaration; implicit reference is found in the conditional language of '*may* have an adverse effect' on biodiversity and/or human health. The chief regulatory technique employed is the 'advanced informed agreement' ('AIA') procedure, trailed in the 1992 CBD but set out in more detail here in Article 7, which is designed to ensure that Contracting Parties are provided with the information necessary to make informed decisions before agreeing to the import of LMOs into their territory. AIA marks the Protocol out from the 'prior informed consent' procedures of the 1989 Basel and 1998 Rotterdam Conventions,[619] which are based on prior multilateral agreement on the hazardous substances to be regulated and which are set out in annexes. Prior informed consent has been applied where substances have already been adjudged

[617] The responsibility clause of draft 5 was dropped from the final text of the CBD.

[618] For coverage of the final negotiating session see (2000) 9:137 *Earth Negotiations Bulletin*, 1–11; see also CBD, *The Cartagena Protocol on Biosafety: A Record of the Negotiations* (Montreal, 2003), hereafter 'Record of the Negotiations'. On the Protocol generally, see Hagan and Weiner, 12 *Georgetown Environmental Law Review* (2002) 697; Burgiel, 11 *RECIEL* (2002) 53; McKenzie et al, *An Explanatory Guide to the Cartagena Protocol on Biosafety*, IUCN Environmental Policy and Law Paper No 46 (Gland, 2003), hereafter 'Explanatory Guide to the Protocol'. On biotechnology more widely see Mackenzie, 13 YbIEL (2002) 97–163; Redgwell, 60 *CLP* (2007); Francioni and Scovazzi (eds), *Biotechnology and International Law* (Oxford, 2006).

[619] The 1998 Rotterdam Convention on Prior Informed Consent expressly excludes LMOs from its scope to eliminate the possibility of conflict arising between it and the 2000 Cartagena Protocol.

hazardous; the primary purpose of the 2000 Cartagena Protocol is to facilitate early assessment by each Contracting Party of the potential risks in accordance with the Protocol. As Stoll observes, the 2000 Cartagena Protocol's 'unique combination between import State control and risk assessment results from the fact that it does not contain an agreed definition of materials that the importing State may refuse without condition or even an agreement that the substances that it regulates are "undesirable"'.[620] Indeed, the flexibility of the rules under the Protocol has led to suggestions that it represents a form of 'treaty-based environmental unilateralism' and that it is a 'prototype of minimum harmonisation legislation'.[621] It establishes principles and procedures to guide national decision-making based on risk assessment and risk management, without mandating a particular outcome.

The AIA procedures must be read with the risk-management provisions for the safe use, handling, and transboundary movement of LMOs;[622] emergency measures in the event of unintentional release of LMOs;[623] and provisions on handling, transport, packaging, and indentification.[624] Illegal transboundary movements are regulated by Article 25, which includes a 'take-back' provision: the country of origin may be requested to dispose of the LMO at its own expense. Similar provisions are found in the 1998 Rotterdam Convention on Prior Informed Consent and the 1989 Basel Convention, for example. To facilitate information exchange each contracting party must designate a national focal point for liaison with the Secretariat and a competent national authority to perform the administrative tasks required in implementing an AIA procedure.[625] Monitoring and reporting, so common in international environmental agreements, is also required under the Protocol (Article 33). It 'piggy-backs' on the institutions established under the 1992 CBD[626] discussed above—including dispute settlement—but does establish its own Biosafety Clearing-House mechanism to facilitate the exchange of scientific, technical, environmental and legal information.[627] This mechanism, combined with its capacity-building provisions,[628] is designed to

620 Stoll, 10 *YbIEL* (1999) 91.

621 Pavoni, X *Italian Yearbook of International Law* (2000) 113, 115–6. But note that Article 14 expressly provides for bilateral, regional and multilateral agreements and arrangements regarding intentional movement of LMOs so long as such arrangements do not provide a lower level of protection than that provided for by the Protocol—either equal protection or in fact a form of bilateral and/or multilateral upward derogation, and certainly precluding 'contracting out' of the Protocol's level of protection. Article 24 also envisages such agreements being concluded between Contracting Parties and non-parties to the Protocol.

622 Article 16. 623 Article 17. 624 Article 18. 625 Article 19.

626 The Protocol relies on the institutions established under the CBD, including the Secretariat (Article 31), the COP which serves as the Meeting of the Parties to the Protocol (Article 29), and any subsidiary bodies under the Convention which the MOP determines may also serve the Protocol (Article 30). It also shares the financial mechanism of the CBD (Article 28).

627 Article 20. This builds on the clearing house mechanism already established under the CBD, as well as establishing a gateway to other biosafety information exchange sites such as UNIDO's Biosafety Information Network and Advisory Service (BINAS) and UNEP's Information Resource for the Release of Organisms (IRRO), as provided for in Article 20(2) of the Protocol.

628 Which in turn are closely linked with Articles 16 (access to and transfer of technology) and 18 (technical and scientific cooperation) of the CBD. Under the Protocol, capacity building is viewed as of particular importance for developing countries without domestic biosafety systems, and is closely linked with Article 28 of the Protocol (financial mechanism and resources).

facilitate developing states' participation. Scientific capacity-building at the national or regional level will 'go a long way in shaping the potential of the GMO revolution used to address local needs and the requirements for sustainable development'.[629] However, the Biosafety Clearing-House mechanism contains far fewer entries regarding decisions taken under AIA compared with risk assessments and under Article 11, the streamlined decision-making procedure in respect of LMOs for food feed and processing.

(b) Public awareness and participation in biosafety decision-making

The AIA approach of the Cartagena Protocol is dependent on the ability of receiving states to conduct some form of risk assessment; for non-contained LMOs this may be part of a broader EIA exercise in which public participation is central. In the biosafety field, consultation will likely embrace a wide range of stakeholders—civil society, research institutes, and the biotechnology industry, for example. The Protocol requires states to ensure that the public is actively consulted on LMOs and biosafety to promote transparency and informed decision-making—but only 'in accordance with their respective laws and regulations' (Article 23). Significant differences in institutional and technical capacity exist between states, differences that are only partly addressed through the Protocol's provisions on capacity building and information sharing through, inter alia, the clearing house mechanism already briefly touched upon. A question arises whether international rules on public participation specifically tailored to biosafety decision-making are necessary.

This question has been faced squarely in the discussion of the role of civil society in biosafety decision-making under the 1998 Aarhus Convention on access to information, public participation in decision-making, and access to justice in environmental matters.[630] When Article 6 was originally concluded, decisions on GMOs (the terminology of the Aarhus Convention) were expressly excluded from its binding requirements on public participation, with the parties required to apply its terms to decisions on whether to permit the deliberate release of GMOs into the environment only 'to the extent feasible and appropriate'. This weak provision resulted from a lack of agreement on the issue between the parties during the negotiation of the Convention, and was clearly going to be revisited once the Convention entered into force.

In May 2005 agreement was reached on an amendment to the Convention which, once it enters into force,[631] will require parties to inform and consult the public in decision-making regarding the deliberate release and placing on the market of GMOs. The public would have the right to submit comments and public authorities would be expected to take these into account in the decision-making process. Once made, the

[629] Kameri-Mbote, 11 *RECIEL* (2002) 62, 73.

[630] Concluded 25 June 1998 and in force 30 October 2001, available at 38 *ILM* (1999) 517.

[631] At the time of writing, the amendment required one further ratification by a State party to the Convention when the amendment was adopted for it to enter into force. In the interim, non-binding Guidelines adopted at MOP-1 in 2002 provide particular inspiration for states without domestic biosafety legislation. See Etty, 2006 *YBIEL* 506 (2007).

decision taken should be publicly available together with the reasons and considerations upon which it is based. Information associated with GMO decisions would be made available to the public, subject to the usual protection for commercially confidential information. However, confidentiality may not be extended to information on the intended uses of the release or regarding assessment of environmental risk. This is clearly intended to prevent abuse of the confidentiality exception, and to ensure full transparency in respect of the use and environmental impact of GMOs and mirrors the language of Article 21(6) of the 2000 Cartagena Protocol. Upward derogation—that is, the flexibility for parties to adopt more expansive measures for public participation and access to information in GMO decision-making[632]—is also provided for. Overall, this compromise embeds national and regional flexibility whilst establishing international minimum standards for public participation in GMO decision-making, and seeks further to fill the biosafety regulatory gap which persists in some Central and East European and newly independent states. For states party to both the 1998 Aarhus Convention and the 2000 Cartagena Protocol (and that have also accepted the amendment and when it has entered into force), these provisions on the pubic right to participate in GMO decision-making will serve as a modest strengthening of the public awareness and participation provisions of Article 23 of the Protocol.

(c) Risk assessment

The AIA procedure set forth in Article 7 of the 2000 Cartagena Protocol is buttressed by provisions addressing notification[633] and decision procedures (Articles 8–10) in which, as was discussed above, there may be a role for public participation. The import of LMOs may be approved by the designated national authority with or without conditions, prohibited, or additional information may be requested. Silence in response to an initial notification from the party of export does not imply consent to transboundary movement (Article 9(4)). There is also provision for review of decisions in the light of new scientific information regarding the potential adverse effects of the LMO (Article 12). The Protocol stresses that lack of scientific certainty due to insufficient information available about the potential negative effects of LMOs on biodiversity, including taking into account risks to human health, will *not* prevent the importing/receiving state from taking decisions in respect of LMOs in order to avoid or minimize potential adverse effects (Article 10(6)). However, such decisions must be taken in accordance with the risk-assessment procedure stipulated in Article 15 and Annex III of the Protocol. And, whilst states are expressly permitted to take action more protective of biodiversity than provided for in the Protocol, such action

632 Access to justice, the third pillar of the Aarhus Convention, is not addressed in the amendment regarding GMOs, though clearly could be embraced in the exercise of such upward derogation.

633 With regard to the information submitted with the notification, confidentiality may be preserved in accordance with Article 21. This includes a list of what is not considered confidential, including '[a] summary of the risk assessment of the effects on the conservation and sustainable use of biological diversity, taking into account risks to human health' (para 6) and information relating to '[a]ny methods and plans for emergency response' (para 7).

must be consistent both with the Protocol *and* with that party's other obligations under international law (e.g. trade obligations). The socio-economic impact of LMOs on biodiversity, especially its value to indigenous and local communities, may also be taken into account by contracting parties, but again to the extent consistent with their other international obligations (Article 26).[634] Thus in both instances—a more stringent approach to LMO regulation, and taking into account in risk assessment non-scientific factors such as the socio-economic impact of LMOs on biodiversity—individual response is conditioned by compliance with wider international obligations, including trade obligations.[635]

During the negotiation of the Protocol there was some divergence between developed and developing states regarding the purpose of risk assessment. One of the most contentious issues was whether to include in the decision-making process the precautionary principle and socio-economic considerations just mentioned. For developed states, in particular those members of the 'Miami Group' keen to facilitate LMO trade,[636] the key point was to ensure that assessments were based on the most up-to-date scientific data (the 'sound science' approach). The inclusion of 'extraneous' matters such as socio-economic impact was viewed as encouraging disguised restrictions on trade.[637] The trade group also favours a minimalist (and less costly) approach to the documentation and labelling requirements of the Protocol.[638] Developing states considered scientific data alone to be insufficient to assess the full range of possible impacts on conservation and sustainable use of biological diversity, socio-economic factors, and risks to agriculture and to human health. This broader approach necessitates a multidisciplinary approach to risk assessment,[639] the implementation of which requires a case-by-case approach. Arguably the flexibility to maintain a multidisciplinary case-by-case approach is provided by the 2000 Cartagena Protocol, whilst also ensuring that possible impacts on human health and on the conservation and sustainable use of biological diversity are an integral part of the risk-assessment process, the 'backbone of the decision-making process' under the Protocol.[640] Precaution is

[634] This concern with non-scientific factors is reflected in the ecosystem approach of the parent 1992 CBD which 'establishes the importance of including the socio-economic dimensions of nature management when implementing the CBD': see 'The Convention on Biological Diversity and the World Summit on Sustainable Development' at http://www.biodiv.org/events/wssd.asp.

[635] This may be compared with, for example, with the original EU implementation legislation, the 2003 GM Food and Feed Regulation in the EU (Regulation 1829/2003, OJ [2003] L268/1). There the legitimate objectives that may be pursued by a system of prior approval embrace not only internal market objectives and concerns for the protection of human life and health and of the environment, but also animal health and welfare and consumer interests in relation to genetically modified foodstuffs in particular. On the other hand, the 2001 Deliberate Release Directive (Directive 2001/18/EC, OJ [2001] L106/1) is addressed only to protection of human health and the environment. See further Scott, 2006 *CLP* 444.

[636] Comprising Argentina, Australia, Canada, Chile, Uruguay, and the US, i.e. the major actual or likely exporters of LMOs. Three of the Miami Group—Argentina, Canada, and the US—launched proceedings under the WTO's dispute settlement procedure challenging the EU's biosafety regime: WT/DS292, WT/DS292, and WT/DS293, *EC—Measures Affecting the Approval and Marketing of Biotech Products*, discussed *infra*, Ch 13.

[637] Burgiel, 11 *RECIEL* (2002) 53, 55.

[638] Etty, 2006 *YBIEL* 499 (2007).

[639] CBD/UNEP, *Record of the Negotiations*, 51.

[640] Kameri-Mbote, 11 *RECIEL* (2002) 62, 63.

an integral part of the AIA decision-making procedure, and socio-economic concerns are catered for to an extent in the provisions permitting taking account of the concerns of indigenous and local communities. But it is clear that decision-making regarding LMOs must be grounded in 'sound science' and that non-scientific factors alone—for example, a generalized consumer concern regarding genetically modified foodstuffs—will not provide unchallengeable grounds for refusal to import LMOs under the Protocol.

The requirement that risk assessments 'shall be carried out in a scientifically sound manner' entails taking account not only of the provisions of the Protocol but also of 'recognized risk assessment techniques'—i.e. those recognized at the national, regional and international levels.[641] There is no definition of 'scientifically sound manner' in the Protocol though similar language may be found in other agreements.[642] 'Sound science' should entail independence, transparency, scepticism, peer review and accountability.[643] While in general terms these are not matters prescribed at the international level but left for domestic or regional implementation, Annex III of the Cartagena Protocol does set forth certain general principles of risk assessment which include the requirement that it 'should be carried out in a scientifically sound and transparent manner' (Article 3). This absence of an agreed definition of 'scientifically sound manner' may give rise to disagreements between states both as to the meaning of the phrase and as to the validity of inevitably diverging scientific views 'about the manner in which an inserted gene is likely to modify characteristics of the organism other than the intended changes, about the interpretation of data, and about the ecological and environmental effects of LMOs'.[644] Part of the difficulty in establishing international minimum harmonized standards for risk assessment, as observed by Australia in the negotiation of the Protocol,[645] is the diverse range of national regulatory measures already in place for undertaking risk assessment. As we saw above, this problem has also beset efforts to draft binding international rules on public participation in GMO decision-making. To address these issues, an Ad Hoc Technical Expert Group on Risk Assessment and Risk Management was established[646] which developed, inter alia, voluntary Guidance on Risk Assessment adopted in 2016.[647]

641 Mackenzie et al, *Explanatory Guide to the Protocol*, 110. On the international level these might include UNEP's *International Technical Guidelines on for Safety in Biotechnology*, which a number of delegations in the Protocol negotiations viewed as a valuable source of guidance. See UNEP/CBD/BSWG/1/4/paras 57–63, and CBD/UNEP, *Record of the Negotiations*, 50.

642 See also the SPS Agreement—'scientific principles' (Article 2(2)); 'scientific justification' (Article 3(3)); and 'scientific evidence' (Articles 2(2) and 5(2)), discussed further *infra*, Ch 13. The provisions on the application of the precautionary approach in the 1995 Straddling Stocks Agreement refer to the 'best scientific information available' (Article 6): see Ch 121.

643 Stirling, *On Science and Precaution in the Management of Technological Risk*, vol 1, EC Institute for Prospective Technological Studies, EUR 19056 EN Spain (1998), cited in Macrory, 54 *CLP* (2001) 640.

644 Mackenzie et al, *Explanatory Guide to the Protocol*, 108.

645 See CBD/UNEP, *Record of the Negotiations.*

646 See Decision BS IV/11 which established an Ad Hoc Technical Expert Group on Risk Assessment and Risk Management, which under Decision BS VIII/12 was considered to have achieved its mandate.

647 CBD/BS/COP-MOP/8/8/Add.1.

There are clearly both benefits and drawbacks to the 2000 Cartagena Protocol's approach to maintaining the diversity of national and regional approaches to living modified organisms. The benefit lies in preserving divergence, albeit consistent with other international obligations, with the principal focus the impact of LMOs on biological diversity which necessarily varies from state to state. Yet the tether for diversity is the application of the precautionary principle, which requires a degree of objectivity in its application. Subjective concerns about the impact of LMOs are left outwith this process, save to the extent that socio-economic impact may be taken into account where impacting on indigenous and local peoples. International regulation of LMOs thus reflects a rationalist faith in the objective application of scientific principles; what Holder has referred to as a 'technocratic approach to environmental problems'.[648] This is well-illustrated by the role of science in the application of the precautionary concept under the 2000 Cartagena Protocol.[649]

This approach may be out of step with recent scientific developments, in particular 'sustainability science'. This is multidisciplinary, combining scientific, economic, legal, and other disciplinary understandings and knowledge. It recognizes the limitations of traditional scientific inquiry in dealing with the complex reality of social institutions interacting with natural phenomena. It is also a recent phenomenon—since 2001 or so—and seeks a rapprochement between science and sustainable development.[650] This multidisciplinary approach is reflected in the IUCN's 2004 report on GMOs and biosafety which identifies the single most important factor in resolving conflict over GMO regulation as the development of 'reliable information and analysis' in a multidisciplinary range of fields—biology, ecology, law, economics, ecosystem management, and social policy.[651] This is also recognized in the 1992 CBD's 2004 Addis Ababa Principles, principle 6 of which stresses the importance of interdisciplinary research for the successful implementation of the 1992 CBD.

(d) Trade implications

Several of the Protocol's provisions have a clear potential for conflict with other international obligations, most notably trade-related obligations. These are discussed in more detail in Chapter 13. For present purposes, it should be noted that the precautionary approach, such a key feature of the Protocol as we have noted,[652] allows importing countries to ban imports because of lack of scientific certainty. Unlike under the Agreement on the Application of Sanitary and Phytosanitary Measures (SPS Agreement), there is no obligation to seek further information to enable a more

[648] Holder, 53 *CLP* (2000) 152. [649] For an EU perspective, see Hervey, 10 *RECIEL* (2001) 321.

[650] Clark and Dickson, 100 *Proceedings of the National Academy of Sciences of the United States of America* (2003) 8061: Kates et al, 292 *Science* (2001) 641–2.

[651] IUCN–The World Conservation Union, *Genetically Modified Organisms and Biosafety: A background paper for decision-makers and others to assist in consideration of GMO issues* (Gland, 2004), 5. It identifies three, often disconnected, strands in GMO discourse, namely: (i) science; (ii) economics; and (iii) socio-cultural issues.

[652] In addition to the preambular provisions and Article 1 cited above, see Articles 10(6), 11(8).

objective, informed assessment of the risk and to review the SPS measure within a reasonable time. Thus a trade-restrictive measure under the 2000 Cartagena Protocol may be of unlimited duration, or at least until the importing country decides that scientific certainty exists regarding the effects of products on biodiversity and human health.[653] The Protocol does address its relationship with trade agreements—a contentious issue during negotiations—in the Preamble,[654] which repeats nearly verbatim the preambular language of the 1998 Rotterdam Convention on Prior Informed Consent. The Preamble to the 2000 Cartagena Protocol recognizes that trade and environment agreements should be mutually supportive with a view to achieving sustainable development. It then emphasizes that 'this Protocol shall not be interpreted as implying a change in rights and obligations of a Party under any existing international agreements' whilst immediately asserting, potentially paradoxically, that this recital 'is not intended to subordinate this Protocol to other international agreements'. There is an obvious contradiction between asserting on the one hand no change in rights and obligations yet on the other rejecting any hierarchy between agreements in the event of conflict. The answers are far from clear and have been the subject of much discussion, though such conflict will only materialize in fact when a decision taken thereunder is challenged as trade restrictive. In the *EC—Biotech Case*, discussed further in Chapter 13, the EU relied on the precautionary principle as articulated in, inter alia, the 2000 Cartagena Protocol, to which it is a party, but the WTO Dispute Settlement Panel did not apply it.[655]

(e) Subsequent developments under the protocol: non-compliance and liability

Owing to the subject matter of the Protocol, it is unsurprising to find that, unlike its parent Convention, provisions were included providing for the subsequent elaboration of rules and procedures on liability and redress (Article 27) and the conclusion of a compliance mechanism (Article 34). A facilitative compliance mechanism has been established, though in common with the mechanisms established under other treaty instruments, the Compliance Committee spent its first meetings elaborating rules of procedures, aided by an assessment of the practice of other environmental agreements' compliance procedures. This process was necessitated by the political compromises embedded in this weak compliance mechanism adopted in 2004, with further elaboration necessary. It is now established that the Compliance Committee may take a number of measures with a view to promoting compliance and addressing cases of non-compliance, including: (a) providing advice or assistance to the Party concerned; (b) making recommendations to the COP-MOP regarding the provision of financial and technical assistance, technology transfer, training and other capacity building measures; and (c) requesting or assisting the Party concerned to develop a

653 See Zarilli, in Francioni (ed), *Environment, Human Rights & International Trade* (Oxford, 2001) Ch 3, esp 57–64; Hagan and Weiner, 12 *Georgetown Environmental Law Review* (2002) 697; Gaston and Abate, 12 *Pace Int'l L Rev* (2000) 107; and *infra*, Ch 13.

654 For thorough analysis see Stoll, 10 *YbIEL* (1999) 91, and Gaston and Abate, ibid.

655 See *infra*, Ch 13 and Ch 1 above.

compliance action plan regarding the achievement of compliance with the Protocol within a timeframe to be agreed upon between the Committee and the Party. It is for the COP-MOP to take decisions on one of more specific measures, upon the recommendations of the Compliance Committee, such as the provision of financial and technical assistance or issuing a caution to the concerned Party. While it has now considered some specific instances of non-compliance submitted to it,[656] the bulk of the Committee's activities have related to general review, including: of compliance with the obligation to designate national focal points and identify competent national authorities, based on information available on the Biodiversity Clearing House;[657] of the operation of the Protocol based on the national reports submitted by the parties;[658] and general overview of compliance with the obligation to submit such reports.[659] This relatively slow uptick in 'business' is a reflection upon the slow rate of implementation of the Protocol, hinging in part on disagreement over key aspects such as risk assessment, discussed above, and lack of progress on liability and redress.[660]

With respect to the latter, at COP-MOP 4 (2008) the parties agreed to draft legally binding rules and procedures for liability and redress for potential damage caused from the transboundary movement of LMOs. Article 27 of the 2000 Cartagena Protocol provided merely an enabling provision, underscoring the divergence in views between developed and developing States as to the desirability of developing such bespoke rules. In 2010 the Nagoya—Kuala Lumpur Supplementary Protocol on Liability and Redress to the 2000 Cartagena Protocol on Biosafety was duly adopted, and entered into force on 5 March 2018. Its purpose is to provide a clearer legal framework for the liability and redress where transboundary movement of LMOs causes transboundary harm. However, in stark contrast with the detailed civil liability regimes discussed in Chapter 4, it constitutes merely 'a text allowing Parties to address LMO damage through existing civil liability systems or through newly developed civil liability mechanisms' under domestic law.[661] It applies to damage resulting from living modified organism which find their origin in a transboundary movement, including damage from unintentional and illegal transboundary movement of LMOs (Article 3). 'Damage' is defined as 'an adverse effect on the conservation and sustainable use of biological diversity that is measurable or otherwise observable and significant, taking also into account risks to human health' (Article 2) with an indicative list of factors

656 Any Party may make a compliance submission in respect of itself, or any Party 'which is affected or likely to be affected, with respect to another Party'. For the most recent overview of individual submissions, see CBD/CP/CC/17/5 17 February 2020 (Note by the Executive Secretary) and CBD/CP/CC/17/6, 17 April 2020.

657 See Review of General Issues of Compliance, CBD/CP/CC/17/4 (2020).

658 See, for example, the Report of the Compliance Committee submitted to COP-MOP 4 (2008) at UNEP/CBD/BS/COP-MOP/4/2; for pertinent decisions of the COP/MOP, see Decisions BS-I/7, BS-II/1, BS-III/1 BS-IV/1.

659 CBD/CP/CC/17/2 16 March 2020.

660 An Ad Hoc Working Group on Liability and Redress was established pursuant to Decision BS-I/8 and met five times between 2005 and 2008. For background on the key liability and redress issues, see the *Report of the Technical Group of Experts on Liability and Redress in the Context of the Cartagena Protocol on Biosafety* UNEP/CBD/BS/TEG-L&R/1/3, 9 November 2004.

661 Telesky, 14 *ASIL Insights* (2011) 10.

that should be used to determine the significance of an adverse effect. A causal link between the damage and the living modified organism must be established (Article 4). States must require the appropriate operator or operators to take response measures in the event of damage resulting from living modified organisms which find their origin in a transboundary movement (Article 5), with response measures defined as 'reasonable actions to prevent, minimize, contain, mitigate or otherwise avoid damage, as appropriate, or reasonable actions to restore biological diversity' (Article 2). The 'operator'—i.e. any person in direct or indirect control of the LMO—must also take response measures where there is a sufficient likelihood that damage will result if timely response measures are not taken. Response measures may also be taken by the competent authority, for example when the operator has failed to do so, but with cost recovery from the operator. Aside from the obligation to provide for response measures, it is for the Parties to develop civil liability rules and procedures to address damage, with the obligation either to continue to apply existing legislation on civil liability or to develop specific legislation concerning liability and redress for material or personal damage associated with damage to the conservation and sustainable use of biological diversity. Consequently, it is difficult to predict not only the precise contours of domestic law LMO liability regimes and to identify common approaches and elements; even more uncertain is whether a coherent international response to the need for liability and redress for damage to biological diversity caused by LMOs will emerge. The delay in the entry into force of the Supplementary Protocol is not an auspicious harbinger for future robust international development of the liability and redress regime.

6(9) NAGOYA PROTOCOL ON ACCESS TO GENETIC RESOURCES AND FAIR AND EQUITABLE SHARING OF BENEFITS ARISING FROM THEIR UTILISATION

As noted above, one of the objectives of the 1992 CBD is the 'fair and equitable sharing of the benefits arising out of the utilisation of genetic resources'[662], with Article 15 obliging the Parties to take legislative, administrative or policy measures with the aim of sharing in a fair and equitable manner with the Party providing such resources the results of R&D and the benefits arising from the utilisation of such resources.[663] This is subject to prior informed consent and for mutually agreed terms to be established.[664] However, implementation of these benefit-sharing objectives was inadequate, with less than half the Parties adequately translating these access and benefit sharing provisions into domestic law.[665] Concerns also continued regarding 'biopiracy' including the 'misappropriation of genetic resources and associated traditional knowledge'.[666] The need

[662] See E Morgera, E Tsioumani and M Buck, *Unravelling the Nagoya Protocol: A Commentary on the Nagoya Protocol on Access and Benefit-sharing to the Convention on Biological Diversity* (Leiden/Boston, 2014).

[663] CBD Article 15(7). [664] CBD Article 15(4) and (5).

[665] As revealed on the ABS measures database, now migrated to the Access and Benefit-Sharing Clearing-House at https://absch.cbd.int/.

[666] UN Environment WCMC, *Access to genetic resources and benefit-sharing: a review of existing frameworks* (Cambridge, 2019) 9.

for further international guidance on how domestically to implement an access and benefit sharing framework was addressed initially in 2002 with the non-binding Bonn Guidelines on Access to Genetic Resources and Fair and Equitable Sharing of the Benefits Arising from their Utilization.[667] Amongst other things, the Bonn Guidelines provided a list of examples of monetary and non-monetary benefits which are reproduced nearly verbatim in Annex I of the 2010 Nagoya Protocol. However, within months of the adoption of the Bonn Guidelines the Johannesburg Plan of Implementation adopted at the 2002 World Summit on Sustainable Development agreed to launch negotiation of an international regime on benefit-sharing. This eventually culminated in the adoption, following six years of intergovernmental negotiations,[668] of a compromise text for adoption at 1992 CBD COP10. This involved some brinksmanship in that the adoption of the Protocol was linked with adoption of the 1992 CBD's Strategic Plan and implementation of the Convention's Strategy for Resource Mobilization. This 'package deal' was made possible by a Japanese compromise text (Japan holding the presidency of the COP) which, in circumstances resonating with the conclusion of its parent Convention at the Rio Conference in 1992, 'did not leave time for. . .rigorous language and legal consistency checks. . .thereby inevitably creating several interpretative questions'[669] regarding a text greeted on its adoption as 'far from perfect'.[670] In a common refrain, many of its provisions are couched in qualified and vague language (eg 'appropriate access to genetic resources' and 'appropriate funding'[671]).[672]

The 'essential goal' of the 2010 Nagoya Protocol 'is realizing fairness and equity among States, as well as between governments and indigenous and local communities, through the sharing of monetary and non-monetary benefits arising from the use of genetic resources and traditional knowledge'.[673] Its provisions reflect the need for effective domestic implementation of rules and procedures on access to genetic resources[674] and the creation of an international access and benefit-sharing regime for genetic resources, including the traditional knowledge associated with such resources.[675] Parties requiring prior informed consent must take measures indicating

[667] UNEP/CBD/COP/6/20, Annex.

[668] See eg Greiber et al, *An Explanatory Guide to the Nagoya Protocol on Access and Benefit Sharing* (IUCN, Gland, 2012); Oberthür and Rosendal (eds), *Global Governance of Genetic Resources: Access and Benefit Sharing After the Nagoya Protocol* (London, 2013); and Morgera, Tsioumani and Buck, *Unravelling the Nagoya Protocol* 17–24.

[669] Morgera et al, ibid, 23.

[670] UNEP/CBD/COP/10/27, paras 98–102. Moreover, certain provisions reflected in the Japanese compromise text were not the product of extensive negotiation, such as the innovative Global Multilateral Benefit-sharing Mechanism in Article 10: ibid. In addition, and like the 2000 Cartagena Protocol, the 2010 Nagoya Protocol also piggy-backs on the institutional and financial arrangements under the Convention.

[671] Article 1 NP.

[672] It has been observed that this provides developing countries in particular 'with policy space to refine the details and find the most adequate way to regulate access and benefit-sharing in accordance with their circumstances': South Centre, *The Nagoya Protocol: Main Characteristics, Challenges and Opportunities* (2015) 18.

[673] Morgera, Tsioumani and Buck, *Unravelling the Nagoya Protocol* 371.

[674] For comparative analysis of some existing arrangements, see UN Environment WCMC, *Access to genetic resources and benefit-sharing: a review of existing frameworks* (Cambridge, 2019).

[675] Article 3.

how to apply for such consent, with evidence of a decision to grant such consent and of the mutually agreed terms provided by a permit or its equivalent.[676] This 'internationally recognized certificate of compliance' thus comprises evidence that genetic resources have been accessed in accordance with the provisions of domestic law.[677]

Significantly, this applies not only in Parties where genetic resources are accessed but also where such resources, accessed in another Party, are utilised. This addresses the fact that bioprospecting, i.e. 'the search for plant and animal species from which medicinal drugs and other commercially valuable compounds can be obtained'—is frequently a transnational activity with genetic resources accessed in one State but utilised in another.[678] Such use is to be monitored to ensure that the domestic law requirements regarding prior informed consent and mutually agreed terms of the Party providing such resources have been complied with.[679]

'Benefits' are widely defined to include both monetary and non-monetary benefits with an indicative list contained in Annex 1.[680] Parties are merely required to 'encourage' users and providers of genetic resources to direct these benefits to conservation of biodiversity and sustainable use of its components.[681] Where indigenous and local communities hold genetic resources, benefits arising from their use are to be shared with the significant caveat that this is only in accordance with domestic legislation regarding their established rights over such resources.[682] As with the 1992 CBD, the 2010 Nagoya Protocol treads carefully with respect to indigenous rights, with no mention of ILO Convention 169 and only preambular reference to the UN Declaration on the Rights of Indigenous Peoples.[683] Benefits arising from the use of traditional knowledge associated with genetic resources 'should' also be shared with indigenous and local communities holding such knowledge, thus providing an intra-State dimension to benefit-sharing.[684]

Key to the Nagoya Protocol's approach is the linkage between access and benefit sharing and the other key objectives of the 1992 CBD—conservation of biological diversity and sustainable use of its components. As the Preamble to the 2010 Nagoya Protocol recognises, 'public awareness about the economic value of ecosystems and biodiversity and the fair and equitable sharing of this economic value with the custodians of biodiversity are key incentives for the conservation of biological diversity and sustainable use of its components'. However, the extent to which benefits are directed to such conservation are largely at the discretion of the provider country and, more broadly, concerns have been expressed about the 'commodification of biodiversity' and market-based approaches to conservation and sustainable use of biodiversity which the Protocol represents.[685]

[676] Article 6(3). [677] Article 17.

[678] Morgera, Tsioumani and Buck, *Unravelling the Nagoya Protocol* 4; Godt in Kamau and Winter (eds), *Genetic Resources, Traditional Knowledge and the Law* (London, 2009) 420.

[679] Article 15. [680] As already noted, this is lifted nearly verbatim from the 2002 Bonn Guidelines.

[681] Article 9. [682] Article 5(2).

[683] See further Morgera et al, *Unravelling the Nagoya Protocol* 35–42, and section 6(3) above.

[684] Article 5(5). [685] Reid, *Transnational Environmental Law* (2013) 217.

7 CONCLUSION

According to a former Executive Secretary of the 1992 CBD, the Convention has been 'quite successful in promoting and leading the development and implementation of the global biodiversity agenda, though not yet at the scale and speed needed to reverse the ongoing crisis and decline of biodiversity'.[686] Agenda-setting it may have been, and doubtless has contributed to greater integration of biodiversity concerns within the UN, as we saw in Chapter 2, and across biodiversity-related treaties, as we saw earlier in this chapter. Undoubtedly the concept of biodiversity, as defined in the Convention, has become the 'organizing' or at least the 'integrating' concept for relating relevant existing agreements, both to bring them into closer relation with each other, by embodying common concepts, and to the aims of the 1992 CBD. Today the 1992 CBD (196 Parties) and the 2000 Cartagena Protocol on Biosafety (170 Parties) enjoy widespread participation, and numbers are growing under the 2010 Nagoya Protocol (126 Parties). A general pattern has emerged under the 1992 CBD of initially hortatory language, in the treaty text and in subsequently adopted strategies, plans and guidelines, supplemented by a ratcheting up of indicators and timetables in non-binding COP decisions and in partnership with a wide range of institutions.[687] Much was learnt from the failure of the First Strategic Plan adopted in 2002 which initially contained no detailed targets,[688] provided too short a time period for implementation, insufficient funding, and failed to address the underlying causes of biodiversity loss.[689]

This is crucial for the success of the 1992 CBD since—as is the case with many MEAs with hortatory, programmatic language—it is dependent on robust and effective national implementation. Two developments here are significant. The first is the increased adoption of National Biodiversity Strategies and Action Plans ('NBSAPs') from 76 Parties in 2000 to nearly all Parties in 2020,[690] with three-quarters of Parties updating their NBSAPs post 2010 to align national biodiversity targets with the Aichi Targets.[691] However, adoption—or 'alignment'—does not necessarily mean effective implementation, and the Aichi Biodiversity Targets will not be met.[692] Part of this may be ascribed to lack of national priority; the same former CBD Executive-Secretary

[686] Dias, former Executive Secretary of the CBD, 31 July 2020.

[687] See for example the Biodiversity Indicator Partnership (BIP) established in 2007 with GEF support, and with UNEP-WCMC acting as secretariat, 'to promote and coordinate development and delivery of the CBD biodiversity indicator suite'. It comprises over forty treaty secretariats, international organizations, and non-State actors. See further https://www.bipindicators.net/ In general, however, measures under the CBD are not 'SMART' (specific, measurable, achievable, relevant, time-bound).

[688] Subsequently adopted at COP7 (2004).

[689] See the Third Global Biodiversity Outlook Report (2010), GBO3, *supra*, n 13.

[690] Cyprus, Libya, Monaco and Palestine remain the outliers.

[691] For detailed analysis see CBD/SBI/3/2/Add.2, 16 March 2020.

[692] For analysis of the NBSAPs presented in national reports, see CBD/SBI/3/2/Add.2. This includes a compilation of all the targets extracted from national reports, which amounts to a global total of 4,107 separate targets. The deadline for the latest (sixth) round of national reports was 31 December 2018 and by March 2020, 156 national reports had been submitted.

laments the lack of heads-of-States engagement with the 1992 CBD framework as compared with the UNFCCC.[693]

The second development of note with respect to the effective implementation of the 1992 CBD is the increasing role of the SBI, which as noted above was created in 2012.[694] In a development typical of the 1992 CBD, however, it was initially toothless and indeed continues to fall short of a robust review mechanism; for example, there is no provision for a mechanism analogous to that under the 2015 Paris Agreement[695] to enhance the level of ambition in national targets to ensure that agreed global biodiversity targets are achieved. That this is needed is vividly underscored by the 2020 assessment of NBSAP and national reports that concludes that both ambition and effort 'have been insufficient to reach the level of ambition set out in the Aichi Targets', thereby confirming the accuracy of the 2019 ISPBES prediction that: 'the implementation of policy responses and actions to conserve nature and manage it more sustainably has progressed, yielding positive outcomes *relative to scenarios of no intervention*, but progress is not sufficient to stem the direct and indirect drivers of nature deterioration. It is therefore likely that most of the Aichi Biodiversity Targets for 2020 will be missed.'[696]

This benchmark of 'no intervention' is a tricky one, as it is notoriously difficult to assess the 'but for' consequences of the 1992 CBD. Take Aichi Biodiversity Target 12, which states that 'By 2020, the extinction of known threatened species has been prevented and their conservation status, particularly of those most in decline, has been improved and sustained'. The 1992 CBD's own mid-term assessment concluded that further extinctions were likely by 2020, but that conservation measures have and will continue to prevent 'some extinctions'.[697] By 2020 the picture of national implementation was a bleak one: of the 143 NBSAP's containing national targets with respect to Aichi Biodiversity Target 12, 79 per cent were either lower or did not contain all of its elements; as for national reports, less than a tenth (7 per cent) had national targets similar to Aichi Biodiversity Target 12 which are on track to be met.[698]

Snapshots must be treated with caution, however, as such extinction prevention as has been attained will not constitute 'conservation success' if all that has been achieved is a slowing of an inexorable decline to extinction.[699] Nor is it merely a question that 'considerably greater efforts are needed to prevent the extinction and improve the status of the 6,413 species currently assessed as Critically Endangered on the IUCN Red List'.[700] Success is achieved where conservation action matches conservation threat for all species, habitat and ecosystems, not only those under threat

693 Dias, *supra*, n 686. 694 CBD COP Decision XII/26. 695 See Chapter 6 *supra*.

696 As quoted in CBD/SBI/3/2/Add.2, 16 March 2020, para 81 (emphasis added); see also GBO-4.

697 CBD (2014). This is borne out by recent analysis of known threatened species during the lifetime of the CBD and of Aichi Target 12, which estimates that 'extinction rates would have been 2.9–4.2 times greater without conservation action' under the CBD and 12–26 times higher since the adoption of Aichi Target 12 in 2010: Bolam et al, *bioRxiv* (12 February 2020).

698 CBD/SBI/3/2/Add.2, 16 March 2020, paras 52–53. 699 Ibid.

700 Bolam, *infra* n 697, citing IUCN, *The IUCN Red List of Threatened Species. Version 2019-3* (2020).

of irremediable degradation or extinction, and we continue to be a long way short of that goal. As noted at the beginning of this chapter, the 2019 IPBES paints a relatively gloomy picture and presents 'compelling evidence of continued deterioration of the state of nature in the face of increasing pressures'.[701] We still await the next phase in the 1992 CBD's development since, owing to the COVID-19 pandemic, the 2020 meeting of the 1992 CBD to agree a Post-2020 Biodiversity Agenda for 'living in harmony with nature' has been postponed to 2021. Given the link between human encroachment, habitat loss and disease vividly underscored by the COVID-19 pandemic, this vision of harmony has a particular resonance, where 'by 2050, biodiversity is valued, conserved, restored and wisely used, maintaining ecosystem services, sustaining a healthy planet and deriving benefits essential for all people'.[702] The task is fulfilling this Agenda, with the record of the 1992 CBD to date suggesting that only renewed national commitment at the highest level will avert the continued acceleration of biodiversity loss—and requires concerted action on the many drivers of such loss within and also beyond the 1992 CBD and the biodiversity-related conventions considered in this chapter.

[701] *Infra* n 15.

[702] OEWG, Post-2020 Global Biodiversity Agenda Zero Draft (13 January 2020).

12

CONSERVATION OF MARINE LIVING RESOURCES

1 INTRODUCTION

1(1) THE PROBLEM

The oceans which cover 70 per cent of the Earth's surface represent its most extensive but least understood ecosystem. Conservation of marine living resources presents complex problems of regulation and management. The need to conserve commercial fisheries and the great whales has long attracted attention but conservation of marine habitats and spawning grounds, including the very rich biodiversity found in coral reefs, seamounts and the deep sea, has only become a significant environmental concern since the 1992 Rio Conference. Coastal development, together with pollution from land-based sources, adds to the destructive impact of modern life on the coastal environment. Recent research has in particular identified the increasing threat to marine life posed by micro-plastics, even in remote areas.[1] Longer-term the biggest threat to the marine environment and its living resources is most probably climate change. The effects of global warming are already evident in the polar ecosystems and in changes in the distribution of marine species. Sea-level rise, higher ocean temperatures, de-oxygenation, and acidification are all caused by climate change and are degrading marine ecosystems such as mangrove swamps, coral reefs, wetlands, and estuaries, threatening the loss or destruction of many marine species, including a third of all coral species.[2] Even the deepest oceanic waters are affected. Unless the

[1] GESAMP, *Reports and Studies No 93: Sources, fate and effects of microplastics in the marine environment: part two of a global assessment* (London, 2016).

[2] FAO, *Fisheries Report No. 870: Report of the FAO Expert Workshop on Climate Change Implications for Fisheries and Aquaculture* (Rome, 2008). See generally UN, *The First Global Integrated Marine Assessment: World Ocean Assessment I* (Cambridge, 2016).

Paris Agreement brings real reductions in greenhouse gas emissions the harmful impacts on the entire marine environment can only increase.[3] The consequences for low-lying states and states dependent on fisheries for their food will be severe.

The rise in fish catches represents another major threat to marine biological diversity and the sustainable use of marine resources. In 1938 the world catch was 15 million tonnes (mt); by 1992 it had stabilized at around 80 mt, where it remains.[4] Fisheries science has traditionally focused on maximising the sustainable yield of specific stocks of fish—generally referred to as 'MSY'. The concept has proved difficult to apply with accuracy, and largely inadequate to the task of conserving fish stocks and minimising the broader ecological effects of fisheries, but it remains embedded in all of the fisheries conventions we consider below.[5] Many fisheries are at or above maximum sustainable utilization.[6] The reasons for this high level of exploitation include rising populations and the growth in fishing by developing states but, above all, the enormous advances in technology for catching and processing fish. Developed sections of the industry use sonar and satellites for locating fish shoals, and factory/freezer vessels which can store and process fish on board and stay at sea for months at a time. The increased capital cost leads in turn to more intensive catching efforts, while older boats are sold on to other users. Fishing methods are often highly destructive. Bottom trawling damages coral reefs and seamounts; blast fishing using explosives destroys them. Nylon driftnets float like a curtain and when lost at sea can trap a variety of species, including seals, turtles and dolphins. Longline fishing attracts and snares seabirds in large numbers. Paradoxically the viability of some stocks is threatened by certain conservation restrictions. Targeting only larger fish alters the genetic diversity of the stock and results eventually in smaller fish. 'Discards', fish thrown away because quotas have been exceeded, add a growing element of waste to the overfishing of traditionally rich fishing grounds. In 'industrial fishing' fish are processed into feed for livestock or aquaculture, or used as fertilizer; it matters little what species are taken or of what size. Such fishing has led to reductions in seabird colonies unable to feed their young.[7]

Nor is the harm caused by overfishing limited to coastal areas. High seas species such as sharks, rays, dolphins, turtles, and various species of tuna are among the many that have suffered steep declines.[8] Not all are directly exploited. Some, such as the albatross and the dolphin, are merely incidental victims of needlessly wasteful fishing

[3] IPCC, *Global warming of 1.5°C: Summary for Policymakers* (Geneva, 2018); CBD, *Technical Series no. 46: Scientific Synthesis of the Impacts of Ocean Acidification on Marine Biodiversity* (Montreal, 2009) 9; IPCC, *Special Report on the Ocean and Cryosphere in a Changing Climate* (2019).

[4] FAO, *The State of World Fisheries and Aquaculture* (Rome, 2016).

[5] The problems were identified in the 1960s. See Johnston, *The International Law of Fisheries: A Framework for Policy Orientated Enquiries* (New Haven, Conn, 1965) 49–51; Hey, 27 *IJMCL* (2012) 763; Kesteven, 21 *Marine Policy* (1997) 73. For a scientific analysis of the concept's limitations see Stafford, 7: 8 *Elementa Science of the Anthropocene* (2019) at https://doi.org/10.1525/elementa.346.

[6] See *infra*.

[7] Smith et al, 333 *Science*, Issue 6046 (2011) 1147–1150

[8] Myers and Worm, 423 *Nature* (2003) 280; WWF, *Living Blue Planet Report* (Gland, 2015).

methods. Many deep-sea stocks such as the Patagonian toothfish or orange roughy are so poorly understood that fishing has resulted in particularly rapid declines because the fish mature and reproduce slowly. In effect they are mined rather than managed. Fisheries science cannot realistically provide enough data about an environment that is still less well known than outer space. Uncertainty abounds, but the old belief that fish stocks recover rapidly has been discredited by the evidence. The once vast cod fishery off Canada's east coast has yet to recover, although some less seriously depleted stocks have slowly been rebuilt.[9] But, if rational management requires good science, it also requires decision-makers to follow scientific advice, which in this field they sometimes do not do, for short-term reasons, with inevitable consequences. The prolonged failure of the Antarctic Marine Living Resources Commission, the Western and Central Pacific Fisheries Commission, and the Indian Ocean Tuna Commission to set quotas in accordance with scientific advice illustrate the problem.[10]

The effect of all these developments on certain species has been devastating. The collapse of whale stocks until the IWCended commercial whaling in 1986 was an early indication of the problem, but many other species are now affected. Not only are fish taken in much larger amounts but the smaller species on which the larger fish, seabirds, and marine mammals predate are also removed, usually as 'by-catch.' The exploitation of marine living resources is thus an environmental problem pre-eminently because it has been pursued unsustainably with broader ecological effects on biodiversity and marine ecosystems.[11]

International policy declarations have recognized the problem. Agenda 21 placed new emphasis, inter alia, on ecosystem and biodiversity protection, application of the precautionary approach, and sustainable use of marine living resources.[12] It noted that the management of high seas fisheries had been inadequate. Problems identified included a failure to adopt, monitor and enforce effective fisheries conservation measures, unreliable data regarding high seas stocks and catches, evasion of controls by re-flagging of vessels, excessive fishing-fleet size, and a lack of sufficient cooperation between states. We will see below the significant developments in international law-making which flowed from the Rio Conference. Twenty-three years later, however, the UN's 2015 SDGs again reiterated the same concerns. SDG 14 committed states to 'effectively regulate harvesting and end overfishing, illegal, unreported and unregulated fishing and destructive fishing practices and implement science-based management plans, in order to restore fish stocks in the shortest time feasible, at least to levels that can produce maximum sustainable yield as determined by their biological characteristics.'[13] This suggests that the extensive changes in fisheries law over the intervening

[9] FAO, *The State of World Fisheries and Aquaculture* (2016) 42–5.

[10] See Bowman et al, *International Wildlife Law*, 146; Guggisberg, *The Use of CITES for Commercially Exploited Fish Species* (Heidelberg, 2015) 139–48.

[11] See UN, *The First Global Integrated Marine Assessment: World Ocean Assessment I*.

[12] *Infra*, section 3.

[13] UNGA Res 70/1 (2015): *Transforming our world: the 2030 agenda for sustainable development*. For a detailed analysis see FAO, *The State of World Fisheries and Aquaculture* (2016) 182–8.

period have not fundamentally changed the overall picture. The FAO's own statistics confirm the point: some 25 per cent of fish stocks were overfished in 1992; by 2013 this figure had increased to 31.4 per cent and only the rate of increase had slowed. Put another way, 'the share of fish stocks within biologically sustainable levels has exhibited a downward trend, declining from 90 percent in 1974 to 68.6 percent in 2013.'[14] To take only one example: 41 per cent of the main tuna stocks were fished at biologically unsustainable levels in 2013 according to the FAO. Overfishing—defined by the FAO as 'stock abundance fished down below the level that can produce MSY'—is not only an environmental problem. It is also an economic one, as an unsustainable fishery will eventually collapse. We are left then with an obvious question: is international law part of the problem, or is it part of the solution?

1(2) AN OVERVIEW OF THE LAW

International law on conservation and sustainable use of marine living resources has developed only slowly. Effective regimes for conservation of marine living resources have to address not only sustainable use of targeted stocks, but also incidental catch of other species, conservation of biological diversity, and protection of the marine ecosystems which provide the main habitat for fish stocks and other species. Some fish species such as tuna are migratory and need protection throughout their range. Regional fisheries treaties in the period before UNCLOS III were more concerned with establishing national quotas for the equitable allocation of high seas fish stocks than with conservation of the marine environment as such. These treaties offered a variety of approaches—some were species specific; others regional; some were both. Some had closed membership, others were open to all interested fishing states. Though regulatory powers of fisheries commissions were often wide in scope—setting a total allowable catch ('TAC'), allocating national quotas, regulating fishing gear and net mesh sizes, establishing closed areas or seasons, etc—the science was sometimes inadequate and it was difficult to secure agreement on conservation measures or to prevent key fishing states opting out of conservation regulations. Not all fisheries were covered by regional agreements and not all states exploiting the fishery were party to those that did exist.

The 1958 Geneva Convention on Fishing and Conservation of the Living Resources of the High Sea was the least successful of the four Geneva conventions because it failed to secure the support of the main distant water fishing states for the modest changes it made to freedom of fishing on the high seas.[15] As we saw in Chapter 3, the salient characteristics of a common-property regime, as applied to the high seas, are that the living resources do not fall within the sovereignty or sovereign rights of any

[14] FAO, *The State of World Fisheries and Aquaculture* (2016) 38. For a good overview of the causes of the decline see Guggisberg, *The Use of CITES for Commercially Exploited Fish Species*, Ch 2.

[15] For a short account of the 1958 Convention see Nelson, in Boyle and Freestone (eds), *International Law and Sustainable Development* (Oxford, 1999) 113–8.

state and are free for use and exploitation by vessels of all nations. Garrett Hardin's description of the 'tragedy of the commons' remains the most compelling analysis of the problem of unsustainability of the classical model of high seas freedom of fishing: free access to a free resource which no one controls, and everyone can exploit, leads inexorably to over-consumption, unrestrained competition, and ultimate ruin for all.[16] Marine living resources present no better proof of the accuracy of this conclusion. The task of international law since the earliest fisheries and whale conservation agreements has been to try to ameliorate this powerful tendency.

The EEZ regime agreed during UNCLOS III and incorporated in Part V of the 1982 UNCLOS was quickly implemented by coastal states. It sought to address the over-exploitation of high seas fish stocks by giving coastal states the exclusive right within the 200-mile EEZ to control access, exploitation, and conservation—the very opposite of high seas freedom for all states.[17] This radical change of approach relied on national self-interest, not international cooperation, to ensure rational and sustainable use. Some 90 per cent of all fish are caught within 200 miles of the coast, and most coastal states now have an exclusive economic zone, or at least an exclusive fisheries zone (EFZ). However, as we explain below, exclusive jurisdiction has not put an end to overfishing, nor does it do away with the need for cooperation. Much depends on whether coastal states make effective use of this opportunity to conserve fisheries on a sustainable basis. It is not always easy to do so, especially for developing states with extensive EEZs. The cost of collecting the necessary data, maintaining surveillance over the zone, and actively enforcing conservation laws is greater the larger the area. Very few states have scientific research vessels. The possibility of arresting violators at sea, or of making use of the right of 'hot pursuit' of offending vessels, requires naval vessels, aircraft, satellites, and trained personnel. This problem can be ameliorated by flag states of distant water fishing vessels doing more to enforce the law, by regional cooperation, by pooling resources with other states, and by provision of technical assistance and advice by international organizations, such as the FAO or regional fisheries commissions. Nevertheless, the FAO estimates that illegal, unreported and unregulated fishing on the high seas and in EEZs takes tens of millions of tonnes of fish annually and is 'a global threat to fisheries resources and marine ecosystems, undermining national, regional and global efforts to manage fisheries sustainably and conserve marine biodiversity.'[18]

That EEZs can be effectively policed even by poorly resourced states is illustrated by the 1992 Niue Treaty on Cooperation in Fisheries Surveillance and Enforcement in the South Pacific Region. This agreement created the South Pacific Forum Fisheries Agency ('SPFFA'), instituted a regional register of vessels licensed to fish, and set minimum terms and conditions, backed by strong aerial and surface surveillance and enforcement capacity, as well as a data and communication network and training.[19]

[16] 162 *Science* (1968) 1243–8. See also Wijkman, 36 *Int Org* (1982) 511.

[17] See *infra*, section 4(2).

[18] da Silva, FAO Director-General, *Agreement on Port State Measures to Prevent, Deter and Eliminate Illegal, Unreported and Unregulated Fishing*, Preamble, (FAO, 2016).

[19] See Lodge, 2 *RECIEL* (1993) 277–83.

The SPFFA has successfully enforced the conservation regulations for highly migratory tuna in its region, where large-scale illegal fishing had previously taken place.[20] However, its success depends heavily on a high level of material support and cooperation from Australia and New Zealand for surveillance patrols, all its other parties being small-island developing states with limited resources. Moreover, even developed states are not always successful in managing and conserving living resources in their EEZs or EFZs and the record of some has been poor.[21] Few fisheries are immune to improvident policies motivated by short-term social and political concerns. FAO statistics point, as we saw, to a general worsening of overfishing and unregulated fishing since 1992. Since most fish stocks now fall within the EEZ regime, it follows that the transfer from a high seas regime has not solved the problem.

The paradox with which international lawyers have had to grapple in this context is that biologically the oceans are an ecosystem, or a series of interlocking ecosystems, while the 1982 UNCLOS has divided them into arbitrary jurisdictional zones whose only merit is that they are easier to plot on maps.[22] Fish stocks and marine mammals frequently migrate through or straddle a variety of jurisdictional zones, including the high seas. It has long been established that where marine living resources remain shared or common property states must negotiate and cooperate in good faith to accommodate equitably their respective rights and interests, to regulate catches in the light of scientific information and take full account of conservation needs.[23] In the *Gulf of Maine*[24] and *Jan Mayen Cases*,[25] EEZ boundaries drawn by the International Court cut across established fishing grounds. Rejecting American arguments in the *Gulf of Maine Case* based on the unity of the marine ecosystem, the court considered that any adverse effects on fisheries would not be sufficiently serious to affect the proposed boundary and that any difficulties could be resolved by cooperation, which had become 'all the more necessary' as a result of its decisions.[26] These cases indicate how cooperation remains necessary, even with an EEZ regime in place. One of the principal challenges in reforming the law on fisheries since 1982 has been to find ways of making that cooperation effective.

[20] Pacific Islands Forum Fisheries Agency, *2016/17 Annual Report*.

[21] See Ulfstein, Andersen, and Churchill, *The Regulation of Fisheries: Legal, Economic and Social Aspects* (Council of Europe, 1986); Johnston, 22 *ODIL* (1991) 199; Beckman and Coleman, 14 *IJMCL* (1999) 491; Saunders, *Policy Options for the Management and Conservation of Straddling Stocks*, Research Paper—Royal Commission on Renewing and Strengthening our Place in Canada (St John's, 2003); EC, *Fishing Opportunities for 2009: Policy Statement from the European Commission*, COM(2008) 331 final.

[22] Diz, *Fisheries Management in Areas Beyond National Jurisdiction*, Ch 4.

[23] *Behring Sea Fur Seals Arbitration*, Moore, I *Int Arb Awards* (1898) 811, reproduced in 1 *IELR* (2000) 43; *Icelandic Fisheries Cases* (*UK v Iceland*) ICJ Reports (1974) 3, paras 72–5 and (*FRG v Iceland*) 175, paras 64–7, on which see Churchill, 24 *ICLQ* (1975) 82, and see now *AO on Fisheries*, ITLOS Reports (2015).

[24] ICJ Reports (1984) 246.

[25] ICJ Reports (1993) 38; Churchill, 9 *IJMCL* (1994) 1.

[26] ICJ Reports (1984) 246, paras 237–41. See also *Barbados/Trinidad Arbitration*, PCA (2006) paras 241, 283–6; Churchill, 17 *Marine Policy* (1993) 44; Hey, *The Regime for the Exploitation of Transboundary Marine Fishery Resources*, 34–5; Antunes, 50 *ICLQ* (2001) 299, 301–16.

Marine mammals (whales, seals, walruses, dolphins, sea otters etc), being larger and warm blooded, reproduce slowly and give birth to live progeny which require nursing, in some cases on land. They are thus more vulnerable to capture and over-exploitation and need special protection of various kinds. Because of their characteristics many marine mammal species are listed under the 1973 CITES or are protected by some of the other conservation conventions discussed in Chapter 11. Although replenishment of some badly affected fish stocks may also take many years, and certain species are increasingly endangered, for political reasons no commercially exploited fish species are currently listed under the 1973 CITES.[27] The argument against is that they can be protected by regional fisheries organisations; this is true but it misses the point that 1973 CITES provides a framework for controlling international trade in endangered species that no regional fisheries agreement can match.[28] However, all marine life is covered by the 1992 CBD;[29] not surprisingly, the COP selected marine and coastal biodiversity as one of the topics for early consideration under that Convention.[30] This has gradually reshaped the Law of the Sea and the law relating to marine living resources by emphasizing the need to protect marine ecosystems and marine species in a more environmentally holistic and coherent legal regime. To reinforce the point, in 2012 the UN called on states 'to effectively apply an ecosystem approach and the precautionary approach in the management, in accordance with international law, of activities having an impact on the marine environment'.[31]

Thus, another challenge in reforming the law has been to find ways of giving effect to this broader ecological perspective in the management of marine living resources. The result is a legal regime which, although still based on the 1982 UNCLOS, has now been further reformed by the 1995 UN Fish Stocks Agreement and by additional instruments adopted by the FAO. We consider these important developments in section 3 below. But the fundamental point is the simplest and most obvious: 'Reducing the killing power/overcapacity of the world's fishing fleets is an essential first step towards ecosystem-based fisheries management'.[32] On this view, a large part of the problem is that we are managing fish stocks without also managing fishing effort: too many big, modern, efficient, fishing boats chasing too few fish. Fishing effort could be reduced in at least two ways: by eliminating subsidies for new fishing boats and by removing endangered fish species or stocks from international trade. Both ideas have met strong political opposition, the first during WTO negotiations, the second during attempts to list endangered fish species on the 1973 CITES appendices.[33]

27 See Franckx, in Freestone, Barnes, and Ong (eds), *The Law of the Sea: Progress and Prospects* (Oxford, 2006) Ch 12; Guggisberg, *The Use of CITES for Commercially Exploited Fish Stocks*, Chs 6–8.

28 *Supra*, Ch 11, section 2(4).

29 See *infra*, section 4.

30 COP, 2nd meeting, 1994; see *Handbook of Biological Diversity* (London, 2001) and *infra*, section 4.

31 *The Future We Want*, UNGA Res 66/288 (2012) annex, para 158.

32 Parsons, 20 *IJMCL* (2005) 421.

33 Hey, 27 *IJMCL* (2012) 765, 768.

2 THE 1982 UN CONVENTION ON THE LAW OF THE SEA

2(1) GENERAL APPROACH

The 1982 UNCLOSa is the foundation for the modern law relating to marine living resources.[34] As we saw in Chapter 9, the 1982 UNCLOS was negotiated and adopted as a 'package deal'. States had to reach compromises on some issues, including living resources, in order to secure agreement on others of particular concern to them. While nominally retaining freedom of fishing on the high seas, UNCLOS responds to pressure from coastal states by removing living resources within the EEZ from a high seas common-property regime.[35] It also adopts special rules for marine mammals and certain species of fish. However, the 1982 UNCLOS does not provide any mechanism for coordinating existing fisheries commissions or the relationship between fisheries conservation and other conservation conventions. Nor does it deal effectively or in detail with the crucial problem of stocks that migrate between zones, though it does address it in general terms. It does not clearly endorse an ecosystem or habitat preservation approach, although its main article on conservation (Article 61) goes some way towards this. Part XII and especially Article 194(5) have provided the basis for the broader approach to ecosystem-based protection of the marine environment adopted in the 1995 UN Fish Stocks Agreement.[36] UNCLOS case law has made the same point, holding that the provisions of Part XII on the protection and preservation of the marine environment are not limited to pollution control but also cover harm to fragile ecosystems, endangered species, and biodiversity.[37]

2(2) COMPETENCE OVER CONSERVATION OF MARINE LIVING RESOURCES UNDER UNCLOS

Although the 1982 UNCLOS reiterates the obligation of states parties to conserve and sustainably utilise marine living resources in the EEZ and on the high seas,[38] the powers and responsibilities of states differ according to whether the stocks in question fall within national jurisdiction or on the high seas.

[34] See Caddell and Molenaar (eds), *Strengthening International Fisheries Law in an Era of Changing Oceans* (Oxford, 2019); Harrison, *Saving the Oceans through Law* (Oxford, 2017) Ch 7; Bowman, Davies and Redgwell, *Lyster's International Wildlife Law* (2nd edn, Cambridge, 2009) Ch 5; Churchill and Lowe, *The Law of the Sea* (3rd edn, Manchester, 1999) Ch 14; Hey (ed), *Developments in International Fisheries Law* (The Hague, 1999); Lucchini and Voeckel, *Le Droit de la Mer* (Paris, 1996); de Yturriaga, *The International Regime of Fisheries: From UNCLOS to the Presencial Sea* (Dordrecht, 1997); Burke, *The New International Law of Fisheries* (Oxford, 1994).

[35] Contrast the 'preferential fishing zone' endorsed in the *Icelandic Fisheries Cases, supra*, n 23.

[36] *Infra*, section 3(3).

[37] *Southern Bluefin Tuna Cases (Provisional Measures)* ITLOS Reports (1999) 280, para 70; *Chagos Marine Protected Area Arbitration*, PCA (2015) paras 320, 538; *South China Sea Arbitration (Jurisdiction and Merits)* PCA (2016) paras 945, 950–83.

[38] Articles 61–7; 117–9.

(a) Living resources in the territorial sea and archipelagic waters

Extending seaward to a distance of 12 nautical miles, the territorial sea which borders every coastal state is often an important marine ecosystem, rich in biodiversity and fish stocks. The same is true of the archipelagic waters which lie behind the baseline drawn around the outer islands of archipelagic states such as Indonesia, the Philippines or several other island states.[39] Within these waters the coastal state can adopt laws and regulations to regulate exploitation of its marine living resources.[40] Unless authorized, foreign vessels must refrain from fishing in the territorial sea and archipelagic waters,[41] although traditional artisanal fishing is allowed, subject to 'reasonable regulation'.[42] Although the fisheries provisions of the 1982 UNCLOS Part V do not apply to the territorial sea or archipelagic waters, as we saw above Articles 192 and 194(5) are relevant to the conservation of living resources throughout the marine environment. In the *South China Sea Case* they were relied on by the tribunal which found that China had failed to protect coral reefs, endangered species, and biodiversity within the territorial sea.[43] Marine protected areas can be established; the only significant constraint is that they must not interfere with innocent passage or archipelagic sea lanes passage by foreign ships.[44]

(b) Living resources in the exclusive economic zone (EEZ)

In allowing coastal states to claim an EEZ not exceeding 200 nautical miles from the baseline,[45] the UNCLOS negotiators sought to provide a more effective basis for conservation and sustainable management of marine living resources. The EEZ is not an area in which the coastal state has territorial sovereignty but a more limited functional zone,[46] in which the coastal state is accorded 'sovereign rights for the purpose of exploring, exploiting, conserving and managing the natural resources, whether living or non-living, of the water superjacent to the seabed and its subsoil'.[47] It also exercises jurisdiction, as provided for in the Convention, with regard to marine scientific research and protection and preservation of the marine environment.[48] Coastal states must have 'due regard' to the rights and duties of other states in the EEZ,[49] but there is no longer either freedom of fishing for other states, nor unfettered freedom of scientific research.[50] Although other states may in certain circumstances have a claim to

39 Articles 46–53. See Tsamenyi and Hanich. 27 *IJMCL* (2012) 783.

40 Article 21(1)(d)-(f); 42(1)(c).

41 Articles 19(2)(i); 42(1)(c); *Chagos MPA Arbitration*, PCA (2015) para 516.

42 Article 51; *South China Sea Arbitration*, PCA (2016) paras 794–809.

43 *South China Sea Arbitration*, PCA (2016) paras 950–83.

44 Articles 24, 44, 54. See *supra*, Ch 9, section 5(1).

45 Articles 55–7. Where an EEZ would otherwise overlap with the maritime zones of an adjacent or opposite state, an equitable boundary is delimited. This will often, but not always, be the median line: see *Gulf of Maine Case*, ICJ Reports (1984) 246 and *Jan Mayen Case*, ICJ Reports (1993) 38.

46 See Barnes, in Freestone, Barnes and Ong (eds), *The Law of the Sea*, Ch 13; Christie, in Hey (ed), *Developments in International Fisheries Law*, 395–419; Burke, *The New International Law of Fisheries*, Ch 2; Attard, *The Exclusive Economic Zone in International Law*, 146–91; Kwiatkowska, *The 200 Mile EEZ in the Law of the Sea*, 45–103.

47 Article 56(1)(a) emphasis added.

48 *Ibid*, (b)–(c) and see *supra*, Ch 9.

49 Article 56(2); *Chagos MPA Arbitration*, PCA (2015) para 518.

50 Articles 58, 62, 246.

share in surplus fish stocks within the EEZ,[51] the coastal state determines the TAC for harvesting the living resources and allocates fishing rights.[52]

Conservation obligations laid down in Part VI of the 1982 UNCLOS seek to qualify the sovereign right to exploit the EEZ's living resources. They are expressed in general terms in Article 61 but create complex obligations.[53] In determining the TAC the coastal state must ensure 'through proper conservation and management measures' that the living resources of the EEZ are not threatened by over-exploitation.[54] In formulating laws and regulations the coastal state must also 'take into consideration' such ecological factors as 'effects on species associated with or dependent upon harvested species' with a view to maintaining or restoring these populations 'above levels at which their reproduction may become seriously threatened'.[55]

This conservation aim, however, is offset by the need to promote 'optimum utilization' and to adopt measures which will maintain or restore populations of harvested species at levels which can produce maximum sustainable yield as qualified by 'relevant environmental *and* economic factors'.[56] A non-exhaustive list of the factors to be taken into account includes the economic needs of coastal fishing communities, special needs of developing states, fishing patterns, the interdependence of stocks, and any 'generally recommended international minimum standards whether sub-regional, regional or global.'[57] These would include any relevant UN General Assembly resolutions and FAO conventions and soft law instruments.[58]

Optimum utilization does not require full utilization, however; the coastal state is not tied to any specific level and could hold back on exploitation in the interests of conservation. Other states cannot insist on access in such circumstances and the declaration of a TAC or a refusal to allocate quotas can be challenged only if arbitrary.[59] There is thus considerable freedom for a coastal state to determine its own policies on conservation and access to EEZ fish stocks, including establishing no-take MPAs on environmental grounds.[60] Disputes over the coastal state's management of EEZ living resources were deliberately excluded from binding the 1982 UNCLOS compulsory dispute settlement.[61] Burke summarises the position as follows: 'Articles 61 and 62 are unequivocal in establishing the exclusivity of coastal State decision making authority, and article 297 both reinforces this exclusive authority and confirms the fact that decision making criteria are solely for the coastal State to determine in any specific instance'.[62]

Clearly, the EEZ regime affords a more generally acceptable approach to conservation than did the 1958 Fisheries Conservation Convention. Although one study

[51] Articles 62(2), 69–70. [52] Article 61(1).

[53] Summarised in the *AO on Fisheries*, ITLOS Reports (2015) paras 96–104,

[54] Article 61(2). [55] Article 61(4). [56] Article 61(3) emphasis added. [57] *Ibid.*

[58] See *infra*, section 3. [59] Article 297(3).

[60] *Chagos MPA Case*, PCA (2015) paras 297–301. See discussion of 'no-take' MPAs, *infra*, section 5.

[61] Article 297(3). See Nordquist (ed), *UNCLOS 1982: A Commentary*, v, 87–94, 105; Klein, *Dispute Settlement in the UNCLOS* (Cambridge, 2005) 175–188.

[62] Burke, 63 *Oregon LR* 73 (1984) 117.

concludes that the failings of the EEZ regime 'render the conservation obligations of States largely illusory',[63] the management of some EEZs has improved.[64] But it is not easy to hold a coastal state to account for mismanagement. A coastal state's 'manifest failure' to ensure that the zone's living resources are not endangered can be submitted to conciliation procedures under Part XV, but not to binding dispute settlement,[65] while the FAO has no power to exercise any kind of oversight.[66] In any event the factors to take into consideration are complex and difficult to assess with certainty, and collection of the necessary data requires a good deal of expensive scientific research.

The role of fisheries commissions has been reduced by the advent of EEZs and EFZs, and this contributed to the evidence of stock collapse in the North-west Atlantic and North Sea. In these areas national EEZs abut each other, and stocks naturally straddle several zones, as well as the high seas. They are not an exclusive resource, but a shared one. Effective cooperation remains necessary for sustainable management, but this is more difficult to achieve now than it had been before UNCLOS under a high-seas regime. The failure of West African states to cooperate in managing their adjacent EEZs appears to be one of the reasons for the request to ITLOS for an advisory opinion.[67] The regulatory structure of most fisheries commissions reflects the privileged status of coastal states' exclusive rights, exemplified by the North-East Atlantic Fisheries Commission ('NEAFC') and North-West Atlantic Fisheries Organization ('NAFO'). Both were reconstituted following the adoption of EEZs or EFZs by the states parties. Both bodies can adopt binding regulations for their high seas regulatory areas, but those regulations will apply to the EEZ within the convention area only with the agreement of the relevant coastal states.[68] All that the 1982 UNCLOS Article 63(1) provides in this respect is that states shall consult and negotiate in good faith in order to 'seek to agree' on measures necessary for coordination and conservation of shared EEZ stocks.[69] The ITLOS *Advisory Opinion* emphasised that for coastal states 'the conservation and development of shared stocks in the exclusive economic zone ..... require from that State effective measures aimed at preventing over-exploitation of such stocks that could undermine their sustainable exploitation and the interests of neighbouring Member States.'[70] The cooperative management of some shared EEZ stocks fulfils these requirements.[71] In others it has been less successful. If, as in the

63 Barnes, in Freestone, Barnes and Ong (eds), *The Law of the Sea*, 234. See also literature cited *supra*, n 21.

64 E.g. the US and Australia. See FAO, *State of the World's Fisheries and Aquaculture 2016*, 44–5.

65 Article 297(3).

66 See Barnes, *loc cit*, 257–60; Churchill, 22 *IJMCL* (2007) 383.

67 *AO on Fisheries*, ITLOS Reports (2015) paras 176–7. See also China's refusal to cooperate in the *South China Sea Arbitration*, PCA (2016).

68 1980 NEAF Convention as amended 2006, Articles 5, 6, and 12; 1978 NAFO Convention as amended 2017, Articles 6(8)-(10) and 14. Contrast 2000 Convention on Conservation of Highly Migratory Fish Stocks in the Western and Central Pacific, Articles 7and 11.

69 Article 63(1), on which see *AO on Fisheries*, ITLOS Reports (2015) paras 192–213.

70 *Ibid*, para 211. ITLOS was not asked to apply the 1995 UN Fish Stocks Agreement, so the advice is given on the basis of UNCLOS alone.

71 See e.g. 1982 Nauru Agreement Concerning Cooperation in the Management of Fisheries of Common Interest; Dahl, 30 *IJMCL* (2015) 120, discussing cooperation between Norway and Russia in the Barents Sea.

South China Sea, coastal states will not cooperate with each other in managing their shared EEZ fish stocks the 1982 UNCLOS Part XV provides no remedy.[72]

(c) Living resources of the high seas

About 400 species are found outside 200-mile zones—including cephalopods, sharks, marine mammals, but also many species of fish, such as tuna, swordfish, halibut, and turbot.[73] The increased scale of high seas fishing beyond 200 miles has put pressure on some of these stocks and shown that some form of integrated management is essential.[74] Many fish migrate between EEZs and the high seas and many species of marine mammals spend a considerable part of their lives there during migrations. Though Part VII of the 1982 UNCLOS recognizes that all states have the right for their nationals to engage in fishing on the high seas,[75] this is subject to existing treaty obligations and to the rights, duties, and interests of coastal states in conserving stocks that migrate between EEZs (or EFZs) and the high seas, as set out in Articles 63–7. Article 63(2) obliges coastal states and states fishing straddling stocks beyond EEZs to cooperate in the same terms as Article 63(1), considered in the previous section,[76] but as we saw there, regional fisheries bodies are given no power to impose conservation regulations on coastal states without their agreement. They are thus left to try to negotiate a coordinated EEZ and high seas regime for straddling or migratory fish stocks with each coastal state.

Articles 117-9 lay down the duty of states to take, or to cooperate with other states in taking, the measures necessary for conservation and management of high seas living resources in terms taken largely from Article 4 of the 1958 Fisheries Conservation Convention. These provisions essentially address the conservation obligations of flag states, which are also required to cooperate in establishing regional and sub-regional fisheries organizations for this purpose but only 'as appropriate'.[77] No harmonized standards for conservation of high seas fish stocks are laid down in UNCLOS; once again conservation measures are meant to maintain or restore MSY, qualified by economic and environmental factors including interdependence of stocks and effects on associated species, and take into account any 'generally recommended international minimum standards'. Thus UN General Assembly resolutions on driftnet fishing,[78] and the FAO's Code of Conduct on Responsible Fishing, including its guidelines on matters such as deep sea fishing,[79] sharks,[80] and longline fisheries,[81] cannot be ignored:

72 UNCLOS Article 297(3) and *Chagos MPA Case*, PCA (2015) paras 297–301.

73 See Stokke (ed), *Governing High Seas Fisheries* (Oxford, 2001); Burke, *The New International Law of Fisheries*, Ch 3; Nelson, in Boyle and Freestone (eds), *International Law and Sustainable Development*, 113–34; Diz, *Fisheries Management in Areas Beyond National Jurisdiction*, 11–33.

74 Saunders, *Policy Options for the Management and Conservation of Straddling Fisheries Resources* (St John's, 2003).

75 Articles 87, 116. Article 119(3) also requires that conservation measures do not discriminate in form or in fact against fishermen of any state on the high seas.

76 See also *AO on Fisheries*, ITLOS Reports (2015) paras 192–213.

77 Article 118. See Molenaar, 20 *IJMCL* (2005) 533–70.

78 *Infra*, n 117.

79 2008 International Guidelines for the Management of Deep-sea Fisheries in the High Seas.

80 2012 International Plan of Action for the Conservation and Management of Sharks.

81 2010 International Plan of Action for Reducing Incidental Catch of Seabirds in Longline Fisheries.

at the very least they are relevant to the interpretation and application of Articles 117-9 and 194(5).[82]

The 1982 UNCLOS neither clarifies the rights of coastal states if agreement on high seas conservation measures is not possible, nor does it address in any detail the broader objectives of ecosystem protection and conservation of biological diversity, although Article 192 and 194(5) go some of the way.[83] More fundamentally, although under UNCLOS flag states have an obligation to regulate fishing by their vessels on the high seas,[84] an obligation to cooperate does not compel them to join regional fisheries bodies nor to ensure that their vessels comply with the rules those bodies establish. Free-riding is thus not excluded. However, the 1995 UN Fish Stocks Agreement and a range of other measures subsequently adopted by the FAO are intended to remedy some of these defects in the UNCLOS text, whose articles must now be interpreted taking these later instruments into account. The 1995 UN Fish Stocks Agreement is considered in more detail below.[85]

(d) Living resources of the continental shelf

Within 200 miles of the coast, the EEZ regime now overlaps with the continental shelf regime in Articles 76-85 of the 1982 UNCLOS. The shelf may, however, extend beyond 200 miles and if so it will then overlap with the high seas regime. While the EEZ or high seas provisions of the 1982 UNCLOS govern fish and marine mammals in the water column, the continental shelf regime governs the sedentary species which inhabit the seafloor,[86] and which can only be harvested with the agreement of the coastal state and in accordance with its conservation laws. This remains true even when the superjacent waters are high seas regulated by a regional fisheries agreement.[87]

Sedentary species (i.e. those that cannot swim) are an important category in ecosystem terms because they include coral reefs which are a rich habitat and spawning ground for marine species of all kinds.[88] Lobsters, and crabs are among the commercially significant sedentary species.[89] Others, such as some giant clam species, are listed on Annex I of the 1973 CITES but are illegally caught and traded in Asia. Although Article 77 says nothing specifically about conservation of sedentary species, coastal states have at least the obligation under Articles 194(5) and 197 to protect

82 On the legal status of FAO soft law see Korseberg, 67 *ICLQ* (2018) 801, and *supra*, Ch 1.

83 See *AO on Fisheries*, ITLOS Reports (2015) para 120; *Southern Bluefin Tuna Cases (Provisional Measures)* ITLOS Reports (1999) 280, para 70; *South China Sea Arbitration*, PCA (2016) paras 945, 956–60.

84 UNCLOS Articles 94, 117; *AO on Fisheries*, ITLOS Reports (2015) paras 108, 116–9.

85 See *infra*, section 3.

86 UNCLOS, Article 77(4). See Mossop, *The Continental Shelf Beyond 200 Nautical Miles* (Oxford, 2016) Chs 2 and 3.

87 See e.g. the 1980 Northeast Atlantic Fisheries Convention, as amended 2006, Articles 6, 8(2), 9(2), which require the consent of the coastal state before NEAFC can regulate the sedentary species which fall within its competence under Article 1(b).

88 *Chagos MPA Arbitration*, PCA (2015) para 304.

89 The inclusion of crabs was accepted by the EU, Norway and Russia in a dispute over the taking of snow crabs on Norway's continental shelf in 2015.

and preserve endangered species and fragile ecosystems, including coral reefs and other habitats on the continental shelf, and to cooperate with other states in doing so.[90] The MPA around the British Indian Ocean Territory (Chagos Archipelago) is an example of coral reef protection within the 200-mile limit, but there may be reef systems extending beyond 200 miles which could also be protected by the relevant coastal state in the interests of biodiversity or sustainable fishing using its continental shelf jurisdiction.[91] The Barents Sea illustrates cooperation between a regional fisheries organisation (NEAFC) and coastal states with jurisdiction over the continental shelf. NEAFC Recommendation 19/2014 on Protection of VMEs is applicable to sedentary species in the Barents Sea insofar as it regulates the harmful impacts of bottom trawling: it was adopted with the consent of Russia and Norway whose shared continental shelf the regulation seeks to protect.

(e) Deep seabed living resources

As we saw in Chapter 9, questions have arisen concerning the legal status of living resources found at great depths in the vicinity of hydrothermal vents and seamounts on the seabed beyond national jurisdiction.[92] Over 200 species of micro-organisms, crustaceans, molluscs, and other species have been identified in these vent areas.[93] Because of their genetic material they have potential pharmaceutical applications.[94] Neither the 1982 UNCLOS nor the 1992 CBD specifically covers their use for pure scientific research or commercial purposes. Nor is research or exploitation of these species constrained by the the 1982 UNCLOS provisions governing the deep seabed in areas beyond national jurisdiction. Those provisions apply only in respect of 'solid, gaseous or mineral resources';[95] this phraseology cannot readily be construed to include living or genetic resources. Although some developing states disagree, deep-seabed species are thus not common heritage resources and do not fall directly within the management responsibilities of the ISA;[96] rather they appear to be EEZ, continental shelf, or high seas living resources depending on where they are found. As such, relevant provisions of the 1982 Convention and customary law will apply.[97] However, the ISA's jurisdiction to regulate pollution from activities in the Area and prevent interference with the ecological balance of the marine environment would cover living organisms if affected by seabed mineral resource activities.[98]

[90] *South China Sea Arbitration*, PCA (2016) paras 945, 956–60. See generally Goodwin, *International Environmental Law and the Conservation of Coral Reefs* (London, 2011) esp. Chs 2–5, 7.

[91] Portugal has done so: see Ribeiro, 25 *IJMCL* (2010) 183.

[92] See Drankier et al, 27 *IJMCL* (2012) 375; de La Fayette, 24 *IJMCL* (2009) 221; Armas Pfirter, *ibid*, 281; Hayes, in Nordquist et al (eds), *Law, Science and Ocean Management* (Leiden, 2007) 683; Millicay, *ibid*, 730; Lodge, 19 *IJMCL* (2004) 299; Scovazzi, *ibid*, 383; Glowka, 12 *Ocean Yb* (1996) 156.

[93] See Imhoff and Hügler, 24 *IJMCL* (2009) 201.

[94] See de la Calle, 24 *IJMCL* (2009) 209.

[95] Articles 133–4.

[96] Articles 136–7, and on common heritage see *supra*, Ch 3, section 3.

[97] Articles 61–2, 77, 117–9, 192–206, 209. See *infra*.

[98] Articles 143, 145. See *supra*, Ch 9, section 6.

The 1992 CBD does not extend to the 'components of biological diversity' in areas beyond national jurisdiction,[99] so the Convention's provisions on sustainable use of those components will not apply.[100] However, the convention does apply to 'processes or activities' carried out under a state's jurisdiction or control in areas beyond national jurisdiction.[101] Thus if biological resources are harvested for use (an 'activity') or affected by seabed mining (a 'process') the other provisions of the 1992 CBD will potentially be applicable, including in situ and ex situ conservation and access to genetic resources. Moreover, given the relationship between the 1992 CBD and the 1982 UNCLOS,[102] the latter's provisions on protection and preservation of the marine environment would be relevant where any fragile ecosystems or endangered species on the deep seabed are threatened.[103] But as the *South China Sea* dispute showed, these provisions will not stop a state determined to break them.

Noting the obvious gaps in the existing law, in 2015 the UN General Assembly initiated further preparatory discussions for a new legal instrument. The conclusion was that a conference should be convened to negotiate a text.[104] This may not be easy, as views remain deeply divided on what the status of deep seabed genetic resources should be, who should regulate them, and who should benefit.[105]

2(3) THE SPECIES APPROACH

It was agreed at UNCLOS III that special regimes should be established for certain species that migrate in various ways. The origins of this approach lie more in allocation of access and jurisdictional rights than in conservation, but the provisions also allocate jurisdiction for this purpose. The 1982 Convention specifically addresses the following categories.

(a) Highly migratory species

As we saw in Chapter 11, the essential point about migratory species is the need to ensure protection throughout their migratory range.[106] For fish and marine mammals the migratory range may include areas within national jurisdiction and the high

99 CBD, Article 4(a).

100 I.e. Articles 5–7, 10–12. Sustainable use is defined by reference to 'use of the components of biological diversity.'

101 CBD, Article 4. See de La Fayette, 24 *IJMCL* (2009) 221.

102 CBD, Article 22, on which see *infra*, section 5.

103 UNCLOS, Article 192 and 194(5); *Chagos MPA Arbitration*, PCA (2015) paras 320, 538; *South China Sea Arbitration*, PCA (2016) paras 945, 956–60. But see Gjerde, 27 *IJMCL* (2012) 839.

104 See Report of the Preparatory Committee established by UNGA Res 69/292, UN Doc A/AC.287/2017/PC.4/2.

105 See Mossop, in Toledo and Tassin (eds), *Guide to the Navigation of Marine Biodiversity Beyond National Jurisdiction* (Belo Horizonte, 2017); Tladi 30 *IJMCL* (2015) 654; Barnes, 31 *IJMCL* (2016) 583; Lodge, Segerson, Squires, 32 *IJMCL* (2017) 427, 442ff, and for southern hemisphere views see various authors, 32 *IJMCL* (2017) 607–796.

106 See Burke, *The New International Law of Fisheries*, Ch 5.

seas. In some cases entire oceans will thus require some form of cooperative conservation and management regime. The migratory species listed in Annex I of the 1982 UNCLOS include various species of tuna, marlin, sailfish, swordfish, dolphin, shark, and whales.[107] The Annex is neither comprehensive (it does not include sea turtles or squid, for example) nor easily amendable. In addition to the other EEZ requirements, Article 64 requires coastal and other states fishing in a region for highly migratory species to cooperate directly or through 'appropriate' international organizations 'with a view' to ensuring and promoting optimum utilization, within *and* beyond the EEZ.[108] Unlike marine mammals (Article 65), highly migratory species are not removed from the requirement of optimum use.

Relevant fisheries organizations cover Atlantic tuna ('ICCAT'),[109] Inter-American tropical tuna ('ITTC'),[110] southern bluefin tuna ('CCSBT');[111] Indian Ocean tuna ('IOTC');[112] South Pacific tuna ('SPFFA');[113] Western and Central Pacific migratory species,[114] and, although outside Annex I, Inter-American sea turtles.[115] If no relevant organization exists, the states involved must cooperate to establish one 'and participate in its work'. Any failure at this stage will mean that some highly migratory species may not be conserved throughout their entire range.[116] Conservation objectives may thus be compromised if no agreement is concluded for high seas areas and if the wide discretion accorded to coastal states within their EEZ undermines the aims of Article 64. The problem of by-catches of dolphins, turtles etc is not directly addressed; the use of driftnets has, however, become such a serious problem that it is the subject of UN General Assembly resolutions and a regional convention.[117]

The weaknesses of Article 64 stem from the US' wish to remove highly migratory species as far as possible from coastal state control in the EEZ and subject their management to international regulation. Developing coastal states, however, wanted to protect their sovereign rights to tuna, etc and had been seeking in the tuna commissions higher quotas for 'resource adjacent nations'. Article 64 tries to accommodate

[107] Although Article 65 protects marine mammals, cetaceans were left on Annex I because small cetaceans are caught incidentally in the nets used by the tuna industry and it falls within the ambit of ICCAT and the ITTC to deal with this problem.

[108] See *AO on Fisheries*, ITLOS Reports (2015) paras 182–213.

[109] See 1966 International Convention for the Conservation of Atlantic Tuna.

[110] See 2003 Antigua Convention for the Strengthening of the Inter-American Tropical Tuna Commission.

[111] 1993 Convention for the Conservation of Southern Bluefin Tuna.

[112] 1993 Agreement for the Establishment of the Indian Ocean Tuna Commission.

[113] 1992 Niue Treaty on Cooperation in Fisheries Surveillance and Enforcement in the South Pacific Region.

[114] 2000 Convention on the Conservation and Management of Highly Migratory Fish Stocks in the Western and Central Pacific Ocean.

[115] 1996 Inter-American Convention for the Protection and Conservation of Sea Turtles.

[116] See Burke, 14 *ODIL* (1984) 283–93.

[117] 1989 Wellington Convention for the Prohibition of Fishing with Long Driftnets in the South Pacific; UNGA Res 44/225 (1989); 45/197 (1990); 46/215 (1991); 59/25 (2004). See FAO, *The Regulation of Driftnet Fishing on the High Seas: Legal Issues* (Rome, 1991); Kaye, *International Fisheries Management*, 188–94; Carr and Gianni, in Van Dyke, Zaelke, Hewison (eds), *Freedom of the Seas in the 21st Century: Ocean Governance and Environmental Harmony* (Washington DC, 1993) 272; Burke, Freeburg, and Miles, 25 *ODIL* (1994) 127.

both views. Following the establishment in 1987 of the SPFFA,[118] a licensing system was introduced for the catching, inter alia, of tuna in the SPFFA area, which comprises the 200-mile zones of participating states and entities, the high seas areas enclosed by these, and certain other specified areas in the Pacific Ocean. The US initially objected but eventually paid a considerable sum to the SPFFA in return for access to a fixed quota of tuna.

The 1995 UN Fish Stocks Agreement makes important changes to the law and Article 64 must now be read in the light of that agreement.[119] As Schram and Tahindro conclude, 'The Agreement put flesh on the bones of the obligation to conserve' and it should be a step towards more adequate management of these stocks if fully implemented.[120] But while some of the tuna conventions have been revised to conform to the requirements of the 1995 UN Fish Stocks Agreement (e.g. the IATTC), others have not, including the ICCAT, the IOTC, and the CCSBT.[121] Given that all these tuna stocks remain heavily overfished, the failure to reform is continuing evidence of institutional failure. Both the Atlantic and the Southern bluefin tuna remain critically endangered; the ICCAT has not been revised and the commission does not act on scientific advice. ICCAT's problems include poor data, the ineffectiveness of previous measures, excess fishing capacity, quotas that exceed catch levels, the harmful ecological effects of fish aggregating devices, the failure of observer schemes, failure to deal with by-catch and discards, and so on.[122] While the US has driven serious reform of the IATTC, in the Atlantic the EU and Japan have not pushed for similar reform. Attempts to end trade in bluefin tuna by listing the species on appendix I of the 1973 CITES have so far failed because of the opposition of Japan and other tuna fishing states. The creation of large-scale no-take MPAs around British Overseas Territories in the South Atlantic and Indian Ocean provides some relief for the tuna, but the fishing can simply move elsewhere. Only in the South Pacific is there evidence of successful management of tuna stocks.[123]

(b) Anadromous species

Anadromous species[124] (mainly salmon) spawn in freshwater but spend the major part of their lives at sea, passing through the territorial sea and EEZ to the high seas before returning to die in the rivers in which they originated. Conservation measures

118 See Swan, in Soons (ed), *Implementation of the Law of the Sea Convention Through International Institutions* (Honolulu, 1990) 318–43, for details of the practice of the SPFFA; see also Tsamenyi, 10 *Marine Policy* (1986) 29, 31–6, 41, who points out the need to retain ambiguity concerning sovereignty over HMS in order to secure an agreement.

119 *Infra*, section 6.

120 Schram and Tahindro, in Hey (ed), *Developments in International Fisheries Law* 251, 285–6.

121 In some cases measures have been adopted that partly implement UNFSA requirements. See e.g. Garcia and Koehler, 2nd *Performance Review of the CCSBT 2009–13* (2014).

122 The problems, and ICCAT's attempt to address them, are set out in ICCAT Recommendation 16/01 on multi-annual conservation and management programme for tropical tunas. See also Song, 24 *IJMCL* (2009) 101.

123 *Supra*, section 1(2).

124 See Burke, *The New International Law of Fisheries*, Ch 4; Birnie, in Hey (ed), *Developments in International Fisheries Law*, Ch 13; Orrego Vicuña, 22 *ODIL* (1991) 133–5; and generally, Kurlansky, *Salmon: A Fish, the Earth, and the History of a Common Fate* (London, 2020).

adopted by the state of origin are rendered useless if the species are over-exploited in the EEZ or on the high seas. Article 66 of the 1982 UNCLOS provides that the state in whose rivers the stocks originate has the *primary* interest in and responsibility for these stocks[125] but, in return, it must ensure their conservation by establishing appropriate regulatory measures for this purpose and for determining access to these stocks landward of the outer boundary of its own EEZ.[126] Anadromous species can only be taken on the high seas in exceptional circumstances,[127] but fishing in other states' EEZs or in the rivers of downstream states is not banned. Where the stock migrates through the EEZ of another coastal state, the parties must cooperate on conservation and management.[128] TACs can be set by the state of origin in consultation with other interested states,[129] but it is not obliged either to do so or to determine its own harvesting capacity. It retains the discretion to adopt other measures that ensure conservation. A major problem for wild salmon is the intermingling with farmed salmon in coastal waters. Not only does this put the wild salmon at risk from disease but it may lead to irreversible genetic change and ecological interactions.[130]

If banning fishing on the high seas causes economic dislocation in other states,[131] the state of origin must consult 'with a view to achieving agreement on terms and conditions of such fishing', including determining the necessary conservation measures. Enforcement must be agreed among the state of origin and the others concerned. The state of origin must also cooperate in minimizing economic dislocation to all other states where fishing has taken place.[132]

Article 66 thus establishes a discrete conservation regime, apart from others in Part V; conservation is the main aim, with the secondary interests of other states balanced by cooperation through consultation. Most fisheries conventions do not apply to salmon and we have to look for evidence of state practice in the species-specific conventions, in particular the 1982 Convention for the Conservation of Salmon in the North Atlantic Ocean[133] and the 1992 Convention for the Conservation of Anadromous Stocks in the North Pacific.[134] With limited exceptions, both agreements ban all high-seas fishing for salmon. The North Atlantic Salmon Conservation Organisation has

[125] UNCLOS, Article 66(1); Article 116(b) also subjects freedom of fishing on the high seas to the rights and interests of coastal states 'as provided in the Convention', i.e. including Article 66.

[126] Article 66(2). [127] Article 66(3)(a). [128] Article 66(4). [129] Article 66(2).

[130] See NASCO, *Ten Year Review of the Atlantic Salmon Conservation Organization* (Edinburgh, 1995); id, *Report of the 17th Annual Meeting of the Council* (Edinburgh, 2000) 271, 285–7; Hansen and Windsor, *Interactions between Aquaculture and Wild Stocks of Atlantic Salmon and other Diadromous Fish Species: Science and Management, Challenges and Solutions* (Trondheim, 2006); 2006 Resolution to Minimise Impacts from Aquaculture, Introductions and Transfers, and Transgenics on the Wild Salmon Stocks, CNL(06)48.

[131] Article 66(3)(a). [132] Article 66(3)(b). E.g. in the EEZ of another coastal state.

[133] The current parties are Canada, Denmark (for Faroe Islands and Greenland), the EU, Norway, Russia, and the US.

[134] The current parties are Canada, Japan, Republic of Korea, Russia, and the US. See Birnie, in Hey (ed), *Developments in International Fisheries Law*, Ch 13. See also 1985 Treaty Concerning Pacific Salmon between Canada and the US. Yanagida, 81 *AJIL* (1987) 577–91, draws attention to the practical difficulties of operating the complex devolved solutions this treaty provides.

developed principles for ensuring a precautionary approach when there is a risk of adverse impacts on salmon stocks and their habitats.[135] These changes evidence the impact of UNCED principles. They also reveal how problems of habitat and biodiversity protection must be addressed in order to ensure conservation and sustainable use.

(c) Catadromous species

Catadromous species are the opposite of the above; they spawn at sea and spend the major part of their lives in rivers and lakes. The species of main interest are eels, which provide a significant export resource in several states; the principal market is in Asia. Overfishing, pollution, habitat loss and climate change have contributed to a sharp decline in eel stocks; the critically endangered European eel is listed on appendix II of the 1973 CITES. The ban on European exports has put additional pressure on eel stocks in Asia and North America, and there is evidence of continued illegal trade.[136]

Article 67 of the 1982 UNCLOS provides that coastal states in whose waters these species spend the major part of their life-cycle are responsible for their conservation and management; they have the primary interest.[137] Exploitation within the EEZ is subject to the provisions of Article 67 and other provisions of the Convention. Exploitation is not permitted beyond the outer limit of the EEZ. Catadromous species which migrate through one state's EEZ but spend the major part of their life-cycle in the coastal waters of another state are to be regulated by agreement between the states concerned so as to ensure rational management, taking account of the special interest of both states. The only relevant agreement to date is the non-binding 2014 Declaration on Collaboration for the Conservation of the Sargasso Sea, signed by the governments of Bermuda, the Azores, Monaco, the UK and the US. The Declaration creates a commission whose task is to coordinate member state proposals for conservation measures within the IMO, the FAO and the fisheries commissions.[138] European eels are believed to breed in the Sargasso Sea, an important high seas ecosystem for many marine species in the North Atlantic.

(d) Sharks, rays and other endangered species

The 1982 UNCLOS lists oceanic sharks as migratory species in Annex I but otherwise says nothing about this ecologically important species.[139] Sharks and rays merit separate treatment here because they are often taken as by-catch in commercial fishing operations on a scale that puts them at risk. The science shows significant declines

135 See 1998 Agreement on Adoption of a Precautionary Approach, CNL(98)46; 2001 Plan of Action for the Application of the Precautionary Approach to the Protection and Restoration of Atlantic Salmon Habitat, CNL(01)51; 2009 Guidelines for the Management of Salmon Fisheries, CNL(09)43; 2010 Guidelines for the Protection, Restoration and Enhancement of Atlantic Salmon Habitat CNL(10)51.

136 See the EU paper on 'Conservation and Trade in Anguilla SPP', submitted to the 17th CITES COP (2016).

137 Article 67(1). Thus, in Europe it is the EU which has primary responsibility.

138 See Freestone in Barrett and Barnes (eds), *Law of the Sea: UNCLOS as a Living Treaty*, 243–65.

139 See generally Techera and Klein, *International Law of Sharks* (Leiden, 2017); *id* (eds), *Sharks: Conservation, Governance and Management* (London, 2014).

in populations of some shark and ray species.[140] Twelve species of shark and eight species of rays are listed on appendix II of the 1973 CITES in order to control international trade, while seven shark species are also listed on appendix I or II of the Bonn Convention on Migratory Species.[141] An MOU adopted under this convention establishes a conservation plan.[142] The growth of marine protected areas (MPAs) has partly been driven by a desire to protect threatened species such as the shark.[143] A number of states have created shark 'sanctuaries' for this purpose.[144]

The FAO has also made efforts to regulate shark catches during fishing operations. An International Plan of Action for the Conservation and Management of Sharks ('IPOA Sharks') was adopted in 1999 as part of the Code of Conduct on Responsible Fishing.[145] The IPOA is non-binding, but like other FAO soft law it may be relevant to interpretation of the 1982 UNCLOS, including Article 64; it has to be taken into account for the purposes of Article 119; and it has to be applied by parties to the 1995 UN Fish Stocks Agreement pursuant to Article 10. It covers all shark and ray species, both as a target catch and as a by-catch, and applies globally, so coastal and flag states are to give effect to its provisions. States are expected to draw up national or regional action plans and to report on progress. The main problem with the IPOA is the poor response of states in implementing it. The main shark fishing states have been particularly slow. One study concludes that 'there is no clear evidence that the IPOA Sharks has delivered improved management of sharks.'[146]

Klein and Techera say that the non-binding status of the IPOA Sharks is 'a central weakness' undermining its effectiveness.[147] It is, however, worth noting what the arbitrators in the *South China Sea Case* said about the 1982 UNCLOS and 'depleted, threatened or endangered' species. In that case the species at risk were sea turtles listed on appendix I of the 1973 CITES and giant clams listed on appendix II, but the judgment could apply equally to other listed species, including sharks:

'.......CITES is the subject of nearly universal adherence, including by the Philippines and China, and in the Tribunal's view forms part of the general corpus of international law that informs the content of Article 192 and 194(5) of the Convention. "[T]he conservation of the living resources of the sea is an element in the protection and preservation of the marine environment," and the Tribunal considers that the general obligation to "protect and preserve the marine environment" in Article 192 includes a due diligence obligation to prevent the harvesting of species that are recognized internationally as being at risk of extinction and requiring international protection.'[148]

'The Tribunal has noted that it considers the duty to prevent the harvest of endangered species follows from Article 192, read against the background of other applicable international law. The Tribunal considers that this general obligation is given particular shape in

140 Myers and Worm, 423 *Nature* 280.
141 *Supra*, Ch 11, sections 3(3–4).
142 See Techera and Klein, *International Law of Sharks*, 43–8.
143 *Supra*, section 5.
144 Techera and Klein, op cit 135–7.
145 *Ibid*, 32–5.
146 Lack, in Techera and Klein (eds), *Sharks: Conservation, Governance and Management*, 48.
147 *Ibid*, 34.
148 *South China Sea Arbitration*, PCA (2016) para 956, footnotes omitted. On giant clams see *ibid*, para 957.

the context of fragile ecosystems by Article 194(5). Read in this context, the Tribunal thus considers that Article 192 imposes a due diligence obligation to take those measures "necessary to protect and preserve rare or fragile ecosystems as well as the habitat of depleted, threatened or endangered species and other forms of marine life." Therefore, in addition to preventing the direct harvesting of species recognised internationally as being threatened with extinction, Article 192 extends to the prevention of harms that would affect depleted, threatened, or endangered species indirectly through the destruction of their habitat.'[149]

This is a particularly far-reaching judgment. Its interpretation of 'depleted, threatened or endangered' species covers at least those listed on appendices I and II of CITES, including sharks, albatrosses, and cetaceans, but could easily extend to fish stocks or species that are treated by the FAO or an RFMO as 'depleted'. Moreover, the treatment of giant clams and coral reefs—both sedentary species—as part of the ecosystem suggests that Articles 194(5) will also cover those parts of the deep seabed that are at risk from seabed mining or bottom trawling. Certainly, it places on all states an obligation to protect coral reefs and other vulnerable marine ecosystems.[150] It is only a short step from there to giving legal effect to the FAO soft law on vulnerable marine ecosystems, sharks, and albatrosses via Articles 192 and 194(5). Klein's assumption that FAO soft law is 'non-binding' looks less convincing from this perspective. The *South China Sea Arbitration* shows that disputes concerning compliance with Articles 192 and 194(5) will fall within the 1982 UNCLOS Part XV compulsory jurisdiction wherever they arise.[151]

3 POST-UNCLOS DEVELOPMENTS

3(1) FAO AND THE CONSERVATION OF HIGH SEAS LIVING RESOURCES

As we saw in Chapter 9, the Rio Conference treated the 1982 UNCLOS as a codification of the existing law relating to the marine environment.[152] While acknowledging that the relevant provisions of the 1982 UNCLOS represented the rights and obligations of states with respect to conservation and sustainable use of high seas living resources, Agenda 21 called for the convening of a UN conference on straddling and highly migratory fish stocks, and for more effective cooperation through regional fisheries organizations and agreements.[153]

149 *Ibid*, para 959. See also para 960.

150 See generally Goodwin, *International Environmental Law and the Conservation of Coral Reefs*, esp. Chs 2–5, 7.

151 PCA (2016) paras 695, 925–38. But note the exclusion of disputes concerning the coastal state's management of EEZ living resources in Article 297(3), on which see *ibid*, para 695.

152 See Harrison, *Saving the Oceans through Law*, 178–82.

153 *Rept of UNCED*, UN Doc A/CONF 151/26/Rev 1, Vol I (1992 Ch 17, paras 44–63.

The Rio Conference thus initiated some important developments in the law relating to marine living resources, including not only the conclusion in 1995 of the UN Fish Stocks Agreement but also the adoption by the FAO of the 1993 Agreement to Promote Compliance with International Conservation and Management Measures by Fishing Vessels on the High Seas,[154] the 1995 Code of Conduct for Responsible Fisheries,[155] the 2001 International Plan of Action on Illegal, Unregulated and Unreported Fishing,[156] and the 2009 Agreement on Port State Measures.[157] In the assessment of one FAO lawyer:

> There can be little doubt that the sum total of the changes introduced has substantially strengthened the regime of the 1982 UN Convention . . . [T]hese instruments have ensured that the importance of the long-term sustainable use of marine living resources has been placed in the forefront of any serious analysis of the legal regime . . .[158]

One consequence is that the traditional concept of high seas freedom of fishing has been substantially altered since the 1995 UN Fish Stocks Agreement entered into force in 2001, if indeed it can be said to have survived at all.[159] Another is that international fisheries law has acquired a stronger environmental dimension, integrating it more closely with Part XII of the 1982 UNCLOS and the 1992 CBD.[160] As Freestone concludes, freedom of fishing is no longer the dominant community interest; instead the protection of the marine environment has become a fundamental element in international fisheries law.[161] However, other studies point to the ineffectiveness of regional fisheries organizations and the inability of too many flag states to ensure that their vessels fish legally and comply with applicable conservation measures.[162] As we shall see below it remains unclear that these changes in the law will significantly affect the uncertain future of marine living resources.[163]

[154] Edeson, in Boyle and Freestone (eds), *International Law and Sustainable Development*, 165. Adopted by FAO to reinforce flag state obligations in respect of high seas fishing, this agreement might be regarded as another UNCLOS 'implementing agreement.'

[155] See Edeson, 11 *IJMCL* (1996) 97.

[156] See Edeson, 16 *IJMCL* (2001) 603. Some states expressed significant reservations when adopting the 2001 Plan of Action: see FAO, *Rept. of the Committee on Fisheries*, 24th Session (2001). See also the 2008 Guidelines for the Management of Deep Sea Fisheries and 2012 Guidelines on Bycatch Management and Reduction of Discards.

[157] See Swan, 31 *IJMCL* (2016) 395; Serdy, *ibid*, 422; Witbooi, 29 *IJMCL* (2014) 290.

[158] Edeson, in Boyle and Freestone (eds), *International Law and Sustainable Development*, 165. See also Edeson, in Nordquist, Moore, Mahmoudi (eds), *The Stockholm Declaration and Law of the Marine Environment* (The Hague, 2003) 165.

[159] See Orrego Vicuña, in Stokke (ed), *Governing High Seas Fisheries*, 23; Örebech et al, 13 *IJMCL* (1998) 140–1.

[160] Freestone and Makuch, 7 *YbIEL* (1996) 3.

[161] In Boyle and Freestone (eds), *International Law and Sustainable Development*, 164.

[162] For an overview see Guggisberg, *The Use of CITES for Commercially Exploited Fish Species*, 149–66.

[163] See Gjerde, in Freestone, Barnes, and Ong (eds), *The Law of the Sea*, Ch 15. For comprehensive studies of high seas fisheries law and governance see articles collected in 19 *IJMCL* (2004) 209–363 and 20 *IJMCL* (2005) 323–629.

3(2) ALTERNATIVE APPROACHES TO MANAGEMENT OF HIGH SEAS FISHERIES

Notwithstanding the very widespread adoption of the 200-mile EEZ, the over-exploitation of fish stocks in the North Pacific, the Behring Sea, the North Atlantic and the North Sea shows that the 1982 UNCLOS strategy for sustainable fishing has not worked as intended.[164] As we saw earlier, one reason for this failure is that some coastal states have failed to ensure sustainable fishing within their own EEZs. Another closely connected problem is that some important fish stocks are not confined to the EEZ but can also be taken on the high seas. Highly migratory species such as tuna clearly fall into this category, but other less-mobile stocks are also found straddling the remaining high seas areas and adjacent EEZs. Fishing effort on the high seas has not been eliminated by the extension of coastal-state jurisdiction, but transferred beyond 200 miles, and competition for stocks made more intense. This has seriously affected the viability of some adjacent EEZ fisheries. Redrawing the boundary between coastal-state jurisdiction and the high seas has not done away with the unavoidable facts of geography: in a divided ocean, most fish are inevitably at least a shared EEZ resource and will in some cases also be a high seas common property resource.

One possible response—the further extension of coastal state jurisdiction—adopted so far only by Chile and briefly by Canada, would destroy the consensus arrived at in the 1982 UNCLOS, and once again generate serious conflict with distant-water fishing states.[165] Another solution would entail the abolition or suspension of high seas exploitation rights, based on a 'precautionary approach' to environmental risks.[166] At its strongest, the precautionary approach may result in a 'preservationist' model of sustainability if, for example, a workable scheme of sustainable exploitation proves impossible to devise. The moratorium on whaling in force since 1986 reflects this form of precaution; so for somewhat similar reasons does the prohibition of sealing or the taking of salmon on the high seas.[167] Limited versions of the same approach are evident in the revival of the high seas abstention doctrine to contain Japanese, Korean, and Taiwanese fishing in the North Pacific,[168] and in the attempt to outlaw mainly Japanese drift-netting in the South Pacific.[169] All of these possibilities were rejected

164 See Ulfstein, Andersen, and Churchill, *The Regulation of Fisheries: Legal, Economic and Social Aspects* (Council of Europe, 1986); Meltzer, 25 *ODIL* (1994) 255; Burke, *The New International Law of Fisheries*.

165 See Orrego Vicuña, 55 *ZAÖRV* (1995) 520; Davies and Redgwell, 67 *BYIL* (1996) 199; Saunders, *Policy Options for the Management and Conservation of Straddling Stocks* (St John's, 2003).

166 See for an example the 1994 Convention on Conservation and Management of Pollock Resources in the Central Bering Sea, *infra*, section 3(3)(c).

167 1982 UNCLOS, Article 66; 1982 North Atlantic Salmon Convention; 1992 Convention for the Conservation of Anadromous Stocks in the North Pacific; Burke, *The New International Law of Fisheries*, Ch 4.

168 Joint Resolution of the 5th Conference on the Conservation and Management of the Living Marine Resources of the Central Bering Sea, 1992; see Meltzer, 25 *ODIL* (1994) 283–90.

169 1989 Convention for the Prohibition of Fishing with Long Drift Nets in the South Pacific.

during negotiation of the 1995 Fish Stocks Agreement in favour of a more moderate version of the precautionary approach, considered below.[170]

A serious weakness of the 1982 UNCLOS negotiations was that they did not address problems of institutional cooperation on fisheries conservation: as a study by Lodge and Nandan showed, the analysis of the failure of RFMOs given by Koers in the early 1970s remains just as pertinent to contemporary analysis of NAFO, CCAMLR, and other post-UNCLOS fisheries commissions.[171] The lesson to be learnt from this experience is self-evident: if a resource allocated on the principle of common property cannot be exploited sustainably without the support of effective institutional arrangements to ensure rational cooperation, then the fundamental problems of regime participation, effective regulation based on adequate scientific information, adequate dispute settlement arrangements, and high seas enforcement need to be addressed once more. Recognition of this elementary lesson is apparent in the UN General Assembly resolution convening the Straddling and Highly Migratory Fish Stocks Conference.[172] Reviewing the work of the second session of the conference, the chairman observed that governments must be flexible and 'not insist on old rules of the game which are no longer appropriate, whether they apply to areas under national jurisdiction or to the resources of the high seas'.[173]

The most radical alternative to 'the old rules of the game' would involve extending the common heritage concept to high seas fisheries. As this would entail surrendering management and regulatory authority to an international body, comparable to the ISA,[174] or to similar regional bodies, it was not a solution proposed either at UNCED or during negotiation of the 1995 UN Fish Stocks Agreement. This is politically understandable, but only at the cost of ignoring the economic logic of separating the right to fish from the right to own or profit from the catch.[175] Without such a separation it will always be in the economic interest of distant-water fishing nations to tolerate unrestrained fishing on the high seas, whatever international law may provide. It is against this economic logic that the 1995 Fish Stocks Agreement must be assessed.

3(3) 1995 AGREEMENT ON STRADDLING AND HIGHLY MIGRATORY FISH STOCKS

The 1995 UN Fish Stocks Agreement represents an attempt to deal with the serious problems of unsustainable fishing by building on the existing provisions of the 1982

170 For an account of the negotiations on this issue see Boyle and Freestone (eds), *International Law and Sustainable Development*, 154; Hewison, 11 *IJMCL* (1996) 301.

171 Lodge and Nandan, 20 *IJMCL* (2005) 345, especially annexes, and. *supra*, Ch 11; cf Koers, *International Regulation of Marine Fisheries* (London, 1973).

172 UNGA Res 47/192 (1992).

173 24 *EPL* (1994) 144.

174 *Supra*, Ch 2, section 5(3). Malta's proposal for a treaty establishing an international agency for this purpose limited it to assuming jurisdiction over the seabed 'as a trustee for all countries': Draft Ocean Space Treaty: Working Paper submitted by Malta, UN Doc AC 138/53, 5 (1973).

175 Compare the 1957 North Pacific Fur Seals Convention, *infra*, section 4(1).

UNCLOS.[176] Nevertheless, the Agreement is in many respects radical in its reform of international fisheries law. It introduces new obligations of sustainable use; requires a precautionary approach to be applied to the conservation and management of stocks and broadens this obligation to include associated ecosystems; seeks to ensure compatibility between EEZ and high seas conservation measures, and places on parties a more extensive obligation of cooperation through regional fisheries bodies, without which they risk losing the right to fish on the high seas. Although the Fish Stocks Agreement is to be interpreted and applied 'in the context of and in a manner consistent with the [1982] Convention' and is without prejudice to the rights, jurisdiction and obligations of parties to the 1982 UNCLOS,[177] in effect it not only amplifies that convention, but amends other regional fisheries treaties covering straddling and highly migratory stocks. Moreover, in accordance with the general rules on interpretation of treaties, the 1995 UN Fish Stocks Agreement can provide guidance on, or confirmation of, the inherently evolutionary meaning of Articles 63 and 116–19 of the 1982 UNCLOS.[178] The fact that it was negotiated and adopted by consensus, including all the major distant water and coastal fishing states, reinforces this conclusion, although not all of these states have subsequently become parties and this may weaken its authority.[179] Of the top 25 maritime fishing states eight remain non-parties, including China, by far the world's biggest fishing state.[180] As we saw in Chapter 1, a treaty cannot realistically be regarded as an agreement on interpretation or as a 'relevant rule applicable in relations between the parties' unless it has the consensus support of all the parties, or there is no objection.[181]

(a) Application of the 1995 Fish Stocks Agreement

The 1995 UN Fish Stocks Agreement as a whole applies only to straddling and highly migratory fish stocks in areas beyond national jurisdiction—i.e. on the high seas.[182]

176 See Anderson, 45 *ICLQ* (1996) 463; Balton, 27 *ODIL* (1996) 125; Freestone and Makuch, 7 *YbIEL* (1996) 3; Davies and Redgwell, 67 *BYIL* (1996) 199; Hayashi, 29 *O&C Man* (1995) 51; Hayashi, in Vidas and Østreng (eds), *Order for the Oceans at the Turn of the Century* (The Hague, 1999) 37; Örebech, Sigurjonsson, and McDorman, 13 *IJMCL* (1998) 119–42. For drafting history see FAO Fisheries Circ 898, *Structure and Process of the UN Conference on Straddling Fish stocks and Highly Migratory Fish Stocks* (Rome, 1995).

177 Article 4. However, a state can be a party to the 1995 Agreement without being party to UNCLOS: in that limited sense it is a 'stand-alone' treaty.

178 See 1969 Vienna Convention on the Law of Treaties, Article 31(3); Freestone, in Boyle and Freestone (eds), *International Law and Sustainable Development*, 160. This argument has not yet surfaced in any of the decided cases.

179 For the reasons see Molenaar, 26 *IJMCL* (2011) 195.

180 See FAO, *Global Capture Production database updated to 2013: Summary information* (Rome, 2013) Table 2. The other seven non-parties are Argentina, Peru, Malaysia, Mexico, Myanmar, Morocco, and Vietnam. In 2012/13 these states and China accounted for 45 per cent of global catches. Few coastal states in West Africa, the Caribbean or Central America have become parties. However, the US, which is not a party to UNCLOS, is a party to the Fish Stocks Agreement.

181 *Supra*, section 2(2). The arguments are reviewed extensively by Pauwelyn, 95 *AJIL* (2001) 535, 575–6; McLachlan, 54 *ICLQ* (2005) 279, 315, para 16, (but note his qualifications at para 17); French, 55 *ICLQ* (2006) 300–7; Boyle, 54 *ICLQ* (2005) 563.

182 Article 3.

Neither the terms 'straddling' nor 'highly migratory' are defined, although most highly migratory species are listed in Annex I of the 1982 Convention. Not all high-seas stocks necessarily fall into one or other of these categories, so the Agreement is not a comprehensive framework for regulating all high seas fisheries. Deep sea fish stocks, for example, are not covered, but following a UN review conference which recommended that they should be, the FAO adopted Guidelines in 2008.[183] These set out recommended governance frameworks intended to ensure conservation and sustainable use. Although the guidelines do not amend the 1995 UN Fish Stocks Agreement they would be relevant to interpretation and application of Articles 117-9 and 194(5) of the 1982 UNCLOS. The key point is that Article 118 of UNCLOS requires states parties to cooperate in the conservation and management of living resources in the high seas—all of them—including discrete stocks and deep-sea species. Thus, although the regime set out in the UN Fish Stocks Agreement would not apply to those two categories, they are not unprotected.

With some limited exceptions, the 1995 UN Fish Stocks Agreement also does not cover stocks which are exclusive to one EEZ or which only straddle other EEZs.[184] However, there are, exceptionally, certain articles which apply to straddling and highly migratory stocks within the EEZ and which thus place some obligations on coastal states with regard to their conservation and management. The essential point is that, within the EEZ, coastal states are required to apply the general principles concerning sustainable use in Article 5, the precautionary approach in Article 6, and to a more limited extent the compatibility provisions of Article 7. These are of course precisely the matters which are most likely to affect fish stocks and other marine species in adjacent EEZs and on the high seas, and to that extent the unity of marine ecosystems is implicitly acknowledged, regardless of boundaries.

In addition to states parties, under Article 1(3) the Agreement applies *mutatis mutandis* to 'other fishing entities whose vessels fish on the high seas'. This novel provision is intended to allow for Taiwanese acceptance of the Agreement, without having to address that country's uncertain international status.[185] It thus addresses for the first time the application of international wildlife conservation agreements to a country whose inability to participate in other treaties such as the 1973 CITES has provided a significant loophole for unregulated trade and fishing. Taiwan ('Chinese Taipei') is now a member of the Pacific fisheries bodies.[186]

[183] 2009 International Guidelines for the Management of Deep-sea Fisheries in the High Seas. See FAO Fisheries and Aquaculture Report No 881, *Report of the Technical Consultation on International Guidelines for the Management of Deep-Sea Fisheries in the High Seas* (Rome, 2008) appendix F. See also UNGA 66/68 (2011) paras 116–165.

[184] UNFSA, Article 3. But see discussion of UNCLOS Article 63(1), *supra*, section 2.

[185] See Edeson, 22 *IJMCL* (2007) 485. However, Taiwan has not yet given its consent to the 'application' of the Fish Stocks Agreement.

[186] 2000 Convention on the Conservation and Management of Highly Migratory Fish Stocks in the Western and Central Pacific Ocean, Annex I; 2003 Antigua Convention for the Strengthening of the Inter-American Tropical Tuna Convention, Article 28; 2009 Convention on the Conservation and Management of High Seas Fishery Resources in the South Pacific Sea, Annex IV; 2012 Convention on the Conservation and Management of High Seas Fisheries Resources in the North Pacific Ocean, Annex.

(b) Conservation, sustainable use and ecosystem protection

Although MSY is reformulated in Articles 61 and 119 of the 1982 UNCLOS in terms which allow for environmental factors and effects on associated or dependent species to be taken into account, conservation measures are still supposed to maximize the allowable catch, having regard, inter alia, to economic considerations and the special needs of developing states. It is far from clear that Article 119 obliges states to fish at sustainable levels.[187] In determining total allowable catches this formulation has proved notoriously open to over-optimistic assessments by fisheries commissions. Not infrequently, scientific advice has been disregarded or uncertainty and inadequate data relied on to justify higher-than-prudent levels of fishing. Some fisheries commissions did not establish conservation measures until the scientific evidence was sufficiently compelling to demonstrate that a stock was under real threat.[188] The Rio Conference recognized that reform was needed.

The 1995 UN Fish Stocks Agreement retains the wording of Article 119, but places 'maximum sustainable yield' within the broader context of a proactive, precautionary, and more environmentally focused approach to conservation and sustainable use.[189] In giving effect to their duty to conserve marine living resources, states are now required by Article 5 to adopt measures designed to ensure 'long-term sustainability........and optimum utilisation' of straddling and highly migratory fish stocks. These include preventing overfishing and removing excess capacity, as well as using more selective, environmentally safe and cost-effective fishing gear. Measures must also be taken to minimize pollution, waste, and catches of other non-target stocks or species. As the chairman of the 1995 conference pointed out: 'the collective interest of the international community must be taken into account if sustainable use of high seas resources was to be secured'.[190] The collective interest in question is the protection and preservation of the marine environment.

Thus, it is not only exploited fish stocks which benefit from the approach outlined in the 1995 UN Fish Stocks Agreement. Recognizing the overriding need for an ecosystem-based approach to fisheries management, the ultimate objectives of Articles 5 and 6 are to protect marine living resources and biological diversity, including non-target stocks and associated and dependent species, and preserve the marine ecosystem in general.[191] There is now an obligation, as there was not under the 1982 UNCLOS,[192]

[187] Freestone, in Boyle and Freestone (eds), *International Law and Sustainable Development*, 146–7.

[188] See e.g, Redgwell's account of the practice of the Commission for the Conservation of Antarctic Marine Living Resources in Boyle and Freestone, op cit, 216.

[189] Articles 5, 6.

[190] Ambassador Satya Nandan, quoted in FAO Fisheries Circular 898, *Structure and Process of the UN Conference etc*, para 4.5.

[191] On ecosystem-based management see FAO, *Fisheries Management: The Ecosystem Approach to Fisheries*, FAO Technical Guidelines for Responsible Fisheries No 4, Suppl 2 (Rome, 2003); Worm et al, 325 *Science* (2009) 578; Diz, *Fisheries Management in Areas Beyond National Jurisdiction* (Leiden, 2013) especially Chs 1, 5 and 6.

[192] Compare 1982 UNCLOS, Article 119(1)(b) which merely requires effects on associated and dependent species to be 'taken into account' when setting a total allowable catch and establishing other conservation measures.

to assess and monitor the impact of fishing on ecosystems, other species and their habitats, and to take and keep under review measures to conserve and protect them. Ecosystem-based management thus looks at cumulative impacts on the marine environment, not simply at the sustainability of the target stock.[193] This is very much in keeping with Article 194(5) of the 1982 UNCLOS, and with the general obligation to protect the marine environment codified in Part XII,[194] but it is the first time it has been spelt out explicitly in a major fisheries agreement. It has been suggested that, as a result, the 1995 UN Fish Stocks Agreement is more important for the protection of marine biological diversity than the 1992 CBD, and that 'sustainability in the Agreement is to be read in ecosystem and biodiversity terms, rather than, as before, in terms of constant food supply.'[195] Most modern regional fisheries agreements reflect this broader environmental perspective.[196]

The FAO uses a variety of soft law instruments to promote implementation of the fisheries conservation provisions of the 1982 UNCLOS and the 1995 UN Fish Stocks Agreement, including the 1995 Code of Conduct on Responsible Fishing,[197] the 2001 Plan of Action on Illegal, Unreported and Unregulated Fishing,[198] the 2003 Guidelines on the Ecosystem Approach to Fisheries,[199] and the 2008 Guidelines for the Management of Deep Sea Fisheries,[200] which also address the protection of vulnerable marine ecosystems from the destruction caused by bottom trawling. The choice of soft law instruments to promote an ecosystem-based approach to fisheries management can partly be explained by the opposition of some states to binding agreements. Another reason, however, is that they are aimed at regional fisheries organizations and the fishing industry as well as states and contain some elements which are unlikely to find their way into treaty form. They are also easier to amend or replace than treaties, requiring simply the adoption of another instrument. Negotiated in the same manner as treaties, and adopted by consensus in the FAO,[201] these non-binding 'voluntary

[193] Diz, *Fisheries Management in Areas Beyond National Jurisdiction*, 4–9.

[194] Freestone, in Boyle and Freestone, *International Law and Sustainable Development*, 148–9, and see *supra*, Ch 9.

[195] Freestone and Makuch, 7 *YbIEL* (1996) 50.

[196] See e.g. 1978 Convention on Cooperation in the Northwest Atlantic Fisheries, as amended 2017, Preambles and Articles II and III; 1980 Northeast Atlantic Fisheries Convention as amended 2006, Preamble and Article 4; 2001 Convention on the Conservation and Management of Fishery Resources in the Southeast Atlantic Ocean, Article III; 2009 Convention on the Conservation and Management of High Seas Fishery Resources in the South Pacific Ocean, Preamble and Articles 2 and 3; 2000 Convention on the Conservation and Management of Highly Migratory Fish Stocks in the Western and Central Pacific Ocean, Preamble and Article 5; 2012 Convention on the Conservation and Management of High Seas Fisheries Resources in the North Pacific Ocean, Preamble and Article 3.

[197] See Edeson, 11 *IJMCL* (1996) 97.

[198] See Edeson, 16 *IJMCL* (2001) 603. See also the International Plans of Action on Longline Fisheries; Conservation and Management of Sharks; and Management of Fishing Capacity, adopted by FAO in 1999.

[199] FAO, *Fisheries Management: The Ecosystem Approach to Fisheries,* FAO Technical Guidelines for Responsible Fisheries No 4, Suppl 2 (Rome, 2003).

[200] See also UNGA 66/68 (2011) paras 116–165, which sets out an agenda for further action by FAO and states parties to protect high seas ecosystems.

[201] However, some states expressed significant reservations when adopting the Plan of Action on IUU Fishing: see FAO, *Rept of the Committee on Fisheries*, 24th Session (2001).

instruments' also seek to promote implementation of elements of the 1995 UN Fish Stocks Agreement by non-parties.

However, regional fisheries organisations carry the main responsibility for adopting measures to 'operationalize' the ecosystem approach to fisheries, which in the view of one FAO official 'is still largely political and conceptual'.[202] The first regional agreement to adopt an ecosystem approach was the 1980 CCAMLR, so the concept is not new, although its application in Antarctic waters has not be easy, and the regime is not an unqualified success.[203] The FAO's technical guidelines encourage states to 'apply an integrated approach to fisheries within ecologically meaningful boundaries', taking into account 'the knowledge and uncertainties about biotic, abiotic and human components of ecosystems and their interactions'.[204] Doing so is a complex task and ecosystem-based management should not be seen as a panacea.[205] Parsons argues that over-exploitation and depletion of stocks 'usually result from failure to apply the scientific advice being given on single species approaches'.[206] He advocates incremental development of existing regimes, building in particular on the experience of 1980 CCAMLR and advice given by ICES and above all, reducing fishing capacity. Most regional fisheries bodies have now adopted measures to protect vulnerable marine ecosystems and assess potential impacts of fishing on the marine environment.[207] They have done less to reduce fishing capacity, although the Fish Stocks Agreement requires parties to do so.[208]

(c) Application of the precautionary approach

Another indication of the 1995 Agreement's environmental perspective is the requirement to apply a precautionary approach to fishing and to the protection of associated ecosystems and species. A precautionary approach may already be implicit in the 1982 UNCLOS,[209] but what this entails is set out explicitly and in some detail by the 1995 UN Fish Stocks Agreement. The moderate version of the precautionary approach incorporated in Article 6 reflects the realization that 'with an imperfect knowledge of fish population and dynamics and an incomplete understanding of socio-economic dynamics', the continued use of maximum sustainable yield as a management target is 'neither efficient nor safe'.[210] In combination with the other measures or agreements

[202] Garcia, in Nordquist et al (eds), *Law, Science and Ocean Management*, 171–216, 173.

[203] For an assessment see Fabra and Gascon, 23 *IJMCL* (2008) 567. See also Howard, 38 *ICLQ* (1989) 135; Redgwell, in, Boyle and Freestone (eds), *International Law and Sustainable Development* (Oxford, 1999) Ch 9; Molenaar, 16 *IJMCL* (2001) 465; Miller, Sabourenkov and Ramm, 19 *IJMCL* (2004) 317.

[204] FAO, *Fisheries Management: The Ecosystem Approach to Fisheries*, 6.

[205] Parsons, 20 *IJMCL* (2005) 381, 419. [206] *Ibid*, 420–1.

[207] *Supra*, n 196 and see Diz, *Fisheries Management in Areas Beyond National Jurisdiction*, 133–157.

[208] Article 5(g). See also 2008 FAO IPOA for the Management of Fishing Capacity.

[209] *Southern Bluefin Tuna Cases*, ITLOS Reports (1999) paras 77–79; *AO on Activities in the Area*, ITLOS Reports (2011) paras 125–35; and *supra*, Ch 9, section 2.

[210] 24 *EPL* (1994) 142. See also Kimball, *Treaty Implementation: Scientific and Technical Advice Enters a New Stage* (Washington DC, 1996).

referred to above, it seeks sustainability through improving data collection and techniques for dealing with risk and scientific uncertainty. These include setting 'precautionary reference points' for specific fish stocks, enhanced monitoring, and broadening the range of factors to be taken into account.

Reference points identify the safe biological limit for harvesting, and other relevant constraints.[211] They are to be determined in advance of using the best scientific information available, but uncertainties are also to be taken into account and the absence of adequate information 'shall not be used as a reason for postponing or failing to take conservation and management measures'. In the case of a new fishery, 'cautious conservation and management measures' are to be adopted until there is enough data to permit assessment of the impact on long-term sustainability.[212] Thus the importance of the precautionary approach is that states are no longer free to ignore conservation until a stock is shown to be under stress. As Freestone points out, 'This represents a major change in the traditional approach of fisheries management which until recently has tended to be reactive to management problems only after they arrived at crisis levels.'[213] Timely action must therefore be taken to ensure that precautionary reference points are not exceeded; if stocks are under threat, conservation and management measures must be reviewed. However, in such cases nothing in the Agreement expressly requires a halt to fishing or a moratorium; as we saw above, the parties rejected the automatic application of such outcomes. This does not mean that fishing of depleted stocks can lawfully continue, merely that what response is appropriate will depend on the circumstances and will be determined by the relevant regional fisheries body.[214]

As we saw in Chapter 3, requiring states to apply a precautionary approach does not of itself determine what measures must be adopted: it merely helps determine when action is necessary. The approach taken in the IWC and in the UN's driftnet resolutions has already been noted. There the onus of proving by scientific evidence that resumption of hunting or fishing will not be environmentally harmful is shifted to the proponents, although in the IWC the burden of formulating an appropriate procedure is delegated to the Scientific Committee. The 1994 Bering Sea Pollock Convention expressly prohibits fishing unless the parties determine that the total biomass of pollock exceeds a stipulated level; only if a stock is above that level can a total allowable catch be set.[215] In effect this agreement specifies a precautionary reference limit in the treaty, and compels a fishing moratorium when that limit is exceeded, whereas the 1995 UN Fish Stocks Agreement leaves parties to negotiate such limits, and the consequences of

211 See Annex II of the 1995 Agreement, and FAO Fisheries Circular 864, *Reference Points for Fisheries Management: Their Potential Application to Straddling and Highly Migratory Resources* (Rome, 1993).

212 Article 6(6).

213 Boyle and Freestone (eds), *International Law and Sustainable Development*, 160.

214 Freestone and Makuch, 7 *YbIEL* (1996) 3, 28; Nelson, in Boyle and Freestone (eds), *International Law and Sustainable Development*, 129.

215 Convention on Conservation and Management of Pollock Resources in the Central Bering Sea. See Balton, in Stokke (ed), *Governing High Seas Fisheries*, 143; Dunlop, 10 *IJMCL* (1995) 114ff.

exceeding them.[216] Since the 1995 Agreement is essentially a framework for the negotiation of regional agreements covering very diverse fisheries, its less robust approach to precautionary measures is understandable. Nevertheless, it does create a presumption in favour of conservation and long-term sustainability,[217] and the parties must apply it accordingly.

(d) Cooperation through regional fisheries bodies

The establishment of regional fisheries commissions, and the gradual enlargement of their powers, was a seminal development in the conservation and sustainable use of ocean fish stocks.[218] As we saw in Chapter 9 they are an important contribution to implementing the 1982 UNCLOS and giving effect to Chapter 17 of Agenda 21 and the 2015 SDGs. Sustainable fisheries management cannot progress without an appropriate scientific basis; the law must respond both to new scientific research and data, and also take account of relevant economic, social, and political factors. Regional fisheries commissions provide the forum in which the necessary negotiations and decisions can take place.[219] Fisheries commissions usually meet annually to set new quotas and revise or adopt other conservation measures. Typically, the more detailed conservation regulations found in annexes or appendices to the older fisheries agreements were amendable by a two-thirds or three-quarters majority without the need for further ratification. This system provided a means of adapting fisheries conventions to changing scientific advice, but its fundamental weakness was that any state could opt out of regulations adopted in this manner.[220] Use of the objections procedure could destroy the ability of such bodies to take effective measures.[221] This element of the system was long overdue for reform.

Beyond requiring states to cooperate in the conservation and management of fish stocks,[222] the 1982 UNCLOS did little to rectify the shortcomings of regional fisheries cooperation; nor, until the adoption of the 1995 UN Fish Stocks Agreement, did the FAO. Underlying the 1995 UN Fish Stocks Agreement, however, is a recognition that

216 Starting in 1991, precautionary limits for toothfish and krill have been agreed by the Commission for Antarctic Marine Living Resources, but Redgwell, in Boyle and Freestone (eds), *International Law and Sustainable Development*, 217, points out the serious difficulty in doing so when there is little data on stocks or their interaction with other species. See also Herr, in Stokke (ed), *Governing High Seas Fisheries*, 304.

217 Boyle and Freestone (eds), *International Law and Sustainable Development*, 158.

218 See Koers, *The International Regulation of Marine Fisheries* (London, 1973); Knight (ed), *The Future of International Fisheries Management* (St Paul, 1975); Hey, *The Regime for the Exploitation of Transboundary Marine Fishery Resources* (Dordrecht, 1989) 133–274; Stokke (ed), *Governing High Seas Fisheries* (Oxford, 2001); Kaye, *International Fisheries Management* (The Hague, 2001); Henriksen, Hønneland, Sydnes, *Law and Politics in Ocean Governance: The UN Fish Stocks Agreement and Regional Fisheries Management Regimes* (Leiden, 2006); Diz, *Fisheries Management in Areas Beyond National Jurisdiction* (Leiden, 2013) Ch 5.

219 For an overview see Guggisberg, *The Use of CITES for Commercially Exploited Fish Species*, 59–75.

220 *Supra*, Ch 4, section 3.

221 See generally Koers, *The International Regulation of Marine Fisheries*. The Canada–Spain dispute over turbot caused by the inability of the North-west Atlantic Fisheries Commission to control Spanish overfishing provides a good example of this problem. See Davies and Redgwell, 67 *BYIL* (1996) 199–217; Joyner and von Gustedt, 11 *IJMCL* (1996) 425.

222 Articles 61(2), 63–5, 66(4), 118.

its objectives can only be achieved through improved regional cooperation between coastal and distant-water fishing states, addressing the historic problems identified above. Like the 1982 UNCLOS, Article 8 spells out the duty of all states fishing on the high seas to cooperate in order to 'ensure effective conservation and management of such stocks'. They can do so directly, or through regional fisheries management organizations (RFMOs), which must if necessary be created. Unlike the 1982 UNCLOS, the 1995 UN Fish Stocks Agreement lays down detailed provisions on the functions of these bodies.[223] Inter alia, Article 10 rather bluntly requires RFMO members to:

agree on and comply with conservation and management measures to ensure the long-term sustainability of straddling fish stocks and highly migratory fish stocks

adopt and apply any generally recommended international minimum standards for the responsible conduct of fishing operations

obtain and evaluate scientific advice, review the status of the stocks and assess the impact of fishing on non-target and associated or dependent species

establish appropriate cooperative mechanisms for effective monitoring, control, surveillance, and enforcement

agree on decision-making procedures which facilitate the adoption of conservation and management measures in a timely and effective manner.

These provisions represent a bold attempt to put some serious content into fishery conservation agreements and to compel member states to adopt and comply with the necessary measures. Compliance is obligatory: arguably, even a state party which opts out of RFMO conservation measures in such a way as to defeat their purpose will not be compliant with Article 10, and the continued use of such opt-outs may itself fail to meet the required standard of timely and effective decision-making. The revised decision-making procedures found in modern fisheries agreements favour consensus decision-making, and allow opt-outs only in limited circumstances, subject to a formal review process.[224] But this process also has problems: the result, according to the FAO, is that 'decision-making is slow, and final binding decisions are often diluted to satisfy the lowest common denominator.'[225]

However, if RFMOs cannot do the job, it seems possible within the terms of Article 10 for 'generally recommended international minimum standards' to be adopted by intergovernmental organizations, including the FAO, the 1992 CBD, and the UN General Assembly,[226] opening up the possibility of these bodies in effect legislating for RFMO member states in the same way that IMO resolutions or IAEA Codes may become binding under Part XII of the 1982 UNCLOS or the 1994 Nuclear

[223] UNFSA, Articles 8–12. See generally *supra*, Ch 2, section 5(2) and Lodge and Nandan, 20 *IJMCL* (2005) 345; Molenaar, ibid, 533; Henriksen, Hönneland and Sydnes (eds), *Law and Politics in Ocean Governance: The UN Fish Stocks Agreement and Regional Fisheries Management Regimes* (Leiden, 2006).

[224] See e.g. 1978 NAFO Convention, as amended 2017, Articles 13–14; 2000 Western and Central Pacific Fisheries Convention, Article 20; 2012 North Pacific Fisheries Convention, Article 9; Diz, *Fisheries Management in Areas Beyond National Jurisdiction*, 127–33. For a comprehensive analysis of alternative approaches to decision-making under Article 10 see McDorman, 20 *IJMCL* (2005) 423.

[225] FAO, *State of the World's Fisheries* (2016) 95.

[226] Lodge and Nandan, 20 *IJMCL* (2005) 365–72.

Safety Convention.[227] This is particularly relevant to the FAO's Code of Conduct on Responsible Fishing,[228] its other guidelines and plans of action,[229] and UN General Assembly resolutions on driftnets.[230] It also provides a possible basis on which the FAO or the 1992 CBD could recommend the creation of high seas protected areas where fishing is banned or severely restricted, or impose a moratorium on certain kinds of fishing, in cases where regional fisheries organisations have failed on their own initiative to take the necessary action. It would still be for the RFMO to 'adopt and apply' whatever the FAO or the 1992 CBD had recommended but a failure to do so would risk being in breach of Article 10.

Article 12 adds the important rider that 'States shall provide for transparency' in the decision-making processes and activities of regional fisheries bodies. It goes on to give NGOs and intergovernmental organizations 'concerned with' straddling or migratory fish stocks a right to participate in meetings and to have timely access to reports and records—an attempt to move fisheries agreements beyond the closed-door world in which some have operated.[231] With a view to updating and amendment, Article 13 requires states to cooperate to strengthen existing subregional and regional fisheries management organizations and arrangements in order to improve their effectiveness.

Where there is an appropriate regional body, states fishing for high seas stocks and relevant coastal states 'shall give effect to their duty to cooperate by becoming members of such organization', or by agreeing to apply its rules.[232] This is a significant strengthening of the 1982 UNCLOS Articles 63, 64, and 118. Failure to do so will entail loss of the right to engage in the high seas fishery,[233] another significant change in the 1982 UNCLOS position. States with a 'real interest' in the fishery have a right to membership on non-discriminatory terms,[234] and new participants can expect to be treated in accordance with factors set out in Article 11, but this does not guarantee them a quota. One problem with these attempts to control or deny access is that they may lead to an increase in IUU fishing. In theory non-parties to the 1995 UN Fish Stocks Agreement are bound by none of these provisions, although states parties have committed themselves to taking measures to deter non-party vessels from undermining the effective implementation of the Agreement.[235] This is likely to involve denial of port access,[236] or of access to EEZ fishing. However, the more important risk that non-parties face is that eventually the 1995 UN Fish Stocks Agreement will come to be regarded as establishing new rules of access to high seas fishing that are no longer based on high-seas freedoms. Once that occurs they will lose altogether the right to fish except in accordance with regional agreements and their vessels might be apprehended if they

[227] *Supra*, Ch 1. Contrast UNCLOS Article 119(1)(a) under which generally recommended international minimum standards need only be taken 'into account'. See generally Korseberg, 67 *ICLQ* (2018) 801.

[228] The 2001 Reykjavik Declaration on Responsible Fisheries is also relevant.

[229] *Supra*, nn 198–200.

[230] *Supra*, n 117.

[231] On transparency see *supra*, Ch 2, section 5(2).

[232] Article 8(3).

[233] Article 8(4).

[234] Article 8(3). See Molenaar, 15 *IJMCL* (2000) 475; *id*, 18 *IJMCL* (2003) 457.

[235] Article 33.

[236] As required by the 2009 FAO Agreement on Port State Measures.

attempt to do so. At that point a new conception of common property on the high seas will finally have emerged.[237]

Since the entry into force of the 1995 UN Fish Stocks Agreement new regional fisheries agreements have been negotiated and most of the older ones have been renegotiated to ensure consistency with the Agreement.[238] There are now very few gaps in their geographical coverage left. Most tuna stocks,[239] together with salmon and certain other high seas fish stocks,[240] are subject to species-specific regional agreements, although as we have seen some of these are inadequate. Further agreements are still needed for the South China Sea and Southwest Atlantic, where there are territorial disputes, and for certain species, including swordfish stocks in the South-eastern Pacific, where Chile and the EU have been in dispute over an access and conservation regime.

Some flag-of-convenience fishing states remain outside applicable regional agreements and the 1995 UN Fish Stocks Agreement.[241] Their vessels will continue to fish unregulated until either access to ports or a market for their fish can be denied,[242] or the 1982 UNCLOS itself can be reinterpreted in accordance with the Fish Stocks Agreement to allow arrest for illegal fishing on the high seas. In this respect it is worth recalling that high seas fishery disputes (and the 1995 UN Fish Stocks Agreement) are subject to compulsory dispute settlement in accordance with Part XV of the 1982 UNCLOS.[243] Since nearly all states are 1982 UNCLOS parties, they can thus be held to account for overfishing or ecosystem destruction on that basis, in a way that coastal states cannot.[244] Protection of the marine environment is an *erga omnes partes* obligation, so any 1982 UNCLOS party would be entitled to initiate proceedings, whether or not they have a 'real interest' in the fishery.[245] However, the 1995 UN Fish Stocks Agreement makes no provision for any form of non-confrontational non-compliance procedure comparable to other MEAs.

While the 1995 UN Fish Stocks Agreement has undoubtedly promoted changes to the architecture of some regional agreements, there remains considerable room for improving accountability mechanisms,[246] since states are understandably reluctant to address the mismanagement of high seas living resources by regional fisheries

[237] See Örebech et al, 13 *IJMCL* (1998) 119.

[238] See those listed *supra*, n 196, and 1949 Agreement for the Establishment of a General Fisheries Council for the Mediterranean, as amended 1997; 1980 Convention on Conservation of Antarctic Marine Living Resources; 1994 Convention on the Conservation and Management of Pollock Resources in the Central Bering Sea; 2006 Southern Indian Ocean Fisheries Agreement. For a review of some of them see Bowman et al, *International Wildlife Law*, 132–48.

[239] *Supra*, section 2(3).

[240] E.g. Pacific halibut, Bering Sea pollock. See Meltzer, 20 *IJMCL* (2005) 571–604.

[241] E.g. Honduras, Equatorial Guinea and Vanuatu. But Cyprus, Liberia, Panama and St Vincent are parties to the Fish Stocks Agreement. These seven are the main FOC states.

[242] But see 2009 FAO Agreement on Port State Measures, *infra*, section (f).

[243] *Supra*, Ch 4, section 4(5). [244] UNCLOS Article 297(3).

[245] *South China Sea Arbitration*, PCA (2016) and *supra*, Ch 4, section 2.

[246] Gjerde, in Freestone, Barnes and Ong (eds), *The Law of the Sea*, 298–301; Lodge and Nandan, 20 *IJMCL* (2005) 357–9.

organisations in adversarial judicial processes.[247] The problems exhibited by ICCAT and some of the other tuna commissions illustrate that there is still some way to go before governance structures for all fish stocks meet the objectives of the 1982 UNCLOS, the 1995 UN Fish Stocks Agreement, and the UN's sustainable development goals.[248]

(e) Compatibility of EEZ and high seas conservation measures

Article 63(2) of the 1982 UNCLOS merely provides that coastal states and those whose vessels fish straddling stocks in adjacent high seas areas[249] shall seek agreement on conservation measures for those high seas areas.[250] Article 64 similarly requires cooperation on the conservation of highly migratory stocks in the EEZ and on the high seas. One of the principal purposes of the 1995 UN Fish Stocks Agreement is to 'ensure that the measures taken for conservation and management in the EEZs and in the adjacent high seas areas are compatible and coherent, in order to take into account the biological unity of the stocks and the supporting ecosystem'.[251] Article 7 thus amplifies Articles 63 and 64 of the 1982 UNCLOS by requiring these states to cooperate to ensure compatibility between the measures adopted for high seas areas and those for areas under national jurisdiction. The article lists various matters to be taken into account in determining compatibility, including the measures adopted by coastal states within their EEZ, the biological unity of the stocks, and the impact on other marine living resources. States whose vessels fish the adjacent high seas are required to ensure that measures they take do not undermine the effectiveness of coastal-state conservation and management measures within the EEZ.[252] Pointedly, Article 7 does *not* say that measures applied in the EEZ and on the high seas should be the same.

The objective of this article is obvious, but it is less clear what happens if the parties cannot agree on compatible measures for the high seas. The 1995 UN Fish Stocks Agreement says only that any of the states concerned may invoke dispute settlement procedures, which include seeking provisional measures and special arbitration by fisheries experts.[253] However, while this may allow an independent tribunal to determine the question and indicate compatible measures if asked to do so,[254] it should be appreciated that not all disputes relating to straddling or highly migratory stocks will

247 FAO does however have a process for reviewing RFMOs, and some RFMOs make provision for dispute settlement: see 2009 Convention on the Conservation and Management of High Seas Fishery Resources in the South Pacific Ocean, Article 17, and Guggisberg, *The Use of CITES* etc, 169–73.

248 For earlier reviews of the UNFSA see reports of the 1st and 2nd Review Conferences, UN Doc A/CONF.210/2006/15 (2006) and A/CONF.210/2010/7 (2010).

249 See Diz, *Fisheries Management in Areas Beyond National Jurisdiction*, Ch 4.

250 But not for the EEZ. The coastal state alone determines these, and its determination cannot be challenged, except in non-binding conciliation: see 1982 UNCLOS, Article 297(3); 1995 UNFSA, Article 32.

251 FAO Fisheries Circular 898, para 4.4, at 15.

252 Article 7(2)(a).

253 Article 7(4)–(5). On settlement of disputes see Articles 27–32, and *supra*, Ch 4, section 4.

254 Provisional measures were sought successfully in the *Southern Bluefin Tuna Cases* (1999) ITLOS Nos 3 and 4. See various authors in 10 *YbIEL* (1999) and Kwiatkowska, 15 *IJMCL* (2000) 1.

necessarily be subject to compulsory jurisdiction.[255] Failing agreement or a third-party determination, can the coastal state unilaterally insist on the non-discriminatory application of its own conservation measures to straddling or highly migratory stocks in adjacent high seas areas? Coastal states did have such a power under Article 7 of the 1958 Geneva Convention on Fisheries Conservation, but there is no comparable article in the 1982 UNCLOS or the 1995 Fish Stocks Agreement, although some authors have argued that Article 116 (b) of the 1982 UNCLOS gives such a priority to the special interests of coastal states.[256] Even if this is correct, coastal states have no power to enforce their own conservation laws by arresting and prosecuting foreign fishing vessels on the high seas, but a number of coastal states have sought to do so indirectly by denying such vessels access to ports. For distant-water fishing vessels this can cause serious supply problems, and it is no idle threat. Arguably, unilateral action of this kind is a violation of the GATT Agreement,[257] provided that the distant-water states have shown their willingness to negotiate in good faith,[258] but this does not solve the problem if the parties still cannot agree and no dispute settlement forum has jurisdiction. This omission remains one of the major uncertainties left over from the 1995 negotiations.

(f) Illegal, unreported and unregulated fishing ('IUU fishing')

Illegal, unreported and unregulated fishing remains one of the biggest challenges to the current legal regime for conservation and sustainable management of ocean fish stocks, whether within the EEZs of coastal states, or on the high seas.[259] Within the EEZ Article 73 provides coastal states with the power to board, inspect, arrest and confiscate vessels where necessary and reasonable to do so in order to enforce compliance with their laws on conservation and exploitation of living resources,[260] but there is no comparable article allowing coastal states to arrest fishing vessels on the high seas, except in cases of hot pursuit from an EEZ.[261]

One of the most important objectives of post-UNCED fisheries law reform has been to improve compliance by fishing vessels. The 2015 ITLOS *Advisory Opinion* emphasised the obligation of flag states to regulate their fishing vessels wherever they fished: 'The flag State is under the "due diligence obligation" to take all necessary measures

[255] See *Southern Bluefin Tuna Arbitration*, ICSID (2000); Boyle, 14 *IJMCL* (1999) 1; Churchill, 22 *IJMCL* (2007) 383. But *Bluefin Tuna* was not followed in the *South China Sea Arbitration (Jurisdiction)*, PCA (2015).

[256] Miles and Burke, 20 *ODIL* (1989) 343, 352. See also Orrego Vicuna, 55 *ZAÖRV* (1995) 520.

[257] On freedom of transit through ports see 1947 GATT, Article V. In 2000 the European Community and Chile initiated parallel proceedings before the WTO and ITLOS after failing to agree on measures to protect straddling swordfish stocks. The cases were eventually settled and withdrawn.

[258] On unilateral action see WTO Appellate Body, *US Import Prohibition of Shrimp and Certain Shrimp Products* ['*Shrimp-Turtle Case*'] 37 *ILM* (1998) 832, *infra*, Ch 13.

[259] See generally FAO Fisheries and Aquaculture Report No. 1106, *Report of the Expert Workshop to Estimate the Magnitude of Illegal, Unreported and Unregulated Fishing Globally* (Rome, 2015).

[260] As interpreted by ITLOS in the *Tomimaru Case*, ITLOS Reports (2007) paras 75–6) and the *Virginia G Case*, ITLOS Reports (2014) paras 252–271.

[261] See UNCLOS Article 111.

to ensure compliance and to prevent IUU fishing by fishing vessels flying its flag.'[262] In the Tribunal's view this required a prohibition of fishing unless authorized, and measures to ensure compliance with conservation and management measures, including investigation, prosecution, with sanctions sufficient to deter violations and deprive offenders of benefits of IUU fishing.[263] On this view of the law, the mere fact that a vessel is fishing illegally does not demonstrate that the flag state is at fault, but a fortiori if it facilitates and protects vessels fishing illegally it will necessarily be in breach of its legal obligations. In the *South China Sea Arbitration* China was found to have violated UNCLOS Article 58(3) when its fisheries enforcement vessels knowingly allowed Chinese vessels to fish illegally in Philippine waters.[264] As this case illustrates, relying on flag state enforcement has not been effective at controlling illegal fishing. Nor have mutual observer schemes.[265] Moreover, flag states do not usually send patrol vessels to accompany their fishing fleets, and fishing vessels have found it easy to evade flag-state control by the simple expedient of re-flagging when necessary, usually to states not party to the relevant regional fisheries agreement.[266] Much of the high seas, especially in the southern hemisphere, is effectively unpoliced. Cooperation thus remains essential for effective law enforcement. Litigation is also an option, however, where the flag state refuses to cooperate or is failing in its duty of due diligence: the *South China Sea Case* shows that such disputes fall within the 1982 UNCLOS Part XV compulsory jurisdiction.[267]

The 1995 UN Fish Stocks Agreement is one of several global and regional treaties creating a stronger enforcement and compliance regime for high seas fishing.[268] The regime has three elements.

First, flag-state regulatory and enforcement responsibility is reiterated in more specific terms in the 1995 UN Fish Stocks Agreement,[269] the FAO Compliance Agreement,[270] the 2001 FAO Plan of Action on IUU Fishing, the 2009 Agreement on Port State Measures,[271] and the 2014 FAO Voluntary Guidelines for Flag State Performance.[272] *Inter alia*, vessels must be licensed and their catches monitored; high-seas fishing must be regulated and violations investigated, prosecuted, and sanctioned effectively. It remains primarily the duty of the flag state to ensure that vessels flying

262 *AO on Fisheries*, ITLOS Reports (2015) paras 124 and 129. See also 1993 FAO Compliance Agreement, Article 3.

263 *AO on Fisheries*, paras 134–9.

264 *South China Sea Arbitration*, PCA (2016) paras 735–57.

265 See e.g. 1980 Convention on the Conservation of Antarctic Marine Living Resources, Article 24.

266 See Birnie, 2 *RECIEL* (1993) 270.

267 *South China Sea Arbitration (Jurisdiction)*, PCA (2015).

268 For innovative provisions in regional treaties, see 1992 Convention for the Conservation of Anadromous Stocks in the North Pacific, Article 5; 1994 Convention on the Conservation and Management of Pollock Resources of the Bering Sea, Article 11; 1992 Niue Treaty on Cooperation on Fisheries Surveillance and Law Enforcement in the South Pacific, Articles 4–6. See generally, Moore, 24 *ODIL* (1993) 197; Edeson, in Boyle and Freestone (eds), *International Law and Sustainable Development*, Ch 8; Joyner, in Hey (ed), *Developments in International Fisheries Law*, Ch 12; Rayfuse, 20 *IJMCL* (2005) 509.

269 Articles 18–19.

270 Articles III-IV. See Birnie, 2 *RECIEL* (1993) 245; Edeson, in, Boyle and Freestone (eds), *International Law and Sustainable Development*, Ch 8.

271 Article 20.

272 See K Erikstein and J Swan, 29 *IJMCL* (2014) 116.

its flag comply with conservation and management measures adopted by regional fisheries organizations and coastal states and it should not authorize vessels to fish if it cannot control them effectively. These provisions are designed not only to strengthen flag state control but also to deter evasive re-flagging of vessels. They essentially amplify and interpret the relevant 1982 UNCLOS articles; as we saw above, the *ITLOS Advisory Opinion* reiterates the same points.

Secondly, port states may take non-discriminatory measures to promote the effectiveness of international conservation and management measures.[273] In the 1995 UN Fish Stocks Agreement this includes a power to inspect vessels in port and to prohibit landing or transhipment of illegally caught stock. If the port state does not prosecute the vessel, it can report its findings to the flag state, which then has a duty to investigate and take action.[274] These powers do not in reality depend on the 1995 UN Fish Stocks Agreement, which merely codifies them. They exist as a matter of customary law by virtue of the port state's sovereignty over its ports and are exercisable by any port state.[275] In 2009 the FAO also adopted an Agreement on Port State Measures.[276] The principal purpose of this measure is to deny illegally caught fish access to world markets. Parties must refuse port entry or access to port services, including landing and transshipment of fish, to foreign-flagged vessels known to have engaged in IUU fishing. Port state control has the obvious merit that it can be applied effectively by states that lack the means to patrol their EEZs or arrest illegal fishing boats at sea. At the same time, it will work only if all the ports in a region are participating,[277] and if WTO rules on access to ports, or applicable regional and bilateral trade agreements, are overridden.[278]

Thirdly, in high seas areas covered by a regional or subregional fisheries organization, inspectors from any member state may board and inspect where there are 'clear grounds' for believing that a fishing vessel has engaged in illegal fishing.[279] The findings are then reported to the flag state. If the flag state does not respond and the violation is serious, for example where the vessel is unlicensed or operating under a false identity, has no catch records, is caught fishing in a closed area, taking prohibited stocks, or using prohibited gear, it may be arrested and brought into port for further enquiry and prosecution by or with the agreement of the flag state.[280]

The power to board and detain is hedged about with extensive safeguards, both to prevent abuse or the use of excessive force, and to protect the position of the flag state.[281] The flag state may at any point require the vessel to be released into its custody and take further proceedings itself.[282] There are also prompt release procedures and limitations on the penalties for arrests within the EEZ,[283] but these do not apply to

[273] UNFSA, Article 23; Compliance Agreement, Article V. See Anderson, in Boyle and Freestone (eds), *International Law and Sustainable Development*, Ch 14; Molenaar, 38 *ODIL* (2007) 225.

[274] UNFSA, Article 19. [275] *Supra*, Ch 9. [276] *Supra*, n 157.

[277] Compare the port state inspection schemes for marine pollution, *supra*, Ch 9, section 5.

[278] See *infra*, Ch 13. [279] UNFSA, Article 21. See Hayashi, 9 *Georgetown IELR* (1996) 1.

[280] UNFSA, Article 21(8)–(11). [281] UNFSA, Article 22. [282] UNFSA, Article 21(12)–(13).

[283] UNCLOS Articles 73(2)–(3) 292. See also *MV Saiga* (1997/9) ITLOS Nos 1 and 2; Mensah, 22 *IJMCL* (2007) 425; Rothwell, 53 *ICLQ* (2004) 171.

high seas arrests.[284] Concerns about high seas arrests may have deterred some states from ratifying the 1995 UN Fish Stocks Agreement. Nevertheless, the Agreement expands significantly the enforcement powers available to members of regional fisheries bodies, and facilitates greater cooperation in this respect between flag, coastal, and port states. For the first time, fishing vessels are no longer immune from non-flag state inspection and arrest on the high seas, and the introduction of compulsory vessel monitoring systems[285] has improved the potential for enforcement through satellite surveillance. Their need for access to ports provides a further instrument of control and supervision of illegal fishing.

4 MARINE MAMMALS

4(1) LEGAL STATUS OF MARINE MAMMALS

Marine mammals were among the first marine species to be regulated by international agreements and international law. Indeed, the first arbitral or judicial decision on any environmental problem is the seminal *Behring Sea Fur Seals Arbitration*.[286] This award helps to understand how modern international law deals with conservation of living resources which are found on the high seas, in coastal waters, and on land. The US contended that because the fur seals lived and gave birth on US territory it had an exclusive right to regulate their conservation and exploitation at sea. It regarded itself as the trustee of the seal herd for the benefit of mankind. Britain (for Canada) argued that seals on the high seas were either *res communis* or *res nullius*, but not the exclusive property of the US. The US countered that the high seas were 'free only for innocent and inoffensive use, not injurious to the just interests of any nation which borders upon it', and that the seals had an *animus revertendi*, returning cyclically to US territory, and should thus be equated to domestic animals, which could be the subject of property rights.[287] The arbitral tribunal rejected the US arguments. It held that neither Russia nor its successor (the US) exercised exclusive rights in the Behring Sea beyond areas of national jurisdiction. Thus, the US had no property rights in the seals, and no right to protect them beyond the three-mile territorial sea limit.[288] Freedom of the high seas was held to be the prevailing doctrine.

The importance of this decision to the development of the law concerning conservation of marine living resources cannot be overstressed. It laid the twin foundations for subsequent developments over the next century. First, it confirmed that high seas freedom of fishing applied to marine mammals, and that no distinction was to be

284 Churchill, 22 *IJMCL* (2007) 402–5.

285 UNFSA, Article 18(3)(g) and Annex 1.

286 Moore, *Int Arb Awards*, I (1898) 811. Reproduced in 1 *IELR* (2000) 43.

287 *Ibid*, 812, 839, 883–4.

288 The 12-mile territorial sea and the 200-mile EEZ were not established until the 1982 UNCLOS was adopted and in force.

made in this respect between fisheries and marine mammals despite their very different characteristics. Secondly, it recognized the need for conservation to prevent over-exploitation and decline of a hunted species, but because of the former finding, it made this dependent on the express acceptance of regulation by participants in the fishery.

The two parties in the case had asked the tribunal, if it found against the US, to recommend the required conservation regulations. Its nine-point plan for conservation provides a model for fishery commissions to this day: a prohibited zone; a closed season in a defined area of the high seas, with specific exceptions for indigenous peoples as long as they hunted for traditional purposes, using traditional methods; a limitation on the type of vessels used; a licensing system to be operated by the governments concerned; the keeping of catch records; exchange of data; governmental responsibility for regulation of crews. Moreover, the tribunal went on to recommend that these regulations be enacted into uniform national laws in *both* states and that national measures be adopted to ensure their enforcement. Finally, a three-year ban on all sealing was recommended, the foundation of the moratorium approach to conservation of marine mammals.

Thus, although it perpetuated high seas freedom of fishing and hence made conservation and enforcement more difficult, the *Behring Sea* arbitral tribunal strongly supported the need for restraint in exploitation, clearly indicated the requisite measures, and recognized that freedom of the seas was not absolute but had to take reasonable account of the interests of other states and the needs of conservation. In these respects, the award is similar to the ICJ's judgments in the *Icelandic Fisheries Cases* some seventy-five years later.[289] The decision failed in the short term because it could be addressed to only two of the four states engaged in hunting the Behring Sea fur seals; Russia and Japan were not involved in the arbitration. US and Canadian vessel owners re-registered under Japanese and other flags to evade the US and Canadian regulations. The decline in seal stocks continued until 1911, when a regulatory treaty between all four states involved in sealing was adopted. The Convention on Behring Sea Fur Seals as revised in 1957 was innovative in several respects, including a ban on pelagic (high seas) sealing, provision for high seas enforcement by any party, and a sharing of the income among all four parties to compensate Canada and Japan for giving up the right of pelagic sealing on the high seas.[290] Only the USSR and US were permitted to continue sealing on land. This separation of the right to exploit a resource from the right to share in the proceeds is arguably the most advanced example of equitable utilization to be found in any wildlife or fisheries convention, and for many years it provided an effective control on over-exploitation. Today Behring Sea fur seals are protected by the 1973 CITES,[291] and by the extension of coastal state jurisdiction to 200 miles, but the basic principles outlined in 1893 continue to inform the law on marine mammals.[292]

289 *Supra* n 23.

290 The 1911 Convention on Behring Sea Fur Seals was replaced in 1957 by the Interim Convention on North Pacific Fur Seals, since terminated. See Lyster, *International Wildlife Law* (1st edn, Cambridge, 1993) 40–9.

291 Listed on Appendix II.

292 See also 1972 Convention for the Conservation of Antarctic Seals.

4(2) UNCLOS AND MARINE MAMMALS

In addition to seals, the category of marine mammals includes the twelve species of great whales, many of which were previously hunted to near extinction, as well as small cetaceans (walruses, dolphins, porpoises, dugongs, manatees) and sea otters. Some of these species are listed in the 1982 UNCLOS as highly migratory and are thus covered by Article 64.[293] However, Articles 65 and 120 allow for stricter protection of marine mammals in the EEZ and on the high seas than is required by Articles 61 and 119.[294] Article 65 provides that:

> Nothing in this Convention restricts the right of a coastal state or international organization, as appropriate, to prohibit, limit or regulate the exploitation of marine mammals more strictly than provided for in this Part. States shall co-operate with a view to the conservation of marine mammals and in the case of cetaceans shall in particular work through the appropriate international organization for their conservation, management and study.

Articles 65 and 120 (which applies Article 65 to the high seas) thus remove all marine mammals from the requirement of optimum utilization that applies to fish stocks; states can prohibit all taking unilaterally or through international organizations if they wish. Most whale species are listed on Appendix I of the 1973 CITES, which prevents all trade; the others are listed on Annex II.[295] At the same time, Articles 65 and 120 do not prohibit the taking of marine mammals or whaling, nor does the 1946 ICRW, the principal treaty under which states cooperate in the management of the marine mammals pursuant to Articles 65 and 120.[296] Non-parties to the 1946 ICRW are thus free to engage in sustainable commercial whaling provided they comply with Articles 61, 65, and 194(5) of the 1982 UNCLOS, and with the 1973 CITES, if applicable.

4(3) 1946 INTERNATIONAL CONVENTION FOR THE REGULATION OF WHALING

Adopted for the purpose of restoring depleted stocks of twelve great whale species to a level that would permit commercial hunting[297], the 1946 ICRW has steadily evolved into an anti-whaling regime because most of its members now oppose commercial

293 See UNCLOS Annex I.

294 For the negotiating history of Articles 65 and 120 see Birnie, in Freestone, Barnes and Ong (eds), *The Law of the Sea*, Ch 14. See generally Jefferies, *Marine Mammal Conservation and the Law of the Sea* (Oxford, 2016).

295 Japan, Norway, Iceland and Palau have made reservations to the listing of some whale species under CITES and are thus free to allow hunting.

296 See also 1990 Bonn Agreement on the Conservation of Seals in the Wadden Sea; 1992 Agreement on Research, Conservation and Management of Marine Mammals in the North Atlantic; 1992 New York Agreement on Conservation of Small Cetaceans of the Baltic and North Seas; 1996 Agreement on Conservation of Cetaceans of the Black Sea, Mediterranean Sea and Contiguous Atlantic Areas; Churchill, in Boyle and Freestone (eds), *International Law and Sustainable Development*, Ch 10.

297 See Birnie, *International Regulation of Whaling*, 2 vols (Dobbs Ferry, 1985); *id*, in Hey (ed), *Developments in International Fisheries Law*, Ch 13; *id*, 12 *IJMCL* (1997) 307, 488; Burke, *The New International Law of Fisheries*, Ch 6; D'Amato and Chopra, 85 *AJIL* (1991) 21; Maffei, 12 *IJMCL* (1997) 287; Bowman et al, *International Wildlife Law*, Ch 6; Fitzmaurice, *Whaling and International Law* (Cambridge, 2015).

whaling.[298] The key to this evolution has been the IWC power to regulate catch quotas, protected species, whaling sanctuaries, and whaling methods by amending the Schedule to the 1946 ICRW when it deems this to be 'necessary .... for the conservation, development and optimum utilization of the whale resources.'[299] A three-quarters majority vote is required, although parties may opt out of any revisions by objecting under Article III.[300] By setting catch quotas for each species at zero, all taking can in effect be suspended. This was how the IWC adopted a moratorium on commercial whaling in 1982. The moratorium remains in force and most stocks are slowly recovering. In effect a treaty originally intended to regulate whaling has through this simple device become a treaty to protect whales. Japan, Norway and Iceland conduct small-scale commercial whaling within their own coastal waters, operating either outside the 1946 ICRW or under reservations to the moratorium.[301]

Separately from the moratorium, commercial whaling is banned in two whale sanctuaries, the Indian Ocean and the Southern Ocean, although Japan continued until 2018 to permit the taking of whales there and in the North Pacific for scientific research under Article VIII of the 1946 ICRW.[302] Other proposals for whale sanctuaries have failed to secure the necessary votes. Several non-binding resolutions whose purpose is to ensure humane killing and deter whaling outside the 1946 ICRW framework have also been adopted. Inter alia, these ban transfer of vessels, equipment, and know-how to non-member states; they also prohibit trading in whales and whale products.[303] Following the model of the Behring Sea Fur Seals Convention, the schedule has been used to permit, exceptionally, aboriginal subsistence whaling in Siberia and Alaska, but only if using traditional, simple means of killing the whales.

The IWC has not regulated (with minor exceptions) small cetaceans.[304] Attempts have instead been made to protect at least some of these species by listing them on the appendices of the Bonn and Berne Conventions and the 1973 CITES.[305] Two regional agreements on small cetaceans have been adopted under the Bonn Convention.[306]

Although IWC regulations must be based on 'scientific findings' (Article V), the IWC's Scientific Committee has developed a strongly precautionary policy on any renewal of commercial whaling. The Revised Management Procedure ('RMP') is the most conservationist of any system currently used for setting quotas. The RMP was

298 Bowman, 29 *Mich JIL* (2007–8) 293; Carlarne, 24 *Virginia Env LJ* (2005) 1.

299 ICRW, Article V.

300 Bowman et al, *International Wildlife Law*, 161–3, and *supra*, Ch 2, section 5.

301 Japan withdrew from the ICRW in 2019; Iceland rejoined in 2001, with a reservation concerning the moratorium. Norway objected to the moratorium.

302 See *Whaling in the Antarctic Case*, ICJ Reports (2014) 226. Although Japan lost this case because its research methodology was poor, a new special permit was issued after revisions to the scientific programme allowed whaling to resume.

303 For texts of these and related resolutions, see Birnie, *International Regulation of Whaling*, ii, 775–97.

304 Birnie, 29 *NRJ* (1989) 903–34; id, 10 *Georgetown IELR* (1997) 1.

305 See *supra*, Ch 11, section 2, and CITES Resolution 11.4.

306 1992 Agreement on Conservation of Small Cetaceans of the Baltic and North Seas; 1996 Agreement on Conservation of Cetaceans of the Black Sea, Mediterranean Sea and Contiguous Atlantic Areas.

based on the view that the available scientific information and population theory are so uncertain that catch quotas could not be set until understanding of whale population dynamics had improved. IWC policy thus provides an example of the application in a wildlife context of a precautionary approach which reverses the burden of proof, so that any state wishing to resume commercial whaling will have to satisfy the Commission that the relevant stock can be exploited sustainably.[307] Iceland, Japan, and Norway have argued that certain stocks and species could be taken without risk.[308] Before any commercial whaling could recommence, however, there would also have to be (i) an effective observation and inspection system, (ii) arrangements to ensure that total catches over time are within prescribed limits, and (iii) incorporation into the Schedule of the requirements of the RMP and the proposed Management Scheme.[309]

Until Japan's departure IWC member states remained deadlocked on proposals to lift the moratorium in return for an end to scientific whaling, nor could they agree on how to revise Article VIII.[310] Revising the convention more comprehensively has also been impossible for the same political reasons. Arguments for a preservationist reinterpretation of the ICRW,[311] giving a special status to whales, must be viewed with scepticism following the ICJ judgment in the *Whaling Case*. That case confirmed that the object and purpose of a convention adopted in the very different circumstances of 1946 cannot be changed by the simple expedient of passing resolutions or amending the schedule, and that 'conservation' even in this context allows for sustainable exploitation.[312] Thus the whaling moratorium could be lifted insofar as the science allows, and a complete ban on whaling will only become definitive if a new or substantially revised treaty can be agreed by a consensus which includes the pro-whaling members. Japan's absence may allow the remaining parties to renegotiate the ICRW. Like other 'charismatic megafauna' there are arguments for banning whaling on ethical grounds,[313] or because it is inherently inhumane,[314] or simply unnecessary in the modern world. Probably the most compelling argument for a complete ban on whaling is that no system of regulation can effectively control the inherent tendency to over-exploit a resource that renews itself only slowly, and about which our scientific knowledge remains poor.

307 Compare the 1995 UNFSA, *infra*, section 4, and on the precautionary approach generally see *supra* Ch 3, section 6.

308 For example, minke whale stocks targeted by Japan in the Southern Ocean and by Norway in the Arctic. Although listed on CITES Appendix I they may not meet the criteria and there have been attempts to downlist them to Appendix II.

309 IWC, *Chairman's Report of the 51st Annual Meeting* (1999) 24. See Bowman et al, *International Wildlife Law*, 164–9.

310 See Telesetsky and Lee, 30 *IJMCL* (2015) 700.

311 See e.g. Bowman et al, *International Wildlife Law*, 152–4.

312 See *Whaling in the Antarctic Case*, ICJ Reports (2014) 226, paras 56–8, and *supra*, Ch 3, section 3(2).

313 See Bowman et al, *International Wildlife Law*, Ch 3; Gillespie, *International Environmental Law, Policy and Ethics* (Oxford, 1997) Chs VII-IX, and *supra*, Ch 11.

314 Harrop, 6 *JIWLP* (2003) 79.

5 CONSERVATION OF MARINE BIODIVERSITY

5(1) EVOLUTION OF THE LAW ON MARINE BIODIVERSITY

The relationship between the 1982 UNCLOS and the 1992 CBD shows how quite distinct treaties can nevertheless contribute to the development of a coherent legal regime.[315] The 1982 Convention makes no reference to biological diversity, although Article 194(5) does require parties to take measures necessary 'to protect and preserve rare or fragile ecosystems as well as the habitat of depleted, threatened or endangered species and other forms of marine life'. It is clear from the totality of Articles 192–6 that Part XII was never intended to be only about pollution, and that it encompasses protection of ecosystems, conservation of depleted or endangered species of marine life, and control of alien species.[316] A decade later the 1992 Rio Conference on Environment and Development adopted the 1992 CBD, whose provisions apply both to terrestrial and marine biodiversity. Clearly, each agreement is relevant for the purpose of interpreting the other. Equally clearly, the increasingly devastating effect of unsustainable fishing on marine biodiversity and ecosystems is a matter that directly affects the1992 CBD. There is thus a possibility that implementing the later treaty could affect rights and obligations under the 1982 UNCLOS. Moreover, Agenda 21 of the Rio Conference, the 1992 CBD and the 1995 UN Fish Stocks Agreement all give a broad reading to the responsibilities of states with regard to protection of the marine environment. In this context conservation and sustainable use of marine living resources, ecosystems, and biological diversity are important elements, and the 1982 UNCLOS must be interpreted and applied accordingly.[317]

5(2) AGENDA 21 AND THE UN SUSTAINABLE DEVELOPMENT GOALS

A more ecological approach to 'Protection of the Oceans and all Kinds of Seas', including their living resources, was first addressed in Chapter 17 of UNCED Agenda 21,[318] the opening paragraph of which asserts that 'the marine environment—including the oceans and all seas and adjacent coastal areas—forms an integrated whole that is an essential part of the global life-support system'. Whilst accepting that international law as reflected in the 1982 UNCLOS provides the basis for pursuing protection and sustainable development of the marine and costal environment, it stresses the need for

[315] See generally, Joyner, 28 *Vand JTL* (1995) 635–87; de Klemm, in Hey (ed), *Developments in International Fisheries Law*, 423–99; Pullen and Warren, 1 *Int Jnl of Biosciences and the Law* (1997) 249; Drankier and Elferink (eds), *Biological Diversity and Governance of Areas Beyond National Jurisdiction*, 27 *IJMCL* (2012) 187–501; de La Fayette, 24 *IJMCL* (2009) 221; Warner (ed), *Conservation and Sustainable Use of Marine Biodiversity: Southern Hemisphere Issues and Approaches*, 32 *IJMCL* (2017) 607–797.

[316] *Chagos Marine Protected Area Arbitration*, PCA (2015) para 538, and *supra*, Ch 9, section 2.

[317] *South China Sea Arbitration*, PCA (2016) paras 945; 959–64; 970; 983. See generally Molenaar, 22 *IJMCL* (2007) 89; Gjerde, 'Ecosystems and Biodiversity in Deep Waters and High Seas', *UNEP Regional Seas Reports and Studies* No 178 (2006).

[318] *Rept of the UNCED*, UN Doc A/CONF 151/26/REV 1, Vol I (1992).

'*new approaches to marine and costal management and development at the national, subregional and global levels, approaches that are integrated in content and are precautionary and anticipatory in ambit*'.[319] States are encouraged to identify marine ecosystems exhibiting high levels of biodiversity and productivity and other critical habitat areas and to establish necessary limitations on the use of such areas through, inter alia, designation of protected areas in coral reef systems, estuaries, and wetlands, including mangroves, seagrass areas, and other spawning and nursery areas, all of which are generally rich providers of biodiversity. The SDGs adopted in 2015 say little about marine biodiversity, but they do reiterate the need to 'sustainably manage and protect marine and coastal ecosystems to avoid significant adverse impacts, including by strengthening their resilience, and take action for their restoration in order to achieve healthy and productive oceans.'[320] The 1992 CBD remains the principal legal instrument for achieving these policy objectives.

5(3) 1992 CONVENTION ON BIOLOGICAL DIVERSITY

The parties to the 1992 CBD identified marine and coastal biodiversity as an early priority for action. A ministerial statement, the Jakarta Mandate on Marine and Coastal Biological Diversity,[321] acknowledged a new global consensus on the importance of this topic, reaffirming the critical need to address conservation and sustainable use of marine and coastal biodiversity and urging parties to initiate immediate action. Based on expert recommendations a programme adopted by COP IV[322] specifically addressed coral bleaching and related biodiversity loss and the special needs of small island states in implementing the programme. Its basic principles include, inter alia, ecosystem-based and precautionary approaches; the importance of science; use of local and indigenous community knowledge; and strong coordination with other relevant bodies. Its five main thematic areas relate to: integrated marine and coastal management; sustainable use of the resources concerned; marine and coastal protected areas; mariculture; and alien species.[323] Operational objectives are set for all these thematic areas.[324] It is noteworthy that COP VII expressed concern about threats to conservation of biodiversity in marine areas beyond national jurisdiction, particularly to vulnerable marine ecosystems.[325] COP IX adopted criteria for selecting representative marine protected areas and identifying ecologically or biologically significant marine areas in need of protection.[326] COP X adopted the so-called 'Aichi targets', setting out strategic priorities for the CBD. These include managing fish stocks sustainably with

[319] Para 17.1, emphasis added.

[320] UNGA Res 70/1 (2015) *Transforming our world: the 2030 Agenda for Sustainable Development*, SDG 14.2. See also UNGA Res 66/288 (2012) *The future we want*, paras 158–77.

[321] See COP Decision II/10.

[322] Decision IV/5 and Annex.

[323] See COP Decision VII/5, Annex I.

[324] For further details see *CBD Handbook*, Sec IV, Guide to Decisions of the Conference of the Parties: Thematic Work Programmes.

[325] See COP Decision VII/5.

[326] See COP Decision IX/20, Annexes I and II.

no adverse impact on other species or ecosystems; reducing anthropogenic pressures on coral reefs and other vulnerable ecosystems; and designating at least 10 per cent of coastal and marine areas important for biodiversity and ecosystem services as marine protected areas.[327]

The Jakarta Mandate goes some way to meet the disappointment expressed by the US in its declaration on adoption of the Convention concerning the limited scope of its obligations respecting the marine environment.[328] Many of the actions required are already within the scope of existing conventions concerned with wildlife conservation, insofar as they list marine protected species or facilitate establishment of marine protected areas.[329] The 1971 Ramsar Convention listings include areas of shallow coastal waters, while the World Heritage List also includes some coral reef areas, including the Great Barrier Reef. All cetaceans and some seals and other marine mammals have been listed on CITES Appendix I and are thus banned from trade. Some species of whales and seals, the dugong, and porpoises are listed in the Bonn Convention, under which several relevant Agreements have now been concluded.[330] There are also agreements providing for conservation of specific species such as Antarctic seals,[331] polar bears,[332] and sea turtles.[333]

Most regional-seas agreements were originally limited to preventing pollution, but as awareness of the importance of the marine environment as a habitat has grown, many of original conventions have been revised to take on a broader role in protecting ecosystems and marine biodiversity.[334] Protocols to protect various species of marine wildlife and establish specially protected areas have been added.[335] Other measures

[327] See COP Decision X/2. [328] Goote, 12 *IJMCL* (1997) 377 and *supra*, Ch 11.

[329] Notably the 1971 Convention on Wetlands of International Importance for Wildfowl Habitat; 1972 Convention for the Protection of the World Cultural and National Heritage Convention; 1973 Convention on International Trade in Endangered Species; 1979 Convention on Migratory Species of Wild Animals (Bonn Convention); 1979 Convention on Conservation of European Wildlife and National Habitats (Berne Convention); and the 1980 Convention on Conservation of Antarctic Marine Living Resources (CCAMLR). See *supra*, Ch 11, section 2; Churchill, in Bowman and Redgwell (eds), *International Law and the Conservation of Biological Diversity*, 71–89.

[330] 1990 Bonn Agreement on the Conservation of Seals in the Wadden Sea; 1992 New York Agreement on Conservation of Small Cetaceans of the Baltic and North Seas; 1996 Agreement on Conservation of Cetaceans of the Black Sea, Mediterranean Sea and Contiguous Atlantic Areas; 1996 Convention on the Conservation of African-Eurasian Migratory Waterbirds; 2001 Agreement on Conservation of Albatrosses and Petrels.

[331] 1972 Convention on the Conservation of Antarctic Seals. See *supra*, section 4.

[332] 1973 Agreement on the Conservation of Polar Bears; 2000 Agreement on the Conservation and Management of the Alaska-Chukota Polar Bear Population. See Bowman et al, *International Wildlife Law*, Ch 11.

[333] 1996 Inter-American Agreement on the Conservation of Sea Turtles; MOU Concerning Conservation Measures for Marine Turtles of the West Coast of Africa.

[334] See *supra*, Ch 9.

[335] See *e.g.* 1995 Protocol Concerning Specially Protected Areas and Biological Diversity in the Mediterranean Sea; 1985 Protocol on Protected Areas and on Wild Fauna and Flora in the East African Region; 1990 Protocol on Specially Protected Areas and Wildlife in the Wide Caribbean Region (SPAW Protocol); 1989 Paipa Protocol for the Conservation and Management of Protected Marine and Coastal Areas in the South East Pacific. The Black Sea Convention concluded a protocol in 2001. See de Klemm, in Hey (ed), *Developments in International Fisheries Law*, 441–7.

have been aimed at maintaining the quality of waters forming the habitat of marine species. The OSPAR Commission adopted the Sintra Statement phasing out certain polluting discharges by 2002, applying new principles for sustainable development and preservation of the marine environment, and adding an annex and appendix on the Protection and Conservation of Ecosystems and Biological Diversity.[336] The Helsinki Commission also took measures aimed at restoring habitats important to fish and sustainable aquaculture.[337] Thus the 1982 UNCLOS and treaties on land-based marine pollution have begun to protect marine ecosystems.

Other developments supporting restoration of marine habitats include a series of measures adopted by IMO. Despite past reluctance to invade the role of other UN specialized agencies and bodies it is now cooperating with many of these.[338] The 1992 CBD has influenced the IMO's agenda in various ways. The 2001 Convention on Control of Harmful Anti-Fouling Systems on Ships restricts the use chemicals that have been particularly harmful to certain marine species.[339] A Convention for the Control and Management of Ships' Ballast Water and Sediments was adopted in 2004 in order to reduce the increasingly serious problem of alien species transported worldwide in ships' ballast water.[340]

The creation of large-scale MPAs is another important development since Rio, intended to promote ecosystem protection and sustainable use of marine resources.[341] The MPA concept has no agreed or generally accepted content but it encompasses, inter alia, conservation of living resources, endangered species, ecosystems such as coral reefs, other types of habitat, and biodiversity.[342] It has quickly become one of the principal tools for protecting the marine environment and its biodiversity in an integrated and holistic way. The contracting parties to the 1992 CBD have agreed a target of ensuring that at least '10 per cent of coastal and marine areas, especially areas of particular importance for biodiversity and ecosystem services, are conserved through effectively and equitably managed, ecologically representative and well connected systems of protected areas and other effective area-based conservation measures' by 2020.[343] This 'Aichi target' was endorsed at the Rio+20 Conference in 2012.[344]

336 *Supra*, Ch 8.

337 *Ibid.* The Helsinki Commission launched an Agenda 21 for the Baltic region in 1996, focusing, inter alia, on fisheries and strengthened relations with the Baltic Sea Fishery Commission.

338 See de La Fayette, 16 *IJMCL* (2001) 155.

339 The Annex currently lists only tributyl.

340 Vallega, 19 *IJMCL* (2004) 411–82, and *supra*, Ch 9, section 4(2).

341 See Techera and Klein, *International Law of Sharks*, Ch 5; Ribeiro (ed), *30 Years After the Signature of UNCLOS* (Coimbra, 2014) 179; Tanaka, *The International Law of the Sea* (3rd edn, Cambridge, 2019) Ch 8; Scovazzi (ed), *Marine Specially Protected Areas: the General Aspects and the Mediterranean Regional System* (The Hague, 1999); Freestone, in Bowman and Redgwell (eds), *International Law and the Conservation of Biological Diversity* (The Hague, 1996).

342 See IUCN, *Guidelines for Marine Protected Areas* (Gland, 1999); CBD, Decision VII/5, para 10; Ribeiro (ed), *30 Years After the Signature of UNCLOS*, 185–91; Diz, *Fisheries Management in Areas Beyond National Jurisdiction*, 159–66.

343 CBD, COP 10 (2010) Decision X/2, Aichi Target 11.

344 *The Future We Want*, UNGA Res 66/288 (2012), para 177. See also UNGA Res 66/231 (2011).

The 1982 UNCLOS itself makes no mention of MPAs, but it does provide a legal basis for them. In particular, Article 194(5) requires states to take measures to 'protect and preserve rare and fragile ecosystems as well as the habitat of depleted, threatened or endangered species and other forms of marine life.'[345] Provided they do not interfere with freedom of navigation or the rights of other states, national MPAs within the EEZ or territorial sea are one means of giving effect to this article and to the 1992 CBD target.[346] The creation of MPAs in the South Atlantic, Pacific, Indian Ocean, and Southern Ocean has gone some way towards fulfilling this target.[347] The UK's overseas territories now constitute the world's largest system of national MPAs whose purpose is to protect marine biodiversity. Various types of MPA have also been created in areas beyond national jurisdiction by IMO,[348] under regional seas agreements,[349] and under fisheries agreements.[350] In 2016 the CCAMLR declared the world's largest high seas MPA in the Ross Sea off Antarctica.[351]

Clearly, there is a need for coordination and integration of these activities. The existing governance system for the marine environment as a whole is undeniably ad hoc and fragmented,[352] confined within artificial boundaries either of a jurisdictional nature or by species or pollutant, whereas conserving marine biological diversity is essentially an ecosystemic challenge. Moreover, enforcement and detailed regulation depend largely on action by national authorities. As noted in a UNEP/FAO Report,[353] the practical implications of regional fishery bodies and regional seas conventions adopting an ecosystem approach have only begun to attract international attention.[354]

345 See also Articles 56 and 211(6); *South China Sea Arbitration*, PCA (2016) paras 945; 959–64; 970; 983, and Ribeiro (ed), *30 Years After the Signature of UNCLOS*, 180–5.

346 Ribeiro (ed), *30 Years After the Signature of UNCLOS*, 192ff

347 The largest national MPAs include the Coral Sea (Australia); Phoenix Islands Protected Area (Kiribati); Marianas Trench Marine National Monument (US); Sala y Gomez Marine Park (Chile); Pacific Remote Islands Marine National Monument (US); Prince Edward Islands MPA (South Africa); South Orkney Islands MPA (UK); British Indian Ocean Territory MPA (UK); Pitcairn Island MPA (UK); Tristan da Cunha, Ascension and St Helena MPA (UK). See UN, *Oceans and Law of the Sea: Report of the Sec Gen* (New York, 1998) esp paras 306–28; Jones, *Governing Marine Protected Areas* (London, 2014) and generally *Chagos Marine Protected Area Arbitration*, PCA (2015).

348 See *supra*, Ch 9, section 5 (PSSAs) and Roberts and Chircop, 25 *IJMCL* (2010) 483.

349 MPAs have been established in high seas areas under the OSPAR and Barcelona Conventions, and see also 2014 Declaration on Collaboration for the Conservation of the Sargasso Sea. See generally Freestone, in Barrett and Barnes (eds), *Law of the Sea: UNCLOS as a Living Treaty* (London, 2016) 231; Scovazzi, in Ribeiro (ed), *30 Years After the Signature of UNCLOS*, 210; Diz, *Fisheries Management in Areas Beyond National Jurisdiction*, Ch 6; Scott, 4 *Asia-Pacific J of Ocean Law and Policy* (2019) 158.

350 See e.g. the system of 'vulnerable marine ecosystems' established by the Northeast Atlantic Fisheries Commission, and Diz, *Fisheries Management in Areas Beyond National Jurisdiction*, Ch 6; Ardron et al, 49 *Marine Policy* (2014) 146.

351 For analysis of the complex legal regime see Cordonnery, Hemmings and Kriwoken, 30 *IJMCL* (2015) 727.

352 See Molenaar, 22 *IJMCL* (2007) 89 and articles collected in 19 *IJMCL* (2004) 209–363.

353 *Report on Ecosystem-Based Management of Fisheries: Opportunities and Challenges for Coordination Between Marine Regional Fishery Bodies and Regional Seas Conventions*, 2nd Meeting of FAO and Non-FAO Regional Fishery Bodies or Arrangements, Rome (2001).

354 Notably at a symposium on 'Ecosystem Effects of Fishing,' convened by ICES in March 1999, and the 2001 Reykjavik Conference on Responsible Fisheries in the Ecosystem. See the 2001 Reykjavik Declaration on Sustainable Fisheries and FAO, *Fisheries Management: The Ecosystem Approach to Fisheries*, FAO Technical Guidelines for Responsible Fisheries No 4 Suppl 2 (Rome, 2003).

As we saw in discussing regional fisheries agreements, however, some progress has been made at broadening their environmental perspective.

5(4) THE RELATIONSHIP BETWEEN UNCLOS AND THE CBD

The 1992 CBD does not give blanket priority to the 1982 UNCLOS.[355] True, Article 22 specifically requires parties to implement the 1992 CBD 'consistently with the rights and obligations of States under the law of the sea'. This suggests that they could not, for example, ignore the rights of ships to freedom of navigation in the EEZ and high seas, whether under the 1982 UNCLOS or under customary law. To that extent Article 22 of the 1992 CBD reinforces the terms of Article 311(3) of the 1982 UNCLOS. Within these limits the 1982 UNCLOS will prevail in any conflict. On the other hand, as Article 237 of the 1982 UNCLOS makes clear, agreements relating to the marine environment do not have to conform to Part XII of the Convention but need only be carried out in a manner consistent with its 'general principles and objectives'. This should allow CBD parties much greater latitude to depart from the terms of Part XII than from other parts of the Convention since, as a *lex specialis,* Article 237 overrides Article 311(3).[356] Subject to Article 22, the CBD regime will therefore prevail over Part XII of the 1982 UNCLOS.

More importantly, however, while Article 22 also provides that existing treaty rights and obligations are not affected by the 1992 CBD, this exclusion does not apply where 'the exercise of those rights and obligations would cause serious damage or threat to biological diversity'. While in general terms the effect of Article 22 is to ensure that the 1982 UNCLOS will normally prevail, states parties to the 1992 CBD cannot rely on UNCLOS to justify—or to tolerate—fishing which causes or threatens serious damage to biodiversity. To that extent the 1992 CBD may have modified the fisheries provisions of the 1982 UNCLOS. Moreover, since conservation of marine living resources and protection and preservation of 'rare or fragile ecosystems' and the habitat of 'depleted, threatened or endangered species and other forms of marine life' are already envisaged by the 1982 UNCLOS,[357] the Convention's objects and purposes can readily be interpreted to include measures aimed at protection of marine biodiversity. Thus, for example, the adoption under the 1992 CBD of marine protected areas intended to reduce serious damage to biodiversity from high seas fishing would not be incompatible with the 1982 UNCLOS and would be consistent with Article 22 of the 1992 CBD. However, such zones would not be opposable to non-parties to the 1995 CBD, whose UNCLOS rights Article 311 expressly protects.[358] Any meaningful attempt to regulate

355 See generally Wolfrum and Matz Luck, 4 *Max Planck YbUNL* (2000) 445.

356 Nordquist (ed), *UNCLOS Commentary*, IV, 423–6.

357 Articles 61, 64–7, 117–20, 194(5).

358 But a recommendation from the CBD that fishing be discontinued in certain high seas areas or using methods harmful to biodiversity would appear to be binding on RFMOs pursuant to Article 10 of the UNFSA, *supra*, section 5(3).

marine biodiversity thus in practice depends principally on the parties to the 1982 UNCLOS, not on the parties to the 1992 CBD. Thus, the most important agreement on marine biodiversity—the 1995 UN Fish Stocks Agreement—is formally an agreement implementing the 1982 UNCLOS, not an agreement implementing the 1992 CBD. We can see from this example how a major law-making treaty such as the 1982 UNCLOS has an ongoing impact on the structuring of later law-making agreements. The range of matters covered by the 1995 UN Fish Stocks Agreement could not have been addressed with the same freedom or priority as an addendum to the 1992 CBD.

A final point is that we can see from the relationship between the 1982 UNCLOS and the 1992 CBD that international law on conservation of marine living resources and ecosystems is not the exclusive preserve of either treaty. A coherent and comprehensive understanding of the present law requires consideration of both treaties together with the related network of FAO agreements and soft law.

6 CONCLUSIONS

Developing a legal regime that provides for sustainable use and conservation of the ocean's living resources and biological diversity within the framework of the general law of the sea has been a problem since the late nineteenth century. Despite very extensive reforms to international fisheries law since the 1970s overfishing and loss of marine habitat have largely continued unabated. A pessimistic report on EU fish stocks concluded that: 'Despite substantial efforts, there are no significant signs of stock recovery nor of reductions in overfishing since 2003. Fisheries management in the EU is not working as it should and the objective of achieving long-term sustainability is not being reached.'[359] This seems an apt summary for the World as a whole. Only the 1946 ICRW has brought real improvements in the state of marine living resources, but that has come about only because commercial whaling effectively ended in 1986 and whale stocks have had thirty years to recover. Even then, some whale species remain seriously depleted by historic standards (e.g. the blue whale).

Whatever may have been true in the past, it is difficult to conclude that further reform of international fisheries law would significantly improve the state of fish stocks. The legal regime now in existence is complex, and not all states are bound by it all, but it does address the major problems. Its focus on ecosystem-based management, taking a precautionary approach, and addressing protection and preservation of the marine environment as a whole, is surely the right one. It is difficult to see how the FAO or the UN could have taken a different direction in their efforts to reform the law. We could perhaps save the oceans by banning commercial fishing, or by internationalizing the

[359] *Fishing Opportunities for 2009: Policy Statement from the European Commission*, COM (2008) 331 final, 5. But there are some signs of improvement: see FAO, *State of the World's Fisheries and Aquaculture 2016*, 44–5.

management of fish stocks on a common heritage basis, but those solutions would be unrealistic and unnecessary. A more prudent policy would renew the focus on reducing fishing effort, eliminating subsidies, extending the protection of ecosystems through large-scale no-take MPAs, and listing endangered fish species on appendix I of the 1973 CITES. More efforts could be made to save coral reefs, both from human interference and from climate change. A precautionary moratorium on seabed mining would also be a significant addition to ecosystem protection, fully justified by the uncertainty surrounding the science and the seriousness of the risk to the marine environment.

These would all be important changes, but they could be achieved within the existing law. Similarly, although some regional fisheries management bodies continue to be dysfunctional, there is no inherent reason why they could not all be reformed along the lines envisaged by the 1995 UN Fish Stocks Agreement. Extending participation to include a broader community of states than those with an interest only in fishing stocks to extinction would further improve the system of regional cooperation envisaged by the 1982 UNCLOS and the 1995 UN Fish Stocks Agreement. Above all, however, the principal weakness of international fisheries law remains what it has always been: coastal states do not manage their EEZ resources adequately and flag states do not manage their fishing fleets effectively. Ensuring that all these states make progress in achieving the 2015 SDGs with respect to management of fishing would potentially make a difference to these problems. Otherwise, the opportunities presented by the 1982 UNCLOS Part XV for putting pressure on poorly performing flag states have been enhanced by the overruling of the *Southern Bluefin Tuna Arbitral Award*,[360] by the non-compliance proceedings brought against Japan in the *Whaling Case*,[361] and by the ITLOS *Advisory Opinion*.[362] Ultimately, however, all these efforts may be wasted unless we grapple successfully with climate change and its increasingly serious effects on the oceans.

360 See *South China Sea Arbitration (Jurisdiction)*, PCA (2015) para 223.

361 *Whaling in the Antarctic Case*, ICJ Reports (2014) 226.

362 *AO on Fisheries*, ITLOS Reports (2015).

13

INTERNATIONAL TRADE AND ENVIRONMENTAL PROTECTION

1 INTRODUCTION: WTO AND INTERNATIONAL TRADE

Promotion and liberalization of free trade in goods and services has been the objective of international trade law since the GATT was first adopted in 1947. That legal regime was substantially revised in 1994 when the WTO was created, but it is still based on the same fundamental principles that, inter alia, trade restrictions must comply with the 'most-favoured nation' rule (GATT Article I), which prohibits discrimination between goods from different countries, the requirement of national treatment (GATT Article III), which prohibits discrimination between domestic and imported goods, and the ban on quantitative restrictions (GATT Article XI).[1] Many states have subsequently become parties to what is now a complex system of international trade agreements based on the 1994 version of GATT and other WTO 'covered agreements'.[2] These agreements are

[1] On WTO law and policy see: Trebilcock, Howse and Eliason, *The Regulation of International Trade* (4th edn, Abingdon, 2013); Jackson, *The World Trading System*, (2nd edn, Cambridge, Mass, 1997); Matsushita, Schoenbaum, Mavroidis and Hahn, *The World Trade Organization: Law, Practice and Policy* (3rd edn, Oxford, 2015); Van den Bossche and Zdouc, *The Law and Policy of the World Trade Organization: Text, Cases and Materials* (3rd edn, Cambridge, 2013).

[2] For texts of the 1994 GATT, the Marrakesh Agreement Establishing the World Trade Organization, the General Agreement on Trade in Services ('GATS'); the Agreement on the Application of Sanitary and Phytosanitary Measures ('SPS), the Agreement on Technical Barriers to Trade ('TBT'); the Agreement on Trade-Related Aspects of Intellectual Property Rights ('TRIPs') and other related agreements, understandings, and decisions, see WTO, *The Legal Texts: The Results of the Uruguay Round of Multilateral Trade Negotiations* (Cambridge, 1999).

administered by the WTO.[3] The WTO provides the principal forum for negotiations on multilateral trading relations among member states, and for the binding settlement of disputes arising under WTO agreements. These institutional and dispute settlement features of the WTO, contrasted with the decentralized and consensual dispute settlement features of international environmental agreements, initially fuelled a 'trade and environment debate' with some arguing that trade and environment disputes would inevitably fall for compulsory adjudication under a trade regime perceived to be inimical to environmental concerns.[4] In practice, however, the supposedly 'centrifugal pull' of the WTO has not resulted in a multitude of cases before the WTO Dispute Settlement Body arising from trade and environment conflicts. Nonetheless, as we discuss below, though few in number, the WTO's trade and environment cases have displayed a more nuanced approach to environmental issues than the pre-WTO GATT panels.[5]

An environmentalist perspective on WTO law requires us to consider whether it (i) may pose difficulties for the implementation of multilateral environmental agreements that use trade restrictions to protect the environment, such as the 1998 Rotterdam Convention on Prior Informed Consent; (ii) may frustrate attempts to protect resources and the environment in areas beyond national jurisdiction (e.g. the oceans), as in the US–Mexico tuna-dolphin dispute, or the similar attempt to protect sea turtles from shrimp fisheries; (iii) prevents states from setting high domestic standards for products, labelling, packaging, and recycling; or (iv) may obstruct efforts to adopt measures necessary for preserving the global environment and preventing climate change. This chapter focuses on these environmental issues: it does not attempt to summarise or survey the whole of WTO law.

Principle 12 of the Rio Declaration called for 'a supportive and open international economic system that would lead to economic growth and sustainable development in all countries, to better address the problems of environmental degradation.' This policy of mutual supportiveness is reflected in the Preamble to the 1994 Marrakesh Agreement Establishing the WTO. The Preamble acknowledges that expansion of production and trade must allow for:

> the optimal use of the world's resources in accordance with the objective of sustainable development, seeking both to protect and preserve the environment and to enhance the means for doing so in a manner consistent with their respective needs and concerns at different levels of economic development.

[3] *Supra*, Ch 2, section 4(6).

[4] For the flavour of this debate following the GATT Panel decisions in *Tuna-Dolphin*, see Weiss and Schoenbaum, 86 *AJIL* (1992) 700.

[5] See *infra*, section 8. On trade and environment generally see: Esty, *Greening the GATT: Trade, Environment, and the Future* (Washington DC, 1994); Wolfrum (ed), *Enforcing Environmental Standards: Economic Mechanisms as Viable Means* (Berlin, 1996); Schoenbaum, 91 *AJIL* (1997) 268; McRae, 9 *Otago LR* (1998) 221; Esty and Gerardin, 32 *JWT* (1998) 5; Trebilcock, Howse, and Eliason, *The Regulation of International Trade* Ch 15; Scott, in Weiler (ed), *The EU, the WTO, and the NAFTA: Towards a Common Law of International Trade* (Oxford, 2000) Ch 5; Sampson, *The WTO and Sustainable Development* (Tokyo, 2005); Goyal, *The WTO and International Environmental Law* (Oxford, 2006); Vranes, *Trade and the Environment—Fundamental Issues in International Law, WTO Law and Legal Theory* (Oxford, 2009); van Asselt in Rajamani and Peel (eds), *The Oxford Handbook of International Environmental Law* (2nd edn, Oxford, 2021) Ch 43.

As we will see below, the reference to 'the objective of sustainable development' has influenced the interpretation of the WTO-covered agreements, including the GATT.[6]

At the same time, Principle 12 of the Rio Declaration also provides that 'Trade policy measures for environmental purposes should not constitute a means of arbitrary or unjustifiable discrimination or a disguised restriction on international trade'. Unilateral actions to deal with 'environmental challenges outside the jurisdiction of the importing country are to be avoided,' and 'environmental measures addressing transboundary or global environmental problems should, as far as possible, be based on an international consensus'.

These are policy preferences, not law, and Principle 12 is not expressed in normative terms, but like the Rio Declaration as a whole it was adopted by consensus of the international community and in part it reflects policies already enshrined in the GATT.[7] As we will see in subsequent sections of this chapter Principle 12 has been influential on the development of WTO case law and the drafting of trade provisions in multilateral environmental agreements. In environmental treaty negotiations 'the potential for conflict with WTO rules is near deal-breaking in new MEA negotiations . . .'[8] Thus, environmental agreements concluded since 1994 have merely exhorted parties to accommodate trade and environmental concerns in preambular language. They have not established any clear priority or principles for conflict resolution. The 2000 Cartagena Protocol, the 1998 Rotterdam Convention on Prior Informed Consent and the 2013 Convention on Mercury are the most recent examples.[9]

WTO law does not give free trade priority over environmental protection, but neither does it endorse any general exception for environmental purposes. While recognizing the potential for conflict between these two objectives,[10] neither the WTO Committee on Trade and Environment ('CTE') nor the member states have been able to negotiate the agreement on trade and environment contemplated by the 2001 Doha Declaration.[11] After twenty years of negotiations progress on this issue and on many others remains blocked by deep divisions between WTO member states.[12]

[6] See in particular, *US—Import Prohibition of Certain Shrimp and Shrimp Products*, WTO Appellate Body Report, WT/DS58/AB/R (1998) paras 12, 17, 67 and 152–3 [hereafter '*Shrimp-Turtle* Case'].

[7] See Young, in Viñuales (ed), *The Rio Declaration on Environment and Development* (Oxford, 2015) 325.

[8] UNEP/IISD, *Environment and Trade: A Handbook* (2000, New York, UNEP/IISD) 62, and Green, 8 *JIEL* (2005) 143.

[9] See infra, section 3, and on the Biosafety Protocol see Safrin, 96 *AJIL* (2002) 606 and *infra*, section 7.

[10] See *Report of the Committee on Trade and Environment*, WT/CTE/4 (1999) and WTO Special Studies, *Trade and Environment* (Geneva, 1999).

[11] WTO Ministerial Declaration WT/MIN(01)/DEC/1(2001), para 31 provides: 'With a view to enhancing the mutual supportiveness of trade and environment, we agree to negotiations, without prejudging their outcome, on: the relationship between existing WTO rules and specific trade obligations set out in multilateral environmental agreements (MEAs). The negotiations shall be limited in scope to the applicability of such existing WTO rules as among parties to the MEA in question. The negotiations shall not prejudice the WTO rights of any Member that is not a party to the MEA in question.'

[12] WTO Ministerial Declaration and Decisions of 19 December 2015, WTO Doc. WT/MIN(15) DEC (2015), para 30.

Consequently it has fallen to the WTO Appellate Body to clarify how the balance between free trade and environmental protection is to be achieved. One look at the case law reviewed in this chapter demonstrates the wisdom of creating an appellate body of generalist international lawyers and trade lawyers. This is a specialised tribunal, but unlike the earlier 1947 GATT panels it is not an insular one and it has done a good job.[13]

2 GATT ENVIRONMENTAL EXCEPTIONS

2(1) GATT ARTICLE XX

Article XX lists various exemptions from the obligations established inter alia by Articles I, II, and XI of the GATT. Although the word 'environment' is not used in Article XX, subsections (b) and (g) may justify environmental constraints on trade. The pertinent wording of Article XX is as follows:[14]

Subject to the requirement that such measures are not applied in a manner which would constitute a means of arbitrary or unjustifiable discrimination between countries where the same conditions prevail, or a disguised restriction on international trade, nothing in this Agreement shall be construed to prevent the adoption or enforcement by any contracting party of measures:

...

(b) necessary to protect human, animal or plant life or health; ...

(g) relating to the conservation of exhaustible natural resources if such measures are made effective in conjunction with restrictions on domestic production or consumption.

The introductory clause in Article XX, set out above but commonly termed the *chapeau,* qualifies the entire catalogue of exceptions under Article XX.[15] Even if a trade 'measure'[16] otherwise falls within one of the exceptions in Article XX, it would be illegal under the *chapeau* if it constitutes (i) arbitrary or unjustifiable discrimination between countries where the same conditions prevail, or (ii) a disguised restriction on international trade. Discriminatory treatment is not necessarily irrational but it will be arbitrary or unjustifiable if its rationale 'bears no relationship to the objective of a measure provisionally justified under one of the paragraphs of Article XX, or goes against that objective.'[17] Thus, treating tyres imported from Mercosur countries more

[13] See *infra*, section 8.

[14] For drafting history see Charnovitz, 25 *JWT* (1991) 37. A virtually identical 'General Exception' appears in Article XIV GATS.

[15] See generally, Bartels, 109 *AJIL* (2015) 95.

[16] By 'measure' is meant the law or rule challenged as inconsistent with WTO/GATT norms: *US—Standards for Reformulated and Conventional Gasoline*, Report of the Appellate Body, WT/DS2/AB/R (1996) at 13–14 ['*US Gasoline Standards Case*'].

[17] *Brazil—Measures Affecting Imports of Retreaded Tyres* ['Brazil Tyres Case'], Appellate Body Report, WT/DS332/AB (2007), para 232.

favourably than those imported from elsewhere could not be justified by reference to the Mercosur Agreement when that agreement itself allowed control of imports on health grounds.[18]

The significance of the *chapeau* was emphasized in the *US Gasoline Standards* Case.[19] This case involved the US Clean Air Act of 1990. The implementing rules of the Environmental Protection Agency established different baselines for foreign and domestic producers and refiners. The Appellate Body found that the implementing rules constituted 'unjustifiable discrimination' and a 'disguised restriction on international trade' contrary to the *chapeau*. The US could have imposed the same baselines on domestic and foreign producers and importers and the Appellate Body rejected the alleged reasons for not doing so. But this was not a case in which trade trumped environmental protection: it was simply a case in which the national regulator sought to give an unjustifiable advantage to national producers that had nothing to do with the objective of environmental protection.

In the *Shrimp-Turtle Case*, the Appellate Body explained that the *chapeau* is (i) a balancing principle to mediate between the right of a member to invoke an Article XX derogation and its obligation to respect the rights of other members; (ii) a qualification making the Article XX exemptions 'limited and conditional'; (iii) an expression of the principle of good faith in international law; and (iv) a safeguard against *abus de droit*, the doctrine that requires the assertion of a right under a treaty to be 'exercised bona fide, that is to say reasonably'.[20] Accordingly, the *chapeau* protects 'both substantive and procedural requirements.'[21]

The Appellate Body's reasoning focused on the manner of application of the US regulations on shrimp harvesting. First, it found that there was 'arbitrary discrimination' because US law required a 'rigid and unbending . . . comprehensive regulatory programme that is essentially the same as the US programme, without inquiring into the appropriateness of that program for the conditions prevailing in the exporting countries'.[22] Second, arbitrary discrimination was also found to exist because the US authorities, in their certification process for shrimp imports, did not comply with basic standards of fairness and due process with regard to notice, the gathering of evidence, and the opportunity to be heard. The Appellate Body held that the GATT requires 'rigorous compliance with the fundamental requirements of due process' with respect to exceptions to treaty obligations.[23] This meant a process that is 'transparent' and 'predictable,' and offers opportunities for the exporting countries concerned 'to be heard, or to respond to any arguments.'[24]

Third, the US regulations applied differing phase-in periods for countries similarly situated and impacted by the import ban.[25] Most importantly, the Appellate Body held that it was also unjustifiable discrimination for the US not to have negotiated seriously with the affected countries: the US statute recognized the importance of

[18] Ibid, paras 233–4. [19] Appellate Body Report, section IV, at 22–29.
[20] *Shrimp-Turtle* Case, Appellate Body, paras 157–8. [21] Ibid, para 160.
[22] Ibid, para 177. [23] Ibid, para 182. [24] Ibid, paras 180–1. [25] Ibid, para 182.

seeking international agreements, and the US had, subsequent to imposing its own restrictions, entered into the 1996 Inter-American Convention for the Protection and Conservation of Sea Turtles with a few of the other states affected. The Appellate Body concluded: 'The Inter-American Convention thus provides convincing demonstration that an alternative course of action was reasonably open to the USA'.[26]

The *Shrimp-Turtle Case* is a well-reasoned decision of great importance for the trade/environment controversy.[27] The Appellate Body, unlike earlier GATT panels in the very similar *Tuna/Dolphin* dispute,[28] went out of its way to emphasize respect for general international law and international environmental agreements. Three important conclusions emerge from its decision.

First, although unilateral trade restrictions are likely to be regarded as arbitrary or discriminatory for the purposes of Article XX if the State concerned has not first sought a cooperative solution through negotiation,[29] the Appellate Body did not condemn all unilateral action or declare it illegal per se as the GATT panels had done. The Appellate Body stated only that '[T]he unilateral character . . . heightens the disruptive and discriminatory influence of the import prohibition and underscores its unjustifiability'.[30] This leaves some room, albeit small, for unilateral measures to protect the environment beyond national jurisdiction. When US measures in the *Shrimp-Turtle Case* were reformulated to meet due process concerns and conditions in other countries, they were upheld, subject to the proviso that the US continued to make 'serious, good faith efforts to reach a multilateral agreement.'[31] If the other states then refused to enter into negotiations, they would be in breach of the principle of good faith,[32] and unilateral measures could then be justified.

Second, *Shrimp/Turtle* also provides a template, if necessary, for carefully focused unilateral trade measures designed to put pressure on states that are not supporting or implementing internationally agreed commitments to protect the global environment, including states whose policies on climate change do not show the degree of ambition required by the 2015 Paris Agreement.[33] This does not mean that the more ambitious states can arbitrarily force their climate change policies on others regardless of their circumstances,[34] but it does mean that they can require the adoption of a nationally determined contribution 'comparable in effectiveness.'[35] Obvious targets

26 Ibid, para 171.

27 See generally Howse, 27 *Columbia JEL* (2002) 491.

28 *US—Restrictions on Imports of Tuna*, Report of the Panel, 30 *ILM* (1991) 1598, (not adopted by the GATT Council) (hereafter, '*Tuna-Dolphin I*').

29 *Shrimp-Turtle*, paras. 168–172. See Bartels, (2012) 23 *EJIL* 429.

30 *Shrimp-Turtle* Case, Appellate Body, para 172.

31 *US—Shrimp, Recourse to Art 21.5 of the DSU by Malaysia*, Report of the Appellate Body, WT/DS58/AB/RW (2001) 49–51. See Young, in Viñuales (ed), *The Rio Declaration etc*, 338–40.

32 And arguably also of its conservation and cooperation obligations under the 1982 UNCLOS: see *supra*, Ch 12.

33 See Mehling et al, 113 *AJIL* (2019) 433. On the Paris Agreement see *supra*, Ch 6, section 4(4).

34 1992 UNFCCC, Article 3(5) reiterates the GATT prohibition on arbitrary or unjustifiable discrimination and disguised restrictions on trade. Moreover, Article 2(2) of the Paris Agreement allows for some degree of policy differentiation 'in light of different national circumstances.' See *supra*, Ch 6, section 4(4).

35 *Shrimp/Turtle (Article 21.5)*, para 144; Mehling et al, 113 *AJIL* (2019) 433, 469; Pauwelyn, in Prevost and Van Calster (eds),*Research Handbook on Environment, Health, and the WTO* (Cheltenham, 2013) 502–3

for trade measures justified by Article XX(g) would be the states that have left the 2015 Paris Agreement or have essentially repudiated it.

Third, the *Shrimp-Turtle* decisions provide a principled basis for upholding multilateral and bilateral environmental agreements under Article XX(b) and (g). By interpreting the requirements of (g) (and impliedly (b)) in an environmentally sensitive manner, it is virtually certain that trade measures under MEAs, as well as in bilateral environmental agreements, would be upheld. They would meet the requirements of the *chapeau* unless they contained substantial flaws or were disguised protectionist measures. Thus, the *Shrimp-Turtle Cases* provide an important new basis for upholding trade-restrictive international environmental agreements.[36] Moreover the Appellate Body also relied upon international environmental agreements not binding on the parties as an aid to the interpretation of existing WTO provisions, not as the applicable law between the parties.[37] This point was emphasized in the *EC—Biotech Case* where the panel considered whether, and how, agreements external to the WTO covered agreements could be taken into account.[38]

2(2) ARTICLE XX(B): PROTECTION OF HEALTH

Article XX(b) of the GATT and the identically worded Article XIV(b) of the GATS can be invoked to protect the domestic environment from risks to the life or health of 'humans, plants, or animals' posed by imported goods.[39] The trade measure in question must be *necessary* for those purposes, and must be applied consistently with the *chapeau*.[40] In the *Asbestos Case*, the Appellate Body held that a measure is 'necessary' if no GATT-consistent alternative is reasonably available and provided it entails the least degree of inconsistency with other GATT provisions.[41] In the *Brazil Tyres Case* the Appellate Body explained that this decision involved 'weighing and balancing' how far an import ban would achieve its objective against its trade restrictiveness in the light of the interests at stake, and, secondly, a comparison of the possible alternatives, including associated risks.[42] As in the *Asbestos Case*, they concluded that the import ban was 'necessary' within the terms of Article XX(b).

In deciding what is 'necessary', WTO law allows considerable freedom to member states, but the test is an objective one, with the burden of proof falling on the defending government to present the evidence supporting its case.[43] Upholding a French ban on

[36] See Scott, 15 *EJIL* (2004) 311. [37] See *infra*, section 8, and *supra*, Ch 1, section 2.

[38] *European Communities—Measures Affecting the Approval and Marketing of Biotech Products*, Panel Report, WT/DS291/R, WT/DS292/R, WT/DS293/R (2006) paras 7.70–7.95 ['*EC-Biotech case*']. See Young, 56 *ICLQ* (2007) 907.

[39] Only to that extent is this an 'environmental' exception, in contrast to the Agreement on Technical Barrier to Trade, Article 2 of which does refer specifically to the environment.

[40] *EC—Measures Affecting Asbestos* ['*EC-Asbestos case*'] WTO Appellate Body WT/DS135/AB/R (2001) paras 155–75.

[41] Ibid, paras 164–75. [42] *Brazil Tyres Case*, para 182; Charnovitz, 10 *JIEL* (2007) 685, 691.

[43] *US—Measures Affecting the Cross-Border Supply of Gambling and Betting Services*, WT/DS285/AB/R (2005), paras 304–10.

imports of products containing asbestos under Article XX(b), the Appellate Body in *EC-Asbestos* held that the defending government may 'rely in good faith, on scientific sources which, at that time, may represent a divergent, but qualified and respected, opinion'.[44] Where there is evidence of a risk to health, 'WTO members have the right to determine the level of protection of health that they consider appropriate',[45] based *either* on the quality of the risk (i.e. is it regarded as socially acceptable) or on the quantity of the risk (i.e. how likely is it).[46] The more vital the common interests or values pursued, the easier it would be to accept as 'necessary' measures designed to achieve those ends;[47] wisely, in the *Brazil Tyres Case* the Appellate Body noted that 'the results obtained from certain actions—for instance, measures adopted in order to attenuate global warming and climate change . . . can only be evaluated with the benefit of time.'[48]

2(3) ARTICLE XX(G): CONSERVATION OF EXHAUSTIBLE NATURAL RESOURCES

Article XX(g) is designed to allow WTO members to take action to conserve 'exhaustible natural resources.' The measures taken must include restrictions on domestic production or consumption; and be applied in conformity with the requirements of the *chapeau* of Article XX.[49] A consistent theory of interpretation of Article XX(g) has been advanced by the Appellate Body in the *US Gasoline Standards Case* and the *Shrimp-Turtle Case*.[50] The latter is particularly relevant because it involved a trade measure similar to the one employed in the *Tuna-Dolphin Cases*. As such it marks the contrasting approach of the WTO Appellate Body and earlier GATT panels.

The first issue that must be addressed under Article XX(g) is whether the particular trade measure relates to the 'conservation of exhaustible natural resources'.[51] The Appellate Body has taken a generous view of this matter, adopting an evolutionary interpretation of the term 'natural resources' which 'must be read by a treaty interpreter in the light of contemporary concerns of the community of nations about the protection and conservation of the environment'.[52] A 'resource' may be living or non-living, and it need not be rare or endangered to be potentially 'exhaustible'. Thus, dolphins, fish, clean air, biological resources, fresh water, and sea turtles all qualify. Under this expansive interpretation, virtually any living or non-living resource would qualify.

The second 'relating to' element of Article XX(g) has proved more difficult to apply. Although a trade measure does not have to be 'necessary' (as in Article XX(b)) for

[44] *EC-Asbestos case*, para 178.

[45] *EC-Asbestos case*, para 168. See Howse and Türk, in Bermann and Mavroidis (eds), *Trade and Human Health and Safety* (Cambridge, 2006) 77, 113.

[46] *EC-Asbestos case*, para 167. [47] Ibid, para 172. [48] Ibid, para 151.

[49] See *US Gasoline Standards case*, where the Appellate Body held that clean air is an exhaustible natural resource.

[50] For discussion of the *Shrimp-Turtle* case see Mann, 9 *YbIEL* (1998) 28; Schoenbaum, ibid, 36; Wirth, ibid, 40.; Musto and Redgwell, in Bjorge and Miles (eds), *Landmark Cases in Public International Law* (Oxford, 2017) Ch 22.

[51] *Shrimp-Turtle* Appellate Body Report, para 127. [52] Ibid, paras 129–31.

natural resource conservation, some WTO/GATT panels have interpreted 'relating to' to mean that it must be 'primarily aimed at' conservation.[53] The question arises whether the 'primarily aimed at' interpretation of 'relating to' is correct. As the Appellate Body in *US Gasoline Standards* pointed out, 'the phrase "primarily aimed at" is not, itself, treaty language and was not designed as a simple litmus test' for Article XX.[54] In *Shrimp-Turtle* the Appellate Body took a more nuanced approach, examining the relationship between the measure in question and the conservation objectives and concluded that the US import ban on shrimp was 'reasonably related' to the turtle conservation measures.[55]

A third requirement of Article XX(g) is that the measure in question must be 'made effective in conjunction with restrictions on domestic production or consumption'. The definitive interpretation of this phrase was given by the Appellate Body in the *US Gasoline Standards Case*:

> [W]e believe that the clause 'if such measures are made effective in conjunction with restrictions on domestic product[ion] or consumption' is appropriately read as a requirement that the measures concerned impose restrictions, not just in respect of imported gasoline but also with respect to domestic gasoline.[56]

As the Appellate Body further pointed out, however, the 'in conjunction with' element requires a certain amount of even-handedness, but not identity of treatment, and restrictions on either domestic production or consumption will be acceptable.[57]

A similar approach was used in the *Shrimp-Turtle Case*.[58] The 'in conjunction with' requirement was satisfied because the US required all shrimp trawlers to use turtle excluder devices in areas and at times when there is a likelihood of intercepting sea turtles. Thus, there were comparable restrictions on the domestic harvesting of shrimp.[59]

The approach to Article XX(g) now mandated by the Appellate Body is substantially different from the interpretations of earlier GATT panels, particularly the *Tuna-Dolphin I* decision. Restrictions on tuna harvesting aimed at dolphin protection could now pass Article XX(g) provided they were non-discriminatory.[60] Dolphins clearly are an exhaustible natural resource; the import ban on tuna harvested by methods that kill dolphins clearly is related to the purpose of cutting dolphin mortality. Equally important, the Appellate Body in the *Shrimp-Turtle Case* gave *extraterritorial* scope to Article XX(g): in that context it applies without distinction to exhaustible

[53] See *US Gasoline Standards*, at 16. [54] *Ibid*, at 19.

[55] *Shrimp-Turtle* Appellate Body Report, para 141. Compare the case law on Article XX(b) in the previous section.

[56] At 20. [57] At 21. [58] *Shrimp-Turtle* Appellate Body Report, paras 138–42.

[59] Ibid, paras 143–5.

[60] See *US-Measures Concerning the Importation, Marketing and sale of Tuna and Tuna Products* ['*Tuna/Dolphin II*'], Appellate Body Report, WT/DS381/AB (2012), where, however, the measures then in place were found to be discriminatory. See *infra*, section 4. In *Tuna/Dolphin I* the measures protecting dolphins also applied to US vessels and fishers.

living resources on the high seas as well as to those within national jurisdiction.[61] In that respect *Shrimp/Turtle* and later cases have firmly rejected the restrictive approach of *Tuna/Dolphin I*.[62]

3 MULTILATERAL ENVIRONMENTAL AGREEMENTS AND TRADE RESTRICTIONS

How does the WTO/GATT system accommodate MEAs that employ trade restrictions?[63] Examples of such MEAs include the 1987 Montreal Protocol,[64] which adopts trade controls that are more restrictive for non-parties than parties; the 1973 CITES,[65] which regulates imports and exports of endangered species of animals and plants and allows trade restrictions to be imposed on non-complying parties; the 1989 Basel Convention,[66] which regulates trade in wastes and prohibits export of hazardous waste to developing countries, and the 1998 Rotterdam Convention on Prior Informed Consent which restricts export of hazardous chemicals and pesticides.[67]

3(1) THE RELATIONSHIP BETWEEN WTO AGREEMENTS AND ENVIRONMENTAL AGREEMENTS

The CTE has endorsed 'multilateral solutions based on international cooperation and consensus as the best and most effective way for governments to tackle environmental problems of a transboundary or global nature'.[68] Attempts have been made without much success to address the relationship with WTO agreements during MEA negotiations,[69] but no party has subsequently challenged the conformity of MEA trade restrictions with GATT. Thus, no WTO dispute-resolution panel has been asked to rule on the question. This is hardly surprising: it would not be persuasive to argue before the Appellate Body that a WTO agreement takes priority over a widely ratified MEA when the complainant state is a party to that MEA. As the CTE rightly observed: 'WTO Agreements and multilateral environmental agreements (MEAs) are representative of efforts of the international community to pursue shared goals, and in the

61 *Shrimp-Turtle,* Appellate Body Report, paras 132–3. But note the qualified terms of this decision: 'We do not pass upon the question of whether there is an implied jurisdictional limitation in Article XX(g), and if so, the nature or extent of that limitation. We note only that in the specific circumstances of the case before us, there is a sufficient nexus between the migratory and endangered marine populations involved and the United States for purposes of Article XX(g).' For a comprehensive review of extraterritoriality see Cooreman, 65 *ICLQ* (2016) 229.

62 See Young, in Viñuales (ed), *The Rio Declaration etc*, 336–41.

63 See Tarasofsky, 7 *YbIEL* (1996) 52; Brack, 9 *YbIEL* (1998) 13; and references supra, n 5.

64 *Supra*, Ch 6, section 3.

65 *Supra*, Ch 11, section 2(4).

66 *Supra*, Ch 8, section 5.

67 *Supra*, Ch 8, section 2.

68 WTO, *Report of the Committee on Trade and Environment*, WT/CTE/1 (1996) para 171.

69 See *infra*, section 3(2).

development of a mutually supportive relationship between them due respect must be afforded to both.'[70]

WTO law is not a closed system.[71] Article 3(2) of the WTO Dispute Settlement Understanding, and the decision of the Appellate Body in the *Shrimp-Turtle Case*,[72] make it clear that WTO agreements must, like any other treaty, be interpreted and applied in accordance with general rules of international law. In effect this means the 1969 VCLT. Without a priority clause, or any provision comparable to Article 311 of the 1982 UNCLOS, the relationship between WTO agreements and other treaties can only be determined in accordance with general rules of international law on treaties, or with the relevant provisions of other treaties. Put another way, there is no requirement for an MEA to conform to the rules of WTO law. The question then is how the two will interact. A *lex specialis* will not be displaced by the more general rules of the GATT, nor will integral treaties from which no derogation is permitted, such as the 1982 UNCLOS and various other MEAs,[73] and on that basis an environmental agreement making specific provision for trade restrictions will usually provide the applicable norm.[74] To say that a state cannot implement an MEA trade restriction that contravenes the GATT is to miss this fundamental point.

The point here is that some treaties seek to create integral regimes for the common benefit of all states, usually reinforced by a prohibition on reservations. It would be counter-productive to allow some states parties in effect to contract out by reference to incompatible agreements such as the GATT. The necessary assumption is of course that the MEA provisions in question are 'integral' agreements for the common benefit of all states, from which derogation *inter se* must be controlled, and that WTO agreements create a network of principally bilateral relations, from which derogation *inter se* will usually be permissible.[75]

Thus the relationship between MEAs and the GATT is primarily one of interpretation rather than precedence.[76] This is an important conclusion. If correct, it means, for example, that Article 30 of the 1969 VCLT will not operate to give general WTO trade rules adopted in 1994 priority as treaty law over more specific trade restrictions in the 1973 CITES or the 1989 Basel Convention, or later agreements such as the 1998 Rotterdam Convention on Prior Informed Consent, the 2000 Cartagena Protocol, or the 2013 Convention on Mercury. If the WTO negotiators in 1994 had intended otherwise they should have said so expressly.

[70] WTO, *Report of the Committee on Trade and Environment*, WT/CTE/1 (1996) para 171.

[71] Pauwelyn, *Conflict of Norms in Public International Law* (Cambridge, 2003); id, 95 *AJIL* (2001) 535.

[72] *Import Prohibition of Certain Shrimp and Shrimp Products*, WTO Appellate Body (1998) WT/DS58/AB/R. See Howse, in, Weiler (ed), *The EU, the WTO and the NAFTA* (Oxford, 2000) 54.

[73] See UNCLOS Articles 309–11; 1992 UNFCCC, Article 24; 1992 CBD, Article 37; 1989 Basel Convention, Article 37; 1973 CITES Convention, Article 23.

[74] VCLT, Aticles 30 and 41 and see Boyle and Chinkin, *The Making of International Law*, Ch 5.

[75] Pauwelyn, *Conflict of Norms in Public International Law* (Cambridge, 2003), 315–24; id, 14 *EJIL* (2003) 907, 925–41. Pauwelyn acknowledges the possibility that some WTO treaty obligations may be collective in character. Equally, some MEA provisions may not be.

[76] Pauwelyn, *Conflict of Norms*, 408; Safrin, 96 *AJIL* (2002) 606.

Even the GATT panel in the *Tuna-Dolphin I Case* noted that dolphins could be protected through 'international cooperative arrangements'.[77] In the *Shrimp-Turtle* case the Appellate Body clearly upheld the right of WTO members to legislate for the protection of natural resources beyond national boundaries, especially if they do so pursuant to an MEA. As we saw earlier, in coming to this conclusion, it adopted an interpretation of GATT Article XX which would permit MEAs in appropriate circumstances to derogate from GATT obligations.[78] The Appellate Body in the *Shrimp-Turtle Case* also encouraged the US to seek international agreement on turtle conservation.[79] Based on this reading of GATT Article XX it seems unlikely that any trade restrictions adopted pursuant to an existing or future MEA would contravene GATT.

3(2) TRADE IN HAZARDOUS CHEMICALS AND PESTICIDES

Clearly a state may bar *imports* of a product that is banned for domestic sale or consumption because it presents a danger to human, animal, or plant life, or health. Can exports of such products also be restricted consistently with the GATT? This question arose during negotiation of the Rotterdam Convention on Prior Informed Consent.[80] The Rotterdam Convention on Prior Informed Consent establishes a prior informed consent (PIC) regime for banned or restricted chemical products and hazardous pesticide formulations that may cause health or environmental problems. During the negotiations there was no consensus on the inclusion of a provision establishing an order of priority between the Convention and the GATT.[81] In the event the Preamble recognizes 'that trade and environmental policies should be mutually supportive with a view to achieving sustainable development'. The Preamble further emphasizes 'that nothing in this Convention shall be interpreted as implying in any way a change in the rights and obligations of a Party under any existing international agreement applying to chemicals in international trade or to environmental protection', whilst at the same time immediately recording the parties' '[u]nderstanding that the above recital is not intended to create a hierarchy between this Convention and other international agreements'. The 2000 Cartagena Protocol (but not the 2001 POPS Convention or the 2013 Convention on Mercury) repeats these preambular provisions virtually verbatim, though it replaces 'hierarchy' with 'subordinate'.[82]

Neither approach is particularly helpful, not least because no specific guidance is given on how 'trade and environment' conflicts are to be resolved should they arise. But given the Appellate Body's reading of Article XX of the GATT in *Shrimp-Turtle* it again seems unlikely that there is any risk of inconsistency between the

[77] *Tuna-Dolphin I*, para 5.28.

[78] *Shrimp-Turtle Case*, Appellate Body Report, paras 171–2.

[79] *Shrimp-Turtle Case*, Appellate Body Report, paras 167–9. On the failure to achieve a negotiated solution, see *US—Shrimp, Recourse to Art 21.5 of the DSU by Malaysia*, Report of the Appellate Body, WT/DS58/AB/RW (2001).

[80] *Supra*, Ch 8, section 2. See further Redgwell, in Kiss, Shelton, and Ishibashi (eds), *Economic Globalization and Compliance with International Environmental Agreements* (The Hague, 2003) Ch 6.

[81] Kummer, 8 *RECIEL* (1999) 322, 325.

[82] See Safrin, 96 *AJIL* (2002) 606.

Rotterdam Convention and the GATT. GATT Article XX(b) allows trade measures (affecting either imports or exports) that are 'necessary to protect human, animal, plant life or health'. Moreover, if Article XX(g) permits a state to conserve exhaustible natural resources on the high seas, i.e. *outside* the territory of that state,[83] then it might be argued that Article XX(b) will similarly justify trade measures designed to protect the health or safety of persons, animals or plants located on the high seas or otherwise outside the territory of that state.[84] The fact that so many states are parties to the Rotterdam Convention on Prior Informed Consent strengthens that argument: these states clearly do accept that the convention has an extra-territorial reach. No comparable argument was available in the *Tuna/Dolphin, Shrimp/Turtle* or *EC-Seals* cases.

3(3) HAZARDOUS WASTE

An export ban on hazardous wastes could be justified under GATT Article XX(b) on the same basis as export restrictions on chemicals. Even a discriminatory export ban may be upheld under Article XX(b) if the discrimination is not 'arbitrary or unjustifiable . . . between countries where the same conditions prevail'. A ban that distinguishes between the OECD and developing countries could pass this test because of the very different conditions in developing countries. Thus the ban amendment to the Basel Convention that came into force in 2019[85] should be justifiable under GATT Article XX(b). Again, with so many parties to the Basel ban, it would be hard to sustain a claim that as between those parties the ban contravened the GATT.

4 TECHNICAL AND SANITARY TRADE RESTRICTIONS

The protection of a nation's domestic environment may involve three different kinds of trade restrictions: (i) import restraints on products or services that do not comply with domestic environmental norms; (ii) regulations on labelling, packaging, and recycling; and (iii) export restrictions to conserve natural resources.

83 *Shrimp/Turtle*, paras 132–3, 168. But note the qualified terms of paragraph 133 with respect to extra-territorial application.

84 But that conclusion was left open in *EC—Measures Prohibiting the Importation and Marketing of Seal Products* ['*EC-Seals*'], Appellate Body Report, WT/DS400 &401/AB/R (2014), where Canada contested the extra-territorial application of Article XX(b).

85 *Supra*, Ch 8, section 5.

4(1) IMPORT RESTRAINTS FOR TECHNICAL, SANITARY AND PHYTOSANITARY PURPOSES

In addition to the requirements of the GATT, import restrictions are also subject to the Agreement on Technical Barriers to Trade ('TBT')[86] and the Agreement on the Application of Sanitary and Phytosanitary Measures ('SPS)'.[87] The TBT and SPS Agreements are mutually exclusive: the SPS Agreement deals with additives, contaminants, toxins, and disease-carrying organisms in food, beverages, and feedstuffs, while the TBT applies to all other product standards.[88] The Agreements restrict non-tariff barriers but allow states reasonable freedom to set their own standards.

The SPS is the more restrictive of the two agreements but it confirms that WTO member states have the right to take trade measures that are 'necessary' for the protection of human, plant and animal life or health.[89] This repeats the language in GATT Article XX(b). In the *Beef Hormones Case*,[90] which involved an EC import ban on hormone fed meat and meat products, the Appellate Body clarified the criteria and the process by which a WTO member can adopt and apply its own sanitary and phytosanitary standards. Six specific requirements must be fulfilled.

First, SPS measures must 'not be more trade-restrictive than required to achieve their appropriate level of . . . protection'.[91] This provision presumes the right of each state to choose *its own level* of protection unilaterally: 'appropriate' is the level of protection deemed appropriate by the member state.[92] A footnote specifies that a measure is not more trade restrictive than required unless there is another measure *reasonably* available (meaning feasible) that would do the job.[93] This elaboration effectively gives the word 'necessary' a flexible interpretation.

Second, any SPS measure shall be applied 'only to the extent necessary' to protect human, animal, or plant life or health.[94] This seems to duplicate partially the first requirement; arguably, it places the emphasis on the obligation not to *apply* a measure so as to cause more trade restriction than necessary for the appropriate level of protection desired. Under this interpretation, the first two requirements are complementary: a state can neither *adopt* nor *apply* a measure that goes beyond its chosen level of protection.

86 See Wolfrum, Stoll, Fohr (eds), *WTO—Technical Barriers and SPS Measures* (Leiden, 2007); Epps and Trebilcock (eds), *Research Handbook on the WTO and Technical Barriers to Trade* (Cheltenham, 2013).

87 See Pauwelyn, 2 *JIEL* (1999) 641 and Scott, *The WTO Agreement on Sanitary and Phytosanitary Measures: A Commentary* (Oxford, 2007).

88 TBT Agreement, Article 1(5); SPS Agreement, Article 1(4).

89 SPS Agreement, Article 2(1)–(2).

90 *EC—Measures Concerning Meat and Meat Products* ['Beef *Hormones Case*'], Rept of the Appellate Body, WT/DS26/AB/R (1997). Two further cases have similarly struck down national food safety measures because of a lack of scientific evidence and the failure to carry out a risk assessment. See *Australia—Measures Affecting the Import of Salmon*, Rept of Appellate Body, WT/DS18/AB/R (1998), and *Japan—Measures Affecting Agricultural Products*, Rept of the Panel, WT/DS76/R (1998).

91 Article 5(6).

92 See Annex A, para 5.

93 SPS Agreement, Article 5(6), n 3.

94 Article 2(2).

Third, a measure must be based upon 'scientific principles' and 'sufficient scientific evidence'.[95] Even without sufficient scientific evidence, the SPS Agreement includes 'precautionary language' that permits standards to be adopted provisionally 'on the basis of available pertinent information'.[96] This does not relieve the state concerned from the continuing obligation 'to obtain the additional information necessary for a more objective assessment of risk' and to review the measure within a reasonable period of time.[97] Nor does it permit a measure to be justified on the basis of the precautionary principle—whatever the international legal status of that principle—if otherwise contrary to the explicit requirements of the SPS Agreement.[98] As we noted in Chapter 11 above, this is a point of potential conflict between the SPS Agreement and the 2000 Cartagena Protocol. The Protocol explicitly adopts the precautionary principle for the regulation of food, feed, and processed LMOs, allowing import regulation even in the face of 'lack of scientific certainty due to insufficient scientific information'.[99] As we saw above, the SPS Agreement allows the precautionary principle to be applied only to measures taken on a provisional basis where there is insufficient scientific evidence.[100] Direct conflict has thus far been avoided and the Panel in the *EC—Biotech Case* did not apply the 1992 CBD and Protocol to its analysis of precaution under the SPS Agreement, thus at the same time raising the hurdle for interpretation of WTO agreements in the light of other instruments.[101]

Fourth, measures must be based upon a risk-assessment process 'taking into account' available scientific evidence and economic factors, including the objective of minimizing negative trade effects.[102] What is a sufficient risk assessment is not defined in the SPS Agreement either substantively or procedurally. A member, therefore, is free to consider both 'available scientific evidence' (Article 5(2)) and 'relevant economic factors' (Article 5(3)). But there must be a 'rational relationship between the trade measure and the risk assessment',[103] and the scientific reports relied upon must rationally support the import restriction. Since the risk assessment in the *Beef Hormones Case* failed these tests, the EC's import restriction was held to violate Article 5(1).

Fifth, Article 2(3) of the SPS Agreement repeats the requirements of the *chapeau* of Article XX, that the measure must not 'arbitrarily or unjustifiably discriminate between members' and must not be a 'disguised restriction on international trade'. Moreover, 'with the objective of achieving consistency', Article 5(5) also prohibits 'arbitrary or unjustifiable distinctions' in the levels of sanitary or phytosanitary protection considered appropriate. In practice and in the case law this provision is the real bite of the agreement.[104] The Appellate Body, interpreting these elements in the

[95] Ibid. For cogent critiques of the use of scientific evidence by WTO panels see Christoforou, 8 *NYUEnvLJ* (2000) 622 and Green and Epps, 10 *JIEL* (2007) 285.

[96] SPS Agreement, Art 5(7); *Beef Hormones* (AB), paras 124–5.

[97] SPS Agreement, Art 5(7). This was one of the points on which EC member state safeguard measures failed in the *EC—Biotech Case*.

[98] *Beef Hormones* (AB), paras 124–5; see Peel, 5 *Melb JIL* (2004) 483, 493.

[99] Article 11(8).

[100] Article 5(7).

[101] See Young, 56 *ICLQ* (2007) 907.

[102] Article 5.

[103] *Beef Hormones Case*, para 193.

[104] See Pauwelyn, 2 *JIEL* (1999) 641.

context of SPS Article 2(3), read Article 5(5) to require a showing of three elements: (i) that a member has adopted its own appropriate levels of SPS protection in several situations; (ii) that those levels of protection do not exhibit arbitrary or unjustifiable differences; and (iii) that these differences are not discriminatory or a disguised restriction on international trade.[105] These three elements are cumulative: arbitrary or unjustifiable differences alone will not violate Article 5(5) unless they also result in discrimination or a disguised restriction on international trade.[106]

Sixth, there is an obligation at least to consider adopting international SPS standards in the interests of achieving harmonization. Such standards are deemed under the SPS Agreement to include those emanating from three international standards-setting organizations—Codex Alimentarius for food safety, the International Office of Epizootics for animal health, and the Secretariat of the International Plant Protection Convention for plant health.[107] In addition, Annex A of the SPS Agreement includes 'appropriate standards' from other international organizations open to membership by all WTO members as identified by the SPS Committee.[108] Yet, the Agreement explicitly permits maintenance of higher standards if they are justified scientifically or required by the member state's own unilaterally determined higher level of protection.[109] Thus, a member may either choose an international SPS standard, or may base its standard on the international standard without conforming to all its requirements, or may set a level of protection wholly its own.[110] When an international standard is used, there is a rebuttable presumption that it is consistent with the SPS Agreement and the GATT.[111] If the national measure is based merely upon the international standard, but not in conformity with it, there is no presumption in its favour, but a complaining member must make a prima facie case in favour of inconsistency. If a member adopts its own level of protection under Article 3(3) of the SPS Agreement, it must be based on a 'risk assessment' (Article 5(1)) and 'sufficient scientific evidence' (Article 2(2)).[112]

The TBT Agreement accepts that member states have the right to regulate 'like' products, but it requires that technical regulations applicable to imported products will 'be no less favourable' than those applicable to domestic products (Article 2(1)),

105 *Beef Hormones Case*, para 214.

106 *Beef Hormones Case*, para 2.44–2.46. See also *Australia—Measures Affecting Importation of Salmon*, Report of the Appellate Body, WT/DS18/AB/R (1998).

107 IPCC standards were cited as the relevant international standards in *Japan—Measures Affecting the Importation of Apples* WT/DS245/AB/R, 75 (2003), para 205; see further *supra*, Ch 11, section 3.

108 See *Tuna/Dolphin II*, paras 363–401, which addresses the same point in the TBT Agreement. See also *EC—Biotech Case* and Young, 56 *ICLQ* (2007) 907.

109 Article 3.

110 *Beef Hormones Case*, paras 165–73. This interpretation is based upon Article 3(1)–(3) of the SPS Agreement. See also WT/DS231/AB/R *EC—Trade Descriptions of Sardines*, Report of the Appellate Body, para 245 (for domestic regulation based on international standards there must be a 'very strong and close relationship').

111 SPS Agreement, Article 3.2; *Beef Hormones Case*, para 170.

112 *Beef Hormones Case*, paras 176–80. Article 2(2) is to be read as informing the risk assessment obligation of Article 5(1). The reasoning of the Appellate Body in the *Beef Hormone Case* was followed by a WTO panel in *Australia—Measures Affecting Importation of Salmon*, Report of the Panel, WT/DS18/R (1998).

and that they will not be 'more restrictive than necessary to fulfil a legitimate objective' (Article 2(2)). 'Legitimate objective' includes 'protection of human health or safety, animal or plant life, or health, *or the environment*'.[113] In principle therefore the TBT Agreement allows the importing state to apply environmental protection measures. Here again, the *level* of protection is up to the individual member state, and a high level of environmental protection can be chosen. Furthermore, although international standards must be used when they exist, a state can employ its own stricter standards if the international technical requirements would be 'ineffective or inappropriate'.[114]

Several conclusions may be drawn from this brief analysis of the SPS and TBT Agreements. First, a WTO member may choose the level of protection it wants to adopt regarding environmental quality, health and safety. However, it must be prepared to justify trade-restricting measures once a prima facie case of violation is made out by a complaining member. Second, the precautionary principle, whatever its status as a general rule or principle of international law,[115] cannot override the specific provisions of the SPS Agreement.[116] Third, harmonization and the adoption of international standards is encouraged, but not required, and would in many cases not be easy.[117] Fourth, only the *means* chosen to implement these domestic policies will be subject to WTO review when they impact international trade, and the tests employed attempt to balance national interests, on the one hand, and the need to police disguised trade restrictions on the other.[118]

4(2) RECYCLING AND PACKAGING

Several countries have introduced mandatory recycling of products and packaging to reduce the generation of waste and the resulting pollution and need for landfills. Germany has led the way, passing the *Verpackungsverordnung* (*Packaging Ordinance*)[119] in 1991, which regulates the packaging of products and sets mandatory recycling requirements for packaging waste. The *Packaging Ordinance* requires the manufacturers of products to take back packaging wastes and to arrange for their recycling. They fulfil this duty by participating in a private waste collection system, which, for a fee, will handle this obligation by collecting waste from consumers. Participating manufacturers may mark their products with a green dot. The *Packaging Ordinance* applies to all products distributed within Germany.[120]

113 TBT Agreement, Article 2(2). See also *EC-Asbestos case*, paras 59–80.

114 TBT Agreement, Article 2(4).

115 See *supra*, Ch 3, section 6.

116 *Beef Hormone Case*, paras 123–5.

117 See Delimatsis (ed), *The Law, Economics and Politics of International Standardisation* (Cambridge, 2015) Ch 5.

118 Nichols, in Stewart (ed), *The World Trade Organization* (Washington DC, 1996) 191.

119 20 August 1991 BGBl I S 1234 *translated in* 21 *ILM* (1992), 1135. For commentary, see Goldfine, 7 *Georgetown IELR* (1994), 309.

120 Bundesministerium für Umwelt, Naturschutz, and Reaktorsicherheit, *The Packaging Ordinance and International Trade* §1(1), 23 June 1993.

Largely because of this German initiative and in order to harmonize member state legal regimes, the EU adopted a Packaging Directive in December 1994.[121] The EU directive sets target ranges for packaging waste recovery and recycling, standardizes methods of analysing product lifecycles and measuring toxicity of packaging components and waste, and sets maximum concentration levels for heavy metals in packaging. The directive applies to the packaging of all products sold in the EU, including imports.[122]

These laws are part of an increasing trend in many industrialized countries to consider the environmental impact of products throughout their lifecycles to the point of their ultimate disposal. The purpose of these laws is to (i) minimize packaging waste, (ii) prohibit the use of toxic and hazardous materials in packaging, and (iii) create incentives or requirements for recycling, reuse, or proper disposal of both the packaging and the products themselves. As we saw in Chapter 8 all these objectives are reflected in UN policy and international law on hazardous waste and toxic products. The growing problem of plastic waste is also beginning to attract international attention.[123]

Life-cycle laws plainly serve important environmental purposes. In principle, product lifecycle and producer responsibility laws are permitted under GATT Article III as long as they apply equally to domestic and foreign producers. They are also subject to the TBT Agreement and must not create 'unnecessary obstacles to international trade' or be 'more restrictive than necessary to fulfil a legitimate objective', including, of course, protection of the environment. These tests ensure that a balancing process will be applied so that restrictive measures are not out of proportion to their benefits.

The most serious problems come from the proliferation of such laws rather than their substantive requirements. If every country adopts its own national (or sub-national) system, trade will be disrupted simply by the burden of satisfying many different national bureaucracies. The problems stemming from proliferation could be alleviated through international harmonization of product life-cycle regulation.

4(3) ECO-LABELS

Another method of raising environmental standards is through eco-labelling. The theory behind eco-labels is that if consumers are informed, the market and consumer choice can be relied upon to stimulate the production and consumption of environmentally friendly products.[124] A great variety of eco-labelling schemes exist, sponsored by governments, private groups, or a combination of the two. They take several

121 Council Directive 94/62 EC, 1994 OJ (L 365) 10. See generally, Haner, 18 *Fordham ILJ* (1995), 2187; Comer, 7 *Fordham ELJ* (1995)163.

122 Council Directive 94/62, para 2(1).

123 See UNEA Resolutions 4/6 and 4/9 (2019). For a comprehensive study see Schäli, *The Mitigation of Marine Plastic Pollution in International Law: Facts, Policy and Legal Implications*, PhD submitted to the University of Bern in 2020.

124 See Ward, 6 *RECIEL* (1997) 139. For a sceptical view, see Menell, 4 *RECIEL* (1995) 304.

forms: mandatory 'negative content' labelling, mandatory 'content neutral' labelling, and voluntary 'multi-criteria' labelling.[125] Eco-labels can show product characteristics and/or process and production methods ('PPMs'). They can operate as a 'seal of approval' or objectively impart information. Well-known examples of eco-labelling plans include Germany's 'Blue Angel' programme and the 'White Swan' mark launched by the Scandinavian countries.[126] In the US a private organization operates a 'Green Seal' programme. Increasingly, governments are adopting such programmes.[127] In 1992 the EU established an eco-label scheme to 'promote the design, production, marketing, and use of products which have a reduced environmental impact during their entire lifecycle, and provide consumers with better information on the environmental impact of products'.[128]

Eco-labelling must comply with WTO/GATT requirements.[129] Even mandatory eco-label requirements on products would be permissible if they are applied on a non-discriminatory basis, adhering to the GATT most favoured nation ('MFN') and national treatment requirements. For example, under the US Energy Policy and Conservation Act,[130] corporate average fuel economy standards for cars must be calculated for domestic manufacturers and importers, and new cars sold in the USA must bear a label stating the estimated miles-per-gallon rate for city and highway use. This programme was the subject of a GATT panel report in the *US Taxes on Automobiles Case*,[131] which upheld the standards except for the separate foreign fleet accounting aspects, which discriminated unfairly against foreign manufacturers.

Even eco-label schemes that pertain to PPMs may be upheld if they adhere to GATT MFN and national treatment norms. On that basis in the *Tuna-Dolphin I Case*, the panel accepted the voluntary 'dolphin safe' labelling scheme for tuna products sold in the US, because they did not make the right to sell tuna or tuna products conditional on the use of specific harvesting methods.[132] But eco-labelling schemes must also comply with Article 2 of the TBT Agreement,[133] and with notice and transparency requirements, including the TBT Code of Good Practice.[134] In *Tuna/Dolphin II*, the Appellate Body concluded that US dolphin-friendly labelling requirements did affect competition in the US market to the detriment of Mexican tuna products and were not 'even-handed in the way in which they address the risks to dolphins arising from different fishing techniques in different areas of the ocean.'[135] Thus, a discriminatory labelling scheme would not be upheld under Article 2 of the TBT Agreement.

125 US Environmental Protection Agency, *Status Report on the Use of Environmental Labels Worldwide* (1993).

126 *See* Staffin, 21 *Col JEL* (1996) 205, 225.

127 Ibid, 230–2.

128 Commission Regulation 880/92, Article I, 1992 OJ (L 99) 1.

129 See Vranes, *Trade and the Environment,* 342–50.

130 17 USC §4001 (1994).

131 *US—Taxes on Automobiles*, DS31/R, 11 Oct 1994 (Not adopted by GATT Council).

132 *Tuna-Dolphin I*, para 5.42.

133 TBT Agreement, Annex I, para 1; *Tuna/Dolphin II.*

134 Ibid, Annex III.

135 *Tuna/Dolphin II*, paras 298–9.

5 TRADE RESTRICTIONS TO IMPROVE THE GLOBAL ENVIRONMENT

In some cases trade restrictions may be aimed at improving the environmental performance of other countries, for example those that are not taking steps to protect the global environment by reducing fossil fuel consumption or conserving forests and biodiversity. There are obvious concerns not just about a failure to take necessary measures, but about free-riders gaining competitive advantages in countries with lax environmental standards which thereby attract investment and facilitate 'leakage' from more stringent controls elsewhere on greenhouse gas emissions or ozone depleting substances. Border tax adjustments may offer one answer to this problem,[136] but the question arises whether the problem can be addressed indirectly through trade restrictions. A comparable argument can be made with respect to labour standards.[137] There are several possible ways of approaching the problem and all risk conflict with applicable WTO law.

5(1) PROCESS AND PRODUCTION METHODS

First, states may try to regulate how a product is produced or manufactured, or how resources are extracted or harvested—commonly referred to as process and production methods ('PPMs').[138] Some PPM regulations are directly related to the characteristics of the product. For example, pesticides used on crops produce residues on food products; cattle raised on growth hormones produce meat with hormone residues; and unsanitary conditions in slaughterhouses result in meat that may be contaminated with disease-causing organisms. Regulation of PPMs such as these is allowed by the SPS and TBT Agreements,[139] provided they are necessary on health or environmental grounds respectively and as long as the same regulations are applied to 'like' products both domestically produced and imported.

The position is less clear when the PPM regulation relates to the method of production or harvesting rather than the inherent characteristics of the product ('non product-related PPMs'). For example, when the US banned import of tuna caught by methods that involved targeting dolphins, GATT dispute-settlement panels declared this action inconsistent with GATT norms on the ground that it discriminated between 'like' products.[140] On this view, a state cannot adopt different treatment for two

136 See next section. 137 Ward, 45 *ICLQ* (1996) 592.

138 OECD, *Processes and Production Methods (PPMs): Conceptual Framework and Considerations on Use of PPM-Based Trade Measures* OCDE/GD(97)137 (Paris, 1997). See generally, Charnovitz, 27 *Yale JIL* (2002) 59; Conrad, *Processes and Production Methods (PPMs) in WTO Law: Interfacing Trade and Social Goals* (Cambridge, 2011); Vranes, *Trade and the Environment*, 319–30.

139 See TBT Agreement, Article 2 and Annex I, para 1; SPS Agreement, Annex A, para 1. See e.g. *EC-Asbestos case*, paras 59–80.

140 *Tuna/Dolphin I*. See generally Choi, *'Like Products' in International Trade Law: Towards a Consistent GATT/WTO Jurisprudence* (Oxford, 2003).

products with the same physical characteristics based upon how the products have been produced or harvested. Even if that is a correct view of the law, however, such a distinction may nevertheless be justifiable under Article XX(g) of GATT, as in *Shrimp/Turtle*, where the US regulation of shrimp fishing addressed only the method of catching shrimp.[141] Similarly, in *Tuna/Dolphin II* the Appellate Body by implication allowed the regulation of catch methods provided it applied the same standard to all tuna fishing where dolphins were endangered.[142] In this case a US regulation requiring that tuna for sale display a dolphin friendly label was found to contravene Article 2 of the TBT Agreement because it applied a stricter standard to areas where only Mexican boats operated, and not to other areas where US and other boats operated.[143] A third such case, *EC-Seals* took a different approach, holding that an import ban on seal products,[144] motivated by public revulsion at the inhumane methods of killing, was not regulated by the 'like product' provisions of the TBT Agreement, and could be justified by Article XX(a) of GATT because it was necessary for the protection of public morals.[145] Thus the cases appear to show that states may regulate trade in order to deter the use of inhumane, wasteful or unsustainable methods of hunting or catching. In all of these cases the fundamental problem is not the unilateral trade ban on 'like products' or its application to extraterritorial activities but the non-transparent and discriminatory character of the ban, and the preferred solution where possible is a multilateral agreement.[146] One study thus concludes that 'within limits npr-PPMs can serve as an alternative to international inaction. Only where the environmental effects on the regulating country would be too indirect, or where environmental concerns find little or no support in the international community, will States be hindered to adopt trade measures based on the extraterritorial nature of the environmental concern'.[147]

Thus the alternative to unilateral regulation of PPMs is to seek international agreement on regulation. The WTO/GATT system, through the TBT and SPS Agreements, and consistently with GATT Article III, relies primarily on encouraging harmonization and the adoption of international standards, while permitting national treatment where there are no such standards. If harmonization of product standards on a worldwide basis has proved difficult, harmonizing PPMs would be more so. There are also economic and environmental arguments for not trying to make PPM standards identical on a worldwide basis.[148]

141 *Supra*, section 2. 142 Young, in Viñuales (ed), *The Rio Declaration etc*, 335–6.

143 *Tuna/Dolphin II*, para 298. See Crowley and Howse, 13 *World Trade Rev* (2014) 321.

144 Under Regulation (EC) No. 1007/2009. For a critical analysis see Marin Duran, 6 *Eur Ybk Int Economic L* (2015) 87. For the history of this dispute see Bowman, Davies and Redgwell, *Lyster's International Wildlife Law* (Cambridge, 2009), Ch 20, and Nollkaemper, 8 *JEL* (1996) 237.

145 *EC-Seals*, paras 289–90. But the ban's discriminatory features contravened the chapeau to Article XX: see para 339.

146 Young, in Viñuales (ed),*The Rio Declaration etc*, 338–40. 147 Cooreman, 65 (*ICLQ*) 229 at 248.

148 See Stewart, 102 *Yale LJ* (1993) 2039, 2051–7.

PPMs can also be addressed through corporate adoption of environmental management systems developed by the International Standards Organization ('ISO').[149] ISO 14001 does not establish specific PPMs, rather, it requires companies to commit themselves to continual improvement of their compliance with applicable laws, but it leaves each company free to implement individual solutions. Although adoption of ISO 14001 is voluntary, governments can provide incentives for its use through enforcement policies and guarantees for companies that implement it.

Another approach to the problem is to tax imported products for environmental purposes, known as 'border tax adjustments', considered in section 6 below.

5(2) CONSERVATION OF NATURAL RESOURCES

Can exports of natural resources be banned on conservation grounds? In principle yes. Such bans would have to qualify either under GATT Article XI(2)(a), which permits an export prohibition or restriction to relieve 'critical shortages', or under Article XX(g), as a measure related to conservation of exhaustible natural resources. Thus, a ban on timber or fish exports in order to conserve forests or fish could be consistent with Article XX(g) but only if non-discriminatory and 'made effective in conjunction with restrictions on domestic production or consumption'.[150] On the same basis, a country could ban or restrict the production of oil or coal in order to conserve the global atmosphere from carbon emissions. Compelling it to do so under an international agreement on climate change would not violate the GATT if given effect on a non-discriminatory basis.

6 ENVIRONMENTAL TAXES

Environmental taxes are based on the principle that resources are under-priced and, therefore, overused. Environmental taxes have three purposes: (i) to discourage the consumption of goods and services that create environmental costs; (ii) to encourage producers to develop alternative production methods and products that are less harmful to the environment; and (iii) to implement the polluter-pays principle.[151] There are three different categories of environmental taxes that governments may use to achieve these purposes. First, taxes can be imposed directly on the sale of a product that has potentially adverse environmental consequences. Second, the tax can be levied on the

[149] See Roht-Arriaza, 22 *ELQ* (1995) 479; ibid, 6 *YbIEL* (1995) 107; Rodgers, 5 *NYU Env LJ* (1996) 181; Morrison and Roht-Arriaza, in Bodansky, Brunnée, and Hey (eds), *The Oxford Handbook of International Environmental Law* (Oxford, 2007) Ch 21; Scott in Rajamani and Peel (eds), *The Oxford Handbook of International Environmental Law* (2nd edn, Oxford, 2021) Ch 26.

[150] *Supra*, section 2.

[151] On the polluter-pays principle see *supra*, Ch 5, section 4 and OECD, Recommendations C(72)128 on Guiding Principles Concerning International Economic Aspects of Environmental Policies; C(74)223 on the Implementation of the 'Polluter Pays' Principle.

use of the resource itself. Examples include charges for the emission of pollutants into the air, discharges into rivers or sewer systems. Third, environmental taxes may be imposed on *inputs* into products. Here, two kinds of measures may be distinguished: taxes on inputs that are physically incorporated into the final product (such as chemical feedstock incorporated into a plastic or petroleum product), and taxes on inputs consumed during production, such as fuel or energy used in making a manufactured product. Environmental taxes will increase the cost of the goods, and may result in import substitution, pulling in imports from countries that do not have comparable taxes. The importing state may then respond by taxing imports from those countries in order to level the playing field, so called 'border tax adjustments' ('BTA').

Taxes on imports raise the issue of their consistency with the WTO system. The GATT distinguishes two principal categories of taxes and charges and submits them to different controls.[152] Article II(1), which applies to customs duties and import charges, prohibits WTO members from imposing higher charges than those specified in their agreed schedules of concessions. Article III, which applies to internal taxes and charges, requires national treatment. To distinguish between the two, Article II(2) (a) provides:

> Nothing in this Article shall prevent any contracting party from imposing *at any time* on the importation of any product:
>
> (a) a charge equivalent to an internal tax imposed consistently with the provisions of paragraph 2 of Article III in respect of an article *from which* the imported product has been manufactured or produced *in whole or in part*. [Emphasis added][153]

BTA allows (i) an internal tax to be imposed on imported products and (ii) the remission of internal taxes on domestic products destined for export.

(i) Taxes on products Environmental taxes levied on products are eligible for BTA as long as they are consistent with the national treatment standards of GATT Article III. In the *US Superfund Case*, the panel made the point that the GATT 'does not distinguish between taxes with different policy purposes'.[154] The GATT requires only that 'like' imported and domestic products be taxed the same. A deposit-and-return system of taxes on products is also permissible under GATT rules. In the *Canada Beer Cases*,[155] panels upheld the Canadian deposit/return system on beer containers

[152] See generally Fauchald, *Environmental Taxes and Trade Discrimination* (The Hague, 1998); Vranes, *Trade and the Environment* 331–41.

[153] The requirements of Article III(2) must be met, so imports cannot be charged more than domestic products. See *Japan—Taxes on Alcoholic Beverages*, WTO Appellate Body Report, WT/DS8/AB/R (1996) [*Japan -Alcoholic Beverages II*].

[154] *US—Taxes on Petroleum and Certain Imported Substances* ['*US-Superfund Case*'] GATT BISD (34th Supp) (1988), 136, para 5.2.8. See to the same effect *Japan-Alcoholic Beverages II*.

[155] *Canada—Import, Distribution, and Sale of Alcoholic Drinks by Canadian Provincial Marketing Agencies*, 22 March 1988, GATT BISD (35th Supp) 37 (1989) (hereafter '*Canada Beer I*'); *Canada—Import, Distribution, and Sale of Alcoholic Drinks by Canadian Provincial Marketing Agencies*, 18 February 1992, GATT BISD (39th Supp) 27 (1993) (hereafter '*Canada Beer II*').

as applied to imports; to meet the national treatment standard, however, the system had to be applied equally without different systems of delivery to points of sale for imported and domestic beer.[156] Thus, GATT norms freely permit BTA with respect to environmental taxes on products.

(ii) Taxes on inputs. The leading case on environmental taxation of physically incorporated inputs is *US Superfund*, which ruled that environmental taxes on inputs that are physically present in some form in the final imported product are properly subject to BTA.[157] This means that BTA can be applied, for example, to CFCs or other ozone-depleting substances incorporated in refrigerators.

The status of taxes on inputs consumed in the production process, such as fossil fuels, is more problematic. The implementation of greenhouse gas reductions under the Paris Agreement could include taxes on energy consumption, or on greenhouse gas emissions. But the GATT is ambiguous about BTA for taxes on inputs consumed during the production process. Article III requires only national treatment, but on one view Article II(2)(a) appears to preclude BTA, since it allows a tax only on inputs 'from which', *not* 'with the help of which', the imported and the like domestic product were produced. In 1970 a GATT Working Party on Border Tax Adjustments noted a divergence of views on whether energy taxes can be imposed on imported products in these circumstances.[158] One recent study of 'border carbon adjustments' (BCA) designed to reduce 'carbon leakage' under the 2015 Paris Agreement concludes that whether BTA could be applied to imported goods for this purpose: '. . . would ultimately depend on how broadly any future WTO dispute settlement body interprets the terms of Article II:2(a) and Article III:2 of the GATT'.[159] The legal issues are too complicated to explore here, but the same study rightly concludes that even if BTA in respect of carbon taxes is not permitted by Articles II or III it could still be justified under GATT Article XX(g) because such taxes clearly relate to the conservation of an exhaustible resource and the implementation of the Paris Agreement.[160] Here is a situation where the mutually supportive outcome envisaged by Rio Principle 12 is obviously called for. As we saw earlier,[161] this would be an important conclusion if parties to the 2015 Paris Agreement ever wish to use trade measures to pressurise those states that are not parties to or are not implementing the Agreement.

156 *Canada Beer II*, ibid, para 5.33. 157 *US Superfund Case*, para 5.2.8.

158 GATT, *Border Tax Adjustments: Report of the Working Party*, L/3464, BISD 18S/97 (1970).

159 Mehling et al, 113 *AJIL* (2019) 433, at 458–59.

160 Ibid, 464ff. See also Pauwelyn, in Prevost and Van Calster (eds),*Research Handbook on Environment, Health, and the WTO* (Cheltenham, 2013).

161 *Supra*, section 2.

7 THE TRIPS AGREEMENT AND THE BIODIVERSITY CONVENTION

The WTO Agreement on Trade-Related Aspects of Intellectual Property Rights ('TRIPs')[162] guarantees recognition and enforcement of intellectual property rights backed by the authority of the WTO's dispute settlement mechanism. As indicated above, the relationship between TRIPS and the environment is one of three areas of focus for the CTE identified in the 2001 Doha Declaration, with two features subsequently dominating CTE discussions: (i) transfer of environmentally friendly technology; and (ii) the general relationship between TRIPS and the Convention on Biological Diversity.[163] As we noted above in Chapter 11, the 1992 CBD provides that the genetic resources of plants and animals are under the sovereignty of the state in which they are located,[164] and developing countries have a right to benefit from the development of these resources as well as from the transfer of technology relevant to the development and use of genetic resources. The 1992 CBD also requires the recognition 'as far as possible and as appropriate' of the rights of 'indigenous and local communities' in 'innovations and practices' relevant to the conservation and use of biological diversity.[165] These two agreements contain the seeds of potential conflicts with vast implications not only for the environment, but also for the biotechnology, pharmaceutical, and agricultural industries. The opportunity to clarify the relationship arose with conclusion of the 2010 Nagoya Protocol[166] which applies to traditional knowledge associated with genetic resources and to the benefits arising from the use of such knowledge. Anticipating the potential for overlap with both TRIPS and WIPO[167]—though neither is explicitly mentioned[168]—implementation of the Nagoya Protocol 'in a mutually supportive manner with other instruments' is required.[169] For Parties to

[162] The text of TRIPS is reprinted in WTO, *The Legal Texts, supra*, n 2.

[163] TRIPS Article 64, with a delayed implementation periods for developing countries which have now expired.

[164] For the particular problem of genetic resources on the deep seabed, see *supra*, Ch 12 and Scovazzi, in Francioni and Scovazzi (eds), *Biotechnology and International Law* (Oxford, 2006) Ch 4.

[165] Articles 3, 8, 10, 15, 16, 19. See also the Nagoya Protocol on Access and Benefit Sharing, Articles 5, 6, 7 and 12.

[166] See further Morgera, Tsioumani and Buck, *Unravelling the Nagoya Protocol* (Leiden/Boston, 2014), sections 1.1 and 4.

[167] 'Due regard' should also be paid to ongoing work in other fora which does not run counter to the objectives of the Protocol. A case in point is work under WIPO, which in 2001 established an Intergovernmental Committee on Intellectual Property and Genetic Resources, Traditional Knowledge and Folklore which has been slowly working towards an international legal instrument relating to intellectual property, genetic resources and traditional knowledge associated with genetic resources. This is expressly 'without prejudice to the work pursued in other fora' eg the TRIPS Council and Nagoya Protocol.

[168] Preambular language referring to the Nagoya Protocol as 'the comprehensive protocol' on ABS and for it to be used as the basis for WIPO's continuing work on the topic was not included in the final text: Morgera, Tsioumani and Buck, 85.

[169] Article 4(3).

the Nagoya Protocol, Article 4 imposes a negative obligation to refrain from developing further instrument(s) which run counter to the objectives of the Convention and Protocol.[170]

The TRIPS Agreement and the 1992 CBD were developed, albeit at the same time, by different delegations, in different forums, with different objectives, and with almost no consultation or even communication between the two negotiations. The same is not true for the 2000 Cartagena Protocol, however, as we have noted, and subsequent developments under the 1992 CBD have seen increased cooperation between, for example, the Biodiversity secretariat and the WTO and WIPO secretariats.[171] Since the 1992 CBD is in force and accepted by 196 States and the WTO/GATT by over 150, conflicts are most likely to arise between nations that have accepted both treaty regimes. In such a case, Article 22 of the 1992 CBD adopts the following rule of priority:

1. The provisions of this Convention shall not affect the rights and obligations of any Contracting Party deriving from any existing international agreement, except where the exercise of those rights and obligations would cause a serious damage or threat to biological diversity.[172]
2. Contracting Parties shall implement this Convention with respect to the marine environment consistently with the rights and obligations of States under the law of the sea.

As we noted above in Chapter 11, this 'serious damage or threat' standard can be interpreted in different ways, and highlights the importance of dispute settlement when concrete issues arise. However, the 1992 CBD provides a flexible dispute settlement mechanism in Article 27: parties are required to negotiate and they may refer the dispute by agreement to mediation, but arbitration or resort to the ICJ are compulsory only if both parties have made a declaration accepting jurisdiction. Since few states have accepted this option, most disputes under the Convention will be resolved by compulsory conciliation, which requires only that the states involved submit their dispute to a conciliation commission and consider the solution proposed by the commission 'in good faith'. This provision also applies to disputes under the 2000 Cartagena and 2010 Nagoya Protocols. It may be contrasted with the dispute resolution mechanism of TRIPS, where disputes are subject to resolution under GATT Articles XXII and XXIII and the WTO's Dispute Settlement Understanding detailed earlier in this chapter and featuring compulsory jurisdiction, a strict timetable, judicialized procedures, and mandatory compliance or punishment in the form of compensation or suspension of concessions.

170 Article 4(2) and (4); see further Pavoni, 'The Nagoya Protocol and the WTO' in Morgera, Buck and Tsioumani (eds), *2010 Nagoya Protocol on Access and Benefit-Sharing in Perspective* (Brill, 2012), Ch 6.

171 See Ch 11 *supra*. While the TRIPS is a covered agreement under the WTO and is concerned with the trade-related aspects of intellectual property rights, the other international conventions referred to in it—on trademarks, copyright, and industrial property for example—are administered by WIPO.

172 In similar terms see also Article 4(1) of the Nagoya Protocol, which goes on explicitly to add that this is not intended to create a hierarchy between the Protocol and other international instruments.

Given these two separate regimes, disputes arising under both the 1992 CBD / Protocols and TRIPS probably will be addressed by the WTO dispute settlement regime. This is because the WTO process is mandatory if either party brings a complaint; the other party will not be able to resist. Thus, conciliation under the 1992 CBD will take place only if both parties involved agree to forego resort to the WTO. In some cases disputes may arise between states that have accepted binding arbitration or adjudication by the ICJ as well as the WTO regime. In such a case a true conflict may arise as to which dispute settlement body has primary jurisdiction.[173]

7(1) ACCESS TO GENETIC RESOURCES

Major industries, such as those relating to biotechnology, pharmaceuticals, and agriculture, are dependent on worldwide access to genetic resources. These and other industries use wild plants and animals in three basic ways. First, a species can be used directly as a source of natural chemicals or compounds for the production of drugs or other products. An example is the use of the Pacific yew tree to produce an anti-cancer drug. Second, a species' natural chemicals can provide information and ideas that can lead to the production of useful synthetic chemicals, drugs, and products. An example is aspirin, a drug developed as a synthetic modification of salicylic acid, which is found in plants. Third, a natural species can be a source of a gene or genetic sequence that can be used to develop new varieties through breeding or a genetically modified organism through implantation. The former process is essential to modern agriculture. Because crops and animals are susceptible to disease and adverse climatic conditions, it is critical to have access to natural gene pools (germ plasm) to develop more productive and disease resistant plants and animals. The latter process is critical to the biotech industry which develops new products through genetic modification and incorporation of genetic materials.

Article 15 of the 1992 CBD authorizes states to limit or place conditions on access to genetic resources.[174] The vague language of Article 15 provides a potential basis for a range of actions, from an export ban to market pricing. However, members of the WTO are required to observe the GATT norms in its implementation. Most notably, export bans or conditions would have to comply with GATT Article XX(g), which requires that export restrictions must relate to the conservation of the resource and must be applied in conjunction with restrictions on domestic production or consumption. In addition, an Article 15 export measure must not employ 'arbitrary or unjustifiable

[173] A precedent for reconciliation of the jurisdiction of different international tribunals is Article 2005 of the North American Free Trade Agreement (NAFTA), which contains a complex regime for deciding when the parties to a trade dispute should go to the World Trade Organization and when the NAFTA dispute settlement provisions should be employed. See Abbott, in Weiler (ed), *The EU, the WTO and the NAFTA: Towards and Common Law of International Trade* (Oxford, 2000) 182–4.

[174] The provisions on access and benefit sharing in the CBD have been elaborated by the SBSTTA and by the Nagoya Protocol: see *supra*, Ch 11 section 6.

discrimination between countries' or be a 'disguised restriction on international trade'. Thus, the vagaries of Article 15 are subject to the discipline of the GATT.

A striking exercise of Article 15 rights is the control regime adopted by Costa Rica, which, in 1992, passed amendments to its Wildlife Conservation Law declaring wildlife to be in the 'public interest' and requiring advance governmental approval for the export of genetic materials and for bio-genetic research.[175] This law is designed to give the Costa Rican government broad discretion in negotiating contracts with foreign firms that wish to employ genetic resources for research. A precursor of this contractual regime was the 1989 contract[176] signed by Merck & Company, the largest US pharmaceutical company, and the Instituto de Biodiversidad Nacional (INBIO), a non-profit institution created by the Costa Rican government. Under this arrangement Merck advanced $1 million to INBIO for the right to develop drugs from Costa Rican plants, insects, or microbes supplied by INBIO, and INBIO and the Costa Rican government will share an amount, reportedly between 1 and 3 per cent, of the revenues from any products developed from INBIO-supplied genetic resources.

GATT would not bar this arrangement or any other that requires compensation in the form of payment or royalties in return for resource use.[177] The GATT does not regulate pricing so that any payment arrangement would be permissible; however, if a state trading enterprise is involved, GATT Article XVII requires that purchases and sales must be in accordance with commercial consideration and must be made on a non-discriminatory basis.[178] Thus, the GATT and Article 15 of the 1992 CBD are prima facie compatible.

Perhaps the most important and troublesome question likely to arise in legislation and contracts implementing Article 15 is whether countries can discriminate against foreign companies, charging them for resource use while exempting domestic firms. The answer to this question depends on whether the charge is levied as a customs charge or an internal tax or charge. A true customs charge must comply only with the most-favoured-nation requirement of the GATT Article I, while an internal charge must comply not only with Article I but also with GATT Article III, which requires national treatment. In the latter case it would be GATT-illegal to exempt domestic firms. Thus, foreign firms that establish and carry on research activities in the country of origin of the biological materials cannot be subjected to a discriminatory pricing arrangement.

While Article 15 is, in principle, compatible with the GATT, it may be difficult for substantial revenues to be derived from Article 15 by developing countries unless they illegally control exports and discriminate against foreign firms. First, only rarely will the biological materials concerned be limited to one country, and availability from multiple sources will reduce the price. For example, Eli Lilly Company produced two

175 See Aseby and Kempenaar, 28 *Vand JTL* (1998), 703.

176 See Reid et al (eds), *Biodiversity Prospecting: Using Genetic Resources for Sustainable Development* (Washington DC, 1993); Powers, 12 *Wis ILJ* (1993) 103, 117–20.

177 For a comprehensive review and analysis of contractual arrangements, see Aseby and Kempenaar, 28 *Vand JTL* (1995) 703.

178 GATT Article XVII(1)–(2).

anti-cancer drugs, vinblastine and vincristine, from periwinkle leaves first obtained in Madagascar. However, the plant grows wild in many areas of the world including Texas, where it is grown commercially. Although Eli Lilly has been criticized[179] for not providing compensation to Madagascar, it is not difficult to see why it did not do so. Second, few new drugs or products are made from unmodified biological resources; more often they will be derivatives or produced purely synthetically.[180] Thus, Article 15 seems to be deficient as a mechanism for achieving the goal of sustainable development.

7(2) PATENTABILITY

Patentability is important for the development of both beneficial biotechnologies and marketable environmental technologies that generate less waste and pollution. The TRIPS Agreement, by strengthening global intellectual property protection, will have a positive effect on both categories by providing incentives for research and development. Under TRIPS Article 27(1) patents must be available for products and processes in all fields of technology. TRIPS Article 8(1) permits 'measures necessary to protect public health and nutrition and to promote the public interest in sectors of vital importance to . . . socio-economic and technological development', but this is qualified by the requirement that such measures must be 'consistent with . . . this Agreement'. It would thus appear that Article 8(1) does not qualify the patentability requirement of Article 27. However, Article 27(2) allows members to exclude from patentability inventions that endanger human, animal or plant life or health, or the environment, but the exclusion must be 'necessary', not 'merely because the exploitation is prohibited by their law'. Article 27(3) also allows plants, animals, and biological processes to be excluded from patentability, but micro-organisms, non-biological and microbiological processes must be patentable.

This formulation ensures that most biotechnological, pharmaceutical, and agricultural biotechnical inventions must be protected by patent law. Naturally occurring plants and animals are not patentable, but genetically modified micro-organisms, animal genes, human DNA sequences, human proteins, and human genes have all been patented in the USA and Europe.[181] Although TRIPS does not require parties to allow the patenting of genetically engineered animals, such as the 'Harvard mouse', an experimental animal developed for the study of breast cancer, the transgenic process by which such animals are developed would be patentable under TRIPS, either as a microbiological or a non-biological process.[182] The US Patent and Trademark Office

[179] See Stone, 256 *Science* (1992) 1624.

[180] Office of Technology Assessment, US Cong, *Biotechnology in a Global Economy*, 75–6 (Washington DC, 1991).

[181] See generally Walden, in Bowman and Redgwell (eds), *International Law and the Conservation of Biological Diversity*, 171; Hedge, 38 *Ind JIL* (1998) 28. In *Diamond v Chakrabarty*, 447 US 303 (1980) the US Supreme Court held that a genetically altered micro-organism was patentable under US law either as a 'manufacture' or a 'composition of matter'.

[182] Genetically altered animals are patentable under US law: see *Ex parte Allen*, 2 USPQ 1425 (1987).

issued a patent in 1988 to the inventors of the 'Harvard mouse' (also known as the 'ONCO mouse'). In contrast, a similar patent granted by the European Patent Office in 1991 was subject to opposition proceedings under Article 53 of the 1973 European Patent Convention, which provides that a patent should not be granted (a) for an invention the exploitation of which would be contrary to *ordre public* or public morality, and (b) for plant or animal varieties, or essentially biological processes for the production of plants or animals. Article 6 of the 1998 EC Directive 98/44/EC on Protection of Biotechnological Inventions retains similar but not identical morality provisions, although its general thrust is to provide for the patentability of biological material in EU member states. Article 1(2) of the Directive explicitly provides that it is without prejudice to member States' obligations pursuant to international agreements, and in particular TRIPS and the Biodiversity Convention.

TRIPS also for the first time requires plant breeders' rights (PBR) to be given world-wide protection. Although naturally occurring plants cannot be patented, TRIPS Article 27(3)(b) provides that 'Members shall provide for the protection of plant varieties either by patents or by an effective *sui generis* system or by any combination thereof'. The *sui generis* system refers to the International Union for the Protection of New Varieties of Plants ('UPOV'), established by the UPOV Convention in Paris in 1961 and periodically revised.[183] States adhering to UPOV undertake to create a system of granting PBRs under their domestic laws. TRIPS supplements UPOV by requiring all WTO member states to grant protection to PBRs, either through UPOV or by admitting their patentability.[184]

The 1992 CBD, in general, is consistent with the patentability provisions of TRIPS and places no limits on protection of genetic resources. The same is the case for the 2010 Nagoya Protocol which does not impose limits on the patentability of biotechnological applications.[185] However, the Convention calls for respect and preservation of the knowledge, innovations, and practices of indigenous and local communities.[186] It is not clear what impact, if any, these provisions were intended to have on intellectual property rights. Presumably, domestic legislation could provide for PBR for traditional societies and certain kinds of knowledge could be protected as trade secrets.[187] Thus, these provisions of the 1992 CBDmay be accommodated under existing categories of intellectual property rights. A similar conclusion may be drawn under the 2010 Nagoya Protocol, which does not impose IPR-related benefit sharing nor does

[183] In 1972, 1978, and 1991. 'UPOV' stands for 'Union Internationale pour la Protection des Obtentions Végétales' and its members include the EC and the USA. On international regimes for plant genetic resources see Rose, in Bowman and Redgwell (eds), *International Law and the Conservation of Biological Diversity*, 145; Duffield, *Intellectual Property Rights, Trade and Biodiversity* (London, 1999); and *supra*, Ch 11, section 6.

[184] See Tilford, 30 *Case WRJIL* (1998) 373.

[185] And see also Article 4 above, on the relationship between the Protocol and other international agreements and instruments.

[186] Articles 8(j), 10(c); and Nagoya Protocol, especially Articles 7 and 12. See Shelton, 5 *YbIEL* (1994) 77, and *supra*, Ch 11, section 6. See also the UNESCO Convention on intangible property rights.

[187] See generally Starr and Hardy, 12 *Stan ELJ* (1993) 85.

it require the mandatory disclosure of the origin of genetic resources (and the indigenous knowledge utilised) when filing for patent protection.[188]

Another problem may be posed by the exception clause of TRIPS Article 27(2). On first reading, this exception seems very broad, freely allowing national exceptions to patentability. However, the two qualifying phrases, 'necessary' and 'not made merely because the exploitation is prohibited by their law' could, if interpreted strictly, mean that only when there is a substantial international consensus in favour of non-patentability and only where no other means is available to protect the environment, will this exception be triggered. As yet the meaning and scope of this Article 27(2) exception has not been clarified.[189]

7(3) ACCESS TO AND TRANSFER OF TECHNOLOGY

The 1992 CBD and the TRIPS Agreement may come into conflict depending on how Article 16 of the Convention is interpreted concerning access to and transfer of technology. TRIPS mandates a private, free-market system for the acquisition and transfer of rights to intellectual property. Article 28 confers on the patent owner the right to prevent the selling or importing of patented products; patent owners also have the exclusive right to assign, transfer or license their patents. The 1992 CBD, in contrast, requires that the contracting parties provide for (i) priority or concessional access for developing countries; (ii) preferential terms for such countries; and (iii) joint research and development efforts by the firms that develop the IPRs and the country supplying the genetic resources.[190]

All of these requirements potentially conflict with the TRIPS regime, which would leave matters to the private sector to decide without governmental interference. For this reason, as we noted above in Chapter 11, the US initially refused to sign the 1992 CBD,[191] and the Clinton administration essentially repudiated all three requirements in its statement supporting the Convention's ratification. President Clinton's Message to the Congress stated that sharing of results of research and benefits 'must take fully into account exclusive rights that a party may possess and that transfers of proprietary technology will take place only at the discretion of the owner of the technology'.[192] Article 16 should be interpreted, the president stated, so 'that in the case of technology subject to patents and other intellectual property rights, such access and transfer shall be provided on terms that are consistent with the adequate and effective protection of intellectual property rights'.[193] The message further holds that:

[188] As noted in Ch 11 above, the only provision is found in the Annex to the Protocol which provides an illustrative, non-exhaustive list of possible benefits including joint ownership of relevant IPRs.

[189] See Harper, 2 *Wm & Mary Envtl L & Pol Rev* (1997) 381.

[190] See Articles 15(7), 16(2)–(3), 19(1)–(2). See *supra*, Ch 11.

[191] See also Chandler, 4 *Col JILP* (1993) 141, 173–5.

[192] Convention on Biodiversity: Message from the President of the US, 103 Cong Treaty Doc 103–20, Nov 1993, XI.

[193] Ibid, XIII.

technology transfer by the US private sector to other countries requires an economic infrastructure in the recipient country that encourages the voluntary transfer of technology and provides sufficient safeguards for investment . . . To be considered adequate and effective, a country's intellectual property system must make protection available for all fields of technology and provide effective procedures for enforcing rights.[194]

These comments appear to disregard the primary requirements of Articles 15, 16, and 19 of the 1992 CBD and would amount to a reservation, should the US move to ratification on this basis. However, no reservations are permitted.[195]

There is, perhaps, one way to reconcile the provisions of the 1992 CBD with the TRIPS Agreement and the protection of intellectual property rights. Articles 20 and 21 of the Convention provide for a 'financial mechanism' and the provision of financial resources to facilitate transfer of technology to developing countries on favourable terms. Nothing in the TRIPS Agreement would prohibit the use of an international financial mechanism to assure access and the transfer of technology. Articles 15, 16, and 19 can be interpreted to mean that transfer of technology should be left to negotiations between private parties, but should be supplemented where needed by the financial mechanism established by the Convention's contracting parties under Articles 20 and 21.[196]

7(4) COMPULSORY LICENSING

An important question that may arise under the 1992 CBD and the TRIPS Agreement is whether a developing country that believes its rights under the Convention are being denied can resort to compulsory licensing. The 1992 CBD contains no specific authorization of compulsory licensing, but it does authorize 'legislative, administrative or policy measures, as appropriate' to gain the rights granted by the access to and transfer of technology and biotechnology provisions.[197] Compulsory licensing by WTO members would be controlled by TRIPS Agreement, which has specific provisions dealing with this issue. Article 30 of TRIPS permits 'limited exceptions to the exclusive rights conferred by a patent, provided [the exceptions] do not unreasonably conflict with the normal exploitation of the patent and do not unreasonably prejudice the legitimate interest of the patent owner . . .'. These conditions make Article 30 of TRIPS a poor vehicle to claim the transfer of technology benefits accorded by the Biodiversity Convention. Article 30 envisages only ad hoc exceptions primarily for experimental purposes.

194 Ibid. According to US Department of State data, the Convention is one of thirty-seven treaties submitted to Senate which have not received its advice and consent to ratification.

195 Article 37.

196 Another possibility might be an Agreement on Implementation analogous to that adopted in 1994 with respect to the 1982 Law of the Sea Convention, which subjects the technology transfer provisions of Part XI on the deep sea bed to GATT disciplines: see Evans, in Evans (ed), *International Law* (5th edn, Oxford, 2018) Ch 21.

197 Articles 15(4), 16(3), 19(1).

Article 31 of TRIPS authorizes compulsory licensing subject to highly restrictive conditions that would seem to make the use of compulsory licensing impractical to achieve the purposes of the 1992 CBD, except in extreme cases. Under TRIPS, the compulsory licensee must be remunerated based upon 'economic value', and it must be preceded by efforts to obtain authorization on 'reasonable commercial terms'. Thus, a developing country could not obtain the 'concessional and preferential terms' provided for by the 1992 CBD through compulsory licensing.[198] However, in 2005 an amendment to Article 31 was adopted to give effect to a waiver granted to make it easier for countries in need to import cheaper generic medicines made under compulsory licensing if unable to manufacture it for themselves.[199] This is the first amendment adopted to one of the 'core' WTO agreements and indicates a potential way forward where the political will to act—in this case to facilitate access to generic drugs for the treatment of HIV/AIDS.

8 INTERNATIONAL TRADE AND INVESTMENT

While the GATT 1947 did not address international investment, one of the WTO covered agreements added by the Uruguay Round is the Agreement on Trade-Related Investment Measures ('TRIMs'). However, it is neither a comprehensive code on international investment nor of the trade-related investment measures employed by States.[200] If measures are not trade-related within the meaning of Articles III or XI of the GATT, they will not come under the TRIMs Agreement (though will of course be subject to any obligations assumed under a BIT or under general international law). In practice this means that the relationship between international investment law and environmental protection is largely regulated outside of the WTO framework.

While Principle 12 of the Rio Declaration directly addresses the relationship between trade and environment, investment is approached more tangentially. Rare mention is contained in Principle 16 of the Rio Declaration on the polluter pays principle, the application of which requires 'due regard to the public interest and without distorting trade and investment'.[201] Such distortion might arise through eg a differential tax regime based on the carbon intensity of products and their end use, or subsidies for carbon efficient

[198] Article 16(2).

[199] A waiver was granted on 30 August 2003 by decision of the General Council (WT/L/540), accompanied by (an interpretative statement by the Chair, to give effect to paragraph 6 of the Doha Declaration on TRIPS and public health. At the Hong Kong Ministerial Meeting in December 2005 an amendment inserted a new Article 31 *bis* and Annex to TRIPs, rendering in binding legal form the 2003 Decision and accompanying Chair's statement upon receipt of instruments of ratification by 2/3 of WTO members: see WT/L/641, 6 December 2005.

[200] For background see Lowenfeld, *International Economic Law* (2nd edn, Oxford, 2008) 105–6.

[201] See *supra*, Ch 5, section 4.

or 'climate-friendly' technologies.[202] Investment arbitration involving challenges to domestic environmental regulation has increased significantly in recent decades.[203]

As discussed in Chapter 3, foreign direct investment as part of the 'green economy' can be a significant contributor to achieving sustainable development.[204] We saw there the purpose of Principle 4 of the Rio Declaration is to ensure that development decisions—including with respect to FDI—do not disregard environmental considerations. This is evident in the investment and lending policies of the World Bank and other multilateral development which banks have sought to integrate environmental assessment into their lending policies.[205] As we discussed earlier, the *Pulp Mills Case* provides clear evidence of the impact this 'greening' of the Bank can have in encouraging governments to take environmental protection seriously when promoting foreign investment in natural resource exploitation.[206] At the same time, global investment has been linked with increasing environmental degradation including deforestation and biodiversity loss.[207] Further detailed exploration of this 'multi-layered and, at times, contradictory'[208] relationship between foreign investment and environmental protection is, however, beyond the scope of this work.

9 WTO DISPUTE SETTLEMENT

One of the successes of the WTO is the system of compulsory binding dispute settlement[209] created by the Understanding on Rules and Procedures Governing the Settlement of Disputes adopted in 1994.[210] The WTO dispute settlement system is

202 Schwartz in Viñuales (ed), *The Rio Declaration etc*, 433; and see generally Viñuales, *Foreign Investment and the Environment in International Law* (Cambridge, 2012); Dupuy and Viñuales (eds), *Harnessing Foreign Investment to Promote Environmental Protection: Incentives and Safeguards* (Cambridge, 2013).

203 See discussion of relevant case law in Ch 5, section 5.; see further Mills in Rajamani and Peel (eds), *The Oxford Handbook of International Environmental Law* (2nd edn, Oxford, 2021) Ch 44 and, generally, Tienhaara, *The Expropriation of Environmental Governance: Protecting Foreign Investors at the Expense of Public Policy* (Cambridge, 2009).

204 See *supra*, Ch 3, section 2(2); and SDG 17.3. and 17.5. On synergies between foreign investment and environmental protection in the climate change and biodiversity contexts, see further Viñuales, *Foreign Investment etc*, 50–58; Virger in Dupuy and Viñuales, *Harnessing Foreign Investment etc*, Ch 7; Pavoni in ibid., Ch 8.

205 See *supra*, Ch 2, section 4(7).

206 Ibid.

207 Maby and McNally, *Foreign Direct Investment and the Environment: From Pollution Havens to Sustainable Development* (WWF, 1999) 3.

208 Miles in Rajamani and Peel (eds),*The Oxford Handbook of International Environmental Law* (2nd edn, Oxford, 2021) 1; see also Miles (ed), *Research Handbook on Environment and Investment* (Cheltenham, 2019).

209 See Petersmann, *The GATT/WTO Dispute Settlement System* (The Hague, 1997); Palmeter and Mavroidis, *Dispute Settlement in the World Trade Organization: Practice and Procedure* (The Hague, 1999); Trebilcock, Howse and Eliason, *The Regulation of International Trade*, Ch 4; Matsushita, Schoenbaum, Mavroidis and Hahn, *The World Trade Organization: Law, Practice and Policy*, Ch 2; Kulovesi, *The WTO Dispute Settlement: Challenges of the Environment, Legitimacy and Fragmentation* (The Hague, 2011).

210 Hereafter the 'DSU'. See also 1947 GATT, Articles XXII–XXIII and 1994 Agreement Establishing the World Trade Organization, Annex 2, in WTO, *Legal Texts, supra*, n 3.

administered by the Dispute Settlement Body ('DSB'). Disputes between members arising under the Multilateral Trade Agreements ('covered agreements') are first remitted to consultations,[211] but if these are not successful, will then be adjudicated by a dispute settlement panel and may be appealed to the Appellate Body.[212] Decisions must be implemented by the parties within a reasonable period of time, normally not more than fifteen months from the date of adoption of a panel or Appellate Body Report.[213] In the event of non-compliance, a member can be subjected to sanctions in the form of compensation and suspension of trade concessions.[214]

This system of dispute settlement is neither self-contained nor static, but it has to be remembered that the jurisdiction of the DSB extends only to disputes arising under the 'covered agreements',[215] not under other treaties or customary international law. At most these other rules of international law are relevant only when interpreting or applying the WTO covered agreements.[216] In interpreting WTO agreements the Appellate Body has followed the general rule codified in Article 31(3) of the 1969 VCLT that account *shall* be taken of 'any relevant rules of international law applicable in the relations between the parties'.[217] Since these rules necessarily develop over time, the interpretation given to some provisions of WTO agreements is not static but evolutionary. Thus, in the *Shrimp-Turtle* decision, the Appellate Body referred, inter alia, to the 1992 Rio Declaration on Environment and Development, the 1982 UNCLOS, the 1973 CITES, the 1979 CMS, and the 1992 CBD. Rather than interpreting the GATT Article XX(g) ('exhaustible natural resources') in accordance with whatever might have been the intention of the drafters in 1947, the Appellate Body took account of these much later and directly relevant agreements to reject Malaysia's argument that only minerals or other non-living resources are covered by Article XX(g). However, in the *EC—Biotech* decision, a Panel interpreted Article 31(3) to cover only those treaties applicable between all parties, and thus declined to take into account the 1992 CBD and 2000 Cartagena Protocol.[218] But even if that is a correct reading of Article 31(3), nothing in the 1969 VCLT stops a court or tribunal from referring to treaties that are not applicable law between the parties as an aid to interpretation, and that is essentially what happened in *Shrimp/Turtle*.[219]

211 DSU, Article 4. Alternative dispute settlement procedures such as conciliation, good offices, mediation, and arbitration also may be employed: see Articles 5, 25.

212 DSU, Articles 6, 17.

213 DSU, Article 21. Reports of the panels and Appellate Body must be adopted unless there is a consensus against.

214 DSU, Article 22. For an assessment of the effectiveness of WTO remedies, see Mavroidis, 11 *EJIL* (2000), 763.

215 DSU, Articles 2–3.

216 See, generally, Pauwelyn, *Conflict of Norms in Public International Law, How WTO Law Relates to other Rules of International Law* (Cambridge, 2003).

217 *Supra*, Ch 1, section 2.

218 Paras 7.70–7.95, and *supra*, section 3. For analysis on this point see Young, 56 *ICLQ* (2007) 907. The arguments are reviewed extensively by Pauwelyn, 95 *AJIL* (2001) 535, 575–6; McLachlan, 54 *ICLQ* (2005) 279, 315, para 16, (but note his qualifications at para 17); French, 55 *ICLQ* (2006) 300–7.

219 See Boyle and Chinkin, *The Making of International Law*, section 4.4.2.

As we saw earlier, Article 3(2) of the WTO Dispute Settlement Understanding expressly provides that the existing provisions of the 'covered agreements' are to be clarified 'in accordance with customary rules of interpretation of public international law'.[220] *Shrimp/Turtle* has made it clear that this means interpreting WTO agreements in accordance with Articles 31–3 of the 1969 VCLT, and not in accordance with the specific GATT canons of interpretation employed by earlier GATT panels. The importance of this change in helping resolve trade-environment conflicts cannot be understated. As one author observes:

> the very decision to follow these general public international law interpretative norms enhances the legitimacy of the dispute settlement organs in adjudicating competing values—because these norms are common to international law generally, including regimes that give priority to very different values, and are not specific to a regime that has traditionally privileged a single value, that of free trade.[221]

The Appellate Body's more consistent and principled approach to interpretation, and the reference to sustainable development in the Preamble to the GATT, [222] have helped it move away from the more rigidly free trade focus of earlier GATT panel awards. It has thus been able to develop the new and more environmentally nuanced jurisprudence considered earlier in this chapter. This is a significant contribution to ensuring that international trade law and international environmental law and agreements interact in the coherent way envisaged by Principle 12 of the Rio Declaration.

10 CONCLUSIONS

Twenty-five years after the WTO system came into operation we can see that neither trade law nor environmental law have trumped each other. Rather, there has been a process of accommodation which is still ongoing. The relatively more transparent and participatory environmental treaty framework has had some impact on WTO, which now allows observer status for IUCN, and accepts increased cooperation with MEA secretariats.[223] At the same time trade provisions in MEAs have largely worked without conflict with WTO law. But WTO law, and the system of compulsory dispute settlement established in 1994, have essentially outlawed unilaterally imposed trade sanctions unless justified by GATT Article XX or other provisions of the WTO covered agreements.

A good illustration of this point is the EU's response to Chile's ban on port access for Spanish fishing vessels in a dispute over conservation of swordfish. By commencing

220 *Supra*, section 3(1).

221 Howse, in Weiler (ed), *The EU, the WTO and the NAFTA* (Oxford, 2000) 54.

222 See *Shrimp/Turtle*, paras 12, 17, 67 and 152–3.

223 See Charnovitz, 10 *JIEL* (2007) 685.

WTO proceedings for a violation of Article V of GATT, and making a counterclaim in the UNCLOS proceedings brought by Chile, the EU derailed Chile's unilateralist policy, and eventually secured a settlement of the dispute through negotiation in accordance with the 1982 UNCLOS.[224] That outcome also reflects Principle 12 of the Rio Declaration. It is of course possible to argue that unilateral trade sanctions for environmental objectives are to be welcomed, since they can be an effective means of pressuring other states. But WTO case law has shown that there is room within WTO law for addressing environmental problems without resort to unilateral trade measures. As in so many environmental disputes, what is needed here is the ability to do international law in a coherent and undogmatic way in order to ensure a mutually supportive outcome.[225]

But this conclusion does not mean that the current policy of encouraging free trade can always be made environmentally friendly or will remain so. We can see the problem if we consider climate change. Free trade and the globalisation of production and transport have exacerbated the difficulty of regulating global GHG emissions. As we noted in Chapter 6, China and India's industrial development has resulted in very greatly increased GHG emissions not regulated by the 1997 Kyoto Protocol.[226] This development has been facilitated by free trade, but its harmful effects have been amplified by the 1992 UNFCCC carbon accounting rules which failed to account for trade effects,[227] and which simply attributed GHG emissions to the country in which goods were produced rather that the country in which those goods were consumed. Free trade also involves transporting goods and agricultural produce over long distances. Thus, it generates additional carbon emissions from shipping, aviation and road transport. An IMO report in 2014 estimated that international shipping emitted 2.2 per cent of the total global anthropogenic CO_2 emissions, that emissions from ships were increasing, and could grow between 50 per cent and 250 per cent by 2050 mainly due to the growth of trade.[228] 2.2 per cent of global emissions makes shipping one of the largest contributors to global warming, only slightly behind Japan.[229] There are large questions here about whether WTO rules on free trade can survive unchanged if we ever want to get serious about implementing the Paris Agreement

[224] See *supra*, Ch 12. See also a similar outcome in the WTO and UNCLOS cases brought by the Faeroe Islands against the EU: *DS469: European Union—Measures on Atlanto-Scandian Herring* (2014) and *Atlanto-Scandian Herring Arbitration*, PCA (2014).

[225] *Supra*, Ch 1, section 2.

[226] *Supra*, Ch 6, section 4.

[227] See 2006 IPCC Guidelines for National Greenhouse Gas Inventories, Vol 1, General Guidance and Reporting, 1.4: 'National inventories include greenhouse gas emissions and removals taking place within national territory and offshore areas over which the country has jurisdiction'.

[228] *3rd IMO GHG Survey* (2014).

[229] Olivier and Peters, *Trends in Global CO_2 and Total Greenhouse Gas Emissions: 2018 Report* (2018). On control of GHG emissions from ships, see *supra*, Ch 9, section 4(3).

on climate change.[230] Moreover, if, as we saw in Chapter 2, one of the key problems with sustainable development as a concept is that there has been too much emphasis on development, and not nearly enough on sustainability, then a policy of promoting free trade is part of that problem. Thus it is difficult to disagree with Young's conclusion: 'The economic growth caused by a supportive and open international economic system has been important for many people and many countries, but Principle 12's hope that this would allow the problems of environmental degradation to be better addressed seems overly simplistic.'[231]

230 See Barrett, *Climate Change and International Trade: Lessons on their Linkage from International Environmental Agreements* (Geneva, CTEI, 2010); UNEP/WTO, *Trade and Climate Change* (Geneva, UNEP/WTO, 2009); Kulovesi, 23 *RECIEL* (2014) 342; Low, Marceau and Reinaud, 46 *JWT* 485 (2012), and *supra*, Ch 6.

231 In Viñuales (ed), *The Rio Declaration etc*, 348.

BIBLIOGRAPHY

Only periodical articles cited in the footnotes are listed here. A full reference for each book and monograph is given when first cited in each chapter.

ABBOTT, K and SNIDAL, D, 'Hard and Soft Law in International Governance', 54 *Int Org* 421 (2000)

ADEDE, AO, 'Utilization of Shared Natural Resources: Towards a Code of Conduct', 5 *EPL* 66 (1979)

AGO, R, 'Nouvelles réflexions sur la codification du droit international', 92 *RGDIP* 532 (1988)

AKEHURST, M, 'Custom as a Source of International Law', 47 *BYIL* 1 (1974–5)

—— 'International Liability for Injurious Consequences Arising out of Acts Not Prohibited by International Law', 16 *NYIL* 8 (1985)

ALDRICH, GH, 'Progressive Development of the Laws of War: A Reply to Criticism of the 1977 Geneva Protocol 1', 26 *VJIL* 693 (1986)

—— 'Prospects for United States Ratification of Additional Protocol 1 to the 1949 Geneva Conventions', 85 *AJIL* 1 (1991)

ALEXANDER, LM, 'Regional Arrangements in the Oceans', 71 *AJIL* 84 (1977)

—— 'Regionalism and the Law of the Sea: The Case of Semi-Enclosed Seas', 2 *ODIL* 151 (1974)

ALLOTT, P, 'State Responsibility and the Unmaking of International Law', 29 *Harv ILJ* 1 (1988)

—— 'Power Sharing in the Law of the Sea', 77 *AJIL* 1 (1983)

ALSTON, P, 'Conjuring up New Human Rights: A Proposal for Quality Control', 78 *AJIL* 607 (1984)

—— 'A Third Generation of Solidarity Rights: Progressive Development or Obfuscation of International Human Rights Law?' 29 *NILR* 307 (1982)

—— 'Making Space for New Human Rights: The Case of the Right to Development', 1 *Harv HRYb* 21 (1988)

ANDERSON, K, 'The Ottawa Convention Banning Landmines, the Role of International NGOs and the Idea of International Civil Society', 11 *EJIL* 91 (2000)

ANNACKER, C, 'Part Two of the ILCs Draft Articles on State Responsibility', 37 *GYIL* 206 (1994)

ANTRIM, L, 'The UNCED Negotiating Process', 18 *O&CM* 79 (1992)

ARDEN, M, 'Water for All? Developing a Human Right to Water in National and International Law', 65 *ICLQ* 771 (2016)

ARDRON, JA, RAYFUSE, R, GJERDE, K, WARNER, R, 'The Sustainable Use and Conservation of Biodiversity in Areas Beyond National Jurisdiction: What Can Be Achieved Using Existing International Agreements?' 49 *Marine Policy* 98 (2014)

ARMAS PFIRTER, FM, 'How Can Life in the Deep Sea be Protected?', 24 *IJMCL* 281 (2009).

ARRANGIO-RUIZ, G, 'Some International Legal Problems of the Civil Uses of Nuclear Energy', 107 *Recueil des Cours* 497 (1962)

AUST, A, 'The Theory and Practice of Informal International Instruments', 35 *ICLQ* 787 (1986)

AYLING, J, 'Serving Many Voices: Progressing Calls for an International Environmental Organisation', 9 *JEL* 243 (1997)

BAKER, J, 'A Substantive Theory of the Relative Efficiency of Environmental

Treaty Compliance: The Case of CITES', 2 *JIWLP* 1 (1999)

Barkenbus, J, 'Nuclear Power Safety and the Role of International Organization', 41 *Int Org* 482 (1987)

—— and Forsberg, C, 'Internationalizing Nuclear Safety', 20 *Ann Rev of Energy and the Environment* 179 (1995)

Barral, V, 'Sustainable Development in International Law: Nature and Operation of an Evolutive Legal Norm', 23 *EJIL* 377 (2012)

—— 'Towards Judicial Coordination for Good Water Governance?' 67 *ICLQ* 931 (2018)

Barrelli, M, 'The Role of Soft Law in the International Legal System', 58 *ICLQ* 957 (2009)

Barnes, R, 'The Proposed LOSC Implementation Agreement on Areas Beyond National Jurisdiction and its Impact on International Fisheries Law', 31 *IJMCL* 583 (2016)

Bartels, L, 'The WTO Legality of the Application of the EU's Emission Trading System to Aviation', 23 *EJIL* 429 (2012)

—— 'The Chapeau of the General Exceptions in the WTO GATT and GATS Agreements: A Reconstruction', 109 *AJIL* 95 (2015)

Baxter, RR, 'International Law in Her Infinite Variety', 29 *ICLQ* 549 (1980)

Bederman, D and Keskar, SP, 'Antarctic Environmental Liability: The Stockholm Annex and Beyond', 19 *Emory Int LR* 1383 (2005)

Beeby, C, 'The South Pacific Nuclear Free Zone Treaty', 17 VUWLR 33 (1987)

Bekhechi, M, 'Une nouvelle étape dans le développement du droit international de l'environnement: la Convention sur la Désertification', 101 *RGDIP* 101 (1997)

Bello, E, 'The African Charter on Human and Peoples Rights: A Legal Analysis', 194 *Recueil des Cours* 1 (1985)

Berman, WH and Hydeman, LM, 'A Convention on Third Party Liability For Damage From Nuclear Incidents', 55 *AJIL* 966 (1961)

Bernhardt, R, 'A Schematic Analysis of Vessel-Source Pollution: Prescriptive and Enforcement Regimes in the Law of the Sea Conference', 20 *VJIL* 265 (1980)

Bernasconi, C, 'Civil Liability resulting from transfrontier Environmental Damage: A case for The Hague Conference?' *Hague YIL* 35 (1999)

Bewers, JM and Garrett, C, 'Analysis of the Issues Related to Sea Dumping of Radioactive Waste', 11 *Marine Policy* 121 (1987)

Beyerlin, U, 'New Developments in the Protection of the Marine Environment: Potential Effects of the Rio Process', 55 *ZAÖRV* 544 (1995)

—— 'State Community Interests and Institution-Building in International Environmental Law', 56 *ZAÖRV* 602 (1996)

—— and Reichard, M, 'The Johannesburg Summit: Outcome and Overall Assessment', 63 *ZAÖRV* 213 (2003)

Bianchi, A, 'The Harmonisation of Laws on Liability for Environmental Damage in Europe: an Italian Perspective', 6 *JEL* 21 (1994)

—— 'Ad Hocism and the Rule of Law', 13 *EJIL* 263 (2002)

Bilder, R, 'Controlling Great Lakes Pollution: A Study in United States/ Canada Environmental Co-operation', 70 *Mich LR* 469 (1972)

—— 'The Settlement of Disputes in the Field of the International Law of the Environment', 144 *Recueil des Cours* 139 (1975)

Birnie, PW, 'The Role of Developing Countries in Nudging the International Whaling Commission from Regulating Whaling to Encouraging Non-consumptive Uses of Whales', 12 *ELQ* 675 (1985)

—— 'International Legal Issues in the Management and Protection of the Whale: A Review of Four Decades of Experience', 29 *NRJ* 903 (1989)

—— 'Environmental Protection and Development', 20 *MelbULR* 66 (1995)

Blix, H, 'The Role and Development of Nuclear Power', 18 *EPL* 142 (1988)

Böckenförde, M, 'The Operationalization of the Precautionary Approach in International Environmental Law Treaties', 63 *ZAÖRV* 313 (2003)

Boczek, BA, 'Global and Regional Approaches to the Protection and Preservation of the Marine Environment', 16 *CWRJIL* 39 (1984)

Bodansky, D, 'Scientific Uncertainty and the Precautionary Principle', 33 *Environment* 5 (1991)

—— 'Protecting the Marine Environment from Vessel-source Pollution: UNCLOS III and Beyond', 18 *ELQ* 719 (1991)

—— 'Managing Climate Change', 3 *YbIEL* 60 (1992)

—— 'The UN Framework Convention on Climate Change', 18 *Yale JIL* 451 (1993)

—— 'Customary (And Not So Customary) International Environmental Law', 3 *Indiana Journal of Global Legal Studies* 105 (1995)

—— 'The Emerging Climate Change Regime', 20 *Ann Rev Energy & Env* 425 (1995)

—— 'Rules vs Standards in International Environmental Law', 98 *Proc ASIL* 275 (2004)

—— 'The Legitimacy of International Governance', 93 *AJIL* 596 (1999)

—— 'The Copenhagen Climate Change Conference: A Postmortem', 104 *AJIL* 230 (2010)

—— 'The Paris Climate Change Agreement: A New Hope?' 110 *AJIL* 288 (2016)

Boehmer-Christiansen, S, 'Environmental Quality Objectives versus Uniform Emission Standards', 5 *IJECL* 139 (1990)

Bolam, FC, 'How many bird and mammal extinctions has recent conservation action prevented?' *bioRvix* (2020)

Bonine, J, 'Environmental Impact Assessment—Principles Developed', 17 *EPL* 5 (1987)

Bookman, P. K, 'Litigation Isolationism', 67 *Stanford LR* 1081 (2015)

Bothe, M, 'The Protection of the Environment in Times of Armed Conflict: Legal Rules Uncertainty, Deficiencies and Possible Developments', 34 *GYIL* 54 (1992)

—— 'International Regulation of Transboundary Movement of Hazardous Waste', 33 *GYIL* 422 (1990)

Bourne, CB, 'International Law and Pollution of International Rivers and Lakes', 6 *UBCLR* 115 (1971)

—— 'Procedure in the Development of International Drainage Basins: The Duty to Consult and to Negotiate', 10 *CYIL* 212 (1972)

—— 'The Right to Utilize the Waters of International Rivers', 3 *CYIL* 187 (1965)

—— 'Procedure in the Development of International Drainage Basins', 22 *UTLJ* 172 (1972)

—— 'The Primacy of the Principle of Equitable Utilization in the 1997 Watercourses Convention', 35 *CYIL* 215 (1997)

Boustany, K, 'The Development of Nuclear Law-making or the Art of Legal "Evasion"', 61 *Nuclear Law Bull* 39 (1998)

Bowett, DW, 'Reservations to Non-Restricted Multilateral Treaties', 48 *BYIL* 67(1977)

Bowman, M, 'Conflict or Compatibility? The Trade, Conservation and Animal Welfare Dimension of CITES', 1 *JIWLP* 9 (1998)

—— 'International Treaties and the Global Protection of Birds', 11 *JEL* 87 and 281 (1999)

—— 'The Ramsar Convention Comes of Age', 42 *Neths ILR* 1 (1995)

—— 'The Multilateral Treaty Amendment Process, A Case Study', 66 *ICLQ* 560 (1995)

—— 'CITES: Trade Conservation and Animal Welfare', 2 *JIWLP* 9 (1999)

—— 'Normalizing the International Convention for the Regulation of Whaling', 29 *Mich JIL* 293 (2007–8)

—— 'A Tale of Two CITES: Divergent Perspectives upon the Effectiveness of the Wildlife Trade Convention', 22 *RECIEL* 228 (2013)

Boyle, AE, 'Marine Pollution Under the Law of the Sea Convention', 79 *AJIL* 347 (1985)

—— 'Nuclear Energy and International Law: An Environmental Perspective', 60 *BYIL* 257 (1989)

—— 'State Responsibility and International Liability for Injurious Consequences of Acts Not Prohibited by International Law: A Necessary Distinction', 39 *ICLQ* 1 (1990)

—— 'Dispute Settlement and the Law of the Sea Convention: Problems of Fragmentation and Jurisdiction', 46 *ICLQ* 37 (1997)

—— 'Problems of Compulsory Jurisdiction and the Settlement of Disputes Relating to Straddling Fish Stocks', 14 *IJMCL* 1 (1999)

—— 'Globalising Environmental Liability: the Interplay of National and International Law', 17 *JEL* 3 (2005)

—— 'Further Development of the 1982 Law of the Sea Convention: Mechanisms for Change', 54 *ICLQ* 563 (2005)

Human Rights or Environmental Rights? A Reassessment 18 *Fordham Env LR.* 471 (2007).

—— 'Human Rights and the Environment: Where Next?', 23 *EJIL* 613 (2012)

—— 'UNCLOS Dispute Settlement: Uses and Abuses of Part XV', 47 *RBDI* 182 (2014)

—— 'Climate Change, the Paris Agreement and Human Rights', 67 *ICLQ* 759 (2018)

—— 'Litigating Climate Change under Part XII of the LOSC', 34 *IJMCL* 458 (2019)

—— 'Progressive Development of International Environmental Law: Legislate or Litigate?' 63 *GYIL* 305 (2020)

—— and Harrison, J, 'Judicial Settlement of International Environmental Disputes: Current Problems', 4 *J Int Dispute Settlement* 245 (2013)

Brack, D, 'The *Shrimp-Turtle* Case: Implications for the Multilateral Environmental Agreement—World Trade Organization Debate', 9 *YbIEL* 13 (1998)

Bradlow, D and Schlemmer-Schulte, S, 'The World Bank's New Inspection Panel', 54 *ZAÖRV* 392 (1994)

Brent, KA, 'The Certain Activities case: what implications for the no-harm rule?', 20 *Asia Pacific JEL* 28 (2017)

Brölmann, C, 'Law-making Treaties: Form and Function in International Law', 74 *Nordic JIL* 383 (2005)

Brown, ED, 'Lessons of the Torrey Canyon', 21 *CLP* 113 (1968)

—— Dispute Settlement and the Law of the Sea: the UN Convention Regime, 21 *Marine Policy* 17 (1997)

Brown Weiss, E, 'The Planetary Trust: Conservation and Intergenerational Equity', 11 *ELQ* 495 (1984)

—— 'Our Rights and Obligations to Future Generations for the Environment', 84 *AJIL* 198 (1990)

Brownell, H and Eaton, SD, 'The Colorado River Salinity Problem with Mexico', 69 *AJIL* 255 (1975)

Brownlie, I, 'Legal Status of Natural Resources in International Law', 162 *Recueil des Cours* 245 (1979)

Brunnée, J, 'Common Interest—Echoes from an Empty Shell? Some Thoughts on Common Interests and International Environmental Law', 49 *ZAÖRV* 791 (1989)

—— and Toope, S, 'Environmental Security and Freshwater Resources: Ecosystem Regime Building', 91 *AJIL* 26 (1997)

—— and Toope, S, 'Environmental Security and Freshwater Resources: A Case for International Ecosystem Law', 5 *YbIEL* 41 (1994)

—— 'Of Sense and Sensibility: Reflections on International Liability Regimes as Tools for Environmental Protection', 53 *ICLQ* 351(2004)

—— and Toope, S, 'International Law and Constructivism: Elements of an Interactional Theory of International Law', 39 *Columbia JTL* 19 (2000)

—— 'COPing with Consent: Law-making Under MEAs', 15 *Leiden JIL* 1 (2002)

—— 'International Legal Accountability Through the Lens of State Responsibility', 36 *NYIL* 21 (2005)

—— 'International Environmental Law and the United States: Living with the Elephant', 15 *EJIL* 617 (2004)

—— 'Procedure and Substance in IEL: Confused on a Higher Level?', 5 *ESIL Reflections* (2016) Issue 6

Brusendorff, A and Ehlers, P, 'The HELCOM Copenhagen Declaration: A Regional Environmental Approach for Safer Shipping', 17 *IJMCL* 351 (2002)

Burgiel, SW, 'The Cartagena Protocol on Biosafety: Taking the Steps from Negotiation to Implementation', 11 *RECIEL* 53 (2002)

Burhenne-Guilmin, F and Casey-Lefkowitz, S, 'The Convention on Biological Diversity: A Hard-Won Global Achievement', 3 *YbIEL* 43 (1992)

Burke, WT, 'Highly Migratory Species in the New Law of the Sea', 14 *ODIL* 273 (1984)

—— 'Anadramous Species and the New International Law of the Sea', 22 *ODIL* 95 (1991)

—— Freeberg, M and Miles, E, 'UN Resolutions on Driftnet Fishing: An Unsustainable Precedent', 25 *ODIL* 127 (1994)

Burns, S, 'The Fukushima Daiichi Accident', 11 *Washington U Glob Studs LR* 739 (2012)

—— 'The impact of the major nuclear power plant accidents on the international legal framework for nuclear power', 101 *NLB* 7 (2018)

Buzan, B, 'Negotiating by Consensus: Developments in Techniques at the United Nations Conference on the Law of the Sea', 75 *AJIL* 324 (1981)

Caddell, R, 'The Integration of Multilateral Environmental Agreements: Lessons from the Biodiversity-Related Conventions', 22 *YbIEL* 37 (2011)

—— 'International Law and the Protection of Migratory Wildlife: An Appraisal of Twenty-Five Years of the Bonn Convention', 16 *Colorado JIELP* 113 (2005)

Caflisch, L, 'Règles générales du droit des cours d'eau internationaux', 219 *Recueil des Cours* 13 (1989)

Cameron, P, 'The Revival of Nuclear Power: An Analysis of the Legal Implications', 19 *JEL* 71 (2007)

Camm, T and Bowles, D, 'Animal Welfare and the Treaty of Rome: A Legal Analysis of the Protocol on Animal Welfare and Welfare Standards in the European Union', 12 *JEL* 197 (2000)

Carlarne, C, 'Saving the Whales in the New Millennium: International Institutions, Recent Developments and the Future of International Whaling Policies' 24 *Va Env LJ* 1 (2005)

Caron, D, 'The International Whaling Commission and the North Atlantic Marine Mammal Commission: The Institutional Loss of Coercion in Consensual Structures', 89 *AJIL* 154 (1995)

—— 'The Legitimacy of the Security Council', 87 *AJIL* 552 (1993)

Carroz, JE, 'International Aspects of Fishery Management Under the New Regime of the Oceans', 21 *San Diego LR* 516 (1984)

Cavers, DF, 'International Cooperation in the Peaceful Uses of Atomic Energy', 12 *Vand LR* 17 (1958)

Ceballos, G, Ehrlich, PR, and Raven, PH, 'Vertebrates on the brink as indicators of biological annihilation and the sixth mass extinction' 117:24 *Proceedings of the National Academy of Sciences of the United States of America* 13596 (2020)

Chandler, M, 'The Biodiversity Convention: Selected Issues of Interest to the International Lawyer', 3 *Colorado JILP* 141 (1993)

Charney, J, 'Third State Remedies in International Law', 10 *Mich JIL* 57 (1989)

—— 'The Persistent Objector Rule and the Development of Customary International Law', 56 *BYIL* 1 (1985)

—— 'Entry into Force of the 1982 UNCLOS', 35 *VJIL* 381 (1995)

—— 'The Implications of the International Dispute Settlement System of the 1982 Convention on the Law of the Sea on International Law', 90 *AJIL* 69 (1996)

—— 'The Marine Environment and the 1982 UNCLOS', 28 *Int Lawyer* 879 (1994)

—— 'Progress in International Criminal Law?' 93 *AJIL* 452 (1999)

Charnovitz, S, 'Exploring the Environmental Exceptions in GATT Article XX', 25 *JWT* 37 (1991)

—— 'The World Trade Organization and the Environment', 8 *YbIEL* 98 (1998)

—— 'Non-Governmental Organizations and International Law', 100 *AJIL* 348 (2006)

—— 'The WTO's Environmental Progress', 10 *JIEL* 685 (2007)

—— 'The Law of Environmental PPMs in the WTO: Debunking the Myth of Illegality' 27 *Yale JIL* 59 (2002)

Chatterjee, SK, 'The Charter of Economic Rights and Duties of States: An Evaluation of 15 Years', 40 *ICLQ* 669 (1991)

Cheng, B, 'The Moon Treaty: Agreement Governing the Activities of States on the Moon and other Celestial Bodies within the Solar System other than Earth', 33 *CLP* 213 (1980)

—— 'United Nations Resolutions on Outer Space: "Instant" Customary Law?' 5 *Indian JIL* 23 (1965)

Cheng, L et al, 'Record-Setting Ocean Warmth Continued in 2019', 37 *Advances in Atmospheric Sciences* 137–42 (2020)

Chinkin, CM, 'The Challenge of Soft Law: Development and Change in International Law', 38 *ICLQ* 850 (1989)

Chircop, A, 'Regional Cooperation in Marine Environmental Protection in the South China Sea: A Reflection on New Directions for Marine Conservation', 41 *ODIL* 334 (2010)

—— 'Ships in Distress, Environmental Threats to Coastal States, and Place of Refuge', 33 *ODIL* 207 (2002)

Choudhury, B, 'Balancing Soft and hard Law for Business and Human Rights', 67 *ICLQ* 961 (2018)

Christian, AC, 'Designing a Carbon Tax: The Introduction of the Carbon Burned Tax (CBT)', 10 *UCLA J Envtl L & Poly* 332 (1992)

Churchill, RR, Kutting, G and Warren, L, 'The 1994 UN ECE Sulphur Protocol', 7 *JEL* 169 (1995)

Churchill, RR, and Ulfstein, G, 'Autonomous Institutional Arrangements in Multilateral Environmental Agreements', 94 *AJIL* 623 (2000)

Churchill, RR, 'Civil Liability Litigation for Environmental Damage by Means of Treaties: Progress, Problems and Prospects', 12 *YbIEL* 3 (2001)

—— and SCOTT, J, 'The MOX Plant Litigation: The First Half-Life', 53 *ICLQ* 643 (2004)

—— '10 Years of the UNCLOS—Towards a Global Ocean Regime? A General Appraisal', 48 *GYIL* 81 (2005)

—— 'The Jurisprudence of the International Tribunal for the Law of the Sea Relating to Fisheries: Is there Much in the Net?' 22 *IJMCL* 383 (2007)

CICIN-SAIN, B and KNECHT, R, 'Implications of the Earth Summit for Ocean and Coastal Governance', 24 *ODIL* 323 (1993)

CIGOJ, S, 'International Regulation of Civil Liability for Nuclear Risk', 14 *ICLQ* 809 (1965)

CLARK, WC and DICKSON, NM, 'Sustainability Science: The emerging research program', 100:14 *Proceedings of the National Academy of Sciences of the USA* 806 (2003)

COASE, R, 'The Problem of Social Cost', 3 *J of Law and Economics* 1 (1960)

COHEN, M, 'The Regime of Boundary Waters: The Canadian–United States Experience', 146 *Recueil des cours* 219 (1975)

COLLIARD, C, 'La Convention de Bruxelles relative à la responsabilité des exploitants de navires nucléaires', 8 *AFDI* 41 (1962)

COMBACAU, J and ALLAND, D, '"Primary" and "Secondary" Rules in the Law of State Responsibility: Categorizing International Obligations', 16 *NYIL* 108 (1985)

CONTINI, P and SAND, PH, 'Methods to Expedite Environmental Protection: International Ecostandards', 66 *AJIL* 37 (1972)

COOMANS, F, 'The Ogoni Case before the African Commission on Human and Peoples Rights', 52 *ICLQ* 749 (2003)

COOPER, C, 'The Management of International Environmental Disputes in the Context of Canada–United States Relations: A Survey and Evaluation of Techniques and Mechanisms', 24 *CYIL* 247 (1986)

COOREMAN, B, 'Addressing Environmental Concerns Through Trade: A Case for Extraterritoriality?' 65 *ICLQ* (2016) 229

CORDONNERY, L, HEMMINGS, AD, and KRIWOKEN, L, 'Nexus and Imbroglio: CCAMLR, the Madrid Protocol and Designating Antarctic Marine Protected Areas in the Southern Ocean', 30 *IJMCL* (2015) 727

COUGHLIN, MD, 'Using the Merck-In Bio Agreement to clarify the Convention on Biological Diversity', 31 *Columbia JTL* 337 (1993)

CRAIK, N, 'The Duty to Cooperate in the Customary Law of Environmental Impact Assessment', 69 *ICLQ* 239 (2020)

CRAWFORD, J, 'Democracy and International Law', 64 *BYIL* 113 (1993)

CROLEY, SP and JACKSON, J, 'WTO Dispute Procedures, Standard of Review, and Deference to National Governments', 90 *AJIL* 193 (1996)

CROWLEY MA, HOWSE, R, 'Tuna - Dolphin II: a legal and economic analysis of the appellate body report', 13 *World Trade Rev* (2014)

CROOK, JR, 'The UN Claims Commission' (1993) 87 *AJIL* 144

—— and MCCAFFREY, SC, 'The United Nations Starts Work on a Watercourses Convention', 91 *AJIL* 374 (1997)

CULLET, P, 'Differential Treatment in International Law: Towards a new Paradigm of Inter-State Relations', 10 *EJIL* 549 (1999)

D'AMATO, A, 'Do We Owe a Duty to Future Generations to Preserve the Global Environment?', 84 *AJIL* 190 (1990)

—— and CHOPRA, SK, 'Whales: Their Emerging Right to Life', 85 *AJIL* 21 (1991)

Dam, S and Tewary, V, 'Polluting Environment, Polluting Constitution', 17 *JEL* 383 (2005)

Davidson N C et al, 'A review of the adequacy of reporting to the Ramsar Convention on change in the ecological character of wetlands', 71 *Marine & Freshwater Research* 117 (2020a)

—— 'Trends in the ecological character status of wetlands reported to the Ramsar Convention', 71 *Marine & Freshwater Research* 127 (2020b)

de Arechaga, J, 'International Law in the Past Third of a Century', 159 *Recueil des Cours* 272 (1978)

de Bruyne, J, 'Liability of Classification Societies: Cases, Challenges and Future Perspectives', 45 *JMLC* 181 (2014)

de La Fayette, LA, 'International Environmental Law and the Problem of Nuclear Safety', 5 *JEL* 31 (1993)

—— 'The ILC and International Liability: a Commentary', 6 *RECIEL* 321 (1997)

—— 'The OSPAR Convention Comes into Force: Continuity and Progress', 14 *IJMCL* 247 (1999)

—— 'The MEPC: The Conjunction of the Law of the Sea and International Environmental Law', 16 *IJMCL* 155 (2001)

—— 'New Approaches to Addressing Damage to the Marine Environment', 20 *IJMCL* 167 (2005)

—— 'A New Regime for the Conservation and Sustainable Use of Marine Biodiversity and Genetic Resources Beyond the Limits of National Jurisdiction', 24 *IJMCL* 221 (2009)

de Kageneck, A and Pinel, C, 'The Joint Convention on the Safety of Spent Fuel Management and the Safety of Radioactive Waste Management', 47 *ICLQ* 409 (1998)

De Mulder, J, 'The Protocol on SEA: A Matter of Good Governance', 20 *RECIEL* 232 (2011)

de Klemm, C, 'Migratory Species in International Law', 29 *NRJ* 932 (1989)

de Sadeleer, N, 'The Precautionary Principle as a Device for Greater Environmental Protection: Lessons from EC Courts', 18 *RECIEL* 3 (2009)

Damro, C and Mendez, PL, 'Emissions Trading at Kyoto', 12 *Environmental Politics* 2 (2003)

Davies, P, 'EC–Canada Fisheries Dispute', 44 *ICLQ* 927 (1995)

Demaret, P and Stewardson, R, 'Border Tax Adjustment under GATT and EC Law and General Implications for Environmental Taxes', 28 *JWT* 5 (1994)

Dennis MJ and Stewart, DP, 'Justiciability of Economic, Social and Cultural Rights', 98 *AJIL* (2004) 462.

Dernbach, J, and Cheever, F, 'Sustainable Development and its Discontents', 2 *Transnational Env L* 247 (2015)

Desai, B, 'Making Sense of the International Environmental Law-Making Process at a Time of Perplexity', 30 *YbIEL* 1 (2020)

—— 'Revitalising International Environmental Institutions: The UN Task Force Report and Beyond', 40 *Ind JIL* 455 (2000)

—— 'Regulating Transboundary Movement of Hazardous Wastes', 37 *Ind JIL* 43 (1997)

Di Leva, C, 'Climate-Related Standards and Multilateral Finance for Development', 4 *Laws* 674 (2015)

Diaz, A, 'Permanent Sovereignty over Natural Resources', 24 *EPL* 157 (1994)

—— 'Private Rights Under the Environment and Labor Agreements', 2 *US-Mex LJ* 11 (1994)

Dickstein, HL, 'International Lake and River Pollution Control: Questions of Method', 12 *CJTL* 487 (1973)

Ditz, D and Tuncak, B, 'Bridging the Divide between Toxic Risks and Global Chemicals

Governance', 23 *RECIEL* (2014) 181–194, 187

DOECKER, G and GEHRING, T, 'Private or International Liability for Transnational Environmental Damage: The Precedent of Conventional Liability Regimes', 2 *JEL* 1 (1990)

DOUMA, WTH, 'Fleshing out the Precautionary Principle by the Court of First Instance', 15 *JEL* (2003) 394

DOUSSIS, E, 'Does International Environmental Law Matter in Sustainable Development?', 28 *YbIEL* 3 (2017)

DRANKIER, P, 'Marine Protected Areas in Areas Beyond National Jurisdiction', 27 *IJMCL* 291 (2012)

——, ELFERINK, AO VISSER, B, TAKACS, T, 'Marine Genetic Resources in Areas beyond National Jurisdiction', 27 *IJMCL* 375 (2012)

DREMLIUGA, R, 'A Note on the Application of Article 234 of the Law of the Sea Convention in Light of Climate Change: Views from Russia', 48 *ODIL* 128 (2017)

DROEGE, C, and Tougas, M.-L. 'The Protection of the Natural Environment in Armed Conflict – Existing Rules and Need for Further Legal Protection', 82 *Nordic JIL* 21 (2013)

DUNLOP, W, 'The Bering Sea: The Donut Hole Agreement', 10 *IJMCL* 114 (1995)

DUNOFF, G, 'From Green to Global: Toward the Transformation of International Environmental Law', 19 *Harv ELR* 241 (1995)

DUPUY, P-M, 'L'affaire des essais nucléaires français et le contentieux de la responsabilité internationale publique', 20 *GYIL* 375 (1977)

—— 'Soft Law and the International Law of the Environment', 12 *Michigan JIL* 420 (1991)

—— 'Où en est le droit international de l'environnement à la fin du XXeme siècle?' 101 *RGDIP* 873 (1997)

—— 'Reviewing the Difficulties of Codification: on Ago's Classification of Obligations of Means and Obligations of Result in Relation to State Responsibility', 10 *EJIL* 371 (1999)

——, 'Impressions - Reviving a Tradition', 30 *EJIL* 1441(2019)

DUVIC-PAOLI, LA, 'The Status of the Right to Public Participation in International Environmental Law: An Analysis of the Jurisprudence', 23 *YbIEL* 80 (2013)

DUYCK, S, 'The Paris Climate Agreement and the Protection of Human Rights in a Changing Climate', 26 *YbIEL* 3 (2015)

EBBESSON, J, 'Innovative Elements and Expected Effectiveness of the 1991 EIA Convention', 19 *EIA Rev* 47 (1999)

—— 'The Notion of Public Participation in International Environmental Law', 8 *YbIEL* 98 (1997)

—— 'A Critical assessment of the 1992 Baltic Sea Convention', 43 *GYIL* 38 (2000)

EBEKU, K, 'The Right to a Satisfactory Environment and the African Commission', 3 *African HR LJ* 149 (2003)

EDESON, W, 'The Code of Conduct for Responsible Fisheries: An Introduction', 11 *IJMCL* 97 (1996)

—— 'The International Plan of Action on Illegal, Unreported and Unregulated Fishing: The Legal Context of a Non-Legally Binding Instrument', 16 *IJMCL* 603 (2001)

—— 'An International Legal Extravaganza in the Indian Ocean: Placing the Indian Ocean Tuna Commission outside the Framework of FAO', 22 *IJMCL* 485 (2007)

EHLERS, P, 'The History of International North Sea Conferences', 5 *IJECL* 3 (1990)

ELDER, PS, 'Legal Rights for Nature: The Wrong Answer to the Right(s) Question', 22 *OsHLJ* 285 (1984)

ELFERINK, AO, 'Environmental Impact Assessment in Areas beyond National Jurisdiction', 27 *IJMCL* 449 (2012)

Elkind, JB, 'Footnote to the Nuclear Test Cases: Abuse of Right—A Blind Alley for Environmentalists', 9 *Vand JTL* 57 (1976)

Elias, O and Lim, C, 'General Principles of Law, Soft Law and the Identification of International Law', 28 *Neths YIL* 3 (1997)

Emond, P, 'Cooperation in Nature: A New Foundation for Environmental Law', 22 *OsHLJ* 323 (1984)

Epiney, A, 'Sustainable Use of Freshwater Resources', 63 *ZAÖRV* 377 (2003)

Ercmann, S, 'The Contribution of the Council of Europe to the Protection of the Environment through Penal Law', 65 *Rev Int de Droit Pénal* 1199 (1994)

Eriksen, HH, and Perrez, FX, 'The Minimata Convention: A Comprehensive Response to a Global Problem', 23 *RECIEL 195* (2014)

Erikstein, K, and Swan, J, 'Voluntary Guidelines for Flag State Performance', 29 *IJMCL* 116 (2014)

Esty, D, 'NGOs and the WTO', 1 *JIEL* 123 (1998)

Etemire, U, 'Insights on the UNEP Bali Guidelines and the Development of Environmental Democratic Rights', 28 *JEL* 393 (2016).

Eze, C, 'The Bamako Convention on the Ban of the Import into Africa and the Control of the Transboundary Movement and Management of Hazardous Wastes within Africa: A Milestone in Environmental Protection', 15 *Afr J Int'l & Comp L* 208 (2007)

Fabra, A and Gascon, V, 'The Convention on the Conservation of Antarctic Marine Living Resources and the Ecosystem Approach', 23 *IJMCL* 567 (2008)

Farrier, D and Tucker, L, 'Wise Use of Wetlands Under the Ramsar Convention', 12 *JEL* 21 (2000)

Faure, M, and Svatikova, K, 'Criminal or Administrative Law to Protect the Environment? Evidence from Western Europe', 24 *JEL* 253 (2012)

Faure, M G and Nollkaemper, A, 'International Liability as an Instrument to Prevent and Compensate for Climate Change', 26 *Stanford Env LJ* 123 (2007)

Fawcett, JJ, 'The Impact of Article 6(1) of the ECHR on Private International Law', 56 *ICLQ* 1 (2007)

Feria Tinta, M, Milnes, S, 'The Rise of Environmental Law in International Dispute Resolution: The Inter-American Court of Human Rights Issues a Landmark Advisory Opinion on the Environment and Human Rights', 27 *YbIEL* 64 (2016)

Finlayson, C M et al., 'The second warning to humanity: providing a context for wetland management and policy', 39 *Wetlands* 1 (2019)

Fitzmaurice, M, 'International Environmental Law as a Special Field', 25 *NYIL* 181 (1994)

—— 'The *Gabčíkovo-Nagymaros Case*: the Law of Treaties', 11 *Leiden JIL* 321 (1998)

——and Redgwell, C, 'Environmental Non-Compliance Procedures and International Law', 31 *NYIL* 35 (2000)

—— 'Public Participation in the North American Agreement on Environmental Cooperation', 52 *ICLQ* 334 (2003)

—— 'General Principles Governing the Co-operation between States in Relation to the Non-navigational Uses of International Watercourses', 14 *YbIEL* 3 (2003)

——'The Human Right to Water', 18 *Fordham ELR* 537 (2007)

Footer, M, 'Intellectual Property and Agro-biodiversity: Towards Private Ownership of Genetic Commons', 10 *YbIEL* 48 (1999)

Fornasier, R, 'La Convention complémentaire à la convention de Paris de 29 Juillet 1960 sur la responsabilité civile dans la domaine de l'energie nucléaire', 8 *AFDI* 762 (1962)

FOSTER C, E, 'New clothes for the Emperor? onsultation of Experts by the ICJ', 5 *JIDS* 139 (2014)

FOSTER, WF, 'The Convention on International Liability for Damage Caused by Space Objects', 10 *CYIL* 136 (1972)

FRAENKEL, A, 'The Convention on Long-range Transboundary Air Pollution: Meeting the Challenge of International Cooperation', 30 *Harv ILJ* 447 (1989)

FRANCKX, E, 'Regional Marine Environment Protection Regimes in the Context of UNCLOS', 13 *IJMCL* 307 (1998)

—— 'The 200-Mile Limit: Between Creeping Jurisdiction and Creeping Common Heritage?' 48 *GYIL* 117 (2005)

FRANCIONI, F, 'International Human Rights in an Environmental Horizon', 21 *EJIL* 41 (2010)

FRANK, E, and WILCOVE, D, 'Long delays in banning trade in threatened species', 363 *Science* 686 (2019)

FRANK, V, 'Consequences of the Prestige Sinking for European and International Law', 20 *IJMCL* 1 (2005)

FREESTONE, D, 'Specially Protected Areas and Wildlife in the Caribbean: The 1990 Kingston Protocol to the Cartagena Convention', 5 *IJECL* 362 (1990)

—— 'The Road from Rio: International Environmental Law After the Earth Summit', 6 *JEL* 193 (1994)

—— and MAKUCH, Z, 'The New International Environmental Law of Fisheries: The 1995 UN Straddling Stocks Convention', 7 *YbIEL* 3 (1996)

FRENCH, D, 'Developing States and International Environmental Law: the Importance of Differentiated Responsibilities', 49 *ICLQ* 35 (2000)

—— 'Treaty Interpretation and the Incorporation of Extraneous Legal Rules', 55 *ICLQ* 281 (2006)

—— 'From the Depths: the Seabed Disputes Chamber's 2011 Advisory Opinion', 26 *IJMCL* 525 (2011)

—— 'Finding Autonomy in International Environmental Law and Governance', 21 *JEL* 255 (2009)

FRIEDMAN, W, 'The Uses of General Principles in the Development of International Law', 57 *AJIL* 279 (1963)

FUENTES, X, 'The Criteria for the Equitable Utilization of International Rivers', 67 *BYIL* 337 (1996)

—— 'Sustainable Development and the Equitable Utilisation of International Watercourses', 69 *BYIL* 119 (1998)

FULLER, L, 'The Forms and Limits of Adjudication', 92 *Harv LR* 353 (1978)

GALIZZI, P, 'Economic Instruments as Tools for the Protection of the International Environment', 6 *Eur Env LR* 155 (1997)

—— 'From Stockholm to New York Via Rio and Johannesburg: Has International Environmental Law Lost Its Way on the Global Agenda?' 29 *Fordham ILJ* 952 (2006)

GASKELL, N, 'Decision Making and the Legal Committee of the IMO', 18 *IJMCL* 155 (2003)

GASSER, HP, 'For Better Protection of the Natural Environment in Armed Conflict: a Proposal for Action', 89 *AJIL* 837 (1995)

GAVOUNELI, M, 'Mediterranean Challenges: between Old Problems and New Solutions', 23 *IJMCL* 477 (2008)

—— 'Access to Environmental Information', 13 *Tulane Env LJ* 303 (2000)

GEHRING, T, 'International Environmental Regimes: Dynamic Sectoral Legal Systems', 1 *YbIEL* 35 (1990)

GIAGNOCAVO, C, and GOLDSTEIN, H, 'Law Reform or World Reform: The Problem of Environmental Rights', 35 *McGill LJ* 345 (1990)

Gjerde, K, 'Challenges to Protect the Marine Environment Beyond National Jurisdiction', 27 *IJMCL* 39 (2012)

Glennon, MJ, 'Has International Law Failed the Elephant?' 84 *AJIL* 1 (1990)

Glowka, L, Complementarities between the CMS and CITES, 3 *JIWLP* 205 (2000)

Glowka, L and De Klemm, C, 'International Instruments and Processes and Non-Indigenous Species: Is a Protocol Necessary?' 26 *EPL* 247 (1996)

Gold, E, 'Vessel Traffic Regulation: The Interface of Maritime Safety and Operational Freedom', 14 *JMLC* 136 (1983)

—— 'Marine Salvage: Towards a New Regime', 20 *JMLC* 487 (1987)

Goldblat, J, 'The Nuclear Non-proliferation Regime: Assessment and Prospects', 256 *Recueil des Cours* 9 (1995)

Goldie, L, 'Concepts of Strict and Absolute Liability and the Ranking of Liability in Terms of Relative Exposure to Risk', 16 *NYIL* 175 (1985)

—— Liability for Damage and the Progressive Development of International Law, 14 *ICLQ* 1189 (1965)

Gondek, M, 'Application of the ECHR: Territorial Focus in an Age of Globalization' 52 *Neths ILR* 349 (2005)

Goote, M 'The Jakarta Mandate on Marine and Coastal Biological Diversity' 12 *IJMCL* 377 (1997)

Graefrath, B, 'Universal Criminal Jurisdiction and an International Court', 1 *EJIL* 67 (1990)

Gray, C, 'Current Developments: *Whaling in the Antarctic*', 109 *AJIL* 589 (2015)

—— and Epps, T, 'The WTO, Science and the Environment', 10 *JIEL* 285 (2007)

Griffith, A, 'The South and UNCED: the Dawn of a Probable Turning Point in International Relations Between States', 18 *O&CM* 55 (1992)

Grubb, M, 'Full legal compliance with the Kyoto Protocol's first commitment period – some lessons', 16 *Climate Policy* 673 (2016)

Green, A and Epps,T, 'The WTO, Science, and the Environment: Moving Towards Consistency', 10 *JIEL* 285 (2007)

Gruchalla-Wesierski, T, 'A Framework for Understanding Soft Law', 30 *McGill* LJ 37 (1984)

Guillaume, G, 'The Future of International Judicial Institutions', 44 *ICLQ* 848 (1995)

——, The Use of Precedent by International Judges and Arbitrators1 *JIDS* 1 (2011)

Gundling, L, 'Our Responsibility to Future Generations', 84 *AJIL* 207 (1990)

Gupta, J, 'The Role of Non-State Actors in International Environmental Affairs', 63 *ZAÖRV* 459 (2003)

Haas, PM, 'Do Regimes Matter? Epistemic Communities and Mediterranean Pollution Control', 43 *Int Org* 377 (1989)

——, Levy, MA and Parson, EA, 'How Should We Judge UNCED's Success?' 34 *Environment* 6 (1992)

Hackett, DP, 'An Assessment of the Basel Convention on the Control of Transboundary Movements of Hazardous Wastes and their Disposal', 5 *AUJILP* 291 (1990)

Hafner, G, 'The Optimum Utilization Principle and the Non-Navigational Uses of Drainage Basins', 45 *Austrian JPIL* 113 (1993)

Hagan, P and Weiner,J,'The Cartagena Protocol on Biosafety: New Rules for International Trade in Living Modified Organisms'., 12 *Georgetown Environmental Law Review* 697 (2002)

Handl, G, 'Marine Environmental Damage: the Compensability of Ecosystem Service Loss in International Law', 34 *IJMCL* 602 (2019)

—— 'The Nuclear Non-Proliferation Regime', 19 *Tulane JICL* 1 (2010)

—— 'The IAEA Safety Conventions: An Example of Successful Treaty Management?', 72 *Nuclear Law Bull* 7 (2003)

—— 'Controlling Implementation of and Compliance with International Environmental Commitments: The Rocky Road From Rio', 5 *Colorado JIELP* 327 (1994)

—— 'The International Law Commission's Draft Articles on the Law of International Watercourses: Progressive or Retrogressive Development of International Law', 3 *Colorado JIELP* 123 (1992)

—— 'Environmental Security and Global Change: The Challenge to International Law', 1 *YbIEL* 3 (1990)

—— and Lutz, R, 'An International Policy Perspective in the Trade of Hazardous Materials and Technologies', 30 *Harv ILJ* 351 (1989)

—— 'Après Tchernobyl: Quelques réflexions sur le programme législatif multilatéral à l'ordre du jour', 92 *RGDIP* 50 (1988)

—— 'National Uses of Transboundary Air Resources: The International Entitlement Issues Reconsidered', 26 *NRJ* 405 (1986)

—— 'Liability as an Obligation Established by a Primary Rule of International Law', 16 *NYIL* 49 (1985)

—— 'State Liability for Accidental Transnational Environmental Damage by Private Persons', 74 *AJIL* 525 (1980)

—— 'The Principle of Equitable Use as Applied to Internationally Shared Natural Resources: Its Role in Resolving Potential International Disputes over Transfrontier Pollution', 14 *RBDI* 40 (1978)

—— 'An International Legal Perspective on the Conduct of Abnormally Dangerous Activities in Frontier Areas: The Case of Nuclear Power Plant Siting', 7 *ELQ* 1 (1978)

—— 'International Liability for the Pollution of International Watercourses: Balancing Interests', 13 *CYIL* 156 (1975)

—— 'Territorial Sovereignty and the Problem of Transnational Pollution', 69 *AJIL* 50 (1975)

Hardy, M, 'Nuclear Liability: The General Principles of Law and Further Proposals', 36 *BYIL* 223 (1960)

—— 'The Liability of Operators of Nuclear Ships', 12 *ICLQ* 778 (1963)

Harrison, J, 'Recent Developments and Continuing Challenges in the Regulation of Greenhouse Gas Emissions from International Shipping' *Ocean Yearbook* 359 (2013)

—— 'Regime Pluralism and the Global Regulation of Oil Pollution Liability and Compensation', 5 *Int J of Law in Context* 379 (2009)

—— 'Reflections on the Role of International Courts and Tribunals in the Settlement of Environmental Disputes and the Development of International Environmental Law', 25 *JEL* 501 (2013)

Harrop, SR, 'From Cartel to Conservation and on to Compassion: Animal Welfare and the International Whaling Commission', 6 *JIWLP* 79 (2003)

Harrop, SR and Pritchard, D, 'A Hard Instrument Goes Soft: The Implications of the Convention on Biological Diversity's Current Trajectory' (2011) 21 *Glob Env Change* 474 (2011)

Hart, D and Wheeler, M, 'Night Flights and Strasbourg's Retreat from Environmental Human Rights', 16 *JEL* 132 (2004)

Hassan, P, 'Toward an International Covenant on Environment and Development', *Proc ASIL* 513 (1993)

Hausfather, Z, et al, 'Evaluating the Performance of Past Climate Model Projections', 47 *Geophysical Research Letters* 1–10 (2019)

HAYASHI, M, 'Toward Elimination of Substandard Shipping: The Report of the International Commission on Shipping', 16 *IJMCL* 501 (2001)

HEPWORTH, R, 'The Independent Review of CITES', 1 *JIWLP* 412 (1998)

HERKENRATH, P, 'The Implementation of the Convention on Biological Diversity: A Non-Government Perspective Ten Years On', 11 *RECIEL* 29 (2002)

HERMITTE, MA, 'La Convention sur la biodiversité biologique', 37 *AFDI* 844 (1991)

HERVEY, T, 'Regulation of Genetically Modified Products in a Multi-Level System of Governance: Science or Citizens?' 10 *RECIEL* 321 (2001)

HEWISON, G, 'The Precautionary Approach to Fisheries Management: An Environmental Perspective', 11 *IJMCL* 301 (1996)

HEY, E, 'The International Regime for the Protection of the North Sea', 17 *IJMCL* 325 (2002)

—— 'Sustainable Development, Normative Development and the Legitimacy of Decision-making', 34 *NYIL* 3 (2003)

—— 'The Persistence of a Concept: Maximum Sustainable Yield', 27 *IJMCL* 763 (2012)

HIGGINS, R, 'The Development of International Law by the Political Organs of the United Nations', *Proc ASIL* 116 (1965)

—— 'A Babel of Judicial Voices?' 55 *ICLQ* 791 (2006)

HILBORN, R, WALTERS, CJ and LUDWIG, D, 'Sustainable Exploitation of Renewable Resources', 26 *Ann Rev Ecol Syst* 45 (1995)

HILLGENBERG, H, 'A Fresh Look at Soft Law', 10 *EJIL* 499 (1999)

HOFFMAN, H, 'Germany's New Environmental Liability Act: Strict Liability for Facilities Causing Pollution', 38 *NILR* 27 (1991)

HOLDER, J, 'New Age: Rediscovering Natural Law', 53 *CLP* 152 (2000)

HONG, GH, and LEE, YJ, 'Transitional Measures to Combine Two Global Ocean Dumping Treaties', 55 *Marine Policy* 47 (2015)

HOWARD, M, 'The Convention on the Conservation of Antarctic Marine Living Resources: A Five Year Review', 38 *ICLQ* 104 (1985)

HOWSE, R, 'The Appellate Body Rulings in the Shrimp/Turtle Case: A New Legal Baseline for the Trade and Environment Debate', 27 *Columbia JEL* 491 (2002)

HUDEC, RE, 'Differences in National Environmental Standards: The Level-Playing Field Dimension', 5 *Minn. J. Global Trade* 1 (1995)

HULME, K, 'Environmental Security: Implications for International Law', 20 *YbIEL* 41 (2010)

HUTCHINSON, DH, 'Solidarity and Breaches of Multilateral Treaties', 59 *BYIL* 151 (1988)

IANNI, RW, 'International and Private Actions in Transboundary Pollution', 11 *CYIL* 258 (1973)

IJLSTRA, T, 'Regional Cooperation in the North Sea: An Inquiry', 3 *IJECL* 181 (1988)

IMHOFF, F and HÜGLER, M, 'Life at Deep Sea Hydrothermal Vents', 24 *IJMCL* 201 (2009)

JACOBSSON, M, 'The French Court of Cassation and the Erika case; some issues relating to civil liability'; 20 *JIML* 18 (2014)

JAECKEL, A, 'An Environmental Management Strategy for the ISBA? The Legal Basis', 30 *IJMCL* 93 (2015)

JENKS, W, 'Liability for Ultra-Hazardous Activities in International Law', 117 *Recueil des Cours* 99 (1966)

JENNINGS, RY, 'What is International Law and How Do We Tell it When We See It', 37 *Ann Suisse DDI* 59 (1981)

—— 'The ICJ After 50 Years' 89 *AJIL* 493 (1995)

—— 'The Judiciary, National and International, and International Law', 45 *ICLQ* 1 (1996)

Jetoo, S and Krantzberg, G, 'The Great Lakes Water Quality Protocol 2012: a focus on the effectiveness of the International Joint Commission', 11 *Int Jo of Sustainability in Economic, Social, and Cultural Context* 1 (2015)

Johnson, P, 'The Post-Fukushima Daiichi Response: The Role of the Convention on Nuclear Safety', 91 *Nuclear Law Bull* 7 (2013)

Joyner, C, 'UN General Assembly Resolutions and International Law: Rethinking the Contemporary Dynamics of Norm Creation', 11 *CWILJ* 446 (1981)

——'Biodiversity in the Marine Environment: Resource Implications for the Law of the Sea', 28 *Vand JTL* 635–687 (1995)

Juda, L, 'IMCO and the Regulation of Ocean Pollution from Ships', 26 *ICLQ* 558 (1977)

—— 'Considerations in Developing a Functional Approach to the Governance of Large Marine Ecosystems', 30 *ODIL* 89 (1999)

Kameri-Mbote, P, 'The development of biosafety regulation in Africa in the context of the Cartagena Protocol: Legal and Administrative Issues' 11 *RECIEL* 62 (2002)

Kamminga, M, 'The IAEA Convention on Nuclear Safety', 44 *ICLQ* 872 (1995)

Kamto, M, 'Les nouveaux principes du droit international de l'environnement', 1 *Rev Jur de l'Environnement* 11 (1993)

Kasoulides, G, 'State Responsibility and Assessment of Liability for Damage Resulting from Ocean Dumping Operations', 26 *San Diego LR* 497 (1989)

Kelson, J, 'State Responsibility and the Abnormally Dangerous Activity', 13 *Harv ILR* 197 (1972)

Kerr, D, 'The 1989 Salvage Convention: Expediency or Equity?', 20 *JMLC* 505 (1989)

Kesteven, GL, 'MSY Revisited: A Realistic Approach to Fisheries Management and Administration', 21 *Marine Policy* 73 (1997)

Keyuan, Z, 'The Common Heritage of Mankind and the Antarctic Treaty System', 58 *NILR* 173 (1991)

Kindt, JW, 'The Effect of Claims by Developing Countries on Law of the Sea International Marine Pollution Negotiations', 20 *VJIL* 313 (1979)

Kingsbury, B, 'The Concept of Compliance as a Function of Competing Conceptions of International Law', 19 *Mich JIL* 345 (1998)

——, Krisch, N and Stewart, R, 'The Emergence of Global Administrative Law', 68 *Law&Cont Problems* 15 (2005)

Kirgis, FL, 'Standing to Challenge Human Endeavors that Could Change the Climate', 84 *AJIL* 525 (1990)

Kiss, AC, 'International Cooperation for the Control of Accidental Marine Pollution', 23 *GYIL* 231 (1980)

—— 'Nouvelles tendances en droit international de l'environnement', 32 *GYIL* 241 (1989)

—— 'Dix ans après Stockholm: une decennie de droit international de l'environnement', *AFDI* (1982) 784

—— 'La Notion de patrimonie commun de l'humanité', 175 *Recueil des Cours* 99 (1985)

—— 'Compliance with International and European Environmental Obligations', *Hague YIL* 45 (1996)

—— and Doumbe-Bille, S,'La Conférence des Nations Unies sur l'environnement et le développement' 38 *AFDI* 823 (1992)

Kitt, JR, 'Waste Exports to the Developing World: A Global Response', 7 *Geo IELR* 485 (1995)

Klabbers, J, 'The Substance of Form: The *Case Concerning the Gabčíkovo-Nagymaros Project*', 8 *YbIEL*32 (1997)

—— 'The Undesirability of Soft Law', 67 *Nordic JIL* 381 (1998)

Knecht, R, 'A Commentary on the Institutional and Political Aspects of Regional Ocean Governance', 24 *O&C Man* 39 (1994)

Knox, J, 'Myth and Reality of Transboundary Environmental Impact Assessment', 96 *AJIL* 291 (2002)

—— 'Linking Human Rights and Climate Change at the UN', 33 *Harv ELR* 477 (2009)

Koester, V, 'The Biodiversity Convention Negotiating Process and Some Comments on the Outcome', 27 *EPL* 175 (1997)

—— 'Review of Compliance Under the Aarhus Convention', 2 *J Eur Env & Plng L* 31 (2005)

Koivurova, T, and Polonen, I, 'Transboundary EIA in the Case of the Baltic sea Gas Pipeline', 25 *IJMCL* 151 (2010)

Konz, P, 'The 1962 Brussels Convention on the Liability of Operators of Nuclear Ships', 57 *AJIL* 100 (1963)

Kopela, S, 'Climate Change, Regime Interaction and the Principle of Common but Differentiated Responsibility: The Experience of the International Maritime Organization', 24 *YbIEL* 70 (2014)

Korsberg, L, 'The Law-making Effects of the FAO Deep-Sea Fisheries Guidelines', 67 *ICLQ* 801 (2018)

Koskenniemi, M, 'Breach of Treaty or Non-Compliance? Reflections on the Enforcement of the Montreal Protocol', 3 *YbIEL* 123 (1992)

—— 'Solidarity Measures: State Responsibility as a New International Order', 72 *BYIL* 337 (2001)

—— 'The Fate of Public International Law', 70 *MLR* 4 (2007)

Kravchenko, S, 'The Aarhus Convention and Innovations in Compliance with MEAs', 18 *Colorado JIELP* 1 (2007)

Kulovesi, K, 'International Trade Disputes on Renewable Energy: Testing Ground for the Mutual Supportiveness of WTO Law and Climate Change Law', 23 *RECIEL* 342 (2014)

Kummer, K, 'The International Regulation of Transboundary Traffic in Hazardous Wastes: The 1989 Basel Convention', 41 *ICLQ* 530 (1992)

—— 'Prior Informed Consent for Chemicals in International Trade: The 1998 Rotterdam Convention', 8 *RECIEL* 322 (1999)

Kummer-Peiry, K, 'The Basel Convention on Control of Transboundary Movements of Hazardous Wastes and their Disposal', 107 *Proc ASIL* 434 (2013)

Kwiatkowska, B, 'Creeping Jurisdictions Beyond 200 Miles in the Light of the 1982 Law of the Sea Convention and State Practice', 22 *ODIL* 153 (1991)

Laly-Chevalier, C, 'Les Catastrophes maritimes et la protection des côtes Françaises', 50 *AFDI* 581 (2004)

Lang, W, 'Compliance Control in International Environmental Law', 56 *ZAÖRV* 685 (1996)

Langlet, D, 'Exporting C02 for Sub-Seabed Storage: The Non-Effective Amendment to the London Dumping Protocol and its Implications', 30 *IJMCL* 395 (2015)

Lawrence, P, 'International Legal Regulation for Protection of the Ozone Layer: Some Problems of Implementation', 2 *JEL* 17 (1990)

Leonard, L, 'Recent Negotiations Toward the International Regulation of Whaling', 35 *AJIL* 90 (1941)

LE MARQUAND, D, 'The International Joint Commission and Changing Canada-United States Boundary Relations', 33 *NRJ* 59 (1993)

LEE, M and ABBOTT, C, 'Usual Suspects? Public Participation Under the Aarhus Convention', 66 *MLR* 80 (2003

LESTER, A, 'River Pollution in International Law', 57 *AJIL* 828 (1963)

LEVY, R, HAAS, P and KEOHANE, M, 'Institutions for the Earth', 34 *Environment* 12 (1992)

LIJNZAAD, L and TANJA, G. 'Protection of the Environment in Times of Armed Conflict: The Iraq-Kuwait War', 40 *NILR* 169 (1993)

LODGE, M, 'Improving International Governance in the Deep Sea', 19 *IJMCL* 299 (2004)

—— 'The Common Heritage of Mankind', 27 *IJMCL* 733 (2012)

—— and NANDAN, S, 'Some Suggestions Towards Better Implementation of the United Nations Agreement on Straddling Fish Stocks etc', 20 *IJMCL* 345 (2005)

—— and SEGERSON, K, SQUIRES, D, 'Sharing and Preserving the Resources in the Deep Sea: Challenges for the ISBA', 32 *IJMCL* 427 (2017)

LOUCAIDES, L, 'Environmental Protection through the Jurisprudence of the ECHR', 75 *BYIL* 249 (2004)

—— 'Determining the Extra-territorial effect of the European Convention: Facts, Jurisprudence and the *Bankovic* Case', *Eur Human Rights LR* 391 (2006)

LOW, P, MARCEAU, G and REINAUD, J, 'The Interface between the Trade and Climate Change Regimes: Scoping the Issues' 46 *JWT* 485 (2012)

LOWE, AV, 'The Enforcement of Marine Pollution Regulations', 12 *SDLR* 624 (1975)

—— 'The Function of Litigation in International Society' 61 *ICLQ* 209 (2012)

MCCAFFREY, S, 'The OECD Principles Concerning Transfrontier Pollution: A Commentary', 1 *EPL* 1 (1975)

—— 'Transboundary Pollution Injuries: Jurisdictional Considerations in Private Litigation Between Canada and the United States', 3 *CWJIL* 191 (1973)

—— and SINJELA, M, 'The 1997 UN Convention on International Watercourses', 92 *AJIL* 97 (1998)

MCCONNELL, M and GOLD, E, 'The Modern Law of the Sea: Framework for the Protection and Preservation of the Marine Environment', 23 *CWRJIL* 83 (1991)

MCDORMAN, TL, 'Implementing Existing Tools: Decision-making Processes of Regional Fisheries Management Organisations', 20 *IJMCL* 423 (2005)

MCDOUGAL, M and SCHLEI, N, 'The Hydrogen Bomb Tests in Perspective: Lawful Measures for Security', 64 *Yale LJ* 648 (1955)

MC GEE, J and STEFFEK, J, 'The Copenhagen Turn in Global Climate Governance and the Contentious History of Differentiation in International Law,' 28 *JEL* 37 (2016)

MCGOLDRICK, D, 'Sustainable Development and Human Rights as an Integrated Conception', 45 *ICLQ* 796 (1996)

MCGRAW, DM, 'The CBD: Key Characteristics and Implications for Implementation', 11 *RECIEL* 17 (2002)

MCINTYRE, O, and MOSEDALE, T, 'The Precautionary Principle as a Norm of Customary International Law', 9 *JEL* 221 (1997)

MCLACHLAN, C, 'The Principle of Systemic Integration in Treaty Interpretation and Article 31(3)(c) of the Vienna Convention', 54 *ICLQ* 279 (2005)

MC RAE, B, 'Entry into force of the Convention on Supplementary Compensation for Nuclear Damage: Opening the umbrella', 95 *NLB* 7 (2015)

McRae, DM, 'Trade and Environment: The Development of WTO Law', 9 *Otago LR* 221 (1998)

—— and Goundrey, DJ, 'Environmental Jurisdiction in Arctic Waters: The Extent of Article 234', 16 *UBCLR* 197 (1982)

Mackenzie, C, 'Lessons from Forestry for International Environmental Law', 21 *RECIEL* 114 (2012)

Mackenzie, R, 'The International Regulation of Modern Biotechnology', 13 *YEL* 97 (2002)

Macrory, R, 'Regulating in a Risky Environment', 54 *CLP* 640 (2001)

Magraw, DB, 'Transboundary Harm: The International Law Commission's Study of International Liability', 80 *AJIL* 305 (1986)

Mahmoudi, S, 'The International Court of Justice and Nuclear Weapons', 66 *Nordic JIL* 77 (1997)

Maljean-Dubois, S, 'La CIJ face aux enjeux de protection de L'environnement', 115 *RGDIP* 39 (2011)

Mann, H, 'Of Revolution and Results: Trade and Environmental Law in the Afterglow of the Shrimp Turtle Case', 9 *YbIEL* 28 (1998)

Mansell, W and Scott, J, 'Why Bother about a Right to Development?' 21 *JLS* 171 (1994)

Margolis, E, 'The Hydrogen Bomb Experiments and International Law', 64 *Yale LJ* 629 (1955)

Marín Durán, G, 'Non-Tariff Barriers and the WTO Agreement on Technical Barriers to Trade: the Case of PPM-based Measures after *US – Tuna II* and *EC – Seal Products*', 6 *Eur Ybk Int Economic L* 87(2015)

Martin-Bidou, P, 'Le Principe de précaution en droit international de l'environnement', 103 *RGDIP* 631 (1999)

Martinez Romera, B, 'The Paris Agreement and the Regulation of International Bunker Fuels', 25 *RECIEL* 215 (2016)

Mayer, B, 'The Applicability of the Principle of Prevention to Climate Change: A Response to Zahar', 5 *Climate Law* 1 (2015)

Maxwell, S L, et al, 'Biodiversity: The Ravages of Guns, Nets and Bulldozers (Comment)' 536 *Nature* 43 (2016)

Mehling, M, et al, 'Designing Border Carbon Adjustments for Enhanced Climate Action', 113 *AJIL* 433 (2019)

—— 'Betwixt Scylla and Charybdis: The Concept of Effectiveness in International Environmental Law', 13 *Finnish YB Intl L* 129 (2002)

Mekouar, MA, 'La Convention Africaine: petite histoire d'une grande renovation', 34 *EPL* 43 (2004)

Meijers, H, 'How is International Law Made? The Stages of Growth of International Law and the Uses of its Customary Rules', 9 *NYIL* 3 (1978)

Meron, T, 'Extraterritoriality of Human Rights', 89 *AJIL* 78 (1995)

Merrills, JG, 'The Mosaic of International Dispute Settlement Procedures: Complementary or Contradictory', 54 *NILR* 361 (2007)

Mensah, T, 'The Tribunal and the Prompt Release of Vessels', 22 *IJMCL* 425 (2007)

Miller, GM, Sabourenkov, EN and Ramm, DC, 'Managing Antarctic Marine Living Resources: The CCAMLR Approach', 19 *IJMCL* 317 (2004)

Minelli, S, Erlewein A, and Castillo, V, 'Land Degradation Neutrality and the UNCCD: From Political Vision to Measurable Targets' *International Yearbook of Soil Law and Policy 2016* 85 (2017)

Molenaar, E, 'The Concept of "Real Interest" and Other Aspects of Co-operation Through Regional Fisheries Management Mechanisms', 15 *IJMCL* 475 (2000)

—— 'CCAMLR and Southern Ocean Fisheries', 16 *IJMCL* 465 (2001)

—— 'Participation, Allocation and Unregulated Fishing: The Practice of Regional Fisheries Management Organisations', 18 *IJMCL* 457 (2003)

—— 'Addressing Regulatory Gaps in High Seas Fisheries', 20 *IJMCL* 533 (2005)

—— 'Port State Jurisdiction: Toward Comprehensive Mandatory and Global Coverage', 38 *ODIL* 225 (2007)

—— 'Managing Biodiversity in Areas Beyond National Jurisdiction', 22 *IJMCL* 89 (2007)

—— 'Current and Prospective Roles of the Arctic Council System within the Context of the Law of the Sea,' 27 *IJMCL* 553 (2012)

—— 'Non-Participation in the Fish Stocks Agreement: Status and Reasons', 26 *IJMCL* 195 (2011)

Morgera, E, 'Significant Trends in Corporate Environmental Accountability: The New Performance Standards of the International Finance Corporation', 18 *Colorado JIELP* 151 (2007)

—— 'Bilateralism at the Service of Community Interests? Non-Judicial Enforcement of Global Public Goods in the Context of Global Environmental Law', 23 *EJIL* 744 (2012)

—— and Savaresi, A, 'A Conceptual and Legal Perspective on the Green Economy' 22 *RECIEL* 14 (2012)

—— 'Justice, Equity and Benefit-Sharing under the Nagoya Protocol to the Convention on Biological Diversity' 24 *Italian Yearbook of International Law* 113 (2015)

—— 'The Need for an International Legal Concept of Fair and Equitable Benefit Sharing', 27 *EJIL* 353 (2016)

Muchlinski, P, 'The Bhopal Case: Controlling Ultra-hazardous Industrial Activities Undertaken by Foreign Investors', 50 *MLR* 545 (1987)

—— 'Corporations in International Litigation: Problems of Jurisdiction and the United Kingdom Asbestos Case', 50 *ICLQ* 1 (2001)

Muller, B, 'Access to the Courts of Member States for NGOs in Environmental Matters under EU Law' 23 *JEL* 505 (2011)

Mushal, RM, 'Reflections Upon American Environmental Enforcement Experience', 19 *JEL* 201 (2007)

Myers, R and Worm, B, 'Rapid Worldwide Depletion of Predatory Fish Communities', 423 *Nature* 280 (2003)

Navid, D, 'The International Law of Migratory Species: The Ramsar Convention', 29 *NRJ* 1001 (1989)

Nollkaemper, A, 'The Rhine Action Programme: A Turning Point in the Protection of the North Sea', 5 *IJECL* 123 (1990)

—— 'Norms in the Law of Marine Environmental Protection', 8 *IJMCL* 1 (1993)

—— 'Agenda 21 and Prevention of Sea-based Marine Pollution', *Marine Policy* 537 (1993)

—— 'Balancing Protection of Marine Ecosystems and the Economic Benefits from Land-based Activities: The Quest for International Legal Barriers', 27 *ODIL* 153 (1996)

—— 'The Distinction Between Non-legal and Legal Norms in International Affairs—with Reference to Protection of the North Sea from Hazardous Substances', 13 *IJMCL* 355 (1998)

Noyes, J, 'The International Tribunal for the Law of the Sea', 32 *Cornell ILJ* 109 (1998)

Nurmukhametova, E, 'Problems in Connection with the Efficiency of the World Bank Inspection Panel', 10 *Max Planck YbUNL* 397 (2006)

Nwobike, JC, 'The African Commission on Human and Peoples' Rights and the Demystification of Second and Third Generation Rights under the African Charter', 1 *African JLS* 129 (2005)

Oda, S, 'The ICJ Viewed from the Bench', 244 *Recueil des Cours* 127 (1993)

—— 'Dispute Settlement Prospects in the Law of the Sea', 44 *ICLQ* 863 (1995)

Okidi, IO, 'Towards Regional Arrangements for Regulation of Marine Pollution: An Appraisal of Options', 4 *ODIL* 1 (1971)

Okowa, P, 'Procedural Obligations in International Environmental Agreements', 71 *BYbIL* 275 (1996)

Ong, D, 'CITES: Implications of Recent Developments', 10 *JEL* 291 (1998)

—— 'The Impact of Environmental Law on Corporate Governance', 12 *EJIL* 685 (2001)

Oppenheimer M and Petsonk, A, 'Article 2 of the UNFCCC: Historical Origins, Recent Interpretations', 73 *Climatic Change* 195 (2005)

Orakhelashvili, A, 'The World Bank Inspection Panel in Context: Institutional Aspects of the Accountability of International Organizations', 2 *Int Orgs LR* 57 (2005)s

Örebech, P, Sigurjonsson, K and McDorman, TL, 'The 1995 United Nations Straddling and Highly Migratory Fish Stocks Agreement: Management, Enforcement and Dispute Settlement', 13 *IJMCL* 119 (1998)

Orrego Vicuña, F, 'International Cooperation in Salmon Fisheries and a Comparative Law Perspective on the Salmon and Ocean Ranching Industry', 22 *ODIL* 133 (1991)

Osterwoldt, R, 'Implementation and Enforcement Issues in the Protection of Migratory Species', 29 *NRJ* 1017 (1989)

Outhwaite, O, 'Neither Fish, nor Fowl: Honeybees and the Parameters of Current Legal Frameworks for Animals, Wildlife and Biodiversity', 29 *JEL* 317 (2017)

Owen, D, 'The Application of the Wild Birds Directive beyond the Territorial Sea of EC Member States', 13 *JEL* 39 (2001)

Panjabi, R, 'From Stockholm to Rio: A Comparison of Declaratory Principles of International Environmental Law', 21 *Den JILP* 215 (1993)

Palchetti, P, 'Opening the International Court of Justice to Third States: Intervention and Beyond', 6 *Max Planck Yb UN Law* 139 (2002)

Pallemaerts, M, 'International Legal Aspects of Long-Range Transboundary Air Pollution', *Hague YIL* 189 (1988)

Palmer, G, 'New Ways to Make International Environmental Law', 86 *AJIL* 259 (1992)

Parsons, S, 'Ecosystem Considerations in Fisheries Management: Theory and Practice', 20 *IJMCL* 381 (2005)

Pauwelyn, J, 'A Typology of Multilateral Treaty Obligations: Are WTO Obligations Bilateral or Collective in Nature?' 14 *EJIL* 907 (2003)

—— 'The Role of Public International Law in the WTO: How Far Can We Go?' 95 *AJIL* 535 (2001)

Pavoni, R, 'Assessing and Managing Biotechnology Risk under the Cartagena Protocol on Biosafety', X *Italian YbIL* 113 (2000)

Payne, C, 'The Limits of Judicial Mechanisms for Developing and Enforcing International Environmental Norms', 109 *Proc ASIL* 193 (2015)

Pearce, D, 'An Intellectual History of Environmental Economics', 27 *Annual Review of Energy and Environment* 57 (2002)

Pedersen, O, 'An International Court and International Legalism', 24 *JEL* 547 (2012)

—— 'European Environmental Human Rights', 21 *Georgetown IELR* 73 (2008)

Peel, J, 'Precaution: A Matter of Principle, Approach or Process', 5 *Melb JIL* 483 (2004)

PELZER, N, 'Safer Nuclear Energy through a Higher Degree of Internationalization', 91 *Nuclear Law Bull* 43 (2013)

PERRAULT, AM and MUFFETT, WC, 'Turning off the Tap: A Strategy to Address International Aspects of Invasive Alien Species', 11 *RECIEL* 211 (2001)

PERREZ, FX, 'The Strategic Approach to International Chemicals Management: Lost Opportunity or Foundation for Brave New World' 15 *RECIEL* 245 (2006)

PETSONK, CA, 'The Role of UNEP in the Development of International Environmental Law, 5 *Am UJILP* 351 (1990)

PHARAND, D, 'Canada's Arctic Jurisdiction in International Law', 7 *Dal LJ* 315 (1983)

PINTO, CW, 'Reflections on International Liability for Injurious Consequences arising Out of Acts Not Prohibited by International Law', 16 *NYIL* 17 (1985)

PISILLO-MAZESCHI, R, 'The Due Diligence Rule and the Nature of the International Responsibility of States', 35 *GYIL* 9 (1992)

PLAKOKEFALOS, I, 'Prevention Obligations in International Environmental Law', 23 *YbIEL* 3 (2013)

—— 'The Pulp Mills Case', 26 *IJMCL* 169 (2011)

PLANT, G, 'International Legal Aspects of Vessel Traffic Services', 14 *Marine Policy* 71 (1990)

PONTECORVO, G, 'The Enclosure of the Marine Commons: Adjustment and Redistribution in World Fisheries', 12 *Marine Policy* 361 (1988)

POPOVIC, NAF, 'In Pursuit of Human Rights: Commentary on the Draft Declaration of Principles on Human Rights and the Environment', 27 *Columbia HRLR* 487 (1996)

POSTIGLIONE, A, 'An International Court for the Environment?' 23 *EPL* 73 (1993)

PULLEN, S and WARREN, L, 'The Biodiversity Convention and its Implementation with Respect to Marine Biodiversity', 1 *Int Jnl of Biosciences and the Law* 269 (1997)

QUÉRÉ, C L et al, 'Global Carbon Budget 2018', 10 *Earth System Science Data* 2141 (2018)

RACHOVITSA, A, 'The Principle of Systemic Integration in Human Rights Law', 66 *ICLQ* 557 (2017)

RAHMAN, R, 'The Law of the Non-navigational Uses of International Watercourses: Dilemma for Lower Riparians', 19 *Fordham ILJ* 9 (1995)

RAJAMANI, L, 'Addressing the Post-Kyoto Stress Disorder', 58 *ICLQ* 803 (2009)

—— 'The Increasing Currency and Relevance of Rights-based Perspectives in the International Negotiations on Climate Change', 22 *JEL* 391 (2010)

—— 'The Making and Unmaking of the Copenhagen Accord' 59 *ICLQ* 824 (2010)

—— 'The Durban Platform for Enhanced Action and the Future of the Climate Regime', 61 *ICLQ* 501 (2012)

—— 'Ambition and Differentiation in the 2015 Paris Agreement: Interpretative Possibilities and Underlying Politics', 65 *ICLQ* 493 (2016)

—— 'The 2015 Paris Agreement: Interplay Between Hard, Soft and Non-Obligations', 28 *JEL* 337 (2016)

—— and BODANSKY, D, 'The Paris Rulebook: Balancing International Prescriptiveness with National Discretion', 68 *ICLQ* 1023 (2019)

—— and WERKSMAN, J, 'The legal character and operational relevance of the Paris Agreement's temperature goal' 376 *Philosophical Transactions of the Royal Society* 1 (2018)

RAUSTIALA, K and VICTOR, D, 'The Regime Complex for Plant Genetic Resources', 58 *Int Org* 277 (2004)

Rayfuse, R, 'From Promoting to Achieving Compliance in High Seas Fisheries', 20 *IJMCL* 509 (2005)

—'Precaution and the Protection of Marine Biodiversity in Areas Beyond National Jurisdiction', 27 *IJMCL* 773 (2012)

—'Climate Change and Antarctic Fisheries: Ecosystem Management in CCAMLR' 45 *ELQ* 53 (2018)

Razzaque, J, 'Linking Human Rights, Development and Environment: Experiences from Litigation in South Asia', 18 *Fordham ELR* 587 (2007)

Read, J, 'The Trail Smelter Dispute', 1 *CYIL* 213 (1963)

Redgwell, C, 'The Greening of Salvage Law', 14 *Marine Policy* 142 (1990)

— 'Environmental Protection in Antarctica: the 1991 Protocol', 43 *ICLQ* 599 (1994)

— 'Universality or Integrity? Some Reflections on Reservations to General Multilateral Treaties', 64 *BYIL* 245 (1993)

— 'Biotechnology, Biodiversity and International Law', 58 *CLP* 543 (2005)

— 'Treaty Evolution, Adaptation and Change: Is the LOSC Enough to Address Climate Change Impacts on the Marine Environment?', 34 *IJMCL* 440 (2019)

Reed, C T, 'Between Priceless and Worthless: Challenges in Using Market Mechanisms for Conserving Biodiversity', *Transnational Environmental Law* 217 (2013)

Reid, E, 'Liability for Dangerous Activities: A Comparative Analysis', 48 *ICLQ* 731 (1999)

Rest, F, 'The Sandoz Conflagration and Rhine Pollution Liability Issues', 30 *GYIL* 160 (1987)

Reyners, P, 'La convention de 1994 sur la sûreté nucléaire', 99 *RGDIP* 605 (1995)

Ribeiro, M, 'The Rainbow: the First National MPA Proposed under the High Seas', 25 *IJMCL* 183 (2010)

Richards, RW and Hahn, KR, 'The Internationalization of Environmental Regulation', 30 *Harv ILJ* 421 (1989)

Ricupero, R, 'Chronicle of a Negotiation: The Financial Chapter of Agenda 21', 4 *Col JIELP* 81 (1993)

Rieu-Clarke, A, 'Notification and Consultation on Planned Measures Concerning International Watercourses: Learning Lessons from the *Pulp Mills* and *Kishenganga* Cases', 24 *YbIEL* 102 (2014)

Rigby, M, Park S, et al, 'Increase in CFC-11 emissions from eastern China based on atmospheric observations,' 569 *Nature* 546 (2019)

riley, s, 'A Weed by any Other Name: Would the Rose Smell as Sweet if it were A Threat to Biodiversity?' 22 *GIELR* 157 (2009–2010)

Riphagen, W, 'From Soft Law to Jus Cogens and Back', 17 *VUWLR* 81 (1987)

Roach, A, 'Today's Customary International Law of the Sea', 45 *ODIL* 239 (2014)

Roberts, A, 'Traditional and Modern Approaches to Customary International Law: A Reconciliation', 95 *AJIL* 757 (2001)

Roberts, J, 'Protecting Sensitive Marine Environments: The Role and Application of Ships' Routeing Measures', 20 *IJMCL* 135 (2005)

—, Chircop, A and Prior, S, 'Area-based Management on the High Seas: Possible Application of IMO's PSSA Concept', 25 *IJMCL* 483 (2010)

Robinson, NA, 'Colloquium: The Rio Environmental Law Treaties: IUCN's Proposed Covenant on Environment and Development', 13 *Pace Env LR* 133 (1995)

— 'International Tends in Environmental Impact Assessment', 19 *Boston Coll Env Aff LR* 591 (1991–2)

Rochette, J and Billé, R, 'Bridging the Gap between Legal and Institutional Developments within Regional Seas Frameworks', 28 *IJMCL* 433 (2013)

RODGERS, KE, 'The ISO Environmental Standards Initiative', 5 *NYU Env LJ* 181 (1996)

ROGERS, B, 'The Nature of Value and the Value of Nature: a Philosophical Overview', 76 *Int Affs*315 (2000).

ROHT-ARRIAZA, N, Shifting the Point of Regulation: The International Organization for Standardization and Global Lawmaking on Trade and the Environment, 22 *ELQ* 479 (1995)

—— 'Private Voluntary Standard Setting: The International Organization for Standardization and International Environmental Lawmaking', 6 *YbIEL* 107 (1995)

ROSENCRANTZ, A, 'The ECE Convention of 1979 on Long Range Transboundary Air Pollution', 75 *AJIL* 975 (1981)

—— 'The Uniform Transboundary Pollution Reciprocal Access Act', 15 *EPL* 105 (1985)

ROSENFELD,F, 'Mass Claims in international law' 1*JIDS* 159 (2013)

ROTHWELL, D, 'Illegal Southern Ocean Fishing and Prompt Release', 53 *ICLQ* 171 (2004)

RUBIN, A, 'Pollution by Analogy: The Trail Smelter Arbitration', 50 *Oregon LR* (1971) 259

RUHL, JB and JEWELL, MJ, 'The Oil Pollution Act of 1990: Opening a New Era in Federal and State Regulation of Oil Spill Prevention, Containment and Clean-up, and Liability', 8 *OGTLR* 234 (1990)

SACHARIEW, K, 'Promoting Compliance with International Environmental Legal Standards: Reflections on Monitoring and Reporting Mechanisms', 2 *YbIEL* 31 (1991)

SACHS, N, 'Beyond the Liability Wall: Strengthening Tort Remedies in International Environmental Law', 55 *UCLALR* 837 (2008)

SAFRIN, S, 'Treaties in Collision? The Biosafety Protocol and the World Trade Organization Agreements', 96 *AJIL* 606 (2002)

SALMON, J, 'La pollution des fleuves et des lacs et le droit international', 58 *Ann Inst DDI* 193 (1979)

SALMON, M, 'From NIEO to Now and the Unfinishable Story of Economic Justice', 62 *ICLQ* 31 (2013)

SÁNCHEZ-BAYO, F, and WYCKHUYS, KAG, 'Worldwide decline of the entomofauna: A review of its drivers', 232 *Biological Conservation* 8 (2019)

SAND, PH, 'International Environmental Law after Rio', 3 *YbIEL* 3 (1992)

—— 'Institution-building to Assist Compliance with International Environmental law: Perspectives', 56 *ZAÖRV* 774 (1996)

—— 'Whither CITES? The Evolution of a Treaty Regime on the Borderland of Trade and Environment', 8 *EJIL* 29 (1997)

——'Information Disclosure as an Instrument of Environmental Governance', 63 *ZAÖRV* 487 (2002)

—— 'Compensation for Environmental Damage from the 1991 Gulf War', 35 *EPL* 244 (2005)

—— 'Environmental Dispute Settlement and the Experience of the UN Compensation Commission', 54 *JYIL* 151 (2011)

SANDS, P, 'The Environment, Community and International Law', 30 *Harv ILJ* 393 (1989)

—— 'International Law in the Field of Sustainable Development', 65 *BYIL* 303 (1994)

—— 'The New Architecture of International Environmental Law', 30 *RBDI* 512 (1997)

——, 'Climate Change and the Rule of Law: Adjudicating the Future in International Law', 28 *JEL* 19 (2016)

SAVARESI, A, 'Traditional Knowledge and Climate Change: A New Legal Frontier?' 9 *JHRE* 32 (2018)

SCANLON, J and IZA, A, 'International Legal Foundations for Environmental Flows', 14 *YbIEL* 81 (2003)

SCHACHTER, O and SERWER, P, 'Marine Pollution Problems and Remedies', 65 *AJIL* 84 (1971)

SCHALL, C, 'Public Interest Litigation Concerning Environmental Matters before Human Rights Courts', 20 *JEL* 417 (2008)

SCHALLY, H, 'Forests: Toward an International Legal Regime?' 4 *YbIEL* 30 (1993)

SCHEIBER, H, 'From Science to Law in Politics: A Historical View of the Ecosystem Idea and its Effects on Resources Management', 24 *ELQ* 631 (1999)

SCHNEIDER, J, 'Codification and Progressive Development of International Environmental Law at the Third UNCLOS: The Environment Aspects of Treaty Review', 20 *Columbia JTL* 243 (1981)

SCHLEMMER-SCHULTE, S, 'The World Bank's Experience with Its Inspection Panel', 58 *ZAÖRV* 353 (1998)

SCHOENBAUM, T, 'International Trade and the Environment: the Continuing Search for Reconciliation', 91 *AJIL* 268 (1997)

—— 'The Decision in the *Shrimp-Turtle* Case', 9 *YbIEL* 36 (1998)

—— 'Liability for Damages in Oil Spill Accidents: Evaluating the US and International Law Regimes in the Light of Deepwater Horizon,' 24 *JEL* 395 (2012)

SCHRAGE, W, BULL, K, KARADJOVA, A, 'Environmental Legal Instruments in the UNECE Region', 18 *YbIEL* (2008) 3.

SCHWARTZ, B, and BERLIN, M, 'After the Fall: An Analysis of Canadian Legal Claims for Damage Caused by Cosmo 954', 27 *McGill LJ* 676 (1982)

SCOTT, J, 'European Regulation of GMOs: Thinking About Judicial Review in the WTO', 58 *CLP* 444 (2005)

—— 'International Trade and Environmental Governance: Relating Rules (and Standards) in the EU and the WTO', 15 *EJIL* 307 (2004)

SCOTT, KN, 'Ocean CO2 Sequestration and the Future of Climate Change', 18 *Geo IELR* 57 (2005)

—— 'Conservation on the High Seas: Developing the Concept of the High Seas Marine Protected Areas', 27 *IJMCL* 849 (2012)

—— 'Area-based Protection Beyond National Jurisdiction: Opportunities and Obstacles', 4 *Asia-Pacific J of Ocean Law and Policy* 158 (2019)

SCOVAZZI, T, 'Some Considerations on the Role of the International Seabed Authority', 19 *IJMCL* 383 (2004)

—— 'State Responsibility for Environmental Harm', 12 *YbIEL* 43 (2001)

SERDY, A, 'The Shaky Foundations of the FAO Port State Measures Agreement', 31 *IJMCL* 422 (2016)

SETTE-CAMARA, J, 'Pollution of International Rivers', 186 *Recueil des Cours* 117 (1984)

SHELTON, D, 'Human Rights, Environmental Rights, and the Right to the Environment', 28 *Stanford JIL* 103 (1991)

—— 'What Happened in Rio to Human Rights?' 3 *YbIEL* 91 (1992)

—— 'The Participation of NGOs in International Judicial Proceedings', 88 *AJIL* 611 (1994)

—— 'Fair Play, Fair Pay: Preserving Traditional Knowledge and Biological Resources', 5 *YbIEL* 77 (1994)

—— 'Decision Regarding Case 155/96', 96 *AJIL* 937 (2002)

SIMMA, B, 'The work of the ILC at its 50th session', 67 *Nordic JIL* 444 (1998)

—— 'From Bilateralism to Community Interest in International Law', 250 *Recueil des Cours* 293 (1994)

—— 'Self Contained Regimes', 16 *NYIL* 111 (1985)

—— 'Foreign Investment Arbitration: A Place for Human Rights', 60 *ICLQ* 573 (2011)

—— 'Universality of International Law from the Perspective of a Practitioner', 20 *EJIL* 265 (2009)

Sindico, F, 'Climate Change: A Security (Council) Issue?' 1 *CCLR* 6 (2007)

Sivakumaran, S, 'The Influence of Teachings of Publicists on the Development of International Law', 66 *ICLQ* (2017) 1.

Skubiszewski, K, 'Enactment of Law by International Organizations', 41 *BYIL* 198 (1965)

Slaughter Burley, AM, 'International Law and International Relations Theory', 87 *AJIL* 205 (1993)

Sloan, B, 'General Assembly Resolutions Revisited', 58 *BYIL* 39 (1987)

Smets, H, 'Le principe de non-discrimination en matière de protection de l'environnement', *Rev Eur Droit de l'Environnement* 3 (2000)

—— 'Le principe pollueur payeur: un principe économique érigé en principe de droit de l'environnement?' 97 *RGDIP* 339 (1993)

Smith, A, et al, 'Impacts of Fishing Low-Trophic Level Species on Marine Ecosystems', 333 *Science* 1147, Issue 6046 (2011)

Snape, W and Lefkovitz, N, 'Searching for GATTs Environmental *Miranda*: Are Process Standards Getting Due Process?' 27 *Cornell ILJ* 777 (1994)

Soares, G and Vargas, V, 'The Basel Liability Protocol', 12 *YbIEL* 69 (2001)

Sohn, L, 'The New International Law: Protection of the Rights of Individuals Rather than States', 32 *AULR* 1 (1982)

—— 'The Stockholm Declaration on the Human Environment', 14 *Harv ILJ* 423 (1973)

—— 'Settlement of Disputes Relating to the Interpretation and Application of Treaties', 150 *Recueil des Cours* 195 (1976)

—— 'Settlement of Law of the Sea Disputes', 10 *IJMCL* 205 (1995)

Somers, E, and Gonsaeles, G, 'The Consequences of the Sinking of the *M/V ERIKA* in European Waters: Towards a Total Loss for International Shipping Law?' 41 *JMLC* 57 (2010)

Song, Y, 'The Efforts of ICCAT to Combat IUU Fishing', 24 *IJMCL* 101 (2009)

Springer, AL, 'Towards a Meaningful Concept of Pollution in International Law', 26 *ICLQ* 531 (1977)

Staffin, E, 'Trade Barrier or Trade Boon? A Critical Evaluation of Environmental Labelling and Its Role in the Greening of World Trade', 21 *Columbia JEL* 205 (1996)

Stafford, R, 'Sustainability: A flawed concept for fisheries management?' 7: 8 *Elementa Science of the Anthropocene* (2019)

Stewart, RB, 'Environmental Regulation and International Competitiveness', 102 *Yale LJ* 2039 (1993)

Stone, C, 'Should Trees Have Standing? Towards Legal Rights for Natural Objects', 45 *Southern Cal LR* 450 (1972)

Streck, C and Scholz, SM, 'The Role of Forests in Global Climate Change: Whence We Come and Whence We Go', 82 *International Affairs* 861 (2006)

—— and Gehring, M, 'Emissions Trading: Lessons from SOx and NOx Emissions Allowance and Credit Systems', 4 *Env Law Reporter* 10219 (2005)

Subedi, S, 'Balancing International Trade with Environmental Protection: International Legal Aspects of Eco-labels', 2 *Brooklyn JIL* 373 (1999)

Sunstein, C, 'Montreal vs. Kyoto: A Tale of Two Protocols', 31 *Harv ELR* 1 (2007)

SWAN, J, 'Port State Measures – From Residual Port State Jurisdiction to Global Standards', 31 *IJMCL* 395 (2016)

SZASZ, P, 'The Convention on the Liability of Operators of Nuclear Ships', 2 *JMLC* 541 (1970)

—— 'The Security Council Starts Legislating', 96 *AJIL* 901 (2002)

TAL, A, and COHEN, JA, 'Bringing "Top-Down to "Bottom-Up": A New Role for Environmental Legislation in Combating Desertification' 31 *Harvard Environmental Law Review* 163 (2007)

TANAKA, Y, 'Zonal and Integrated Management Approaches to Ocean Governance', 19 *IJMCL* 483 (2004)

—— 'Regulation of Land-based Marine Pollution in International Law: A Comparative Analysis Between Global and Regional Legal Frameworks', 66 *ZAÖRV* (2006) 535

TARASOFSKY, R, 'Ensuring Compatibility Between Multilateral Environmental Agreements and GATT/WTO', 7 *YbIEL* 52 (1996)

—— 'Legal Protection of the Environment During International Armed Conflict', 24 *NYIL* 17 (1993)

TELESETSKY, A and LEE, SK, 'After Whaling in the Antarctic: Amending Article VIII to Fix a Broken Treaty Regime', 30 *IJMCL* 700 (2015)

TEMPLETON, J, and KOHLER, P, 'Implementation and Compliance under the Minamata Convention on Mercury', 23 *RECIEL* (2014) 211–220, 219.

THORNTON, J and TROMANS, S, 'Human Rights and Environmental Wrongs', 11 *JEL* 35 (1999)

TINKER, C, 'Environmental Security in the United Nations: Not a Matter for the Security Council', 59 *Tennessee LR* 787 (1992)

TLADI, D, 'The Proposed Implementing Agreement: Options for Coherence and Consistency in the Establishment of Protected Areas beyond National Jurisdiction', 30 *IJMCL* 654 (2015)

TOMCZAK, M, 'Defining Marine Pollution: A Comparison of Definitions Used by International Conventions', 8 *Marine Policy* 311 (1984)

TONHAUSER, W and WETHERALL, A, 'The International Atomic Energy Agency and the International Legal Framework for Nuclear Safety', 56 *JYIL* 283 (2013)

TRIBE, L, 'Ways Not to Think About Plastic Trees: New Foundations for Environmental Law', 83 *Yale LJ* 1315 (1974)

TRINDADE, AC, 'Coexistence and Coordination of Mechanisms of International Protection of Human Rights', 202 *Recueil des Cours* 9 (1987)

TROUDET, J, et al, 'Taxonomic bias in biodiversity data and societal preferences', 7(1) *Scientific reports* 9132 (2017)

TRÜEB, HR, 'Natural Resource Damages: A Swiss Perspective', 27 *EPL* 58 (1997)

TSAMENYI, M, 'The South Pacific States, The USA and Sovereignty over Highly Migratory Species', 10 *Marine Policy* 29 (1986)

—— and HANICH, Q, 'Fisheries Jurisdiction under the Law of the Sea Convention: Rights and Obligations in Maritime Zones under the Sovereignty of Coastal States', 27 *IJMCL* 783 (2012)

TSIMPLIS, M, 'Alien Species Stay at Home: The International Convention for the Control and Management of Ships Ballast Water', 19 *IJMCL* 411 (2004)

—— 'The Bunker Pollution Convention 2001: completing and harmonizing the liability regime for oil pollution from ships?', *LMCLQ* 83 (2005)

Tsioumani, E, 'Minamata Convention on Mercury – An Overview of the Agreed Text', 43 *EPL* 90 (2013)

Tully, SR, 'The Contribution of Human Rights to Freshwater Resource Management', 14 *YbIEL* 99 (2003)

Usuki, T, 'Measures to Ensure Compliance with the Montreal Ozone Protocol', 43 *Jap Ann IL* 19 (2000)

Vallega, A, 'The Regional Scale of Ocean Management and Marine Regional Building', 24 *O&C Man* 17 (1994)

—— 'Management of Ships' Ballast Water and Sediments 2004', 19 *IJMCL* 411 (2004)

VanderZwaag, DL, 'The Precautionary Approach and The International Control of Toxic Chemicals: Beacon of Hope, Sea of Confusion and Dilution', 33 *Houston JIL* 605 (2010–11)

—— 'The 2013 Minamata Convention and Protection of the Arctic Environment: Mercurial Promises and Challenges', *China Oceans LR* 208 (2015)

—— and Powers, A, 'Protection of the Marine Environment from Land-Based Pollution and Activities: Gauging the Tides of Global and Regional Governance', 23 *IJMCL* 423 (2008)

van Hooydonk, E, 'The Obligation to Offer a Place of Refuge to a Ship in Distress' *CMI Yearbook* 329 (2003)

van der Mensbrugghe, Y, 'Legal Status of International North Sea Conference Declarations', 5 *IJECL* 15 (1990)

van Heijnsbergen, P, 'The Pollution Concept in International Law', 5 *EPL* 11 (1979)

van Reenen, W, 'Rules of Reference in the New Convention on the Law of the Sea', 12 *NYIL* 3 (1981)

Vignes, D, 'La valeur juridique de certaines règles, normes ou pratiques mentionnées au TNCO comme généralement acceptées', *AFDI* 712 (1979)

Vinogradov, S, 'Observations on the ILC Draft Rules on Non-Navigational Uses of International Watercourses: Management and Domestic Remedies', 3 *Colorado JIELP* 235 (1992)

—— 'Marine Pollution Via Transboundary Watercourses: Regimes in the Wider Black Sea Region', 22 *IJMCL* 585 (2007)

—— 'The Impact of Deepwater Horizon: The Evolving International Legal Regime for Offshore Accidental Pollution Prevention, Preparedness and Response', 44 *ODIL* 335 (2013)

Viñuales, JE, 'Legal Techniques for Dealing with Scientific Uncertainty in Environmental Law', 43 *Vand JTL* 437 (2010)

—— 'Access to Water in Foreign Investment Disputes', 21 *Georgetown ELR* 733 (2008–9)

—— 'The Contribution of the ICJ to the Development of International Environmental Law', 32 *Fordham ILJ* 232 (2008–9)

Virally, M, 'Valeur juridique des recommandations', *AFDI* 66 (1956)

Voigt, 'The Paris Agreement: What is the standard of conduct for parties?' 3 *Questions of International Law* 17 (2016)

Von Bar, C, 'Environmental Damage in Private International Law', 268 *Recueil des Cours* 303 (1997)

Waelde T, and Kolo, A, 'Environmental Regulation, Investment Protection and Regulatory Taking in International Law', 50 *ICLQ* 811(2001)

Wandesforde-Smith, G, 'Looking for Law in All the Wrong Places? Dying Elephants, Evolving Treaties and Empty Threats', 19 *JIWLP* 365 (2016)

WANG, CP, 'A Review of the Enforcement Regime for Vessel Source Oil Pollution Control', 16 *ODIL* 305 (1986)

WARD, H, 'Common but Differentiated Debates: Environment, Labour and The World Trade Organisation', 45 *ICLQ* 592 (1996)

—— 'Trade and Environment Issues in Voluntary Eco-labelling and Life Cycle Analysis', 6 RECIEL (1997) 139

——'Some Lessons from the Thor Chemical and Cape PLC Cases', 12 *YbIEL* 105 (2001)

—— 'Beyond the Short Term: Legal and Institutional Space for Future Generations in Global Governance', 22 *YbIEL* 3 (2012)

WARNER, R, 'Oceans beyond Boundaries: Environmental Assessment Frameworks', 27 *IJMCL* 481 (2012)

WATTS, AD, 'The Convention on the Regulation of Antarctic Mineral Resource Activities 1988', 39 *ICLQ* 169 (1990)

WEE, L, 'Debt-for-Nature Swaps, A Reassessment of their Significance in International Environmental Law', 6 *JEL* 1 (1994)

WEIL, P, 'Towards Relative Normativity in International Law?' 77 *AJIL* 413 (1983)

WERKSMAN, J, 'Compliance and Transition: Russia's Non-Compliance Tests the Ozone Regime' 36 *ZAÖRV* 750 (1996)

—— 'Consolidationg Governance of the Global Commons: Insights from the GEF', 6 *YbIEL* 27 (1995)

—— 'Compliance and the Kyoto Protocol: Building a Backbone into a Flexible Regime', 9 *YbIEL* 47 (1998)

WETTESTAD, J, 'Science, Politics and Institutional Design: Some Initial Notes on the Long-Range Transboundary Air Pollution Regime', 4 *J Env & Devmnt* 165 (1995)

WIERSEMA, A, 'CITES and the Whole Chain Approach to Combating Illegal Wildlife Trade', 20 *JIWLP* 207 (2017)

WIJKMAN, PM, 'Managing the Global Commons', 36 *Int Org* 511 (1982)

WILLHEIM, E, 'Private Remedies for Transfrontier Environmental Damage: A Critique of Equal Right of Access', 7 *AYIL* 174 (1976)

WILLIS, FM, 'Economic Development, Environmental Protection and the Right to Health', 9 *Georgetown IELR* 195 (1996–7)

WILLIAMS, C, and DAVIS, B, 'Land-based Activities: What Remains to Be Done', 29 *O&CM* 207 (1995)

WILSON, EO, 'A global biodiversity map', 289 *Science* 2279 (2000)

WINTER, G, 'Patent Law Policy in Biotechnology', 2 *JEL* 167 (1992)

WIRTH, D, The Rio Declaration on Environment and Development: Two Steps Forward and One Step Back, or Vice Versa, 29 *Georgetown LR* 599 (1995)

—— 'Some Reflections on Turtles, Tuna, Dolphin and Shrimp', 9 *YbIEL* 40 (1998)

WITBOOI, E, 'The Port State Measures Agreement in Context', 29 *IJMCL* 290 (2014)

WOLFRUM, R, 'Means of Ensuring Compliance with and Enforcement of International Environmental Law', 272 *Recueil des Cours* 110 (1998)

—— and MATZ LUCK, N, 'The Interplay of the UNCLOS and the Convention on Biological Diversity', 4 *Max Planck YbUNL* 445 (2000)

WOOD, H, 'The United Nations World Charter for Nature: The Developing Nations Initiative to Establish Protections for the Environment', 12 *ELQ* 977 (1985)

WORM, B, et al, 'Rebuilding Global Fisheries', 325 *Science* 578 (2009)

WRIGHT, A and DOULMAN, D, 'Drift Net Fishing in the South Pacific: From Controversy to Management', 15 *Marine Policy* 303 (1991)

WU, C, 'Liability and Compensation for Bunker Pollution', 33 *JMLC* 553 (2002)

YANAGIDA, J, 'The Pacific Salmon Treaty', 81 *AJIL* 577 (1987)

YANG, T and PERCIVAL, R, 'The Emergence of Global Environmental Law', 36 *Ecol LQ* 615 (2009)

YEATER, N and VASQUEZ, J, 'Demystifying the Relationship Between CITES and the WTO', 10 *RECIEL* 271 (2002)

YOSHIDA, O, 'Soft Enforcement of Treaties: The Montreal Non-Compliance Procedure and the Functions of Internal International Institutions', 10 *Colorado JIELP* 95 (1999)

YOUNG, MA, 'The WTO's Use of Relevant Rules of International Law: An Analysis of the Biotech Case', 56 *ICLQ* 907 (2007)

ZHU, X, and HE, J, 'International Court of Justice's Impact on International Environmental Law: Focusing on the *Pulp Mills* Case', 23 *YbIEL* 106 (2013)

ZIHUA, G, VOIGT, C and WERKSMAN, J, 'Facilitating Implementation and Promoting Compliance With the Paris Agreement Under Article 15: Conceptual Challenges and Pragmatic Choices', 9 *Climate Law* 65 (2019)

INDEX